WITHDRAWN

HANDBOOK OF
LATIN AMERICAN STUDIES:
No. 65

A Selective and Annotated Guide to Recent Publications in
Anthropology, Economics, Geography, Government and Politics,
International Relations, Political Economy, and Sociology

VOLUME 66 WILL BE DEVOTED TO THE HUMANITIES:
ART, HISTORY, LITERATURE, MUSIC, AND PHILOSOPHY

EDITORIAL NOTE: Comments concerning the *Handbook of Latin American Studies* should be sent directly to the Humanities or Social Sciences Editor, *Handbook of Latin American Studies*, Hispanic Division, Library of Congress, Washington, D.C. 20540-4851.

HANDBOOK OF LATIN AMERICAN STUDIES: NO. 65

SOCIAL SCIENCES

Prepared by a Number of Scholars
for the Hispanic Division of The Library of Congress

TRACY NORTH, *Social Sciences Editor*
KATHERINE D. McCANN, *Humanities Editor*

2010

UNIVERSITY OF TEXAS PRESS   *Austin*

International Standard Book Number: 978-0-292-72263-7
International Standard Serial Number: 0072-9833
Library of Congress Catalog Card Number: 36-32633
Copyright © 2010 by the University of Texas Press.
Printed in the United States of America.

Requests for permission to reproduce material
from this work should be sent to:
Permissions, University of Texas Press,
Box 7819, Austin, Texas 78713-7819

First Edition, 2010

The paper used in the publication meets the minimum requirements of American
National Standard for Information Sciences—Permanence of Paper for Printed
Library Materials, ANSI Z39.48-1984. ⊚

CONTRIBUTING EDITORS

SOCIAL SCIENCES

Juan M. del Aguila, *Emory University*, GOVERNMENT AND POLITICS
Enrique Desmond Arias, *The City University of New York (CUNY)*, GOVERNMENT
  AND POLITICS
Melissa H. Birch, *University of Kansas*, ECONOMICS
Christian Brannstrom, *Texas A&M University*, GEOGRAPHY
Jacqueline Anne Braveboy-Wagner, *The City University of New York (CUNY)*,
  INTERNATIONAL RELATIONS
Charles D. Brockett, *Sewanee: The University of the South*, GOVERNMENT AND
  POLITICS
Luis René Cáceres, *Inter-American Development Bank*, ECONOMICS
Roderic A. Camp, *Claremont-McKenna College*, GOVERNMENT AND POLITICS
María Esperanza Casullo, *Universidad de Río Negro, Argentina*, SOCIOLOGY
César N. Caviedes, *University of Florida, Gainesville*, GEOGRAPHY
Thomaz Guedes Da Costa, *National Defense University*, INTERNATIONAL
  RELATIONS
María Amparo Cruz-Saco, *Connecticut College*, ECONOMICS
Bartholomew Dean, *University of Kansas*, ANTHROPOLOGY
David W. Dent, *Towson University*, GOVERNMENT AND POLITICS
Duncan Earle, *Wake Forest University*, ANTHROPOLOGY
Scott M. Fitzpatrick, *North Carolina State University*, ANTHROPOLOGY
Michael Fleet, *Marquette University*, GOVERNMENT AND POLITICS
Daniel W. Gade, *The University of Vermont*, GEOGRAPHY
Mario A. González-Corzo, *The City University of New York (CUNY)*, ECONOMICS
Clifford E. Griffin, *North Carolina State University*, GOVERNMENT AND POLITICS
Daniel Hellinger, *Webster University*, POLITICAL ECONOMY
John Henderson, *Cornell University*, ANTHROPOLOGY
Peter H. Herlihy, *University of Kansas*, GEOGRAPHY
Eric Hershberg, *American University*, POLITICAL ECONOMY
Joan F. Higbee, *Hispanic Division, Library of Congress*, GOVERNMENT AND POLITICS
Daniel Hilliard, *Georgetown University*, SOCIOLOGY
Silvia María Hirsch, *FLACSO Argentina*, ANTHROPOLOGY
Jonathan Hiskey, *Vanderbilt University*, POLITICAL ECONOMY
Keith Jamtgaard, *University of Missouri*, SOCIOLOGY
Arthur A. Joyce, *University of Colorado at Boulder*, ANTHROPOLOGY
Barbara Kotschwar, *Georgetown University*, POLITICAL ECONOMY
José Antonio Lucero, *University of Washington, Seattle*, GOVERNMENT AND
  POLITICS
Markos J. Mamalakis, *University of Wisconsin-Milwaukee*, ECONOMICS

Ana Margheritis, *University of Florida, Gainesville*, POLITICAL ECONOMY
Daniel Masís-Iverson, *American University*, POLITICAL ECONOMY
Kent Mathewson, *Louisiana State University*, GEOGRAPHY
Philip Mauceri, *University of Northern Iowa*, GOVERNMENT AND POLITICS
Betty J. Meggers, *Smithsonian Institution*, ANTHROPOLOGY
Mary K. Meyer McAleese, *Eckerd College*, INTERNATIONAL RELATIONS
Frank O. Mora, *National War College*, INTERNATIONAL RELATIONS
Donna J. Nash, *University of Illinois at Chicago*, ANTHROPOLOGY
Andrew Orta, *University of Illinois at Urbana-Champaign*, ANTHROPOLOGY
Jason Pribilsky, *Whitman College*, SOCIOLOGY
René Salgado, *Independent Consultant*, GOVERNMENT AND POLITICS
Joseph Leonard Scarpaci, Jr., *Virginia Military Institute*, GEOGRAPHY
David W. Schodt, *St. Olaf College*, ECONOMICS
Jörn Seeman, *Universidade Regional do Cariri, Brazil*, GEOGRAPHY
Andrew D. Selee, *Woodrow Wilson International Center for Scholars*,
    INTERNATIONAL RELATIONS
Peter M. Siavelis, *Wake Forest University*, POLITICAL ECONOMY
Russell E. Smith, *Washburn University*, ECONOMICS
Anthony Peter Spanakos, *Montclair State University*, POLITICAL ECONOMY
Pamela K. Starr, *University of Southern California*, POLITICAL ECONOMY
Steven L. Taylor, *Troy University*, GOVERNMENT AND POLITICS
Brian Turner, *Randolph-Macon College*, GOVERNMENT AND POLITICS
Antonio Ugalde, *The University of Texas at Austin*, SOCIOLOGY
Aldo C. Vacs, *Skidmore College*, INTERNATIONAL RELATIONS
Hannah Wittman, *Simon Fraser University*, SOCIOLOGY
Robin M. Wright, *University of Florida, Gainesville*, ANTHROPOLOGY

HUMANITIES

Maureen Ahern, *Ohio State University*, TRANSLATIONS
Diana Álvarez-Amell, *Seton Hall University*, LITERATURE
Severino J. Albuquerque, *University of Wisconsin-Madison*, LITERATURE
Félix Ángel, *Inter-American Development Bank*, ART
Dain Borges, *University of Chicago*, HISTORY
John Britton, *Francis Marion University*, HISTORY
Jürgen Buchenau, *University of North Carolina*, HISTORY
Francisco Cabanillas, *Bowling Green State University*, LITERATURE
Jorge L. Chinea, *Wayne State University*, HISTORY
Don M. Coerver, *Texas Christian University*, HISTORY
Jerry W. Cooney, *Professor Emeritus, University of Louisville*, HISTORY
Wilfredo H. Corral, *California State University, Sacramento*, LITERATURE
Edward L. Cox, *Rice University*, HISTORY
Sandra Cypess, *University of Maryland, College Park*, LITERATURE
Paula De Vos, *San Diego State University*, HISTORY
Jennifer L. Eich, *Loyola Marymount University, Los Angeles*, LITERATURE
Darío A. Euraque, *Instituto Hondureño de Antropología e Historia*, HISTORY

César Ferreira, *University of Wisconsin-Milwaukee*, LITERATURE
John D. Garrigus, *University of Texas at Arlington*, HISTORY
Gilberto Gómez-Ocampo, *Wabash College*, LITERATURE
Robert Haskett, *University of Oregon*, HISTORY
José M. Hernández, *Professor Emeritus, Georgetown University*, HISTORY
Christine Hunefeldt, *University of California, San Diego*, HISTORY
Regina Igel, *University of Maryland, College Park*, LITERATURE
Clara Jalif de Bertranou, *Universidad Nacional de Cuyo, Mendoza, Argentina*,
    PHILOSOPHY
Héctor Jaimes, *North Carolina State University*, LITERATURE
Gwen Kirkpatrick, *Georgetown University*, LITERATURE
John Koegel, *California State University, Fullerton*, MUSIC
Jill S. Kuhnheim, *University of Kansas*, LITERATURE
Erick D. Langer, *Georgetown University*, HISTORY
Hal Langfur, *The State University of New York at Buffalo*, HISTORY
Dana Leibsohn, *Smith College*, ART
Alfred E. Lemmon, *Historic New Orleans Collection*, MUSIC
Peter S. Linder, *New Mexico Highlands University*, HISTORY
Maria Angélica Guimarães Lopes, *Professor Emerita, University of South Carolina*,
    LITERATURE
Cristina Magaldi, *Towson University*, MUSIC
Carol Maier, *Kent State University*, TRANSLATIONS
Claire Martin, *California State University, Long Beach*, LITERATURE
Frank D. McCann, *Professor Emeritus, University of New Hampshire*, HISTORY
Karen Melvin, *Bates College*, HISTORY
Elizabeth Monasterios, *University of Pittsburgh*, LITERATURE
Naomi Hoki Moniz, *Associate Professor Emerita, Georgetown University*,
    LITERATURE
José M. Neistein, *Independent Scholar, Washington, DC*, ART
Suzanne B. Pasztor, *Humboldt State University*, HISTORY
Daphne Patai, *University of Massachusetts, Amherst*, TRANSLATIONS
Valentina Peguero, *University of Wisconsin, Stevens-Point*, HISTORY
S. Elizabeth Penry, *Fordham University*, HISTORY
Charles A. Perrone, *University of Florida*, LITERATURE
José Promis, *University of Arizona*, LITERATURE
Susan E. Ramírez, *Texas Christian University*, HISTORY
Jane M. Rausch, *University of Massachusetts-Amherst*, HISTORY
Jonathan Ritter, *University of California, Riverside*, MUSIC
Humberto Rodríguez-Camilloni, *Virginia Polytechnic Institute*, ART
Kathleen Ross, *New York University*, TRANSLATIONS
Oscar D. Sarmiento, *State University of New York, Potsdam*, LITERATURE
William F. Sater, *Professor Emeritus, California State University, Long Beach*,
    HISTORY
Jacobo Sefamí, *University of California-Irvine*, LITERATURE
Joan Supplee, *Baylor University*, HISTORY
Barbara A. Tenenbaum, *Hispanic Division, Library of Congress*, HISTORY
Juan Carlos Torchia Estrada, *Independent Scholar, Washington DC*, PHILOSOPHY
Lilián Uribe, *Central Connecticut State University*, LITERATURE
Thomas Whigham, *University of Georgia*, HISTORY

CONTENTS

ECONOMICS

GEOGRAPHY

GOVERNMENT AND POLITICS

INTERNATIONAL RELATIONS

POLITICAL ECONOMY

SOCIOLOGY

INDEXES

EDITOR'S NOTE

I. GENERAL AND REGIONAL TRENDS

As the first decade of the 21st century comes to a close, much of the research being published and reviewed in the *Handbook* continues to grapple with the theme of globalization. The most striking perspective on themes of globalization relate to indigenous peoples and their inclusion in society, politics, and the economy. Definitions of mestizaje and indigeneity abound, with no clear consensus on what it means to be a citizen or how the concept reflects national identity or autonomy (item **520**). The concept of "neoliberal multiculturalism" has entered the discourse. Arguably as a direct result of the 1994 Chiapas uprising, the Mexican government recently published a response in which they outlined official constitutional changes increasing cultural, legal, educational, language, and other rights of indigenous individuals, at the same time swiftly replacing the traditional exclusionary paradigm of mestizaje (item **527**). The Zapatista movement continues to attract the attention of scholars, but the published materials generally lack academic rigor. One notable exception is the massive, comprehensive tome by Maya Lorena Pérez-Ruiz in which she documents the history of the movement, its relationship with other indigenous movements in Chiapas and in Mexico, and the interaction between the Zapatistas and the Mexican government (item **1480**).

Ethnographic research into contemporary indigenous communities reveals a focus on rights, within which ethnic identity is explored. Likewise, indigenous political participation and mobilization are explored throughout the region. At long last, there appears to be "a respect for cultural differences" in Latin American policy-making (Earle, p. 76). It is refreshing to report that several introductory essays note "the increasing representation of indigenous scholars engaged in research that documents and often participates in these [policy] developments" (Orta, p. 116). In 2005, Evo Morales was elected as Bolivia's first indigenous president, and works listed in *HLAS 65* begin to address the impact of his presidency on the nation and the region, ranging from biographies of Morales and his vice-president, Alvaro García Linera, to analyses of indigenous politics and social movements. Illustrating this trend toward indigenous political participation, Donna Lee Van Cott's notable 2005 monograph on ethnic political movements examines their success or failure as they attempt to transform from social movements to institutionalized political parties; she concludes that "the emergence of ethnic parties in South America has been positive for democratic institutions in the region, while having mixed results for indigenous peoples and their cultures" (item **1438**, p. 264). Another article published that same year, "Indigenous Parties and Democracy in Latin America," assesses the growing importance of indigenous parties in the process of democratization in Latin America "by improving the representation of the party system and reducing political violence" (item **1422**, p. 261).

Political violence and corruption are explored in several areas in Latin

America, including Colombia, Venezuela, and the Caribbean. In Peru, former president Alberto Fujimori was convicted of abuse of authority in 2007 and sentenced to six years in prison. In 2008, he stood trial for human rights violations, including crimes against humanity, and in April 2009, the Corte Suprema of Peru convicted Fujimori and sentenced him to 25 years in prison. The shadow of Fujimori continues to be cast over Peruvian politics. One article analyzes population policies during his regime and concludes that they targeted poor indigenous women, reinforcing racial and gender stereotypes (item **1687**). On a related note, gender is a recurring theme for Central America, with one article examining how and why women in Nicaragua and El Salvador participated in revolutionary armies (item **2605**).

Violence of another sort dominates the literature on Central America. Youth and gang violence continue to attract the attention of scholars, whose focus has shifted from quantitative reports toward qualitative examinations of the root and structural causes of the violence (Wittman, p. 496). One article argues that the proliferation of youth gangs is a result of the lack of socioeconomic support structures and disenfranchisement precipitated by neoliberal economic reforms (item **2593**).

Several studies look at miscegenation and racism in Latin American society. It is interesting to note that in Lowland South America, "the dynamics of mestizaje (item **613**) are not between whites and Indians, but between two different indigenous groups, the Chané (Arawak origin) and the Guaraní" (Hirsch, p. 99). One study of race in Mexico concludes that indigenous women have the least access to citizenship (item **2489**). Other studies of gender and politics indicate that, while advances have been made in terms of furthering women's participation and access to democratic institutions and structures, difficulties remain in gaining equal rights for women throughout the region. One important study on Mexico concludes that electoral accountability and political participation are integral components for enabling democracy to increase human rights protections (item **1448**). A disappointing related topic is that of voter abstentionism, which is echoed in contributions on voting and political participation throughout the Americas. One exception is the case of Brazil, where participatory budgeting has re-engaged the populace.

Although *HLAS* does not cover education or indigenous languages per se, a corollary to the topic of indigenous rights is bilingual education—or "ethnoeducation"—about which several research efforts appear in this volume. A study from Mexico explains the efforts of the government to map popular culture in the country by examining indigenous language, food, and art (item **1056**). Another study focuses on Mexican immigration, discussing the benefits of international migration in terms of language acquisition (item **2502**). It is no surprise that relations between indigenous and non-indigenous peoples continue to be of interest to scholars. One contribution in particular investigates the tragic story of the impact of a Protestant mission on the Nukak of Colombia (item **581**).

Turning the clock back to the precontact era, social archeology remains a popular research area in which scholars have attempted to recreate the everyday life of precolumbian civilizations. Topics of research include spatial organization, gender roles and identity, and religion. Specifically, analyses of Maya texts and the Maya calendar provide updated understandings of their political structures, economy, and ways of life. Studies on mortuary customs and rituals of the Aztecs appear in greater number in this *HLAS* volume. Interregional interaction is examined throughout the Americas, shedding new light on human mobility and trade routes. Likewise, land settlement patterns continue to be fodder for research projects examining the availability—or scarcity—of resources. Scholars caution against a reliance on analysis of goods such as pottery and ceramics for determining material culture, noting that once Europeans arrived in the New World, many factors impacted the production and circulation of goods. Similarly, the debate continues within Brazil as to whether humans were able to domesticate their environments if they were dissatisfied with the available resources—or if they were simply forced to relocate.

It is worthwhile to note the increase in publications on Caribbean archeology in recent years. Scholars are making efforts to publish their findings in more widely disseminated journals with the goal of encouraging greater exchange of ideas among regions. Several monographs on the Taíno were published during this review period (items **258**, **271**, and **280**). A fascinating scholarly debate regarding Taíno chiefdoms in the Caribbean continues to draw attention. Luis Antonio Curet (item **257**) and William F. Keegan (*HLAS 61:233* and item **268**) have engaged in a published discussion about the political and social structure of precolumbian societies, disagreeing over rules of succession and rules of descent that may or may not have varied across islands and communities. The topic of land use has permeated archeological studies on the Caribbean, noting the problematic outcome of coastal erosion due to archeological excavations.

A recent current of research in the field of South American archeology has been the efforts of scholars to document "the development of the discipline and its practices, such as collection and exposition, as well as noting the influence of key individuals to their respective regions of research" (Nash, p. 47). Understanding the evolution of research methodology within the field will surely benefit future investigations. One fabulous example is a publication celebrating the 50th anniversary of the Centro de Estudos e Pesquisas Arqueológicas (CEPA) in which 15 archeologists discuss their early careers in Brazil (item **338**). Also coming out of Brazil is a publication that offers a panorama of the field of Brazilian anthropology today (item **559**).

As has been the case in recent *HLAS* Social Science volumes, several topics appear as research interests across disciplines, notably the environment and water rights. According to Peter H. Herlihy, "the importance and complexity of water management makes it one of the most significant resource issues of the 21st century" (p. 198). Climate change is being investigated from various disciplinary perspectives, ranging from land use by precolumbian civilizations to current indigenous practices of fishing and land management. One study in the Geography chapter looks at gender and the environment in the Andean region in relation to biodiversity and environmental policy (item **1080**). In a similar vein, Juanita Sundberg looks at the intersection of human-environment relations, noting that "racial arguments are a powerful factor in shaping identities and defining places" (item **968**). The subfield of environmental geography has expanded within the last decade in response to growing concern about environmental degradation and conservation. Aspects analyzed include the social costs of conservation, ethnographic relationships with rural development, and land use. These studies are reviewed in *HLAS* by both geographers and sociologists alike.

Another fascinating arena has arisen as a major topic in recent literature on land use in Brazil: "smallholder land uses, road construction, land violence, and unofficial road building" (Brannstrom, p. 240). Several articles discuss the deforestation in the Amazon as a result of smallholders rather than large-scale ranchers; the impact of road-building on rainforests, local climate, and communities; and the "land war" in Pará using GIS analysis to attempt to explain rural violence as a result of disputes over land use.

Economic policy-making has clashed with environmental concerns in cases where countries are exploring new ways of generating economic activity. For example, in Ecuador there have been demonstrations opposing the new mining law. At the same time, the government has been engaged in international efforts to curtail detrimental petroleum exploitation without negatively impacting the economy (item **785**). A complementary publication looks at a region in Peru where mining has occurred on and off since colonial times (item **821**). Turning to Chile, one publication brings together 10 essays discussing the environmental impact of rural-to-urban migration on the greater metropolitan area of Santiago (item **809**). Likewise in Bolivia, "natural resources provide much of Bolivia's prosperity and are also a source of great political contention, both internal and external" (Kotschwar, p. 447).

The intersection of indigenous groups and the environment is evident in the studies of various national parks and reserves throughout Mexico and Central America. The management of forest resources and protected areas is a dominant theme in this *HLAS* volume. The interdisciplinary nature of these studies can be seen in the methodologies applied to the research projects: some monitor land use via remote sensing and GIS, while others apply econometric modeling and analysis to land cover change in an effort to detect the complex variability of land use over time. Studies of land use include analyses of forests (i.e., community forestry, deforestation, reforestation) based on agricultural practices, conservation efforts, and ecotourism. The recurring element of education is discussed in terms of disseminating information about parks and reserves to those communities whose livelihoods are tied to reserves; one article demonstrates that neighbors who visit the protected sites increase their knowledge and valuation of the area (item **1004**). In Ecuador, voters approved a progressive constitution in 2008 which included provisions to uphold *sumac kawsay*, an indigenous concept meaning "living well" which stipulates harmonious relationships between people, their immediate surroundings, and the environment (Pribilsky, p. 511).

The 150th anniversary of the death of Alexander von Humboldt spurred worldwide interest in his scientific explorations, a theme that is reflected in the historical geography literature reviewed for this *HLAS* volume. At the beginning of the 19th century, Humboldt traveled widely in Latin America. In 2002, exactly 200 years after Humboldt arrived in Peru, a symposium on his activities took place in the country (item **1137**). Some of his previously unpublished diaries from his travels in Ecuador were published in 2006 (item **940**). Karl S. Zimmerer, in his 2006 article from *Geographical Review* entitled "Humboldt's Nodes and Modes of Interdisciplinary Environmental Science in the Andean World," argues that the Andean region was an excellent location for Humboldt to continue his scientific exploration of previously unstudied phenomena, while also serving as a place where he "integrated his thinking about nature and culture" (item **1082**). Similarly, his travelogues from visiting Cuba were used to explore the cultural geography of the island (item **986**).

Most of the studies reviewed in the international relations chapter deal with regionalism and regional integration as a consequence of globalization. Few works seem to address foreign policy-making or comparative foreign policy analysis, although in-depth research on Mexico's foreign policy appears to be an exception. More perspectives from within Latin America and the Caribbean as well as from

Europe are being published. Critical views of neoliberalism continue to appear, as do critiques of free trade initiatives. It is worthwhile to note that the regional response to globalization includes a shift of geopolitics and a reconsideration of hegemonic powers; Mercosur and the Andean Community illustrate a shift from North-South regionalism to one in which neighbors in the Southern Hemisphere join together politically and economically to counterbalance the overwhelming forces of globalization. To that end, Brazil has emerged as a hemispheric leader in trade negotiations and regional economic integration. Subregional arrangements are appearing "with the goal of lessening dependency and promoting development" (Meyer McAleese, p. 364). At the same time, there has been a noticeable increase in studies examining interregional and transregional ties being forged with nontraditional partners in Europe, Asia (China, in particular), and even Africa. Continuing the themes echoed throughout the volume, two studies look at the role of inter-American institutions in protecting indigenous peoples' rights and the environment (items **1948** and **1981**).

Within the overarching arena of globalization, a number of contributions look at changes to the market and how these changes impact economic and political development. There appears to be a rift in the scholarship between "those who see the region's increasing economic integration and turn toward market-based development strategies as an obstacle to Latin American prosperity, and those who see these phenomena as essential to the region's economic development" (Hiskey, p. 415). Two economic studies on Chile consider the effects of globalization on the salmon (item **789**) and wine (item **802**) industries. As an aside, a thought-provoking contribution by Hugo Fazio Vengoa argues that the effect of globalization cannot and should not be measured for a specific economy at a certain point in time, but rather must be examined "as a longer-term evolutionary process that stretches back to the colonial period" (item **2326**). One intriguing study looks at small coffee producers in Peru, arguing that globalization and specifically the fair trade market, along with cooperativism, have vastly boosted the development of the industry despite limited state support (item **2318**). Geographers are also contributing to this corpus of literature by examining the impact of market liberalization on small-scale and local producers. The impact of neoliberal land reforms on water rights, another consequence of globalization, will need further investigation by geographers, particularly as property rights shift and long-standing land use patterns begin to change.

Globalization, or a reliance on global markets, appears to have a more dramatic impact on smaller states that rely on the stronger economies of developed countries. A case in point is the reaction within Latin America to the global financial crisis of 2008. Some scholars have argued that Latin American economies are more vulnerable to international instability. However, others seem to be optimistic in their assessment that Latin American as a region has weathered the storm with its relative economic stability. Future research will determine which of these opposing camps may have been more accurate. The studies that appear in this volume offer a more nuanced approach to the impact of globalization on the countries in the region. For example, Carmen Diana Deere's paper explores the growth in women's participation in agriculture as a by-product of neoliberalism (item **2183**). A striking development in recent studies is the examination of the outcomes of market-based reforms in concrete terms rather than the general emotional assessments for or against globalization. The consensus is for countries to focus on domestic economic policy first, and then look to the international financial markets for possibilities of economic growth. For example, one can imagine that the major theme to emerge in publications about Argentine political economy is the attempt to explain the causes and implications of the 2001 economic crisis. A corollary to research on the aftermath of the economic crisis is a re-examination of the social landscape within the country. Several sociological contributions espouse a pessimistic tone, no doubt due to the perceived "permanent" social crisis (Casullo, p. 518).

Despite deep economic reforms and market-driven policies, poverty continues to plague Latin America. Several studies examine causes for the persistence of poverty, while others focus on the role of education as a means for overcoming poverty and fostering economic growth. A number of countries have instituted antipoverty and social protection programs. A recurring theme seen in the publications reviewed here is social inclusion/exclusion. Many countries are re-examining their social policies with an eye toward distribution of income and greater attention to the needs of the lower middle class populations. This topic is woven throughout studies within each discipline covered in *HLAS*. In Brazil, "a tradition has developed of emphasizing not only social inclusion, but social networks" in the political economy literature (Spanakos, p. 469). Two studies on Ecuador look at the effects of the cut flower industry on poverty in the country (items **782** and **784**). It is certain that more studies of this industry, its growth in South America, and its effect on economic development will appear in the future. One study focused on Mexico examines political participation among the poor and finds that economic reforms result in short-term increases in participation but in the long term, lower income citizens will drop out of the political process (item **2219**).

Research on Mexico's political economy has shifted away from analyses of the reform process and toward the economic performance of the reforms, specifically examining microeconomic activity in the country. Studies on globalization focus on three levels of analysis: the global economic system, state-level policies and reforms, and individuals. Two contributions on Mexico stand out for their acute examinations of individual policymakers (items **2204** and **2218**).

Several economic analyses examine the labor market, specifically looking at gender and racial discrimination and the repercussions of free trade agreements on labor market regulations. Studies of maquilas in Mexico and Central America consider labor relations, wages and benefits, education/training, and gender. Kirsten Sehnbruch's comprehensive monograph on the labor market in Chile is a welcome addition to the literature (items **810** and **2335**). For Brazil, three works look at the labor market, labor conditions, and labor relations in various industries throughout the country (items **880, 894,** and **901**).

The inaugural issue of *EspacioTiempo: Revista Latinoamericana de Ciencias Sociales y Humanidades* was published in 2008 by the Universidad Autónoma de San Luis Potosí in Mexico. The contents of the journal are focused on discussing theory, methodology, and themes of geographic research, and the first issue, from which two articles were reviewed in *HLAS 65*, focuses on indigenous peoples, cultural geography, and the environment (items **1029** and **1072**). Turning to geographic research developments in Colombia, the first Geography PhD program in the Andes was established in 2008 at the Universidad Nacional de Colombia in Bogotá. This initiative reflects a commitment to institutionalizing the exploration of serious scholarly research for the field of geography in the region.

A relatively new trend in the social science literature is the exploration of peoples of African descent, mainly in Mexico and the Atlantic Coast of Nicaragua.

Luis Sánchez, in his article "Splitting the Country: The Case of the Atlantic Coast of Nicaragua," suggests that "dissatisfaction with the core-periphery relations has meant the resurgence of separatist feelings among the populations of the two autonomous regions on the Atlantic Coast" (item **1026**). To illustrate this argument, an excellent study by a team of Nicaraguan and European scholars examines the move toward regional autonomy within the Atlantic Coast, offering a historical account of the movement based on extensive interviews and observation (item **1530**). An example of research on Afro-descendant populations is the study of an Afro-Caribbean population of turtle fishermen that settled on the Caribbean coast of Costa Rica in the early 19th century, looking at how their "identity practices" and their embrace of Afro-Caribbean heritage and Rastafarianism have attracted tourism (item **1001**). For the first time, sociological studies of Afro-Mexicans have been published. Contributions from a 1997 symposium describe African cultural influences in Mexico (item **2527**); an article on santería describes the existence of this Afro-Cuban religion in Mexico City (item **2505**); and a chapter from the book *Neither Enemies Nor Friends: Latinos, Blacks, Afro-Latinos* (2005) discusses why there is not an evident black culture in the Pacific coastal region (item **2547**). Another chapter from that same book looks at Afro-Ecuadorians and their experience with racism (item **2637**).

Migration continues to attract the attention of scholars from different disciplinary backgrounds. Within the realm of geography, one noteworthy contribution is the Spanish translation of an original French research report on fieldwork from the 1990s in Bolivia (item **1164**). The study examines the dilemma of Andean peasants: whether to stay on their farms, where they have been unable to sustain a rewarding livelihood, or to migrate to urban areas within and outside of Bolivia in search of work. The emphasis of the work is on the strong ties that migrants maintain with their home communities. Daniel W. Gade, the long-time contributing editor for the Western South American Geography section, points out that more research needs to be done on the effect of migration on home communities, including "its effects on the zones of departure in terms of declining villages, abandoned land, and changing land-use" (p. 212). From an international relations perspective, one monograph analyzes US immigration policy in the Caribbean, focusing on the domestic and foreign policies of the host countries (item **2076**). Sociological studies on migration have shifted from demographic to ethnographic in nature.

The publication of *HLAS 65* comes during a year when terrible natural disasters have occurred in Latin America. Devastating earthquakes struck in Haiti, Chile, and Mexico, and mudslides forced the relocation of thousands living in favelas on the outskirts of Rio de Janeiro. Even Corcovado National Park, home of O Cristo Redentor and recently declared one of the New Seven Wonders of the World, was forced to close temporarily. The catastrophic earthquake that hit Haiti on January 12, 2010, destroyed vast sections of the capital city of Port-au-Prince. Over 200,000 people perished in the earthquake, and many more were injured and/or lost their homes, businesses, schools, etc. The United Nations, national governments, and NGOs including universities and libraries throughout the world scrambled to the aid of the poorest nation in Latin America, with citizens from around the globe donating food, clothing, and even cash donations via cutting-edge cellular phone technology. Joan Higbee, contributing editor for Francophone Caribbean government and politics and Specialist in the Caribbean Area in the Hispanic Division of the Library of Congress, quickly responded to the devastating quake by attempting to contact her Haitian colleagues and, with their guidance, selected over 200 Web sites to be archived by the Library of Congress for future research and study. Not surprisingly, it was the existing rural organizations within Haiti that emerged as leaders in the post-earthquake relief environment, as Haitians fled the city and sought refuge in rural areas in droves. In her essay introducing the Caribbean government and politics section, Higbee mentions two cybercasts from a day-long event at the Library of Congress in 2009 in which the Haitian peasant movement is documented: *http://www.loc.gov/today/cyberlc/feature_wdesc.php?rec=4799* and *http://www.loc.gov/today/cyberlc/feature_wdesc.php?rec=4804*. These valuable sites and others that are available on the Internet will continue to disseminate details about the rich tradition and valuable heritage of Haitian rural peasant organizations and agronomers' histories for future research.

II. CLOSING DATE

With some exceptions, the closing date for works annotated in this volume was 2009. Publications received and cataloged at the Library of Congress after that date will be annotated in the next social sciences volume, *HLAS 67*. In consultation with the *HLAS* Advisory Board, in recent years the *Handbook* has begun to pay closer attention to publication dates of materials considered for review. We are more stringent about including only works published in the previous five years.

III. ELECTRONIC ACCESS TO THE *HANDBOOK*

Web Site

The *Handbook's* Web site, *HLAS Online*, continues to offer, free of charge, all bibliographic records corresponding to *HLAS* volumes 1–65. Records that did not appear in a print volume may or may not be annotated, and newer records are in a preliminary editorial stage. The Web site also includes a list of *HLAS* subject headings, a list of journal titles and the corresponding journal abbreviations found in *HLAS* records, tables of contents for volumes 50–63 and linked introductory essays for volumes 50–57 (*http://www.loc.gov/hlas/contents.html*), as well as introductory essays for volumes 1–49, which are searchable in the database by using the phrase "general statement." The web address for *HLAS Online* is *http://www.loc.gov/hlas/*. The site is updated weekly. *HLAS Online* is an OpenURL source, allowing seamless linking from *HLAS* entries to related electronic resources available at your local institution, including full text access to articles if they are available and part of a subscription resource at your institution. One major improvement to the *HLAS* citations is the inclusion of the full journal title for articles. We hope this additional piece of information helps patrons and librarians alike in locating materials.

HLAS Web

HLAS records from volumes 50 onward may also be searched through *HLAS Web*. Searches may be limited by language, publication date, place of publication, and type of material (book or journal article). The address for *HLAS Web* is *http://hlasopac.loc.gov/*, and it is also linked from the *HLAS Online* home page. In addition, selected bibliographic records in the Library of Congress Online Catalog (*http://catalog.loc.gov/*) contain *HLAS* annotations.

CD-ROM

Volumes 1–55 (1935–96) of the *Handbook* are available on the *Handbook of Latin American Studies: CD-ROM: HLAS/CD (v. 2.0)*. This retrospective version is produced by the Fundación Histórica TAVERA (Madrid) and distributed for them by DIGIBIS. For ordering information, contact DIGIBIS:

DIGIBIS Producciones Digitales
Calle Claudio Coello, 123, 4a planta
28006 Madrid SPAIN
Tel. 00 34 91 581 20 01
Fax. 00 34 91 581 47 36
http://www.digibis.com/colecciones_cd_referencia.htm

IV. CHANGES FROM PREVIOUS SOCIAL SCIENCES VOLUME

Anthropology

William Keegan, the Caribbean Archeology contributing editor, passed the baton to Scott Fitzpatrick, North Carolina State University, beginning with Vol. 65. Donna Nash, University of Chicago, joined Betty J. Meggers of the Smithsonian Institution to collaborate on the South American Archeology section. Robin Wright, University of Florida, Gainesville, has rejoined *HLAS* as the contributing editor for Brazilian Ethnology. He shares the workload of the South American Lowlands with Bartholomew Dean and Silvia María Hirsch.

Economics

Volume 65 is the final volume in which the Economics chapter will appear. To that end, there are gaps in coverage as we transition the coverage of these materials to other chapters, mainly Political Economy but also Geography and Sociology, among others. Luis René Cáceres from the Inter-American Development Bank graciously reviewed General works in addition to continuing his coverage of Central America.

Geography

In addition to covering Central America, Peter H. Herlihy, University of Kansas, took on the task of reviewing materials on Mexican Geography. With this volume, Joseph Scarpaci began reviewing materials on Caribbean Geography. Christian Brannstrom of Texas A&M University demonstrated a masterful comprehensiveness in his compilation of the section on Brazilian Geography.

Government and Politics

Charles Brockett, Sewanee: The University of the South, is now handling the Central America Government and Politics section.

International Relations

Following in G. Pope Atkins footsteps, Mary Meyer McAleese of Simmons College began coverage of the General International Relations section.

Political Economy

Barbara Kotschwar, Research Associate at the Peterson Institute for International Economics and Adjunct Professor at Georgetown University, canvassed materials on Political Economy of Bolivia and Peru. Ana Margheritis of the University of Florida, Gainesville, ably reviewed Political Economy materials on Argentina, Uruguay, and Paraguay.

Sociology

Notwithstanding a tight timeline, Daniel Hilliard, Executive Director of the Zoo Conservation Outreach Group and Adjunct Assistant Professor at the Georgetown Public Policy Institute, waded through a large amount of materials on Brazil, along with assistance from *HLAS* Humanities Editor Katherine McCann. Hilliard's connection with his PhD advisor and former *HLAS* contributing editor for Brazilian Sociology, J. Timmons Roberts (vols. 59 and 61), is evident in the high quality of his submission. He also enjoyed the subject expertise and editorial assistance of his colleague at Tulane University, Meredith Dudley.

V. ACKNOWLEDGMENTS

As with each *HLAS* volume, Volume 65 presented unique challenges to staff and contributing editors alike. In the *HLAS* office, we have a revolving door of interns and temporary staff members who demonstrate a keen sense of awareness of the goals and direction of this massive undertaking; they are bright, inquisitive, helpful, and dedicated. Contributing editors, pressed for carving out time in their busy lives in a way that seems unprecedented, have responded to our requests for a rapid turn-around of materials by suppplying us with outstanding, comprehensive submissions that together present a clear picture of the current state of research and publishing for Latin America.

Volume 65 marks the end of *HLAS* tenure for two distinguished contributing editors, David W. Dent, Professor Emeritus, Towson University, and Daniel W. Gade, Professor Emeritus, The University of Vermont. Both continued their service to *HLAS* after retirement from their university obligations. We are grateful for their decades-long commitment to this annotated bibliography.

Tracy North, *Social Sciences Editor*

ANTHROPOLOGY

GENERAL

1   Chamanismo y sacrificio: perspectivas arqueológicas y etnológicas en sociedades indígenas de América del Sur. Edición de Jean-Pierre Chaumeil *et al.* Bogotá: Fundación de Investigaciones Arqueológicas Nacionales: Banco de la República: Instituto Francés de Estudios Andinos, 2005. 368 p.: bibl., ill. (some col.). (Travaux de l'Institut francais d'études andines; 179)

The collected works in this volume present a number of themes related to shamanism, ritual, and myth based on archeological, ethnographic, and ethnohistoric sources from Colombia, Ecuador, and Peru. Authors address a number of themes related to the role of shamans, the transition of shamanism to priesthood, sacrifice, transformation, offerings, astronomy, and calendrical observances. [D. Nash]

2   Extraordinary anthropology: transformations in the field. Edited by Jean-Guy A. Goulet and Bruce Granville Miller. Preface by Johannes Fabian. Lincoln: Univ. of Nebraska Press, 2007. 456 p.: bibl., index.

A gripping collection of 16 cases where anthropologists became lost and transformed by their field experiences, where the separations made by anthropologists from their subjects and their field experience are eroded by the intensity of direct experience and their emotional responses to it. Tells the tales not told in the standard ethnography. [D. Earle]

3   Feminist anthropology: past, present, and future. Edited by Pamela L. Geller and Miranda K. Stockett. Philadelphia: Univ. of Pennsylvania Press, 2006. 226 p.: bibl., index.

Thorough discussion of feminist anthropological thinking in both the past and present. The future trajectory of feminist research in anthropology is also considered. Contributors include representatives from the archeological, cultural, and biological subdisciplines of anthropology. Focal issues include heteronormativity, performativity, materiality, pedagogy, identity, and difference. Important contribution on the practice and politics of feminist anthropology. [A. Joyce]

4   Historia de un olvido: la expedición científica del Pacífico (1862–1865): Museo de América, diciembre 2003—mayo 2004. Spain: Ministerio de Educación, Cultura y Deporte, 2003. 237 p.: bibl., col. ill., col. maps.

This exposition catalog celebrates La Expedición Científica del Pacifico (1862–1865) conducted by a group of naturalists from Spain. The volume illustrates ethnographic and archeological materials collected during the expedition from several South American countries. The introductory material details the expedition as well as other Spanish scientific explorations of interest to historians of the era. [D. Nash]

ARCHEOLOGY
Mesoamerica

JOHN HENDERSON, *Professor of Anthropology, Cornell University*
ARTHUR A. JOYCE, *Associate Professor of Anthropology, University of Colorado at Boulder*

SOCIAL ARCHEOLOGY—emphasizing interpretation of the social dimensions of ancient Maya societies using anthropological models, often focusing on the everyday practices of social life, remains a popular conceptual approach among Maya archeologists. Interpretation of the social relations of craft production (items **122, 124, 149, 158,** and **170**) is an increasingly popular focus; spatial organization (items **172, 206,** and **215**) and gender roles (items **136** and **213**) continue to be well represented.

Despite the long-standing and intensifying trend toward social perspectives in Maya studies, descriptive work remains strong, especially in Mexico and Central America (items **153, 160, 161, 175, 184, 197,** and **199**). Descriptive reports on field investigations—excavation projects (items **143, 153, 160, 165, 175,** and **179**); settlement pattern studies (items **130, 137, 167,** and **221**); analyses of ancient environments, agriculture, and ecology (items **155** and **216**); studies of ancient technology and sources of raw material (items **125, 148,** and **149**)—are well represented. Traditional problems in cultural history, notably the Maya "collapse" (items **22, 155,** and **171**), continue to be a major theme, though social dimensions are often emphasized.

Ancient Maya political geography (items **132, 156, 167,** and **190**), the institutions surrounding kingship in Maya states (items **98** and **236**), and ritual and belief (item **13**) are enduring concerns in Maya studies. The human body, especially its mortuary treatment, is a major emphasis in terms of both reconstructing ancient Maya beliefs and employing bioarcheological approaches (items **57, 80, 139, 163, 193, 194,** and **222**).

Epigraphic analyses of ancient Maya texts (items **233** and **239**) are increasingly nuanced in reconstructing grammar and syntax. The Maya calendar has re-emerged as a focus, bringing new understandings of grammar and syntax to bear on calendar recording as well as its political uses (items **98** and **226**). Traditional approaches to interpretation of meaning (item **13**) also continue to be represented.

The recent inclination to think of archeological research and writing and archeological remains in relation to living peoples is intensifying, and collaborations between archeologists and descendant communities are increasingly common (items **18, 102,** and **218**).

The effects of looting, collecting, and the antiquities market and the ethical implications of archeologists' use of unprovenienced material are, remarkably, hardly reflected in the literature (item **168**). [JSH]

NORTHERN MESOAMERICA

Important themes in recent publications on the archeology of northern Mesoamerica include research on religion, ideology, and politics; gender and identity; interregional interaction; economy and subsistence; and artifact-based studies, as well as more general regional and site-based syntheses. There has been a decline in publications on landscape, space, and settlement during the period under review.

University presses continue to be important publication venues for the archeology of northern Mesoamerica. The presses that publish extensively on northern Mesoamerican archeology include the University Press of Colorado, the University of Texas Press, and the University of Utah Press. Important monograph series are published by the Cotsen Institute of Archaeology at the University of California at Los Angeles, the University of Pittsburgh, and the University of Michigan. In Mexico, the *Colección Científica* series of the Instituto Nacional de Antropología e Historia (INAH) publishes many important field reports and monographs. Important professional journals focusing on Mesoamerican archeology are *Latin American Antiquity, Ancient Mesoamerica, Arqueología,* and *Mexicon. Arqueología Mexicana* publishes short accessible articles on Mexican archeology for a more popular audience.

Diverse general overviews of northern Mesoamerican archeology include regional summaries on the states of Guanajuato (items **17** and **78**), Guerrero (item **104**), and classic-period Veracruz (item **23**), as well as the Sayula Basin, Jalisco (item **10**), the Otopame of Central Mexico (item **36**), the Huasteca (item **58**), the Mixteca (items **67** and **108**), the southern Highlands and Pacific Coast (item **71**), epiclassic Central Mexico (item **96**), and Aztec city-states (item **106**). Blomster (item **5**) edits an important volume on the Oaxacan postclassic (also see item **84**); Lowe and Pye (item **7**) edit a volume in honor of Gareth Lowe that focuses on the Formative period; Pollard (item **93**) presents a model for the development of the Tarascan state; and Pool (item **94**) presents a comprehensive overview of the Olmec. *Arqueología Mexicana* published a series of brief overviews of Mesoamerican archeology by time period, including the Paleo-Indian and Archaic (item **43**), early and middle preclassic (item **44**), late preclassic (item **89**), classic (item **69**), and epiclassic (item **79**). Marrow and Gnecco (item **85**) summarize Paleo-Indian archeology in the Americas, including Mexico. Site-based summaries have been written on Tula (item **24**), Chalco (item **72**), Teotihuacán (item **28**), San Lorenzo (items **29** and **142**), Tututepec (item **62**), Cerro de la Estrella (item **90**), La Organera-Xochipala (item **97**), Cerro de las Minas (item **118**), El Polvorín (item **176**), Ranas and Toluquilla (item **182**), Chapultepec (item **150**), and Yucundaa (item **202**). Valencia Cruz (item **35**) discusses issues of cultural patrimony and preservation in Querétero; Vásquez León (item **114**) critically examines archeological discourse and practice in Mexico; Geurds (item **154**) discusses community-based archeology in Oaxaca; and Winter (item **119**) discusses the life and work of Ronald Spores.

There has been a rise in publications concerning religion, ideology, and politics over the last several years. A major focus of research has drawn on archeological, iconographic, and ethnohistorical evidence to investigate the politics, religious belief, and ritual of the late postclassic and early colonial period Aztec (items **12, 33, 48, 49, 68, 75, 82, 83, 100, 111, 144, 223, 224, 228,** and **229**). General studies of religion and ritual in other regions include the Huaxteca (items **42** and **61**), Olmec (items **47, 50,** and **110**), and colonial period Chiapas (item **164**). Another major topic of study is mortuary ritual represented by publications on the shaft tombs of West Mexico (items **15, 16, 70, 128, 131, 174,** and **177**), the Moon Pyramid sacrifices at Teotihuacán (items **133, 200, 209,** and **220**), skulls recovered from the Cueva de la Calendaria in central Mexico (items **135** and **189**), and early cremation burials in Oaxaca (item **146**), as well as general regional studies of funerary customs in the Gulf Coast (item **25**) and human alterations of mortuary remains (item **183**). Studies that focus on ritual also include the origins of the central Mexican Old God of Fire and the Storm God (item **19**), the history of the Volador ritual (item **112**), Middle Formative ritual feasting in the Soconusco (item **101**), ball courts at the site of Cantona (item **120**), and the early colonial period Zapotec calendar (item **244**), as well as edited volumes on commoner ritual and ideology (item **26**) and the relationship between ritual and economy in Mesoamerica (item **76**). De la Cruz published a major study of Zapotec (Binnigula'sa') religion, worldview, and calendrics that synthesizes archeological, ethnohistoric, linguistic, and ethnographic evidence (item **32**). Other themes include research on the symbolic significance of petroglyphs in northern and western Mexico (items **105** and **115**), as well as iconographic studies from Chalcatzingo (item **27**) and Las Higueras (item **240**) and potbelly sculptures of Pacific coastal Guatemala and El Salvador (item **212**).

There has been an increase in research on the Mixtec codices addressing issues of religion and political history (items **230** and **245**), including a special issue of the journal *Desacatos* (items **231, 232, 234, 242, 243,** and **246**) and a major edited volume (item **238**). Other important epigraphic studies include a study of the history of the word cacao (item **235**) and a study of the Spearthrower Owl Hill toponym from Teotihuacán, which has important implications for contacts with the Maya Lowlands (item **241**). Rodríguez Martínez *et al.* present an important article on Olmec inscriptions that represent the earliest writing yet discovered in the New World (item **99**).

Works that focus on political organization and process include Beekman's study of corporate power strategies in the Tequila Valleys (item **15**), Haskell's consideration of political hierarchy in the Tarascan state (item **52**), Elson's study of a secondary administrative center in the Oaxaca Valley (item **34**), and the study of the political significance of Teotihuacán's Moon Pyramid by Sugiyama and Cabrera Castro (item **210**). Important edited volumes include a collection of articles on the political significance of palaces by Christie and Sarro (*HLAS 63:14*) and the edited volume by Cyphers and Hirth in honor of David Grove, which focuses on ideology and society in Formative Period Mesoamerica (item **59**). Warfare in ancient Mexico has been another important research theme with debates concerning the nature, scale, causes, and effects of conflict (items **53, 60, 66, 92,** and **201**).

Publications on social identity, especially gender, have increased. General overviews of gender in prehispanic Mesoamerica include Arden (item **8**) and Joyce (item **63**) as well as chapters in an edited volume on feminist anthropology (item **3**); gender and households (item **45**); and gender, ritual, and sustainability in rural Tlaxcala (item **46**). Begun considers figurines as markers of ethnic identity in Michoacán (item **127**).

Research on interregional interaction continues as an important theme in northern Mesoamerican publications. Recent research includes the impact of Teotihuacán in northern Yucatán (item **107**), the impact of the Olmec in Chiapas (item **117**), the Protohistoric Tarascan-Aztec frontier (item **54**), isotopic studies of human mobility (item **185**), ceramic exchange in southern Veracruz (item **208**), and world systems-based studies (items **6** and **21**). Trade routes are examined for Highland Mesoamerica (item **20**) and between Oaxaca and the Gulf Coast (items **40** and **51**). Studies of exchange based on obsidian source analyses continue to be important (items **134, 188,** and **198**).

Research on economy and subsistence continues to focus on craft production involving ceramics (items **9, 31, 38, 55, 138, 151, 178, 186,** and **211**), textiles (item **41**), obsidian (items **30** and **56**), copper (item **73**), and shell artifacts (item **214**), as well as more general overviews of craft production (item **74**). Studies of prehispanic subsistence include agricultural practices in the Gulf Coast (items **64** and **109**) and the exploitation of aquatic resources in the basin of Mexico (items **86** and **87**). Perry *et al.* report on the use of starch fossils to identify chili peppers (item **91**) and Adrian-Morán and McClung de Tapia (item **121**) look at wood use at Teotihuacán. King considers the social significance of domestic food sharing in coastal Oaxaca (item **166**). Minc proposes methods for examining market systems in ancient Mesoamerica with a focus on the Aztec (item **77**). Research involving the intraregional exchange of ceramics and political economy include studies in the Gulf Coast (items **95** and **205**) and the Valley of Oaxaca (item **147**).

Artifact-based studies continue, although there is a decline in publications on ceramic typologies and chronologies. Lithic studies include an overview of uses of obsidian in Mesoamerica (item **181**) and a comprehensive edited volume on lithic artifacts and industries in prehispanic Mexico (item **187**). Sax *et al.* determine that two purportedly prehispanic crystal skulls are fakes (item **191**). Other studies include research on bitumen use among the Olmec (items **116** and **219**), iconographic research on Zapotec effigy vessels (item **195**), and a study of artifacts with representations of urban architecture (item **192**). Barba presents an important summary of research on chemical residues from plaster floors (item **11**).

Publications dealing with landscape, space, and settlement declined considerably in recent years. Significant publications include Kowalewski's (item **65**) review of regional settlement pattern studies, while Stark and Garraty (item **204**) assess the effects of topography, vegetation, and surface visibility on surface survey results in Veracruz. Parsons (item **88**) presents results of settlement survey in the Zumpango region of the Valley of Mexico. Borejsza (item **129**) examines the history of agricultural terracing and land-use at La Laguna, Tlaxcala.

I would like to thank Jessica Hedgepeth and Sarah Jennings for assistance with the annotated bibliography. [AAJ]

GENERAL

5 **After Monte Albán: transformation and negotiation in Oaxaca, Mexico.** Edited by Jeffrey P. Blomster. Boulder, Colo.: Univ. Press of Colorado, 2008. 438 p.: bibl., ill., index, maps. (Mesoamerican worlds)

Chapters discuss the sociopolitical transformations and continuities after the late classic collapse of states in Oaxaca. Case studies consist of polities in the Valley of Oaxaca, Mixteca Alta, and the Lower Río Verde Valley. Authors draw on a variety of data, including ethnohistoric documents, codices, architecture, ceramics, and other forms of material culture. Volume emphasizes the central role of Oaxaca in inter-regional networks of the postclassic period and the cultural inventiveness which characterized Oaxacan polities at this time. [AAJ]

6 **Alexander, Rani T.** The world according to Robert: macroregional systems theory in Mesoamerica. (*J. Anthropol. Res.*, 64:3, Fall 2008, p. 383–394)

Reviews Robert Santley's approaches to understanding Mesoamerican issues, including the spread of Teotihuacán material culture to other areas of Mesoamerica and macroregional economic systems. Outlines unresolved questions in the archeological use of world-systems theory as applied to Mesoamerica. Discusses how recent research on trade diasporas applies to the data from Matacapan and considers new directions for research. [AAJ]

7 **Archaeology, art, and ethnogenesis in Mesoamerican prehistory: papers in honor of Gareth W. Lowe.** Edited by Lynneth S. Lowe and Mary E. Pye. Provo, Utah: New World Archaeological Foundation, Brigham Young Univ., 2007. 362 p.: bibl., ill., maps. (Papers of the New World Archaeological Foundation; 68)

Collection of papers in honor of Gareth W. Lowe presented at an SAA symposium in Salt Lake City in 2005. Volume begins by discussing his life and research. Remaining contributions focus on the archeology of Chiapas, the Guatemalan coast, the Isthmus of Tehuantepec, Morelos, and the Northern Maya lowlands. Archeological studies examine topics such as the origins of civilization in central Chiapas, Archaic Period subsistence, and formative period interaction, monuments, and material culture. [AAJ]

8   Arden, Traci. Studies of gender in the prehispanic Americas. (*J. Archaeol. Res.*, 16:1, March 2008, p. 1–35, bibl.)

Defines key concepts and identifies three major themes within gender studies in Mesoamerica: gender in native cosmologies, intersections of gender and the body, and studies of work and specializations. Discusses contributions of engendered archeology to the broader field and makes suggestions for linkages with queer studies and indigenous feminism. [AAJ]

9   Arnold, Dean E. Social change and the evolution of ceramic production and distribution in a Maya community. Boulder: Univ. Press of Colorado, 2008. 351 p.: bibl., graphs, index, maps, photos, tables. (Mesoamerican worlds)

An ethnoarcheological study of the changes in ceramic production at the community of Ticul from 1965–97. Chapters focus on the shifts which occurred at each stage of the production process, including clay procurement, temper procurement, clay composition, forming methods, and firing technology. Social changes in the Ticul potter community and shifts in the consumption and distribution of ceramics are also investigated. Book has important implications for archeological studies of ceramic specialization. [AAJ]

10   Arqueología de la Cuenca de Sayula. Edición de Francisco Valdez, Otto Schöndube, y Jean Pierre Emphoux. Guadalajara, Mexico: Univ. de Guadalajara; Mexico City: Institut de recherche pour le développement, 2005. 473 p.: bibl., ill., maps.

Analysis of the distinctive occupational stages of Sayula, one of the biggest lacustrine basins in Jalisco. Principle objective is to understand economic and political development of the local population, from the first settlement of the Sayula region to the Spanish conquest. Chapters present analyses of cultural remains recovered from the basin, focusing on the social transformations of landscape, architecture, and funerary patterns. A useful regional overview of the sociocultural makeup of the Mexican Occidental region. [AAJ]

Baquedano, Elizabeth. El oro azteca y sus conexiones con el poder, la fertilidad agrícola, la guerra y la muerte. See *HLAS 64:190.*

11   Barba, Luis A. Chemical residues in lime-plastered archaeological floors. (*Geoarchaeology/New York*, 22:4, April 2007, p. 439–452, bibl., ill., map)

Discussion of the study of chemical residues in stuccoes, specifically lime-plastered floors such as those used in Mesoamerica after the classic period. Details the ethnoarcheological research of UNAM's Laboratorio de Prospección Arqueológica designed to understand the distribution of chemical residues in archeological floors. [AAJ]

12   Barrera Rodríguez, Raúl and **Gabino López Arenas.** Hallazgos en el recinto ceremonial de Tenochtitlan. (*Arqueol. Mex.*, 16:93, sept./oct. 2008, p. 18–25, ill., photos)

Reviews recent investigations of the building Donceles 97 and discusses how the associated sculptures have led researchers to propose that the structure was used as a training ground for religious officials. [AAJ]

13   Bassie-Sweet, Karen. Maya sacred geography and the creator deities. Norman: Univ. of Oklahoma Press, 2008. 359 p.: bibl., ill., index, maps.

Synthesizes Maya worldview and beliefs about the supernatural as they are reflected in precolumbian imagery and hieroglyphic texts and especially in the *Popol Vuh*, a colonial-period Quiche book of myth and legendary history. Argues that events described in classic period (AD 300–1000) texts and imagery from the Maya lowlands as well as those in the *Popol Vuh* refer to a specific location in the Lake Atitlan area of highland Guatemala. [JSH]

14   Beekman, Christopher Stockard. The chronological context of the central Jalisco shaft tombs. (*Anc. Mesoam.*, 17:2, July 2006, p. 239–249)

Details the elaborate characteristics of shaft tombs in the Tequila Valleys that have led some to view the Tequila Valleys as the "core" of the shaft tomb tradition. Reviews Weigand's 1960s settlement survey that utilized surface artifacts and materials from looters' pits to associate ceramics with tombs and public architecture. Discusses current research on the ceramic chronology of the eastern Tequila Valleys. [AAJ]

15   Beekman, Christopher Stockard. Corporate power strategies in the late formative to early classic Tequila Valleys of central Mexico. (*Lat. Am. Antiq.*, 19:4, Dec. 2008, p. 414–434, bibl., ill., map, table)

Examines aspects of corporate political strategies among early complex societies in the Tequila Valleys of West Mexico. Data derived from excavations of multiple sites in the region suggest that corporate, lineage groups competing for power can leave distinct archeological patterns. [AAJ]

16   Beekman, Christopher Stockard and **Luis Javier Galván Villegas.** The shaft tombs of the Atemajac Valley and their relationship to settlement. (*Anc. Mesoam.*, 17:2, July 2006, p. 259–270, bibl., ill., map)

Reviews the excavation of unlooted shaft tombs in the Valley of Guadalajara, Jalisco, which form the primary sample of a shaft tomb cemetery known from western Mexico. Summarizes findings in light of more recent work and argues that the Tabachines cemetery, in particular, provides evidence for significant social inequalities and social changes part way through the Tabachines phase, and that the mortuary ritual practiced in the tombs shares some commonalities with other areas of Mesoamerica. [AAJ]

17   Braniff C., Beatriz. Guanajuato en la historia. (*Arqueol. Mex.*, 16:92, julio/agosto 2008, p. 28–35)

Traces the history of Guanajuato, beginning with early hunter gatherers and ending with the founding of the city of Tula. [AAJ]

18   Breglia, Lisa. Monumental ambivalence: the politics of heritage. Austin: Univ. of Texas Press, 2006. 242 p.: bibl., index. (Joe R. and Teresa Lozano Long series in Latin American and Latino art and culture)

Uses case studies of Chichen Itzá and Chunchucmil, Maya sites in Yucatán, to explore the interests of local communities, workers at archeological sites, archeologists, government agencies, and the Mexican state in cultural patrimony. Concludes that privatization—informal as well as formal—is a growing threat to cultural heritage. [JSH]

Brotherston, Gordon et al. Por ti América: arte pré-colombiana. See item **295**.

19   Carballo, David M. Effigy vessels, religious integration, and the origins of the central Mexico pantheon. (*Anc. Mesoam.*, 18:1, March 2007, p. 53–67, bibl., ill., map, photo, table)

Argues that the origins of two central Mexican deities—the Old God of Fire and the Storm God—can best be understood through contextual analysis of effigy vessels depicting them during later formative periods. By using new examples of such effigy vessels and contemporary counterparts from other central Mexican sites, one can better understand the formative religious integration of the region and its legacy for later Mesoamerican societies. [AAJ]

20   Carballo, David M. and **Thomas Pluckhahn.** Transportation corridors and political evolution in highland Mesoamerica: settlement analyses incorporating GIS for northern Tlaxcala, Mexico. (*J. Anthropol. Archaeol.*, 26:4, Dec. 2007, p. 607–629, bibl., graphs, ill., tables)

Reports investigations of natural transportation corridors in highland central Mexico using GIS. Examines inter-regional exchanges and the evolution of early ceremonial centers, Teotihuacán's territorial expansion through the region, political balkanization following the collapse of Teotihuacán, and the establishment of small, independent polities encountered by the Spanish. Also contributes quantitative measures relevant to assessing the systemic integration of the region and the social value of the corridor during different chronological phases. [AAJ]

21 Carmack, Robert M. and Silvia Salgado González. A world-systems perspective on the archaeology and ethnohistory of the Mesoamerican/lower Central American border. (*Anc. Mesoam.*, 17:2, July 2006, p. 219–229, bibl., map, photos, tables)

Using Spanish colonial sources and archeological information, argues that indigenous peoples along the Pacific Coast of Central America, from El Salvador to the Nicoya Peninsula, were part of the Mesoamerican world-system periphery during the late postclassic. Posits that Central American peoples south of Nicoya formed both a chiefly world-system of their own and part of the Mesoamerican frontier by engaging in networks of trade with the coastal Mesoamericans in Nicoya and Nicaragua. [AAJ]

22 Chase, Diane Z. and Arlen F. Chase. Framing the Maya collapse: continuity, discontinuity, method, and practice in the Classic to Postclassic Southern Maya Lowlands. (*in* After collapse: the regeneration of complex societies. Edited by Glenn M. Schwartz and John J. Nichols. Tucson: Univ. of Arizona Press, 2006, p. 168–187, ill., map)

Discussion of the transformation of lowland Maya societies in the terminal classic period (AD 800–1000). Attributes such features of postclassic (AD 1000–1500) Maya city-states as the absence of architecture and carved monuments designed to celebrate dynastic kings as a rejection of autocratic trends of terminal classic kings and the development of alternative political institutions emphasizing shared power. For review of entire volume, see item **292**. [JSH]

23 Classic period cultural currents in southern and central Veracruz. Edited by Philip J. Arnold III and Christopher A. Pool. Washington, D.C.: Dumbarton Oaks Research Library & Collection; Cambridge, Mass.: Harvard Univ. Press, 2008. 381 p.: bibl., ill., index, maps.

Multidisciplinary study of classic period lifeways in central and southern Veracruz. Contributions include studies by

archeologists, art historians, and linguists on topics including sociopolitical developments, iconography and writing, as well as the relationship between local sites and outside influences. Authors examine sites such as Matacapán, Cerro de las Mesas, Tres Zapotes, and El Tajín. Volume questions the assumption that Veracruz was peripheral to major classic period developments in Mesoamerica. [AAJ]

24 Cobean, Robert H. and Luis M. Gamboa Cabezas. Investigaciones recientes en la zona monumental de Tula, 2002–2006. (*Arqueol. Mex.*, 14:85, mayo/junio 2007, p. 36–41)

Spanning 70 years, the work at Tula has been impressive and is reviewed here. Also discusses the next steps to preserve the site. [AAJ]

25 Coloquio Internacional de Antropología Física "Juan Comas," 11th, Orizaba, Veracruz-Llave, Mexico, 2001. Prácticas funerarias en la costa del Golfo de México. Recopilación de Yamile Lira López y Carlos Serrano Sánchez. Xalapa, Mexico: Univ. Veracruzana, Instituto de Antropología; México: UNAM, Instituto de Investigaciones Antropológicas; Asociación Mexicana de Antropología Biológica, 2004. 229 p.: bibl., ill., maps.

Collection of papers presented at the 11th Coloquio Internacional de Antropología Física "Juan Comas" in Orizaba, Veracruz (2001). Chapters discuss the ancestral funerary customs of prehispanic peoples primarily in the Centro de Veracruz. Burials analyzed in sites including El Tajín, Tabuco, Las Higueras Quiahuiztlan, Chachalacas, el Valle de Maltrata, El Zapotal, El Manatí, and the Tierra Alta in Tamaulipas. Editors encourage the development of interdisciplinary collaboration between archeologists and physical anthropologists. [AAJ]

26 Commoner ritual and ideology in ancient Mesoamerica. Edited by Nancy Gonlin and Jon C. Lohse. Boulder, Colo.: Univ. Press of Colorado, 2006. 304 p.: bibl., index. (Mesoamerican worlds)

Volume discusses the ritual practices of commoners in Mesoamerica. Case studies span the formative through postclassic periods and concern regions including the Valley of Oaxaca, Teotihuacán, Copán,

Cholula, Morelos, and the Naco Valley in Honduras. Authors employ several lines of material evidence to demonstrate commoner status and to investigate the relationship between status and ideational expression. Contributors emphasize that ideology is not confined to elites and the ritual practices of commoners occur both inside and outside the domestic realm. [AAJ]

27   **Córdova Tello, Mario** and **Carolina Meza Rodríguez.** Chalcatzingo, Morelos: un discurso sobre piedra. (*Arqueol. Mex.*, 15:87, sept./oct. 2007, p. 60–65)

Discusses three variants found in the decorations of the monuments at Chalcatzingo, which are considered to be the only representations dating to the middle preclassic in the central highlands. [AAJ]

28   **Cowgill, George L.** An update on Teotihuacan. (*Antiquity/Cambridge*, 82:318, Dec. 2008, p. 962–975, bibl.)

Discusses recent work and research goals at Teotihuacán. Provides information about the people who inhabited Teotihuacán as well as new data on the rise of the city. [AAJ]

29   **Cyphers, Ann.** Surgimiento y decadencia de San Lorenzo, Veracruz: del Ojochi al Nacaste. (*Arqueol. Mex.*, 15:87, sept./oct. 2007, p. 36–42)

Discusses how San Lorenzo was the ideal setting for the growth and development of the Olmec culture and the role of sculpture in the religious and cultural identities of the Olmec people. [AAJ]

30   **Darras, Véronique.** Estrategias para la producción de navajas de obsidiana en la región de Zacapu y la vertiente del Lerma (Michoacán, México) entre el epiclásico y postclásico tardío. (*Anc. Mesoam.*, 19:2, Sept. 2008, p. 243–264, bibl, ill, tables)

Discusses changes in the production of obsidian artifacts from the classic to the late postclassic, highlighting form changes and proposing causes for those changes. [AAJ]

31   **Darras, Véronique** and **Brigitte Faugère.** La cerámica de la cultura Chupícuaro. (*Arqueol. Mex.*, 16:92, julio/agosto 2008, p. 64–69)

Discusses recent archeological findings that provide insight into the economy and technology of fine paste Chupícuaro ceramics. [AAJ]

32   **de la Cruz, Víctor.** El pensamiento de los binnigula'sa': cosmovisión, religión y calendario con especial referencia a los binnizá. México: Instituto Nacional de Antropología e Historia: Centro de Investigaciones y Estudios Superiores en Antropología Social (CIESAS): Casa Juan Pablos; Santa María Ixcotel, Oaxaca: Instituto Estatal de Educación Pública de Oaxaca, 2007. 544 p.: bibl., ill. (Publicaciones de la Casa Chata)

A comprehensive study of Zapotec (Binnigula'sa') culture, religion and calendrics using archeological, ethnohistoric, linguistic, and ethnographical evidence. Traces the history of Zapotec religion and the calendar from the classic period to the time of the Spanish conquest. [AAJ]

33   **Diel, Lori Boornazian.** Till death do us part. (*Anc. Mesoam.*, 18:2, Sept. 2007, p. 243–264, bibl., photo)

Examines marriage statements in Aztec histories that reveal the standardized political nature of matrimony for elite Nahua rulers in late postclassic-period central Mexico. This article focuses on four case studies of unconventional marriages: two which violated established political alliances and two in which aggressions were taken out against royal wives. The case studies reveal increasing political tensions in the Aztec empire that are not obvious when looking at conquest history, as well as the largely hidden role of noblewomen in Aztec politics. [AAJ]

Dull, Robert A. Evidence for forest clearance, agriculture, and human-induced erosion in precolumbian El Salvador. See item **1006.**

34   **Elson, Christina M.** Excavations at Cerro Tilcajete: a Monte Albán II administrative center in the Valley of Oaxaca. Ann Arbor, Mich.: Museum of Anthropology, Univ. of Michigan, 2007. 138 p.: bibl., ill., maps. (Prehistory and human ecology of the Valley of Oaxaca; 14) (Memoirs / Museum of Anthropology, University of Michigan; 42)

Reports excavations at Cerro Tilcajete in the Valley of Oaxaca. Argues that after defeating the Tilcajete region, Monte Albán created a new administrative center at Cerro Tilcajete. Discusses the nature of Cerro Tilcajete's ties to Monte Albán, especially between elite families. [AAJ]

35   El estudio y la conservación del patrimonio histórico de Querétaro. Coordinación de Daniel J. Valencia Cruz. Querétaro, Mexico: Centro INAH Querétaro, 2005. 133 p.: bibl., ill., map.

A short study of issues relating to the research and conservation of cultural patrimony in the state of Querétaro in central Mexico. Chapter topics include prehispanic iconography, Querétaro museums, perceptions of cultural patrimony, and the conservation of La Virgen de los Dolores del Templo de Santa Rosa de Viterbo. Argues that the Museo Regional de Querétaro is an essential entity for the continuity of historical memory. [AAJ]

36   Estudios de Cultura Otopame. No. 5, 2006. Coordinación de Yolanda Lastra y Ana María Salazar. México: UNAM, Instituto de Investigaciones Antropológicas. 317 p.: bibl., ill.

A diverse collection of anthropological, archeological, and ethnohistorical studies on the history and culture of Otopame peoples. Contributions range from an archeological study of prehispanic burials in Hupalcalco, Hidalgo, to an investigation of modern, public gender relations in the Valle del Mezquital, located in Central Mexico. [AAJ]

37   European Maya Conference, 7th, British Museum, 2002. Jaws of the underworld: life, death, and rebirth among the Ancient Maya: 7th European Maya Conference, The British Museum, London, November 2002. Edited by Pierre R. Colas, Geneviève LeFort, and Bodil Liljefors Persson. Markt Schwaben, Germany: Anton Saurwein, 2006. 112 p.: bibl., ill., maps. (Acta Mesoamericana; 16)

Collection of papers on beliefs about death and rebirth among the Maya. Emphasizes evidence from precolumbian imagery and hieroglyphic texts. Also includes a summary of archeological evidence for mortuary practice in the Maya world and an analysis of the effect of colonial period disease and famine on Maya beliefs about death. [JSH]

38   Feinman, Gary M. and Linda Nicholas. La producción artesanal en Oaxaca. (*Arqueol. Mex.*, 14:80, julio/agosto 2006, p. 36–43)

Examines domestic production of a variety of products for exchange at the sites of Ejutla and El Palmillo in Oaxaca. [AAJ]

39   Feinman, Gary M.; Linda M. Nicholas; and Edward F. Maher. Domestic offerings at El Palmillo. (*Anc. Mesoam.*, 19:2, Sept. 2008, p. 175–194, bibl., ill., map, photos, tables)

Examines the internal organization and interconnectedness of the classic-period settlement of El Palmillo, in the valley of Oaxaca. Discusses investigations of domestic offerings from both commoner and elite residence, revealing both hierarchical and non-hierarchical variations among assemblages. Concludes that El Palmillo barrios may have been defined by ideological concepts as well as economic realities. [AAJ]

Filini, Agapi. Agencia y relaciones intra-elites en la cuenca de Cuitzeo durante el periodo clásico. See *HLAS 64:218.*

40   Flannery, Kent V. and Joyce Marcus. Las sociedades jerárquicas oaxaqueñas y el intercambio con los olmecas. (*Arqueol. Mex.*, 15:87, sept./oct. 2007, p. 71–76)

Discusses the exchange of material goods and ideas between the Olmec and Oaxaca. [AAJ]

41   Follensbee, Billie. Fiber technology and weaving in formative-period Gulf Coast cultures. (*Anc. Mesoam.*, 19:1, March 2008, p. 87–110, bibl, ill.)

Examines the importance of textiles in early Mesoamerican cultures such as the formative-period Olmec. While poor preservation has left minimal fiber evidence, additional evidence of textiles is available through other material culture, such as the pictorial record of fibers and cloth shown in Olmec sculpture, textile-related ceramics, greenstone elite textile making tools, and "heirloom caches." Argues that the Olmec already held not only textiles but textile making in high esteem. [AAJ]

42   Fuente, Beatriz de la. La escultura huaxteca. (*Arqueol. Mex.*, 14:79, mayo/junio 2006, p. 38–41)

Reviews the stone sculptures of the Huastec culture as a fountain of information on their cosmological views and the physical characteristics of their population. [AAJ]

43 García-Bárcena, Joaquín. Etapa lítica: 30000–2000 A.C. (*Arqueol. Mex.,* 15:86, julio/agosto 2007, p. 30–33)

Traces the history of hunter-gatherer groups in Mesoamerican prehistory. [AAJ]

44 García Moll, Roberto. Preclásico temprano y medio, 2500–400 A.C. (*Arqueol. Mex.,* 15:86, julio/agosto 2007, p. 34–39)

Article traces the history of agricultural development in Mesoamerica and the impact it had on the inhabitants. [AAJ]

45 Gender, households, and society: unraveling the threads of the past and the present. Edited by Cynthia Robin and Elizabeth M. Brumfiel. Malden, Mass.: Blackwell; Arlington, Va.: American Anthropological Association, 2008. 124 p.: bibl., ill., maps. (Archeological papers of the American Anthropological Association; 18)

Chapters examine gender roles, gender identities, and the organization of domestic labor in Mesoamerican, Andean, and North African archeological sites including Teotihuacán, Maya, Oaxaca, and coastal Guatemala. The volume's central argument is that models of prehistoric societies tend to posit an inflexible, binary gender system. [AAJ]

46 Género, ritual y desarrollo sostenido en comunidades rurales de Tlaxcala. Coordinación de Pilar Alberti Manzanares. México: Colegio de Postgraduados, Área de Género—Mujer Rural: Plaza y Valdés, 2004. 305 p.: bibl., ill., map.

Multidisciplinary study of the role of women in ritual and agriculture in the rural community of Santa Maria Nativitas, Tlaxcala. Volume integrates agronomy, anthropology, and archeology and focuses on issues of race and sustained development. Explores the relationship between women's roles in present-day Tlaxcala to those of women in the prehispanic archeological sites of Xochitecatl and Cacaxtla. [AAJ]

47 Gonzalez Lauck, Rebecca B. El complejo A: La Venta, Tabasco. (*Arqueol. Mex.,* 15:87, sept./oct. 2007, p. 49–54)

Explores the cultural and ritual importance of Complex A, not only in terms of the tribute found underneath the platform, but in the complex construction of the platform itself. [AAJ]

Gordon R. Willey and American archaeology: contemporary perspectives. See item 298.

48 Graulich, Michel. Autosacrifice in ancient Mexico. (*Estud. Cult. Náhuatl,* 36, 2005, p. 301–329, bibl.)

A detailed analysis of the practice of autosacrifice in ancient Mesoamerica. Discusses the mythical origins of autosacrifice, participants in the ritual, instruments used, and contexts in which autosacrifice took place. Also examines the political, social, and symbolic significance of the act. Focuses on Aztec autosacrificial practices. Argues that autosacrifice was conducted by humans in order to conciliate the gods. For ethnohistorian's comment, see *HLAS 64:225.* [AAJ]

49 Graulich, Michel. Le sacrifice humain chez les Aztèques. Paris: Fayard, 2005. 415 p.: bibl.

Comprehensive examination of human sacrifice among the Aztecs. Chapters discuss the myths behind human sacrifice, the festivals or other contexts in which it was practiced, the social positions of victims and sacrificers, and the customs involved in the rite itself. Emphasis is on understanding human sacrifice as a state-sponsored practice which facilitated societal integration. [AAJ]

50 Grove, David C. Cerros sagrados olmecas: montañas en la cosmovisión mesoamericana. (*Arqueol. Mex.,* 15:87, sept./oct. 2007, p. 30–35)

Highlights the significance of mountains in the prehistory of Mesoamerica, particularly in creation stories where they are thought to be the places where ancestors and spirits reside. [AAJ]

51 Gutiérrez Mendoza, Gerardo. De los valles centrales de Oaxaca al Golfo de México. (*Arqueol. Mex.,* 14:81, sept./oct. 2006, p. 32–36)

Geographic and archeological analysis demonstrates that a complex web of prehispanic routes, rather than one direct route, led from the central valleys of Oaxaca to the coastal plain of the Gulf of Mexico, corresponding with historic and modern roads. [AAJ]

52 Haskell, David L. The cultural logic of hierarchy in the Tarascan state. (*Anc. Mesoam.*, 19:2, Sept. 2008, p. 231–241, bibl, ill, table)

Proposes that the historical narrative contained in the Relación de Michoacán is concerned with legitimizing the rule of the Tarascan royal dynasty through the cultural logic of hierarchy. Outlines a model of elite interaction and the development of the Tarascan state in which the royal dynasty sought to monopolize foreign trade goods, thus materially constructing its own identity as a possessor of legitimate authority while at the same time, creating a class of status markers that could be shared with the lesser nobility, conferring legitimacy on them while preserving the legitimacy of the royal dynasty. [AAJ]

53 Hassig, Ross. La guerra en la antigua mesoamérica. (*Arqueol. Mex.*, 14:84, marzo/abril 2007, p. 32–40)

Discusses the history of war in Mesoamerica and examines how there is no one single underlying cause of its various occurrences. [AAJ]

54 Hernández, Christine L. and Dan M. Healan. The role of late classic precontact colonial enclaves in the development of the postclassic Ucareo Valley, Michoacán, Mexico. (*Anc. Mesoam.*, 19:2, Sept. 2008, p. 265–282, bibl., ill., photos, tables)

Discusses information from ethnohistoric sources that northeastern Michoacan was a multi-ethnic region when it was incorporated into the eastern frontier of the Tarascan Empire in the mid-1400s. Reports data from recent investigation in the Ucareo-Zinapecuaro source area that uncovered evidence of an earlier foreign enclave consisting of two settlements in the Ucareo Valley. Considers the implications of these data alongside Ucareo obsidian exploitation and its role in the construction of the Protohistoric Tarascan-Aztec frontier, along with results of preliminary chronometric dating. [AAJ]

55 Hirshman, Amy J. Tarascan ceramic production and implications for ceramic distribution. (*Anc. Mesoam.*, 19:2, Sept. 2008, p. 299–310, bibl, photos, tables)

Argues that markets and political economies are part of the continuum of strategies used by elites to create the larger political economy of a state. Considers the contradiction between ethnohistoric evidence suggesting that Tarascan state ceramics were produced under central control and the lack of direct evidence for ceramic production in the Tarascan core. Argues that ceramic data from Urichu, Michoacán, indicate that ceramic production was not under centralized political control. Ceramics were produced locally and distributed using the market mechanisms of the larger mix of economic strategies on the part of the Tarascan political elite. [AAJ]

56 Hirth, Kenn. The economy of supply: modeling obsidian procurement and craft provisioning at a central Mexican urban center. (*Lat. Am. Antiq.*, 19:4, Dec. 2008, p. 385–406, bibl., ill., maps, tables)

Authors suggest that by using multiple lines of evidence, various forms of craft provisioning can be differentiated. The author uses the results of source and technological analysis of obsidian from domestic workshops at Xochicalco, Mexico to argue that independent, domestic craft specialists were the foundation of the Mesoamerican economy and were responsible for the procurement of raw resources and the distribution of final products without the involvement of elite institutions. [AAJ]

57 Houston, Stephen D.; David Stuart; and Karl Taube. The memory of bones: body, being, and experience among the classic Maya. Austin: Univ. of Texas Press, 2006. 324 p.: bibl., index.

Explores Maya thought, imagery, and writing through concepts relating to the body: body parts, body modifications, body adornment and costume, bodily functions, sensory experience, and indiectly related notions including emotions, honor, music, speech and its characterization. Focuses on classic period (AD 250–900) texts and imagery, but draws on later historical and ethnographic sources to extend interpretation. [JSH]

58 La Huasteca, un recorrido por su diversidad. Coordinación de Jesús Ruvalcaba Mercado, Juan Manuel Pérez Zevallos y Octavio Herrera. Mexico: CIESAS: El Colegio de San Luis, A.C.: El Colegio de

Tamaulipas, 2004. 380 p.: bibl., ill., index. (Col. Huasteca)

Collection of papers presented at the 10th Encuentro de Investigadores de la Huasteca at the Univ. Autónoma de Tamaulipas in 1998. Presents a study of the cultural and environmental diversity of the Huastec region in northeast Mexico. Chapters explore the life and scholarly research of Guy Stresser-Péan; the Huastec natural environment and agricultural practices; and the history, identity, and culture of Huastec peoples during the prehispanic and post-contact eras. Volume aims to use the insights of this diachronic study to ameliorate the negative impacts of world-wide economic expansion on indigenous peoples in Mexico. [AAJ]

59   Ideología política y sociedad en el periodo formativo: ensayos en homenaje al doctor David C. Grove. Edición de Ann Cyphers y Kenneth G. Hirth. México: UNAM, Instituto de Investigaciones Antropológicas, 2008. 442 p.: bibl., ill., maps.

Volume contributions focus on sociopolitical topics of formative period archeology which served as the focus of David C. Grove's academic research. Chapters consider the structure and ideology of formative society. Authors principally examine sites from Veracruz, Honduras, and the Puebla-Tlaxcala region such as San Lorenzo, Chalcatzingo, and Copán. [AAJ]

60   Jiménez Garcia, Esperanza Elizabeth. Iconografía guerrera en la escultura de Tula, Hidalgo. (*Arqueol. Mex.*, 14:84, marzo/abril 2007, p. 54–59)

Examines sculpture of Tula and how it exemplified the Toltec warrior culture that spread throughout most of Mesoamerica. [AAJ]

61   Johansson, Patrick. Erotismo y sexualidad entre los huastecos. (*Arqueol. Mex.*, 14:83, enero/feb. 2007, p. 58–64)

Reviews the archeological expressions of Huasteco eroticism and sexuality. [AAJ]

62   Joyce, Arthur A. and **Marc N. Levine.** Tututepec, Yucu Dzaa: un imperio del posclásico en la mixteca de la costa. (*Arqueol. Mex.*, 15:90, marzo/abril 2008, p. 44–47)

Presents an overview of the Mixtec imperial center of Tututepec and discusses its history and social organization through a consideration of domestic excavations, survey, and analyses of the codices. [AAJ]

63   Joyce, Rosemary A. Gender and Mesoamerican archaeology. (*in* Worlds of gender: the archaeology of women's lives around the globe. Edited by Sarah Milledge Nelson. Lanham, Md.: AltaMira Press, 2007, p. 191–217, bibl.)

Presents the history of gender studies in Mesoamerican archeology. Begins by discussing the pioneers who first question androcentric models such as Tatiana Proskouriakoff (1960–61, 1963–64) and Clemency Coggins (1975). Traces the development of gender studies to the present day, in which archeologists no longer take categories such as "male" and "female" for granted. Argues that opposition must still be faced from those who continue the view that the subordination of women is a characteristic of all complex societies. Nevertheless, gender studies have resulted in positive and irrevocable shifts in Mesoamerican archeology. [AAJ]

64   Killion, Thomas J. Cultivating, farming, and food containers: reflections on formative subsistence and intensification in the southern Gulf Coast lowlands. (*J. Anthropol. Res.*, 64:3, Fall 2008, p. 367–382)

Reviews Santley's study of formative period agriculture and settlement in the Sierra de los Tuxtlas, Veracruz. Discusses how Santley's work linked land use and food preparation practices to ceramic vessel use in a study of early and middle formative ceramics from the central Tuxtlas. Suggests that Santley's work resonates well with recent research on agriculture and the variable role of wild and cultivated food resources among Olmec and pre-Olmec societies of the Gulf Coast lowlands. [AAJ]

65   Kowalewski, Stephen A. Regional settlement pattern studies. (*J. Archaeol. Res.*, 16:3, Sept. 2008, p. 225–285, bibl.)

Reviews regional settlement pattern archeology from the last decade as a productive approach. Discusses importance of regional studies to resource/heritage databases and understanding Paleolithic and Holocene foragers, the reciprocal relations between Neolithic communities and regional societies, and states and empires. Argues that research designs should rely on comparisons, macroregional analysis to look at long-term change, and alternative pathways, while specifying systematic coverage at the regional scale and carry out spatial analysis in which social groups are the primary focus. [AAJ]

66 Latin American indigenous warfare and ritual violence. Edited by Richard J. Chacon and Rubén G. Mendoza. Tucson: Univ. of Arizona Press, 2007. 293 p.: bibl., ill., index, maps.

A multidisciplinary study of indigenous violence in Latin America from the prehispanic era to modern times. Chapters examine the causes, magnitude, and effects of warfare and ritualized violence among Mesoamerican groups such as the Aztec, Maya, and Zapotec as well as South American and Chacoan peoples. Authors present archeological, ethnographic, historical, osteological, and forensic evidence. Emphasis is on the deep antiquity of violence in Latin America. [AAJ]

67 Lind, Michael. Arqueología de la mixteca. (*Desacatos*, 27, mayo/agosto 2008, p. 13–32, bibl., ill., maps, photos, tables)

Overview and summary of the archeology of the Mixtec region of Oaxaca with a focus on the postclassic period. [AAJ]

68 López Austin, Alfredo. Los mexicas ante el cosmos. (*Arqueol. Mex.*, 16:91, mayo/junio 2008, p. 24–35)

Details the cosmovision of the Mexica culture and examines beliefs about supernatural powers that may have affected their relations with other groups. [AAJ]

69 López Luján, Leonardo. Clásico: 150–600/650 D.C. (*Arqueol. Mex.*, 15:86, julio/agosto 2007, p. 44–49)

Examines the classic period in Mesoamerica and the rise of the first true city: Teotihucán. [AAJ]

70 López Mestas Camberos, Lorenza and Jorge Ramos de la Vega. Some interpretations of the Huitzilapa shaft tomb. (*Anc. Mesoam.*, 17:2, July 2006, p. 271–281, bibl., ill., maps)

Examines excavations of an unlooted shaft tomb at site of Huitzilapa in central Jalisco. The Teuchitlan tradition provides the most detailed information to date on the funerary customs of the late formative period. Evaluates the place of Huitzilapa in local and regional settlement patterns and examines whether the evidence supports the existence of stratified societies in central Jalisco during the late formative period. [AAJ]

71 Love, Michael. Recent research in the southern highlands and Pacific Coast of Mesoamerica. (*J. Archaeol. Res.*, 15:4, Dec. 2007, p. 275–328, bibl., maps, table)

Reviews recent research on the southern highlands and Pacific Coast of Mesoamerica, including studies of the development of social complexity, hunter/gatherer subsistence patterns, early sedentism, the origins of food production, the development of the state, migration, the construction of social identity, political economy, the collapse of complex societies, human paleoecology, theories of social change, and identity. [AAJ]

72 Un lugar de jade: sociedad y economía en el antiguo Chalco = Place of jade: society and economy in ancient Chalco. Edited by Mary G. Hodge. México: Instituto Nacional de Antropología e Historia; Pittsburgh, Pa.: Univ. of Pittsburgh, 2008. 506 p.: bibl, graphs, ill., maps, photos. (Arqueología de México)

Chapters present the results of the Chalco Archaeological Project including studies of ceramics, lithics, ceramic and obsidian raw material sourcing, faunal remains, botanical remains, spindle whorls and textile production, figurines, and human remains. Examines the changing community, politics, and economy of Chalco from the classic to postclassic periods. [AAJ]

73 Maldonado, Blanca E. A tentative model of the organization of copper production in the Tarascan state. (*Anc. Mesoam.*, 19:2, Sept. 2008, p. 283–297, bibl, ill, photos)

Using archeological and ethnohistorical data, proposes a model for examining copper production and its role as wealth finance in the late postclassic Tarascans state. [AAJ]

74 Manzanilla, Linda. La producción artesanal en Mesoamérica. (*Arqueol. Mex.*, 14:80, julio/agosto 2006, p. 28–35)

Uses examples to demonstrate that understanding artisan production allows one to consider broader aspects of social organization in Mesoamerica. [AAJ]

75 Matos Moctezuma, Eduardo and **Felipe Solís.** El Calendario azteca y otros monumentos solares. México: Consejo Nacional para la Cultura y las Artes: Instituto Nacional de Antropología e Historia: Grupo Azabache, 2004. 164 p.: ill.

A short study of the Aztec calendrical monument and other associated solar monuments. Chapters discuss the iconography of the monuments, the cultural contexts in which they were used, and the worldviews which characterized the cult of the sun. [AAJ]

76 Mesoamerican ritual economy: archaeological and ethnological perspectives. Edited by E. Christian Wells and Karla L. Davis-Salazar. Boulder, Colo: Univ. Press of Colorado, 2007. 336 p.: bibl., index. (Mesoamerican worlds from the Olmecs to the Danzantes)

Volume investigates the relationship between religious ritual and the procurement, production, distribution, and consumption of raw materials in ancient Mesoamerica. Contributors draw on archeological and ethnological data to explore ritual economy among groups such as the classic Maya, Aztecs, and inhabitants of the Lower Río Verde Valley of Oaxaca. Authors problematize the notion that materialism is the sole factor behind economic processes of the past. [AAJ]

77 Minc, Leah D. Monitoring regional market systems in prehistory: models, methods, and metrics. (*J. Anthropol. Archaeol.*, 25:1, March 2006, p. 82–116, bibl., graphs, maps, tables)

Argues that market systems are key factors in the development and integration of many complex societies, but are inadequately researched. Proposes methods that focus on the distribution and movement of goods in various market systems, allowing predictions of distinct patterns of commodity distribution. Metrics for monitoring exchange based on artifact assemblage similarity are proposed and applied as a case study to the regional market system in the Aztec heartland. [AAJ]

78 Nalda, Enrique. La arqueología de Guanajuato: trabajos recientes. (*Arqueol. Mex.*, 16:92, julio/agosto 2008, p. 36–43)

Provides a history of the state of Guanajuato based on recent architectural and ceramic findings. [AAJ]

79 Nalda, Enrique. Epiclásico: 650–900 D.C. (*Arqueol. Mex.*, 15:86, julio/agosto 2007, p. 50–53)

Documents the fall of Teotihuacán and the consequences for areas surrounding the city. [AAJ]

80 New perspectives on human sacrifice and ritual body treatment in ancient Maya society. Edited by Vera Tiesler and Andrea Cucina. New York: Springer, 2007. 319 p.: bibl., ill., index, maps. (Interdisciplinary contributions to archaeology)

Collection of papers focusing on archeological evidence for human sacrifice and references to human sacrifice in imagery and hieroglyphic texts in the Maya lowlands during the classic (AD 300–1000) and postclassic (AD 1000–1500) periods. [JSH]

81 Nuevas ciudades, nuevas patrias: fundación y relocalización de ciudades en Mesoamérica y el Mediterráneo antiguo. Recopilación de Ma. Josefa Iglesias Ponce de León, Rogelio Valencia Rivera, y Andrés Ciudad Ruiz. Madrid: Sociedad Española de Estudios Mayas, 2006. 404 p.: bibl., ill., maps. (Publicaciones de la S.E.E.M.; 8)

Collection of papers comparing the processes of city foundation in Mesoamerica and the ancient Mediterranean. Mesoamerican coverage emphasizes lowland Maya cities of the classic period (AD 300–1000), but includes consideration of later Maya cities, and those of Oaxaca and central Mexico. [JSH]

82 Olivier, Guilhem. Los "2000 dioses" de los mexicas: politeísmo, iconografía y cosmovisión. (*Arqueol. Mex.*, 16:91, mayo/junio 2008, p. 44–49)

A study of the many gods in the mexica pantheon and how they can help investigators better understand the social and political organization of these ancient people. [AAJ]

83 Olko, Justyna. Turquoise diadems and staffs of the office: elite costume and insignia of power in Aztec and early colonial Mexico. Warsaw, Poland: Ośrodek Badań nad Tradycją Antyczną w Polsce i w Europie Środkowo-Wschodniej, 2005. 561 p.: bibl., ill., maps, tables.

Comprehensive analysis of Aztec elite apparel and power insignia during the late postclassic and 16th century. Area of study includes the Valley of Mexico, other provinces of the Aztec empire, and nearby independent territories such as Tlaxcala. Examines 16th and 17th century Spanish documents, Nahuatl manuscripts, sculpture, and other media. Combines a semiotic approach with the "iconographical analysis" model of Panofsky. Argues that among the Aztec, costumes served as tools of visual communication concerning rank and identity. During the early colonial period, Aztec elite incorporated status insignia of the Spanish into their own repertoire. For ethnohistorian's comment, see *HLAS 64:276.* [AAJ]

Olko, Justyna. Turquoise diadems and staffs of the office: elite costume and insignia of power in Aztec and early colonial Mexico. See *HLAS 64:276.*

84   Oudijk, Michel R. Mixtecos y zapotecos en la época prehispánica. (*Arqueol. Mex.,* 15:90, marzo/abril 2008, p. 58–62)

Examines the false historical dichotomy that the Zapotecs had the choice of either paying tribute to the Mixtecs or abandoning the Valley of Oaxaca. [AAJ]

85   Paleoindian archaeology: a hemispheric perspective. Edited by Juliet E. Morrow and Cristóbal Gnecco. Gainesville: Univ. Press of Florida, 2006. 368 p.: bibl., index.

Chapters discuss Late Pleistocene habitation sites in North, Central, and South America. Emphasis is on the creation of dialogue between different theoretical viewpoints rather than consensus— both traditional perspectives on Clovis colonization of the Americas and evidence for earlier occupations are presented. Chapter topics include single-site studies, comparisons of archeological evidence of North and South America, radiocarbon dating, the Clovis drought, South American fluted points, and criticisms of Paleo-Indian archeology. Volume argues for a "hemispheric

perspective" on the peopling of the Americas. [AAJ]

86   Parsons, Jeffrey R. Beyond Santley and Rose (1979): the role of aquatic resources in the prehispanic economy of the basin of Mexico. (*J. Anthropol. Res.,* 64:3, Fall 2008, p. 351–366, bibl., ill., map, photos, table)

Expands on Santley and Rose's 1979 consideration of algae in prehispanic diet and demography to incorporate a more varied diet, including aquatic insects. Argues that algae and aquatic insects were part of a suite of resources in postclassic Mesoamerica that were complementary to seed-based agriculture and that together with maguey formed the functional equivalent of pastoralism in the absence of domestic herbivores. [AAJ]

87   Parsons, Jeffrey R. The last pescadores of Chimalhuacán, Mexico: an archaeological ethnography. Ann Arbor, Mich.: Univ. of Michigan Museum of Anthropology, 2006. 377 p.: bibl., ill., index, maps. (Anthropological papers/Museum of Anthropology, Univ. of Michigan; no. 96)

Examines the role of aquatic resources in the urbanized societies of ancient Mesoamerica. Presents the results of an ethnographic study of traditional aquatic economy in Chimalhuacán in southeastern Lake Texcoco conducted by the author in 1992. Ethnographic data are used in a comparative approach which also draws on historical, botanical, and zoological data. Goal is to build analogies relating to how ancient exploitation of aquatic resources is manifested archeologically. Argues that wetland resources served as key protein sources in ancient economies, especially in the absence of domestic herbivores. [AAJ]

88   Parsons, Jeffrey R. Prehispanic settlement patterns in the northwestern Valley of Mexico: the Zumpango region. Ann Arbor, Mich.: Museum of Anthropology, Univ. of Michigan, 2008. 438 p.: bibl., ill., maps. (Memoirs; 45)

Presents data from a systematic regional archeological survey carried out over an area of ca. 600 square kilometers. Six principal occupational cycles are identified. [AAJ]

89   Pérez Campa, Mario A. Preclásico tardío: 400 A.C.-200 D.C. (*Arqueol. Mex.*, 15:86, julio/agosto 2007, p. 40–43)

Examines the late preclassic period in Mesoamerica and the initial developments that would later spawn centers like Cuicuilco and Teotihuacán. [AAJ]

90   Pérez Negrete, Miguel. El Cerro de la Estrella: unidades políticas de la cuenca de México, periféricas a Teotihuacan y la transición al Epiclásico. (*Arqueología/México*, 34, sept./dic. 2004, p. 38–61, bibl., ill., maps, photos)

Article examines the classic period development of El Cerro de la Estrella, located in the Basin of Mexico, and the site's transition into the epiclassic. Discusses the relationship of the site with Teotihuacán and other populations at the periphery of the basin. Examines the architectural sequence of El Santuario, the civic-ceremonial center of El Cerro de la Estrella, and discusses the culture history of the Iztapalapa peninsula. Argues that El Cerro de la Estrella grew into a regional center for Teotihuacán, while at the same time maintaining local traditions. [AAJ]

91   Perry, Linda et al. Starch fossils and the domestication and dispersal of chili peppers (Capsicum spp. L.) in the Americas. (*Science/Washington*, 315:5814, Feb. 16, 2007, p. 986–988)

Reports that a genus-specific starch morphotype provides a means to identify chili peppers from archeological contexts and trace both their domestication and dispersal. Argues that maize and chilies were an ancient and widespread neotropical plant food complex that predates pottery in some regions. [AAJ]

92   Pohl, John M. La guerra entre los zapotecos. (*Arqueol. Mex.*, 14:84, marzo/abril 2007, p. 48–53)

Discusses the history of war in the Valley of Oaxaca, reviewing likely motives and its role as impetus to the development of the state. [AAJ]

93   Pollard, Helen Perlstein. A model of the emergence of the Tarascan state. (*Anc. Mesoam.*, 19:2, Sept. 2008, p. 243–264, bibl, ill, tables)

Uses archeological, ecological, and ethnohistoric research to propose a model of the emergence of the Tarascan state. Examines why Tarascan state formation occurred, why secondary state formation was "delayed" for more than 1,000 years, why it occurred in the Lake Patzcuaro Basin, and the role of Purepecha ethnicity in the process. [AAJ]

94   Pool, Christopher A. Olmec archaeology and early Mesoamerica. Cambridge; New York: Cambridge Univ. Press, 2007. 354 p.: bibl., ill., index, maps. (Cambridge world archaeology)

A comprehensive study of Olmec social and cultural evolution from Archaic period roots to collapse in the late formative period. Book focuses on the power relations and interactions between Olmec leaders and those of other formative polities, arguing for a position between the "Mother Culture" and "Sister Culture" models of early sociopolitical development. Author examines the interaction between politics and the local environmental setting in the process of cultural evolution and diachronic changes and continuities in Olmec culture. [AAJ]

95   Pool, Christopher A. and Wesley D. Stoner. But Robert, where did the pots go?: ceramic exchange and the economy of ancient Matacapan. (*J. Anthropol. Res.*, 64:3, Fall 2008, p. 411–424)

Paper assesses Santley's central-place systems model of economies of Teotihuacán's dependents in light of recent data on ceramic production and exchange in the Tuxtlas region. Yields a more informed view of political economy that does not easily fit any one central-place model. [AAJ]

96   Reacomodos demográficos: del clásico al posclásico en el centro de México. Edición de Linda Manzanilla. México: UNAM, Instituto de Investigaciones Antropológicas, 2005. 324 p.: bibl., ill.

Collection of papers presented at the 26th Mesa Redonda de la Sociedad Mexicana de Antropología (Zacatecas, 2001). Contributions discuss the cultural and demographic changes which occurred during the classic-to-postclassic transition in central Mexico. Geographic areas considered in the volume include Zacatecas, Michoacán, el Bajío, the Toluca Valley, the Basin of Mexico, and the Puebla-Tlaxcala Valley. Authors use modern osteological techniques to infer migration, such as strontium isotope analysis. Volume offers novel data on the complexity of inter-regional interaction during the epiclassic. [AAJ]

97 Reyna Robles, Rosa María. La Organera, Xochipala, Guerrero. (*Arqueol. Mex.*, 14:82, nov./dic. 2006, p. 42–46)

Examines archeological investigations at the site of La Organera, Xochipala. [AAJ]

98 Rice, Prudence M. Time, power, and the Maya. (*Lat. Am. Antiq.*, 19:3, Sept. 2008, p. 275–298)

Reviews theoretical approaches to time in anthropology and history, and examines relationships between calendar systems and political organization in the Maya lowlands. Argues that the power of Maya kings stemmed in large part from their success in presenting themselves as in control of time and calendars. Suggests that the may cycle of 13 katuns that structured the shifting of political power in the northern lowlands in the postclassic period (AD 1000–1500) was also a feature of earlier political organization in the Maya world. [JSH]

Rodríguez-Alegría, Enrique. Eating like an Indian: negotiating social relations in the Spanish colonies. See *HLAS 64:289.*

99 Rodríguez Martínez, María del Carmen et al. Oldest writing in the new world. (*Science/Washington*, 313:5793, Sept. 15, 2006, p. 1610–1614, bibl., ill., map, photos)

Reports on a block with a hitherto unknown system of writing from the Olmec heartland of Veracruz, Mexico. Argues that stylistic and other dating of the block places it as the oldest writing in the new world, with features that firmly assign it to the Olmec civilization. [AAJ]

100 Romero, Laura E. La noción de persona: la cosmovisión de los nahuas de la Sierra Negra de Puebla. (*Arqueol. Mex.*, 16:91, mayo/junio 2008, p. 62–66)

Discusses the Nahua view of the cosmos and how their beliefs influenced their daily lives. [AAJ]

101 Rosenswig, Robert M. Beyond identifying elites: feasting as a means to understand early middle formative society

on the Pacific Coast of Mexico. (*J. Anthropol. Archaeol.*, 26:1, March 2007, p. 1–27, bibl., graphs, maps, photos, tables)

Discusses material patterns resulting from feasting involving intra-site variability in food preparation, presentation, and consumption at Cuauhtémoc in the Soconusco region of southern Mexico. Expectations are evaluated by comparing ceramic, ground stone, obsidian, and faunal data recovered from Conchas phase elite and village midden deposits. Argues that elite feasting created political cohesion as socially stratified and politically hierarchical societies emerged. [AAJ]

102 Ruins of the past: the use and perception of abandoned structures in the Maya lowlands. Edited by Travis W. Stanton and Aline Magnoni. Boulder: Univ. Press of Colorado, 2008. 364 p.: bibl., index. (Mesoamerican worlds)

Collection of 10 papers exploring ways the precolumbian lowland Maya modified, terminated, abandoned, and re-used buildings. Emphasizes reconstructing how the ancient Maya thought about the past, harnessed it to political agendas, and made use of it in constructing identities. [JSH]

103 Schávelzon, Daniel. Las ciudades mayas: un urbanismo de América latina. Buenos Aires, Argentina: Ediciones FADU: Nobuko, 2008. 162 p.: bibl., ill., maps. (Serie Difusión; 19)

Overview of the history of thought about ancient Maya cities and settlement patterns in the lowlands of Guatemala, Mexico, and Belize form the 18th century to the present. [JSH]

104 Schoenburg, Paul Schmidt. La época prehispánica en Guerrero. (*Arqueol. Mex.*, 14:82, nov./dic. 2006, p. 28–37)

Overview of archeological research in Guerrero. Examines the origins and development of complex societies. [AAJ]

105 Seminario de Petrograbados del Norte de México, 1st, Mazatlan, Sinaloa, Mexico, 2003. Los petroglifos del norte de México: memoria del Primer Seminario de Petrograbados del Norte de México. Coordinación de Víctor Joel Santos Ramírez y Ramón Viñas Vallverdú. Culiacán, Mexico:

Instituto Nacional de Antropología e Historia: Dirección de Investigación y Fomento de Cultura Regional, 2006. 192 p.: ill.

Collection of papers presented at the first Seminario de Petrograbados del Norte de México in Mazatlan, Sinaloa, in 2003. Contributors examine petroglyphs recovered from northern Mexico, which constitute 70 percent of the country's recorded examples. Authors discuss the dating, cultural affiliation, function, and interpretation of petroglyphs. Petroglyphs from areas farther south, such as Guerrero and Jalisco, are also presented. [AAJ]

106 Smith, Michael Ernest. Aztec city-state capitals. Gainesville: Univ. Press of Florida, 2008. 255 p.: bibl., ill., index, maps. (Ancient cities of the new world)

Examines Aztec cities outside Tenochtitlán dating between the 12th and 15th centuries AD. Chapters focus on four aspects of urbanism: urban form, life, function, and meaning. Analysis draws on a wide variety of data including archeology, ethnohistory, and codices. Emphasizes how the political ideologies of Aztec rulers shaped urban environments. [AAJ]

107 Smyth, Michael P. Beyond economic imperialism: the Teotihuacan factor in northern Yucatan. (*J. Anthropol. Res.*, 64:3, Fall 2008, p. 395–410)

Explores the Teotihuacán factor in the northern plains at Dzibilchaltun, Acanceh, and Yaxuna and in the Puuc region at Chac II and Oxkintok. The article addresses questions of chronology, economic process, and Robert Santley's legacy of investigating Teotihuacán's role in Classic Mesoamerica. [AAJ]

108 Spores, Ronald. La mixteca y los mixtecos. (*Arqueol. Mex.*, 15:90, marzo/abril 2008, p. 28–33)

Highlights the Mixtec culture of Pueblo and Oaxaca and shows that this region is rich in both natural and cultural resources. [AAJ]

109 Stark, Barbara L. and **Alanna Ossa.** Ancient settlement, urban gardening, and environment in the Gulf lowlands of Mexico. (*Lat. Am. Antiq.*, 18:4, Dec. 2007, p. 385–406, bibl., graphs, ill., maps, tables)

Examines both the symbolic and practical functions of gardens at the urban settlements of the Lower Papaloapan River Basin in the Gulf coast lowlands. Settlements were preferentially orientated along lower lying elevations suited towards a mix of rainy season farming, recessional agriculture, and pot irrigation. Argue that this type of agrarian settlement is part of the continuum of Mesoamerican forms of urbanism and is not the exception. [AAJ]

110 Taube, Karl A. La jadeíta y la cosmovisión de los olmecas. (*Arqueol. Mex.*, 15:87, sept./oct. 2007, p. 43–48)

Explores the Olmec mastery of jade carving and the themes depicted in the carvings; considers what they meant to their creators and the people who used them. [AAJ]

111 Umberger, Emily. The metaphorical underpinnings of Aztec history: the case of the 1473 civil war. (*Anc. Mesoam.*, 18:1, March 2007, p. 11–29)

Discusses the 1473 civil war between the two polities that formed the capital of the Aztec empire, Tenochtitlán and Tlatelolco, as presented in the *Codex Durán*. Argues that the literal, European-style rendition of the events of the war includes remnants of preconquest symbolic thought, which indicate that the war was staged to follow the outlines of the story of the battle between the gods Huitzilopochtli and Coyolxauhqui at Coatepetl. This story is an allegory for the rise and fall of powerful rulers. Contends that the enemy king and his second in command, after being thrown from the Templo Mayor, were buried in the funerary vessels beside the Great Coyolxauhqui Stone which was discovered in 1978 at the base of the Tenochtitlán Templo Mayor. For art historian's comment, see *HLAS 64:42*. [AAJ]

112 Urcid, Javier. Antigüedad y distribución de la danza de los Voladores: águilas que descienden, corazones que ascienden. (*Arqueol. Mex.*, 14:81, sept./oct. 2006, p. 70–74)

Discusses the uncertain origins and spread of the Mesoamerican Volador ritual as well as its symbolic role in representing space and time. [AAJ]

113 Valdez, Francisco et al. Late formative archaeology in the Sayula Basin
of southern Jalisco. (*Anc. Mesoam.*, 17:2,
July 2006, p. 297–311, bibl., ill., map, tables)
Presents habitation and mortuary
deposits of two late formative sites in the
Sayula Basin, Jalisco, Mexico. Also discusses the possible subsistence patterns in
the region that combined agriculture with
the seasonal exploitation of salt deposits,
suggesting that these subsistence patterns
were the basis of daily interaction in a developing rank society. [AAJ]

114 Vázquez León, Luis. El leviatán arqueológico: antropología de una tradición científica en México. 2. ed. Mexico:
CIESAS: M.A. Porrúa, 2003. 385 p.: bibl.
(Sociedades, historias, lenguajes)
A sociocultural anthropological study
of the scientific discipline of archeology as it
is practiced in Mexico. Uses an ethnometh-
odological and critical framework to examine topics such as professional discourse,
daily practices, and theoretical principles of
Mexican archeologists. Argues that Mexican archeology is firmly intertwined with
a nationalist agenda which insulates the
discipline from the public. [AAJ]

115 Viramontes Anzures, Carlos. El lenguaje de los símbolos: el arte rupestre
de las sociedades prehispánicas de Querétaro. Santiago de Querétaro, Mexico: Gobierno del Estado de Querétaro, 2005. 424 p.:
bibl, ill. (Historiografía Querétana; v. 15)
A formal analysis of rock art recovered from the semiarid state of Querétaro.
Discusses the anthropology, archeology, and
ethnohistory of the area's groups and the
worldviews which informed their symbolic
representations. Study relates to both agricultural and hunting and gathering societies. [AAJ]

116 Wendt, Carl J. Las olmecas: los primeros petroleros. (*Arqueol. Mex.*, 15:87,
sept./oct. 2007, p. 56–59)
Examines evidence that Olmecs were
the first Mesoamericans to harness the
power of petroleum, which they used for
decoration, knife handles, and as a construction material. [AAJ]

117 Whiting, Thomas A. Lee. Los olmecas en Chiapas. (*Arqueol. Mex.*, 15:87,
sept./oct. 2007, p. 66–70)

Explores the Olmec influence in the
state of Chiapas through discussion of economic, political, and genetic links. [AAJ]

118 Winter, Marcus. Cerro de las Minas:
arqueología de la Mixteca Baja. 2. ed.
Oaxaca, Mexico: Centro INAH Oaxaca,
2007. 112 p.: bibl., ill. maps. (Arqueología
oaxaqueña. Serie popular; 1)
Second edition of this overview of
Ñuiñe culture in the Mixteca Baja region
of Oaxaca. Discusses insights from an archeological study conducted at the site of
Cerro de las Minas. Focuses on the culture,
history, environmental characteristics,
social organization, religion, and ideology of
Ñuiñe centers. [AAJ]

119 Winter, Marcus. Ronald Spores y los
años tempranos en la Mixteca: una
semblanza. (*Desacatos*, 27, mayo/agosto
2008, p. 193–198, photos)
Biographical sketch of Ronald Spores
and his more than five decades of archeological, ethnohistoric, and ethnographic
research in the Mixteca Alta, Oaxaca. [AAJ]

120 Zamora Rivera, Mónica. Ubicación,
descripción y análisis de los juegos de
pelota en Cantona, Puebla. (*Arqueología/
México*, 34, sept./dic. 2004, p. 62–74, bibl.,
maps, photos)
Analysis of 25 ball courts found at the
site of Cantona, Puebla. Describes the location and architectural features of each court
and presents a preliminary chronology. Also
discusses the occupational phases of the
city of Cantona. Evidence indicates that the
ball courts date from the late formative to
the early postclassic. [AAJ]

FIELDWORK AND ARTIFACTS

**121 Adriano-Morán, Carmen Cristina
and Emily McClung de Tapia.** Trees
and shrubs: the use of wood in prehispanic
Teotihuacán. (*J. Archaeol. Sci.*, 35:11, Nov.
2008, p. 2927–2936)
Discusses how charcoal from excavations in the Teotihuacán Valley was used
to evaluate changes in the use of wood over
time in prehistory. Multiple taxa of trees
and shrubs were identified and variations in
the proportions of taxa suggest continuities
in utilization and management of vegetation. [AAJ]

122   Aoyama, Kazuo. Elite artists and craft producers in Classic Maya society: lithic evidence from Aguateca, Guatemala. (*Lat. Am. Antiq.*, 18:1, March 2007, p. 3–26)

Summarizes evidence for manufacture and use of lithic tools at the classic period (AD 600–800) Maya city in the Petexbatun region in Guatemala. Production of utilitarian tools and objects for elite consumption—including stela-carving as well as fabricating bone and shell ornaments—was concentrated in and around elite residences in the core of the city. [JSH]

123   Aoyama, Kazuo. La guerra y las armas de los Mayas clásicos: puntas de lanza y flecha de Aguateca y Copán. (*Estud. Cult. Maya*, 28, 2006, p. 27–49, bibl., ill., map, photo)

Summarizes evidence for production and use of spear and arrow points at the two classic period (AD 300–800) lowland Maya cities. The bow and arrow was in use in the Maya lowlands earlier than usually believed. Points, along with other stone tools, were manufactured and used by the elite of Aguateca. [JSH]

124   Aoyama, Kazuo. Preclassic and classic Maya obsidian exchange, artistic and craft production, and weapons in the Aguateca region and Seibal, Guatemala. (*Mexicon/Germany*, 30:4, 2008, p. 78–86)

Overview of obsidian and chert tool manufacture and craft production at two cities in the Petexbatun region of the Maya lowlands. Notes chert tool production and manufacture of bone and shell artifacts for elite consumption were concentrated in central Aguateca. Suggests that the concentration of spear and dart points in this sector, along with the burning of elite residences at the time Aguateca was abandoned early in the 9th century, indicates that warfare focused on elites and their dwellings. [JSH]

125   Arnold, Dean E. *et al.* Sourcing the palygorskite used in Maya blue: a pilot study comparing the results of INAA and LA-ICP-MS. (*Lat. Am. Antiq.*, 18:1, March 2007, p. 44–58)

Reports results of chemical analyses of source samples of the special clay that, combined with indigo, produced the famous Maya Blue pigment used in painting pottery, murals, and sculpture. The results establish a baseline characterization of sources that can be used to determine whether palygorskite was mined from a single source area and exchanged widely or obtained from multiple sources. [JSH]

126   Ball, Joseph W. and Jennifer T. Taschek. Sometimes a "stove" is "just a stove": a context-based reconsideration of three-prong "incense burners" from the western Belize valley. (*Lat. Am. Antiq.*, 18:4, Dec. 2007 p. 451–470)

Analysis of composite ceramic vessels consisting of a base with three upright prongs that supported a dish or jar from late and terminal classic period (AD 600–1000) Maya sites in western Belize. Argues on the basis of the contexts in which they are found and the patterning of traces of burning and residues that these vessels were not incense burners, as the conventional interpretation would have it, but braziers normally used for food preparation. [JSH]

127   Begun, Erica. The many faces of figurines. (*Anc. Mesoam.*, 19:2, Sept. 2008, p. 311–318, bibl., ill, maps, tables)

Discusses how the figurines of Michoacán can be used as markers of ethnic identity and ethnic continuity in the Lake Pátzcuaro basin. Presents a preliminary typology for the figurines to support the idea that a distinctly Michoacán style is visible in decorative and production styles throughout the sequence. Argues that this continuity supports the hypothesis that the ethnic origins of the Michoacán people may reach back to the late preclassic/early classic period. [AAJ]

128   Benz, Bruce F.; Lorenza López Mestas C.; and **Jorge Ramos de la Vega.** Organic offerings, paper, and fibers from the Huitzilapa shaft tomb, Jalisco, Mexico. (*Anc. Mesoam.*, 17:2, July 2006, p. 283–296, bibl., photos, tables)

Organic materials from the Huitzilapa shaft tomb were examined to identify the burial accoutrements and offerings found with six interments. Food analyses have produced only class or kingdom level identifications, while fibers analyses have identified cotton and agave textile fibers. A piece of amate paper is the earliest organic evidence of paper in Mesoamerica. The presence of cotton suggests it was a high-status item, while the predominance of agave fibers indicates that maguey was a utilitarian fiber. Argues that late formative inhabitants of Huitzilapa recognized status differences and observed class differentiation and craft specialization. [AAJ]

129 Borejsza, Aleksander et al. Agricultural slope management and soil erosion at La Laguna, Tlaxcala, Mexico. (*J. Archaeol. Sci.*, 35:7, July 2008, p. 1854–1866, bibl., ill., photo, table)

Investigates chronology of agricultural terracing at the site of La Laguna and reconstructs sequence of land use at the site from the formative through modern times. Discusses risks of dating agricultural features by ceramic association and the complex relationships between demographic variables, agricultural intensity, and terracing. [AAJ]

130 Borgstede, Greg and **James R. Mathiew.** Defensibility and settlement patterns in the Guatemalan Maya highlands. (*Lat. Am. Antiq.*, 18:2, June 2007, p. 191–211, bibl., ill., maps, photos, tables)

Analysis of settlement location, layout, and architectural features contributing to defensibility in Maya sites in the western highlands of Guatemala. Concludes that defensive features are as common in the classic period (AD 300–1000) as in the postclassic period (AD 10–1500), casting doubt on the orthodox view that warfare increased markedly in the postclassic. [JSH]

131 Cabrero García, María Teresa and **Carlos López Cruz.** The shaft tombs of El Piñon, Bolaños Canyon, State of Jalisco, México. (*Anc. Mesoam.*, 18:2, Sept. 2007, p. 239–257, bibl., ill., map, photos, tables)

Discusses excavation of a group of three unlooted shaft tombs at the site of El Piñon in Bolaños Canyon of northern Jalisco and southern Zacatecas. Includes discussion of chronology, the presence of local and trade goods, osteological analysis, and addresses the question of sequential versus single interment. [AAJ]

132 Canuto, Marcello A. and **Ellen E. Bell.** The ties that bind: administrative strategies in the El Paraíso Valley, Department of Copan, Honduras. (*Mexicon/ Germany*, 30:1, 2008, p. 10–20)

Summary of recent work at El Paraíso and El Cafetal in western Honduras, on the fringe of the area dominated by the Maya city of Copan in the late classic period (AD 600–800). In contrast with local styles of artifacts and buildings at El Cafetal, El Paraíso closely resembles Copan. This, along with reduced construction at El Paraíso during the mid-8th century when Copan suffered a major political setback, suggests considerable variability in political affiliation and cultural identity in the hinterlands of Maya cities. [JSH]

133 Carballo, David M. Implements of state power. (*Anc. Mesoam.*, 18:1, March 2007, p. 173–190, bibl., ill., maps, table)

Recent excavations at the Moon Pyramid at Teotihuacán demonstrate that the large-scale manufacture of weaponry and the production of ceremonial items were undertaken next to the monument, as evidenced by obsidian dart points and eccentrics linked to militarism and sacrificial practices. These craft production activities were likely overseen by state functionaries and the finished products served as means of directing military coercion and symbolic reification of state authority, materialized through the militaristic offering complexes. [AAJ]

134 Carballo, David M.; Jennifer Carballo; and Hector Neff. Formative and classic period obsidian procurement in central Mexico: a compositional study using laser ablation-inductively coupled plasma-mass spectrometry. (*Lat. Am. Antiq.*, 18:1, March 2007, p. 27–43, bibl., graphs, ill., map, photo, tables)

Reports on the use of laser ablation-inductively coupled plasma-mass spectrometry (LA-ICP-MS) to source obsidian in central Mexico. Study revealed a shift in the middle formative from a 50/50 reliance on sources from both the Mesa Central and the Sierra Madre Oriental to a full reliance on sources from the Mesa Central. The shift coincided with the development of large regional centers in Tlaxcala-Puebla, indicating increased interactions with the Mesa Central economic sphere, including the Basin of Mexico. Examines obsidian from a Teotihuacán workshop dump, which reveals a continued, but diversified reliance on Mesa Central sources one thousand years later with preferential utilization of sources depending on the tools being manufactured. [AAJ]

135 **Catálogo gráfico de los cráneos de la cueva de La Candelaria.** Edición de Arturo Romano Pacheco. México: Instituto Nacional de Antropología e Historia, 2005. 117 p.: bibl., ill. (Col. Científica; 478. Serie Antropología física)

An illustrated catalog of skulls recovered from the Central Mexican cave of La Candelaria. Presents 39 feminine skulls and 45 masculine skulls, each photographed at six different views (right lateral, left lateral, posterior, anterior, superior, and basal). Summarizes cultural and environmental contexts. Discusses the cave's chronology, and presents morphological, craneometric, and paleopathological data. [AAJ]

136 **Chase, Arlen F.** *et al.* Textiles and the Maya archaeological record: gender, power, and status in classic period Caracol, Belize. (*Anc. Mesoam.*, 19:1, March 2008, p. 127–142)

Documents textile production at the classic period (AD 300–800) Maya city in Belize. The contexts of spindle whorls, needles, pins and other textile-related tools in women's burials, especially elite women, confirms the association of textile production with women and suggests that it was a high-status activity. [JSH]

137 **Colas, Pierre Robert** *et al.* Sites and sinkholes: archaeological investigations of terminal classic Maya society on the northern Vaca plateau, Belize. (*Mexicon/ Germany*, 30:6, 2008, p. 126–135)

Summary of mapping and surface investigations at Ix Chel, in western Belize. Also reports exploration and excavation in several caves in the region used for burials and ritual activities. These data reflect late and terminal classic period (AD 600–1000) occupation in the region. [JSH]

138 **Crider, Destiny** *et al.* In the aftermath of Teotihuacán: epiclassic pottery production and distribution in the Teotihuacán Valley, Mexico. (*Lat. Am. Antiq.*, 18:2, June 2007, p. 123–143, bibl., ill., map, photos, tables)

Results of instrumental neutron activation analysis of epiclassic Coyotlatelco

and early postclassic Mazapan ceramics from the Teotihuacán Valley suggesting that the pottery was locally made with few imports. Evidence reflects an "inward" economic orientation of basin polities following the decline of the Teotihuacán state. Includes discussion of models of postclassic political economy and the classic to postclassic transition. [AAJ]

139 **Cucina, Andrea; Allan Ortega;** and **Vera Tiesler.** When the East meets the West: biological affinities between coastal populations in the Yucatan peninsula during the postclassic period. (*Mexicon/Germany*, 30:2, 2008, p. 39–43)

Reports analysis of dental morphology from skeletal material from late (AD 1000–1500) Maya sites along the coast of Yucatán. Samples from East Coast sites show more differences among the samples than expected, suggesting that the pattern of relationships among coastal centers was complex and varied. [JSH]

140 **Cuddy, Thomas W.** Political identity and archaeology in Northeast Honduras. Boulder, Colo.: Univ. Press of Colorado, 2007. 206 p.: bibl., index.

Re-analyzes data from field research in the early 20th century and proposes political-cultural units on the basis of stylistic distributions. [JSH]

141 **Culbert, T. Patrick** and **Robert L. Rands.** Multiple classifications: an alternative approach to the investigation of Maya ceramics. (*Lat. Am. Antiq.*, 18:2, June 2007, p. 181–190)

Advocates multiple independent pottery typologies based on paste, form, surface treatment, and decoration instead of the single type-variety approach common in analyses of ancient Maya pottery. [JSH]

142 **Cyphers, Ann.** Escultura olmeca de San Lorenzo Tenochtitlán. México: UNAM, Coordinación de Humanidades, Programa Editorial, Instituto de Investigaciones Antropológicas, 2004. 293 p.: bibl., ill.

Study of 159 Olmec sculptures from the regional center of San Lorenzo as well as four other Olmec sites, including Tenochtitlán, El Remolino, Loma del Zapote, and Estero Rabón. Monument descriptions provide data on sculpture material, local name, dimensions, surface treatment, and current location. Aim of sculptural study is to gain information on Olmec culture, settlement hierarchy, communications of governors and priests, and ideological changes. [AAJ]

143 Dahlin, Bruce H. *et al.* In search of an ancient Maya market. (*Lat. Am. Antiq.*, 18:4, Dec. 2007, p. 363–384)

Proposes that a leveled open area at the intersection of several ancient causeways near the core of Chuchucmil in Yucatán served as the city's marketplace in the early classic period (AD 300–600). Chemical analysis of soil from the hypothetical marketplace reveals concentrations of phosphorus and zinc, a pattern also found in food preparation and produce sales areas in a modern market in Antigua, Guatemala. [JSH]

144 de la Cruz, Isabel *et al.* Sex identification of children sacrificed to the ancient Aztec rain gods in Tlatelolco. (*Curr. Anthropol.*, 49:3, June 2008, p. 519–526, bibl., photo, table)

Recent excavation of an Aztec rain god temple in Tlatelolco, Mexico, recovered remains of 37 children and six adults, which resulted from a single sacrificial ritual. DNA was successful in determining the sex of victims, while morphometrics analyses proved less reliable. The majority of victims were male and likely served as living impersonators of the rain god. [AAJ]

145 deFrance, Susan D. and Craig A. Hanson. Labor, population movement, and food in sixteenth-century Ek Balam, Yucatán. (*Lat. Am. Antiq.*, 19:3, Sept. 2008, p. 299–316)

Reports on excavations in an early colonial period residence at Ek Balam in the northern Maya lowlands of Yucatán. Analysis of animal bone shows that the Maya residents were strongly affected by the colonial environment, raising pigs, chickens and other European animals and hunting less native game because of their restricted mobility. [JSH]

146 Duncan, William N. *et al.* Human cremation in Mexico 3,000 years ago. (*Proc. Natl. Acad. Sci. U.S.A.*, 105:14, 2008, p. 5315–5320, ill., photos)

Argues for the presence of cremation

burials dating to the early formative period at the site of Tayata in the Mixteca Alta region, Oaxaca. These would be the earliest cremations discovered in Mexico. [AAJ]

147 Elson, Christina M. and R. Jason Sherman. Crema ware and elite power of Monte Albán: ceramic production and iconography in the Oaxaca Valley, Mexico. (*J. Field Archaeol.*, 32:3, Fall 2007, p. 265–282, bibl.)

Examines ceramic data from the terminal formative Zapotec capital of Monte Albán, along with data from secondary centers in the Oaxaca Valley. Analysis suggests that crema-paste ceramics were produced at Monte Albán as prestige goods and distributed to local elites at administrative sites throughout the valley. While local elites acquired some crema vessels from elites at the capital, local elites also sponsored the production of crema vessels. Local production would have subverted attempts by elites at the capital to control both the distribution of prestigious ceramics and the subordinate elites who desired them. [AAJ]

148 Emery, Kitty F. Techniques of ancient Maya bone working: evidence from a classic Maya deposit. (*Lat. Am. Antiq.*, 19:2, June 2008, p. 204–221)

Documents a rich assemblage of bone from a residence near the center of the late and terminal classic (AD 600–1000) Maya city of Dos Pilas in the Petexbatun region of Guatemala. The assemblage is unusual in that it includes waste material and partly finished artifacts, representing all phases of bone tool manufacture. Suggests that the techniques and processes represented in this household provide a good model for precolumbian bone tool manufacture throughout the Maya lowlands. [JSH]

149 Emery, Kitty F. and Kazuo Aoyama. Bone, shell, and lithic evidence for crafting in elite Maya households at Aguateca, Guatemala. (*Anc. Mesoam.*, 18:1, March 2007, p. 69–89)

Detailed analysis of evidence for the manufacture of bone and shell tools at the late classic period (AD 600–800) city in the Petexbatun region of the Maya lowlands in Guatemala. The distribution manufacturing implements, waste material, and finished products indicates that bone and shell objects were manufactured by the nobility in their residences. [JSH]

150 Espinosa Rodríguez, Guadalupe. Investigaciones recientes en Chapultepec. (*Arqueol. Mex.*, 13:77, enero/feb. 2006, p. 62–66)

Details recent studies on the Teotihuacano presence in Chapultepec, the Christian cemeteries in Jardín de Leones and the analysis of trash recovered from the Mayor and Minor lakes. [AAJ]

151 Fargher, Lane F. A microscopic view of ceramic production: an analysis of thin-sections from Monte Albán. (*Lat. Am. Antiq.*, 18:3, Sept. 2007, p. 313–323, bibl., ill., map, tables)

Presents results of a petrographic study of Monte Albán gray-ware pottery which demonstrate that the organization of gray-ware production changed greatly through time. During the late-terminal formative, the majority of gray wares consumed at Monte Albán were imported from some distance, with small-scale part-time specialists engaged in production. During the classic period the organization of gray-ware production changed dramatically and nearly all of the gray wares recovered from Monte Albán were probably produced there through specialized production. [AAJ]

152 Galindo Trejo, Jesús. Un análisis arqueoastronómico del edificio circular Q152 de Mayapán. (*Estud. Cult. Maya*, 29, 2007, p. 63–81, bibl., maps, photos, tables)

Analyzes the orientations of architectural features of a round structure at the late postclassic (AD 1200–1500) Maya city in Yucatán that is often interpreted as a counterpart of the Caracol, a documented observatory at the earlier city of Chichén Itzá. Alignments point to positions of the sun corresponding to beginnings, days of divisions of the calendar, as well as to bright stars. [JSH]

García Barrios, Ana. Confrontation scenes on Codex-style pottery: an iconographic review. See *HLAS 64:221*.

153 García Moll, Roberto. Pomoná: un sitio del clásico maya en las colinas tabasqueñas. México: Inst. Nacional de Antropología e Historia, 2005. 161 p.: bibl.,

ill., maps. (Colección Científica; 481. Serie Arqueología)

Detailed summary of investigations at the classic period (AD 300–800) Maya city in the Lower Usumacinta region of Mexico. Includes description of pottery, architecture, burials, and sculpture. [JSH]

154 Geurds, Alexander. Grounding the past: the praxis of participatory archaeology in the Mixteca Alta, Oaxaca, Mexico. Leiden, The Netherlands: CNWS Publications, 2007. 367 p.: bibl., ill., index. (CNWS Publications; 150)

A critical study of the practice of field archeology in the communities of Santiago Tilantongo and Santiago Apoala in the Mixteca Alta, Oaxaca. Initial chapters present an archeological study involving surface survey, mapping, and analysis of recovered artifacts dating from the late formative to the postclassic. Second part of book employs reflexive analysis to investigate how archeological knowledge may be better integrated with indigenous perspectives on monuments and landscape. Argues that a reflexive approach is necessary to facilitate collaboration with indigenous communities. [AAJ]

155 Gill, Richardson Benedict et al. Drought and the Maya collapse. (*Anc. Mesoam.*, 18:2, Sept. 2007, p. 283–302)

Reviews evidence for a long period of drought affecting the Maya lowlands between AD 760 and 930. Argues that drought peaks within this period correspond to stages of the collapse of Maya city-states and that the climatic change was a major causal factor. [JSH]

156 Golden, Charles W. et al. Piedras negras and Yaxchilan: divergent political trajectories in adjacent Maya polities. (*Lat. Am. Antiq.*, 19:3, Sept. 2008, p. 249–274)

Preliminary report of archeological survey in the middle Usumacinta region of the Maya lowlands in the hinterlands of the Maya cities of Yaxchilan and Piedras Negras. In the late formative period (300 BC–AD 300) both had emerged as political and economic centers, along with several other sites, and both grew into seats of royal dynasties in the early classic period (AD 300–600). In the late classic period (AD 600–800), Yaxchilan maintained close control of subsidiary administrative centers in the hinterland, while Piedras Negras did not. Both cities collapsed in the 9th century and the region was subsequently abandoned. [JSH]

Guernsey, Julia. Ritual & power in stone: the performance of rulership in Mesoamerican Izapan style art. See *HLAS 64:28.*

157 **Haines, Helen R.; Phillip W. Willink; and David Maxwell.** Stingray spine use and Maya bloodletting rituals: a cautionary tale. (*Lat. Am. Antiq.*, 19:1, March 2008, p. 83–98)

Argues that stingray spines used in Maya bloodletting ritual were likely cleaned of tissue and venom since tissue death is a likely outcome of the use of fresh spines. Suggests that stingray spines or replicas were used in preference to other bloodletting implements in rituals involving transformation of royal power or states of being. [JSH]

158 **Halperin, Christina T.** Classic Maya textile production: insights from Motul de San José, Peten, Guatemala. (*Anc. Mesoam.*, 19:1, March 2008, p. 111–125)

Analyzes the distribution of spindle whorls and other spinning and weaving tools at the late classic Maya city in northern Guatemala. Concludes that textile production was concentrated in large elite residences, indicating that it was an elite activity, not a tribute obligation of lower status households. [JSH]

Hamann, Byron. Seeing and the Mixtec screenfolds. See *HLAS 64:29.*

Headrick, Annabeth. The Teotihuacán trinity: the sociopolitical structure of an ancient Mesoamerican city. See *HLAS 64:30.*

159 **Helmke, Christophe et al.** Burial BVC88-1/2 at Buenavista del Cayo, Belize: resting place of the last king of Puluul? (*Mexicon/Germany*, 30:2, 2008, p. 43–49)

Describes a late classic period (AD 800–1000) elite burial from a palace building at the Maya city in western Belize. A carved bone buried with the individual, a male about 45–50 years of age, bears a hieroglyphic text with a series of titles ending with a variant of the Emblem Glyph title that may designate the polity as Puluul. [JSH]

Herring, Adam. A borderland colloquy: Altar Q, Copán, Honduras. See *HLAS 64:47.*

160 **Inomata, Takeshi.** Warfare and the fall of a fortified center: archaeological investigations at Aguateca. Nashville, Tenn.: Vanderbilt Univ. Press, 2006. 331 p.: bibl. (Vanderbilt Institute of Mesoamerican Archaeology; 3)

Report on mapping, survey, and some of the excavations in the center of the Maya city in the Petexbatun region of the Maya lowlands in Guatemala. Results of intensive excavation of structures in the site center are considered in the discussion of social and political disruption in the terminal classic period (AD 800–1000), a major focus of the Vanderbilt Univ. project, but detailed consideration of those data is reserved for a later volume in the series. Presents clear evidence for construction of the defensive wall system during the late classic period, suggesting increasing warfare in the period prior to the collapse, and for the rapid abandonment of the city early in the 9th century as the result of military attack. [JSH]

161 **Investigaciones arqueológicas en Ciudad Vieja El Salvador: la primigenia villa de San Salvador.** Recopilación de Roberto Gallardo y William R. Fowler. San Salvador: Dirección de Publicaciones e Impresos, Consejo Nacional para la Cultura y el Arte, 2002. 143 p.: bibl., ill., maps. (Col. Antropología e historia; 1)

Detailed report on mapping and excavation at the site of the first stable location of the colonial period capital in the 16th century. Ciudad Vieja is one of the few cities founded soon after the Spanish invasion of Central America that is well preserved and not buried by later construction. [JSH]

162 **Iwaniszewski, Stanislaw and Jesús Galindo Trejo.** La orientación de la estructura 33 de Yaxchilán: una reevaluación. (*Estud. Cult. Maya*, 28, 2006, p. 15–26, bibl., ill., photos, tables)

Re-analyzes the orientation of one of the major buildings of Bird Jaguar, the 8th century king of the Maya city on the Usumacinta river. Concludes that earlier suggestions that the building was built so that the rising sun on the summer solstice would illuminate a statue of the king just inside the central doorway are incorrect. [JSH]

163 Janaab' Pakal of Palenque: reconstructing the life and death of a Maya ruler. Edited by Vera Tiesler and Andrea Cucina. Tucson: Univ. of Arizona Press, 2006. 219 p.: bibl., index.

Collection of 11 papers focusing on an assessment of the skeletal remains of Pakal, the 7th century king of the lowland Maya city of Palenque. Analyses of his skeletal remains using modern techniques resolves the controversy over his age that arose from the discrepancy between earlier skeletal assessments and his age as recorded in hieroglyphic inscriptions. Includes a retrospective essay by Arturo Romano, one of the original analysts. Also reports analysis of the remains of the "Red Queen," buried in a tomb in an adjacent building, and consideration of comparative information on lowland Maya royal biographies, especially from Yaxchilan. [JSH]

164 Josserand, J. Kathryn and Nicholas A. Hopkins. Tila and its Black Christ: history, pilgrimage, and devotion in Chiapas, Mexico. (*Mesoamérica/Antigua,* 28:49, 2007, p. 82–113, bibl., ill., map, photo)

Provides a synthesis of linguistic, ethnographic, ethnohistoric, and archeological sources to shed light on the development of the Mexican pilgrimage cult of the Black Christ. [AAJ]

165 Kaplan, Jonathan. Hydraulics, cacao, and complex developments at Preclassic Chocolá, Guatemala. (*Lat. Am. Antiq.,* 19:4, Dec. 2008, p. 399–413)

Describes an extensive system of canals built in the late middle and late formative periods (500 BC–AD 300) at the Maya city in the piedmont zone of southern Guatemala. Suggests that the water system was used for intensive cultivation, perhaps of cacao, given its documented importance in the region in later times. [JSH]

166 King, Stacie M. The spatial organization of food sharing in early postclassic households: an application of soil chemistry in Ancient Oaxaca, Mexico. (*J. Archaeol. Sci.,* 35:5, May 2008, p. 1224–1239, bibl., graphs, maps, tables)

Investigates relationship between food sharing, commensality, and household social organization at the site of Río Viejo in coastal Oaxaca, Mexico through a study of soil chemical residues in contemporaneous occupation surface and floor deposits in two residential neighborhoods dating to the early postclassic. [AAJ]

167 Laporte, Juan Pedro; Héctor E. Mejía; and Jorge E. Chocón. Reconocimiento arqueológico en zona de frontera: la cuenca del río Chiquibul en Petén, Guatemala. (*Mesoamérica/Antigua,* 27:48, 2006, p. 1–46, ill., maps, tables)

Reports results of archeological investigations in an area along the Belize border in northeastern Guatemala. Identifies seven independent polities in the region in the late classic (AD 600–800) and describes the sites associated with each. [JSH]

168 Loughmiller-Newman, Jennifer A. Canons of Maya painting: a spatial analysis of Classic Maya polychromes. (*Anc. Mesoam.,* 19:1, March 2008, p. 29–42)

Analysis of the placement of human figures and hieroglyphic texts in the design layout of Maya polychrome painted pottery of unknown provenience but likely dating to the classic period (AD 300–800). Suggests that spatial relationships on the pottery reflect social status relationships. [JSH]

169 Lucero, Lisa J. Classic Maya temples, politics, and the voice of the people. (*Lat. Am. Antiq.,* 18:4, Dec. 2007, p. 407–427)

Analysis of six temples at Yalbac, a small late classic (AD 600–800) Maya city in Belize. Argues that variation in construction features and associated artifacts indicate that the temples were built by different groups, perhaps for the worship of different deities, and that they were sites of competition among social segments for status and power. [JSH]

170 Luke, Christina and Robert H. Tykot. Celebrating place through luxury craft production. (*Anc. Mesoam.,* 18:2, Sept. 2007, p. 315–328)

Documents the production of carved marble vessels at Travesía in the Ulúa valley of northern Honduras in the late to terminal classic period (AD 600–900) and the procurement of marble from local quarries. Argues that centralized production of these luxury vessels functioned more in enhancing the status of Travesía than in the creation of political authority. [JSH]

171 Masson, Marilyn A.; Timothy S. Hare; and Carlos Peraza Lope. Postclassic Maya society regenerated at Mayapán. (*in* After collapse: the regeneration of complex societies. Edited by Glenn M. Schwartz and John J. Nichols. Tucson: Univ. of Arizona Press, 2006, p. 188–207, ill., map)

Examines the transformation of lowland Maya city-states and political organization in the terminal classic period (AD 800–1000) through the lens of the new political order that emerged at Mayapán in the late postclassic period (AD 1200–1500) and its material correlates, which reflect both continuity and rejection of former patterns. Identifies competition among leading families for political power, expanded priestly roles, and intensification of long-distance exchange as key organizational innovations. For review of entire volume, see item 292. [JSH]

172 McCafferty, Sharisse D. and Geoffrey G. McCafferty. Spinning and weaving tools from Santa Isabel, Nicaragua. (*Anc. Mesoam.*, 19:1, March 2008, p. 143–156)

Analysis of a large assemblage of spindle whorls and bone needles, picks and other weaving tools at the early postclassic site on the shore of Lake Nicaragua. Weaving tools were concentrated in one sector of the site, suggesting that textile production was a specialized activity, while the general distribution of spindle whorls indicates that spinning was not. [JSH]

173 Milbrath, Susan et al. Effigy censers of the Chen Mul modelled ceramic system and their implications for Late Postclassic Maya interregional interaction. (*Mexicon/Germany*, 30:5, 2008, p. 104–112)

Overview of the distribution and contexts of large ceramic effigy incense burners from late (AD 1000–1500) sites in the Maya lowlands. The focus is on Mayapán in Yucatán, where these effigy incense burners are most common. Argues that their broad geographic distribution implies shared religious belief and practice and that analysis of their regional variability will be required to elucidate the mechanisms responsible for that sharing. [JSH]

174 Mountjoy, Joseph B. and Mary K. Sandford. Burial practices during the late formative/early classic in the Banderas

Valley area of coastal west Mexico. (*Anc. Mesoam.*, 17:2, July 2006, p. 313–327, bibl., ill., map, photos, tables)

Reports on the excavation of multiple, late preclassic and early classic shaft-and-chamber tombs in the Banderas Valley of coastal West Mexico. Details the multiple sources of data obtained from the excavations, which lend support to the idea that the Ameca River and the Banderas Valley formed an area of intermixing between two distinct prehispanic cultural traditions. [AAJ]

175 Nalda, Enrique. Kohunlich: emplazamiento y desarrollo histórico. México: Inst. Nacional de Antropología e Historia: Plaza y Valdés, 2004. 185, 11 p.: bibl., ill. (some col.), maps. (Serie Arqueología) (Col. científica)

Detailed report on mapping at the Maya city in the central Maya lowlands of Yucatán. Includes large-scale maps of classic period (AD 300–1000) architectural groups and a summary of excavations, with tabulation of the pottery recovered. [JSH]

176 Ojeda Mas, Heber and Vicente Suárez Aguilar. El polvorín de Campeche, México. (*Rev. Arqueol. Am./México*, 23, 2004/2005, p. 291–333, bibl., ill., photos, tables)

Article describes the archeological findings from the salvage of El Polvorín, a 17th-century munitions storehouse built in the vicinity of Campeche in the Yucatán peninsula. Describes the historical context and architecture of three buildings, including the kitchen and storeroom, guard station, and gunpowder warehouse. Archeological excavations at the site have uncovered a prehispanic occupation extending from 300 BC to AD 1450, as indicated by ceramic remains. Presents the ceramic sequence and discusses other material culture from this early occupation. [AAJ]

177 Oliveros Morales, J. Arturo. El Opeño: un antiguo cementerio en el occidente mesoamericano. (*Anc. Mesoam.*, 17:2, July 2006, p. 251–258, bibl., map, photos)

Discusses excavations at the cemetery site of El Opeño, a possible precursor to the shaft tomb tradition of western Mexico. Considers material remains found within the tombs that point to connections with groups outside of the region. [AAJ]

178 Otis Charlton, Cynthia L. and Thomas H. Charlton. Artesanos y barro: figurillas y alfarería en Otompan, estado de México. (*Arqueol. Mex.*, 14:83, enero/feb. 2007, p. 71–77)

Article looks at a late postclassic ceramic production center and specifically the excavation of a ceramic figurine workshop. [AAJ]

179 Palenque: recent investigations at the classic Maya center. Edited by Damien B. Marken. Lanham, Md.: Altamira Press, 2006. 335 p.: bibl., index.

Collection of papers summarizing recent investigations at the classic period (AD 300–800) Maya city in Mexico. Emphasizes reconnaissance in the hinterland; refining the city's chronology; exploration of architecture, especially the temples of the Cross Group; and new insights from hieroglyphic texts. [JSH]

180 Paris, Elizabeth H. Metallurgy, Mayapan, and the Postclassic Mesoamerican world system. (*Anc. Mesoam.*, 19:1, March 2008, p. 43–66)

Documents the casting of copper bells, rings, and tweezers from imported raw materials at the late postclassic (AD 1200–1500) Maya city in northern Yucatán. Although production was localized in two elite residential complexes, metal artifacts were not restricted to the elite. [JSH]

181 Pérez Campos, Elizabeth Mejía and Alberto Herrera Muñoz. La obsidiana en Mesoamérica. (*Arqueol. Mex.*, 14:80, julio/agosto 2006, p. 49–54)

Reviews prehispanic uses of obsidian, including domestic, medical, artisan, military, and religious contexts. [AAJ]

182 Pérez Campos, Elizabeth Mejía and Alberto Herrera Muñoz. El sur de la Sierra Gorda: Ranas y Toluquilla. (*Arqueol. Mex.*, 13:77, enero/feb. 2006, p. 38–41)

Reviews the investigations of the two sites of Ranas and Tolquilla including chronology, urban plan, and the nature of life for its inhabitants. [AAJ]

183 Perspectiva tafonómica: evidencias de alteraciones en restos óseos del México prehispánico. Edición de Carmen Maria Pijoan Aguadé y Xabier Lizarraga Cruchaga. Mexico: Instituto Nacional de Antropología e Historia, 2004. 219 p.: bibl., ill., maps. (Serie antropología física) (Col. científica; 462)

Short collection of papers presented at the 15th Mesa Redonda de la Sociedad Mexicana de Antropología in San Luis Potosí in 1998. Contributions discuss the detection, analysis, and interpretation of the processes which impact human mortuary remains. Topics include mummification, thermal alterations to bones, human sacrifice, tzompantli rituals, cranial trauma, indicators of status on human mandibles, and other forms of osteological impact. Remains from major centers such as Teotihuacán and La Quemada are detailed. An important contribution on the methodology of physical anthropologists. [AAJ]

184 La población maya costera de Chac Mool: análisis biocultural y dinámica demográfica en el clásico terminal y el posclásico. Coordinación de Lourdes Márquez Morfín, Patricia O. Hernández Espinoza, y Ernesto González Licón. México: Programa de Mejoramiento del Profesorado: Consejo Nacional para la Cultura y las Artes: Instituto Nacional de Antropología e Historia: Escuela Nacional de Antropología e Historia, 2006. 231 p.: bibl., ill.

Describes results of archeological investigations at the terminal classic and postclassic period (AD 800–1500) Maya city on the east coast of Yucatán. Emphasizes analysis of skeletal remains in relation to demography, disease and health status, indicators of activity and status, and modification of skulls and teeth. [JSH]

185 Price, T. Douglas *et al.* Strontium isotopes and the study of human mobility in ancient Mesoamerica. (*Lat. Am. Antiq.*, 19:2, June 2008, p. 167–180, bibl., graphs, ill., map, table)

Reports on the analysis of strontium isotopes from both modern and archeological samples of shell, bone, and dental enamel from across Mesoamerica. The significant isotopic variation among the samples suggests that it can be very useful in identifying the location of childhood residence and tracking human mobility as further evidenced by the results of five case studies from different areas in Mesoamerica. [AAJ]

186 La producción alfarera en el México antiguo. Coordinación de Beatriz Leonor Merino Carrión y Angel García Cook. México: Instituto Nacional de Antropología e Historia, 2005. 1 v.: bibl., ill. (Col. Científica; 484. Serie arqueología)

First installment of a five-volume series synthesizing research on ancient ceramics of Mexico. Volume begins with general topics such as ceramic analysis methodology and the beginnings of ceramic production in Mexico. Majority of volume includes ten typological discussions of formative period ceramics from areas such as Guerrero, Chiapas, Morelos, Puebla-Tlaxcala, the Yucatán peninsula, and others. [AAJ]

187 Reflexiones sobre la industria lítica. Coordinación de Leticia González Arratia y Lorena Mirambell. México: Instituto Nacional de Antropología e Historia, 2005. 354 p.: bibl., ill., maps. (Col. Científica; 475) (Serie Arqueología)

Volume aims to present an overview of theory, methodology, analytical criteria, and terminology behind lithic studies in Mexican archeology. Chapters focus on the analysis of flint and obsidian, and examine topics including lithic production and distribution, the ideology behind lithic industries, and the control of raw materials. Authors investigate lithic industries dating from 35,000 years ago to the late postclassic period in Hidalgo, Michoacán, Tamaulipas, and other areas. [AAJ]

188 Rivero-Torres, Sonia E. et al. Characterization of archaeological obsidians from Lagartero, Chiapas, Mexico by PIXE. (*J. Archaeol. Sci.*, 35:12, Dec. 2008, p. 3168–3171, bibl., graph, map, table)

Obsidian samples from the archeological site of Lagartero, Chiapas, and from other Mexican and Guatemalan sources were analyzed by proton induced X-ray emission. Statistical analysis identified Lagartero samples as originating from two obsidian sources in Guatemala and one in Mexico, indicating contact between areas. [AAJ]

189 Romano Pacheco, Arturo. Los restos óseos humanos de la cueva de La Candelaria, Coahuila: craneología. México: Instituto Nacional de Antropología e Historia, 2005. 93 p.: bibl., ill. (Col. Científica; 477. Serie Antropología física)

Original, unmodified Master's thesis of Arturo Romano Pacheco, completed in 1956. Important early contribution to craniological studies in physical anthropology. Using a series of detailed cranial measurements, examines human remains rescued from a cave in La Candelaria, located in central Mexico. Thesis objective was to study the biological distance of the Candelaria population to other American groups to address the larger question of the peopling of the Americas. Concluded that remains had biological affinity with indigenous groups in Texas, Baja California, New York, and populations in South America. [AAJ]

190 Rosenswig, Robert M. and Douglas J. Kennett. Reassessing San Estevan's role in the Late Formative political geography of northern Belize. (*Lat. Am. Antiq.*, 19:2, June 2008, p. 123–145)

Summarizes the results of excavations in the core of the city in the Maya lowlands of northern Belize. Documents the beginning of monumental architectural projects about the beginning of the Common Era, and suggests that the city was the focus of a small independent polity, not a dependency of neighboring cities, at that time. [JSH]

191 Sax, Margaret et al. The origins of two purportedly pre-Columbian Mexican crystal skulls. (*J. Archaeol. Sci.*, 35:10, Oct. 2008, p. 2751–2760, bibl., ill., photo)

Investigates the history, technology and material of the British Museum crystal skull and another larger white quartz skull, donated recently to the Smithsonian Institution. Mesoamerican artifacts were used as comparative items. Findings suggest that both skulls are modern creations and fakes. [AAJ]

192 Schávelzon, Daniel. Treinta siglos de imágenes: maquetas y representaciones de arquitectura en México y América Central prehispánica. Buenos Aires: Fundación Centro de Estudios para Políticas Públicas Aplicadas, 2004. 255 p.: bibl., ill.

Analysis of 100 prehispanic artifacts from Mesoamerica and South America which contain representations or models of urban architecture. Majority of chapters examine Mesoamerican artifacts from centers in Oaxaca, central Mexico, the Maya region, and other areas. Emphasizes that representations of architecture can provide insight into how past peoples saw themselves. [AAJ]

193   Scherer, Andrew K.; Lori E. Wright; and Cassady J. Yoder. Bioarchaeological evidence for social and temporal differences in diet at Piedras Negras, Guatemala. (*Lat. Am. Antiq.*, 18:1, March 2007, p. 85-104)

Reports chemical and macroscopic analysis of skeletal material from the classic period (AD 300–800) Maya city in the lowlands of northern Guatemala. Results indicate heavy reliance on maize and relatively little difference among social groups. Beginning in the 8th century, bone chemistry indicates much more variability in diets, probably reflecting disruption of subsistence strategies at the time of the collapse of the political system. [JSH]

194   Seidemann, Ryan M. and Heather McKillop. Dental indicators of diet and health for the Postclassic Maya on Wild Cane Cay, Belize. (*Anc. Mesoam.*, 18:2, Sept. 2007, p. 303-313)

Analysis of wear, caries and other indications of health and diet on teeth from postclassic period (AD 1000–1500) burials at the Maya site in Belize. Results indicate that inhabitants of the island enjoyed better dental health than their inland contemporaries, in part because of the greater proportion of marine protein and lower proportion of maize, a factor consistent with faunal remains from the site. [JSH]

195   Sellen, Adam T. El cielo compartido: deidades y ancestros en la vasijas efigie zapotecas. Mérida, Mexico: UNAM, 2007. 400 p.: bibl., ill. (Monografías; 4)

A study of the iconography of Zapotec effigy vessels used primarily in elite tombs from the late formative to the classic period. Most examples are from the Oaxaca Valley. [AAJ]

196   Shaw, Justine M. White roads of the Yucatán: changing social landscapes of the Yucatec Maya. Tucson: Univ. of Arizona Press, 2008. 226 p.: bibl., index.

Documents large-scale construction of causeways at two sites in Yucatán during the Terminal Classic period. Argues that the roads enhanced the ability of centers to integrate dispersed populations, allowing them to flourish during a time of political turmoil. Includes comparative analysis of causeways in the Maya world, emphasizing their varied functions. [JSH]

197   Sheseña, Alejandro. Pinturas mayas en cuevas. San Roque, Tuxtla Gutiérrez, Chiapas, Mexico: Gobierno del Estado de Chiapas: Consejo Estatal para la Cultura y las Artes de Chiapas, 2006. 230 p.: bibl., ill. (Biblioteca Popular de Chiapas; 113. Estudios mayística)

Overview of caves with precolumbian paintings in the Maya lowlands of Guatemala, Belize, and Mexico. Includes classification of imagery by theme. [JSH]

198   Smith, Michael Ernest *et al.* Sources of imported obsidian at postclassic sites in the Yautepec Valley, Morelos: a characterization study using XRF and INAA. (*Lat. Am. Antiq.*, 18:4, Dec. 2007, p. 429–450, bibl., graphs, map, photos)

Presents the results of obsidian characterization of a large sample (N=390) of obsidian blades recovered from middle and late postclassic sites in the Yautepec Valley of Morelos, central Mexico. Using both X-ray fluorescence and instrumental neutron activation analysis the samples were sourced to a quarry location. Discusses complementarity of the two techniques and their utility as tools used for examining issues such as production and exchange. [AAJ]

199   Smyth, Michael P. and D. Ortegón Zapata. A preclassic center in the Puuc region: a report on Xcoch, Yucatan, Mexico. (*Mexicon/Germany*, 30:3, 2008, p. 63–68)

Preliminary report of investigations at the Maya city in the Puuc hills of western Yucatán indicating that it had become a substantial community with monumental architecture before 500 BC. The city continued to flourish during the early classic period (AD 300–600), but was largely abandoned by the time of the regional florescence beginning in the 9th century. [JSH]

200   Spence, Michael W. and Grégory Pereira. The human skeletal remains of the Moon Pyramid, Teotihuacán. (*Anc. Mesoam.*, 18:1, March 2007, p. 147–157, bibl., ill., photos, tables)

Examines data resulting from excavation of human sacrificial offerings at the Moon Pyramid in Teotihuacán. [AAJ]

201 Spencer, Charles S. *et al.* Ceramic microtypology and the territorial expansion of the early Monte Albán state in Oaxaca, Mexico. (*J. Field Archaeol.*, 33:3, Fall 2008, p. 321–341, bibl., graphs, ill., maps, tables)

Authors present a new microtypology of G.12, gray-ware bowls which are characteristic of the late and terminal formative, early Monte Albán state. This microtypology is based upon excavations at three sites south of Monte Albán and yields a finer-grained chronology that the authors argue elucidates the territorial expansion of the emergent Monte Albán state. [AAJ]

202 Spores, Ronald and **Nelly Robles García.** A prehispanic (postclassic) capital center in colonial transition: excavations at Yucundaa Pueblo Viejo de Teposcolula, Oaxaca, Mexico. (*Lat. Am. Antiq.*, 18:3, Sept. 2007, p. 333–353, bibl., ill., map, photos, tables)

Authors present results of archeological investigations of the postclassic and early colonial Mixtec City of Yucundaa, Pueblo Viejo de Teposcolula, Oaxaca. They argue that as the first project in Oaxaca to focus specifically on a major prehispanic city and its dramatic transformation during the first three decades of the colonial period, it demonstrates the utility of a well-planned excavation program and useful model for the study of other Mesoamerican urban settlements. [AAJ]

203 Stanton, Travis W.; M. Kathryn Brown; and **Jonathan B. Pagliaro.** Garbage of the gods?: squatters, refuse disposal, and termination rituals among the ancient Maya. (*Lat. Am. Antiq.*, 19:3, Sept. 2008, p. 227–247)

Reviews examples of deposits in lowland Maya cities that have been interpreted as evidence of ritualized termination of buildings and sites and/or as refuse generated by squatters following the abandonment of sites. Argues that careful attention to the nature of these deposits is required to differentiate between these possibilities. Suggests that evidence of intense burning, intentional destruction of buildings, and sometimes intentional placement of deposits of white marl or other special materials differentiates termination deposits from refuse. [JSH]

204 Stark, Barbara L. and **Christopher P. Garraty.** Parallel archaeological and visibility survey in the western Lower Papaloapan Basin, Veracruz, Mexico. (*J. Field Archaeol.*, 33:2, Summer 2008, p. 177–196, bibl., graphs, ill., map, photos, tables)

Evaluates intensive Gulf lowland surveys in western Lower Papaloapan Basin, Veracruz, to assess the effects of topographic and ground visibility as well as vegetation types on the archeological information recovered. Survey focused on individual archeological features such as earthen mounds and monumental earthen architecture. Estimates that although 3,690 features were recorded, a substantial number (between 1,056 and 1,327 features) may have gone undetected due to a variety of vegetation and visibility conditions. [AAJ]

205 Stark, Barbara L. *et al.* Inter-regional and intra-regional scale compositional variability in pottery from south-central Veracruz. (*Lat. Am. Antiq.*, 18:1, March 2007, p. 59–84, bibl., graphs, ill., maps, tables)

Reports on the study of chemical compositional analysis of several types of classic period pottery from the western Lower Papaloapan Basin of the Gulf lowlands. Neutron instrumental activation results suggest trade at intraregional scale, but little at the inter-regional scale. Also analyzed sand sources in the region to examine whether temper was a source of differentiation among compositional groups. [AAJ]

206 Stockett, Miranda K. Performing power: identity, ritual, and materiality in a Late Classic southeast Mesoamerican crafting community. (*Anc. Mesoam.*, 18:1, March 2007, p. 91–105)

Analyzes the distribution of ceramic figurines and incense burners Las Canoas, a late to terminal classic period (AD 600–1000) site in western Honduras. Interprets the distribution as a reflection of ritual performances in civic space designed to enhance the prestige and power of subgroups within the community. [JSH]

207 **Stone houses and earth lords: Maya religion in the cave context.** Edited by Keith M. Prufer and James E. Brady. Boulder, Colo.: Univ. Press of Colorado, 2005. 392 p.: bibl., ill., index, maps. (Mesoamerican worlds)

Collection of papers on the archeology of caves in the Maya lowlands and their roles in Maya belief and ritual, particularly mortuary ritual and disposal of the dead. [JSH]

208 **Stoner, Wesley D.** *et al.* Exchange of coarse orange pottery in the middle classic Tuxtla Mountains, Southern Veracruz, Mexico. (*J. Archaeol. Sci.*, 35:5, May 2008, p. 1412–1426, bibl., graphs, maps, photos, tables)

Reports results of instrumental neutron activation analysis and petrographic point-counting analysis on coarse orange sherds sampled from various localities in the southwestern Tuxtla Mountains. Uses data to understand intensive ceramic production industries in the region, as well as the modes and nature of exchange. Advocates use of both point mineralogical and bulk chemical techniques to more accurately determine compositional data of ceramic samples. [AAJ]

209 **Sugiyama, Saburo** and **Leonardo López Luján.** Dedicatory burial/offering complexes at the Moon Pyramid, Teotihuacán. (*Anc. Mesoam.*, 18:1, March 2007, p. 127–146, bibl., ill.)

Details discovery of burial and offering complexes found in association with seven superimposed monumental constructions at the Moon Pyramid, including artifacts made of obsidian, greenstone, shell, pyrite, ceramics, wood, and textile, as well as abundant skeletal remains of sacrificed animals and human. Argues that the artifacts were buried in the temple to communicate sociopolitical information, serving as symbols of the ideology of sacred rulership. [AAJ]

210 **Sugiyama, Saburo** and **Rubén Cabrera Castro.** The Moon Pyramid project and the Teotihuacán state polity. (*Anc. Mesoam.*, 18:1, March 2007, p. 109–125, bibl., ill., photos, tables)

Reviews recent work at the Moon Pyramid at Teotihuacán, including excavations around and tunnel operations within its nucleus that have discovered seven overlapping monumental constructions, five burial complexes of sacrificed individuals, and sacred animals associated with rich offerings. Discusses excavations in nearby structures and the three-dimensional mapping of the Moon Plaza complex that provide information about the ideology of leadership at Teotihuacán. [AAJ]

211 **Sullivan, Kristin S.** Specialized production of San Martín orange ware at Teotihuacán, Mexico. (*Lat. Am. Antiq.*, 17:1, March 2006, p. 23–53, bibl., graphs, ill., map, photos)

Discusses surface collections and the partial excavation of one apartment compound and ceramic workshop in the Tlajinga district of Teotihuacán to consider the organization of specialized production. Results suggest that Tlajinga district pottery production was maximally organized at the community level, with individual apartment compounds forming the basic production units. [AAJ]

212 **Thompson, Lauri McInnis** and **Fred Valdez, Jr.** Potbelly sculpture: an inventory and analysis. (*Anc. Mesoam.*, 19:1, March 2008, p. 13–27)

Documents the distribution of potbelly sculptures, mainly dating to the late formative period (400 BC–AD 300) in eastern Mesoamerica and tabulates their stylistic features. Argues that posture and adornment indicate that they represent kingly figures, perhaps specific ancient rulers. [JSH]

213 **Triadan, Daniela.** Warriors, nobles, commoners and beasts: figurines from elite buildings at Aguateca, Guatemala. (*Lat. Am. Antiq.*, 18:3, Sept. 2007, p. 269–293)

Reports on a unique sample of ceramic figurines—human and animal effigies excavated on the floors of rapidly abandoned residences where they were actually used as well as in garbage deposits—from the late classic (AD 600-800) city in the Petexbatun region of the Maya lowlands. The distribution of figurines in residential structures, particularly in areas with food storage, food preparation and weaving implements, often was associated with women, so that the figurines may reflect women's perspectives on social roles. [JSH]

214 Velázquez Castro, Adrián. Arqueología experimental: producción de objetos de concha en el Templo Mayor. (*Arqueol. Mex.*, 14:80, julio/agosto 2006, p. 44–45)

Demonstrates the use of experimental archeology to understand the process used to produce shell artifacts recovered at the Templo Mayor. [AAJ]

215 Villamil, Laura P. Creating, transforming, rejecting, and reinterpreting ancient Maya urban landscapes: insights from Lagartera and Margarita. (*in* Negotiating the past in the past: identity, memory, and landscape in archaeological research. Edited by Norman Yoffee. Tucson: Univ. of Arizona Press, 2007, p. 183–214)

Interprets spatial organization at two Maya cities in the northern lowlands of Mexico as aspects of contrasting elite strategies of creating social distinctions that served to maintain and enhance their status and power. Lagartera's core emphasized the construction of monumental buildings and formal civic spaces during the late formative and early classic periods (300 BC–AD 600), while Margarita's late classic (AD 600–800) elite building programs focused on creating elaborate residential compounds adjacent to civic spaces. [JSH]

216 Wahl, David et al. A paleoecological record from a Late Classic Maya reservoir in the north Petén. (*Lat. Am. Antiq.*, 18:2, June 2007, p. 212–222)

Reports analysis of a sediment core from an artificial reservoir in the Maya lowlands of northern Guatemala. Pollen from the core reflects maize farming during the late classic period (AD 700–850) followed by the cessation of farming and regeneration of the forest in the terminal classic and postclassic (AD 850–1500). [JSH]

217 Weeks, John M. El sistema de la Misión Mercedaria en Santa Bárbara de Tencoa, Honduras. (*Yaxkin/Tegucigalpa*, 24:2, 2008, p. 29–49, ill.)

Overview of the organization of the Mercedarian missions in the Tencoa region of western Honduras. Summarizes archeo-

logical survey data on precolumbian and colonial period settlement patterns in the region. [JSH]

218 Wells, E. Christian. La arqueología y el futuro del pasado en las Islas de la Bahía. (*Yaxkin/Tegucigalpa*, 33:1, 2008, p. 66–81)

Brief summary of the history of archeological work on the Bay Islands of Honduras with commentary on poorly understood aspects of the prehistory of the region. Emphasizes the discovery of a collection of precolumbian ceramics from the islands and their return to Honduran authorities. [JSH]

219 Wendt, Carl J. and Ann Cyphers. How the Olmec used bitumen in ancient Mesoamerica. (*J. Anthropol. Archaeol.*, 27:2, June 2008, p. 175–191)

Analyses of archeological, ethno-archeological, and experimental data of bitumen from Mesoamerica's Gulf Coast region provide insights on the organization of Olmec bitumen processing activities. Archeological data from investigations at two early formative period Olmec sites—El Remolino and Paso los Ortices—suggests that bitumen processing was organized as a specialized activity, involving multiple production stages, but not necessarily having elite involvement or control. [AAJ]

220 White, Christine D.; T. Douglas Price; and Fred J. Longstaffe. Residential histories of the human sacrifices at the Moon Pyramid, Teotihuacán. (*Anc. Mesoam.*, 18:1, March 2007, p. 159–172, bibl., graphs, maps, tables)

Reports the results of analysis of tooth enamel and bone from sacrificial burials at the Moon Pyramid at Teotihuacán using oxygen- and strontium-isotope ratios. Data indicates that most of the sacrificed individuals appear to have been born in a foreign location. This data is compared with data from the Feathered Serpent Pyramid victims, identified groups of isotopically distinct individuals at each pyramid. Argues that Moon Pyramid victims appear to have arrived in the city recently, but that the Feathered Serpent Pyramid victims had lived in Teotihuacan for a long time before death. [AAJ]

221 Wölfel, Ulrich and **Lars Frühsorge.** Archaeological sites near San Mateo Ixtatán: hints at ethnic plurality. (*Mexicon/ Germany*, 30:4, 2008, p. 86–93)

Describes classic and postclassic period (AD 300–1500) Maya sites in the highlands of western Guatemala. Combines documentary sources with the fact that local Chuj residents identify some, but not all, sites with ancestors to suggest that the region was a frontier between the Chuj and other Mayan-speaking groups in precolumbian times. [JSH]

222 Wright, Lori E. Diet, health, and status among the Pasión Maya: a reappraisal of the collapse. Nashville, Tenn.: Vanderbilt Univ. Press, 2006. 256 p.: bibl. (Vanderbilt Institute of Mesoamerican Archaeology monograph series; 2)

Analysis of human skeletal remains burial practices in the Petexbatun region of the Maya lowlands in Guatemala. Focuses on chemical and macroscopic analyses of bone to reconstruct the diet and helath status of ancient Maya populations in the region, especially the time of the major social and political disruption that affected the Maya world in the terminal classic period (AD 800–1000), a major focus of the Vanderbilt Univ. excavation project. Concludes that diets vary considerably from site to site, with no pattern of intensified reliance on maize or deteriorating health that would suggest environmental pressures as a major causal factor in the collapse. [JSH]

NATIVE SOURCES AND EPIGRAPHY

223 Asselbergs, Florine Gabriëlle Laurence. Conquered conquistadors: the *Lienzo de Quauhquechollan;* a Nahua vision of the conquest of Guatemala. Leiden, The Netherlands: CNWS Publications, 2004. 312 p.: bibl., ill., index, maps (some col.).

An analysis of the *Lienzo de Quauhquechollan*, a Nahua pictographic account of the conquest of Guatemala from AD 1523 to 1527. Chapters focus on presenting the cultural and historical context of the document and interpreting its message. Comparative material is drawn from other native pictographic histories of the Spanish conquest. Author reveals that instead of representing battles which occurred in central Mexico, the *Lienzo de Quauhquechollan* describes the alliance of Quauhquecholteca warriors to Spanish conquistadores in the Guatemalan invasion. Book has important implications for predominant perceptions of the Spanish conquest. For ethnohistorian's comment, see *HLAS 62:197*. [AAJ]

224 Batalla Rosado, Juan José. The scribes who painted the *Matrícula de Tributos* and the *Codex Mendoza.* (*Anc. Mesoam.*, 18:1, March 2007, p. 31–51, bibl., ill., map)

Article presents an analysis of scribes who participated in the production of the *Matrícula de Tributos* (a precolumbian document that recorded the tribute paid to the Mexica empire by conquered towns) and the *Codex Mendoza* (a document created to be sent to the Spanish emperor) using comparative analysis of some elements of the iconography and logosyllabic writing in the two documents. Analysis suggests the *Matrícula de Tributos* was probably painted during the last decade of the rule of Moctezuma II and shows the work of at least six scribes. Its content was copied by one of the six scribes 20 years later as the second part of the *Codex Mendoza.* [AAJ]

225 Bíró, Péter. Las piedras labradas 2, 4 y 5 de Bonampak y los reyes de Xukalnah en el siglo VII. (*Estud. Cult. Maya*, 29, 2007, p. 31–61, bibl., photos)

Suggests a new chronological placement in the 7th century for three monuments with hieroglyphic texts from the Maya city in the lowlands of eastern Mexico. Also proposes Xukalna, possibly the name of an unknown ancient city, as a title used by the lords of Bonampak. [JSH]

226 Fuls, Andreas. The calculation of the lunar series on classic Maya monuments. (*Anc. Mesoam.*, 18:2, Sept. 2007, p. 273–282)

Analysis of information about the moon recorded in classic period (AD 300–1000) Maya hieroglyphic inscriptions. Proposes that lunar information was determined by formula rather than observation and suggests that the formula and the count of lunar months varied across the Maya world and through time. [JSH]

227 **García Barrios, Ana.** El dios Chaahk en el nombre de los gobernantes mayas. (*Estud. Cult. Maya*, 29, 2007, p. 15–29, bibl., photos)

Explores the use of Chaahk, the name of a god of lightning and rain in the northern Maya lowlands of Yucatán in the 16th century, in rulers' names recorded in hieroglyphic texts of the classic period (AD 300–1000). [JSH]

228 **García Quintana, María José.** La confesión auricular: dos textos. (*Estud. Cult. Náhuatl*, 36, 2005, p. 331-357, bibl.)

Translates two texts from the *Florentine Codex* into modern Spanish which were originally recorded in Castilian. Author precedes the translation with an interpretation and historical background of the texts as well as an overview of previous research conducted on them. The first text discusses the characteristics of and rituals pertaining to the goddess Tlazolteotl and describes the repentant procedures necessary for those who have committed sexually-related sins. The second text is a rhetorical speech given by the tonalpouhqui to Tezcatlipoca. For ethnohistorian's comment, see *HLAS 64:222*. [AAJ]

229 **Hamann, Byron.** Chronological pollution: potsherds, mosques, and broken gods before and after the conquest of Mexico. (*Curr. Anthropol.*, 49:5, Oct. 2008, p. 803–836, bibl., photos)

Considers how historical understandings are shaped by the exclusion ("matter out of time") or inclusion of certain objects ("matter in time"). Suggests the status of matter in time is cultural categorization, not a physical process. Uses "pollution" of objects (matter) in both time and space as a method for understanding the interconnected histories of Old and New Worlds of the 15th and 16th centuries. [AAJ]

230 **Hermann Lejarazu, Manuel A.** Los códices de la mixteca alta: historias de linajes y genealogías. (*Arqueol. Mex.*, 15:90, marzo/abril 2008, p. 48–52, ill., photos)

Reports on how the Mixtec codices relate rich histories and genealogical information from postclassic culture. Provides a valuable glimpse of the political structure of Mixtec society. [AAJ]

231 **Hermann Lejarazu, Manuel A.** Los libros parroquiales como fuentes complementarias para la historia de la mixteca. (*Desacatos*, 27, mayo/agosto 2008, p. 187–190, photos)

Brief discussion of the importance of parish records (e.g., birth, marriage, death, and sacrament records) in historical studies of the Mixteca. [AAJ]

232 **Hermann Lejarazu, Manuel A.** Religiosidad y bultos sagrados en la mixteca prehispánica. (*Desacatos*, 27, mayo/agosto 2008, p. 75–94, bibl., ill., photos, tables)

Study of the form, contents, symbolism and uses of sacred bundles through research on early colonial Mixtec and Spanish documents along with comparative data from other parts of Mesoamerica. Expands views of variability in the nature and uses of sacred bundles and their broader significance in Mixtec religion. [AAJ]

233 **Josserand, J. Kathryn.** The missing heir at Yaxchilán: literary analysis of a Maya historical puzzle. (*Lat. Am. Antiq.*, 18:3, Sept. 2007, p. 295–312)

Reanalyzes a hieroglyphic text from the Maya city on the Usumacinta river in eastern Mexico taking into account reconstructed literary conventions, identifying the name of a hitherto unknown son of Shield Jaguar, the 8th century king of the city. The existence of a son by Shield Jaguar's principal wife may explain the puzzling 10-year lag between his death and the accession of Bird Jaguar, Shield Jaguar's son, by a later wife. [JSH]

234 **Joyce, Arthur A.** Reflecciones críticas sobre el estudio de la escritura pictográfica en México. (*Desacatos*, 27, mayo/agosto 2008, p. 139–146, bibl., photos)

Review of the articles in this special issue of *Desacatos* on Mixtec pictographic writing. Emphasizes the importance of analogy in the determination of meanings in the ancient texts. [AAJ]

Just, Bryan R. Modifications of ancient Maya sculpture. See *HLAS 64:5*.

235 **Kaufman, Terrence** and **John Justeson.** The history of the word for cacao in ancient Mesoamerica. (*Anc. Mesoam.*,

18:2, Sept. 2007, p. 193–237, bibl., ill., map, tables)

Argues that the word kakaw(a) (cacao) originated in the Mije-Sokean language family and not from Nawa as argued by Dakin and Wichmann (2000). Also discusses the linguistic data on various cacao related topics that are pertinent to issues of inter-group interaction in precolumbian Meso-america, but does not shed light on the nature or the cultural context of the diffusion of cacao in Mesoamerica, or on its uses. [AAJ]

236 **Martin, Simon** and **Nikolai Grube.** Chronicle of the Maya kings and queens: deciphering the dynasties of the ancient Maya. Rev. ed. London: Thames & Hudson, 2008. 240 p.: bibl., ill. (some col.), index, maps (some col.).

Comprehensive revision of compendium of dynastic histories of 11 classic period (AD 300–800) Maya lowland cities, incorporating results of new archeological and epigraphic research. For review of first edition, see *HLAS 59:302.* [JSH]

237 *Mayab: Sociedad Española de Estudios Mayas.* Vol. 20, 2008. Madrid: Mayab.

Collection of papers presented at the International Congress of Americanists in Seville (2006), focusing on the combination of material evidence and epigraphic evidence bearing on issues in the archeology of the Maya lowlands during the classic period (AD 300–1000). In some cases the two lines of evidence are entirely compatible and complementary; in others they are at variance. [JSH]

238 **Mixtec writing and society: escritura de Ñuu Dzaui.** Edited by Maarten E.R.G.N. Jansen and Laura N.K. van Broekhoven. Amsterdam: Koninklijke Nederlandse Akademie van Wetenschappen, 2008. 444 p.: ill., index. (Verhandelingen der Koninklijke Nederlandse Akademie van Wetenschappen. Afdeling Letterkunde; 191)

Comprehensive analysis of the development of the Mixtec writing system from its inception to the present. Initial chapters reflexively consider the construction of scholarly knowledge and the images of indigenous peoples perpetuated in inter-cultural communication. Chapters from

second portion of book investigate the social setting and historical development of native histories and communication systems. Case studies include sites from the Mixtec highlands and lowlands in northern Oaxaca as well as the western coast. [AAJ]

239 **Mora-Marín, David F.** Full phonetic complementation, semantic classifiers, and semantic determinatives in ancient Maya hieroglyphic writing. (*Anc. Mesoam.,* 19:2, Sept. 2008, p. 195–213)

Detailed analysis of phonetic complements in ancient Maya hieroglyphic writing. Includes discussion of their relationship with semantic classifiers. [JSH]

240 **Morante López, Rubén B.** La pintura mural de Las Higueras, Veracruz. Xalapa, Veracruz, Mexico: Univ. Veracruzana, 2005. 224 p.: bibl., ill.

An analysis of a painted mural salvaged from the late classic site of Las Higueras, on the Gulf Coast of Veracruz. Painting contains multiple, superimposed layers spanning three centuries, allowing the author to examine the diachronic changes in style, techniques, and methods involved in the creation of the pictorial message. Iconographic analysis and discussion of Mayan and Teotihuacán influence. Ultimate goal is to elucidate information regarding the daily life, ritual practices, and worldviews of the inhabitants of Las Higueras. [AAJ]

241 **Nielsen, Jesper** and **Christophe Helmke.** Spearthrower Owl Hill: a toponym at Atetelco, Teotihuacán. (*Lat. Am. Antiq.,* 19:4, Dec. 2008, p. 459–474, bibl., ill., maps)

Article begins with an examination of the polychrome murals 2 and 3 from Portico 1 of the North Patio of the Atetelco residential compound at Teotihuacán, which depict a row of toponymic hill signs. Repeated toponymic references to "Spearthrower Owl Hill" in murals are contemporaneous with hieroglyphs from the Mayan region that record a Teotihuacano named "Spearthrower Owl" who was a key figure in the Teotihuacán entrada at Tikal. Authors go on to suggest that the toponymic symbol and the historical person share the name of a common forebearer, possibly a previously unidentified deity that has similarities to the Mexica god, Huitzilopochtli. [AAJ]

242 Oudijk, Michel R. De tradiciones y métodos: investigaciones pictográficas. (*Desacatos*, 27, mayo/agosto 2008, p. 123–138, bibl., ill., maps)

Argues that there have been five schools of thought in the study of Mixtec pictrographic documents, each with its own objectives and methods. Reviews strengths and weaknesses of each approach. [AAJ]

243 Rodríguez Cano, Laura. Los signos y el lenguaje sagrado de los 20 días en el calendario ritual de la mixteca y los códices del noroeste de Oaxaca. (*Desacatos*, 27, mayo/agosto 2008, p. 33–74, bibl., ill., maps, photos, tables)

Study of pictographic writing from the Mixteca Baja, addressing the list of 20 day names in the 260-day ritual calendar. Shows that there was considerable variation in the alphabetic glosses for particular day names, perhaps due to differences in the way that spoken Mixtec was recorded alphabetically or as a result of dialetical variability. [AAJ]

244 Távarez, David Eduardo and John Justeson. Eclipse records in a corpus of colonial Zapotec 260-day calendars. (*Anc. Mesoam.*, 19:1, March 2008, p. 67–81, bibl., photos, tables)

Paper translates and analyzes references to eclipses in two 17th-century Zapotec calendrical booklets which were part of a campaign against traditional indigenous ritual practices conducted in the province of Villa Alta in northern Oaxaca. The booklets contain a complete day-by-day representation of the Zapotec 260-day divinatory calendar, with annotations in Zapotec. Analysis by authors suggests that colonial Zapotec calendar specialists monitored and perhaps also anticipated the occurrence of eclipses in terms of the patterns of eclipse recurrence in particular parts of the 260 day calendar. [AAJ]

245 Van Doesburg, Sebastián. Los documentos pictográficos de la Mixteca Baja. (*Arqueol. Mex.*, 15:90, marzo/abril 2008, p. 53–57)

Presents a history of the little-studied Mixteca Baja region using pictographs that provide detail on genealogy, land ownership, and the production of salt. [AAJ]

246 Van Doesburg, Sebastián. Documentos pictográficos de la Mixteca Baja de Oaxaca: el Lienzo de San Vicente el Palmar, el Mapa Núm. 36 y el Lienzo Mixteca III. (*Desacatos*, 27, mayo/agosto 2008, p. 95–122, bibl., ill., maps, photos)

Article uses both indigenous and Spanish alphabetic documents and mapas from the late 16th to 18th centuries along with studies of modern geography and toponyms to infer that the *Lienzo de San Vicente del Palmar* originated in the cazicazgo of Ihualtepec in the western Mixteca Baja. Identification of place of origin of this lienzo allows it to be better contextualized historically. Concludes that the document may have been produced as part of an agreement among early colonial rulers. [AAJ]

Caribbean Area

SCOTT M. FITZPATRICK, *Associate Professor of Archaeology, North Carolina State University*

THERE HAS BEEN A STEADY INCREASE in the number of publications related to circum-Caribbean archeology in recent years. This increase applies especially to books, edited volumes, and special issues of journals, most of which focus on islands in the Greater Antilles and northern Lesser Antilles. Some examples include a general review of Caribbean prehistory (item **290**), a volume on current subjects in precolumbian archeology (item **255**), applications of geographic information systems (item **250**), biological resource use by Amerindians (item **279**), and several works on the Taíno (items **258, 271,** and **280**).

Of particular note is a movement of Caribbean scholars publishing in more widely disseminated journals accessible to a larger readership. This development is encouraging, for it will certainly help to highlight the contribution that the Caribbean area can make to discussions of culture contact, island adaptations, and the rise of social complexity, for example. As was also noted in the previous *HLAS* volume, there is a growing emphasis on human impacts to island environments for which the Caribbean will play an increasingly important role.

RECENT DOCTORAL DISSERTATIONS

Bonnissent, Dominique M.C. "Archéologie précolombienne de l'île de Saint-Martin, Petites Antilles (3300 BC–1600 AD)," Univ. de Provence—Aix-Marseille, 2009.

Copper, Jago. "Island interaction in the prehistoric Caribbean: an archaeological case study from northern Cuba," Univ. College London, 2007.

Knippenberg, Sebastiaan. "Stone artefact production and exchange among the northern Lesser Antilles," Leiden Univ., 2006.

Lammers-Keijsers, Yvonne Marie Jacqueline. "Tracing traces from present to past: a functional analysis of pre-Columbian shell and stone artefacts from Anse à la Gourde and Morel, Guadeloupe, FWI," Leiden Univ., 2007.

Rodríguez Ramos, R. "Puerto Rican precolonial history etched in stone," Univ. of Florida, 2007.

Waal, Maaike S. de. "Pre-Columbian social organisation and interaction interpreted through the study of settlement patterns: an archaeological case-study of the Pointe des Châteaux, La Désirade and Les Îles de la Petite Terre microregion, Guadeloupe, F.W.I.," Leiden Univ., 2006.

LOWER CENTRAL AMERICA

247 Fonseca Z., Oscar M. and **Sergio Chávez Chávez.** Contribución al estudio de la historia antigua del pacífico sur de Costa Rica: El sitio Java (Cat. U.C.R. No. 490). (*Cuad. Antropol./San José*, 13, dic. 2003, p. 21–62, bibl., graphs, ill., maps)

Summary of archeological investigations at the Java site on the south Pacific coast of Costa Rica. Authors describe the systematic survey and analysis of remains found, particularly a large array of petroglyphs and stone sculptures along with a myriad of other cultural remains, such as pottery, stone tools, and various anthropomorphic and zoomorphic objects. The site helps decipher social relations in this region in which the household is the basic unit of production.

CARIBBEAN ISLANDS

248 Allsworth-Jones, Philip. Pre-Columbian Jamaica. Tuscaloosa: Univ. of Alabama Press, 2008. 320 p.: bibl., ill., index, maps. (Caribbean archaeology and ethnohistory)

The first major synthesis of prehistoric archeology in Jamaica. An enclosed CD-ROM serves as a valuable source of supplementary information about the colonization and settlement of the island since AD 600.

249 Ancient Borinquen: archaeology and ethnohistory of native Puerto Rico. Edited by Peter E. Siegel. Tuscaloosa: Univ. of Alabama Press, 2005. 423 p.: bibl., index.

A nice collection of papers that examines the diversity and complexity of native Amerindians inhabiting Puerto Rico. Divided into 10 chapters written by many well-known Caribbean scholars. Touches on subjects related to the manufacturing of lithic tools, analysis of animal remains and diet, symbolic and functional use of the landscape, rock art, and the impact to traditional culture vis-à-vis European colonialism.

250 Archaeology and geoinformatics: case studies from the Caribbean. Edited by Basil A. Reid. Tuscaloosa: Univ. of Alabama Press, 2008. 234 p.: bibl., ill., index, maps. (Caribbean archaeology and ethnohistory)

Although archeologists in the Caribbean are increasingly using remote sensing techniques and geographic information systems (GIS) in their research, this collection of papers is the first major synthesis of their applications in the region. Divided into four major sections dealing with visibility models in colonization, cultural resource management strategies, satellite imagery and aerial photography, and geophysics. Covers prehistoric and historic periods on several islands in the Greater and Lesser Antilles.

251 Berman, Mary Jane and Deborah M. Pearsall. At the crossroads: starch grain and phytolith analyses in Lucayan prehistory. (*Lat. Am. Antiq.*, 19:2, June 2008, p. 181–203, bibl., maps, photos, tables)

Documents the presence of maize and other domesticated plants in the Bahamas ca. AD 800, centuries earlier than previously thought. The recovery of botanical remains from smaller stone tools, similar to those recorded elsewhere which were used for plant processing, suggests they functioned in much the same way. This result indicates a more widespread and long term use of plant foods by Caribbean peoples.

252 Callaghan, Richard T. On the question of the absence of Archaic age sites on Jamaica. (*J. Island Coastal Archaeol.*, 3:1, Jan. 2008, p. 54–71, bibl., ill., maps, tables)

One of the more unusual phenomena to occur prehistoricallly in the Caribbean is why Jamaica does not appear to have been settled until very late in time, in contrast to nearby islands such as Cuba and Hispaniola that were settled by Archaic people thousands of years ago. Using computer simulations of voyaging, Callaghan demonstrates that this situation might be related to navigational difficulties, hurricanes, and changes in sea-level that inhibited movement between the islands. Only when canoes became more sophisticated later on was the island able to be settled.

253 Callaghan, Richard T. Prehistoric settlement patterns on St. Vincent, West Indies. (*Caribb. J. Sci.*, 43:1, June 2007, p. 11–22, bibl., maps, tables)

Summarizes the first major survey of the island of St. Vincent in the southern Lesser Antilles. Over 25 new sites were located and compared with various environmental indicators to examine settlement patterns. Results indicate a preference for coastal habitation, particularly in the southwest part of the island during initial settlement by Saladoid peoples, but not near existing reefs as is common elsewhere in the region.

254 Carder, Nanny; Elizabeth J. Reitz; and John G. Crock. Fish communities and populations during the post-Saladoid period (AD 600/800–1500), Anguilla, Lesser Antilles. (*J. Archaeol. Sci.*, 34:4, April 2007, p. 588–599)

Based on analysis from two sites, the authors propose that humans did not adversely impact fish populations during the Late Ceramic Age despite increased population growth and sociopolitical complexity. This finding is in contrast to other sites in the region which show evidence of overharvesting marine resources through time prehistorically, suggesting that this outcome may not always be a given.

255 Crossing the borders: new methods and techniques in the study of archaeological materials from the Caribbean. Edited by Corinne L. Hofman, Menno L.P. Hoogland, and Annelou L. Van Gijn. Tuscaloosa: Univ. of Alabama Press, 2008. 293 p.: bibl., ill., index, maps. (Caribbean archaeology and ethnohistory)

The goal of this volume is to provide a synopsis of Caribbean archeological materials and the diversity of ways in which researchers are analyzing them in the field and laboratory. Consists of chapters by leading authorities in the field which discuss the investigation of starch residues and phytoliths, stable isotopes, experimental archeology, ethnoarcheology, geochemistry, and DNA from mostly prehistoric contexts.

256 Curet, Luis Antonio. Caribbean paleodemography: population, culture history, and sociopolitical processes in ancient Puerto Rico. Tuscaloosa: Univ. of Alabama Press, 2005. 271 p.: bibl., graphs, index, maps.

One of the most challenging exercises archeologists face is trying to determine the size of a given prehistoric population and how settlement patterns may have changed over time using disparate sources of archeological and historical data. Curet does a commendable job of tackling this issue in Puerto Rico using various lines of evidence, including mortuary behaviors, population migration and expansion, construction of agricultural features, and changing levels of social stratification. Among other results, he suggests that interaction between island populations was fairly constant.

257 Curet, Luis Antonio. Missing the point and an illuminating example: a response to Keegan's comments. (*Ethnohistory/Columbus*, 53:2, Spring 2006, p. 393–398, bibl.)

Author expands on critique and discussion by Keegan (item **268**) of his previously published paper "The Chief is Dead, Long Live. . . Who?" (see *HLAS 61:233*). Reinforces the notion that Caribbean researchers have perpetuated ideas of kinship relations without adequate historical or archeological research—especially the idea of matrilineal descent—and that researchers have too often applied perceived social relations seen in one place to another. The argument is that rules of succession are not the same as rules of descent and that these likely differ dramatically between island populations.

258 The earliest inhabitants: the dynamics of the Jamaican Taíno. Edited by Lesley-Gail Atkinson. Kingston: Univ. of the West Indies Press, 2006. 215 p.: bibl., ill., maps.

The 14 chapters in this volume provide one of the most recent and comprehensive looks at the archeology of Jamaica. Subjects covered include reviews of some of the more well-known excavated sites on the island, Taíno exploitation and use of the

environment and their changing subsistence strategies through time, artifact production (particularly ceramics), and artistic representations as observed in petroglyphs and carvings. Examines Jamaican prehistory from a holistic perspective that helps contextualize the island within the larger sphere of precolumbian societies.

259 Fitzpatrick, Scott M. A critical approach to 14C dating in the Caribbean: using chronometric hygiene to evaluate chronological control and prehistoric settlement. (*Lat. Am. Antiq.*, 17:4, Dec. 2006, p. 389–418, bibl., map, tables)

First major review of radiocarbon dates from archeological sites in the West Indies. Author examines known dates and discards those that are ambiguous or required additional information to place them into a more secure cultural context. Suggests a need to examine dates more closely, concluding that the collection of dates does not support the traditional model of a northward stepping stone migration of prehistoric peoples into the Caribbean through the Lesser Antilles from South America.

260 Fitzpatrick, Scott M. and **William F. Keegan.** Human impacts and adaptations in the Caribbean islands: an historical ecology approach. (*Earth Environ. Sci.*, 98, 2007, p. 29–45, bibl., ill., map)

A synthesis of long term human impacts to environments in the prehistoric Caribbean through time. Couched in a historical ecology perspective, the authors examine differences in technologies and subsistence strategies between the Archaic, Ceramic, and Historic periods and how increased levels of population through the Holocene led to the overexploitation of resources.

261 Fitzpatrick, Scott M. *et al.* Evidence for inter-island transport of heirlooms: luminescence dating and petrographic analysis of ceramic inhaling bowls from Carriacou, West Indies. (*J. Archaeol. Sci.*, 36:3, March 2009, p. 596–606, bibl., ill., map, tables)

Examines the discrepancy between the age of ancient drug paraphernalia and that of the archeological context in which they were found. Petrographic analysis of three ceramic inhaling bowls are shown to be exotic to the island, suggesting that they were made elsewhere. Results indicate that they may have been kept within family groups for generations as heirlooms and then transported to other islands as people migrated.

262 Fitzpatrick, Scott M.; Michiel Kappers; and Quetta Kaye. Coastal erosion and site destruction on Carriacou, West Indies. (*J. Field Archaeol.*, 31:3, Fall 2006, p. 251–262, ill., map, photos)

The Caribbean's archeological record is actively being destroyed by a host of factors, including development, agriculture, and natural processes. The authors provide a case study from one of the smaller southern islands in the Grenadines, showing how one of the largest archeological sites in the region is being eroded at an average rate of one meter per year, primarily due to sand mining by locals.

263 Funes Funes, Roberto. Camagüey en la arqueología aborigen de Cuba. Camagüey, Cuba: Editorial Ácana, 2005. 77, 34 p.: bibl., ill. (Col. Suma y reflejo)

Provides a primer on aboriginal peoples of Cuba, also known as the Camagüey. Includes multiple short sections on common vocabulary used, cave paintings, archeological research, cultural relations during different time periods, general types of prehistoric sites found on the island (including those that are burial or ceremonial in nature), and the use of caves.

264 Harlow, George E. *et al.* Pre-Columbian jadeite axes from Antigua, West Indies: description and possible sources. (*Can. Mineralogist*, 44:2, April 2006, p. 305–321, bibl., ill. maps, tables)

Archeologists have been finding jadeite artifacts on Antigua for years, but their origin was unknown. This paper describes an attempt to source 10 samples through mineralogical analysis dating to the early Saladoid period. Results suggest that the unique composition of the stone may have come from Guatemala, although other nearby sources in the Greater Antilles cannot be discounted.

265 Hofman, Corinne Lisette *et al.* Attractive ideas, desirable goods: examining the Late Ceramic Age relationships between Greater and Lesser Antillean societies. (*J. Island Coastal Archaeol.*, 3:1, Jan. 2008, p. 17–34, bibl., ill., map, photos)

There is a growing corpus of data suggesting that interactions between island populations in the Caribbean were frequent, but also intensified through time. The authors review such evidence, emphasizing the movement of objects and spiritual belief systems from the Greater Antilles southward into the Lesser Antilles, focusing on concepts related to incorporation, exchange, and appropriation.

266 *Journal of Caribbean Archaeology.* Vol. 1, special issue, 2006, Historic archaeology in the French Caribbean. Edited by Kenneth Kelly. Gainesville: Univ. of Florida, Florida Museum of Natural History.

Six papers detailing the generally understudied historic period of the French Caribbean, including Martinique, Guadeloupe, Marie Galante, and French Guyana. Recognizes the growing interest in historical archeology in the region and highlights a variety of topics within the field such as industrialism, plantations, ethnoarcheology, and survey methodologies.

267 *Journal of Caribbean Archaeology.* Vol. 2, special issue, 2008, An exploratory study into the chemical characterization of Caribbean ceramics. Edited by Christophe Descantes *et al.* Gainesville: Univ. of Florida, Florida Museum of Natural History.

This compilation of 10 papers represents the first concerted effort by researchers to establish a chemical compositional database of ceramics in the Caribbean. Initiated by researchers at the Missouri Univ. Research Reactor, the papers examine the manufacturing techniques and provenance of both prehistoric and historic period pottery from numerous islands using instrumental neutron activation analysis (INAA). This development is significant as prior to this special issue, very few Caribbean researchers had undertaken studies dealing with the bulk composition of ceramics.

268 Keegan, William F. All in the family: descent and succession in the proto-historic chiefdoms of the Greater Antilles; a comment on Curet. (*Ethnohistory/Columbus*, 53:2, Spring 2006, p. 383–392, table)

Archeologists and historians have long engaged in debates about how pre-columbian societies were structured politically and socially. The author responds to one such attempt to address these issues with the Taíno by examining a paper written by Curet, "The Chief is Dead, Long Live... Who?" (see *HLAS 61:233*). He argues that most scholars are correct in their assertion that these societies were matrilineal, but that while succession and descent need not be the same, they most likely were.

269   Keegan, William F. Archaic influences in the origins and development of Taino societies. (*Caribb. J. Sci.*, 42:1, April 2006, p. 1–10, bibl., map)

Pottery production in the Caribbean was long assumed to have been restricted to Arawak (Saladoid) peoples who colonized the islands from South America. Keegan examines emerging evidence that Archaic peoples in the Greater Antilles had been making pottery all along. Pottery production systems during the two thousand years before European contact should be reevaluated.

270   Keegan, William F. Central plaza burials in Saladoid Puerto Rico: an alternative perspective. (*Lat. Am. Antiq.*, 20:2, June 2009, p. 375–385, bibl., ill., map)

Central plazas in the Caribbean have often been considered the *axis mundi*, functioning as ceremonial places where the dead interact with the living as part of ancestor veneration. The author proposes an alternative hypothesis, suggesting that burial patterns may be reflective of clan members from one village who had moved elsewhere being returned to their clan village for burial as an effort to maintain social cohesion between villages.

271   Keegan, William F. Taíno Indian myth and practice: the arrival of the stranger king. Foreword by Jerald T. Milanich. Gainesville: Univ. Press of Florida, 2007. 230 p.: bibl., ill., index, maps. (Ripley P. Bullen series)

Using the almost universal concept of the "stranger king" in which a foreigner weds a chief's daughter and then overthrows the ruler, the author explores how this scenario may have played out when Christopher Columbus landed in the Caribbean and encountered the Taínos. A combination of ethnohistorical data, oral histories, and archeological data is fused together to provide a robust analysis of how this pivotal event may have transpired during the colonization of the New World.

272   Keegan, William F. *et al.* The role of small islands in marine subsistence strategies: case studies from the Caribbean. (*Hum. Ecol.*, 36:5, Oct. 2008, p. 635–654, bibl., ill., map, table)

Argues that there has been a bias toward examining larger islands in the Caribbean in terms of subsistence quality and quantity. Suggests that in many cases, smaller islands contained a greater abundance of marine resources, had ritual spaces that were isolated, and could be defended more easily. The downside is that small islands were also more susceptible to environmental degradation.

273   Late ceramic age societies in the Eastern Caribbean. Edited by André Delpuech and Corinne L. Hofman. Oxford, England: Archaeopress: Hadrian Books, 2004. 329 p.: bibl., ill., maps. (BAR international series; 1273. Paris monographs in American archaeology; 14)

This tome is divided into five sections with 17 chapters dealing with the latter stages of prehistoric settlement in the Caribbean. Written by some of the leading scholars in Caribbean archeology on topics as diverse as cultural history, the rise of sociopolitical complexity, inter-island contacts and exchange, and linkages of these ceramic-making peoples with South America. Includes a preface in both English and French and two chapters in French. For review of one chapter from the book on the Guianas, see *HLAS 63:587*.

274   LeFebvre, Michelle J. Zooarchaeological analysis of prehistoric vertebrate exploitation at the Grand Bay Site, Carriacou, West Indies. (*Coral Reefs*, 4, 2007, p. 931–944, bibl., maps, tables)

Presents the first in-depth analysis of vertebrate remains from an island in the Grenadines. Sample dating to the late Ceramic Age demonstrates the importance of reef fish to the Amerindian diet and also indicates the importance of using a sampling strategy that involves wet screening sediments with fine mesh. In this case, had it not been done, overall biomass of remains would have been underestimated by 95 percent.

275   Lugo Romera, Karen Mahé and
Sonia Menéndez Castro. Barrio de Campeche: tres estudios arqueológicos. La Habana, Cuba: Fundación Fernando Ortiz, 2003. 151 p.: ill. (La Fuente viva; 27)

Briefly documents three historical sites in Cuba and subsequent archeological investigation and archival research. The first study examines contacts between Cuba and Mesoamerica and the establishment of the Campeche neighborhood; the second discusses excavation of a residence in Havana prior to reconstruction and renovation; and the third looks at archeological excavation undertaken at the church of San Francisco de Paula. These sites all serve to contextualize part of the early historical period in Cuba based on the analysis of archeological materials.

276   Martinón-Torres, Marcos *et al.* Metals, microanalysis and meaning: a study of metal objects excavated from the indigenous cemetery of El Chorro de Maíta, Cuba. (*J. Archaeol. Sci.*, 34:2, Feb. 2007, p. 194–204, bibl., maps, photos, tables)

Metal beads and other artifacts recovered from the largest prehistoric cemetery yet found on Cuba were analyzed chemically to determine their composition and provenance. Elite members possessed beads produced from gold found locally along with other beads made from silver, gold, and copper native to South America. Brass European lacetags were also present, lending insight into Taino relationships with colonial powers.

277   Milanich, Jerald T. Laboring in the fields of the Lord: Spanish missions and southeastern Indians. Gainesville: Univ. Press of Florida, 2006. 210 p.: bibl., index.

Fascinating portrayal of Spanish missionary life in Florida between the 16th and 18th centuries. Organized into eight chapters that deal with issues ranging from early colonial perceptions of native North American groups to the establishment of Franciscan missions, conflicts that arose as traditional belief systems were eroded and eradicated, detailed accounts of individual friars traveling throughout La Florida and immersing

themselves in exotic cultures, and the eventual decline of Spanish influence.

278   Montenegro, Ernesto. Los karibes y los fantasmas medievales. (*Catauro/ Habana*, 5:9, 2004, p. 63–81, bibl.)

The word "Carib" has been used as a blanket term to describe precolumbian peoples in the Caribbean, a function of its historical context. However, the author notes that Carib peoples were extremely diverse sociopolitically and religiously and as such, he argues that this term is misused and inaccurate on many different levels. Additionally, he challenges the negative connotation by historic chroniclers and explorers that these peoples were barbarians and cannibals which fueled domination and exploitation of indigenous Amerindians, quickly leading to their demise at the hands of Europeans.

279   Newsom, Lee Ann and **Elizabeth S. Wing.** On land and sea: Native American uses of biological resources in the West Indies. Tuscaloosa: Univ. of Alabama Press, 2004. 323 p.: bibl., ill., index, maps.

An extremely useful guide to the history of resource use by Amerindians in the Caribbean over the past several thousand years. The authors tap into a growing corpus of archeological data to provide a synthesis of when humans colonized the West Indies, the plant and animal resources they began exploiting locally, and those that were brought in to supplement their diet and other needs. Using numerous case studies from different islands, they show a trend of resource use through time, but with local and regional differences. Well-crafted tables and a clear writing style make reading and referencing fairly effortless.

280   Oliver, José R. Caciques and Cemí idols: the web spun by Taíno rulers between Hispaniola and Puerto Rico. Tuscaloosa: Univ. of Alabama Press, 2009. 306 p.: bibl., ill., index, maps. (Caribbean archaeology and ethnohistory)

The author discusses the relationship between Taino caciques (chiefs) and cemis (objects imbued with supernatural power) in the 500 years before European contact. Also illustrates perceptions of the use of cemis by historical chroniclers and their pivotal role in sociopolitical relations.

281 Peros, Matthew C.; Elizabeth Graham; and Anthony M. Davis. Stratigraphic investigations at Los Buchillones, a coastal Taino Site in north-central Cuba. (*Geoarchaeology/New York*, 21:5, June 2006, p. 403–428, bibl., ill., maps, tables)

The site of Los Buchillones is one of the most significant Taino sites found to date, partly due to the presence of preserved wooden structures submerged along the coastline. Geoarcheological investigations at the site reveal that similar to what is seen elsewhere in the Caribbean, sea level stabilized during the Late Holocene. An unusual case of at least one structure built over the water is presented and an overall assessment of site selection suggests access to multiple resources was considered by local inhabitants.

282 Reid, Basil A. Myths and realities of Caribbean history. Tuscaloosa: Univ. of Alabama Press, 2009. 154 p.: bibl., ill., index, maps. (Caribbean archaeology and ethnohistory)

An interesting review of some of the misconceptions that scholars and laymen alike have had regarding prehistoric Amerindian populations in the Caribbean. Using case studies from throughout the region, Reid debunks many of these popular myths and in doing so, lends important insight about Amerindian groups who had been living in the Caribbean for thousands of years before Europeans arrived.

283 Rodriguez Alvarez, Angel. Astronomía en la prehistoria del Caribe Insular: arqueoastronomía de las plazas megalíticas antillanas. Ed. rev. y aum. Puerto Rico: Editorial Nuevo Mundo, 2008. 291 p.: bibl., ill.

Comprehensive review of ancient astronomical features in the Caribbean islands. The author looks at the use of ceremonial plazas in the Americas, making comparisons with those found in the West Indies and explores these structures in more detail at the sites of Tibes and Caguana on Puerto Rico. Proceeds to establish relations of how these features were constructed and aligned with cyclical and seasonal events. Provides interesting insight into the realm of religious and supernatural beliefs by Caribbean Amerindians.

284 Rodríguez Ramos, Reniel and Jaime Pagán Jiménez. Interacciones multi-vectoriales en el Circum-Caribe precolonial: un vistazo desde las Antillas. (*Caribb. Stud.*, 34:2, July/Dec. 2006, p. 99–139, bibl.)

How and why Amerindian populations migrated into the Lesser and Greater Antilles from areas around the Circum-Caribbean and their levels of interaction through time have been at the forefront of archeological inquiry regionally. The authors note the importance and influence that came from interaction with the surrounding continents, particularly South America, but also the Southeast US. Rather than providing hard data on the extent to which these spheres of influence developed through time, they propose hypotheses that can be used to test directional modes of transaction and movement of cultural modes of behavior.

285 Rodríguez Ramos, Reniel et al. The pre-Arawak pottery horizon in the Antilles: a new approximation. (*Lat. Am. Antiq.*, 19:1, March 2008, p. 47–63, bibl., ill., map)

It has long been traditionally thought that the first ceramics in the Caribbean were introduced by Saladoid migrants from South America, despite pottery often being found in earlier contexts. The authors show that the evidence now suggests otherwise and that changes that occur in terms of technology and decoration in pottery after 500 BC may have roots deeper in antiquity.

Santos, Danilo de los. Memoria de la pintura dominicana: impulso y desarrollo moderno, 1920–1950. See *HLAS 64:80.*

286 Saunders, Nicholas J. Peoples of the Caribbean: an encyclopedia of archeology and traditional culture. Santa Barbara, Calif.: ABC-CLIO, 2005. 399 p.: bibl., ill., index, maps.

A comprehensive and useful guide of the peoples who inhabited the Caribbean islands over the last 7000 years. Includes descriptions of people, languages, cultural periods, significant archeological sites, historical figures, islands, and important events, among many other topics.

287 Steadman, David W. and Sharyn Jones. Long-term trends in prehistoric fishing and hunting on Tobago, West Indies.

(*Lat. Am. Antiq.*, 17:3, Sept. 2006, p. 316–334, bibl., ill., maps, tables)

Authors compare prehistoric bone assemblages between two sites on Tobago—one preceramic (Archaic) and the other ceramic. Results suggest that fishing intensified through time and that earlier occupants hunted a wider variety of lizards, birds, and mammals. This finding may be related to a combination of food preferences, collection techniques, and environmental setting.

288 Steadman, David W. et al. Asynchronous extinction of late Quaternary sloths on continents and islands. (*Proc. Natl. Acad. Sci. U.S.A.*, 102:33, 2005, p. 11763–11768, bibl., ill., map, photos, tables)

Debate continues as to whether humans, climate change, or a combination of both led to the extinction of megafauna in the New World. This study suggests that the extinction of sloths in the Caribbean did not occur until thousands of years after the end of the last interglacial period. This argument provides evidence that the extinction of sloth populations was related to the arrival of humans prehistorically and not caused by changing environmental conditions.

289 Turvey, Samuel T. et al. Late Holocene extinction of Puerto Rican native land mammals. (*Biol. Letters*, 3:2, 2007, p. 193–196, bibl., ill., map, photos, table)

Over 100 land animals have gone extinct in the West Indies during the Late Quaternary, with Puerto Rico being the only island in the Greater Antilles to have lost all land mammals, including sloths, shrews, and various rodents, prior to human arrival. New radiocarbon dates on animal remains suggest that Puerto Rico underwent two major episodes of extinction with smaller sized animals surviving up until the time of European contact.

290 Wilson, Samuel M. The archaeology of the Caribbean. New York: Cambridge Univ. Press, 2007. 209 p.: bibl., ill., index, maps. (Cambridge world archaeology)

A review of Caribbean prehistory by one of the leading scholars on the subject. Purposefully shortened to make it accessible for students and researchers alike, this book summarizes some of the major events which occurred over the past roughly 7000 years of human occupation. Highlights major colonization events, including the movement of horticultural and ceramic-making Saladoid peoples around 500 BC, the socially complex Taíno groups found in the Greater Antilles, and what happened to indigenous peoples after Europeans arrived.

291 Wilson, Samuel M. The prehistory of Nevis, a small island in the Lesser Antilles. With contributions by Laura Kozuch et al. Foreword by Irving Rouse. New Haven, Conn.: Dept. of Anthropology, Yale Univ.: Division of Anthropology, Peabody Museum of Natural History, 2006. 248 p.: bibl., ill., index, maps. (Yale University publications in anthropology; 87)

A synopsis of archeological fieldwork on Nevis. Author provides a background of Caribbean prehistory and research conducted on the island, with chapters written by specialists which detail the analysis of ceramics, plant, and animal remains found at sites excavated by the author.

South America

BETTY J. MEGGERS, *Research Associate, Department of Anthropology, National Museum of Natural History, Smithsonian Institution*
DONNA J. NASH, *Adjunct Assistant Professor of Anthropology, University of Illinois at Chicago*

SOUTH AMERICA

RECENT YEARS IN SOUTH AMERICAN ARCHEOLOGY have seen developments in many theoretical areas. Several regions have become the focus of intensive research programs and much information has become available through the publication of survey results and excavation reports (items **304, 422,** and **449**). While ongoing research in South America is as diverse as its prehistoric past, a number of significant themes run through the work, likely a result of the increasing interaction promoted by multinational conferences and symposia (items **316, 445,** and **460**). Many investigators are concerned with the processes and material changes affiliated with growing complexity and centralization, changes resulting from cultural confrontations such as the expansion of states or colonial era contact between indigenous groups and foreign intruders. Strikingly, over the past few years many scholars have been concerned with documenting the development of the discipline and its practices, such as collection and exposition, as well as noting the influence of key individuals to their respective regions of research.

One such theme is complexity. Many researchers are working at a number of scales to describe the organization of complex societies (items **306** and **313**) and their attributes (item **292**), or have drawn together several lines of evidence to link material remains to increasing complexity (item **313**). Perhaps the most prominent among these is the construction and use of public ceremonial spaces, such as the early center of Caral in Peru's Supe Valley (item **462**), the highland center of Chavín (items **434** and **454**), or the Formative Period center of Tulán in Chile's Atacama Basin (item **410**). Survey projects documenting significant shifts in settlement patterns have also linked the use or scarcity of specific resources as stimulants for social stratification (items **401** and **425**). Several programs of research in Northwest Argentina examine changes from the Formative to Regional Development Periods (items **302, 317, 325,** and **326**). Some of which have focused particularly on the design of public spaces as both an indicator of and a mechanism leading to growing sociopolitical complexity (items **313** and **328**). Likewise archeologists have used the design of monumental spaces to discuss changes in political activity on Peru's north coast (item **448**).

As large examples of material culture, settlement organization (item **322**), details of building form (item **333**), and the placement of sites and structures on the landscape can be informative means of defining groups because buildings and landscape features can have an active role in the production of identity and its maintenance through time (items **414**). Portable goods such as pottery can play a role in reproducing group identity (items **429** and **469**) with producers of such goods active in the reproduction of ideology (item **447**). The objects themselves, especially in the case of the Moche tradition, can provide a glimpse of the different identities operative in a particular society (items **436, 444,** and **448**). Often pottery and other portable goods are key indicators for archeologists to recognize group identity and common practices among some societies, and thus are used to link sites to polities (item **463**). Nevertheless, a few studies suggest that elements of style can also be idiosyncratic and representative of individuals during some time periods (item **414**). The production and use of material culture has also been used to chart continuity and change over long time periods (item **419**), but some scholars warn that such goods may not be the best medium for studying important social or economic changes (item **427**), especially during the colonial era when many factors impacted the production and circulation of goods.

Change based on such cultural confrontations is a prominent topic of research in which archeology overlaps with history. Several multidisciplinary collaborative or comparative studies in Argentina (items **307, 318,** and **327**), Bolivia (item **330**), Chile (item **315**), Colombia (items **419, 420,** and **427**), and Peru (items **446** and **449**) examine the experiences of indigenous groups and the subsequent changes and continuities in material culture, ritual, and economy, among other attributes. Researchers are also examining similar processes resulting from Inca expansion in the Late Horizon (items **312, 315, 400, 402,** and **442**), as well as the impact that Formative Period and Middle Horizon interaction with contemporary groups had on the character of the Tiwanaku state and its development (item **334**), Tiwanaku's relations with autochthonous communities (items **403** and **411**), or both (items **300, 311, 334,** and **407**). Interactions also figure prominently in hypotheses of change from the north coast of Peru to the south coast of Chile (items **321** and **406**).

Interaction as a historical process lends diversity to the archeological record: likewise unique historical situations and interactions in regions and countries of South America have created differences in the discipline and practice of archeology. Over the past few years several edited volumes, monographs, and journal articles focus on documenting the history of collecting (item **4**), changing interpretations (item **458**), general theoretical and methodological developments (items **418, 426, 430,** and **470**) and the contributions of individuals (items **453** and **465**) or groups (item **461**). Recent publications discuss important issues for the future such as site conservation (items **440, 441,** and **451**), museum exhibition, and community involvement with the protection of archeological remains (item **294**). Such self-reflection demonstrates a strong, mature professionalism that promises future developments and positive contributions from the South American research area in archeological theory. [DJN]

BRAZIL AND THE GUIANAS

The focus of archeological research in Brazil has changed greatly during the past two decades, both in the goal of fieldwork and the interpretation of the evidence. The majority of archeologists are now conducting salvage investigations rather than basic research. Although this shift has the advantage of providing information on previously ignored regions (items **343, 344, 384,** and **396**), it limits the amount of excavation, analysis, and resulting publication.

Increased attention has been devoted to analysis of human skeletal remains from both recent and ancient sites and from cemeteries, providing information on trauma, sexual differences, diet, and disease (item **299**). A particularly significant contribution to the peopling of the hemisphere is made by Walter Neves *et al.*, who have identified a pre-mongoloid population that is less well represented in North America (see *HLAS 63:475* and item **376**). Lithic evidence of Paleo-Indians has been identified in open sites and rock shelters on the upper Tocantins (item **339**) and faunal remains have been described from a rock shelter in Rio Grande do Sul (item **388**). A detailed description of the contents of the Santa Elina rock shelter in Mato Grosso with an initial radiocarbon date of 24,000 BP is noteworthy (item **383**).

Stimulated by the 50th anniversary of the founding of the Centro de Estudos e Pesquisas Arqueológicas, the Universidade Federal do Paraná invited 15 senior archeologists to describe the support they received from the CEPA during their early careers (items **338** and **367**). Biographical sketches have been published on Peter Paul Hilbert (item **358**), João Alfredo Rohr (item **392**), and José Loureiro Fernandes (item **342**).

The most controversial recent development in Amazonian archeology is the application of historical ecology theory to the interpretation of prehistoric cultural development. This approach posits that if humans are not satisfied with the resources of their environment, they can domesticate it. According to Clark Erickson, the principal proponent, archeologists have demonstrated that much of the lowlands was occupied by urban societies practicing intensive agriculture, although he fails to document any examples (item **349**) and none of the evidence for environmental limitations provided by ecologists, biologists, paleoclimatologists, geologists, and other specialists is addressed (items **369** and **370**). His theme is shared by José Oliver (item **379**) and Michael Heckenberger (items **354**, **355**, **356**, and *HLAS 63:834*), but Eduardo Neves provides a more balanced view of the theory (item **374**). [BJM]

GENERAL

292 After collapse: the regeneration of complex societies. Edited by Glenn M. Schwartz and John J. Nichols. Tucson: Univ. of Arizona Press, 2006. 336 p.: bibl., index.

Brings together a collection of articles on the collapse and regeneration of complex societies. Using case studies from numerous world regions, the volume develops an alternative evolutionary perspective focusing on social fragmentation, reformation, and rise of second-generation states. Contributions are comparative, diachronic studies intended to delineate patterns of sociocultural and historical change. For reviews of two individual chapters, see items **22** and **171**. [DJN]

293 Aproximaciones a la paleopatología en América Latina. Coordinación de Hugo A. Sotomayor Tribín y Zoilo Cuéllar-Montoya. Bogotá: Convenio Andrés Bello: Academia Nacional de Medicina de Colombia: Asociación Latinoamericana de Academias nacionales de Medicina, España y Portugal, 2007. 290 p.: bibl., ill. (chiefly col.), index, maps.

Contributors consider paleopathology through human remains and depictions in various media, precolumbian medicinal practices, mortuary behavior, cranial modification, and related topics. The sections of the volume cover Argentina, Bolivia, Colombia, Ecuador, Mexico, Paraguay, and Peru. Chapters are authored by medical doctors, anthropologists, and archeologists and include diverse data illustrated with color photographs. [DJN]

294 Archaeological site museums in Latin America. Edited by Helaine Silverman. Foreword by Paul Shackel. Gainesville: Univ. Press of Florida, 2006. 301 p.: bibl., index. (Cultural heritage studies)

The volume describes issues surrounding museum representation of archeological sites in the context of Latin America. The authors describe site museums in several Latin American countries with regard to local, national, and international involvement, politics, funding, and collaboration. Provides a wide array of case studies in archeological outreach through the medium of the site museum. [DJN]

295 Brotherston, Gordon et al. Por ti América: arte pré-colombiana. Rio de Janeiro: Centro Cultural, Banco do Brasil, 2005. 303 p.: bibl., ill., maps.

Color illustrations of ca. 350 gorgeous pottery, gold, stone, and textile objects from Mesoamerica, the Circum-Caribbean, Lowland South America and the Andes selected for exhibition in the Brazilian cities of Rio de Janeiro, Brasília, and São Paulo, to create awareness among the Brazilian public of the intellectual, cultural, and technological sophistication of precolumbian societies of the Americas. [BJM]

296 Cardich, Augusto. Hacia una prehistoria de Sudamérica: culturas tempranas de los Andes Centrales y de Patagonia. Buenos Aires: Univ. de La Plata, 2003. 686 p.: bibl., ill., maps.

A massive and erudite tome on the archeology of early cultures of the Central Andes and Patagonia. The text covers such topics as Lauricocha, Ranracancha, and

Cajamarca in Peru and Los Toldos and the rock paintings of El Ceibo in Patagonia. [S. Ramírez]

Gender, households, and society: unraveling the threads of the past and the present. See item 45.

297 González Lens, Daniel and **Betty J. Meggers.** Coeficiente Brainerd Robinson: ¿panacea real o ilusoria?; una revisión de las bases utilizadas para criticar la seriación como método para reconstruir la reocupación de sítios en las tierras bajas amazónicas. (*Int. J. South Am. Archaeol.*, 4, 2009, p. 15–28, bibl., tables)

Provides a detailed demonstration that use of the Brainerd Robinson Coeficient by DeBoer, Kintigh, and Rostoker (published in *Latin American Antiquity* in 1996) to refute the validity of pottery seriation for identifying prehistoric settlement behavior fails to recognize the limitations of statistical analysis for interpreting archeological remains. [BJM]

298 Gordon R. Willey and American archaeology: contemporary perspectives. Edited by Jeremy A. Sabloff and William L. Fash. Norman: Univ. of Oklahoma Press, 2007. 256 p.: index.

Colleagues and students of Gordon Willey provide informative personal accounts of his pioneering contributions to the expansion of the focus of archeological fieldwork and resulting interpretation in Mesoamerica and Peru during the last half of the 20th century. [BJM]

299 Nossa origem: o povoamento das Américas: visões multidisciplinares. Organização de Hilton P. Silva e Claudia Rodrigues-Carvalho. Prefácio de Francisco M. Salzano. Rio de Janeiro: Vieira & Lent, 2006. 230 p.: bibl., ill., maps.

Nine chapters by Brazilian specialists provide linguistic, genetic, parasitological, fossil, facial reconstruction, morphological, physical anthropological, and biodiversity perspectives on reconstructions of the peopling of South America and suggest their relevance to the evaluation of current models. An important contribution to the topic. [BJM]

Paleoindian archaeology: a hemispheric perspective. See item 85.

300 Torres, Constantino Manuel. Imágenes legibles: la iconografía Tiwanaku como significante. (*Bol. Mus. Chil. Arte Precolomb.*, 9, 2004, p. 55–73, bibl., ill., photos)

Considers the iconography of Tiwanaku as a dynamic, context-specific communicative medium. Examines a snuff tablet from the Denver Art Museum collection and discusses the variations of Tiwanaku style objects from several regions to support the hypothesis that Tiwanaku iconography did not have fixed meanings but rather was adapted to be meaningful in different local contexts. [DJN]

ARGENTINA

301 Anglorama, Carlos Ignacio. Acerca de incas y metales en Humahuaca: producción metalúrgica en Los Amarillos en tiempos del Tawantinsuyu. (*Relac. Soc. Argent. Antropol.*, 29, 2004, p. 39–58, bibl., ill., maps, photos)

Presents evidence of the production of metal objects during the Inca era occupation of Los Amarillos, Humahuaca Basin, Jujuy, Northwest Argentina. Metal was imported to the site, refined, and formed using molds. Based on features and materials recovered, the author describes the steps in the production process. [DJN]

302 Baldini, Lidia et al. Los desarrollos regionales en el valle Calchaquí central, Salta. (*Relac. Soc. Argent. Antropol.*, 29, 2004, p. 59–80, bibl., ill., maps, table)

The authors present results from a survey of a segment of the Calchaquí Valley between the Cachi and Molinos rivers to understand the nature of the Regional Development Period in the region. They consider the agricultural potential, production, settlement attributes, evidence of goods exchange, and mortuary practices to describe economic and sociopolitical developments. [DJN]

303 Bollini, Gabriel A. et al. Antropología dental de una serie prehistórica de araucanos provenientes de la Patagonia Argentina. (*Rev. Arqueol. Am./México*, 23, 2004/2005, p. 385–406, bibl., tables)

Describes the dental characteristics of 36 individuals from the collections of the

Museo de La Plata, Argentina, from central Chile (Araucanos or Mapuche) of the protohistoric period. Results show that the homogeneous sample exhibits interesting differences from other indigenous samples in the region. [DJN]

304 Callegari, Adriana Beatriz. Las poblaciones precolombinas que habitaron el sector central del valle de Vinchina entre el 900–950 y 1600–1650 d.C. (*Relac. Soc. Argent. Antropol.*, 29, 2004, p. 81–110, bibl., graphs, maps, photos, tables)

Callegari presents survey results pertaining to the Aguada and Sanagasta occupation of the La Rioja prov., Argentina. Site organization, ceramic distributions, and radiocarbon dates from several sites suggest that the Aguada and Sanagasta occupations overlapped in time with Sanagasta located in the valley bottom and Aguada in foothill canyons (*rincones*). [DJN]

305 Durán, Víctor et al. Estudio de fuentes de aprovisionamiento y redes de distribución de obsidiana durante el Holoceno Tardío en el sur de Mendoza, Argentina. (*Estud. Atacameños*, 28, 2004, p. 25–43, graphs, ill., maps, photos, tables)

Authors describe five sources of obsidian located in Mendoza, Argentina, and central Chile, along with their chemical signatures. They also present analysis of obsidian artifacts from archeological sites to understand the movement of obsidian through time in the region as well as the sources of obsidian used in Mendoza. [DJN]

306 Elías, Alejandra Mercedes. Informalidad: un acercamiento a la tecnología lítica de momentos tardíos a partir de las características de diseño de los instrumentos relevados en dos sitios de Antofagasta de la Sierra (Prov. Catamarca, Argentina): la alumbrera y campo cortaderas. (*Hombre Desierto*, 12, 2005, p. 47–71, bibl., map, tables)

Discusses the lithic technology observed at two sites, La Alumbrera y Campo Cortaderas, of the Regional Development Period (1100–450 BP) to understand reduction strategies and the use of local materials among sedentary groups in the region. Author considers the location of source material, basic forms, size, platform type, and reduction techniques to show that

complex societies were using an expedient or utilitarian lithic production strategy. [DJN]

307 Entre médanos y caldenes de la pampa seca: arqueología, historia, lengua y topónimos. Compilación de Ana M. Aguerre y Alicia H. Tapia. Buenos Aires: Univ. de Buenos Aires, Facultad de Filosofía y Letras, 2002. 338 p.: bibl., ill., maps.

The edited volume is a multidisciplinary work on the Pampa Seco region of Argentina. Archeological research includes a survey of the West Pampa, landscape studies and rock art in the zone. Studies of historical documents, the records of earlier travelers, and language detail the interethnic interaction and change in the 18th and 19th centuries. [DJN]

308 Escola, Patricia S. Variabilidad en la explotación y distribución de obsidianas en la Puna Meridional argentina. (*Estud. Atacameños*, 28, 2004, p. 9–24, maps, tables)

Escola presents the distribution of obsidian from two sources based on artifacts from 20 sites dating from 2200 BP to 600 BP in Catamarca and Salta, Northwest Argentina. Although material from the Cueros Purulla source is superior in quality, obsidian from the Ona source was found to be more widely distributed, especially after 1800 BP, demonstrating that a number of sociopolitical factors affected the distribution of obsidian. [DJN]

309 Fabra, Mariana. Producción tecnológica y cambio social en sociedades agrícolas prehispánicas: Valle de Ambato, Catamarca, Argentina. Oxford, England: Archaeopress, 2007. 200 p.: bibl., ill., maps. (BAR international series;1723)

The author compares ceramic technology, production investment, and diversity to determine if craft specialization was related to growing complexity between the Formative and Regional Integration Period Aguada society. Analysis of pottery from El Altillo (AD 100–600) and Piedras Blancas (AD 600–1000) demonstrates that early diversity gave way to fewer Aguada forms, however technology changed little and some Formative wares exhibited high investment related to their ritual use. [DJN]

310   **Fernández Distel, Alicia A.** ¿Arte
rupestre o graffiti?: los grabados con
leyendas de Abra Colorada, Jujuy; una vision
interdisciplinaria. (*Hombre Desierto*, 12,
2005, p. 7–21, bibl., ill., photo)

Article describes the site of Abra Colorada, Dept. of Tumbaya, Jujuy, Argentina,
which includes both traditional designs
considered by most to be rock art, as well
as letters, words, and phrases described as
graffiti. The authors consider the important
differences between the two and discuss the
distinction with regards to archeological
enquiry. [DJN]

311   **González, Alberto Rex.** La arqueología del Noroeste argentino y las culturas formativas de la cuenca del Titicaca.
(*Relac. Soc. Argent. Antropol.*, 29, 2004,
p. 7–38, bibl., ill., photos)

Article examines interaction between
Northwest Argentina and the Titicaca
Basin in the Formative Period (Pukara) and
the Middle Horizon through iconography
on stone stela, metal plaques, and textiles.
The author suggests that Tiwanaku and
Aguada cosmology had a common origin in
the Formative and that some aspects of this
common tradition were part of later Inca
religion. [DJN]

312   **González, Luis R.** and **Myriam N.
Tarrago.** Vientos del sur: el valle de
Yocavil, Noroeste Argentino, bajo la domi-
nación incaica. (*Estud. Atacameños*, 29,
2005, p. 67–95, ill.)

Article describes the regional complexity before Inca intrusion and the selective placement of Inca installations in the
Yocavil valley, Northwest Argentina. Relations between local elites and Inca officials
seem to have permitted many population
centers to remain intact with Inca sites
being selectively placed to control metal
production, the extraction of minerals, and
to maximize other features of local production. [DJN]

313   **Gordillo, Inés.** Arquitectos del rito:
la construcción del espacio público
en la Rinconanda, Catamarca. (*Relac. Soc.
Argent. Antropol.*, 29, 2004, p. 111–136, bibl.,
ill., maps, photos, tables)

Describes the spatial design of La
Rinconada, an Aguada site, Dept. of Ambato, Catamarca, Argentina. The author
analyzes the public space with a number of
techniques and emphasizes the importance
of the platform/plaza complex as part of the
developing sociopolitical complexity during
the Regional Integration Period. [DJN]

314   **Haber, Alejandro F.** Una arqueología
de los oasis puneños: domesticidad,
interacción e identidad en Antofalla, primer
y segundo milenios D.C. Córdoba, Argentina: Jorge Sarmiento Editor, Universitas
libros, 2006. 422 p.: bibl., ill.

Haber presents survey information
from Tebenquiche Chico as a case study to
characterize the Antofalla oasis landscape
in the Atacama Puna, Argentina. He considers the theoretical models and history of
research in the region and reconsiders the
area using the domestic, community, and
regional scales to describe social formations
dating to the fourth through 12th centuries.
[DJN]

315   **Hernández Llosas, María Isabel.**
Inkas y españoles a la conquista
simbólica del territorio Humahuaca: sitios,
motivos rupestres y apropiación cultural del
paisaje. (*Bol. Mus. Chil. Arte Precolomb.*,
11:2, 2006, p. 9–34, bibl., maps, photos)

Examines rock art in the Quebrada de
Humahuaca, Argentina, as part of the cultural landscape to understand the symbolic
aspects of territorial expansion. Discusses
four periods of imperial intrusion, first by
the Inca (AD 1480–1535), and then three by
the Spanish (AD 1535–1650). [DJN]

316   **Jornadas de Arqueología e Historia de
las Regiones Pampeana y Patagónica,
3rd, Luján, Argentina, 2003.** Signos en el
tiempo y rastros en la tierra. Recopilación
de Mariano Ramos y Eugenia Néspolo.
Luján, Argentina: Univ. Nacional de Luján,
2003. 336 p.: bibl., ill., maps.

The majority of the conference papers focus on different aspects of historical
archeology: dating, site formation processes,
and ways of managing written sources. The
remaining sections are more diverse in
composition and are loosely grouped into
frontier studies, urban archeology, the Patagonia region, the Pampas region, and the
Near East. [DJN]

317   **Laguens, Andrés G.** Arqueología de
la diferenciación social en el valle
de Ambato, Catamarca, Argentina (S. II–VI

d.C.): el actualismo como metodología de análisis. (*Relac. Soc. Argent. Antropol.*, 29, 2004, p. 137–161, bibl., tables)

Examines the transformation in Ambato from Condorhuasi-Alamito and Ciénaga to Aguada. While some elements of continuity are identified, in general new types of capital (social, economic, political, or symbolic) and new fields of social interaction for diversifying populations are viewed as a revolutionary change in kind rather than of scale. [DJN]

318 Local, regional, global: prehistoria, protohistoria e historia en los valles calchaquíes. Dirección académica de Maj-Lis Follér. Recopilación de Per Cornell & Per Stenborg. Göteborg: Inst. Iberoamericano, Univ. de Göteborg, 2003. 460 p.: bibl., ill. (some col.). (GOTARC. Series C, Arkeologiska skrifter; 54) (Anales; nueva época, 6) (Etnologiska studier; 46)

The collected works focus on the theme of edges, borders, and frontiers from the Formative Period to the modern era. Studies range in scale from the walls that divide interior and exterior spaces to the boundaries and interaction between regions. Several articles also examine situations of contact and change, particularly during colonial times. [DJN]

319 Mondini, Mariana. La comunidad de predadores en la Puna durante el Holoceno: interacciones bióticas entre humanos y carnívoros. (*Relac. Soc. Argent. Antropol.*, 29, 2004, p. 183–209, bibl., maps, tables)

Mondini presents a detailed analysis of archeofauna and carnivore excrement to assess the taphanomic effects of carnivore activity on hunter-gatherer sites in Northwest Argentina. Using two sites, Inca Cueva 4, Jujuy, and Quebrada Seca 3, Catamarca, the author determined that the taphanomic effects in both regions were minimal and did not have a serious impact on the archeological deposits. [DJN]

320 Muscio, Hernán Juan. Aproximación evolutiva a la complejidad y al orden social temprano a través del estudio de representaciones rupestres de la quebrada de Matancillas (Puna argentina). (*Estud. Atacameños*, 31, 2006, p. 9–30, bibl., graphs, ill., map, photos)

Examines petroglyphs and geoglyphs of Matancillas, Puna, of Salta, Argentina, as extensions of the human phenotype. The author takes a Darwinian perspective and interprets the glyphs as artifacts that transmit cultural information, reproducing group life and institutionalizing the social order. [DJN]

321 Neme, Gustavo A. Cazadores-recolectores de altura en los Andes meridionales: en alto valle del río Atuel, Argentina. Oxford, England: Archaeopress, 2007. 152 p.: bibl., ill., maps. (BAR international series; 1591)

Examines the Upper Atuel Valley, Mendoza, from its first settlement by hunter-gatherers (ca. 9000 BP) until the period of European contact. Neme suggests a significant shift in the subsistence economy around 2000 BP, in which intensification corresponds with the appearance of ceramics and exotic imports, perhaps indicating reduced mobility and increased trade in the following periods. [DJN]

322 Nielsen, Axel E. Plazas para los antepasados: descentralización y poder corporativo en las formaciones políticas preincaicas de los Andes circumpuneños. (*Estud. Atacameños*, 31, 2006, p. 63–89, bibl., ill., maps, photos, tables)

Presents archeological evidence from two Late Intermediate Period sites, Los Amarillos in the Quebrada de Humahuaca and Laqaya in north Lipez, Argentina. The author considers the use of public space in order to understand the social organization of these communities. [DJN]

323 Podestá, María Mercedes. El arte rupestre de Argentina indígena. Noroeste. Prólogo de Rodolfo A. Raffino. Colaboración de Fermín Fèvre. Textos de María Mercedes Podestá, Diana S. Rolandi, y Mario Sánchez Proaño. Coordinación de Rodolfo A. Raffino. Buenos Aires: Grupo Abierto Comunicaciones: Union académique internationale: Academia Nacional de la Historia, 2005. 115 p.: bibl., col. ill., col. maps. (Corpus antiquitatum Americanensium. Argentina; 5)

This colorful, well-illustrated book, with text in English and Spanish, discusses the different designs represented in rock art throughout the Northwest region of Argentina. The volume covers representations on rock (incised and painted) from the earliest human colonization of South America to the early Spanish colonial period. [DJN]

324 Reunión Anual de Etnología, 20th, Museo Nacional de Etnología y Folklore, 2006. Memorias. La Paz: MUSEF Editores, 2007. 2 v.: bibl., ill.

This published proceeding includes a wide array of current research in archeology, ethnohistory, ethnography, linguistics, migration studies, popular culture studies, and sociocultural anthropology. The archeological research is found in vol. 1 and includes rock art studies as well as examinations of Tiwanaku and the Inka. Together the volumes contain 113 articles that demonstrate the vibrant and growing research tradition in South America today. [DJN]

325 Seldes, Verónica. Bioarqueología de poblaciones prehistóricas de la quebrada de Humahuaca (Jujuy, Argentina). (*Estud. Atacameños*, 31, 2006, p. 47–61, bibl., maps, tables)

Compares the nutritional stress, functional stress, diet, and trauma of samples from several sites spanning three time periods: the late Formative, the Regional Development I, and the Regional Development II, to assess changes in subsistence, resources consumed, and population health. The author relates these changes to developing social complexity to show how bioarcheological study can contribute to understanding social change. [DJN]

326 Sempé, María Carlota. Contextos temáticos funerarios de las tumbas Aguada Gris Grabado del cementerio Aguada Orilla Norte, Catamarca. (*Relac. Soc. Argent. Antropol.*, 29, 2004, p. 275–295, bibl., ill., tables)

Describes icons and motifs on pottery associated with graves from the Aguada type site, Aguada Orilla Norte, Dept. of Belén, Catamarca, Argentina, and examines changes between the earlier and later phases. The author suggests that early variation with different groups appropriating different symbols gave way to a later phase of less ideological differentiation. [DJN]

327 Signorile, Analía and Griselda Benso. Comechingones y los primeros españoles en Calamuchita. Córdoba: Ediciones del Boulevard, 2006. 170 p.: bibl., ill., maps.

Describes the cultural history of the Comechingones, indigenous people of the Sierra de Calamuchita, Argentina. A brief review of the archeological sites of the region is followed by descriptions of the first encounters between locals and Spanish conquistadors, the subsequent era of encomiendas, and the early colonial population. [DJN]

328 Tarrago, Myriam Noemí and Luis R. González. Arquitectura social y ceremonial en Yocavil, Catamarca. (*Relac. Soc. Argent. Antropol.*, 29, 2004, p. 297–315, bibl., maps, photos, table)

Authors consider the quality, circulation, visibility, modification of natural space, and use of colored stone in the ceremonial architecture at the site of Rincón Chico, Catamarca, Northwest Argentina. They suggest that public space was designed to situate elites in a position of power between traditional sources of power (ancestors and mountains) and the populace during the Regional Development Period. [DJN]

329 Vila, Assumpció; Alicia Casas; and Oriol Vicente. Mischiuen III, un contexto funerario singular en el Canal Beagle, Tierra del Fuego. (*Rev. Esp. Antropol. Am.*, 36:1, 2006, p. 47–61, bibl., map, photos)

Describes a funerary context from the site of Mischiuen III, in Yámana territory, north coast of the Beagle Canal, Argentina. Remains of two individuals were uncovered and registered in a GIS. The authors emphasize the importance of carefully documenting funerary contexts to understand these important social settings. [DJN]

BOLIVIA

330 Cruz, Pablo. Mundos permeables y espacios peligrosos: consideraciones acerca de punkus y qaqas en el paisaje altoandino de Potosí, Bolivia. (*Bol. Mus. Chil. Arte Precolomb.*, 11:2, 2006, p. 35–50, bibl., maps, photos, table)

Presents ethnographic notions of landscape features called Punku and Qaqa, which are typically associated with modern votive rites. Several examples of such places are associated with archeological remains such as rock art or mortuary monuments. The author relates cosmological ideas of the present with the significance of these spaces in the past. [DJN]

331 Erickson, Clark L. and **William Balée.** The historical ecology of a complex landscape in Bolivia. (*in* Time and complexity in historical ecology: studies in the neotropical lowlands. Edited by William Balée and Clark L. Erickson. New York: Columbia Univ. Press, 2006, p. 187–233, bibl., ill., map, tables)

Topographic mapping of the Ibibate mound complex, consisting of two connected mounds 16–18 in elevation, and detailed inventory of vegetation composition provide evidence for "massive pre-Hispanic human disturbance." No excavations were conducted and pottery is limited to small surface samples. Detailed inventories are provided for the composition of the vegetation and the chemical content of the soil. [BJM]

332 Historia de Bolivia. Coordinación de Ximena Medinaceli Gonzáles. La Paz: Fundación del Banco Central de Bolivia, 2006. 1 v.: bibl., ill. (some col.).

Offers a general introduction to the cultural history of different regions of Bolivia. Summarizes recent archeological research conducted by Bolivian and foreign scholars. The final section briefly describes ethnohistoric groups as well as modern ethnographic populations. [DJN]

333 Kesseli, Risto and **Martti Pärssinen.** Identidad étnica y muerte: torres funerarias (*chullpas*) como símbolos de poder étnico en el altiplano boliviano de Pakasa, 1250–1600 d.C. (*Bull. Inst. fr. étud. andin.*, 34:3, 2005, p. 379–410, bibl., maps, photos)

Article describes chullpa mortuary monuments from the Pakasa (Pacaje) area of the Bolivian altiplano. Variation between different areas during the Late Intermediate Period and later Inca *chullpa* suggests that the Pacaje *señorio* consisted of several ethnic groups, each with a distinguishable form of *chullpa* construction. [DJN]

334 Ponce Sanginés, Carlos. Tiwanaku y su fascinante desarrollo cultural: ensayo y síntesis arqueológica. v. 3, La cultura tiwanaku y el sistema sociocultural prehispánico. La Paz: Producciones Cima: Univ. Americana, 2003. 1 v. (525 p.): bibl., ill. (some col.).

This volume in the 4-volume series focuses on the sociocultural system of Tiwanaku and external political relations. The author discusses Tiwanaku's urban character, social classes, and demography, as well as several elements of dress and ornamentation. He also considers Tiwanaku's relationship with contemporary societies such as Pukara, Moche, Nazca, and Wari. [DJN]

BRAZIL

335 Alfonso, Marisa Coutinho and **Camila Azevedo de Moraes.** O sítio Agua Branca: interações culturais dos grupos ceramistas no norte do estado de São Paulo. (*Rev. Mus. Arqueol. Etnol.*, 15/16, 2005/2006, p. 59–71, bibl., ill., tables)

Describes a site with pottery affiliated with the Aratu/Sapucai Tradition with a TL date of 205 ± 20 BP. [BJM]

336 Araujo, Astolfo Gomes de Mello. A tradição cerâmica Itararé-Taquara: características, área de ocorrência e algumas hipóteses sobre a expansão dos grupos Jê no sudeste do Brasil. (*Rev. Arqueol./São Paulo*, 20, 2007, p. 9–38, bibl., maps, tables)

Provides a detailed overview of the definition, distribution, antiquity, and regional differences in pottery assigned to the Itararé-Taquara tradition, associated archeological features, and affiliation with contemporary Kaingang and Xokleng groups. Although the earliest radiocarbon dates are from Rio Grande do Sul, these distributions suggest derivation of the pottery from the Una Tradition in northern Minas Gerais. [BJM]

337 Araujo, Astolfo Gomes de Mello *et al.* Human occupation and paleoenvironments in South America: expanding the notion of an "archaic map." (*Rev. Mus. Arqueol. Etnol.*, 15/16, 2005/2006, p. 3–35, bibl., ill., map)

Comparison of the frequency of radiocarbon dates by 500-year intervals from 12,000 BP to the present from archeological sites and pollen cores in coastal Brazilian states reveals significant reductions in frequency during the middle Holocene, implying a decline in human population density attributable to the impact of severe drought. [BJM]

338 Arqueologia. 4, Número Especial, 2007. Curitiba, Brazil: Univ. Federal do Paraná, Centro de Estudos e Pesquisas Arqueológicas (CEPA).

Reminiscences by 15 senior archeologists of the impact of the Centro on their early professional development provide a personalized insight into the significant role it played in the history of Brazilian archeology during the past 50 years. [BJM]

339   Bueno, Lucas de Melo Reis. As indústrias líticas da região do Lajeado e sua inserção no contexto do Brasil central. (*Rev. Mus. Arqueol. Etnol.*, 15/16, 2005/2006, p. 37–57, bibl., ill., map, tables)

Survey along the middle Tocantins identified 110 open sites and 20 rock shelters with lithic artifacts consisting of amorphous unifacial flakes. Twenty-six radiocarbon dates extend from 10530 to 510 BP. [BJM]

340   Caldarelli, Solange Bezerra; Fernanda de Araújo Costa; and Dirse Clara Kern. Assentamentos a céu aberto de caçadores-coletores datados da transição Pleistoceno final/Holoceno inicial no Sudeste do Pará. (*Rev. Arqueol./São Paulo*, 18, 2005, p. 95–108, bibl., ill., maps, tables)

The lower levels of two ceramic sites on the east bank of the Tocantins at Tucuruí produced cores, flakes, and complete and unfinished stone artifacts. Five radiocarbon dates range from 9510 ± 70 to 4890 ± 50 BP. [BJM]

341   Os ceramistas tupiguarani. Vol. 1, Sínteses regionais. Recopilação de André Prous e Tania Andrade Lima. Belo Horizonte, Brazil: Belo Horizonte, Sigma, 2008. 216 p.

Seven chapters describe archeological sites and ceramics attributed to the Tupiguarani Tradition in Amazonia, northeastern Brazil, southeastern Brazil, southern Brazil, the states of São Paulo and Mato Grosso do Sul, and Argentina, providing the first overview of the coastal distribution of the tradition. Authors express disagreements concerning the correlations between the Painted (Tupi) and Corrugated (Guarani) subtraditions and speakers of Tupi and Guarani languages, directions of migration, environmental contexts, and other differences. Abundant illustrations of decoration and vessel shapes, as well as lists of 14C dates and extensive bibliographies, make this a useful reference. [BJM]

342   Chmyz, Igor. José Loureiro Fernandes e a arqueologia brasileira. (*Arqueologia/Curitiba*, 10, 2006, p. 43–105, bibl., ill.)

Provides a detailed account of the profound impact of José Loureiro Fernandes on the creation of cultural institutions, legislation protecting archeological sites, the training of archeologists, and promoting fieldwork in Paraná, with repercussions on the professionalization of archeology elsewhere in Brazil. [BJM]

343   Chmyz, Igor and Eliane Maria Sganzerla. Patrimônio arqueológico da área da rodovia BR 156: trecho Rio Preto—Laranjal do Jari, Estado do Amapá. (*Arqueologia/Curitiba*, 9, 2006, p. 17–40, bibl., ill., map)

Environmental impact survey along BR 156 identified ten sites with ceramics, three neobrazilian and seven preceramic, one of a latter rockshelter. A radiocarbon date of 4130 BP was obtained from one of the open sites and a date of 3350 BP from the rock shelter. [BJM]

344   Chmyz, Igor et al. A arqueologia da área da LT 750kV Ivaiporã-Itaberá III, Paraná—São Paulo. (*Arqueologia/Curitiba*, 5, 2008, p. 1–305, bibl., ill.)

Survey along a power line transect 272 km long by 100 m wide identified 335 sites representing 19 Preceramic occupations (four in rock shelters) of the Umbu Tradition, 62 habitation sites of the ceramic Itararé Tradition, one Casa de Pedra, and 46 Tupiguarani. Maps showing location and descriptions of soil, site dimensions, excavations, burials, pottery types, and lithics are provided for all sites. [BJM]

345   Dantas, Vladimir José and Tania Andrade Lima. Pausa para um banquete: análise de marcas de uso de vasilhames cerâmicos pré-históricos do Sítio Justino, Canindé do São Francisco, Sergipe. Canindé do São Francisco, Brazil: MAX, Museu de Arqueologia de Xingó, 2006. 147 p.: bibl., ill.

Provides detailed descriptions of surface conditions on seven complete and 23 restored undecorated bowls associated with burials dating between ca. 2000 and 3000 BP, including soot, oxidation, fire clouds, pits, and surface finish. Comparing interpretations of the origin of these phenomena with observations of the behavior of local Xocó Indians indicates these vessels were used for preparation of funerary feasts and then interred with the deceased. [BJM]

346 Dias, Adriana Schmidt. Novas perguntas para um velho problema: escolhas tecnológicas como índices para o estudo de fronteiras e identidades sociais no registro arqueológico. (*Bol. Mus. Para. Emílio Goeldi Sér. Ciênc. Hum.*, 2:1, jan./abril 2007, p. 59–76, bibl.)

Detailed analysis of the raw materials, lithic technology, artifact morphology, and location of sites of the preceramic Umbu Tradition in the Rio dos Sinos valley, Rio Grande do Sul, identifies regional complexes with social and chronological significance. [BJM]

347 Dias, Ondemar F. As estruturas arqueológicas de terra no estado do Acre—Amazônia ocidental, Brasil: um caso de resiliência? (*in* Estudos contemporâneos de arqueologia. Recopilação de Ondemar Dias, Eliana Carvalho e Marcos Zimmermann. Palmas, Brazil: UNITINS/IAB, 2006, p. 59–168, bibl., ill., maps, tables)

One of the participants of a Brazilian national program on the coast (PRONAPA) and in Amazônia (PRONAPABA) describes sites in eastern Acre consisting of ditches of various diameters. Excavations at the site of Los Angeles identified four areas with different functions occupied discontinuously between 2900 and 1400 BP. The author provides a provocative critique of efforts to reconstruct the social organization responsible for these and other complex archeological sites. [BJM]

348 Dias, Ondemar F. and Eliana de Carvalho. Arqueologia da Amazônia ocidental: descrição sumária das características da Tradição Quinari, alto curso do Rio Purus. (*in* Estudos contemporâneos de arqueologia. Recopilação de Ondemar Dias, Eliana Carvalho e Marcos Zimmermann. Palmas, Brazil: UNITINS/IAB, 2006, p. 169–205, bibl., ill., tables)

Describes the sites and ceramics differentiating five phases assigned to the Quinari Tradition. [BJM]

349 Erickson, Clark L. Amazonia: the historical ecology of a domesticated landscape. (*in* Handbook of South American archaeology. Edited by Helaine Silverman and William H. Isbell. New York: Springer, 2008, p. 157–183, bibl., ill.)

Erickson argues that rather than adapt to environmental limitations, "Ama- zonian people created, transformed, and managed those very environments" and cites the existence of earthworks (mounds, raised fields, causeways), black soil, anthropogenic forests, and large permanent settlements as evidence of their impact. To provide examples, he ignores the traditional definition of Amazônia and extends its geographical limits as far as the headwaters of all the tributaries where very different conditions exist. He also ignores the multitude of articles and books describing climatic, edaphic, ecological, chemical, and biological evidence, as well as archeological and ethnographic evidence, that contradict his interpretations. Readers impressed with his argument should keep these deficiencies in mind. [BJM]

350 Gaspar, Maria Dulce et al. Sambaqui (shell mound) societies of coastal Brazil. (*in* Handbook of South American archaeology. Edited by Helaine Silverman and William H. Isbell. New York: Springer, 2008, p. 319–335, bibl., ill., map)

Provides a useful synthesis of the distribution, regional variation, chronological changes, subsistence differences, and evidence for social, ritual, and ideological behavior among shell middens that extend along most of the coast of Brazil. [BJM]

351 Gomes, Denise Maria Cavalcante. The diversity of social forms in precolonial Amazonia. (*Rev. Arqueol. Am./ México*, 25, 2007, p. 187–223, bibl., ill.)

Argues that the increasing acceptance by archeologists of Roosevelt's estimates of the existence of dense prehistoric populations and permanent occupation with hierarchical social organization in Amazônia is not supported by archeological evidence and ignores significant similarities between the ceramic iconography and shamanistic practices and beliefs. Various kinds of evidence from the Santarém region are provided in support of this critique. [BJM]

352 Gomes, Denise Maria Cavalcante. Padrões de organização comunitária no baixo Trapajós: o formativo na área de Santarém, Brasil. (*in* Pueblos y paisajes antiguos de la selva amazónica. Edited by Gaspar Morcote Ríos, Santiago Mora Camargo, and Carlos Franky Calvo. Bogotá: Univ. Nacional de Colombia, 2006, p. 237–251, ill., map)

Parallel transects across a 36 sq. km sector on the left bank of the Tapajós 100 km upriver from Santarém identified 10 ceramic sites of different dimensions in different environmental settings implying different functions. All the pottery was assigned to the Incised Rim Tradition. Small sites dating between 3800–3600 BP, attributed to semi-sedentary communities, were replaced by larger sites occupied by more sedentary groups with more diverse vessel shapes and decoration between 1300–900 BP. There was no evidence of significant influence from Santarém. [BJM]

353 Guapindaia, Vera. Prehistoric funeral practices in the Brazilian Amazon: the Maracá urns. (in Handbook of South American archaeology. Edited by Helaine Silverman and William H. Isbell. New York: Springer, 2008, p. 1005–1026, bibl., ill., map)

Although rockshelters containing cylindrical anthropomorphic pottery urns were first reported more than a century ago, a recent survey in the headwaters of the Igarapé do Lago, a tributary of the Rio Maracá in southern Amapá has identified 13 cemeteries in rockshelters and three habitation sites containing pottery fragments and polished stone tools. A single radiocarbon date of 360 BP was obtained from one of the habitation sites. [BJM]

354 Heckenberger, Michael J. History, ecology, and alterity: visualizing polity in ancient Amazonia. (in Time and complexity in historical ecology: studies in the neotropical lowlands. Edited by William Balée and Clark L. Erickson. New York: Columbia Univ. Press, 2006, p. 313–340, bibl., ill.)

Argues that complex societies existed in prehistoric Amazônia, but that they are difficult to recognize because their sociopolitical organization was based on social and symbolic factors that are not reflected in differences in settlement size and composition. [BJM]

355 Heckenberger, Michael J. et al. The legacy of cultural landscapes in the Brazilian Amazon: implications for biodiversity. (Philos. Trans., 362:1478, 2007, p. 197–208, bibl., ill., maps)

Argues that the existence of plazas surrounded by ditches in the upper Xingu indicates that the region was occupied by a dense population with complex social organization between AD 1250 and European contact and implies that the subsistence resources were exploited intensively in a sustainable way. [BJM]

356 Heckenberger, Michael J. et al. Pre-Columbian urbanism, anthropogenic landscapes, and the future of the Amazon. (Science/Washington, 321:5893, Aug. 29, 2008, p. 1214–1217, bibl., ill., maps)

Repeats previous arguments that circular ditches in the upper Xingu region identify "plaza towns" of various sizes that are connected by networks of roads to form "galactic clusters" and constitute a form of prehistoric urbanism. [BJM]

357 Hemming, John. Tree of rivers: the story of the Amazon. Maps by Martin Lubikowski. New York: Thames & Hudson, 2008. 368 p.: bibl., ill. (some col.), index, maps.

A detailed and readable history of European exploration, colonization, and commercialization of the Amazon from the first contact to the present time based on extensive consultation of bibliographic sources and first-hand acquaintance with the region. Highly recommended. [BJM]

358 Hilbert, Klaus. Uma biografia de Peter Paul Hilbert: a história de quem partiu para ver a Amazônia. (Bol. Mus. Para. Emílio Goeldi Sér. Ciênc. Hum., 4:1, jan./abril 2009, p. 135–154, bibl., ill.)

A lively personal account of the pioneering accomplishments of German scholar Peter Hilbert, who conducted archeological investigations along the Amazon between 1948 and 1961, written by his son. [BJM]

359 Hilbert, Klaus. "Cave canem!": cuidado com os "Pronapianos"!: em busca dos jovens da arqueologia brasileira. (Bol. Mus. Para. Emílio Goeldi Sér. Ciênc. Hum., 2:1, jan./abril 2007, p. 117–130, bibl.)

Argues that rejection by the current generation of Brazilian archeologists of the methodology and theoretical perspective of the Programa Nacional de Pesquisas Arqueológicas (PRONAPA) is based on the invalid assumption that they ignore the social aspect of cultural change. [BJM]

360 Lessa, Andrea. Reflexões preliminares sobre paleoepidemiologia da violência em grupos ceramistas litorâneos: (I) Sítio Praia da Tapera—SC. (*Rev. Mus. Arqueol. Etnol.*, 15/16, 2005/2006, p. 199–207, bibl., ill., tables)

Analysis of 71 skeletons from a habitation site occupied by the Itararé Tradition, representing 36 males and 35 females, identified evidence of violence on five males and one female. Three males had corporal injuries inflicted by projectile points and two males and the female had cranial fractures. An earlier and later occupation at the site showed no evidence of violence. Possible motivations are discussed. [BJM]

361 Lima, Luiz Fernando Erig. Investigações arqueológicas nas áreas de interflúvio entre os rios Negro e Solimões, Amazônia central, Brasil. (*in* Pueblos y paisajes antiguos de la selva amazónica. Edited by Gaspar Morcote Ríos, Santiago Mora Camargo and Carlos Franky Calvo. Bogotá: Univ. Nacional de Colombia, 2006, p. 211–235, ill., map)

The eastern part of the peninsula between the Lower Negro and the Solimões was divided into 2x2 km units from which seven were selected for systematic sampling. Eighteen sites were identified on the terra firme and 11 adjacent to the varzea. The former were 100-300 m in diameter and represented the Manacapuru, Paredaõ, and Guarita traditions; the latter were more than 600 m in diameter and produced mainly pottery of the Guarita Tradition. Although the relative antiquity of sites of the same tradition was not established, it is assumed that the region was densely populated after the adoption of pottery ca. 300 BC. [BJM]

362 Lima, Tania Andrade. Teoria arqueológica em descompasso no Brasil: o caso da arqueologia darwiniana. (*Rev. Arqueol./São Paulo*, 19, 2006, p. 125–141, bibl.)

Distinguishes the Darwinian concept of cultural evolution as transformation from the traditional perspective as progress and traces its increasing impact on the interpretation of prehistoric cultural development

since the 1970s throughout the world, except in Brazil. [BJM]

363 Machado, Juliana Salles. Processos de formação: hipóteses sobre a variabilidade do registro arqueológico de um montículo artificial no sítio Hatahara, Amazonas. (*Rev. Arqueol./São Paulo*, 18, 2005, p. 9–24, bibl., ill., map)

Excavation in one of the 10 mounds that compose a semi-circle in the Hatahara site on the left bank of the Lower Solimões revealed complex stratigraphy consisting of layers alternating natural soil and terra preta, with abundant pottery fragments and complete vessels attributed to the Paredão and Guarita phases, as well as skeletal remains. After considering various interpretations, Machado suggests the mound was constructed by the Guarita Phase using earlier Paredão habitation refuse and that the dense layers of large sherds may have reduced the penetration of moisture and contributed to the preservation of the skeletal remains. [BJM]

364 Machado, Lilia Maria Cheuiche. Sítio cemitério dos Pretos Novos: análise biocultural, interpretando os ossos e os dentes humanos. (*in* Estudos contemporâneos de arqueologia. Recopilação de Ondemar Dias, Eliana Carvalho e Marcos Zimmermann. Palmas, Brazil: UNITINS/IAB, 2006, p. 11–58, bibl., ill., tables)

Detailed analysis of skeletal remains of 31 individuals from a previously unknown slave cemetery in Rio de Janeiro dating between AD 1770–1830 includes age, sex, caries, dental wear, pathology, intentional tooth modification, and other characteristics compatible with a West African origin. [BJM]

365 Mann, Charles C. Ancient earth movers of the Amazon. (*Science/Washington*, 321:5893, August 29, 2008, p. 1148–1152, ill., map)

Describes "geoglyphs" in the southwestern Brazilian state of Acre consisting of ditches one to seven meters deep defining circular or rectangular areas up to 350 m in diameter. Although few are associated with pottery or other cultural materials, they are assumed to imply the existence of large populations with complex social organization. [BJM]

366   Martins, Gilson Rodolfo. Arqueologia do Planalto Maracaju-Campo Grande. Brasília: Ministério da Integração Nacional, Secretaria de Desenvolvimento do Centro-Oeste; Campo Grande, Brazil: UFMS, 2003. 255 p.: bibl., ill. (some col.), col. maps. (Col. Centro-Oeste de estudos e pesquisas; 2)

Provides a detailed description of percussion flaked cores, flakes, and artifacts from a rockshelter in central Minas Gerais with a radiocarbon date of 610 ± 50 and a TL date of 830 ± 80 BP. [BJM]

367   Meggers, Betty J. A contribuição do Brasil à interpretação da linguagem da cerâmica. (*Arqueologia/Curitiba*, 4, 2007, p. 31–56, bibl., ill.)

History of the origin and accomplishments of the Programa Nacional de Pesquisas Arqueológicas (PRONAPA), which coordinated systematic archeological surveys and interpretation along the coast of Brazil between 1965 and 1970, creating a time-space framework for the region. [BJM]

368   Meggers, Betty J. Mid-Holocene climate and cultural dynamics in Brazil and the Guianas. (*in* Climate change and cultural dynamics: a global perspective on Mid-Holocene transitions. Edited by David G. Anderson, Kirk A. Maasch and Daniel H. Sandweiss. New York: Elsevier, 2007, p. 117–155, bibl., maps)

Paleoclimatic evidence indicates that both Amazonia and the Brazilian coast were cooler and drier prior to ca. 7000 14C yr BP and the similarity of the vegetation is reflected in the existence of similar subsistence remains and artifacts in sites in both regions from the inception of human occupation. Development of Holocene conditions and culmination of sea level rise created new terrestrial and aquatic resources; however, although these ameliorations permitted larger and more sedentary communities, inherent limitations to intensive food production placed a ceiling on population concentration throughout the lowlands. [BJM]

369   Meggers, Betty J. Sustainable intensive exploitation of Amazonia: cultural, environmental, and geopolitical perspectives. (*in* World system and the earth system. Edited by Alf Hornborg and Carole L. Crumley. Walnut Creek, Calif.: Left Coast Press, 2007, p. 195–209, bibl., ill., map, table)

Provides archeological, ethnographic, climatic, and historical evidence for the existence of the population density, settlement pattern, and social behavior characteristics of surviving traditional communities throughout the tropical lowlands prior to European contact. [BJM]

370   Meggers, Betty J. and **Eurico Th. Miller.** Evidencia arqueológica para el comportamiento social y habitacional en la Amazonía prehistórica. (*in* Pueblos y paisajes antiguos de la selva amazónica. Edited by Gaspar Morcote Ríos, Santiago Mora Camargo and Carlos Franky Calvo. Bogotá: Univ. Nacional de Colombia, 2006, p. 325–348, ill., maps, table)

Quantitative analysis and seriation of pottery from habitation sites along the Tocantins and the Jamarí identified the territories of prehistoric communities and indicated that they were composed of matrilocal moieties that reoccupied their own sites and avoided sites occupied by earlier communities. Review of the behavior of surviving indigenous communities supports the validity of these interpretations. [BJM]

371   Miller, Eurico Theófilo. História da cultura indígena do Alto-Médio-Guaporé: Rondônia e Mato Grosso. Rondônia, Brazil: Porto Velho, Editora da Univ. Federal de Rondônia, 2007. 338 p.

Survey along the right bank of the Guaporé identified two groups of habitation sites bounded by ditches on the inland side. Classification of the pottery revealed significant differences in decoration, implying the existence of independent communities separated by an unoccupied region. Detailed descriptions of the sites and ceramics, as well as the environmental potential, post-contact history, and cultural interpretation make this a significant reference. [BJM]

372   Monticelli, Gislene. O céu é o limite: como extrapolar as normas rígidas da cerâmica Guarani. (*Bol. Mus. Para. Emílio Goeldi Sér. Ciênc. Hum.*, 2:1, jan./abril 2007, p. 105–115, bibl., ill.)

Speculations on the significance of the unusual frequency of innovations in surface treatment on pottery from U-470, a site of the Guaraní Tradition on the northern border of Rio Grande do Sul. [BJM]

373 Morais, José Luiz de; Silvia Cristina Piedade; and Eliete Pythagoras Brito Maximino. Arqueologia da *Terra Brasilis*: o engenho São Jorge dos Erasmos, na capitania de São Vicente. (*Rev. Arqueol. Am./México*, 23, 2004/2005, p. 349–384, bibl., photos, tables)

Excavation of the cemetery associated with an abandoned 18th century mill revealed 19 skeletons and 14 clusters of long bones. Remains are described and illustrated, but were not excavated. Shovel-shaped incisors identified several as mestizos and skull shape identified one as African. [BJM]

374 Neves, Eduardo Góes. Ecology, ceramic chronology and distribution, long-term history, and political change in the Amazonian floodplain. (*in* Handbook of South American archaeology. Edited by Helaine Silverman and William H. Isbell. New York: Springer, 2008, p. 359–379, bibl., ill.)

Reviews conflicting interpretations of the origins and distributions of the Zoned Hachure, Incised Rim, Polychrome, and Incised-punctate pottery traditions and their linguistic associations for reconstructing cultural development along the Amazon after about 2000 BC. Concludes that the latest societies were cyclical, alternating periods of political centralization and decentralization. [BJM]

375 Neves, Eduardo Góes and James B. Peterson. Political economy and pre-columbian landscape transformations in central Amazonia. (*in* Time and complexity in historical ecology: studies in the neotropical lowlands. Edited by William Balée and Clark L. Erickson. New York: Columbia Univ. Press, 2006, p. 279–309, bibl., ill., map, tables)

Archeological investigations at two sites on the left bank of the lower Solimões occupied between 1200 and 900 BP indicate that subsistence resources were sufficiently abundant to permit long-term occupation of large settlements and that abandonment was provoked by political conflict and resulting fission of communities. [BJM]

376 Neves, Walter A. and Luís Beethoven Piló. O povo de Luzia: em busca dos primeiros americanos. São Paulo: Editora Globo, 2008. 334 p.: ill., maps.

Brazil's leading paleoanthropologist provides an authoritative and readable account of the peopling of the Americas and his role in the excavation and interpretation of early human remains in rockshelters in the Lagoa Santa region of Minas Gerais, which identify a premongoloid immigration. [BJM]

377 Neves, Walter A. and Maria Mercedes Martinez Okumura. Afinidades biológicas de grupos pré-históricos do vale do rio Ribeira de Iguape (SP): uma análise preliminar. (*Rev. Antropol./São Paulo*, 48:2, julho/dez. 2005, p. 525–557, bibl., tables)

Comparison of craniometric data on 12 skeletons from fluvial shell middens dating between 6000 and 1200 BP with those on 225 skeletons from various coastal and interior sites indicates biological affinity of the former with coastal rather than interior populations. [BJM]

378 Noelli, Francisco Silva and Lúcio Menezes Ferreira. A persistência da teoria da degenerção indígena e do colonialismo nos fundamentos da arqueologia brasileira. (*Hist. Ciênc. Saúde Manguinhos*, 14:4, 2007, p. 1239–1264, bibl.)

Argues that the use by Meggers of environmental limitations on intensive agriculture to explain the failure of the indigenous inhabitants of Brazil and other regions in the Americas to develop permanent settlements and social stratification perpetuates the colonial assessment of their inherent inferiority. [BJM]

379 Oliver, José R. The archaeology of agriculture. (*in* Handbook of South American archaeology. Edited by Helaine Silverman and William H. Isbell. New York: Springer, 2008, p. 185–216, bibl., ill., map)

Argues that prehistoric humans did not adapt to nature in Amazonia, but created the environment they wanted, that they could not have cleared slash-and-burn fields with stone axes, that house gardens were widespread by 8000 BP, that they intentionally created anthropogenic black soil for cultivation, and that they produced elaborate pottery throughout the lowlands by 4500 BP, among other accomplishments. [BJM]

380 Pereira, Edithe. Historia de la investigación sobre el arte rupestre en la Amazonia brasileña. (*Rev. Arqueol. Am./ México*, 24, 2006, p. 67–98, bibl., photos)

Summarizes publications on rock art from the 18th century to the present and recognizes three regional styles: North of the Amazon similar to Colombia, Venezuela, and the Guianas; Northern Pará, a unique variant; and Southern Pará, similar to the west-central lowlands. [BJM]

381 *Pesquisas Antropologia*. No. 65, 2007. Almas, corpos e especiarias: a expansão colonial nos rios Tapajós e Madeira. Textos de Doris Cristina Castilhos de Araujo Cypriano. São Leopoldo, Brazil: Instituto Anchietano de Pesquisas.

Analysis of 17th and 18th century Jesuit documents provides detailed evidence for the ability of the indigenous population to incorporate advantageous concepts of missionary doctrine while perpetuating traditional customs and beliefs in secret. [BJM]

382 *Pesquisas Antropologia*. No. 66, 2008. Diversidade morfológica craniana, micro-evolução e ocupação pré-histórica da costa brasileira. Textos de Maria Mercedes Martinez Okumura. São Leopoldo, Brazil: Instituto Anchietano de Pesquisas.

Detailed morphological analysis of skulls from shell middens identifies two coastal populations, one in Rio de Janeiro and São Paulo and the other in Santa Catarina, with intermediate characteristics in Paraná. [BJM]

383 Pré-história do Mato Grosso. Vol. 1, Santa Elina. Vol. 2, Cidade de Pedra. Organização de Agueda Vilhena Vialou. São Paulo: EDUSP, 2005–2006. 2 v.: bibl., ill. (some col.), maps (some col.).

The first substantive description of investigations in a rockshelter occupied intermittently from 25,000 BP to the present, these volumes provide details on geomorphology, geology, sedimentology, Pleistocene fauna, lithic technology, rock art, dating methods, paleobotany, and fieldwork by specialists. [BJM]

384 Pré-história no Vale do Rio Manso— MT. Coordenação de Sibeli Aparecida Viana. Goiânia, Brazil: IGPA, Instituto Goi-

ano de Pré-história e Antropologia: Editora da UCG, 2006. 402 p.: bibl., ill. (some col.), maps (some col.). (Série Preservando o patrimônio cultural; 2)

Survey of a 427 sq. km region identified 81 archeological sites, including lithic accumulations, rock art, and habitation sites with pottery. Detailed descriptions are provided of excavations and artifacts at 27 sites, 18 of which produced pottery of the Uru Tradition. [BJM]

385 Prous, André. O Brasil antes dos brasileiros: a pré-história do nosso país. Rio de Janeiro: Jorge Zahar Editor, 2006. 141 p.: bibl., ill. (Nova biblioteca de ciências sociais)

One of Brazil's leading archeologists provides a brief popular discussion of the peopling of Brazil, followed by chapters on the prehistory of the southern and central/ northeastern regions, the expansion of Tupiguarani speakers, and the late ceramic traditions of Amazonia. [BJM]

386 Rincón, Beatriz Eugenia and Alessandro Martínez. La gente de Maicura y Omé: una imagen dentro del contexto arqueológico amazónico. (*in* Pueblos y paisajes antiguos de la selva amazónica. Edited by Gaspar Morcote Ríos, Santiago Mora Camargo and Carlos Franky Calvo. Bogotá: Univ. Nacional de Colombia, 2006, p. 261–280, ill., map)

Describes pottery decorated by painting, fine incision, appliqué, modeling, and impressed rim from two sites dating between AD 800–1300 on the Río Purité, a tributary of the Lower Putumayo near the Brazilian border, and compares it with Amazonian traditions. [BJM]

387 Rogge, Jairo Henrique and Pedro Ignácio Schmitz. Pesquisas arqueológicas em São Marcos, RS. (*Pesqui. Antropol.*, 67, 2009, p. 23–132, bibl., ill., maps, tables)

Detailed inventory of pithouses, mounds, open sites, and rockshelters on the planalto of northeastern Paraná associated with pottery and lithics of the Taquara Tradition. [BJM]

388 Rosa, André Osorio. Análise zooarqueológica do sítio Garivaldino (RS-TA-58) Municipio de Montenegro, RS. (*Pesqui. Antropol.*, 67, 2009, p. 133–172, bibl., tables)

Classification and interpretation of amphibian, reptile, bird, mammal, and fish remains from a preceramic rock shelter occupied ca. 9000 BP. [BJM]

389 Schaan, Denise Pahl. Uma janela para a história pré-colonial da Amazônia: olhando além—e apesar—das fases e tradições. (*Bol. Mus. Para. Emílio Goeldi Sér. Ciênc. Hum.*, 2:1, jan./abril 2007, p. 77–89, bibl., ill., map)

Argues that the use of differences in temper and decoration to define ceramic phases and traditions on Marajó during initial archeological investigations in 1948 obscures similarities with social and cultural significance that imply local development rather than successive episodes of settlement by immigrant populations. [BJM]

390 Schaan, Denise Pahl. Manejo ecológico e o desenvolvimento de sociedades compexas na ilha de Marajó, Brasil. (*in* Pueblos y paisajes antiguos de la selva amazónica. Edited by Gaspar Morcote Ríos, Santiago Mora Camargo and Carlos Franky Calvo. Bogotá: Univ. Nacional de Colombia, 2006, p. 349–365, ill., map)

Mapping and excavations in 34 mounds along the Camutins in central Marajó identified three clusters of habitation mounds, two associated with larger ceremonial or elite mounds. Total population is estimated at 2000. The proximity of natural or artificial ponds that would have retained water during the dry season implies that intensive fishing was a major subsistence resource, most likely supplemented by palm starch. Artifacts and decorated pottery were restricted to the large mounds. Excavation of 24 burials identified the oldest as primary and the most recent as secondary or cremations. Differences in abundance and quality of artifacts do not appear to reflect prestige and power, suggesting that personal qualities were more important indicators of status. [BJM]

391 Schaan, Denise Pahl et al. Geoglifos da Amazônia occidental: evidencia de complexidade social entre povos da terra firme. (*Rev. Arqueol./São Paulo*, 20, 2007, p. 67–82, bibl., ill., tables)

Geometric geoglyphs consisting of circular and rectangular ditches bounded on the exterior by ridges were discovered in eastern Acre during archeological investiga-

tions between 1977–80 by Ondemar Dias, who published preliminary descriptions in 1988 and 2006 (see *HLAS 51:490* and item 347). They were rediscovered in 1999 and intensive subsequent exploration has identified more than 130 examples. This article summarizes the data provided by Dias, including TL dates extending from 500 BC and AD 1000. Although no new archeological excavations have been conducted and the function of the geoglyphs is unknown, the authors speculate that they were created by large populations with hierarchical social organization. [BJM]

392 Schmitz, Pedro Ignácio. João Alfredo Rohr: um jesuíta em tempos de transição. (*Pesqui. Antropol.*, 67, 2009, p. 9–22)

Padre Rohr (1908–84) made a remarkable contribution to the development of archeology in Brazil. He studied natural history while undergoing training as a Jesuit, and continued this interest after being sent to teach at a Jesuit school on the coast of Santa Catarina. There he became interested in archeology, beginning with cemeteries and shell-middens along the coast and continuing with pit houses and habitation sites in the interior. He became a careful excavator and documenter of skeletal remains and artifacts, and produced at least 50 publications. The addition of posthumous publication of his unfinished manuscripts makes the prehistory of the state of Santa Catarina one of the best known regions in Brazil. [BJM]

393 Schmitz, Pedro Ignácio et al. Aterros da tradição Pantanal nas fazendas Sagrado Coração de Jesus e Bodoquena, Corumbá, MS. (*Pesqui. Antropol.*, 67, 2009, p. 321–374, bibl., ill., tables)

An inventory of ca. 400 sites was undertaken with the goal of establishing whether size and location were correlated with resources, water level, permanence of occupation, and other characteristics that would suggest differences in social significance. [BJM]

394 Schmitz, Pedro Ignácio et al. Taió, no Vale do rio Itajaí, SC: o encontro de antigos caçadores com as casas subterrâneas. (*Pesqui. Antropol.*, 67, 2009, p. 185–320, bibl., ill., maps, tables)

Describes 25 open sites and one site with 12 pit houses associated with a single

mound. Dates of 8000 and 4000 BP were
obtained from open sites; dates of 1300,
1200, and 650 BP were obtained from the
pit houses. No pottery was encountered,
but stemmed projectile points of the Umbu
Tradition were abundant and are illustrated
in 43 plates. [BJM]

395 **Sganzerla, Eliane Maria** and **Igor
    Chmyz.** Patrimônio arqueológico no
espaço do projeto de reflorestamento Felipe
2, na Gleba Gavião, Laranjal do Jarí, Amapá.
(*Arqueologia/Curitiba*, 9, 2006, p. 41–65,
bibl., ill.)
    Describes and illustrates vessel
shapes and decoration on pottery from
four habitation sites, one with a radiocarbon date of 350 ± 60 BP and another with
a date of 1990 ± 50 BP. [BJM]

396 **Sganzerla, Eliane Maria; Igor Chmyz;
    and Jonas Elias Volcov.** Patrimônio
arqueológico da área da rodovia EAP-070:
trecho Santa Luiza do Pacuí-Foz do Rio
Gurijuba, Amapá. (*Arqueologia/Curitiba*, 9,
2006, p. 67–106, bibl., ill., maps)
    Survey identified nine sites, seven
prehistoric and two neobrasilian. The pottery was classified into undecorated and
decorated types and decoration and reconstructed vessel shapes are described and
illustrated by site. [BJM]

397 **Vergne, Cleonice.** Cemitérios do
    Justino: estudo sobre a ritualidade fu-
nerária em Xingó, Sergipe. Canindé do São
Francisco, Brazil: MAX, Museu de Arqueologia de Xingó, Univ. Federal de Sergipe,
2004. 209 p.: bibl., ill. (some col.), col. maps.
    Provides age, sex, orientation, posi-
tion, and pathology of 185 skeletons in four
cemeteries of different ages; describes associated lithic artifacts; and suggests their
sociopolitical significance. [BJM]

398 **Vieira Junior, Almir Souza** and **José
    Arnaldo Vasconcelos Palmeira.**
Grupos pré-históricos de Xingó: um estudo
cranioscópico e craniométrico. Canindé
do São Francisco, Brazil: MAX, Museu de
Arqueologia de Xingó, Univ. Federal de Sergipe, 2006. 130 p.: bibl., ill., maps.
    Provides detailed measurements on
the skulls and mandibles of 203 skeletons
from the Justino and São José II cemeteries
on the lower Rio São Francisco dating between 9000 and 1280 BP. [BJM]

399 **Workshop Arqueológico de Xingó,
    2nd, *Canindé de São Francisco,
Brazil, 2002*. Anais.** Organização de José
Alexandre Felizola Diniz *et al.* Canindé
de São Francisco, Brazil: MAX, Museu de
Arqueologia de Xingó, 2002. 130 p.: bibl., ill.,
maps.
    Twenty abstracts with bibliographies
discuss historic and prehistoric sites, rock
art, shell-middens, human skeletal remains,
and other topics in Bahia, Paraíba, Maranhão, Sergipe, Pernambuco, and Rio Grande
do Norte. [BJM]

CHILE

400 **Adán A., Leonor** and **Mauricio
    Uribe R.** El dominio inca en la loca-
lidad de Caspana: un acercamiento al pensamiento político andino, río Loa, norte
de Chile. (*Estud. Atacameños*, 29, 2005,
p. 41–66, ill., map, photos)
    The authors describe five late prehis-
panic settlements in the Caspana located in
the upper Loa Valley, Chile (Atacama Desert) and the evidence of Inca control in the
region. They present different types of Inca
control and relate these to different Inca
power strategies. [DJN]

401 **Agüero P., Carolina.** Aproximación
    al asentamiento humano temprano
en los oasis de San Pedro de Atacama. (*Estud. Atacameños*, 30, 2005, p. 29–60, maps,
tables)
    The article presents new survey data
for the Vilama Basin and the oasis south of
San Pedro de Atacama, on the northern margin of Salar, Chile. Given shifts in population and settlement location, the author
presents new interpretations of Formative
development in the region. [DJN]

402 **Chacama Rodríguez, Juan.** Patrón de
    asentamiento y uso del espacio: pre-
cordillera de Arica, extremo norte de Chile,
siglos X–XV. (*Bull. Inst. fr. étud. andin.*,
34:3, 2005, p. 357–378, bibl., ill., maps, tables)
    Describes the Late Intermediate Pe-
riod and Late Horizon settlement pattern for
the upper tributaries of Arica. Comparisons
are made between these two periods and
change consists of an Inca overlay of administrative centers to manage the existing
pattern of dispersed settlement and agricultural production. [DJN]

403 Costa J., Maria Antonietta; Walter Alves Neves; and Mark Hubbe. Influencia de Tiwanaku en la calidad de vida biológica de la población prehistórica de San Pedro de Atacama. (*Estud. Atacameños*, 27, 2004, p. 103–116, maps, tables)

Presents an analysis of 161 individuals from three cemeteries in San Pedro de Atacama during four phases (pre-Tiwanaku, Tiwanaku apogee, late Tiwanaku, and post Tiwanaku) to assess the relative health of populations during the period of Tiwanaku influence. Concludes that populations in San Pedro had a greater quality of health during the Tiwanaku period. [DJN]

404 De Souza, Patricio. Cazadores recolectores del arcaico temprano y medio en la cuenca superior del río Loa: sitios, conjuntos líticos y sistemas de asentamiento. (*Estud. Atacameños*, 27, 2004, p. 7–43, graphs, ill., map)

Describes Archaic Period sites and materials from the upper Loa Valley, Chile. Based on site distribution and chronology, the author suggests three phases of settlement systems in the archaic (10,500–6,000 BP). Finds that over time groups became less mobile, perhaps in response to more arid conditions and the restricted habitat of camelids. [DJN]

405 Dillehay, Tom D. Monuments, empires, and resistance: the Araucanian polity and ritual narratives. Cambridge; New York: Cambridge Univ. Press, 2007. 484 p.: bibl., index. (Cambridge studies in archaeology)

The leading authority on the archeology, history, and culture of the Araucanian population of southern Chile draws on three decades of research to describe how they resisted Spanish conquest by altering their ideologies while preserving the continuity with the past. [BJM]

406 Dillehay, Tom D. and Ximena Navarro H. Explotación y uso de los recursos marinos y patrones de residencia entre los mapuches: algunas implicaciones preliminares para la arqueología. (*Maguaré/Bogotá*, 17, 2003, p. 260–273, bibl., map)

Describes Mapuche resource use on the central south coast of Chile to understand archeological populations. The authors present the relationship between resource abundance and differences in use rights between family, lineage, and common access. Areas with abundant resources may have been exploited by multiple groups in the past and may have been points of interaction, promoting intra-group cohesion. [DJN]

407 Horta T., Helena. Iconografía del formativo tardío del norte de Chile: propuesta de definición e interpretación basada en imágenes textiles y otros medios. (*Estud. Atacameños*, 27, 2004, p. 45–76, ill., map)

Considers a large sample of Formative Period textile iconography from coastal and highland areas of northern Chile with comparisons to the Titicaca region and southern Peru. Analysis suggests that three common themes were widely distributed, the "rayed head front facing person," the isolated "rayed head," and the stepped pyramid, which compose a late Formative (500 BC–AD 600) horizon style in the southern Andes. [DJN]

408 Magaña, Edmundo. Astronomía de algunas poblaciones quechua-aymara del Loa Superior, norte de Chile. (*Bol. Mus. Chil. Arte Precolomb.*, 11:2, 2006, p. 51–66, bibl., maps, photos)

Conveys indigenous conceptions of astronomy (movement of the sun, eclipses, comets, the moon, the Milky Way, stars, and constellations), the ritual calendar, meteorology, and the significance of animals and landscape features. These phenomena are related to the cults of saints and virgins (and their affiliated indigenous supernaturals), the agricultural and pastoral cycles, climatic occurrences, and auspicious times for different rites of passage. [DJN]

409 Muñoz Ovalle, Iván. Espacio social y áreas de actividad en asentamientos agrícolas prehispánicos tardíos en la sierra de Arica. (*Bull. Inst. fr. étud. andin.*, 34:3, 2005, p. 321–355, bibl., maps, photos, tables)

Describes three sites located in the upper tributaries of Arica, Huaihuarani, Lupica, and Saxamar. Surface mapping and excavations provide information about habitation areas, production, agricultural zones, corrals, storage, and other features to characterize the organization of activities and daily life in the region. [DJN]

410 Núñez, Lautaro et al. El templete de Tulán y su relaciones formativas panandinas (norte de Chile). (*Bull. Inst. fr. étud. andin.*, 34:3, 2005, p. 299–320, bibl., ill., map, photos)

Describes the general features of the Formative Tilocalar phase in the Quebrada Tulán, southeast Atacama Basin, and details an early temple complex at the site of Tulán (900–400 BC). The temple is interpreted as an early ceremonial center promoting group cohesion and specific ritual traditions pertaining to the religious tradition of the Tilocalar pastorlists. [DJN]

411 Uribe R., Mauricio. Acerca de la cerámica Tiwanaku y una vasija del valle de Azapa, Arica, Norte Grande de Chile. (*Estud. Atacameños*, 27, 2004, p. 77–101, bibl., ill., map)

Reexamines the nature of Tiwanaku expansion into the Azapa Valley. Presents a ceramic analysis that emphasizes a vessel depicting the Tiwanaku front-faced deity, currently the only one of its kind. The patterns of ceramic production and iconography suggest Tiwanaku presence in Azapa but not necessarily colonial occupation. [DJN]

COLOMBIA

412 Aceituno, Francisco Javier and Nicolás Loaiza. Domesticación del bosque en el Cauca medio colombiano entre el Pleistoceno final y el Holoceno medio. Oxford: Archaeopress, 2007. 138 p.: bibl., ill., index, maps. (BAR international series; 1654)

Examines how early hunter-gatherers altered the forest in the Porce and Cauca valleys of the Cordillera Central. Suggests that early groups inhabiting the area were experimenting with plant species and changed the character of the forest through their activities and domesticated their environment. [DJN]

413 Boada Rivas, Ana María. The evolution of social hierarchy in a Muisca chiefdom of the northern Andes of Colombia = La evolucíon de jerarquía social en un cacicazgo Muisca de los Andes septentrionales de Colombia. Pittsburgh, Pa.: Univ. of Pittsburgh, Dept. of Anthropology; Bogotá: Instituto Colombiano de Antropología e

Historia/ICANH, 2007. 250 p.: bibl., ill., maps. (University of Pittsburgh memoirs in Latin American archaeology; 17)

Examines roles of prestige and resource control in the evolution of social hierarchy at El Venado ca. AD 800–1600. Surface collection and excavations yield archeological evidence of inequities in household wealth accumulation. The long occupational sequence demonstrates numerous power strategies, including competition, exchange, and control over knowledge and resources. [DJN]

414 Escallón, María Fernanda. Decoración, cronología y territorio: un estudio comparativo de la cerámica Herrera del altiplano cundiboyacense. Bogotá: Univ. de Los Andes, Facultad de Ciencias Sociales, Depto. de Antropología: Ediciones Uniandes, 2005. 208 p.: bibl., ill. (Col. Prometeo)

This report describes decorations present on Herrera pottery (ca. 400 BC–AD 1000), a pre-Muisca style predominantly from the Dept. of Cundinamarca. Escallón considers samples from seven sites: Mosquera, Zipaquirá, Duitama, Tunja, Madrid, Pubenza, and Iza, and concludes that design motifs on pottery likely pertain to individual identity within communities rather than group expressions among communities or regions. [DJN]

415 Gnecco, Cristóbal. Contra el reduccionismo ecológico en la arqueología de cazadores-recolectores tropicales. (*Maguaré/Bogotá*, 17, 2003, p. 65–82, bibl., tables)

Suggests that many researchers examining hunters and gatherers in the tropics reduce culture to the strategies people use to adapt to their environment. Uses two sites from the Popayán Valley, Colombia—San Isidro and Elvira—to show that hunter-gatherers make significant changes to their environment rather than merely changing their life ways to adapt to the environments they encounter. [DJN]

416 Marchant, Robert et al. Vegetation disturbance and human population in Colombia: a regional reconstruction. (*Antiquity/Cambridge*, 78:302, Dec. 2004, p. 828–838, bibl., maps)

Pollen data from 42 sites in Colombia are used to identify "vegetation degradation," a proxy for human disturbance or cultivation. While changes are primarily linked to human activity, climate is also considered an important factor. Significant changes in human occupation are traced from low to high altitudes over time. [DJN]

417 Mora Camargo, Santiago. Amazonía: pasado y presente de un territorio remoto: el ámbito, la historia y la cultura vista por antropólogos y arqueólogos en la Amazonía. Bogotá: Univ. de Los Andes, Facultad de Ciencias Sociales-CESO, Depto. de Antropología: Fondo de Promoción de la Cultura del Banco Popular, 2006. 249 p.: bibl., ill.

The author considers anthropological models derived from ethnographic studies applied to understand the occupational history and cultural development in the Colombian Amazon. He evaluates these models based on the existing archeological evidence of the region to understand some of the exceptional characteristics of the Amazon. [DJN]

418 El mundo Guane: pioneros de la arqueología en Santander. Textos de Justus W. Schottelius y Martín Carvajal. Recopilación de Alicia Dussán de Reichel Dolmatoff y Armando Martínez Garnica. Santander, Colombia: Gobernación de Santander: Univ. Industrial de Santander, 2005. 175 p.: bibl., ill. (Col. Temas y autores regionales)

Discusses Justus Schottelius, a pioneer in the archeology of Santander, Colombia. Some of Schottelius' reports on his visits to Cueva de los Indios and Cueva de los Santos are reprinted here. Commentaries discuss Schottelius' contributions to methodology, the early years of Colombian archeology, and the current state of research in the country. [DJN]

419 Ome, Tatiana. De la ritualidad a la domesticidad en la cultura material: un análisis de los contextos significativos del tipo cerámico guatavita desgrasante tiestos entre los periodos prehispánico, colonial y republicano—Santa Fe y Bogotá. Bogotá: Univ. de los Andes, Facultad de Ciencias Sociales, Depto. de Antropología, CESO: Ediciones Uniandes, 2006. 253 p.: bibl., ill., maps. (Col. Prometeo)

Examines how a type of pottery, GDT (Guatavita desgrasante tiestos), was used

during the Muisca period (AD 1000–1600) in the Cundiboyacense Altiplano and how the use, production, and circulation of this type of material culture changed through the Santa Fé colonial period, and the Bogotá republic. [DJN]

420 Pineda Camacho, Roberto. Historia, metamorfosis y poder en la orfebrería prehispánica de Colombia. (Bol. Hist. Antig., 92:830, julio/sept. 2005, p. 635–657, bibl., photos)

Reviews the history of religious art in Colombia from Spanish contact to the present day. Describes connections between ethnographic work and archeological recoveries, and emphasizes the importance of preserving indigenous culture to better understand the past. [DJN]

421 Rodríguez Cuenca, José Vicente. Las enfermedades en las condiciones de vida prehispánica de Colombia. Bogotá: Univ. Nacional de Colombia, Facultad de Ciencias Humanas, Depto. de Antropología, 2006. 299 p.: bibl., ill. (some col.).

Offers a comprehensive view of health and illness in the prehispanic populations of Colombia's different environments. Reviews current knowledge on ecology, diet, and demographic stress. Discusses evidence of disease and trauma using dental and skeletal evidence found in prehispanic populations. The accompanying photographs make this book a valuable reference. [DJN]

422 Rodríguez Cuenca, José Vicente and **Arturo Cifuentes Toro.** Un yacimiento formativo ritual en el entorno de la antigua laguna de La Herrera, Madrid, Cundinamarca. (Rev. Mex. Cienc. Polít. Soc., 47:194, mayo/agosto 2005, p. 103–131, bibl., photos)

Details the results of rescue excavations of a Formative Period Herrera site uncovered during construction in Madrid, Cundinamarca, Colombia. The site included ritual architecture with mortuary contexts. Analysis of the remains included attributes of human skeletal remains, ceramics, lithic material, fauna, and shell artifacts. [DJN]

423 Rodríguez Cuenca, José Vicente; Sonia Blanco; and **Pedro José Botero Zuluaga.** Comunidad prehispánica de El Cerrito, Valle del Cauca: medio ambiente, prácticas funerarias y condiciones de vida. Bogotá: Univ. Nacional de Colombia, Sede Bogotá, Facultad de Ciencias Humanas, Depto. de Antropología: Unibiblos, 2005. 138 p.: bibl., ill. (some col.), maps.

Reports on excavations at Hacienda la Cristalina y Tarento, located in El Cerrito, which lies between the areas of Malagana and late Quimbaya occupation. Research uncovered 24 individuals and associated funerary materials, dating to the 4th century BC to the 5th century AD. Analysis describes health, mortality, and affiliated material culture, which relates to sites such as Malagana, Coronado, and Santa Bárbara. [DJN]

424 Rosique, Javier; Paula A. Gallego; and Claudia I. Ospina. Determinación del sexo en cráneo y mandíbula en una muestra contemporánea de Medellín. (*Rev. Mex. Cienc. Polít. Soc.*, 47:194, mayo/agosto 2005, p. 213–232, bibl.)

Based on a sample of 70 modern exhumations from the Medellín area, the authors compare methodologies for assessing sexual dimorphism based on features of the cranium and mandible. They conclude that the Medellín population exhibits less sexual dimorphism than a modern population from Bogotá (Rodríguez Cuenca 2002). [DJN]

425 Sánchez, Carlos A. Constricción social y estrategias productivas agrícolas prehispánicas en el Alto Magdalena. (*Rev. Mex. Cienc. Polít. Soc.*, 47:194, mayo/agosto 2005, p. 149–166, bibl., maps)

Presents a hypothesis relating increasing social complexity to the differential access to land in the Alta Magdalena. Reviews the distribution of elaborate funerary monuments and settlement patterns through the Formative Period to show correlations between the occupation of arable land and the material indicators of status differences. [DJN]

426 Simbolismo y ritual en los Andes septentrionales. Recopilación de Mercedes Guinea. Quito: ABYA YALA: Editorial Complutense, 2004. 187 p.: bibl., ill.

This volume reviews the early history and development of Colombian archeology. It describes early explorers, collectors, and excavators, Colombian archeological expositions on the world stage of the late 1800s, and the important Colombian collections currently held in European museums. The book also describes the recent developments of a scientific research program and the establishment of the Museo del Oro. [DJN]

427 Therrien, Monika; Lina Jaramillo Pacheco; and María Fernanda Salamanca. Política cultural en la significación de la casa: contextos de reflexión sobre las cerámicas arqueológicas; escenario: Santa Fé, Nuevo Reino de Granada, Colombia. (*Rev. Arqueol. Am./México*, 22, 2003, p. 137–164, bibl., facsim., ill.)

Considers changes in the configuration of residential space during the 16th and 17th century in the early colonial city of Santa Fé, Colombia, examining changing local practices. The authors present examples based on historical records and consider ceramics as material culture that may be difficult to correlate to "acculturation" or "resistance" in complex colonial settings. [DJN]

ECUADOR

428 Arellano López, A. Jorge. Culturas prehispanicas del Napo y El Aguarico, amazonía ecuatoriana: transecta Yuturi-Lago Agrio. Lima: Centro Cultural José Pío Aza, Misioneros Dominicos, 2009. 321 p.: bibl., ill., maps.

Provides the first detailed time-space framework for the prehistoric occupation of northeastern Lowland Ecuador based on a survey along a 143 km powerline transect extending from the Napo to the Aguarico. Sites are allocated to five traditions, which are subdivided into phases based on differences in seriated ceramic sequences. Detailed pottery type descriptions are accompanied by illustrations of decoration and vessel shapes. The identification of a Corrugated Tradition, characterized by extremely complicated types of corrugated surface treatment, marks the northern limit of this technique, which is otherwise represented only in southern Brazil. [BJM]

429 García Caputi, Mariella. Las figurinas de Real Alto: reflejos de los modos de vida Valdivia. Quito: Abya Yala, 2006. 262 p.: bibl., ill.

Examines the Valdivia figurines from the site of Real Alto in Ecuador from a social perspective in an effort to show how they relate to gender relations within the community and the gender roles pertaining to men and women in Valdivia society. Theoretical consideration is accompanied by description and illustration of the figurines. [DJN]

430 Gartelmann, Karl Dieter. Las huellas del jaguar: culturas antiguas en el Ecuador. 2. ed. Quito: Trama, 2006. 406 p.: bibl., ill. (some col.).

This catalog offers a historical perspective of the archeological discoveries in Ecuador. It outlines the details of different research programs and includes photographs of excavations and high-quality museum collections. The book is fairly comprehensive in scope highlighting different ancient Ecuadorian societies and their relationships with other South American groups. [DJN]

431 Jara Chávez, Holguer. Tulipe y la cultura yumbo: arqueología comprensiva del subtrópico quiteño. Quito: Fondo de Salvamento del Patrimonio Cultural de Quito, 2006-07. 2 v.: bibl., col. ill., col. maps, index. (Biblioteca básica de Quito; 11)

This two-volume set is a beautifully illustrated survey report describing the archeological remains in the subtropical area around Quito, including Nanegal, Nanegalito, Gualea, and Pacto (the Northwest region of Pichincha). Vol. 1 provides the ecological background and discusses sites of the formative period (Tolas). Vol. 2 details remains in Tulipe and the Yumbo culture. [DJN]

THE GUIANAS

432 Rostain, Stéphen. Agricultural earthworks on the French Guiana coast. (in Handbook of South American archaeology. Edited by Helaine Silverman and William H. Isbell. New York: Springer, 2008, p. 217–233, bibl., ill., map)

Descriptions and excellent photographs of four types of precolumbian raised fields constructed by Arauquinoid immigrants, intensively exploited between AD 700 and AD 1400, and abandoned after European contact. [BJM]

433 Versteeg, Aad H. Barrancoid and Arauquinoid mound builders of coastal Suriname. (in Handbook of South

American archaeology. Edited by Helaine Silverman and William H. Isbell. New York: Springer, 2008, p. 303–318, bibl., ill., map)

Describes raised fields along the coast constructed beginning ca. AD 300 by immigrants from the Mabaruma Phase of western Guyana and amplified by Araquinoid intruders ca. AD 700. [BJM]

PERU

434 Ardito Vega, Giuliano. Análisis de los elementos y los ciclos naturales presentes en el Obelisco Tello. (Bol. Lima, 28:147, 2007, p. 58–71, graph, ill., table)

Examines the Tello Obelisk, a carved stone stela from the Early Horizon site of Chavín de Huantar in northern Peru. Looks at individual figures to determine the animal species depicted and postulates that the figures shown demonstrate that the Chavín authors of the stela commanded knowledge of seasonal cycles and astronomical phenomena. [DJN]

435 Ayca Gallegos, Oscar Raúl. Historia regional: Tacna, Moquegua, Puno. Vol. 2, Tacna prehispánica. Arequipa, Peru: Instituto de Estudios Andinos del Sur, 2006. 124 p.: bibl., ill. (Espacio, tiempo y origen)

This small book focuses on the prehistory of the Dept. of Tacna. Includes b/w photographs of artifacts, architectural features, and sites. Reviews literature from recent archeological research and provides a great introduction to the archeological record and cultural history of Tacna. [DJN]

436 Bourget, Steve. Sex, death, and sacrifice in Moche religion and visual culture. Austin: Univ. of Texas Press, 2006. 258 p.: bibl., index.

Explores the relationships between sexuality, death, and sacrifice through the detailed and realistic art of the Moche, comparing representations with archeological evidence. Describes key Moche characters and themes as background to an analysis of different sexual scenes depicted on Moche ceramic vessels. [DJN]

437 Bueno Mendoza, Alberto. Investigaciones arqueológicas en Tumshukayko (Caraz, Ancash). (Investig. Soc./San Marcos, 15, dic. 2005, p. 43–76, bibl., photos, tables)

Report describes general excavation results from the site of Tumshukayko, Callejón de Huaylas, Peru. Based on characteristics of large shaped stones in two monumental curved walls, the author relates the preceramic occupation (2500–1600 BC) to the Sechin Complex of coastal Casma. The site was also occupied later during the Early Intermediate Period (300 BC–AD 500). [DJN]

438 Campana D., Cristóbal. Chan Chan del Chimo: estudio de la ciudad de adobe más grande de América antigua. Lima: Editorial Orus, 2006. 409 p.: bibl., ill. (some col.).

Presents a synthesis of the current knowledge of the North Coast Chimu polity accompanied by many illustrations and photographs of Chimu sites, features, technology, and artifacts. The final section focuses on the capital of Chan Chan with an iconographic analysis of the city's adobe friezes. [DJN]

439 Cárdenas Martin, Mercedes and Judith Vivar Anaya. Restos humanos de la ocupación precerámica en las Pampas de Salinas de Chao. (*Bol. Lima*, 24:129, 2002, p. 43–62, bibl., ill., maps, photos, tables)

Presents skeletal analysis of six individuals from the coastal area of Salinas de Chao. Five individuals are from Los Morteros (site 7), dating to the Cotton Preceramic, and one individual from site 141 pertains to the earlier precotton period. Remains are fragmentary but comparisons between the two periods suggest interesting changes through time. [DJN]

440 Carreño Collatupa, Raúl. Conjuntos arqueológicos y peligros naturales en el Valle Sagrado de los Incas, Cusco. (*Bol. Lima*, 28:144, 2006, p. 21–50, bibl., map, photos, tables)

Describes geological processes that can damage archeological remains in the Sacred Valley, Cuzco. Presents study results from sites such as Calca, Chinchero, Moray, Pisaq, Ollantatambo, among others, and details existing problems. In general geological destruction is slow, whereas human activity is accelerating such processes and is the major source of potential damage in the future. [DJN]

441 Carreño Collatupa, Raúl. Patrimonio cultural prehispánico y peligro geodinámico en el valle de Huatanay—Cusco.

(*Bull. Inst. fr. étud. andin.*, 34:1, 2005, p. 35–57, bibl., maps, photos)

Assesses how geological processes and land management practices may endanger archeological remains in Cuzco. Examines the sites of Saqsayhuaman, Chakán, K'enqo, Pukapukara, Tambumachay, among others, and concludes that human activity is the cause of most recent damage. [DJN]

442 Covey, R. Alan. How the Incas built their heartland: state formation and the innovation of imperial strategies in the Sacred Valley, Peru. Ann Arbor: Univ. of Michigan Press, 2006. 333 p.: bibl., ill., index, maps. (History, languages, and cultures of the Spanish and Portuguese worlds)

Covey addresses Inca state formation and imperial expansion in terms of processes rather than singular events. He synthesizes archeological and ethnohistorical data from the Cuzco region ca. AD 1000–1532 to describe the political, economic, and social contexts of Inca state formation. These structures and institutions emerged long before imperial expansion. [DJN]

443 Descripción de los quipus del Museo de Sitio de Pachacamac: Proyecto Quipu. Dirección de Hugo Pereyra Sánchez. San Borja, Lima, Peru: Consejo Nacional de Ciencia, Tecnología e Innovación Tecnológica: Proyecto Especial Arqueológico Caral-Supe / INC, 2006. 176 p.: bibl., ill. (some col.).

Detailing the characteristics of the collection of quipus from the site of Pachacamac held by the Site Museum of Pachacamac, located near Lima, the book includes one or more color photos of all 32 quipus described. Pereyra Sánchez explains the significance of different quipu features and research methods. [DJN]

444 Donnan, Christopher B. Moche portraits from ancient Peru. Austin: Univ. of Texas Press, 2004. 88 p.: bibl., ill. (some col.), index, maps (some col.). (Joe R. and Teresa Lozano Long series in Latin American and Latino art and culture)

This illustrated volume explores the Moche portrait vessel tradition. Donnan, an expert on the Moche, describes vessel production and discusses the diversity of Moche society through the portraits' dress and ornamentation. The vessels depict some individuals through different phases of life:

young, old, warriors, captors, and possibly as dead ancestors. [DJN]

445 Eeckhout, Peter. La sombra de Ychsma: ensayo introductorio sobre la arqueología de la costa central del Perú en los periodos tardíos. (*Bull. Inst. fr. étud. andin.*, 33:3, 2004, p. 403–423, bibl., tables)

Author offers comments on a conference organized to understand Ychsma society, which occupied the central coast of Peru before and during the Inca period. Reviews the existing literature on Pachacamac and affiliated sites. Emphasizes the importance of testing models generated by ethnohistory and encourages scholars to study the technical and stylistic elements of ceramics, architecture, textiles, etc., in order to define Ychsma sociopolitical organization. [DJN]

446 Fernández Valle, Juan. Los ruricancho: orígenes prehispánicos de San Juan de Lurigancho. Lima: Fondo Editorial del Congreso del Perú, 2007. 205 p.: bibl., ill., maps.

Discusses the cultural history of the Ruricancho, the original name of the area now known as San Juan de Lurigancho, located in the Lower Rimac Valley and once part of the Ychsma-Pachacamac señorío. Reviews the archeological information from sites in the zone and describes changes during the colonial period using documentary sources. [DJN]

447 Gallardo Ibáñez, Francisco. Un ensayo sobre cultura visual y arte Chimú: costa norte del Perú. (*Bol. Mus. Chil. Arte Precolomb.*, 9, 2004, p. 35–54, bibl., photos)

Examines the artistic restraints placed on artisans of the Chimú empire in an atmosphere of mass production and speculates how artisans responded to production demands. Suggests that artists were active agents responding with creative solutions to satisfy demand and create objects of prestige. [DJN]

448 Gamboa Velásquez, Jorge. Continuidad y cambio en la organización de los espacios arquitectónicos de Huaca de la Luna y Plataforma A de Galindo, costa norte del Perú. (*Bull. Inst. fr. étud. andin.*, 34:2, 2005, p. 161–183, bibl., maps)

Reconsiders the features of Platform 1 of Huaca de la Luna and Platform A of Galindo in light of new dates that suggest that the two Moche complexes may have been contemporary. Suggests that Platform 1 may have served as a model for the construction of Platform A, however with some significant design modifications that might be related to changing political and economic circumstances. [DJN]

449 Hampe Martínez, Teodoro. La última morada de los incas: estudio histórico-arqueológico del Real Hospital de San Andrés. (*Rev. Arqueol. Am./México*, 22, 2003, p. 101–135, bibl., facsim., map)

Describes the veneration of royal Inca mummies in Cuzco, the history of royal mummies under Spanish rule, and the circumstances that brought a few surviving mummies to the hospital of San Andrés in Lima. A recent ground-penetrating radar survey of the hospital revealed several promising locations that may hold the remains of the royal Inca mummies. [DJN]

450 Hocquenghem, Anne Marie and **Luisa Vetter Parodi.** Las puntas y rejas prehispánicas de metal en los Andes y su continuidad hasta el presente. (*Bull. Inst. fr. étud. andin.*, 34:2, 2005, p. 141–159, bibl., graphs, photos)

Describes the Sicán (ca. AD 900) innovation of arcenic bronze, specifically the production of agricultural implements that are found widely in northern Peru and southern Ecuador. Similar tools are made of iron or steel and in use today in parts of Ecuador and northern Peru, and likely are related to tools used in the central highlands of Peru. [DJN]

451 Hostnig, Rainer and **Raúl Carreño Collatupa.** Los petroglifos de Pusharo, Madre de Dios, Perú: consideraciones arqueológicas y geológicas. (*Bol. Lima*, 28:143, 2006, p. 112–144, bibl., maps, photos)

Describes the petroglyphs of Pusharo, in the middle Palotoa valley, in Manu National Park, Peru. The petroglyphs appear in three primary clusters. These areas are subject to several destructive processes and a conservation plan is important for the preservation of the petroglyphs. [DJN]

452 León Canales, Elmo. Orígenes humanos en los Andes del Perú. Lima: Univ. de San Martín de Porres, Escuela Profesional de Turismo y Hoteleria, 2007. 328 p.: bibl., ill., maps.

This book takes a comprehensive look at the peopling of the Americas and considers Paleo-Indian and archaic occupations from the perspective of Peruvian archeological remains. It reviews the lithic technology, human remains, diet, and other lines of evidence. Site photographs and artifact illustrations make this a valuable reference resource. [DJN]

453 Lumbreras, Luis Guillermo. Arqueología y sociedad. Recopilación de Enrique González Carré y Carlos del Águila. Lima: IEP Ediciones: Instituto Nacional de Cultura: INDEA, 2005. 320 p.: bibl., ill. (Historia andina; 30)

Offers a general introduction to the method and theory of archeology as an anthropological science. Lumbreras discusses his theoretical perspective and how it changed throughout his career. He also describes empirical methods of data collection, reviews notions of state-level society, and summarizes archeology as a profession in Peru. [DJN]

454 Lumbreras, Luis Guillermo. Chavín: excavaciones arqueológicas. Lima: UAP, Univ. Alas Peruanas, 2007. 2 v. (753 p.): bibl., ill. (some col.).

This two-volume set reports on excavations from the site of Chavín de Huantar. Both volumes include color photographs and high-quality artifact illustrations. Vol. 1 describes the physical setting and excavations in the Lanzón Atrium, the Circular Plaza, and the Ofrendas Gallery along with an analysis of the materials recovered. Vol. 2 is dedicated to Chavín and imported pottery styles. [DJN]

455 Machupicchu: historia, sacralidad e identidad. Cusco, Peru: Instituto Nacional de Cultura, 2005. 166 p.: bibl., ill., map (chiefly col.).

This colorful volume presents different perspectives on Machu Picchu. A general overview of the main features of the site is supplemented by a formal and thorough building-by-building description. Authors describe the pottery, human remains, architectural designs, sacred stones, and the significance of the monument to the people of Peru and the world. [DJN]

Manners, R.B.; F.J. Magilligan; and P.S. Goldstein. Floodplain development, El Niño, and cultural consequences in a hyperarid Andean environment. See item **1140**.

456 Mayer Center Symposium, 1st, Denver Art Museum, 2001. Andean textile traditions: papers from the 2001 Mayer Center Symposium at the Denver Art Museum. Edited by Margaret Young-Sánchez and Fronia W. Simpson. Denver, Colo.: Denver Art Museum, 2006. 192 p.: bibl., ill. (some col.), maps.

This edited volume includes interesting details about textile production, design, and meaning ranging from the Early Intermediate Period (AD 0–600) to modern times. Several types of textiles are discussed. Each chapter includes photographs, many in color, and other illustrations. The collected works offer a broad corpus of information for the textile expert, the archeologist, and the historian. [DJN]

457 Olivera Alegre, Gloria. Tejidos precerámicos de las Salinas de Chao. Lima: Univ. de San Martín de Porres, Facultad de Ciencias de la Comunicación, Turismo y Psicología, 2006. 156 p.: bibl., ill. (some col.). (Patrimonios. Cultura; 2)

Introduces early techniques in textile production and describes late preceramic textiles (ca. 2500–1800 BC) from the Salinas de Chao, located between the Rivers Santa and Virú on the coast of Peru. Pieces from four sites are compared with contemporary sites throughout the Andes. [DJN]

458 Pachacamac. San Borja, Peru: INC, Instituto Nacional de Cultura, 2006. 128 p.: bibl., ill. (some col.).

This edited volume is a collection of reprinted publications on the ethnohistory and archeology of the central coast site of Pachacamac, Peru. It includes an excerpt of a letter by Hernando Pizarro describing the pilgrimage center and its shrine at the time of contact. Other articles were originally published between 1923 and 1985. [DJN]

459 Reindel, Markus; Johny Isla; and Karsten Lambers. Los geoglifos de Palpa: documentación, analisis y perspectivas. (*Bol. Lima*, 28:143, 2006, p. 73–111, bibl., maps, photos)

Describes a survey of the Palpa geoglyphs, Peru. Early glyphs (ca. 400 BC) in the region were built on hill slopes and visible from great distances. Later Nazca period glyphs were placed on plains and were less visible. Middle Nazca glyphs were built with nearby platform structures and wooden posts, exhibiting evidence of ritual activity and offerings among the glyphs. [DJN]

460 Round Table on Ancash Sierra Archaeology, *1st, Cambridge, England, 2003*. La complejidad social en la Sierra de Ancash: ensayos sobre paisaje, economía y continuidades culturales. Recopilación de Alexander Herrera, Carolina Orsini, y Kevin Lane. Milan, Italy: Civiche Raccolte d'Arte Aplicada del Castello Sforzesco; Lima: PUNKU Centro de Investigación Andina, 2006. 197 p.: bibl., ill., maps.

Volume of conference papers examines different intermontane valleys in the Ancash region from a number of perspectives and time periods to understand the development of social complexity in the north-central highlands of Peru. Chapters (in English and Spanish) touch upon three themes: social identity, material culture, and continuity and change. [DJN]

461 Salazar-Soler, Carmen. La presencia de la antropología francesca en los Andes peruanos. (*Bull. Inst. fr. étud. andin.*, 36:1, 2007, p. 93–107, bibl.)

Reviews the influence and contributions of French anthropology and French anthropologists to the anthropology of Peru since the 1940s. Discusses early research, changes in the 1960s and 1970s, ethnohistoric research, structuralism, ethnicity, and recent trends in current studies, emphasizing the progress on research in both France and Peru resulting from the interchange of ideas between the two countries. [DJN]

462 Shady Solís, Ruth. Caral-Supe y su entorno natural y social en los orígenes de la civilización. (*Investig. Soc./San Marcos*, 14, mayo 2005, p. 89–120, bibl., graphs, ill., maps, photos)

Offers a synthesis of the early ceremonial centers and associated sites in the Supe Valley, Peru, with a detailed description of Caral. Presents a model of early state organization associated with Caral and describes the settlement pattern, economy, religion, and political organization of the early Supe civilization. [DJN]

463 Silva Sifuentes, Jorge E. and Cecilia Jaime Tello. Etnoarqueología del Bajo Rímac y el Callao prehispánico. (*Investig.*

Soc./San Marcos, 15, dic. 2005, p. 29–42, bibl., ill.)

Describes cultural remains encountered in the urban zone of Lima, La Perla. Based on ceramic styles, the authors associate these modest deposits with small villages of the Maranga (Malanga) polity of the central coast in the Late Intermediate and Inca periods. [DJN]

464 Solanilla i Demestre, Victòria. Textiles de las antiguas culturas andinas: colección F. Cervera. Barcelona: Arqueología Clásica, 2006. 173 p.: bibl., ill. (chiefly col.).

Catalog illustrates 62 textiles, mostly Chancay, as well as a weaving basket. Each piece is described in detail. The introduction is written for the lay person, describing the climate, geography, sources of textile fiber, and other important Andean resources. Also contains a simple explanation of Andean spinning and weaving techniques. [DJN]

465 Tello, Julio César. Vida y obra de Julio C. Tello. Introducción, notas y selección de textos de César A. Ángeles Caballero. Lima: Arteidea Editores, 2007. 270 p.: bibl., ill., 1 map, ports.

Describes the life and works of Julio Tello and includes a bibliography of his publications as well as a listing of his unpublished papers held by the Univ. de San Marcos, Lima. Several of Tello's classic works are reprinted such as his writings on Chavin, Paracas, and Andean mythology. [DJN]

Ugent, Donald and **Carlos M. Ochoa.** La etnobotánica del Perú: desde la prehistoria al presente. See item **1155**.

466 Valdez, Lidio M. Los vecinos de Nasca: entierros de la tradición Huarato del valle de Acarí, Perú. (*Bull. Inst. fr. étud. andin.*, 35:1, 2006, p. 1–20, graph, map, photos, table)

Reports on burial practices from the Early Intermediate Period Acarí Valley, southern coastal Peru. Describes four burial types, including one exclusive to infants, as well as burial contexts, body positioning, and orientation. Huarato burial practices are compared to Nazca to demonstrate their contrasting cultural traditions. [DJN]

467 Vargas Paliza, Ernesto. Kusikancha: morada de las momias reales de los Inkas. Cusco, Peru: Instituto Nacional de Cultura, Dirección Regional INC-C, Sub Dirección de Investigación, 2007. 339 p.: bibl., ill. (some col.).

Examines architectural and ethnohistoric documents to identify buildings and their locations and uses in Cuzco. Suggests that the area called Kusikancha near the Qorikancha contained special houses for the mummified remains of the early Inka kings and queens, and may have been established by Pachakuti during his reorganization of the city. [DJN]

468 Velázquez Castro, Adrián; Emiliano Melgar Tísoc; and Anne Marie Hocquenghem. Análisis de las huellas de manufactura del material malacológico de Tumbes, Perú. (*Bull. Inst. fr. étud. andin.*, 35:1, 2006, p. 21–35, maps, photos, table)

Reports on a collaborative experimental-archeological analysis of lithics from a workshop at Rica Playa, near Tumbes. Analysts generated different use-wear assemblages and examined them through scanning electron microscopy. Results show archeological lithics were used for working shell materials. Discusses implications for site production activities and the value of experimental archeology. [DJN]

Wernke, Steven A. Negotiating community and landscape in the Peruvian Andes: a transconquest view. See *HLAS 64:1168.*

VENEZUELA

469 Antczak, María Magdalena and Andrzej Antczak. Los ídolos de las islas prometidas: arqueología prehispánica del archipiélago de los Roques. Caracas: Editorial Equinoccio, 2006. 630 p.: bibl., col. ill.

Considers the figurines from the archipelago de los Roques in archeological and ecological contexts to understand their production, use, and meaning. The beautifully illustrated book includes many color photographs of the figurines and associated material culture, which facilitate the discussion of interaction between ethnohistorically recorded groups during late prehispanic times. [DJN]

470 Navarrete Sánchez, Rodrigo. El pasado con intención: hacia una reconstrucción crítica del pensamiento arqueológico en Venezuela (desde la colonia al siglo XIX). Caracas: Facultad de Ciencias Económicas y Sociales, Univ. Central de Venezuela: Fondo Editorial Tropykos, 2004. 258 p.: bibl.

Offers a synthetic consideration of trends and developments in Venezuelan archeological method and theory in relation to European and North American traditions. Discusses the major schools of thought and key figures in the unique history of the Venezuelan discipline from a critical perspective, promoting self-reflection in archeology. [DJN]

471 Oliver, José R. and Charles S. Alexander. Ocupaciones humanas del Pleistoceno terminal en el occidente de Venezuela. (*Maguaré/Bogotá*, 17, 2003, p. 83–246, bibl., maps, photos, tables)

Reviews the Paleolithic sites of western Venezuela and evaluates the dating of the geological terrace strata in the El Jobo Basin in the Pedregal Valley in the state of Falcón. Suggests an alternative chronology for the early lithic traditions from the region based on new dates and an examination of its geological formation. [DJN]

472 Quero, Arturo Jaimes. El Vano: una nueva localidad paleo-india en el noroccidente de Venezuela. (*Maguaré/Bogotá*, 17, 2003, p. 46–64, bibl., maps, photos)

Describes preliminary findings from the Paleo-Indian site of El Vano, Lava, Venezuela. The site consists of projectile points of El Jobo type and faunal remains from Megaterio, which exhibit marks and are arranged in a manner that appear to result from human activity. The locale is interpreted as a consumption site. [DJN]

ETHNOLOGY
Middle America

DUNCAN EARLE, *Associate Professor of Anthropology, Wake Forest University*

It is a wincing irony of our times that the contemporary indigenous Maya, so much in the vanguard of the indigenous movements for rights, respect, and autonomy in Middle America, have been suddenly thrust into the public eye by the dubious reputation of their ancestors as purported cosmic predictors of doom. It seems the global imaginary has grasped hold of an upcoming calendar date (a date many centuries after the Long Count calendar fell into general disuse and was forgotten) as the time for the end of everything, Hollywood style. The impending arrival of late 2012 as characterized by the digitalized cinematic spectacle has generated unending questions and theories regarding the significance of the Baktun cycle ending for Winter Equinox, 21.12.2012—this number is our calendar's version of the Long Count period ending date for a chunk of time of almost 52 centuries. Not that there is a whit of evidence the ancient Maya thought this date to be the last; some of their calendars go millions of years further into the future. Some opportunistic people have seized this date to scare the general public for fun and profit—usually at the expense of either consulting with specialists in the areas of the claims (astronomers, seismologists, archeologists) or consulting with living indigenous people. In contrast to the disturbing and ill-informed picture painted by the appropriation of Maya cultural heritage for alien and distressing contemporary purposes, Maya endings seem to engender new beginnings, the old cycle dying to bring on the new, based on their cyclical view of time; one era ends, another starts, and the new era brings lessons from the previous one, in a kind of cumulative creation. This explanation is a good metaphor for the following analysis.

Four issues that touch on the Maya and their neighbors, none of them having to do with disasters or outer space, come to mind as being of growing or continuing importance in the recent ethnographic record, and all of them are tied to the notion of endings and beginnings. The first topic is the shift in national and global discourse towards respect for indigenous people and their rights, rights to exist and constitute distinct communities apart from acculturative nationalist projects. The second issue area, a growing trend in the literature for some time, is indigenous voices who alone or in collaboration with (other) ethnographers have shifted from being subjects of study to being studying subjects, increasing their space within the ethnographic universe. Outsider hegemony ends, and indigenous voices are heard. A third research interest is the complexity of ethnic identity when it meets politics and power, especially with the recent shift towards state and constitutional recognition of indigenous rights. Acculturation is officially repudiated, to give space for policies of diversity.

The last ending and starting issue is the environment and ending the isolation of subfields such that environmental topics now are often woven together with other subjects of more traditional ethnographic activity, reflecting the growing acceptance of green solutions in the face of an impending global ecological crisis. To follow the metaphor, ending would be a wasteful, unsustainable society, in a destructive relationship with nature, and beginning would be a new covenant with nature and a new appreciation for the tribal and traditional wisdom regarding viable, sustainable alternatives to the current situation.

A major sign of momentous change in this region—like a new "sun" or creation in its own right—can be found in the subject of indigenous rights, especially in Mexico, where progress has brought us to the point where indigenous subjects, such as rights to autonomous self-governance, or the right to cultural difference in practices and language, have become official canon, displacing the old paradigm of the cosmic race of mestizaje (item **527**). The amount of change in most of the Americas is remarkable, where increasingly as a region the official position (if not all of the public perception) regarding indigenous people and rights has shifted, and notions of pluri-ethnic nations, indigenous rights, and respect for cultural difference are real. The gaps between that which is said and done remain substantial, but this change represents a major shift in the way the state conceives of its relationship with a nation's indigenous people, a form of legal recognition that moves towards official acknowledgement of the veracity of their complaints and an acknowledgement of historic wrongs done to them. In ways inconceivable less than a generation ago, there is now the legal right to being Indian in Hueyapan (whatever that really is, see below) and this has meant the state no longer backs up the acculturative posture embraced in Mexico since nationhood, which has for generations been the paternalistic position that "our" Indians need to be brought in under the big, Spanish-speaking mestizo tent, leaving their quaint culture behind. Surely many people continue to see acculturation as the solution to the "Indian problem," but tacit government support for this position has largely evaporated, and the implications of this dramatic change are rippling through society at a good clip. For example, the census numbers for the indigenous exceed their rates of growth, as the fence-sitters and prior deniers come back to their indigenous roots by embracing their hidden identity, to re-identify with being indigenous. This reflects and reinforces a change in how notions of indigenous identity are viewed in the social landscape, while complicating identity concerns.

Mexico's complex reaction and response(s) to the indigenous-based uprising in Chiapas in 1994 included legal flurries of multi-ethnic rights legislation and some constitutional modifications, and many of these are working their way (unevenly) into the larger landscape. Suddenly being indigenous, individually and collectively, raises complicated new legal issues, governance questions, jurisdiction concerns, and more. Constitutional notions of equality under the law confront distinctions in legal status for those considered or not considered Indian. Indigenous identity may also provide an unprecedented kind of social capital and political leverage, making it more difficult to marginalize, repudiate, or silence. Although the reforms of the San Andrés Accords were weakened by the Mexican Senate so as to deny the Zapatistas constitutional backing for obligatory collective rights, other reforms which were approved, and the momentum brought on by such unprecedented events as indigenous leaders talking inside the Mexican Congress, has opened up irreversible political space, similar to the legal situation of the territory of the Zapatista movement that still holds in the state of Chiapas. Mexico's response has brought the indigenous rights questions to the forefront of national consciousness, and sent the political scientists and philosophers back to work figuring out what it all means—is this postmodern or premodern, anarchism or Liberation Theology, nationalist, pan-indigenous solidarity, or intergalactic dignity? Arguments abound and no hegemony has arisen.

Guatemala, under intense international observation in the shadow of the monstrous rural massacres, as well as after the ensuing refugee crisis and later, the efforts at official UN-aided return of refugees, signed on to cultural rights language in the 1996 Peace Accords in resonance with some of these rights changes going on next door. The language of these accords has provided a boost for notions of Maya cultural and language rights and animated indigenous voices across that nation, with some even taking up government posts as self-identified Mayas. This shift is reflected in indigenous and "cultural revindication" writings from there, as well as from Chiapas, Oaxaca, and elsewhere in Mexico and Central America. Here appears an opening for a new political engagement across lines of ethnicity, but one where power relations must be profoundly rethought and reworked in light of indigenous rights law and informed indigenous voices.

The legal shift into acknowledging the rights of indigenous people to enjoy respect for their culture and their civil rights, and even some degree of their own political autonomy (hotly debated is how much), reflects a paradigm shift. The Indian who would become mestizo for the good of the nation now is displaced by a pluralist multiculturalism with indigenous difference as the good, as part of the wealth and heritage of a nation, with the civil right to exercise that difference without prejudice, without derogation. Racism is now a crime. In the past race was not even part of the assimilation project vocabulary, but now it has been thrust into the open—and governments have, under international pressure, embraced diversity with great verbosity: truly a new era.

Some voices in the list below are troubled by the facile shift from erasure to heralding of indigenousness, and are willing to ask, above and beyond the long-awaited official approval for indigenous multiculturalism, what we now mean by "indigenous"—and note how the category evolves and shifts with time, setting, and policy, excluding and including more or less people depending on non-indigenous factors. Once to be Indian was thought of as backward, inferior, and unclean. The new paradigm is to celebrate (while documenting) indigenous culture, but critics claim that this shift has happened without having fully theorized what we mean by Indian, indigenous, native, and so on. Such identity questions are the complaint of Carmen Martínez Novo, in her work, *Who Defines Indigenous?* (item **520**)—following in the line of analysis of her principle professor Judith Friedlander, whose classic book, *Being Indian in Hueyapan,* has reemerged with updates (item **498**). The question these scholars raise becomes complicated by diverse social landscapes onto which identities are now deployed, often self-consciously and strategically, by competing actors with complex and situational identity claims. Now leaders and organizations are in a position to promote their visions of indigenous identity, of who is and is not an Indian, for the criteria of belonging. The same can be said for government and businesses whose interests are in supporting tourism. Some events posing as empowering the indigenous may in fact be the opposite, an opportunity for outside control; and some forms of organization in communities may not succeed by using local cultural practices and customs (for example if those customs are not democratic nor inclusive).

Along similar lines, Virginia Tilley's *Seeing Indians* examines the new emphasis in El Salvador on identifying and promoting its indigenous heritage, after years of denial and repression, with seeming mixed results (item **546**). Also critiquing standard categories of ethnicity, but in a different way, Maria Mosquera Saravia, in her book *Lógicas y racionalidades,* questions the veracity of linguistic hegemony in labeling ethnicity in Guatemala, claiming one township (Rabinal) is ethnically distinct from other places and people as a whole, based on other, nonlinguistic grounds, a unity which includes its mestizos or Ladinos, and this is demonstrated by the author through an extensive look at the way midwifery operates in the region (item **525**). Certainly identity politics are complex and often mutable to match changing social circumstances, but they do find power in organizing during situations and epochs of major displacement, as the social glue. Research on migrants and refugees from indigenous towns in Guatemala and Mexico show how identity can become multiple, situational, segmented, and flexible, where presentation of self varies with each social situation, and certain members of households opt out into other larger social categories.

Like the Civil Rights era in US history, Middle America participates in the renewed efforts at establishing, maintaining, and defending indigenous collective rights recently reaffirmed by the United Nations. The legal basis of this effort rests predominantly upon the International Labor Organization's Convention 169, adopted in Geneva in 1989 and ratified by 17 nations so far, including Mexico, Guatemala, Honduras, and Costa Rica. ILO 169 and many similar accords emphasize the linkages between indigenous people and their natural resources, as an economic but also cultural basis of their history, their current situation, and their future. Some scholars applaud this complexity in terms of political rights vis-à-vis the state, but others do not, finding it ambiguous and even contradictory to the modern nation-state. These are familiar arguments raised in any discussion about the state exercising its authority to protect minorities against the majority, whether on ethnic/racial grounds, or as can be seen in the US today regarding marriage rights. This arena of thought will no doubt continue to produce a rich harvest of work. Take the example of *Dissident Women: Gender and Cultural Politics in Chiapas*, where indigenous and women's rights are extensively explored by both anthropologists and indigenous women (item **490**).

The appearance of ethnoecological studies, both more traditional ethnoscience approaches and ones challenging Western botanical hegemony, are part of a larger emergence of works with environmental themes, from sacred geographies (item **478**) to the marvels of "ethnoagroecology" (item **483**) and how people in Mesoamerica traditionally fish. Studies that link the environment to local and global change are on the ascent, as issues such as global climate change become harder to ignore. We also see a return to regional studies that are holistic in terms of methods and theoretical focus, incorporating beliefs and worldview along with economics, environment, and technological changes, and that look at land management issues. Other themes represented in this review include studies of migration and transnationalism, the psychological effects of violence, medical anthropological themes, and ethnographies promoted by the local people themselves. Finally a handful of works question how ethnography is done, decrying the distances of the old paradigm and encouraging new forms of subjectivity, a shift from interviews and words to images and sensation, from objective observation to intersubjective relations (items **2** and **513**).

As the world enters the second decade of this new century, we see in sum works situated within very traditional and nontraditional ethnographic frameworks, resurgences of old ideas such as regional studies and new ones like collaborative ethnographies with indigenous communities, making for a rich and textured postmodern whole. Moreover, the original tenets of ethnography still hold, both of single case studies and team-based or comparative ones: it is of vital importance to collect and assess field data, from what people say and do, to what they make and opine. Indigenous rights is part of a larger decolonizing project, where the asymmetries of society are no longer reinforced in communication and action, and the unheard indigenous, women, youth, poet voice is able to be heard.

Thus the importance of those works listed below that allow many of their pages to be covered with the words of the local people themselves, in small bits and in long bibliographic accounts, stories of love and violence, tales of ancient heroes and animal companions, long journeys and elaborate cures, of Giants and Serpents in mountains, by rivers, by water. Highly abstract notions of law, rights, religion, and so on are exemplified and embodied by the fieldwork and assessments of those who witness these concepts embodied in daily life, and sometimes over significant amounts of time. This old story is given new life by new voices and new ways of presenting that voice and making it heard.

473 **Acuña Delgado, Angel.** La construcción cultural del cuerpo en la sociedad Rarámuri de la Sierra Tarahumara. Quito: Abya-Yala, 2006. 453 p.: bibl., ill.

An ethnographic exploration into Raramuri culture through examining the social and cultural constructions of the male and female body, as seen through the temporal prism of life cycle stages; also through diet; through notions of body, space, and landscape; through wellness, illness, and healers and, in some detail, through their sports, games, and dances. The author concludes that these dances generate identity as they tie people socially, connect them with the mystical elements of earth and sky, and allow them to fulfill sacred and social obligations to the group, such that their dances profoundly embody their culture.

474 **Acuña Delgado, Angel.** Etnología de la carrera de bola y ariweta rarámuris. México: Centro de Investigaciones y Estudios Superiores en Antropología Social, 2006. 300 p.: bibl., ill. (Publicaciones de la casa chata)

An engaging ethnography focused on the social and symbolic meanings behind gendered race-running practices of the Raramuri (Tarahumara) of Chihuahua, Mexico. Strongly methodological as well as theoretical, the work places these long foot races in their larger community contexts of sociocultural significance; it also provides local children's drawings depicting the races in an annex, as part of an effort to provide local imaginary.

475 **Adams, Walter Randolph.** Health care in Maya Guatemala: confronting medical pluralism in a developing country. Norman: Univ. of Oklahoma Press, 2007. 268 p.: bibl., ill., index, maps.

Via students placed in three Maya communities, the authors explore specific medical anthropological topics—midwifery, nutrition, dentistry, depression—in search of a more efficacious integration of a Maya worldview and the Western allopathic paradigm. Shows the use of annual summer field schools as a means to gather ethnographic data.

476 **Alarifes, amanuenses y evangelistas: tradiciones, personajes, comunidades y narrativas de la ciencia en México.** Coordinación de Mechthild Rutsch y Mette Marie Wacher. México: Instituto Nacional de Antropología e Historia: Univ. Iberoamericana, 2004. 461 p.: bibl., ill., maps, ports. (Seria Antropología / Instituto Nacional de Antropología e Historia) (Col. científica; 467)

A collection of anthropological, historical, and archeological articles derived from a conference in 2001 by UNAM's Instituto de Investigaciones Antropológicas. Of interest are several narratives on the formation of anthropology and anthropologists, such as Angel Palerm, and an article on legal anthropology touching on some of the problems associated with clashes between law and indigenous custom.

477 **Alfaro Telpalo, Guillermo.** El trasluz de la diferencia: consideraciones sobre pueblos indígenas y diversidad cultural en México. México: Univ. Iberoamericana, Dirección de Servicios para la Formación Integral, Programa de Reflexión Univeristaria, 2006. 135 p.: bibl.

An essay about the long history of poor understanding across ethnic lines, in an era when Mexico has been invited to transform ideas of the indigenous as an embarrassment and an exemplification of underdevelopment into an active and respect-worthy partner in the inventing of the new multi-ethnic Mexican nation. It casts doubt upon this national project, in that it would profoundly transform what Mexico is in relation to what most non-indigenous imagine it currently to be, especially regarding notions of the modern and of national unity through state uniformity. To really embrace the new laws, it suggests, requires a major transformation of the historically situated non-indigenous views of the indigenous.

Arnold, Dean E. Social change and the evolution of ceramic production and distribution in a Maya community. See item **9.**

478 Barabas, Alicia. Dones, dueños y santos: ensayo sobre religiones en Oaxaca. México: Instituto Nacional de Antropología e Historia: Miguel Angel Porrúa, 2006. 288 p.: bibl., maps.

After years of vibrant study of the symbolic and religious traditions of numerous ethnic groups in the state of Oaxaca, Mexico, this collection of nine essays revisits and deeply explores notions of symbolic territoriality and religious expression across diverse groups in this same region. Of particular interest are chapters on territorial rights (etnoterritorialidad) and the pluricultural state, on life cycle rituals and gifting, and on the ways religious conversions still maintain familiar cultural attitudes and beliefs.

479 Bonfiglioli, Carlo. La epopeya de Cuauhtémoc en Tlacoachistlahuaca: un estudio de contexto, texto y sistema en la antropología de la danza. México: Casa Abierta al Tiempo, Univ. Autónoma Metropolitana, 2004. 430 p.: bibl., ill. (Cultura universitaria; 78. Serie Ensayo)

Focusing on one of three main regions of "diffusion" of the Dance of the Conquest within Mexico, in the state of Guerrero (Costa Chica region), the author places the study in the context of dance theory, then gives a detailed ethnographic context, followed by detailed accounting of the dance phase (including a choreographic notation for each dance step set), and a social and symbolic analysis of the significance of the dance in its context. It is also compared with some other variations in the Gulf region, Guerrero and Oaxaca, and the dance is subjected to a structural assessment of its symbolic expressions in a variety of cases.

480 Brockmann, Andreas. La pesca indígena en México. México: UNAM, Instituto de Investigaciones Antropológicas, 2004. 173 p.: bibl., ill., maps.

A comparative examination of indigenous fishing and fish-taking practices in Mexico based on available ethnographic material, with emphasis on the Valley of Mexico, the Seris, the Tarahumara, the Huaves, and the Tarascan region. The author seriates types of fishing by category and applies it to a broad database, seeking a diffusion model, and also does some ethnoscience comparisons between Tzeltal and Tarascan fish naming. Includes a brief discussion of economics, social change and religious significance of fish and fishing, and its role in Mesoamerica from prehispanic times forward. Exemplifies the ethnological use of prior ethnographic data to create comparative understandings across cultural and physical geographies of seemingly similar types of concerns and practices in different Mesoamerican cultures. It also illuminates fish as a cultural category.

481 Cabrera Pérez-Armiñán, María Luisa. Violencia e impunidad en comunidades mayas de Guatemala: la masacre de Xamán desde una perspectiva psicosocial. Guatemala: Equipo de Estudios Comunitarios y Acción Psicosocial (ECAP): F&G Editores, 2006. 349 p.: bibl., ill.

Using the 1995 massacre of 11 indigenous Guatemalans and the subsequent prosecution process as a case study, the author presents a complex psychosocial and politico-legal analysis to illuminate the problems of violence and impunity at a critical moment in the "post-war" period (including organized returning refugees and UN-mediated peace accords). Based on extensive, culturally sensitive surveys and interviews by field teams, the study identifies post-traumatic stress and its negative social impacts, as well as the positive implications of the judicial process for victimized communities and groups, advancing therapeutic social memory even when justice is not achieved.

482 Carrillo Trueba, César. Pluriverso: un ensayo sobre el conocimiento indígena contemporáneo. México: UNAM, 2006. 132 p.: bibl. (Col. La pluralidad cultural en México; 11)

Begins by noting global conservation focus has shifted increasingly to indigenous lands, assessing good and bad land management practices through a decidedly Western science lens, neglecting to entertain epistemic pluralism. The author suggests that different histories of plant and animal domestication, and environmental modification, gave birth to differently situated sciences, while delightfully outlining many specifics of the Mesoamerican maize tradition. Following the shift in anthropological theorizing of the last two decades in Mexico, and the neo-Zapatista rhetoric of philosophical pluralism revindicating indigenous cultures and rights, the text makes an eloquent argument for ceasing to privilege Western knowledge conceits based on their scale or force, and elevating indigenous rights as regards the concrete to those regarding the philosophical, with the advocacy of a "pluriverse"—a multilensed and anthropologically situated process.

483 Castro Pérez, Francisco. Colapsos ambientales, transiciones culturales. Coyacan, Mexico: UNAM: Instituto de Investigaciones Antropológicas: Benemérita Univ. Autónoma de Puebla, 2006. 475 p.: bibl., ill., map. (Col. Posgrado; 33)

Unpacking and applying his theoretical, holistic concept of ethnoagroecology to a series of mestizo and indigenous communities in the Altipano Central of Mexico (Acolhuacan), the author links variables of worldview, environmental knowledge, economic rationality, and agricultural technologies to compare and contrast communities along ethnic and other historically and ecologically grounded bases, and documents their changes especially in the last 20 years of Mexico's economic globalization and environmental change. He provides a robust understanding of the material and social factors that promote or erode the campesino (peasant) lifestyle in areas of proximity to urbanism and under ecosystemic stress. He also reveals the sustainable aspects of indigenous land use, and identifies many complex threats to it, cosmological, ethnoecological, and in terms of alternatives in technology and economic logics. An important work for understanding the socioecological and economic conditions under which peasant adaptations are sustainable.

484 Celestino, Eustaquio. Gotas de maíz: jerarquía de cargos y ritual agrícola en San Juan Tetelcingo, Guerrero. México: Centro de Investigaciones y Estudios Superiores en Antropología Social, 2004. 311 p.: bibl., ill. (Antropologías Ciesas)

A detailed reporting of the community-wide cargo system that mediates three important agricultural rituals in a village in Guerrero, despite the religious divisions between Catholic and Protestant, and assures the maintenance of relations with critical elements of nature, with ancestors, and with indigenous identity. In an era when many civil-religious hierarchies have declined or fallen, for both secular and religious reasons, the manner by which this system continues to enjoy municipality-wide moral authority and efficacy teaches much about the institution and its followers.

485 Centeno García, Santos. Adhesión étnica. Tegucigalpa: Editorial Universitaria, Univ. Nacional Autónoma de Honduras, 2004. 268 p.: bibl., ill. (Col. Realidad nacional)

A clarion call for inclusion of the "autochthonous ethnicities" in a renewed national dialogue about being Honduran, along with an effort at their description, including Tolupanes, Pech, Garifias, Lencas, Misquitos, Tawahkas, Chortis, and African Hondurans (who together make up 12 percent of the population). The book provides a solid critique of the actual situation of marginalization, due to ignorance.

486 Chevalier, Jacques M. The hot and the cold: ills of humans and maize in native Mexico. Toronto; Buffalo, N.Y.: Univ. of Toronto Press, 2003. 301 p.: bibl., ill., index. (Anthropological horizons; 24)

Using southern Veracruz as a case area, the author explores the clash and mesh of medical traditions arising from indigenous traditions (Nahua, Popoluca), Catholicism, humoralism, and biomedicine, with a goal of reiterating the resiliency of the native system, both in human health and certain agricultural concerns. Balance, cyclical movements of increase and decline, and directionality of life provide a cultural logic juxtaposed to exogenous ones, and woven into cornfields, tales, and religious practice.

487 Ciudadanías diferenciadas en un estado multicultural: los usos y costumbres en Oaxaca. Textos de Graciela Ángeles Carreño *et al.* Prólogo por Víctor Manuel Durand Ponte. Coordinación de Jorge Hernández-Díaz. México: Siglo XXI Editores: Univ. Autónoma Benito Juárez de Oaxaca, 2007. 388 p.: bibl. (Sociología y política)

An ample collection of articles exploring and debating community cultural politics in the indigenous Oaxaca state, in the wake of the post-Zapatista federal support for community rights and law based on "uses and customs", and the uneven, creative, conflictive and contradictory employment of the same. Oaxaca has taken the lead in this area due to their new laws reflecting the federal constitutional changes championing indigenous self-governance and tradition-based authority, and in these essays we find varied cases of what happens when such changes are given space by state authorities. Their collective results say much about what a politically multicultural landscape would look like in Mexico and beyond.

488 Comunidades en movimiento: la migración internacional en el norte de Huehuetenango = Konob'laq yin ek'jab'ahilal: B'eytzejtoqb'ahil b'ay juntzanoqxa konob'laq yuj heb' kajan ajelb'a ajtoq Chinab'jul. Edited by Manuela Camus. Guatemala: Instituto Centroamericano de Desarrollo y Estudios Sociales (INCEDES): Centro de Documentación de la Frontera Occidental de Guatemala (CEDFOG), 2007. 223 p.: bibl., ill.

First in a proposed series of studies on (im)migration, based in a border region of Guatemala (with Mexico). Framed with the term "communities in movement," this well-introduced compilation serves to both describe and exemplify in diversely situated cases the complexity of emergent transnationality of communities once defined as and confined to small "traditional" spaces, and now strung across nation and continent.

489 18 de julio no se olvida!: identidad y cultura popular e indígena. Coordinación de Marco A. Anaya Pérez *et al.* Chapingo, Mexico: Univ. Autónoma Chapingo, Dirección General de Investigación y Posgrado, Dirección General de Difusión Cultural y Servicio, 2004. 140 p. (Serie Identidad y cultura popular e indígena; 1)

Twelve prize-winning research works by students from the Univ. Autónoma Chapingo on the cultural and social particulars of their own communities. Asked to carry out ethnographic research rather than just read it, the student works have qualities of enthusiasm, of personal engagement in the interest of the larger communities they represent, and a quality of return to understandings and reflections upon the meanings of things previously taken for granted or discarded as antiquated or insignificant.

490 Dissident women: gender and cultural politics in Chiapas. Edited by Shannon Speed, R. Aída Hernández Castillo, and Lynn M. Stephen. Austin: Univ. of Texas Press, 2006. 280 p., 12 p. of plates: bibl., ill., index, map. (Louann Atkins Temple women & culture series; 14)

A diverse collection of materials and articles assembled to document and comment upon the emergence of indigenous women as new social and political actors, by anthropologists and advocates with significant field experience in Chiapas, Mexico. Critiquing Mexico's "exclusionary discourse of liberal citizenship" that erased the importance of indigenous collective political and cultural rights, the authors follow the ways Zapatistas and other indigenous women have cultivated their own cultural citizenship concepts, allowing for their spaces of difference within the larger nation and within their cultural traditions. Their engagement with rights debates have covered a wide arena of issues, including alcoholism and domestic violence, women's political participation, land rights, arranged marriages, rights to housing, education, medical attention, and employment, as well as women's participation in previously male traditional domains. Provides rich insights into how indigenous women construct a distinct feminism based on their daily struggles from urban feminism, and how this challenges the latter's conceptualizations and actions.

491 Early, John D. The Maya and Catholicism: an encounter of worldviews. Gainesville: Univ. Press of Florida, 2006. 311 p.: bibl., ill., indexes, map.

Former Jesuit and Harvard Chiapas Project-trained anthropologist who began his studies on religion, but went on to publish on concrete issues of medical anthropology, demography, and mortality in Guatemala and elsewhere, the author returns to his first subject in this marvelous study of comparative Maya religion (across time and space) and its long-complicated relationship to Catholicism. Superb comparative discussion of core Maya theological concepts, the role of Maya saints as replacements for specific prehispanic deities in past strategic appropriations of Catholic icons and institutions, and the history of Maya relations with the Church from its earliest presence to current times. Makes crystal clear why Maya appropriations are neither unconscious syncretism nor an imposed conversion to an alien God, and "revindicates" the prehispanic origins of contemporary Maya "shamanic" saint worship.

492 Estudios antropológicos de los pueblos otomíes y chichimecas de Querétaro. Coordinación de María Elena Villegas Molina. Querétaro, Mexico: Centro Regional INAH en Querétaro, 2005. 160 p.: bibl., ill., maps.

A rambling collection of diverse archeological (3), historical (2), and ethnographic (6) articles focused generally on the Querétaro region of north-central Mexico; the state is about 3 percent indigenous, mostly Otomí. Subjects include rock art, ancient funerary practices, a lost convent, historic indigenous characters, pilgrimages, ethnographic photography, water use, and language use.

Ethnic identity in Nahua Mesoamerica: the view from archaeology, art history, ethnohistory, and **contemporary ethnography.** See *HLAS 64:217.*

493 Etnicidad, autonomía y gobernabilidad en América Latina. Recopilación de Salvador Martí i Puig y Josep Ma. Sanahuja. Salamanca, Spain: Ediciones Univ.

de Salamanca, 2004. 398 p.: bibl., ill. (Acta Salmanticensia) (Biblioteca de América; 29)

A broad collection of essay chapters addressing how the rise in political awareness of indigenous spaces and legal claims has altered profoundly the Latin American political landscape, a terrain in which indigenous ethnicity in the past rarely was a serious consideration—and certainly not one to animate dialogue on real political autonomy. With three Ecuador cases, three from Guatemala, and three from Nicaragua, and a number of synthesizing chapters addressing the whole region, the book squarely addresses the issues confronting the state when contemplating indigenous self-governance and autonomy, and raises many fascinating questions about the politics of governance.

494 Etnomedicina en Guatemala. Compilación de Elba Marina Villatoro. Guatemala: Editorial Universitaria, Univ. de San Carlos de Guatemala, 2005. 296 p.: bibl., ill. (Col. Historia nuestra)

Republished (from first printing in 1984), this classic book is a collection of very distinct articles on the subject of ethnomedicine, from a substantial essay summarizing much of what is known about hallucinogens in Mesoamerica, to early documents on native and Spanish colonial medicine, contemporary Maya midwife practices, and two semi-applied articles promoting the study, assessment, and use of native medicine in rural health care.

495 Euraque, Darío A. Conversaciones históricas con el mestizaje y su identidad nacional en Honduras. San Pedro Sula, Honduras: Centro Editorial, 2004. 279 p.: bibl.

One effect of the Chiapas rebellion in 1994 was to bring before the Honduran national consciousness its own racial and ethnic history, both indigenous and African, a subject rarely in open discussion previously, in the wake of a Lenca march on the capital. This book explores this subject and its history, as well as the many meanings and understandings of mestizo and mestizaje.

496 Fábregas, Andrés. Chiapas: culturas en movimiento. Tuxtla Gutiérrez, Chiapas Mexico: Viento al Hombro, 2006. 103 p.: bibl., ill., 1 map, ports.

A small handbook of indigenous peoples and languages, including Zoque, Lacandon, Chol, Tojolabal, Chuj, Jacaltek, Tzotzil, and Tzeltal. It ends with an epilogue championing more research on change, on mestizo or Ladino culture, and the impacts of the outside world on local indigenous culture.

Farr, Marcia. Rancheros in Chicagoacán: language and identity in a transnational community. See item **2485.**

497 Fortalecimiento de la participación política de las mujeres mayas. Investigación de María Estela Jocón González. Chimaltenango, Guatemala: Asociación Maya Uk'u'x B'e, 2005. 167 p.: bibl., ill. (some col.). (Serie Oxlajuj baqtun)

A small handbook designed to strengthen indigenous women's political participation, in light of the signing of the Guatemalan Peace Accords and its social contract for inclusive political participation, written from a Maya woman's perspective. Written within the paradigm of Maya cultural renovation and revival, it employs such elements as the 260-day calendar and daily cultural practices to strengthen the position of the female in political life. It also draws on colonial and recent history to situate women's struggle and suffering, their role in nonviolent and armed resistance, in refugee organizations in Mexico, and other groupings of women inside and outside the country. It lays out the rights spelled out for indigenous women in the Peace Accords, and makes a long series of recommendations for strengthening the position of women and Mayas generally in Guatemala, including the spiritual dimension.

498 Friedlander, Judith. Being Indian in Hueyapan. A rev. and updated ed. New York: Palgrave Macmillan, 2006. 287 p.: bibl., ill., index.

The author updates this classic text and adds a chapter to bring the polemic of the earlier work into contemporary times reflect the renewed interest in the rights of the indigenous in Mexico. She expresses concern that state-promoted "Indianness" may be as problematic as state-promoted mestizo nationalism of 30 years ago.

499 Geist, Ingrid. Liminaridad, tiempo y significación: prácticas rituales en la Sierra Madre Occidental. México: Instituto Nacional de Antropología e Historia, 2005. 322 p.: bibl., ill., index. (Col. Científica;) 471. Serie Antropología

Using detailed ethnographic data from a Huichol and a Cora community, the author approaches ritual practice from the standpoint of the liminal state (re. V. Turner) created by performance, a state that both reiterates and dissolves the cosmic order.

500 Gonzáles Enríquez, J. Les Yaqui: Mexique septentrional, un manuel d'ethnographie appliquée. Paris: Harmattan, 2007. 164 p.: bibl. (Recherches Amériques latines)

Conversations with Yaquis from almost a dozen distinct locales punctuated with observation, analysis and discussions of the application of traditional forms of understanding (cosmovision, myth, ritual) to contemporary applied issues, such as healing and health—with the heuristic message that to help in other cultural settings you have to understand how different worlds are culturally and practically constituted. Introduces many Middle American and Yaqui cultural concepts and terms to French readers.

501 González Ortiz, Felipe. Estudio sociodemográfico de los pueblos y comunidades indígenas del Estado de México. Colaboración de Reyes Alvarez Fabela *et al.* Zinacantepec, Mexico: El Colegio Mexiquense, A.C.; Toluca, Mexico: Consejo Estatal para el Desarrollo Integral de los Pueblos Indígenas del Estado de México, 2005. 243 p.: bibl., ill., maps.

Reflecting on indigenous identity, ethnic division, and acculturation in a region highly and unevenly urbanized (adjacent to sprawling Mexico City), the study both challenges and promotes an ethnography of field complexity, rural and urbanizing, traditional and economizing. The work includes an excellent discussion of traditional devotional sodalities of "spenders" who underwrite annual religious ceremony.

502 González Ortiz, Felipe and **Ivonne Vizcarra Bordi.** Mujeres indígenas en el Estado de México: vidas conducidas desde sus instituciones sociales. Zinacantepec, Mexico: El Colegio Mexiquense, A.C.; Toluca, Mexico: Univ. Autónoma del Estado de México, 2006. 247 p.: bibl., ill., maps.

Addressing how indigenous women have the double burden of their marginalization as an ethnic group and the situations of social power asymmetry within the indigenous society, itself embedded in a non-indigenous society of great asymmetry, the author examines quantitatively and qualitatively women, especially indigenous women, in the state of Mexico (the state surrounding the capital city). They take on the gender symbolic complementarity issue by assessing Aztec and Otomi cultures at contact as patriarchal, reinforced by the privileging of warriors (gods and men) and the use of elite women for alliance currency, despite dual gendered gods. Family, kinship, and cargo systems conspire to subordinate women via symbolic means, which is reinforced as women encounter other institutions, including those of the state.

503 Gordillo y Ortiz, Octavio. El EZLN: una aproximación bibliográfica. México: Editorial Praxis, 2006. 284 p.: index.

A rich and broad 50 page bibliographic essay followed by an unannotated bibliography of social and political works published on the Chiapas uprising, mostly through about 2002.

504 Granados Pérez, Victoria. Los costos de la modernidad: transformaciones económicas en un pueblo rarámuri. Chihuahua, Mexico: Instituto Chihuahuense de Cultura, 2006. 253 p.: bibl., ill. (Col. Solar. Serie Ensayos)

Bases on a study of a Taraumara community on the edge of Copper Canyon in the municipality of Batopilas, Chihuahua, the author asks why this indigenous group has lost much of its former economic resilience, as documented up to the second half of the last century, such that now migration and salaried work have come to play an ever more dominant role in the local economy. Her answers involve the role of government, major impacts of narcotrafficking operations, and other forms of penetration of the locale.

505 Gutiérrez Avila, Miguel Angel; José C. Tapia Gómez; and Marguerite Bey. Multipartidismo y poder en municipios indígenas de Guerrero. Coordinación de

Daniele Dehouve, Víctor Franco Pellotier, e Aline Hémond. México: Centro de Investigaciones y Estudios Superiores en Antropología Social: Univ. Autónoma de Guerrero, 2006. 406 p.: bibl., maps.

A team-based five-year political study of 12 municipalities in the northeast and eastern part of Guerrero, Mexico, looking at the rise of alternative political parties after 1989 as they are lived out in very local politics, but also under the many and uneven impacts of recent government programs. One of the many values of this comparative, regional, coordinated study is its thoughtful examination of the political and social effects (such as isolation) of government assistance programs in the wake of national neoliberal restructuring. Few studies martial such rich data from so many places of such similarity over such an amount of time, with its controlled forms of comparison. A political anthropology goldmine.

506 Guzmán Medina, María Guadalupe Violeta. Una nueva mirada hacia los mayas de Yucatán: identidad, cultura y poder. Mérida, Mexico: Univ. Autónoma de Yucatán, 2005. 475 p.: bibl., ill. (some col.), maps, plans. (Tratados)

A discussion of academic thinking on identity and its application to the indigenous people of Yucatán. Captivating discussion of relations between power and religion, the legitimization of authority, indigenous appropriation of alien cultural material, and comparisons between different Maya regions, as in Motul versus Valladolid. Also of note is the emphasis on daily life as cultural practices of resistance and identity.

507 Hernández Díaz, Jorge. Grupos indígenas en Oaxaca: situación sociodemográfica. Oaxaca, Mexico: Instituto de Investigaciones Sociológicas de la Univ. Benito Juárez de Oaxaca: Plaza y Valdés, 2005. 139 p.: bibl., ill.

A look at the demographic and language changes for indigenous people in the last century in the Mexican state of Oaxaca, noting a relative loss of monolingualism and the loss of native tongues to Spanish. These language shifts do not represent great change in equitable integration locally, and the author insists that if the state wishes now to promote inter-ethnic cultural respect, they need to focus on educating local non-indigenous people who currently express much of the cultural prejudice, and also on bilingual education for everyone.

508 Higgins, Nicholas P. Understanding the Chiapas rebellion: modernist visions and the invisible Indian. Austin: Univ. of Texas Press, 2004. 259 p.: bibl., ill., index, map.

A significant if simplified, historically and politically grounded analysis of Mexico seeking explanation for the 1994 Chiapas rebellion in efforts by the state to "make invisible" indigenous people who do not fit within the modernist vision(s) of the Mexican nation. In his cultural humanism the author captures Zapatista political counterpoint to the state as expressed by its leadership and literature, and reiterates anew other scholars' observations about native resistance through time as expressed through strategic appropriation (and reworking) of externally imposed institutions, symbols, and sources of legitimacy.

509 Historia y etnografía entre los chontales de Oaxaca. Coordinación de Andrés Oseguera. México: Instituto Nacional de Antropología e Historia, 2006. 337 p.: bibl., ill., maps. (Col. Etnografía de los Pueblos Indígenas de México. Serie Estudios monográficos)

A fine if uneven collection of work on the Chontal, including the reprinting in Spanish of Carrasco's 1960 classic article, "Pagan Rituals and Beliefs among the Chontal Indians of Oaxaca, Mexico" (see *HLAS 27:889*), a long linguistic piece by Loretta O'Connor, and another major article on Chontal historical and territorial narratives by Danny Zborover. History, archeology, and other ethnographic issues are also addressed, making it a rich and informative starting place for understanding the Chontal of Oaxaca.

510 Hooft, Anuschka van 't. The ways of the water: a reconstruction of Huastecan Nahua society through its oral tradition. Leiden: s.n., 2003. 273 p.: bibl., map.

Translation of a 2003 work shedding light on the relationship between Nahua texts and Huasteca regional context (especially Xochiatipan) in eastern Mexico, with a large and well-analyzed corpus of Nahua oral literature, based on ten years

of fieldwork in the native tongue. Most of the oral tradition discussed pools around themes of water, rivers, snakes, and mythic beings associated with water, and spiritual danger/healing as it relates to water. He also demonstrates the ties between oral performance and indigenous language retention and identity.

511 Hunn, Eugene S. A Zapotec natural history: trees, herbs, and flowers, birds, beasts, and bugs in the life of San Juan Gbëë. Tucson: Univ. of Arizona Press, 2008. 261 p.: bibl., ill., index, 1 CD-ROM.

Years of fieldwork are reflected in this "natural history" that is so much cultural heritage, where children seem precociously predisposed to learn the culture's 150+ plant vocabulary, complete with information on flowering time, plant part use, and location where they likely occur, and so on, some by the age of only seven. Such early adult knowledge not only suggests their deep plant and ecological "literacy" but also exposes our own culture's nature knowledge deficit. The accompanying CD-ROM has the plant, animal, and fungi categories for the region, with a catalog of photographs and some sound recordings of village life.

512 Ixtepec: historia viva. Coordinación de Emma Yanes Rizo. México: Instituto Nacional de Antropología e Historia: Fundación para la Investigación Social y Ambiental de México y sus Regiones, 2006. 182 p.: bibl., ill.

After a devastating flood in 1999, an internet site was set up to document the struggles by the local people of the Sierra Norte de Puebla to recover (Totonacs). However, the site continued to get material and slowly evolved into a forum for local information, a "living file" that began to gather voices. From this arose a whole series of reflections, and eventually a broad panorama emerged, including discussion of education, health, traditions of the Totonacs, even municipal financial reports in the interest of municipal transparency. This evolution was joined to commentaries by the editors to make this book the first in a series derived from the project.

513 Kahn, Hilary E. Seeing and being seen: the Q'eqchi' Maya in Livingston, Guatemala, and beyond. Austin: Univ. of Texas Press, 2006. 242 p.: bibl., index.

Lyrical account of ethnic encounters between Q'eqchi' Mayas and Ladinos and Garifunas (and gringos) in and around the Caribbean town of Livingston, and the identity complexity engendered in this setting. Using videos and other reflexive techniques, weaving theory and methodological concerns together in a sensory-focused ethnography that undermines the boundaries of the differences under study, we have a thoroughly personalized and historicized view of the current identity landscape. Kahn vividly constructs a Q'eqchi' symbolic morality in terms of the visible, social reciprocities, notions of respect, complexities of ownership and even commentaries on consumption. Effects of globalization also make an appearance, as do the contradictions of unity and difference between and among groups, all within a frame that questions the hegemony of word and text over seeing and symbolizing, movement and relationship, perception and the unseen but nonetheless real.

514 Knab, Timothy J. The dialogue of earth and sky: dreams, souls, curing, and the modern Aztec underworld. Tucson: Univ. of Arizona Press, 2004. 179 p.: bibl., index.

Distilling the ethnographic information from the work he previously modeled his factual fiction "War of Witches" (1995) upon in the Sierra de Puebla Nahua villages, this work lays out brilliantly a contemporary cosmological model, explains the role of dreams, and describes in detail the geography of the non-ordinary realms like Talocan, and the work of prayer and of healers who work in this realm to cure and protect. Insightful regarding conflict resolution through ritual.

515 Kyle, Chris. Feeding Chilapa: the birth, life, and death of a Mexican region. Norman: Univ. of Oklahoma Press, 2008. 269 p.: bibl., index.

This smart and accessible work reinvigorates the old call for regional economic study in ethnography, as a more useful, effective explanatory framework than community-based studies or ones that make recourse to "resistance" to the state. It examines the ups and downs of rural and urban people in this region across centuries, especially agricultural productivity and rural-urban relations, and explores the prob-

lematic impacts of changes in economic and political conditions and policies up to very recent times. The study informs a distinct perspective on what motivates economic and related social behavior in regional areas of Mexico, including such things as diet, reforestation, agriculture, migration, and responses to government welfare programs in regions economically transformed by globalization.

León Portilla, Miguel. Obras de Miguel León-Portilla. See *HLAS 64:504.*

516 Lillo Macina, Vincenza. El temazcalli mexicano: su significación simbólica y su uso psicoterapéutico pasado y presente. México: Plaza y Valdés Editores, 2007. 270 p.: bibl., ill., maps.

The spiritual and medical uses of the Mesoamerican sweat bath or sauna (*temascal*) are examined here historically and in terms of current use by indigenous and mestizo people in Mexico. Interesting study showing the indigenous influences on people who do not identify as indigenous.

517 López Bárcenas, Francisco. Autonomía y derechos indígenas en México. Bilbao, Spain: Univ. de Deusto, 2006. 116 p.: bibl. (Cuadernos Deusto de derechos humanos; 39)

A clear and experienced indigenous voice presenting legal and political implications of the many impacts upon Mexican law and practice of the Chiapas rebellion and the reforms it inspired, especially for the rights of indigenous people—and how much further things will have to go before the paper matches political practice on the ground in most parts of Mexico. With an excellent understanding of the Zapatista innovations in community governance and defensive organization, the author traces the central problems hobbling the enacting of indigenous autonomy within a power framework still bedeviled by the colonial and Liberal national project, and furthermore challenges the Mexican state to fully allow local indigenous people to decide their own future, in the area of rights but also development.

518 López Moreno Chapoy, Andrés Iván. La construcción de los pueblos indígenas de México. Tuxtla Gutiérrez, Chiapas, Mexico: Centro Estatal de Lenguas, Arte y

Literatura Indígenas: Gobierno del Estado de Chiapas, 2007. 300 p.: bibl. (Ts'ib-jaye: textos de los pueblos originarios) (Pensamiento contemporáneo)

A discussion of the complexity of the term "indigenous peoples" (pueblos indígenas) in the social and political discourse in Mexico, starting with historic notions of nation and how this has changed with the rise of indigenous and ethnic "nations without states," under multiple influences and understandings of the rights of indigenous peoples, especially after the constitutional changes of the 1990s. Demonstrates (and complains about) the contradictions raised for multi-ethnic states between assimilationist nationalism and self-determination of indigenous groups (pluriculturalism) historically denied power and autonomy by the state—and how Mexico has attempted to address (and avoid) this contradiction.

519 Macías Guzmán, Eugenia. Sentido social en la preservación de bienes culturales: la restauración en una comunidad rural: el caso de Yanhuitlán, Oaxaca. México: Plaza y Valdés: INAH, 2005. 171 p.: bibl., ill. (Antropología)

After doing historic preservation work in Yanhuitlán, the project decides it must bring the community into the process more, and embraces the goal to turn over the restoration activities to the community, when it becomes possible, as part of a larger development vision. The book describes the work at the site and discusses how the community became involved. Also explains what the project tells us about the social dimension of cultural preservation work.

520 Martínez Novo, Carmen. Who defines indigenous?: identities, development, intellectuals, and the state in northern Mexico. New Brunswick, N.J.: Rutgers Univ. Press, 2006. 187 p.: maps.

A study of migrant Mixtecs and other indigenous in Tijuana and nearby agricultural regions, examining businesses, as well as ethnic, social, and labor conditions—but most fundamentally interrogating notions of indigenous as an identity, and how such identifications are used by non-indigenous as well as indigenous people themselves. The author points to the interests of those in power in promoting indigenous identity, which ironically many migrants wish to

downplay, as low status and as promoting racism, in their work ambit. Racism, paternalism, maternalism and other mechanisms of asymmetry are deployed by power against the interests of those now labeled inclusively as indigenous in this schema.

521 Mendoza Castelán, Guillermo; Roque Lugo Pérez; and Humberto Tehuacatl Cuaquehua. Ipehualyo in temazcalyo = Fundamentos del temazcalli. Chapingo, Mexico: Univ. Autónoma Chapingo, Depto. de Fitotecnia, Programa Universitario de Medicina Tradicional y Terapéutica Naturista: San Miguel Tlaixpan, Mexico: Centro de Estudios Integrados y Formación Comunitaria "Caltepehtlatocan," Consultorio de Medicina Tradicional Indígena "Quetzalpapalotl", 2004. 669 p.: bibl., ill.

This book presents what is primarily a modern ethnographic study of temazcallis in the Texcoco region and (to an extent) Mesoamerica more generally. The authors include an interesting discussion of the traditional plants used in temazcalli rituals. [R. Haskett/S. Wood]

522 Mentinis, Mihalis. Zapatistas: the Chiapas revolt and what it means for radical politics. London; Ann Arbor, Mich.: Pluto Press, 2006. 201 p.: bibl., index.

Not really an ethnography, although the author did interviews and fieldwork in Chiapas, this smart, deep treatise on political philosophy asks its readers to place the Zapatista movement in the larger field of radical politics, and critiques a variety of political interpretations of Zapatismo from the left, finding them all wanting. Elevates Zapatista political theory to new heights, based on an extensive interpretation of Maya epistemology, indigenous metaphysics, shamanism, masks, naguals, new forms of intersubjectivity in language—and similar issues not typically the subjects of political theory.

Midré, Georges. Opresión, espacio para actuar y conciencia crítica: líderes indígenas y percepción de la pobreza en Guatemala. See item **2577.**

523 Molesky-Poz, Jean. Contemporary Maya spirituality: the ancient ways are not lost. Austin: University of Texas Press, 2006. 224 p.: bibl., index.

A participant-observer perspective on the contemporary traditional Maya religious views and practices in Highland Guatemala, in light of the emerging pan-Maya spiritual movement, with a detailed focus on the daykeeper/diviner (ajq'ijab), the 260-day calendar, everyday spiritual practice, sacred geography, rituals, and the issue of cultural rights to practice Maya religion in the face of prejudice and converts. Provides a nuanced description of spiritual and cultural differences from the West, with a strong grounding in psychology and comparative religion, as well as in ethnic cultural politics.

524 Montejo, Victor. Maya intellectual renaissance: identity, representation, and leadership. Austin: Univ. of Texas Press, 2005. 236 p.: bibl., ill., index. (The Linda Schele series in Maya and pre-Columbian studies)

A collection of 11 essays, most previously published, by a Maya anthropologist addressing issues of identity, representation, self-representation, and indigenous leadership, within the framework of the Guatemalan pan-Maya movement. Discusses problems of Maya leadership, the implications and problems of implementing the Peace Accords, and ends by advocating dialogue between Mayas and non-indigenous Guatemalans.

525 Mosquera Saravia, Maria Teresa. Lógicas y racionalidades entre comadronas y terapeutas tradicionales. Guatemala: Instituto de Estudios Interétnicos, Univ. de San Carlos de Guatemala, 2006. 314 p.: bibl., ill.

This study explores the indigenous logic and rationality applied to midwifery and related healing practices in the Rabinal (Achi) region of Guatemala. The author makes a compelling argument for cultural unity of logics in Rabinal, even across language and "ethnic" lines, in a challenge to the linguistic hegemony of current views on who is what kind of Indian. All midwives operate the same way, indigenous and Ladino. She also argues for a different approach to medical anthropology from what has been dominant since the 1980s, building an understanding of the therapeutic tradition out of the contexts of cultural logics

from whence it is generated (e.g., symbolic healing), and not from Western biomedical or ethnobotanical perspectives, or from only those places where traditions cross paths.

Münch Galindo, Guido. Una semblanza del Carnaval de Veracruz. See item **2518**.

526 Muñoz Ramírez, Gloria. The fire and the word: a history of the Zapatista movement. Translated by Laura Carlsen with Alejandro Reyes Arias. San Francisco, Calif.: City Lights Books, 2008. 339 p.: ill.

A product of long-term accompaniment of Zapatistas by a journalist, the text covers the 20 years from the creation of the movement to the formation of the Good Government Boards in 2003, plus an update/epilogue that moves the discussion up to 2007, covering the Other Campaign and the Sixth Declaration. Displays the same rebellious creativity as the "sub" (who gets the second 20 p. of the book) presenting with much color the story of Zapatismo according to the leadership the author interviews, and the experiences she shares. The text served as a piece of popular supportive literature during the course of the EZLN Other Campaign, travelling around "unknown Mexico" at the time of the Mexican presidential elections, and is iconic of that historic moment, and for those who seek to understand it.

527 Una nueva relación: compromiso con los pueblos indígenas. México: Fondo de Cultura Económica: Comisión Nacional para el Desarrollo de los Pueblos Indígenas, 2005. 214 p.: bibl., ill. (Col. editorial del gobierno del cambio)

Produced by the administration of former Mexican President Vicente Fox, via the National Commission for the Development of Indigenous Peoples, this text is an official response to the changes in nationwide perspective on indigenous people brought about in Mexico by the Chiapas uprising. Serves to demonstrate the transformation of official views toward indigenous peoples in the last ten years, and outlines the changes in the constitution (based on a modification of the San Andrés peace accords) that increase the cultural, legal, educational, language, and other rights of indigenous individuals, and provides testimonies by various indigenous people helped by new government efforts, mostly from Chiapas and Oaxaca. Also applauds Mexico's renewed efforts to strengthen and support international accords that address indigenous issues, and its government programs fashioned to address indigenous needs and concerns, and as a political document further codifies the shift from nationalistic notions of Mexican ethnic unity to one of apparent appreciation for cultural pluralism and the rights of ethnic minorities.

528 Oliva Martínez, J. Daniel. La cooperación internacional con los pueblos indígenas: desarrollo y derechos humanos. Madrid: CIDEAL, 2005. 382 p.: bibl.

A view from Spain of the indigenous rights questions (and ties to development) raised by the ascent of indigenous and tribal rights in the EU and global arenas, and especially focused on the indigenous of Latin America. It reviews indigenismo, questions of power relations with the state, assimilation versus integration, EU and other international ties to indigenous groups, alternative approaches to development such as "self-development"—and examines many questions regarding legal relations between a number of prominent international organizations on one hand, and both indigenous people and their host states, on the other.

529 Olmos Aguilera, Miguel. El viejo, el venado y el coyote: estética y cosmogonía: hacia una arquetipología de los mitos de creación y del origen de las artes en el noroeste de México. Tijuana, Mexico: El Colegio de la Frontera Norte: Fondo Regional para la Cultura y las Artes del Noroeste, 2005. 330 p.: bibl.

A border-crossing collection of Gran Chichimeca region oral texts of myth, legend, and fable, placed neatly within a general cultural system and its many variations within the region. Included are tales from the Baja California Yumanos, the Yoreme, Mayo, Yaqui, Raramuri/Tarahumara, Comcaac/Seri, Makurawe/Guarijios, O'oba/Pima, and the O'odham/Papago. Arising from these many stories of creation and heroics one sees a common ontological thread, very much expressing its intertwined cultural location between Mesoamerica and the southern edges of the American Southwest, and also showing the ways in which European tales are appropriated for local indigenous symbolic themes and messages.

530 Paredes, Carlos A. Te llevaste mis palabras. Guatemala: Equipo de Estudios Comunitarios y Acción Psicosocial (ECAP), 2006. 2 v.: bibl. (Col. Psicología social ECAP; 4)

The work explores the origins and history of political and land tenure conflicts in the Polochic region of Guatemala, starting with the 1978 Panzos Massacre, and carrying through the terrible militarization and "internal war" period, and assesses the psycho-social impacts of such things as terror, violence and fear, torture, disappearance and accusation, as well as truth and collective memory. It provides a nuanced description of the profound changes caused by state-sponsored and locally enforced violence.

531 Patiño, Juan Carlos. Tradición y desarrollo: las estrategias productivas de los mazahuas de Ixtlahuaca. Toluca: Univ. Autónoma del Estado de México, 2006. 202 p.: bibl. (Col. Elucidario)

A detailed study of Masahua indigenous economics; it moves between discussions of traditional agricultural strategies with hereditary lands, and creative encounters with the newly developed market and labor alternatives the Masahua have adopted—including temporal migration as an indigenous economic diversification tactic. Rich in migration field data, the complicated socioeconomic pushes and pulls on Masahua familial and community structures the author documents reveal a perspective grounded in family-based domestic production, and yet one sensitive to global impacts as they are locally interpreted, costed and lived out.

532 Pérez López-Portillo, Raúl. Los Mayas: historia de un pueblo indómito. Madrid: Silex Ediciones, 2007. 419 p.: bibl., ill., maps. (Serie Historia)

Journalist's rendering of the whole span of Maya history, from its Olmec antecedents through the colonial trauma and up to the present time, lightly.

533 Perezgrovas Garza, Raúl. La Lana del Tunim Chij, el "venado de algodón." San Cristóbal de las Casas, Chiapas, Mexico: Univ. Autónoma de Chiapas, Instituto de Estudios Indígenas, 2005. 365 p.: bibl., ill. (some col.). (Serie Monografías; 8)

As the title suggests, this study details the local indigenous knowledge of sheep and wool management and production in two Tzotzil-speaking municipalities of Chiapas renown for their wool weaving. In describing in Spanish and Tzotzil with numerous photos, charts, terms, and testimony the entire production process and how it fits into the larger household economy/ecology and society, it provides the depth of study useful for both ethnographic scholarship and informed applied work. The author reviews how his team-based study has implications for rural Chiapas development, for animal husbandry extension, for working with Tzotzil women to better their life conditions, and for an overall appreciation for the validity, power, and importance of understanding indigenous knowledge as a prerequisite to effectively helping people improve their communities.

534 Pineda, Baron L. Shipwrecked identities: navigating race on Nicaragua's Mosquito Coast. New Brunswick, N.J.: Rutgers Univ. Press, 2006. 280 p.: bibl., index, map.

Historical ethnography traces the life of a port town of Bilwi, now Puerto Cabezas, in Atlantic Coast Nicaragua, to explore the identity claims and imaginaries of the blacks, mestizos, and Miskitos through time. Another in the trend of examining identity claims, notions of authenticity, and the changes in identity claims tied to changes in how outsiders see identity labels and construct identities. Provides a historical context to current identities and unpacks the identity politics of the region.

535 Reyes Couturier, Teófilo. Campesinos, mercado de tierras y globalización en México: el caso del ingenio, El Potrero. México: Plaza y Valdés, 2006. 206 p.: bibl., ill., maps.

A case study from a sugar-producing ejido region of the Gulf Coast of Mexico, looking at the new land market in former ejido lands, and the mechanisms of neoliberalism that push peasants to either become "modern farmers" or join the ranks of the rural proletariat or petit entrepreneurs. Takes the contested position that for the area studied the sale of ejido lands appears in some cases progressive, at the same time

as explaining from the standpoint of rural development economics why it is that as of the date of the study, not much ejido land has been sold, nor will be any time soon.

536 Reyes Montes, Laura. Estudio antropológico de una región agrícola al norte del Estado de México. Toluca, Mexico.: Univ. Autónoma del Estado de México, 2006. 155 p.: bibl., charts, maps. (Cuadernos de Investigación. Cuarta época; 46)

Socioeconomic, political, and environmental study of four communities in the valley of Ixtlahuaca, focused on rural households' efforts to adapt to changing conditions over time, especially traditional subsistence farmers who have increased commercial production and confronted the ecological, economic, and political limitations, as well as shifting social relations that this change has brought. It ties involvement with traditionally produced cash crops to topics such as access to national and regional markets, intergenerational relations, migration, customary social obligations, dynamics within households, and adaptation to globalization and political/economic change.

537 Reyes Valdez, Jorge Antonio. Los que están benditos: el mitote comunal de los tepehuanes de Santa María de Ocotán, Durango. México: Instituto Nacional de Antropología e Historia, 2006. 246 p.: bibl., ill. (Col. Etnografía de los pueblos indígenas de México. Serie Estudios Monográficos)

Rigorous fieldwork elaborates emblematic rituals of the Tepehuanes del Sur at one of the seven ancestral settlements in northwest Mexico. The author places the community within the larger region ("Gran Nayar") and its other indigenous groups (e.g., Cora, Huichol), and places their elaborate rituals within the context of legitimization of authorities, enactments of the cosmic conflict of underworld and solar domains, as well as links to agricultural cycles and to Church influences.

538 Riverstone, Gerald. Living in the land of our ancestors: Rama Indian and Creole territory in Carribbean Nicaragua. Managua: ASDI, 2004. 186 p.: bibl., col. ill., index, maps (chiefly col.).

This focused ethnography captures the current situation of the Rama people of the Southeast Atlantic coast of Nicaragua, as well as of the Creole minority in this same location, especially in regard to indigenous land rights issues, Protected Natural Areas, and the state's new Indigenous Land Demarcation Law. Working closely with local people to give their views adequate voice, it assesses the many threats to ethnic territorial rights, such as the advancing agricultural frontier, plans for pipelines, roads, and other development under the Plan Puebla-Panamá and similar neoliberal policies, as well as commercial logging, hunting, and fishing. Recent violence against indigenous leaders to drive them off their land suggests a growing threat by land speculators seeking to profit by tourism development, abetted by local authorities. Alternative territorial proposals are assessed, with their potential for success linked to environmental management.

539 Roads to change in Maya Guatemala: a field school approach to understanding the K'iche'. Edited by John P. Hawkins and Walter Randolph Adams. Norman: Univ. of Oklahoma Press, 2005. 249 p.: bibl., index.

Explores the virtues of such an approach, for both teaching fieldwork and using undergraduate research to inform ethnography, uncommon in the discipline. Topics include details of the field school structure and operations in rural Guatemala, as well as changes in traditions, marriage practices, gender relations, weaving, education, religion, and development.

540 Romero López, Laura Elena. Cosmovisión, cuerpo y enfermedad: el espanto entre los nahuas de Tlacotepec de Díaz, Puebla. México: Instituto Nacional de Antropología e Historia, 2006. 303 p.: bibl., ill., maps. (Obra diversa)

Prize-winning medical anthropology ethnography that demonstrates how the medical system is a subset of the indigenous view of the world, and that the theo-geography of the Other World of the spiritual, the ethnogeography of the body, and the etiology of disease and infirmity are tightly interwoven. In assessing ritual fright or soul loss (espanto), the author demonstrates these ties eloquently, and shows how the malady has general quali-

ties of the Mesoamerican phenomenon and elements unique to the immediate region of Tlacotepec. The passing of fright sickness from mother to fetus and breast-fed infant, for example, is one specific she relates as an aspect of her discussion of espanto cause, vulnerability, symptoms, diagnosis, and healing procedures for soul retrieval and wellness recovery. Also of special interest is the description of curer lucid dream work—with the soul of the patient—dream work later confirmed through the exchanging of mutual dream experience with the client!

541 Roque, Consuelo. Cultura lenca de Guatajiagua, Consuelo Roque y Manuel Antonio Ramírez Suárez. El Salvador: Univ. de El Salvador, 2004. 102 p.: bibl.

A small heuristic ethnography based on the requests of a Lenca (Poton)-speaking community in El Salvador to have documentation of their social organization, ceremonies, traditions, dances, stories, crafts, and beliefs. Half the book is set up to teach the local school children how to speak and write "Poton Piau," the Lenca language of the area, with a dictionary annex; this book is part of the larger El Salvador project of rediscovering their indigenous cultures.

542 The sacred mushrooms of Mexico: assorted texts. Edited by Brian P. Akers. Lanham, Md.: Univ. Press of America, Inc., 2007. 175 p.: bibl., index.

A reprinting and translating of classic studies on the subject of hallucinogenic mushrooms used in religious contexts by native peoples (L. Reyes, A. Lopez, R. Ravicz, W. Miller, F. Benitez), plus an article about a 1961 television broadcast on the subject, in which the journalists go to Oaxaca to see native mushroom use and then eat the same mushrooms on national television. The book takes advantage of the sustained popularity (in English) of ethnomycological research on indigenous use of mind-altering drugs to make these classics available.

543 Seminario Permanente de Estudios de la Gran Chichimeca, 2nd, Aguascalientes, Mexico, 2004. Diversidad cultural y sobrevivencia: la frontera chichimeca, una visión desde el siglo XXI. Coordinación de Andrés Fábregas Puig, Mario Alberto Nájera Espinoza, y José Alfredo Ortiz Garza. Guadalajara, Mexico: Univ. de Guadalajara

CUCSH, CUAAD, CUCIÉNEGA, 2007.
301 p.: bibl., ill.

Articles derived from the Second
Encounter of the Permanent Seminar of
Studies of the Gran Chichimeca, in 2004,
examining topics associated with cultural
diversity, change, and persistence in oral
tradition, history, cultural ecology, ethnomusicology, and archeology, among other
anthropological topics.

544 Simbolismo y poder. Coordinación
de María Eugenia Olavarría. México:
Univ. Autónoma Metropolitana, Unidad
Iztapalapa: Miguel Angel Porrúa, 2007.
182 p.: bibl., ill. (Las Ciencias Sociales.
Segunda década)

Six studies unified by a focus on the
intersection of symbolism and power, noting in diverse ethnographic contexts how
symbolism can serve to subordinate and
serve hegemonic ends outside the apparent.
Here human rights encounters indigenous
rights, complicates the construction of citizenship and the conflicts between political
elites and community agents of change, and
creates tensions between indigenous identity and symbolic structures.

545 Taggart, James M. Remembering
Victoria: a tragic Nahuat love story.
Austin: Univ. of Texas Press, 2007. 144 p.:
bibl., ill., index.

Emerging from his long study of the
town of Huitzilán, the story of the life, love,
and tragic death of the wife of a villager, told
to him in Nahuat by her husband, is the basis
of this book. It is also an effort to understand
the political violence that led to her and
many more deaths, and how the town came
apart and came back together, as viewed from
narratives and the commentaries of the long-
time anthropological observer.

546 Tilley, Virginia Q. Seeing Indians: a
study of race, nation, and power in El
Salvador. Albuquerque: Univ. of New Mexico Press, 2005. 297 p.: bibl., index.

Insightful exploration into the complexities of "being Indian" in El Salvador
since the 1932 violence (La Matanza). Contrasted with excellent ethnographic detail
from indigenousness typical of Guatemala,
the author explores the evolution of the
state project of Indian denial, its historical antecedents, and its halting, externally

promoted turn around in the 1990s towards
a reimagined pluricultural national identity. Transnational indigenous movements,
reactions against assimilationist ideologies
and policies proclaimed at defining international meetings, and an emerging global
indigenous hegemony have reanimated and
complicated indigenousness in El Salvador,
and the author explores this problematic extensively and credibly, always asking who it
is that defines indigenousness and towards
what end.

547 Trejo, Leopoldo. Los que hablan
la lengua: etnografía de los zoques
chimalapas. México: Instituto Nacional
de Antropología e Historia, 2004. 165 p.:
bibl., ill. (Col. Etnografía de los pueblos
indígenas de México. Serie Estudios
monográficos)

Lively ethnography of two Tehuantepec Zoque municipalities, exploring the
underlying dualism in many aspects of
their culture, including myth, public ritual,
religion, social organization, and ethnogeography. Of equal interest is the description
of the history of different migrants to this
jungle region, both indigenous and mestizo,
and the conflicts and collaborations this has
created, facing issues of deforestation, development, boundary disputes, cattle ranching
and logging interests, and more.

548 Urieta Donoso, Esther. La represa del
río Bayano: estudio antropológico de
los efectos generados por los grandes proyectos nacionales sobre los grupos humanos.
Panamá: Editorial Portobelo Librería El
Campus, 2004. 210 p.: bibl., maps. (Pequeño
formato; 221. Antropología-indigenismo-
sociología)

A study of the more than two decade
impact of human relocation associated with
a dam project in rural Panama, especially
on the indigenous populations (Choco,
Cuna). The work describes complex problems in cultural maintenance, sustainable
adaptation to new tropical settings, youth
education, and support for community
organizations. The study finishes with
recommendations for ameliorative actions
addressed to the government.

549 Vázquez Jiménez, Antonio. Ayudando
de sanar: biografía del J'ilol Antonio
Vázquez Jiménez. Zona Centro, Chiapas,

Mexico: Programa de Investigaciones Multi-disciplinarias sobre Mesoamérica y el Sureste, UNAM, 2006. 237 p.: bibl., ill., port. (Científica; 12)

The biography of a famous and respected healer from Chenalho, Chiapas, who became a founding member of the Organization of Indigenous Doctors of the State of Chiapas (OMIECH) before his death. The book was conceived as a method of teaching the non-indigenous more about how the traditional system of healing medicine works, inasmuch as there are new official and NGO efforts to bring the two systems together. After a rigorous introduction to local cosmology and the region, the edited transcript of hours of interviews begins, first in Spanish (over 100 pages), and then in Tzotzil. Such a lengthy oral biography of an important community leader is rare; the more so in Tzotzil, but this second text is very important for the growing literate Tzotzil community, and especially those associated with the healing arts. Represents the first in a planned series of oral biographies of healers.

550 Visiones de la diversidad: relaciones interétnicas e identidades indígenas en el México actual. Vol. 1. Coordinación de Miguel Alberto Bartolomé. México: Instituto Nacional de Antropología e Historia, 2005. 1 v.: bibl., ill., maps. (Col. Etnografía de los pueblos indígenas de México. Serie Ensayos)

Six related chapters focused largely on Northern Mexican indigenous groups (Yaquis, Mayos, O'odham, Raramuri, Guajirios, others) and questions of ethnic, inter-ethnic, and national identity, in the face of diverse forms of change and efforts at cultural maintenance in rural and urban settings.

551 Ya hnini ya jä'itho Maxei = los pueblos indios de Querétaro. Coordinación de Diego Prieto Hernández y Beatriz Utrilla Sarmiento. Textos de Luis Enrique Ferro Vidal *et al.* México: Comisión Nacional para el Desarrollo de los Pueblos Indígenas, 2006. 325 p.: bibl., ill. (Antropología social)

A team-based fieldwork examining Otomi communities in Querétaro state, with accounts of ethnographic details, such as identification of the sacred regional landscapes and explanations for how they are tied to myths and traditional uses of the environment. Also explored are issues of ethnic identity, history, religion, and current social conditions.

South America
Lowlands

BARTHOLOMEW DEAN, *Associate Professor of Anthropology, University of Kansas and Profesor Invitado, Graduate Program in Amazonian Studies/Maestría en Estudios Amazónicos, Universidad Nacional Mayor de San Marcos, Lima, Peru*
SILVIA MARÍA HIRSCH, *Professor, FLACSO, Buenos Aires, Argentina*
ROBIN M. WRIGHT, *Associate Professor of Religion, University of Florida, Gainesville*

A CURSORY REVIEW OF REPRESENTATIVE CONTRIBUTIONS to the ethnology of Lowland South America reveals a diverse set of topics of scholarly inquiry, mimicking the region's rich sociocultural mosaic and astonishing biodiversity. To wit, authors explore stalwart themes of anthropological inquiry—social organization, ritual life, shamanism, cosmology, and mythopraxis—as well as probing recent concerns with identity politics, market integration and transformations in resource use, medical anthropology, and efforts to understand the complex relationships among indigenous and non-indigenous peoples, not to mention agents of the self-aggrandizing "developmentalist" state driven by paradigms of neoliberal *modernization.* This latter point is illustrated by a number of scholarly contributions that assess the supra-local factors shaping indigenous peoples' communities, such as the special issue of *Íconos* that assesses the character of globalized linkages in Amazonia (item **592**), Rubenstein's survey of the changing symbolic import of Shuar *tsantsas* (the shrunken heads of foes slain in warfare) (item **600**), or Killick's trenchant review of land titling among the Ashéninka of the Peruvian Amazon (item **594**). Emphasizing a positivist approach, Lu's research among Ecuadorian indigenous peoples demonstrates the need to employ multiple variables of both household production and consumption when ascertaining levels of market integration.

Particularly noteworthy recent ethnographic iterations include the Whittens' remarkable text *Puyo Runa: Imagery and Power in Modern Amazonia* (item **605**) and Jonathan Hill's masterful collection entitled *Made-from-Bone* (item **583**). *Puyo Runa* represents the fruits of more than four decades of fieldwork conducted among the Canelos Quichua of Ecuador, and yields critical insight into the character of ethnogenesis, and local understandings of ecology, cosmology, and shamanism. While attending to the intricacies of mythopraxis, the Whittens situate the Canelos Quichua's political engagements within the wider non-indigenous world. For its part, Hill's *Made-from-Bone* is a beautifully crafted ethnographic depiction of the Wakuénai peoples of Venezuela's mythic past and "audioscapes." In addition to drawing attention to their continuing enmeshment in the structural ambiguities of everyday life, Hill's provocative work adeptly provides meaning to the esthetic and poetic facets of Wakuénai narratives.

While the aforementioned ethnographic accounts highlight the cosmological veracity and "health" of indigenous societies, analysts continue to document the destructive impact of the postcolonial encounter. Predicated on both field research conducted among the Nukak peoples of Colombia and on primary archival documents, Cabrera Becerra's valuable text, for example, recounts the tragic legacy that Protestant mission activity (New Tribes Mission) has had for indigenous peoples (item **581**). Notwithstanding recognition of the detrimental influence outsiders have historically had for native cosmologies and performed ritual life, the spiritual and ontological aspects of indigenous sociality remain key concerns of ethnographers of Lowland South America. This notion is evident in Rosengren's incisive evaluation of the dynamics of human-spirit interactions among the Matsigenka of southeastern Peru (item **599**), or Zent's welcome study illustrating the cosmological, as well as the ecological, vitality of hunting among the Jotï of the Venezuelan Guayana (item **587**). While Santos-Granero explores the nature of sociality and alterity by providing a sustained analysis of the concept of "friendship" in indigenous Amazonia (item **601**), others have emphasized the violent expression of social life in Lowland South America. On this point, Beckerman and Valentine have produced a seminal collection on the widespread phenomena of revenge noted among 14 indigenous groups of Lowland South America (item **552**). This collection complements the 2004 publication *In Darkness and Secrecy: The Anthropology of Assault Sorcery and Witchcraft in Amazonia* (see *HLAS 63:825*).

In the arena of medical anthropology, research in Lowland South America has minimized the putative divide between Occidental biomedicine and indigenous health systems. Scholars such as Calvet-Mir, Reyes-García, and Tanner underscore the prominence of medical pluralism in the region, and describe the innovative collaboration among local healers and medical practitioners (see item **609**). Similarly, Lewis' findings affirm the efficacy of Western psychotherapists assisting *ayahuasca* imbibers: psychotherapists can provide ritual participants with meaning for the emotional anguish they experience during shamanic rituals (item **595**). Indication of the concern with global health challenges is evidenced by a number of research projects, such as Martínez Silva's work in Colombia's northwest Amazonian frontier (item **585**). Martínez Silva endeavors to situate illness narratives about HIV-AIDS, while concomitantly interrogating the theoretical categories underpinning biomedicine itself.

An allied concern of medical anthropology is the enduring interest in plants and people, which has given rise to a number of innovative studies, such as Wilson's investigation of manioc selection among the Colombian Tukanoans (item **607**), Heckler and Zent's work on manioc's function as a social mediator among the Piaora of Venezuela (item **582**), or the scholarly review of the deleterious impact global forces have had on "traditional" knowledge systems, such the Yuquí of Bolivia. Yet, research among the Yuquí demonstrates how the tourist trade for bows and arrows has had a positive impact on the retention of customary knowledge associated with the use of "black beeswax" as arrow cement (item **628**). Continued attention to the use of psychotropic plants in Lowland South America is manifested by studies on Banisteriopsis caapi consumption, while advances in ethnobotany are evident in Jernigan's pioneering research on Aguaruna chemosensory clues for their identification and classification of woody plants in the Peruvian rainforest (item **593**).

In trying to comprehend how environmental transformations have influenced the historical trajectories of human societies, Rival calls for a methodological embrace of historical ecology (item **598**). This approach is elaborated by Schjellerup *et al.*'s comprehensive text on the Chilchos Valley of Peru, which provides excellent insight into the complex nature of human adaptations to various biomes, including the area's ecologically vulnerable montane forests (item **597**). Interest in human-environment interactions is showcased in Cepek's analysis of Cofán environmental discourses and practices (item **588**). Instead of rendering environmentalism as merely instrumentalist responses to transnational identity politics, Cepek reveals the substantive ties between the Cofán peoples' cultural identity and their traditional territories. Likewise, Garcés' comparative study of the Achuar, Shuar and Kichua of Ecuador reveals the role that management of natural resources has in influencing the very nature of gender relations (item **590**).

The political nature of indigenous cultural performances is recognized by many analysts of the human topography of the region. For instance, Veber's astute analysis of Ashéninka leader's narrative accentuates the politically charged nature of the interplay between individual and communal interests in the Peruvian Amazon (item **603**). Struggles for greater administrative and cultural autonomy from the state take center stage in Viatori and Ushigua's study of the Zápara case of Ecuador, which highlights how language revalorization initiatives have been critical to local efforts at securing self-determination (item **605**). In a somewhat similar vein, Stronza's study of ecotourism in the Peruvian Amazon stresses the growth of local efforts to actively promote linguistic survival and enhanced interest in indigenous cultural heritage, particularly in the face of an influx of tourists and all of their accoutrements of modernity (item **602**).

Debates over the performance and meanings of indigeneity are common themes surfacing in the sociopolitical lives of contemporary indigenous peoples of Lowland South America. For example, Valdivia's study of the distinctive performances of indigeneity among three native political organizations (FEINCE, OISE, and FOISE) in the Ecuadoran Amazon is useful for assessing the legal case against Chevron Texaco (see *HLAS 63:869*). Moreover, by outlining how indigenous federations have endeavored to garner supra-local support for their claims, Valdivia demonstrates how identity politics and transnational social networks are themselves mutually implicated in the formation of organizations that putatively represent indigenous peoples. In a similar fashion, Jaramillo's text not only provides insight into the sociopolitical lives of the Embera of Colombia, but it also shows how local conceptions of sociological constructs (i.e. "community," "territorially," and "identity") are embedded in supra-local interactions and processes (item **584**). Likewise, Alarcón Puentes adopts a political anthropological approach to account for the transformations of power noted among the Wayúu and their fractious relations with the Venezuelan state and broader national society (item **580**). Finally, Lucero's comparative study of two indigenous political federations in Bolivia (CONAMAQ) and Ecuador (FEINE) is a somber reminder that indigeneity is a product of localized "grassroots" mobilization, as well as a result of "opportunity structures" located beyond the community that collude to privilege some voices over others (see *HLAS 63:861*). In the face of global and local alterations associated with the predominance of neoliberalism and the ongoing challenges to the cultural survival of indigenous societies, additional research is warranted that effectively links multiple levels of analysis capable of understanding the radically transformed modalities of sociocultural existence in Lowland South America. [BD]

BRAZIL

The publications selected for review in this issue can be grouped into six themes which are, in order of importance: (1) indigenous experiences and views of contact phenomena; (2) ethnographies of indigenous peoples of Northeast Brazil and other, little-known peoples; (3) the fields of Brazilian anthropology and ethnology; (4) aspects of symbolism in indigenous religious traditions; (5) indigenous education; and (6) Brazilian mestizo populations.

The first and perhaps the most dynamic of the themes is, in part, a result of the trend in Brazilian ethnology toward understanding more deeply indigenous views, perspectives, and experiences of contact. One of the important sources of theoretical stimulus in this direction is the "Nucleus for [the study of] Indigenous Transformations," coordinated by the Brazilian ethnologist Eduardo Viveiros de Castro at the National Museum in Rio de Janeiro, and his ex-advisees and colleagues. This "school" has produced innovative studies of indigenous identity in the contact situation (item **576**), indigenous perspectives on "the civilizing process" (item **553**), and indigenous understandings of, and relation to, money and merchandise (item **564**), which previously would have been classified under the rubric of "economic anthropology." These studies have in common a determination to take seriously indigenous perspectives and experiences of contact and to explore how categories of indigenous ontology (being and becoming) are transformed in the process. Methodology is based in phenomenology of perception and the poststructuralist school of "perspectivism." Other ways of understanding religious phenomena in historical situations of contact are based on a combination of symbolic anthropology and ethnohistory and have produced important studies, such as Wright on prophetic movements (item **579**) and conversion movements (item **575**). Both trends complement each other and should not be seen as mutually exclusive; other areas where such approaches can be extended include gender studies and shamanism.

The second theme includes ethnographies of the ways of life and cultures of such little-known peoples as the Caxixó of Minas Gerais—one of the "newly-emergent" or "resistant" peoples (item 571), the Kambiwá and Pipipã of the Northeast (item 556), the Guarani of Rio de Janeiro state (item 569), the Bakairi (item 557) of the Xingu; and isolated peoples of the southern Amazon known only by the exquisite craftsmanship of their arrows (item 570). Each of these contributes in different ways to ethnographic approaches: the relation of discourse and culture in the case of "newly-emergent" peoples; the regional importance of ritual forms, such as the Toré, to the resistant peoples of the Northeast (item 574); an insider's view by an ethnographer married to a Bakairi political leader; and inter-tribal encounters amongst the Guarani, Pataxo, and Indians of the US Southwest when each presented their own cultural ways to the other.

Thirdly, over the past decade, Brazilian anthropologists have taken stock of their field's diversification as it has grown and matured. One collection provides a general panorama of Brazilian anthropology (item 559); another, its methods in fieldwork (item 567), or, developing codes of ethics for different kinds of fieldwork (item 554); and finally, documenting the role of the ethnologist in the process of land definition for indigenous peoples (item 555).

A fourth area extends anthropological research on religious traditions with studies of the Tikuna's understanding of astronomy, meteorology, ritual, and myth (item 563), and recovering the meaning of Bororo ritual items that had long been stored in mission museums (item 558). To a certain extent, these studies overlap with the first trend mentioned above, insofar as each seeks to understand the parameters of subjectivity in native thought, and how "artifacts" partake of their creator's subjectivity.

One area that has produced numerous workshops and conference sessions, but is underrepresented in this issue of the *HLAS*, is ethno-education. Under discussion are the parameters of a "differentiated education" specific to native peoples (item 561), which raises methodological questions and innovative ethnographies of indigenous children (item 560) and how their subjectivities are formed.

Finally, another underrepresented area is the study of mestizo populations of Brazil, such as the Amazonian caboclo (item 573) and the caicara population of the southeastern coast (item 577). The latter is simply a re-edition of a "classic" study but needs updating; and the former seems to be searching for new approaches to modernization among Amazonian caboclos.

In the future we expect to see studies of sustainable development projects organized and administered by native and rural peoples, discussing how such projects are perceived by subjects; the future of shamanism among native peoples, an institution that is rapidly transforming if not disappearing, at least in its traditional forms; and discussions of the protection of traditional knowledge and heritage sites which, in Brazil, unlike the US, has barely begun. [RMW]

ARGENTINA, BOLIVIA, AND PARAGUAY

The works reviewed in this volume include an increase in the number of publications on gender, a topic on which there had been significant production in other regions, but had been neglected in the lowlands of Argentina, Bolivia, and Paraguay. The publication of a collection of essays on indigenous women in Argentina (item 625) introduces an array of perspectives that range from symbolic and performative analysis of initiation, life cycles, gender violence, mothering, and the sexual division of labor, among Toba, Wichi, Guaraní, and Mapuche people. Other studies (item 619) focus on women's knowledge of their environment, their gathering practices, and how notions of personhood (item 615) are constitutive of gender and gender relations.

Ethnohistorical studies not only continue to be the focus of scholarship in the area but also constitute a contribution to unravelling the complex processes of inter-ethnic relations and the process of mestizaje among different indigenous groups. In fact, the dynamics of "mestizaje" (item 613) are not between whites and Indians, but between two different indigenous groups, the Chané (Arawak origin) and the Guaraní. The study questions how this process has been described in the literature, and illustrates the cultural and political influences of an Arawak group on the Guaraní (item 614), hereby changing the point of view of previous studies. The ethnohistorical dimension of inter-ethnic relations and of the social and political organization of lowland groups is a fundamental component of several studies (621, 622, and 626). The publication of an edited volume (item 624) on the impact of the Chaco War is a major contribution to the study of the displacements and transformations undergone by indigenous peoples caught in the middle of a political confrontation between two states.

In Lowland South America, the study of political systems is part of a genealogy of works by ethnographers which range from Nordenskiold to Clastres. Several publications describe current political systems with a historical perspective, while focusing on the changes and the emergence of new forms of leadership among numerous lowland groups of the Chaco region. These works show a nuanced approach to the relations among leaders, kinship, social organizations, and inter-ethnic relations. Braunstein, in his collection based on a conference organized in the Chaco province in Argentina, explores the complexity of the new forms of leadership that are present in indigenous communities (item 623). In this venue, several authors in the volume address the role of religious leaders, such as evangelical pastors and shamans, and the new leadership roles imposed by governmental agencies, who are seeking intermediaries in their relations with the communities. Moreover, the study of Mbya Guaraní leadership (item 620) illustrates a paradigmatic case in which the changes in the political system, in addition to the pressures exerted by the Catholic Church and the government, undermine the role of traditional leaders and give rise to new political authorities. These new leadership roles help in connecting the communities to the municipal and national centers, and provide a means for channeling resources, but create conflicts in terms of authority and representation and frequently divide the political loyalty of the communities.

Interdisciplinary projects have addressed collaborative research with native peoples and in so doing have produced ethnographic descriptions (item 618, 621, and 622) written in an accessible language. These ethnographies provide useful data on understudied groups which have been "invisibilized" as a result of their subaltern relation with the larger society. The new ways in which identities reemerge and contest the state's representation and defy commonly held ideas of who are indigenous is represented in several contributions (items 610 and 617).

Several works included in this volume reflect innovative and in-depth symbolic (item 630) and reflexive accounts on religion and religious conversion (item 611), shamanism, and dreaming. In addition, the growing field of anthropology of the body, which explores dances, rituals, and music and how the body is constitutive of these practices, is represented by a study conducted among the Toba Indians (item **612**).

The conflictive and tense relations between indigenous peoples and the state and the impact of the latter's policies on the internal life of communities have been a continuing focus of research (items **608** and **610**). New scholarship is based on a comparative perspective on these relations at the regional and provincial levels, focusing on the development of laws and policies and the politics of ethnicity put forward by indigenous peoples. [SMH]

GENERAL

552 Beckerman, Stephen. Revenge in the cultures of lowland South America. Gainesville: Univ. Press of Florida, 2007. 314 p.: bibl., index.

This exceptional collection of essays is dedicated to assessing the nature of insult, vengeance, and the complex dynamics of revenge found among 14 indigenous societies of Lowland South America. Contributors review various manifestations of vengeance, from dramatic examples of blood revenge, to the more mundane or prosaic aspects of this universal social phenomena, such as the naming of infants and the attribution of illness and misfortune. In addition to exploring what triggers vengeance, the contributors examine its multiple manifestations and sociocultural implications, spanning from cosmology and ritual life, to the actual reproduction of society. [BD]

BRAZIL

553 Andrello, Geraldo. Cidade do índio: transformações e cotidiano em Iauaretê. São Paulo: Editora Unesp: Instituto Socioambiental; Rio de Janeiro: NUTI, Núcleo Transformações Indígenas, 2006. 447 p.: bibl., ill., maps.

This is an historical ethnography about the emergence of the large indigenous town of Iauaretê on the Uaupés River, Northwest Amazon. Since the early 20th century, this town was an important center of the Salesian missions in the region, with boarding schools for indigenous children, a trading post, and an airstrip for the Brazilian Air Force. Over the past few decades, Iauaretê has been transformed from a mission center to a large multi-ethnic urban center, mainly of Tariana Indians—the

town's original occupants—but also of Tukano Indians whose language predominates as the lingua franca in the region. Andrello summarizes the history of contact in the Uaupés region, focusing on the mission period until the 1980s, then provides an ethnography of life in the neighborhoods and how values have been transforming. Finally, he discusses the mythical origin of the two main ethnic groups that comprise the town's population. [RMW]

554 Antropologia e ética: o debate atual no Brasil. Organização de Ceres Víctora. Niterói, Brazil: Editora da Univ. Federal Fluminense, 2004. 207 p.: bibl.

An important collection of articles by well-known Brazilian anthropologists on the state of the current discussions on ethics in research methodology. It is the result of a series of discussions initiated by the former president of the Brazilian Anthropological Association, Ruben Oliven. With the growing diversification of anthropology as a field, there is an urgent need to develop clear codes of ethical conduct for diverse kinds of anthropological research. The volume covers the areas of health, indigenous anthropology, and multidisciplinary research. [RMW]

555 Antropologia e identificação: os antropólogos e a definição de terras indígenas no Brasil, 1977–2002. Organização de Antonio Carlos de Souza Lima e Henyo Trindade Barretto Filho. Rio de Janeiro: LACED, Laboratório de Pesquisas em Etnicidade, Cultura e Desenvolvimento: Contra Capa, 2005. 444 p.: bibl., ill., maps.

This is an important review and update of the role of the anthropologist in changes in procedures and legislation regarding land definitions in Brazil between the years 1977–2002. The year 1977 marks the beginning of systematic involvement by anthropologists in the official process of identifying, delineating, and demarcating indigenous lands in Brazil. The papers in this volume seek to broaden the sociological understanding of the legal-administrative practice of indigenous land identification. The authors reflect on what has changed and what has remained the same in this process in relation to the political contexts of the constitutional assembly and subsequent political developments; also, they discuss how the anthropologist has increasingly assumed the role of political actor. [RMW]

556 Barbosa, Wallace de Deus. Pedra do encanto: dilemas culturais e disputas políticas entre os Kambiwá e os Pipipã. Rio de Janeiro: LACED: Contra Capa, 2003. 199 p.: bibl., ill., map. (Territórios sociais; 10)

This ethnography of the Kambiwá and Pipipã Indians of the Serra Negra region of the Pernambucan backlands raises important questions for a theory of culture with its focus on native conceptions of discourse and culture, and the historical constitution of a native cultural heritage. It is also one of the few monographs about the cultural and political dynamics of the indigenous peoples of the Brazilian Northeast, who have long been neglected in the classic ethnography of Brazil. [RMW]

557 Barros, Edir Pina de. Os filhos do sol: história e cosmologia na organização social de um povo Karib, os Kurâ-Bakairi. São Paulo: EDUSP, 2003. 385 p.: bibl., ill. (some col.), maps.

This monograph is about the Carib-speaking Bakairi Indians of the upper Xingu region of central Brazil, until now a little-known group in the anthropological literature. The author's depth of knowledge comes from having lived for years in the region as the wife of an Indian agent of the Indian Assistance Post, or FUNAI. The monograph presents in fine detail indigenous history, kinship and social organization, economy, and cosmology. Social processes of group formation and fission are articulated with their ceremonial life, which is presented in all its beauty and complexity. Pan-community rituals are intercalated with seasonal alternation, but they have also selectively adapted to the

new human environment, populated by "civilized people." [RMW]

558 Brandão, Aivone Carvalho. O museu na aldeia: comunicação e transculturalismo no diálogo museu e aldeia. Campo Grande, Brazil: UCDB Editora, 2006. 237 p.: bibl., ill. (chiefly col.), col. maps.

The author's approach is based on the semiotics of culture which are applied to the Bororo of Mato Grosso. The supposition is that cultural codes are based in linguistic codes that make social communication possible. These linguistic codes operate in conjunction with "hypo-linguistic" codes that govern the processes of transmission of information to the biological level. Thus, semiosis occurs before human consciousness. Concretely, numerous workshops were realized in which various cultural objects of importance were recreated by the Bororo. Many of these objects had been stored in the Salesian Museum of Dom Bosco for decades. For the Bororo, all cultural objects have subjectivity, so the workshops revitalized the living links between the Bororo creator and cultural artifact—live creation. The extraordinary richness of Bororo artwork and ritual life come alive through the presentation of the workshops and through the recovery of sacred items which had for so long been stored in the museum, however much the present context differs from the original. [RMW]

559 O campo da antropologia no Brasil. Organização de Wilson Trajano Filho e Gustavo Lins Ribeiro. Rio de Janeiro: ABA: Contra Capa, 2004. 269 p.: bibl.

This is an excellent panorama of the discipline and profession of anthropology as exercised in Brazil today. The articles are written by some of the foremost leaders in the field, with years of experience in national and state research foundations that support anthropological work. The field has become incredibly professionalized over the past few decades, as seen in the increasing number of members of the Brazilian Anthropological Association, new journals in the field, and the growing recognition of Brazilian anthropologists on the international scene. This volume is one of the first major assessments of the field in recent times. [RMW]

560 Crianças indígenas: ensaios antropológicos. Organização de Aracy Lopes da Silva, Angela Nunes e Ana Vera Lopes da Silva Macedo. São Paulo: Global: MARI, 2002. 280 p.: bibl., ill., map. (Série antropologia e educação)

As the title suggests, the central theme of this volume is native children in Brazilian indigenous cultures, a theme that has rarely been explored in the literature. The studies present a critique of concepts used since the beginning of the 20th century for understanding childhood in historical and social contexts. All of the articles seek to present epistemological critiques and then treat a wide gamut of themes such as rituals, corporality, religiosity, life conditions, environment, and daily life. Thus, as a whole, the volume explores the ways in which children of different language families (especially Gê and Guaraní) experience and express themselves in social life. Relevant to burgeoning interest in indigenous education. [RMW]

561 Dalmolin, Gilberto Francisco. O papel da escola entre os povos indígenas: de instrumento de exclusão a recurso para emancipação sociocultural. Rio Branco, Brazil: EDUFAC, 2004. 423 p.: bibl. (Série Dissertações e teses)

The focus of this book is the emerging field of indigenous education in Brazil. The author examines the perception of indigenous leadership in the region of Acre and Amazonas and the new role played by schools in indigenous struggles for autonomy. In these regions, this study is particularly relevant given the great cultural diversity. For the indigenous schools to be effective, it is important to create a dialogue among diverse areas of knowledge, their logic and forms of production, allowing the indigenous teachers space and freedom to make cultural negotiations. The study is based on numerous interviews and the author's participation in numerous meetings of indigenous leaders, teachers, and indigenous organizations. [RMW]

562 Diniz, Edson Soares. Etnologia indígena da Amazônia brasileira. Belém, Brazil: Gráfica Editora Meridional, 2005. 454 p.: bibl., ill., maps.

A collection of short articles by the Brazilian ethnologist Edson Soares Diniz.

Many of the articles were originally published in journals that are difficult to find, over a period from 1962–2002. Many are in the form of notes based on short field-stays among a variety of peoples, mostly from northern Brazil. Topics range from kinship to culture change. [RMW]

563 Faulhaber, Priscila. "As estrelas eram terrenas": antropologia do clima, da iconografia e das constelações Ticuna. (Rev. Mex. Caribe, 9:18, 2004, p. 379–426, bibl., photos, tables)

The author presents the interesting results of her studies of the significance of astronomical and atmospheric phenomena in Ticuna myths and rituals, as well as the importance of artistic representations of these phenomena for the social practices of Amazonian indigenous peoples. Among the Ticuna of the Upper Solimões, celestial bodies depicted in the iconography of artifacts used in girls' puberty rites can be related to several aspects of their mythology, cosmology, and ecology. [RMW]

564 Gordon, Cesar. Economia selvagem: ritual e mercadoria entre os índios Xikrin-Mebêngôkre. São Paulo: Editora UNESP: Instituto Socioambiental; Rio de Janeiro: Núcleo de Transformações Indígenas, 2006. 452 p.: ill., maps.

The central questions that emerge from this study include: how can anthropology explain the desires of an indigenous population for money and merchandise? In fact, this question affects nearly all researchers who work with Lowland South American indigenous peoples. How can anthropology explain when indigenous consumption does not answer the needs of material production or subsistence and appears, at first, to be a sort of "consumerism"? What are the effects of the circulation of industrialized goods on native political economy? Gordon's detailed ethnography and analysis of Kayapo-Xikrin "economy" shows that indigenous desire for objects is not exotic, spurious, or inauthentic. It is the expression of an objective and specifically indigenous history, with deep connections to cosmology, the ritual system, and kinship. [RMW]

Grünberg, Georg. Os Kaiabi do Brasil Central: história e etnografia. See *HLAS 64:345.*

565 Koch-Grünberg, Theodor. Do Roraima ao Orinoco. Vol. 1, Observa-
ções de uma viagem pelo norte do Brasil e
pela Venezuela durante os anos de 1911 a
1913. Tradução de Cristina Alberts-Franco.
São Paulo: Editora UNESP, 2005. 374 p.:
bibl., ill.

First complete Portuguese translation
of vol. 1 of the German ethnological classic
about Amazonia by Theodor Koch Grünberg, *Vom Roroíma zum Orinoco: Reisen in
Nordbrasilien und Venezuela in den Jahren
1911–1913*, originally published in 1917.
Illustrated with contemporary photographs.
[F. Obermeier]

566 McCallum, Cecilia and **Ana Paula
dos Reis.** Childbirth as ritual in Brazil: young mothers' experiences. (*Ethnos/
Stockholm,*) 70:3, Sept. 2005, p. 335–360, bibl.

This is a very innovative approach
to studies of personhood in the context of
the institutional practice of women giving
birth. The location of the study is the state
hospital in Bahia. The authors seek to apply
a ritual model to understand the transformations of the individual patient from the
time she enters the hospital to the time she
leaves. The so-called dynamics of labor and
delivery in hospitals do resemble "religious"
rituals in "traditional societies." [RMW]

Mello, Marco Antonio da Silva and **Arno
Vogel.** Gente das areias: história, meio
ambiente e sociedade no litoral brasileiro,
Maricá, RJ, 1975 a 1995. See item **1354**.

567 Mindlin, Betty. Diários da floresta.
São Paulo: Editora Terceiro Nome,
2006. 240 p.

For a fieldworker, the most precious
instrument that s/he has is his/her field
notebook. In it, the ethnographer creates records of everyday life which at first
may not make any sense but later, when
their meaning becomes clear, are the most
important sources of information on the
flow of life and the things that matter
for the villagers. Field diaries are rarely
published, unfortunately, thus Mindlin's
contribution of her notes is a valuable
ethnography in itself as a document of her
relationship with the Indians and the day-
to-day struggles that occupied both anthropologist and village members. Sadly, no
photos. [RMW]

**568 Moitará, 1st, Itatiaia, Rio de Janeiro,
Brazil, 1978.** O simbolismo nas culturas indígenas brasileiras. Organização
de Carlos Amadeu Botelho Byington. São
Paulo: Paulus, 2006. 326 p.: bibl., ill.

The title refers to a traditional type of
get-together in the Xingu, but was adapted
by the Brazilian Society for Analytical Psychology to refer to a multidisciplinary study
of symbolism in Brazilian indigenous cultures. The volume's theoretical inspiration,
however, derives from the meetings held
in Eranos, Switzerland, in the 1930s when
leading scholars (such as Eliade and Jung)
gathered to discuss great themes of culture.
This volume presents the results of the first
"moitará" in Brazil in 1978, which covered
such topics as ethno-astronomy, shamanism, myths, rock art, and death. [RMW]

**569 Museu de arte e origens: mapa das cul-
turas vivas guaranis.** Organização de
Dinah Guimaraens. Rio de Janeiro: Contra
Capa Livraria, 2003. 319 p.: bibl., ill., maps.

This is a valuable book presenting the
Guarani culture of southern Brazil. Very
little of the vast literature on the Guarani
actually presents the communities in Rio
de Janeiro state. In this work, a collaboration of the Brazilian Museum of Fine Arts,
the Ministry of Culture, and the Catholic
Univ. of Rio de Janeiro, the Guarani present
themselves as they are today, highlighting
their history, present-day culture, and especially their artwork. Also interesting are
the connections they have forged with the
Pataxo, original inhabitants of Bahia state,
with the Northwest Amazon, and the indigenous peoples of the North American Southwest whom Guarani leaders visited. [RMW]

570 Nossa, Leonencio. Homens invisíveis.
Edição e revisão de texto de Neri
Vitor Eich. Rio de Janeiro: Editora Record,
2007. 264 p.: bibl., col. ill., maps.

This book narrates the voyage of
3 1/2 months through the territory of un-
contacted and unknown indigenous peoples
in the backwater regions of the Jurua River
on the border of Brazil and Colombia/Peru.
The headwaters of the Jutai and Jandaiatuba
rivers are one of the most remote and, until
today, unexplored regions of the planet.
These are the lands of a tribe which is only
known for its skill in making arrows; they

have rarely been seen, but they do not hesitate to fight off intruders into their territory. Since they are "isolated," it is not known how many they are nor what language they speak. Their situation is highly uncertain since attacks either from them or by intruders could spell their end. [RMW]

571 Santos, Ana Flávia Moreira and João Pacheco de Oliveira Filho. Reconhecimento étnico em exame: dois estudos sobre os Caxixó. Rio de Janeiro: LACED: Contra Capa, 2003. 207 p.: bibl., ill. (Territórios sociais; 9)

The analysis presented in this book is specifically focused on the Caxixó Indians of the state of Minas Gerais, a group of "recently-emerged" indigenous people known in the field of indigenism for having a way of life indistinguishable from the rural peasants of the area. The book raises larger questions, such as: Which definition of "indigenous" is useful for the practice of indigenism? One that applies to a people who, through numerous adaptive strategies, have tried to preserve shared values and have constructed a sociability and project for the future based on their relationship to their past. [RMW]

572 Silva, Orlando Sampaio. Eduardo Galvão: índios e caboclos. São Paulo: Annablume, 2007. 417 p.: bibl., maps.

Provides a detailed analysis and critique of the theoretical and methodological content of the publications by Brazil's pioneering ethnologist Galvão and their impact on the development of the discipline between 1940 and 1970. [B. Meggers]

573 Sociedades Caboclas Amazônicas: Modernidade e Invisibilidade, *Univ. de São Paulo*, 2002. Sociedades caboclas amazônicas: modernidade e invisibilidade. Edição de Cristina Adams, Rui Murrieta e Walter Neves. São Paulo: Annablume, 2006. 362 p.: bibl., ill., maps (some col.).

The papers of this volume are the result of a workshop on "Amazonian Caboclo Societies: Modernity and Invisibility" held at the Univ. de São Paulo in 2002. The papers present a diversity of approaches used over the past 15 years in the anthropological study of the Amazonian peasant population. Critical of previous approaches, the authors seek to develop a set of new analytical tools

and concepts with which to understand caboclo society that go beyond the folk culture model or "positivist" systems of interaction with the environment. A multidisciplinary study involving anthropologists, historians, ecologists, health specialists, and development specialists. [RMW]

574 Toré: regime encantado do índio do nordeste. Organização de Rodrigo de Azeredo Grünewald. Recife, Brazil: Fundação Joaquim Nabuco, Editora Massangana, 2005. 328 p.: bibl., ill.

This is a valuable collection by anthropologists and ethnomusicologists of the indigenous peoples of Northeastern Brazil, on the most important ritual performances of all native peoples of the region. Native peoples of this region were the hardest-hit by the advance of civilization; with their societies destructured, many fled to the backlands to escape further persecution, where eventually they were relocated to mission settlements. With the demise of the missions, native peoples were left on their own and, by the mid-19th century, state Indian policy ignored the existence of any Indians in the backlands declaring that these had been totally assimilated to national society. The reverse was true, however; native peoples in the late 20th century began to reaffirm their ethnic identity. One of the principal ways they did so was through performance of the Toré ritual, connecting the ancestral spirits to their living descendants. This remarkable story is richly presented in this important collection. [RMW]

575 Transformando os deuses. Vol. 2, Igrejas evangélicas, pentecostais e neopentecostais entre os povos indígenas no Brasil. Organização de Robin M. Wright. Campinas, Brazil: Editora UNICAMP, 2004. 1 v.: bibl., ill., maps.

This is the second volume of a series, organized since 1993, on the indigenous transformations of the various forms of Christianity which have been introduced amongst them by diverse Christian missionary organizations. The cases in this volume include several from the Amazon region, but the majority is from the southern regions of Brazil. Thus, one of the differences from the first volume is that non-Amazonian peoples are included. Relations to Christian missions vary from a total transformation of Christianity to meet the social and spiritual needs of the native people, to a rejection of Christian doctrine and acceptance of material and health assistance. The introductory essay seeks to advance theories of conversion by understanding the global and local historical contexts in which conversion occur. [RMW]

576 **Vilaça, Aparecida.** Quem somos nós: os Wari' encontram os brancos. Rio de Janeiro: Editora UFRJ, 2006. 607 p.: bibl., ill., index, maps (some col.).

From the author's dissertation advisor, "this ethnography focuses on the cosmological dynamics of the relation between the Wari' Indians of Rondonia and the surrounding society; it is one of the first book-length analyses of the problem of indigenous meaning given to the relation between themselves and the national society. These relations have been traditionally presented as though they were constituted by notions such as the national dynamics of the dominant capitalist economic pole, colonialist policy, frontier in expansion, leaving to the indigenous pole the alternatives of submission or resistance. Seen essentially as 'constructed' by the national society in both the objective and conceptual senses, the Indians were typically conceded the trifle of being able to relatively 'construct' this first construction, that is, of 'adapting to' or 'manipulating' the conditions of contact imposed from outside. The book shows with great richness of detail and analytical penetration how history is different when we seek to tell it as the Indians tell it" (Eduardo Viveiros de Castro). This topic, of course, has been a theme in various, previously published North American ethnographies of Lowland South American Indians. [RMW]

577 **Willems, Emílio.** Ilha de Búzios: uma comunidade caiçara no sul do Brasil. Colaboração de Gioconda Mussolini. Tradução de Ana Maria Lopes Pontifex. São Paulo: Hucitec/NUPAUB/CEC, 2003. 185 p.: bibl., ill., map. (Ecologia e cultura; 4)

This is the Portuguese translation of the anthropological classic by Emilío Willems and Gioconda Mussolini published in 1945 on the peoples and cultures of the island of Buzios, off the shores of Rio de

Janeiro and São Paulo states, Brazil. The peoples are known as "caiçaras" or "fisherfolk," the descendants of a mix of rural, peasant populations who have inhabited the coastal shores for centuries. The monograph is still a classic despite the disappearance of the original caiçara population, now replaced by a new generation of "caiçaras," given its identification of a relatively homogeneous "caiçara" population and the profound transformation that the original caiçara population was undergoing at the time of research. [RMW]

578 **Woortmann, Klaas.** O selvagem e o novo mundo: ameríndios, humanismo e escatologia. Brasília: Editora UnB, 2004. 300 p.: bibl.

An erudite and fascinating study of the history of an "idea"—"savagery" in Western thought. The notion all too frequently served to use native peoples of the hemisphere as a sort of mirror for Western civilization—they are those whom we are not. The author shows how this notion developed from ancient Greco-Roman civilization through the European Middle Ages. The arrival of Europeans to the New World deeply disturbed European cosmological and theological thought; the notion of "savagery" was applied to natives even before they came to be known; thus, they were seen as a critique of the West, as objects of political projects, in eschatological terms, and in terms of history. [RMW]

579 **Wright, Robin M.** História indígena e do indigenismo no Alto Rio Negro. Campinas, Brazil: FAEP, UNICAMP; Mercado de Letras; São Paulo: Instituto Socioambiental, 2005. 319 p.: bibl., ill., maps.

This is a collection of articles written over 20 years since the author completed his PhD dissertation. Its main theme is the history of the prophetic movements among the native peoples of the Northwest Amazon. Four of the book's eight chapters are dedicated to demonstrating the continuity of the prophetic tradition from its beginning in the mid-19th century to the second half of the 20th century. Two other chapters focus on oral narratives of warfare, internal among the phratries, and external against the invading white man. A valuable historical bibliography completes the work along with the author's perspective for the immediate future of the Indians of the Upper Rio Negro region. [RMW]

Zanotti, Laura and **Janet Chernela.** Conflicting cultures of nature: ecotourism, education and the Kayapó of the Brazilian Amazon. See item **1412.**

COLOMBIA, VENEZUELA, AND THE GUIANAS

580 **Alarcón Puentes, Johnny.** Las relaciones de poder político en el pueblo wayuu. Zulia, Venezuela: Univ. del Zulia, Ediciones del Vice Rectorado Académico, 2007. 115 p.: bibl., ill. (Col. Textos universitarios)

Emphasizing political anthropology, this pithy text is an ethnographic account of a Wayúu community in Venezuela. The text explores the transformations of political power among the Wayúu, studies the interrelation between the practices and representations of the group, and reviews Wayúu relations with the Venezuelan state and national society. [BD]

581 **Cabrera Becerra, Gabriel.** Las Nuevas Tribus y los indígenas de la Amazonia: historia de una presencia protestante. Bogotá: G. Cabrera Becerra, 2007. 224 p.: bibl., ill., maps.

Paying special attention to Colombia, this valuable work discusses the impact of Protestantism in Amazonia. Following a historical review of their role in South America, the text turns its attention to the influence that the New Tribes Mission has had upon the social lives of "isolated" indigenous groups. Book assesses the presence and actions of the New Tribes Mission of Colombia, which were established in the mid-1940s by Sofia Müller, among the indigenous peoples of Colombia's frontier zone with Venezuela and Brazil. Based on the combination of primary source documents and fieldwork research conducted among the indigenous Nukak peoples, text chronicles the tragic history of indigenous contact with missionaries and other outsiders. [BD]

582 **Heckler, Serena** and **Stanford Zent.** Piaroa manioc varietals: hyperdiversity or social currency? (*Hum. Ecol.*, 36:5, Oct. 2008, p. 679–697)

This paper explores the remarkable diversity of "folk" varieties of manioc cultivated by the Piaroa of the Venezuelan Amazon who recognize 113 distinctive types. Qualitative analysis demonstrated the symbolic significance and vital role manioc has in Piaroa social life. Based on nearly two decades of research, authors assert that Piaroa agro-biodiversity must be understood through a multifaceted approach, taking into consideration practical and ecological elements, the multiplicity of ways in which the manioc is processed, and sociocultural factors which highlight manioc's role as a social mediator among the Piaroa. [BD]

583 **Hill, Jonathan David.** Made-from-bone: trickster myths, music, and history from the Amazon. Urbana: Univ. of Illinois Press, 2009. 195 p.: bibl., ill., index, maps. (Interpretations of culture in the new millennium)

Made-from-Bone is an ethnographic collection that depicts the mythic past and "audioscapes" or musical-scapes of the Wakuénai peoples of Venezuela. Author skillfully gives meaning to a masterful rendering of the esthetic and poetic dimensions of Wakuénai narratives, while drawing attention to their ongoing embeddedness in the localized struggles and structural ambiguities of contemporary life. The pivotal character during the primordial mythical times is a trickster-originator, called "Made-from-Bone," who manages to stay alive despite a number of mortal attacks. The mythical narratives are complemented by ethnohistorical, musical, and ethnographic observations. Foundational myths, such as the source of cooking with hot peppers, the story of origin of night, and the battle between Made-from-Bone and the First-Woman frame this memorable account of ethnography and Amazonian mythogenesis. For a different view on the topic, see Wright's 1998 volume, *HLAS 59:965.* [BD]

584 **Jaramillo Salazar, Pablo.** El jaibaná en la encrucijada: ritual, territorio y política en una población embera. Manizales, Colombia: Editorial Univ. de Caldas, 2006. 275 p.: bibl., ill. (Col. Ciencias jurídicas y sociales)

This intellectually provocative book is a contribution to the ethnography of identity politics in the context of the indigenous rights movement and the Colombian state's articulation of multiculturalism. Based on careful analysis of ethnographic fieldwork conducted over a four year period among an Embera community in the resguardo of La Albania, this book questions conventional models of ritual and their theoretical relationship to the politics of identity. The author provides a novel way of thinking about these phenomena via the concept of what he deems "ritual digression." The nuanced text provides wonderful insight into the sociopolitical lives of the Embera, and critically explores the local meanings of sociological constructs such as "community," "territorially," "ethnicity," and "identity," which are persuasively demonstrated to be embedded in contentious supralocal historical forces. [BD]

Koch-Grünberg, Theodor. Do Roraima ao Orinoco. See item **565**.

585 Martínez Silva, Pablo Andrés. Colonización y VIH/SIDA: una narrativa de malestar de la Amazonia colombiana. (*Antípoda*, 3, julio/dic. 2006, p. 179–198)
    By exploring the subjectivity of the theoretical categories used by medical anthropology, as well as the practice of biomedicine itself, a new framework for action is developed in this essay. The author provides an analysis of narratives about HIV-AIDS that were collected during fieldwork conducted along Colombia's northwest Amazonian frontier. This effort in turn yields the contextual framework for understanding the historical, social, and economic issues that have emerged at the local level, which enables the author to reflect on the broader issues of global public health. [BD]

586 Rodd, Robin. Reassessing the cultural and psychopharmacological significance of *Banisteriopsis caapi*: preparation, classification and use among the Piaroa of southern Venezuela. (*J. Psychoactive Drugs*, 40:3, Sept. 2008, p. 301–307)
    This article strives to provide information on the key cultural contexts, meanings, and modalities of B. caapi consumption among snuff-using indigenous societies, namely the Piaroa of Venezuela, who interestingly do not use N,N-dimethyltryptamine (DMT) admixtures in their B. caapi's hallucinogenic concoctions (yopo). While the Piaroa recognize at least five different types of B. caapi, their shamans rely only on B. caapi's

cambium, and stress this plant's value in amplifying empathic states of awareness. Some Piaroa also point to a number of nonshamanic uses for B. caapi, such as a stimulant, as well as an aid in the art of hunting. Given the psychopharmacological intricacy of harmala alkaloids coupled with the widespread ethnographic reports of its diverse uses, the essay concludes by encouraging subsequent investigation of B. caapi's cultural legacies and its psychopharmacological uses, focusing on the plant's stimulant and antidepressant-like traits. [BD]

587 Zent, Eglée L. The hunter-self: perforations, prescriptions, and primordial beings among the Jotï, Venezuelan Guayana. (*Tipití*, 3:2, Dec. 2004, p. 35–76)
    Emphasizing the cosmological as well as ecological vitality of Jotï society in the Venezuelan Guayana, this ethnographic account illustrates the social and cultural significance of hunting. The author's symbolic analysis, which emphasizes ritual and myth, suggests that hunting is an essential component of Jotï cultural life. [BD]

PERU AND ECUADOR

588 Cepek, Michael. Essential commitments: identity and the politics of Cofán conservation. (*J. Lat. Am. Caribb. Anthropol.*, 13:1, April 2008, p. 196–222)
    Article examines the nature of indigenous discourses by exploring the role environmentalism plays in the daily lives and political agendas of the Cofán peoples of Ecuadorian Amazonia. Rather than rendering Cofán environmental discourses and practices as merely instrumentalist responses to transnational identity politics, the author notes Cofán peoples' valorization of the substantive links between their cultural identity and their traditional lands. This in turn shapes Cofán involvement in their struggle for self-determination that predicates "political rights on conservationist commitments." [BD]

589 Estudios sobre la Amazonía. Contribuciones de Elena Burga Cabrera *et al.* Lima: Fondo Editorial de la Facultad de Ciencias Sociales UNMSM, 2005. 176 p.: bibl., ill., maps. (*Cuadernos MacArthur*; 2)
    The second of the Cuadernos MacArthur series, this welcome collection represents six diverse studies of the Peru-

vian Amazon that ponder the historical transformations experienced by indigenous societies of the region. Essays evaluate a wide spectrum of topics, including the challenges for promoting sustainable development, land management, and the transformations wrought by the market economy. Essays of note are devoted to understanding the cosmological life of the Aguaruna and the Ashaninka in the context of shamanism and the sociocultural construction of knowledge and power. [BD]

590 Garcés, Alicia. Relaciones de género en la amazonía ecuatoriana: estudios de caso en comunidades indígenas Achuar, Shuar y Kichua. Quito: Ediciones ABYA-YALA: CEDIME: DED, 2006. 116 p.: bibl.

Written in part as a policy analysis for NGO projects involved in enhancing gender equity and indigenous community well-being, this useful text is a comparative study of gender relations among the Achuar, Shuar, and Kichua communities of the Ecuadorian Oriente. Moreover, the author assesses the role that natural resource management plays in shaping contemporary and future gender relations in indigenous Amazonian communities. [BD]

591 Gray, Clark L. et al. Indigenous land use in the Ecuadorian Amazon: a cross-cultural and multilevel analysis. (*Hum. Ecol.*, 36:1, Feb. 2008, p. 97–109)

In an effort to determine household and community factors shaping local land use patterns, this essay provides "regional-scale survey" data on five indigenous populations in the Northern Ecuadorian Amazon and multilevel statistical models. The authors note the relatively small areas cultivated by indigenous households in comparison to neighboring mestizo colonists in the study sites. Research findings underscore the significance of "market integration" as a primary force transforming land use practices in indigenous territories. For geography specialist's comment, see item **1119**. [BD]

592 ICONOS. No. 25, 2006. Quito: FLACSO Ecuador.

This special issue surveys the role of globalized linkages in Amazonia. A number of contributing authors explore the role of economic, institutional, and social agents in shaping the historical trajectories of this vast region. This issue includes essays by specialists animated by the need to effectively address the multinational challenges posed by advances in the Amazonian mining and agricultural frontiers. To wit, Guillaume Fontaine provides an "Andean" perspective on globalization, whereas Delfina Trinca's cogent contribution describes the Venezuelan case. For his part, Richard Pasquis discusses the immense impact soya cultivation has had on the Brazilian Amazon. Francisco Neira's essay describes various discursive representations of "nature" in the Ecuadorian Amazon. Collectively, these essays explore strategies local and regional official bodies can use in mitigating the environmental threats posed by the encroaching extractive frontiers. The special issue is complemented by the visual artistry of Marcelo Aguirre, who provides a graphic depiction of the hypnotic world of Naporuna myths. [BD]

593 Jernigan, Kevin A. The importance of chemosensory clues in Aguaruna tree classification and identification. (*J. Ethnobiol. Ethnomed.*, 4:12, May 2008, p. 1–7, bibl., map, photos)

This article reveals the significance of odor among the Aguaruna's taxonomy and identification of woody plants. The odor of bark, resin, flowers, leaves, and fruit are all vital signs that allow the Aguaruna to ascertain the interrelatedness of trees found in their environs. In contrast, taste for the Aguaruna appears to play a more limited role in classifying plants. Focusing on the Aguaruna's category of númi (those trees excepting palms), the author recounts how the Aguaruna of the Peruvian Amazon most often classify as related (kumpají) to those trees that have a similar smell collectively. In the study, Aguaruna subjects seldom referenced tree odors in a non-botanical fashion, whereas taste was most often employed to designate those trees with edible fruits. The author found that trees classified by the Aguaruna were almost always matching members of the same botanical family. [BD]

594 Killick, Evan. Creating community: land titling, education, and settlement formation among the Ashéninka of Peruvian Amazonia. (*J. Lat. Am. Caribb. Anthropol.*, 13:1, April 2008, p. 22–47)

Through a detailed assessment of the process and consequences of land titling among Ashéninka communities of Peruvian Amazonia, this essay deftly evaluates the connection between nation-states and indigenous peoples. In so doing, the article demonstrates the multiplicity of relationships characterizing indigenous peoples' relationships to the state. In addition to assessing cases of Ashéninka communities obliged to battle for their land rights, the author explores examples where indigenous communities have endeavored to gain official recognition of their lands through formal, legal channels. The article illustrates how some Ashéninka groups formed communities and subsequently sought formal recognition of their communities in an effort to obtain state-backed education for their family members. Rather than serving as the driving force for the Ashéninka's assertion of their rights to native territories, the essay notes that communal identities and collective action can be correlated with official state recognition of land rights claims. [BD]

595   Lewis, Sara. Ayahuasca and spiritual crisis: liminality as space for personal growth. (*Anthropol. Consciousness*, 19:2, 2008, p. 109–133)

Essay tackles the controversy surrounding Amazonian Ayahuasca tourism by noting that many outsiders who participate in such ceremonies run the risk of psychological distress, which the author deems as "spiritual emergencies." Three examples of North Americans who participated in Ayahuasca ceremonies in Peru are proffered as case studies of people negotiating "spiritual emergencies." Relying on Victor Turner's concept of liminality, ethnographic data on shamanic novitiates is examined in order to comprehend the spiritual experiences accompanying Ayahuasca use, and to assert the utility of Western psychotherapists assisting Ayahuasca consumers in providing meaning to their emotional distress. [BD]

596   Lu, Flora E. Integration into the market among indigenous peoples: a cross-cultural perspective from the Ecuadorian Amazon. (*Curr. Anthropol.*, 48:4, Aug. 2007, p. 593–602, bibl., graphs, map, tables)

Essay asserts that indigenous peoples' systematic integration into market economies has received scant attention in the body of scholarship on Lowland South America. Prior research has emphasized market involvement in terms of factors like extent of forest clearance, indices of well-being, and ecological knowledge, but studies differ immensely in their evaluation of the metrics of market involvement, and typically have used only a few or only one of the aforementioned measures. This essay reviews data from five indigenous groups located in the northern Ecuadorian Amazon and illustrates that there is minimal correlation between various measures of incorporation into the market. Importantly, the essay points to the value of employing a variety of measures of both household production and consumption to evaluate the level of market integration among indigenous peoples. [BD]

Millones, Luis. Ser indio en el Perú: la fuerza del pasado; las poblaciones indígenas del Perú, costa y sierra. See *HLAS 64:353.*

597   Redescubriendo el Valle de los Chilchos: condiciones de vida en la Ceja de Selva, Perú = The Chilchos Valley revisited: life conditions in the Ceja de Selva, Peru. Contribuciones de Inge Schjellerup *et al.* Copenhagen: The National Museum of Denmark, 2005. 424 p.: bibl., ill. (chiefly col.). (*Ethnographic monographs;* 2)

Focusing on the Chilchos Valley of Peru, this comprehensive book underscores how human habitation over the past 500 years has transformed the montane forests (Ceja de Selva). Relying on a wide range of data, including archeological, ethnohistorical, and ethnographic information, the work demonstrates a major decline in population during the colonial epoch, followed by a period of socioeconomic and ecological change over the past century as the result of the area's colonization by Andean migrants. Work provides insight into the complex nature of human adaptations to various biomes. [BD]

598   Rival, Laura. Amazonian historical ecologies. (*J. Royal Anthropol. Inst.*, 12:1, March 2006, p. 79–94)

Taking models of ecology as a point of departure for understanding the social organization of Lowland South America's foraging bands with restricted access to cultivated foods—a position associated with the *Handbook of South American Indians* published roughly five decades ago under Julian Steward's direction—the article argues for an historical ecology. The essay asserts that a "diachronic analysis of living ecological system" will enable us to reconceptualize our understanding of the poorly understood nature of human occupation in Amazonia. Rather than a paradigm, the author suggests that historical ecology is akin to a research method that examines precisely how environmental transformations influence the historical trajectories of human societies. Article closes by considering the significance of human reliance on resources produced in the past, which the author suggests could be a common feature of Upper Amazonian foraging or "trekking groups." [BD]

599 Rosengren, Dan. Transdimensional relations: on human-spirit interaction in the Amazon. (*J. Royal Anthropol. Inst.*, 12:4, Dec. 2006, p. 803–816, bibl.)

Taking its cue from both the long-standing scholarly interest in, as well as recent contributions to the study of animism, this article examines notions of the human-spirit relationship—or what the author deems "transdimensional." Based on ethnographic fieldwork conducted with the Matsigenka of southeastern Peru, a society that stresses the cultural import of conviviality and egalitarian ideals of sharing and mutual trust, the author assesses the dynamics of human-spirit interactions. The essay contends the aforementioned qualities undermine the formation of indigenous social hierarchy and inform the Matsigenka's contentious associations with spirit beings. [BD]

600 Rubenstein, Steven. Circulation, accumulation, and the power of Shuar shrunken heads. (*Cult. Anthropol.*, 22:3, August 2007, p. 357–399)

Essay explores the ongoing relevance of tsantsas for the Shuar peoples of Ecuador. Rebuffing simplistic distinctions between the tropes of savagery and civilization, this engaging article explores the shifting symbolic import of Shuar tsantsas, the shrunken heads of foes slain in warfare. The author affirms that prior to colonization Shuar headhunting formed part of a broader

system of sociopolitical power, one which was exemplified by the complex circulation of its constituent parts. Yet when Ecuadorian officials banned warfare in the 1950s the Shuar had in fact exchanged all of their tsantsas with European and North American collectors in return for barter items. The "customary" circulation of tsantas was ruptured when they became permanent accoutrements of Western museums and private collections. At this historical juncture the meaning of the shrunken heads became secondary to a structure whereby Shuar power was now vested in what the author deems "the accumulation of values." The year 1995 marked the repatriation of a number of heads to Ecuador by the National Museum of the American Indian. Following their absence, the shrunken tsantsas have now come to represent "distance," according to the author, specifically the detachment of contemporary Shuar from their history as well as the great expanse between Shuar representatives and their federation constituents. [BD]

601 Santos-Granero, Fernando. Of fear and friendship: Amazonian sociality beyond kinship and affinity. (*J. Royal Anthropol. Inst.*, 13:1, March 2007, p. 1–18)

The author investigates the character of sociality and alterity by providing a sustained analysis of the concept of "friendship" in indigenous Amazonia. The article demonstrates the role of friendship as an alternative to merely kinship and affinity in the constitution of indigenous societies. Through study of Amazonian trading partnerships, mystical associations, and shamanic complexes, the essay explores how the formation of "spaces of trust" is a way in which antagonistic relations in non-kin-based social networks can be altered into relations of sociality. [BD]

602 Stronza, Amanda. Through a new mirror: reflections on tourism and identity in the Amazon. (*Hum. Organ.*, 67:3, Fall 2008, p. 244–257)

Based on a study of an ecotourist "lodge" co-owned and operated by a pluriethnic community in the Peruvian Amazonia, this article provides ethnographic insight into "tourists' expectant gazes and locals' reactions to them." Analysis reveals that local residents have begun to alter their awareness of indigenous authenticity. In response to the influx of tourists, local peoples have shown renewed interest in their indigenous heritage and a heightened sensitivity about the challenges indigenous cultural assertions carry with them. This is illustrated by an intensified local desire for the elders to teach indigenous languages, recount stories of the ancient ones, and to sing sacred songs. [BD]

603 Veber, Hanne. Merits and motivations of an Ashéninka leader. (*Tipití*, 5:1, June 2007, p. 9–31)

Highlighting personal motives for becoming an indigenous advocate, this article provides a subtle analysis of the autobiographical narrative of an Ashéninka leader of the Peruvian Amazon. While drawing from recollections of the past, close study of the leader's narrative underscores the interconnection between individual and communal interests, and in turn gives meaning to Ashéninka struggles for indigeneity and claims for cultural autonomy. [BD]

604 Viatori, Maximilian and Gloria Ushigua. Speaking sovereignty: indigenous languages and self-determination. (*Wicazo Sa Rev.*, 22:2, 2007, p. 7–21)

Essay reviews the function that language has served in indigenous efforts at obtaining self-determination. Authors pay close attention to how the Zápara of Ecuador have used language revalorization efforts to assert their demands for greater administrative and cultural autonomy from Ecuador's government. [BD]

605 Whitten, Norman E. and Dorothea S. Whitten. Puyo runa: imagery and power in modern Amazonia. Urbana: Univ. of Illinois Press, 2008. 304 p.: bibl., index.

Written by an astonishing couple credited with pioneering the development of modern Ecuadorian anthropology, this text is a welcome addition to the ethnological literature of Western Amazonia. Based on intensive ethnographic fieldwork spanning more than four decades among the Canelos Quichua of Ecuador, this marvelous collection of essays provides an invaluable contribution to our understanding of foundational themes long occupying the interest of Lowland South American specialists: e.g., the

nature of ethnogenesis; the (em)powerment of ecological knowledge; indigenous cosmologies; and shamanic practices. This lucidly written text frames and gives deep meaning to the nature of Amazonian esthetics, imagery, and cultural performance. Similarly, the collection explores the relationship among anthropologically robust topics—myth, history, and ritual—not to mention providing vitally important context for understanding the Canelos Quichua's contemporary political engagements with the broader nonindigenous world(s). [BD]

606 Wilson, Patrick. Neoliberalism, indigeneity and social engineering in Ecuador's Amazon. (*Crit. Anthropol.*, 28:2, 2008, p. 127–144)

Foregrounding the consequences of neoliberal state reforms, this sensible essay evaluates a state-sanctioned hacienda invasion by indigenous peoples in the Ecuadorian Amazonian. The case-study demonstrates the role of the municipal government, which encouraged the land invasion while concomitantly providing members of the newly created community with improved access to basic social services. The author suggests that the case under review is a manifestation of a change in Ecuador's process of governmental decentralization, which ostensibly accompanies the prospects for increased state services. While transformations in Ecuador's neoliberal policies may in fact facilitate novel forms of state domination in Amazonia, the essay indicates that this comes at the cost of buttressing racist discourses associated with "modernizing nationalisms." [BD]

607 Wilson, Warren. Ethnobotanical evidence for cultivar selection among the Tukanos: manioc *manihot esculenta crant* in the Northwest Amazon. (*Cult. Agric.*, 28:2, 2006, p. 122–130)

The objective of this brief essay is to establish which qualities of manioc the Tukanoans of Colombia think are the most significant as cultivars. In light of the presumed resistance of high-cyanide containing manioc to the ravages of insects and pathogens, it was hypothesized that the Tukanoans' penchant for high-cyanide containing types of manioc (which account for over 80 percent of their daily caloric intake) would be justified in terms of their perceived higher yields relative to low-cyanide cultivars planted in their food gardens. Nevertheless, the research found that while higher yields may indeed be factors shaping Tukanoan selection of manioc cultivars, the principal consideration is based on what sort of foods can be prepared from each type of manioc cultivar. [BD]

PARAGUAY, ARGENTINA, AND BOLIVIA

608 Bonifacio, Valentina. Ciudadanos trabajadores: breve historia del Pueblo Maskoy, la Empresa Carlos Casado S.A. y la Iglesia Católica en Puerto Casado, Chaco, Alto Paraguay. (*Supl. Antropol.*, 43:1, junio 2008, p. 387–432)

Study of the incorporation of Maskoy Indians as workers in the tannin industry in the Paraguayan Chaco, their struggle to obtain the lands and the changes these processes encompassed.The social and political organization of the Maskoy was transformed by the action of government agencies, the Church, and their settlement in the expropriated lands. Author describes emergence of new forms of leadership in the celebration of traditional dances. Contributes to the study of the impact of private companies and government policies on indigenous peoples. [SMH]

609 Calvert-Mir, Laura; Victoria Reyes-García; and Susan Tanner. Is there a divide between local medicinal knowledge and Western medicine?: a case study among native Amazonians in Bolivia. (*J. Ethnobiol. Ethnomed.*, 4:18, Aug. 2008, p. 1–11, bibl., graphs, table)

This article relates the results of a study of the interactions between localized and biomedical knowledge among the Tsimane' of the Bolivian Amazon. A number of research methodologies (participant observation, free-listing, semi-structured interviews, pile-sorting and surveys) were employed by the investigators to elicit whether the Tsimane' incorporate local healing knowledge with Occidental models of biomedicine. In spite of the fact that the Tsimane' did not in fact mention biomedical treatments in their free-lists, researchers found that they do, nevertheless, rely on

both "ethnomedical" as well as biomedical healing modalities. The article's findings stand in stark contrast to those studies that accentuate a radical divide between "Western" biomedicine and indigenous healing systems, and points to novel efforts at promoting "synergistic" collaboration among healers and physicians. [BD]

610 Cartografías argentinas: políticas indigenistas y formaciones provinciales de alteridad. Recopilación de Claudia Briones. Buenos Aires: EA: GEAPRONA, 2005. 349 p.: bibl.

Collection of essays which focus on the political, economic, and ideological determinants of provincial states in designing policies and implementing practices. Authors in this edited volume explore how specific provincial state policies of inclusion and exclusion have created indigenist policies and notions of alterity. [SMH]

611 Ceriani Cernadas, César. Nuestros hermanos lamanitas: indios y fronteras en la imaginación mormona. Buenos Aires: Editorial Biblos, 2008. 285 p.: bibl., map. (Culturalia) (Desde América)

Excellent analysis of Mormonism among the Toba Indians of Argentina. Study focuses on the history of Mormon settlement in Argentina and the process of proselytism. The author analyzes the ways in which the Mormons have constructed and invented "the lamanites," referring to the indigenous inhabitants of the Americas. Focuses on Mormonism as a colonial narrative of the frontier. [SMH]

612 Citro, Silvia V. Cuerpos significantes: travesías de una etnografía dialéctica. Buenos Aires: Editorial Biblos, 2009. 351 p.: ill. (Culturalia) (Desde América)

This study is framed in the anthropology of the body, and how the body constitutes a site of cultural significance. The author incorporates a dialectic approach, using philosophy, psychoanalysis, and ethnography, in exploring the meaning of ritual dances, curing practices, and esthetic representations among the Toba Indians of Argentina. [SMH]

Combès, Isabelle. Alto y Bajo Isoso: géographie et pouvoir dans le Chaco bolivien. See item **1161.**

613 Combès, Isabelle and **Diego Villar.**
Os mestiços mais puros: representações Chiriguano e Chané da mestiçagem. (*Mana/Rio de Janeiro*, 13:1, 2007, p. 41–62)

Authors compare the process of miscegenation among the Isoseño Indians of Bolivia and Chané of Argentina. Taking an ethnohistorical and ethnographic perspective, article explores how notions of "mestizaje" are redefined by Indians in terms of purity. Inter-ethnic marriages currently reflect a scale of values, which is the result of the ambivalence of these groups regarding miscegenation. Contributes to the study of "mestizaje" among indigenous peoples. [SMH]

614 Combès, Isabelle and **Kathleen Lowrey.** Slaves without masters?: Arawakan dynasties among the Chiriguano, Boliviano Chaco, sixteenth to twentieth centuries. (*Ethnohistory/Columbus*, 53:3, Summer 2006, p. 689–714, bibl.)

Based on ethnohistorical and ethnographic data, article explores the ways in which the Chiriguano, who are the result of the fusion of Guaraní and Chané (Arawak), but are not predominantly Guaraní, have been influenced by Arawak culture. By focusing on political organization, authors demonstrate the persistence of Arawak political systems, which are defined as Guaraní. Contributes to the study of leadership among Lowland groups and inter-ethnic dynamics. [SMH]

615 Córdoba, Lorena. Ideología, simbolismo y relaciones de género en la construcción de la persona chacobo. (*Anthropos/Freiburg*, 101, 2006, p. 145–158)

Explores the notions of womanhood and personhood among the Chacobo of the Bolivian Amazon. The author analyzes womanhood as the result of progressive stages and the construction of the self. Focuses on the analysis of female initiation, procreation processes, mythic representation of sexuality, and the practice of couvade. [SMH]

616 Escobar, Ticio. The curse of Nemur: in search of the art, myth, and ritual of the Ishir. Translated by Adriana Michele Campos Johnson. Foreword by Michael Taussig. Pittsburgh, Pa.: Univ. of Pittsburgh Press, 2007. 303 p.: bibl., ill., index, map.

(Illuminations: cultural formations of the Americas)

English translation of Escobar's rendering of the Tomáraho, a subgroup of the Ishir (Chamacoco) of Paraguay, and their belief system, narratives, myths, rituals, feather decoration, dream songs, and shamanism. Focuses on the Tomaráho's esthetic representations including their drawings and use of color. [SMH]

617 Escolar, Diego. Los dones étnicos de la nación: identidades huarpe y modos de producción de soberanía en Argentina. Buenos Aires: Prometeo, 2007. 249 p.: bibl., ill. (Col. miradas antropológicas)

Author provides an in-depth analysis of the ethnic reemergence of the Huarpe Indians of Argentina. Resorting to historical and ethnographic research, the book traces the "disappearance" of the Huarpe for over 200 years, and how this is linked to a discourse and practice embedded in notions of hegemonic national sovereignty. This process in turn renders invisible the presence of indigenous peoples and at times of crisis and of particular political opening allows the emergence of subaltern groups. [SMH]

618 La fiesta del 30 de agosto entre los mocovíes de Santa Fe. Textos de Modesto González *et al.* Documentación y análisis de Silvia Citro. Buenos Aires: Univ. de Buenos Aires, Facultad de Filosofía y Letras, Instituto de Lingüística, 2006. 173 p.: bibl., ill. (Col. Nuestra América. Serie Documentos)

Description of the ritual cycle of the Mocoví, includes data on the music, dances, and rituals. Focuses on a feast called "30 de agosto" and analyzes how this was practiced and how it constitutes a marker of Mocoví ethnicity and a way of congregating dispersed communities. Important contribution to an understudied group. [SMH]

619 Gómez, Mariana Daniela. Las formas de interacción con el monte de las mujeres tobas. (*Rev. Colomb. Antropol.*, 44:2, 2008, p. 373–408)

Author focuses on Toba women's knowledge of the bush and their food-gathering practices. By resorting to the notion of embodiment, the author explains how women perceive, experience, act, and relate to the bush as part of a knowledge system that is socially and culturally transmitted, marked by gender, age, and ethnic differences. Contributes to the scarce literature on gender in lowland areas. [SMH]

620 Gorosito Kramer, Ana María. Liderazgos guaraníes: breve revisión histórica y nuevas notas sobre la cuestión. (*Avá,* 9, agosto 2006, p. 11–27, bibl.)

Author describes the traditional forms of Guaraní leadership, and how the imposition of new forms of leadership give rise to internal conflicts in the communities. The emergence of new leaders is linked to external intervention and resources from state agencies, NGOs, the Church, etc. However, new leaders lack leadership qualities held to be legitimate by the community, but are able to channel minimal external resources. [SMH]

621 Hirsch, Silvia María. El pueblo tapiete de Argentina: historia y cultura. Buenos Aires: Univ. de Buenos Aires, Facultad de Filosofía y Letras, Instituto de Lingüística, 2006. 143 p. (Col. Nuestra América)

Ethnography of the Tapiete of Argentina includes an ethnohistorical description of the origins of the group, the process of migration to Argentina, their work on the sugar-cane plantations, conversion to Pentecostalism, and settlement in an urban community. Contributes to the scarce ethnographic data on this group. [SMH]

Lehm Ardaya, Zulema. Bolivia: estrategias, problemas y desafíos en la gestión del territorio indígena Sirionó. See item **1169.**

622 Lengua, cultura e historia mocoví en Santa Fe. Textos de Teresa Coria *et al.* Documentación y análisis de Beatriz Gualdieri y Silvia Citro, con la colaboración de María Hellemeyer y Marta Krasan. Buenos Aires: Instituto de Lingüística, Facultad de Filosofía y Letras, Univ. de Buenos Aires, 2006. 238 p.: bibl., ill. (some col.). (Serie Documentos. Col. Nuestra America)

Ethnographic and linguistic study of the Mocoví Indians of Argentina. Based on ethnographic, archival, and oral history research, this book contributes to the scarce bibliography on this group. Includes a sociolinguistic description and texts in Mocoví and Spanish. [SMH]

623 Liderazgo, representatividad y control social en el Gran Chaco. Recopilación de José Braunstein et Norma Meichtry. Corrientes, Argentina: Editorial Universitaria de la Univ. Nacional del Nordeste, 2008. 313 p.: bibl., ill., maps.

Consists of 19 articles addressing different forms of representation of political and religious leadership in the Gran Chaco region. Introductory essay by Braunstein reviews concepts and categories of leadership among Chaco Indians, including a typology of different leadership roles in relation with the sociopolitical and kinship organization of the groups. Contributes to the study of political systems and the process of continuity and change of leadership roles. [SMH]

624 Mala guerra: los indígenas en la Guerra del Chaco, 1932–1935. Recopilación de Nicolas Richard. Asunción: ServiLibro: Museo del Barro; Paris: CoLibris, 2008. 421 p.: bibl., ill., maps.

Excellent collection of articles on the impact of the Chaco War between Bolivia and Paraguay (1932–35) on indigenous peoples of Bolivia, Argentina, and Paraguay. Includes an introductory essay that critiques the absence of native peoples in the ethnographic record and reviews the literature on the war. The articles address the consequences of the war for indigenous peoples, particularly on their social and political organization, and the relationship with the army and the nation-state. [SMH]

625 Mujeres indígenas en la Argentina: cuerpo, trabajo y poder. Coordinación de Silvia María Hirsch. Textos de Guadalupe Barúa et al. Buenos Aires: Editorial Biblos, 2008. 254 p.: bibl., ill., maps. (Culturalia) (Desde América)

Edited volume on indigenous women in Argentina, based on articles written by anthropologists working among a wide range of groups (Toba, Wichi, Mbya, Mapuche and Guaraní). Articles explore reproduction, cultural construction of womanhood, socialization of indigenous children, work, and gender relations. Important contribution to an understudied area of research. [SMH]

626 Saignes, Thierry. Historia del pueblo chiriguano. Compilación, introducción y notas de Isabelle Combès. Lima: Instituto Francés de Estudios Andinos; La Paz: Embajada de Francia en Bolivia: Plural

Editores, 2007. 332 p.: bibl., ill., maps. (Travaux de l'Institut français d'études andines; 226)

Collection of previously published essays on the Chiriguano of Bolivia by ethnohistorian Saignes, compiled and annotated by Combès. The chapters reflect Saignes' primary areas of research: mestizaje, Jesuit and Franciscan missions, war, identity, and ethnic borders. Provides in-depth analysis into the main issues addressed by Saignes in his thorough reading of historical sources. [SMH]

627 Spadafora, Ana María and Marina Matarrese. Cambios territoriales y conocimiento medioambiental entre los pilagá, Chaco central. (*Ankulegi*, 11, 2007, p. 101–119)

Authors review and critique cultural ecology studies which analyze the relationship between nature and culture. Article addresses the case of the Pilaga Indians of Argentina, their changing use of their environment, and their link to the pressures of the surrounding society. [SMH]

628 Stearman, Allyn MacLean et al. Stradivarius in the jungle: traditional knowledge and the use of "black beeswax" among the Yuquí of the Bolivian Amazon. (*Hum. Ecol.*, 36:2, April 2008, p. 149–159, bibl., graphs, table)

Article investigates the use of so-called black beeswax among the Yuquí of the Bolivian Amazon to fletch their hunting arrows. This intriguing study explores the special properties of the wax-resin cerumen, which is derived from stingless bees (Meliponini), and serves as a superb arrow cement. Authors discuss Yuquí formulation and application of wax-resin to arrows, as well as the results of infra-red spectroscopy

comparison of cooked and raw samples of cerumen. Essay concludes by exploring the deleterious impact global forces have had on the retention of Yuquí's "traditional" knowledge system. However, the customary knowledge surrounding arrow cement continues to survive, due in part to the tourist market for Yuquí bows and arrows. For geography specialist's comment, see item **1179**. [BD]

629 Torres, Graciela F.; Mirta E. Santoni; and Liliana N. Romero. Los Wichi del Chaco Salteño: ayer y hoy: alimentación y nutrición. Salta, Argentina: Crisol Ediciones, 2007. 389 p., 3 leaves of plates: bibl., ill. (some col.), maps.

Thorough study of the foodstuffs collected and consumed by the Wichi of northern Argentina. Includes oral accounts of hunting and gathering and fishing practices as well as knowledge on plants and animals. Describes foods consumed during different life cycles (menstruation, pregnancy) and a study of the nutritional status of several communities. [SMH]

630 Wright, Pablo Gerardo. Ser-en-el-sueño: crónicas de historia y vida toba. Buenos Aires: Editorial Biblos, 2008. 270 p.: bibl., ill. (some col.), 1 map. (Culturalia)

An insightful anthropological and historical study on the way of life of the Toba Indians of Argentina, focusing on historical memory, the role of the state in constructing the Indian identity, cosmology and religious conversion, and dreams as a realm of experience. By resorting to reflexivity, the author examines the ways in which ethnographic fieldwork among indigenous peoples in Argentina is constituted and how intersubjectivity influences the ethnographer. [SMH]

Highlands

ANDREW ORTA, *Associate Professor of Anthropology, University of Illinois at Urbana-Champaign*

THE SELECTION OF WORKS FOR THIS SECTION of the *Handbook* reflects the complementarity of two recently established trends in regional ethnography. On the one hand are studies documenting the unfolding impact of a set of coordinated processes deriving from democratization, neoliberal economic and political reforms, as well as burgeoning indigenous movements in all of the Andean nations. On the other hand is the increasing representation of indigenous scholars engaged in research that documents and often participates in these developments.

Recent years have seen the publication of subtle ethnographies of now advanced neoliberal societies. Side-by-side, these works set in relief some of the comparative dimensions of turn-of-the-century developments in the region. Gustafson's excellent monograph, focused on bilingual education in Bolivia, points to themes of education and literacy as spaces for the unfolding of interculturalism and related forms of cultural decolonization (item **639**; see also item **636**). Informative assessments of decades of sociopolitical changes, often linked to shifting models of local participation in development planning, are available for Bolivia (item **640**), Ecuador (item **656**), and Peru (items **661** and **665**). The positioning and repositioning of indigenous territorial claims and practices in new national policy contexts concerned with the management of national environmental and cultural resources is evident in cases from Colombia (item **647**) and Peru (item **660**). Other studies annotated here examine the history of indigenous political mobilization in contexts of shifting state policies fostering official multiculturalism (items **632, 643, 645,** and **646**).

The best of these studies begin to unsettle classical binary constructions of top-down state power and indigenous resistance. Zapata (item **646**), for instance, draws attention to a "new Indian subject" in Chile, positioned as an engaged national citizen (see also item **633**). Gustafson similarly complicates critical dismissals of official multiculturalisms as co-opting indigenous rights movements, suggesting that the compromises and partial victories achieved by his Guarani consultants working within the parameters of the Bolivian educational reform should be seen not as a failure to escape from the state, but rather as steps toward an alternative Guarani imagining of the Bolivian state. The flexibility of indigenous institutions across a range of social, political, and economic environments throughout the history and geography of the Andean region remains a salient regionalist lesson today (items **631** and **640**). Colloredo-Mansfeld's re-examination of the highlands "community" is a particularly notable contribution to this discussion (item **649**).

In a similar way, some of the studies work to complicate long-standing racial and ethnic binaries that have defined much of highlands ethnography. Barragán (item **634**) and De la Cadena (item **659**) each return to the complex category of "mestizo." Working in La Paz, Bolivia, Barragán suggests a resignification of the category to coordinate with shifting rural-urban connections and the intensifying salience of the urban milieu as the primary point of reference for a range of socioeconomic identities. Writing in a more genealogical vein, De la Cadena unpacks the category of mestizo in Peru to reveal the accretion of competing conceptualizations of mestizaje deriving from colonial and republican periods. In the tensions between these understandings of mestizaje, she argues, are spaces for alternative mestizo subject positions.

A related development, evident in these selections, is a shift in ethnographic focus toward other actors in the region and to spaces of cultural activity beyond rural communities or peri-urban contexts. Lyons (item **652**) and Goudsmit (item **638**) address the history and contemporary circumstances of *hacendados* in Ecuador and Bolivia, respectively, illuminating the ways in which rural social hierarchy and privilege have been reproduced and transformed in different historical periods. (For another record of hacienda life, see item **654**.) Goodale's ethnography of legal practices examines provincial professional elite in Norte de Potosí, Bolivia (item **637**). His ethnography takes up challenging questions concerning the universalism of discourses of legal rights also pursued in an Ecuadorian context by Clavero (item **648**). In different ways, Broad and Orlove, Gustafson, Jackson and Ramírez, and Vergara each address national and transnational policy-makers as historically and culturally embedded actors in the region.

In their study of the 1997–98 El Niño event, Broad and Orlove analyze a range of representations in the Peruvian media of a global climate phenomena (item **658**). In this effort, they join other works in this selection in an ethnographic focus on media. Garcés (item **636**) analyzes a Quechua language newspaper and the politics of literacy and orality in Bolivia (see also item **644**). Schiwy (item **641**) focuses on indigenous video production, examining the ways in which these expressive media create new spaces for indigenous modes of storytelling and knowledge transmission.

A final thread to be highlighted in these introductory remarks is a turn—in some cases a return—to highly local and even intimate contexts of highland life. I note here some classical ethnographic themes, such as mortuary practices (items **635** and **650**), as well as a number of works in this selection focused on household level activities. Lozano (item **663**), for instance, examines household level economic strategies, and Bolin (item **657**) offers an ethnography of child rearing practices. This last theme is developed in additional ways by the work of Leinaweaver (item **662**) and Walmsley (item **655**) on the circulation and adoption of children across households in Peru and Ecuador, respectively, as well as Roberts' study of the cultural politics of cryogenic embryo storage in *in vitro* fertilization clinics in Ecuador (item **654**). As these works powerfully demonstrate, the intimate spaces of life in the highlands are far from insular. And, lest we think these new directions in research reflect radically new dimensions of life in the region, two life histories of indigenous women (items **654** and **656**) help us to keep in focus a long history of engagement and transformation across multiple sites in the highlands.

GENERAL

631 Korovkin, Tanya. Indigenous movements in the Central Andes: community, class, and ethnic politics. (*Lat. Am. Caribb. Ethn. Stud.*, 1:2, Sept. 2006, p. 143–163, bibl.)

Comparative examination focused on indigenous movements in Bolivia, Ecuador, and Peru, drawing principally from other published sources. Core argument is that longstanding and intertwined issues of class and ethnicity have found different forms of expression under the banners of 20th-century "peasant" politics and in the contemporary contexts of political democracy and economic neoliberalism. A correlated argument concerning the continuing salience of indigenous territorial community is suggestive but undeveloped.

Olsen, Dale Alan. The chrysanthemum and the song: music, memory, and identity in the South American Japanese diaspora. See *HLAS 64:2615.*

632 Quijano, Aníbal. Estado-nación y "movimientos indígenas" en la región andina: cuestiones abiertas. (*Obs. Soc. Am. Lat.*, 7:19, enero/abril 2006, p. 15–24, photos)

Brief comparative examination of the state of indigenous political mobilization in Ecuador, Peru and, with slightly more detail, Bolivia. The challenges of indigenous political participation and various projects to construct pluricultural or plurinational nations are considered in the light of continuing forms of socioeconomic domination that the author considers to be integral to the relatively uncontested framework of the nation-state.

633 Seminario Regional "Participación Política, Democracia y Movimientos Indígenas en los Andes," La Paz, Bolivia, 2003. Participación política, democracia y movimientos indígenas en los Andes. La Paz: Fundación PIEB: Embajada de Francia; Instituto Francés de Estudios Andinos (IFEA), 2005. 181 p.: bibl., ill. (Actes & memoires; 2)

A collection of 11 chapters ranging from brief academic papers to transcripts of remarks by local indigenous leaders discussing contemporary indigenous movements in the Andes. Cases are drawn from Bolivia, Ecuador, Colombia, and Peru, though seven of the 11 chapters deal with Bolivia. Many of the chapters share a focus on recent experiences of empowerment and participation in local and national governance.

ARGENTINA

Giraudo, Silvia and Patricia Arenas. Científicos europeos en el altiplano boliviano-argentino: antropología, expediciones y fotos. See *HLAS 64:1363.*

BOLIVIA

634 Barragán Romano, Rossana. Más allá de lo mestizo, más allá de lo aymara: organización y representaciones de clase y etnicidad en La Paz. (*Am. Lat. Hoy/Salamanca*, 43, agosto 2006, p. 107–130, bibl., graphs, map, tables)

A rethinking of ethnic and class identities in the urban context of La Paz based upon surveys and interviews with market and street vendors. Building upon an informative description of the day-to-day associational milieu of urban street vendors, including social hierarchies and organization structures of the the multiple vendors' associations, the article focuses on vendors' perceptions of different class and ethnic identities. Overlapping and generally favorable traits associated with the "middle" class and the "popular" class and generally negative characterization of the "poor" and the "rich" (including a category of "rich Aymara" understood by urban vendors to reside in rural areas) undergird the main argument that social identifications such as "mestizo," which have classically been understood with reference to putatively stable

rural identities and national cultural projects, have been resignified in the current Bolivian context to reflect an intermediate position in a spectrum of socioeconomic identities.

635 Fernández Juárez, Gerardo. *Apxatas de difuntos en el altiplano aymara de Bolivia.* (*Rev. Esp. Antropol. Am.,* 36:1, 2006, p. 165–182, bibl., photos)

Close examination of rituals commemorating the dead in Aymara communities in the vicinity of Lake Titicaca. After a cursory review of some colonial sources, the author focuses on altars constructed to receive the souls of the dead during All Souls rites. The construction of the altars, the activities around them linking grieving families, visitors and ritual specialists, and the decomposition of the altar are described in detail to support an analysis keyed on the structural boundaries represented by the altar and the potential abundance associated with the dead and experienced by other participants through eating and drinking over the course of the rites.

636 Garcés V., Luis Fernando. De la voz al papel: la escritura quechua del periódico *CONOSUR ñawpaqman.* Cochabamba, Bolivia: CENDA; La Paz: Plural, 2005. 210 p.: bibl., ill.

Taking the case of a Quechua language newspaper (the *CONOSUR ñawpaqman*) that began publication in the early 1980s, this book documents an evolving effort to create a written register of Quechua oral culture. The work spans discussions of the politics of literacy and orality, the sociolinguistics of contemporary Bolivian Quechua, and recent political history of Bolivian social movements to contextualize the goals and practices of the newspaper and its relation to its readers. Includes numerous textual examples from the paper.

Giraudo, Silvia and Patricia Arenas. Científicos europeos en el altiplano boliviano-argentino: antropología, expediciones y fotos. See *HLAS 64:1363.*

637 Goodale, Mark. Dilemmas of modernity: Bolivian encounters with law and liberalism. Stanford, Calif.: Stanford Univ. Press, 2009. 245 p.: bibl., ill., index, maps.

Theoretically ambitious ethnography of law in Bolivia, approaching law as a vaguely defined set of discourses and practices participating in an ever emergent Bolivian modernity. The interplay of Bolivian legal practices and institutions, discourses of law deriving from transnational organizations, and more quotidian senses of law for everyday Bolivians is part of the situation being examined here. Fieldwork in Sacaca yields a number of interesting observations about town life in the area of Northern Potosí, but little detailed ethnography to anchor the diffuse framing of the problem.

638 **Goudsmit, Into A.** Exploiting the 1953 agrarian reform: landlord persistence in northern Potosí, Bolivia. (*J. Lat. Am. Caribb. Anthropol.*, 13:2, Nov. 2008, p. 361–386)

Interesting reexamination of the impact of the 1953 agrarian reform, focusing on the area of Northern Potosi, Bolivia. At a moment when the Bolivian state has been creating new opportunities for rural communities to establish juridical personhood with recognized territorial rights, the author observes that this process in Northern Potosi is benefiting local landlords. This is the point of departure for an examination of the limited results of the 1953 reforms, routinely hailed as displacing the landlord class in places like this. A historical review of the region underscores the interdependence of rural landlords and indigenous ayllu communities of the region. This not only made the structural change of the reforms difficult to implement completely, but it also created new opportunities for landlords to reproduce their dominance in the post-1953 context.

639 **Gustafson, Bret Darin.** New languages of the state: indigenous resurgence and the politics of knowledge in Bolivia. Durham, N.C.: Duke Univ. Press, 2009. 331 p.: bibl., ill., index, maps. (Narrating native histories)

A subtle and illuminating ethnography of the interactions and intersections of grassroots and official projects of interculturalism in Bolivia. The primary case is the Guarani and various initiatives and experiences linked to bilingual intercultural education. Field research spans Guarani

communities, rural school rooms, and the offices of the Ministry of Education in La Paz. For political scientist's comment, see item 1654.

Lazar, Sian. El Alto, rebel city: self and citizenship in Andean Bolivia. See item 1660.

Postero, Nancy Grey. Now we are citizens: indigenous politics in postmulticultural Bolivia. See item 1669.

640 **Raqaypampa: una experiencia de control territorial; crisis agrícola y soberanía alimentaria.** Coordinación Jhonny Limbert Ledezma Rivera y Gonzalo Vargas. Cochabamba, Bolivia: Centro de Comunicación y Desarrollo Andino, 2005. 210 p.: bibl., col. ill.

Multifaceted study of the Indigenous District of Raqaypampa in Mizque province of the Department of Cochabamba. In part a chronicle of two decades of local sociopolitical changes, in part a presentation of a series of statistical snapshots comparing agricultural productive practices at the household and regional levels in 1986, 2003 and, for some data sets, in the late 1990s, the book presents a case study of the community and household level impacts of a series of challenges to people in the region stemming from droughts, population pressure, and the decentralizing of many state functions over this period. Limited summary analysis documents the flexibility of indigenous institutions for the control of territory and management of economic practices, and underscores a set of continuing challenges for the people of Raqaypampa. More than 100 tables and graphs.

641 **Schiwy, Freya.** Indigenous media and the end of the lettered city. (*J. Lat. Am. Cult. Stud.*, 17:1, March 2008, p. 23–40, photos)

Focusing on indigenous media in Bolivia, and particularly through an analysis of a representative video production, this essay argues that such expressive practices create spaces for indigenous modes of storytelling and knowledge transmission, and so unsettle simplistic oppositions that rigidly contrast the lettered sophistication of modern expressive genres with rural indigeneity. Rather than signaling its end, such practices are presented as compelling a new understanding of the "lettered city."

CHILE

Bengoa, José. La memoria olvidada: historia de los pueblos indígenas de Chile. See *HLAS 64:325.*

642 González P., José Antonio. Los pueblos originarios en el marco del desarrollo de sus derechos. (*Estud. Atacameños,* 30, 2005, p. 79–90)

Review of the history of state indigenous policy in Chile from independence through the 1990s, contextualizing a recent focus on indigenous rights in post-1989 Chile with respect to a longer state project that has, at certain times, pursued a comparable vision of juridical equality for indigenous Chilean citizens.

643 Haughney, Diane. Neoliberal economics, democratic transition, and Mapuche demands for rights in Chile. Gainesville: Univ. Press of Florida, 2006. 310 p.: bibl., index.

Examines the shifting position of Mapuche political movements in the context of the post-1990 transition from dictatorship in Chile, focusing on the ways the neoliberal social and economic models of the Concertación government compelled new political strategies and goals on the part of Mapuche. Chapters focused on the Mapuche movement from the early 20th century and during the Pinochet dictatorship set the stage for a closer examination of struggles over the Concertación government's Indigenous Law of 1993. A set of case studies, focused principally on conflicts over environmental and territorial rights, illustrates emerging alliances and strategies of mobilization as well as the tensions between Mapuche demands for collective rights and the "individualistic political values" reinforced by a neoliberal policy environment.

644 Mamani Morales, Juan Carlos. Los rostros del aymara en Chile: el caso de Parinacota. La Paz: Plural Editores: PINSEIB: PROEIB Andes, 2005. 245 p.: bibl., ill.

Sociolinguistic study of Aymara speakers in two communities of northern Chile, one more closely tied to urban centers, the other more remote and characterized by a smaller population. Core of the study is a fine-grained description of levels of Aymara use among differently positioned speakers, the different contexts in which Aymara is used, and the pragmatic functions of different uses of the Aymara language. These data, along with a discussion of the factors contributing to the diminishing use of Aymara, present a rich portrait of the Aymara as a minority language group in contemporary Chile.

645 Vergara, Jorge Iván; Hans Gundermann; and Rolf Foerster. Legalidad y legitimidad: Ley Indígena, Estado chileno y pueblos originarios, 1989–2004. (*Estud. Sociol./México,* 24:71, mayo/agosto 2006, p. 331–361, bibl.)

Thoughtful analysis of the unfolding of indigenous policy within the process of redemocratization in Chile since 1990. The authors reject polemical/strawman views of indigenous policy as either threatening the integrity of the Chilean nation state or coopting indigenous social movements through a superficial official multiculturalism, suggesting that these frame the problem as a struggle between two abstractions. Instead, the authors offer a close reading of a Chilean indigenous policy and the actors and institutions involved in its making, to understand policy as the contingent outcome of the work of historically embedded actors.

646 Zapata S., Claudia. Atacameños y aymaras: el desafío de la "verdad histórica." (*Estud. Atacameños,* 27, 2004, p. 169–187)

Examines the work of Chile's "Historical Truth and New Deal Commission," focusing on the politics of history. The discussion turns on the tension between the discourse of "historical truth" and a rhetoric of ethnic revindication that, the author argues, overlooks the complexities of Aymara and Atacameño engagement with Chilean citizens, who have attempted to assert a more coherent and discrete "new Indian subject." Includes a review of Chilean indigenous policies and practices and analysis of excerpts of the Commission's documents.

COLOMBIA

647 Jackson, Jean E. and María Clemencia Ramírez. Traditional, transnational, and cosmopolitan: the Colombian Yanacona look to the past and to the future.

(*Am. Ethnol./Washington*, 36:3, Aug. 2009, p. 521–544)

A thick description of a conflict in southwestern Colombia involving Yanacona, the Colombian government, and organizations responsible for the management of a UNESCO-recognized Archeological Park. The events of 2006–07 involved an occupation of a portion of the park, the construction of a road and a communal house, and a series of protests and meetings at which various sides voiced their claims and interests. The article contextualizes the position of the Yanacona, who have recently established formal recognition as an indigenous group in Colombia. The analysis addresses the assertion of multiple notions of indigeneity by indigenous groups as they mobilize in encounters and conflicts with state and transnational actors.

ECUADOR

648 **Clavero, Bartolomé.** Antropologías normativas y derechos humanos: ¿multiculturalismo constituyente en el Ecuador? (*Rev. Vasca Adm. Pública*, 74, enero/abril 2006, p. 103–141)

Thoughtful reflection on the tension between universal ideals of human rights and cultural particularity, taking the situation of Ecuador and the 1998 Ecuadorian Constitution as a point of departure. What does it mean to have a right to a collective, cultural identity? The author finds little guidance in the national constitution, nor in the United Nations Universal Declaration of Human Rights, which too often position culture as a resource of national or universal patrimony. The appeal instead is for a more robust sense of culture as anchored in communities which are the spaces of meaningful socialization and interactions of individual subjects.

649 **Colloredo-Mansfeld, Rudolf Josef.** Fighting like a community: Andean civil society in an era of Indian uprisings. Chicago, Ill.: Univ. of Chicago Press, 2009. 233 p.: bibl., ill., index, maps.

A rich ethnography of contemporary indigenous social movements in the Ecuadorian highlands wedded to a rethinking of "community" in the Andes. Examining two Ecuadorian cases, the author presents rural communities as at once sites and sources of conflicts and as institutions for managing such tensions, sites for the achievement of coordinated action that in certain circumstances can be scaled up and linked to broader frames of action and identity.

650 **Corr, Rachel.** Death, dice and divination: rethinking religion and play in South America. (*J. Lat. Am. Caribb. Anthropol.*, 13:1, April 2008, p. 2–21)

Detailed discussion of funeral wakes in Salasaca, Ecuador, focusing on ritual games. Rich connection to comparative material from elsewhere in the Andes and beyond. Useful for a wealth of ethnographic details and an informed comparative overview.

651 **DeTemple, Jill.** (Re)production zones: mixing religion, development and desire in rural Ecuadorian households. (*J. Lat. Am. Caribb. Anthropol.*, 13:1, April 2008, p. 115–140)

Wide ranging rethinking of the highland Ecuadorian/Andean household. Core of the argument concerns the complexity of the highland household as a production zone integrating different local and trans-local discourses and a range of positioned subjects. This complicates representations of the household in the discourses of development and evangelization (and academic anthropology), and establishes the household as a potent site to examine the intersection of multiple influences in highland life. Expansive ambitions of the article limit the detailed pursuit of any single theme.

652 **Lyons, Barry J.** Remembering the hacienda: religion, authority, and social change in highland Ecuador. Austin: Univ. of Texas Press, 2006. 350 p.: bibl., ill., index, maps. (Joe R. and Teresa Lozano Long series in Latin American and Latino art and culture)

Rich historical ethnography examining hacienda life in Chimborazo, Ecuador, between 1880 and 1962. Detailed oral historical interviews support a nuanced analysis focused on a complex social field encompassing indigenous laborers, overseers, the Catholic Church (which owned the hacienda), and a string of renters who operated the hacienda over the years. A brief concluding section takes up land reform, the emergence of liberation theology, and ethnic resurgence in the region.

653 Roberts, Elizabeth F.S. Extra embryos: the ethics of cryopreservation in Ecuador and elsewhere. (*Am. Ethnol./ Washington*, 34:1, Jan. 2008, p. 181–199)

A fine study of regionally varying ethical orientations to the cryopreservation of human embryos in Quito and Guayaquil. Based upon field research with staff and patients in in-vitro fertilization clinics, the article contrasts the attitudes manifest in Guayaquil, where the preference is to cryopreserve extra embryos, citing Catholic ethical teachings about embryos as a form of human life, with those in Quito, where the preference is to destroy embryos rather than freeze them. The Quiteño logic is grounded in an orientation to the embryo as potential kin, with cryopreservation seen as a form of abandonment more lamentable than the destruction of the embryonic "child."

654 Rodas Morales, Raquel. Dolores Cacuango: gran líder del pueblo indio. Quito: Banco Central del Ecuador, 2005. 179 p.: bibl., ill., index. (Biografías ecuatorianas; 3)

Celebratory biography of Dolores Cacuango, a leader and organizer of indigenous communities in Ecuador through much of the 20th century. Drawing upon interviews with family and associates, archival and published materials, as well some recorded reflections by Cacuango herself, the work traces her early life experiences on an hacienda near Cayambe, her emergence as an indigenous leader and founder of the Federación Ecuatoriana de Indios, and other achievements. An informative vantage on key moments in 20th century Ecuadorian history through the experiences of a history-making indigenous leader.

655 Walmsley, Emily. Raised by another mother: informal fostering and kinship ambiguities in Northwest Ecuador. (*J. Lat. Am. Caribb. Anthropol.*, 13:1, April 2008, p. 168–195)

A study of child circulation in the city of Esmeraldas. Recognizing a variety of types of informal fostering, the discussion details the ways in which new bonds of connectedness are forged between children and foster families as well as the continuing relevance of consanguineal links to biological mothers.

656 Yáñez del Pozo, José. Mi nombre ha de vivir: y yo me he de ir a mi destino (Tránsito Amaguaña), género, producción y aprendizaje intercultural en los pueblos andinos. Quito: CEDERENA: Abya Yala: Asociación Agroartesanal "Tránsito Amaguaña": GEF: UNDP, 2005. 175 p.: bibl., ill.

Interesting evaluation of a local agricultural development project in the community of Chimba, near Cayambe, Ecuador, twining together three different discussions. One concerns a description of the various agricultural activities undertaken by a local women's organization with particular attention to gendered productive practices and the implications for local indigenous categories of changing agricultural practices. A second is an evaluation of the intercultural dimensions of the project based upon reflections on the interactions between local women and a group of university-trained technical advisors who worked with them. The third strand is a brief life history a local woman, Tránsito Amaguaña, whose story reflects the struggles of indigenous communities in the region, and particularly of indigenous women in these communities, against domination from haciendas and for autonomous development. The local women's organization featured here is named in honor of Amaguaña.

PERU

657 Bolin, Inge. Growing up in a culture of respect: child rearing in highland Peru. Austin: Univ. of Texas Press, 2006. 214 p.: bibl., index.

A richly detailed, somewhat idealized, ethnography of childhood and child rearing in the highlands herding community of Chillihuani, Department of Cuzco, Peru. From conception and contraception, childbirth and infancy, through adolescence, the discussion focuses on embedded experiences of family, community, and traditions of respect as these contribute to the formation of confident, caring, and curious children and young adults. The thrust of the argument is to contrast these data with practices and results of child rearing in the US and with stereotypes of highlands herders in Peru; engagement with other literature on child rearing is minimal.

658   Broad, Kenneth and **Ben Orlove.** Channeling globality: the 1997–98 El Niño climate event in Peru. (*Am. Ethnol./ Washington,* 34:2, May 2007, p. 285–302)

Examines the early forecasts and detection of the 1997–98 El Niño and the responses of the Peruvian state, the media, and sectors of the public. Taking the climate event and its status as an object of international scientific scrutiny as a global phenomenon, the authors are interested in the country-level activities of different Peruvian actors (in particular then-President Alberto Fujimori) as the global event takes on meaning in more regional and local contexts. There is a thoughtful discussion of other literature on globalization and its local articulations, to which the authors want to add the metaphor of "channeling."

Bunker, Stephen G. The snake with golden braids: society, nature, and technology in Andean irrigation. See *HLAS 64:1301.*

659   Cadena, Marisol de la. Are mestizos hybrids?: the conceptual politics of Andean identities. (*J. Lat. Am. Stud.,* 37:2, May 2005, p. 259–284)

A genealogical revisiting of the concept of mestizaje and the identity position mestizo, focusing on the uneasy accretion of colonial discourses of hybridity anchored in universalist Christian beliefs and 19th-century "scientific" discourses of race and policies aimed at ameliorating indigenous racial difference through the production of mestizos through education. Within the tensions of this official and hybrid orientation to mestizaje, argues the author, can be found complex spaces for alternative mestizo subject positions.

660   Kent, Michael. The making of customary territories: social change at the intersection of state and indigenous territorial politics on Lake Titicaca, Peru. (*J. Lat. Am. Caribb. Anthropol.,* 13:2, Nov. 2008, p. 283–310)

Multifaceted discussion of emerging territorial claims by Uros living on the shores of Lake Titicaca in the vicinity of Puno, Peru. The author evokes a dynamic sociopolitical field involving Uros, other lakeshore communities, and agents of the Peruvian state including specialists managing the region as part of a national biological reserve. The shifting, and sometimes violent relations among these groups reflect different claims of territorial legitimacy and customary or ancestral use in a region that has long been shared and marked by flexible, permeable borders. Tourism clearly plays a role in these shifting and contentious territorial practices, but it is mentioned only in passing in this discussion.

661   Landa Vásquez, Ladislao. Waqamuwanku haykumuyku Nos llaman y entramos: los modos de participación en el espacio rural: Cusco y Apurímac. Lima: Instituto de Estudios Peruanos, 2004. 153 p.: bibl. (Serie Estudios de la sociedad rural; 27)

An ethnography of local rural democracy focusing on three cases of "concertación"—local planning involving systematic participation of citizen groups—from the departments of Cuzco and Apurimac. An early chapter is devoted to specifying the concept of concertación as a specific mode of governance, linking local government offices (e.g., mayor) and NGOs in an orientation to establishing new kinds of participatory relationships with civil society, and reviewing some of the obstacles to achieving this in the rural Peruvian context. Brief case studies include summary overviews of the case, critical analysis, along with observations of specific activities, such as meetings. The discussions include excerpts from interviews with participants.

662   Leinaweaver, Jessaca B. On moving children: the social implications of Andean child circulation. (*Am. Ethnol./ Washington,* 34:1, Jan. 2008, p. 163–180)

Discusses the circulation of children across different family households as a practice that creates and strengthens connections of kinship while also creating benefits for the child and participating households. Focusing on a few cases from Ayacucho, Peru, the practices are placed in historical context by noting that the violence of the conflict with Sendero Luminoso displaced many people and created a new social geography for child circulation. Orphanages, some participating in transnational adoption networks, have become a new component in this system of child circulation.

663 Lozano, Marco. Elementos para una clasificación de estrategias familiares campesinas en el alto Tambopata. (*Debate Agrar.*, 40/41, julio 2006, p. 85–98)

A sketchy examination of economic strategies pursued by peasant families in northeastern Puno, Peru. In an area characterized primarily by commercial coffee and fruit cultivation, the study looks at the ways that factors such as availability of labor through familial and social networks, dominant strategies in micro-regions in the area of study, and home-regional orientation of migrant peasant families impact strategic decisions that balance subsistence and growth for peasant producers.

Millones, Luis. Ser indio en el Perú: la fuerza del pasado; las poblaciones indígenas del Perú, costa y sierra. See *HLAS 64:353.*

Montoya, Rodrigo. De la utopía andina al socialismo mágico: antropología, historia y política en el Perú. See *HLAS 64:1338.*

664 Montoya, Rodrigo. Elogio de la antropología. Lima: Fondo Editorial de la Facultad de Ciencias Sociales UNMSM; Cusco, Peru: Instituto Nacional de Cultura, Dirección Regional de Cultura de Cusco, 2005. 492 p.: bibl., col. ill.

Written by a renowned Peruvian anthropologist, this monograph has a strong autobiographical underpinning. It is divided into three themes: 1) anthropology as a science, to understand a multilingual and multicultural reality and how anthropology relates to other disciplines and fieldwork; 2) a reading of the multilayered relationships between culture and power structure; 3) newspaper articles written by the author in response to crisis situations in the country. Seeks to identify the links between Peru's geographical and cultural sites to produce unity and autonomy. Lima is not Peru, but Peru is not Peru without Lima. [C. Hunefeldt]

665 Oré Vélez, María Teresa. Yakunchik: concertando la gestión del agua después de la violencia. (*Allpanchis/Cuzco,* 37:67, primer semestre 2006, p. 15–35)

An informative discussion of the Yakunchi Platform: an effort to coordinate the perspectives and interests of multiple stakeholder groups concerned with water management in a region of Huamanga, Peru. The author details the local contexts and challenges of environmental resource management and development and examines the interactions of state agencies, NGOs, businesses, municipalities, and representatives of indigenous communities in this process.

Salazar-Soler, Carmen. La presencia de la antropología francesca en los Andes peruanos. See item **461.**

ECONOMICS

GENERAL

LUIS RENÉ CÁCERES, *Inter-American Development Bank, Washington, DC*

666 **El área de libre comercio de las Américas (ALCA).** Coordinación de Jorge Witker. México: UNAM, 2004. 295 p. (Serie Estudios jurídicos; 62)

Collection of essays from a symposium that took place at UNAM in 2003. Papers address a wide array of topics, such as intellectual property, antidumping measures, market access, and investment rules of origin. Particularly informative are the papers on the status of the ministerial negotiations and the main issues faced, and the lessons from NAFTA to the Latin America Free Trade Area.

667 **Cáceres, Luis René.** Reforma económica, inversión y estancamiento en América Latina. (*Comer. Exter.*, 56:1, enero 2006, p. 6–65, bibl., graphs, tables)

Explains the lower economic growth rates experienced by the Latin American countries in the 1990s, compared to the previous decades, in terms of the reductions in public investment that took place since the 1980s. Explores the causality chain from public to private investment and hence to economic growth. Other explanations are formulated with respect to the role of economic openings experienced in the 1990s, which displaced domestic production, leaving little room for new private investment directed at the production of tradable goods. Concludes by presenting an argument in favor of undertaking development efforts that rely on human capital and promote social equity and justice. Includes an extensive literature review on the impact of reform on development in Latin America.

668 **Cáceres, Luis René.** Variables determinantes del índice de desarrollo humano en América Latina. (*Comer. Exter.*, 58:6, junio 2008, p. 420–430, bibl., graphs, tables)

Estimates econometric equations to quantify the determinants of the human development index in 18 Latin American countries, using cross-sectional data for the 2002–04 period. Findings indicate that the level of education, social expenditures as percentage of GDP, per capita income, and an indicator of income distribution explain a large percentage of the variance of the index of human development. Further analysis reveals that the most significant variable is the level of education. An analysis is conducted of El Salvador's index of human development at the municipal level, finding that there are patterns specific to regions, which indicates that the territory is a valid variable in the analysis of social development.

Challenges to fiscal adjustment in Latin America: the cases of Argentina, Brazil, Chile, and Mexico. See item **792.**

669 **Comisión Económica para América Latina y el Caribe (CEPAL).** Foreign investment in Latin America and the Caribbean: 2004 report. Santiago: CEPAL, 2004. 156 p.: bibl., graphs, maps, tables.

Presents an overview of direct foreign investment into Latin America and the Caribbean during 2004, covering a wide range of areas, including economic sectors, geographic location, and technology. Conducts analyses of several countries, exploring trends in foreign investment and implications for export capacity and aggregate supply. Interesting discussion of emerging transnational companies in Latin America.

670 **Coraggio, José Luis.** La gente o el capital: desarrollo local y economía del trabajo. Quito: Centro de Investigacio-

nes CIUDAD: ILDIS-FES: Abya Yala, 2004.
258 p.: bibl.

Collection of essays on sundry topics of regional and urban planning from a heterodox perspective. Topics covered include informal sector, urban solidarity, popular economy, globalization, and income distribution. Interesting discussion of principles, framework, and circuits of popular economy and of exchange networks in a framework of solidarity.

671 Daly Gimón, Carlos Eduardo. Vigencia de la conversión de deuda externa en inversión extranjera. Caracas: Comisión de Estudios de Postgrado, Facultad de Ciencias Económicas y Sociales, Univ. Central de Venezuela: Fondo Editorial Tropykos, 2002. 162 p.: bibl., ill.

Presents an overview of mechanisms designed to effect the conversion of external debt into investments in several Latin American countries during the 1980s and part of the 1990s. Several issues are analyzed, particularly the legal and inflationary implications, as well as monitoring requirements. Develops mathematical formulae to determine costs and benefits of debt conversion operations in Chile, Argentina, Mexico, and Venezuela.

672 Desarrollo de las economías rurales en América Latina y el Caribe. Recopilación de Ruben G. Echeverría. Washington: Banco Interamericano de Desarrollo, 2001. 256 p.: bibl., ill.

Collection of essays on recent approaches to rural development in Latin America. Essays are based on the premise that the economies have undergone structural reforms and are more susceptible to the international economy. The main topic is the analysis of poverty in rural areas, but also considers technology transfer, financial mechanisms, human and social capital, and land reform. Attention is given to the analysis of labor markets in the context of rural poverty reduction.

673 Evolución e impacto de la financiación de vivienda en Iberoamérica: experiencias de Argentina, Brasil, Colombia, España, México y Venezuela. Textos de Omar de Jesús Montilla Galvis et al. Cali, Colombia: Univ. del Valle, Facultad de Ciencias de la Administración: AUSBANC Internacional, 2005. 298 p.: bibl., ill.

Presents a review of the evolution of housing finance in several Latin American countries. Each country study covers the history of housing finance from colonial times to the present, and includes evaluations of financial mechanisms that have been implemented over the years, examining shortcomings and institutional aspects. Interesting discussion of impacts on housing finance resulting from devaluations, financial crisis, currency meltdowns, and globalization.

674 Financing for development in Latin America and the Caribbean. Edited by Andrés Franco. Tokyo; New York: United Nations Univ. Press, 2001. 206 p.: bibl., ill., index.

Collection of papers written under the context of the UN International Conference on Financing for Development, focusing on the particular needs of Latin American and Caribbean countries. Topics covered include flows of foreign direct investment and its determinants, particular characteristics of subregional financial institutions, determinants of country risk, and the reform of the international financial architecture. Quality is even throughout the book and analysis is timely and thought-provoking.

675 Garza Toledo, Enrique de la. La formación socioeconómica neoliberal: debates teóricos acerca de la reestructuración de la producción y evidencia empírica para América Latina. México: Univ. Autónoma Metropolitana, Unidad Iztapalapa: Plaza y Valdés, 2001. 202 p.: bibl. (Col. CSH)

Presents a review of economic theories, from the classics to the institutionalists, as the scenario for the analysis of the main currents of development thinking in Latin America, thus covering import substitution, structuralism, dependency theory, neoliberalism, and neostructuralism. Case studies of several countries are presented, emphasizing the performance of labor markets during different time periods.

676 Globalización y alternativas incluyentes para el siglo XXI. Coordinación de Jorge Basave et al. México: Porrúa, 2002. 766 p.: bibl., ill. (Col. Jesús Silva Herzog)

Collection of papers on the impact of globalization on Latin America, and particularly on Mexico. A wide variety of topics are covered, and emphasis is placed on regional economic integration, institutions and development, information technology, equity, and social development. Includes interesting discussions and proposals of appropriate economic and social policies in a post-neoliberal environment.

677 Guerrero Amparán, Juan Pablo and **Helena Hofbauer Balmori.** Transparencia presupuestaria en cinco países de América Latina: resultados en 2001. México: Miguel Angel Porrúa: Centro de Investigación y Docencia Económica, 2004. 167 p.: bibl.

Describes the methodology for setting up a mechanism to assess the transparency of central government budgets, explaining in detail aspects related to the assessment of civil society participation, auditing, monitoring, and evaluation. Applies methodology to cases studies in Chile, Brazil, Argentina, Mexico, and Peru. Provides useful and clear elements to design systems to deliver higher levels of transparency in public sector functions.

678 Inequality in Latin America: breaking with history? Washington: The World Bank, 2004. 380 p.: bibl., ill., index. (World Bank Latin American and Caribbean studies. Viewpoints)

Latin America is the region with the highest indexes of income inequality in the world. This book seeks and offers a series of explanations for this situation. Using macro- and microeconomic analyses, and resorting to history and the development of institutions, the authors identify the original factors that gave rise to inequality and the mechanisms of vicious circles that have made inequality so persistent in the region. Recommendations are presented to ameliorate high income inequality, in a framework that emphasizes the expansion of education opportunities, strengthening institutions, and promoting access to productive assets. A solid case is made that the region can "break with history."

679 Latin American macroeconomic reforms: the second stage. Edited by José Antonio González *et al.* Chicago: Univ. of Chicago Press, 2003. 442 p.: bibl., ill., indexes.

Collection of essays on Latin American countries' economic reforms enacted in the 1980s and 1990s, emphasizing the identification of reforms still pending. Among the topics covered, special relevance is taken by inflation targeting, risk management, institutional aspects of central bank independence, and tax reform. Also includes interesting country studies on the determinants of financial crises and policies for their avoidance.

680 López Valdés, José Manuel and **Francisco Jiménez Holguín.** La regulación bancaria en América Latina. Santo Domingo: Asociación de Bancos Comerciales de la República Dominicana, 2002. 194 p.: bibl.

Presents an analysis of several topics related to banking supervision and regulation in Latin America, particularly capital requirements, deposit insurance, risk management, presentation of financial results, credit risk, and portfolio diversification. Interesting cross-country comparison of capital adequacy and accounting standards.

681 Luis Socas, Jaime. Areas monetarias y convergencia macroeconómica: Comunidad Andina. Caracas: Univ. Católica Andrés Bello: Banco Central de Venezuela, 2002. 254 p.: bibl., ill.

Presents an extensive review of theories of monetary integration and examines the conditions that should be met by candidates for integration, so that the benefits of a monetary union outweigh the costs. Applies these criteria to the case of Andean countries to measure their degree of readiness for the creation of a monetary union in the region. Proposes an action plan for the harmonization of economic policies that would contribute to the successful creation of an Andean monetary union.

682 Microcrédito contra la exclusión social: experiencias de financiamiento alternativo en Europa y América Latina. Textos de Giovanni Beluche *et al.* San José: Red Aura: FLACSO Costa Rica, 2005. 268 p.: bibl., ill., map.

Presents an overview of the financing of microenterprises in several Latin American countries, with emphasis on financial instruments, organization, intermediation institutions, and development impact. Cases of microfinance lending in Italy are discussed as well, which offers a point of comparison and places the Latin American cases in an international context. Interesting analysis of Grameen Bank-type experiences in the region.

683 The microeconomics of income distribution dynamics in East Asia and Latin America. Edited by Francois Bourguignon, Francisco H.G. Ferreira, and Nora Lustig. Washington: World Bank; New York: Oxford Univ. Press, 2004. 416 p.: bibl., ill., index.

Collection of essays on three Asian and four Latin American countries (Argentina, Mexico, Colombia, and Brazil), on the determinants and changes in income distribution and poverty. Studies are of even quality and despite complexity of analytical techniques employed, presentations are clear and concise. Finds that the relevant variables in the evolution of inequality are education, place of residence, and labor force participation, particularly of women. Insightful and didactic use of microeconomics in the analysis of poverty.

684 Portocarrero Maisch, Felipe; Álvaro Tarazona Soria; and Glenn D. Westley. Cómo deberían financiarse las instituciones de microfinanzas? Lima: Instituto de Estudios Peruanos; Washington: Banco Interamericano de Desarrollo, División de Micro, Pequeña y Media Empresa, Depto. de Desarrollo Sostenible, 2006. 271 p.: bibl., ill. (Análisis económico; 23)

Collection of essays on the situation and perspectives of microfinance in Latin America, based on data and case studies from 61 microfinance institutions, mainly from Bolivia, Peru, and Paraguay. Analysis is structured around four means of funding microfinance institutions: deposits, lines of credit, issuance of bonds, and selling of equity. Offers a detailed analysis of project assessment techniques and the risks related to sector, country, and finance. Very relevant case studies on growth of operations, funding, and diversification of lending instruments.

685 Portrait of the poor: an assets-based approach. Edited by Orazio Attanasio and Miguel Székely. Washington: Inter-American Development Bank; Baltimore, Md.: Johns Hopkins Univ. Press, 2001. 266 p.: bibl., ill.

Collection of essays on the determinants of poverty in a sample of Latin American countries. Studies emphasize the contributions of productive assets in enabling households to escape—or avoid falling into—poverty, examining also the roles exerted by variables such as work experience, city of residence, age, and economic sector of employment. The role of human and social capital in the design of poverty reduction strategies is highlighted throughout the essays.

686 Prácticas prometedoras en finanzas rurales: experiencias de América Latina y el Caribe. Recopilación de Mark D. Wenner, Javier Alvarado y Francisco Galarza. Lima: Centro Peruano de Estudios Sociales; Washington: Banco Interamericano de Desarrollo; San José: Academia de Centroamérica, 2002. 401 p.: bibl., ill. (some col.).

Presents the theoretical basis for the new mechanisms and the criteria for the financing of microenterprises in the region, analyzing in detail aspects of financial deepening, asymmetric information, and financial liberalization. The analysis is placed in the context of the financial structure of specific countries. The second part of the book covers the experience of financial institutions that have been successful in assisting urban and rural microenterprises.

687 Salazar, Juan Carlos. Amenazas y oportunidades en los tratados de Libre Comercio y el ALCA: una mirada desde la ciencia y la tecnología. Bogotá: Convenio Andrés Bello, 2004. 87 p.: bibl., ill. (Papeles CAB)

After a review of the state of the art of science and technology in each of the member countries of the Convenio Andrés Bello, the author compares the countries' current capacity with the demands that would arise from the trade and technology pacts that are under consideration as part of the hemispheric trade and integration programs. Recommends the adoption of specific policies to alleviate current shortcomings and to place the countries in a better position to confront the challenges posed by closer integration links across the region.

688 Sana, Mariano and Douglas S. Massey. Household composition, family migration, and community context:

migrant remittances in four countries. (*Soc. Sci. Q.*, 86:2, June 2005, p. 509–529, bibl., tables)

Comparative study of the determinants of families receiving remittances in Mexico, Dominican Republic, Nicaragua, and Costa Rica. Finds that the principal determinant is having the male head of household living abroad, whereas a female head living abroad has no effect on the reception of remittances. A daughter residing abroad has more effect on the family receiving remittances than a son residing abroad. Interesting discussion and testing of recent theories on transnational migration based on data from these countries.

689 Seminario "El Trabajo y la Producción de la Pobreza en Latinoamérica y el Caribe: Estructura, Discursos y Actores," Santa Cruz, Bolivia, 2004. Trabajo y producción de la pobreza en América Latina. La Paz: CEDLA, Centro de Estudios para el Desarrollo Laboral y Agrario, 2004. 473 p.: bibl., ill.

Collection of essays on poverty in several Latin American countries, from the perspective of sociological theories that rest on exclusion, class, and social capital. Essays probe the causes of poverty and raise questions about the lack of social mobility in the region, and on the short term vision of public policies. In-depth analysis of the theory of Popular Economy, the implications of solidarity, as well as the economic implications of child labor.

690 Seminario Internacional sobre "Comercialización de Microfinanzas," Asunción, Paraguay, 2001. Microfinanzas: nuevas technologías crediticias en América Latina. Textos de J.D. Von Pischke *et al.* Compilación de Dionisio Borda. Asunción: Banco Central del Paraguay; Centro de Análisis y Distribución de la Economía Paraguaya, 2002. 239 p.: ill. (Serie Políticas públicas)

Collection of essays presented at an international conference on microfinance (Asunción, 2001). Topics are related to financial intermediation, regulatory framework, information systems, and technology. Most essays are based on case studies from Bolivia, Paraguay, and Uruguay, while others present surveys of specific aspects of microfinance in Latin America. Good discussion

of best practices on project analysis, preparation, and follow-up.

691 Skipper, Susan. La matriculación en la educación secundaria en América Latina: la importancia de las instituciones. (*Comer. Exter.*, 57:11, nov. 2007, p. 890–897, bibl., graphs, tables)

Presents an econometric model estimated with a cross section of Latin American countries to explain a country's secondary school enrollment as a function of education expenditures as percentage of GDP, and several indexes of institutional capacity. Finds that institutions explain a large percentage of the variance of secondary school enrollment. Shows that strengthening institutional capacity is a more efficient mechanism to increase education outcomes than relying solely on expenditures. Excellent review of the literature on the role of institutions on economic and social development.

692 Sztulwark, Sebastián. El estructuralismo latinoamericano: fundamentos y transformaciones del pensamiento económico de la periferia. Argentina: Instituto de Industria, Univ. Nacional de General Sarmiento, 2003. 123, 13 p.: bibl. (Col. Investigación. Serie Informes de investigación; 16)

Presents a review of the evolution of ECLAC's development thinking, from the early structuralism to more recent neostructuralist positions. Provides a critique of the main ideas of structuralism, such as the deterioration of terms of trade and import substitution, as well as of newer thinking associated with technological development, indicating shortcomings and comparing them to more established classical and neoclassical theories. Gives the impression that a fusion or convergence of economic theories is taking place in the region.

693 Zúñiga Quevedo, Javier. La contribución de la Corporación Andina de Fomento al desarrollo de la Comunidad Andina de Naciones. Madrid: Servicio de Publicaciones de la Univ. Autónoma de Madrid, 2003. 158 p.: bibl., ill. (Cuadernos de apoyo; 9)

Presents a review of the subregional integration process in the Andean countries from the late 1960s until 1998, covering aspects such as the negotiation of treaties, common external tariffs, and the institutional framework. The creation and development of operations of the Andean Development Corporation are also analyzed, examining the dynamism of operations, economic sectors of concentration, financial results, and resources obtained from international and regional markets. An attempt is made to quantify the impact of its operations on the generation of employment, but methodology and results are unclear.

CENTRAL AMERICA

LUIS RENÉ CÁCERES, *Inter-American Development Bank, Washington, DC*

ALL THE STUDIES WITHIN THE GENERAL SECTION cover topics related to economic integration. Cáceres (item **696**) presents an exhaustive balance of progress and constraints in the Central American economic integration program, emphasizing the institutional weaknesses that have blocked further progress. This author also provides an in-depth analysis of the economic interdependence between El Salvador and Guatemala, and concludes that their economies are so interlocked they should be considered a single economy (item **694**). The role of institutions in promoting economic integration is discussed by Cáceres (item **695**) who introduces the concept of the institutional multiplier of economic growth which results from improvements in institutions. He shows that this effect is as important as the multiplier resulting from autonomous expenditures. A final paper in this section presents an evaluation of the impacts of DR-CAFTA on each of the member countries' economies (item **697**).

Poverty is a topic that is present in the literature on several countries. In Costa Rica, Herrero *et al.* (item **701**) analyze the causes for the persistence of poverty, while Slon and Zúñiga (item **700**) describe the dynamics of poverty, finding that education is a strong anchor to prevent falling into poverty. In the case of El Salvador, Skipper (item **713**) analyzes the role of education in the determination of poverty and in promoting economic growth, while in Honduras, Fuentes (item **717**) describes the contributions of remittances to poverty reduction.

Migration is another topic that occupies an important place in this volume. In El Salvador, Cáceres (items **705** and **706**) and Cáceres and Saca (item **707**) discuss the macroeconomic impacts of remittances; Andrade-Eekhoff (item **703**) presents a broad description of migrants and the geographical destination of remittances, while Márquez, Cuéllar, and Guevara (item **709**) discuss the effects of remittances on the expansion of the services sector in El Salvador, a theme also discussed by Montesinos Castro (item **711**). For Panama, Sánchez Saavedra presents the case of internal migration among the peoples of the Darien (item **727**).

Studies on the geographical aspects of development are included in this volume. In El Salvador, Argueta (item **704**) discusses the benefits of adopting the property tax and the implications on decentralization, while Quiteño and Vega (item **712**) review the regional planning efforts undertaken in the last 10 years. The changing landscape in Panama in response to trade and investment is discussed by Castillero Calvo (item **725**).

Topics on agricultural development are presented in several countries. Fernández Alvarado and Granados Carvajal (item **699**) analyze the changes that took place in Costa Rica's agricultural sector and in its institutions resulting from the structural reforms undertaken since the 1980s, while Faure and Samper (item **698**) discuss the effects of import liberalization on agriculture. The repercussions from DR-CAFTA on agriculture in Honduras and Nicaragua are analyzed by Suazo (item **718**) and Acevedo and Vogl (item **721**), respectively. The effects of land tenure on agricultural production in Nicaragua are discussed by Bainville (item **722**) and Bandiera (item **723**).

There are four noteworthy labor market studies: Martínez (item **710**) studies the incidence of gender discrimination in the labor market and its repercussions on economic growth in El Salvador; Fuentes Garcia (item **715**) analyzes racial discrimination in Guatemala's labor market; Evangelos (item **726**) looks at determination of wages in Panama; and Van der Laat Echeverría (item **702**) analyzes the repercussion of DR-CAFTA on Costa Rica's labor market regulations.

UCA's Departamento de Economía study covers the themes of national economies and short-term economic perspectives in El Salvador (item **714**).

In contrast to previous volumes, there are few studies on micro enterprises, the industrial sector and on tourism. Reference can be made to Suriol's (item **719**) diagnostic of the petroleum sector in Honduras; Luoto, McIntosh, and Wydick's (item **716**) study of the effects of a credit information system in Guatemala; Bilbao Ercoreca's (item **724**) study of maquila established in a rural area of Nicaragua; and Schloegel's (item **728**) analysis of sustainable tourism in Panama. Two energy studies are present in this volume: Lara López's (item **708**) quantification of the benefits resulting from the privatization of the electric utilities in El Salvador and Zelaya Aguilar's (item **720**) analysis of the potential benefits of increasing hydropower generation in Honduras.

GENERAL

694 Cáceres, Luis René. Exportaciones, inversión y crecimiento económico en Centroamérica. (*Trimest. Econ.*, 74:295, julio/sept. 2007, p. 719–743, bibl., graphs, tables)
Presents a bi-national integration model for El Salvador and Guatemala, which includes the macroeconomic variables GDP, investment, and exports. Finds that significant spillover effects from El Salvador to Guatemala exist so that the former's economic variables exert significant repercussions on the latter's. The author argues that cross border macroeconomic interdependence should lead to the adoption of a coordination framework for economic and social policies, which would result in faster economic growth, higher levels of human development and greater credibility for the integration process. Extensive discussion of literature on exports and economic growth.

695 Cáceres, Luis René. Instituciones e integración económica: el caso de Centroamérica. (*Comer. Exter.*, 58:10, oct. 2008, p. 708–719, bibl., graphs, tables)

Estimates gravity equations for bilateral trade flows between the Central American countries, including among its determinants indexes of institutional capacity. It is found that these indexes are significant only for the equations representing trade with Panama, which is not a member of the integration program. Argues that economic integration among developing countries offers advantages not present in unilateral trade liberalization, since the design of national institutions can be carried out on a regional framework and according to regional consensus and timetables, so that change can be gradual, taking into consideration the national and regional contexts. Extensive review of the literature on institutions and trade, and insightful arguments on the multiplier effects exerted by institutions.

696 Cáceres, Luis René. Los retos de la integración centroamericana. (*Comer. Exter.*, 57:1, enero 2007, p. 55–68, bibl., graphs, tables)
Analyzes the evolution of Central America's integration efforts in recent

years. Describes the significant progress achieved in the commercial aspects and the weaknesses in the institutional areas. Proposes models and mechanisms to make the integration framework useful in the promotion of national social development goals and in the modernization of national and regional institutions. Interesting argument of social development as a global public good.

697 DR-CAFTA: impacto sobre sectores sociales menos favorecidos en América Central. Recopilación de Nehemías Obed López Carrión. Textos de Doris Osterlof Obregón *et al.* Managua: Fundación Friedrich Ebert, Representación en Nicaragua, 2004. 299 p.: bibl., ill.

Collection of essays, each one on the implications of CAFTA-DR on the respective country economic development perspectives. Each country study analyzes the different sector performances and identifies the variables that may impact their future development. Emphasis is placed on small industry, maquila, small scale agriculture and gender issues. Recommendations are directed to strengthening several areas, particularly human capital, labor standards and agriculture.

COSTA RICA

698 Faure, Guy and **Mario Samper.** Veinte años de apertura económica: el porvenir comprometido de la agricultura familiar en el norte de Costa Rica. (*Anu. Estud. Centroam.*, 30:1/2, 2004, p. 7–26, bibl., maps, tables)

Describes the perspectives faced by agricultural production in the Huetar Norte region, in Costa Rica's northern frontier with Nicaragua, under the constraints and opportunities resulting from import liberalization. Different scenarios are discussed, assessing their effects depending on farm size and product orientation, in both internal and external markets. Authors recommend a national policy to promote efficient use of land without sacrificing the equity gains generated by traditional forms of production.

699 Fernández Alvarado, Luis Fernando and **Rafael Evelio Granados Carvajal.** Hacia una nueva institucionalidad en Costa Rica: desafíos para el sector agropecuario. Heredia, Costa Rica: EUNA, 2002. 235 p.: bibl., ill.

Within the context of the structural reforms undertaken in Costa Rica since the 1980s, this book traces the changes undergone by the agricultural sector in terms of poverty, infrastructure, exports, and employment. It depicts the trade liberalization and privatization processes, their impact on the agricultural sector and on the public sector entities charged with the development of agriculture. Interesting overview of the evolution of sectoral institutional changes as macroeconomic changes were taking place.

700 Slon, Pablo and **Edwin Zúñiga.** Poverty dynamics in Costa Rica with panel data from cross-sections. (*CEPAL Rev.*, 89, Aug. 2006, p. 165–178, bibl., graphs, tables)

Constructs a panel of data from annual household surveys to analyze the dynamics of poverty in Costa Rica during the 2000–06 period. Finds that although the macroeconomic environment remained stable and the national poverty rate remained constant in that period, 60 percent of the poor households remained poor and 40 percent escaped poverty, while 88 percent of the non-poor households remained nonpoor and 12 percent slipped into poverty. Those who fell into poverty were identified as having low education levels, residing in rural areas, and having women as heads of household. Clear and didactic presentation of methodologies to analyze poverty dynamics.

701 Taller de Expertos para la Superación de la Pobreza Costa Rica 2005–2015, 2005. Pobreza: talón de Aquiles del desarrollo costarricense. Recopilación de Fernando Herrero Acosta y Gladys González Rodríguez. San José: Procesos, 2006. 178 p.: bibl., ill.

Costa Rica has experienced relatively low levels of poverty but this has proven to be persistent, falling only 3 percent in the 20 years between 1984–2004. This study presents a collection of essays that analyzes the causes of poverty and the reasons for its persistence. Contains proposals on conditioned transfers, regionalization, investments in infrastructure, and human capital.

Interesting analysis of how the deterioration of income distribution affects the persistence of poverty.

702 van der Laat Echeverría, Bernardo. Las obligaciones laborales del CAFTA y Costa Rica: evaluación inicial. (*Integr. Comer.*, 10:25, julio/dic. 2006, p. 171–205, bibl.)

Presents an extensive diagnostic of challenges that may be confronted by Costa Rica's judiciary sector in the event of Costa Rica entering the CAFTA-DR. The author reviews a wide sample of issues where progress has been made, as well as those where advance is still pending, mainly in the process phase of justice administration, and offers comments on how they could be resolved. Considers that CAFTA-DR's labor regulations would not run counter to existing regulations and could even strengthen them.

EL SALVADOR

703 Andrade-Eekhoff, Katharine. Mitos y realidades: el impacto económico de la migración en los hogares rurales. San Salvador: FLACSO Programa El Salvador: FundaUngo, 2003. 131 p.: bibl., ill.

Remittances represent close to 18 percent of El Salvador's GDP. This book provides information on who El Salvador's migrants are, where they originated, where they are currently located, how much they send home each month, and how the resources are used. Analyzes the social consequences of migration, especially in terms of fractured families, loss of skilled manpower, and school desertion. Good source of data on migration and remittances.

704 Argueta, Lorena. Impuesto predial y descentralización fiscal del estado. (*ECA/San Salvador*, 61: 697/698, nov./dic. 2006, p. 1181–1200, bibl., tables)

Extensive study of the property tax in El Salvador, with references to the experiences of other developed and developing countries. The benefits associated with this form of taxation are discussed in detail, particularly its incidence in preventing urban sprawl. The importance of designing a simple system for its management is stressed, as well as the need to seek consensus on the use of its revenues. Interesting discussion of fiscal decentralization in the context of the Latin American countries.

705 Cáceres, Luis René. El destino de las remesas en El Salvador. (*Comer. Exter.*, 58:1, enero 2008, p. 27–40, bibl., graphs, tables)

Investigates how and to what degree remittances contribute to the acceleration of economic growth in El Salvador. Analyzes the impact of remittances on imports, national savings, investment, and trade balance. Results indicate that, overall, the contributions of remittances are questionable. Concludes by pointing out the necessity of increasing investments in human capital, and by discussing mechanisms that could be employed to increase the amounts of remittances directed towards capital formation.

706 Cáceres, Luis René. Remesas y macroeconomía en El Salvador. (*Comer. Exter.*, 56:7, julio 2006, p. 592–607, bibl., graphs, tables)

Presents a general economic model to assess the effects of remittances on national macroeconomic variables, such as inflation, interest rate, economic growth, investment, and external accounts. Author estimates econometric equations to quantify repercussions of remittances on El Salvador's economy, finding that effects are not significant for most variables, except for a weak effect on interest rates, which may decrease the rate of economic growth. Interesting presentation of mechanisms to invest remittances in productive projects.

707 Cáceres, Luis René and **Nolvia Saca.** El mecanismo de transmisión de los efectos de las remesas en El Salvador. (*Comer. Exter.*, 56:10, oct. 2006, p. 875–885, bibl., graphs, tables)

Presents the estimation of a VAR model to analyze, for the case of El Salvador's economy, the response of money supply, inflation rate, exports, imports, and international reserves to an inflow of remittances. Results indicate that increasing remittances gives rise to increases in imports and hence to lower economic growth rate. These results could be the reflection of the high degree of openness of the economy. Recommends the adoption of policies to increase the generation of high quality human capital as the foundation of future economic development.

708 Lara López, Edgar. Impactos sociales y económicos de la privatización de la distribución de la energía eléctrica en El Salvador. San Salvador: Fundación Nacional para el Desarrollo, 2005. 69 p.: bibl., ill. (Cuaderno de análisis y propuesta / Global Policy Network y Fundación Nacional para el Desarrollo)

Presents an evaluation of the benefits resulting from the privatization of the electric utility companies in El Salvador in 1996–98. Analysis covers several areas, particularly quality of service, cost of electricity, reliability of service, and labor relations. Author concludes that results have been disappointing, but an assessment of the sector leaves out the examination of a broad range of benefits.

709 Márquez, Marielos; Amelia E. Cuéllar; and Miguel A. Guevara. Economía de remesas del trabajo: eficiencia de la racionalidad solidaria. (*ECA/San Salvador*, 61:695, sept. 2006, p. 851–867)

Presents an approach to the study of emigration and remittances in El Salvador based on family decisions and bonds of solidarity. Argues that remittances should be accounted in economic statistics as part of balance of rent, instead of being recorded as current transfers, which would provide a more precise representation of the domestic economy. Authors establish a parallel between annual increases in remittances and the changes in economic structure towards the tertiary sector. Their estimation of the multiplier of remittances on GDP is implausibly large (3.03) which may be explained by not taking into account lagged effects and leakage processes.

710 Martínez, Julia Evelin. Los retos de la competitividad de la economía salvadoreña, desde una perspectiva de género. (*ECA/San Salvador*, 60, 681/682, julio/agosto 2005, p. 593–612, bibl., photos, tables)

Describes the different ways in which gender discrimination has incidence on economic growth. Covers areas related to nonpaid household work, difficulties in obtaining credit, stereotypes about career preferences, and the devastating effects of economic recessions on women. Argues

that gender asymmetries at the workplace give rise to costs, both human and economic, whose eradication would redound in gains in competitiveness in the national economy.

711 Montesino Castro, Mario Salomón. Enfoque teórico de la economía abierta de servicios y la economía de remesas del trabajo. (*ECA/San Salvador*, 61:695, sept. 2006, p. 829–849, bibl., graphs, table)

Offers an explanation for the emigration flows from El Salvador in terms of the over-exploitation of the labor force, analyzing other points such as the role of remittances on the consumption of services and the resulting stagnation of agricultural and manufacturing sectors. Presents a discussion of the maquila sector as a manifestation of labor services instead of as a true export sector. Arguments would have been strengthened by the presentation of data and statistical verification of proposed behavior relationships.

712 Quiteño, Gloria and Lilian Vega. El territorio: del planteamiento a la práctica. (*ECA/San Salvador*, 61: 697/698, nov./dic. 2006, p. 1157–1179, bibl., graphs, map, tables)

Describes the efforts undertaken in El Salvador in the field of regional planning in the last 10 years. Looks at the institutional aspects, the financial mechanisms, the coordination instances that have been created, and the role of foreign aid. Presents a detailed discussion on the national social investment fund, the national plan for local development, and the mechanisms for joint planning by municipalities.

713 Skipper, Susan. Desarrollo del capital humano y reducción de la pobreza en El Salvador. (*Comer. Exter.*, 56:11, nov. 2006, p. 968–979, bibl., graphs, tables)

After a review of the social and economic benefits of increasing education levels in developing countries, the author computes the acceleration of economic growth that El Salvador's economy would experience as a result of increasing the average level (in years) of education of its population. Finds that if investment in education were increased considerably—so that an additional year of educational attainment were gained every seven years—the resulting increases in GDP would be substantial, reaching three times the value that results from the average investment tendency after 20 years. Interesting and pedagogical discussions of the impact of education level on economic growth and of mechanisms to finance education.

714 Universidad Centroamericana José Simeón Cañas. Departamento de Economía. Análisis de la coyuntura económica. Primer semestre de 2006. (*ECA/San Salvador*, 61:695, sept. 2006, p. 799–827, graphs, tables)

Detailed analysis of economic developments and issues in El Salvador during the first semester of 2006. Emphasis is placed on the assessment of employment and wages, production, inflation, and the external sector. Interesting examination of the determinants of trade, current and capital accounts balances.

GUATEMALA

715 Fuentes García, Alberto. La discriminación y su relación con la diferencia de ingresos en el mercado laboral guatemalteco. (*Perf. Latinoam.*, 13:27, enero/junio 2006, p. 141–167, bibl., graphs, tables)

Presents an in-depth study of discrimination in Guatemala's labor market based on the application of Oaxaca and Blinder's model of labor discrimination, using the 2002 household survey. The significant variables in explaining salaries are education level, experience, gender, urban/rural place of residence and indigenous/non-indigenous divide. Results indicate that discrimination is significant, but it mainly adheres to gender differences, which are more significant than ethnicity differences. Also finds that increasing human capital levels of the indigenous population is very effective in decreasing wage discrimination, as is the existence of labor contracts and access to training. Very rigorous and clear methods of analysis.

716 Luoto, Jill; Craig McIntosh; and Bruce Wydick. Credit information systems in less developed countries: a test with microfinance in Guatemala. (*Econ. Dev. Cult. Change*, 55:2, Jan. 2007, p. 313–334, graphs, maps, tables)

Guatemala introduced an electronic

credit bureau system in 2002 which was to serve the needs of the country's microfinance institutions. This study presents the results of an evaluation of a group of financial institutions that used the system. The results show that large benefits were generated by the credit bureau in terms of reductions in missing payments and loan delinquency rates. An analysis of the return on the investment in the credit system indicated that benefits surpassed the costs by a considerable margin.

HONDURAS

717 Fuentes, Luis Alberto. Pobreza, emigración y transferencias de dinero (remesas) en Honduras. (*Rev. Centroam. Econ.*, 11:67/68, 2006, p. 1–47, bibl., index, tables)

Using data from national household surveys, the author presents a detailed assessment of the characteristics and nature of Honduras' emigration flows. Reveals that the main reason for emigrating is having a relative who resides abroad. The age structure of migrants show a marked concentration in the younger strata, those between 5 and 28 years old. The author explains consequences of migration flows in terms of losses of human capital and the resulting impairment of development prospects.

718 Suazo, Javier. Honduras: RD-CAFTA y los pequeños productores de granos básicos. (*Rev. Centroam. Econ.*, 11:67/68, 2006, p. 92–122, bibl., graphs, tables)

Examines possible impacts of RD-CAFTA on the production of basic grains in Honduras. Proposes policies and programs that should be implemented to strengthen domestic production which will face competition from imports.

719 Suroil, Inc. Estudio de la industria de los productos derivados del petróleo en Honduras. (*Rev. Centroam. Econ.*, 11:67/68, 2006, p. 123–170, appendices, graphs, tables)

Extensive analysis of the gas and petroleum industry in Honduras, covering issues related to market structure, competition, regulation, and pricing mechanisms. Identifies areas where improvements can be made. Excellent discussion of market structure and prices.

720 Zelaya Aguilar, Mario Rubén. Generación hidroeléctrica: una alternativa para propiciar el desarrollo en Honduras. (*Rev. Centroam. Econ.*, 9:63/64, 2004, p. 76–96, bibl., graphs, map, tables)

Presents a review of changes in electricity generation in Honduras since the early 1990s. Author documents the costs of relying on thermal electric generation in lieu of hydro power, specifically in terms of imported fuel costs, increasing pollution, and power insecurity.

NICARAGUA

721 Acevedo Vogl, Adolfo José. Impactos potenciales del Tratado de Libre Comercio Centroamérica-Estados Unidos en el sector agrícola y la pobreza rural de Nicaragua. Managua: Coordinadora Civil y Comité de Servicio de los Amigos, 2004. 118 p.: bibl., ill.

Analyzes the agricultural sector in Nicaragua to assess its capacity to compete with imports that will result from the free trade pact with the US. Diagnostic covers several aspects, particularly technology, land conservation, productivity, credit, and human capital. Concludes that the agricultural sector is in a weak position to confront competition.

722 Bainville, Sebastién et al. La pobreza de las explotaciones familiares nicaragüenses: ¿atraso tecnológico o falta de tierras? (*Anu. Estud. Centroam.*, 30:1/2, 2004, p. 67–86, bibl., graphs, map, tables)

Study based on the analysis of 10 farming communities in Nicaragua, conducted to shed light on the capacity of three types of farms (worked by owners and their families, owners and hired workers, and only by hired workers), in terms of employment and the generation of value added. Results indicate the significant benefits resulting from family farming. Authors recommend programs to support family farming as a means to generate employment. Extensive literature review of agrarian policies in Nicaragua.

723 Bandiera, Oriana. Land tenure, investment incentives, and the choice of techniques: evidence from Nicaragua. (*World Bank Econ. Rev.*, 21:3, May 2007, p. 487–508, bibl., table)

Investigates the determination of farmers' choice of cultivation technique in Nicaragua. The results are based on the estimation of econometric models that indicate that the technique depends on tenure status, with true crops less likely to be grown on rented plots than on owner-cultivated plots.

724 Bilbao E., Jon Ander; Magdalena Mayorga Gaitán; and Olga Rocha Ulloa. Sébaco, Nicaragua: el impacto de la maquila en una zona campesina. Managua: UCA-Nitlapán, 2006. 264 p.: bibl., ill., col. maps.

Study based on interviews of 46 employees of textile maquila firm established in Sébaco, in north central Nicaragua. The first chapter presents a historical overview of maquila investments and operations in the country, and subsequently the results of interviews are presented. These results shed light on topics of labor relations, wages and benefits, education requirements, training, and gender issues.

PANAMA

725 Castillero Calvo, Alfredo. Ciclos y coyunturas en la economía panameña, 1654–1869; interpretación sumaria (segunda parte). (*Tareas*, 120, mayo/agosto 2005, p. 113–130, bibl.)

Vivid account of commerce and trade along the Panama isthmus during the second half of the 19th century, stressing the comparison between the domestic economy and the phenomenal increase in imports for reexport. Author depicts the role of technological improvements in transportation in increasing trade flows, as well as the impacts of new traded products, gold, and coffee, among others, in determining the volume of interoceanic commerce through Panama. Good use of references to original British and US sources on trade, investment, and migration in Panama. For review of first part of article, see *HLAS 64:851.*

726 Falaris, Evangelos M. A quantile regression analysis of wages in Panama. Newark: Univ. of Delaware, Dept. of Economics, 2004. 26 p.: bibl., tables. (Working paper; 2004–01)

Applies quantile regression methods to determine how wages are influenced by public sector employment, firm size, and labor union membership. Results indicate that, for both men and women, public sector employment and employment at a large firm increase wages at the lower quantiles of wage distribution, but men at the highest quantile who work in the public sector suffer a high penalty. The presence of a union at the workplace increases wages of men at the lower quantiles. Higher education and experience affect men positively at the higher quantiles, but the effects of these two variables on wages of women do not vary across quantiles. Clear presentation of econometric approach and literature on labor economics and wage determination.

727 Sánchez Saavedra, Kevin Evandro.
Migración transfronteriza indígena en Darién, Panama. (*ECA/San Salvador*, 62:699/700, enero/feb. 2007, p. 63–88, graph, map, photo)
Analysis of the migration patterns of the Embera and Wounaan tribes from Panama to Colombia, identifying the causes that, over time, have motivated such flows in both directions. References are made to influences of family, age, economic down and upturns, and to violence. Reveals the importance of family factors and the tendency to move for groups that have characterized migration patterns. For sociologist's comment, see item **2599**.

728 Schloegel, Catherine. Sustainable tourism: sustaining biodiversity? (*J. Sustain. For.*, 25:3/4, 2007, p. 247–264, bibl., graphs, tables)
Analysis of the potential of sustainable tourism in Panama. Considers the attractiveness, existing supply and demand, and limitations existing in modalities such as carbon offset and scientific research tourisms. Recommends undertaking promotion campaigns and upgrading existing facilities.

CUBA

MARIO A. GONZÁLEZ-CORZO, *Assistant Professor of Economics, Accounting, and Business Administration, Lehman College, The City University of New York (CUNY), Department of Economics and Business*

THE LITERATURE ON THE CUBAN ECONOMY has experienced some significant changes since the announcement of Fidel Castro's "temporary" retirement on July 31, 2006. Some of the changes that have taken place in Cuba as the need to transform the current economic system has moved to center stage have influenced the public and official discourse (with regards to economic matters mostly) within the island in recent years.

Raul Castro's "July 26" (2007) speech increased the public's expectations about the possibilities of economic change. It ushered in an era of greater official "openness" (and willingness) to "debate" real (economic) issues and problems in the public sphere. The Cuban people were encouraged to (openly, but always within the boundaries of what is officially permitted) discuss and exchange ideas and propose solutions to daily economic problems, to address and improve (even rationalize) the allocation and utilization of resources. The public "debates" were organized by state-sponsored mass organizations (*organizaciones de masas*) and took place in factories, offices, schools, and other places of work.

The primary objectives of these officially sponsored "debates" were to reinvigorate and reactivate Cuban socialism by adopting a more "participative" form and using it to (gradually) replace the bureaucratic constraints and rigidities associated with the "classical" system; expose the internal causes (e.g., excessive bureaucratic constraints, lack of discipline and worker motivation, inefficiency, low productivity, waste, etc.) of Cuba's economic problems; and identify and propose viable solutions or strategies to address the issues and challenges confronting the Cuban economy, always "within Socialism" (*"dentro del socialismo"*).

In recent years, and possibly as a result of the limited expansion of some "alternative spaces," Cuban intellectuals and scholars have made noteworthy contributions to the recent literature on the Cuban economy. The principal themes (or topics) addressed in the recent economic literature produced in Cuba include: the evolution of the Cuban economy, existing challenges and opportunities, and possible policy measures to improve current economic conditions (items **747** and **765**), strategies to transform the agricultural sector (items **736**, **749**, **750**, and **753**), recent developments in the tourism industry (item **759**), measures to improve the housing sector (item **759**), and the need for the gradual elimination of the dual currency system (items **767** and **770**). In addition, some Cuban scholars have written extensively about the situation and potential role of foreign direct investment (FDI) in Cuba (item **762**), the impact of inflation and monetary dualism on the purchasing power of pensions and salaries (item **771**), and the relationship between property forms, efficiency, and labor productivity.

The publications on the Cuban economy that have been produced outside Cuba since 2006 address important topics like the structural characteristics of the Cuban economy (item **742**), the evolution of the Cuban economy since the beginning of the Special Period (item **772**), the agricultural sector (items **729** and **743**), the external sector (item **758**), monetary dualism and income inequality in contemporary Cuba (items **735** and **739**), and health care in Cuba and the export of medical services (item **764**).

Finally, one positive and recurring trend in the recent literature on the Cuban economy is the increased and improved availability of statistical information and Cuba's principal demographic and socioeconomic indicators through the official Web site of the *Oficina Nacional de Estadísticas—ONE* (*http://www.one.cu/*). Four noteworthy publications in this category are the comprehensive statistical yearbook (item **732**), the demographic yearbook (item **731**), the annual social and economic statistical report (item **755**), and a newly created publication known as the "Panorama territorial" (2008), which facilitates regional comparisons of key demographic and socioeconomic indicators (item **756**).

729 Álvarez, José. Privatization of state-owned agricultural enterprises in post-transition Cuba. (*Probl. Post-Communism*, 53:6, Dec. 2006, p. 30–45, tables)

Discusses the theoretical framework of privatization methods in post-socialist economies, and applies it to the (possible) privatization of Cuba's state-owned agricultural enterprises during the (possible) transition to a market-oriented economy.

730 Álvarez González, Elena. La apertura externa cubana. (*Cuba Siglo XXI (on-line)*, 55, julio 2005, p. 1–24, bibl., tables)

Examines the principal characteristics of Cuba's efforts to expand its external sector and reinsert itself into the global economy during the post-Soviet era. The topics discussed include: the conceptual framework (to analyze a country's external sector openness), main aspects of Cuba's external sector dependency, Cuba's external trade model until 1989, the challenges confronting Cuba's external sector after 1989, and the main characteristics of Cuba's efforts to open its external sector since the disintegration of Eastern European and Soviet Socialism in the early 1990s.

731 Anuario Demográfico de Cuba. 2007. La Habana: Dirección de Estadísticas de Población, Dirección General de Estadística, JUCEPLAN.

This comprehensive demographic year book is divided into seven chapters. Chapter 1 provides general information about the Cuban population, such as: population by age, place of residence, gender, population density by province and territory, and economically active population. Chapter 2 presents, detailed fertility data by province, age of the mother, and other demographic indicators. Chapter 3 presents similar data for deaths; Chapter 4 for marriages; Chapter 5 for divorces; Chapter 6 for domestic (internal) migration; and Chapter 7 offers international comparisons of select demographic indicators. The 2007 demographic yearbook also provides a very useful glossary of demographic terms and concepts.

732 Anuario Estadístico de Cuba. 2007. La Habana: Oficina Nacional de Estadísticas.

Most recent volume of the national statistical yearbook. Contains a wide range of socioeconomic statistics, mostly covering the 2002–07 period. National account series remain questionable given recent (2001) changes in the methodology used to estimate gross domestic product (GDP) (at constant prices), and the increased role of the service sector in the Cuban economy. Coverage of external sector statistics has been expanded to include merchandise exports and imports according to their corresponding Standard International Trade Classifications (SITC), as well as balance of payments and external debt statistics. The current version (2007) is available online through the official Web site of the Oficina Nacional de Estadísticas (http://www.one.cu/).

733 Barbería, Lorena. Remesas, pobreza y desigualdad en Cuba. (*Espacio Laical*, 4:14, abril/junio 2008, p. 18–21, bibl., tables)

Provides a brief overview of the impact of remittances on income inequality and poverty in Cuba during the "Special Period."

734 Becerra Lois, Francisco Ángel and **Jesús René Pino Alonso.** Evolución del concepto de desarrollo e implicaciones en el ámbito territoral: experiencia desde Cuba. (*Econ. Soc. Territ.*, 5:17, enero/abril 2005, p. 85–119, bibl., table)

Examines the concept of development from an economic perspective, and explores the regional impact of economic development in Cuba. Focuses on the role of the state in reducing regional inequalities, and on the role of localities in promoting their own economic development.

735 Blue, Sarah A. The erosion of racial equality in the context of Cuba's dual economy. (*Lat. Am. Polit. Soc.*, 49:3, Fall 2007, p. 35–68, graphs, tables)

Analyzes the impact of Cuba's "post-Soviet" economic reforms (1993–95) on racial inequality. Focuses on the effects of self-employment and family remittances on the distribution of income across racial groups, and explores the relationship between educational attainment and income. Concludes that even though equal access to education and employment reduced the structural means of racial discrimination during the 1959–89 period, the economic transformations of the 1990s have contributed to higher racial inequality in contemporary Cuba.

736 Bu Wong, Ángel and **Idanis Rego Sánchez.** Cuba: producción, transformación y comercialización de productos agropecuarios. (*Agroalimentaria*, 12:25, julio/dic. 2007, p. 13–32, bibl., graphs, tables)

Analyzes the implementation of policies and the implementation of enterprise improvement techniques in Cuba's agrofood system, and discusses the principal challenges and restrictions that limit the production and distribution of domestically produced food products in Cuba.

737 Cuba: evolución económica durante 2007 y perspectivas para 2008. México: Comisión Económica para América Latina y el Caribe (CEPAL), 2008. 55 p.: appendix, ill., tables.

Discusses the most significant trends in the Cuban economy during the 2003–07 period, and economic prospects for 2008. The topics discussed include: (1) recent evolution of the Cuban economy, (2) the external sector, (3) economic policies (e.g., fiscal policy, monetary policy, exchange rate policy, and commercial policy), (4) output, employment and prices, and, (5) outlook for 2008.

738 *Cuba in Transition: Papers and Proceedings of the . . . Annual Meeting of the Association for the Study of the Cuban Economy,* Vol. 18, 2008. Washington, D.C.: Assn. for the Study of the Cuban Economy.

Includes more than 30 papers and commentaries covering a wide range of topics dealing with Cuba's (future) transition to a market economy such as: Cuba's current socioeconomic situation, institutions and economic performance, agriculture, energy, real estate, tourism, the external sector, and international relations. Copies of papers and commentaries from earlier meetings of the Association are also available in both physical and electronic (PDF) format.

739 **Eckstein, Susan.** Dollarization and its discontents: remittances and the remaking of Cuba in the post-Soviet era. (*Comp. Polit./New York,* 36:3, April 2004, p. 313–330, tables)

Analyzes the influence of state policies and societal changes on the influx of remittances to Cuba during the post-Soviet era (1990–2004); and compares (where appropriate) trends in remittances flows to Cuba with flows to El Salvador and the Dominican Republic. Concludes that in a socialist country like Cuba remittances are likely to undermine productivity and erode the state's control over economic activities. Remittances also contribute to higher income inequality, affect the social and cultural fabric of Cuban society, and plant the seeds of economic transformation, while leaving the formal polity intact.

740 **Feinsilver, Julie.** Médicos por petróleo: la diplomacia médica cubana recibe una pequeña ayuda de sus amigos. (*Nueva Soc.,* 216, julio/agosto 2008, p. 107–122)

Examines Cuba's "medical diplomacy" in the Western hemisphere and in select regions of the world. Argues that the export (or assignment) of Cuban doctors abroad serves an economic and political purpose simultaneously. On the economic front, it provides Cuba with a steady source of foreign exchange receipts and/or with bartered goods and services (e.g., Venezuelan oil in exchange for Cuban medical

personnel). It also provides doctors and other health care professionals with an opportunity to earn hard currency income and bring items for personal consumption from abroad. On the political front, Cuba's "medical diplomacy" offers invaluable benefits: it allows Cuba to gain international good will and acceptance; enhances its status as a "medical power" (*potencia medica*); and provides it with a valuable tool of political leverage and influence.

741 **Galbraith, James K.; Laura Spagnolo; and Daniel Munevar.** Inequidad salarial en Cuba durante el período especial. (*Am. Lat. Hoy/Salamanca,* 48, abril 2008, p. 109–138, bibl., graphs, tables)

Analyzes the evolution of wage inequality in Cuba during the 1990–2004 period. Concludes that wage inequality has increased dramatically during the Special Period, particularly when strategic, export-oriented sectors like tourism are compared with the rest of the Cuban economy.

742 **García Díaz, Manuel.** La economía cubana: estructuras, instituciones y tránsito al mercado. Granada, Spain: Univ. de Granada, 2004. 286 p.: bibl., ill. (Monográfica. Biblioteca de ciencias económicas y empresariales; 41)

Analyzes the principal characteristics of the Cuban economy, with a particular emphasis on the institutional framework that governs the behavior and interactions between the key economic actors in Cuba's centrally planned economy, and their roles in a (possible) market-oriented transition. The principal topics discussed include: (1) characteristics of the Cuban population and the labor market, (2) labor productivity in Cuba, (2) capital and productivity, (3) total factor productivity in the Cuban economy, (4) the external sector, (5) the institutional framework, and (6) basic elements for a market-oriented transition in Cuba.

743 **Hagelberg, G.B. and José Álvarez.** Cuba's dysfunctional agriculture: on the eve of reform? (*Cuban Aff.,* 2:4, Oct. 2007, p. 1–25, bibl., tables)

Analyzes the recent performance of Cuba's agricultural sector with a particular emphasis on key indicators such as: physical output in the sugar and non-sugar sectors, labor productivity, foreign trade (i.e., exports and imports), and the state-operated procurement system, Acopio. Concludes that the most pressing issue concerning (the transformation of) Cuba's agricultural sector is the need to improve efficiency and productivity, and increase production.

744 Marcelo, Luis; Adriano García; and Oscar U-Echevarría. Reflexiones sobre la empresa estatal cubana. (*Cuba Siglo XXI (online)*, 70, oct. 2006, p. 1–20, bibl., ill., tables)

Describes the social roles and functions of state-owned enterprises (SOEs) in Cuba, and describes their contributions to the domestic economy and the external sector.

745 Marquetti Nodarse, Hiram. Cuba: una nueva etapa del desarrollo industrial. (*Bol. Cuatrimestral*, abril 2009, p. 1–38, bibl., ill, tables)

Examines the structural transformation experienced by Cuba's industrial sector from 1990 to the present, with a particular emphasis on the role of Cuba-Venezuela relations and their impact on the efforts to reactivate the island's industrial sector. Argues that the process of de-industrialization experienced by Cuba during the Special Period (1990–2007) requires a comprehensive set of industrial policies designed to modernize the country's industrial sector and improve its efficiency and competitiveness.

746 Mesa-Lago, Carmelo. La economía cubana en la encrucijada: el legado de Fidel, el debate sobre el cambio y las opciones de Raúl. Madrid: Real Instituto Elcano de Estudios Internacionales y Estratégicos, 2008. 43 p.: bibl., tables. (Documento de trabajo; 19/2007)

Analyzes Cuba's current economic situation, examines the debate that emerged after Raúl Castro's July 26, 2007 speech, and explores possible policy transformations. The topics discussed include: analysis of recent economic developments (domestic economy and external sector), the internal economic and social debate, policy options, and prospects for the future.

747 Monreal González, Pedro. El problema económico de Cuba. (*Espacio Laical*, 4:14, abril/junio 2008, p. 1–3, bibl., tables)

Examines Cuba's principal economic problems from a structural perspective. Concludes that economic reforms should be considered as the primary structural changes in Cuba, and that the main economic problem confronting the island at the present is the inability of the (current) economic system to promote economic development.

748 Nova González, Armando. El actual mercado interno de los alimentos. (*Cuba Siglo XXI (online)*, 89, julio 2008, p. 1–9, bibl., graphs)

Presents a detailed description of the multiple sources (i.e., suppliers) that operate in Cuba's highly fragmented food market, the economic forces and institutional framework governing their operations, and the principal distortions and disequilibria caused by such segmentation. Argues that the unification of the food market (or more accurately the sources that supply the food market) is an essential requirement to address these distortions and improve the current situation.

749 Nova González, Armando. La agricultura en Cuba: actualidad y transformaciones necesarias. (*Cuba Siglo XXI (online)*, 90, agosto 2008, p. 1–11, bibl., tables)

Describes recent developments in Cuba's agricultural sector (2004–07) and possible policy measures to transform this vital sector of the Cuban economy.

750 Nova González, Armando. La agricultura en Cuba: evolución y trayectoria, 1959–2005. La Habana: Editorial de Ciencias Sociales, 2006. 310 p.: bibl., ill. (Economía)

Analyzes the economic evolution of Cuba's agricultural sector during the 1959–2005 period. The principal topics discussed include: (1) the historical evolution of Cuba's agricultural sector, (2) necessary changes and transformations to improve agricultural production in Cuba, (3) new production relationships in Cuba's agricultural sector, with an emphasis on the newly created productive units, agricultural markets, and other intermediaries, (4) Cuba's internal food market, (5) the role of cooperatives in sugar and nonsugar agriculture, (5) food availability and food security in contemporary Cuba, (6) the agricultural sector's contribution to the Cuban economy, and (7) recent trends and developments in Cuban agriculture (2000–05).

751 Nova González, Armando. La agroindustria bioenergética de la caña de azúcar y la producción de alimentos. (*Bol. Cuatrimestral*, agosto 2007, p. 1–11, bibl.)

Presents a high level overview of Cuba's sugarcane-related biofuels production. Concludes that given its high energy contents, and other environmental benefits (e.g., contributions to the reduction of carbon dioxide (CO_2) and other greenhouse gasses through the release of oxygen into the atmosphere), sugarcane has the potential of playing a critical role in reducing global dependency on hydrocarbons. With its natural endowments, and history of sugarcane production, Cuba can emerge as one of the principal beneficiaries of this trend.

752 Nova González, Armando. La integración de la agroindustria azucarera y el turismo en Cuba: relaciones con el Caribe. (*Bol. Cuatrimestral*, dic. 2007, p. 1–12, bibl., graphs, tables)

Examines recent trends in the integration of tourism and agriculture in Cuba, with a particular emphasis on the "spillover effects" of tourism-related foreign direct investment (FDI), particularly the transfer of technologies and new production techniques, on Cuba's agricultural sector.

753 Nova González, Armando. El microcrédito en las nuevas condiciones de la agricultura. (*Bol. Cuatrimestral*, dic. 2008, p. 1–4, bibl., tables)

Discusses the possible role of microloans (or microcredit) to small farmers in Cuba, and the potential role of these loans in stimulating agricultural output and eventually reducing Cuba's reliance on food imports.

754 Nova González, Armando. La UBPC, mercado y propiedad. (*Bol. Cuatrimestral*, dic. 2007, p. 1–16, bibl.)

Discusses the principal challenges confronting Cuba's Cooperative Units of Basic Production ("Unidades Básicas de Producción Cooperativa"—UBPCs), and agricultural markets. Outlines a series of policy measures to confront these challenges and improve conditions in Cuba's agricultural sector.

755 Panorama económico y social: Cuba 2008. La Habana: Oficina Nacional de Estadísticas, 2008. 55 p.: ill., tables.

Summarizes and compares Cuba's principal socioeconomic indicators in 2007 and 2008. The data presented include: gross domestic product (GDP), the state budget, composition of the labor force, select tourism and physical output indicators, transportation, art and culture, education, science, technology, women in Cuban society, and a comparison between Cuba and select Latin American and Caribbean countries.

756 Panorama territorial: Cuba 2008. Havana: Oficina Nacional de Estadísticas, 2008. 68 p.: ill., tables.

Presents Cuba's principal socioeconomic indicators during the 2001–08 period by province or territory. The data presented are designed to facilitate territorial comparisons, and include: demographic indicators (or statistics), physical output indicators for the non-sugar agriculture and housing sectors, investment, retail sales, human development and health indicators (e.g., live births, infant weight at birth, life expectancy, doctors per capita, dentists per capita), and educational attainment indicators (e.g., literacy rate, student-teacher ratio, school enrollment, graduates by grade and field of specialization, etc.).

757 Pérez-López, Jorge F. The rise and fall of private foreign investment in Cuba. (*Cuban Aff.*, 3:1, Feb. 2008, p. 1–30, bibl., graphs, tables)

Presents an overview of the evolution of foreign direct investment (FDI) in Cuba from the early 1980s to the present. Argues that Cuba's opening to FDI has positively impacted the country's balance of payments (BOP); has contributed to the growth and expansion of vital sectors like tourism, oil production, and nickel mining; has opened foreign markets to Cuban goods and services; and has played a critical role in promoting the transfer of (foreign) technologies and managerial techniques and practices in select areas of the Cuban economy. However, in recent years private foreign investment has been gradually replaced by government investment. Since the latter is based on political, rather than economic, considerations, this trend does not bode well for the future of the Cuban economy.

758 Pérez-López, Jorge F. Tiempo de cambios: tendencias del comercio exterior cubano. (*Nueva Soc.*, 216, julio/agosto 2008, p. 168–179, bibl., tables)

Examines Cuba's foreign trade patterns during the 2001–2006 period. Concludes that even though the structure and patterns of Cuban foreign trade have changed in recent years, with merchandise trade being eclipsed by services, and the emergence of a new set of trading partners—namely China and Venezuela—Cuba's commercial balance is still in the red.

759 Pérez Villanueva, Omar Everleny. Apuntes sobre la vivienda en Cuba. (*Bol. Cuatrimestral*, dic. 2008, p. 1–12, graphs, tables)

Summarizes historical trends in Cuba's housing sector, with a particular emphasis on the post-1959 period. Describes the current condition of Cuba's housing stock, using the 2002 Housing and Population Census, and discusses possible policy measures to address the country's chronic housing shortage.

760 Pérez Villanueva, Omar Everleny. Apuntes sobre las importaciones cubanas desde Estados Unidos. (*Econ. Press Serv.*, 5, marzo 2009, p. 1–7, graphs)

Examines the recent evolution of US agricultural exports to Cuba from 2002 to the present. Sales (exports) of US agricultural products are analyzed by year, total value (in US dollars), product category, and total share of Cuban food imports.

761 Pérez Villanueva, Omar Everleny. La economía en Cuba: un balance actual y propuestas necesarias. (*Bol. Cuatrimestral*, agosto 2008, p. 1–24, bibl., graphs)

Describes recent developments and trends in the Cuban economy, and explores some possible areas that can be improved and/or transformed. The topics discussed include: macroeconomic trends and developments, the external sector, prices, salaries, and employment, fiscal policy, demographic and population trends, principal challenges and future outlook, and possible areas for economic improvements and transformations.

762 Pérez Villanueva, Omar Everleny. La inversión directa en Cuba: vientos a su favor? (*Bol. Cuatrimestral*, agosto 2008, p. 1–9, graphs)

Provides a high level overview of foreign investment in Cuba and discusses the particular characteristics of Cuba as a foreign investment destination.

763 Sánchez Egozcue Jorge Mario and Juan Triana Cordoví. An overview of the Cuban economy: the transformations underway and the challenges it faces. Madrid: Real Instituto Elcano de Estudios Internacionales y Estratégicos, 2008. 42 p.: graphs, tables. (Documento de trabajo; 31/2008)

Presents a detailed overview of the Cuban economy from the early 1990s to the present, and the principal economic challenges confronting contemporary Cuba. The topics discussed include: the economic transformations of the 1990s, sectors of the Cuban economy that are likely to be reformed, interactions associated with economic changes and transformations, economic relations with the European Union (EU), and recent developments in US-Cuba relations and the prospects for the future.

764 Spiegel, Jerry and Annette Yassi. Lessons from the margins of globalization: appreciating the Cuban health paradox. (*J. Public Health Policy*, 25:1, 2004, p. 85–110, bibl., graphs, ill., tables)

Examines recent health policies in Cuba with a particular emphasis on vertical and horizontal integration, prevention, primary care, and nonmedical determinants of health. Argues that Cuba's experience challenges the assumption that national wealth is a fundamental condition for improving health; countries around the world may want to learn how alternative public policy approaches to health care, such as those used in Cuba, may be effectively applied to improve their health services delivery and coverage.

765 Triana Cordoví, Juan. De los desequilibrios a las distorsiones: como crecer en el futuro inmediato. (*Bol. Cuatrimestral*, abril 2008, p. 1–11, tables)

Presents a brief analysis of the principal economic distortions and the sources of the imbalances (or disequilibrium) af-

fecting the Cuban economy. Offers three
essential (gradual) policy measures to address these imbalances: (1) using economic
incentives to improve factor productivity
and efficiency; (2) allowing the formation
and expansion of privately operated and
cooperative-based small and medium enterprises (SMEs); and (3) attracting foreign
investment to nontraditional sectors of the
Cuban economy, particularly agriculture.

766 Vidal Alejandro, Pavel. La disyuntiva
actual de la política económica cubana. (*Econ. Press Serv.*, 18, sept. 2008,
p. 1–4)
Examines recent macroeconomic
developments (2007–2008) in Cuba, and
how the devaluation of the convertible peso
(CUC) can be used to confront the economic
shocks that affected the Cuban economy in
the aftermath of two devastating hurricanes
in 2008 (Ike and Gustav), lower prices for
key Cuban exports (e.g. nickel, sugar, and
tobacco), and a higher import bill.

767 Vidal Alejandro, Pavel. La encrucijada de la dualidad monetaria. (*Nueva
Soc.*, 216, julio/agosto 2008, p. 90–106, table)
Analyzes the origins and objectives
of the implementation of a system of monetary dualism in Cuba as a response to the
economic crisis of the 1990s, and recent
changes in Cuban monetary policy. Discusses possible policy measures to elimi-
nate the system of monetary dualism, but
warns that improved economic efficiency
and labor productivity are essential requirements to achieve this goal.

768 Vidal Alejandro, Pavel. La macroeconomía cubana en 2008: datos de cierre
de año. (*Econ. Press Serv.*, 1, enero 2009,
p. 1–8, tables)
Uses official Cuban statistics and
figures compiled by CEPAL to summarize
the principal economic developments in
2008. Particular emphasis is given to general macroeconomic indicators (e.g., GDP,
the fiscal deficit, and monetary aggregates),
and select external sector indicators (e.g., exports, imports, and the balance of payments).

769 Vidal Alejandro, Pavel. Relación
comercio-crecimiento en Cuba:
estimación con el filtro de Kalman. (*Rev.
CEPAL/Santiago*, 94, abril 2008, p. 101–120,
bibl., graphs, ill., tables)

Uses coefficients that change over
time to analyze a model of economic growth
with balance of payments (BOP) constraints.
Argues that exports have been a determining factor in the postcrisis recovery of the
Cuban economy since 2005, particularly
as a result of the growing importance of
service exports, which tend to have a larger
multiplier effect.

770 Vidal Alejandro, Pavel. Los salarios,
los precios y la dualidad monetaria.
(*Espacio Laical*, 4:14, abril/junio 2008,
p. 22–26)
Presents a high-level account of the
origins and objectives of monetary dualism
in Cuba, and its impact on prices and the
real purchasing power of Cuban workers and
households. Concludes that, while monetary
dualism represented a viable (and necessary)
policy response to the economic crisis of the
1990s, it has outlived its purpose and usefulness. The elimination of the system of monetary dualism, combined with more flexible
salaries (to reflect the cost of living and the
productivity of labor), along with a series of
structural changes, would be beneficial for
Cuba's economic development.

771 Vidal Alejandro, Pavel and **Saira Pons
Pérez.** Determinantes de la inflación
en Cuba: una modelación estructural. (*Bol.
Cuatrimestral*, agosto 2008, p. 1–22, bibl.,
graphs, tables)
Uses a structurally oriented econometric model, based on the *Taylor Rule* and
the *Phillips Curve* to identify the principal
determinants of inflation in Cuba. Concludes that the principal determinants of
inflation in Cuba include: the income received by the population, the productivity of
labor, and the exchange rates that prevail in
the economy.

772 Xalma, Cristina. Cuba, ¿hacia dónde?:
transformación política, económica y
social en los noventa: escenarios de futuro.
Barcelona: Icaria Editorial, 2007. 205 p.:
bibl., ill., index, tables. (Icaria antrazyt; 258.
Análisis contemporáneo)
Examines the policy measures implemented in Cuba as a response to the economic crisis the 1990s, and analyzes recent
socioeconomic developments and conditions
in Cuba. Topics discussed include: (1) the
economic reforms of the 1990s; (2) the inter-

national context and its economic impact; (3) the domestic situation; and (4) possible future scenarios.

773 Yera, Yoel del Risco and Lluís Mundet I. Cerdan. El turismo como estrategia de desarrollo en Cuba. (*Estud. Geogr./Madrid*, 66:258, enero/junio 2005, p. 293–318, bibl., graphs, tables)

Examines recent developments in Cuba's tourism sector, and the relationship between tourism and economic development. Argues that in the Cuban context, tourism is generally perceived as a source of foreign exchange receipts and employment. However, despite the importance of this sector in the Cuban economy, the substitution of sugar production with tourism and other export-oriented services represents a significant economic challenge, which merits careful analysis and revision. For geography specialist's comment, see item **992**.

ECUADOR

DAVID W. SCHODT, *Professor of Economics, St. Olaf College*

THE DOLLARIZATION of the Ecuadorian economy in 2000, which helped to resolve a growing economic crisis (analyzed in *La Banca Central en el entorno de la crisis financiera del Ecuador* (item **783**)), and the subsequent increase in the world price of petroleum contributed to improved economic performance in the early years of the new century. The rate of GDP growth, which was only 3 percent in 2000, had risen to a peak of 8 percent by 2004. Inflation had fallen from nearly 100 percent in 2000 to a low of 3 percent by 2004. The current account balance moved from negative to positive over the same period.

However, sustained and equitable growth of the Ecuadorian economy remains heavily dependent on the price of petroleum. Efforts to diversify the economy away from its reliance on petroleum have met with limited success, although the articles by Sawers (item **784**) and Korovkin (item **782**) document the growth of the cut-flower industry as a notable exception. Sawer's article, in particular, examines the interplay of domestic policy and international factors behind the rapid growth of this industry. Although he does not develop the argument, his observation of parallels between the development of the cut-flower industry and the earlier banana industry merits further exploration. Korovkin's work complements that of Sawers by examining the implications of the industry for poverty reduction.

One consequence of dollarization is that external shocks, such as the recent fall in the price of petroleum, are swiftly translated into reductions in real output unless offset by other inflows of foreign exchange. Remittances, which had helped to fill this gap and which had accounted for up to 8 percent of GDP, have declined and are expected to fall sharply in 2009 as the world recession cuts into migrant workers' employment and earnings. The article "Remittances, Liquidity Constraints, and Human Capital Investments in Ecuador" (item **774**) examines how families make use of this income and therefore documents what might be the social cost of its decline, reminding us that remittances, while providing foreign exchange, also have immediate benefits for recipient families (also see the complementary work, *La migración en el Ecuador: oportunidades y amenazas* (item **2625**)).

Ecuador's need to diversify its economy, and to develop additional sources of foreign exchange, has raised questions about the environmental impacts of these policies. Recent demonstrations against Ecuador's new mining law and the government's efforts to persuade the international community to pay Ecuador for not exploiting petroleum in an environmentally sensitive area of the Amazon, are different expressions of these concerns. Two works address these questions: *La "huella ecologica" de la dolarización* (item **778**) explores the effects of dollarization on the sustainability of the Ecuadorian economy, while *La estructura biofísica de la economía ecuatoriana* (item **785**) applies a Material and Energy Flow Accounting (MEFA) methodology to analyzing the environmental costs of Ecuador's exports.

Tourism, particularly the growing ecotourism sector, has been viewed as an environmentally friendly industry, a means of diversifying the economy, and a source of foreign exchange. *Una interpretacíon mesoeconómica del turismo en Ecuador* (item **780**), makes an important contribution to our understanding of this sector by bringing to public attention the Central Bank's efforts to create satellite accounts for tourism (unfortunately that work was suspended in 2003).

774 Calero, Carla; Arjun S. Bedi; and Robert Sparrow. Remittances, liquidity constraints, and human capital investments in Ecuador. (*World Dev.*, 37:6, June 2009, p. 1143–1154)

Remittances sent to Ecuador in recent years have been the second largest source of foreign exchange earnings after petroleum, yet this topic has received very little attention from researchers. This important article evaluates empirically the direct article of remittances to investments in human capital, and the effects of shocks on these investments. It finds that remittances increase school enrollment and decrease the incidence of child work, particularly for girls and in rural areas of Ecuador. It also finds that economic shocks are associated with increased work, while remittances are used to smooth educational investments. In addition, remittances are found to be associated with a net substitution from public to private (higher quality) schooling.

775 Colloredo-Mansfeld, Rudolf Josef and Jason Antrosio. Economic clusters or cultural commons?: the limits of competition-driven development in the Ecuadorian Andes. (*LARR*, 44:1, 2009, p. 132–157, bibl., graphs)

This article by two anthropologists examines state policies to promote competitive advantage in the Ecuadorian highland communities of Atuntaqui and Otavalo. While there are many studies of the weaving industry in Otavalo, this may be the first academic study of local economic development in the town of Atuntaqui. The authors see the latter community as a successful example of state policies supporting an increasingly competitive local textile industry. Despite what economists might view as an excess of anthropological jargon, and some confusion about economic concepts (such as wage costs and unit costs), this article will hold interest for those interested in local economic development policy in the context of macroeconomic liberalization. There are virtually no published studies of this kind for Ecuador.

776 Comercio exterior: alternativas para Ecuador. Recopilación de Javier Ponce Leiva. Quito: Abya-Yala: FLACSO, Sede Ecuador, 2005. 455 p.: bibl., ill. (Ágora)

This is a collection of essays resulting from collaboration between representatives of Ecuador's Foreign Service and academics, the purpose of which was to reexamine the country's trade policy. The first essay, for example, by Diego Ramírez surveys efforts to diversify exports. Another provides an overview of Ecuador's growing trade with Pacific-Rim countries. The volume contains little original research, but does provide perspectives on Ecuador's trade policy that are not frequently encountered in the literature.

777 Economía ecuatoriana. Compilación de Falconí Benítez Fander y Julio Oleas Montalvo. Quito: FLACSO, Sede Académica de Ecuador, 2004. 405 p.: bibl., ill. (Antología)

This is a valuable collection of articles on the Ecuadorian economy, by both national and international authors. Most of the articles have been published elsewhere previously, but their publication in a single volume performs a useful service. The collection spans the period 1992–2003, focusing on the economic crisis of the late 1990s, the dollarization in 2000, and the subsequent performance of the economy. The first article, "Antología de la economía ecuatoriana 1992–2003" contains an overview of domestic sources of research and publication that should be essential reading for anyone beginning work on the Ecuadorian economy. Other articles are by local and international economists, such as Fidel Jaramillo, Nader Nazmi, Doug Southgate, and Morris Whitaker, who are recognized authorities on the Ecuadorian economy.

778 Falconí Benítez, Fander. La "huella ecológica" de la dolarización. (*Ecuad. Debate*, 66, dic. 2005, p. 21–38, bibl., graphs, tables)

Economist Fander Falconí (who assumed the position of Foreign Minister in the Correa administration in 2008) examines the effects of dollarization on the sustainability of the Ecuadorian economy, arguing that this has led to both a renewed emphasis on primary products and a growing export concentration. In turn, he sees the growth of primary product exports under dollarization leading to unsustainable environmental costs. While the questions raised are important ones, there is little effort to demonstrate the linkages empirically. It would have been interesting, for example, to know how much of the environmental effect can be attributed to dollarization, and how much may be due to other factors, such as the growth of Chinese demand and the low productivity of Ecuador's manufacturing sector.

779 Gray, Clark L. Environment, land, and rural out-migration in the southern Ecuadorian Andes. (*World Dev.*, 37:2, Feb. 2009, p. 457–468)

Marginal agricultural conditions in southern Ecuadorian Andes have long made this region a source of internal migration to both the country's urban centers and to its frontier areas. This empirical study uses 2006 household survey data collected by the author from nearly 400 households in Loja province to explore the effects of land ownership and environmental conditions on three types of out-migration: local (within the province); internal (to other areas in Ecuador); and international. The author uses a multinomial discrete-time event history model. He finds that the determinants of out-migration differ strongly by type of migration. Local and internal migration is negatively associated with land ownership, while international migration is positively associated. Negative environmental characteristics (such as decreased rainfall) increased out-migration; those effects were weakest for international migrants.

780 Una interpretación mesoeconómica del turismo en Ecuador. Edición de Salvador Marconi Romano y Juan Falconí Morales. Prólogo de Rocío Vázquez Alcázar. Contribuciones de Consuelo Aguinaga C. et al. Quito: Publicaciones Económicas, Banco Central del Ecuador, 2005. 415 p.: ill., CD-ROM.

Tourism in Ecuador has grown dramatically in recent years (accounting for 4.2 percent of GDP in 2003) and the inflow of foreign visitors is an important source of foreign exchange earnings. However, apart from anecdotal evidence, little has been know about the economic impact of tourism. In 1993, the Central Bank developed a satellite account for tourism to complement their national input-output accounts. This account was computed from 1993–2003, after which its compilation was suspended. The accounts, nevertheless, are an invaluable resource for analyses of the tourism sector. One finding, for example, is that domestic tourism has a larger weight in the Ecuadorian economy than foreign tourism.

781 Jácome, Hugo. Microfinanzas en la economía ecuatoriana: una alternativa para el desarrollo. Edición de Hugo Jácome. Contribuciones de Hugo Jácome, Emilia Ferraro y Jeannette Sánchez. Quito: FLACSO: Presidencia de la República del Ecuador, 2004. 146 p.: bibl., ill. (Agora)

This book contains three studies of microfinance in Ecuador. The first, which forms the bulk of the book, argues that microfinance has not made a significant contribution to economic growth nor to poverty reduction but that it has been important in channeling credit to the informal sector, estimated at 41 percent of GDP. It draws these conclusions from an empirical analysis of the microfinance sector. The study also provides a useful overview of the microfinance sector in Ecuador. The second, shorter, study offers a case study of microfinance lending in one community, and focuses on the social context of this lending.

782 Korovkin, Tanya. Creating a social wasteland? Non-traditional agricultural exports and rural poverty in Ecuador. (*Rev. Eur. Estud. Latinoam. Caribe,* 79, Oct. 2005, p. 47–67, bibl., tables)

This article, which looks at the poverty effects of Ecuador's cut flower industry, is an interesting complement to Larry Sawers work on the same industry (see item **784**). The research is based on surveys conducted by the author in 2001 and 2002 in the canton of Pedro Moncayo. This is a fine-grained study that argues "Ecuador's flower export production hampers, rather than helps, the efforts to alleviate poverty." It does find that the rural poor are "probably not as poor as before," but they face "mounting problems of insecurity and lack of participation." The question of an appropriate counterfactual is not addressed. It is difficult to determine whether the effects observed are a necessary concomitant of this industry, or may be more attributable to a lack of supportive public policies.

783 Marchán Romero, Carlos. La Banca Central en el entorno de la crisis financiera del Ecuador: factores que la originan y son causa de su profundización, 1995–1999. Quito: Banco Central del Ecuador, 2005. 211 p.: bibl.

This publication will be valuable for those seeking an Ecuadorian perspective on the antecedents to the economic crisis of the late 1990s, which ultimately led to the decision to dollarize. The author is well placed to offer a good account of the role of the Central Bank in the crisis. Written from the perspective of 2005, the account argues that the crisis originated in the dependency of the public sector on petroleum revenues, the fragility of the financial system along with a rapid expansion of credit

in the mid-1990s, and banks' knowledge that the Central Bank would bail them out. The author's investigation is distinguished by its use of data from the Superintendence of Banks, something which has not figured in most other analyses of the period.

784 Sawers, Larry. Nontraditional or new traditional exports: Ecuador's flower boom. (*LARR,* 40:3, 2005, p. 40–67, bibl., tables)

This article examines the sources of the post-1987 boom in Ecuador's cut flower exports, during which period the industry expanded from less than 0.2 to 9 percent of the country's nonpetroleum exports. The question examined-whether the industry responded primarily to macroeconomic policy reforms or to changes in the international flower market-is an important one, with relevance to Ecuador as well as to other Latin American countries. It provides a useful survey of Ecuadorian macroeconomic and trade policy prior to and during the period. The author argues that the success of this nontraditional export was due to both policy changes as well as to changes in the international economy that provided local entrepreneurs with a profitable opening. One specific stimulus appears to have been the growing political unrest in Columbia, which undermined that country's cut flower industry and brought both capital and technological expertise to Ecuador. Valuable.

785 Vallejo G., María Cristina. La estructura biofísica de la economía ecuatoriana: el comercio exterior y los flujos ocultos del banano. Quito: Abya-Yala: FLACSO-Ecuador, 2006. 218 p.: bibl., ill., map.

This interesting study draws on ecological economics for its analytical framework, and makes an argument for ecologically unequal exchange. It employs a methodology of Material and Energy Flow Accounting (MEFA) associated with the Institute of Social Ecology in Vienna to analyze material flow associated with international trade in the Ecuadorian economy from 1980 to 2003. It also provides a more detailed analysis of the banana sector, arguing that monetary flows alone obscure the large environmental costs of this export for Ecuador. Complements the study by Fander Falconí.

CHILE

MARKOS J. MAMALAKIS, *Professor Emeritus of Economics, University of Wisconsin-Milwaukee*

EVER SINCE CHILE DECLARED INDEPENDENCE from Spanish colonial rule on September 18, 1810, all of its political movements and governments have attempted to overcome what distinguished Chilean historian Francisco Encina described, in his classic *Nuestra inferioridad economica: sus causas, sus consequencias,* as its economic inferiority.

In his *Mensaje al Congreso Pleno* (Message to Congress) of May 21, 2005, President Ricardo Lagos made the claim that Chile has left behind a history, as described by Anibal Pinto, of frustrated growth *(desarrollo frustrado)* and started down the path of overcoming its economic inferiority.

President Salvador Allende's 1970–73, relatively brief, strategic attempt to end Chile's economic inferiority through a socialist-Marxist model of state sovereignty and government intervention unleashed centrifugal forces of chaotic self destruction unprecedented in Chile's history. On 11 September 1973, a military coup put an end to Allende's socialist experiment. A radically new economic policy which was procedurally and consequentially linked to individual sovereignty and economic freedom was formulated and implemented by a team directed by Sergio de Castro, and became, during the dictatorial Augusto Pinochet presidency (1973–1980), the strategic cornerstone of a relentless effort to overcome Chile's inherited, seemingly insurmountable, debilitating, economic inferiority.

Almost all documents reviewed in this essay accept the unique, benevolent nature of the prevailing economic structure. Furthermore, almost all of them recognize that Chile's collective services market, always the central engine of growth, must become more efficient through an increased recognition and satisfaction of the seven, complementary, moral collective needs for safety, security, protection of life, political freedom, economic freedom(s), equal treatment by the government, and social harmony and environmental sanctity. Such an improvement in the allocative, consequentialist efficiency of the collective services output market could lead to significant progress in overcoming the inequality, extreme poverty, gender discrimination, environmental decay, and other socioeconomic pathologies associated with Encina's economic inferiority.

1. THE COLLECTIVE NEED, SERVICE, AND MARKET FOR SAFETY, SECURITY, AND PROTECTION OF LIFE

The most widely used indicator measuring the degree of recognition and satisfaction of the moral collective need for individual and collective well-being, or, for safety, security, and protection of life, is the level and rate of growth of per capita income and output. Additional direct and indirect indicators of well-being include price stability, a low rate of unemployment, and the satisfaction of other moral collective needs.

Since 1973, the Chilean government has pursued the goal of price stability through, first, a highly independent, anti-inflationary, macro, monetary economic policy. As a consequence, the average annual rate of inflation during 1990–2007 has been only 6 percent (UNICEF). Furthermore, the inflation rate, as measured by the GDP deflator (annual percent) was 4.6 in 2000, 5.6 in 2005, 12.4 in 2006 and 4.9 in 2007 (World Bank). Second, it pursued the goal of price stability through an equally disciplined fiscal policy, complementary to the monetary, macro, balanced budget. As a consequence, the Chilean government run a cash surplus/deficit (percent of GDP) of −0.7 in 2000, 4.5 in 2005, 7.7 in 2006, and 8.8 in 2007 (The World Bank Group). As a result of extremely successful monetary and fiscal macroeconomic policies, GNI (Gross National Income) per capita, Atlas method (current US dollars) increased from 4,840.0, in 2000, to 8,190.0 in 2007 (The World Bank Group). Measured in Purchasing Power Parity (PPP), in current international dollars, Chilean GNI per capita increased from 8,910, in 2000, to 12,339, in 2007 (The World Bank Group). Life expectancy at birth, total (years) was 69 in 2007 (The World Bank Group). And the mortality rate, under 5 (per thousand), had fallen to 68 in 2007 (The World Bank Group).

The following studies make significant contributions to our understanding of the degree of efficiency of the collective output submarket where the collective need for safety, security, and protection of life is recognized and satisfied: the relevance of intangible assets in financial analysis (item **812**); the inadequate nature of Chile's production structure as a basis for more complex, sustainable, economic, and technological development (item **787**); effects of government policy, freedom of trade, globalization, and a new entrepreneurial climate-spirit on the Chilean wine industry (item **802**); an excellent analysis of the specialization patterns in the Chilean economy during the period of fastest growth, taking into account its relative abundance of natural resources (item **788**); an estimate of the economic value of reductions in mortality rates between 1980 and 1997 (item **799**); a review of the strengths and weaknesses of the Chilean takeoff in the mid 1980s (item **795**); the relationship between institutions and regulation of labor, the functioning of labor markets and economic growth, as well as of the need for systems of labor protection, and presentation of evidence that major improvements in growth and well-being would come from increases in productivity, labor participation, and improvement in human capital (item **786**); and an analysis of strengths, weaknesses, and recommendations for improvement of the financial market (item **800**).

2. THE COLLECTIVE NEED, SERVICE, AND MARKET FOR POLITICAL FREEDOM(S)

The segment of the Chilean collective output market where the moral collective need for political freedom had to be recognized and satisfied was highly imperfect when socialist President Salvador Allende was elected in 1970. During the ill-fated 1970–73 Allende presidency, the conception of how political power should be used differed radically between the Socialist-Marxist Left, the Right and all the other political groups in between. There existed no consensus—political, social, economic or otherwise—of how political groups could gain access to state power or how it could or should be used. During the 1973–90 military dictatorship of General Augusto Pinochet Ugarte, the moral collective need for political freedom was neither recognized nor satisfied. The essence of the collective services market was controlled by the military. The military also decided which collective needs were to be recognized and satisfied. With sustainable democracy and civil society missing, collective well-being and welfare suffered. A spectacular increase in economic well-being materialized after 1990, when democracy and the "political freedom" collective market, the mother of all moral collective markets, were restored, and recognition and satisfaction of the moral collective need for political freedom regained its historical centrality.

3. THE COLLECTIVE NEED, SERVICE, AND MARKET FOR ECONOMIC FREEDOM(S)

The complementary goals of a high rate of growth of per capita income, price stability, low rate of unemployment and a fair distribution of income, could never have been attained in Chile without the parallel pursuit of the mesoeconomic policies—complementary to macro monetary and fiscal—satisfying the seven fundamental, moral, collective needs. Indeed, what is widely considered as a Chilean developmental success story, can be perceived as the consequence not only of prudent monetary and fiscal macroeconomic policies, but also more importantly, of the unprecedented, in Chilean economic history, recognition and satisfaction of the moral (to many) collective needs of individuals (households), of private and state-owned enterprises (corporations), and nonprofit institutions, for economic freedom(s).

Ironically, the unprecedented transformation of the "political" collective services market in 1973, from democracy (recognition of the collective need for political freedom) to dictatorship (suppression of the collective need for political freedom), initiated a parallel, equally unprecedented transformation in other collective services markets. First and foremost is the globally unique recognition and satisfaction of the collective need for economic freedom in all individual (food, clothing, and shelter) and semipublic (health, education, and welfare) final output markets; in all intermediate value-added markets; and in all labor, capital, and land factor markets. The mesoeconomic determination of value largely by government fiat, of the Allende years, was completely replaced by the mesoeconomic determination of value, in free product, value added and factor markets, guided by the principles of individual, consumer, and producer sovereignty.

The overall vibrancy of the "economic freedom" collective-service market during 1973–2010 is unique in Chilean history. It has become a powerful, shining beacon at the peak of an economic freedom pyramid with an ever wider and deeper base encompassing all final, intermediate output, and factor markets.

The degree of recognition and satisfaction of the composite moral collective need for economic freedom increased steadily during the Democratic presidencies of Patricio Aylwin Azócar (1990–94), Eduardo Frei Ruiz-Tagle (1994–2000), Ricardo Lagos (2000–2006), and Michelle Bachelet (2006–2010).

The summary rating of the degree of recognition and satisfaction of the collective need for economic freedom, in Chile, increased from 5.56 (out of a maximum of 10.0) in 1980, to 6.93 in 1990, to 7.28 in 2000 and 7.98 in 2006, the most recent year for which there is information available. Furthermore, Chile's rank in the degree of satisfaction of the moral collective need for economic freedom rose from 45, in 1980, to 8, in 2005, and a truly impressive 6 in 2006 (CATO 2008 Report, p. 68). In terms of recognizing and satisfying the collective need for freedom to trade internationally, Chile is ranked 5th in the world in 2006, up from 27th in 1995 and 7th in 2005 (CATO 2008 Report, p. 68).

The reciprocal relationship between economic freedom and development is explored by outstanding studies focusing on the development, strengths, and weaknesses of financial markets (item **800**); market efficiency in electricity production (items **790** and **808**); institutional changes in artisan fishing of austral cod (item **807**); political, legal, social, cultural, and, especially, environmental dimensions of the globalization of salmon production (item **789**); and the impact of freedom of trade and globalization on the wine industry (item **802**).

4. THE COLLECTIVE NEED, SERVICE, AND MARKET FOR EQUAL TREATMENT BY GOVERNMENT

Unequal treatment by government of households-individuals, enterprises and nonprofit institutions has been endemic in Chile. The collective output market where the moral collective need for equal treatment by government is satisfied has improved over time, but by no means enough. A high degree of poverty in the consumption-satisfaction of the moral collective need for equal treatment by government remains an important obstacle to attaining the goals of sustainable democracy, economic growth, and civil society. In pursuit of this goal, since 1973 and, especially, since the restoration of democracy in 1990, widespread mesoeconomic government policies have been introduced to improve access of low income households to education, health, and welfare, pivotal services for upward social, economic, and political mobility.

The following publications provide rich insights into the production efficiency of the collective output market for equal treatment by government. The articles examine labor market reform in an effort to equalize the playing field for all workers (item **786**); improving the quality of financial markets (item **800**); managing urbanization (item **809**); a description of the failings of the collective output market producing the moral collective need for equal treatment by government (item **796**); challenges created by the liberalization of the spot market of the electricity industry (item **790**); the need for reforms that increase productivity (item **813**); sources of inequality in the relative distribution of income (item **805**); integration of smallholders into commercial structures (item **803**); protection of natural resources under common property (item **807**); increasing the neutrality of the tax system (item **811**); provision of equally protected pensions to affiliates (item **804**); elimination of gender discrimination in labor markets (item **791**); the need for gender equity in antipoverty and antihunger programs (item **794**); development of equalized human capabilities (item **810**); and increased importance of satisfying human needs based on principles of solidarity and justice (item **798**).

5. THE COLLECTIVE NEED, SERVICE, AND MARKET FOR SOCIAL HARMONY

Without an efficiently functioning "social harmony" collective output market, it is impossible to achieve the goals of sustainable democracy, economic growth, and civil society. The sharply declining level of social harmony during the Allende presidency unleashed the uncontrollable centrifugal forces that largely precipitated the military dictatorship of General Pinochet. The degree of efficiency of the collective social harmony market depends on the actions of all institutional units, namely, households-individuals, enterprises, nonprofit institutions and government units. Furthermore, the degree of success in satisfying the moral collective need for social harmony has been as much a function of specific social harmony-promoting mesoeconomic policies, especially after 1990, as the post-1973, anti-inflationary, ultimately income-raising and unemployment-reducing macro monetary and fiscal policies.

An inadequate level of social harmony has historically characterized Chile, as demonstrated by the extreme inequality in its relative distribution of income. During 1995–2005, the percent share of household income of the poorest (lowest)

40 percent was 11 percent, while the highest (richest) 20 percent received a 60 percent share (UNICEF). According to The World Bank Group, the relative distribution of income was even worse. The income share held by the lowest 20 percent was only 3.5 percent in 2000, and 4.1 percent in 2006 (World Bank Group).

Chile is, however, the only country in Latin America which has achieved satisfactory results in respect to poverty reduction. It has complied with the first goal established in the Development Objectives of the Millennium, to reduce by half the persons living under conditions of absolute poverty between 1990 and 2015. Since the return to democracy in 1990, the proportion of the population which receives incomes below the poverty line, has fallen from 38.6 percent to 18.8 percent in 2003 (item **794**). In addition, during the same period, it reduced extreme poverty by a third, from 12.9 percent in 1990, to 4.7 percent in 2003. Despite these successes, the eradication of extreme poverty remains a priority challenge. Chile still had, in 2004, 2.9 million persons with incomes below the poverty line. Of these, 728,000 were indigents.

The vital role of the social harmony collective services submarket is revealed by the following excellent studies exploring the need for systems of labor protection as a means of improving the functioning of labor markets, and advancing growth and well-being through increases in productivity, labor participation, and improvement in human capital (item **786**); inequality in the relative distribution of income (item **805**); institutional evolution of artisan fishing of austral cod (item **807**); fairness of taxation through a transition from an enterprise income tax towards a tax on cash flows (item **811**); the changing morphology of the Santiago megalopolis (item **809**); precariousness of contractual relations of temporary, agricultural female workers (item **791**); rectitude of fiscal policy linked to concentration of policy making powers on the executive branch of government (item **792**); and the central role of well-being of humans in both labor and development policies (item **810**).

6. THE COLLECTIVE NEED, SERVICE, AND MARKET FOR SAFETY, SECURITY, AND PROTECTION OF PRIVATE PROPERTY AND PRICE STABILITY

The collective need for sanctity of private property of individuals-households, enterprises and nonprofit institutions is linked to their moral collective need for safety, security, and protection of human *cum* legal life-existence. As life needs to be protected, so too does the income earned by one's labor and related factor services. An institutional unit's labor and other income, and the parallel property, can be sacrosanct, as they should be, only as long as their inseparable, human nature-based moral collective needs for sanctity of life, and of its product, private property, are satisfied through production of the moral collective services in the corresponding collective services output markets. Much of the historically unprecedented growth of income and output in Chile since 1990 can be explained in terms of the equally unprecedented, synchronous, satisfaction of the interconnected collective needs for sanctity of natural as well as legal life-existence, and its byproduct, namely income and private property.

The Chilean post-1973 collective market of "privatization," i.e., where the moral collective need for private property, and by extension, for price stability, is recognized and satisfied, is a cause célèbre at a global level. Studies pertaining to the moral collective need for sanctity of private property analyze the following topics: the role of intangible assets in evaluating enterprises (item **812**); globalization of the wine industry (item **802**); specialization patterns in Chilean industry (item **788**); the post-mid-1980s economic takeoff (item **795**); labor market efficiency (item **786**); the phenomenal growth of Chile's financial system (item **800**); the growth of Greater Santiago (item **809**); the electricity industry (item **790**); volatility of productivity growth (item **813**); inequalities in the distribution of income (item **805**); the wholesale electricity market (item **808**); creation, destruction, and rotation of employment (item **814**); tax system reform (item **811**); private pension system (item **804**); salmon export industry (item **789**); system of contractors in Chilean agriculture (item **791**); fiscal rectitude (item **792**); exploitation of benthic resources (item **806**); and a critique of the Chilean privatization experiment (item **798**).

7. THE COLLECTIVE NEED, SERVICE, AND MARKET FOR ENVIRONMENTAL SANCTITY, SAFETY, SECURITY, AND PROTECTION

The environment is affected by the production, consumption, investment, leisure, and other activities of all institutional units and sectors. Furthermore, environmental sanctity can be endangered by the rate, as well as the nature, of economic growth. In turn, the impact of the environment on the quality of human life is indisputable. Thus, recognition and satisfaction of the moral collective need for environmental sanctity, through the "environmental" collective market, is a necessary precondition for the attainment of sustainable democracy, growth, and civil society.

An efficient market satisfying the collective need for environmental sanctity has gained special importance in Chile because of its rapid economic growth, urbanization, and dependence on agriculture-, mining-, and sea-based exports with undeniable environmental repercussions. Fundamental mesoeconomic environmental policies have thus become an important complement to successful macro monetary and fiscal policies in determining aggregate well-being.

The "environmental collective output submarket" has had uneven results. The percentage of population with access to improved water source was 86 in 2007 (The World Bank Group). CO_2 emissions (metric tons per capita) were 4.1 in 2000 and 4.5 in 2005 (The World Bank Group). Improved urban sanitation facilities (percentage of urban population with access) was 77 in 2000 and 78 in 2006 (The World Bank Group).

Studies focusing on the degree of recognition and satisfaction of the moral collective need for environmental protection cover the following topics: environmental impact of urbanization and centralization of population (item **809**); exploitation of mobile natural resources under common property (item **807**); the marijuana market (item **801**); benefits and costs, including environmental ones, of the salmon export industry (item **789**); research, development and innovation in the collective market producing the collective service of environmental sanctity (item **793**); and extraction and cooperation rules in the management and exploitation of benthic resources (item **806**).

What renders Chilean economic historiography unique, partially since 1973, but especially since 1990, is not so much the determination of "value" in shaping collective well-being through the division of political authority into the legislative, executive and judiciary powers, as advanced by Montesquieu, but the use of state power to largely (or rarely not) recognize and satisfy the seven, complementary, moral collective needs through their respective collective output markets. Although these collective output market values have unleashed the historically unprecedented centripetal forces forging Chile's current political, social, and economic dynamism, and phenomenal progress, it is still far too early to claim that they have reached the strength and sustainability level needed to permanently overcome Chilean economic inferiority.

786 Albagli, Elías. Mercado laboral y crecimiento económico: recomendaciones de política para Chile. (*Estud. Públicos*, 99, invierno 2005, p. 135–164, bibl., graphs, tables)

A review of the theoretical and empirical relationship between institutions and regulation of labor, the functioning of labor markets, and economic growth. In view of the implications on efficiency and welfare, and the structural characteristics of the Chilean labor market, Albagli proposes measures to increase labor efficiency and participation under a vision that legitimizes systems of labor protection. The major ones include: substitution of financing labor protection from a system of compensation towards unemployment insurance; increased flexibility in working hours and types of contracts; creation of a rule of adjustments of minimum wage in agreement with indicators of macroeconomic performance; fair compensation for childcare by parents between men and women; creation of a system of certification of abilities; and increased incentives for training by enterprises. The major improvements in growth and well-being would come from increases in productivity, labor participation, and improvement in human capital.

787 Albala-Bertrand, José Miguel. Cambio de la estructura productiva en Chile, 1986–1996: producción e interdependencia industrial. (*Rev. CEPAL/Santiago*, 88, abril 2006, p. 167–181, bibl., tables)

Albala-Bertrand carefully analyzes the changes in the Chilean production structure between 1986 and 1996 and, in general, until 2000, using input-output methodology. He concludes that, despite the notable rates of growth during the period examined, the Chilean economy still appears relatively weak as a base for a sustainable, more complex, economic and technological development.

788 Álvarez, Roberto and **Rodrigo Fuentes.** Pautas de especialización en una economía de rápido crecimiento: el caso de Chile. (*Trimest. Econ.*, 73:292, oct./dic. 2006, p. 749–781, bibl., graphs, tables)

Álvarez and Fuentes carefully analyze specialization patterns in the Chilean economy during the period of fastest economic growth, taking into account its relative abundance of productive factors. They describe the three major findings which are relevant for fast growing economies with an abundance of natural resources. First, even if there is a high degree of heterogeneity in output and productivity growth across economic activities, the most dynamic sectors are those more intensive in natural resources. In contrast, the labor intensive sectors are more likely to experience economic contraction. Second, consistent with international evidence, the results suggest that significant changes in Chilean specialization patterns are possible only if the economy increases substantially the investment in both physical and human capital. Third, the authors do not find evidence that the tradable sector is necessarily an engine of growth. In fact, during much of the period under analysis, the non-tradable sector experienced more rapid output and productivity growth than the tradable sector. This finding would be consistent with a number of structural reforms (privatization and liberalization of foreign direct investment) that favored expansion in the non-tradable sectors.

789 Aravena, Antonio. La industria del salmón en Chile: ¿crecimiento social o explotación laboral? (*Alternativa/Santiago*, 11:24, dic. 2006, p. 8–35, graphs, table)

The phenomenal growth of the Chilean salmon industry has been an integral component of rapid globalization. The value of salmon exports, which in 2005 reached 1.7 billion US dollars, is projected to reach 2.0 billion US dollars by 2010, and possibly even 3.0 billion US dollars. In addition to the economic and narrow production dimensions, there exist also major political, legal, social, cultural, and especially environmental factors that shape the collective and individual well-being of Chileans. Aravena's provocative study demonstrates the need to provide a balanced assessment of the multiple benefits and costs of the salmon export industry by considering such aspects as social harmony, income distribution, equal and fair (in terms of health, security, gender, compensation) treatment of those providing labor services, environmental sanctity, and political and economic freedoms.

790 Arellano, M. Soledad. Reformando el sector eléctrico chileno: diga no a la liberalización del mercado spot. (*Estud. Públicos,* 99, invierno 2005, p. 63–96, bibl., graphs, tables)

In this article, Arellano claims that liberalization of the spot market of the Chilean electricity industry is not a recommendable policy alternative because there exists an ample potential for the exercise of market power. In particular, the national electric company, ENDESA (Empresa Nacional de Electricidad, Sociedad Anonima), would distort the inter-temporal allocation of water, thus forcing an increase in the spot price, especially during periods of less elastic demand. In addition, two policies are analyzed which could serve to mitigate the competition problem: the sale of assets on the part of ENDESA and the obligation to sell part of the production through contracts. Although both alternatives would effectively attain a reduction of the market power problem, neither constitutes in practice a guarantee that the problem mentioned would not arise. The first alternative has a problem of practical feasibility, while the functioning of the second cannot be guaranteed in the medium and long term.

791 Caro Molina, Pamela and **Catalina de la Cruz Pincetti.** Contratistas e intermediación laboral en la agricultura de exportación. Santiago: CEDEM, Centro de Estudios para el Desarrollo de la Mujer, 2005. 217 p.: bibl., ill.

The theme and ideas in this book sprang from a research project carried out between March 2003 and May 2004 about the system of contractors in Chilean agriculture. The project was described as follows: "from diagnosis to action. A prospec-

tive study of the situation of precariousness of contractual relations of temporary, agricultural female employment: An analysis of the system of recruiters (enganchadores)." The first chapter examines the phenomenon of labor intermediation in the agricultural sector. The second provides a characterization of male and female employees of agro exports in the Maule Region and the province of Curicó in Chile. The third chapter presents the perspectives of the four actors involved: the contractors themselves, the enterprises, the markets, and the state through the inspection of labor (inspección del trabajo), and the organizations. It analyzes and characterizes the diverse types of labor intermediaries encountered and the motivations of each agent for participating in the system, his form of operating in practice, the advantages, disadvantages, and projections. The fourth chapter presents the tendencies found in relation to the labor conditions in which the direct or subcontracted workers find themselves. The last chapter of this excellent study contains a presentation and evaluation of the central features of the labor submarket in this predominantly agro-export area of Chile as well as recommendations for improvement.

792 Challenges to fiscal adjustment in Latin America: the cases of Argentina, Brazil, Chile, and Mexico. Edited by Luiz R. de Mello. Paris: Organisation for Economic Co-operation and Development, 2006. 166 p.: bibl., ill.

In the excellent chapter on Chile, José Pablo Arellano discusses the driving forces behind Chile's strong fiscal performance. He argues that fiscal rectitude owes much to the progressive concentration of policy-making powers in the executive branch of government, including over subnational finances. The ban on revenue earmarking is highlighted as a means of rendering fiscal management more flexible. Structural reform since the return to democracy in 1990 was facilitated by a high degree of political cohesiveness. The use of fiscal policy as a demand management instrument is due to the introduction of mechanisms to deal with the impact of fluctuations in copper prices on the budget and the business cycle, an achievement that is underpinned by Chile's low level of public indebtedness.

793 Chile: OECD reviews of innovation policy. Paris: OECD, 2007. 218 p.: bibl., ill. (OECD reviews of innovation policy) http://www.sourceoecd.org/9264037519

Chile's economy displays a low R&D intensity (0.67 percent of GDP in 2002). This excellent study outlines the strengths, weaknesses, opportunities, and threats of the Chilean national innovation system. Strengths include a stable macroeconomic framework and well-functioning product markets, international openness, reliable regulatory and legal frameworks, political commitment to increased support to innovation, among others. Weaknesses, in addition to the fragmented, low level of business R&D, include an underdeveloped and outdated infrastructure for technology diffusion, a low supply of seed and risk capital, and severe bottlenecks in the supply and mobility of human resources. Opportunities include the greater exploitation of value-added innovation in the resource-based industries, the ability to build innovative clusters around existing dynamic export-oriented industries, and an important potential of the service sector, from low-skilled jobs to knowledge-intensive business services. Finally, some threats discussed in these papers include loss of human and social capital if the current level of inequalities is not reduced, and the deterioration of misused capabilities, notably in engineering sciences.

794 Chile solidario y los desafíos de la igualdad. Recopilación de Verónica Riquelme y María Elena Valenzuela. Santiago: Oficina Internacional del Trabajo: Programa de las Naciones Unidas para el Desarrollo, 2005. 280 p.: bibl., ill. (Género, pobreza y empleo en América Latina)

The first Millennium Development Goal of the UN is to Eradicate Extreme Poverty and Hunger. Target 1: halve, between 1990 and 2005, the proportion of people whose income is less than 1 dollar a day. Target 2: achieve full and productive employment and decent work for all, including women and young people. Target 3: halve, between 1990 and 2015, the proportion of people who suffer from hunger. One of the most important initiatives of the Chilean government in its effort to eradicate extreme poverty and hunger

is the *Chile Solidario* (mutually binding) System of Social Protection (Sistema de Protección Social Chile Solidario). This useful monograph aims to strengthen the incorporation of gender equity into the actions of this program and, thereby, support efforts of contributing to the eradication of absolute poverty and attainment of an effective exercise of citizen rights of poor women. By providing a common knowledge base, which permits meeting the challenges intrinsic to overcoming extreme poverty, hunger, unemployment and gender inequality, it hopes to advance the well-being of men and especially women. Its first chapter analyzes the overlapping patterns of class and gender inequality and identifies the areas which Chile Solidario must advance to guarantee an effective equality of opportunities. The second provides a review of the assumptions and design of actions and makes innovative recommendations for strengthening the integration of the gender dimension. The third provides background information about the needs and abilities of the families targeted by Chile Solidario. The fourth constitutes a counterpoint to the analysis of the program. Based on empirical and background information, it describes the visions of the providers and beneficiaries. The ultimate goal is to create labor markets which, by being free of gender inequality and discrimination, can create high quality, "decent," well protected and compensated, work.

795 De Gregorio, José. Crecimiento económico en Chile: evidencia, fuentes y perspectivas. (*Estud. Públicos*, 98, otoño 2005, p. 19–86, bibl., graphs, tables)

A solid review of the Chilean growth experience with special emphasis on the rapid growth which started in the mid-1980s, when the economy was recovering from the crisis of 1982, to become more moderate by the end of the 1990s. It also analyzes the evidence with respect to growth and activity, reviewing strengths and weaknesses of the economic takeoff of Chile and the elements which sustain future growth. Finally, it presents estimates for the long term potential economic growth of the Chilean economy. For political economy specialist's comment, see item **2325**.

796 Fazio R., Hugo. TLC: el amarre del modelo. Santiago: LOM Ediciones: Univ. Academia de Humanismo Cristiano, 2004. 172 p.: bibl., ill. (Ciencias humanas. Economía)

Hugo Fazio Rigazzi, a truly prolific author, who served as vice president of the Central Bank and as representative of Chile to the Inter-American Development Bank during the 1970–73 Allende presidency, provides a detailed critique of Chile's (June 4th, 2004) free trade agreement with the US. Fazio argues that the agreement subordinates Chilean democracy and sovereignty to the interests of the US.

797 Gómez-Lobo, Andrés and Aldo González. El financiamiento de gastos generales mediante las tarifas aeronáuticas en Chile: una crítica económica. (*Estud. Públicos,* 102, otoño 2006, p. 211–236, graphs, tables)

Aeronautic rates and fees are the prices paid by the users of the national aeronautic system for the diverse services provided by the sector. In Chile, it was announced that by the end of 2005 there would be an increase in the passenger embarkation fee for international flights from the prevailing level of 26 US dollars per passenger to 30 US dollars. The collected revenues would be used to finance campaigns abroad promoting Chile as a tourist destination, as well as to support the Fund for a Campaign against Poverty within the framework of Chilean participation in UN Peace Campaigns. This article presents a comparison of the aeronautic rates in various countries of the world using a non-parametric technique of comparative efficiency. The results suggest that the rates in Chile are, on average, relatively lower given the levels of traffic and the quality level of the sector. Despite that finding, the article argues that financing the non-aeronautic activities with rates and fees of the sector is not commendable for the following reasons: First, it is an expensive form of financing public expenditure in comparison with other alternatives. Second, it would be fairer and more efficient for the tourist industry to finance the campaigns of promoting Chile abroad. Third, by increasing travel costs, the increase in the embarkation fees becomes counterproductive as a means of promoting Chile as a

tourist destination. Among international travelers, the tourist segment is the most price-sensitive.

798 Gonzalorena Döll, Jorge. Transformaciones de la economía chilena en el siglo XX. (*Ciclos Hist. Econ. Soc.,* 15:30, segundo semestre 2005, p. 95–132, bibl.)

This is a highly informative survey of Chile's economic history since Independence from a broad dependency perspective. Chile's challenge, according to the author, consists in reversing the individualist and socially disintegrating course of late capitalism imposed today upon its economic activity, by creating a new framework that effectively guards the interest of the society, as expressed in a total of fundamental values and objectives. This can be achieved only through a New International Economic and Political Order, which satisfies human needs based on principles of solidarity and justice, thus giving rise to a dignified, comfortable, and secure life for all.

799 Gutiérrez Casa, Luis Enrique. Potencial de desarrollo y gestión de la política regional: el caso de Chihuahua. (*Front. Norte,* 19:38, julio/dic. 2007, p. 7–35, bibl., graphs, maps, tables)

Between 1979 and 1999, general mortality rates in Chile fell from 6.8 to 5.4 per thousand while infant (one year of age or younger) mortality rates decreased from 75 to 38 per thousand of live births. The authors present a methodology to determine the value of the reductions in the mortality rates based on a model in which agents choose consumption and leisure, facing survival rates. Their results indicate that changes in the mortality rates between 1980 and 1997 can be valued at 270 percent of Chilean GDP in 1998.

800 Hernández, Leonardo and Fernando Parro. Sistema financiero y crecimiento económico en Chile. (*Estud. Públicos,* 99, invierno 2005, p. 97–134, bibl., graphs, tables)

The financial system of Chile is one of the largest among emerging economies. Still, it is not equal to the size of developed countries or of some of the emerging economies of Asia. This study presents a brief description of the degree of development of the financial markets in Chile, in comparison with other countries. After summarizing the principal financial reforms implemented in the country in recent decades, it points out the most important weaknesses and strengths of the financial markets in Chile. In continuation, it analyzes the urgent problems, in particular the liquidity of the stock market, the market of financial derivatives and the market of risk capital, and discusses whether recent reforms and proposals adequately resolve these problems.

801 Hurtado, Paula. Determinantes del consumo de marihuana en Chile: análisis de los datos de autorreporte. (*Estud. Públicos*, 102, otoño 2006, p. 147–177, bibl., table)

This study models the demand for marijuana in Chile and estimates it by using data from the last national survey about narcotics in the general population. The results reveal that when the monetary price increases and perceived risk rises, the proportion of the population that decides to consume the drug declines. The effect of the prices of other substances over the decision to consume marijuana suggests that substitution dominates between it and legal drugs (tobacco and alcohol), while in relation to cocaine (in the form of hydrochloride or pasta base) the predominant effect is one of complementarity.

802 Morel-Astorga, Paulina. The Chilean wine industry: its technological transformation and new export orientation. (*Iberoamericana/Stockholm*, 31:2, 2001, p. 85–101, ill., table)

In this fascinating, well-documented essay, Morel-Astorga discusses the effects of government policy, the globalization process, and a new entrepreneurial climate-spirit, on the Chilean wine industry. During the 1938–73 era of interventionism, the Chilean state aimed to promote the wine industry through numerous direct measures, including confiscation and formation of new co-operative enterprises. The 1973–2009 era is characterized by liberalization of markets, elimination of prohibitions, technology transfer, creation of Centers of Business Development and active promotion of exports. Globalization of the wine industry leads to technological transformation, export orientation and changing production

and consumption patterns. Implementation of new technology, global market possibilities, and multiple innovations reinforce the reciprocal links between the wine industry, and the imitative, as well as the innovative, entrepreneurship, giving birth to the Chilean wine miracle.

803 OECD review of agricultural policies: Chile. Paris: OECD, 2008. 153 p.: bibl., col. ill.

Chile's agricultural sector has played an important role in the country's economic development, helping raise incomes and reduce poverty. The sector has benefited from a stable macroeconomic climate and an open trading environment, and exports have grown rapidly, notably for high value products such as wine and fruits. A current priority of the Chilean government is to broaden the basis of agricultural growth by successfully integrating the country's smallholders into commercial structures. This extremely well researched and documented review measures the level and composition of support provided to Chilean agriculture, and evaluates the effectiveness of current measures in attaining their objectives. The study finds that Chile provides much lower support and protection to its agricultural sector than most OECD countries, even though government expenditures on the sector have trebled in real terms over the past ten years. About half of that spending is on public goods such as infrastructure and irrigation, while the other half consists mostly of measures that seek to make Chile's poorer farmers more competitive. The report suggests ways in which the effectiveness of these policies might be enhanced, including by systematic evaluation of policy performance, by closer co-ordination across government agencies and by framing policies for smallholders and salaried farm workers in an economy-wide context, so that agricultural policies can focus on potentially competitive farmers and be effectively distinguished from other development and social policies.

804 Ortiz H., Roberto; Salvador Zurita L.; and Gustavo Genoni. Riesgos de inversión y empleo en el sistema de pensiones chileno. (*Trimest. Econ.*, 73:290, abril/junio 2006, p. 575–609, bibl., graphs, tables)

The Chilean private pension system is one of defined contribution. Thus, the future pension of its affiliates is uncertain. In this paper, the authors study two factors that influence the level of pensions that an affiliate can expect to receive at retirement: temporary unemployment (and the consequent lack of contributions) and the investment risk of the pension assets themselves. They model the wage curve over time of a representative Chilean affiliate, but do not add risk to it. Instead they focus on the risk of unemployment, which they model as a Markov process with two states: employed and unemployed. Furthermore, they model the investment risk assuming that the pension assets follow a geometric Brownian motion. They use the model to estimate the probability distribution of pensions at retirement age. This allows them to estimate the likely impact of changes in the aggregate unemployment rate and the risk and return on the future pensions. They find that the future pensions of Chilean affiliates are more sensitive to investment risks than to unemployment risks. Also, female affiliates are more vulnerable than male affiliates, and married male affiliates are more vulnerable than single ones.

805 Palma, Alexis. Explaining earnings and income inequality in Chile. Göteborg: Göteborg Univ., 2007. 1 v.: bibl., ill. (Economic studies/Dept. of Economics, School of Business, Economics and Law, Göteborg Univ., 169)

Distribution of income has been a central topic in public discourse in Chile since colonial times. In the four essays of his PhD dissertation, Palma focuses on the inequality of the relative distribution of income in Chile between 1970 and 2003. Essay I examines the levels, trends, and explanations of income inequality. Essay II focuses on the size, significance, and sources of recent income inequality changes. Essay III analyzes the occupational structure and earnings inequality in Chile, 1992–2000. And essay IV describes the price and composition effects on the rise and fall of inequality in Santiago. This well-researched study makes a valuable contribution to the literature of Chilean economic development in respect to the relative distribution of income.

806 Palma, Mario and **Carlos Chávez.** Normas y cumplimiento en áreas de manejo de recursos bentónicos: estudio de caso en la región del Bío-Bío. (*Estud. Públicos*, 102, otoño 2006, p. 237–276, tables)

This highly informative study describes forms of organization and norms of functioning in areas of management and exploitation of benthic resources in the Bío-Bío region. In addition, on the basis of a special survey applied to the fishermen members of their organizations, a report is provided on the results of an evaluation of the observance of extraction and cooperation rules. Concludes that even if the areas considered present similar organization and functioning aspects, differences exist in relation to the systems of vigilance used and rules of distribution of economic benefits. The results of the survey indicate that while 18 percent of the fishermen declare themselves as violators of the rules restricting the extraction of resources, 43 percent admit to transgressing rules of cooperation. Also analyzes the socioeconomic profiles of the offending artisan fishermen, their perception in respect to the legitimacy of the regulation and the leaders, and their sense of membership to their organizations.

807 Peña-Torres, Julio; R. Javier Bustos; and **Claudio Pérez.** Mercados informales y control vertical: comercialización de producción perecible. (*Estud. Públicos*, 101, verano 2006, p. 239–282, graphs)

This is an excellent study of the institutional changes that have occurred since the end of the 1990s in artisan fishing of austral cod (merluza austral = Merluccius australis), a species of high export value captured between the X and XII Region. The institutional evolution of this fishing during the last decade represents a pioneering and virtually unique process in Chile, and without doubt exceptional at the world level, considering productive sectors that exploit mobile natural resources under common property. A total of artisan fishermen communities, which operate in these fisheries, have attained an organizational success in order to control the extractive effort of the distinct artisan fleets in operation. And this, despite the fact that this extractive activity has important atomization and the fishing resource is *de jure* under common property.

The institutional innovations introduced have involved systems of actions and fishing control with important self government spaces for the fishing communities. This study examines aspects of industrial organization which have conditioned the interchange patterns prevailing in this sector. Standing out are the significant persistence of industrial concentration in the wholesale commercialization of the exported production, as well as the use of different mechanisms of vertical control in the interchange between wholesale merchants, exporters, processors, and intermediate agents who contract the haul with the fishermen. Contractual aspects being analyzed include: use of informal transactions, multidimensional exchanges with the same commercial opposite side, the provisional specificity in the value of the exchange as a result of the perishableness of the product, the use of different vertical control mechanisms and the influence of an increasing industrial concentration to the extent that there is an advance in the wholesale commercialization chain towards final export markets.

808 Rudnick, Hugh. Un nuevo operador independiente de los mercados eléctricos chilenos. (*Estud. Públicos*, 101, verano 2006, p. 213–238, graph)

The wholesale electricity market of each of the interconnected systems of Chile is administered by the Center for the Economic Load Dispatch (Centro de Despacho Económico de Carga-CDEC), an organization charged with the physical, economic and commercial operation of the system. The functioning of the CDEC is one of the most discussed and analyzed aspects of regulation, and its reorganization has been proposed on various occasions. The article reviews the ideal characteristics which this organization needs to realize, according to international standards, and how CDEC does or does not meet them. An analysis is provided of how changes in its structure and mode of operation have been gradually introduced. Finally, suggestions are made of how this reform can be advanced to establish an effective, independent operator.

809 Santiago en la globalización: una nueva ciudad? Edición de Carlos A. de Mattos *et al.* 2. ed.Santiago: Ediciones SUR: Eure Libros, 2004. 294 p.: bibl., ill., maps.

This truly impressive collection of ten excellent essays focuses on the multiple, and up to now little analyzed, dimensions of the rapidly changing morphology of Santiago, the capital-metropolitan city-region of Chile.

810 Sehnbruch, Kirsten. The Chilean labor market: a key to understanding Latin American labor markets. New York: Palgrave Macmillan, 2006. 339 p.: bibl., ill., index.

In this highly informative book, Sehnbruch argues that, after years of high and stable economic growth combined with targeted social policies, the Chilean labor market could not generate good jobs. With this book, Sehnbruch hopes to make a contribution to the debate of whether the Chilean experience reflects a "Model Performance or Precarious Employment" first, by placing labor policy at the center of the development policy agenda and human beings and their well-being at the center of labor policy; second, by offering a different theoretical approach to the issues—not tarnished with the ideological fervor of either neoliberalism or its opponents; third, by replacing the simplistic focus of labor market analysis on the unemployment rate with a more comprehensive measure of the quality of employment which could be replicated in other countries with limited data; and, fourth, by presenting detailed information on such aspects of the Chilean labor market as its politics, empirical evidence, and policies. Chap. 1 provides an interesting, human-capabilities-focused, introduction to the overall theme of the book. Chap. 2 provides the author's justification for adopting the capability approach. Chap. 3 shows how Chile's three post-Pinochet democratic governments maintained and refined the labor market model that they inherited as a consequence of the unprecedented structural transformation process carried out during Pinochet's lengthy military dictatorship. Chaps. 4–5 discuss such aspects of the labor market as the type of contract, occupational position, social security, size of company, employment, poverty and income distribution, unionization, and regulatory enforcement. Chaps. 6–7 discuss Chile's new unemployment insurance, vocational training, and institutional structure. Chap. 8 presents a model of a quality of employment indicator as a complement, in policy debate, to the unemployment rate. Sehnbruch's self-professed constructive conclusion is that her approach goes beyond judging Chile's development process in the rather simplistic language of economic growth, unemployment, or poverty rates by instead discussing it from a perspective of the development of human capabilities. For comment by political economist, see item **2335**.

811 Serra, Pablo. La reforma al sistema tributario chileno: una tarea inconclusa. (*Estud. Públicos*, 101, verano 2006, p. 187–212, graphs, tables)

In recent years, there have been introduced diverse modifications in the tax system which brought it closer to a tax on expenditure. This solid article by Pablo Serra proposes to complete this road, suggesting the gradual elimination of limits to the saving incentive mechanisms, and substitution of the enterprise income tax by a tax on cash flows (IFC=impuesto a los flujos de caja). If it were impossible to establish the IFC, Serra proposes that the enterprise tax be applicable only to distributed profits while, at the same time, the accelerated depreciation be eliminated. It is also proposed that the state take bids for mineral resources and that part of the revenue is used to remunerate their discoverers. Finally, it is proposed to freeze tax collection as a percentage of GDP (Gross Domestic Product), the aim being to concentrate on effectiveness of public expenditure.

812 Valenzuela D., Elena. Consideración de los intangibles en la evaluación de acciones por los analistas financieros. (*Rev. Mex. Econ. Finanz.*, 3:2, junio 2004, p. 101–126, bibl., graphs, tables)

Traditionally, financial information has dominated investment decisions. However, analysis of intangible assets has assumed increasing importance. The objective of this thoroughly researched, excellent, study by Valenzuela D. is to establish the relevance of intangible assets that financial analysts assign in studying firms and recommending actions. Valenzuela carefully describes the variables serving as inputs in such decisions and their weights in evaluating firms of different economic sectors. The study includes a survey of 76.1 percent of local stockbrokers in Santiago, Chile. The evidence demonstrates the use of nonfinan-cial information in the recommendations of stock purchases and the differences according to economic sector.

813 Vergara, Rodrigo. Productividad en Chile: determinantes y desempeño. (*Estud. Públicos*, 99, invierno 2005, p. 23–62, bibl., graphs, tables)

The objective of this careful study is to analyze the determinants of productivity in Chile between 1960 and 2004. It also presents a discussion of the strengths and weaknesses existing in this material. Productivity in Chile during these years has been very volatile and has also been strongly correlated with the economic cycle. The longest period of sustained growth and elevated productivity was during 1986–97, which is referred to as the "golden age of the Chilean economy." In order to recover this growth process, Vergara argues that it is necessary to emphasize reforms which permit attainment of improvements in those variables which have a significant effect on productivity and in which currently Chile is relatively weaker.

814 Vergara M., Sebastián. Dinámica laboral de la industria en Chile. (*Rev. CEPAL/Santiago*, 86, agosto 2005, p. 147–166, bibl., graphs, tables)

This solid study analyzes the labor dynamics of industry in Chile through descriptive and parametric information, at the level of industrial plants, between 1979 and 2000. It examines the creation, destruction, and rotation of employment and investigates its link to the economic cycle, the sectoral characteristics, and the size of the plants. It finds evidence of procyclical employment creation and countercyclical employment destruction; of countercyclical labor rotation inversely related to plant size; of strong heterogeneity among sectors; of great importance of managerial demographics in the evolution of employment and the primary responsibility of large enterprises in the labor flows. Subsequently, it examines the impact of trade liberalization, the exchange rate and comparative advantages on sectoral employment flows. It concludes that a decrease in custom duties increases the destruction and, for that reason, the employment rotation, and that comparative advantages and an increase in the exchange rate have a positive effect on employment creation and labor rotation.

PERU

MARÍA AMPARO CRUZ-SACO, Professor of Economics, Connecticut College

THE CONTRIBUTIONS REVIEWED FOR *HLAS 65* can be grouped into four categories. The first category includes works that analyze macroeconomic issues such as sustained economic growth (item **815**), management of the external debt (item **818**), and the role of minimum wages (item **817**). The second category reflects an interest in gaining a better understanding of the role of micro and small enterprises, particularly with newly enacted legislation designed to assist with professional development needs and enhance commitment to corporate social responsibility (items **823** and **825**). The third category is represented by contributions that study capacity building in the areas of international trade negotiation and competitiveness in textile and apparel production (items **820** and **822**). And finally, the fourth category includes two unique volumes: one examines the complexities associated with assigning a value to the contributions of the "culture" industry (item **816**) and the other analyzes the political economy of foreign direct investment and the socioeconomic implications of the carbon mine of Goyllarisquizga in Cerro de Pasco, Peru (item **821**).

815 Cinco años: crecimiento económico sostenido y recuperación democrática: el gobierno de Alejandro Toledo Manrique, 2001–2006. Recopilación e investigación de Patricia Arévalo, con asistencia de edición e investigación de Michelle Salcedo Teullet. Lima: Presidencia del Consejo de Ministros, 2006. 397 p.: col. ill., col. map.

Comprehensive overview of the institutional and economic achievements of President Alejandro Toledo's administration in 2001–2006. The book is presented by President Toledo and it covers a wide range of critical areas including the strengthening of democracy, respect of human rights, independence of state institutions and anticorruption policies, state reform, efforts to decentralize public administration, economic recovery and sustainable growth, poverty reduction, and attainment of millennium development goals. The book concludes with a list of pending issues and an agenda for the future in which poverty eradication and sustained economic growth are highlighted as key objectives. Prepared by the technical staff of Pedro Pablo Kuczynski, prime minister (Presidente del Consejo de Ministros) and minister of finance, the book uses abundant official statistics, in most cases publicly available, and other primary sources. Clearly written and carefully edited, this source should

become an important reference book for readers interested in Peru's recent development process.

816 El impacto económico de la cultura en Perú. Equipo del Instituto de Investigación de la Escuela Profesional de Turismo y Hotelería de la Universidad de San Martín de Porres. Bogotá: Convenio Andrés Bello, 2005. 265 p.: bibl., ill. (Economía & cultura; 11)

Original study that measures the economic impact of "culture." To measure the value of the culture industry, the authors acknowledge the complexities involved in valuing the economic contribution of culture to society. These concerns aside, however, they select the following industries for their study: publishing and magazine industry, performing arts, radio and television broadcasting, music and film industry, handicrafts, museums, and the marketing industry. For each of these, they provide contextual information, a brief historical review, an estimate of their relative share in gross domestic product (for formal activities only), and an economic analysis. For certain industries, the authors provide calculations of the value of black market sales. The study is based on data collected by institutions such as the Cámara Peruana del Libro, Cultural Center of the Catholic Univ.,

Peruvian-Japanese Cultural Center, National Institute of Culture, and interviews with experts and managers in the culture industry. The authors emphasize that satellite accounts can be used to supplement the national accounting system thereby helping to measure the economic contributions of these activities. They also offer a note of caution regarding free trade agreements that promote the globalization of culture for massive markets and in the process negatively affect the creation and sustainability of a native or indigenous culture.

817   Jaramillo, Miguel and **Kristian López.** Cómo se ajusta el mercado de trabajo ante cambios en el salario mínimo en el Perú?: una evaluación de la experiencia de la última década. San Isidro, Peru: Grupo de Análisis para el Desarrollo (GRADE): Consorcio de Investigación Económica y Social (CIES), 2006. 70 p.: bibl. (Documento de trabajo; 50) (Serie Diagnóstico y propuesta; 26)

Econometric analysis of the impact of the minimum wage on work income and employment in both the formal and informal sectors in 1996–2004. It uses data from the national household surveys (1996–2000) and the permanent survey on employment for Metropolitan Lima (2003–04). The minimum wage has been administered erratically, influencing income distribution in the informal sector when the minimum salary is low, and both the informal and formal sectors when it is set at a relatively higher level. In the short-term, an increase in the minimum wage increases the income of the small portion of workers in the formal sector who are paid an income that falls in the vicinity of the new minimum wage. But changes in the minimum wage negatively affect the probability of maintaining the employment of salaried workers who earn from 1.2 to 2 minimum wages and have no impact on the informal sector. Here, it appears as if the transfer from formal salaried workers to the informal sector increases competition which may lead to job losses among informal workers. An important implication of the study is that Peru's recent experience with the administration of the minimum wage suggests that it is not an instrument that can be used to increase the equity of the distribution of work income.

818   Lezama Coca, Hugo. Deuda externa Peruana 1969–2004: atrapados sin salida? Lima: Univ. Nacional Mayor de San Marcos, Facultad de Ciencias Económicas, 2007. 185 p.: bibl., ill.

Analysis of the evolution of the external debt crisis in 1969–2000 by four consecutive regimes: the Military Junta (1969–79), Acción Popular (1980–85), APRA (1986–90), and Cambio 90 (1991–2000). The first two used external debt to fund their development agendas. The APRA government under Alan García defaulted on the service of the external debt, and Fujimori contracted external debt and attracted foreign direct investment as part of the liberalization process. Peruvian creditors varied from international financial organizations (to fund infrastructure projects and reconstruction efforts following the natural disasters from El Niño) to the Russian government (that provided financial support for the purchase of armament and weaponry) and Japanese suppliers (for mining projects). In the early 1980s, the international external debt payment crisis motivated a series of refinancing cycles among a large number of developing countries with their creditors, including Peru. The author, who was director of the office of public credit with the ministry of finance, presents evidence on the various refinancing models, the Paris Club negotiations, and projections of debt service payments. Critical review of the 1999 International Monetary Fund facility, external debt policies of Fujimori and Toledo, and of the various schemes to reduce payment through bond conversions and Paris Club negotiations. Policy recommendations are formulated at the end. The relevant data presented and the first-hand observations by the author make this book an important reference for readers interested in this topic.

819   More Palacios, Raúl; Emma Zevallos Aguilar; and **Arturo Granados Mogrovejo.** Pequeño comercio y desarrollo económico social. Recopilación de Raúl More Palacios y Vicente Otta Rivera. Jesús María, Peru: EDAPROSPO, Equipo de Educación y Autogestión Social, 2003. 199 p., 5 folded leaves of plates: bibl., ill., col. maps. (Serie Economía popular; 1)

Examines street vending and petty commerce (*comercio ambulatorio*) in five districts of Metropolitan Lima (Comas, Carabayillo, Ate-Vitarte, Santa Anita, and San Juan de Lurigancho) with a focus on commercial conglomerates, location, and differentiation among vendors (by More Palacios); gender relationships (by Zevallos Aguilar); and municipal policies regarding street vending (Granados Mogrovejo). More Palacios argues that street vending reflects the structural inability of the economy to generate productive and decent jobs for a large proportion of the working age population. Most of this type of commerce is conducted by females which is transforming gender relationships at home that need further analysis. Street vending often generates conflictive relationships among neighbors, vendors and town officials. But relocating street vendors and consolidating them into commercial conglomerates in designated spaces has not reduced the level of municipal tension and extensive presence of this type of commerce in urban centers. An integrated strategy with effective labor market interventions is required. The most important component of this vision should be the forging of productive linkages, creation of job opportunities, and stable domestic markets.

820 More Palacios, Raúl; Mirtha Villanueva Rodríguez; and Teresa Morales Bayro. Identificación de demandas y desarrollo de capacidades en el pequeño comercio. Peru: EDAPROSPO, Equipo de Educación y Autogestión Social: COPEME, 2006. 158 p.: bibl., ill. (Serie Economía popular; 2)

Identifies the needs for professional development of small businesspeople in commerce as well as beneficiaries of EDAPROSPO. This study is based on 452 surveys including 315 businesspeople in commerce, 30 managers of small stores (mostly food, cleaning, health and beauty products), and 60 EDAPROSPO beneficiaries. The book discusses the relationship between barriers that microenterprises face and the need for capacity building in the area of entrepreneurship development; goals, methodology, survey design and samples for the empirical study; the main features of the sample for both businesspeople in commerce and EDAPROSPO beneficiaries, and a description of the supply of and revealed demand for professional development for

businesspeople and beneficiaries (through the survey). Findings about the perceived demand for capacity building through entrepreneurship development are presented at the end. Included is a chapter by Mirtha Villanueva Rodríguez and Teresa Morales Bayro on adult education and services for developing entrepreneurial skills among small businesspeople.

821 Muñasqui Hurtado, Teófilo. Goyllarisquizga: explotación del carbón y la voracidad del imperialismo yanqui. Jesús María, Peru: Editorial San Marcos, 2006. 625 p.: bibl., ill., maps.

This book combines an historical review of the formal creation of the town of Goyllarisquizga (translated from Quechua as "the fallen star" because ancient inhabitants recollect how a meteor struck a nearby field) with narratives about the struggles of Peruvian peasants and mining workers in the department of Cerro de Pasco. Social exclusion and marginalization of indigenous communities began in colonial times with the extensive Spanish exploitation of gold and silver. The encomienda system used by Spanish colonizers forced the native indigenous labor to work in exchange for their Christianization and survival. Peru's political independence from Spain in the early 1820s did not transform the system of oppression of the Indian population now in the hands of both national and foreign-owned mining firms. In 1881, Peru was occupied by the Chilean army after losing the Pacific War (1979) and ceding the vast and nitrate rich territory of Antofagasta to Chile. Abusive labor contracts for mining workers and the negative environmental effect of the carbon industry continued at Goyllarisquizga when the Cerro de Pasco Cooper Corporation bought the land in 1901, heavily invested in the mining "enclave" to extract minerals, and shipped them out of the country until the closing of the carbon mine in 1970. The mine was reopened in 1978 by the state-owned firm Centromin-Peru with similar negative consequences on the health status of the labor force and on the environment. The author argues that the use of the dialectical materialism approach is most appropriate for understanding the history of mining production and labor relationships in a dependent society. He illustrates the resilience and strength of the indigenous Quechua population with references to the work of local labor union leaders and other brave community members. He further highlights the contributions of Marxist leaders such as José Carlos Mariátegui and reports on his own work as an active community organizer.

822 Muñoz Marticorena, William. Perú, tradición textil y competitividad internacional. Colaboración de Carmen Valdivia y María Albujar. Lima: Fondo Editorial de la Univ. Católica Sedes Sapientiae, 2006. 151 p.: bibl.

This study shows that the production of apparel has the potential for promoting growth, manufactured exports, and creating productive and stable jobs. Precolonial weavers and handicrafters worked with cotton and wool (alpaca and vicuña in particular), and organic dyes. The authors argue that this tradition can be supported by appropriate macroeconomic policies that should create new institutions, leadership, and entrepreneurship, development of clusters, and upward value chain movements among national producers. Accompanied by increased research and development as well as investment, new production chains should raise productivity and thus, the competitiveness of Peruvian textiles and apparel. Peru ranks low in competitiveness as measured by the Growth Competitiveness Index 2005 and using a systemic approach, such as the Porter competitiveness model, a national plan for textiles and apparel should be formulated. The authors analyze special markets for Peruvian textiles and apparel and make recommendations on ways to increase competitiveness.

823 Portocarrero S., Felipe; Bruno Tarazona; and Luis Camacho. Situación de la responsabilidad social empresarial en la micro, pequeña y mediana empresa en el Perú. Lima: Univ. del Pacífico, Centro de Investigación, 2006. 94 p.: bibl., charts. (Documento de trabajo; 75)

This pioneer study on corporate social responsibility among micro-, small-, and medium enterprises in Peru is based on a survey of 150 firms in manufacturing, commerce, and services, of which half employed less than 50 workers and the other

half, more than 50 workers. This study was part of a regional project sponsored by the IADB, which included Argentina, Brazil, Chile, Colombia, El Salvador, Mexico, and Venezuela. Three categories of corporate social responsibility were identified: external (supporting sports, cultural activities, health and well-being, education, vulnerable groups, public life), internal (supporting the health and well-being of workers, their professional development, work and family balance, equal opportunities, good corporate governance), and the environment (environmental impact of firm's activities; efficiency of energy and water consumption, trash disposal and recycling programs, integrated environmental systems, environmental certification of providers). Survey results show that corporate social responsibility is still a novel initiative among Peruvian firms. External and environmental social responsibility is almost non-existent and if it exists, it is an isolated and sporadic event. There is, however, commitment to the well-being and professional development of workers due in part to the goal of enhancing the workplace climate. Even among informal businesses that do not comply with labor regulations, businesspeople grant acknowledgements and incentives from monetary bonuses to educational opportunities. Due to size and greater managerial capacity, medium-size enterprises are more likely to follow more consistent internal and environmental social responsibility strategies. Promotion and guidance through appropriate macro policies can potentially lead to the development of social responsibility in the future.

824 Tópicos de negociaciones comerciales internacionales: metodologías y aplicaciones relevantes para el Perú. Edición de Fernando González Vigil *et. al.* Lima: Univ. del Pacífico, Centro de Investigación, 2006. 561 p.: bibl., ill.

This volume brings together selected studies on international trade negotiations that were conducted in 2004–05 by graduates from Universidad del Pacífico under the supervision of Fernando González Vigil. The motivation for the development of capacity building in this area was prompted by negotiation of free trade agreements (FTA), notably with the US, at the intergovernmental level with technical support from a business council on international negotiations (Consejo Empresarial de Negociaciones Internacionales). Contributions are grouped in two parts: analysis of preferential trade agreements and analysis of issues in international trade negotiations. The first part includes six contributions on the Peru-China FTA; Peru, the Andean Community of Nations (CAN) and the European Union (EU); impact on CAN from the creation of a free trade zone with Mercosur; impact on the bilateral trade between Peru and Chile from an agreement on economic integration (Acuerdo de Complementación Económica, ACE); impact of preferential trade agreements on foreign direct investment in the CAN; and opportunities and challenges from a Peru-Singapore FTA. Issues covered in part two include: an analytical survey of non-tariff measures that Peru's exporters face; unanticipated application of safeguards; test data protection for Peruvian pharmaceuticals under the Peru-US FTA; rules of origin and trade in the economic integration agreement between Peru and Chile and in the Chile-US FTA; and impact of intellectual property protection on medicine imports n Peru.

825 Vildoso Chirinos, Carmen. Dos años en el Ministerio de Trabajo: agenda, micro y pequeñas empresas. Lima: s.n., 2004. 188 p.: bibl.

Analysis of the genesis and legislative approval of the law that promotes and legalizes small and micro-enterprises on June 5, 2002 (Ley de Promoción y Formalización de la Micro y Pequeña empresa). This new law aimed at increasing the competitiveness of these enterprises, and enhancing working conditions for their workers. It provided parameters to define a small or micro-enterprise, and delineated five instruments to support their future development. The law affected more than half of the salaried labor force, estimated in 2002 at three million workers and another half million of nonsalaried workers. The law created an organization, CODEMYPE, at the highest ministerial level with representation from diverse stakeholders and a focal point with the Ministry of Labor and Employment Promotion. CODEMYPE was responsible for the planning, coordination and harmonization of sectoral policies, access to financial services and technical assistance, statistical monitoring and assessment of the development of this sector. The author, who held the position of deputy minister for social promotion in the Ministry for Labor and Social Promotion, was directly involved in the passing of the law. Sections in the book are rich personal testimony of her experience as a policymaker and as a participant in negotiations among political parties, labor unions, private sector representatives and other stakeholders.

PARAGUAY

MELISSA H. BIRCH, *Associate Professor and Director, Center for International Business Education and Research, University of Kansas*

THE SURGE IN RESEARCH AND PUBLICATION of economics literature that occurred immediately after the fall of the Stroessner dictatorship seems to have run its course. In the last few years, there has been a noticeable drop in publications by Paraguayan authors writing about the Paraguayan economy, while the literature published in the US on the Paraguayan economy continues to be slim. What is conspicuous in this year's collection is the presence of funded research studies sponsored by foreign or international agencies and realized by a combination of Paraguayan and international scholars. The topics are widely varied but often have a policy focus.

826 Algunos enfoques sobre el empleo y el capital social en el Paraguay: resultado de investigaciones. Asunción: Asociación Paraguaya de Estudios de Población, 2005. 214 p.: bibl., ill. (Serie de investigaciones—población y desarrollo; 2)

The volume contains four studies sponsored by the UN's Fund for Population Studies and conducted in 2005. The two studies that focus on employment come from sociological and economic perspectives, respectively. The social capital studies focus on the role of education in the formation of social capital and the connection between social capital and community violence. All are well done academic papers with ample data, mostly from the Encuesta de Hogares.

827 Cohn, Patricia J.; Matthew S. Carroll; and Jo Ellen Force. So happy together or better off alone?: women's economic activities, cooperative work, and empowerment in rural Paraguay. (*Community Dev.*, 34:1, Jan. 2003, p. 57–74, bibl.)

This study examines the income-generating activities of women in a small town in Caaguazu. The authors' conclusion that many of the women in this community preferred to work alone is striking given the current interest globally in microfinance based on the village banking model. The authors' identify difficulties in the transition from income-generating activity to community engagement and recommend specific measures tailored to the characteristics of the community.

828 Davis, Robyn. Social capital among small urban enterprise in Asunción. Toronto: Univ. of Toronto, Centre for International Studies, Programme on Latin America and the Caribbean, 2006. 59 p.: bibl., tables. (CIS/CADEP Working Paper; 10)

The study seeks to analyze the impact of Paraguayan political and social history on current expressions of social cohesion and cooperation and to identify social capital variables associated with successful entrepreneurial performance. The study finds that the transition to democracy has increased social capital formation but that uncertainty and lingering distrust

limit its growth. The study makes specific suggestions for government intervention to enhance social capital formation and business success.

829 Economía y empleo en el Paraguay. Recopilación de Dionisio Borda. Asunción: Centro de Análisis y Difusión de la Economía Paraguaya, 2007. 448 p.: bibl., ill.

This volume reports the results of a major research project funded by Canada's International Development Research Center and led by economist Albert Berry. The individual chapters are written by well-known Latin American social scientists and focus on the factors that have led to limited economic growth and low levels of job creation. The studies include both urban and rural labor markets and factors such as education, technology, investment, and small business development.

830 Memorándum para el gobierno, 2008–2013. Recopilación de Dionisio Borda. Asunción: Centro de Análisis y Difusión de la Economía Paraguaya, 2008. 237 p.: bibl., ill.

This volume comprises the results of a series of individual policy studies undertaken in advance of the 2008 presidential election with the goal of contributing to and enhancing the quality of the discussion of public policy issues. The papers have been prepared by some of Paraguay's best social scientists and cover the following topics: economic growth and employment, governance and governability, housing and environment, education, poverty and inequality, and international relations. Each paper contains a brief analysis of the situation and a set of specific recommendations. For political science specialist's comment, see item **1802**.

831 Security in Paraguay: analysis and responses in comparative perspective. Texts by James L. Cavallaro *et al.*, Cambridge, Mass.: International Human Rights Clinic, Human Rights Program Harvard Law School, Harvard Univ. Press; Asunción: Univ. Columbia del Paraguay, 2008. 186 p.: bibl., ill. (Human Rights Program practice series)

This book examines public safety

(insecurity) in Paraguay and the state's response. Based on extensive in-country interviews by an accomplished international team, the report finds that reforms in the judicial system, and particularly the criminal code, are not responsible for increases in crime. The team identifies prison overcrowding, institutional corruption, and the privatization of security as issues of concern and makes concrete policy recommendations for the police and criminal justice system.

832 Weber, Wagner Enis. El sinceramiento de la economía paraguaya. Asunción: El Lector, 2005. 105 p.: bibl.

This small volume by a Brazilian author provides commentary on the national income accounts as well as short chapters focusing on measures of poverty, the size of the state, and Paraguayan trade in the Mercosur context. Idiosyncratic, but a useful quick read by a foreign scholar whose goal is to be constructive in improving economic measurement.

BRAZIL

MELISSA H. BIRCH, Associate Professor and Director, Center for International Business Education and Research, University of Kansas
RUSSELL E. SMITH, Professor and Associate Dean, School of Business, Washburn University

THE LITERATURE REVIEWED FOR THIS VOLUME reflects the concerns of a Brazil that has moved past the crises and challenges that marked the 1980s and 1990s. These included the debt crisis, endemic inflation, the process of redemocratization, and the challenges of international trade and increased competition. Even the successful Real Plan and the 1999 devaluation are almost outside of the concerns of the present period. The neoliberal reforms of the state and privatizations of the 1990s, including the opening of the economy and the politics of Mercosul, now seem part of the background, or are of technical or historical interest. Instead of analyses of crisis, one finds heightened interest in the dynamics of a working market economy that has become open to the world, that allocates activities across Brazil in accord with market forces and local rather than national policies, and that is far enough removed from its recent past that numerous retrospective efforts are in order.

Brazil's openness to the world is reflected in works that consider trade and investment across borders and the rules, mechanisms, and policies that guide these activities. The sudden success of Brazilian exports, including ethanol (item **853**) and soy (item **838**), has attracted considerable attention, leading authors to examine more closely the entire supply chain in an effort to understand the phenomena and make appropriate policy recommendations (items **839** and **892**). The research seeks to explain the origin and destination of exports (items **883** and **920**), the finance and logistics required to support them, and the importance of the origin of capital (item **875**) and the size of the firm (item **877**; also see item **904**) in the determination of export success. Also considered are the developmental safeguards that are part of trade law (item **845**) and the new role of civil society groups in the formulation of trade policy (item **917**). It is these mechanisms that allow Brazil to respond to globalization and the open economy and ultimately to influence the allocation of activities geographically now that protective barriers are down.

The literature reviewed includes a large number of items about the economic experience of specific regions, states, and more local units, reflecting perhaps both the dispersion of economic activity as well as the increased dispersion of the researchers. While recent economic performance has been shaped by liberalizing reforms of the 1990s, it also has been influenced by the previous pattern of economic activity, investment, and development, including the general historical pattern of economic development starting in the coastal cities, and also the movement of actors, by choice and by policy, to extend the region of economic development to the west and to the north. The cases in the literature reviewed here reflect both the historical pattern of development and also the allocation of economic activities in response to the more open economy.

Consistent with both a development trajectory and the newly opened economy, the literature exhibits a clear concern with the idea of a service economy, both as a post-industrial next step and as part of the idea of a global city based on high-value, knowledge-intensive service in a global system of such cities. In a set of papers linked by the theme of innovation and services in the context of the knowledge-based economy, the role of innovation, technology, and services for the future of the Brazilian economy is explored (items **836** and **862**). A mostly theoretical discussion of the service (tertiary) sector in industrial and postindustrial economies finds that with industrial restructuring, Brazil's increasing service activities are predominantly low-skill rather than the technology rich, sophisticated services characteristic of the developed economies (item **878**). In the concrete case of São Paulo, the service economy discussion interacts with the migration of manufacturing activities since the 1970s from the city to the metropolitan region and to other areas of the state and country in search of lower costs. It is argued that the new prominence of service industries reflects outsourcing of services by manufacturing, as well as the migration of manufacturing, but does not indicate that São Paulo is becoming a global city disconnected from manufacturing (item **905**).

Viewing São Paulo from a regional perspective and starting from an apparent "reversal of polarization" that shifts manufacturing activity from the São Paulo Metropolitan Region to Porto Alegre, Curitiba, and Belo Horizonte, researchers ask whether the forces of disagglomeration leading to dispersion of manufacturing dominate the forces of agglomeration retaining centralization in São Paulo. They conclude that what was seen as a dispersion of manufacturing to low-cost areas outside the city, or even outside of the state, is now seen as the expansion of a system of manufacturing that retains the control, innovation, and knowledge-based functions within São Paulo. The new, lower-cost locations of manufacturing are not seen as having the research and intellectual capital base to be autonomous centers. On the service side, a portion of the service activity in São Paulo is seen as a result of outsourcing and not associated with an emerging center in the world city or world system framework (item **879**). Global city or not, the restoration of the central region of the city of São Paulo since 2000 is explored thoroughly elsewhere in the literature (item **846**).

Emblematic both of the thread of the westward movement of Brazil and also of globalization is the recent development of the state of Goias in the center-west, an agricultural frontier region that grew consistently through recent decades, even as the manufacturing-driven cities of the coast stagnated. Illustrative is the case of Catalão in southeastern Goias, which benefited from the boom in modern agriculture by becoming a regional center for agricultural services and eventually, after several stages and with economies of agglomeration, a center for manufacturing often by outside firms. The conclusion is that small cities on the periphery can grow to connect the region to the wider world, even while remaining relatively small (item **858**).

Emblematic in a different way is the restructuring and new growth in the state of Rio de Janeiro, which also experienced major deindustrialization in the Rio de Janeiro Metropolitan Region in the 1990s. Several works report localized manufacturing growth in the interior of the state, which is not connected to the capital city and its previous manufacturing activity. For example, one study reports on the success of "local productive arrangements" (APLs) for 13 industries rooted in regions across the state outside of the Rio de Janeiro Metropolitan Region (item **844**). A similar study looked at "configurations of local production" (CPLs), which are groupings of small and medium firms and agencies and institutions of support in four small cities (item **857**). Taking up the question of the city of Rio de Janeiro as an emerging center of high-value services, a third study finds that the city has experienced a substantial out-migration of the highly qualified workers needed for advanced services to cities in adjacent states and especially to São Paulo (item **912**).

Studies of parts of Brazil outside of the larger states are very much in evidence in the literature reviewed, including studies from the agricultural economy, the southern states, and from export agriculture generally (item **853**). The growth of these regions, and the power of the agribusinesses that are so important to their transformation, is changing the way politics are "done" in Brazil (item **889**). With the dispersion of activities in the textile industry in response to the opening of the economy, the Southeast is found to still be first in spinning, weaving, and clothing and the South is first in cotton production, while the Northeast leads in growth in all areas (item **847**). Another case of South-Northeast links is the outsourcing of shoe and garment production from Rio Grande do Sul to Ceará in response to labor and fiscal incentives, resulting in excessively bad labor conditions (item **880**). Labor conditions in large-scale projects are discussed for the construction of Brasília in the late 1950s (item **901**) and more recently in metal mining in Pará state (item **894**).

The sense of having moved into a new era is reinforced by the number of volumes which demonstrate, with a combination of economic history and development studies, how far Brazil has come (items **897** and **914**). Other retrospective volumes include those on the economic and social conditions of urban workers from 1930 to the present (item **916**), and on capital markets over 50 years (item **854**), and on the 30th anniversary of FUNCEX, the trade promotion agency (item **870**). A less sanguine study might be the volume that focuses on the evolution of government policy on hydrocarbons (item **865**).

Some studies, despite their retrospective focus, include a forward-looking, policy-oriented component (items **860**, **893**, and **900**). These volumes tend to state explicitly that they will begin their analysis after the creation of the *real* or after the devaluation of 1999. In fact, these studies may be the beginnings of a new macroeconomic literature for Brazil: an examination of the economy in the context of relative stability and the under the policy priorities of Lula's government. Among those reviewed here are an analysis of the tax reform started by the Lula government (item **919**), volumes that examine the public debt (item **860**) and central bank autonomy (item **907**), and studies of the present performance of privatized firms (item **834**) and labor markets and institutions (item **843**). Another branch of this literature examines the articulation of business groups and policy toward business (item **859**) in the wake of globalization. The common thread of these studies is the focus on preserving monetary stability while promoting economic growth, distribution of wealth, and social inclusion. These are the issues for so many countries, developed and developing, suggesting that the outlook for the future contribution of Brazil's evolving economic literature is bright.

833 Agronegócio paranaense: potencialidades e desafios. Organização de Marina Silva da Cunha, Pery Francisco Assis Shikida e Weimar Freire da Rocha Júnior. Cascavel, Brazil: EDUNIOESTE, 2002. 280 p.: bibl., ill., maps.

The 11 papers in this volume analyze various aspects of agribusiness in Parana in the context of the state's proximity to major markets in Brazil, access to the world market, and the declining share of agribusiness in state GDP in spite of productivity increases and greater attention to processing. Individual papers include industry studies and specific issues such as foreign investment, exports, land ownership, living conditions, and migration.

834 Anuatti-Neto, Francisco. et al. Os efeitos da privatização sobre o desempenho econômico e financeiro das empresas privatizadas. (*Rev. Bras. Econ./Rio de Janeiro*, 59:2, abril/junho 2005, p. 151–175, bibl., charts)

This paper examines the impact of privatization on firms privatized since 1991 using 15 measures of performance and controlling for other factors such as macroeconomic conditions, economic sector, listing on the stock exchange, etc. The authors find an increase in profitability and operational efficiency but the impact on investment, production, and payment of dividends and taxes is unclear.

835 Araújo Turolla, Frederico et al. Competição, colusão e antitruste: estimação da conducta competitiva de companhias aéreas. (*Rev. Bras. Econ./Rio de Janeiro*, 60:4, out./dez. 2006, p. 425–459, bibl., graph, tables)

Analyzes econometrically whether there was evidence of price fixing among air carriers on the Rio de Janeiro to São Paulo route. The study was able to reject the hypothesis of collusive behavior, but was not able to reject the hypothesis of competitive behavior.

836 Arbix, Glauco; Mario Sergio Salerno; and João Alberto de Negri. O impacto da internacionalização com foco na inovação tecnológica sobre as exportações das firmas brasileiras. (*Dados/Rio de Janeiro*, 48:2, 2005, p. 395–441, appendix, bibl., tables)

Innovative firms with international linkages tend to be larger, more efficient, and more intensively engaged in trade, exporting items with more value added and providing higher quality jobs. The study finds that such firms spend relatively more on training and hire more educated workers who are more productive and better paid.

837 Arraes, Ronaldo A. and Zilah Maria Oliveira Barros. Atributos individuais e distorções no mercado de trabalho regional brasileiro. (*REN Rev. Econ. Nordeste*, 36:3, julho/set. 2005, p. 338–357, bibl.)

Study attempts to identify the variables that determine the inequality of income and of educational attainment in the Southeast (São Paulo) and Northeast (Ceará). Findings show that both factors can be seen as the determinant of the other and that race and gender are important determinants of both, with race being more important in the Southeast and gender more important in the Northeast.

838 Barbosa, Marisa Zeferino and Luis Henrique Perez. Evolução das exportações brasileiras de farelo de soja por portos de embarque e estados de origem, 1996 a 2004. (*Inf. Econ./São Paulo*, 35:11, nov. 2005, p. 24–35, bibl., graph)

Brazil has become the second largest exporter of soy in the world. This article provides a wealth of data on the sources (by state) and destination countries of processed soy exports.

839 Bekerman, Marta and Santiago Rodríguez. Cadeias produtivas no processo de integração regional: o caso dos móveis de madeira no Mercosul. (*Rev. Bras. Econ./Rio* *de Janeiro*, 59:1, jan./março 2005, p. 72–82, bibl., graph)

The characteristics of the furniture industries in Argentina and Brazil suggest that trade benefits could result from developing international supply chains to overcome market failures in a single country. The authors identify a need for policy intervention to realize the complementarities that would lead to greater competitiveness in the regional furniture industry.

840 Belluzzo, Walter; Francisco Anuatti-Neto; and Elaine T. Pazello. Distribuição de salários e o diferencial público-privado no Brasil. (*Rev. Bras. Econ./Rio de Janeiro*, 59:4, out./dez. 2005, p. 511–533, bibl., graphs)

Studies the public-private wage differential in Brazil, finding state and local public salaries are higher than private salaries in the lower end of the distribution, but the contrary in the upper end. Federal salaries are generally higher when compared with private sector salaries.

841 Bertucci, Janete Lara de Oliveira; Patrícia Bernardes; and Mônica Mansur Brandão. Políticas e práticas de governança corporativa em empresas brasileiras de capital aberto. (*Rev. Adm./São Paulo*, 41:2, abril/junho 2006, p. 183–196, bibl.)

This analysis of the Brazilian stock market focuses on how it helps or hinders the implementation of policies and practices of corporate governance. Survey and interview data from four sets of stakeholders reveal that they are in different stages of implementing best practices of corporate governance and that both a formal apparatus and the strategic behavior of economic agents are required to reduce the asymmetry of information.

842 Bezerra, Márcia Maria de Oliveira. Turismo e financiamento: o caso brasileiro à luz das experiências internacionais. Campinas, Brazil: Papirus Editora, 2005. 160 p.: bibl., ill. (Col. Turismo)

This book examines the evolution of the tourism industry in Brazil and the role of public policies in the growth and development of the national industry. Examined in the context of global trends and the experiences of other countries, the author studies the business of tourism and the financing of government incentives for the Brazilian tourism industry.

843 Brasil, o estado de uma nação. Rio de Janeiro: Instituto de Pesquisa Econômica Aplicada, 2006. 1 v.: col. ill., col. maps.

Second in the series, *Brasil, o estado de uma nação*, reports the recent macroeconomic, labor force, labor institution, and post-labor market social welfare and retirement experience since roughly 1999. Chapters are essentially long essays and include "Monetary Effort and Stability," "The Brazilian Labor Force," "Education in Brazil," "Labor Institutions and Labor Market Performance," "Recent Labor Market Performance," "Technology, Exportations, and Employment," "Public Employment, Labor, and Income Policies," and "Social Security and Social Assistance in Brazil."

844 Britto, Jorge. Arranjos produtivos locais: perfil das concentrações de atividades econômicas no Estado do Rio de Janeiro. Niterói, Brazil: UFF; Rio de Janeiro: FUNCEX: UFRJ, Instituto de Economia: SEBRAE/RJ, 2004. 241 p.: bibl., col. ill., col. maps. (Série Estudos)

Reports on the distribution and dynamic of small-scale "Local Produtive Arrangements" ("Arranjos Produtivos Locais") for 13 industries across the regions in the state of Rio de Janeiro based on 2001 data from the Relação Annual de Informações Sociais (Rais) and the Censo Cadastro do IBGE. The concepts of local productive arrangements and concentration of activities are used to describe a dynamic portion of the economic restructuring that followed the deindustrialization of the 1990s.

845 Brogini, Gilvan Damiani. OMC e indústria nacional: as salvaguardas para o desenvolvimento. São Paulo: Aduaneiras, 2004. 295 p.: bibl.

Written by a specialist in international trade law, the book examines the use of safeguards by the World Trade Organization and in international trade treaties to protect the interests of developing countries over the course of many GATT rounds. The author proposes modifications in the way safeguards are used in such treaties, which would result in improving the ability of developing countries to use trade policy for effective industrial restructuring.

846 Caminhos para o centro: estratégias de desenvolvimento para a região central de São Paulo. Coordenação geral de Alvaro A. Comin e Nadia Somekh. São Paulo: EMURB, Prefeitura de São Paulo: CEBRAP, Centro Brasileiro de Análise e Planejamento: Centro de Estudos da Metrópole, 2004. 420 p.: bibl., ill., maps.

A collection of 13 papers discussing the decline and restoration of the downtown and central neighborhoods in the city of São Paulo, especially during the administration of Mayor Marta Suplicy. Provides a concrete and detailed understanding of the region and redevelopment activities that have restored the area since 2000, particularly following activities by previous administrations that promoted growth to the southwest.

847 Campos, Antônio Carlos de and Nilson Maciel de Paula. A indústria têxtil brasileira em um contexto de transformações mundiais. (*REN Rev. Econ. Nordeste*, 37:4, out./dez. 2006, p. 592–608, graphs, tables)

Analyzes the competitive dynamic of the world and Brazilian textile industry. Notes the chains and complexes of the sector, including new forms of organization and the changes within the Brazilian industry. The Southeast still leads in spinning, weaving, and clothing, while the South is the leader in cotton production; however the Northeast leads in growth in all areas.

848 Cardoso, Adalberto Moreira and Telma Lage. A inspeção do trabalho no Brasil. (*Dados/Rio de Janeiro*, 48:3, 2005, p. 451–489, bibl., tables)

Analysis of federal system of labor inspectors in the Ministry of Labor in Brazil. Considers the incentives and disincentives for employers to comply with workplace legislation, the history and details of the system, its efficacy, efficiency, and effectiveness, and improvements in recent years.

849 Carisio, Maria Clara Duclos. A política agrícola comum e seus efeitos sobre o Brasil. Brasília: Instituto Rio Branco: Fundação Alexandre de Gusmão, 2006. 310 p.: bibl. (Teses CAE)

Analyzes the evolution of the European Union's Common Agricultural Policy (CAP) over time from its beginning with six members in 1956 to the present with 25 members. Discusses the dynamic between member states and costs and benefits, as well as external negotiations through the GATT and the WTO. Considers Brazil's position and how much Brazil and other developing countries could benefit from the liberalization of the CAP. Also considers Brazil's negotiating strategy in Mercosul and the WTO.

850 Carneiro, Francisco Galrão and Andrew Henley. Las reformas a la seguridad social y el comportamiento del mercado laboral en Brasil. (*Trimest. Econ.*, 73:289, enero/marzo 2006, p. 87–124, bibl., graphs, tables)

Using aggregate time series data for the period 1985–2002, estimates the elasticity of impact of labor costs on employment in the formal and informal sectors. Because of high elasticity of demand in the formal sector, argues that social security coverage would be best increased by measures to make covered, formal sector employment more attractive.

851 Castilho, Marta Reis. Regional integration and the labour market: the Brazilian case. (*CEPAL Rev.*, 87, dic. 2005, p. 147–165, bibl.)

Analyzes the potential employment impacts on Brazil of successful completion of trade negotiations of which Brazil is a part: the Mercosul—European Union negotiation, the Free Trade Area of the Americas (FTAA), and the two together. All three options would generate between 225,000 and 240,000 jobs for an increase in employment of 0.4 percent, with the FTAA creating the most jobs. Those workers with the lowest skills would benefit the most.

852 Castro, Eduardo Rodrigues de. Efeito da desvalorização cambial na oferta, no preço de insumos e na relação entre os fatores na cultura do café. (*Rev. Econ. Sociol. Rural*, 43:4, out./dez. 2005, p. 421–441, bibl., tables)

Analyzes the effect of the 1999 devaluation on the prices of coffee and intermediate inputs, and on the supply of coffee. Found that the devaluation increased coffee supply by 19.75 percent without considering inputs and by only 17.69 percent when imported inputs were considered as well.

853 Costa, Cinthia Cabral da; Heloisa Lee Burnquist; and Joaquim José Martins Guilhoto. Impacto de alterações nas exportações da açúcar e álcool nas regiões Centro-Sul e Norte-Nordeste sobre a economia do Brasil. (*Rev. Econ. Sociol. Rural*, 44:4, out./dez. 2006, p. 611–630, graphs, tables)

Using an inter-regional input-output matrix of the Brazilian economy, the authors examine the impact on production and employment of an increase in the external demand for sugar and ethanol. They find the impacts are larger for sugar than ethanol and that the shock is felt first in the North-Northeast of Brazil, and that the impact on production and employment is greater than when it begins in the Center-South.

854 Costa, Roberto Teixeira da. Mercado de capitais: uma trajetória de 50 anos. São Paulo: Imprensa Oficial, 2006. 475 p.: bibl., ill., map.

Part memoir and part historical record, this book traces 50 years of capital market activity in São Paulo. Written by the former chief of the financial market regulatory agency, the book includes more photographs than tables but does provide data on the historical levels of capital market activity.

855 Crescimento econômico e distribuição de renda: prioridades para ação. Organização de Jacques Marcovitch. Textos de Erminia Maricato *et al.* São Paulo: Edusp: Editora Senac, 2007. 231 p.: bibl., ill. (some col.), col. maps.

A collection of papers addressing the ten priorities previously identified by the 2006 Latin American Roundtable of the World Economic Forum: education, health, employment, housing, social protection, infrastructure, tax reform, innovation, international trade, and financial services. Organized in three groups, papers recommended government actions to create infrastructure to fight poverty, economic and financial conditions to reduce inequity, and enduring conditions for a redistribution of income.

856 Cury, Samir; Alexandro Mori Coelho; and Carlos Henrique Corseuil. A computable general equilibrium model to analyze distributive aspects in Brazil with a trade policy illustration. (*Estud. Econ./São Paulo*, 35:4, out./dez. 2005, p. 739–765, bibl., tables)

Presents the result of a Computable General Equilibrium (CGE) simulation with an external trade policy shock on the distribution of income using 1996 data. The policy shock is to restore the tariffs in effect in 1990, on the eve of accelerated trade liberalization. Found welfare losses of this "partial closing of the economy" for all families, with greater losses for rural and urban poor families.

857 O desenvolvimento local no estado do Rio de Janeiro: estudos avançados nas realidades municipais. Organização de Yves-A. Fauré e Lia Hasenclever. Rio de Janeiro: E-papers, 2005. 460 p.: bibl., maps.

Reports the results of a three-year study of "configurations of local production" (CPL) in four municipalities—Campos de Goytacazes, Itaguai, Macae, and Nova Friburgo—in the state of Rio de Janeiro. CPLs are made up of groups of medium and small firms, municipalities, agencies of support, and institutions and customs generally. Study looked at agencies of support as a driving force, the role of macroeconomic restrictions, and sources of successful local economic transformation, as well as differences in the evolution of industrial structures, the role of mercantile and non-mercantile institutions, and other factors.

858 Deus, João Batista de. O sudeste goiano e a desconcentração industrial. Brasília: Ministério da Integração Nacional, Secretaria de Desenvolvimento do Centro-Oeste; Goiânia, Brazil: UFG, 2003. 243 p.: bibl., ill. (chiefly col.). (Col. Centro-Oeste de estudos e pesquisas; 12)

A study of changing position of southeastern Goias in the Brazilian economy in the context of the general thrust of movement west and the industrial decentralization of the 1980s and 1990s. Through the case of Catalão, a small city in a micro region of the same name, finds that traditional agriculture was replaced with modern agriculture, especially livestock, which in turn stimulated the local manufacturing of inputs, processing equipment, and eventually, with economies of agglomeration, other manufacturing, all of these often by outside firms. Concludes that small cities on the periphery can grow to be regional centers providing a wide range of activities and connecting the region to the wider world, even while remaining relatively small.

859 Diniz, Eli and Renato Raul Boschi.
Empresários, interesses e mercado: dilemas do desenvolvimento no Brasil. Belo Horizonte, Brazil: Editora UFMG; Rio de Janeiro: IUPERJ, 2004. 241 p.: bibl., ill. (Humanitas; 110)
This is a detailed analysis of Brazilian industrial policy with special reference to the role of business organizations and the evolving representation of business since 1930. The authors are particularly interested in the impact of the major liberalization policies of the 1990s on business organization and business-government relations.

860 A dívida pública brasileira. Relação de Félix Mendonça. Coordenação de Alberto Pinheiro de Queiroz Filho e Edilberto Carlos Pontes Lima. Brasília: PLENARIUM, 2005. 199 p.: bibl., col. ill. (Série Cadernos de altos estudos; 2)
A report commissioned by the Brazilian Chamber of Deputies to examine the origin and sustainability of Brazilian public debt, this volume contains many tables and charts along with a precise discussion of public debt, in theory and practice. The aim of the volume is to provide this information in accessible language (for example, a glossary is provided) and includes essays by major players in Brazilian economic policy such as Delfim Netto and João Sayad.

861 Enge, Leonardo de Almeida Carneiro.
A convergência macroeconômica Brasil-Argentina: regimes alternativos e fragilidade externa. Brasília: Instituto Rio Branco: Fundação Alexandre Gusmão, 2005. 164 p.: ill. (Col. Rio Branco)
Examines fiscal and monetary policy in Argentina and Brazil between 1989 and 2003 to determine whether macroeconomic convergence is occurring as a product of Mercosur. A combination of theory and empirical work, the author seeks to identify a set of optimum policies that would promote not only convergence, but also sustainable development and reduce Brazil's vulnerability to international or global economic events. The volume was the author's MA thesis at the Instituto de Rio Branco and he now serves as a Brazilian diplomat in Argentina.

862 Estrutura e dinâmica do setor de serviços no Brasil. Organização de João Alberto de Negri e Luis Claudio Kubota. Brasília: IPEA, 2006. 501 p.: bibl., ill. (some col.), col. maps.
Survey of Services by the IBGE. The papers are linked by the theme of innovation and services in the context of the knowledge-based economy. The central role of innovation, technology, and services for the future of the Brazilian economy is explored. The book is the third in a series on the theme of innovation.

863 Expansão do setor de microfinanças no Brasil. Supervisão de Angela M.M. Fontes. Rio de Janeiro: Ford Foundation: IBAM, 2003. 203 p.: bibl., ill., maps.
This is the second of two studies financed by the Ford Foundation examining microfinance in Brazil. This study focuses on the challenges to expanding microfinance, including insufficient capital, the continental expanse of the region to be served, and differing definitions of what constitutes microfinance.

864 Faria, Luiz Augusto Estrella. A chave do tamanho: desenvolvimento econômico e perspectivas do Mercosul. Porto Alegre, Brazil: UFRGS Editora: FEE, Fundação de Economia e Estatística Siegfried Emanuel Heuser, 2004. 197 p.: bibl. (Série Estudos e pesquisas)
A discussion of economic development, generally from a structuralist perspective, drawing from regulationist and systems approaches, and focusing in the end on the prospects of Mercosul. Chapters consider the evolution of economic systems, economies over space and time with special regard to the Southern Cone, and the process of integration in Mercosul. In spite of structural barriers, Faria is generally optimistic about the ability of Mercosul to further economic development in the face of problems brought by neoliberalism.

865   Ferolla, Sergio Xavier and Paulo
       Metri. Nem todo o petróleo é nosso.
Prefácio de Carlos Lessa. São Paulo: Paz e
Terra, 2006. 267 p.: bibl., ill.
       The book examines the changes in
government policy toward hydrocarbons,
beginning with the 1988 Constitution. The
analysis centers on petroleum and the early
role of Petrobras in identifying and developing the country's resources. The book
decries the growing role of foreign players in
the energy sector.

866   Ferraz, João Carlos; David Kupfer;
       and Mariana Lootty. Industrial com-
petitiveness in Brazil: ten years after economic liberalization. (CEPAL Rev., 82, April
2004, p. 91–117, bibl., graphs, tables)
       Based on data collected by the Minis-
try of Development, Industry, and External
Trade, the authors analyze changes in industrial competitiveness since their previous
study in 1996. They find that, unlike other
developing countries, few new economic
activities were added or subtracted in Brazil. Instead, changes were observed in the
management of production processes and in
the patterns of ownership, with the role of
foreign capital increasing.

867   Ferreira, Assuéro. O nordeste no Bra-
       sil: integração e crescimento recente.
(REN Rev. Econ. Nordeste, 37:4, out./dez.
2006, p. 471–492, graphs, tables)
       Analyzes the growth of the Northeast
of Brazil and its relationship to the national
economy for the period 1985 to 2002. Found
strong integration with the national economy for most of the period as growth patterns moved together and the Northeast lost
share in the whole. Only after 2000 did the
Northeast gain in share and demonstrate
some autonomy relative to the national
economy.

868   Ferreira, Pedro Cavalcanti and Os-
       mani Teixeira de Carvalho Guillén.
Estrutura competitiva, produtividade industrial e liberalização comercial no Brasil.
(Rev. Bras. Econ./Rio de Janeiro, 58:4, out./
dez. 2004, p. 507–532, bibl., tables)
       This paper examines the impact of
trade liberalization on industry productivity and estimates the markup of different
industrial sectors before and after trade
liberalization, revealing non-competitive

practices in most sectors. While significant
increases in productivity are found in the
majority of sectors, there was no decline in
market power, suggesting the existence of
forces other than global competition driving
productivity changes.

869   Fonseca, Marcos Wagner da. Impactos
       diferenciados da política monetária:
um estudo para o Brasil. Cascavel, Brazil:
Edunioeste, 2003. 165 p.: bibl., ill. (Col.
Thésis)
       Using the case of the 1995 Real Plan,
analyzes the effects of monetary policy
on the various regions of Brazil, identifying availability of credit, interest rate, and
exchange rate as transmission mechanisms.
Some evidence of differentiation was found
in what appeared to be greater impact in the
North, Northeast, and Center West via the
rate of interest.

870   Fonseca, Roberto Giannetti da. Fun-
       cex: 30 anos de apoio ao comércio ex-
terior brasileiro. (Rev. Bras. Comér. Exter.,
20:86, jan./março 2006, p. 2–3, table)
       A short editorial note from the presi-
dent of Funcex with a retrospective commentary on the 30th anniversary of this
export promotion agency.

871   Frey, Márcia Rosane and Milton
       Luiz Wittmann. Gestão ambiental
e desenvolvimento regional: uma análise
da indústria fumageira. (EURE/Santiago,
32:96, agosto 2006, p. 99–115, bibl., graphs,
map, tables)
       A study of the environmental prac-
tices of the tobacco-growing industry of the
Vale do Rio Pardo in the state of Rio Grande
do Sul, Brazil. After developing a theoretical institutional context, presents the industry as a case of environmentally sound
management.

872   Gomes, Marília F. Maciel. Mudança
       na produtividade dos fatores de pro-
dução da cafeicultura nas principais regiões
productores do Brasil. (Rev. Econ. Sociol.
Rural, 43:4, out./dez. 2005, p. 633–656, bibl.,
tables)
       Studies the change in factor produc-
tivity in coffee production in the states of
São Paulo and Minas Gerais over the period
1975–2001. Found that unit costs fell while
productivity increased. In São Paulo it was

found that all factors: rent of land, machine operations, labor, and other inputs, were substitutes for each other in accord with economic theory. In Minas Gerais, all factors were complements to land, while being substitutes for each other.

873 Guimarães, Nadya Araujo. Caminhos cruzados: estratégias de empresas e trajetórias de trabalhadores. São Paulo: Curso de Pós-Graduação em Sociologia, Univ. de São Paulo: Editora 34, 2004. 405 p.: bibl., ill.

Grounded in the theory of the sociology of work and empirically in a case study of chemical and petrochemical industries of Bahia, this volume studies the processes and labor relations, under conditions of rapid change, in the production chains of these industries. The circumstances of the workers who continue in the industry are considered, as well as what happens to those who have to leave the industry.

874 Guimarães, Nadya Araujo et al. Desemprego—mercados, instituições e percepções: Brasil e Japão numa perspectiva comparada. (*Tempo Soc./São Paulo*, 16:2, nov. 2004, p. 257–287, bibl., graphs, tables)

A comparative study of unemployment in São Paulo and Tokyo, including a discussion of the labor markets, the different characteristics unemployment takes, and the institutions of unemployment, policies of the firms, and family organization. The form, duration, and selectivity of unemployment are considered, as well as the normative plane of institutions that intervene on behalf of the population and the subjective plane, including the experience of unemployment.

875 Hiratuka, Célio and Fernanda de Negri. The influence of capital origin on Brazilian foreign trade patterns. (*CEPAL Rev.*, 82, April 2004, p. 119–135, bibl., graph, tables)

This article examines the geographical pattern of external trade of foreign-owned and domestic Brazilian firms using panel data from a representative set of enterprises for the years 1989, 1997, and 2000. The authors find that intra-firm trade is an important determinant of the difference in the pattern observed and, as in previous studies, the impact is greater on imports than exports. This latter pattern is especially pronounced when the technological content of the product is taken into account.

876 Jacinto, Paulo de Andrade. Diferenciais de salários por gênero na indústria avícola da Região Sul do Brasil: uma análise com micro dados. (*Rev. Econ. Sociol. Rural*, 43:4, out./dez. 2005, p. 529–555, bibl., tables)

Using individual data from the Relação Annual de Informações Sociais (RAIS) for 1998, analyzes wage differences by gender in the chicken-processing industry in the Região Sul of Brazil. After controlling for education and occupation, finds evidence of discrimination in favor of men.

877 Klotzle, Marcelo Cabus and Cristiane Caires Thomé. Fatores associados ao desempenho exportador de micros, pequenas e médias empresas brasileiras. (*Rev. Adm./São Paulo*, 41:3, julho/set. 2006, p. 339–346, bibl., tables)

Based on an email survey of 80 micro-, small-, and medium-sized Brazilian exporting firms, the authors identified four statistically significant factors that contribute to export strategy success: length of time in international markets, existence of a specialized export department, utilization of export finance programs, and quality of product.

878 Kon, Anita. Economia de serviços: teoria e evolução no Brasil. Consultação editorial de Honório Kume. Rio de Janeiro: Editora Campus, 2004. 269 p.: bibl., ill.

Presents analysis of the evolution of the service (tertiary) sector of industrial and post-industrial economies, and also contemporary developing economies. Distinguishes between traditional low-skill service activities and advanced services that are often rich in skill, technology, and information. In the case of Brazil, finds that with industrial restructuring, service activities have increased, but are predominantly of the low-skill variety rather than in the technology rich, sophisticated services that are characteristic of the developed economies.

879 Lemos, Mauro Borges et al. Capacitação tecnológica e *catching up:* o caso das regiões metropolitanas emergentes

brasileiras. (*Rev. Econ. Polít.*, 26:1, jan./
março 2006, p. 95–118, bibl., tables)

Analyzes the apparent "reversal of polarization" where Brazilian manufacturing
activity has become less concentrated in the
São Paulo Metropolitan Region with a shift
of manufacturing activity to Porto Alegre,
Curitiba, and Belo Horizonte. Asks whether
the economies of agglomeration or disagglomeration are dominant. Concludes that
São Paulo continues to experience economies of agglomeration in activities incorporating emerging and advanced technologies
and that the other cities, beneficiaries of
the migration of traditional activities, need
to develop more research and development
capacity to truly catch up.

880   Lima, Jacob Carlos. Novos espaços
produtivos e novas-velhas formas de
organização do trabalho: as experiências
com cooperativas de trabalho no Nordeste
brasileiro. (*Rev. Crít. Ciênc. Sociais*, 73, dez.
2005, p. 91–110, bibl.)

Discusses the use of state and
employer-sponsored worker "cooperatives,"
in the interior of Ceara in the late 1990s.
Made up of the associated autonomous
workers, the cooperatives provided labor
to shoe and garment firms attracted to the
region by the state tax incentives promoted
during guerra fiscal as part of attempts to
avoid the labor legislation and lower costs of
globalization. The firms provided technology and access to markets. Extreme labor
exploitation in the tightly managed system
led to its end in the early 2000s.

881   Lopes, Alexsandro Broedel. Financial
accounting in Brazil: an empirical
examination. (*Lat. Am. Bus. Rev.*, 6:4, 2005,
p. 45–68, bibl.)

Seeks to test country-specific aspects
of the relationship between accounting numbers and market variables (prices and returns)
for the 1995–99 period. As an important
emerging market economy using code law,
Brazil offers an interesting site to test theories about the relationship. The author finds
that, adjusting for scale effects, value relevance is low. He also finds that the earnings-
return relationship is weak in Brazil.

882   Magalhães, João Paulo de Almeida.
Nova estratégia de desenvolvimento
para o Brasil: um enfoque de longo prazo.

(*Rev. Econ. Polít.*, 26:2, abril/junho 2006,
p. 186–202, bibl.)

Argues for a new, long-term development strategy for Brazil, replacing recent
neoliberal approaches and based on an
understanding of the market, not the availability of savings, as the precondition for
development policies. Argues that globalization in its present form is unacceptable and
proposes a model of globalization directed
by underdeveloped countries.

**883   Markwald, Ricardo A. and Fernando
Ribeiro.** Análise das exportações
brasileiras sob a ótica das empresas, dos
produtos e dos mercados. (*Rev. Bras. Comér.
Exter.*, 19:85, out./dez. 2005, p. 3–85, bibl.,
graphs)

This article seeks to explain the recent rapid growth of Brazilian exports, a
divergence from the prior 20 years of weak
exports, by examining the producers, the
products, and the markets. It concludes that
recent success results from new foreign exchange rate policy, expanding world markets
and the boom in commodity prices.

**884   Martins, Ricardo S.; José Augusto de
Souza; and Luiz Astoni Kloh.** Análise
dos impactos de investimentos nos sistemas
de transporte na logística do complexo soja
brasileiro: os casos Ferronorte e Hidrovia do
Araguaia-Tocantins. (*REN Rev. Econ. Nordeste*, 36:3, julho/set. 2005, p. 411–429, bibl.,
graphs, tables)

This logistics study uses an optimiza-
tion model to evaluate the new geographic
distribution of soybean production in Brazil
with respect to investments in transportation systems. It finds that traditional production in Paraná remains competitive in
all scenarios considered, while competition
occurs with the expansion zone. The results
of this linear model would not suggest that
expansion of ports at Santos or Paranagua is
recommended.

885   Matos, Jéferson Daniel de. Distribuição de renda: fatores condicionan-
tes e comparação entre as regiões metropolitanas pesquisadas pela PED. Porto Alegre,
Brasil: Secretaria da Coordenação e Planejamento, Fundação de Economia e Estatística
Siegfried Emanuel Heuser, 2005. 56 p.: bibl.,
ill. (Documentos FEE; 62)

Presents the results of a study of the

inequality of labor earnings (from principal employment) in metropolitan areas of Porto Alegre, São Paulo, Belo Horizonte, Salvador, and Recife using 2002 data from the Pesquisa de Emprego e Desemprego (PED). Found the higher measures of earning inequality were associated with greater educational inequality.

886   Morais, Igor Alexandre C. de and Vanessa Frainer. Uma investigação sobre o ciclo dos negócios na indústria da Bahia. (REN Rev. Econ. Nordeste, 36:3, julho/set. 2005, p. 378–410, bibl., graphs, tables)

The authors use the Stock and Watson methodology to produce an industrial index for the state of Bahia and estimate the business cycles in recent years. They find an average period of recession lasts two months while growth periods last about nine months, however growth rates are much smaller than the declines registered during recession.

887   Okediji, Tade O. The dynamics of race, ethnicity and economic development: the Brazilian experience. (J. Socio-Econ./New York, 33:2, 2004, p. 201–215, bibl., tables)

Analyzes the relationship between region, race, education, and income in Brazil using cross-section data from 1998–1999. Finds a strong correlation between color, educational attainment, and earnings in Brazil, and that nonwhites are able to obtain higher earnings in the relatively whiter and industrialized regions of Brazil. Argues for government policies to combat these inequalities to further economic development.

888   Oliveira, Cristiano Aguiar de. Externalidades espaciais e o crescimento econômico das cidades do Estado do Ceará. (REN Rev. Econ. Nordeste, 36:3, julho/set. 2005, p. 319–337, bibl., tables)

Studies the economic growth of the cities of Ceará in the 1990s. Finds the presence of spatial dependence in that the cities that grew the most were those with neighbors that also grew, although without convergence of income per capita. Highlights the importance of human capital and urbanization in the promotion of the knowledge spillovers.

889   Ortega, Antonio César. Agronegócios e representação de interesses no Brasil. Prefácio de José Graziano da Silva. Uberlândia, Brazil: EDUFU, 2005. 269 p.: bibl., ill.

Noting the increasing strength of local politics in Brazil over the last decade and the weakening of policy-making at the national level, the author asks how agricultural interests find representation in this new political setting. He argues that local agencies in partnership with agro-professional associations are forging new policies.

890   Pavia, Paulo de Tarso Almeida and Simone Wajnman. Das causas às conseqüências econômicas da transição demográfica no Brasil. (Rev. Bras. Estud. Popul., 22:2, julho/dez. 2005, p. 303–322, bibl., graphs)

Analyzes the relationship between population and economic development in the context of the demographic transition in Brazil, in particular with reference to the decline in the dependency ratio from the 1960s to 2020. Notes that this demographic bonus creates a window of opportunity in the policy area, making recommendations in a number of areas.

891   Pereira, Fernando Batista and Marco Crocco. Metas sociais de programas de microcrédito financeiramente viáveis. (Anál. Econ./Porto Alegre, 22:42, set. 2004, p. 149–183, bibl., tables)

This analysis of the microcredit program at Banco Popular de Ipatinga finds that the social goals of the microcredit program are constrained and subordinated by the financial feasibility of the program.

892   Pereira, Lia Valls. Os acordos Sul-Sul assinados pelo Mercosul: uma avaliação sob a ótica brasileira. (Rev. Bras. Comér. Exter., 20:86, jan./março 2006, p. 1–11, tables)

In recent years Brazil has given priority to trade agreements with other developing countries. This paper seeks to evaluate the potential of these treaties for developing supply chain linkages through intra-industry trade more typical of trade among developed countries. The author examines the trade treaties with India and with South Africa and finds little scope for such trade development.

893 Perspectivas para a economia brasileira: inserção internacional e políticas públicas. Organizacão de Luiz Fernando de Paula, Léo da Rocha Ferreira e Milton Pereira de Assis. Rio de Janeiro: EdUERJ, 2006. 409 p.: bibl., ill.

Written on the 75th anniversary of the founding of the Faculdade de Ciencias Economicas at UERJ, the 17 chapters of the book examine the performance of the Brazilian economy after the creation of the real. The book seeks to identify the appropriate public policy to preserve monetary stability while addressing issues of economic growth, distribution of wealth, and social inclusion.

894 Pont Vidal, Josep. Trabajo y relaciones laborales en los enclaves minero-metalúrgicos de la Amazonia oriental. (*Rev. Eur. Estud. Latinoam. Caribe*, 84, April 2008, p. 37–59, bibl., tables)

A study of labor relations in the metal-mining enclaves of eastern Pará state presented in a world-systems framework. Finds substantial differences between large and subcontractor firms in terms of labor rights, working conditions, and precariousness of employment, with labor gains won over the years being lost under pressure for Washington Consensus policies. In general, found that the production and wage structures in the large firms were not formal enough to be called "Fordist," or even "Periphery Fordist."

895 PIB da Bahia: 30 anos em análise. Salvador, Brazil: SEI, 2006. 180 p.: bibl. (Série Estudos e pesquisas; 72)

Reports the performance of the economy of the state of Bahia annually through the state domestic product data from 1975 through 2004. Annual sections include a macroeconomic analysis as well as subsections on manufacturing, construction, mining, public utilities, agriculture, commerce, and other services.

896 Rangel, Inácio. Obras reunidas. Vol. 1. Organização de Inácio Rangel e César Queiroz Benjamin. 2a. ed. Rio de Janeiro: Contraponto, 2005. 1 v.: ill.

First of a two-volume collection, brings together various texts from the author's thesis, books, and monographs, mostly from the 1950s and 1960s, though

running to 1985. Topics covered include Brazilian economic development, development planning, dualism, idle resources, inflation, and economic long cycles.

897 Rangel, Inácio. Obras reunidas. Vol. 2. Organização de Inácio Rangel e César Queiroz Benjamin. 2a. ed. Rio de Janeiro: Contraponto, 2005. 1 v.: ill.

Second of a two-volume collection, brings together the author's published articles. Topics covered include the agrarian question (1955–89), Brazilian national economic issues (1960–61), technological cycle and growth (1969–81), and Brazilian economy in the 1983–87 period. A mixed final section brings together articles on dualism, inflation, industrial policy, economic crises and cycles, among other topics.

898 Ratton Brandi, Vinicius et al. Foreign exchange volatility and trading volume of derivatives instruments: evidence from the Brazilian market. (*Lat. Am. Bus. Rev.*, 8:1, 2007, p. 65–82, tables)

Investigating the empirical relationship between trading volume and volatility, the author finds a positive contemporaneous relationship between unexpected volume and volatility, suggesting simultaneous influence at the arrival of relevant information. A better understanding of market microstructure may provide useful guidance for policy intervention.

899 Raupp, Fabiano Maury and **Ilse Maria Beuren.** O suporte das incubadoras brasileiras para potencializar as características empreendedoras nas empresas incubadas. (*Rev. Adm./São Paulo*, 41:4, out./dez. 2006, p. 419–430, bibl., tables)

Based on an email survey of 179 incubators in Brazil, the authors describe the kinds of services offered by incubators and the characteristics developed in the incubated firms.

900 Reis, Eustáquio J. A economia brasileira no século XX. (*in* Retratos do Brasil. Organização de Elisa P. Reis and Regina Zilberman. Porto Alegre, Brazil: EDIPUCRS, 2004, p. 15–38, bibl., graphs)

Discusses the broad trends in the Brazilian economy, including the cycles of growth, the relationship with the inflationary process, rates of savings and investment, and the role of the state. Provides a basis to consider the challenges faced by the Lula administration.

901 Reis, Maurício Cortez. Os impactos das mudanças na demanda por trabalho qualificado sobre o desemprego por nível de qualificação durante os anos noventa no Brasil. (*Rev. Bras. Econ./Rio de Janeiro*, 60:3, julio/set. 2006, p. 297–319, bibl., graph, tables)

Using PNAD data from 1990 and 1999, analyzes the impact of changes in demand on unemployment by skill level. Finds that aggregate demand shocks increased unemployment of skilled workers relatively more due to wage rigidity. Changes in relative demand favoring high-skilled workers did reduce unemployment of that group, although not as much as expected due to increased labor supply.

902 Resende, Marcelo and **Ricardo Wyllie.** Aglomeração industrial no Brasil: um estudo empírico. (*Estud. Econ./São Paulo*, 35:3, julho/set. 2005, p. 435–459, bibl., graphs)

This article measures industrial agglomeration in the Brazilian manufacturing industry in 1995 and 2001. Using new measures developed by Ellison and Glaeser, Maurel and Sedillot, and Devereux *et al.*, the data indicated that substantial heterogeneity was present across the different sectors and reflects substantial changes in agglomeration patterns between 1995 and 2001.

903 Ribeiro, Gustavo Lins. El capital de la esperanza: la experiencia de los trabajadores en la construcción de Brasilia. Buenos Aires: EA, 2006. 247 p.: bibl., ill., maps.

Studies the experience of workers, including the camp, the work, and conflict, in the construction of Brasilia in the period 1956–1960 in what was then isolated wilderness. Places the Brasilia experience in the context of other large-scale, rapid construction projects managed by a single company under isolated, construction camp circumstances.

904 Ruiz, Fernando J. Exportações brasileiras: fatores explicativos da participação das micro e pequenas empresas. São

Paulo: Editora Senac São Paulo, 2007. 147 p.: bibl., ill., index.

A rigorous study of the motivation to export of micro and small firms and the obstacles they encounter. Based on survey research, supplemented with a handful of in-depth interviews, and a review of the existing data on small business exporting, the study provides useful recommendations both for firms wanting to increase exports and government policy.

905 Santos Acca, Rogério dos. A dinâmica produtiva recente da metrópole paulista: das perspectivas pós-industriais á consolidação do espaço industrial de serviços. (*Dados/Rio de Janeiro*, 49:1, 2006, p. 119–157, bibl., graphs, tables)

Argues that the present shift of manufacturing activity from the city of São Paulo to the interior of the state and the new prominence of service industries, many of them linked to globalization, does not mean that São Paulo was becoming a global, service city disconnected from manufacturing. Rather the process represents outsourcing of services still linked to manufacturing on the one hand and the movement of some manufacturing activities in the production chain to micro-regions on the other near to São Paulo.

906 Seminário a Pequena Produção e o Modelo Catarinense de Desenvolvimento, *Florianópolis, Santa Catarina, Brazil, 2001.* A pequena produção e o modelo catarinense de desenvolvimento. Organizacão de Paulo Freire Vieira. Textos de Ademir Antônio Cazella *et al.* Florianópolis, Brazil: APED Editora, 2002. 310 p.: bibl., ill.

The published papers from a conference analyzing small-scale production in the state of Santa Catarina. Individual papers consider family agriculture, the third sector of cooperatives and similar associations, industrial restructuring and local clusters, high technology and software, tourism, and sustainable development. Considers the historical roots of the economy of the state and argues that it constitutes a model different from other regions of Brazil.

907 Seminário Banco Central: Autonomia x Independência, *Brasília, Brazil, 2003.* Banco Central: autonomia x independência. Brasília: Centro de Documentação e Informação, Coordenação de Publicações, 2004. 124 p.: bibl., ill. (Série Ação parlamentar; 284)

Reports the discussion from a seminar sponsored by a committee of the Brazilian House of Deputies on Central Bank autonomy motivated by the question of a possible inverse relationship between degree of autonomy and the rate of inflation. Includes the original discussion paper and the full discussion of the participants.

908 Seroa da Motta, Ronaldo. Economia ambiental. Rio de Janeiro: FGV Editora, 2006. 225 p.: bibl., ill.

An introductory textbook for environmental economics, the book is notable for its inclusion of four case studies on topics ranging from strategies to reduce urban waste to measuring the costs of deforestation of the Amazon. Also includes chapters outlining standard microeconomic analysis relevant to environmental issues.

909 Silva, José Carlos Domingos da and Fabiano Silvio Colbano. Uma nova especificação para as relações das exportações brasileiras. (*Rev. Bras. Comér. Exter.*, 20:89, out./dez. 2006, p. 35–45, bibl., graphs, tables)

An econometric analysis of the recent performance of Brazilian exports which includes an unusual variable, the profitability of exports. The authors find that the exchange rate plays a determinant role in the profitability of exports, but that export performance seems to depend heavily on the level of world exports.

910 Silva Júnior, Luiz Honorato da and Yony Sampaio. O perfil do pobre e da pobreza rural nordestina: um estudo para os anos 1990. (*REN Rev. Econ. Nordeste*, 36:4, out./dez. 2005, p. 559–576, bibl., graphs)

Constructs a profile of rural poverty in the states of the Northeast of Brazil using data for the years 1992, 1995, and 1999. Found that education is the principal determinant of the probability that a person will be poor, followed by gender, age, and occupation. Race and state of residence had a smaller impact. Makes policy recommendations.

911 Silveria Neto, Raul da Mota. Quão pró-pobre tem sido o crescimento econômico no Nordeste?: evidências para o

período 1991–2000. (*REN Rev. Econ. Nordeste*, 36:4, out./dez. 2005, p. 483–507, bibl., map, tables)

Using census data from 1991 and 2000, analyzes the extent to which economic growth as experienced in the Northeast is pro-poor. Finds that in the Northeast growth was less pro-poor relative to other regions in Brazil. Suggests that the lower increase in income reflects inequality in the distribution of human capital and land.

912 Simões, André Geraldo de Moraes. Reorganização do espaço produtivo e a "recuperação" da economia fluminense: uma análise a partir dos migrantes altamente qualificados. (*Rev. Bras. Estud. Popul.*, 21:1, jan./junho 2004, p. 67–82, bibl., tables)

Analyzes population shifts and industrial restructuring in the state of Rio de Janeiro in the 1990s using the migration of highly qualified workers as a major indicator. Notes the decline in manufacturing in the Rio de Janeiro Metropolitan Region and the increase in the medium-sized cities in the interior. Finds migration of highly qualified workers important to advanced services in São Paulo in particular but also Belo Horizonte and Brasilia.

913 Soluções do mercado de capitais para o crescimento sustentado. Organização de Carlos Antonio Rocca *et al.* Rio de Janeiro: IBMEC Mercado de Capitais; José Olympio Editora, 2004. 186 p.: bibl., ill. (Estudos Ibmec; 3)

A summary of the conference II Encontro Codemec (Comitê para o Desenvolvimento do Mercado de Capitais) in 2003 on capital market solutions for renewed growth. The panels of specialists made a number of recommendations for the better functioning of market mechanisms.

914 Souza, Nilson Araújo de. A longa agonia da dependência: economia brasileira contemporânea, JK-FH. São Paulo: Editora Alfa-Omega, 2004. 759 p.: bibl. (Biblioteca Alfa-Omega de cultura universal. Série 2a; 71. Col. Atualidade)

From a dependency theory point of view, reports in great detail the economic and political experience of Brazil from the late 1950s through the early 2000s. In the end proposes a "Brazilian road" (caminho brasileiro) model of development that harkens back to economic transformation interrupted by the military takeover in 1964.

915 Takeda, Tony; Fabiana Rocha; and **Márcio I. Nakane.** The reaction of bank lending to monetary policy in Brazil. (*Rev. Bras. Econ./Rio de Janeiro*, 59:1, jan./ março 2005, p. 107–126, bibl., graphs, tables)

Analyzes the relevance of the bank lending channel for monetary policy in Brazil using monthly data from Dec. 1994 to Dec. 2001 and also considers other instruments of monetary policy. Finds evidence to support the relevance of the bank lending channel. Also finds that the reserve requirement is especially relevant under certain conditions.

916 Trabalhadores urbanos: ocupação e queda na renda. Organização de Alexandre Guerra *et al.* São Paulo: Cortez Editora, 2007. 143 p.: bibl., ill., col. maps. (Atlas da nova estratificação social no Brasil; 2)

Recounts the evolution of the urban working class in the context of political and economic history from the 1930–80 period of national industrialization through to the present. Presents substantial employment, income, and consumption data, as well as state-level maps identifying municipios by percent participation of urban workers in the economically active population.

917 Veiga, Pedro da Motta. Formulação de políticas comerciais no Brasil: a mudança do padrão de relacionamento entre o Estado e a sociedade civil. (*Rev. Bras. Comér. Exter.*, 20:86, jan./março 2006, p. 9–26, bibl.)

The author argues that while trade policy was previously the purview of a single government agency, in the 21st century there are numerous civil society organizations that have an impact, particularly on implementation and operation of trade policies, but to a lesser extent also on trade policy strategy.

918 Viapiana, Luiz Tadeu. Economia do crime: uma explicação para a formação do criminoso. Porto Alegre: Age Editora, 2006. 175 p.: bibl., ill.

Explores the changes in crime in Brazil over the last century and explores the possible causes empirically, using economic analysis. The data tend to be from Brazil, although the analysis makes heavy use of international comparisons.

919 Werneck, Rogério L. Furquim. An evaluation of the 2003 tax reform effort in Brazil. (*Rev. Econ. Polít.*, 26:1, jan./ março 2006, p. 75–94, bibl., table)

This paper provides an assessment of the 2003 Brazilian tax reform. While ambitious in its conceptualization, it faced considerable resistance. Unable to reach consensus, the more modest reform passed is analyzed here and future tax policy challenges are discussed.

920 Xavier, Clésio Lourenço and **Emerson Fernandes Marçal.** O impacto da composição setorial, dos fluxos intra-setoriais e da abertura comercial na participação de mercado das exportações brasileiras. (*Anál. Econ./Porto Alegre*, 22:41, março 2004, p. 81–99, bibl., tables)

This paper seeks to identify the determinants of the market share of Brazilian exports. Using panel data for the period 1981–97, the model tests the impact of three sets of variables: degree of Brazilian market openness, relative importance of product in world trade, and degree of intra-industry trade and finds that they contribute to explaining the patterns observed.

921 Xavier, Clésio Lourenço and **Sabrina de Cássia M. de Souza.** Especialização comercial após a liberalização da economia brasileira: uma análise dos setores de insumos básicos. (*Ensaios FEE*, 27:1, 2006, p. 57–92, graphs, tables)

Analyzes the impact of trade liberalization in Brazil after the 1980s on trade specialization within the steel and paper and celulose industries. Found that the liberalization resulted in greater intra-industry specialization with Brazil specializing in the lower valued-added activities even though Brazil has a comparative advantage, a phenomenon termed "regressive intra-industry trade specialization."

GEOGRAPHY

GENERAL

KENT MATHEWSON, *Associate Professor, Department of Geography and Anthropology, Louisiana State University*
JÖRN SEEMANN, *Assistant Professor, Departamento de Geociências, Universidade Regional do Cariri, Brazil*

PUBLICATIONS DURING THIS BIENNIUM on the geography of Latin America as a whole, or works that do not neatly fit into one of the regional groupings, fall into a number of categories. Urban and economic themes continue to be a staple in the literature, though no single theoretical perspective can be said to be dominant. With the shortcomings or outright failure of neoliberal programs being increasingly demonstrated, advocacy as well as critique of this strain of development thought and practice is somewhat paradoxically less intense. Yet, geographers or those writing from a geographical standpoint—and this is an increasingly larger cohort among economists and development specialists—have seemingly not taken measure of the next wave, whether it be contemporary forms of populism or some variation of the globalization-is-good-and-inevitable ("world is flat") camp (items **941** and **942**). Since at least the mid-1960s, questions of development have occupied a central place in the Latin Americanist geography literature. This is not likely to change in the coming decade, though some axes and poles of the debates have shifted considerably over time. Emphasis on issues such as grassroots participation and social movements (items **926, 929, 947,** and **961**), sustainability (item **965**), environmental efficacy (items **953** and **963**), human and indigenous rights (item **968**) continues to have equal if not greater voice than strictly economic weights and measures.

Space- and place-related studies in neighboring areas such as anthropology, literature, and architecture deal with identity, public space, and literary representations, and have become increasingly fashionable (items **922, 952, 957, 962,** and **964**).

As with most of geography's subdisciplinary fields that formerly were constituted as largely synchronic, analytical, and quantitative enterprises, population and migration studies have undergone a significant shift toward more cultural, historical, and critical orientations. Perhaps the most active arena at present within this domain is the topic of transnationalism. A term borrowed from political economy referring to multinational corporations, it has been adapted to refer to the circuits of migration, often tracked at the individual level. Accordingly, there has been a shift away from positivist models of population and migration to more humanistic perspectives centered on questions of identity and mobility (items **948** and **951**).

The expansive category "environment," continues to command the attention of many geographers. While most Latin Americanist work is pitched at scales less than the realm as a whole, there are exceptions. Until recently, neither historical geographers nor environmental historians have attempted hemispheric-wide surveys. This is beginning to change (items **927** and **954**). One of the historical environmental topics enjoying increased attention is hazards and disasters (item **935**). The relationship between historical geography and environmental history is also under inspection (item **967**) The interstices of these two subfields has provided fertile grounds for work reaching well beyond academic audiences (item **949**). Research and writing falling into the domain of environmental historical geography, pioneered by Carl Sauer and his associates and students in the Berkeley school, promises to continue to be one of Latin Americanist geography's most productive sites.

The history of geography pertaining to Latin America is another increasingly active area of research and publication. New studies of perennially important figures such as Sauer and Alexander von Humboldt continue to appear. Sauer's work is also being introduced to a new generation of Latin American geographers (item **931**). Translation and publication of his writings into Portuguese and Spanish are being carried out by geographers in Brazil, Mexico, and Panama. Humboldt's (previously unpublished) journals of his New World travels (mostly written in French) are being translated into German and published in Germany (item **940**). Studies of geographic exploration, as part of the larger enterprise of Hispanic colonial science, engage both historians and literary scholars (items **930** and **966**). This is part of a much larger current within contemporary scholarship in the humanities and social sciences wherein geographic knowledge and concepts (place, space, landscape) have gained new wide appreciation and application. Latin Americanist geography and geographical themes in particular are enjoying wider use.

922 **Aparicio, Juan Ricardo** and **Mario Blaser.** The "lettered city" and the insurrection of subjugated knowledges in Latin America. (*Anthropol. Q.*, 81:1, Fall 2008, p. 59–94)

Discusses the changing role and scope of academic intellectuals in Latin America in view of the paradigmatic shift from modernity to alternative ideas that emphasize social movements, mobility, and local knowledge.

923 **Barton, Jonathan R.** Eco-dependency in Latin America. (*Singap. J. Trop. Geogr.*, 27:2, July 2006, p. 134–149)

Presents a political economy reading of dependency theories for natural resources and environmental issues. Introduces the term "eco-dependency" to characterize the relations of socioeconomic aspects and export-oriented exploitation of natural resources in Latin America.

924 **Bebbington, Anthony.** Latin America: contesting extraction, producing geographies. (*Singap. J. Trop. Geogr.*, 30:1, March 2009, p. 7–12)

Anticipates a deepening of extraction industries in the near future as well as greater state control over mining in Latin American countries.

925 **Biles, James J.** Informal work in Latin America: competing perspectives and recent debates. (*Geogr. Compass*, 3:1, 2009, p. 214–236)

Up-to-present overview of the recent debates and controversies surrounding informal work in Latin America.

926 **Bosco, Fernando J.** The geographies of Latin American social movements. (*in* Placing Latin America: contemporary themes in human geography. Edited by Edward L. Jackiewicz and Fernando J. Bosco.

Lanham, Md.: Rowman & Littlefield, 2008, p. 177–190, bibl., photos)

Defines and contextualizes social movement mobilizations and considers the geographical scales at which they emerge and are articulated. The example of the Mothers of the Disappeared movement in Argentina is used. For comments on other chapters in this book, see items **929, 941, 945, 948,** and **950.**

927 Brailovsky, Antonio Elio. Historia ecológica de Iberoamérica. Vol. 1, De los Mayas al Quijote. Vol. 2, De la independencia a la globalización. Buenos Aires: Ediciones Le Monde diplomatique, El Diplo: Ediciones Kaicron: Capital Intelectual, 2006–2009. 2 v.: bibl. (Monde Diplomatique "El Dipló"; 24, 40)

Survey of environmental conflicts and their social impacts through time and space. The first volume describes the situation on the Iberian Peninsula and in Latin America from precolumbian times to the 18th century. The second volume analyzes environmental aspects from the period of independence to present-day globalization.

928 Bringel, Breno and **Alfredo Falero.** Redes transnacionais de movimentos sociais na América Latina e o desafio de uma nova construção socioterritorial. (*Cad. CRH/Salvador,* 21:53, 2008, p. 267–286)

Emphasizes the importance of transnational networks and social movements as key factors in spatial processes. Presents the examples of landless movements and housing cooperatives from Brazil and Uruguay.

929 Brown, J. Christopher. NGOs and ongoing changes in Latin American society. (*in* Placing Latin America: contemporary themes in human geography. Edited by Edward L. Jackiewicz and Fernando J. Bosco. Lanham, Md.: Rowman & Littlefield, 2008, p. 159–176, bibl.)

Discusses the role of NGOs in a variety of contexts in contemporary Latin America. For comments on other chapters in this book, see items **926, 941, 945, 948,** and **950.**

930 Cañizares-Esguerra, Jorge. Nature, empire, and nation: explorations of the history of science in the Iberian world.

Stanford, Calif.: Stanford Univ. Press, 2006. 230 p.: bibl., ill., index.

Collection of essays exploring two traditions of interpreting and manipulating nature in the early-modern Iberian world: instrumental/imperial and patriotic/national. The patriotic narratives underwrote the first modern representations of the racialized body, Humboldtian theories of biodistribution, and views of the landscape as a historical text representing different layers of historical memory.

931 Carl Sauer on culture and landscape: readings and commentaries. Edited by William M. Denevan and Kent Mathewson. Baton Rouge: Louisiana State Univ. Press, 2009. 458 p.: bibl., index.

Collection of Sauer's writings with introductory commentaries and critical essays. Features several of Sauer's Latin Americanist publications along with commentary on Sauer as a Latin Americanist geographer.

932 Carney, Judith Ann. Una valoración de la geografía y la diáspora africana. (*Tabula Rasa,* 4, enero/junio 2006, p. 145–163, bibl., photo)

Reviews the work of geographers on the transfer of African elements of material culture, especially plants, to the New World. Transatlantic diffusion of these elements forms another way to understand the African diaspora and the African contribution to the cultural landscape of Latin America. [D. Gade]

933 Cities and urban geography in Latin America. Edited by Vicent Ortells Chabrera, Robert B. Kent and Javier Soriano Martí. Castellón de la Plana, Spain: Publicacions de la Univ. Jaume I, Servei de Comunicació i Publicacions, 2005. 200 p.: bibl., ill., index. (Col. Amèrica; 5)

Collection of eight essays (in English or Spanish) on a range of urban geographic issues. Case studies from Brazil, Peru, Argentina, and the US-Mexican border discuss colonial towns, urban squares, migration processes, and urban planning. For comment by historian, see *HLAS 64:381.*

934 Denevan, William M. Traditional versus new directions: the first meeting of the Conference of Latin Americanist

Geographers, 1970. (*J. Lat. Am. Geogr.*, 7:2, 2008, p. 155–162)

Historical inquest into, and memoir of, the origins of CLAG and its first general meeting.

935 El Niño, catastrophism, and culture change in ancient America. Edited by Daniel H. Sandweiss and Jeffrey Quilter. Washington, D.C.: Dumbarton Oaks Research Library and Collection; Cambridge, Mass.: Distributed by Harvard Univ. Press, 2008. 290 p.: bibl., ill., index, maps.

Collection of ten essays on the El Niño phenomenon and other catastrophic natural events in prehistoric times and during the Columbian encounter. Emphasizes the human-environment interactions in light of climate change and variability, and political and social complexity.

936 Encuentro de Geógrafos de América Latina, *10th, Universidade de São Paulo, 2005*. América Latina—cidade, campo e turismo. Organização de Amalia Inés Geraiges de Lemos, Mónica Arroyo e María Laura Silveira. Buenos Aires: CLACSO; São Paulo: Univ. de São Paulo, 2006. 378 p.: ill. (Col. Edição e distribuição cooperativa. Série por uma geografia latino-americana)

Second volume of essays presented at the 10th Encontro de Geógrafos da América Latina in 2005. Discusses contemporary issues on the production of urban and rural spaces and tourism geography.

937 Ethno- and historical geographic studies in Latin America: essays honoring William V. Davidson. Edited by Peter H. Herlihy, Kent Mathewson, and Craig S. Revels. Baton Rouge, LA: Geoscience Publications, 2008. 346 p.: bibl.

Volume of papers celebrating William V. Davidson's geographical career. Emphasis on Honduras and Central America, but also contributions set in South America.

938 Gade, Daniel W. Irreverant musings on the dissertation in Latin Americanist geography. (*in* Ethno- and historical geographic studies in Latin America: essays honoring William V. Davidson. Edited by Peter H. Herlihy, Kent Mathewson, and Craig S. Revels. Baton Rouge, La.: Geoscience Publications, 2008, p. 29–59, bibl.)

Survey of Latin Americanist geog-

raphy dissertations with observations on trends, shifts in topical emphasis, quality, and quantity.

939 Geography education: Pan American perspectives. Edited by Osvaldo Muñiz-Solari and Richard G. Boehm. San Marcos, Tex.: Grosvenor Center for Geographic Education, 2009. 280 p.: ill., tables.

Collection of essays on the state of art of geography education in a range of countries in North, Central, and South America.

940 Humboldt, Alexander von. Über einen Versuch den Gipfel des Chimborazo zu ersteigen: mit dem vollständigen Text des Tagebuches "Reise zum Chimborazo." Herausgegeben und mit einem Essay versehen von Oliver Lubrich. Berlin: Eichborn, 2006. 195 p.: ill., graph.

Previously unpublished diary entries on Alexander von Humboldt's expedition to the Chimborazo volcano with biographical sketch and additional comments.

941 Jackiewicz, Edward L. and Linda Quiquivix. Eras and errors: a historical and geographical overview of Latin America's economic and political development. (*in* Placing Latin America: contemporary themes in human geography. Edited by Edward L. Jackiewicz and Fernando J. Bosco. Lanham, Md.: Rowman & Littlefield, 2008, p. 17–30, bibl.)

Brief overview of modern economic eras (modern/liberal, import substitution, neoliberal) with speculation on what might follow neoliberalism. For comments on other chapters in this book, see items **926, 929, 945, 948,** and **950.**

942 *Journal of Latin American Geography. Special Issue: Globalization: linking scales of analysis.* Vol. 6, No. 2, 2007. Austin: Univ. of Texas Press.

Special journal issue that presents six empirical case studies on globalization and Latin American geography and the interactions of local and global processes. Topics include small-scale agriculture, medical tourism, food retailing, informal urban work, and land reform movements. Case studies are situated within the broader framework of economic, political, and cultural globalization. Four articles examine Mexico (Biles *et al.* on traditional markets in the Yucatán, Judkins on medical tourism since NAFTA, Harner on food retailing in Guadalajara in the face of big-box discounters, and Gravel on small-food production in light of multinational competition in a post-NAFTA environment). Two essays focus on South America: Schroeder describes the rise of indigenous politics in a pre-Evo Morales' Bolivia (item **1177**), while Whitson argues that informal work in Argentina in the early 2000s should be conceptualized as formal enterprises that contribute to the national economy and not as fleeting informal endeavors (items **1214** and **2398**).

943 Kay, Cristóbal. Land, conflict, and violence in Latin America. (*Peace Rev.*, 19:1, 2007, p. 5–14)
Brief overview of the processes that have led to violent conflicts about land in several Latin American countries.

944 Keeling, David J. Latin America's transportation conundrum. (*J. Lat. Am. Geogr.*, 7:2, 2008, p. 133–154, bibl., maps, photos, tables)
Review of literature on Latin America's transportation geography. Examines the relationship between development and transportation and proposes strategies for future research.

945 Klak, Thomas. Neoliberal exports and regional vulnerability: overview and critical assessment. (*in* Placing Latin America: contemporary themes in human geography. Edited by Edward L. Jackiewicz and Fernando J. Bosco. Lanham, Md.: Rowman & Littlefield, 2008, p. 31–49, bibl., photos)
Looks at selected examples of neoliberal export strategies for economic development, particularly for the Caribbean, but also with applications in other parts of Latin America. Among these are: bananas, non-traditional crops, maquiladoras, online gambling, and off-shore financial services. For comments on other chapters in this book, see items **926, 929, 941, 948,** and **950.**

946 Livi-Bacci, Massimo. The depopulation of Hispanic America after the conquest. (*Popul. Dev. Rev.*, 32:2, June 2006, p. 199–232, bibl., maps, tables)
Discusses the reasons for the depopulation of indigenous peoples in the Americas following the Columbian encounter. The

author de-emphasizes the lethal effects of diseases brought by the Europeans, and seeks a plurality of explanations such as harsh labor conditions, social and economic dislocation, and war.

947 Madrid, Raúl L. The rise of ethnopopulism in Latin America. (*World Polit.*, 60:3, April 2008, p. 475–508)
Relates the increasing influence of ethnically based political parties in Latin America. The author's main argument is that these groups achieve political power through the use of inclusive strategies and not exclusionary ethnic appeal. Presents a case study of the Movimento al Socialismo in Bolivia.

948 Mains, Susan P. Transnational communities, identities, and moving populations. (*in* Placing Latin America: contemporary themes in human geography. Edited by Edward L. Jackiewicz and Fernando J. Bosco. Lanham, Md.: Rowman & Littlefield, 2008, p. 205–234, bibl., photos)
Discusses the concept of transnationalism in the context of migration and population geography, and offers two case studies—on Mexico and Colombia. For comments on other chapters in this book, see items **926, 929, 941, 945,** and **950.**

949 Mann, Charles C. 1491: new revelations of the Americas before Columbus. New York: Knopf, 2005. 465 p.: bibl., ill., index, maps.
Revisionist look at evidence of human occupation of the Americas on the eve of the Columbian invasion, with special emphasis on precolumbian demography, antiquity of humans in the New World, and pre-European landscape modifications.

950 Mathewson, Kent. Drug geographies. (*in* Placing Latin America: contemporary themes in human geography. Edited by Edward L. Jackiewicz and Fernando J. Bosco. Lanham, Md.: Rowman & Littlefield, 2008, p. 137–158, bibl.)
Considers the geographies of drug substances (both licit and illicit) in cultural-historical perspective and their roles in the cultural, political, and economic history of Latin America. For comments on other chapters in this book, see items **926, 929, 941, 945,** and **948.**

951 McSweeney, Kendra and Brad Jokisch. Beyond rainforest: urbanisation and emigration among lowland indigenous societies in Latin America. (Bull. Lat. Am. Res., 26:2, April 2007, p. 159–180, table)

Presents refreshing perspectives on the migration of indigenous populations to urban areas. The text contends that these groups remain attached to particular rural landscapes, and seeks to stimulate research on the dynamics and mechanisms of these migrations that differ from other forms of rural-urban flows.

952 Melendez, Mariselle. The cultural production of space in colonial Latin America: from visualizing differences to the circulation of knowledge. (in The spatial turn: interdisciplinary perspectives. Edited by Barney Warf and Santa Arias. London: Routledge, 2008, p. 173–192)

Book chapter that combines literary studies and critical human geography in order to discuss how indigenous populations (re)imagined their territorialities and local spaces under the influence of 18th-century Enlightenment philosophy. Case study of a group of Peruvian intellectuals in the late 1700s.

953 Milani, Carlos R.S. Ecologia política, movimentos ambientalistas e contestação transnacional na América Latina. (Cad. CRH/Salvador, 21:53, 2008, p. 289–303)

Discusses recent tendencies in the debate on environment, ethics, and international policies in Latin America. Main focus is on the internationalization of environmental issues and the resulting critique by Latin American environmentalists.

954 Miller, Shawn William. An environmental history of Latin America. New York: Cambridge Univ. Press, 2007. 257 p.: bibl., ill., index, maps. (New approaches to the Americas)

Survey of human and environmental interactions from the time of European conquest to the present. Employs short historical episodes to narrate this five-century progression. Actors include Amerindians, Africans, and Europeans as well as commodified plants, animals, substances (silver and guano), events (hurricanes), and processes (erosion).

955 Morrone, J.J. Biogeographic areas and transition zones of Latin America and the Caribbean islands based on panbiogeographic and cladistic analyses of the entomofauna. (Annu. Rev. Entomol., 51, 2006, p. 467–494)

Proposes a new regionalization of biogeographical areas and their respective subdivisions in Latin America that is based on a panbiogeographical and cartographic approach to the distribution of insect taxa. The author describes three distinct regions and two transition zones.

956 Naturraum Lateinamerika: geographische und biologische Grundlagen. Herausgegeben von Axel Borsdorf und Walter Hödl. Münster, Germany: LIT, 2006. 429 p.: graph, ill. (Atención, 10)

Collection of 20 essays on a wide range of physical geographic aspects of Latin America. The book merges traditional themes such as climate, geology, vegetation, and biodiversity with more contemporary issues of human-environment interactions, exploring the tropical rain forest, coffee and coca plantations, and ownership of genetic resources.

957 Ordinary places, extraordinary events: citizenship, democracy and public space in Latin America. Edited by Clara Irazábal. London; New York: Routledge, 2008. 254 p.: bibl., ill., index. (Planning, history and environment series)

Collection of ten essays on the social construction of public space and the struggle for citizenship in light of emerging democratic and protest movements. The volume presents empirical case studies on town squares, museums and historical centers in a range of Latin American cities.

958 Placing Latin America: contemporary themes in human geography. Edited by Edward L. Jackiewicz and Fernando J. Bosco. Lanham, Md.: Rowman & Littlefield, 2008. 276 p.: bibl., ill., index, maps.

Collection of commissioned essays on selected topics by Latin Americanist geographers. Themes include: neoliberal export economics; urbanization, migration, and employment; architectural icons and urban form; tourism; drugs; NGOs; social movements; urban environmental politics;

transnationalism; cinema. Six of the essays are singled out for individual citation and annotation (items **926, 929, 941, 945, 948,** and **950**).

959 **Price, Marie D.** and **Catherine W. Cooper.** Competing visions, shifting boundaries: the construction of Latin America as a world region. (*J. Geogr.*, 106, 2007, p. 113–122)
Short article on the construction of Latin America as a world region for teachers and educators. Discusses different mechanisms of regionalization and presents suggestions for classroom exercises.

960 **Questões territoriais na América Latina.** Organização de Amalia Inés Geraiges de Lemos, María Laura Silveira e Mónica Arroyo. Buenos Aires: CLASCO, 2006. 293 p.: bibl., maps. (Col. Edição e distribuição cooperativa)
First volume of essays presented at the 10th Encontro de Geógrafos da América Latina in 2005. Discusses contemporary issues on territoriality, spatial dynamics, identity, and medical geography in Latin America.

961 **Radcliffe, Sarah A.** Latin American indigenous geographies of fear: living in the shadow of racism, lack of development, and antiterror measures. (*Ann. Assoc. Am. Geogr.*, 97:2, June 2007, p. 385–397)
Analyzes the shifting geopolitical perception of Latin American indigenous populations after the 9/11 attacks from a postdevelopmental viewpoint. Concludes that indigenous people are classified as security risks, rather than as victims of discrimination and marginalization in light of international antiterror measures.

962 **Ramirez, Luz Elena.** British representations of Latin America. Gainesville: Univ. Press of Florida, 2007. 212 p.: bibl., index.
A survey of Americanist literature with significant geographical content. This includes Schomburgk's 1848 edition of Raleigh's *Discovery of Guiana*, the rhetoric of Andean development in Joseph Conrad's *Nostromo*, science and commerce in Arthur Conan Doyle's *The Lost World*, and Graham Greene's *Americanist vision: Mexico, Argentina, and Panama.*

963 **Risiko und Vulnerabilität in Lateinamerika.** Herausgegeben von Rainer Wehrhahn. Kiel: Geographisches Institut der Universität, 2007. 314 p.: bibl., ill., maps. (Kieler geographische Schriften, Bd. 117)
Collection of 14 essays and three shorter contributions on the geographic dimensions of risk and vulnerability. The publication entails theoretical discussions and case studies from different Latin American regions, ranging from the emergence of new agrarian spaces to the impacts of eucalyptus plantations on indigenous land resources and urban planning.

964 **Rosenberg, Fernando J.** The avant-garde and geopolitics in Latin America. Pittsburgh, PA: Univ. of Pittsburgh Press, 2006. 211 p.: bibl., index. (Illuminations)
Examines the canonical Latin American avant-garde texts of the 1920s and 1930s in novels, travel writing, journalism, and poetry, and presents them in a new light as formulators of modern Western culture and precursors of global culture.

965 **Saffache, Pascal; Jean Valéry Marc;** and **Colette Ranély Vergé-Depré.** Les dégradations environnementales en Amérique Latine: état des lieux et perspectives. (*Acta geogr.*, 179:1527, 2007, p. 29–50)
Discusses degradation processes of Latin American environments in the past and the present, from precolumbian and colonial times to contemporary phenomena such as deforestation and urbanization.

966 **Safier, Neil.** Measuring the new world: enlightenment science and South America. Chicago: Univ. of Chicago Press, 2008. 387 p.: bibl., ill., index, maps.
Study of how geographic knowledge (cartographic, geodetic, ethnographic, botanical) was collected, constructed, and transferred to Europe, with particular emphasis on La Condamine.

967 **Sluyter, Andrew** and **Kent Mathewson.** Intellectual relations between historical geography and Latin Americanist geography. (*J. Lat. Am. Geogr.*, 6:1, 2007, p. 25–41, bibl., graphs, tables)
This analysis of the intellectual relationship among historical geographers demonstrates the lack of intellectual con-

nectivity between the Latin Americanist Specialty Group (LASG) and the Historical Geography Specialty Group (HGSG), resulting from the fact that historical geographers of the US and Canada dominate the HGSG and they do not focus on the literature related to the historical geography of Latin America, suggesting the need to rekindle these connections. [P. Herlihy]

968 **Sundberg, Juanita.** Placing race in environmental justice research in Latin America. (*Soc. Nat. Resour.*, 21:7, Aug. 2008, p. 569–582, graphs, map, photos)

Approaches the issue of environmental injustice through the lens of human-environment relations and stresses that racial arguments are a powerful factor in shaping identities and defining places.

THE CARIBBEAN

JOSEPH LEONARD SCARPACI, JR., *Professor of Marketing, Department of Economics and Business, Virginia Military Institute, and Professor Emeritus of Geography, Virginia Polytechnic Institute*

THE LITERATURE UNDER REVIEW emphasizes the fragility of the physical environment as studied by local scholars of the Caribbean (items **970, 971, 973, 974, 975, 976, 977, 978, 979, 981, 983, 988,** and **992**). Also evident are interdisciplinary studies that weave myriad social science perspectives on place, landscape, and heritage with elements from the humanities (items **980, 986,** and **987**) and environmental (items **969, 985,** and **990**) and commodity histories (item **984**). These literatures should serve as a benchmark for the international community as it focuses on Haiti in the aftermath of the January 12, 2010, earthquake and begins to rethink development policy (item **982**) and the changing role of the peasantry (item **989**) across the Caribbean.

969 **Beyond sun and sand: Caribbean environmentalisms.** Edited by Sherrie L. Baver and Barbara Deutsch Lynch. New Brunswick, N.J.: Rutgers Univ. Press, 2006. 210 p.: bibl., index.

Argues that the trappings of the region's tourism conceal the real underpinnings of a Creole environmentalism—a construct linked by multiple paradigms with cultural and subregional variations. Local actors must connect with North-South movements. Most of the chapters deal with Puerto Rico, but there are also chapters on Martinique, Cuba, the Dominican Republic, and New York City.

970 **Cámara Artigas, Rafael; Jose Ramón Martínez Batlle; and Fernando Díaz del Olmo.** Desarrollo sostenible y medio ambiente en República Dominicana: medios naturales, manejo histórico, conservación y protección. Sevilla: Consejo Superior de Investigaciones Científicas, Escuela de Estudios Hispano-Americanos, Univ. de Sevilla, 2005. 280 p.: bibl., ill., map.

Comprehensive cataloging of the Dominican Republic's physical geography, including biogeography, soils, and climatic variation. Aims to link the nation's (and island of Hispaniola's) physical backdrop against historical and contemporary resource management, defined as sugar production, ranching, tobacco, and fishing. Argues that contemporary environmental stewardship must be ramped up even though public and private management of resources are not covered in great depth, nor are there insights into achieving sustainable development.

971 **Cepero, Eudel Eduardo.** Crítica a la ecosofía de la Revolución. (*Encuentro Cult. Cuba.*, 43, invierno 2006/2007, p. 131–144, photo)

Critical appraisal of revolutionary Cuba's environmental policy and philosophy. Uses statements by Fidel Castro and geographer Antonio Núñez Jiménez to demonstrate misguided proposals like the draining of Zapata Swamp and problems of elevated roads (pedraplanes) through mangroves and marshes separating the northern keys, poor forest management (despite the rise in forested and reforested areas), and salt-water intrusion island-wide.

972 Congreso-Taller Internacional de Ética Ecológica, *Universidad de Puerto Rico, Recinto de Cayey, 2003.* Ética y ecología: la crisis ética de los movimientos ecologistas contemporáneos: actas del Congreso-Taller Internacional de Ética Ecológica: perspectivas humanistas sobre el medio ambiente, Univ. de Puerto Rico, Recinto de Cayey, 29–31 de octubre de 2003. Recopilación de Luis Galanes Valldejuli, Antonio Aledo Tur, y José Andrés Domínguez Gómez. San Juan: Editorial Tal Cual, 2004. 152 p.: bibl.

A collection of essays on Puerto Rico, the Panama Canal, the Caribbean, and other regions debunks the romantic myth of all ecological NGOs championing the rights of the downtrodden. Instead, illustrates how NGOs often take aim at developing nations and indigenous groups in questionable ways. Incorporates an animal-rights and ecofeminist perspective in two chapters.

973 Contreras Pérez, José B.; Carmen Leticia Mendoza; and Arismendis Gómez. Determinación de metales pesados en aguas y sedimentos del Río Haina. (*Cienc. Soc./Santo Domingo*, 29:1, enero/marzo 2004, p. 38–71, bibl., graphs, tables)

Nine samples from the Haina River in Santo Domingo were measured for heavy-metal (copper, nickel, lead iron, arsenic, cadmium, chrome, and zinc) and sediment levels. Although most metals (except iron and copper) fell within acceptable levels, traces of all metals were present, with heavier amounts of chrome, lead, iron, nickel, and copper.

974 Cotilla-Rodríguez, Mario Octavio. Estudio geomorfológico del carso en la región Gibara-Banes de Holguín, Cuba. (*Rev. Geogr./México*, 134, julio/dic. 2003, p. 5–22, bibl., maps, tables)

Field research coupled with panchro-matic and satellite imagery of the Gibara-Banes region at 1:100,000 scale identifies 22.4 percent as a karstic formation, of which about two-thirds is in the plains and the balance is in uplands. Siting a nuclear power plant in the study area should be reassessed in light of the geomorphology of the region.

975 Cotilla Rodríguez, Mario Octavio *et al.* La red fluvial de Cuba y su interpretación moroestructural. (*Rev. Geogr./México*, 134, julio/dic. 2003, p. 23–50, bibl., maps, tables)

Classifies watersheds and rivers throughout Cuba according to primary and secondary streams. Produces stream-classification maps of first to fourth-order levels at a scale of 1:250,000. Identifies the largest watershed extending from Cape San Antonio in the west to Maisí headwaters in the east. Delineates watersheds using the pre-1975 provincial political divisions.

976 Espinal, Georgina and Sócrates Nivar. Estudio comparativo de las condiciones ambientales al interior de las viviendas en dos barrios de la capital dominicana. (*Cienc. Soc./Santo Domingo*, 29:2, abril/junio 2004, p. 213–242, bibl., graphs, tables)

Compares and contrasts two different socioeconomic neighborhoods—Arroyo Hondo Viejo and Barrio Duarte de Herrera—in Santo Domingo, to define the conditions of house interiors by their residents. The former neighborhood had a superior interior that was also better preserved. Environmental variables assessed included levels of NO_2, SO_2, air particulates, and volatile organic compounds. Poorer interior environmental quality correlates directly with smaller homes that use inferior building materials.

977 Espinal, Georgina and Sócrates Nivar. Estudio de la contaminación ambiental al interior de las viviendas en tres barrios de la capital dominicana. (*Cienc. Soc./Santo Domingo*, 29:2, abril/junio 2004, p. 167–212, bibl., graphs, tables)

Interior air quality and noise levels were examined in three neighborhoods in Santo Domingo. Variables measured included levels of CO, CO_2, NO_2, suspended particles, and noise pollution. Findings showed that the overall quality of housing influences the indoor quality of the home which, in turn, reflects residents' comfort, safety, and health levels.

978 **Funes Monzote, Reinaldo.** From rainforest to cane field in Cuba: an environmental history since 1492, Translated by Alex Martin. Chapel Hill: Univ. of North Carolina Press, 2008. 357 p.: bibl., ill., index, maps. (Envisioning Cuba)

Despite the title and subtitle, examines mainly colonial and earlier national periods of sugar cane production and deforestation in Cuba.

979 **Funes Monzote, Reinaldo.** *El asiento de su riqueza*: los bosques y la ocupación del este de Cuba por el azúcar, 1898–1926. (*Anu. IEHS*, 19, 2004, p. 231–253, graph, table)

Documents the pace of deforestation in Camagüey and Oriente provinces in Cuba in the first half of the 20th century due to US investment in sugar plantations and plantings.

980 **Huish, Robert L.** and **W. George Lovell.** Under the volcanoes: the influence of Guatemala on José Martí. (*Cuba. Stud.*, 39, 2007, p. 25–43)

Ideas and writings of José Martí, Cuban patriot and Pan-American thinker, inspired not only a decolonization of the island and Caribbean Basin region, but also had an impact in Guatemala (and Guatemalan President Justo Rufino Barrios influenced him when he was exiled there in 1877 and 1878).

981 **Jaffe, Rivke.** A view from the concrete jungle: diverging enviromentalisms in the urban Caribbean. (*NWIG*, 80:3/4, 2006, p. 221–243, bibl., table)

Ethnographic research at local and supralocal levels in Curacao and Jamaica reveals locals' coherent folk ecologies which have implications for the ways green professionals, especially environmental nongovernmental organizations (ENGOs), allocate aid.

982 **Klak, Thomas.** Development policy drift in Central America and the Caribbean. (*Singap. J. Trop. Geogr.*, 30:1, March 2009, p. 12–17)

Outlines the emergence of a developmentalist state in the region that departs from the schema proposed by Venezuela's Hugo Chávez.

983 **Lézy, Emmanuel.** La Guyane, un territoire de légendes, en marge de toutes les cartes. (*Cah. Am. lat.*, 43, 2003, p. 39–65, bibl., graphs, maps, photos)

Questions the traditional conceptualization of Guyana in the geographical imagination, and draws on the works of Neil Whitehead on the country's central savannahs to delineate an indigenous Guyana.

984 **Mandelblatt, Bertie.** A transatlantic commodity: Irish salt beef in the French Atlantic world. (*Hist. Workshop J.*, 63, 2007, p. 18–47, bibl., ill.)

Explores and deepens the discussion of the Creolization of foods. Shows how salt beef links slaves' consumption to the expansion of French sugar production in the 18th century throughout networks between Europe (France and Ireland) to Saint-Domingue, Guadeloupe, and Martinique.

985 **Ryder, Roy.** Local soil knowledge and site suitability evaluation in the Dominican Republic. (*Geoderma*, 111, 2002, p. 289–305)

Enlists a survey of 80 farmers to understand the source of knowledge about soils and crop adaptability and concludes that even though their soil taxonomy is unsophisticated, a participatory approach to agriculture can be enhanced by consulting with peasants. In turn, local assessment of soil suitability can be matched against more empirical constructs.

986 **Scarpaci, Joseph L.** and **Armando H. Portela.** Cuban landscapes: heritage, memory, and place. New York: Guilford Press, 2009. 216 p.: bibl., ill., index, maps. (Texts in regional geography)

A cultural geographic exploration of the meaning of Cuban identity, or *cubanidad*, manifested through 19th-century landscape portraits, poetry, music, Afro-Cuban heritage, television, film, and national and international heritage sites. Traces the evolution of thinking about Cuba as a place from 19th-century travel logs, 20th-century popular culture, and postrevolutionary interpretations both inside and outside the island.

987 **Sheller, Mimi.** Virtual islands: mobilities, connectivity, and the New Caribbean spatialities. (*Small Axe*, 24: 2007, p. 16–33)

The Caribbean's long-standing interconnectivity with the world means that today the region is being reconceptualized in the form of neocolonial fantasies. Neoliberalism reestablishes new relationships between these fragmented territories with expatriate communities across the Atlantic. Examples draw on architectural design, Atlantis in Paradise Island in the Bahamas, and curatorial representations of the Turks and Caicos.

988 Théry, Hervé. Une Guyane brésilienne? (*Cah. Am. lat.*, 43, 2003, p. 103–119, bibl., maps)

Long considered culturally and physically remote from the more heavily populated portion of Guyana, the southern part of the nation is increasingly becoming more integrated with the rest of the nation due to transportation and communication developments.

989 Weis, Tony. The rise, fall and future of the Jamaican peasantry. (*J. Peasant Stud.*, 33:1, Jan. 2006, p. 61–88, bibl.)

A cogent historical review of the vicissitudes of the Jamaican farmers who face mounting pressures from importing foodstuffs, international lending agencies, market irregularities, and limited inputs. Land reform and creative policies must protect this vulnerable class to nurture the island's beleaguered agricultural landscape for future generations.

990 "What is the earthly paradise?": ecocritical responses to the Caribbean. Edited by Chris Campbell and Erin Somerville. Newcastle, U.K.: Cambridge Scholars Pub., 2007. 173 p.: bibl., index.

This collection of 11 essays explores the cross-disciplinary meanings of the environmental condition of the region expressed in literature and the environmental histories of several islands. It traces ecofeminist and historical interpretations of precolumbian, colonial, and post-colonial landscapes among the English- and French-speaking islands. Examines the work of renowned writers such as Derek Walcott, Sam Selvon, Patrick Chamoiseau, among others.

991 Whittle, Daniel and Orlando Rey Santos. Protecting Cuba's environment: efforts to design and implement effective environmental laws and policies in Cuba. (*T'inkazos*, 21, dic. 2006, p. 73–103, bibl.)

A policy and rhetorical review of the national government of Cuba's response to environmental policies, laws, and regulation since the Rio Summit of 1992. Focuses upon the workings of one ministry in particular (CITMA, Ministry of Science, Technology and the Environment) and especially Law 81, the 1997 Law of the Environment.

992 Yera, Yoel del Risco and Lluís Mundet I. Cerdan. El turismo como estrategia de desarrollo en Cuba. (*Estud. Geogr./Madrid*, 66:258, enero/junio 2005, p. 293–318, bibl., graphs, tables)

Descriptive overview of four stages of the island's tourism from the 1920s to the new millennium. Emphasizes traditional roles of Havana and Varadero while also warning about the negative social and environmental impacts in northern coastal and archipelago sites. For economist's comment, see item **773**.

CENTRAL AMERICA AND MEXICO

PETER H. HERLIHY, *Associate Professor of Geography, University of Kansas*

THE GEOGRAPHICAL RESEARCH reviewed on Mexico and Central America maintains a broad sample of thematic, theoretical, and methodological perspectives. About one-third of the literature sampled from the 2004–08 period is annotated here, with about half the entries on Mexico. Cultural-historical geography, protected areas management, and the indigenous/Afro-descendant populations continue as strong interests, with new emphasis on forests, water, and land reforms reflecting societal concerns about the use and misuse of natural resources, as well as the emergence of solid waste management as a serious environmental issue impacting both urban (item **1032**) and rural areas. As in the past, the cultural side is much more heavily represented than the physical side of the discipline and there are only a small number of strictly physical geography entries. The literature reflects, however, that geographers are increasingly using multifaceted research methodologies that combine both physical and cultural information with GIS and remote sensing for understanding human-environmental interactions.

This biennium two significant centers of geographic scholarship have developed in Mexico and merit notation here. The Universidad Autónoma de San Luis Potosí (UASLP) established the Coordinación de Ciencias Sociales y Humanidades (CCSyH) in 2002 with its founding director geographer Miguel Aguilar Robledo subsequently forming the Department of Geography. In 2008, the UASLP and CCSyH began the journal *EspacioTiempo: Revista Latinoamericana de Ciencias Sociales y Humanidades* to serve as a platform for discussion and reflection of distinct theoretical stances, methodological approaches, and themes. Geographic research is well represented in their first edition, entitled "Cultura y medio ambiente en la Huasteca: la población indígena y su entorno natural" (items **1029** and **1072**). The other, the Morelia Academic Unit of the Institute of Geography at the Universidad Nacional Autónoma de México (UNAM) established the Centro de Investigaciones en Geografía Ambiental (CIGA) in 2007 at the Morelia campus. CIGA researchers, including two of the founding geographers Gerardo Verdinelli Bocco and Narciso Barrera Bassols, aim at high-quality research to contribute to land-use planning and natural resource management through an integrated academic program of research, education, and outreach (items **1031**, **1034**, and **1071**).

Many research trends identified previously in *HLAS 61* and *63* continue today. A strong interest remains in cultural-historical geography and ethnogeography combining archival and field research. Many geographers studied the vernacular complexes of the contemporary cultural landscape, including the architecture of Q'eqchi' Maya in Guatemala (item **1008**), the concrete block landscape in Mexico (item **1044**), the grid pattern of street layout in Honduras (item **1021**), and the mesquite economy of the US-Mexican Borderlands (item **1070**).

A Spanish translation of E.G. Squier's important treatise on the geography of mid-19th century Honduras and El Salvador was published by the Colección Cultural de Centro América by the Fundación VIDA in Nicaragua, with critical annotations by geographer William V. Davidson (item **997**). In Mexico, Aguilar-Robledo reconstructed the environmental history of the Valles Jurisdiction in the Huasteca region from the mid-16th to early 19th century (item **1029**); equally exemplary, Alfred Siemens and colleagues studied past and present landscape changes caused by the expansion of Mexico's principal port of Veracruz (item **1069**). Mack completed an outstanding study showing how colonial Omoa in Honduras lost its strategic importance due to changing coastal geomorphology and declining economic importance (item **1017**), while Revels shows what place-names reveal about historical mahogany trade in Honduras (item **1020**).

The study of indigenous and Afro-descendant populations included a variety of themes and methodological approaches. Geographer George Lovell provides a vivid and poignant narrative of the injustices of the indigenous experience in Guatemala (item **1010**). A study of the Mayanga of Nicaragua details their settlement dislocation and subsequent reoccupation in their once war-torn homelands, explaining current efforts to delimit and protect their homelands (item **1027**). To the east, there is a resurgence of separatist feelings among the Miskitu populations on the country's Atlantic Coast (item **1026**). Geographers have also reflected on their own research and representation of indigenous peoples (items **1010** and **1018**) and an insightful treatise of bioprospecting in Mexico contains lessons for all working among peasant and indigenous societies (item **1053**).

How indigenous peoples interact with their environment and with protected areas also remains a focus. Geographers studied contemporary Yucatec Maya farmers' knowledge, use, and management of their landscapes (items **1031** and **1071**), and their past and present use of the dooryard orchard-garden (item **1054**). In Honduras, shifting cultivation is still very much part of the Miskito economy in the Río Plátano Biosphere Reserve (item **1016**) and Lenca settlements exploit forest resources within the limits of the Guajiquiro Cloud Forest Reserve (item **1015**).

Geographers have also studied the social construction of space and how ethnic identity is constructed and maintained. One study shows how government agencies map indigenous language, regional cooking, and popular art to register popular cultures in Mexico (item **1056**). Others demonstrate that the ritual landscape is crucial in defining the territoriality of the indigenous Teenek in the Huasteca region (item **1072**) and that Garífuna identity in coastal Belize is symbolized and maintained by specific "markers" that carry their identity (item **998**). Related research among an Afro-Caribbean population in Costa Rica demonstrates how revitalized "identity practices" can attract tourism (item **1001**) or define the spatial identity of a region like the Olancho in Honduras (item **1014**). Today, indigenous K'iche' extend transnational linkages between their homelands, Houston, and Los Angeles (item **1011**).

A sizable body of research focuses on the management of forest resources and protected areas. An excellent paleoecological analysis records past human occupancy and forest disturbance in El Salvador (item **1006**). Contemporary land-use/land cover studies use remote sensing and GIS to document changes in the Toledo District of Belize (item **999**), in the northern Petén of Guatemala (item **1009**), and in the Huasteca region of Mexico (item **1067**). Econometric modeling and analysis of land cover change around Cerro Celaque National Park in Honduras demonstrates the complex and multidirectional nature of land-use changes (item **1019**), with results from Costa Rica showing similar variability over time (item **1003**).

Researchers have documented the complexities of managing the Monarch Butterfly Biosphere Reserve of Mexico, the hibernation habitat of millions of the butterflies each year, which is both a conservation priority and a spectacular tourist attraction, pointing out that strategies have overemphasized the capacity of the state (items **1035** and **1061**). In the Calakmul region, invasive bracken fern creates a destructive "perturbation" invading agricultural lands (item **1068**), while government development programs there sometimes do and sometimes do not cause deforestation (item **1066**). Such research begins to question core conservation management practices and Hecht and Saatchi show the significant implications that "woodland resurgence" should have for tropical conservation (item **1007**).

Given the variability and multidirectional nature of land-use/land cover change over time, perhaps it is not surprising that debate still exists over parks-and-people versus protectionist approaches to conservation management. One study compared the "conventional park" of La Amistad in Costa Rica to a "parks-and-people" park of Cerro Azul Meambar National Park in Honduras (item **996**). Another documented the factors behind settler land-use and forest clearing in the Sierra de Lacandón National Park, a core conservation zone of the Maya Biosphere

Reserve in Guatemala (item **1009**). Study shows that environmental education of residents in communities around Costa Rica's La Selva increases knowledge and valuation of the reserve (item **1004**).

A significant collection by Bray, Merino-Pérez, and Barry (item **1039**) focuses on community-based forestry in Mexico, with the consensus being that community benefit and control leads to better use and protection of forest and other natural resources. Decentralized municipal and community development of forestry resources is common in Honduras where indigenous communities form effective agroforestry groups (item **1022**). A critique of the Nicaraguan portion of the Mesoamerican Biological Corridor, however, suggests only a limited role of the local governments and impacted populations (item **1024**), but the country's forestry law and politics do not promote municipal control over, or community development of forest resources (item **1025**). A look at forest policy in Costa Rica calls for "hybrid" management with both market-oriented and state-interventionist approaches (item **1002**).

Geographers focus more today on issues tied to globalization and neoliberal economic changes. An excellent volume shows how these forces impact women's mobility, employment, and political activism along the US-Mexico Borderlands (item **1073**). Market liberalization has brought supermarket chains to Guadalajara that privilege wealthy over poor (item **1051**) and the reconfiguration of food retailing networks in the Yucatán has been detrimental for small-scale chile and beef producers (item **1033**). Global volatility of coffee prices has led local producer in Veracruz to experiment with state livelihood diversification programs, or to migrate and sell their land (item **1052**). Geographers also focused on the environmental impact of the electricity sector in Mexico (item **1050**), and on the political economy of the extractive petroleum and mining industries in Guatemala (item **1012**). With petroleum reserves dwindling in Mexico, great potential exists for renewable energy resources such as sun and wind energy, but also biomass, water, and geothermal (item **1060**).

New trends in the literature include investigation of some of the region's most pressing environmental and social problems, such as water resources, municipal autonomy, and migration (item **1041**). Neoliberal property regimes are quietly changing ancestral patterns of communal tenure and resource use. Mexico has undergone the most dramatic changes through a gargantuan land certification program that is transforming the country's social property into private property, with tremendous consequences for land and natural resource use. This legal certification of communal ejido and agrarian community lands brings multiple outcomes (item **1065**). An exceptional book explains how campesinos of central Veracruz forge their identity with agrarian reforms, ejido politics, and sugar/coffee cultivation playing defining roles in their uncertain futures (item **1063**). Scholars have also looked at these changes in the Tuxtlas region (item **1058**) and in the Yucatán (item **1043**) where the state's role in sustaining the chicle industry has divided indigenous territories. Research has also focused on the incorporation of ejido lands into the urban area of Guadalajara (item **1038**), and on the irregularities of tenancy and the applications of land legalization programs in Tijuana (item **1030**). In Guatemala, land-use and tenure problems at the municipality level point to the inadequacy of the country's property regime (item **1013**).

The importance and complexity of water management makes it one of the most significant resource issues of the 21st century. Two edited volumes, one based on a benchmark conference in 2001, introduce the key issues related to water use in Mexico. The work includes contributions from academics and public officials on water use in cities, in agriculture, and its extraction from subterranean reserves, with consideration given to community use, development, privatization, conservation, and indigenous water rights (item **1048**). Scholars examined how past mid-20th century agrarian reforms and irrigation projects of the "Green Revolution" created water access disputes in the Mayo and Yaqui valleys of Sonora (items **1042** and **1059**), but the impacts of contemporary neoliberal land reforms on water use needs more study. Furthermore, the excellent edited collection, *La gestión del agua urbana en Mexico: retos, debates y bienestar*, demonstrates the inadequacies of the country's contemporary water systems and services, warning of the overexploitation and contamination of more than half the country's aquifers (item **1047**). Researchers also considered water management at the municipality level in Aguascalientes (item **1037**) and along the US-Mexican Borderlands (item **1036**).

Finally, geographers have demonstrated that the destructive impacts set in motion by hurricane disasters in Mexico and Central America, such as Paulina in 1997 and Mitch in 1998, are dependent on the social and geographical context in which they occur (items **998**, **1023**, and **1040**). One hundred twenty-nine natural disasters struck Central America between the 16th and 20th centuries and 28 hit the east coast of Mexico over the past century, which should condition development in the region (items **995** and **1049**). Indeed, the gap between population growth and economic possibilities increased in Central America during the military conflicts of the 1980s and natural disasters of the 1990s (item **993**).

CENTRAL AMERICA: GENERAL

993 Alonso Santos, José Luis. América Central: contrastes entre el proceso demográfico, el crecimiento económico y el mercado de trabajo. (*Estud. Geogr./Madrid,* 66:259, julio/dic. 2005, p. 373–406, bibl., graphs, tables)

The gap between population growth and economic and social possibilities in Central American countries increased during the 1980s due to military conflicts, and in the 1990s due to natural disasters, hurricanes, and earthquakes, resulting in emigration and huge population movements with remittances becoming an important source of income.

994 Castro Soto, Gustavo. El movimiento social en Mesoamérica por la defensa de los recursos naturales. (*Obs. Soc. Am. Lat.,* 6:17, mayo/agosto 2005, p. 41–51, bibl., photos)

Resistance to dams was central in the development of the Mesoamerican movement for the defense of natural resources; conflicts over water resources may be central in the future.

Horton, Lynn. Grassroots struggles for sustainability in Central America. See item **2570**.

Klak, Thomas. Development policy drift in Central America and the Caribbean. See item **982**.

995 Petit-Breuilh Sepúlveda, María Eugenia. Desastres naturales y desarrollo sostenible en Centroamérica: un desarrollo de futuro. (*Rábida/Huelva,* 23, 2004, p. 47–53, bibl., graph)

The fact that 129 natural disasters struck Central America between the 16th and 20th centuries, including significant earthquakes, volcanic eruptions, droughts, and floods (associated with hurricanes), should condition development throughout the region, as the experience with Hurricane Mitch in 1998 has demonstrated.

996 Schelhas, John and **Max John Pfeffer.** Saving forests, protecting people?: environmental conservation in Central America. Lanham, Md.: AltaMira Press, 2008. 310 p.: bibl., ill., index, maps. (Globalization and the environment series; 10)

The authors introduce the volume with an overview of forest conservation and protected area management, and discussion of the conflicts in conservation philosophies of protectionist versus parks-and-people approaches, recognizing conservation usually involves a combination of these together with other efforts on private lands. They contrast these two management styles with in-depth case studies from the "conventional park" of La Amistad International Park in Costa Rica and from the "park-and-people" Cerro Azul Meambar National Park in Honduras, using excerpts from their own transcribed interviews together with questionnaire results to give voice to the communities living in or near them.

997 Squier, Ephraim George. Apuntamientos sobre Centro América: Honduras y El Salvador: su geografía, topografía, clima, población, riqueza, producciones, etc., etc., y el propuesto Ferrocarril de Honduras. Traducción por León Alvarado. Notas actualizadas por William V. Davidson. Nicaragua: Fundación Vida, 2004. 423 p.: bibl., ill., index, maps. (Serie Viajeros; 5)

This translation of the diplomat, traveler, writer, and businessman E.G. Squier's important treatise on the geography of mid-19th century Honduras and El Salvador is a significant addition to the Spanish literature on the historical geography of these two countries. The work is particularly valuable given the addition of 300 annotations by geographer Davidson that provide critical understanding of the human and environmental observations made by Squier.

BELIZE

998 Bass, Joby. Ethnic landscapes, ethnic ecology: place attachment and ethnic identity following a Caribbean hurricane. (in Ethno- and historical geographic studies in Latin America: essays honoring William V. Davidson. Edited by Peter H. Herlihy, Kent Mathewson, and Craig S. Revels. Baton Rouge, La.: Geoscience Publications, 2008, p. 105-127, bibl., maps, photos)

Exploring Garífuna ethnicity from a case study of the villages of Hopkins and Sittee River in the Stann Creek District of Belize, the author demonstrates how group identity is symbolized and maintained by "markers" specific to that group that can become "carriers" of their ethnic identity.

999 Emch, Michael et al. Forest cover change in the Toledo District, Belize from 1975 to 1999: a remote sensing approach. (Prof. Geogr., 57:2, May 2005, p. 256-267, bibl., maps, tables)

This research used Landsat Multispectral Scanner (MSS) and Enhanced Thematic Mapper Plus (ETM+) imagery with supervised and subpixel classification methods to document forest cover change in the Toledo District of southern Belize. The results showed a 10 percent forest loss between 1975 and 1999 with deforestation expanding significantly in the most populous Mayan areas in the center of the district (with a growing Maya population) and in the west along the Guatemalan border (with a growing immigrant population, mainly from Guatemala); the most densely forested area remains in the Maya Mountains to the north.

1000 Frutos, Ramón. Six hydrologic indices to evaluate the state of aridity in Belize, El Petén, Guatemala and Yucatán. (Belizean Stud., 28:1, April 2006, p. 17-30, bibl., maps, tables)

The researcher uses a computer software designed to input monthly weather data and other parameters like potential evapotranspiration, humidity, and radiation to better define areas prone to aridity in Belize. Shows the country to have a humid climate overall, but with areas of the Cayo, Belize, Orange Walk, and Corozal districts with more dry months and with higher annual water deficits confined to the latter two northern districts.

COSTA RICA

1001 Anderson, Moji. Arguing over the "Caribbean": tourism on Costa Rica's Caribbean coast. (Caribb. Q./Mona, 51:2, June 2005, p. 31-52, bibl.)

The village of Cahuita on Costa Rica's Caribbean coast southeast of Limon was founded by Afro-Caribbean turtle fisherman in the early 19th century; it remained agricultural until the 1970s when villagers began to focus on tourism. Tourism has brought the "Caribbeanising" of Cahuita and locals now embrace certain "identify practices" that recognize their Afro-Caribbean heritage and attract tourists, including elements of Rastafarianism.

1002 Brockett, Charles D. and **Robert R. Gottfried.** State policies and the preservation of forest cover: lessons from contrasting public-policy regimes in Costa Rica. (*LARR*, 37:1, 2002, p. 7–40, bibl.)

This survey of forest policy in Costa Rica characterizes three periods: "laissez-faire," with largely unrestrained deforestation; "interventionist," with new regulatory policies aimed, with mixed results, at protection of wildlands; and, most recently, "hybrid" with both market-oriented and state interventionist approaches that ideally combine effective regulations with market incentive.

1003 Joyce, Armond T. Land use change in Costa Rica as influenced by social, economic, political and environmental factors: 1966–2006. San José: Litografía e Impr. LIL, 2006. 272 p.: bibl., ill.

Dividing Costa Rica into five regions, this impressive study, spanning 40 years, details land-use change in each, focusing on deforestation or reforestation, conservation, government policies, laws, and market economics. Results are grounded in observations on 32 land-use change study sites from around the country monitored by the author from 1966 to 2006, showing the variability of land use change at each site. Concludes that the uncertainties associated with land-use decisions makes predictions beyond five years questionable.

1004 Moorman, Randall S. Benefits of local residents visiting La Selva Biological Station, Costa Rica. (*Environ. Conserv./Cambridge*, 33:3, Sept. 2006, p. 89–99, bibl., graphs, map, tables)

Addressing a conservation axiom that environmental education programs in neighboring communities help reduce local threats to protected areas, this research suggests that visiting does provide an educational experience that may increase residents' knowledge and valuation of their nearby protected area, but with on-going environmental education programs at La Selva since 1985, more study is needed.

1005 Quirós Arias, Lilliam. Agricultura orgánica y desarrollo rural: la naranja orgánica en Costa Rica. (*Rev. Geogr./México*, 137, enero/junio 2005, p. 5–33, bibl., graphs, maps, tables)

Organic orange production has risen steadily since 1999 and now accounts for 4 percent of orange production in the country. Grown in northern Costa Rica by three groups of producers, they use new methods and cultivation systems that conform to international certification requirements.

EL SALVADOR

1006 Dull, Robert A. Evidence for forest clearance, agriculture, and human-induced erosion in precolumbian El Salvador. (*Ann. Assoc. Am. Geogr.*, 97:1, March 2007, p. 127–141, bibl., ill., maps, tables)

This paleoecological analysis of a lacustrine sediment sequence from Laguna Chalchuapa in the Upper Río Paz Valley of El Salvador reveals past human disturbance through maize and weed pollen, microscopic charcoal, magnetic susceptibility, and sediment flux. Results show intensive maize cultivation occurred about 3700 BP, followed by anthropogenic disturbance up to the present, interrupted by two periods when Ilopango volcano erupted (AD 430) and again after the arrival of Europeans, with the greatest disturbances from 3700–1600 BP and 1350–1000 BP.

1007 Hecht, Susanna B. and **Sassan S. Saatchi.** Globalization and forest resurgence: changes in forest cover in El Salvador. (*BioScience*, 57:8, Sept. 2007, p. 663–672, bibl., graphs, maps, tables)

While globalization has been linked to forest loss, fragmentation, and environmental degradation, this research shows "woodland resurgence" in El Salvador, resulting from processes related to the civil war, the retraction of the agricultural frontier, and international migration with associated remittances, as well as agrarian reform, structural adjustment, and emerging environmental ideas. The implications for tropical conservation are significant.

GUATEMALA

1008 Blanco Sepúlveda, Rafael and **Francisco Enríquez Narváez.** El desarrollo rural y la transformación del patrimonio arquitectónico tradicional: el caso de la aldea indígena Plan Grande Quehueche, Izabal, Guatemala. (*Estud. Geogr./Madrid*, 66:259, julio/dic. 2005, p. 407–434, bibl., ill., tables)

This study looks at changes to the vernacular architecture of 60 Q'eqchi' Maya families of Plan Grande Quehueche in the Dept. of Izabal, finding economic development in the community brings the use of modern construction materials. Work will be necessary to protect traditional forms.

1009 Carr, David L. Forest clearing among farm households in the Maya Biosphere Reserve. (*Prof. Geogr.*, 57:2, May 2005, p. 157–168, bibl., map, tables)

This research examines factors behind settler land use and forest clearing among 241 farm households in eight communities in the Sierra de Lacandón National Park, which is the core conservation zone of the Maya Biosphere Reserve with most of the remaining forests in Guatemala's northern Petén. Farmers cleared forest for subsistence cultivation and increasingly for pasture and the results showed household size, Q'eqchí Maya ethnicity, land owned in previous residence, farm size, land title, and the cropping of velvet bean cover were factors positively related to forest clearing, while education, off-farm employment, and farm distance from road were negatively related to farm-level deforestation.

Huish, Robert L. and **W. George Lovell.** Under the volcanoes: the influence of Guatemala on José Martí. See item **980**.

1010 Lovell, W. George. At peace in the corn: Maya narratives and the dynamics of fieldwork in Guatemala. (*Gend. Place Cult.*, 15:1, 2008, p. 75–81)

An insightful essay on the experience of one Maya family from the K'iche' area whose members were victims of the civil war (1961–96) and the injustices of the indigenous experience in Guatemala, providing an authoritative look at research issues related to representation and fieldwork.

1011 Moran-Taylor, Michelle J. Crafting connections: Maya linkages between Guatemala's *altiplano* and *el norte*. (*Estud. Front.*, 5:10, julio/dic. 2004, p. 91–115, bibl., table)

Based on 15 months of field research in Guatemala using participant observation, the author examines how indigenous K'iche' at home and abroad develop transnational connections at a local level using communication networks and hometown associations to forge linkages between their Guatemalan

homelands and their primary destinations of Houston, Texas and Los Angeles, California in *el norte*.

1012 Solano, Luis. Guatemala: petróleo y minería en las entrañas del poder. Guatemala: Inforpress Centroamericana, 2005. 169 p.: bibl., index, maps.

This journalistic volume systematizes the recent political economy of extractive petroleum and mining industries in Guatemala, strongly focusing on 1977–83, to reveal recurrent and not always positive associations between business and military, and between Guatemalan and US officials, within the anticommunist and militarily charged political environment of the time.

1013 Thillet de Solórzano, Braulia. Tierras municipales en Guatemala: un desafío para el desarrollo local sostenible. Guatemala: FLACSO, Sede Académica Guatemala, 2003. 425 p.: bibl., ill., maps.

Land use and tenure problems of ejido and municipal lands in Guatemala relate to the legal uncertainty about the possession, use, and ownership of the land, to the lack of land-use planning, and to the inadequacy of the country's property regime. The author provides suggestions for future studies and for the formation of public policies aimed at sustainable development.

HONDURAS

1014 Bonta, Mark. On Olancho: geographers, spatial identities, and the construction of a region. (*in* Ethno- and historical geographic studies in Latin America: essays honoring William V. Davidson. Edited by Peter H. Herlihy, Kent Mathewson, and Craig S. Revels. Baton Rouge, La.: Geoscience Publications, 2008, p. 193–206, bibl., photos)

Reviving an old tradition of landscape and region study in Latin Americanist geography, the author aims at capturing the spatial identity of the Olancho Department of eastern Honduras, showing Olancho and its peoples as independent and distinct from the rest of the country, separating the real and the *faux mythos* that attracts some and repels others.

1015 Brady, Scott. Exploring the *archivo municipal* to understand recent patterns of forest use in Guajiquiro, Honduras. (*in* Ethno- and historical geographic studies in Latin America: essays honoring William V. Davidson. Edited by Peter H. Herlihy, Kent Mathewson, and Craig S. Revels. Baton Rouge, La.: Geoscience Publications, 2008, p. 161–176, 2008, bibl., ill., tables)

Author combines archival and field research to understand changing forest use and regulation in Guajiquiro, a municipality in southwestern Honduras. The area is inhabited by the indigenous Lenca people who reside in numerous settlements within the problematic limits of the Guajiquiro Cloud Forest Biological Reserve where they clear forest for agriculture, cut timber for house construction, but need forest for local water needs.

1016 Cochran, David M. Who will work the land?: national integration, cash economies, and the future of shifting cultivation in the Honduran Mosquitia. (*J. Lat. Am. Geogr.*, 8:1, 2009, p. 57–84, bibl., maps, tables)

Beyond the frontier and road access in the Mosquitia rainforest corridor of eastern Honduras, shifting cultivation is still a core element of the Miskito communities on the Río Patuca, but its future remains uncertain. Results detail household subsistence and cash-earning activities showing only 16.6 percent of the 227 households sampled focus entirely on land-based subsistence activities.

Gareau, Brian J. Ecological values amid local interests: natural resource conservation, social differentiation, and human survival in Honduras. See item **2567.**

1017 Mack, Taylor E. Failed site and situation, Omoa, Honduras, 1744–1800. (*in* Ethno- and historical geographic studies in Latin America: essays honoring William V. Davidson. Edited by Peter H. Herlihy, Kent Mathewson, and Craig S. Revels. Baton Rouge, La.: Geoscience Publications, 2008, p. 207–222, bibl., maps)

Excellent study of how the colonial fortress designed by Diez Navarro to protect trade routes and end the contraband trade lost its strategic importance due to its changing site and situation, resulting from coastal geomorphology and the emerging economic importance of Puerto Cortés.

1018 McSweeney, Kendra. Portrait, landscape, mirror: reflections on return fieldwork. (*in* Ethno- and historical geographic studies in Latin America: essays honoring William V. Davidson. Edited by Peter H. Herlihy, Kent Mathewson, and Craig S. Revels. Baton Rouge, La.: Geoscience Publications, 2008, p. 145–160, bibl., photos)

Photographs of Tawahka villagers taken in the Honduran Mosquitia by the Strong Expedition of 1933 are used to elicit their descendants' thoughts about changes in their social and biophysical environment. The geographer also reflects on the value of returning again and again to the same peoples and landscapes for study.

1019 Munroe, Darla K.; Jane Southworth; and Catherine M. Tucker. Modeling spatially and temporally complex land-cover change: the case of western Honduras. (*Prof. Geogr.*, 56:4, Nov. 2004, p. 543–559, bibl., graph, maps, tables)

An econometric modeling and analysis of land-cover change in La Campa near the Cerro Celaque National Park demonstrates that land-use change is a complex, multidirectional process of human-environment interactions. With deforestation due to logging no longer a major factor during the 1987–96 study period, results show that the effect of elevation outweighed any other independent variable in land cover change, with both recent growth and recent clearings more likely at higher elevations due to the abandonment of marginal maize-bean areas and to the recent clearing for coffee, respectively.

1020 Revels, Craig S. Banks and booms in the mid-day sun: place names and the Honduran mahogany trade. (*in* Ethno- and historical geographic studies in Latin America: essays honoring William V. Davidson. Edited by Peter H. Herlihy, Kent Mathewson, and Craig S. Revels. Baton Rouge, La.: Geoscience Publications, 2008, p. 223–235, bibl., maps)

This research traces place names specific to mahogany extraction in 18-19th century Honduras, showing the small but important legacy that the English-speaking cutters left in their "mahogany toponyms," such as banks, booms, and creeks.

1021 Tillman, Benjamin Farr. Not always oriented: Honduran plaza-church locational relations. (*in* Ethno- and historical geographic studies in Latin America: essays honoring William V. Davidson. Edited by Peter H. Herlihy, Kent Mathewson, and Craig S. Revels. Baton Rouge, La.: Geoscience Publications, 2008, p. 177–192, bibl., maps, photos, tables)

The grid-pattern of street layout, modeled in textbook illustrations, with the characteristic plaza, church, and government buildings, was found in only 52 percent of the municipal capitals of Honduras.

1022 Vallejo Larios, Mario and **Iván Guillén Coronado.** Descentralización de la gestión forestal en Honduras: mirando hacia el futuro. La Paz: CIFOR; Ottawa, Canada: IDRC, 2006. 83 p.: bibl., map.

Recent legislation combines with favorable political and institutional conditions to promote decentralized municipal and community development of forestry resources; hundreds of "agroforestry groups," including indigenous communities, work with the state forestry agency and municipal authorities to develop forest resources, but support of community forestry is limited.

1023 Zarco, Ismael Ahamdanech; Joaquín Bosque Sendra; and **Esther Pérez Asensio.** Una propuesta metodológica para medir la vulnerabilidad de un territorio ante los peligros naturales: el caso de Honduras tras el paso del Huracán Mitch. (*Estud. Geogr./Madrid,* 65:255, abril/junio 2004, p. 229–254, bibl., graph, map)

Analysis of UN data on the impact of Hurricane Mitch in the country's 18 departments supports the assertion that natural disasters of this magnitude can have differing impacts on a country depending on socioeconomic conditions. The authors develop a statistical model that separates departments into two different groups based on variables of literacy and malnutrition with one highly vulnerable to such natural disasters and the other more capable of resisting them.

NICARAGUA

1024 Finley-Brook, Mary. Green neoliberal space: the Mesoamerican Biological Corridor. (*J. Lat. Am. Geogr.,* 6:1, 2007, p. 101–124, bibl., maps, table)

This less than optimistic critique of the Nicaraguan portion of the Mesoamerican Biological Corridor, and the Atlantic Biological Corridor component of it, suggests only a limited role in decision-making on the part of local governments and the impacted populations, yet cites examples of the local populations' resilience and reworking or resistance to donor activities.

1025 Larson, Anne M. Los grupos marginados, la descentralización y el sector forestal en Nicaragua. La Paz: CIFOR; Ottawa, Canadá: IDRC, 2006. 82 p.: bibl., ill.

Nicaraguan Forestry Law and politics do not promote decentralized municipal government control over or community development of forest resources; nevertheless some interesting examples exist.

1026 Sánchez, Luis. Splitting the country: the case of the Atlantic coast of Nicaragua. (*J. Lat. Am. Geogr.,* 6:1, 2007, p. 7–23, bibl., map, tables)

The cultural history of the Atlantic coast of Nicaragua, with its black and indigenous populations, is quite different from the Pacific coast experience. Dissatisfaction with existing core-periphery relations has meant the resurgence of separatist feelings among the populations of the two autonomous regions on the Atlantic Coast.

1027 Smith, Derek A. Ethnogeography of the Mayangna of Nicaragua. (*in* Ethno- and historical geographic studies in Latin America: essays honoring William V. Davidson. Edited by Peter H. Herlihy, Kent Mathewson, and Craig S. Revels. Baton Rouge, La.: Geoscience Publications, 2008, p. 85–104, 2008, bibl., maps)

A concise culture history of the Mayangna documenting the changing spatial distribution of the indigenous population. Shows past and present threats to their lands and current efforts to delimit and protect their homelands.

PANAMA

1028 Castro H., Guillermo. Ganado y galeones: elementos para una historia ambiental de Panamá. (*Anu. IEHS,* 19, 2004, p. 191–229, bibl., tables)

A broad overview of the environmental history of the Panamanian isthmus spanning from the arrival of the first humans to the present and focusing on the changing populations and ecosystems over time.

MEXICO

1029 Aguilar-Robledo, Miguel. Archival, ethnohistorical, and cartographic re-construction of the environmental history of the Valles jurisdiction, eastern New Spain, mid-16th to early 19th century. (*EspacioTiempo*, 1:1, primavera/verano 2008, p. 72–91, appendices, bibl., maps)

An insightful reconstruction of the environmental history of the colonial jurisdiction of Santiago de los Valles de Oxitipa in the Huasteca Potosina from the mid-16th to early-19th century, using the *Relaciones Geográficas*, the *Suma de visitas* (including 52 reports that provided information on most major towns), the *Mercedes*, and a variety of colonial maps. Results show colonial environmental change was, perhaps not surprisingly, local in character, characterized by "environmental continuity," and reflecting the remarkable stability and resilience of a mosaic environment that did not experience the deep environmental change of modernization until the 20th century.

1030 Alegría Olazábal, Tito and Gerardo Ordóñez Barba. Legalizando la ciudad: asentamientos informales y procesos de regularización en Tijuana. Tijuana, Mexico: Colegio de la Frontera Norte, 2005. 176 p.: bibl., ill., maps.

This is an important study of the irregularities of tenancy of urban lands and their legalization in Tijuana, Mexico. It maps and details with original data over 300 "irregular properties," plotting their external polygons and characteristics in a GIS analysis to understand the actions of federal, state, and municipal organizations and the "regularization" or legalization processes they use on these populated places.

1031 Barrera-Bassols, Narciso and Víctor Manuel Toledo. Ethnoecology of the Yucatec Maya: symbolism, knowledge and management of natural resources. (*J. Lat. Am. Geogr.*, 4:1, 2005, p. 9–41, bibl., graph, map, tables)

An excellent ethnoecological study of contemporary Yucatec Maya farmers' knowledge, use, and management of their landscapes, based on a detailed literature review including results from 60 communities. The authors consider the long-term permanence of the Yucatec Maya populations by examining their multiple-use strategy and their concept of land health. They identify the core of their resilience capacity and its inextricable link to a matrix of their beliefs (*kosmos*), knowledge (*corpus*), and management (*praxis*) of natural resources.

1032 Bernache, Gerardo. Cuando la basura nos alcance: el impacto de la degradación ambiental. México: CIESAS, 2006. 551 p.: bibl., ill. (Publicaciones de la Casa Chata) (Antropologías)

The eight chapters detail the problems related to the production, management, and final disposal of municipal solid wastes in urban Mexico. The author focuses on case studies from Mexico City and Guadalajara, combined with research results from other cities across the country, to describe the components and problems of the municipal solid waste, including its public and private collection, its household contaminants and sanitary wastes, and its separation ("sustainable management") and disposal in land fills.

1033 Biles, James J. et al. Globalization of food retailing and transformation of supply networks: consequences for small-scale agricultural producers in southeastern Mexico. (*J. Lat. Am. Geogr.*, 6:2, 2007, p. 55–73, bibl., graph, maps, photo)

Small-scale producers in the Yucatán, such as those involved in chile habanero and beef production, have not benefited from the reconfiguration of food retailing supply networks.

1034 Bocco, Gerardo et al. La cartografía de los recursos naturales. (*in* Patrimonio cultural y turismo. Cuadernos 8. Cartografía de recursos culturales de Mexico. México: Consejo Nacional para la Cultura y las Artes (CONACULTA), 2004, p. 137–151, photo)

An overview essay on the development and use of standard cartographic information in the study and management of natural resources and biodiversity in Mexico.

1035 Brenner, Ludger and Hubert Job. Actor-oriented management of protected areas and ecotourism in Mexico.

(*J. Lat. Am. Geogr.*, 5:2, 2006, p. 7–27, graph, maps, tables)

An outstanding study of the Monarch Butterfly Biosphere Reserve (56,259 ha) that houses the most important hibernation habitat of the organism at the boundary between Michoacán and Mexico states. A spectacular tourist attraction with millions of the bright orange butterflies concentrated in small areas of the reserve, much of the land inside the reserve is currently owned by *ejidatarios* and *comuneros* from the 59 ejidos and 13 *comunidades indígenas*, with only 21 small private properties. Despite conservation priorities, woodcutting groups linked to the timber processing industry and furniture producers cause the greatest damage. With only four communities presently allowed to provide tourist services and no visitor plan, the authors show how the large number of actors with conflicting interests have not favored a more integrated and participatory approach to either reserve management or tourism development.

1036 Brown, J. Christopher. New directions in binational water resource management in the U.S.-Mexico Borderlands. (*Soc. Sci. J./New York*, 40:4, 2003, p. 556–572, bibl.)

This is a concise discussion of constructive actions being taken for transboundary water management in the US-Mexican Borderlands, such as increased public participation and watershed approaches, also considers institutional dynamics and the potential for reallocating water resources among users.

1037 Caldera Ortega, Alex Ricardo. Agua, participación privada y gobernabilidad: cambio institucional en el servico de agua potable y alcantarillado en la ciudad de Aguascalientes, 1989–2001. (*Caleidoscopio/ Aguascalientes*, 8:16, julio/dic. 2004, p. 7–39, bibl., graphs, tables)

Insightful analysis of the policies and practices of potable water management in the Municipio of Aguascalientes, Mexico, showing that many of the decisions taken by the government over the 12-year study period did not reflect the public agenda of the city's population, which has experienced water shortages since the 1970s.

1038 Chong Muñoz, Mercedes Arabela. La metropolización de una comunidad rural: San José del Castillo. (*Estud. Jalisc.*, 63, feb. 2006, p. 43–55)

This essay details how urban expansion puts different pressures on ejidos and agricultural communities that must change their consumption and redefine their identities to participate in the market economy. The author describes the changes—led by industrial development and land-use change from agricultural to residential—that occurred in the rural community of San José del Castillo as it was absorbed by the city of Guadalajara.

1039 The community forests of Mexico: managing for sustainable landscapes. Edited by David B. Bray, Leticia Merino-Pérez, and Deborah Barry. Austin: Univ. of Texas Press, 2005. 372 p.: bibl., ill., maps.

This collection focuses on the community forestry sector in Mexico, and brings together the distinct contributions of some of the most important researchers and practitioners on community-based forestry. The 14 chapters examine the phenomenon from historical, policy, economic, ecological, sociological, and political perspectives, with an excellent concluding chapter by the lead editor presenting 20 lessons learned from over 25 years of the community forestry enterprise sector in Mexico.

1040 La construcción social de riesgo y el huracán Paulina. Coordinación de Virginia García Acosta. México: CIESAS, 2005. 256 p.: bibl., ill., maps. (Antropologías) (Publicaciones de la Casa Chata)

The essays by García Acosta, Vera Cortés, and Villegas Delgado detail the disaster set in motion by Hurricane Paulina on the Pacific Coast of Mexico in 1997, especially in the port of Acapulco and in the Pochutla District of Oaxaca, demonstrating how the impacts of hurricane disasters are dependent on the social and geographical context in which they occur.

1041 Diversidad rural: estrategias económicas y procesos culturales, Coordinación de Beatriz Canabal Cristiani, Gabriela Contreras Pérez y Arturo León López. México: Univ. Autónoma Metropolitana, Unidad Xochimilco: Plaza y Valdés, 2006. 435 p.: bibl.

Sixteen essays, most by social scientists at the Universidad Autónoma Metropolitana, Unidad Xochimilco, are divided into three sections (Strategies of Survival, Campesina Production and Globalization, and Identity and Power) to portray the changing rural life of Mexico, focusing on critical issues of water, indigenous rights, municipal autonomy, and migration.

1042 Evans, Sterling. La angustia de La Angostura: consecuencias socioambientales por la construcción de presas en Sonora. (*Signos Hist.*, 16, julio/dic. 2006, p. 46–78, maps)

Neoliberal agrarian development experience of the Yaqui Valley employed agrarian reform and large-scale irrigation, including the development of the La Angostura Reservoir, to benefit some, but not others, nor the environment.

1043 Forero, Oscar A. and **Michael R. Redclift.** The role of the Mexican state in the development of chicle extraction in Yucatán, and the continuing importance of coyotaje. (*J. Lat. Am. Stud.*, 38:1, Feb. 2006, p. 65–93, bibl.)

Ejido land reforms and the state's role in sustaining the chicle industry, including coyotaje or illegal and exploitative activities of intermediaries, has divided indigenous territories and had a great impact on the Yucatecan Maya.

1044 Fry, Matthew. Mexico's concrete block landscape: a modern legacy in the vernacular. (*J. Lat. Am. Geogr.*, 7:2, 2008, p. 35–58, maps, photos)

Mexico's rural and urban concrete block landscapes reflect a century-long history of their use and manufacturing and, while replacing past architectural styles, they have their own vernacular meanings such as how they reflect families who are "living incrementally, slowly building toward a perceived future."

1045 García Barrios, Raúl et al. Rescatando el Salto de San Antón: una historia reciente de construcción institucional. (*Econ. Mex.*, 16:2, segundo semestre 2007, p. 307–336, bibl., ill., map, table)

The authors chronicle the history of a local environmental movement to halt further degradation in San Antón, a community along the Apatlaco River now within the urban area of Cuernavaca.

Garza Merodio, Gustavo G. Technological innovation and the expansion of Mexico City, 1870–1920. See *HLAS 64:665.*

1046 La gestión del agua en México: los retos para el desarrollo sustentable. Coordinación de Marco Antonio Jacobo Villa y Elsa Saborío Fernández. México: Miguel Angel Porrúa: Univ. Autónoma Metropolitana, Unidad Iztapalapa, 2004. 375 p.: bibl. (Las Ciencias Sociales, segunda década)

This collection, named after the 2001 conference, includes the participation of representatives from both academic and public sectors working on water resources management in Mexico. The 22 essays are divided into four sections—planning and technology, institutional processes, use and management, and economy and society—that introduce the reader to the broad array of significant water resource issues that affect both rural and urban populations, with important contributions on water use in agriculture, in cities, and especially in subterranean reserves.

1047 La gestión del agua urbana en México: retos, debates y bienestar. Coordinación de David Barkin. Guadalajara, Mexico: Univ. de Guadalajara, 2006. 336 p.: bibl., charts, maps.

The contributors to this significant collection examine the evolution of water services in nine Mexican cities and two states, providing a sad prognosis for the future. The 15 chapters, including an introduction and epilogue, document a profound environmental crisis occurring in urban Mexico. The introduction by economist David Barkin combines with the first chapter that he co-authored with geographer Daniel Klooster to provide an excellent understanding of urban water management issues. The chapters demonstrate the limitations and inadequacies of the systems of water management and the overexploitation and contamination of more than half the aquifers in the country. An excellent epilogue by Jorge Legoretta details succinctly the transformation of hydrology of the Valley of Mexico.

1048 Gestión y cultura del agua. Coordinación de Denise Soares Moraes *et al.* México: Instituto Mexicano de Tecnología del Agua; Montecillo, Estado de México: Colegio de Postgraduados en Ciencias Agrícolas, 2006. 1 v.: ill.

A diverse collection on the human use and management of water, including 12 articles written mainly by social scientists that focus on Mexico, with one on Chile and another on Argentina. The specific focus is on privatization, protection, and community use and development of water, as well as water conflicts, indigenous water rights, and attitudes toward water—reflecting the complexity of managing the resource.

1049 Gómez Ramírez, Mario and **Karina Eileen Álvarez Román.** Ciclones tropicales que se formaron al este de las Antillas menores e impactaron los estados costeros del litoral oriental de México de 1900 al 2003. (*Rev. Geogr./México,* 137, enero/junio 2005, p. 57–80, bibl., graphs, maps, tables)

Mapping and analyzing the trajectory of the 28 tropical cyclones that struck the eastern coast of Mexico in either the Caribbean Sea or Gulf of Mexico over the 103 year study period shows their origins in the southwest North Atlantic Ocean. Mexico's coast of Quintana Roo was most directly impacted and no cyclone dissipated while crossing the Yucatán Peninsula.

1050 González Ávila, María E. *et al.* Evaluación de impacto ambiental del sector eléctrico en el norte de México: evolución histórica e implicaciones para la sostenibilidad. (*Econ. Soc. Territ.,* 6:21, mayo/agosto 2006, p. 219–263, bibl., graphs, map, tables)

Analysis of Evaluation Reports on Environmental Impact (Reportes de Evaluación de Impacto Ambiental) for electricity projects in northern Mexico over the past three decades reveals the need for new evaluation formats specific to the electric sector.

1051 Harner, John P. Globalization of food retailing in Guadalajara, Mexico: changes in access equity and social engagement. (*J. Lat. Am. Geogr.,* 6:2, 2007, p. 34–53, bibl., maps, tables)

Market liberalization has brought about a rapid increase in the number of supermarket chains in Guadalajara. Their locations privilege access for the wealthy over the poor, while public markets endure.

1052 Hausermann, Heidi and **Hallie Eakin.** Producing "viable" landscapes and livelihoods in central Veracruz, Mexico: institutional and producer responses to the coffee commodity crisis. (*J. Lat. Am. Geogr.,* 7:1, 2008, p. 109–131, bibl., graph, map, photos, table)

Recent volatility in coffee prices has led some producers to try state-directed livelihood diversification programs while others respond in different ways through migration or even land sale.

1053 Hayden, Cori. When nature goes public: the making and unmaking of bioprospecting in Mexico. Princeton: Princeton Univ. Press, 2003. 284 p.: bibl., index. (In-formation series)

"Bioprospecting" refers to corporate drug development based on medicinal plants and customary knowledge, mostly in biodiversity-rich regions on the developing world. Based on extensive field and documentary research, this is an insightful treatise of the rocky road of bioprospecting in Mexico and it broader international implications.

1054 Herlihy, Peter H. and **Frederick M. Wiseman.** Ethnogeography of the dooryard orchard-garden of the indigenous Yucatecan Maya. (*in* Ethno- and historical geographic studies in Latin America: essays honoring William V. Davidson. Edited by Peter H. Herlihy, Kent Mathewson, and Craig S. Revels. Baton Rouge, La.: Geoscience Publications, 2008, p. 63–83, bibl., ill., tables)

Multi-tiered, fruit-producing "agroforests" filled dooryards of different Maya populations in prehispanic times. Geographic, archeological, and archival research combine to demonstrate a cultural importance so great to the Yucatecan Maya that the Spaniards adopted a scorched-earth policy in the Yucatán to enable town formations (*reducciones*).

1055 Hurley, Andrew. Aqueducts and drains: a comparison of water imperialism and urban environmental change in Mexico City and Los Angeles. (*J. West/ Manhattan,* 44:3, Summer 2005, p. 12–21)

Well-illustrated comparison/contrast of water issues affecting the two cities. The rapid growth of both cities in the 20th century resulted from their ability to divert large quantities of water over great distances. The author concludes that "hydraulic modification" in both cities reflected cultural demands as much as biological needs. The cities passed on much of the environmental costs of water imperialism to rural areas. [D. Coerver]

1056 Iturriaga de la Fuente, José N. Trabajos cartográficos relativos a las culturas populares en México. (*in* Patrimonio cultural y turismo. Cuadernos 8. Cartografía de recursos culturales de Mexico. México: Consejo Nacional para la Cultura y las Artes (CONACULTA), 2004, p. 153–161, photo)

The author examines three of the diverse manifestations of popular cultures in Mexico that have been registered cartographically by the Dirección General de Culturas Populares e Indígenas and the Consejo Nacional para la Cultura y las Artes: indigenous languages, regional cooking, and popular art.

1057 Klooster, Daniel and **Shrinidhi Ambinakudige.** The global significance of Mexican community forestry. (*in* Community forests of Mexico: managing for sustainable landscapes. Austin: Univ. of Texas Press, 2005, p. 305–334)

An overview of the importance of community forestry experiences from around the world illustrating that the Mexican model is fairly successful because of community ownership and tenure over forested lands (including the rights to harvest and sell trees), and because of the central role the community plays in forest management.

1058 Léonardo, Éric. Frontière interne, gouvernance locale et production de la culture politique en milieu rural mexicain: la réforme agraire dans le Sud-Veracruz, 1920–2000. (*Cah. Am. lat.*, 45, 2004, p. 51–73, bibl., maps)

Excellent overview of agrarian reform and changing sociodemographic and territorial organization through ejido formation, administration, reformations, and changing governance in the Tuxtlas region.

1059 Lorenzana Durán, Gustavo. Tierra y agua: una historia política de los valles del Mayo y del Yaqui, 1934–1940. Hermosillo: Depto. de Historia y Antropología, Inst. de Investigaciones Históricas, Univ. de Sonora, 2006. 127 p.: bibl., ill., maps. (Cuadernos del Departamento de Historia y Antropología; 6)

A study of the mid-20th century agrarian land reform and water rights in the historic agricultural development of these two dry valleys of Sonora, detailing the property regime and access to water changes and disputes, including the significant involvement of the Richardson Construction Company.

1060 Mendoza Martínez, Emma. Energías renovables en México dentro del marco de APEC: estado actual y perspectivas, formación de recursos humanos. (*Estud. Int./Santiago*, 39:153, abril/junio 2006, p. 95–118, bibl., graphs, tables)

With proven petroleum reserves lasting only decades into the future, Mexico will need to dedicate funding for the development of its huge potential of renewable energy resources, especially from sun and wind, but also from biomass, water, and geothermal, that can be promoted through the Cooperación Economica Asia-Pacífico (APEC).

1061 Merino Pérez, Leticia and **Mariana Hernández Apolinar.** Destrucción de instituciones comunitarias y deterioro de los bosques en la reserva de la Biosfera Mariposa Monarca, Michoacán, México. (*Rev. Mex. Sociol.*, 66:2, abril/junio 2004, p. 261–309, bibl., graphs)

This case study of the land use, land tenure, social capital, and organization of two communities, Cerro Prieto and Domiciano Ojeda, with significant areas of their communities within the buffer zone and nucleus of the Monarch Butterfly Biosphere Reserve. The differences between just these two communities underlie the complexities of managing this important monarch sanctuary and the authors contend that the design of conservation strategies have overemphasized the capacity of the state.

1062 Miranda Correa, Eduardo. Del Querétaro rural al industrial, 1940–1973. México: H. Cámara de Diputados, LIX

Legislatura: Univ. Autónoma de Querétaro: M.A. Porrúa, 2005. 478 p.: bibl., ill., maps. (Conocer para decidir)

This is a detailed study of the industrialization of Querétaro and of its change from an agricultural to a modern industrial center and of the actors, politics, and programs of federal and state government that made it possible. The government used its economic and political resources, developing roads, electricity, water and drainage systems, industrial zones, training, and public offices to attract private investors, both local and foreign.

1063 Nuñez Madrazo, María Cristina.
Ejido, caña y café: política y cultura campesina en el centro de Veracruz. Xalapa, Mexico: Univ. Veracruzana, 2005. 365 p.: bibl., ill., maps. (Biblioteca/Univ. Veracruzana)

An important narrative of how the Mexican ejido of Chiltoyac in Vera Cruz constructed its identity through diverse strategies and responses within the context of contradictory relationships with the Mexican state. Campesinos forged their identity around the ejido, pottery-making, and agricultural work, with agrarian reform, ejido politics, and cultivation of sugarcane and coffee playing defining roles. Now, neoliberal land reforms (PROCEDE) and the complexities of sugar and coffee markets paint an uncertain future.

1064 Pando Moreno, Marisela et al. Comparación de métodos en la estimación de erosión hídrica. (*Invest. Geogr./México,* 51, agosto 2003, p. 23–36, bibl., graphs, maps, tables)

Indirect methods for measurement of soil erosion produced different results and are tested against direct field measurements in a small drainage basin study area of the Río Potosí in southeast Nuevo Leon, Mexico, including two physiographic provinces of the Gulf Coastal Plain and Sierra Madre Oriental.

1065 Perramond, Eric P. The rise, fall, and reconfiguration of the Mexican ejido. (*Geogr. Rev.,* 98:3, July 2008, p. 356–371)

The legal certification of communal lands of ejido and other agrarian communities in Mexico, through the PROCEDE

program, will bring multiple outcomes as locals adapt the neoliberal process to their own socioeconomic circumstances.

1066 Reyes-Hernández, Humberto et al.
Efecto de los subsidios agropecuarios y apoyos gubernamentales sobre la deforestación durante el período 1990–2000 en la región de Calakmul, Campeche, México. (*Invest. Geogr./México,* 51, agosto 2003, p. 88–106, bibl., graphs, maps, tables)

A sophisticated GIS analysis of 39 ejidos shows the varying impacts of the Mexican government development programs on deforestation, including the Programa de Apoyo Directo al Campo (PROCAMPO), Crédito a la Palabra, and Alianza para el Campo. The results demonstrate, for example, that the program Crédito a la Palabra accelerated regional and local deforestation during its initial years of operation (1990–93), but subsequently (1994–98) had an opposite effect at a regional level. The authors acknowledge deforestation is the result of many factors.

1067 Reyes Hernández, Humberto et al.
Spatial configuration of land-use/land-cover in the Pujal-Coy project area, Huasteca potosina region, México. (*Ambio/Stockholm,* 37:5, 2008, p. 381–389, bibl., maps, tables)

Four satellite images from 1973, 1985, 1990, and 2000 were used to define five land-use/land-cover categories of forest, pasture, crop, secondary shrublands, and secondary forests, and to show their changing distributions in the Pujal-Coy project area of the Huasteca Potosina region. The researchers detail the relationship between these changes and the environmental conditions in the area, showing that the initial increase of area devoted to state-supported agriculture induced through the Pujal-Coy project has changed and the current distribution of agricultural activities is determined by soils, slope, irrigation, and climate, affirming the accumulated knowledge of local residents. Conversion of agricultural area to grazing lands and forage crops for cattle raising has also resumed.

1068 Schneider, Laura C. Invasive species and land-use: the effect of land management practices on bracken fern invasion in the region of Calakmul, Mexico. (*J. Lat. Am. Geogr.*, 5:2, 2006, p. 92–107, bibl., tables)

With deep rhizomes resistant to fire and drought, bracken fern easily spreads over agricultural and other deforested lands. Present in 72 of the 115 communities in the study region of Southwestern Quintana Roo and southeastern Campeche, it is seen as a destructive "perturbation" that farmers must decide when and how to control.

1069 Siemens, Alfred H.; Patricia Moreno-Casasola; and Clorinda Sarabia Bueno. The metabolization of dunes and wetlands by the city of Veracruz, Mexico. (*J. Lat. Am. Geogr.*, 5:1, 2006, p. 7–29, bibl., maps, photo, table)

An excellent study documenting historic landscape change caused by the expansion of Mexico's principal port of Veracruz. Shows how the enlargement of the port's installations and new commercial facilities, as well as residential expansion, have occurred over a large area of dunes and wetlands that are now part of the city. Concludes that there is a dire need to increase awareness about wetlands destruction.

1070 Taylor, Matthew J. The mesquite economy in the Mexican-American borderlands. (*J. Lat. Am. Geogr.*, 7:1, 2008, p. 133–149, bibl., map, photos, tables)

The use of Sonoran mesquite for charcoal and firewood production for US markets coupled with local household use brings landscape changes to the Borderlands.

1071 Toledo, Víctor Manuel et al. Uso múltiple y biodiversidad entre los mayas yucatecos. (*Interciencia/Caracas*, 33:5, May 2008, p. 345–352, bibl., graphs, maps, table)

Based on a literature review and field research in the Mayan community of Punta Laguna, the authors characterize the diverse and dynamic multiple-use strategy of the Mayan communities of the Yucatán Peninsula. It combines agricultural *milpa* (shifting cultivation) and *huerto* (dooryard orchard-gardens) with beekeeping, forestry, hunting and fishing, exploiting a rich biodi-

versity of 300 plant and 500 animal species, producing a landscape mosaic that partly explains the resilience of the nature-culture system and that should inform discussions of both its past and future.

Trujillo Bolio, Mario A. El Golfo de México en la centuria decimonónica: entornos geográficos, formación portuaria y configuración marítima. See *HLAS 64:714.*

1072 Urquijo, Pedro S. Naturaleza y religión en la construcción de la identidad de los teenek potosinos: la perspectiva de paisaje. (*EspacioTiempo*, 1:1, primavera/verano 2008, p. 19–30, bibl., photos)

The ritual landscape is an indispensable component of indigenous Teenek territoriality in the Huasteca Potosina, who see their territory, *Teenek Tsabaal*, which translates as land, territory, or terrain, not with precise limits, but where certain mountains, caves, and other physical features help define its extension that covers all the area where the language is spoken and the culture is practiced, regardless of political boundaries or social discontinuities.

Viajes al desierto de la soledad: un retrato hablado de la Selva Lacandona. See *HLAS 64:841.*

1073 Women and change at the U.S.-Mexico border: mobility, labor, and activism. Edited by Doreen J. Mattingly and Ellen R. Hansen. Tucson: Univ. of Arizona Press, 2006. 231 p.: bibl., ill., index, map.

The 11 chapters by US and Mexican social scientists provide an insightful and up-to-date picture of the lives and agency of women in the Borderlands. The collection is divided into three sections: women's daily and longer-term mobility (three articles), women's employment (three articles), and women's political activism (four articles). The volume leaves us with images of women from both sides of the border deeply engaged in ways to empower themselves and their communities.

Zanetta, Cecilia. The influence of the World Bank on national housing and urban policies: the case of Mexico and Argentina during the 1990's. See item **1215.**

WESTERN SOUTH AMERICA

DANIEL W. GADE, *Professor Emeritus of Geography, The University of Vermont*

OF THE FIVE ANDEAN COUNTRIES canvassed for this cycle, the quality and quantity of geographical scholarship on Colombia stands out. At several administrative levels, Colombia has emphasized planning its space, an activity that carries with it analyses of a geographical nature. It also has a vigorous culture of publishing and a well developed system of universities. In 2008 the Universidad Nacional de Colombia in Bogotá established the first doctoral program in geography in the Andes. In comparison with Venezuela and Colombia, Ecuador, Peru, and Bolivia have received more research attention from foreign scholars. Several themes transcend country boundaries, most notably lowland deforestation, political ecology of resource exploitation, peasant out-migration, shantytown evolution around cities, and natural disaster management.

Three substantive studies of Andean pastoralism are flagged in this essay, one in Peru's Huancavelica Department (item **1145**) and two on the Altiplano of Peru and Bolivia (items **1135** and **1162**). A data-rich tome on altitudinal gradients in biogeography, an important concept for understanding Andean diversity, also merits mention here (item **1118**). Questions of environmental impact find a focus in the shambolic town that has formed below Machu Picchu (item **1139**). Two works on Andean migration point to the various scales with which that phenomenon can be investigated (items **1074** and **1164**). Two stimulating studies in historical geography include one on Apurimac Department, Peru, that reproduces colonial documents (item **1136**) and another that provides a cartographically rich account of the grid-pattern town in Ecuador as an idea brought from Spain (item **1124**). A postmodern approach to the Andean past suggests the insights that representation can provide (item **1152**). The history of geography is enriched by attention to two seminal figures: the natural scientist Francisco José de Caldas in a work that includes his exquisite maps (item **1109**) and Alexander von Humboldt in the Andes (items **1082** and **1137**).

Though professionally a much smaller field than history, geography is the least hermetic of the social sciences and that inclusiveness has turned it into an exceptionally sprawling discipline. At the same time, as in other domains of knowledge, the grip of intellectual fashion has marginalized many themes. Twenty years of canvassing Western South America for the *HLAS* point to certain lacunae in the knowledge quest of geographers. Rural depopulation has been going on apace in many parts of the Andes since the 1950s, yet little is recorded of its effects on the zones of departure in terms of declining villages, abandoned land, and changing land-use. The study of soil erosion based on diachronic fieldwork would shed light on an insidious process about which still too little is known. More research on production of export commodities would fill gaps in knowledge about the local effects of globalization. Historically oriented investigations that use increasingly organized and accessible archives to reconstruct past geographies offer a perspective that could also be incorporated into how regions emerge and consolidate. Once a staple of the discipline, regional geography will at some point again assert an important role to meet the demand for knowledge about places at various scales. Out of detailed knowledge about regions well informed by the past can emerge theoretical strands about place and the interplay of space and time.

On another front, each Andean country holds extraordinary diversity that offers settings for research on biophysical processes. Since the arrival of Alexander von Humboldt to the New World in 1799, many geographers from different parts of the world have been enchanted with the environments of Andean countries. When foreign and national scholars collaborate to form circles of affinity, a variety of benefits accrue for all concerned.

GENERAL

1074 The Andean exodus: transnational migration from Bolivia, Ecuador and Peru = El éxodo andino: la migración transnacional desde Bolivia, Ecuador y Peru. Edited by Ton Salman and Annelies Zoomers. Amsterdam: Centre for Latin American Research and Documentation, 2002. 121 p.: bibl., ill. (Cuadernos del Cedla; 11)

Five chapters on the movement of peoples within and out of Andean countries: Peru transnationalism (by K. Paerregaard); migration networks from highland Ecuador (D. Kyle); pendular migration of Bolivian peasants (G. Cortes); peasants from Tarija, Bolivia, in northern Argentina (A. Hinojosa Gordonava); and Bolivian immigrations in metropolitan Buenos Aires (S. Sassone). For additional comment, see *HLAS 61:3351.*

1075 Bradley, Raymond S. *et al.* Threats to water supplies in the tropical Andes. (*Science/Washington,* 312:5781, June 23, 2006, p. 1755–1756)

Presents a greenhouse warming model that predicts rising temperatures in the Andean region that are already starting to melt glaciers with potential grave consequences for water supplies.

1076 Camélidos sudamericanos domésticos: investigaciones recientes. Coordinación de Carlo Renieri, Eduardo Frank, y Óscar Toro. Lima: Desco, Centro de Estudios y Promoción del Desarrollo, 2006. 355 p.: bibl., ill.

Compendium of recent studies on llamas and alpacas covering their food behavior, fiber and meat, improvement, physiology, and commercialization. European, especially Italian, scientists are now active in researching these animals.

1077 Castillo, Óscar R. Jalones sobre la modernización y descentralización en el área andina: la perspectiva de los servicios de agua y saneamiento en Perú y Bolivia.

Sevilla, Spain: Consejo Superior de Investigaciones Científicas, Escuela de Estudios Hispano-Americanos, 2005. 241 p.: bibl.

Compares and contrasts the implementation of water and sewage services in Peru and Bolivia. In the former, government agencies have been in charge and the water supply infrastructure has had many problems. In Bolivia, a decentralization policy in effect has placed municipalities in charge of implementing these services. Both countries have rejected the private sector in the provisioning of these services.

1078 Después del consenso de Washington: dinámica de cambios político-económicos y administración de recursos naturales en los países andinos. Edited by Yusuke Murakami. Kyoto, Japan: Center for Integrated Area Studies, Kyoto Univ., 2007. 122 p.: bibl., col. ill., maps. (CIAS discussion paper; 2)

Six papers from a conference in Japan on the Peruvian political economy from 1990–2006; social and political crises in Bolivia; comparison of political parties in the Central Andean countries; the economic relationship between the Andean region and the US; governance of forests in the Bolivian Amazon; and the Uros Indians of Titicaca.

1079 Medio ambiente y desarrollo sostenible. Recopilación de Elizabeth López. Oruro, Bolivia: CEPA: FOBOMADE: Latinas Editores, 2005. 232 p.: bibl., ill., maps.

Collection of essays on environmental questions and indigenous peoples in the Andes in general, as well as more specifically on Peru, Ecuador, and Bolivia. The two most substantive chapters focus on the impact of large-scale mining in Cajamarca Dept., Peru.

1080 Seminario Internacional Tejiendo Redes entre Género y Ambiente en los Andes. *Lima, 2006.* Tejiendo redes entre género y ambiente en los Andes. Recopilación de Susan V. Poats, Masría Cuvi Sánchez, y Adriana Burbano Tzonkowa. Quito: Corporación Grupo Randi Randi; Lima: Flora Tristán, Centro de la Mujer Peruana; Quito: Abya Yala, 2007. 223 p.: bibl., ill.

Fifteen scholars from different countries discuss in largely theoretical terms gender-oriented networks that relate to environmental questions.

1081 Stadel, Christoph. Entwicklungsperspektiven im ländlichen Andenraum. (*Geogr. Rundsch.*, 58:10, Okt. 2006, p. 64–72, bibl., graphs, map, photos)

In spite of poverty and out-migration in the Central Andean realm, the author is optimistic that human potential will be unleashed to turn this region, one of Latin America's problem areas, toward economic, political, and social development.

1082 Zimmerer, Karl S. Humboldt's nodes and modes of interdisciplinary environmental science in the Andean World. (*Geogr. Rev.*, 96:3, July 2006, p. 335–360)

Argues that Alexander von Humboldt's three years in the Andean region formed a seminal place for him to spread his scientific wings on a range of hitherto unstudied phenomena, but also served as a central place where he integrated his thinking about nature and culture. For review of entire journal issue, see *HLAS 63:1463*.

VENEZUELA

1083 Jugo Burguera, Luis. Ríos y municipios como proyectos socio-ambientales: Mérida, ciudad educativa, ciudad parque: el caso de la ciudad y el río Albarregas por el desarrollo sostenible local. 2a ed. actualizada y ampliada. Mérida, Venezuela: IMMECA: Decanato de la Facultad de Arquitectura y Arte de la Univ. de Los Andes: Comisión Universitaria de Asuntos Ambientales de la Univ. de Los Andes: Asociación Cultural Amigos del Museo de Escultura Latinoamericano al Aire Libre "Mariano Picón Salas" y el Complejo Cultural "El Tisure," Consejo Nacional de la Cultura, 2006. 258 p.: bibl., ill., indexes, maps.

By planning its environmental future following the ecological framework of river basins, the author proposes solutions to the chaotic growth that Mérida has experienced over the past half century.

1084 López-Hernández, Danilo; Rosa Mary Hernández-Hernández; and Michel Brossard. Historia del uso reciente de tierras de las sabanas de América del Sur: estudios de casos en Sabanas del Orinoco. (*Interciencia/Caracas*, 30:10, Oct. 2005, p. 623–630, bibl., tables)

In the Orinoco Llanos of Venezuela and Colombia, extensive cattle raising continues to dominate the land use. Yet the soil has substantial potential for crop production as demonstrated by an equivalent tropical grassland, the Cerrado of Brazil.

1085 Moreno Merlo, Fátima. Cuencas hidrográficas e inversiones extranjeras. Caracas: Cendes-UCV, 2005. 85 p.: bibl., maps. (Serie Mención publicación)

Characterization of 47 hydrographic basins in eastern Venezuela oriented toward the Caribbean, with comments on foreign investments.

1086 Reserva Forestal Imataca: ecología y bases técnicas para el ordenamiento territorial. Recopilación de José Luis Berroterán. Venezuela: Ministerio del Ambiente y de los Recursos Naturales: Dirección General de Planificación y Ordenación del Ambiente: Dirección General del Recurso Forestal: Laboratorio de Ecología de Paisajes y Agroecología—IZT: Facultad de Ciencias UCV: Fundación UCV, 2003. 208 p.: bibl., ill., maps.

In this work, the Imataca forest reserve in the Guayana region of Venezuela is inventoried not just for vegetation, ecology, climate, biotic conservation, and forestry resource, but also for the mining of gold and diamonds that is carried out within the boundaries of people who live within the reserve. Report offers suggestions to address this incompatibility.

1087 Rodríguez, Iokiñe. Pemon perspectives of fire management in Canaima National Park, southeastern Venezuela. (*Hum. Ecol.*, 35:3, June 2007, p. 331–343)

Agrees that burning the savanna vegetation is an important tool of indigenous land management in Canaima National Park, yet criticizes the fire control program that has been in place since 1981.

1088 Rojas Salazar, Andrés. La geografía poblacional venezolana entre dos censos: un final de siglo y el comienzo de otro. (*Rev. Geogr. Venez.*, 46:2, 2005, p. 181–193, bibl., tables)

Discusses demographic trends in Venezuela for the period 1950–2001. Since 1971, Bolivar, Miranda, Carabobo, Barinas, and Aragua have grown almost twice as fast as Caracas (Distrito Federal). Suggests how petroleum revenues and federalist thinking affect demography.

1089 Santaella Yegres, Ramón. Geografía: diálogo entre sociedad e historia. Caracas: Fundación Cátedra Pio Tamayo, Centro de Estudios de Historia del Pueblo, Univ. Central de Venezuela, 2005. 364 p.: bibl., ill., maps.

Short essays by a historical geographer from Caracas on a variety of themes: fieldwork, pedagogy, cartography, globalization, capitalism, geohistory, methodology for studying cities, petroleum and society, and statistics.

1090 Soto Sánchez, Oscar David. La cuestión agrária en Venezuela. Mérida, Venezuela: Univ. de Los Andes, Consejo de Estudios de Postgrado, Facultad de Ciencias Jurídicas y Políticas, Maestría en Desarrollo Agrario, 2006. 2 v.: bibl.

This two-volume collection reflects the renewed call in the Chávez administration for the structural transformation of Venezuelan agriculture, land use, and land tenure. Topics of discussion include land and the peasantry in comparison with elsewhere in the world, the land reform process, and different types of agricultural activity. Suggests ways that the different institutions in Venezuela can promote the process. Annex includes a list of all large private and public rural properties in the country.

COLOMBIA

1091 Cambios ambientales en perspectiva histórica. Vol. 2, Ecología histórica y cultura ambiental. Compilación de Carlos E. López, Martha C. Cano y Diana M. Rodríguez. Pereira, Colombia: Grupo Gestión de Cultura y Educación Ambiental, Facultad de Ciencias Ambientales, Univ. Tecnológica de Pereira, 2006. 1 v.: bibl., ill., maps.

Presents 16 chapters on historical changes in different Colombian environments, five of which are in and around Pereira. Andrés Guhl's contribution on landscape change is especially noteworthy.

1092 Carreira, Ana María. De las perturbadoras y conflictivas relaciones de los bogotanos con sus aguas. (*Tabula Rasa*, 6, enero/junio 2007, p. 263–285, bibl., map, photo)

Thought-provoking article on the place of water in the imagination and behavior of citizens of Bogotá, whose relationship with this resource has been viewed indifferently or disrespectfully through much of the city's history.

1093 Carrizosa, Julio. Desequilibrios territoriales y sostenibilidad local: conceptos, metodologías y realidades. Bogotá: Univ. Nacional de Colombia, Sede Bogotá, Instituto de Estudios Ambientales, 2006. 174 p.: bibl., ill., map.

Embedded in the theoretical discourse about sustainability, environmentalism, and other broad themes are astute observations about the growth of Colombian cities, especially the concentration of power in Bogotá.

1094 Ciudad Región Eje Cafetero: hacia un desarrollo urbano sostenible. Recopilación de Gladys Rodríguez P. y Oscar Arango G. Pereira, Colombia: Univ. Tecnológica de Pereira: Corporación Alma Mater, Red de Universidades Públicas del Eje Cafetero, 2003. 363 p.: bibl., maps., tables.

The "Eje Cafetero" is a region that comprises all or parts of five departments dominated by three metropolitan areas—Manizales, Pereira, and Armenia—and 12 other smaller clusters with a combined population of more than 1.8 million people. Maps and tables of social, demographic, and economic information reveal a highly urbanized region.

1095 Construcción de lugares-patrimonio: el Centro Histórico y el humedal de Córdoba en Bogotá. Recopilación de Adriana Párias Durán y Dolly Cristina Palacio Tamayo. Bogotá: Instituto Colombiano para el Desarrollo de la Ciencia: COLCIENCIAS: Univ. Externado de Colombia, 2006. 479 p.: bibl., graphs, ill., maps. (Colciencias)

Authors in several disciplines discuss the cultural and natural patrimony of Bogotá that includes ideas about gender and cultural capital, gentrification and public policy, and a critical analysis of the urban planning process.

1096 Desastres de origen natural en Colombia, 1979–2004. Recopilación de Michel Hermelín. Medellín, Colombia: Univ. EAFIT, Grupo de Geología Ambiental e Ingeniería Sísmica: Cali, Colombia: Univ. del Valle, Observatorio Sismológico del Suroccidente, 2005. 247 p.: bibl., ill., maps.

Collection of 15 chapters by geologists, engineers, and geographers on natural disasters in Colombia between 1979 and 2002 that includes tsunamis, earthquakes, volcanic eruptions, landslides, floods, and El Niño events. Both the science and socioeconomic effects are taken into account. Good bibliographies.

1097 (Des)territorialidades y (no)lugares: procesos de configuración y transformación social del espacio. Recopilación de Diego Herrera Gómez y Carlo Emilio Piazzini Suárez. Medellín, Colombia: La Carreta: Escuela de Gobierno y Políticas Públicas de Antioquia Guillermo Gaviria Correa: INER, Instituto de Estudios Regionales, Univ. de Antioquia, 2006. 259 p.: bibl., ill., maps. (La Carreta social)

Brings together 13 postmodernist essays from social scientists representing several disciplines including human geography. Topics include discussions on questions of time, space, territoriality, violence, boundaries, alterity and ethnicity. Most chapters focus on Colombia.

1098 Domínguez, Camilo A. Amazonia colombiana: economía y poblamiento. Bogotá: Univ. Externado de Colombia, 2005. 330 p.: bibl., ill., maps.

Contains useful information on the Colombian Amazon region about rubber gathering, river transport, colonization, distribution of population, and petroleum exploitation.

1099 Duque Fonseca, Claudia Alexandra. Territorios e imaginarios entre lugares urbanos: procesos de identidad y región en ciudades de los andes colombianos. Manizales, Colombia: Editorial Univ. de Caldas, 2005. 259 p.: bibl., ill. (Col. Ciencias jurídicas y sociales)

Though disorganized, this study of the meaning of the shopping center in Colombian cities offers a postmodernist Latin American perspective on a modern phenomenon. Included in the analysis is a revealing chapter on Antioqueño identity.

1100 Etter, Andrés; Clive McAlpine; and Hugh Possingham. Historical patterns and drivers of landscape change in Colombia since 1500: a regionalized spatial approach. (*Ann. Assoc. Am. Geogr.*, 98:1, March 2008, p. 2–23)

High level generalizations about 500 years of land-use change in Colombia based on human population estimates and broad economic changes. Estimates that in the time span discussed, the human-modified landscape increased from 15 million hectares to 42 million hectares. To test these extrapolations, future research could be undertaken on this topic at a series of larger scales of specific locales and regions.

1101 Geografía de Antioquia: geografía histórica, física, humana y económica. Recopilación de Michel Hermerlin. Medellín, Colombia: Fondo Editorial, Univ. EAFIT; Antioquia, Colombia: Academia Colombiana de Ciencias Exactas, Físicas y Naturales, Capítulo de Antioquia, 2006. 338 p.: bibl., ill., maps.

Assemblage, uneven in quality, of 28 chapters by 31 different authors on Antioquia, the second most populous department in Colombia and one-third of whose inhabitants live in Medellín. Eleven of the chapters focus on physical geography; eight cover human geography; five address economic geography; and four discuss historical geography.

1102 Gordillo Bedoya, Fernando. Hábitat transitorio: vivienda para emergencias por desastres en Colombia: lineamientos y percepciones. Bogotá: Univ. Nacional de Colombia, Sede Bogotá, 2006. 247 p.: bibl., ill., maps. (Punto aparte)

Using examples mainly from Colombia, this risk management analysis of natural disasters discusses emergency housing needs to shelter victims.

1103 Guerra, sociedad y medio ambiente. Recopilación de Martha Cárdenas y Manuel Rodríguez Becerra. Bogotá: Foro Nacional Ambiental, 2004. 545 p.: ill.

Multi-authored work on the ravages that guerrilla warfare has inflicted upon the environment in Colombia, including deforestation and reforestation, policy of protected areas and cultivation of illicit crops, effects of fumigation of standing drug plants, and petroleum exploitation.

1104 Guerrero Rincón, Amado Antonio and **Laritza Páez Martínez.** Poblamiento y conflictos territoriales en Santander. Bucaramanga, Colombia: Univ. Industrial de Santander, Escuela de Historia, 2005. 162 p.: bibl., ill., maps.

Historical geography of the Depto. de Santander (capital: Bucaramanga) from the perspective of jurisdictional and environmental limits. Provides information to suggest the need for another model of development than the one currently in place.

1105 Herrera Angel, Marta. Las bases prehispánicas de la configuración territorial de la provincia de Popayán en el período colonial. (*J. Lat. Am. Geogr.*, 5:2, 2006, p. 53–73, bibl., maps)

The emergence of Popayán as a province was determined in the early archeological findings and analysis of precolumbian structures. In the colonial period, Popayán had a mediating role between the Viceroyalty of Nueva Granada in Bogotá and the Audiencia of Quito.

1106 Itinerarios urbanos: París, La Habana, Bogotá: narraciones, identidades y cartografías. Recopilación de Nicolás Gualteros Trujillo. Bogotá: Pontificia Univ. Javeriana, 2006. 168 p.: bibl., ill., index. (Cuadernos Pensar en público; 2)

Wide-ranging study on the city as representation with major attention on Bogotá that includes essays on the sense of belonging to that city and how it is described in travel guides of the 1930s.

1107 León Sicard, Tomás Enrique. Medio ambiente, tecnología y modelos de agricultura en Colombia: hombre y arcilla. Bogotá: Instituto de Estudios Ambientales, Univ. Nacional de Colombia: Ecoe Ediciones, 2007. 287 p.: bibl. (Ideas (Series) (Universidad Nacional de Colombia. Instituto de Estudios Ambientales); 8) (Col. Textos universitarios. Area Ecología y medio ambiente)

Discusses Colombian agriculture in the aggregate: ecological principles, sustainability ideas, development models for Colombia, transgenetic issues, agricultural potential and problems. Like most pedagogically oriented materials, not much is new in these pages, but the organization offers a valuable perspective.

1108 Mogollón Gómez, María Paulina. Path dependence and civil society: irrigation district performance in Colombia. (*Rev. Planeac. Desarro.*, 36:2, julio/dic. 2005, p. 237–308, bibl., graphs, maps, tables)

Author compares three irrigation districts in the Caribbean coastal region formed after the land reform of the 1960s. In spite of several fundamental similarities, two of the three failed. Using Putnam's social capital model, author attributes this difference to the development of a peaceful and organized civil society.

1109 Nieto Olarte, Mauricio. La obra cartográfica de Francisco José de Caldas. Con la participación de Santiago Muñoz Arbelaez, Santiago Díaz-Piedrahita, y Jorge Arias de Greiff. Bogotá: Univ. de los Andes: Academia Colombiana de Historia: Academia Colombiana de Ciencias Exactas, Físicas y Naturales: Instituto Colombiano de Antropología e Historia—ICANH, 2006. 182 p.: bibl., ill., maps.

Magnificent tome about a scientific giant of the Spanish colonial period born in Popayán in 1768, including reproductions of much of his cartography. Three essays on Caldas as a geographer, cartographer, and botanist and scientific traveler are followed by Caldas' *Atlas de Nueva Granada*, cross-section profiles of the Andes, maps of rivers and expeditions, and military maps.

1110 Palacio, Germán. Fiebre de tierra caliente: una historia ambiental de Colombia, 1850–1930. Bogotá: ILSA: Univ. Nacional de Colombia, Sede Amazonia, 2006. 183 p.: bibl., ill. (Col. En clave de sur)

Two strands, historical geography and political ecology, complement each other in this wide-ranging book that probes two main themes: the past perception of the highland-lowland divide in Colombia, and the geopolitics of 19th-century cinchona and rubber extraction in Caquetá. A recurring theme throughout the book is the idea that landscape change is both symbolic and material.

1111 Pérez Álvarez, Alexánder. Maniobras de la sobrevivencia en la ciudad: territorios de trabajo informal infantil y juvenil en los espacios públicos del centro de Medellín. Medellín, Colombia: Ediciones Escuela Nacional Sindical, 2005. 185 p.: bibl., ill. (Ensayos laborales; 14)

In this volume, children and teens who work in street commerce in the city of Medellín conceptualize their social spaces and discuss their plight. Though lack of maps clouds understanding, this work offers an original perspective on a Latin American phenomenon.

1112 Región, ciudad y áreas protegidas: manejo ambiental participativo. Recopilación de Felipe Cárdenas Támara, Hernán Darío Correa y Claudia Mesa. Bogotá: FESCOL: ECOFONDO: Acción Ambiental: CEREC, 2005. 564 p.: bibl.

Empirical and theoretical chapters on Colombian cities, environment, and territory, and how these three phenomena interconnect in such topics as parks, recreation, cultural landscapes, and ecological impacts.

ECUADOR

1113 Abbott, J. Anthony. Counting beans: agrobiodiversity, indigeneity, and agrarian reform. (*Prof. Geogr.*, 57:2, May 2005, p. 198–212, bibl., graphs, map, tables)

The dynamics of agrobiodiversity in a peasant society is revealed in this field inquiry of the kinds of beans that farmers grow in the Vilcabamba Valley of southern Ecuador. Astute commentary about diversity in farming systems and the modern forces that are chipping away at that diversity.

1114 Aguirre, Milagros; Fernando Carrión; and Eduardo Kingman. Quito imaginado. Bogotá: Univ. Nacional de Colombia: Convenio Andrés Bello: Taurus; Quito: FLACSO Ecuador, 2005. 220 p.: ill., maps.

Gracefully written and beautifully illustrated, this book captures the flavor of Quito as a city of neighborhoods.

1115 Congreso de Conservación de la Biodiversidad de los Andes y la Amazonía, 2nd, Universidad Técnica Particular de Loja, 2003. Memorias del II Congreso de Conservación de la Biodiversidad de los Andes y Amazonía y IV Congreso Ecuatoriano de Botánica: Universidad Técnica Particular de Loja del 25–30 de agosto del 2003. Recopilación de Pablo Lozano, Rainer Bussmann & Hugo Navarrete. Organización de la Fundación Ecuatoriana para la Investigación y Desarrollo de la Botánica (FUNBOTANICA) en colaboración con el Herbario Reinaldo Espinosa (LOJA) y la Universidad Técnica Particular de Loja. Loja, Ecuador: FUNBOTANICA, 2005. 693 p.: bibl., ill., maps.

Papers from a 2003 conference in Loja on conservation management, ethnobotany, flora and vegetation, plant taxonomy, mammals and insects. Of the 34 papers, most focus on the Amazon and the southern highlands of Ecuador.

1116 Fadiman, Maria G. Use of *mocora, Astrocaryum standleyanum* (Arecaceae), by three ethnic groups in Ecuador: differences, similarities and market potential. (*J. Ethnobiol.*, 28:1, Spring/Summer 2008, p. 92–109, bibl.)

One plant in the Mache-Chindul ecological reserve in northwestern Ecuador is mocora, a spiny palm with fronds used to weave mats, make cordage, and fashion seeds into jewelry. Each of three ethnic groups—the indigenous Chachi people, Afro-Ecuadorians, and mestizos—have their own distinctive styles in using this plant.

1117 Farley, Kathleen A. Grasslands to tree plantations: forest transition in the Andes of Ecuador. (*Ann. Assoc. Am. Geogr.*, 97:4, Dec. 2007, p. 755–771, bibl., graph, map, table)

Wood scarcity has led Ecuadorians to plant exotic trees in the non-forested páramos zone. Based on a Monterey pine plantation northwest of the Cotopaxi volcano, this research recorded how planted and spontaneous trees differ in their human uses and needs and how that change has brought about a loss of soil carbon, nitrogen, and water retention capacity.

1118 Gradients in a tropical mountain ecosystem of Ecuador. Edited by Erwin Beck *et al.* Berlin: Springer, 2008. 525 p.: bibl., ill., index, maps. (Ecological studies; 198)

Extraordinary concentration of environmental knowledge about Ecuador's neotropical montane forest that runs through the Reserva Biológica San Francisco between Loja and Zamora. Thirty-six papers on this hot spot of biodiversity feature gradients along altitudes in climate, soils, vegetation, flora and fauna, as well as water relations and nutrient fluxes.

1119 Gray, Clark L. et al. Indigenous land use in the Ecuadorian Amazon: a cross-cultural and multilevel analysis. (*Hum. Ecol.*, 36:1, Feb. 2008, p. 97–109)

Statistical analysis of land use among five indigenous populations (Huarorani, Cofán, Shuar, Secoya and Kichwa) in the northern part of the Ecuadorian Amazon, though focused more on theoretical and methodological commentary than empirical results. Argues for restructuring petroleum extraction activities in the region that impinge on the lives of these indigenous peoples. For ethnology specialist's comment, see item **591**.

1120 Grenier, Christophe. Conservación contra natura: las islas Galápagos. Traducción de María Dolores Villamar, con la colaboración de Alejandra Adoum y Cristina Carrión. Lima: Instituto Francés de Estudios Andinos, 2007. 463 p.: bibl., ill., maps.

Translation of a French university geography thesis on the Galápagos archipelago. Covers its history, essential character as a space, migration, tourist impacts, integration into the Ecuadorian state, and the failure of the natural park to thrive in spite of an active conservation network. Full of astute observations about a unique place.

1121 Keating, Philip L. Fire ecology and conservation in the high tropical Andes: observations from northern Ecuador. (*J. Lat. Am. Geogr.*, 6:1, 2007, p. 43–62, bibl., maps, photos, tables)

Concludes that the effect of fire on the páramo grasslands does not reduce species diversity. Asserts that top-down policies that aim to suppress fire are neither feasible nor desirable.

1122 Keese, James R.; Thomas Mastin; and David Yun. Identifying and assessing tropical montane forests on the eastern flank of the Ecuadorian Andes. (*J. Lat. Am.*

Geogr., 6:1, 2007, p. 63–84, bibl., maps, tables)

Authors calculated that 88 percent of the vegetation on the eastern side of the Ecuadorian Andes between Sangay and Podocarpus National Parks was still in either montane forest or páramo grassland. However, vegetation clearing in three areas of this potential conservation corridor presents a hindrance to the movement of organisms between the two protected areas.

1123 Messina, Joseph P. and Mark A. Cochrane. The forests are bleeding: how land use change is creating a new fire regime in the Ecuadorian Amazon. (*J. Lat. Am. Geogr.*, 6:1, 2007, p. 85–100, bibl., map, tables)

Using remote sensing and sample methods, authors describe persistent deforestation in the northeastern part of Ecuador's Amazon region. Microclimatic data showed that, as a result, daytime temperatures have increased and relative humidity decreased compared to primary forest.

1124 Ortiz Crespo, Alfonso; Matthias Abram; and José Segovia Nájera. Damero. Quito: FONSAL, 2007. 207 p.: bibl., ill., maps.

"Damero" in this context refers to the grid-pattern arrangement of towns and cities imposed by Spanish authorities on the New World. The main focus of this well-illustrated book is on old maps of Quito at various scales, but comments are also included on other Ecuadorian cities. This splendid volume may well stimulate a flow of research ideas.

1125 Ospina, Pablo. Galápagos, naturaleza y sociedad: actores sociales y conflictos ambientales en las islas Galápagos. Quito: Corporación Editora Nacional, 2006. 230 p.: bibl., maps. (Biblioteca de ciencias sociales/Universidad Andina Simón Bolívar; 55)

Views the Galápagos from the perspective of tourism, fishing, and conservation, and investigates the forces of modernization at work in all three realms. An annex contains an array of data on these islands.

1126 Pohle, Perdita and Andrés Gerique. Traditional ecological knowledge and biodiversity management in the Andes of southern Ecuador. (*Geogr. Helv.*, 61:4, 2006, p. 275–285, bibl., maps, photos)

Evaluates differences in traditional knowledge of wild and cultivated plants and forms of land use among two indigenous groups. Authors judged the Shuar of the Nangaritza valley as more knowledgeable about their environment than the Saraguro people. Mestizos who have colonized the area are seen as the least sustainable in their use of the environment.

1127 Sirén, Anders Henrik. Population growth and land use intensification in a subsistence-based indigenous community in the Amazon. (*Hum. Ecol.*, 35:6, Dec. 2007, p. 669–680, bibl., graphs, maps)

Disputes the argument that increasing population among the Kichwa slash-and-burn farmers in Pastaza province has led to serious deforestation. However, an increase in population density in that area has contributed to land scarcity and caused other problems.

1128 Tapia, Luis. Territorio, territorialidad y construcción regional amazónica. Quito: Abya Yala, 2004. 136 p.: bibl.

Thoughtful perspective on the Ecuadorian Amazon that covers indigenous territory, regionalization, urbanization, globalization, decentralization planning and development.

1129 Tendiendo puentes entre los paisajes humanos y naturales: la investigación participativa y el desarrollo ecológico en una frontera agrícola andina. Recopilación de Robert E. Rhoades. Quito: SANREM CRSP: Abya-Yala, 2001. 416 p.: bibl., ill., maps.

Multi-authored sustainable development study begun in 1993 by USAID of the Nanegal area in Pichincha province. Includes chapters on local history, migrations, environmental perceptions, ecological diversity, land use change, sugar cane cultivation, livestock raising, agricultural strategies, gender relations, and the political ecology of aguardiente. Offers suggestions for development planners on the community and sustainability.

PERU

1130 Los Andes y el reto del espacio mundo: homenaje a Olivier Dollfus. Recopilación de Jean-Paul Deler y Evelyne

Mesclier. Lima: IFEA: IEP: République française, Embajada de Francia, 2004. 419 p.: bibl., ill., maps.

Collection of 22 short and rather hermetic essays from French and Peruvian scholars on climate, land use, cities, transportation, and tourism. Seven other essays discuss the contributions of Olivier Dollfus (1931–2005), who himself wrote on geomorphology, territory, globalization, and other themes.

1131 Bury, Jeffrey. Mining migrants: transnational mining and migration patterns in the Peruvian Andes. (*Prof. Geogr.*, 59:3, Aug. 2007, p. 378-389, bibl., graph, map, tables)

Excellent article on the impact of an intrusive transnational gold mining operation in the Cajamarca region on two kinds of migration patterns. One is of Peruvians whose arrival has been a household livelihood strategy; the other are highly skilled international migrants who have created a typical enclave pattern. The old city of Cajamarca has become a new boom town of international gold mining.

1132 Chambers, Bill. The *barriadas* of Lima: slums of hope or despair? problems or solutions? (*Geography/London*, 90:3, Autumn 2005, p. 200–224, bibl., maps, tables)

A grand sweep on the evolution of barriadas around Lima over half a century. The author lived in one of the settlements in 1965–66 and has witnessed their remarkable transformation.

1133 Comités de gestión: construyendo gobernanza para las áreas naturales protegidas del Perú. Recopilación de Bruno Monteferri. Textos de Maritza Mayo *et al.* Lima: Sociedad Peruana de Derecho Ambiental, 2006. 204 p.: bibl., ill., maps.

Discussion of the present state of committees organized to manage protected natural areas in Peru. Presents models of different types of committees and a detailed case study and recent management history of the Reserva Nacional Pacaya Samiria.

1134 Crews-Meyer, Kelley A. Temporal extensions of landscape ecology theory and practice: examples from the Peruvian Amazon. (*Prof. Geogr.*, 58:4, Nov. 2006, p. 421–435, photos, tables)

Uses Iquitos as a case study to address a methodology that incorporates the time factor into landscape ecology.

1135 Del Pozo-Vergnes, Ethel. De la hacienda a la mundialización: sociedad, pastores y cambios en el altiplano peruano. Prólogo de Maurice Godelier. Lima: Instituto Francés de Estudios Andinos: IEP, Instituto de Estudios Peruanos, 2004. 283 p.: bibl., ill. (Serie Estudios de la sociedad rural; 23)

Excellent study of changes in the land tenure in the pastoral society of Melgar province around the town of Ayaviri. Describes the old hacienda system that President Velasco replaced in the early 1970s with the SAIS program. Between 1976–99, a collective, self-managed property called "Rural Kolkeparque" prevailed until that failed when the state abandoned it and wool prices fell. Now several features of the old hacienda system have reappeared in this zone.

1136 Hostnig, Rainer; Ciro Palomino Dongo; and Jean-Jacques Decoster. Proceso de composición y titulación de tierras en Apurímac-Perú, siglos XVI–XX. Cusco, Peru: Instituto de Investigaciones Jurídicas y Asesoramiento: Asociación Kuraka: Instituto de Estudios Históricos sobre América Latina, Univ. de Viena, 2007. 2 v. (961 p.): bibl., ill., index.

Reconstructs the historical geography of communities, ayllus, villages, land use and haciendas in the Dept. of Apurimac, beginning in the 16th century, copied from various archives in Lima, Cuzco, and Abancay. Many old hand-drawn maps are reproduced. Includes information about land titles, property boundaries, land measurements, and such topics as usurpation of lands by hacendados. Five essays help put all these documents into perspective. Interesting photographs of remote locations are included. A source of rich information about a little-known part of the Peruvian Sierra.

1137 El legado científico de Alexander von Humboldt en el Perú. Dirección de José María Sesé. Coordinación de Teodoro Hampe Martínez. Piura, Peru: Univ. de Piura, Facultad de Ciencias y Humanidades, Depto. de Humanidades, 2005. 175 p.: bibl. (Cuadernos de humanidades; 9)

Papers originally presented at a Humboldt symposium in 2002 in Ayabaca (Dept. of Piura). Peruvian-based scholars contribute studies to the worldwide surge of interest in Alexander von Humboldt. Of the four essays on Humboldt in Piura stands an outstanding piece by Hampe Martínez.

1138 Ludeña Urquizo, Wiley. Ciudad y patrones de asentamiento: estructura urbana y tipologización para el caso de Lima. (*EURE/Santiago,* 32:95, mayo 2006, p. 37–59, bibl., maps)

Typologies of the building stock of Greater Lima based on the types and quality of structures that constitute neighborhoods, shantytowns included.

1139 Machupicchu: auditorías de gestión ambiental y de patrimonio cultural. Peru: Embajada Real de los Países Bajos: Contraloría General de la República, 2005. 328 p.: bibl., ill.

This official Peruvian government report lays out the serious environmental degradation around Machu Picchu, especially the chaotic settlement and pollution on the Urubamba valley floor below the ruins and the overused Inca trail leading to the site. A host of recommendations are proposed; implementation will be a challenge to a site that has become an enormous, lucrative venture for the Peruvian government.

1140 Manners, R.B.; F.J. Magilligan; and P.S. Goldstein. Floodplain development, El Niño, and cultural consequences in a hyperarid Andean environment. (*Ann. Assoc. Am. Geogr.,* 97:2, June 2007, p. 229–249, bibl., graphs, maps, photos, tables)

Draws a connection between the erosive power of contemporary floods in the Rio Moquegua Valley associated with cyclical periods of heavy El Niño rainfall that destroyed water delivery systems for irrigated agriculture. From that point, the authors extrapolate how prehistoric societies in the first millennium AD must have experienced those same kinds of floods and how the floods affected the decline of irrigation-dependent human occupation. Suggests an environmental factor as causative in the prehistoric collapse of the society.

1141 Moreau, Marie-Annick and Oliver Coomes. Structure and organization of small-scale freshwater fisheries: aquarium fish collection in Western Amazonia. (*Hum. Ecol.*, 36:3, June 2008, p. 309–323)

Comparative analysis of contrasting practices in the specialized aquarium fish collecting trade in the Peruvian Amazon. Using three communities on the Ucayali River, authors show that local conditions give rise to different outcomes even when the same fish species is targeted.

1142 Ohl-Schacherer, Julia et al. Indigenous ecotourism in the Amazon: a case study of "Casa Matsiguenka" in Manu National Park. (*Environ. Conserv./ Cambridge*, 35:1, March 2008, p. 14–25, bibl., graph, map, tables)

German aid established a community-based ecotourism lodge in Manu Park owned by the indigenous Matsiguenka tribe. Authors assert that a flawed business plan accounts for its economic insustainability; however, in economic and political ways, the lodge has helped the local community of this tribe.

1143 Pajuelo, Ramón. Medioambiente y salud en La Oroya: sistematización de un programa de intervención. Lima: Cooper-Acción, Acción Solidaria para el Desarrollo, 2005. 130 p.: bibl., maps.

Water and air pollution have been a fact of life in La Oroya since 1922 when the Cerro de Pasco Corporation started operation of a metallurgical complex. La Oroya has a serious lead contamination problem caused by the foreign-owned complex. Discovery of high concentrations of lead in the blood of local children and nursing mothers in the 1990s raised awareness of this serious health issue in this city of 25,000 people. More recent findings released in 2005 showed high levels of lead in people, but also air, water, and soil contamination. A good study of the toxic effects of mining.

1144 Peters, Paul A. and Emily H. Skop. Socio-spatial segregation in metropolitan Lima, Peru. (*J. Lat. Am. Geogr.*, 6:1, 2007, p. 149–171, bibl., maps, tables)

Using indicators of education, employment, and tenancy, the authors proceed to show the high degree of segregation in metropolitan Lima of the elites, middle class, and poor. Yet, they find that segregation is highly fragmented, so that at a local level, these socioeconomic classes often live in close proximity.

1145 Postigo, Julio C.; Kenneth R. Young; and Kelley A. Crews. Change and continuity in a pastoralist community in the high Peruvian Andes. (*Hum. Ecol.*, 36:4, Aug. 2008, p. 535–551)

Evaluation of the land use, landscape, and economy of Pilpichaca, Dept. of Huancavelica, at elevation of 4,000 m above sea level, where inhabitants raise llamas, alpacas, and sheep. Shows how this community changes in order to maintain its economic and cultural equilibrium. Fine cultural-ecological study of Andean pastoralism.

1146 Ramírez Bautista, Bernardino. Desarrollo urbano y desigualdad en el área periurbana de Carabayllo. (*Investig. Soc./San Marcos*, 18, junio 2007, p. 313–344, bibl., tables)

Discussion of Carabayllo, the fifth largest *barriada* in the northern part of metropolitan Lima, in terms of population growth, housing, health services, and the economic situation of its inhabitants.

1147 Ravines Ruiz, Juana. El volcán Ubinas y el cielo de Arequipa. (*Bol. Lima*, 28:144, 2006, p. 51–70, bibl., map, photos, tables)

Lays out the eruptions of Ubinas volcano from the prehistoric past to the present in the larger context of the volcanic activity in the Arequipa region and beyond. Also discusses risk to aircraft of eruptions.

1148 Reece, Carl A. and Kam-biu Liu. Inter-annual variability in pollen dispersal and deposition on the tropical Quelccaya ice cap. (*Prof. Geogr.*, 57:2, May 2005, p. 185–197, bibl., graphs, maps, photos, table)

Grains of pollen deposited on the Quelccaya Ice Cap, the largest glacier in Peru, receives wind-transported pollen for which the authors assert the geographical source can be identified. In a normal year, pollen comes from the forested lands to the east, but when the El Niño weather system is in place, this circulation breaks down and the transported pollen comes from the Altiplano. Signals another way to reconstruct El Niño events in the absence of other records.

1149 Richter, Michael and **Michaela Ise.** Monitoring plant development after El Niño 1997–98 in northwestern Peru. (*Erdkunde/Bonn*, 59:2, April/Juni 2005, p. 136–155, bibl., graphs, tables)

Heavy rainfall accompanying El Niño events in the coastal desert brings a new luxuriant growth of plants. Using study sites in the Dept. of Piura, the authors assess what happened in the establishment of spontaneous flora and vegetation before, during, and after the 1997–98 event. Study has broad-ranging implications for everything from goat raising to knowledge of vegetation succession.

1150 Robles Mendoza, Román. Explotación de recursos en la cordillera Huayhuash: la minería y el turismo. (*Investig. Soc./San Marcos*, 16, agosto 2006, p. 93–126, bibl., photos)

The serene beauty of the Cordillera Huayhuash, so attractive to tourists, now faces the prospect of mining enterprises seeking to exploit a dozen minerals. The largest, Proyecto Pallca, controlled by the Mitsui Company, raises questions of environmental contamination. Formerly ignored, indigenous communities are now parties to decisions about these developments.

1151 Salaverry, José A. Macro-ecología de los Andes peruanos: situatión actual y dinámica de cambio en los últimos 20.000 años. Lima: Consejo Nacional de Ciencia, Tecnología e Innovación Tecnológica: Instituto Francés de Estudios Andinos, 2006. 312 p.: bibl., ill., maps. (Travaux de l'Institut français d'études andines; 232)

Highly illustrated discussion of past changes in climate, hydrology, and vegetation, and how the timing of these shifts affected prehistoric human settlement. Its pedagogical tone, frequent errors, and ignorance of much recent research weakens its contribution.

1152 Scott, Heidi V. Rethinking landscape and colonialism in the context of early Spanish Peru. (*Environ. Plann. D Soc. Space*, 24:4, 2006, p. 481–496)

Embedded in a dense prose is the author's main point: to understand the colonial landscapes of the Andes, it is necessary to consider not only the Spaniards' encoun-

ter with the physical environment, but also to look beyond and behind the dramatic events and focus instead on the mundane everyday activities of colonial life.

1153 Spelucín, Juan and **Víctor Hugo Giraldo.** Minería y salud ambiental en Camisea. Lima: CIES, Consorcio de Investigación Económica y Social: Observatorio del Derecho a la Salud; Cusco, Peru: CBC, Centro Bartolomé de las Casas, 2007. 110 p.: bibl., ill. (Serie Diagnóstico y propuesta; 30) (Estudios y debates regionales andinos; 3101)

Discovery in 1980 of Peru's most important natural gas reserve in the jungles of the Lower Urubamba Valley led to Proyecto Camisea, signed in the year 2000 to build a separation plant in the area and to construct a gas pipeline to the coast. Exploitation of this resource has not respected the rights of the Machiguenga people in the area.

1154 Sueiro, Juan Carlos; Astrid M. Cornejo; and **Paula Castro.** La zona costera peruana, recursos, usos y gestión. Elaboración de CooperAcción, Acción Solidaria para el Desarrollo. Lima: CooperAcción, 2005. 137 p.: bibl., ill.

Straightforward presentation of factual information on the 10 departments that comprise Peru's coastal desert. Deals with relief, hydrography, climate, protected areas, population, port facilities, and economic activities. Comments on the integrated management of the entire area.

1155 Ugent, Donald and **Carlos M. Ochoa.** La etnobotánica del Perú: desde la prehistoria al presente. Lima: Consejo Nacional de Ciencia, Tecnología e Innovación Tecnológica, CONCYTEC, 2006. 379 p.: bibl., ill., indexes.

Distressingly incomplete, this work on the main native useful plants of Peru nevertheless has its real application as a guide to those species identified from the prehistoric record.

1156 Ypeij, Annelou and **Elayne Zorn.** Taquile: a Peruvian tourist island struggling for control. (*Rev. Eur. Estud. Latinoam. Caribe*, 82, April 2007, p. 119–128, bibl.)

Account of recent changes in tourism on Taquile, a island in Lake Titicaca populated with indigenous peoples who lost control of the tourist economy and are now seeking ways to regain it.

1157 Zúñiga Rojas, Marcelo G. Espacio y ciudadanía: teoría y práctica, ciudad de Huacho. Lima: Univ. Nacional Federico Villarreal; Huacho, Peru: Univ. Nacional José Faustino Sánchez Carrión, 2006. 228 p.: bibl., ill.

Perspective on the coastal city of Huacho that includes history, demography, services, culture and identity, social organizational and municipal administration. Local economy is not analyzed.

BOLIVIA

1158 Assies, Willem. Land tenure legislation in a pluri-cultural and multi-ethnic society: the case of Bolivia. (*J. Peasant Stud.*, 33:4, Oct. 2006, p. 569–611, bibl., table)

Provides a lucid overview of land tenure systems and the failure of 20th-century reform legislation. Macroeconomic politics of the 1953 land reform did not help the highland campesino; in the eastern lowlands, the same reform actually consolidated and expanded large holdings. Pressures from commercial agricultural interests in Santa Cruz led to the failure of the 1996 reform.

1159 Blanes Jiménez, José. Bolivia: las áreas metropolitanas en perspectiva de desarrollo regional. (*EURE/Santiago*, 32:95, mayo 2006, p. 21–36, bibl., maps, tables)

Examines Bolivia's demographic structure in which two-thirds of the urban population lives in the metropolitan areas of La Paz, Cochabamba, and Santa Cruz, each with different functions. One-half of the indigenous population of Bolivia now lives in these cities.

1160 Coarite Huañapaco, Felipe. Pobreza y contaminación en la ciudad de El Alto. El Alto, Bolivia: Editorial Pirámide, 2005. 145 p.: bibl., ill. (Col. Economía y medio ambiente)

El Alto is now a city of 650,000 people, of whom 82 percent are indigenous. Poverty and water and soil pollution are major problems. Much information provided about this city goes beyond the book's title.

1161 Combès, Isabelle. Alto y Bajo Isoso: géographie et pouvoir dans le Chaco bolivien. (*Mappemonde*, 78, 2005, bibl., maps, http://mappemonde.mgm.fr/num6/articles/art05201.html)

Isoso is a little-known region in the Bolivian Chaco where most settlement is along the Rio Parapetí. Article sheds light on the distinction made between the Upper and Lower Isoso in the past and present.

1162 Conservación y desarrollo sostenible en el suroeste de Potosí, Bolivia. Recopilación de Manuel Olivera A., Patricia Ergueta S., y Mercedes Villca Sanjines. La Paz: Prefectura del Depto. de Potosí: Trópico, 2006. 419 p.: bibl., ill., map.

Excellent collection of 35 chapters on the southeastern quadrant of Potosí, organized around the themes of culture and society, nature, economy, institutional management, conservation, and sustainable development. Presence of strategic minerals and ecotourism have brought this highly traditional region to greater world attention.

1163 Conway-Gómez, Kristen. Market integration, perceived wealth and household consumption of river turtles (*Podocnemis* spp.) in eastern lowland Bolivia. (*J. Lat. Am. Geogr.*, 7:1, 2008, p. 85–103, bibl., graph, maps, photos, tables)

Demonstrates how complicated the forces are that explain degrees of wildlife exploitation in the Amazon basin and that these forces cannot be reduced only to economic factors.

1164 Cortes, Geneviève. Partir para quedarse: supervivencia y cambio en las sociedades campesinas andinas (Bolivia). La Paz: Plural Editores: IRD: IFEA, 2004. 474 p.: bibl., ill., maps.

Translation from the French of a book whose fieldwork was carried out in the 1990s in three communities north of Tarata in the Valle Alto of Cochamba. The title "leaving to stay" captures the essence of the Andean peasant dilemma: unable to derive a rewarding enough livelihood from their farm plots, many men from these communities have migrated for work, usually to urban areas. In this instance, they have gone either to the Chapare to grow coca leaf or to Argentina, the US, or even Israel. Excellent account of the complexities of migration and how people maintain strong ties to their home bases.

1165 Gade, Daniel W. Old World agricultural transfers: the case of treevines in the Bolivian Andes. (*in* Conference of Latin Americanist Geographers, Benicásim, Spain, 2001. Bridging cultural geographies: Europe and Latin America. Edited by Robert B. Kent, Vicent Ortells Chabrera, and Javier Soriano Martí. Castelló de la Plana, Spain: Univ. Jaume I, 2005, p. 59–80, bibl., facsim., map, photo)

The spread of agricultural technology from Spain to Western South America in the early colonial period included everything connected to viniculture. Discusses reasons for the survival in the Cinti Valley of southern Bolivia of the practice once common in the Iberian Peninsula of using trees as supports for grapevines. For review of entire volume, see *HLAS 64:383.*

1166 Gil Montero, Raquel. Despoblamiento diferencial en los Andes Meridionales: Sud Chichas y la Puna de Jujuy en el siglo XIX. (*Bull. Inst. fr. étud. andin.,* 35:1, 2006, p. 55–73)

Mortality brought on by drought, war, and epidemics explained the general 19th-century decline in the population of 10 parishes on both sides of the Bolivian-Argentine border, though it was much more accentuated in the Puna de Jujuy on the Argentine side.

1167 Informe Bolivia 2005: progreso en la implementación de los objetivos de desarrollo del milenio referidos a la pobreza, la sostenibilidad ambiental y la gobernanza. Elaboración del informe y punto focal de Teresa Flores Bedregal. La Paz: LIDEMA, 2005. 170 p.: ill.

Discusses the progress in Bolivia on poverty reduction, environmental sustainability, and governance—three of the eight objectives of the UN-sponsored development plan for the millennium. Concludes that no strong commitment exists in Bolivia to meet the goals laid out in the plan.

1168 Kaup, Brent Z. Negotiating through nature: the resistant materiality and materiality of resistance in Bolivia's natural gas sector. (*Geoforum/New York,* 39:5, Sept. 2008, p. 1734–1752)

Examines the conflicts and paradoxes surrounding Bolivia's natural gas resource from the viewpoint of the material obstacles to its exploitation, need for large-scale investment, social regulations imposed by the government, effects of popular uprisings at a local and regional scale, and the nationalization by Evo Morales of the gas resource in 2004. One of the best of many articles that have now appeared on this subject.

1169 Lehm Ardaya, Zulema. Bolivia: estrategias, problemas y desafios en la gestión del territorio indígena Sirionó. En colaboración con Wendy Townsend, Hugo Salas y Kantuta Lara. Trinidad, Bolivia: CIDDBENI; Copenhagen, Denmark: IWGIA, Grupo International de Trabajo Sobre Asuntos Indígenas, 2005. 232 p.: bibl., ill.

Anthropogeography of the Sirionó people, most of whom live in two communities 60 km from the city of Trinidad in eastern Bolivia. Includes information on social organization, territorial issues, resource management—especially forests, livestock raising, and the challenges of managing the Sirionó territory. Enormous changes have occurred since Holmberg's classic research there in 1939–41.

1170 Madrid, Emilio L. *et al.* Historia de la minería de oro en Bolivia: la lucha de Collapata (Oruro). (*Ecol. Polít./Barcelona,* 28, 2004, p. 91–102, bibl.)

Addresses the conflict that began in 1993 between the Canadian-Bolivian consortium that wanted to mine gold near Challapata (Oruro Dept.). Describes the interests of the indigenous inhabitants of the area and the evolution of a new peasant perception of their rights.

1171 May, Jan-Hendrik. Geomorphological indicators of large-scale climatic changes in the Eastern Bolivian lowlands. (*Geogr. Helv.,* 61:2, 2006, p. 120–134, bibl., maps, tables)

Using remote sensing data, author identifies the landforms of eastern Bolivia at macro and micro scales. Evokes past climatic changes to explain the geomorphological evolution of this region.

1172 Müller, Robert *et al.* Lineamientos estratégicos para la conservación de la biodiversidad en los Yungas de La Paz:

subcorredor Cotapata Cotacajes—Corredor
Vilcabamba—Amboró. Bolivia: Asociación
Boliviana para la Conservación: Conservación Internacional Bolivia, 2005. 54 p.: bibl.,
ill., maps.

Conservation issues in the part of
the eastern slope of the Cordillera Oriental
between 1,500 and 3,500 m above sea level
include worn out land, burning of vegetation, use of insecticides, wood extraction,
loss of plant and animal species, trash, and
contaminated rivers. Several protected areas
in the region, including the Cotapata National Park, also have to deal with several of
those problems.

1173 Perreault, Thomas J. Custom and
contradiction: rural water governance
and the politics of *usos y costumbres* in
Bolivia's irrigators' movement. (*Ann. Assoc.
Am. Geogr.*, 98:4, 2008, p. 834–854)

Using Cochabamba department as his
study area, the author analyzes the implementation of traditional water management
among Bolivian peasants who irrigate their
fields. The cultural politics of *usos y costumbres*, whose logic is quite different from
atomizing neoliberalism, has successfully
influenced the governance of water in this
region.

1174 Perrier Bruslé, Laetitia. The front and
the line: the paradox of South American frontiers applied to the Bolivian case.
(*Geopolitics/London*, 12, 2007, p. 57–77,
maps)

Argues that even though the border
areas are increasingly integrated into Bolivian territory, Bolivians have a hermetic view
of their territorial space, which has deprived
the country of "any possible autonomous
evolution." Dubious assertions and lack of
clarity mar this study.

1175 Ribera, Marco Octavio and **Máximo
Liberman.** El uso de la tierra y los
recursos de la biodiversidad en las áreas
protegidas de Bolivia: un análisis crítico con
propuestas para su conservación y manejo
sostenible. La Paz: Servicio Nacional de
las Áreas Protegidas, SERNAP; New York:
Proyecto GEF-II, Banco Mundial, 2006.
520 p.: bibl., ill., maps.

In 2006, Bolivia had 21 protected
areas divided among national parks, natural
and biological reserves, natural areas, and

indigenous territories. This World Bank-
sponsored study describes each of their
biological identities, but also discusses
human activities, population, accessibility,
and environmental impact.

1176 Rodríguez Rodríguez, Mario. Martín
Cárdenas, el eximio botánico y natu-
ralista de América. La Paz: PROINPA, 2005.
539 p.: bibl., ill.

Martín Cárdenas (1899–1973), one of
Bolivia's eminent scientists of the 20th century, had an unusually productive lifetime
in plant sciences. He classified ca. 6,500 species of Bolivian plants. Eight chapters relate
to his botanical explorations throughout Bolivia. His research on different plant groups,
herbarium visits, biographical sketch, list
of all publications, and the herbarium and
botanical garden he started in Cochabamba
are all collected into this volume.

1177 Schroeder, Kathleen. Economic globalization and Bolivia's regional divide. (*J. Lat. Am. Geogr.*, 6:2, 2007, p. 77–98,
bibl., maps, tables)

Analyzes the roots of the growing
political and economic divide between the
highlands and the lowlands. Dissects the
voting pattern by department of the 2004
natural gas referendum and the 2005 municipal elections as well as the 2005 presidential election results by province. Political
differences in Bolivia may be characterized
by ethnic differences but they are fueled
by resource disparities and the struggle
of departments to control the benefits for
themselves rather than for the country as a
whole.

**1178 Seminario Internacional "Conflicto
y Colaboración en el Manejo de Re-
cursos Naturales," Tarija, Bolivia, 2003.**
Conflicto y colaboración en el manejo de
recursos naturales: experiencias de Bolivia
y Argentina. Coordinación de Carlos Vaca-
flores R. Textos de Fernando Antezana *et al.*
Compilación y edición de Pavel López Flores. San José: Programa CyC-UPAZ IDRC,
Univ. para la Paz; Cochabamba, Bolivia:
CESU, UMSS; Buenos Aires: Grupo de
Estudios Rurales, Instituto Gino Germani,
Facultad de Ciencias Sociales de la Univ. de
Buenos Aires; Tarija, Bolivia: Comunidad
de Estudios JAINA; La Paz: Plural Editores,
2005. 288 p.: bibl., ill.

Of the 13 chapters, seven focus on Bolivia: natural gas conflicts in Tarija, role of unions and communities in Potosí, indigenous territories and oil companies, and water privatization issues in Cochabamba.

1179 Stearman, Allyn MacLean et al.
Stradivarius in the jungle: traditional knowledge and the use of "black beeswax" among the Yuquí of the Bolivian Amazon. (*Hum. Ecol.*, 36:2, April 2008, p. 149–159, bibl., graphs, table)

Beeswax made from stingless bees has been used as an adhesive to affix feathers to arrows. This article reports on many interesting details of this aspect of traditional knowledge that is not likely to survive acculturation of this indigenous group. For ethnography specialist's comment, see item **628**.

1180 Urioste Fernández de Córdova, Miguel and **Cristóbal Kay.** Latifundios, avasallamientos y autonomías: la reforma agraria inconclusa en el Oriente. La Paz: Fundación TIERRA, 2005. 62 p.: bibl., map.

Santa Cruz may be Bolivia's richest department, but nevertheless it has 70 percent of its population in poverty and 32 percent in extreme poverty. In spite of the 1953 land reform and soybean exports, much unproductive latifundia exists to account for some of that poverty. Questions the autonomy agenda of Santa Cruz Dept. when 100,000 Bolivian peasants are without land.

1181 Urquizo Huici, Carlos Fernando. La Paz: saco de aparapita o metrópoli andina? La Paz: Friedrich Ebert Stiftung-ILDIS, 2006. 134 p.: bibl., ill., maps.

Perspective on metropolitan La Paz that includes La Paz, El Alto, Viacha, Mecapaca, Achocalla, and Laja. Includes sections on history and urban development, population dynamics, economic activity, citizen participation, and cultural creativity.

1182 Zeballos Hurtado, Hernán. Agricultura y desarrollo sostenible. La Paz: Superintendencia General, Sistema de Regulación de Recursos Naturales Renovables: COSUDE: Plural Editores, 2006. 285 p.: bibl., ill., CD-ROM.

A broad sweep of information about Bolivian agriculture, the way the government has organized its agencies related to it, the production chains of crops and livestock, and agricultural exports.

THE SOUTHERN CONE

CÉSAR N. CAVIEDES, *Professor of Geography, University of Florida, Gainesville*

SUSTAINABLE DEVELOPMENT CONTINUES to be a preferred theme of Southern Cone economists and environmentalists, who often employ an improper concept of this paradigm as exposed in a critical article by Peter Klepeis and Paul Laris (item **1240**). Following a trend established at the end of the 1990s, the consideration of water as a high-priced commodity essential for development and much coveted by governments, private enterprises, and individual cultivators continues to be a subject of great interest (item **1184**). A third theme garnering great attention is the examination of the economic agendas and advantages sought by each country participating in the Mercosur, particularly in view of the rapid globalization of regional economies (item **1186**).

As Anglo-American and European scholars gradually withdraw from research on Southern Cone countries, national scientists are filling the gap with a great degree of competence and originality. This phenomenon is particularly evident when considering the quality of the papers published in the two major specialized journals from Chile, *Revista de Geografía Norte Grande* and *Informa-*

ciones Geográficas. The publications from Chilean geographers demonstrate a modernity of approach and innovative methodologies and, as a result, the reputations of the journals are attracting contributors from Brazil, Argentina, and Europe. Unfortunately, a similar statement cannot be made about the state of Argentine geography. With regret one notices the discontinuity of the *Boletin de Estudios Geográficos* (Mendoza)—once the leading Argentine geographical journal—and the vanishing of *Meridiano* (Buenos Aires), in whose pages lively theoretical discussions were held and radical interpretations were debated.

In contrast with the small number of items included in previous issues of *HLAS*, research from North American scholars has increased noticeably. There are five articles on Argentina published in the highly visible *Journal of Latin American Geography* (items **1190**, **1195**, **1200**, **1213**, and **1214**), one paper on Chile (item **1264**), and one on Paraguay (item **1268**), which reverse the neglect for the Southern Cone evidenced during the last two decades. It can be hoped that promised changes in attitude by the present government in Washington will further stimulate the academic interest in this region of the continent.

GENERAL

1183 Brasil y Chile: una mirada hacia América Latina y sus perspectivas. Coordinación y edición de Rose Cave. Santiago: RiL Editores/Instituto de Estudios Internacionales/Embajada de Brasil, 2006. 291 p.: bibl., ill., tables.

Nineteen essays grouped in four sections (economics, culture, politics, and social interaction) are authored by noted intellectuals of Brazil and Chile. Each contribution focuses on a particular country, without pointing out similarities among them, a fact that not even the conclusion underlines. The reader is left with compartmentalized glimpses of each country which do not allow an understanding of how relations between Chile and Brazil could serve as a binational model for other nations in the continent.

1184 Los dueños del río, la hidrovía Paraguay-Paraná: el negocio de los recursos en América Latina. (*Ecol. Polít./ Barcelona*, 31, 2006, p. 27–39, maps, photos)

Severe indictment of the utilization of water from the Paraná and Paraguay rivers by large agro-businesses. Interesting document to illustrate the discrepancies between environmentalists and governmental water managers in Argentina and Paraguay with regards to this "commodity."

1185 Laciar, Mirta Elizabeth. Medio ambiente y desarrollo sustentable: los desafíos del Mercosur. Buenos Aires:

Editorial Ciudad Argentina, 2003. 338 p.: bibl.

The attainment of sustainable development and environmental conservation within the legal framework of Mercosur is the major theme of this volume. The inclusion of statistical data and maps pinpointing places under discussion would have added value to this volume.

1186 Saludjian, Alexis. Critiques du régionalisme ouvert à partir de l'économie géographique appliquée au Mercosur. (*J. Lat. Am. Geogr.*, 4:2, 2005, p. 77–96, bibl., graphs, tables)

More an analysis than a "critique," this work by an economist seeks to prove that Mercosur is a trade arrangement that has encouraged the insertion of the participating countries into the larger world trade entities (open regionalism) instead of being a tool to promote regional economic integration (closed regionalism).

1187 Territorios rurales: movimientos sociales y desarrollo territorial rural en America Latina. Edición de José Bengoa. Santiago, Chile: Centro Latinoamericano para el Desarrollo Rural/Editorial Catalonia, 2007. 613 p.: bibl., tables.

This lengthy volume is the result of a project sponsored by the Centro Latinoamericano para el Desarrollo Rural over several years. Twenty-five collaborations whose only commonality ought to be the rural setting are supposed to provide a coherent view of the problems that rural societies face. Unfortunately, the disparity of themes and an awkward definition of territory ("un conjunto de lazos producto de la interacción social que se materializa en un determinado espacio") confuses the issues and blurs the answers to the question of how social movements and modes of exploitation shape rural territories in the continent. A final chapter that might have tied together the numerous unconnected themes is sorely missing, as is a guiding thread of the heterogeneous contributions by the coordinator.

ARGENTINA

1188 Abihaggle, Carlos E. and Jorge A. Day. Agua y sociedad: un ensayo económico sobre la política hídrica. Mendoza, Argentina: EDIUNC, 2004. 252 p.: bibl. (Serie Estudios/El agua; 35)

Rudimentary presentation about the role of water resources in the agricultural development of the semi-arid belt of the province of Mendoza. A higher degree of sophistication and less verbosity in the treatment of this element crucial for the semi-arid agrarian economies of the continent would have been expected from two academic writers.

1189 Almirón, Analía; Claudia Troncoso; and Carla Lois. Promoción turística y cartografía: la Argentina turística en los mapas de la Secretaría de Turismo de la Nación, 1996–2004. (*Invest. Geogr./México*, 62, abril 2007, p. 138–154, bibl., ill., photos)

Description of the content of tourist maps issued by the governmental Secretaría de Turismo which unfortunately does not utilize the proper interpretive content-analysis principles nor modern techniques of cartographic representation.

1190 Barsky, Andrés. Problem of access to land for Bolivian horticultural producers in the transitional zone of western Greater Buenos Aires. (*J. Lat. Am. Geogr.*, 5:2, 2006, p. 127–131, bibl., graphs)

Bolivian guest workers in the Moreno borough of Greater Buenos Aires maintain green gardens, usually owned by Portuguese immigrants, to provide vegetables to local markets in the outskirts of Buenos Aires city. The native Argentine urban dwellers' views on these activities by foreign workers are divided.

1191 Bohn, Vanesa Yael; Gerardo Miguel Eduardo Perillo; and M. Cintia Piccolo. Calidad y aprovechamiento del agua de la laguna Unamuno (Buenos Aires, Argentina). (*Pap. Geogr.*, 40, julio/dic. 2004, p. 173–184, bibl., graphs, tables)

The physical characteristics of the coastal lake of Unamuno are described on the basis of chemical composition and its potential uses for agriculture and cattle ranching. No interpretation is made of the implications of the findings for human occupation.

1192 Calmels, Augusto Pablo and Silvio Alberto Casadío. Compilación geológica de la provincia de La Pampa. Santa Rosa, Argentina: Ediciones Amerindia, 2004. 322 p.: ill., maps.

Conventional description of the stratigraphy of the arid province of La Pampa. While useful for local geologists, this text fails to insert the region into the general geology of Argentina and in the geotectonic framework of southernmost South America.

1193 Carbone, Maria Elizabeth; María Cintia Piccolo; and Beatriz V. Scian. Análisis de los períodos secos y húmedos en la cuenca del arroyo Claromecó, Argentina. (*Pap. Geogr.*, 40, julio/dic. 2004, p. 25–35, bibl., graphs, maps, table)

The influence of droughts on the water budget of a small watershed is detected utilizing Palmer's aridity indices. There is no mention of the relationship of these droughts to the climate oscillations documented for southeastern South America.

1194 Carbone, Maria Elizabeth; María Cintia Piccolo; and Gerardo Miguel Eduardo Perillo. Evaluation of the surface waters of the Claromeco River basin for supplementary irrigation. (*Rev. Geogr./ México*, 137, enero/junio 2005, p. 81–100, bibl., graphs, tables)

Repetitious description of the physical characteristics of the waters of the Claromecó River (see item **1193**) without geographical insights or mention of the effects on human occupance and livestock/ agricultural land use.

1195 Carter, Eric D. Malaria, landscape, and society in northwest Argentina in the early twentieth century. (*J. Lat. Am.*

Geogr., 7:1, 2008, p. 7–38, bibl., graph, maps, photos, tables)

Malaria was once widespread in the northwest of Argentina. Advances in sanitary installations and planned drainage eradicated this scourge from urban centers, but the strain persisted in the neighboring wetlands to compound the already miserable conditions of agricultural workers.

1196 Catullo, María Rosa. Ciudades relocalizadas: una mirada desde la antropología social. Buenos Aires: Editorial Biblos, 2006. 255 p.: maps. (Sociedad Editorial Biblos)

The completion in 1985 of the Salto Grande dam across the Río Uruguay forced the relocation of two towns in Entre Ríos and on the Uruguayan bank, respectively. The sociological disarticulation for the relocated populations is thoroughly detailed.

1197 Cortés, Rosalía and Fernando Groisman. Migrations, the labour market and poverty in Greater Buenos Aires. (*CEPAL Rev.*, 82, April 2004, p. 171–190, bibl., graphs, tables)

Competition for low-paying jobs and the use of public services among rural migrants from Argentina and undocumented workers from Bolivia, Paraguay, and Chile are indications of the hostile relations between these two groups in peripheral Buenos Aires.

1198 Falasca, Silvia and Ana Ulberich. El agua disponible de los suelos del sudeste bonaerense, República Argentina. (*Rev. Geogr./México*, 140, julio/dic. 2006, p. 7–17, bibl., maps, tables)

Repetitious article on the water balance of soils in a southern sector of the province of Buenos Aires. A mere survey, the paper makes no geographical inferences, nor does it address the implications for land use and settlements.

1199 Formiga, Nidia. El derecho a la ciudad y la cuestión del espacio público: experiencias en la ciudad de Bahía Blanca. (*J. Lat. Am. Geogr.*, 6:1, 2007, p. 173–196, bibl., maps, photos)

A lengthy discussion of the meaning of "public spaces" defined by various Latin American urban scholars is followed by a case study of the planned modern city of Bahía Blanca. The enquiry is based on qualitative surveys of residents from different sectors of the city.

1200 García, Susana and Marcela Guerrero. Indicadores de sustentabilidad ambiental en la gestión de espacios verdes: parque urbano Monte Calvario, Tandil, Argentina. (*Rev. Geogr. Norte Gd.*, 35, julio 2006, p. 45–57, bibl., map, tables)

The vegetation in a park in the town of Tandil is used as a testing ground to determine the sustainability of natural resources within urban settings.

1201 Gil Montero, Raquel. Despoblamiento diferencial en los Andes Meridionales: Sud Chichas y la Puna de Jujuy en el siglo XIX.

See item **1166** for discussion of the decline in population along the Argentina-Bolivia border.

1202 Gómez Lende, Sebastián; Jorge Osvaldo Morina; and Guillermo Ángel Velázquez. Reestructuración productiva y diferenciación regional: exportaciones provinciales y desempleo en el Noroeste Argentino, 1991–2000. (*Estud. Geogr./Madrid*, 66:259, julio/dic. 2005, p. 533–556, bibl.)

Verbose article states that the northwestern provinces of Catamarca, Jujuy, La Rioja, Santiago del Estero, Salta, and Tucumán—whose economies hinge on exports from the primary sector—exhibit high unemployment and therefore high out-migration rates.

1203 Gorenstein, Silvia; Martín Napal; and Mariana Olea. Territorios agarios y realidades rururbanas: reflexiones sobre el desarrollo rural a partir del caso pampeano bonaerense. (*EURE/Santiago*, 33:100, dic. 2007, p. 91–113, bibl., maps, tables)

Increasing urbanization in the central Pampa raises the question of whether these places should be called rural or urban, or "rururban" as the authors propose. Not discussed is the reality that a reconfiguration of the functions and the economically active population of the Argentine Pampa is occurring.

1204 Neoliberalismo y problemáticas regionales en Argentina: interpretaciones geográficas. Edición de Jorge Osvaldo

Morina. Luján, Argentina: Grupo de Investigación en Geografía Económica y Regional de la Argentina, División Geografía, Departamento de Ciencias Sociales, UNLu, 2006. 316 p.: bibl., ill., maps.

A group of geographers set out to criticize the economic backsliding and social decay of Argentina since 1976, placing the blame on international neoliberalism and globalization. The book does not mention the role played by inept politicians, greedy economists, and corrupt administrators in this dismal situation.

1205 Ottmann, Graciela. Agroecología y sociología histórica desde Latinoamérica: elementos para el análisis y potenciación del movimiento agroecológico: el caso de la provincia argentina de Santa Fé. Córdoba, Argentina: Univ. de Córdoba, Servicio de Publicaciones, 2005. 224 p.: bibl., ill.

Even though this is an analysis of rural labor employed in latifundia of the Argentine Chaco and the province of Santa Fé, the author tries to generalize the situation to all the peasants working on large holdings and for agribusinesses in Latin America. Despite this disputable generalization, the volume is an adequate introduction to understanding the intricate relationships among organized agricultural workers, latifundia, and international capitalism.

1206 Pengue, Walter A. Deuda ecológica con la agricultura: sustentabilidad débil y futuro incierto en la Pampa argentina. (*Ecol. Polít./Barcelona*, 29, 2005, p. 55–73, bibl., graphs, tables)

Generalities about the agricultural development in Argentina based on the assumption that the Pampa was a region of inexhaustible resources, thus disregarding any sort of conservation measures. The revealing statistics presented are not followed, however, by interpretive elaborations.

1207 Prieto, María del Rosario; Teresita Castrillejo; and Patricia Dussel. El proceso de contaminación hídrica en un oasis andino: la vida y la muerte por las acequias de Mendoza, Argentina, 1880–1980. (*Signos Hist.*, 16, julio/dic. 2006, p. 112–151, maps, tables)

Water for irrigation and consumption in Greater Mendoza originates from Andean streams. Unfortunately, in their lower courses, contamination is widespread due to open sewage lines and industrial discharges that are only loosely controlled by governmental bureaucrats.

1208 Ramos, María Belén and **Alicia M. Campo.** Caracterización de estados de tiempo en el suroeste bonaerense, Argentina. (*Rev. Geogr. Norte Gd.*, 40, sept. 2008, p. 85–97, bibl.)

First original Argentine study on the characterization of weather types around Bahía Blanca and their linkages with synoptic situations over the southern tip of South America. The approach was first used by C. Caviedes in 1969 to characterize the weather sequences in Central Chile, based on models developed in the 1950s by German meteorologists. It is rewarding to see this approach applied in other regions of the continent.

1209 Región pampeana bonaerense: desarrollo sustentable con equidad. La presente investigación fue realizada por el equipo de trabajo del Centro de Estudios para el Desarrollo Territorial y la Gestión de la Infraestructura, bajo la coordinación del Dr. Juan A. Roccatagliata; con la colaboración de la Organización TECHINT. Buenos Aires: Docencia: Fundación Hernandarias, 2005. 2 v. (1115 p.): bibl., ill., maps.

Ambitious compilation of existing knowledge about the natural and human conditions in the pampa. In a work of this extent, the quality of the chapters necessarily varies. The two volumes offer a mosaic in which the reader in search of pertinent information has a lot to sift through.

1210 Ríos, Diego Martín. Planificación urbana privada y desastres de inundación: las urbanizaciones cerradas polderizadas en el municipo de Tigre, Buenos Aires. (*Econ. Soc. Territ.*, 5:17, enero/abril 2005, p. 63–83, bibl.)

Riverside gated communities and developers' speculations have driven the occupation of riverine land into areas of Tigre that are very prone to catastrophic flooding.

Seminario Internacional "Conflicto y Colaboración en el Manejo de Recursos Naturales," *Tarija, Bolivia, 2003.* Conflicto y colaboración en el manejo de recursos naturales: experiencias de Bolivia y Argentina. See item **1178.**

1211 Valenzuela de Mari, Cristina Ofelia. La desarticulación de lógicas territoriales: el sector agrícola del Chaco entre 1994 y 2004. (*Rev. Geogr./México*, 139, enero/junio 2006, p. 103–129, bibl., graph, map, tables)

Largely discursive and conventional presentation of the regional transformations of the Chaco between 1994 and 2004 as a result of the export of cotton, soybeans, and sunflower seeds.

1212 Valenzuela de Mari, Cristina Ofelia. Transformaciones agrarias y desarrollo regional en el nordeste argentino: una visión geográfica del siglo XX. Buenos Aires: Editorial La Colmena, 2006. 186 p.: bibl., ill.

Compiling a series of publications on the impoverished provinces of northeastern Argentina, this prolific geographer has condensed her findings in a volume shaded by a radical interpretive tilt.

1213 Vidal-Koppmann, Sonia. Fragmentación socio-espacial en la periferia de la región metropolitana de Buenos Aires. (*J. Lat. Am. Geogr.*, 8:1, 2009, p. 79–97, bibl., graphs, map)

The suburban fringe of Greater Buenos Aires has undergone a major transformation since the 1990s. The former radial expansion of the urban area has changed to a multi-center sprawl. Each of these centers differs in terms of income level, social status, and quality of life, exacerbating the tensions among the inhabitants of the suburban fringe.

1214 Whitson, Risa. Beyond the crisis: economic globalization and informal work in urban Argentina. (*J. Lat. Am. Geogr.*, 6:2, 2007, p. 121–136, bibl.)

Informal work in Argentina peaked in 2002 due to the worsening of internal economic conditions and the insertion of the country into the global financial order. For political economy specialist's comment, see item **2398.**

1215 Zanetta, Cecilia. The influence of the World Bank on national housing and urban policies: the case of Mexico and Argentina during the 1990's. Aldershot, England; Burlington, Vt.: Ashgate, 2004. 307 p.: bibl., ill., index. (Ashgate economic geography series)

Critical analysis of the policies endorsed by the World Bank to assist family housing projects in Mexico and Argentina during the 1980s and 1990s. The procedures implemented in Mexico seem to have been more successful than those pursued in Buenos Aires, where the expectations of would-be owners were more sophisticated.

1216 Zulaica, Laura and **Juan Pablo Celemín.** Análisis territorial de las condiciones de habitabilidad en el periurbano de la ciudad de Mar del Plata (Argentina), a partir de la construcción de un índice y de la aplicación de métodos de asociación espacial. (*Rev. Geogr. Norte Gd.*, 41, dic. 2008, p. 129–146, bibl., maps, tables)

Using six indicators and 11 variables, an "index of inhabitation" is computed to characterize the popular sectors in the urban fringe of Mar del Plata. As expected, poor neighborhoods are defined by low social levels, deteriorating quality of life, and environmental vulnerability.

CHILE

1217 Acevedo Arce, Ramón Ángel. El viaje de Rakar: travesía por 67 pueblos olvidados de la V Región de Chile. Santiago de Chile: RiL editores, 2006. 302 p.: ill., maps.

Collection of artistic images of landscapes, roads, dwellings, and human types in the province of Valparaíso. Each photograph has captions taken from poems of *Les Fleurs du Mal*, by Charles Baudelaire, also known as "the cursed poet." A very distinct travel guide to rather unknown exotic places.

1218 Andrade, Belisario; Federico Arenas; and Rodrigo Guijón. Revisión crítica del marco institucional y legal chileno de ordenamiento territorial: el caso de la zona costera. (*Rev. Geogr. Norte Gd.*, 41, dic. 2008, p. 23–48, bibl., maps, tables)

Land use along the seafront is assessed in view of existing regulations and the legal framework of coastal management. Few rules are implemented, nor are existing rules enforced by the authorities, and the national coastal management plan is rarely respected.

1219 Araos, José; María Angélica Godoi; and Rubén Carvallo. Variaciones recientes del lóbulo Zapata Sur, Glaciar Tyndall: Campo de Hielo Patagónico Sur (Chile). (*Rev. Geogr. Norte Gd.*, 37, junio 2007, p. 75–84, bibl., graphs, maps, tables)

A glacial lobe at the Patagonian Ice Field South has thinned by 2.6 m since 2003, revealing the impact of global warming upon the maritime high latitudes of the southern hemisphere.

1220 Araya-Vergara, José. Geomorfología glacial y paraglacial de la cuenca andina del Mapocho, Andes de Santiago, Chile. (*Invest. Geogr./Santiago*, 40, 2008, p. 21–48, bibl., graphs, maps, photos, tables)

Valley shape and periglacial features in the upper reaches of the Mapocho River above 2750 m point to glacial modelling processes active since the last southern hemispheric glacial period and to several minor glacial readvances during the Holocene.

1221 Bähr, Jürgen and Kerstin Meyer-Kriesten. Santiago de Chile—eine fragmentierte Stadt?: eine faktorenanalytische Untersuchung der Stadtstruktur in 2002 im Vergleich zu 1970, Mit 6 abbildungen und 6 Tabellen. (*Erdkunde/Bonn*, 61:3, Juli/Sept. 2007, p. 258–276, graphs, maps, tables)

After establishing socioeconomic categories based on factor analysis, the authors compare the situation of Greater Santiago in 1970 and in 2002. The study shows that the patterns have not changed considerably: the wealthy continue to live in attractive natural settings, while the poor dwell in the unattractive locations at the north and west ends of the city.

1222 Camus, Pablo. Ambiente, bosques y gestión forestal en Chile, 1541–2005. Santiago: DIBAM: LOM Ediciones: Centro de Investigaciones Diego Barros Arana, 2006. 374 p.: bibl., ill. (Col. Sociedad y cultura; 40)

This history of the principles that have ruled forest conservation and the management of artificial woodlands in Chile brings to the front page the environmental perceptions prevailing in the country. The book suffers from extremely poor quality printing.

1223 Camus, Pablo and María Eugenia Solari. La invención de la selva austral: bosques y tierras despejadas en la cuenca del río Valdivia, siglos XVI–XIX. (*Rev. Geogr. Norte Gd.*, 40, sept. 2008, p. 5–22, bibl., graphs, map)

Interesting depiction of the deforestation in the surroundings of Valdivia since the arrival of the Spaniards up to the massive land opening by European colonists in the 19th century, based on historical texts and early photographs.

1224 Castro, Luis C. Sequedad y destierro: la expropiación de las aguas de regadío a los campesinos del Valle de Quisma (norte de Chile), 1912–1224. (*Allpanchis/Cuzco*, 37:67, primer semestre 2006, p. 59–90)

The struggle for water supply to the port cities of northern Chile goes back to the time before the region's annexation by Chile in 1881. In the 1920s, tapping of the scant water resources of the Quebrada de Quisma (Pica) oasis prompted most of the native cultivators to leave.

1225 Chile litoral: diálogo científico sobre los ecosistemas costeros. Edición de Ronald G. Hellman y Rodrigo Araya Dujisin. Santiago de Chile: FLACSO-Chile; New York: ACSS, 2005. 406 p.: ill., maps.

Collection of papers about ecosystem management presented at a meeting entitled "Governance, Science and Regional Economic Development in Chile's Coastal Zone Ecosystems," in 2002. Among the subjects addressed are salmon farming in southern Chile and the operation of several ports along the central coast.

1226 Chile sustentable: propuesta ciudadana para el cambio. Edición de Sara Larraín, Karím Palacios y María Paz Aedo. Santiago: Programa Chile Sustentable, 2003. 211 p.: ill.

Pamphlet presents the main points of the non-governmental *Programa Chile*

Sustentable to assure sustainable development throughout the diverse regions of the country. A program of sectorial reforms to attain equality and social justice is also included.

1227 Daude, Jean Hervé. Easter Island: the lost forest. Québec: Private publication, 2008. 171 p.: bibl., ill., photos.

English version of the thesis presented in item **1228**, complemented by additional information from articles published in English-language journals. This version emphasizes the vegetational changes on the island due to climate variability.

1228 Daude, Jean Hervé. Méga El Niño et déforestation de l'Île de Pâques: l'effet combiné d'un dérèglement climatique et de l'action de l'homme. Québec: Private publication, 2008. 169 p.: bibl., photos.

Synthesizing research published by Easter Island specialists, the author interprets the isolation of its pre-European natives as the consequence of decimating droughts caused by "Mega El Niños" (an extremely debatable statement) and blames the relentless foraging of rats for destroying the scarce wood species that could have provided timber for the building of canoes. In his view, climate variations and reckless deforestation lie at the root of the collapse of this eastern outpost of Polynesian culture in the Pacific.

1229 Emilfork, Leónidas. Pasaje al Nuevo Mundo. Santiago, Chile: RiL Editores, 2004. 215 p.: ill., maps.

This Chilean intellectual offers musings about places, peoples, and personalities of Latin America and outlines customs and temperaments that distinguish New World inhabitants from their European counterparts.

1230 Exiliados, emigrados y retornados: chilenos en América y Europa, 1973–2004. Coordinación de José del Pozo. Santiago: RiL Editores, 2006. 211 p.: bibl.

Revealing surveys of Chilean exiles in Sweden, France, Brazil, Mexico, and Canada from 1973 to 2004. The information comes from individuals who left their home country for political reasons, and from others who sought better living conditions abroad. This appropriate outline of the hopes and achievements of Chilean immigrants in the mentioned countries stems from a Chilean exile who is now residing in Canada.

1231 Externalidades de la agricultura chilena. Edición de Alberto Valdés y William Ellis Foster. Santiago: Ediciones Univ. Católica de Chile: Food and Agriculture Organization of the United Nations, 2005. 290 p.: bibl., ill. (Investigaciones)

In this interesting volume, several agronomers defend the position that the agricultural sector of the Chilean economy has contributed to the flourishing exports of the country. Their theses are backed by quantitative analyses, a methodological technique not frequently found in the works of detractors of the social benefits of growth in that sector of the economy.

1232 Farías, Salvador; Martín Castro Avaria; and Consuelo Castro Avaria. Variabilidad de la temperatura superficial del mar, identificación de surgencias costeras y su relevancia en un área marina costera protegida del desierto de Atacama, Chile. (*Rev. Geogr. Norte Gd.*, 41, dic. 2008, p. 49–61, bibl., graphs, map)

Satellite images of sea surface temperatures reveal active foci of upwelling whose intra-annual variablities are regulated by the cold (La Niña) and warm (El Niño) phases of the Southern Oscillation, and thereby tied to thermal variations in the southeastern Pacific.

1233 Galetovic P., Alexander and **Pablo Jordán.** Santiago: ¿dónde estamos? ¿hacia dónde vamos? (*Estud. Públicos*, 101, verano 2006, p. 87–146, graphs, map)

Controversial article on the growth of Greater Santiago and the problems claimed to be associated with it. The density of inhabitants per square hectare has not substantially increased since 1940 and the growth of the city has occurred at the expense of agricultural land. The authors claim that pollution and congestion are also not so bad and that, if anybody is to blame for these "perceived" problems, it is the Ministry for Housing and Urbanism and the Regulating Plan of Santiago that opened the doors for uncontrolled sprawl. See also item **1259**.

1234 Gallardo G., Felipe *et al.* Geografía y fiestas religiosas: análisis a los procesos de territorialización de cuatro fiestas en Chiloé. (*Invest. Geogr./Santiago*, 40, 2008, p. 49–66, bibl., graphs, maps, photos)

The territorial significance of place and the symbolisms involved in the religious festivities of four Chiloé urban centers reveal the influence of ethnos and religious acculturation in this southern island. Original contribution to the geographical dimensions of popular religious manifestations.

1235 González Leiva, José Ignacio. Primeros levantamientos cartográficos generales de Chile con base científica: los mapas de Claudio Gay y Amado Pissis. (*Rev. Geogr. Norte Gd.*, 38, dic. 2007, p. 21–44, bibl., graphs, maps)

Two European naturalists, Claudio Gay (1830) and Amado Pissis (1848), are credited with drawing the first accurate maps of Chile at the onset of its independent republican life. These maps superseded previous ones executed by Spanish surveyors at smaller scales.

1236 González Pizarro, José Antonio. La conquista de una frontera: mentalidades y tecnologías en las vías de comunicación en el desierto de Atacama. (*Rev. Geogr. Norte Gd.*, 40, sept. 2008, p. 23–46, bibl., maps, tables)

Historical study about the use of the notion of "border" with reference to the Atacama Desert, from colonial times to the time after the seizure of this territory by Chile following the War of the Pacific (1879–1884).

1237 Harrison, Stephan *et al.* Quantifying rates of paraglacial sedimentation: an example from Chilean Patagonia. (*Z. Geomorphol.*, 49:3, Sept. 2005, p. 321–334, bibl., maps, tables)

Deglaciation at the northern edge of the Patagonian Ice Field North since 1863 has resulted in the build-up of alluvial fans and debris cones at the margins of the Neff Glacier. The results of this survey are not compared with those obtained by Argentine and Chilean glaciologists in the Patagonian Ice Fields North and South. The unqualified disregard for South American research is further punctuated by the absence of bibliographical entries in any other language than English.

1238 Henríquez, Cristián; Gerardo Azócar; and Mauricio Aguayo. Cambio de uso del suelo y escorrentía superficial: aplicación de un modelo de simulación espacial en Los Ángeles, VIII Región del Biobío, Chile. (*Rev. Geogr. Norte Gd.*, 36, dic. 2006, p. 61–74, bibl., maps, tables)

Using a probabilistic Markovian model, the runoff conditions on lands converted to urban use in the city of Los Angeles, Chile, are computed. The paper represents a well-designed method of analysis and a plausible interpretation of the findings.

1239 Hidalgo D., Rodrigo; Axel Borsdorf; and Rafael Sánchez. Hacia un nuevo tejido rurbano: los megaproyectos de ciudades valladas en la periferia de Santiago de Chile. (*Ciudad Territ. Estud. Territ.*, 39:151, primavera 2007, p. 115–135, bibl., map, photos, tables)

The changes introduced to the morphology of Santiago by gated communities developed in affluent neighborhoods are mapped and interpreted according to previous models developed by Axel Borsdorf.

1240 Klepeis, Peter and Paul Laris. Contesting sustainable development in Tierra del Fuego. (*Geoforum/New York*, 37:4, July 2006, p. 505–518)

A failed logging project in Tierra del Fuego illustrates how decision-making processes about sustainable development require exchange of information, pertinent collective learning about regional environment and development, and proper identification of the environmental and societal issues at stake. Excellent article on an overand misused concept.

1241 Klepeis, Peter and Paul Laris. Hobby ranching and Chile's land reform legacy. (*Geogr. Rev.*, 98:3, July 2008, p. 372–414, bibl., maps, photos, tables)

Former ranches that were distributed among their workers in the course of the 1970s land reform in Tierra del Fuego have been acquired by absentee owners as leisure properties or by middle class individuals as a form of investment. The traditional sheep-raising estancias of the past have disappeared and the grazing practices on the remaining small farms have accelerated land degradation in this rather fragile ecosystem.

1242 Mardones, María; Julius Jara; and José Vargas. El patrón hidrográfico de la cuenca del río Blanco: control tectónico y geomorfológico. (*Rev. Geogr. Norte Gd.*, 38, dic. 2007, p. 79–98, bibl., graphs, maps, tables)

Recent tectonics, climatic oscillations, and geomorphologic variabilities are identified in a study of the geometry and watershed dynamics in the Río Blanco basin during postglacial times. Good application of remote sensing techniques.

1243 Martínez, Carolina and Carolina Cortez. Características hidrográficas y sedimentológicas en el estuario del río Aconcagua, Chile Central. (*Rev. Geogr. Norte Gd.*, 37, junio 2007, p. 65–75, bibl.)

Sediments collected at the mouth of the Aconcagua River and its coastal fringe give clues about the deposition processes dominating the fluvial system and the impact of coastal currents on subshore sediments.

1244 Martinić, Mateo. El monte Fitz Roy, hito natural en la frontera chileno-argentina, descripción geográfica e historia de la delimitación internacional. (*Rev. Chil. Hist. Geogr.*, 168, 2004/2005, p. 89–109, maps)

Mount Fitz Roy is the only natural marker on the often-disputed boundary of Argentina and Chile in the Andes of western Patagonia. The article describes the pristine beauty of the mountain and details the discovery process of this landmark.

1245 Meneses, Claudio and Germán Luebert. Desarrollo turístico en sectores aledaños a las zonas protegidas: el caso de la comunidad Orilla de Río en la Reserva Nacional Río Clarillo. (*Invest. Geogr./Santiago*, 40, 2008, p. 99–112, bibl., graphs, maps, tables)

A riverside community created in the proximity of a forest preserve south of Santiago city illustrates the positive aspects of integrating human occupancy with nature at the periphery of a forest conservation project.

1246 Muñoz, María Dolores et al. Los paisajes del agua en la cuenca del río Baker: bases conceptuales para su valoración

integral. (*Rev. Geogr. Norte Gd.*, 36, dic. 2006, p. 31–48, bibl., photos)

Theoretical and practical considerations about the contribution of water bodies as scenic elements that heighten landscape perception and increase the appeal of tourist attractions in northern Patagonia. The article is illustrated with evocative photographs of peaceful lakes and swirling streams.

1247 Murray, Warwick E. Neo-feudalism in Latin America?: globalisation, agribusiness, and land re-concentration in Chile. (*J. Peasant Stud.*, 33:4, Oct. 2006, p. 647–677, bibl., graph, tables)

A New Zealand geographer rejects the notion that agribusinesses provide work to rural dwellers in Chile's Norte Chico. In his politically biased view the expansion of agribusiness has led to a renewed concentration of landholdings and to the emergence of neofeudalism in Latin America.

1248 Paz Castro, Carmen; Olivia Henríquez; and Rodolfo Freres. Posibilidades de aplicación de lodos o biosólidos a los suelos del sector norte de la Región Metropolitana de Santiago. (*Rev. Geogr. Norte Gd.*, 37, junio 2007, p. 35–45, bibl., graphs, maps, tables)

Interesting article on the accumulation of biosolids (decanted in sewage treatment plants) containing metal traces and pathogens that will prove toxic when reaching cultivated soils and seeping into construction sites.

1249 Peña-Cortés, Fernando et al. Determinación del nivel de antropización de humedales como criterio para la planificación ecológica de la cuenca del lago Budi, IX Región de La Araucanía, Chile. (*Rev. Geogr. Norte Gd.*, 36, dic. 2006, p. 75–91, bibl., maps, tables)

Assesses various parameters of the land-use changes and the impact of human occupancy on scenic Lake Budi, in coastal Araucanía. The article closes with a pertinent and thoughtful discussion about the destruction of pristine landscapes.

1250 Peña-Cortés, Fernando et al. Morfología y dinámica dunaria en el borde costero de la Región de La Araucanía en Chile: antecedentes para la conservación y gestión territorial. (*Rev. Geogr. Norte Gd.*, 41, dic. 2008, p. 63–80, bibl., graphs, tables)

Survey of coastal dune fields in the Araucanía Region from 1994 to 2004 reveals the stabilization of sand accumulations despite increased human activity and the encroachment by forestry exploitations.

1251 Quintanilla Pérez, Víctor. Estado de recuperación del bosque nativo en una cuenca nordpatagónica de Chile, perturbada por grandes fuegos acaecidos 50 años atrás (44°–45° S). (*Rev. Geogr. Norte Gd.*, 39, mayo 2008, p. 73–92, bibl., graphs, maps, photos, tables)

Forest fires in the region of Aisén ignited by colonists clearing land for pastures reduced southern rain forests by 50 percent between 1936 and 1956. Although there has been some regeneration, the stands of southern beech (Nothofagus) were severely affected.

1252 Quintanilla Pérez, Víctor and Juan Matute. Retroceso y degradación del bosque nativo en una isla de la región de Chiloé: el caso de la isla Lemuy. (*Rev. Geogr. Norte Gd.*, 33, julio 2005, p. 113–130, bibl., graphs, photos)

Basic description of the natural stands and introduced species on the island of Lemuy, in eastern Chiloé.

1253 Riffo Rosas, Margarita and Carol Retamales. Dinámica de cambios en el patrón de asentamiento de la población rural: región de Maule. (*Invest. Geogr./Santiago*, 39, 2007, p. 62–90, bibl., graphs, maps, tables)

Varying degrees of "rurality" and "urbanity" in the municipalities of Curicó, El Romeral, and Sagrada Familia reveal that proximity to cities or towns reinforces the urban character of their inhabitants while persistent isolation perpetuates rural life styles in smaller places.

1254 Riffo Rosas, Margarita et al. Condiciones de accesibilidad de los nuevos asentamientos rurales surgidos en el contexto de la modernizacion productiva en la Región del Maule. (*Invest. Geogr./Santiago*, 40, 2008, p. 113–140, bibl., graphs, maps, tables)

Study on the role played by roads in

determining whether settlements remain traditional or become modernized due to improved access to services and sources of employment.

1255 Rodríguez, Jorge and Daniela González. Redistribución de la población y migración interna en Chile: continuidad y cambio según los últimos cuatro censos nacionales de población y vivienda. (*Rev. Geogr. Norte Gd.*, 35, julio 2006, p. 7–28, bibl., graphs, map, tables)

Data from the population censuses in 1970, 1982, 1992 and 2002 suggest the patterns and dimensions of internal migrations in Chile. Greater Santiago has by far the largest net increases in national and international immigrants. The regions of Coquimbo, O'Higgins, and Los Lagos have grown at higher rates than Santiago, but the actual number of immigrants there has decreased.

1256 Rodríguez, Laura et al. La desestructuración de un barrio industrial en la crisis de la modernidad valdiviana, Chile. (*Rev. Geogr. Norte Gd.*, 40, sept. 2008, p. 59–76, bibl., photos, tables)

An industrial borough of Valdivia created by German immigrants is historically analyzed to illustrate the rise and fall of industrial Valdivia during the second half of the 20th century. Revealing photographs showcase the industrial pulse of Valdivia in the past.

1257 Rodríguez Vignoli, Jorge. Dinámica sociodemográfica metropolitana y segregación residencial: ¿qué aporta la CASEN 2006? (*Rev. Geogr. Norte Gd.*, 41, dic. 2008, p. 81–102, bibl., graphs, tables)

Using creditable data from the 2006 survey of CASEN (Caracterización Socioeconómica Nacional), the author posits that the central area of Greater Santiago is becoming a region of net outmigration, which runs counter to the assumption that the core of the metropolis is the preferred goal of immigrants. In fact, districts in the outskirts have become the magnets of intrametropolitan migration.

1258 Sagredo B., Rafael. Chile, del orden natural al autoritarismo republicano. (*Rev. Geogr. Norte Gd.*, 36, dic. 2006, p. 5–30, bibl., ill.)

Verbose article by a Chilean historian trying to explain that Chile became an authoritarian state after its independence from Spain because of its people's belief that the country was an "idyllic copy of Eden."

1259 Santiago: dónde estamos y hacia dónde vamos. Edición de Alexander Galetovic. Planos de Iván Poduje. Santiago, Chile: Centro de Estudios Públicos, 2006. 579 p.: bibl., ill., indexes, maps.

Attractive in its presentation and stimulating in its theses, this volume is an alternative response to the question posed by Chilean urban experts about the declining quality of life and the limits to be imposed on the uncontrolled expansion of Santiago. Written by authoritative specialists, this work is a primer for judging city sprawl during the second half of the 20th century, and a warning for the future.

1260 Schiappacasse C., Paulina. Segregación residencial y nichos étnicos de los inmigrantes internacionales en el Área Metropolitana de Santiago. (*Rev. Geogr. Norte Gd.*, 39, mayo 2008, p. 21–38, bibl., graphs, tables)

Around two percent of Santiago's inhabitants in 2002 were foreign-born. The author details jobs, education, and living quarters of Peruvians, Argentines, Koreans, Bolivians, and North Americans. They live in five districts of choice with no obvious patterns of segregation.

1261 Sillano, Mauricio; Margarita Greene; and Juan de Dios Ortúzar. Cuantificando la percepción de inseguridad ciudadana en barrios de escasos recursos. (*EURE/ Santiago*, 32:97, dic. 2006, p. 17–35, bibl., graphs, maps, photo, tables)

Revealing article on the sense of insecurity experienced by the inhabitants of low-income neighborhoods in Santiago due to the rising levels of crime and lack of police protection. Rampant crime occurrence has become the main existential concern for these popular segments.

1262 Soto, Maria Victoria and Joselyn Arriagada. Características dinámicas de ensenadas estructurales de Chile central: Maitencillo-Cachagua y Papudo, región de Valparaíso. (*Rev. Geogr. Norte Gd.*, 38, dic. 2007, p. 99–112, bibl., graphs, maps, tables)

Two "headland bay beaches" have been modeled by tectonic displacements along active fault lines and fine-tuned by wave erosion and rip-current effects.

1263 Soto, Maria Victoria et al. Carta geomorfológica de la sección central y occidental de la Región Metropolitana de Santiago. (*Invest. Geogr./Santiago*, 39, 2007, p. 28–61, bibl., maps)

Different structural landforms and minor geomorphological features, such as slopes, glacis, colluvial depositions, and stream terraces, are surveyed and presented in a large scale chart of the Central Valley and the coastal range covering the western half of the Metropolitan Region of Santiago. The quality of the geomorphological chart is excellent.

1264 Stackhouse, Jill. Urban land use and the entrepreneurial state: a case study of Pudahuel, Santiago, Chile during the military regime, 1973–1989. (*J. Lat. Am. Geogr.*, 8:1, 2009, p. 99–127, bibl., graph, maps, photos)

During the Pinochet regime, the outskirts of Pudahuel in Greater Santiago became a showcase for the housing and urban development policies introduced by military rule. Social housing programs, population densification, municipal realignment, and public-private partnerships were promoted by the state producing significant landscape changes on this northern urban fringe.

1265 Van Dam, Chris. Empresas forestales y comunidades rurales en el Centro-Sur de Chile: externalidades sociales de un modelo "exitoso." (*Debate Agrar.*, 40/41, julio 2006, p. 225–243)

Critique of the forestry sector of the Chilean economy which, in the view of the author, in its search for new land has short-changed modest peasants and Mapuche Indians.

1266 Vidal Rojas, Rodrigo. El Método de los Valores Tipológicos (MVT): ideas para un método de identificación y de pre-valoración cualitativa de áreas a urbanizar. (*Rev. Geogr. Norte Gd.*, 39, mayo 2008, p. 39–58, bibl., graphs, maps, tables)

Generalities about the spatial distribution of land prices in Santiago de Chile using a "typological value index" derived from 22 parameters which are supposed to provide a price gauge according to accessibility and location attractiveness.

PARAGUAY

1267 Fogel, Ramón B. La cuestión socioambiental en el Paraguay. Asunción: Centro de Estudios Rurales Interdisciplinarios (CERI), 2006. 220 p.: bibl., ill., maps.

The eradication of two native communities from open lands in northern Paraguay is used to plead the case for the preservation of natives' traditional lands and their exemption from environmental laws. Author claims that Brazilian soy growers are dislodging Paraguayan natives from their ancestral lands. For additional comment, see item **2645**.

1268 Gade, Daniel W. Paraguay 1975: thinking back on the fieldwork movement. (*J. Lat. Am. Geogr.*, 5:1, 2006, p. 31–49, bibl., map)

Author prizes fieldwork as a true source of geographical inquiry. Citing his experience in Paraguay in 1975, he purports that fieldwork stimulates geographical imagination and allows landscape analysis and interpretation that is not found in the travelogues of journalists or travelers.

1269 Ramírez, Juan Isidro. La paz del Chaco: la defensa de la línea de hitos. Asunción: [s.n.], 2005. 370 p.: maps.

Detailed presentation of juridical documentation supporting the adjudication of large tracts of Chaco territory to Paraguay after the war with Bolivia (1935–39). Interest-

ing work on the boundary disputes between the two countries.

1270 Vázquez, Fabricio. Territorio y población: nuevas dinámicas regionales en el Paraguay. Asunción: Fondo de Población de las Naciones Unidas: GTZ: Asociación Paraguaya de Estudios de Población, 2006. 194 p.: bibl., ill., maps. (Serie Investigaciones—población y desarrollo; 3)

Original treatise on the regional units of Paraguay and the dynamics of the relations between the centers of political or economic power and the several "peripheries" of the country. This first study on the internal linkages in this rather dysfunctional country is illustrated with original flow diagrams and modern display materials.

URUGUAY

1271 Luque Azcona, Emilio José. Ciudad y poder: la construcción material y simbólica del Montevideo colonial, 1723–1810. Madrid: Consejo Superior de Investigaciones Científicas, Escuela de Estudios Hispano-Americanos; Sevilla: Univ. de Sevilla: Diputación de Sevilla, 2007. 356 p.: bibl., ill., maps. (Col. americana/Univ. de Sevilla; 31) (Serie Nuestra América; 22)

Interesting historical monograph about the Spanish colonial authorities' attempt to construct and solidify a bulwark on the eastern margin of the Río de la Plata estuary with the purpose of deterring European rivals from establishing bridgeheads in this geopolitically sensitive corner of the Spanish empire.

BRAZIL

CHRISTIAN BRANNSTROM, *Associate Professor of Geography, Texas A&M University*

ALTHOUGH THE AMAZONIAN ENVIRONMENT-DEVELOPMENT THEME, noted in *HLAS 61* and *HLAS 63*, continued to be well represented in the 2005–2008 census period, new areas in geographical scholarship have appeared. The work of Valladares (item **1405**) displays a new approach to the study of Brazil's favelas or shantytowns. Valladares, who has numerous publications on favelas dating from the mid-1960s, is concerned with how favelas were "invented" by elite observers, urban planners, social scientists, and others. She draws special attention to the work of French priest Louis-Joseph Lebret, and his alliance with Bishop Helder Câmara in the 1950s, and the more recent construction of "virtual" favelas. Another important contribution to urban geography is Leite's (item **1344**) work on the gentrification of the Old Recife neighborhood. Adapted from the author's PhD dissertation completed at the Universidade de Campinas (UNICAMP), Leite details the political and social aspects of historic preservation in Recife. He is especially interested in how culture is commodified and "counter-uses" of urban space by the area's poor people. Sánchez (item **1390**) touches on the themes that Leite covers by analyzing Curitiba and Barcelona in comparative context. Based on her 2001 PhD dissertation completed in geography at the Universidade de São Paulo, her discussion of Curitiba's takes readers to the inner workings of urban planning and city-marketing.

The historical-environmental theme was strongly represented. Espindola's treatment of the regional historical geography of a relatively unknown area (item **1317**) is the product of the author's PhD dissertation in economic history at the Universidade de São Paulo. Drawing significant inspiration from geographic literatures, Espindola focuses on the idea of the Rio Doce, in Minas Gerais and Espírito Santo, as an invented "sertão" or hinterland serving as a geographical "Other." He reconstructs government attempts during the 1800s to establish fluvial transport on the Doce; this transport imperative fomented the state's many violent confrontations with Botocudo peoples, and set the stage for 20th century attempts to build railroads into the Rio Doce. Ricardo Ribeiro's two-volume work on the Cerrado of Minas Gerais, based on his doctoral dissertation completed at the Universidade Federal Rural de Rio de Janeiro's interdisciplinary Development, Agriculture, and Society graduate program, are beautifully illustrated and passionately written. Volume one (item **1380**), which ends in the mid 1800s, is based on archival and published sources. The strengths are his treatment of indigenous peoples and discussion of the Cerrado as a rebellious space in which various groups opposed to Brazilian and Portuguese authorities sought refuge. Ribeiro's second volume (item **1381**) is based on ethnographic work in various communities in the Cerrado of Minas, in which he argues that traditional resource users have been threatened by private property owners interested in commercial crops or livestock, and by environmental laws that criminalize traditional uses of flora and fauna.

Amazonian topics attracted significant attention on three fronts. First, numerous journal articles represent continued work on smallholder land uses, road construction, land violence, and unofficial road building (items **1277**, **1296**, and **1399**). Geographic implications of land uses and government policies are another major theme (items **1322** and **1363**), complemented by studies of frontier agricultural dynamics (items **1287**, **1293**, **1302**, **1335**, **1356**, and **1388**).

Second, Drummond and Pereira's book on Amapá state represents the return of a familiar topic to Amazonian studies, but, in this case, with a different approach. Their focus on a mining firm that worked on manganese deposits since the mid-1950s stresses how government benefited from royalties. They argue that Amapa's strong performance in socioeconomic indicators is fruit of wise application of royalties, and their research pays careful attention to both ICOMI, the Brazilian firm that partnered with US mining, and state-generated data. Third, Becker's new work on Amazonian geopolitics (item **1284**) aims to establish a new way of thinking about the topic, by arguing that the legal Amazon represents a new role in Brazil, compared to the 1970s and 1980s; she also argues that areas that were used by low-intensity systems are now being used more intensively. Her book emphasizes that the region's new actors, such as traditional peoples and state governments, exert considerably more power than a decade ago.

The 20th-century history of Brazilian geography received a major contribution from Heliana Angotti Salgueiro's edited collection on French geographer Pierre Monbeig (item **1342**) (also see *HLAS 51:3279* for Monbeig). In 2001, Salgueiro organized a conference on Monbeig's work and contribution to Brazilian geography; her edited collection includes various papers that situate Monbeig in terms of his scholarly production and his broader context. The book also reproduces some of Monbeig's previously unpublished photographs held in France's Centre National de la Recherche Scientifique. The collection also includes an essay on Monbeig's archive, which was donated to the Universidade de São Paulo in 1990.

1272 Abordagens geográficas de Goiás: o natural e o social na contemporaneidade. Organização de Maria Geralda de Almeida. Textos de Antônio Teixeira Neto *et al.* Goiânia, Brazil: Gráfica UFG, 2002. 260 p.: bibl., maps.

Edited volume covering the tourist development of Goiás, demographic change, urban-economic dynamics, and conservation units in the state, among other topics.

1273 Abordagens teórico-metodológicas em geografia agrária. Organização de Glaucio José Marafon, João Rua, and Miguel Angelo Ribeiro. Rio de Janeiro: EdUERJ, 2007. 329 p.: bibl., ill., maps.

Edited volume attempting to provide a description of state-of-the-art agricultural geography, with chapters focusing on the recent development of the field, social movements, and family farming. Notable chapters cover artisanal cachaça production in Minas Gerais and the "faxinal" system of forest extraction in an Araucaria region of Paraná.

1274 Açaí (Euterpe oleracea Mart.): possibilidades e limites para o desenvolvimento sustentável no estuário amazônico. Edição de Mário Augusto Gonçalves Jardim, Leila Mourão, and Monika Grossmann. Belém, Brazil: Museu Paraense Emílio Goeldi, 2004. 274 p.: bibl., ill. (Col. Adolpho Ducke)

Edited volume covering various aspects of Açaí palm ecology, cultivation, and marketing with respect to the eastern Amazon. Chapters cover cases of Açaí commercialization, stressing achievements and difficulties.

1275 Acevedo Marin, Rosa Elizabeth. Julgados da terra: cadeia de apropriação e atores sociais em conflito na Ilha de Colares, Pará. Belém, Brazil: Univ. Federal do Pará, 2004. 260 p.: bibl., ill. (some col.), maps (some col.).

Detailed case study of an Afro-Brazilian community, originating from a Quilombo settlement, near Marajó Island in Pará state. Discusses access to land, rural production, and demographic dynamics. Land conflicts with large producers are emphasized. Historical background on the Quilombo is provided.

1276 Agroecologia e sustentabilidade no meio rural: experiências e reflexões de agentes de desenvolvimento local. Organizacão de Paulo Emílio Lovato e Wilson Schmidt. Chapecó, Brazil: Argos Editora Universitária, 2006. 151 p.: bibl. (Col. Debates)

Edited volume covering the experiences of agroecology as practiced on small farms, especially in southern states of Paraná, Santa Catarina, and Rio Grande do Sul. Chapters cover agroecological farmers' markets, medicinal plants, and civil society organizations promoting agroecology.

1277 Aldrich, Stephen P. et al. Land-cover and land-use change in the Brazilian Amazon: smallholders, ranchers, and frontier stratification. (*Econ. Geogr.*, 82:3, July 2006, p. 265–288, bibl., maps, tables)

Argues that recent deforestation in study area is mostly the result of smallholders rather than the creation of large pasture by large-scale ranchers. Study analyzes satellite data and panel data obtained from land users in Uruará, Pará, in 1996 and 2002.

1278 L'Amazonie brésilienne et le développement durable: expériences et enjeux en milieu rural. Sous la direction de Christophe Albaladejo et Xavier Arnauld de Sartre. Préface de Philippe Léna. Paris: L'Harmattan, 2005. 286 p.: bibl., ill., maps. (Coll. Recherches Amériques latines)

Edited book focusing on sustainable development using ethnographic approaches to frontier settlement in peasant and traditional communities.

1279 Araújo, Severina Garcia de. Assentamentos rurais: trajetórias dos trabalhadores assentados e cultura política. Natal, Brazil: EDUFRN, 2005. 272 p.: bibl.

Case study of one agrarian reform settlement in Rio Grande do Norte. Trade-union politics and social movement struggles are detailed.

1280 Arima, Eugenio Y. et al. Fire in the Brazilian Amazon: a spatially explicit model for policy impact analysis. (*J. Reg. Sci.*, 47:3, 2007, p. 541–567, bibl., graphs, maps, tables)

Uses modeling to argue that prices for beef and soy received by Amazonian farmers and ranchers are positively correlated with increased occurrence of fire. Posits that improved protection of conservation units could reduce fire.

1281 Arrais, Tadeu Pereira Alencar. Geografia contemporânea de Goiás. Goiânia, Brazil: Editora Vieira, 2004. 164 p.: bibl., ill., maps.

Regional geography of Goiás, with several useful maps of Goiânia's urbanization and discussion of global aspects of the state's economic geography. Ends with an essay on what the author refers to as the "three Brasílias" as a means to understand the federal district's distinct territories.

1282 Baptista, Sandra R. Metropolization and forest recovery in southern Brazil: a multiscale analysis of the Florianópolis city-region, Santa Catarina state,

1970 to 2005. (*Ecol. Soc. (online)*, 13:2, Dec. 2008, http://www.ecologyandsociety.org/vol13/iss2/art5/, bibl., graphs, maps, photo)

Analyzes land change in the Florianópolis region of Santa Catarina, detailing how forest cover has increased while coastal plains have been urbanized during a 35-year period. Key factors driving change include economic development, environmental policies, and new value given to forest-covered lands.

1283 Baptista, Sandra R. and Thomas K. Rudel. A re-emerging Atlantic forest?: urbanization, industrialization and the forest transition in Santa Catarina, southern Brazil. (*Environ. Conserv./Cambridge*, 33:2, June 2006, p. 195–202, bibl., map, tables)

Study argues that forest cover in Santa Catarina has increased because of urbanization and industrialization, in addition to an increase in planted forests. Notes that the "new" Atlantic forest is less diverse biologically than the former Atlantic forest.

1284 Becker, Bertha K. Amazônia: geopolítica na virada do III milênio. Rio de Janeiro: Garamond, 2004. 168 p.: bibl., ill., maps. (Terra mater)

Important work by well-known scholar focuses on new trends in Amazonian geopolitics, such as inter-regional economic dynamics, government investment plans for infrastructure, and the impact of new technologies. Identifies new and emerging regions and subregions. Argues that new frontiers are active in the Amazon, the region is a major player in global "natural capital," and the Amazon must be considered in its international dimensions.

1285 Belém: a cidade e o rio na Amazônia. Organização de Saint-Clair Cordeiro da Trindade Júnior and Marcos Alexandre Pimentel da Silva. Belém, Brazil: CFCH: Editora UFPA, 2005. 171 p.: bibl., ill., map.

Edited collection focusing on diverse topics, ranging from social aspects of rural Afro-Brazilian residents to urban land use.

1286 Betts, Richard A.; Yadvinder Malhi; and J. Timmons Roberts. The future of the Amazon: new perspectives from climate, ecosystem and social sciences. (*Philos. Trans.*, 363:1498, 2008, p. 1729–1735, bibl.)

Lead essay in a special journal issue devoted to the interaction between humans and the environment in the Amazon. Argues that Amazon deforestation threatens local climate and global carbon cycles, but that policy and governance challenges in dealing with deforestation are large.

1287 Bicalho, Ana Maria de Souza Mello and Scott William Hoefle. On the cutting edge of the Brazilian frontier: new (and old) agrarian questions in the South Central Amazon. (*J. Peasant Stud.*, 35:1, Jan. 2008, p. 1–38, photos)

Uses models from Lenin and Kautsky to interpret recent agrarian change in southern Amazonas state. Argues that farmers in Cerrado areas are following a Leninist model, while farmers in riverine areas are following a Kautskian model, with the latter possibly reverting to a Leninist model because of federal environmental policies.

1288 Bombardi, Larissa Mies. O bairro reforma agrária e o processo de territorialização camponesa. São Paulo: Annablume, 2004. 395 p.: bibl., ill., maps. (Geografias e adjacências)

Detailed study of a land-reform unit near Campinas, São Paulo state, covering the expropriation of the landholding, settlement of small farmers, and micro-level study of individual farming and land-use practices in time and space.

1289 Brandão, Paulo Roberto Baqueiro. Geografias da presença galega na cidade da Bahia. Salvador, Brazil: EDUFBA, 2005. 144 p.: bibl., maps.

Studies the migration of natives of Galicia, Spain, to the city of Salvador, Brazil. Focuses on the specific places in the city where Galicians located, the business they established, and the social networks they created. Verifies the continued presence of Galician-owned hotels and restaurants in Salvador.

1290 Brannstrom, Christian. Decentralising water resource management in Brazil. (*Eur. J. Dev. Res.*, 16:1, Spring 2004, p. 214–234, bibl., map, table)

Discusses decentralization in terms of actors, powers, and accountability using case-study material from the states of Bahia, São Paulo, and Paraná. Concludes that major differences exist among experiences of decentralization.

1291 Brannstrom, Christian et al. Land change in the Brazilian savanna (cerrado), 1986–2002: comparative analysis and land-use policy implications. (*Land Use Policy*, 25:4, Oct. 2008, p. 579–595)

Comparison of two Cerrado regions, in eastern Mato Grosso and western Bahia states, based on interpretation of satellite imagery. Finds that Cerrado land cover is similar in either region, but fragmentation is more severe in eastern Mato Grosso. Findings suggest ways to better implement Brazil's forest policy.

1292 Brasília, controvérsias ambientais. Organização de Aldo Paviani and Luiz Alberto de Campos Gouvêa. Brasília: Editora UnB, 2003. 316 p.: bibl., ill., maps. (Col. Brasília)

Edited book covering Brasília's environmental issues. Chapters discuss urban growth patterns, environmental psychology, environmental quality, and land-use zoning processes.

1293 Browder, John O. et al. Revisiting theories of frontier expansion in the Brazilian Amazon: a survey of the colonist farming population in Rondônia's post-frontier, 1992–2002. (*World Dev.*, 36:8, Aug. 2008, p. 1469–1492, bibl.)

Presents analysis of a major study that collected panel data from 240 farms in Rondônia over a 10-year period. Tests results against three major theoretical approaches, finding that none adequately explains their observations. Indicates as major issues socioeconomic stratification, increase in value of farm production, and the rising importance of urban centers.

1294 Brown, J. Christopher et al. Multitemporal, moderate-spatial-resolution remote sensing of modern agricultural production and land modification in the Brazilian Amazon. (*GIScience Remote Sensing*, 44:2, April/June 2007, p. 117–148)

Discussion of new methods based on analysis of remote-sensing data with high temporal spatial resolution and moderate spatial resolution. Argues that method provides near real-time monitoring of deforestation in addition to discrimination of land uses, such as double-cropping, that replace forest cover.

1295 Cabral, Diogo de Carvalho and **Susana Cesco.** Árvores do rio, floresta do povo: a instituição das "madeiras-de-lei" no Rio de Janeiro e na ilha de Santa Catarina (Brasil) no final do período colonial. (*Luso-Braz. Rev.*, 44:2, 2007, p. 50–86, graph, tables)

Aims to understand the "madeiras-de-lei" institution that developed in the colonial period because of interactions between state officials and forest users. Contributes to debate on this topic that began with Dean's *With Broadax and Firebrand: The Destruction of the Brazilian Atlantic Forest* (1995) and Miller's *Fruitless Trees: Portuguese Conservation and Brazil's Colonial Timber* (see *HLAS 60:3189*).

1296 Caldas, Marcellus M. *et al.* Theorizing land cover and land use change: the peasant economy of Amazonian deforestation. (*Ann. Assoc. Am. Geogr.*, 97:1, March 2007, p. 86–110, bibl., graphs, maps, tables)

Develops theoretical model from von Thünen and Chayanov applied to the household scale to explain and predict land-cover and land-use change. Model is applied to the case of Uruará, Pará state. Concludes that household-scale variables must be included in future modeling efforts, and that explanations stressing market factors are incomplete since they overlook dynamics within households.

1297 Campos Júnior, Carlos Teixeira de. A construção da cidade: formas de produção imobiliária em Vitória. Ilha de Vitória, Brazil: Flor & Cultura Editora, 2002. 161 p.: bibl., ill., maps.

Analysis of the construction of the built environment of Vitória, Espírito Santo, from the 1950s to the 1970s. Stresses the accumulation of capital to elites resulting from civil construction. Also covers labor relations in construction work.

1298 Carlos, Ana Fani Alessandri. O espaço urbano: novos escritos sobre a cidade. São Paulo: Contexto, 2004. 154 p.: bibl.

Collection of essays—mainly covering metropolitan São Paulo—by one of the country's leading urban geographers. Identifies several processes, including new forms

of urban planning and governance as well as new forms of relationships between the state and urban space. Housing is a major topic covered.

1299 Carvalho, Otamar de and **Cláudio Antonio Gonçalves Egler.** Alternativas de desenvolvimento para o nordeste semi-árido. Fortaleza, Brazil: Banco do Nordeste do Brasil, 2003. 204 p.: bibl., col. maps.

Proposal for alternative development strategies for Brazil's semi-arid northeastern region. Discussion focuses on ways to deal with water scarcity in terms of technology for irrigation and water management. Proposes the creation of a new agency that would be responsible for economic development in the entire semi-arid region.

1300 Castellanet, Christian *et al.* Des alliances internationales pour préserver la production de soja non génétiquement modifié au Brésil: enjeux et perspectives. (*Rev. Tiers monde*, 47:188, oct./déc. 2006, p. 755–772, bibl.)

Reviews the debate on genetically modified soy in Brazil during the 1990s, making reference to European policies. Focuses on the work of civil society organizations in southern Brazil and in Europe to establish a trade in non-GM soybeans to France.

1301 Cavenaghi, Airton José. O território paulista na iconografia oitocentista: mapas, desenhos e fotografias, análise de uma herança cotidiana. (*An. Mus. Paul.*, 14:1, jan./junho 2006, p. 195–241, bibl., ill., maps, photos)

Study of 19th-century cartographic representations of São Paulo state. Identifies key maps and other images pertaining to the state. Emphasizes how cartographers adjusted to local conditions.

1302 Caviglia-Harris, Jill L. and **Daniel W. Harris.** Integrating survey and remote sensing data to analyze land use at a fine scale: insights from agricultural households in the Brazilian Amazon. (*Int. Reg. Sci. Rev.*, 31:2, April 2008, p. 115–137)

Studies land-use decision making in Rondônia state, focusing on the creation of pasture. Argues that households with higher household income, lower soil fertility, and less use of hired labor tend to have more of their lands in pasture. Concludes that policies aiming to reduce deforestation among newly arrived settlers will be more effective than continuing to promote the same policies in long-settled areas.

1303 Ceccato, Vânia; Robert Haining; and **Tulio Kahn.** The geography of homicide in São Paulo, Brazil. (*Environ. Plann. A*, 39:7, 2007, p. 1632–1653, bibl., maps, tables)
Investigation of spatial patterns of homicide in São Paulo. Concludes that key factors in variations include poverty, land-use differences, drug markets, and firearm availability.

1304 Chase, Jacquelyn. Their space: security and service workers in a Brazilian gated community. (*Geogr. Rev.*, 98:4, Oct. 2008, p. 476–495, bibl., maps, photos)
Studies Belo Horizonte gardeners who maintain green spaces of elite residences on a daily basis. Argues that gardeners live in rural communities surrounding the gated residences, and that their daily gardening is essential to reduce fear of crime among inhabitants of the gated communities.

1305 Cidade de Manaus: visões interdisciplinares. Organização de José Aldemir de Oliveira, José Duarte Alecrim, and Thierry Ray Jehlen Gasnier. Manaus, Brazil: EDUA, 2003. 295 p.: bibl., ill.
Edited multidisciplinary volume focusing on various urban issues in Manaus, such as housing, vulnerability, urban gardens, and health.

1306 Coelho, Marco Antônio Tavares. Os descaminhos do São Francisco. Ilustrações de Maria Helena Andrés. São Paulo: Paz e Terra, 2005. 272, 16 p.: bibl., ill. (some col.), map.
Historical geography of the São Francisco River Valley, stressing human settlements near the river, human impacts on the river, and various government programs aimed at generating hydroelectricity or supporting irrigated agriculture. Criticizes inter-basin water transfer plans that would channel part of the São Francisco river's water toward the arid north.

1307 Colóquio Internacional sobre Justiça Ambiental, Trabalho e Cidadania, Niterói, Rio de Janeiro, 2001. Justiça ambiental e cidadania. Organização de Henri Acselrad, Selene Herculano e José Augusto Pádua. Rio de Janeiro: Relume Dumará, 2004. 315 p.: bibl.
Edited volume on environmental justice, mostly focusing on Brazilian cases. Key chapters report cases of Afro-Brazilians in environmental conflicts and civil society movements against pollution or large infrastructure projects. Some chapters cover North American topics.

1308 Compans, Rose. Empreendedorismo urbano: entre o discurso e a prática. São Paulo: Editora UNESP: ANPUR, 2005. 303 p.: bibl.
Studies urban governance in Rio de Janeiro. Covers trends in North America and Europe and focuses on Rio's Barra da Tijuca.

1309 Coy, Martin. Gated communities and urban fragmentation in Latin America: the Brazilian experience. (*GeoJournal/Boston*, 66:2, 2006, p. 121–132)
Analyzes gated communities in Brazil as resulting from the action of real estate companies, target groups who expect security in housing, and public officials. Describes phases of expansion, internal structure, and consequences for urban planning.

1310 Cruzando fronteiras disciplinares: um panorama dos estudos migratórios. Organização de Helion Póvoa Neto and Ademir Pacelli Ferreira. Rio de Janeiro: FAPERJ, Fundação Carlos Chagas Filho de Amparo à Pesquisa do Estado do Rio de Janeiro: Editora Revan, 2005. 421 p.: bibl., ill.
Edited volume covering various aspects of migration. Case studies cover internal and international migration, as well as themes such as identity, subjectivity, and power.

1311 Debaixo da lona: tendências e desafios regionais da luta pela posse da terra e da reforma agrária no Brasil. Organização de Antonio Maurílio Alencar Feitosa, Janete Aparecida Gomes Zuba, and João Cleps Junior. Goiânia, Brazil: Editora da UCG, 2006. 277 p.: bibl., ill., maps.
This appropriately titled edited volume details the experiences of small farmers and landless workers to obtain secure

land title and rural credit. Cases focus on the expulsion of traditional peoples from eucalyptus plantations, the education policies of the landless movement (MST), and various attempts to secure land in Minas Gerais and the Federal District.

1312 Desenvolvimento sustentável e gestão ambiental nas cidades: estratégias a partir de Porto Alegre. Organização de Rualdo Menegat e Gerson Almeida. Textos de David Satterthwaite *et al.* Porto Alegre, Brazil: Editora da UFRGS, 2004. 422 p.: bibl., ill., index.

Covers various aspects of urban sustainability. Major topics include urban planning, democratic politics, greenspace management, and green construction standards. The case of Porto Alegre is offered as a case-study example. Global perspectives are highlighted.

1313 Diversidade, espaço e relações étnico-raciais: o negro na geografia do Brasil. Organização de Renato Emerson dos Santos. Belo Horizonte, Brazil: Autêntica, 2007. 203 p.: ill., maps. (Cultura negra e identidades)

Edited book focusing on geographical aspects of Afro-Brazilians, considering racial segregation in urban areas and runaway slave communities, among other topics. One chapter of the book is dedicated to a discussion of a 2003 law mandating the teaching of Afro-Brazilian history and culture.

1314 Drummond, José Augusto and Mariângela de Araújo Póvoas Pereira. O Amapá nos tempos do manganês: um estudo sobre o desenvolvimento de um estado amazônico 1943–2000. Rio de Janeiro: Garamond, 2007. 498 p.: bibl., ill., maps. (Col. Terra Mater)

Studies the economic development of Amapá, focusing on the mining of manganese at the Serra do Navio site. Argues that improvements in the state's economic and social development between 1970 and 1996 are largely the result of a private mining firm and its relations with the state.

1315 Durigan, Giselda; Marinez Ferreira de Siqueira; and Geraldo Antonio Daher Correa Franco. Threats to the Cerrado remnants of the state of São Paulo, Brazil. (*Scientia Agrícola*, 64:4, July/Aug. 2007, p. 355–363, bibl., graphs, table)

Considers pasture, sugarcane, and roads as main threats to Cerrado vegetation. Based on field evaluation of 81 fragments of Cerrado.

1316 Ecologia de pescadores da Mata Atlântica e da Amazônia. Organizacão de Alpina Begossi. São Paulo: Editora Hucitec: NEPAM/UNICAMP: NUPAUB/USP: FAPESP, 2004. 332 p.: bibl., ill. (some col.), col. maps. (Ecologia e cultura; 6)

Edited book covering various aspects of the cultural ecology of fishing communities. Ethnobotany, eating taboos, fisheries management systems, and conservation implications are included, among other topics.

1317 Espindola, Haruf Salmen. Sertão do Rio Doce. Governador Valadares, Brazil: Editora Univale; Bauru, Brazil: EDUSC; Aimorés, Brazil: Instituto Terra, 2005. 485 p.: bibl., maps. (Col. História)

Study of the 19th-century environmental history of the Vale do Rio Doce. Analyzes various state policies aimed at effective occupation and natural resource extraction and describes the resistance of indigenous peoples. For historian's comment, see *HLAS 64:1606.*

1318 Estudos de geografia regional: o urbano, o rural e o rurbano na região de Passo Fundo. Organização de Ana Maria Radaelli da Silva *et al.* Passo Fundo, Brazil: Univ. de Passo Fundo, UPF Editora, 2004. 282 p.: bibl., ill., maps.

Edited book on the geography of Passo Fundo in north-central Rio Grande do Sul covering urban and agricultural geography. Notable chapters cover areas that are considered to be rural-urban hybrids and the growth of new economic activities in both urban and rural areas.

1319 Ewers, Robert M. and William F. Laurance. Scale-dependent patterns of deforestation in the Brazilian Amazon. (*Environ. Conserv./Cambridge*, 33:2, June 2006, p. 203–211, bibl., graphs, maps, photos, tables)

Paper confirms hypothesis that small-scale farmers and large-scale soy farmers create different deforestation patterns.

1320 Expansão e trajetórias da pecuária na Amazônia: Pará, Brasil. Brasília: Editora UnB, 2004. 161 p.: bibl., maps.

Studies causes and consequences of expansion of beef and dairy cattle herds in Pará. Focuses on reasons that ranchers expand herds and choose certain pasture-management strategies. Highly ranked factors include the low-risk nature of cattle herds, good conditions of market access within Brazil, and favorable conditions for forming and maintaining pasture. Suggests that current environmental laws are too rigid to encourage compliance among ranchers.

1321 Falconi, Luiz Carlos and **José Nicolau Heck.** A depredação das áreas de preservação permanente e de reserva legal florestal do bioma Cerrado como causa de desapropriação da propriedade rural por interesse social. (*Rev. Inf. Legis.*, 42:168, out./dez. 2005, p. 75–99, bibl., tables)

Argument for the expropriation of farmland in which Permanent Protection and Legal Reserve areas are being cleared, which is prohibited under Brazilian law. The legal case hinges on the "social function" of land, as enshrined in Brazil's 1988 Constitution.

1322 Fearnside, Philip Martin. Brazil's Cuiabá-Santarém (BR–163) Highway: the environmental cost of paving a soybean corridor through the Amazon. (*Environ. Manag.*, 39:5, May 2007, p. 601–614, bibl., maps)

Enumerates various estimated environmental costs, mainly increased deforestation, of proposed road paving in the Amazon. Argues that road paving should begin after lawlessness and impunity is reduced in the region of the BR-163 highway.

1323 Fearnside, Philip Martin and **Paulo Maurício Lima de Alencastro Graça.** BR-319: Brazil's Manaus-Porto Velho Highway and the potential impact of linking the arc of deforestation to Central Amazonia. (*Environ. Manag.*, 38:5, Nov. 2006, p. 705–716, bibl., maps)

Argues that proposed repaving of a key road in the Amazon would increase deforestation. Proposes that several policies for conservation be undertaken before repaving, and encourages delaying the project.

1324 Fernandes, Edésio. Implementing the urban reform agenda in Brazil. (*Environ. Urban.*, 19:1, April 2007, p. 177–189)

Describes urban reform process beginning with the 1988 Constitution. Argues that legal reform, institutional change, and social mobilization are still required to overcome spatial and social exclusion in Brazilian cities.

1325 Formiga-Johnsson, Rosa Maria; Lori Kumler; and **Maria Carmen Lemos.** The politics of bulk water pricing in Brazil: lessons from the Paraíba do Sul Basin. (*Water Policy*, 9:1, 2007, p. 87–104)

Reports on the factors responsible for the successful implementation of bulk water pricing in a major river basin of southeastern Brazil. Study focuses on the combination of state and market forces, as well as public participation.

1326 Freeman, James. Great, good, and divided: the politics of public space in Rio de Janeiro. (*J. Urban Aff.*, 30:5, 2008, p. 529–556)

Uses ethnographic methods in analysis of a public beach in Rio de Janeiro's Zona Sul area as a contested space between socioeconomic classes. Focuses on the influence of transport and constructed notions of class and privilege.

1327 Garcia, Ricardo Alexandrino and **Adriana de Miranda-Ribeiro.** Movimentos migratórios em Minas Gerais: efeitos diretos e indiretos da migração de retorno—1970–1980, 1981–1991 e 1990–2000. (*Rev. Bras. Estud. Popul.*, 22:1, jan./junho 2005, p. 159–175, bibl., graphs, maps, tables)

Focuses on migrants who return to Minas Gerais and finds that they outnumber people leaving the state. The higher rate of return migration is attributed to the return of migrants to Minas from São Paulo.

1328 Garcia, Ricardo Alexandrino; Mauro Borges Lemos; and **José Alberto Magno de Carvalho.** As transformações das áreas de influência migratória dos pólos econômicos brasileiros nos períodos 1980–1991 e 1991–2000. (*Rev. Bras. Estud. Popul.*, 21:2, julho/dez. 2004, p. 259–281, bibl., maps, tables)

Examines internal migration and regional dynamics over a 20-year period from 1980–2000, concluding that major changes have occurred during this time period. Using a gravity model, study divides

Brazil into 84 economic centers that attract migrants, and authors track changes over time.

1329 Garmany, Jeff. The spaces of social movements: o Movimento dos Trabalhadores Rurais Sem Terra from a sociospatial perspective. (*Space Polity,* 12:3, Dec. 2008, p. 311–328)

Uses ideas of spatial production from Henri Lefebvre to analyze settlements of the MST in Ceará state. Considers representations of space, spatial practices, and spaces of representations. Argues that the success of the MST may result from the movement's attention to social space.

1330 Geografia, meio ambiente e desenvolvimento. Organização de Márcia Siqueira de Carvalho. Londrina, Brazil: Univ. Estadual de Londrina, 2003. 205 p.: bibl., ill., maps.

Collection of essays, produced by students in the geography graduate program at the Univ. Estadual de Londrina, detailing environment-population issues in Paraná state. Papers address topics such as agrarian reform settlement, urban planning, and watershed management.

1331 Geografia: temas sobre cultura e espaço. Organização de Zeny Rosendahl e Roberto Lobato Corrêa. Rio de Janeiro: EdUerj, 2005. 226 p.: bibl. (Col. Geografia cultural; 12)

Edited volume aiming to synthesize current work in cultural geography in Brazil. Essays cover monuments, cinema, place names, relegion, and gender.

1332 Geografias das metrópoles. Organização de Ana Fani Alessandri Carlos and Ariovaldo Umbelino de Oliveira. São Paulo: Editora Contexto, 2006. 540 p.: bibl., ill., maps.

Edited book by two renowned geographers at Univ. de São Paulo. Chapters cover a wide range of urban topics relating mainly to the city of São Paulo. Some essays are broad, covering 450 years of urban change, while others focus on issues such as housing and the banking sector in particular districts of the city.

1333 Geografias entrelaçadas: ambiente rural e urbano no sul de Santa Catarina. Organização de Luiz Fernando Scheibe,

Sandra Maria de Arruda Furtado, and Maria Dolores Buss. Florianópolis, Brazil: Editora da UFSC; Criciúma, Brazil: Editora da Unesc, 2005. 419 p.: bibl., ill., maps.

Edited volume on southern Santa Catarina covering physical and human geography topics. Detailed case studies covering rice production, hydrogeology, agrochemical contamination, Pinus plantations, ceramic tile production, and urban change in the city of Criciúma, among others.

1334 Globalização e estrutura urbana. Organização de Sueli Ramos Schiffer. Textos de Csaba Deák *et al.* São Paulo: Editora Hucitec: FAPESP, 2004. 305 p.: bibl., ill., CD-ROM. (Arte e vida urbana; 8)

Edited collection on globalization processes affecting São Paulo city. Chapters cover inter-state fiscal conflicts, urban labor markets, urban growth dynamics, and infrastructure and public services.

1335 Hecht, Susanna B. Factories, forests, fields and families: gender and neoliberalism in extractive reserves. (*J. Agrarian Change,* 7:3, July 2007, p. 316–347, bibl., tables)

Paper studies women's role in a forest-products industry in the Amazon. Argues that invisible work by women was not contemplated by proponents of a development project.

1336 Hoefle, Scott William. Twisting the knife: frontier violence in the Central Amazon of Brazil. (*J. Peasant Stud.,* 33:3, July 2006, p. 445–478, bibl., graphs, map, photos, tables)

Studies frontier violence in Roraima and Amazonas states using a variety of methods. Concludes that violence is a product of conflict over resources, and most common in areas where agriculture has replaced forest, rather than in areas settled for several decades.

1337 Hogan, Daniel Joseph. Mobilidade populacional, sustentabilidade ambiental e vulnerabilidade social. (*Rev. Bras. Estud. Popul.,* 22:2, julho/dez. 2005, p. 323–338, bibl., table)

Argues that major intra-regional population movements continue to occur, with corresponding impacts on natural resources that demand attention. Meso-

and micro-scale land-use zoning is proposed as a policy tool to manage the continuing migratory processes.

1338 Impactos dos assentamentos: um estudo sobre o meio rural brasileiro. Textos de Sérgio Leite *et al.* Brasília: Ministério do Desenvolvimento Agrário, INCRA: NEAD; São Paulo: Editora UNESP, 2004. 391 p.: bibl., col. ill., col. maps. (Estudos NEAD; 6)

Significant country-wide survey of agrarian reform settlements. Topics covered include state provision of infrastructure, social relations within settlements, crop and livestock production of settlements, and access to credit and technology. Study concludes that agrarian-reform settlements have had a positive impact on livelihoods and local markets.

1339 Itinerários geográficos. Organização de Flávio Rodrigues do Nascimento. Textos de Amélia Cristina Alves Bezerra, Claudio Ubiratan Gonçalves *et al.* Niterói, Brazil: EdUFF, 2007. 358 p.: ill., tables.

Collection of essays produced by students at the Univ. Federal Fluminense covering urban and rural topics. Notable essays cover celebrations in northeastern Brazil, regionalist politics in Rio Grande do Sul, and new socioeconomic territories in Goiás.

1340 Jepson, Wendy E. Private agricultural colonization on a Brazilian frontier, 1970–1980. (*J. Hist. Geogr.*, 32:4, Oct. 2006, p. 839–863, maps, tables)

Argues that private firms settled large numbers of farmers from southern Brazil in Mato Grosso's Cerrado lands, against prevailing interpretations of state-led settlement.

1341 Jepson, Wendy E. Producing a modern agricultural frontier: firms and cooperatives in eastern Mato Grosso, Brazil. (*Econ. Geogr.*, 82:3, July 2006, p. 289–316, bibl., graph, maps, tables)

Uses an institutional approach to study two organizations that led agricultural colonization during the 1970s and 1980s to the Cerrado region. Concludes that the organizations reduced production costs and allowed farmers to respond to challenges of crop production in frontier conditions.

1342 Jornada Internacional Pierre Monbeig, Universidade de São Paulo, 2001. Pierre Monbeig e a geografia humana brasileira: a dinâmica da transformação. Organização de Heliana Angotti Salgueiro. Bauru, Brazil: Pró-Reitoria de Cultura e Extensão Universitária: FAPESP: EDUSC, 2006. 342 p.: bibl., ill. (some col.), maps. (Território & cidade)

Important edited volume contemplating the work of French geographer Pierre Monbeig and his influence on human geography in Brazil. Contains a valuable bibliography, which includes his scholarly work and his numerous newspaper articles, and a chronology.

1343 Klink, Carlos A. and **Ricardo B. Machado.** Conservation of the Brazilian Cerrado. (*Conserv. Biol.*, 19:3, June 2005, p. 707–713, bibl., tables)

Synthesizes key threats to Cerrado biodiversity and the relatively modest efforts to establish conservation units.

1344 Leite, Rogério Proença. Contra-usos da cidade: lugares e espaço público na experiência urbana contemporânea. Campinas, Brazil: UNICAMP; Aracaju, Brazil: Editora Univ. Federal de Sergipe, 2004. 342 p.: bibl., ill. (some col.), map.

Focuses on social implications of historic preservation in Recife. Discusses state politics of preservation and the gentrification process. Uses ethnographic approaches to argue that gentrified spaces constitute places for which people create meaning.

1345 Lemos, Maria Carmen and **João Lúcio Farias de Oliveira.** Can water reform survive politics?: institutional change and river basin management in Ceará, Northeast Brazil. (*World Dev.*, 32:12, Dec. 2004, p. 2121–2137, bibl., graph, map)

Studies the implementation of policies that decentralized water-resources management in Ceará state.

1346 Lima, Eirivelthon *et al.* Florestas familiares: um pacto sócio-ambiental entre a indústria madeireira e a agricultura familiar na Amazônia. Belém, Brazil: Instituto de Pesquisa Ambiental da Amazônia, 2003. 106 p.: bibl., col. ill., col. maps.

Reports on community–industry partnerships in forestry in the Amazon region. Argues that stimulating partnerships leads to cheaper, more effective, and socially just forest-management instead of favoring the growth of the timber industry. Also argues that forest certification schemes could strength partnerships.

1347 Macedo, Joseli. Urban land policy and new land tenure paradigms: legitimacy vs. legality in Brazilian cities. (*Land Use Policy*, 25:2, April 2008, p. 259–270)

Reviews urban land-tenure policies, especially the 2001 City Statute. Argues for policies that move away from legality and toward legitimacy as a way to improve land-tenure security for the urban poor.

1348 Magalhães Júnior, Antônio Pereira. Indicadores ambientais e recursos hídricos: realidade e perspectivas para o Brasil a partir da experiência francesa. Rio de Janeiro: Bertrand Brasil, 2007. 686 p.: bibl., ill., maps.

Study of Brazil's recent decentralization of water management, focusing on theoretical principles of water management, the formation of watershed committees in Brazil, and a case of the Rio Paraopeba committee in Minas Gerais state. Offers several suggestions to improve the current water-management system.

1349 Maslin, Mark et al. New views on an old forest: assessing the longevity, resilience and future of the Amazon rainforest. (*Trans. Inst. Br. Geogr.*, 30:4, 2005, p. 477–499, bibl., graphs, ill.)

Argues that the Amazon rainforest has existed for approximately 55 million years, but that current climatic conditions have no parallel record in the past, and thus warmer and drier conditions could adversely affect the forest.

1350 Mazzarollo, Juvêncio. A taipa da injustiça: esbanjamento econômico, drama social e holocausto ecológico em Itaipu. 2a ed., rev. e ampliada. Curitiba, Brazil: CPT-PR, Comissão Pastoral da Terra do Paraná; São Paulo: Edições Loyola, 2003. 203 p.: bibl., ill., map.

Studies the social impacts of the construction of the Itaipú hydroelectric dam in Paraná state. Details the implications of the removal of thousands of rural people from around the reservoir feeding the dam during the 1970s and 1980s. Pays special attention to the struggles of small farmers and indigenous peoples to obtain new parcels of land after being evicted.

1351 McCormick, Sabrina. The governance of hydro-electric dams in Brazil. (*J. Lat. Am. Stud.*, 39:2, May 2007, p. 227–261, map)

Studies the work of the state and civil society in competing positions regarding the ability of civil society groups to participate in discussions on hydroelectric dams. Studies six collaborative research projects that aim to improve participation of civil society groups.

1352 McGrath, David G. et al. Constructing a policy and institutional framework for an ecosystem-based approach to managing the Lower Amazon floodplain. (*Environ. Dev. Sustain.*, 10:5, 2008, p. 677–695)

Reports on land-tenure policies implemented by the National Institute for Colonization and Agrarian Reform that are thought to enable better co-management of resources in the Lower Amazon. Focuses on issues regarding fisheries and grazing of livestock on floodplain grasslands.

1353 Meireles Filho, João Carlos. O livro de ouro da Amazônia: mitos e verdades sobre a região mais cobiçada do planeta. Rio de Janeiro: Ediouro, 2004. 397 p.: bibl., ill. (some col.), index, maps. (Livros de ouro)

Aims to portray the "real" Amazon by debunking several "myths" and promoting "truths" about topics as varied as indigenous peoples, historical dynamics, land-occupation policies, natural resources, and current policies. Includes photographic essay by Araquém Alcântara.

1354 Mello, Marco Antonio da Silva and Arno Vogel. Gente das areias: história, meio ambiente e sociedade no litoral brasileiro, Maricá, RJ, 1975 a 1995. Niterói, Brazil: EdUFF, Univ. Federal Fluminense, 2004. 419 p.: bibl., ill., maps.

Study of cultural ecology of a fishing village north of Niterói in Rio de Janeiro state. Major topics include health care, intra-family relations, and fishing ecology of residents.

1355 Mendes, Felipe. Economia e desenvolvimento do Piauí. Teresina, Brazil: Prefeitura Municipal de Teresina, Projeto Cultural A. Tito Filho: SETUT: Fundação Cultural Monsenhor Chaves, 2003. 456 p.: bibl., ill.

Economic geography of Piauí state. Emphasizes the possibilities for economic growth yet describes environmental and bureaucratic difficulties. Argues that Piauí has had few economic development plans. Presents a nine-point plan for the state's various regions that stresses targeted investment by federal and state governments.

1356 Merry, Frank; Gregory Amacher; and Eirivelthon Lima. Land values in frontier settlements of the Brazilian Amazon. (*World Dev.*, 36:11, Nov. 2008, p. 2390–2401)

Analyzes data obtained from households along the TransAmazon Highway in development of an estimation model for land value. Finds that land value is determined by the length of time settlers occupy the lot, amount of land under cultivation, and the value of homes on the lot.

1357 Mistry, Jayalaxshmi et al. Indigenous fire management in the Cerrado of Brazil: the case of the Krahô of Tocantíns. (*Hum. Ecol.*, 33:3, June 2005, p. 365–386, bibl., map, tables)

Analysis of burning by an indigenous group, outlining the reasons for burning at particular times during the year.

1358 Moreira, Clarissa da Costa. A cidade contemporânea entre a tabula rasa e a preservação: cenários para o porto do Rio de Janeiro. São Paulo: ANPUR, Associação Nacional de Pós-Graduação e Pesquisa em Planejamento Urbano e Regional: Editora UNESP, 2005. 142 p.: bibl., ill. (some col.), map.

Analyzes the tensions between historic preservation and new construction in Rio de Janeiro, paying particular attention to a project aimed at Rio's port.

1359 Moreira, Roberto José. Terra, poder e território. São Paulo: Expressão Popular, 2007. 360 p.: bibl.

Book of essays originating in conference proceedings or Brazilian journals. Theoretical chapters focus on issues such as land rent and sustainability, while empirical chapters consider rural development in the state of Rio de Janeiro, the inclusion of rural areas in municipal master plans, required in Brazil, and the work of the author's research center over the past decades.

1360 Mota, Ana Elizabete; Marcela Valença; and Maria das Graças e Silva. Política ambiental e reciclágem: o lugar invisível dos catadores de "lixo." (*Cad. Estud. Sociais*, 20:1, jan./junho 2004, p. 71–86, bibl.)

Argues that the rise of recycling of urban waste is creating a wage-labor force replacing an informal activity. Pays special attention to garbage collectors in Recife.

1361 Mourão, Fernando Augusto Albuquerque. Os pescadores do litoral sul de São Paulo: um estudo de sociologia diferencial. São Paulo: Editora Hucitec: NUPAUB; Iguape, Brazil: CEC, 2003. 264 p.: bibl., ill. (Ecologia e cultura; 3)

Study of fish marketing and social organization among fishermen between Santos and Paranaguá. Reports results of fieldwork carried out in the late 1960s and 1970s, a time of transition in the fishing communities, but serves as an important baseline study for future work.

1362 Natureza, fronteiras e territórios: imagens e narrativas. Organização de Gilmar Arruda. Londrina, Brazil: Eduel, 2005. 312 p.: bibl., ill. (some col.), maps (some col.).

Edited volume on human-environment interactions, mainly focusing on Brazil. Key chapters cover the agricultural settlement of Paraná state, the "invention" of the Brazilian South, and perceptions of nature among Brazilian elites.

1363 Nepstad, Daniel C.; Claudia M. Stickler; and Oriana T. Almeida. Globalization of the Amazon soy and beef industries: opportunities for conservation. (*Conserv. Biol.*, 20:6, Dec. 2006, p. 1595–1603, bibl., graphs)

Argues that increased awareness among global consumers for environmental standards may be translated to improved environmental management among Amazon farmers and ranchers. Highlights the rise of beef and soy exports from the Amazon as key drivers of deforestation.

1364 Nygaard, Paul Dieter. Planos diretores de cidades: discutindo sua base doutrinária. Porto Alegre, Brazil: UFRGS Editora, 2005. 287 p.: bibl., ill., maps.

Analysis of urban planning processes with special attention to Porto Alegre. Traces the development of Porto Alegre's Plano Diretor from the late 1950s to the 1970s and criticizes shortcomings. Also identifies the ideology informing various aspects of the Plano Diretor.

1365 Olhares geográficos: meio ambiente e saúde. Organização de Helena Ribeiro. São Paulo: Editora Senac São Paulo, 2004. 222 p.: bibl., ill. (some col.), maps (some col.).

Edited volume covering diverse topics such as local use of resources in the Serra da Bocaina National Park and on the Rio-São Paulo border, environmental issues arising from the participation of firms in the ISO 14001 environmental management standards, and human health issues in metropolitan São Paulo.

1366 Oliveira, Antônio Tadeu de and **André Geraldo de Moraes Simões.** Deslocamentos populacionais no Brasil: uma análise dos Censos Demográficos de 1991 e 2000. (*Cad. Estud. Sociais*, 20:1, jan./junho 2004, p. 87–106, bibl., tables)

Considers country-wide population data, finding considerable inter- and intra-regional migration in the 1990s. In the northeast, migration is more common among poorly skilled workers, while in the southeast, highly skilled workers are more likely to migrate.

1367 Paula, Elder Andrade de. (Des)envolvimento insustentável na Amazônia Ocidental: dos missionários do progresso aos mercadores da natureza. Rio Branco, Brazil: EDUFAC, 2005. 376 p.: bibl., ill., maps. (Série Dissertações e teses)

Account of land occupation of Acre, stressing conflicts and cooperation between INCRA and a rural trade union over access to land. Covers the 1970s and 1980s period of state-organized land settlement and the recent turn to sustainable development and decentralized land settlement schemes. Uses the term "playing the game" to describe how state agencies facilitated private appropriation of nature, and argues that the game must be ended to facilitate nature conservation.

1368 Perfil dos municípios brasileiros: meio ambiente, 2002. Rio de Janeiro: IBGE, 2005. 388 p.: bibl., col. ill., col. maps.

Book produced by a partnership between the Instituto Brasileiro de Geografia e Estatística (IBGE) and Ministry of the Environment to report municipal-level data for a variety of environmental variables. Text, tables, and maps illustrate phenomena such as the local Agenda 21, collection of agro-chemical containers, and conservation units.

1369 Perz, Stephen G. *et al.* Road building, land use and climate change: prospects for environmental governance in the Amazon. (*Philos. Trans.*, 363:1498, 2008, p. 1889–1895, bibl.)

Reviews ideas predicting a "die-back" of Amazonian rainforests, the role of road construction in causing land change, and prospects for governance of environmental resources. Indicates a promising model based in southwestern Amazon, where paving of the Inter-Oceanic Highway is occurring, which builds on the actions of a grassroots social movement to reduce the negative environmental consequences. .

1370 Perz, Stephen G. *et al.* Road networks and forest fragmentation in the Amazon: explanations for local diferences with implications for conservation and development. (*J. Lat. Am. Geogr.*, 7:2, 2008, p. 85–104, bibl., graphs, maps, tables)

Studies cases of road networks in Uruará, Pará state, and Sinop, Mato Grosso state, arguing that major differences are apparent in terms of the networks and forest fragmentation. Major explanatory factors include differences in initial settlement, topography, and size of rural properties.

1371 Perz, Stephen G.; Robert T. Walker; and Marcellus M. Caldas. Beyond population and environment: household demographic life cycles and land use allocation among small farms in the Amazon. (*Hum. Ecol.*, 34:6, Dec. 2006, p. 826–849, bibl., tables)

Paper focuses on household demographics over time, based on data collected in 1996 in Uruará, Pará, along the Transamazon Highway. Argues that changes in household demographics affect land use and land cover, with age structure of households having a strong effect on annual crops.

1372 Política de habitação popular e trabalho social. Organização de Maria de Fátima Cabral Marques Gomes and Ana Izabel de Carvalho Pelegrino. Textos de Ana Clara Torres Ribeiro *et al.* Rio de Janeiro: DP&A Editora, 2005. 240 p.: bibl., ill.

Edited volume on housing issues mainly in Brazil. Notable chapters cover favelas in Rio de Janeiro and Belém and housing policies developed by the Caixa Econômica.

1373 Polizelli, Demerval Luiz; Liége Mariel Petroni; and Isak Kruglianskas. Gestão ambiental nas empresas líderes do setor de telecomunicações no Brasil. (*Rev. Adm./São Paulo,* 40:4, out./dez. 2005, p. 309–320, bibl., tables)

Studies the "greening" of five telecommunications firms, concluding that the environmental policies undertaken were motivated by legislation, certification, and research and development initiatives. Affirms that environmental behavior of the firms studied represents an important advance.

1374 Population and environment in Brazil: Rio + 10. São Paulo: CNPD, Comissão Nacional de População e Desenvolvimento: ABEP, Brazilian Association of Population Studies: NEPO, Population Studies Center, 2002. 311 p.: bibl., ill., maps.

Edited volume explores changing population and environment issues in the post-Rio 1992 Conference era. Chapters focus on ecoregions and on particular themes, such as sustainable consumption, agrarian reform, and urbanization.

1375 Processos de territorialização: entre a história e a antropologia. Organização de Marlon Salomon, Joana Fernandes Silva and Leandro Mendes Rocha. Goiânia, Brazil: ABEU: Editora de UCG, 2005. 309 p.: bibl., ill., map.

Collection of essays focusing on the many ways that people create territories in Brazil, with special attention to territories claimed by indigenous peoples. Chapter also cover the mid-19th-century discussions of

an interior capital and territorial conflicts surrounding large dam and mining projects in the Amazon.

1376 Questões contemporâneas da dinâmica populacional do nordeste. Organização de Lára de Melo Barbosa. Natal, Brazil: EDUFRN, Editora da UFRN, 2006. 252 p.: bibl., ill., maps.

Edited volume on demographic aspects of northeastern Brazil. Chapters cover fertility trends, self-definitions of ethnicity, mortality rates and causes, and migration.

1377 Rangel, Thiago F.L.V.B. *et al.* Human development and biodiversity conservation in Brazilian Cerrado. (*Appl. Geogr.,* 27:1, 2007, p. 14–27, bibl., graphs, maps, tables)

Study spatially correlates socioeconomic variables with diversity patterns of endemic Anura (Amphibia) in the Cerrado, finding that species richness correlated positively with modern agricultural and cattle-ranching systems. Urges consideration of socioeconomic variables for Cerrado conservation planning and management.

1378 Reflexões sobre a geografia física no Brasil. Organização de Antonio Carlos Vitte and Antonio José Teixeira Guerra. Rio de Janeiro: Bertrand Brasil, 2004. 280 p.: bibl., ill., index, maps.

Edited volume aiming to outline key trends in physical geography. Essays cover climate change, biogeography, sustainability, watershed processes, urban landslides, and soil erosion. Chapters present syntheses of findings from case studies.

1379 Restauração florestal: fundamentos e estudos de caso. Recopilação de A. Paulo M. Galvão and Vanderley Porfírio-da-Silva. Colombo, Brazil: Embrapa Florestas, 2005. 143 p.: bibl., ill. (some col.).

Edited volume covering legal and ecological aspects of forest restoration in Brazil's Atlantic Forest and Cerrado regions. Case studies indicate the results of specific restoration initiatives, with significant attention devoted to the challenges of establishing seedlings.

1380 Ribeiro, Ricardo Ferreira. Florestas anãs do sertão: o cerrado na história de Minas Gerais. Belo Horizonte, Brazil: Autêntica, 2005. 472 p.: bibl., ill., maps.

First volume of a 1,200-page PhD dissertation covers the history of the Cerrado of Minas Gerais, from prehistorical times to the mid-1800s.

1381 Ribeiro, Ricardo Ferreira. Sertão, lugar desertado: o cerrado na cultura de Minas Gerais. Belo Horizonte, Brazil: Autêntica, 2006. 373 p.: bibl., col. ill.

Second volume on cultural ecology of various communities living in the Cerrado of Minas Gerais. Aims to show how the Sertão or backlands of Minas is occupied by groups in close contact with the Cerrado's flora and fauna. Concludes that the traditional people of the Cerrado provide an alternative to the ongoing clearing of the ecoregion. For review of vol. 1, see item **1380**.

1382 Ring, Irene. Integrating local ecological services into intergovernmental fiscal transfers: the case of the ecological ICMS in Brazil. (*Land Use Policy*, 25:4, Oct. 2008, p. 485–497)

Evaluates Brazil's ecological value-added tax (ICMS-E) in terms of ability to compensate municipal governments for protected areas and other environmental services provided. Describes methods used to distribute the ICMS-E, focusing on Paraná state and protected areas. Argues that the ICMS-E has positively affected the creation of protected areas.

1383 Rio de Janeiro: formas, movimentos, representações: estudos de geografia histórica carioca. Organização de Maurício de Almeida Abreu. Rio de Janeiro: Da Fonseca Comunicação, 2005. 254 p.: bibl., ill., maps.

Edited volume covering Rio's historical geography. Chapters focus on visual representations of the city, struggles over territorial control, attempts to control prostitution, Carnival celebrations, and the development of favelas.

1384 Rio Grande do Sul: paisagens e territórios em transformação. Organização de Roberto Verdum, Luis Alberto Basso and Dirce Maria Antunes Suertegaray. Porto Alegre, Brazil: UFRGS Editora, 2004. 319 p.: bibl., ill., maps.

Edited volume covering geomorphology, environmental issues, urban and political geography, and agricultural geography of Rio Grande do Sul. Notable chapters cover environmental and urban dynamics of Porto Alegre and territories that the state's indigenous peoples have created outside of Rio Grande do Sul.

1385 Ross, Jurandyr Luciano Sanches. Ecogeografia do Brasil: subsídios para planejamento ambiental. São Paulo: Oficina de Textos, 2006. 208 p.: ill., maps.

Creates environmental-economic regions within Brazil with aim to apply concepts of land-use zoning, or "zoneamento ecológico-econômico" (ZEE) as it is known in Brazil. Case study treats the Vale do Ribeira in coastal São Paulo. Argues that geographers should play a major role in developing ZEE plans in Brazil.

1386 Rossi, Eliana C.; Jonathan V. Beaverstock; and Peter J. Taylor. Transaction links through cities: "decision cities" and "service cities" in outsourcing by leading Brazilian firms. (*Geoforum/New York*, 38:4, July 2007, p. 628–642)

Analyzes production services by leading Brazilian firms to study São Paulo as a "gateway city." Concludes that São Paulo is dominant, but that many firms bypass the gateway, thus evidencing a dispersion of economic activity.

1387 Rückert, Aldomar Arnold. O estado do Rio Grande do Sul—Brasil como um território de internacionalização segmentada do espaço nacional. (*Invest. Geogr./México*, 51, agosto 2003, p. 125–143, bibl., map)

Study argues that Rio Grande do Sul has positioned itself as a vital territory in the Mercosul economic union owing to state reforms and federal macroeconomic policy.

1388 Salisbury, David S. and Marianne Schmink. Cows versus rubber: changing livelihoods among Amazonian extractivists. (*Geoforum/New York*, 38:6, Nov. 2007, p. 1233–1249)

Rubber tapper livelihoods in Acre are the focus of this paper. The study indicates that cattle and crops have increased in the area, while the importance of rubber tapping in livelihoods has declined. Paper indicates that small cattle herds are important for livelihoods of former rubber tappers.

1389 Sanches, Rosely Alvim. Caiçaras e a Estação Ecológica de Juréia-Itatins: litoral sul de São Paulo. São Paulo: Annablume, 2004. 207 p.: bibl., ill., maps. (Selo universidade; 285.

Meio ambiente) Focuses on the cultural ecology of a community of "caiçaras," traditional people who are the equivalent of "caipiras" or "caboclos" elsewhere in Brazil, living in an ecological reserve in coastal São Paulo state. Study identifies key historical moments in the community's history, social organization, and use of natural resources. Aims to improve management of the ecological reserve by improved knowledge of the caiçaras.

1390 Sánchez, Fernanda. A reinvenção das cidades para um mercado mundial. Chapecó, Brazil: Argos, Editora Universitária, 2003. 589 p.: bibl., ill., maps. (Série Debates)

Analyzes the marketing of Curitiba and Barcelona as "model cities." Includes detailed discussion of Curitiba's model-city campaign as "ecological capital" between 1970 and 2001, and argues that the model diffused globally.

1391 Schmertmann, Carl P.; Joseph E. Potter; and Suzana M. Cavenaghi. Exploratory analysis of spatial patterns in Brazil's fertility transition. (*Popul. Res. Policy Rev.*, 27:1, Feb. 2008, p. 1–15, bibl., graphs, maps, tables)

Study analyzes census data at the microregion scale from 1970 to 2000, finding that spatial variations in fertility are associated with electricity availability, child mortality rates, and female education rates.

1392 Schneider, Sergio. A pluriatividade na agricultura familiar. Porto Alegre, Brazil: UFRGS Editora, 2003. 254 p.: bibl., ill., map. (Série Estudos rurais)

Analyzes the multiple strategies among small farmers in southern Brazil for improving livelihoods. Focuses on on- and off-farm activities. Concludes that small farmers are able to adapt to changing economic circumstances by adjusting their productive strategies.

1393 Selwyn, Ben. Labour process and workers' bargaining power in export grape production, North East Brazil. (*J.*

Agrarian Change, 7:4, Oct. 2007, p. 526–553, bibl., graph, map, tables)

Uses global commodity chain approach to study labor relations in the production of export-oriented grapes. Workers have capitalized on increasing demands for quality among consumers by obtaining major concessions from grape farmers.

1394 Seminário Nacional Região Metropolitana: Governo, Sociedade e Território, *Universidade do Estado do Rio de Janeiro, 2003.* Metrópole: governo, sociedade e território. Organização de Catia Antonia da Silva, Désirée Guichard Freire, e Floriano José Godinho de Oliveira. Textos de Adolfo Guichard Freire *et al.* Rio de Janeiro: DP&A Editora: FAPERJ, 2006. 504 p.: bibl., ill., maps. (Col. Espaços do desenvolvimento)

Edited volume includes papers delivered at a national urban studies meeting in 2003. Numerous cities are covered (São Paulo, Rio de Janeiro, Belém, Fortaleza, Goiânia, and Belo Horizonte). Major themes include urban growth dynamics, urban governance, and social movements.

1395 Silva, Alexandre Marco da *et al.* Historical land-cover/use in different slope and riparian buffer zones in watersheds of the state of São Paulo, Brazil. (*Scientia Agrícola,* 64:4, July/Aug. 2007, p. 325–335, bibl., graphs, maps, tables)

Uses 1997 satellite imagery to study seven river basins in São Paulo, with special attention to the 30-meter strip around rivers. Shows that pasture covers 50 percent of the total area and 25 percent of riparian vegetation is preserved. Cost estimates for reforestation of riparian vegetation are provided.

1396 Silva, Joana Aparecida Fernandes *et al.* Spatial heterogeneity, land use and conservation in the Cerrado region of Brazil. (*J. Biogeogr.,* 33:3, March 2006, p. 536–548, bibl., maps, tables)

Presents spatial classification of biodiversity in the Cerrado. Argues that the conversion of Cerrado to agriculture is a key threat to biodiversity conservation. Findings indicate ways to improve the establishment of protected areas.

1397 Silva, Rosemiro Magno da. A luta dos posseiros de Santana dos Frades. Aracaju, Sergipe, Brazil: Editora UFS,

Univ. Federal de Sergipe: Fundação Oviêdo Teixeira, 2002. 349 p.: bibl., ill., maps.

Studies land conflicts in Sergipe state in which the key actors are indigenous peoples, small farmers, the Catholic Church, rural trade unions, and the state land-reform agency. Identifies causes for the appearance of groups opposed to agrarian reform.

1398 Silveira, Rogério Leandro Lima da.
Cidade, corporação e periferia urbana: acumulação de capital e segregação espacial na (re)produção do espaço urbano. Santa Cruz do Sul, Brazil: EDUNISC, 2003. 242 p.: bibl., ill., maps.

Traces urban expansion of Santa Cruz do Sul, in the center of Rio Grande do Sul state, from the 1840s to the present. Focuses on the development of tobacco production and the reliance of peripheral settlements as housing for the workforce. Argues for a direct relationship between the internationalization of the tobacco sector and the urban growth of Santa Cruz.

1399 Simmons, Cynthia S. *et al.* The Amazon land war in the south of Pará. *(Ann. Assoc. Am. Geogr.*, 97:3, Sept. 2007, p. 567–592, bibl., maps, photos, tables)

Analyzes land violence in southern Pará using GIS analysis and contentious politics theory. Uses the idea of place to discuss the various explanations for the high incidence of rural violence. Argues that violence is a place-based phenomenon, and not the result of the frontier process; thus, the closure of the frontier is not likely to end land-related violence.

1400 Simpósio Nacional de Geografia Urbana, 7th, *Universidade de São Paulo, 2001.* Dilemas urbanos: novas abordagens sobre a cidade. Organização de Ana Fani Alessandri Carlos e Amália Inês Geraiges Lemos. São Paulo: Editora Contexto, 2003. 430 p.: bibl.

Edited volume of conference papers covers a wide range of urban issues. Major sections include urban cultural issues, labor relations, urban politics, and urban environmental issues. Many chapters are informed by case-study findings in major cities, such as São Paulo, Salvador, and Belo Horizonte.

1401 Sioli, Harald. Gelebtes, geliebtes Amazonien: Forschungsreisen im brasilianischen Regenwald zwischen 1940 und 1962. Edited by Gerd Kohlhepp. München, Germany: Verlag Dr. Friedrich Pfeil, 2007. 228 p.: ill., maps (some col.).

Collected writings about Amazonia by German geographer Gerd Kohlhepp describe his expeditions and research in the region. [F. Obermeier]

1402 Skop, Emily H. *et al.* Chain migration and residential segregation of internal migrants in the metropolitan area of São Paulo, Brazil. *(Urban Geogr.*, 27:5, 2006, p. 397–421, bibl., maps, tables)

Studies internal migration in São Paulo, arguing that spatial segregation occurs as migrant communities cluster in particular neighborhoods, resulting in increased segregation.

1403 Soares-Filho, Britaldo Silveira *et al.* Modelling conservation in the Amazon basin. *(Nature/London,* 440, March 23, 2006, p. 520–523, maps)

Uses two scenarios, "governance" and "business-as-usual," to model land change in the Amazon. Estimates that agricultural land uses will cover 40 percent of the Amazon by the year 2050. Proposes that improved protection of conservation areas and private conservation reserves would reduce projected deforestation.

1404 Sociedade e natureza na visão da geografia. Organização de Lucia Helena de Oliveira Gerardi and Magda Adelaide Lombardo. Rio Claro, Brazil: Programa de Pós-Graduação em Geografia-UNESP: Associação de Geografia Teorética-AGETEO, 2004. 296 p.: bibl., ill., maps.

Edited volume of graduate student work produced in one of Brazil's top geography departments, at the Univ. Estadual Paulista in Rio Claro. Chapters cover a wide range of topics in physical and human geography.

1405 Valladares, Licia do Prado. A invenção da favela: do mito de origem a favela.com. Rio de Janeiro: Editora FGV, 2005. 204 p.: bibl., ill.

Analyzes the processes by which the favela was "invented" and transformed into a "problem." Approaches to favelas by observers such as Euclides da Cunha are included, in addition to a discussion of the work of Peace Corps volunteers in favelas. Virtual favelas are also described. Concludes that the term *favela* has become a dogma of urban social science and fails to represent adequately the actual processes in these urban spaces.

1406 Vasconcellos, Eduardo Alcântara de. Transport metabolism, social diversity and equity: the case of São Paulo, Brazil. (*J. Transport Geogr.*, 13:4, 2005, p. 329–339)

Studies origin-destination data from 1997 in the city of São Paulo, finding that low-income populations have low mobility, even though they spend a relatively high proportion of income on transport, while higher income populations create large transport externalities because of their reliance on automobiles.

1407 Watson, Kelly and Moira Laura Achinelli. Context and contingency: the coffee crisis for conventional small-scale coffee farmers in Brazil. (*Geogr. J./London*, 174:3, Sept. 2008, p. 223–234, bibl., graphs, map, photo)

Studies small-scale coffee producers in Minas Gerais, focusing on the negative effects of neoliberal economic policies. Finds that coffee farmers have become economically marginalized and soils have become degraded as a result of neoliberalism.

1408 WinklerPrins, Antoinette M.G.A. Jute cultivation in the Lower Amazon, 1940-1990: an ethnographic account from Santarém, Pará, Brazil. (*J. Hist. Geogr.*, 32:4, Oct. 2006, p. 818–838, graphs, map)

Production of jute by Japanese immigrants is studied, with focus on labor relations and marketing. Argues that evidence of the boom is still present in the landscapes of the region.

1409 Wolford, Wendy. Environmental justice and the construction of scale in Brazilian agriculture. (*Soc. Nat. Resour.*, 21:7, Aug. 2008, p. 641–655, graphs, map, photos)

Studies the processes by which large-scale soybean production developed in the Cerrado, detailing the policies that favored this development trajectory. Uses concepts of distributional equity and procedural equity.

1410 Wolford, Wendy. Land reform in the time of neoliberalism: a many-splendored thing. (*Antipode*, 39:3, June 2007, p. 550–570, bibl.)

Juxtaposes the World Bank's neoliberal agrarian program with that offered by Brazil's landless movement (MST) in terms of a case study of the northeastern region. Argues that the approaches of the World Bank and the landless movement differ in terms of the original cause of land-labor conflicts.

1411 World Social Forum, *2nd, Porto Alegre, Brazil, 2002*. Reforma agrária e meio ambiente. Organização de Neide Esterci e Raul Silva Telles do Valle. São Paulo: Instituto Socioambiental, 2003. 191 p.: bibl., ill.

Edited volume focusing on the intersection of Brazilian environmental law with its agrarian reform process. Legal aspects are covered, and regional cases from the Amazon and Atlantic Forest regions are discussed.

1412 Zanotti, Laura and Janet Chernela. Conflicting cultures of nature: ecotourism, education and the Kayapó of the Brazilian Amazon. (*Tour. Geogr.*, 10:4, Nov. 2008, p. 495–521)

Analysis of a university-level study-abroad course among the Kayapó, stressing flows of information and capital among the Kayapó community, course organizers, and student-tourists.

1413 Zeilhofer, Peter and Valdinir Piazza Topanotti. GIS and and ordination techniques for evaluation of environmental impacts in informal settlements: a case study from Cuiabá, central Brazil. (*Appl. Geogr.*, 28:1, Jan. 2008, p. 1–15)

Analysis of environmental impacts of informal settlements, finding that the most severe cases were in areas prone to flooding.

GOVERNMENT AND POLITICS

GENERAL

DAVID W. DENT, *Professor Emeritus of Political Science, Towson University*

THE PUBLICATIONS REVIEWED in this section on Government and Politics reveal that certain themes from the past continue to dominate the literature from the region while a few new subjects have emerged that may fascinate those interested in Latin American political conditions. Studies of democracy, political parties, subnational political institutions, decentralization, and civil-military relations continue as subjects of interest to scholars who publish on the region. There seems to be less interest in populism, drug trafficking, theory building, state-society relations, guerrilla movements, revolutionary groups, and the role of intellectuals than in previous *Handbook* volumes. The newer subjects of interest to emerge in this volume include the politics of indigenous movements, crime and security, presidential impeachment, and gender politics. Scholars are devoting more attention to local-level politics as democracy is strengthened throughout the region. The general country studies that once dominated the literature have disappeared from the publication map of Latin America, leaving a void for those interested in the macropolitical view of government and politics. The low level of attention paid to Latin America by the George W. Bush administration is reflected in the literature as most scholars have little to say about the US as a forceful actor in the domestic politics of the region.

As in previous editions, the larger Latin American countries—Argentina, Brazil, Colombia, Mexico, and Venezuela—receive more research attention than the smaller countries in the Western Hemisphere. In addition, more research attention is focused on areas where controversial leaders are in power and countries are undergoing political and economic changes. The following dominant themes appear in this edition of the *HLAS*.

Democracy and Authoritarianism. Studies of democracy and democratic institutions and practices continue to grow with scholars focused on how to better understand democratic rule in Latin America. Van Cott's study of ethnic political movements highlights the success or failure of ethnic party formation, showing that these fledgling parties have been positive for democratic institutions in key South American countries (item **1438**). Helmke and Levitsky examine in considerable detail the importance of informal institutions by focusing on the rules of the game within a comparative framework (item **1420**). Canache and Allison examine the survival of democratic institutions; their findings indicate that citizens continue to favor democracy as a form of government despite their awareness of and opposition to corruption (item **1415**). Notwithstanding the declining strength of the military in many parts of Latin America, security concerns persist and democracies remain fragile. Hence, there will be a continuing role for the military in many Latin American societies (items **1418** and **1430**). In a comparison between Argentina and Venezuela, Pion-Berlin and Trinkunas find that democratic governments can rely on the military in times of social crisis without fear of negative retribution (item **1431**).

Political Parties. Political parties and electoral politics continue as important topics for those interested in the government and politics of the region. The growing power of leftist parties and leftist social movements is part of this trend (item **1423**), which, along with Regalado's study (item **1433**), focuses on the growing political power of popular movements, leftist political parties, and indigenous movements (item **1422**).

Political Instability and Accountability. As Latin American governments struggle to survive in a world of increasing tensions generated by emerging groups and failing economic conditions, studies of instability and accountability remain popular and important. While the power of the courts appears to be on the rise in Latin America (item **1437**), presidential impeachment has become the major instrument for deposing of unpopular rulers in times of crisis and instability (item **1428**).

Gender Politics. The role of women in Latin American politics and government continues to be a subject of interest due to the election of several female presidents. Studies of women's movements and rights have also appeared in this biennium (item **1419**). While considerable advances have been made in securing the rights of women, significant difficulties remain.

While several studies indicate the importance of US policy for understanding the government and politics of Latin America, there appears to be declining interest in the US as a major actor in the political game. The G.W. Bush administration did not address key problems in US-Latin American relations. Moreover, American foreign policy in this age of globalization, energy dependence, and the growing number of Latin American hot spots related to the global war on terrorism may be the reasons many Latin American governments continue to distance themselves from Washington and its policies, many rooted in a Cold War mind set. Although a handful of works investigate US involvement in the region (items **1427** and **1435**), there is a glaring absence of research interest in how the US shapes the government and politics of the region.

1414 **Alemán, Eduardo.** Policy gatekeepers in Latin American legislatures. (*Lat. Am. Polit. Soc.,* 48:3, Fall 2006, p. 125–155, bibl., tables)

An examination of agenda-setting rules in 26 Latin American legislatures attempts to demonstrate the theoretical importance of institutional structure for policy-making. The gatekeeping power remains critical for understanding the nature of lawmaking and agenda setting in many parts of the region.

Arceneaux, Craig L. and **David Pion-Berlin.** Issues, threats, and institutions: explaining OAS responses to democratic dilemmas in Latin America. See item **1936**.

Cameron, John. Struggles for local democracy in the Andes. See item **1643**.

1415 **Canache, Damarys** and **Michael E. Allison.** Perceptions of political corruption in Latin American democracies. (*Lat. Am. Polit. Soc.,* 47:3, Fall 2005, p. 91–112, bibl., graphs, tables)

Using data from Transparency International's CPI Index and opinion data from the World Values Survey, authors find that Latin Americans are quite aware of the scope of corruption in their countries and are prepared to hold their authorities and institutions accountable for public misconduct. More important for the survival of democratic institutions is the finding that perceptions of corruption have not soured mass opinion on democracy as a form of government.

1416 Cepeda Ulloa, Fernando. Financiación política y corrupción. Epílogo de Humberto de la Calle. Bogotá: Ariel, 2004. 347 p.: ill. (Ariel ciencia política)

Interesting study of the economics and politics of corruption with particular emphasis on the causes of corruption and its consequences for governability in Latin America. Author draws heavily from his extensive experience with Colombia and international financial organizations.

1417 Consejo Latinoamericano de Ciencias Sociales. Asamblea General. *21st, Havana, 2003.* La construcción de la democracia en el campo latinoamericano. Recopilación de Hubert C. de Grammont. Buenos Aires: CLACSO, 2006. 365 p.: bibl., ill., map. (Col. Grupos de trabajo)

Based on a conference of social scientists held in Havana, Cuba, in 2003, 14 authors examine the connection between democracy and rural development. Authors conclude that governments that fail to cultivate the organization and productivity of small producers in the countryside will find it extremely difficult to avoid revolutionary ferver and reduce the existence of extreme poverty in Latin America.

1418 Democracias frágiles: las relaciones civiles-militares en el mundo ibero-americano. Recopilación de José A. Olmeda. Valencia, Spain: Tirant lo Blanch, 2005. 806 p.: bibl., maps.

Two-part study of the role of the military in Latin American democracies. Using a comparative case-study approach, different authors provide insights into the politics of civil-military relations in Argentina, Bolivia, Brazil, Central America, Colombia, Chile, Ecuador, Mexico, Venezuela, and Peru. Despite the declining strength of the military in many parts of Latin America, democracies remain fragile and security concerns dictate a continuing role for the military in Latin American societies. An important work for understanding civil-military relations.

1419 Gender and the politics of rights and democracy in Latin America. Edited by Nikki Craske and Maxine Molyneux.

Houndmills, England; New York: Palgrave, 2002. 226 p.: bibl., index.

Edited volume on the recent evolution of women's movements in Latin America with specific emphasis on the comparative study of women's rights. Can greater gender justice come from the post-authoritarian democracies or are the complexity and politics of the issue bound to limit the potential for change in the region? Authors find considerable advances, but also note significant difficulties on the road ahead.

1420 Informal institutions and democracy: lessons from Latin America. Edited by Gretchen Helmke and Steven Levitsky. Baltimore, Md.: Johns Hopkins Univ. Press, 2006. 351 p.: bibl., ill., index.

Conceptual and theoretical framework for understanding how formal and informal institutions interact in new democracies. Based on two conferences on informal institutions in 2002 and 2003, the contributors examine the "rules of the game" in Chile, Brazil, Ecuador, Honduras, Argentina, and Mexico. Study offers interesting insights for advancing the future study of informal institutions in Latin America and beyond.

1421 La lucha por los derechos indígenas en América Latina. Recopilación de Nancy Grey Postero y León Zamosc. Quito: Ediciones Abya Yala, 2005. 329 p.: bibl., ill.

Edited volume based on a conference devoted to understanding indigenous struggles in Guatemala, Colombia, Ecuador, Venezuela, Mexico, Bolivia, and Peru. Key topics include human rights, legal structures, race relations, and how different governments address the indigenous question in the political arena.

1422 Madrid, Raúl L. Indigenous parties and democracy in Latin America. (*Lat. Am. Polit. Soc.*, 47:4, Winter 2005, p. 161–179, bibl.)

A positive assessment of the growing importance of indigenous parties in improving the operation of democracy in Latin America by improving the representation of the party system and reducing political violence. Article focuses mainly on the Movimiento al Socialismo (MAS) in Bolivia and Pachakutik in Ecuador, the two most important indigenous parties to emerge in Latin America in recent years.

1423 Movimientos y poderes de izquierda en América Latina. Coordinación de Bernard Duterme. Madrid: Editorial Popular, 2005. 220 p.: bibl. (o a la izquierda; 20)

Edited volume devoted to the growing power of the political left in Latin America over the past decade with emphasis on socialist parties and leftist social movements. At the core of the study is the struggle against neoliberalism and its consequences for recent politics and development in Latin America.

1424 Multiculturalism in Latin America: indigenous rights, diversity, and democracy. Edited by Rachel Sieder. Houndmills, England; New York: Palgrave Macmillan, 2002. 280 p.: bibl., index. (Institute of Latin American Studies series)

Edited volume based on a 1999 conference devoted to multiculturalism and its impact on state and society in Mesoamerica and the Andes. An important study linking the rise of indigenous organizations to the politics of development in the region.

1425 Negretto, Gabriel L. Minority presidents and democratic performance in Latin America. (*Lat. Am. Polit. Soc.*, 48:3, Fall 2006, p. 63–92, bibl., graphs, tables)

Important study of the factors involved in measuring conflict in presidential regimes. Author finds that three variables— the policy position of the president's party, the president's capacity to sustain a veto, and the legislative status of the parties included in the cabinet—affect the level of interbranch cooperation. The quantitative analysis suggests that scholars of presidential democracies need a new research agenda to properly understand legislative-executive conflict.

1426 Operaciones conjuntas civiles y militares en la política de defensa. Textos de José Huerta *et al.* Lima: Instituto de Defensa Legal, 2006. 419 p.: ill. (some col.). (Serie Democracia y fuerza armada; 65)

Papers based on a conference organized by the Instituto de Defensa Legal (Lima, 2005) that address current civil-military relations in Latin America. Authors attempt to understand the "new military" that has emerged in Latin America and the need to understand the military as a key actor on the political stage.

1427 Paredes, Alejandro. La Operación Cóndor y la guerra fría. (*Universum/ Talca*, 19:1, 2004, p. 122–137, bibl.)

Brief article devoted to the impact of military dictatorships and Operation Condor on the governments of Argentina, Brazil, Chile, Paraguay, and Uruguay. In a three-part analysis, author examines the factors that sparked the dictatorships, the purpose of Operation Condor, and the postreconstruction efforts to rebuild democratic regimes. Importantly, the article demonstrates the key responsibility of the US in the Condor process.

1428 Pérez-Liñán, Aníbal S. Presidential impeachment and the new political instability in Latin America. New York: Cambridge Univ. Press, 2007. 241 p.: bibl., ill., index. (Cambridge studies in comparative politics)

An important study of how presidential impeachment has become the major instrument employed by civilian elites to depose unpopular rulers in times of crisis and instability. Based on comparative research in five countries, author explains crisis without breakdown as the dominant form of political instability and posits why some presidents are removed from power and others survive. Study offers interesting insights for political communication, democratization, and institutional breakdown in the absence of traditional military coups in the region.

1429 Pérez-Liñán, Aníbal S. Television news and political partisanship in Latin America. (*Polit. Res. Q.*, 55:3, Sept. 2002, p. 571–588, bibl., tables)

Using survey data for eight Latin American countries, author attempts to measure the connection between television news and political partisanship. Results suggest that television news encourages party identification in the short run, although broadcasting television news may weaken Latin American political parties in the long run. The notion that exposure to television may encourage partisanship serves to question prior assumptions about partisan attitudes.

1430 Pion-Berlin, David. Authoritarian legacies and their impact on Latin America. (*Lat. Am. Polit. Soc.*, 47:2, Summer 2005, p. 159–170, bibl.)

Review essay of three books devoted to military authoritarian legacies in which scholarly research indicates that military institutions are still relevant and some of the assumptions about the rationale for the "dirty wars" in key Latin American countries need to be corrected in the ongoing search for plausible explanations about these horrible past events. For *HLAS* reviews of two of the three works, see *HLAS 63:1843* and *HLAS 63:2012*.

1431 Pion-Berlin, David and **Harold Trinkunas.** Democratization, social crisis and the impact of military domestic roles in Latin America. (*J. Polit. Mil. Sociol.*, 33:1, Summer 2005, p. 5–24, bibl.)

Key article on civil-military relations in two Latin American cases: Argentina and Venezuela. Research finds that democratic governments can enlist the help of their militaries domestically without the risk of regime interference, even in times of social crisis. The crisis-based findings may provide incentives for weak democracies to rely on the military without fear of negative retributions. The Argentina-Venezuela comparison confirms the importance of civilian control in sustaining democratic regimes during times of crisis rather than provoking regime change as was so frequent in the past.

1432 Reformas políticas en América Latina. Edited by Wilhelm Hofmeister. Rio de Janeiro: Konrad Adenauer Stiftung, 2004. 440 p.: bibl., ill.

Comparative case studies of the impact of democratic rule over the past 25 years reveal continuing problems that seem unsolvable with democratic reform governments. Twelve countries are examined in terms of democratic governability and political reform.

1433 Regalado Álvarez, Roberto. Latin America at the crossroads: domination, crisis, social struggle and political alternatives for the left. Melbourne; New York: Ocean Press, 2007. 263 p.: bibl.

Cuban scholar examines the issues underlying the prevailing conflict between Latin America and the US. With emphasis on the recent electoral victory of Evo Morales in Bolivia and the tensions between Washington and Venezuela's President Hugo Chávez, author provides important insights into the growing political power of popular movements and leftist political parties in Latin America. His conclusion argues that "the use of some type of revolutionary violence will be inevitable, because those holding power in the world will cling to it to the very end."

1434 Reid, Michael. Forgotten continent: the battle for Latin America's soul. New Haven, Conn.: Yale Univ. Press, 2007. 384 p.: bibl., index.

Sweeping survey of the importance of further reform—not revolution—in Latin America as a strategy for building democratic politics and liberal economic structures. Book presents an argument that the world outside of Latin America needs to pay more attention to the region or some Latin American countries may turn to China as a serious alternative. Author calls for some optimism, and patience, in judging the progress and problems the Latin Americans have faced in their struggle for development.

1435 Seguridad y reforma policial en las Américas: experiencias y desafíos. Coordinación de Lucía Dammert y John Bailey. México: Siglo XXI Editores; Chile: FLACSO Chile; [s.n.]: Naciones Unidas, ILANUD, 2005. 379 p.: bibl., ill. (Criminología y derecho)

Important edited volume devoted to the problems of security in the Americas. Analysis focuses on the politics of public security and police reform in the US, Mexico, El Salvador, Colombia, Brazil, Chile, and Argentina. This Spanish edition of *Public Security and Police Reform in the Americas* (2006; see *HLAS 63:1882*) opens this valuable study to a broader segment of the scholarly community.

1436 Staats, Joseph L.; Shaun Bowler; and Jonathan T. Hiskey. Measuring judicial performance in Latin America. (*Lat. Am. Polit. Soc.*, 47:4, Winter 2005, p. 77–106, bibl., tables)

Cross-national analysis of judicial performance in 17 Latin American countries. By establishing a more valid assessment of the performance of judiciaries in the region, authors seek to advance efforts to better understand the causes and consequences of effective judicial reform. The findings may lead scholars to pay less attention to legislative and executive institutions and focus more on the impact of law and the courts on Latin American politics.

1437 Taylor, Matthew M. Beyond judicial reform: courts as political actors in Latin America. (*LARR*, 41:2, 2006, p. 269–281)

Review essay of six recent books on the political, economic, and social implications of law and legal systems on the evolution of Latin American politics. Author demonstrates the importance of courts as political actors in the new democracies in the region. The works reviewed offer many insights for research into the power of courts in Latin American societies. For *HLAS* reviews of two of the books considered in this article, see *HLAS 63:1853* and *HLAS 63:2370*.

1438 Van Cott, Donna Lee. From movements to parties in Latin America: the evolution of ethnic politics. Cambridge, England; New York: Cambridge Univ. Press, 2005. 276 p.: bibl., ill., index.

Important study of the formation and performance of ethnic political movements as they have evolved into ethnic political parties capable of competing in the national political arena. Van Cott addresses a broad range of theoretical concerns in order to understand how Latin American societies' most advantaged groups managed to achieve autonomous representation in political office. The comparative case studies—Bolivia, Peru, Ecuador, Argentina, Colombia, and Venezuela—highlight the reasons for the success or failure of ethnic party formation. In an important conclusion, the author states that "the emergence of ethnic parties in South America has been positive for democratic institutions in the region, while having mixed results for indigenous peoples and their cultures."

1439 Vial, Alejandro. "Enlatados" o modelos propios: una hipótesis sobre el estancamiento latinoamericano. (*Nueva Soc.*, 200, nov./dic. 2005, p. 25–37, bibl.)

The central argument is that traditional modes of clientelism and patrimonialism that have negative effects on development in Latin America are resilient because of their indigeneity to the region's political systems. To get past these problems, the author argues for building a citizenship not on imported models but rather from the experience of Latin Americans. [D. Arias]

MEXICO

RODERIC A. CAMP, *Professor of Government, Claremont-McKenna College*

SCHOLARSHIP ON MEXICAN POLITICS has followed several well-established trends beginning with *HLAS 59*. The most important development that began with that volume, and that accompanied the changing context of Mexican politics, was a strong interest in electoral politics. While this interest reflects a natural shift and is highly relevant for understanding what is happening in Mexico in the 2000s, it is being pursued to the neglect of many other equally relevant topics. Furthermore, most of this literature has become repetitive and rarely is characterized by originality or significant research, especially field research which would complement what are otherwise merely analyses of voting statistics.

Some notable exceptions to this general conclusion about the weaknesses in voting studies can be found. Broadly speaking, Alba Vega's edited work *Regionalismo y federalismo*, because of its revealing comparisons with other countries including Yugoslavia, Germany, and Spain, is such a case (item **1488**). Not only is regionalism the single most important variable that emerges from the 2006 presidential election, but a number of authors in the selection of works below explore these issues through their analyses of relevant cultural and historical patterns. Additionally, Klesner (item **1466**), like Alejandro Moreno from Mexico, who has been analyzing Mexican elections for more than two decades, focuses on regional alignments since the 1990s, offering interpretations about the consequences of geographic and other shifts in the partisan loyalties of the electorate in his empirical analysis of national election data.

Other scholars too have addressed the issue of political participation in broader, imaginative ways. For example, Somuano Ventura (item **1489**), in her essay "Más allá del voto," examines nonvoting forms of political participation using extensive survey research from the World Values Surveys since the 1980s as well as the recent national political culture survey produced by Mexico's Secretariat of Government. She discovers opposing trends of participation among ordinary citizens. Perhaps the most original approach to understanding the outcome of the electoral process, an area which has received no attention since Camp's collection, *Polling for Democracy, Public Opinion and Political Liberalization in Mexico* (1996; see *HLAS 57:3101*), is Rottinghaus and Alberro's "Rivaling the PRI: the Image Management of Vicente Fox and the Use of Public Opinion Polling in the 2000 Mexican Election" (item **1483**), based on interviews with many of the key media advisers on Fox's campaign staff. They demonstrate unequivocally that Fox understood the importance of the information provided by polls and used that information to tailor his campaign to Mexican voters. His attitude toward polling in contrast to that of his leading opponent, PRI's Francisco Labastida, contributed crucially to his electoral victory. Finally, Hiskey, who has pursued Klesner's scholarly approach, authoring numerous articles rather than monographs, brings his analysis, true of much of his work, to the local level, to determine whether democratic politics affects public policy, specifically the ability of communities to solve poverty through demand-based programs (item **1463**).

Democratic institutions, deserving of much greater attention from Mexicanists, continue to be largely neglected in the literature from both sides of the border. Nevertheless, the judiciary continues to receive some attention. Báez Silva (item **1444**), following the lead of judicial scholars of the US, analyzes Mexican Supreme Court decisions from 1995–2002. He also demonstrates the federal court system's expansion since the 1980s, dramatically increasing citizens' potential access to judicial institutions. At the local level, Beer, whose earlier book on state legislatures was a major work, has shifted her emphasis, but continuing on the state and local level, to the judiciary. In her first article, "Judicial Performance and the Rule of Law in the Mexican States" (item **1447**), she uses case studies of Aguascalientes and Guanajuato to provide insights into the effectiveness of the judicial process on the rule of law. Beer also looks at the impact of other variables nationwide, such as the extent of participation in the judicial system. In a second essay on human rights, another topic on which little scholarly literature exists for Mexico, she tests numerous variables and their impact on the relationship between democratic behavior and the protection of human rights (item **1448**). She discovers that electoral accountability and citizen participation are crucial explanations for democracy's ability to improve human rights. For a darker view of the rule of law and the inability of police reforms to bring about change under a democratic government, see the essay by Diane Davis (item **1456**). Her previous book on governance in the Federal District offered numerous insights about decision-making, but her article provides evidence to suggest that democratic efforts at reform have actually undermined the rule of law and democracy itself.

In *HLAS 63*, scholars paid increased attention to the legislative branch. Unfortunately, this emphasis has not continued into *HLAS 65*. The one study which stands out on Congress is Béjar Algazi's analysis of the issue of party discipline's role in influencing legislation and its relationship to executive-initiated legislation and its passage through Congress (item **1449**). She reveals how each party's respective rules for congressional comportment affect their interactions with each other and with the executive branch.

Other influential political actors outside of governmental institutions include business groups, intellectuals, the media, unions, NGOs, the Catholic Church, and antisystem actors, such as the Zapatistas. Few of these actors have attracted serious scholarly efforts. Indeed, we did not encounter any significant individual contributions on unions, the Church, or NGOs, suggesting declining interest in these topics. Schneider authored a major essay on the business-government relationship (item **1486**). He is a non-Mexicanist who published an outstanding book on this topic in Brazil. His "Why is Mexican Business so Organized?" is an important analysis on the leading influential business organization, the Consejo Mexicano de Hombres de Negocios, and other "peak" business organizations, and their relationship to the executive branch. Hughes, one of the few serious scholars of the media, produced *Newsrooms in Conflict: Journalism and the Democratization of Mexico* (item **1464**), an outstanding analysis of newspapers' role in Mexico's democratic transformation, complementing the equally important earlier monograph by Chappell Lawson. Her book is based on extensive interviews with leading journalists, benefitting strongly from her own career as a reporter for the *Miami Herald* as well as her journalistic career in Mexico.

Intellectuals rarely receive any attention among Mexicanists, especially their relationship to government and politics. Brewster's wonderful book contributes to a better understanding of this relationship through her analysis of four leading Mexican figures, Octavio Paz, Carlos Fuentes, Carlos Monsiváis, and Elena Poniatowska (item **1451**). She evaluates the impact of their writings on politics from the student massacre in Tlatelolco Plaza in 1968 through Ernesto Zedillo's election. The Zapatistas continue to attract scholarly attention, but as has been the case previously, few contributions are truly noteworthy. The exception to this is Pérez-Ruiz's massive, 788-page book which should be viewed as an essential source on the Zapatistas, analyzing every aspect of the movement before and after it emerges, both within and outside of Chiapas (item **1480**). This is an outstanding work of scholarship. An interesting essay by Guillén (item **1461**), which focuses on governance in Chiapas, not the EZLN itself, provides numerous, relevant insights into why such a movement would emerge in Chiapas, and explains the failure of the Chiapas government to mold institutions and processes that would have increased citizen access, including indigenous populations, to government.

Several helpful edited collections, which do address some of these and other important political actors, have appeared since *HLAS 63*. The earliest of these is Middlebrook's, *Dilemmas of Political Change* (item **1458**), an outstanding collection that includes essays on executive-legislative relations, civil-military relations, and business and politics by many leading scholars from both sides of the border. These essays cover the period of the late 1990s. The second edited collection is

Tulchin and Selee's, *Mexico's Politics and Society in Transition* (item **1472**), which includes a range of political topics and actors, including labor, the military, and the Zapatistas, as well as women, who have been significantly neglected during this period of scholarship. The third collection, edited by Peschard-Sverdrup and Rioff (item **1471**), also analyzes similar institutions, including the legislative branch, the judicial branch, civil-military relations, and the media, but also includes an equally neglected actor, the Catholic Church and the religious relationship between church and state, in an excellent essay by González Schmal.

The one new institutional actor that continues to receive deserved attention since the beginning of the democratization process are political parties. Shirk's outstanding book on the Partido Acción Nacional (PAN) is based on field research that focuses on the many internal conflicts over the party's strategy to defeat the PRI in the electoral arena (item **1487**). Shirk's book complements Mizrahi's earlier work. The PRD has fared even better than PAN with two new books worthy of attention. Vivero Ávila's *Desafiando al sistema la izquierda política en México: Evolución organizativa, ideológica y electoral del Partido de la Revolución Democrática, 1989–2005* is an excellent examination of the party's internal conflicts (item **1494**), updating Bruhn's classic work. Martínez González offers the most detailed analysis of the career experiences and political origins of the party's various leadership factions to date, a book essential to understanding the party's evolution since 1989 (item **1469**).

Finally, one feature of predemocratic Mexico continues to attract scholarly attention: clientelism. Schedler examines the continuation of this traditional feature of Mexican politics during the initial years of the Fox administration (item **1485**). He concludes, based on his extensive interviews with rural Mexicans, that most citizens actually are opposed to these social and cultural relationships, and that democratization has produced that opposition. The most important policy issue in Mexico today, other than crime and violence, which strangely has received little attention, is poverty. The collection *Alternancia, políticas sociales y desarrollo regional en México* explores poverty and social policy in the region, providing many comparisons with Mexico (item **1440**). It incorporates a number of case studies and evaluates leading antipoverty programs and strategies.

1440 Alternancia, políticas sociales y desarrollo regional en México. Coordinación de Gerardo Manuel Ordóñez Barba *et al.* Tijuana, Mexico: El Colegio de la Frontera Norte; Tlaquepaque, Mexico: Inst. Tecnológico y de Estudios Superiores de Occidente; Guadalajara, Jalisco, Mexico: Univ. de Guadalajara, 2006. 527 p.: bibl.

The most important issue in Mexico today is poverty, and how government can decrease its presence. This book takes a comprehensive look at poverty and social policy in Latin America, comparing Mexico to other countries, and examining the impact of government programs on poverty reduction generally. It also incorporates several individual case studies and evaluates leading programs and strategies, including Oportunidades.

1441 Anaya, Alejandro. Autonomía indígena, gobernabilidad y legitimidad en México: la legalización de los usos y costumbres electorales en Oaxaca. México: Univ. Iberoamericana: Plaza y Valdés, 2006. 176 p.: bibl. (Política)

An examination of numerous facets of economic and political influence in the evolution of indigenous rights in the southern state of Oaxaca which argues, among other conclusions, that indigenous political challenges to the PRI explain the advancement of indigenous beliefs and practices, not ethnic cultural debates.

1442 Aparicio, Ricardo and **David H. Corrochano.** El perfil del votante clientelar en México durante las elecciones de 2000. (*Estud. Sociol./México*, 23:68, mayo/agosto 2005, p. 375–396, bibl.)

In this well-researched essay, the authors attempt to determine the ideal clientelistic voter in Mexico during the 2000 election, within the context of the larger body of theoretical literature. They confirm that the typical image of this voter as poor and uneducated is true. They also determine, however, the important finding that a voter's place of residence is not intrinsically linked to his/her clientelism.

1443 Assies, Willem; Luis Ramírez Sevilla; and **María del Carmen Ventura Patiño.** Autonomy rights and the politics of constitutional reform in Mexico. (*Lat. Am. Caribb. Ethn. Stud.*, 1:1, April 2006, p. 37–62, bibl.)

Since the Zapatista rebellion, autonomy rights, as is the case elsewhere in Latin America, have become a popular topic of scholarly research. The authors evaluate the extent of reforms directed at municipal autonomy before and after 1994, following their own experiences in the state of Michoacán. In short, this essay provides interesting insights into the reform process from the pragmatic reforms themselves.

1444 Báez Silva, Carlos. Cambio político y poder judicial en México. (*Espiral/ Guadalajara*, 11:32, enero/abril 2005, p. 51–91, bibl., graphs, tables)

The study of the Mexican judiciary requires much more attention among social scientists, a lacunae which Báez Silva attempts to contribute in his helpful analysis of Supreme Court decisions in the Zedillo era and the first two years of the Fox administration. The essay contributes helpful data on the types of decisions the court made during this period, as well as the unanimity of the justices' votes. Báez Silva also provides evidence of the growth of the federal judiciary per capita, having reduced the ratio of courts per citizen by half from 1980 to 2000.

1445 Bailey, John and **Pablo Paras.** Perceptions and attitudes about corruption and democracy in Mexico. (*Mex. Stud.*, 22:1, Winter 2006, p. 57–82)

Survey dealing with how respondents encounter corruption, how various groups react to corruption, and how corruption affects satisfaction with and support for democracy. Authors conclude that the concept of "corruption" had different meanings to different respondents; that the government was seen as only slightly more corrupt than society at large; that only a minority of the respondents had directly experienced bribery; and that corruption negatively affects perceptions of democracy. [D. Coerver]

1446 Barracca, Steven. Devolution and the deepening of democracy: explaining outcomes of municipal reform in Mexico. (*J. Lat. Am. Stud.*, 37:1, Feb. 2005, p. 1–28, tables)

Barracca explores the 1983 municipal reform in three Mexican states—Chihuahua, Oaxaca, and Yucatán—specifically the transfer of municipal services from the state to local governments. He discovered a number of unexpected relationships, including the fact that opposition-controlled municipalities did not fare better than their peers, which he attributes to gubernatorial discretion. He offers some useful recommendations for improving the original reforms.

1447 Beer, Caroline C. Judicial performance and the rule of law in the Mexican states. (*Lat. Am. Polit. Soc.*, 48:3, Fall 2006, p. 33–61, bibl., tables)

In addition to her outstanding essay in this volume on human rights in the states (item **1448**), Beer offers a second article on the effectiveness of the judicial system and the rule of law. On the basis of case studies in Guanajuato and Aguascalientes with empirical statistical data from all the Mexican states, she discovers that a more open export-oriented economy, the level of poverty, and the extent of political participation all have an impact on citizen access to the judicial process and on its effectiveness.

1448 Beer, Caroline C. and **Neil J. Mitchell.** Democracy and human rights in the Mexican states: elections or social capital? (*Int. Stud. Q./Oxford*, 48:2, June 2004, p. 293–312, bibl., maps, tables)

Beer, whose previous excellent work examines the role of legislative politics at the state level, continues her emphasis on understanding political behavior at the provincial level. She tests a number of empirical variables which explain democracy to determine what impact, if any, they have on improvements in human rights. She concludes that electoral accountability and an electorally active citizenry are crucial to increasing protections in human rights.

1449 Béjar Algazi, Luisa. Representación y disciplina en los grupos parlamentarios: el caso mexicano. (*Estud. Polít./ México*, 3, sept./dic. 2004, p. 153–194, appendices, tables)

Béjar offers a thoroughly researched essay on the impact of legislative party discipline in the Mexican Congress. She specifically explores the differences in party discipline among PAN, PRD, and PRI in the 48th legislative session, the first in the Fox presidency. She assesses each party's respective rules and how they impact actual behavior in the Chamber of Deputies as well as consequences for democratization.

1450 Bolívar Meza, Rosendo. El proceso de aglutinamiento de la izquierda en México. (*Estud. Polít./México*, 1, enero/abril 2004, p. 185–226, bibl.)

An interesting analysis of the Mexican left from the 1980s through 2000 which explores the role of the PRD as the central actor in bringing together the radical and moderate left. Describes various features of this process and among his conclusions, Bolívar Meza argues that the strategy of the left often does not square with its ideology, thus creating additional obstacles to unity.

1451 Brewster, Claire. Responding to crisis in contemporary Mexico: the political writings of Paz, Fuentes, Monsiváis, and Poniatowska. Tucson: Univ. of Arizona Press, 2005. 265 p.: bibl., index.

This thoroughly researched study helps to fill a gap in the scholarship on the relationship between intellectuals and politics. The author analyzes how four leading Mexican figures, Octavio Paz, Carlos Fuentes, Carlos Monsiváis, and Elena Poniatowska, have used and influenced the written medium in Mexican politics from 1968 to 1995.

Camp, Roderic Ai. Mexico's military on the democratic stage. See *HLAS 64:745.*

1452 Cansino, César and **Israel Covarrubias.** Muerte y resurrección del populismo en México. (*Metapolítica/México*, 9:44, nov./dic. 2005, p. 79–111, bibl., photos)

A new wave of populism has spread across Latin America and César Cansino and Israel Covarrubias attempt to place Mexico's own version of neopopulism and populism within a larger political context. This is a worthy effort because typically Mexico has been left out of this discussion by other Latin Americanists. The authors believe that Fox and López Obrador both represent contradictory versions of populism, and that as a political option, populism is likely to play a role in the near future.

1453 Castillo Peraza, Carlos. El porvenir posible: obras selectas. Estudio introductorio y selección de Alonso Lujambio y German Martínez Cázares. México: Fondo de Cultura Económica: Fundación Rafael Preciado Hernández, 2006. 668 p.: bibl., ill. (Vida y pensamiento de México)

Compilation of selected essays and articles by the late Carlos Castillo Peraza, one of the leading and most admired figures in the National Action Party (PAN). Provides a chronological evolution of his political interpretations from the 1970s through 2000, representative of this important generation in the development of the party and Mexico's political opposition.

1454 Castro, Hugo. Una lenta agonía: los modelos de la globalización y las elecciones en México. México: Ediciones Gernika, 2006. 391 p.: bibl. (Col. Ciencias políticas; 59)

A critical evaluation of the role of global influences on Mexican elections, which devotes far more attention to the global models and to Mexico generally, with little attention to elections, with the exception of a chapter on the 2006 presidential election.

1455 Concepción Montiel, Luis Enrique. El discurso presidencial en México: el sexenio de Carlos Salinas de Gortari. Prologo de Lorenzo Meyer. Mexicali: Univ. Autónoma de Baja California, 2006. 632 p.: bibl.

This is an extraordinarily detailed analysis of the presidential speeches during the Carlos Salinas administration, which incorporates copious notes. It is particularly useful for understanding the president's publicly stated views on neoliberalism.

1456 Davis, Diane E. Undermining the rule of law: democratization and the dark side of police reform in Mexico. (*Lat. Am. Polit. Soc.*, 48:1, Spring 2006, p. 55–86, bibl.)

Davis, who has provided us with the most detailed and revealing analysis of governance in the Federal District to date, explores a topic which needs much more attention, the rule of law, and specifically, the impact of police reform on that goal. She presents a well-supported and argued pessimistic picture of the failure of democracy to come to grips with adequate reforms. Indeed, she concludes that democratic efforts have actually undermined the rule of law, thus undermining democracy itself.

1457 Diálogos por México. México: Nuevo Siglo Aguilar: Televisa, 2006. 361 p.: bibl., ill.

A useful work for anyone wanting a basic source of information about the views of the 2006 presidential candidates. This book provides a complete transcript of interviews with the candidates during seven programs televised by Televisa in Jan.–Feb. 2006. All the candidates were asked the same questions. The answers are followed by a section in which leading Mexican scholars and intellectuals analyze their responses.

1458 Dilemmas of political change in Mexico. Edited by Kevin J. Middlebrook. London: Inst. of Latin American Studies, Univ. of London; San Diego: Center for U.S.-Mexican Studies, Univ. of California, 2004. 570 p.: bibl., ill., index.

An outstanding collection of essays on all facets of Mexican politics which explores the role of numerous actors, from the perspective of leading American and Mexican scholars, on the transformation of Mexican society to a democratic model in the mid to late 1990s. The topics include executive-legislative relations, legal reforms, business and politics, civil-military relations, among others.

1459 Espinosa, Mario. Historia y cultura política de la participación ciudadana en la Ciudad de México: entre los condicionamientos del sistema y el ensueño cívico.

(*Andamios*, 1, otoño/invierno 2004, p. 9–50, bibl.)

The author provides a careful, deeply researched overview of the evolution of citizen participation in the Federal District from 1929 to 2000, and provides an extensive bibliography on this topic for the capital. His approach focuses on the impact of political culture as an obstacle to developing a participatory role, and the heritage of structures in the present day which were established under different norms of political culture.

Favela Gavia, Diana Margarita. Cambios en el sistema político y en la protesta social en México, 1946–2000: interacción entre instituciones y acción social. See item **2486**.

1460 Gonzalbo Escalante, Fernando. Los años amargos: las ideas políticas en México a fines del siglo XX. (*Hist. Polít.*, 11, 2004, p. 153–174, bibl.)

This analysis of political ideas and language makes the controversial argument that the fundamental change in beliefs in Mexican political culture occurred during the Salinas presidency; that is, the government adopted the language of the opposition, including democracy, liberty, and civil society, implementing some of these beliefs in the religious reforms to the constitutions in 1992 and the Federal Electoral Institute. The author suggests that by legitimizing this language, the government enhanced anti-state beliefs.

1461 Guillén, Diana. Chiapas y el arte de gobernar: apuntes sobre una historia reciente, 1973–1993. (*Secuencia/México*, 59, mayo/agosto 2004, p. 173–198, bibl.)

Guillén pursues an imaginative approach in analyzing the "art of governance" in the state of Chiapas in the two decades before the Zapatista uprising. She offers a number of interesting hypotheses, and her exploration of the failures of the governance process which produced this major political event sheds light on the Chiapan context. She believes, among other conclusions, that Chiapas lacked the fundamental institutions for reinforcing access to government and legitimizing public policies.

1462 Hernández Castillo, Rosalva Aída. The indigenous movement in Mexico: between electoral politics and local resistance. (*Lat. Am. Perspect.*, 33:2, March 2006, p. 115–131)

Beginning with the Aug. 2005 meeting of indigenous groups organized by the Zapatistas, the author examines the failure of the principal political parties to understand fully the indigenous peoples and analyzes the tensions existing between local forms of resistance and the national political strategies proposed by the Zapatistas ("the other campaign"). [D. Coerver]

1463 Hiskey, Jonathan T. Demand-based development and local electoral environments in Mexico. (*Comp. Polit./New York*, 36:1, Oct. 2003, p. 41–59, graph, tables)

Hiskey has published a series of important essays in the last several years, most of which analyze various aspects of electoral politics, especially in local contexts. In this article, he attempts to determine what effect, if any, democracy has on demand-based approaches to poverty alleviation in Mexico, that is, empowering local governments and constituencies to submit proposals. He concludes that much more research needs to be done on this relationship and that meaningful local elections do not guarantee successful project outcomes.

1464 Hughes, Sallie. Newsrooms in conflict: journalism and the democratization of Mexico. Pittsburgh, Pa.: Univ. of Pittsburgh Press, 2006. 286 p.: bibl., index.

Hughes provides an outstanding analysis of the role of the media in the democratic transformation of Mexico, which complements Chappell Lawson's broad interpretation of electronic media. This exploration is based on numerous interviews with leading journalists in the field, and her own career as a journalist in Mexico and for the *Miami Herald*.

1465 Jiménez Badillo, Margarita. Coaliciones parlamentarias en México: éxito del Presidente en un gobierno compartido. (*Rev. Inst. Elect. Estado Méx. Apunt. Elect.*, 4:13, julio/sept. 2003, p. 63–100, bibl., graphs, tables)

Jiménez Badillo explores the relationship between a president's party and the opposition Congress from 1982, when Miguel de la Madrid was inaugurated, through 2003. Despite the increased control of the opposition parties, especially under Fox, she discovers that substantial collaboration occurred on most legislation, contrary to the perception that the opposition-controlled 48th session blocked Fox's legislative agenda.

1466 Klesner, Joseph L. Electoral competition and the new party system in Mexico. (*Lat. Am. Polit. Soc.*, 47:2, Summer 2005, p. 103–142, bibl., tables)

Klesner, one of the leading authors of empirical electoral analysis of Mexican elections, explores the regional alignments that evolved in the 1990s. He makes the major argument that a pro-regime—anti-regime cleavage has developed in the electorate as a result of the dealignments which have resulted from increasing electoral competition, and the major parties have developed into "catch all" organizations, attempting to appeal to broader and ill-defined social bases. Many other interesting findings are included from his review of survey data. For historian's comment, see *HLAS 64:780*.

1467 Macías Vázquez, María Carmen. El impacto del modelo neoliberal en los sindicatos en México. Prólogo de Néstor de Buen Lozano. México: Editorial Porrúa: UNAM, Inst. de Investigaciones Jurídicas, 2005. 322 p.: bibl. (Serie Doctrina jurídica; no. 222)

Essentially a legalistic appraisal on the impact of economic globalization on organized labor in Mexico.

1468 Martin, JoAnn. Tepoztlán and the transformation of the Mexican state: the politics of loose connections. Tucson: Univ. of Arizona Press, 2005. 276 p.: bibl., index.

The author examines popular movements in Tepoztlán, which Robert Redfield and Oscar Lewis examined in detail in early eras, thus shedding fresh light on the evolution of this interesting community. Her work focuses specifically on the changing land tenure situation, and the interactions between domestic and international actors, as globalization reaches this town.

1469 Martínez González, Víctor Hugo. Fisiones y fusiones, divorcios y reconciliaciones: la dirigencia del Partido de la Revolución Democrática (PRD), 1989–2004. México: Plaza y Valdes, 2005. 272 p.: bibl., ill.

This is the most detailed analysis to date of the political origins of the multiple wings and factions within the PRD leadership. An essential work for anyone wishing to understand how these factions emerged and the patterns that have evolved since the party's formation in 1989.

1470 Metapolítica. Vol. 7, No. 30, julio/ agosto 2003. México 2003: El miedo a la democracia. México: Centro de Estudios de Política Comparada.

Metapolítica has become an excellent source of articles on Mexican politics. This special issue devoted to the fear of democracy gathers a number of leading specialists and intellectuals who offer observations on the state of democratic consolidation mid-way through the Fox administration. A useful collection.

1471 Mexican governance: from single- party rule to divided government. Edited by Armand B. Peschard-Sverdrup and Sara R. Rioff. Washington, D.C.: CSIS Press, Center for Strategic and International Studies, 2005. 317 p.: bibl., index. (Significant issues series; v. 27, no. 2)

An excellent edited volume by seven leading Mexican scholars (or scholars who reside in Mexico) which surveys the leading institutions and issues undergoing dramatic changes in a consolidating democracy in Mexico, including Congress, state reform, judicial reform, security policy, Church and state relations, and the media.

México, democracia ineficaz. See item **2223.**

1472 Mexico's politics and society in transition. Edited by Joseph S. Tulchin and Andrew D. Selee. Boulder, Colo.: L. Rienner, 2003. 373 p.: bibl., ill., index.

Tulchin and Selee have achieved a useful collection of essays which examine the most pressing issues in Mexican politics or in the bilateral relationship with the US shortly after Fox began his administration. Among the issues which this collection explores are NAFTA, immigration, Mexican rural development, security, labor, the role of women, and the Zapatista movement.

1473 Morales Ramírez, Rafael. Nuevos campos de juego: mecanismos de acuerdo para el federalismo mexicano. (*Foro Int./México*, 45:3, julio/sept. 2005, p. 466– 488, bibl.)

Morales Ramírez provides a detailed overview of the problems of federalism in Mexico, while focusing on recent efforts by the federal government to decentralize its control over certain policy areas and resources. The author concludes that these questions have not been addressed with much originality and that one of the central weaknesses is that state governments rarely have the institutional capacity to take over tasks previously performed at the national level.

1474 Municipio y buen gobierno: expe- riencias del ímpetu local en México. Coordinación de Tonatiuh Guillén López, Pilar López Fernández e Pablo Rojo Calzada. Mexico: Centro de Investigación y Docencia Económicas, 2006. 502 p.: bibl., ill., maps.

This work is edited by Tonatiuh Guillén López, a leading student of local politics in Mexico, and consists of numerous case studies at the municipal level that reveal how governments function, followed by three sections of contributions, which make recommendations for improving municipal administration, reinforcing democratic practices, and strengthening intergovernmental relations.

1475 Pacheco Méndez, Guadalupe. Democratización, pluralización y cambios en el sistema de partidos en México, 1991– 2000. (*Rev. Mex. Sociol.*, 65:3, julio/sept. 2003, p. 523–564, bibl., graphs)

The author analyzes significant changes in Mexico's party system during the crucial period of democratic transition from 1991 through 2000, as the PRI began losing its dominant electoral position. She focuses on electoral volatility and the impact of pluralization by examining four fundamental variables. She concludes that the electorate during this period was seeking out an alternative strategic means of defeating the PRI while simultaneously viewing all parties with disdain.

1476 Pacheco Méndez, Guadalupe. Geografía de la oleada panista, 1991–2000. (*Veredas*, 4/5, 2002, p. 201–223, bibl., graphs, tables)

This is a worthwhile analysis with much statistical information of the geographic evolution by districts and regions of the voting strength of PAN from 1991 through 2000. For example, Pacheco illustrates that in 1991, half of the districts won by PAN were on the northern border. In the mid- to late 1990s, their geographic success shifted to the west. By 2000, PAN's overwhelming strength had shifted to the Federal District, México, and Morelos, followed by the Gulf states.

1477 Pacheco Méndez, Guadalupe. El PRI ante la pérdida del poder y la búsqueda de un nuevo liderazgo interno: el interregno de julio de 2000 a febrero de 2001. (*Veredas*, 7, segundo semestre 2003, p. 100–130, bibl.)

A narrowly focused but revealing account of how PRI elites, divided into two opposing groups, resolved their differences within the National Political Council in the critical period after their presidential defeat from July 2000 through February 2001. Despite their tentative resolution, Pacheco believes they will face serious challenges in establishing insider control of the party.

1478 Palma, Esperanza. Las bases políticas de la alternancia en México: un estudio del PAN y el PRD durante la democratización. Azcapotzalco, Mexico: Univ. Autónoma Metropolitana, División de Ciencias Sociales y Humanidades, 2004. 303 p.: bibl. (Serie Sociología)

An extensively researched analysis of the evolution of electoral opposition in Mexico from 1988 through 1997, based on the author's PhD dissertation from the Univ. of Notre Dame in 2000. She concludes that the evolution of the opposition's role since 1988 explains Vicente Fox's victory, and that it should not be viewed as a surprise.

1479 Pérez Calleja, David. Aguascalientes, la sucesión 2004: alternancia o continuidad? Mexico: Tall. Gráf. de La Universal, 2004. 307 p.: bibl., ill., maps.

A detailed analysis of the gubernatorial candidates that includes insights about the competing candidates, the distribution of electoral support, and an assessment of recent governors and their political networks and positions.

1480 Pérez-Ruiz, Maya Lorena. Todos somos zapatistas!: alianzas y rupturas entre el EZLN y las organizaciones indíge-

nas de México. México: Inst. Nacional de Antropología e Historia, 2005. 788 p.: bibl., maps. (Col. Científica; 474. Serie Antropología)

This comprehensive, solidly researched and detailed work will be viewed as an essential source on the Zapatistas. It analyzes every aspect of the movement, both pre-EZLN and the EZLN's role within the larger context of indigenous movements generally in Chiapas and in Mexico. The author also provides an extensive discussion of the Fox administration's interactions and difficulties meeting the Zapatista demands.

1481 Reynoso, Diego. Distritos electorales y representación bicameral en México. (*Rev. Mex. Sociol.*, 66:3, julio/sept. 2004, p. 537–564, bibl., tables)

Reynoso provides a comparative analysis of the impact of the 1996 electoral reform laws on the upper and lower houses of Congress. He tests the relationship empirically of the distortion between state populations and the fixed representation in the Senate and House both with and without plurinominal senators and deputies. His findings are carefully placed within the larger comparative context.

1482 Reynoso, Diego. Federalismo y democracia: las dos dinámicas de la transición mexicana. (*Rev. Mex. Sociol.*, 64:1, enero/marzo 2002, p. 3–30, bibl., tables)

Although this essay does not raise any new arguments about the contradictions introduced by an increasing emphasis on federalism as a result of the democratization process, it is valuable for the clarity of its arguments, the carefulness of its research, and the objectivity of its conclusions.

1483 Rottinghaus, Brandon and **Irina Alberro.** Rivaling the PRI: the image management of Vicente Fox and the use of public opinion polling in the 2000 Mexican election. (*Lat. Am. Polit. Soc.*, 47:2, Summer 2005, p. 143–158)

This is an outstanding, original article on a little researched topic which clearly established the role and impact of public opinion surveys on Fox's electoral success in 2000. It demonstrates that Fox understood the value of the insights such polls could provide and used that information to enhance his appeal, while in contrast Labastida ignored similar information provided by his pollsters. For historian's comment, see *HLAS 64:818.*

1484 Saltalamacchia, Homero R. and Alicia Ziccardi. Las ciudades mexicanas y el buen gobierno local: una metodología para su evaluación. (*Rev. Mex. Sociol.*, 67:1, enero/marzo 2005, p. 31–97, bibl.)

This is essentially an article about developing an adequate methodology for evaluating the performace of local governments. The authors develop detailed proposals for testing five indicators of governmental performance: efficiency, responsibility, effectiveness, responsiveness to requests, and encouraging civic participation. Their series of recommendations would be useful to scholars contemplating field research that relies on a survey questionnaire.

Sánchez González, José Juan. Reforma, modernización e innovación en la historia de la administración pública en México. See *HLAS 64:513.*

1485 Schedler, Andreas. "El voto es nuestro": cómo los ciudadanos mexicanos perciben el clientelismo electoral. (*Rev. Mex. Sociol.*, 66:1, enero/marzo 2004, p. 57–97, bibl.)

Schedler, who recently has written several contributions that are important to understanding Mexican politics, provides a detailed exploration of the state of clientelism at the initiation of the Fox administration. He concludes, on the basis of extensive personal interviews in rural Mexico, that, contrary to what many scholars believe, most respondents oppose clientelism, and that these reactions stem from new values introduced by democratic politics.

1486 Schneider, Ben Ross. Why is Mexican business so organized? (*LARR*, 37:1, 2002, p. 77–107, bibl.)

The relationship between business and government in Mexico is one of the most neglected topics in recent political science research. Ben Ross Schneider has explored this relationship in a major book on Brazil, but in this article, he focuses on the single most important business organization in Mexico, the elite capitalist Consejo Mexicano de Hombres de Negocios. He provides numerous valuable insights

into the interactions between the state and the leading business organizations, as well as the interactions among those same organizations.

1487 Shirk, David A. Mexico's new politics: the PAN and democratic change. Boulder, Colo.: L. Rienner, 2005. 279 p.: bibl., index.

An outstanding work on the evolution of the National Action Party (PAN) during the recent decades of democratization. Provides numerous insights into the internal conflicts within PAN, the strategies it used to achieve control over the executive branch, and the conditions which have limited its partisan expansion.

1488 Simposio Internacional "Regionalismo-Federalismo. Aspectos Históricos y Desafíos Actuales en México, Alemania y Otros Países Europeos," *Colegio de México y Facultad de Filosofía y Letras de la Univ. Nacional Autónoma de México, 2001.* Regionalismo y federalismo: aspectos históricos y desafíos actuales en México, Alemania y otros países europeos. Coordinación de León E. Bieber. México: Colegio de México; Bonn, Germany: Servicio Alemán de Intercambio Académico; México: UNAM, Facultad de Filosofía y Letras, 2004. 486 p.: bibl., ill.

This excellent collection addresses the most important issue which emerges from the voting patterns in the 2006 presidential election: regionalism. The value of this work is that it offers interesting comparisons with Germany, Spain, the European Union, and Yugoslavia, and more importantly, goes beyond the issues of federalism, and explores cultural and historical patterns. Carlos Alba Vega offers an insightful analysis of the impact of NAFTA on Jalisco.

1489 Somuano Ventura, María Fernanda. Más allá del voto: modos de participación política no electoral en México. (*Foro Int./México*, 45:1, enero/marzo 2005, p. 65–88, bibl., graphs, tables)

One of the neglected areas of analysis are the methods of increasing political participation outside of voting. The author, using the World Values Surveys and the excellent culture survey from the Secretariat of Government, compares the evolution of these forms of behavior from 1980 to 2001. She argues that while nonvoting participation has increased in Mexico, true in postindustrial societies, it has only increased in some aspects, for example, signing petitions, while actually declining in others.

Tejada, Luis Angel. La historia del PRI en Durango, 1929–2005. See *HLAS 64:834.*

1490 Temkin Yedwab, Benjamín; Rodrigo Salazar Elena; and Gustavo Ramírez Pedroza. Explorando la dinámica del "abstencionismo ilustrado": ¿un caso de demasiada o poca cultura democrática? (*Rev. Inst. Elect. Estado Méx. Apunt. Elect.*, 5:19, enero/marzo 2005, p. 9–44, bibl., graphs, tables)

Abstentionism has long interested analysts of Mexican electoral politics. In this essay, the authors use two major surveys by the Mexican government in 2001 and 2003 to empirically analyze those variables which explain why people do not go to the polls. They conclude that Mexican voters in 2003 did not vote in large numbers because they remained unconvinced by the parties that the elections warranted their participation, rather than because they lack a democratic culture.

1491 Treinta años de cambios políticos en México. Coordinación de Antonella Attili. México: Miguel Ángel Porrúa, 2006. 418 p.: bibl. (Conocer para decidir) (Las ciencias sociales)

This edited collection surveys institutional and procedural changes in Mexican politics during the last 30 years. Many of the contributions are lacking in-depth scholarly research, but three contributions stand out: "Parties and the Party System in Mexico," "The Transformation of Local Government," and most notably, María Eugenia Valdés Vega's chapter on "Radio and Television in the Mexican Transition."

1492 Veloz Espejel, Víctor. Notas para la reforma del Estado mexicano. (*Rev. Inst. Elect. Estado Méx. Apunt. Elect.*, 5:19, enero/marzo 2005, p. 71–93, bibl.)

This essay on the reform of the state is not an analysis of the politics of the reform; rather it focuses primarily on the content of the reforms and what they might actually mean for democratic governance.

It is an extremely well researched effort with an outstanding bibliography that offers pragmatic policy conclusions about governance relationships and the beliefs that such reforms truly suggest the possibility of citizen power, rather than institutional power alone.

1493 Vivero Ávila, Igor. Comportamiento del sistema de partidos mexicano en el proceso de cambio democrático, 1985–2003. (*Rev. Inst. Elect. Estado Méx. Apunt. Elect.*, 4:14, oct./dic. 2003, p. 128–143, bibl., graphs, tables)

This brief work is worthy of mention because it provides a detailed empirical analysis with tables and data to measure the impact of the party system in Mexico and in Latin America on the level of volatility and fragmentation. The conclusions, however, are not monumental, and suggest that Mexico is following the path of other countries shifting from an hegemonic to a pluralistic, competitive system.

1494 Vivero Ávila, Igor. Desafiando al sistema la izquierda política en México: evolución organizativa, ideológica y electoral del Partido de la Revolución Democrática, 1989–2005. México: Univ. Autónoma del Estado de México, Facultad de Ciencias Políticas y Administración Pública: Miguel Ángel Porrúa, 2006. 368 p.: bibl., charts. (Las ciencias sociales)

This is an excellent study of the PRD, particularly from an electoral perspective and on the party's internal conflicts and composition, which updates the original work of Kathleen Bruhn to 2005. The author concludes that much more research needs to be undertaken on the PRD at the local level.

1495 Wuhs, Steven T. Democratization and the dynamics of candidate selection rule change in Mexico, 1991–2003. (*Mex. Stud.*, 22:1, Winter 2006, p. 33–55)

In a democratizing environment, party leaders must balance competing goals of electoral growth and organizational development in determining candidate-selection rules. More-open rules help nominate electable candidates, but more-closed rules help to build stronger party organizations. Author concludes that the mixed electoral system in Mexico permits party leaders to have it both ways: to preserve their influence, pacify party activists, and enjoy the advantages of more-open rules. [D. Coerver]

1496 Yaworsky, William R. At the whim of the state: neoliberalism and non-governmental organizations in Guerrero, Mexico. (*Mex. Stud.*, 21:2, Summer 2005, p. 403–427)

Examination of the relationship between the state (more specifically the Se-cretaría de Desarrollo Social (SEDESOL) and NGOs) in the Chilapa region of Guerrero. Author maintains that the government has successfully co-opted the NGOs into serving as promoters of neoliberal reforms. Instead of encouraging regional autonomy, the NGOs are part of a network allocating government subsidies and helping to integrate the communities into the global economy. [D. Coerver]

CENTRAL AMERICA

CHARLES D. BROCKETT, *Professor of Political Science, Sewanee: The University of the South*

AS A SURE SIGN of continuing democratic consolidation in Central America, much of the literature surveyed here assesses the normal themes associated with relatively stable political systems, such as the functioning of political institutions and electoral processes and results. A good number of other works analyze political culture and attitudes, again with much of the analytic focus and findings befitting consolidating democracies. A happy number of these are impressive in their combination of theoretical ambition and empirical rigor, some from scholars within the region, others from outside either in Europe or the US. At the same time, the region's troubled past is also represented in a set of works providing a mix of perspectives and sophistication.

Institutional relations—and conflict—are front and center in two very good studies that also highlight the conditioning role of party systems. Vargas (item **1509**) examines the consequences of party fragmentation for executive-legislative relations in Costa Rica, while Miranda (item **1515**) analyzes the impact of party-based legislative coalitions on presidential power in El Salvador. More broadly, a team of European scholars (item **1519**) provides perhaps the best account of the contemporary Guatemalan political system, synthesizing across a broad swath of scholarship. Pursuing a narrower focus but equally outstanding, a mixed Nicaraguan-European team (item **1530**) portrays the course of the move toward regional autonomy for the Atlantic half of Nicaragua. Finally, the increasing subordination of security forces to civilian authority is well traced for the four countries from Nicaragua north by Millett and Pérez (item **1500**), and by Caumartin for Panama (item **1536**).

With democracy comes regular elections, followed by just as regular analyses by journalists and scholars. Standing out among the many electoral studies surveyed for this volume is the contribution by Vorst (item **1502**). Analyzing the growth of voter abstentionism in Costa Rica, the collection provides a plethora of great graphics elucidating the differing types of abstainers identified. An excellent examination of the broader context for understanding such trends is offered by Booth and Seligson (item **1505**) in their empirical examination of the relationship in Costa Rica between political participation and legitimacy. Seligson is also associated with two other outstanding works on political culture produced as part of the ongoing series of studies from the Latin American Public Opinion Project at Vanderbilt University, one on Honduras (item **1523**) and the other on Nicaragua (item **1528**). Both examine a wide array of political attitudes from recent national surveys, interpreted in light of both similar surveys throughout Latin America and related social science theory. The implications for democratic consolidation are a concern of all of these works, as well as for two other good studies that also standout for their comparative nature, Pérez's (item **1501**) on public attitudes toward crime in El Salvador and Guatemala and Martí i Puig and Santiuste's (item **1499**) on congressional deputies in these two countries as well as Nicaragua.

Numerous works continue to be produced on the region's political violence, especially the past years of most intense conflict, a good number by political participants themselves. Perhaps the most important study, though, is by a novelist and about a more contemporary crime. The 1998 murder of Guatemalan Catholic Bishop Juan José Gerardi and its aftermath is closely and artfully portrayed by Goldman (item **1518**). The Guatemalan state terrorism that Bishop Gerardi was so instrumental in documenting is also examined by Brockett (item **1498**) along with the parallel violence in El Salvador. Both this work and Almeida's (item **1510**) on El Salvador create extensive protest events databases to examine the relationship between popular protest and regime violence, contributing to the scholarship on social movements.

Looking at this literature as a whole, the extensive interdisciplinary and sometimes interregional collaborations stand out as positive elements. In addition, many scholars continue to make good use of the great advantages provided by Central America for comparative work. Of this, we can hope for more. It would also be beneficial to see more comprehensive, sophisticated social science work on individual countries, that is, solid empirical studies that are meaningfully informed by appropriate theory. At this point the political system best studied is that of Costa Rica, followed by El Salvador, with Honduras as the least studied.

GENERAL

1497 Allison, Michael E. The transition from armed opposition to electoral opposition in Central America. (*Lat. Am. Polit. Soc.*, 48:4, Winter 2006, p. 137–162, bibl., tables)

Helpful comparative summary of armed oppositions in El Salvador, Nicaragua, Guatemala, and Honduras. Also examines their subsequent successes as political parties in capturing votes and seats in executive and legislative elections. Attributes relative success of the transition from armed opposition to political parties in El Salvador and Nicaragua to organization and popular support rather than electoral rules.

1498 Brockett, Charles D. Political movements and violence in Central America. Cambridge; New York: Cambridge

Univ. Press, 2005. 380 p.: bibl., index, maps. (Cambridge studies in contentious politics)

In-depth analysis of the impact of three decades of state violence on contentious political movements in Central America, particularly El Salvador and Guatemala. Based on extensive events database for both countries, resolves repression-protest paradox while addressing controversies related to political process model for studying contentious movements.

1499 Martí i Puig, Salvador and **Salvador Santiuste Cué.** ¿Consolidación o, simplemente, persistencia democrática?: análisis de las percepciones de las élites políticas en Nicaragua, El Salvador y Guatemala. (*ECA/San Salvador*, 60:684, oct. 2005, p. 961–984, bibl., tables)

Data from surveys of political attitudes of congressional deputies in Nicaragua and Guatemala in late 1990s and El Salvador in early 2000s allow for fascinating comparisons between party elites and countries along with good theorizing about implications for democratic consolidation.

1500 Millett, Richard L. and **Orlando J. Pérez.** New threats and old dilemmas: Central America's armed forces in the 21st century. (*J. Polit. Mil. Sociol.*, 33:1, Summer 2005, p. 59–79, bibl.)

Good separate explanations of lessening role of militaries and their increasing subordination to civilian authorities in El Salvador, Honduras, Nicaragua, and Guatemala with the degree of progress in that order. The obstacles to future progress come from new threats, such as the drug trade combined with the weakness of civilian institutions, rather than from military intransigence.

1501 Pérez, Orlando J. Democratic legitimacy and public insecurity: crime and democracy in El Salvador and Guatemala. (*Polit. Sci. Q.*, 118:4, Winter 2003/04, p. 627–644, graphs, tables)

Useful description of public attitudes toward crime in El Salvador and Guatemala and the impact on political attitudes. The work is based on national surveys from the late 1990s and related Latinobarómetro surveys. According to the surveys, fear of crime heightens insecurity, reducing public support for democracy.

COSTA RICA

1502 Abstencionistas en Costa Rica: quiénes son y por qué no votan? Contribuciones de Ciska Raventós Vorst et al. San José: Editorial de la Univ. de Costa Rica: Tribunal Supremo de Elecciones: IIDH/CAPEL: Inst. de Investigaciones Sociales, 2005. 278 p.: bibl., col. ill., col. maps.

After staying steady from 1962 through 1994, abstentionism in Costa Rican presidential elections took a big jump in 1998 and 2002. This collaboration between the Tribunal Supremo de Elecciones and researchers at the Universidad de Costa Rica provides a sophisticated portrayal of who abstained and why, highlighting substantial

variation among the patterns identified. Great graphics.

1503 Alfaro Redondo, Ronald. Elecciones nacionales 2006 en Costa Rica y la recomposición del sistema de partidos políticos. (*Rev. Cienc. Polít./Santiago*, 26:1, 2006, p. 125–137, bibl., graphs, map, table)

Better than most articles in this series of election results descriptions, author does a good job of placing the 2006 Costa Rican election results in longitudinal context with several particularly useful time-series tables.

1504 Argilés Marín, José Manuel and **Raquel Ornat Clemente.** El perro del hortelano: políticas públicas, institucionalidad y pueblos indígenas en Costa Rica. (*Cuad. Antropol./San José*, 15, dic. 2005, p. 25–44, bibl.)

Survey of changes in Costa Rican public policy toward indigenous peoples since the 1940s. Particularly good analysis through the 1980s. Based on fieldwork from the early 2000s, finds that policies need to deal better with indigenous heterogeneity and wariness of those who purport to represent them.

1505 Booth, John A. and **Mitchell A. Seligson.** Political legitimacy and participation in Costa Rica: evidence of arena shopping. (*Polit. Res. Q.*, 58:4, Dec. 2005, p. 537–550, bibl., graph, tables)

Costa Rica's well consolidated democracy and respect for human rights allow for a significant test of the impact of attitudes toward political legitimacy on political participation by two of the best scholars writing on the region. Utilizing a national survey conducted in 2002, they find seven dimensions of legitimacy that provide every possible relationship with four dimensions of political participation.

1506 Contreras, Gerardo. La historia no es color de rosa: a propósito del setenta y cinco aniversario de la fundación del Partido Comunista de Costa Rica. Sabanilla, Costa Rica: Ediciones Perro Azul, 2006. 206 p.: bibl., ill.

One of several books on the Partido Comunista de Costa Rica by a historian at the Universidad de Costa Rica, this is a friendly account written in recognition of the party's three-quarters of a century existence and what is portrayed as its positive role in strengthening democracy in the country.

1507 La democracia del nuevo milenio: transformaciones políticas e institucionales en la Costa Rica contemporánea. San José: PNUD Costa Rica: FLACSO Costa Rica, 2006. 204 p.: bibl., ill., maps.

Separately authored chapters examine possible reforms in areas of national and local government, representation, and public accounting. Originally prepared as basic documents for approximately 40 researchers considering reforms for the country, published in *Desafíos de la democracia: una propuesta para Costa Rica* (2005). Perhaps of most lasting value is the chapter on local government, particularly the GIS maps.

1508 Furlong, William Leon. Evolución de la democracia costarricense: partidos políticos y campañas electorales, 1982–2006. San José, Costa Rica: Editorial UCR, 2008. 302 p.: bibl., ill.

Compilation of two sets of writings by long-time US observer of Costa Rican affairs. Each election since 1986 is given a chapter-length treatment with an epilogue bringing in 2006 and continuing trends of dealignment and disenchantment. Second set examines Costa Rican foreign policy.

1509 Vargas Céspedes, Jean Paul. El ocaso del presidencialismo costarricense. San José: Fundación Arias para la Paz y el Progreso Humano, 2008. 366 p.: bibl.

Reads at times like the dissertation turned into book that it is, but overall a sophisticated, in-depth examination of the implications of party fragmentation for executive-legislative relations. Especially good are the case studies such as an important one about the fate of the Instituto Costarricense de Electricidad (ICE).

EL SALVADOR

1510 Almeida, Paul. Waves of protest: popular struggle in El Salvador, 1925–2005. Minneapolis: Univ. of Minnesota Press, 2008. 298 p.: bibl., ill., index, map. (Social movements, protest, and contention; 29)

Outstanding empirical and theoretical account of popular struggle in El

Salvador across eight decades, focuses on four waves of protest, right up to 2002–2003 campaign against health care privatization. Based on impressive events database as well as interviews with over 200 protestors going back to 1970s actions.

1511 Arana, Rubí Esmeralda and María Santacruz Giralt. La participación política de las mujeres: una mirada desde la opinión pública. (*ECA/San Salvador*, 60, 681/682, julio/agosto 2005, p. 659–676, bibl., graphs, photo, tables)

Good analysis of results of 2003 national public opinion survey by Instituto Universitario de Opinión Pública on attitudes, especially female, concerning political role of women. Employment for women outside the home is crucial explanatory variable, along with age, education, and urban residency. Especially striking is variation in identifying machista culture as the principle barrier to women gaining elected office.

1512 Canales, Tirso. Schafik Hándal: por la senda revolucionaria. San Salvador: Editorial Memoria, 2007. 260 p.: bibl., ill.

Following Schafik Hándal's death in 2006 this volume was compiled by a noted author and long-time associate on the Salvadoran left. Offers interesting details about their political struggles during decades prior to the civil war as well as a summary of key events through mid-1990s, providing context for a series of interviews and other statements by Hándal from 1978 through 2006.

1513 Córdova Macías, Ricardo. Cultura política en torno a los gobiernos locales y la descentralización en El Salvador: informe final de la encuesta. San Salvador: FLACSO-Programa El Salvador; [s.l.] Funda-Ungo, 2000. 142, 10, 41 p.: ill.

Contains the extensive results of 1999 national public opinion survey of Salvadoran political attitudes, especially as related to local government and decentralization issues.

1514 Handal, Schafik Jorge. Una guerra para construir la paz. Argentina: Ocean Sur: Editorial Morazán, 2006. 151 p.: bibl.

Compilation of seven statements from 1996 through 2006 by former long time head of Communist Party of El Salvador and

2004 presidential candidate of Farabundo
Martí National Liberation Front. Of interest
not just for his critique of country's then
rightist government but especially for his
view of accomplishments of historic 1992
peace accords.

1515 Miranda Baires, Danilo Alberto. La
contribución de las alianzas a los
poderes del presidente. (*ECA/San Salvador*,
61:696, oct. 2006, p. 939–956, bibl., tables)
Good examination of presidential
power in El Salvador since 1984, including
both formal powers and varying legislative
political support. Valuable for the regional
comparisons that are made.

**1516 Proceso electoral 2006: una mirada
feminista a la participación política
de las mujeres.** San Salvador: Colectiva Feminista para el Desarrollo Local, 2007.
138 p.: bibl., col. ill.
Descriptive account of the gender
dimensions of the 2006 Salvadoran elections by the Colectiva Feminista para el
Desarrollo Local includes an interesting
study of gendered media campaign accounts. Contains ample data on gender
breakdown of party lists and election results
at various levels, supplemented by some
interviews.

GUATEMALA

Berger, Susan A. Guatemaltecas: the wom-
en's movement, 1986–2003. See item **2558**.

1517 Brett, Roderick Leslie. Social movements, indigenous politics and democratization in Guatemala, 1985–1996.
Boston: Brill, 2008. 229 p.: bibl., ill., index,
map. (*Cedla Latin America studies*; 95)
Seeks to explain patterns of collective
action emerging during Guatemala's process of democratization between 1985 and
1996 through case studies of El Consejo de
Comunidades Étnicas—Runujel, La Coordinadora Nacional Indígena y Campesina,
and La Defensoría Maya. Based on extensive
field research, each case gives a good account of the organization's evolution, identity, objectives, and strategies.

1518 Goldman, Francisco. The art of political murder: who killed the Bishop?
New York: Grove Press: Distributed by

Publishers Group West, 2007. 396 p.: bibl.,
ill. index.
In an important work of impressive
investigative journalism, novelist Goldman
carefully examines 1998 murder of Guatemalan Catholic Bishop Juan José Gerardi,
the ensuing trial and conviction of army
officers, and bizarre judicial aftermath.
Gerardi's murder occurred just days after
his release of a lengthy report clarifying
that the country's security forces were
responsible for most of the extraordinary
political violence of prior decades. That
violence is an ever-present context for the
brave team of murder investigators and for
Goldman's own multi-year effort.

**1519 Perfil de gobernabilidad de Gua-
temala.** Edicion de Instituto Inter-
universitario de Iberoamérica y Portugal.
Salamanca: Ediciones Univ. Salamanca: Red
Eurolatinoamericana de Gobernabilidad
para el Desarrollo, 2005. 188 p.: bibl., ill.
(*Aquilafuente*; 89)
One of the best books on the political
system of contemporary Guatemala, covering each major aspect in separate chapters
pulling together best research in concise
fashion. Well written by team at Universidad de Salamanca as part of a series on Latin
American countries under auspices of the
Red Eurolatinoamericana de Gobernabilidad
para el Desarrollo.

1520 Sánchez, Omar. Guatemala's party
universe: a case study in underinstitutionalization. (*Lat. Am. Polit. Soc.*, 50:1,
Spring 2008, p. 123–151, bibl., tables)
Party structures often perform essential democratic functions, but this
well-executed study finds that this is not
so in Guatemala where the degree of party
underinstitutionalization stands out for
the region. Examining volatility levels,
societal links, ideological coherence, party
discipline, and party organization, neither
does it find evidence of slow improvement
predicted by some theories.

1521 Short, Nicola. The international politics of post-conflict reconstruction in
Guatemala. New York: Palgrave Macmillan,
2007. 188 p.: bibl., ill., index, maps.
After presenting its Gramscian perspective and the historical background to
the case, there remain only 46 pages of text

on the subject of the title. Still, the book does provide a useful account of the Guatemalan peace process and the problematic implementation of the peace accords.

1522 Vela Castañeda, Manolo E. Guatemala, 1954: las ideas de la contrarrevolución. (*Foro Int./México*, 45:1, enero/marzo 2005, p. 89–114, bibl.)

As the author notes, much has been written on the 1954 overthrow of Guatemalan government, but little has been written on its aftermath. Article provides useful identification of major themes of ideology of the counter-revolution, well-captured in its slogan of "Dios, Patria y Libertad," but with little examination of the key figures' own texts.

HONDURAS

1523 Cruz, José Miguel; José René Argueta; and Mitchell A. Seligson. Cultura política de la democracia en Honduras: 2006. San Salvador: IUDOP, Inst. Univ. de Opinión Pública: FOPRIDEH, Fed. de Org. Privadas de Desarrollo de Honduras, 2007. 246 p.: bibl., ill. (Americas barometer)

Part of the data and theory rich series produced by Latin American Public Opinion Project at Vanderbilt Univ., providing excellent account of political attitudes in Honduras based on national surveys in 2004 and 2006, along with comparable data from throughout the hemisphere.

1524 Sierra Fonseca, Rolando and Álvaro Cálix. La gobernabilidad democrática local en Honduras: estudio en 16 municipios. Tegucigalpa: CIPRODEH: AMHON: COSUDE, 2005. 175 p.: bibl., ill.

Useful description of decentralization occurring in Honduras with democratization, reinforced by the Ley de Municipalidades of 1990, and data-rich comparison of sixteen municipios. Findings indicate potential tension between higher levels of local political stability and lower levels of participation and provision of services.

1525 El sistema penitenciario hondureño: un diagnóstico a la luz de los derechos humanos. Contribuciones de Lucas Valderas *et al.* Coordinación de Joaquín A. Mejía Rivera. Tegucigalpa: Equipo de Reflexión, Investigación y Comunicación (ERIC), 2005. 181 p.: bibl.

Lays out in-depth relevant aspects of Honduran and international law relevant to terrible plight of those housed in Honduran prisons, the most overcrowded in Latin America with second highest level of prisoners not yet sentenced. Sharp, critical evaluation but focuses more on legal code and less a study of actual conditions.

1526 Taylor-Robinson, Michelle M. La política hondureña y las elecciones de 2005. (*Rev. Cienc. Polít./Santiago*, 26:1, 2006, p. 114–124, bibl., table)

After describing the results of the 2005 Honduran elections, a new electoral system for Congress leads the author to conclude that the results have a potential for dramatic political changes, particularly in the relations between the executive and legislative branches, providing a beginning point for understanding the constitutional crisis that exploded in 2009.

NICARAGUA

1527 Bautista Lara, Francisco Javier. Policía, seguridad ciudadana y violencia en Nicaragua: breves ensayos y un testimonio. 2a. ed. Managua, Nicaragua: Ediciones de PAVSA, 2005. 206 p.: bibl., index.

Twelve and a half short essays present a useful history of Nicaragua's Policía Nacional, from its founding with the defeat of the National Guard in 1979. Written by a founding member who rose to one of the top positions. Includes interesting thoughts on why Nicaragua's violent crime rate is lower than that of its northern neighbors and lower than socioeconomic indicators predict.

1528 Cultura política de la democracia en Nicaragua. Managua: USAID, 2006. 1 v.: ill.

Outstanding examination of Nicaraguan political attitudes based on national survey in 2006, along with longitudinal trends as well as cross-national comparisons. As with others in this series produced by Latin American Public Opinion Project at Vanderbilt Univ., discussion is enlightened by concise presentation of relevant theoretical work.

1529 Cupples, Julie. Espacialidades de género y legados revolucionarios en una Nicaragua neoliberal: una interpretación geográfica de la transición de estado. (*Polít. Gest.*, 10, 2007, p. 125–155, bibl.)

Based on interviews with 33 politically active women from just one locality, still a worthy article as interviews are repeated one decade later in 2001 and due to its theoretical richness. Especially interesting in its portrayal of revolutionary women struggling to integrate their critical reactions to Sandinista leadership.

1530 Frühling, Pierre; Miguel González; and Hans Petter Buvollen. Etnicidad y nación: el desarrollo de la autonomía de la Costa Atlántica de Nicaragua, 1987–2007. Guatemala: F&G Editores, 2007. 428 p.: bibl.

Broader than its title, this is an excellent work on the Atlantic half of Nicaragua. Close examination of evolution of regional autonomy is placed in the context of an even-handed historical account, including conflicted early 1980s, and along with discussion of contemporary socioeconomic features. Based on observation and extensive interviews going back more than 20 years as well as an extensive bibliography.

1531 Lacayo Oyanguren, Antonio. La difícil transición nicaragüense en el gobierno con Doña Violeta. Nicaragua: Colección Cultural de Centro América, 2005. 751 p.: ill., index. (Serie Ciencias humanas; no. 12)

In-depth inside view of Doña Violeta Chamorro's 1990 election victory and her six-year Nicaraguan presidency by the person best situated to tell—her campaign manager, top presidential assistant, and son-in-law. More of a from-the-diary account than a stand-back reflection, provides often fascinating details of this historic transition.

1532 Ortega Hegg, Manuel. Nicaragua 2006: el regreso del FSLN al poder. (*Rev. Cienc. Polít./Santiago*, vol. especial, 2007, p. 205–219, tables)

Brief article on the 2006 elections which returned Daniel Ortega to the presidency.

1533 Pérez, Justiniano. Los albores de la resistencia nicaragüense: la Legión 15 de septiembre y la lucha indígena. Miami, Fl.: ORBIS, 2006. 159 p.: bibl., ill., maps.

Interesting participant account by an ex-National Guardsman of the founding of the anti-Sandinista forces that would become the contras but by then the author had resigned due to US-Argentine imposed leadership changes. Soon thereafter he became a military adviser to the anti-Sandinista indigenous Miskito forces. Includes valuable maps and documents.

1534 Saballos, Ángela. Elecciones 2006: todos los otros somos nosotros mismos. Managua: A. Saballos, 2006. 247 p.: ill.

Journalist Saballos has produced an informative book centered on the presidential election of 2006. Interview transcripts include a dozen political analysts, the outgoing president, the five vice-presidential candidates, and each of the presidential candidates except for the winner, Daniel Ortega, who did not respond. Good questions lead to broader topics than just the election itself.

PANAMA

1535 Castillo Candanedo, Janio. Ruta de tránsito, utopía transitista y la formación panameña, 1980–1999: el caso de los Partidos Arnulfista y Revolucionario Democrático. San Salvador: Postgrado Centroamericano, FLACSO-El Salvador, 2004. 149 p.: bibl. (Col. Cuadernos de maestría)

History of the importance of cross-isthmus transit to the national project of dominant Panamanian groups from 19th century up to the two dominant contemporary political parties.

1536 Caumartin, Corinne. "Depoliticisation" in the reform of the Panamanian security apparatus. (*J. Lat. Am. Stud.*, 39:1, Feb. 2007, p. 107–133)

Thorough description of the demilitarization, professionalization, and depoliticization of Panamanian security forces following the US invasion of 1989 based, in part, on interviews with key figures such as former President Ernesto Pérez Balladares (1994–1999).

1537 Guevara Mann, Carlos. Sistemas electorales y estilos de campaña: los diputados panameños y el voto personalista. (*Rev. Cienc. Polít./Santiago*, 26:2, 2006, p. 209–230, tables)

Clear explanation of Panama's complex hybrid legislative electoral system, arguing that it leads to personalistic, clientilistic politics, reinforcing the image of what others have claimed to be the region's country with the least programmatic politics.

1538 Sánchez, Peter Michael. Panama lost?: U.S. hegemony, democracy, and the Canal. Gainesville: Univ. Press of Florida, 2007. 251 p.: bibl., index.

Solid survey of US hegemonic relationship with Panama from 19th into 21st century with a focus on ramifications for Panamanian political development. Drawing on in-country experience through military service in mid-1980s and Fulbright year in late 1990s, the author finds that the US is often retarding democratic development in Panama in pursuit of its own short-term narrowly construed interests.

THE CARIBBEAN AND THE GUIANAS (EXCEPT CUBA)

CLIFFORD E. GRIFFIN, *Associate Professor, Department of Political Science, School of Public and International Affairs, North Carolina State University*
JOAN F. HIGBEE, *Specialist in the Caribbean Area, Hispanic Division, Library of Congress*

THE INTERRELATED ISSUES of governance, development, and viability in an increasingly globalized world continue to resonate within and among Caribbean countries as they have attempted to respond and adjust to the profound impacts of the global recession. The maintenance of good governance, together with the role of civil societies, migration, citizenship, economic growth and development, crime, HIV/AIDS, culture, and identity continue to strongly impact these countries as they cope with the impact of the ongoing global recession. Indeed, it is at this historical moment of global economic downturn, when countries the world over have been turning to their governments for more effective leadership, that the Caribbean Community and Common Market (CARICOM), the region's international governmental organization (IGO) that is responsible for regional governance, is facing its most strident criticism.

The article "Bye Caricom & WI Cricket," penned in the October 27, 2009, edition of the Barbados *Nation News* newspaper by retired (Barbados) diplomat and social commentator, Peter Laurie, contained a rather blistering attack against CARICOM. This attack registered the most high-level criticism of the quality of governance within this international governmental organization (IGO). Laurie opined that "CARICOM has exhausted itself. Caribbean regionalism is not so much in retreat as it is irrelevant. CARICOM leaders have absolutely no interest in regional integration other than what petty benefits each can gouge out of it. Most of them, except for the cheapskates and freeloaders, are slowly realizing that they get out less than they put in. CARICOM is no longer a win-win situation, but a zero-sum game . . . In a globalised world economy, we're all better off fending for ourselves. CARICOM has become a drag on the progress of its member states. . . ." These sentiments capture the mood of many thinkers across the Caribbean, and speak to a large extent to the challenges, if not the failures of governance across the region.

However, there are many opposing views, including that presented by Patsy Lewis in *Surviving Small Size: Regional Integration in Caribbean Ministates* (item **1551**). She argues that culture provides the most important noneconomic grounds for regional unity, and since Caribbean countries share many common cultural traits, political union (regional integration) "may become a possibility if these countries were to emphasize a shared West Indian identity, a democratic process, and a need to act as a sovereign entity to combat globalization and economic weakness." There is an intellectual and historical basis for this claim. Peter Manuel, for example, in his edited volume, *Creolizing Contradance in the Caribbean* (item **1544**), undertakes a pan-regional analysis of the diverse forms of contradance and quadrille, the most popular, widespread and important genres of Creole Caribbean music and dance in the 19th century, and demonstrates how these forms constituted sites for interaction of musicians and musical elements of different racial, social, and ethnic origins, which forged musical genres like the Cuban danzoacuten and son, the Dominican merengue, and the Haitian mereng.

Contradicting this cultural commonality argument is Prem Misir's edited volume, *Cultural Identity and Creolization in National Unity: The Multiethnic Caribbean* (item **1546**), which contends that because slavery separated similar linguistic and cultural groupings, it produced a creolized population, whose "commonality" is an embrace of a variant of European culture. More important than the common variant of European culture is the fact that the Caribbean population is "a multiethnic mosaic," which exhibits centripetal forces. It is, therefore, these centripetal forces that endanger national unity, good governance, and political stability in the region. This perspective is also borne out in Viranjini Munasinghe's *Callaloo Or Tossed Salad? East Indians and the Cultural Politics of Identity in Trinidad* (item **1579**), which examines how Indo-Trinidadian leaders in Trinidad have come to challenge the implicit claim that their ethnic identity is antithetical to their national identity as they seek to change the national image of Trinidad to one with Indo-Trinidadian culture portrayed equally alongside those of the dominant Afro-Caribbean (Creole) culture.

The multiethnic mosaic is consistent with the existence of latent separatist/secessionist tendencies in a number of multi-island states. These tendencies are captured by Douglas Midgett in *Pepper and Bones: The Secessionist Impulse in Nevis* (see *HLAS 63:2067*) in which he suggests that "Nevisian predilection for separation from its sister island in the two-island state of St. Kitts-Nevis is born less of some collective identity formation and more of a growing intolerance of what Nevisians regard as continued bondage in an unworkable state structure." This is also one aspect of CARICOM's "dysfunctionality" that Laurie advances in his contention that the regional governance institution has become irrelevant.

Further, as Laurie contends, nostalgia, combined with an unwillingness to admit the dysfunctionality of CARICOM, have resulted in the constituent units failing to develop at their respective pace and abilities, as he points to exhibit number one: "Everybody knows the Secretariat should not be in Georgetown, [Guyana] but nobody will bell the cat." For exhibit number two, Laurie contends that "the Regional Negotiating Machinery has been emasculated for purely political reasons." This is confirmed by Jessica Byron, in "Singing from the Same Hymn Sheet" (item **1540**), who points out that that "Caribbean countries have often found themselves defending minority positions in multilateral negotiations." Byron is much more diplomatic than the former ambassador, who noted that "when we (CARICOM) get to sit at the table with the Americans or the Europeans, we end up presenting a laundry list of petty complaints and begging for pittances. How humiliating." Peter Clegg, in *Banana Splits and Policy Challenges* (item **1542**), underscores this point by demonstrating how the cozy relationship that once existed between the Caribbean banana interests and the UK government began to unravel in the mid-1980s under the influence of an increasingly powerful European Community. Similar perspectives are captured in the volume, *The Diplomacy of Small States: Between Vulnerability and Resilience,* edited by Andrew F. Cooper and Timothy M. Shaw (item **2062**).

The governance issue remains rather complex as the question of political status is treated differently by the various political units across the region. Clegg and Pantojas-Garcia, in *Governance in the Non-independent Caribbean* (item **1549**), address three fundamental issues affecting non-independent countries across the region: the effectiveness and fairness of governance arrangements in place between the territories and their metropolitan centers; their economic position and the possibilities for future development; and the patterns of migration and settlement between the territories and each metropole. Pedro Malavet, commenting on Puerto Rico's status in *America's Colony: The Political and Cultural Conflict Between the United States and Puerto Rico* (item **1575**), contends that "the Puerto Rican cultural nation is under the sway of US imperialism, which compromises both the island's sovereignty and Puerto Ricans' citizenship rights." But this issue is treated differently by de Jong and Kruijt from the perspective of "extended statehood" (item **1547**) as opposed to non-independence, which gives agency to these political entities rather than viewing them from the perspective of colonial holdovers in an increasingly independent and democratic world.

Governance also impacts upon the issue of crime (item **1566**), particularly the extent to which a close relationship continues to manifest itself between politics, political patronage, and drug violence, as indicated by Anthony Harriott in *Organized Crime and Politics in Jamaica* (item **1567**). This phenomenon, long associated with the more impoverished sections of Kingston, including the evolution of certain constituencies into garrison communities, is increasingly manifesting itself across the region, as events in Trinidad and Tobago, Guyana, and St. Kitts and Nevis, for example, demonstrate the provision of political patronage among the most marginalized, and the separation between politics and drug violence over the past 20 years that has witnessed locally produced ganja replaced by Colombian cocaine.

Other governance issues, such as maritime boundary delimitation, overlapping maritime jurisdictions, fisheries, and hydrocarbons, are captured in *Intervention, Border and Maritime Issues in CARICOM* edited by Kenneth Hall and Myrtle Chuck-A-Sang (item **1568**), and in Clifford E. Griffin's *The Race for Fisheries and Hydrocarbons in the Caribbean Basin: The Barbados-Trinidad and Tobago Maritime Dispute—Regional Delimitation Implications* (item **2068**). Criticisms of CARICOM's deficiency in governance also extend into the area of gender relations and gender equity (item **1555**). As the European Union continues to deepen its integration process, the question that will continue to be on the minds of thinkers, scholars, politicians and pundits alike is whether governance across the region can improve without meaningful change in CARICOM. [CEG]

Although the Constitution of 1987 in force in Haiti envisions bottom-up representation, political attention directed toward the country remains focused upon the president and to some extent the Parliament. National institutions remain undeveloped. In the period 2008–2009, the Parliament of Haiti removed two prime ministers. A third recently confirmed prime minister, still in place in January 2010, has announced that his goal will be to establish an environment favorable to investors and job creation. The jobs most frequently mentioned are those of garment assembly workers earning some three dollars per day. The US Congress passed the Hope II Act that allows clothing assembled in Haiti to enter the US duty free. Former President Clinton was appointed United Nations Special Envoy to Haiti; he has since brought an international body of potential investors to the country. UN forces remain in Haiti. The Haitian Police Force has expanded.

In light of accomplishments made by peasant environmental movements and leaders, the agrarian future of rural Haiti is emerging as a story of exceptional interest. Born and nurtured from within the country, created and led by Haitians, there are multifaceted human development initiatives that offer a fresh approach—respectful of culture and context—to economic development, environmental protection and individual survival. A part of that story is told in lectures at the Library of Congress by leaders of the Peasant Movement of Papay (MPP), available on the LC Web site: *http://www.loc.gov/today/cyberlc/feature_wdesc .php?rec=4799* and *http://www.loc.gov/today/cyberlc/feature_wdesc.php?rec=4804.*

Since at least 1804, it has been possible to rely upon the "Francophone" Caribbean to address the deepest issues of human identity. Aimé Cesaire died in 2008. From his homeland of Martinique come two works that continue the tradition of questioning identity (items **1570** and **1572**) and a third that illuminates it (item **1571**). [JFH]

GENERAL

1539 Barnes, Natasha. Cultural conundrums: gender, race, nation, and the making of Caribbean cultural politics. Ann Arbor: Univ. of Michigan Press, 2006. 226 p.: bibl., ill., index.

This book focuses on the social passions invested in the Caribbean cultural arena, in the metaphors—political, social, and economic—that the expressive performance is made to bear and is thus concerned with capturing the manner in which contemporary histories of Caribbean phenomena converge and cauterize upon each other to provide a "new" understanding of Caribbean reality. [CEG]

1540 Byron, Jessica. "Singing from the same hymn sheet": Caribbean diplomacy and the Cotonou Agreement. (*Rev. Eur. Estud. Latinoam. Caribe,* 79, Oct. 2005, p. 3–25, bibl.)

This paper seeks to add to the stack of documented diplomacy on Caribbean perspectives on the Cotonou Treaty of 2000 given that Caribbean countries have often found themselves defending minority positions in multilateral negotiations and there are few recorded accounts of either their strategies or the outcomes. [CEG]

1541 Canterbury, Dennis. Caribbean agriculture under three regimes: colonialism, nationalism and neoliberalism in Guyana. (*J. Peasant Stud.,* 34:1, Jan. 2007, p. 1–28, bibl., tables)

An avowed study of problem creation under cover of "solutions" in the area of agricultural policy within Guyana during the colonial, nationalist, and neoliberal periods. Author concludes that laissez faire is an economic policy aimed at marketization and not an agricultural development program. He suggests that Guyana and the Caribbean must identify ways to return to an agricultural development program that allows the state "to promote the development of the agrarian sector in the country." Useful, lengthy bibliography. [JFH]

1542 Clegg, Peter. Banana splits and policy challenges: the ACP Caribbean and the fragmentation of interest coalitions. (*Rev. Eur. Estud. Latinoam. Caribe,* 79, Oct. 2005, p. 27–45, bibl.)

This paper demonstrates how an increasingly influential supranational organization, the EC, challenged the close ties that existed between the Caribbean banana interests and the UK government beginning in the mid-1980s. [CEG]

1543 Collier, Michael Wayne. Political corruption in the Caribbean basin: constructing a theory to combat corruption. New York: Routledge, 2005. 255 p.: bibl., ill., index. (Studies in international relations)

This book argues that while factors such as colonialism, neoimperialism, multinational corporations, foreign businesses, and drug trafficking contribute to the Caribbean's continuing political corruption problems, the main cause is the local governing elite, who manipulate society's political and economic development and plunder state resources for their own benefit at the expense of the citizenry. [CEG]

1544 Creolizing contradance in the Caribbean. Edited by Peter Manuel. Philadelphia, Pa.: Temple Univ. Press, 2009. 288 p.: bibl., index. (Studies in Latin American and Caribbean music)

This book undertakes a pan-regional analysis of the diverse forms of contradance and quadrille, the most popular, widespread and important genres of creole Caribbean music and dance in the 19th century, and demonstrates how these forms constituted sites for interaction of musicians and musical elements of different racial, social, and ethnic origins, which forged musical genres like the Cuban danzoacuten and son, the Dominican merengue, and the Haitian mereng. [CEG]

1545 Crichlow, Michaeline A and **Patricia Northover.** Globalization and the post-Creole imagination: notes on fleeing the plantation. Durham, N.C.: Duke Univ. Press, 2009. 305 p.: bibl., ill., index.

This book examines sociocultural, political, and economic transformations in the Caribbean and theorizes creolization as a concept that speaks to how individuals from historically marginalized groups refashion self, time, and place in multiple ways, from creating art to traveling in search of homes. [CEG]

1546 Cultural identity and creolization in national unity: the multiethnic Caribbean. Edited by Prem Misir. Lanham, Md.: Univ. Press of America, 2006. 216 p.: bibl., ill., index.

Slavery, by design, separated similar linguistic and cultural groupings and produced a creolized population that embraced and exhibited a variant of European cul-

ture. It is this cultural legacy, argues this collection of essays, that ignores the reality of the Caribbean multiethnic mosaic that endangers national unity, good governance, and political stability in the Caribbean. [CEG]

The diplomacies of small states: between vulnerability and resilience. See item **2062**.

1547 Extended statehood in the Caribbean: paradoxes of quasi colonialism, local autonomy, and extended statehood in the USA, French, Dutch, and British Caribbean. Edited by Lammert de Jong & Dirk Kruijt. Amsterdam: Rozenberg Publishers, 2005. 206 p.: bibl., ill.

This book seeks to promote a new look at "extended statehood" among the non-independent Caribbean while raising a number of questions relating to these entities, including: What are their objectives? What is their mission: How are they organized? How do they operate? What are the advantages and what are the disadvantages? Are there any Gordian knots that cannot be resolved? [CEG]

1548 Governance, conflict analysis & conflict resolution. Edited by Cedric Grant and Mark Kirton. Miami, Fla.: Ian Randall Publishers, 2007. 522 p.

The book is divided into eight sections and offers diverse views on conflict, conflict resolution, and governance. [CEG]

1549 Governance in the non-independent Caribbean: challenges and opportunities in the twenty-first century. Edited by Peter Clegg and Emilio Pantojas-Garcia. Kingston, Jamaica: Ian Randle Publishers, 2009. 280 p.

This book offers an interdisciplinary and international set of contributions that provide an assessment of how the rather forgotten but important non-independent Caribbean territories are facing the challenges of globalization through a particularly interesting and unusual set of governance arrangements. [CEG]

1550 King, Cheryl L.A. Michael Manley & democratic socialism: political leadership and ideology in Jamaica. Eugene, Ore.: Resource Publications, 2003. 72 p.: bibl., index.

This monograph focuses on Prime Minister Michael Manley's leadership from

1972 to 1980 and his leadership model based on democratic socialism. [CEG]

1551 Lewis, Patsy. Surviving small size: regional integration in Caribbean ministates. Barbados: Univ. of the West Indies Press, 2002. 278 p.: bibl., index, map.

This book argues that culture provides the most important non-economic grounds for regional unity. Consequently, political union may become a possibility if these countries were to emphasize a shared West Indian identity, a democratic process, and a need to act as a sovereign entity to combat globalization and economic weakness. [CEG]

1552 Maingot, Anthony P. and Wilfredo Lozano. The United States and the Caribbean: transforming hegemony and sovereignty. New York: Routledge, 2005. 175 p.: bibl., ill. (Contemporary inter-American relations)

This book focuses on the transformation of relations with the US ushered in by the following interrelated events: the change in the foreign policies of Latin American and Caribbean states which resulted from the transition from authoritarianism, the continent-wide depression of the 1980 and consequent shift toward more open market economies, and the end of the Cold War. [CEG]

1553 Palmer, Colin A. Eric Williams and the making of the modern Caribbean. Chapel Hill: Univ. of North Carolina Press, 2006. 354 p.: bibl., index.

This book provides Eric Williams' perspective on a number of Caribbean issues, including: intellectual decolonization, the challenge of political and economic integration, the golden handshake, courting Grenada, bleeding Guyana, Africa and Africans, and the economics and politics of race. [CEG]

1554 Thomas-Hope, Elizabeth M. Freedom and constraint in Caribbean migration and diaspora. Jamaica: Ian Randle Publishers, 2009. 430 p.: bibl., index.

This book explores the contemporary nature of migration and the socioeconomic, political, and cultural impact of movements across and outside the Caribbean region. The collection highlights and examines varying discourses on race, transnational-

ism, and the emerging concept of "diaspora," providing insight for the academic, decision maker, student, or anyone interested in migration studies. [CEG]

1555 Vassell, Linnette. Bringing the broader context home: gender, human rights and governance in the Caribbean. (*Caribb. Q./Mona,* 52:2/3, June/Sept. 2006, p. 51–65, bibl.)

Although the development of the democratic process requires the transformation of gender and social relations towards equality, equity, human empowerment, and development, this paper argues that confronting barriers of gender inequality is challenging for leaders and citizens, especially women, in Caribbean democracies. [CEG]

DOMINICAN REPUBLIC

1556 Foro sobre Desarrollo Humano, 2nd, Instituto Tecnológico de Santo Domingo, 2006. Descentralización y poder local en el desarrollo humano: el proceso de descentralización dominicano, ¿crea ciudadanía o fomenta el clientelimso y el caciquismo? Santo Domingo: Oficina de Desarrollo Humano, Programa de las Naciones Unidas para el Desarrollo (PNUD), 2007. 167 p.: bibl., ill., col. map. (Foro sobre Desarrollo Humano; 2)

Focusing on decentralization in government, looks to local and regional development as an effective means of enhancing human development and inhibiting the growth and expansion of national bureaucracies that institutionalize inefficiencies and stunt growth. [J. del Aguila]

HAITI

1557 Avril, Prosper. La justice face au pouvoir politique en Haïti, 2001–2004. Port-au-Prince: P. Avril, 2005. 280 p.: bibl., index.

Prosper Avril, the former dictator accused of human rights violations and arrested in June of 2001, uses his first-hand knowledge of the penal system to discuss arbitrary and abusive conduct within the Haitian judiciary. Substantial portions of the book are devoted the author's depiction of his personal experience. [JFH]

1558 Dumas, Pierre-Raymond. La transition d'Haïti vers la démocratie: essais sur la dérive despotico-libérale. v. 1, 7 février 1986–7 février 1991, un départ raté. Port-au-Prince: Imprimeur II, 1997. 1 v. (Coll. "Pacte pour la réforme et la démocratie")

Vol. 1 of this 3-vol. collection on politics in Haiti begins in Feb. 1986, when the military ousted then-president Jean-Claude Duvalier. Albeit tenuous, the transition to democratic rule began during this time period. Vol. 2 covers the 7 months of the Aristide-Préval government in 1991. For citation of vol. 3, see item **1559**. [Ed.]

1559 Dumas, Pierre-Raymond. La transition d'Haïti vers la démocratie: essais sur la dérive despotico-libérale. v. 3, Le retour d'Aristide (Ipokrit yo sézi) 15 octobre 1994–7 février 1996; suivi d'un index des partis politiques, groupements et associations socio-professionnelles. Port-au-Prince: Imprimeur II, 2006. 431 p.: bibl. (Coll. "Pacte pour la réforme et la démocratie")

A depiction of Haiti under Aristide during the period of Oct. 15, 1994, to Feb. 7, 1996, this volume offers extensive lists of civil society organizations present in name or name and substance during the timeframe. Also provides a list issued by the Ministry of Justice of official political parties. [JFH]

1560 Dupuy, Alex. The prophet and power: Jean-Bertrand Aristide, the international community, and Haiti. Lanham, Md.: Rowman & Littlefield Publishers, Inc., 2007. 239 p.: bibl., index. (Critical currents in Latin American perspective)

The author examines the rise of Jean-Bertrand Aristide, charismatic priest of liberation theology, and his fall from the position of transformed, empowered secular leader. Dupuy conducts his analysis within a broad framework: "It is a study of the structures and relations of power between Haiti and the core countries and the institutions and resources they control, the relations and conflicts between dominant and subordinate classes and the social forces struggling for and against social change in Haiti." Chapter topics are "Globalization, the New World Order Imperialism and Haiti," "Class Power," "State Power and the Duvalier Dictatorships, 1957–1990," "The Popular Movement for Democracy and the Rise of Jean-Bertrand Aristide," "The First Lavalas Government and Its Overthrow," "The Political Opposition and the Low-Intensity War Against Aristide," and "The Second Overthrow of Aristide and the Pacification of Haiti." [JFH]

1561 Fatton, Robert. The roots of Haitian despotism. Boulder, Colo.: Lynne Rienner Publishers, 2007. 269 p.: bibl., index.

Speaking of the relationship between this text and his earlier study, *Haiti's Predatory Republic* (see *HLAS 61:2170*), the author states that "this new work is more ambitious, a work of excavation; it seeks to understand the social origins of Haitian despotism and why, since its inception, the country has had a persistent history of dictatorial regimes lording it over an exploited majority." He adds that, since the 1990s, Haiti has had such a dependence upon external financial sources that its sovereignty "has become a legal fiction." Chapter topics are "Habitus, Political Culture, and African Legacies," "Social Hierarchies and Authoritarian Legacies," "Presidential Monarchism," "The Empire Arrives: The Road to the US Occupation," "Imperialism and Authoritarianism," and "From Duvalier to the Unending Democratic Transition." [JFH]

1562 Gaspard, Fritzner. Haïti: ajustement structurel et problèmes politiques. Préface de François Houtart. Paris: L'Harmattan, 2008. 153 p.: bibl., ill.

This work presents a detailed analysis of the impact upon and outcomes of structural adjustment programs imposed upon Haiti from the time of Jean-Bertrand Aristide's return in 1994. It examines political instability fostered by the application of external economic theories to unrelated internal social realities. [JFH]

1563 Hippolyte-Manigat, Mirlande. Entre les normes et les réalités: le parlement haitien, 1806–2007. Port-au-Prince: L'Imprimeur II, 2007. 540 p.: bibl., index.

In a period when President René Préval of Haiti has experienced in rapid sequence the removal by Parliament of two prime ministers, a detailed work depicting the history and formation of the legislative branch is valuable indeed. This is a careful, in-depth study of a critical but rarely understood component of the government of Haiti. [JFH]

1564 Péan, Leslie Jean-Robert. Haïti: économie politique de la corruption. v. 4, L'ensauvagement macoute et ses conséquences, 1957–1990. Préface de Jacques Chevrier. Paris: Maisonneuve et Larose, 2007. 812 p.: bibl. (Littératures d'Afrique et de la Caraïbe)

This detailed exploration of corruption in Haiti, primarily from the ascension of François Duvalier to the departure of Jean-Claude Duvalier, is accompanied by an extensive bibliography and footnotes. [JFH]

JAMAICA

1565 Charles, Christopher A.D. An analysis of the type and content of TV ads in the 2002 Jamaican General Election. (*Caribb. Q./Mona*, 53:3, Sept. 2007, p. 1–15, bibl., tables)

This paper reflects exploratory work on the role of the mass media in determining electoral fortunes in Jamaica by seeking to explain the types and contents of ads aired on CVM Television and Television Jamaica during the 2002 general election. [CEG]

1566 Clarke, Colin G. Politics, violence and drugs in Kingston, Jamaica. (*Bull. Lat. Am. Res.*, 25:3, July 2006, p. 420–440, maps)

This paper examines the characteristics of the downtown, impoverished sections of Kingston, Jamaica, including the evolution of certain constituencies into garrison communities, the provision of political patronage among the most marginalized, and the separation between politics and drug violence over the past 20 years that has witnessed locally produced ganja replaced by Colombian cocaine. [CEG]

1567 Harriott, Anthony. Organized crime and politics in Jamaica: breaking the nexus. Jamaica: Canoe Press, 2008. 214 p.: bibl., ill., index.

This book attempts to bridge the nexus between politics and crime by analyzing the rise of organized crime in Jamaica, its internationalization, and efforts to consolidate its hold in the cities and towns of Jamaica. [CEG]

1568 Intervention, border and maritime issues in CARICOM. Edited by Kenneth O. Hall and Myrtle Chuck-A-Sang. Kingston; Miami, Fla.: Ian Randle, 2007. 486 p.: bibl.

A collection of articles, offering a variety of perspectives on key CARICOM issues such as sovereignty with respect to territory boundary delimitation (maritime and land-based) and the potential for intervention (military and otherwise) that is part of the colonial legacy of these countries. [CEG]

1569 Tafari-Ama, Imani. Blood, bullets and bodies: sexual politics below Jamaica's poverty line. Edited by I. Jabulani Tafari. Photographs by Imani M. Tafari-Ama. Cover art by Elgo. Cover design and layout by I. Jabulani Tafari. [S.l.]: Multi Media Communications, 2006. 480 p.: bibl., ill., index, ports.

This book explains how and why Jamaica's two main political parties have both provided ballistic weapons to their supporters living in garrison communities. Highlights the island's evolution into the major transshipment locale in the middle of a new criminal triangular trade involving the movement of drugs, guns, money, and illegal migrants between South America, North America, and Europe. [CEG]

LESSER ANTILLES
French Caribbean

1570 Glissant, Édouard and **Patrick Chamoiseau.** Quand les murs tombent: l'identité nationale hors-la-loi. Paris: Galaade: Institut du tout-monde, 2007. 26 p.

The authors explore identity that is fluid and in evolution with an emphasis upon national identity. A colonizing nation's imposition of values and proclamation of a unique source of origin is explored as a catalyst of anticolonial struggle. Uniform fixed identity, identity through interrelationships, and simple ethnic or cultural juxtaposition are contrasted as ways of existing in the world relevant to social and political issues within Martinique. See also item **1572**. [JFH]

1571 Léotin, Marie-Hélène. Habiter le monde: Martinique, 1946–2006. Matoury, Guyane: Ibis Rouge Editions, 2008. 110 p.: bibl. (Espace outre-mer)

The author explores social and conceptual worlds created within Martinique during the following periods: 1946–58, 1959–73, 1974–2006. The work opens with a discussion of law no. 46–451 of March 19, 1946, by which "old colonies" of France—Guadeloupe, Martinique, Réunion and French Guiana—became departments of France. Employing substantial citation of period texts the author depicts, within the population of Martinique, the transition away from goals of assimilation and equality with white citizens of France. She illuminates currents that led François Mitterand to proclaim in 1954 "Algeria is French" while, in 1957, Camille Sylvestre, speaking on behalf of the Communist Party of Martinique, declared "We are finished with the politics of assimilation." Léotin perceives the year 1959 to offer an opening into the modern era. There is global awareness of the impact of the Algerian War upon France and of the victory in Cuba of Fidel Castro and Che Guevara. For Martinique it is the beginning of the end for a sugar-based economy; rural workers have started to migrate toward Fort-de-France. Social and racial tensions intensify as a significant number of French citizens who have left the Maghreb go to Martinique. Franz Fanon evokes Martinique in rebellion against assimilation in an article published in *El Moudjahid* in Jan. of 1960; the years 1970–73 see the growth on-island of an independence movement. A new period opens in 1974. Workers strike driven by consumer price increases for food, gas, and transportation. With new emphasis upon solving problems of Martinique within Martinique come the words of Aimé Césaire warning of genocide by substitution. This work examines complex forces that have shaped the contemporary society of Martinique. It presents a modern society self-consciously exploring its distinct identity through Creole language and literature capable of expressing the imagination, experience, history, and geography of an evolving culture derived from the interrelationship of multiple ancestries. [JFH]

1572 Monchoachi. Le monde tel qu'il est. Martinique: Lakouzémi, 2007. 59 p.
Martinique poet Monchoachi replies to the worldview expressed by Edward Glissant and Patrick Chamoiseau in their joint work *Quand Les Murs Tombent* (item **1570**). The seminal issue behind Monchoachie's articulation of a profoundly different perception of culture and society is identified as having also motivated the publication of *Quand Les Murs Tombent:* immigration. As founder of the journal *Lakouzémi*, Monchoachie created a space for debate inclusive of the issue of independence for Martinique. In keeping with his emphasis upon the need to closely examine and debate matters fundamental to identity, Monchoachie opens here a counter discourse on culture and immigration with references to effects of globalization. [JFH]

PUERTO RICO

1573 Bayrón Toro, Fernando. Historia de las elecciones y los partidos políticos de Puerto Rico; incluye, Catálogo de gobernadores y legisladores de Puerto Rico. 7. ed., ampliada sustancialmente. Mayagüez, Puerto Rico: Editorial Isla, 2008. 575 p.: bibl., ill., maps, ports. (Col. Puerto Rico)
Offers many facts and figures on politics in Puerto Rico as well as a broad historical account of parties and elections. One of the most comprehensive sources of political information, political party behavior, and electoral results available for Puerto Rico. [J. del Aguila]

1574 Hacia la libre asociación: el futuro. Recopilación de Angel Ortiz Guzmán. Prólogo de Néstor R. Duprey Salgado. Puerto Rico: EMS Editores, 2006. 358 p.: bibl.
Comprehensive volume discusses options for Puerto Rico's political future: nationhood, continued association with the US, or statehood. Data from opinion surveys and plebiscites regarding these alternatives is included, as are brief accounts of the intellectual legacy of Luis Muñoz Marín. An indispensable text for anyone interested in Puerto Rican political and governmental affairs. [J. del Aguila]

1575 Malavet, Pedro A. America's colony: the political and cultural conflict between the United States and Puerto Rico. New York: New York Univ. Press, 2004. 242 p.: bibl., index. (Critical America)
This book offers a critique of Puerto Rico's current status and its treatment by the legal and political systems of the US,

and argues that because the Puerto Rican cultural nation is under the sway of US imperialism, both the island's sovereignty and Puerto Ricans' citizenship rights are compromised. [CEG]

1576 Rezvani, David A. The basis of Puerto Rico's constitutional status: colony, compact, or "federacy"? (*Polit. Sci. Q.*, 122:1, Spring 2007, p. 115–140)

This paper argues that Puerto Ricans, with a distinct history and a dissimilar history from the US, have much of the same sense of nationalistic distinctiveness from the US that areas in, for instance, the former Yugoslavia had as that state was breaking up in the mid-1990s. [CEG]

TRINIDAD AND TOBAGO

1577 Abraham, Sara. Labour and the multiracial project in the Caribbean: its history and its promise. Lanham: Lexington Books, 2007. 242 p.: bibl., ill., index. (Caribbean studies)

This book argues that the Caribbean provides a case study of unity because, unlike metropolitan countries, the major population groups share relatively equal power bases. Trinidad & Tobago and Guyana in the 1930s, 1960s–70, and the 1980s are examined to support this hypothesis. [CEG]

1578 Guilbault, Jocelyne. Governing sound: the cultural politics of Trinidad's Carnival musics. Chicago: Univ. of Chicago Press, 2007. 343 p., 16 p. of plates: ill., music, 1 CD (4 3/4 in.). (Chicago studies in ethnomusicology)

In-depth study of the cultural politics and forms of agency imbedded in Trinidadian calypso and its musical offshoots. Chapters include "Calypso's Historical Entanglements," "Independence, Innovation, and Authenticity," and "Soca, Nation, and Discrepant Diasporas." Author examines forms within different periods "because they contrast with each other in their different arrangements of power, and they foreground the different hegemonic cultural politics that marked the conditions in which calypso and its musical offshoots emerged, changed, and mattered." [JFH]

1579 Munasinghe, Viranjini. Callaloo or tossed salad?: East Indians and the cultural politics of identity in Trinidad. Ithaca, N.Y.: Cornell Univ. Press, 2001. 315 p.: bibl., index, maps.

The book examines how Indo-Trinidadian leaders in Trinidad have come to challenge the implicit claim that their ethnic identity is antithetical to their national identity. Their political and cultural strategy seeks to change the national image of Trinidad by introducing Indian elements alongside those of the dominant Afro-Caribbean (Creole) culture. [CEG]

1580 Pantin, Raoul A. Days of wrath: the 1990 coup in Trinidad and Tobago. Lincoln, Neb.: iUniverse, 2007. 163 p.: ill., index.

A first-hand account by a journalist held hostage during the 1990, six-day occupation of the Trinidad and Tobago television station by members of the Jamaat al Muslimeen. The armed assault depicted also encompassed the country's Parliament. For historian's comment, see *HLAS 64:1118.* [JFH]

CUBA

JUAN M. DEL AGUILA, *Associate Professor of Political Science, Emory University*

Several books on Cuban Politics and Government make important contributions to the vast literature on Cuban studies, specifically studies on corruption, a possible transition after the Castro brothers are gone, and one study on gender and political representation. A highly recommended and well documented study on *Corruption in Cuba: Castro And Beyond* by Sergio Díaz and Jorge Pérez-López looks at public corruption from a historical perspective, including new material on sources of institutional corruption in socialist Cuba (item **1584**). One of the more impressive findings is how and why corruption flourishes as more and more state enterprises are organized to do business with foreign investors and entrepreneurs.

Ilja Luciak looks at *Gender and Democracy in Cuba* from a feminist standpoint (item **1585**), examining female representation in state and Communist Party organs to support her argument. She also provides data comparing the percentage of men and women in professional occupations and decision-making positions. Luciak interviewed women from different generations and generally found younger cohorts more discontented with their lives than older women, mainly due to permanent material hardships and poor access to goods and services. When asked about changes in the medium term, those she interviewed offered guarded and often contradictory opinions on what is both probable and desirable.

In *Changes in Cuban Society since the Nineties,* editor Joseph Tulchin and several scholars from Cuba and the US provide a credible work on the development of civil society in Cuba since the collapse of the Berlin Wall (item **1582**). The book includes fine chapters on religion and Church-state relations, on sources of "new thinking" regarding prospects for liberalization, on an evolving concept of rights, and on the limits faced even by those "working for change from within" by the intransigent response of a one-party state. Still, it is a good contribution to the study of civil society in late-totalitarian regimes like Cuba's.

Amado Rodríguez's *Cuba: clamor del silencio* is a reliable account of political imprisonment in Cuba under the revolutionary regime (item **1583**). The book offers evidence of how the penal system is run and organized, of the horrible abuses committed against political prisoners and common criminals alike well into this decade, and on how the Cuban government continues to hide such practices from the outside world. Former political prisoners provide first-hand accounts of their experiences, and prominent dissidents like Marta Roque and Gerardo Fariña denounce the systematic mistreatment they suffered at the hands of penal authorities. This is still another primary source of information for anyone interested in revealing and denouncing the systematic violations of human rights carried out on defenseless prisoners by agents of the Cuban government.

Finally, Hans Dieterich asks the proverbial rhetorical question in *Cuba después de Fidel: ¿podrá sobrevivir la revolución?* (item **1581**). The short text includes Fidel Castro's perspective on how the successor generation will behave after its founders are gone. One striking observation from the leader is his warning that the Revolution cannot be destroyed from the outside, but that it could indeed collapse from its own blunders and "lack of revolutionary conscience." Former Foreign Minister Felipe Pérez Roque contributed to the book, and in a profoundly hypocritical statement argued "the people need to know that their leaders do not have privileges except a strong sense of service and sacrifice." In another instance of the regime turning on its own "disloyal" members, Pérez Roque would subsequently be summarily dismissed from all governmental and Communist Party responsibilities in 2009, in a major purge affected by the Castro brothers precisely against corrupt leaders who "enjoy the honeys of power."

Three books focusing on important issues in regional politics add to a growing, formal literature on the politics and government of Puerto Rico and the Dominican Republic. Angel Ortiz edited *Hacia la libre asociación: el futuro,* a comprehensive volume where the three alternatives facing Puerto Rico are discussed: nationhood, continued association with the US, and statehood (item **1574**). Data from opinion surveys and plebiscites regarding these alternatives is included, as are brief accounts of the intellectual legacy of Luis Muñoz Marín. This is an indispensable text for anyone interested in Puerto Rican political and governmental affairs. A second book on Puerto Rico, offering a broad historical account of parties and elections, is Fernando Toro's *Historia de las elecciones y los partidos políticos de Puerto Rico* (item **1573**). As a seventh edition, it is with little doubt one of the most comprehensive sources of political information, political party behavior, and electoral results available.

The pressing issue of decentralization in the Dominican Republic is the main subject of *Descentralización y poder local en el desarrollo humano,* a short publication from the Foro Sobre Desarrollo Humano (item **1556**). This report focuses on local and regional development as an effective means of enhancing human development and inhibiting the growth and expansion of national bureaucracies that institutionalize inefficiencies and stunt growth.

1581 Castro, Fidel; Felipe Pérez Roque; and Heinz Dieterich. Cuba después de Fidel: ¿podrá sobrevivir la revolución? Coordinación de Rafael Ceballos, Atienza y Francisco Toro Ceballos. Alcalá la Real, Jaén, Spain: Alcalá Grupo Editorial, 2007. 189 p. (Col. Adveniat; 1)

In this piece, Fidel Castro gives his perspective on the country's future. He warns that the Revolution cannot be destroyed from the outside, but that it could indeed collapse from within. Former Foreign Minister Felipe Pérez Roque contributes to the book, and in a profoundly hypocritical statement argues that "the people need to know that their leaders do not have privileges except a strong sense of service and sacrifice."

1582 Changes in Cuban society since the nineties. Edited by Joseph S. Tulchin with the collaboration of Elizabeth Bryan. Washington, D.C.: Woodrow Wilson International Center for Scholars, Latin American Program, 2005. 291 p.: bibl. (Woodrow Wilson Center reports on the Americas; 15)

Discusses the development of Cuban civil society. Topics covered include religion and Church-state relations, sources of "new thinking" regarding prospects for liberalization, rights, and the limits faced by those "working for change from within."

1583 Cuba, clamor del silencio: presidio político cubano: testimonios. Recopilación de Amado J. Rodríguez Fernández. Miami, Fla.: Ediciones Memorias, 2005. 456 p.: ill., maps.

Describes political imprisonment in Cuba under the revolutionary regime.

Provides evidence of how the penal system is run and organized, of the horrible abuses committed against political prisoners and common criminals alike well into the 2000s, and on how the Cuban government continues to conceal such practices from the outside world. Former political prisoners provide first-hand accounts of their experiences and prominent dissidents like Marta Roque and Gerardo Fariña denounce the systematic mistreatment they suffered at the hands of penal authorities. A primary source of information for anyone interested in the violations of human rights in Cuba.

1584 Diaz-Briquets, Sergio and Jorge Pérez-López. Corruption in Cuba: Castro and beyond. Austin: Univ. of Texas Press, 2006. 286 p.: bibl., index.

Looks at public corruption from a historical perspective, including new material on sources of institutional corruption in socialist Cuba. Discusses how and why corruption flourishes as state enterprises manage increased foreign investment. A balanced assessment of the pervasive and damaging consequences of corruption points out that "curbing corruption in a future Cuba will depend on ethical political leaders committed to the national interest and the welfare of their fellow citizens rather than their own."

1585 Luciak, Ilja A. Gender and democracy in Cuba. Gainesville: Univ. Press of Florida, 2007. 143 p.: bibl., index. (Contemporary Cuba)

Finds that Cuba (and other Marxist, revolutionary regimes) promote "an exaggerated sense of the country's achievements regarding substantive gender equality." From a feminist but critical standpoint, Luciak looks at female representation in state and Communist Party organs to support her argument, and provides data comparing the percentage of men and women in profes- sional occupations and decision-making positions. Luciak interviewed women from different generations and generally found younger cohorts more discontented with their lives than older women, due to perma- nent material hardships and poor access to goods and services.

COLOMBIA

STEVEN L. TAYLOR, *Associate Professor of Political Science, Troy University*

INSTITUTIONAL DEVELOPMENT AND VIOLENCE continue to be the domi- nant themes within the scholarly literature on Colombian government and poli- tics. In terms of institutional development the main foci are on questions of the political legacy of Álvaro Uribe (items **1601** and **1615**), the evolution of the party system, and general questions of governance. The ubiquity of the violence contin- ues to fuel discussion of the on-again, off-again peace process as well as the study of specific belligerents.

Two important issues regarding political developments in need of serious study are the long-term implications of the presidency of Álvaro Uribe and the effects of the 2003 electoral reforms. The literature reviewed for this *Handbook* volume only begins to address these issues. Uribe's democratic security policies are worthy of investigation and his overall political trajectory merits further ex- amination due to the lasting implications for Colombia.

In regards to Uribe, Jaramillo (item **1599**) discusses re-election, while Mede- llín (item **1601**) and Torre (item **1615**) more broadly address Uribe's effects on the presidency and Colombian politics. Understudied in this topic area is Uribe's ef- fect on the evolution of the party system. He has run twice as an independent, but never has formed his own party formally, and yet a number of pro-Uribe political parties have emerged to support him. Ceballos does address the political role of several pro-Uribe parties in local elections (item **1591**), while Ungar also examines these pro-Uribe parties in the context of the 2002 elections (item **1616**).

In regards to political parties, several works add to the literature on the development of the party system, such as those by Gutiérrez (item **1594**) and Guzmán (item **1595**). Both are of interest, although Guzmán's especially so as it focuses on regional and local development, which is a topic in need of deeper study. Within the general scope of political parties and worthy of individual note is Ayala's book on the Alianza Nacional Popular (ANAPO) and the 1970 presiden- tial election (item **1587**). While the focus is on political history rather than con- temporary party behavior, the work is useful for understanding the trajectory of the party system, both historically as well as within the new electoral rules, espe- cially since some current political actors involved in party formation have legacies linked to ANAPO. Along the lines of the reform, Posada-Carbó contributes a key piece on the effect of reform on legislative elections (item **1609**).

Alongside these specific political themes, the broader issues of institution- alization of the state, citizenship, and corruption continue as key topics in the literature. Such discussions underscore the ongoing difficulties of governance in Colombia. Unfortunately, however, recent publications on these topics have not offered original research or perspectives to further innovative discussion. All too often these publications are mere descriptions augmented with a list of prescriptions, rather than useful analyses of the problems at hand (e.g., items **1589** and **1592**).

Beyond studies of political conditions and state capacity, violence remains a key theme. The evolution of the FARC (Fuerzas Armadas Revolucionarias de Colombia) continues to be a central topic in the literature. Of note are works by Kline (item **1600**) and Cadena (item **1588**) on Andrés Pastrana's (1998–2002) peace initiative and Duran and Peceny's analysis of the effects of US antidrug policies on the guerrilla violence (item **1606**). Noteworthy, too, is Vargas' work on the ELN (Ejército de Liberación Nacional), if only because the ELN is understudied relative to the FARC (item **1617**). Aviles' piece on paramilitarism is also worth noting (item **1586**).

A book that deserves special attention is the edited volume by Welna et al. (item **1604**). One of the most comprehensive examinations of Colombian politics published in English in some years, this work includes contributions by several prominent observers of Colombian politics (e.g., Herbert Tico Braun, Daniel García-Peña, Eduardo Pizarro, and Matthew Shugart, to name a few). Another text worthy of singling out is the collection edited by Leal, which offers an analysis of current political conditions in Colombia (item **1593**).

Moving forward, the implications of Uribe's tenure in office will be a major area in need of scholarly attention, as will the long-term evolution of the political party system. Beyond these key issues, a number of areas warrant deeper study, including the fortunes of the FARC in the wake of several dramatic events in 2007–2009, as well as the long-term evolution of paramilitary groups.

1586 Aviles, William. Paramilitarism and Colombia's low-intensity democracy. (*J. Lat. Am. Stud.*, 38:2, May 2006, p. 379–408, table)

This article provides a useful review of the basic background for paramilitarism in Colombia. Beyond that, it attempts to ascribe political explanations for the growth of the phenomenon in the 1990s, linking it to the loss of formal power by local politicians as a result of the 1991 constitutional reforms. The piece examines the Gaviria, Samper, Pastrana, and early Uribe administrations.

1587 Ayala Diago, César Augusto. El populismo atrapado, la memoria y el miedo: el caso de las elecciones de 1970. Medellín: Carreta Editores; Bogotá: Univ. Nacional de Colombia, Depto. de Historia, Facultad de Ciencias Humanas, Sede Bogotá, Línea de Investigación en Historia Política y Social, 2006. 318 p.: bibl., ill. (La Carreta histórica)

This book details the development of ANAPO (Alianza Nacional Popular) political party from 1968 to the infamous 1970 election. The book also examines the broader politics of the day, including substantial treatments of Conservative candidates Misael Pastrana and Belisario Betancur. In addition, it analyzes the general issue of populism in Colombian politics during the era in question, including the role played by gaitanismo. The text includes photos, campaign material, and data from the elections.

1588 Cadena Montenegro, José Luis. La geografía y el poder: territorialización del poder en Colombia—el caso de las FARC—, de Marquetalia al Caguán. (*Estud. Polít./México*, 1, enero/abril 2004, p. 153–183, bibl.)

An analysis of the *zona de distención* granted by the Pastrana administration to the FARC. The piece applies geostrategic logic to the policy and is critical of the policy, noting that while such a policy was intended to create opportunities for reconciliation, it accomplished the opposite. Of interest because the FARC and ELN both continue to request similar zones for the purpose of future negotiations.

1589 El capital social en Colombia: teorías, estrategias y prácticas. Consultación de Luis Jaime Vázquez Caro. Investigación de Camilo Cristancho Mantilla *et al.* Bogotá: Contraloría General de la República, 2006. 351 p.: bibl., ill.

This book, published by the Colombian government, is part of a broad ongoing trend in literature focused on the question of enhancing the capacities of Colombian civil society, which seeks to enhance the legitimacy of the government and general levels of societal trust. Of most interest to those studying the issue of corruption.

1590 Cárdenas Santa-María, Mauricio; Roberto Junguito; and Mónica Pachón. Political institutions and policy outcomes in Colombia: the effects of the 1991 Constitution. New York: Inter-American Development Bank, Latin American Research Network, 2006. 92 p.: bibl., ill. (Research Network working paper; R-508)

This monograph provides a useful overview of institutional change in Colombia as a result of the 1991 constitutional reform. The broader theme of the work is the linkage between institutional change and policy performance. The piece argues that new institutional parameters have altered outcomes in both fiscal and monetary policy.

1591 Ceballos, Marcela. The country behind the ballot box: the impact of political reform in Colombia during a humanitarian crisis. With the collaboration of Iván Romero. London: Crisis States Programme, Development Research Centre, 2005. 23 p.: bibl., tables. (Crisis States Programme working papers series. 1,1740–5807; 74)

Examines local elections in the context of the 2003 electoral reforms and the ongoing political violence. Also studies the influence of Uribe and Uribe-allied groups on Colombian political behavior at the local level. In addition to an overview of local elections, there is specific attention paid to the following municipalities: Arauca, Barrancabermeja, Barranquilla, and Pasto.

Cepeda Ulloa, Fernando. Financiación política y corrupción. See item **1416.**

1592 Colombia. Contraloría General de la República. Transparencia contra la corrupción. Textos de Antonio Hernández Gamarra. Bogotá: Contraloría General de la República, 2006. 185 p.: ill.

A publication of the Colombian government (Contraloría General de la Repúlica) detailing programs aimed at decreasing corruption. Useful in that it documents the official government view on the subject. Also includes data on various budget outlays at they pertain to expenditures for specific policy sectors.

1593 En la encrucijada: Colombia en el siglo XXI. Recopilación de Francisco Leal Buitrago. Bogotá: Grupo Editorial Norma, 2006. 574 p.: bibl., graphs. (Col. Vitral)

This collection of essays by leading academics in Colombia analyzes the state of Colombian politics at the mid-decade point in the 21st century. The essays are organized into three categories: institutional actors, social actors, and public policy (the latter focusing mainly on security issues).

1594 Gutiérrez Sanín, Francisco. Lo que el viento se llevó?: los partidos políticos y la democracia en Colombia, 1958–2002. Bogotá: Grupo Editorial Norma, 2007. 518 p.: bibl., ill., indexes. (Col. Vitral)

This book traces the development of the party system from the Frente Nacional until the last election held prior to the 2003 electoral reform. It attempts to place the study of Colombia's political parties in the broader classic literature on parties. A great deal of attention is paid to the Partido Liberal, given its electoral dominance in the post-Frente Nacional period. Also discusses the fragmentation of the party system in the 1990s and early 2000s.

1595 Guzmán Mendoza, Carlos Enrique. Política, descentralización y subsistemas regionales de partidos en Colombia, 1988–2000: una explicación teórica y un análisis empírico. Ibagué, Colombia: Univ. de Ibagué, 2005. 413 p.: bibl., ill., maps.

This book examines the development and behavior of Colombia's parties at the regional/local level. As such, the text sets itself apart from much of the literature on the subject which tends to acknowledge the importance of regional politics without fully exploring it. This study is rooted firmly in the electoral studies/institutions literature. It spans the entire history of Colombia's mainstream parties, although most of the analysis is focused on the 1980s and 1990s.

1596 Hernández Becerra, Augusto. Regulación jurídica de los partidos políticos en Colombia. (*in* Regulación jurídica de los partidos políticos en América Latina. Coordinación de Daniel Zovatto. México: UNAM: International IDEA, 2006, p. 331–365, bibl.)

This chapter details the evolution of the legal regulation of political parties in Colombia from the post-independence period to the mid-2000s. It is one of the most comprehensive attempts at describing the subject available on this understudied topic.

Holmes, Jennifer S.; Sheila Amin Gutiérrez de Piñeres; and Kevin M. Curtin. Drugs, violence, and development in Colombia: a department-level analysis. See item **2280**.

1597 Hunt, Stacey. Languages of stateness: a study of space and *el pueblo* in the Colombian state. (*LARR*, 41:3, 2006, p. 88–121, bibl.)

This article examines a common question: whether the Colombian state should be considered "failed" or not. Rather than answering that question specifically, the article looks at the issue of "stateness" itself and the role of both smaller units (such at the town) and the multiple meanings of el pueblo. The politics of language is central to the discussion as is the concept of "shadow states" in the context of the ongoing violence.

1598 Isaza Gómez, Omar; Juan Diego Restrepo Echeverri; and Sandra Miled Hincapié Jiménez. Estrategias de la corrupción en Colombia: discursos y realidades. Medellín: IPC de la Corporación de Promoción Popular, 2005. 429 p.: bibl.

An attempt at an academic approach to the question of corruption. Part of that attempt is a "reconceptualization" of the practice, although the degree to which that is accomplished by the text is debatable. Of more use is an examination of the question of corruption specifically in the 1990s

during the Gaviria and Samper administrations. The book also includes case studies focusing on Medellín (transit and education policy).

1599 Jaramillo, Juan Fernando. La reelección presidencial inmediata en Colombia. (*Nueva Soc.*, 198, julio/agosto 2005, p. 15–31, bibl.)

Examines the significance of the 2004 reform that allowed for immediate reelection of the president for the first time in Colombian history for over a century. The article places the concept in a regional and historical context and examines the contemporary politics of the reform.

1600 Kline, Harvey F. Chronicle of a failure foretold: the peace process of Colombian president Andrés Pastrana. Tuscaloosa: Univ. of Alabama Press, 2006. 229 p.: bibl., index.

An extensive look at the negotiations between the FARC and the administration of Andrés Pastrana (1998–2002). Includes some discussion of the policies of the Samper administration (1994–98). A continuation of the work Kline started in his 1999 book, *State Building and Conflict Resolution in Colombia, 1986–1994* (see *HLAS 61:2253*).

1601 Medellín Torres, Pedro. El presidente sitiado: ingobernabilidad y erosión del poder presidencial en Colombia. Bogotá: Planeta, 2006. 394 p.: bibl., ill.

This work is a critique of presidential power in Colombia. While the analytical focus is on the Uribe administration, Medellín Torres casts a broad theoretical and historical net in his analysis of the institution, ranging as far back as the early 1800s.

1602 Monsalve Solórzano, Alfonso. Legitimidad y soberanía en Colombia 1958–2003. Medellín, Colombia: Univ. de Antioquia, Instituto de Filosofía: Univ. Pontificia Bolivarina, Escuela de Derecho y Ciencias Políticas, 2004. 448 p.: bibl., ill. (Serie Estudios políticos)

The book addresses an ongoing theme in the literature on Colombia: the question of legitimacy for the Colombian state. This text seeks to define the subject and examine it within the broad context of Colombian politics from the Frente Nacional through the first Uribe term.

1603 Moreno, Erika and **Maria Escobar-Lemmon.** Mejor solo que mal acompañado: political entrepreneurs and list proliferation in Colombia. (*in* Pathways to power: political recruitment and candidate selection in Latin America. Edited by Peter M. Siavelis and Scott Morgenstern. University Park: Pennsylvania State Univ. Press, 2008, p. 119–142, tables)

Examines candidate recruitment for Colombian legislative elections and looks at how the electoral rules that were in place until 2003 led to an atomized party system and therefore to political entrepreneurialism rather than cohesive party organization. Focuses on the 1958–2002 period. This chapter is part of a broader study of candidate selection processes in Latin America.

1604 Peace, democracy, and human rights in Colombia. Edited by Christopher Welna and Gustavo Gallón. Notre Dame, Ind.: Univ. of Notre Dame Press, 2007. 455 p.: bibl., ill., index.

This collection of essays represents one of the most up-to-date volumes available in English that covers the wide array of key issues of Colombian politics. The book is divided into sections that correspond to the book's title. Specific topics include the drug trade, the peace process, and political reform.

1605 Pécaut, Daniel. Crónica de cuatro décadas de política colombiana. Bogotá: Grupo Editorial Norma, 2006. 543 p.: bibl., maps. (Col. Vitral)

This is an expanded edition of Pécaut's classic work, *Crónica de dos décadas de política colombiana, 1968–1988* (indeed, the bulk of the book is a reprint of the 1989 edition). The original material is augmented by reprints of several essays that cover the 1990–2003 period. The newer material is not as comprehensive as the 1968–88 material.

1606 Peceny, Mark and **Michael Durnan.** The FARC's best friend: U.S. antidrug policies and the deepening of Colombia's Civil War in the 1990s. (*Lat. Am. Polit. Soc.*, 48:2, Summer 2006, p. 95–116, bibl., table)

Argues that many US antidrug policies, even when deemed successful, had the unintended consequence of driving coca production into areas of the country under FARC control. Also discusses the security politics of both the Bush and Uribe administrations and the behavior of other groups such as the AUC (Autodefensas Unidas de Colombia).

1607 Pinto Borrego, María Eugenia. El dividendo de paz en Colombia. (*Rev. Planeac. Desarro.*, 35:2, julio/dic. 2004, p. 719–792, bibl., graphs, tables)

Asks whether a "peace dividend" can be generated from a reduction in military spending. More interestingly, however, the piece examines Colombian military spending over several decades (some sections range back into the 1990s, others farther back than that). The annex of the work is especially interesting as it summarizes basic military policy from 1930 to the present, divided into specific eras (e.g., "Liberal Republic," "la Violencia," etc.). Of special interest to those studying civil-military relations or fiscal policy issues.

1608 Políticas públicas para Colombia: empleo, educación, política agraria, salud, régimen político, distribución del ingreso, deuda, economía pública, regionalización. Textos de Adriana Rodríguez Castillo *et al.* Coordinación académico de Miguel Cárdenas y Ricardo Bonilla. Dirección de Hans R. Blumenthal. Bogotá: Friedrich Ebert Stiftung en Colombia, 2006. 189 p.: bibl., ill.

A collection of essays by academics of various disciplines that examines social policy in Colombia in the early 2000s. The overarching theme is poverty alleviation. Topics include: labor reform, agrarian policy, health care, corruption, and decentralization. Each chapter provides a description of the state of the problem, details about government policy, and a recommendation for future policy.

1609 Posada-Carbó, Eduardo. Colombia hews to the path of change. (*J. Democr.*, 17:4, Oct. 2006, p. 80–94)

An excellent summation of the 2006 election results and the changes to the party system brought about by recent political reforms. Also discusses the long-term trends that led to the changes.

1610 Posada-Carbó, Eduardo. Language and politics: on the Colombian "Establishment." (*LARR*, 42:2, 2007, p. 111–135)

Looks at "how issues of language impinge on political processes" by specifically examining the growing usage of the term "establishment" in the Colombian context. The author notes the usage of the term by both counter-state actors (specifically the FARC) as well as by mainline political actors including members of major political parties such as the Conservatives and the Liberals as well as the Polo Democrático Alternativo political alliance.

1611 Richani, Nazih. Multinational corporations, rentier capitalism, and the war system in Colombia. (*Lat. Am. Polit. Soc.*, 47:3, Fall 2005, p. 113–144, bibl.)

The article builds on Richani's earlier work on the war system in Colombia by examining the role that multinational corporations played in that system. Here he focuses on extractive industries (oil, coal, and gold) and private security corporations. For political economy specialist's comment, see item **2292**.

1612 Salamanca, Manuel Ernesto. Violencia política y modelos dinámicos: un estudio sobre el caso colombiano. Guipúzcoa, Spain: Diputación Foral de Gipuzkoa, Depto. para los Derechos Humanos, el Empleo y la Inserción Social, 2007. 253 p.: bibl., ill. (Col. Derechos humanos; 9)

Rather than the typical descriptive work concerning political violence in Colombia, this work attempts to identify systematically key aspects of that violence and to place it into an analytical model. The study examines guerrilla and paramilitary violence as well as government action.

1613 Taylor, Steven L.; Felipe Botero; and Brian F. Crisp. Precandidates, candidates and presidents: paths to the Colombian presidency. (*in* Pathways to power: political recruitment and candidate selection in Latin America. Edited by Peter M. Siavelis and Scott Morgenstern. University Park: Pennsylvania State Univ. Press, 2008, p. 271–291, appendix, graph, tables)

Examines candidate recruitment for Colombian executive elections by looking at post-Frente Nacional presidential elections (1974–2002). Studies how different candidates sought specific nomination processes that were to their advantage and how these nomination mechanisms changed both over time and by party. This chapter is part of a broader study of candidate selection processes in Latin America.

1614 Tickner, Arlene B. La securitización de la crisis colombiana: bases conceptuales y tendencias generales. (*Colomb. Int.*, 60, julio/dic. 2004, p. 12–35, bibl.)

Examines how Colombia's neighbors conceptualize the security threat created by Colombia's internal security problems. Tickner argues that the domestic politics of the given state are more relevant than the actual threat posed by the Colombian border spillover of guerrilla, paramilitary, and drug trafficking violence in explaining how the given state perceives the threat and the proper response to it.

1615 Torre, Cristina de la. Álvaro Uribe, o, El neopopulismo en Colombia. Medellín, Colombia: Carreta Editores, 2005. 184 p.: bibl. (Col. La carrera política)

This book analyzes the Uribe administration (first term) in the context of Latin American neopopulism and in the broader context of neoliberalism. The discussion deals broadly with the general politics of the period and is not focused solely on Uribe.

1616 Ungar Bleier, Elisabeth and Carlos Arturo Arévalo. Partido y sistema de partidos en Colombia hoy: ¿crisis or reordenación institucional? (*in* Partidos políticos en la Región Andina: entre la crisis y el cambio. Lima: International IDEA: Asociación Civil Transparencia, 2004, p. 51–69, appendix)

Provides an overview of the Colombian party system as of the mid-2000s— after the 2002 elections, but before those of 2006. Also gives an overview of the party system from 1958 to 2004 and discusses the Partido Liberal, Partido Conservador, Polo Democrático Independiente (now known as the Polo Democrático Alternativo or PDA) and the Uribista bloc of parties.

1617 Vargas Velásquez, Alejo. Guerra o solución negociada: ELN: origen, evolución y procesos de paz. Bogotá: Intermedio, 2006. 343 p.: bibl.

The book deals with the origins, development, and behavior of the ELN (Ejército de Liberación Nacional). The book is useful, if anything, because it focuses on the ELN, whereas most discussions of the guerrillas tend to discuss only the FARC. The book consists of lengthy quotes from primary source materials (e.g., newspapers, letters, other documents) as well as connecting material. Some portions contain more original work than others. Perhaps most useful for the section on ELN-government talks in the early 2000s.

VENEZUELA

RENÉ SALGADO, *Independent Consultant, Gaithersburg, Maryland*

IN AN INTERVIEW with the Colombian daily *El Tiempo* (September 26, 2009), former US President Jimmy Carter expressed disappointment and concern about the performance and increasing authoritarianism of the Chávez government. Carter echoed a perception that many people inside and outside Venezuela share, and which reverberates in the literature on Venezuelan politics. This literature used to spread over a wide range of themes in the past, but during the last few years, Chávez and Chavismo have become the ubiquitous topic in books, essays, and articles, often with undercurrents of criticism and disenchantment.

The current literature adumbrates the distinguishing attributes of a system where electoral means and processes seem to have been used to advance and entrench personalistic politics while undermining institutions and democracy. The result has been an increased power concentration linked to a decline in horizontal accountability—or checks and balances—intertwined with weakened local and state governmental authority—or vertical accountability. Chávez prefers to label his personalistic style "participatory democracy" and, at times, he appears to purposefully undermine middle layers of government by the creation of ad-hoc structures (committees and *consejos comunales*) to deal with local population needs and demands. Meanwhile, the cult to the leader is reinforced through several means, which include the use and abuse of state TV and radio for Chávez's propaganda campaigns, and the forced broadcasting of a large proportion of his political speeches during electoral periods.

Strong state intervention in the economy is another feature of Chavismo. More money from high oil prices has allowed the chief executive to trumpet nationalism while acquiring all or most assets of several foreign corporations operating in the country. Often, loyal military officers run state enterprises with much less concern for efficiency than for job opportunities for political affiliates. This problem becomes evident in the case of service-delivery companies, such as happens with potable water and electricity: power blackouts and water restrictions, sometimes for more than a day at a time, have become a constant occurrence in Caracas and other places.

The government's application of administrative, judiciary, and openly repressive tools to undermine the development of strong opposition, is another hallmark of Venezuela's contemporary politics. These devices include administrative procedures that prevent a leader from running for formal office; opening of penalty causes that force opposition leaders into exile; incarceration without trial; deployment of lynching mobs; and the enforcement of rules leading to the closing or harassment of radios and TV stations that cover dissenting voices. In addition, the government has also resorted to expropriation of private enterprises suspected of providing support to political rivals, thereby creating an economic uncertainty that impinges negatively on goods supply. This is reflected in an (official) accumulated inflation of around 31 percent in 2008—the highest in Latin America.

With the erosion of political pluralism and tolerance, such themes as parties and electoral behavior, which used to be essential components of Venezuela's politics and policy literature—have virtually disappeared as areas of enquiry. A notable exception is Morgan (item **1631**) with a retrospective view of party politics and explanations about the weakening of parties and party systems in the late 1990s, which corroborates prevalent views on traditional parties' decay, notably, their inability to channel people's demands and expectations.

The discussion of civil-military relations has gained increased prominence. A most interesting and illuminating discussion is provided by Irwin, Buttó, and Lange (item **1625**). This is a critical overview of civil-military relations theories, accompanied by a longitudinal analysis of such relations in 20th-century Venezuela and a thorough discussion of key features of Chávez's political performance. Another piece coauthored by Irwin (item **1626**) provides a rather unorthodox account about the role of the military in the political system from the 1960s through the late 1990s, and an argument is made in favor of the notion that their influence was larger than suggested in the conventional literature. Meanwhile, the analysis offered by Sepúlveda (item **1635**) shows how military personnel are currently playing a larger role in policy arenas and organizations previously under the control of civilians.

Another set of writings explores additional facets of Chávez's performance, including policy priorities, nature and quality of the regime, accountability, transparency, responsiveness, and the rule of law. On broad features of Chávez's policy-making—including foreign policy—the most encompassing account is the book edited by Maihold (item **1637**), which contains interesting discussions by Boersner, Corrales, Kornblith, Werz and Winkens. The collection of essays under the coordination of Acosta Espinosa (item **1619**) also touches on different facets of the Chávez government. The outstanding article in this compilation is the one by Professor Oscar Reyes, who argues, with provocative insight, about the limited usefulness of best-known democratic performance scales in Chávez's case where electoral mechanisms are systematically used to undermine institutions and components of liberal democracy. His perception about Venezuela's head of state increasing authoritarianism is shared by McCoy (item **1629**), Lalander (item **1627**), and Ramos Jiménez (item **1634**). These authors also offer expressions of disappointment and frustration with the politics of polarization and exclusion, generally regarded as features of contemporary Venezuelan politics.

The weakening of social movements and organizations' autonomy vis-à-vis the government, and the concomitant undermining of a truly vigorous civic scene, are the subjects of the rather rigorous empirical exploration offered in Hawkins and Hansen (item **1624**), and also in the study by Arenas (item **1618**). Their findings are complemented by Penfold-Becerra (item **1633**), which deals with government control of social organizations, clientelism, and links to corruption. Meanwhile, Valdivieso López (item **1636**) discusses increasing media polarization resulting from government-opposition dynamics.

Chávez's treatment of political opponents is illustrated in the pieces by Giacalone (item **1623**) and Lepage (item **1628**). The first centers on the government's increasing animosity and hostility against dissidents, and the latter on Chávez's coarse language and aggressive verbosity, which have become typical ingredients of his public speeches. Some analysts suggest that such attitude and behavior by the head of state contribute to violence, which has become a major problem particularly in large cities, as shown in the book by the Observatorio Venezolano de Violencia (item **1638**).

Finally, Ochoa-Antich (item **1632**) and Escovar Salom (item **1619**), the first an ex-minister of defense and the second an ex-attorney general, share their broad reflections on Venezuela's contemporary evolution. Ochoa-Antich provides a detailed witness account of the violent events of February 4, 1992.

1618 Arenas, Nelly M. Chávez: el mito de la comunidad total. (*Perf. Latinoam.*, 15:30, julio/dic. 2007, p. 153–184, bibl.)

Discusses some of the salient characteristics of social organizations created by the central government, which the author regards as attempts to conquer social and institutional spaces in the name of the poor, social reform, and revolutionary logic at the expense of liberal democracy.

1619 Coloquio de Historia y Sociedad, *1st, Instituto de Investigaciones Históricas (Bolivarium) de la Universidad Simón Bolívar, 2004.* La cultura política del venezolano. Textos de Nelson Acosta Espinosa *et al.* Caracas: Editorial Equinoccio, Univ. Simón Bolívar: Univ. Católica Andrés Bello, 2005. 315 p.: bibl., ill., maps.

The book contains 14 essays by professors and researchers from the Univ. Simón Bolívar and Univ. Católica Andrés Bello centered on government and politics in contemporary Venezuela. A most interesting article by Oscar Reyes offers a concise and useful discussion of ancient and contemporary tools and approaches to distinguish authoritarian from democratic regimes. Shows how the most popular contemporary criteria and scales—such as those offered by Dahl and O'Donnell—are unable to effectively capture Venezuela's contemporary political realities, where mechanisms of formal democracy—such as electoral contests—exist amid a systematic deterioration of institutional quality and fairness. This system includes both subtle and open harassment of opponents when international observation is limited. Author advocates for the creation of new scales of democratic performance (or "*baremos*"). The article is clearly written, at times using a Venezuelan conversational tone.

1620 Corrales, Javier. In search of a theory of polarization: lessons from Venezuela, 1999–2005. (*Rev. Eur. Estud. Latinoam. Caribe*, 79, Oct. 2005, p. 105–118, bibl.)

Argues that Chavismo looks like 20th-century populism, rather than 21st-century socialism, but does not provide a clear explanation of these terms. Defends the notion that increases in oil prices since 2003 have facilitated Chávez's winning of elections and enhancement of institutional controls.

1621 Ellner, Steve. Revolutionary and non-revolutionary paths of radical populism: directions of the *Chavista* movement in Venezuela. (*Sci. Soc.*, 69:2, April 2005, p. 160–190, bibl.)

Without defining the term "radical populism," offers a discussion of political tendencies within the Chávez movement, which the author labels as hard liners and soft liners. Argues that hard liners are for conflict escalation and the disappearance of all earlier forms of political organization, while the latter favor the increased penetration and domination of old structures.

1622 Escovar Salom, Ramón. Los demonios de la democracia. Caracas, Venezuela: Libros de El Nacional, 2006. 370 p.: bibl. (Col. Ares; 69. Fuera de serie)

Book of nearly 400 pages, written by the now-deceased Ramón Escovar Salom who, during his tenure as Venezuela's attorney general, initiated court proceedings (in 1993) against former President Carlos Andrés Pérez on corruption charges. Contains historical and philosophical reflections about the country's politics in an attempt to provide a balance of the rights and wrongs of Venezuelan leaders before Chávez—who the author regards as an incarnation of communist authoritarianism, in the garb of universal suffrage and democracy. The book suggests that poverty is an important component of Chávez's authoritarian populism, which his government manipulates with the promise of a better life. Book concludes with the optimistic message that people prefer democracy in Venezuela and will not allow the consolidation of a new dictatorship.

1623 Giacalone, Rita. The impact of neo-populist civilian-military coalitions of regional integration and democracy: the case of Venezuela. (*J. Polit. Mil. Sociol.*, 33:1, Summer 2005, p. 25–38, bibl.)

Author argues that Venezuela's government sees leaders of opposing political parties as enemies, rather than as legitimate political alternatives. This view, in turn, leads to the systematic use of de-legitimizing strategies that essentially prevent the normal development of party leaders, and obliterate the possibility of strengthening and institutionalizing these organizations. Article advocates the notion that opposition parties seem to be condemned to become de-institutionalized and personalistic.

1624 Hawkins, Kirk A. and **David R. Hansen.** Dependent civil society: the Círculos Bolivarianos in Venezuela. (*LARR*, 41:1, 2006, p. 102–132, bibl., graph, tables)

A very useful and balanced analysis of the modus operandi of the Círculos Bolivarianos, which the author uses as examples of organizations created by government. The essay shows that although some of the Círculos have helped the poor with their basic needs, they have been involved in the administration of programs that granted their goods and services with conditions— understood as a variety of active and passive sanctions which reinforce clientelistic relationships between Chávez and voters. Concludes that the Círculos lack the autonomy needed to make any meaningful and lasting contribution to civil society development.

1625 Irwin G., Domingo. Control civil y pretorianismo en Venezuela: ilusiones y realidades históricas. Edición de Domingo Irwin G., Luis Alberto Buttó, y Frédérique Langue. Caracas: Univ. Pedagógica Experimental Libertador: Univ. Católica Andrés Bello, 2006. 228 p.: bibl.

Book of five chapters dealing with the subject of civil-military relations mainly in Venezuela, the first two chapters being the most important. Chapter one, written by Domingo Irwin, a professor at the Universidad Pedagógica Experimental Libertador, constitutes a critical analysis and evaluation of the usefulness of various approaches and conceptual categories proposed by scholars of civil-military relations, including Samuel Huntington and Morris Janowitz. The chapter explains how the latter's approach is more appropriate and useful for the understanding of Venezuela's political developments since the early 20th century. Chapter two, written by Luis Alberto Buttos, a professor at Universidad Simón Bolívar, discusses the utilization of electoral mechanisms by current authoritarian leaders to legitimize their authority, noticing that once in power, they proceed to weaken institutions, repress the opposition, and engage in actions that undermine democracy. The chapter is based on Venezuelan sources—books, essays, and newspaper articles—about Chávez's politics and decision making.

1626 Irwin G., Domingo and **Frédérique Langue.** Militares y democracia: ¿el dilema de la Venezuela de principios de siglo XXI? (*Rev. Indias*, 64:231, mayo/agosto 2004, p. 549–560, bibl.)

Authors argue that during much of the second half of the 20th century, Venezuela lived under the illusion of civilian control over the military and that the military's political influence was significant during much of the pre-Chávez era. In their view, military power was manifested both in the presence of an active military as defense minister, and in the absence of civilian responsibilities in defense and national security, as well as in the selection of top military officers to run key state corporations, such as PDVSA (oil) and CVG (aluminum and steelmaking).

1627 Lalander, Rickard. La descentralización venezolana y el chavismo: transformaciones del sistema político partidista. (*Rev. Venez. Cienc. Polít.*, 26, julio/dic. 2004, p. 29–74, bibl., tables)

Author is a researcher at the Latin American Institute, Stockholm, Sweden. The article contains a thorough discussion of political developments since 1989, and explains how Chávez's basic understanding of political power and revolution are in conflict with both democracy and decentralization. Defends the notion that administrative decentralization and reinforcement of local and state institutions are true components of local political participation and democracy.

1628 Lepage, Freddy. En el nombre de la revolución. Venezuela: Debate, 2006. 212 p.: bibl., ill. (Col. Actualidad)

Highlights the disqualifying style, coarse language, and insults with which Chávez refers to those who criticize the government or have a different way of thinking. Devotes sections to the cases of ex-army high-ranking officials who dared to oppose the president and were incarcerated without trial, such as Ramírez-Uzon and Baduel. These are army generals who earlier worked for Chávez, the first as finance minister and the second as minister of defense. Concludes that Venezuela will continue to experience democratic decay and further personalization of political power.

1629 McCoy, Jennifer L. One act in an unfinished drama. (*J. Democr.*, 16:1, Jan. 2005, p. 109–123, bibl.)

Discusses different facets of Chávez's political performance. Argues that the combination of highly centralized decision-making, erosion of public institutions and political accountability, and strong dependence on oil prices, constitute very shaky grounds for sound public policy.

1630 Mires, Fernando. Al borde del abismo: el chavismo y la contrarrevolución antidemocrática de nuestro tiempo. Caracas: Debate, 2007. 303 p.: bibl. (Col. Actualidad)

Author, a Chilean, is a political science professor at the German Univ. of Oldenburg. The book is a compilation of several articles on Venezuela written between 2006 and 2007. Defends the notion that Western political history depicts the evolution of a democratic revolution, whose course, albeit constantly interrupted, continues to move forward. Author recounts that his understanding of world history is radically different from the interpretations of Chávez and Castro, whose models are 20th-century totalitarian regimes.

1631 Morgan, Jana. Partisanship during the collapse of Venezuela's party system. (*LARR*, 42:1, 2007, p. 78–98, graph, tables)

Broad discussion on the virtual disappearance of Venezuela's party system, usually regarded as one of the most institutionalized in Latin America. Looks into factors contributing to its decay in the 1990s as reflected in the 1998 elections, notably, parties reduced capacity to deal with the demands of the people.

1632 Ochoa Antich, Fernando. Así se rindió Chávez: la otra historia del 4 de febrero. Caracas, Venezuela: Los Libros de El Nacional, 2007. 348 p.: bibl., ill. (Col. Ares; 87. Fuera de serie)

Author served as minister of defense under President Carlos Andrés Pérez, when the latter was victim of the failed military coup of Hugo Chávez on February 4, 1992. Book provides a witness account of events. Highlights the fact that, while directing the operation, Chávez was well hidden and protected at the Military Museum.

1633 Penfold-Becerra, Michael. Clientelism and social funds: evidence from Chávez's *misiones*. (*Lat. Am. Polit. Soc.*, 49:4, Winter 2007, p. 63–84, bibl., graphs, table)

The author is a former visiting professor at the Latin American Studies Program, Columbia Univ. Article offers an empirical study of Chávez's clientelistic politics. It shows how, in a context of weak institutional constraints and a relatively large number of electoral contests, the government has used increased oil resources to openly manipulate large sections of the electorate, particularly the poor, via selective distribution of funds. Comments that a large proportion of such resources were managed by the Unified Social Fund—operating outside regular administrative structures and under Chávez's direct control—which soon proved to be corrupt and inefficient.

1634 Ramos Jiménez, Alfredo. De la democracia electoral a la democracia plebiscitaria: elecciones y referendos en la Venezuela de Chávez. (*Rev. Venez. Cienc. Polít.*, 29, enero/junio 2006, p. 7–37, bibl.)

Contends that the Venezuelan political system has become increasingly exclusive and authoritarian and that periodic electoral processes and contests have increasingly become exercises designed to proclaim legitimacy of authorities vis-à-vis the international world.

1635 Sepúlveda, Isidro. Hugo Chávez: pretorianismo y predestinación. *(Polít. Exter./Madrid,* 22:122, marzo/abril 2008, p. 149–160)

Book discusses some salient features of Chávez's politics, notably appointments of military personnel in top government positions. Explains how loyalty is a key selection criterion, as more often than not, the designated individuals lack any knowledge and experience relevant to the job. Military appointees have become increasingly responsible for policy design in a variety of areas, including those previously under the control of civilians, such as academic institutions, social policy, public health, and housing and urban development.

1636 Valdivieso López, Ángela. De la hegemonía política a la hegemonía de mediática: problemas en la ciudadanía venezolana. *(Am. Lat./Santiago,* 5, primer y segundo semestres 2005/2006, p. 165–200, bibl.)

Discusses the role of media in the political process and its increasing political polarization. Claims there is currently a distorted role of the media that has transformed it into a surrogate of either the government or the opposition, rather than a reflection of public opinion.

1637 Venezuela en retrospectiva: los pasos hacia el régimen chavista. Edición de Günther Maihold. Madrid: Iberoamericana; Frankfurt am Main: Vervuert, 2007. 346 p.: ill. (Bibliotheca Ibero-Americana; 118)

This is a compilation of 16 essays on the characteristics of the Hugo Chávez regime. Offers a retrospective review that interprets the problem today while seeking to provide analytical inputs on the political evolution of Venezuela over its recent history. Interesting accounts and reflections are provided in the essays by Corrales, Kornblith, Werz and Winkens, and Boersner. Corrales' piece focuses on government-opposition relationships, and advocates the notion that it would be better for Chávez to deal with his opponents in a more demo-

cratic fashion, as it is easier to govern with lesser degrees of antagonism. Kornblith's article, on elections and referendums, is less hopeful than Corrales'. It actually concludes that Chávez has a utilitarian view of the electoral process, with no commitment to democratic rules, and no respect for pluralism and the rule of law. Werz and Winkens' essay focuses on Chávez's relations with the media, noting that strong media opposition to presidential politics and aggressive language have not led to changes in Chávez's confrontational style. Demetrio Boersner's article focuses on foreign policy and highlights the fact that Venezuela's government combines aggressive speech with behaviors that please strategic oil interests in the developed world. Concludes that the typical ambiguities of Chávez's foreign policy discourse are leading Venezuela to growing isolation and weakness within the international community.

1638 Violencia en Venezuela: informe del Observatorio Venezolano de Violencia 2007. Edición de Roberto Briceño-León y Olga Ávila Fuenmayor. Caracas: Laboratorio de Ciencias Sociales, 2007. 326 p.: bibl., ill.

This book was prepared by members of the Observatorio Venezolano de Violencia, an institution created by academics and social researchers from different Venezuelan universities, which emerged in early 2005 when the government restricted journalists and academics from access to data on violence in the country. The Observatorio disseminates data and information along with recommendations for violence prevention. Chapter 6 provides quantitative information on different forms and types of violence in several cities, including Caracas. The capital city used to have homicide rates of less than 10 per 100,000 in the 70s and 80s, significantly lower than the current rate of almost 150 homicides per 100,000 inhabitants. The study explains how in the early 90s violence rates in the capital city rose significantly following coup attempts by the military. It points out that, ironically, Chávez—who led one such coup—established in 2007 the governmental award "February 4" with the objective of "exalting the heroism, selflessness and patriotism of civilians and military."

BOLIVIA

JOSÉ ANTONIO LUCERO, *Assistant Professor of International Studies, University of Washington, Seattle*

THE 2005 ELECTION OF EVO MORALES is widely acknowledged as a landmark event in Bolivian politics. For some, the election heralded the dawn of a democratic revolution and a break with neoliberal technocracy. For others, Morales is a populist caudillo whose policies have only further polarized the country. Of course, Bolivian political dynamics are much more complex than either of these two perspectives suggest, and the works reviewed for this volume of *HLAS* address the following general concerns: the crisis of the old political system, the Evo Morales and Alvaro García Linera administration, the politics of indigeneity and plurinationalism, the politics of Santa Cruz, and gender dynamics. Most are academic works, but some are primary documents providing the voices of important political protagonists.

Many works examine the collapse of pre-existing political and economic orders. Several authors see this political shift as a result of the corruption of the narrow "pacted democracy" and the rise of powerful social movements that played key roles in the resource wars (over water, gas, and taxes) during the first years of the century (items **1647**, **1648**, **1655**, **1656**, and **1658**). Other works recognize the problems of the older system, but are not necessarily optimistic about the prospects for governability and democracy under the new Morales-led order (items **1646**, **1651**, **1659**, and **1678**). There is also an interesting debate about whether, and to what extent, the new government truly is "revolutionary" (items **1644**, **1649**, **1656**, and **1680**). Other authors explore the crisis of state and current political transformation at the local level, examining such key sites of contention as El Alto, Santa Cruz, Cochabamba, or smaller local municipalities (items **1641**, **1643**, **1654**, **1660**, **1662**, **1668**, and **1679**).

Though many works examine the new structures and configurations of power, there is understandably much attention on the individuals at the center of this transformation, especially President Morales and Vice President García Linera. There have been several biographies of Evo Morales (item **1676**, among them) and there are also a few books that provide a view of the intellectual trajectory of the vice president (items **1652** and **1679**). Perhaps inevitably, there is a growing number of works that are extremely critical of the Morales administration, texts that portray his success as the product of the work of foreign powers and NGOs and his rule as responsible for an escalating number of deaths in social confrontations (item **1663** and **1678**). A more reasoned academic critique suggests severe gender blind spots in Morales' revolutionary program (item **1644**).

Given the historic nature of the 2005 election of Bolivia's first indigenous president, it is not surprising that indigenous politics are a central concern of many of the works reviewed for *HLAS 65*. Several works explore the trajectories of indigenous social movements (items **1639** and **1656**), the history of indigenous representation in the public sphere (item **2644**), and the politics of indigenous languages and bilingual education (items **1654**, **1657**, and **2643**). Bolivians followed an often difficult path to a constituent assembly, but nevertheless approved a new constitution that provides pathways for new indigenous rights and autonomy. Several works examine the new legal architecture and the challenges ahead for "plurinational" Bolivia (items **1640** and **1646**). While the constitution is one arena for the government's project of "decolonization," another is the economic realm in which Bolivia seeks to redefine its relationship to the world, especially in terms of the hydrocarbon sector (items **1646**, **1648**, **1650**, and **1651**).

Of course, the political and economic changes underway are not without their critics and one of the centers of anti-Morales sentiment is the department and city of Santa Cruz, the subject of many works. Many scholars provide historical discussions of the rise of Santa Cruz (items **1667** and **1675**), while others take as their focus the construction of autonomy discourse and *camba* identity (items **1661**, **1673**, and **1683**). Waldmann (item **1682**) provides an especially helpful and multidimensional ethnographic look at the city of Santa Cruz, while Postero (item **1669**) and Gustafson (item **1654**) offer important insights into Guarani territories in (and beyond) Santa Cruz.

Finally, several important works look at the politics of gender in Bolivia. The work of Mujeres Creando, perhaps the best known feminist activist group in the country, is receiving growing attention (items **1647** and **2642**). The work of Mujeres Creando (2009) can also literally be read on the walls of Bolivia as graffiti has become their main form of political and artistic intervention (item **1666**). There is also an increasing number of female politicians in the Movimiento al Socialismo (MAS) Party who are making their voices heard (item **1664**). Canessa (item **1644**) braids discussions of masculinity and femininity in his exploration of the campaign of Evo Morales and the history of gender dynamics in the Bolivian countryside. Mujeres Creando (item **1666**) launches sharp critiques against the machismo of both the government and the lowland opposition. As Morales has won re-election and the opposition regroups, the walls and bookstores of Bolivia will continue to offer new readings of the drama of politics.

1639 Albó, Xavier. Movimientos y poder indígena en Bolivia, Ecuador y Perú. La Paz: CIPCA, 2008. 294 p.: bibl. (Cuadernos de Investigación; 71)

Yet another valuable synthesis by the leading scholar of indigenous movements in the Andes. Albó offers excellent overviews of the histories of indigenous movements in Bolivia, Ecuador, and Peru, as well as a review of more and less successful transnational indigenous articulations. Avoiding simple generalizations, this work illustrates how demography, class dynamics, gender, and varieties of indigenous nationalisms constitute complex indigenous projects.

1640 Albó, Xavier and **Franz Xavier Barrios Suvelza.** Por una Bolivia plurinacional e intercultural con autonomías. La Paz: PNUD, 2007. 351 p.: bibl., ill. (some col.), maps. (Cuaderno de futuro; 22)

Two leading social scientists provide a blueprint of possibilities for autonomies in the wake of the new Bolivian constitution. Concerned largely with the prospects for indigenous autonomies, this work discusses other forms of autonomies and also examines the experience of other states (like Belgium, Spain, South Africa, and Colombia) for lessons that could be applied to Bolivia.

1641 Alem Rojo, Roberto and **Ramón Rocha Monroy.** ¡Nunca más!: a un año del 11 de enero. Santa Cruz de la Sierra, Bolivia: Editorial El País, 2008. 309 p.: ill.

This book accompanies a documentary of the same title and provides a detailed view of the Jan. 11, 2007 conflict in Cochabamba. Drawing on a wide range of interviews with participants from both sides of the conflict and including additional reading and a transcript of the documentary, this is a valuable sourcebook.

1642 Bautista S., Rafael. Pensar Bolivia: del estado colonial al estado plurinacional. La Paz: Rincón Ediciones, 2009. 483 p.

Though sorely undercited, presented here are interesting ruminations of a young Bolivian social scientist and newspaper columnist on the media, the constituent assembly, lowland autonomy movements, decolonization, and modernity. As a collection of short essays that seem to have originally been newspaper columns, it can be best read as a kind of primary document of the Bolivia of Evo Morales.

1643 Cameron, John. Struggles for local democracy in the Andes. Boulder, Colo.: FirstForumPress, Inc., 2009. 382 p.: bibl., index.

An excellent comparative treatment of local governance in Bolivia, Ecuador, and Peru. While some recent works have emphasized the agency of local leaders (see item **1679**), Cameron makes a compelling argument for the importance of the structure of local power relations. The book offers insightful analysis of the workings of capitalism, ethnicity, and development on the local level.

1644 Canessa, Andrew. Sex and the citizen: barbies and beauty queens in the age of Evo Morales. (*J. Lat. Am. Cult. Stud.*, 17:1, March 2008, p. 41–64, bibl., photos)

In this lively and insightful article, Canessa offers a gender analysis of the campaign and presidency of Evo Morales as well as an exploration of gender dynamics in rural and urban Bolivia. A particularly effective critique of the remarkably conservative gender politics of the current Bolivian "revolution."

1645 Canessa, Andrew. Todos somos indígenas: towards a new language of national political identity. (*Bull. Lat. Am. Res.*, 25:2, April 2006, p. 241–263)

Tracing the difference in the framing of Indianness in the discourses of Evo Morales, Felipe Quispe, and rural Aymara community members, this article explores the changing patterns of identification in Bolivia. Exploring the tensions between the different discourses, Canessa illustrates

new possibilities for reconfiguring indigeneity in the Andes.

1646 Crabtree, John and **Laurence Whitehead.** Unresolved tensions: Bolivia past and present. Pittsburgh, Pa.: Pittsburgh Press, 2008. 309 p.: bibl., graphs, index, maps, tables. (Pitt Latin American series)

An excellent collection of essays by leading experts on the cultural, political, regional, constitutional, economic, and international challenges facing contemporary Bolivia. Ably framed by essays by the editors, the authors include leading social scientists from Bolivia, Europe, and the US.

1647 Dangl, Benjamin. The price of fire: resource wars and social movements in Bolivia. Edinburgh; Oakland, Calif.: AK Press, 2007. 226 p.: bibl., ill., index, maps.

A lively journalistic account from the left, this is an accessible and celebratory account of popular resistance in Bolivia. The author does not disguise his sympathies or antipathies, but does paint a complex portrait of Bolivian events that include resource wars, Aymara hip hop, female graffiti artists, and the rise of Evo Morales.

1648 Democracy Center. Interpreting Bolivia's political transformation. Cochabamba, Bolivia: The Democracy Center, 2007. 19 p. http://www.democracyctr .org/pdf/Interpreting_Bolivia_Political _Transformation.pdf

A response to Gamarra's *Bolivia on the Brink* (item **1651**), this document elaborated by a Cochabamba-based research organization suggests that changes in Bolivia are less apocalyptic than many claim. Emphasizing the broad popular support that Morales enjoys and the caution taken even in "radical" reforms like the so-called nationalization of the hydrocarbon sector, this report suggests that Bolivia is hardly on the brink. Subsequent crises may test this optimism, but nevertheless a useful perspective.

1649 Dunkerley, James. Evo Morales, the "two Bolivias" and the third Bolivian revolution. (*J. Lat. Am. Stud.*, 39:1, Feb. 2007, p. 133–166, table)

A bold and sweeping synthesis of much of the polarized writing on the rise of Evo Morales by a leading historian of Bolivia. Provides a reconsideration of the current phase of Bolivian history as a "revolutionary" and "plebeian" process given the many "bottom-up" processes at work both before and after the election of Evo Morales.

1650 Fernández Terán, Roberto. Gas, petróleo e imperialismo en Bolivia. La Paz: CESU UMSS: IBP: Plural Editores, 2009. 109 p.: bibl., ill.

A brief but illuminating account of the role of natural gas and petroleum in the various development models in 20th and 21st century Bolivia. Examining the relationship between state and foreign capital, the author describes an emergent shift away from "neocolonial" development schemes.

Galindo, María and **Sonia Sánchez.** Ninguna mujer nace para puta: análisis feminista de la prostitución. See item **2642.**

1651 Gamarra, Eduardo A. Bolivia on the brink. New York: Council on Foreign Relations, 2007. 51 p.: bibl., map. (CSR; 24)

A leading US-based political scientist offers view of Bolivia's present state and offers recommendations for US policy makers. The report urges more constructive engagement between Bolivia and the US, but offers a perhaps overly pessimistic account of Bolivian politics in the time of Evo Morales. For a nuanced response, see item **1648.**

Garcés, Fernando. ¿Colonialidad o interculturalidad?: representaciones de la lengua y el conocimiento quechuas. See item **2643.**

1652 García Linera, Álvaro. La potencia plebeya: acción colectiva e identidades indígenas, obreras y populares en Bolivia. Antología y presentación de Pablo Stefanoni. Buenos Aires: CLACSO: Prometeo Libros, 2008. 412 p.: bibl. (Col. Pensamiento crítico latinoamericano)

Ably introduced by Argentine political analyst Pablo Stefanoni, this work gathers some of the key writings of García Linera, a key Bolivian intellectual and vice president of the Republic. As a kind of intellectual biography, this volume provides a useful view of the trajectory of García Linera's early engagements with Marx and workers' movements to his more recent analysis of indigenous social movements and politics (influenced by the work of Charles Tilly and Pierre Bordieu).

1653 García Linera, Álvaro. Las vías de emancipación: conversaciones con Álvaro García Linera. Recopilación de Pablo Stefanoni, Franklin Ramírez y Maristella Svampa. México: Ocean Sur, 2008. 99 p.: bibl. (Col. Contexto latinoamericano)

Framed by an excellent if brief introduction by the editors, this series of conversations with Evo Morales' vice president, Álvaro García Linera, does not disappoint. The interviews reproduced here take place before and after the historic 2005 election and provide fascinating reflections on García Linera's multiple lives as a former EGTK guerrilla, an intellectual, and politician.

1654 Gustafson, Bret Darin. New languages of the state: indigenous resurgence and the politics of knowledge in Bolivia. Durham, N.C.: Duke Univ. Press, 2009. 331 p.: bibl., ill., index, maps. (Narrating native histories)

Grounded ethnographically in the Guarani territories of south-eastern Bolivia, this is an exceptionally well-researched and innovative argument for seeing education as a terrain of struggles in which state and social actors contest the meanings of citizenship, development, and decolonization. This book is an important contribution to the study of indigenous politics. For anthropologist's comment, see item **639.**

1655 Gutiérrez Aguilar, Raquel. Los ritmos de Pachakuti: movilización y levantamiento indígena-popular en Bolivia. Buenos Aires: Tinta limón, 2008. 382 p. (Pensar en movimiento; 6)

A Mexican intellectual who along with Álvaro García Linera and Felipe Quispe formed part of the armed group EGTK, Gutiérrez offers a philosophically informed account of the critical 2002–2005 juncture in Bolivia. Looking at various moments of mobilization (over gas, water, coca, territory), she examines both the political consequence of each as well as the "interior horizons" of possibilities as expressed by the protagonists of the movements.

Himpele, Jeffrey D. Circuits of culture: media, politics, and indigenous identity in the Andes. See item **2644.**

1656 Hylton, Forrest and **Sinclair Thomson.** Revolutionary horizons: past and present in Bolivian politics. Prologue by Adolfo Gilly. London; New York: Verso, 2007. 177 p.: bibl., ill., index, maps.

An ambitious and impressively synthetic analysis of Bolivian history from 1781 to 2006, this book provides a *longue durée* account of indigenous and popular struggles. It sets forth a provocative conceptualization of revolution which sees the Evo Morales presidency as the culmination, not the start, of revolutionary processes in the country.

1657 Interculturalidad critica y descolonización. La Paz: Convenio Andrés Bello-Instituto Internacional de Integración, 2009. 183 p.: bibl.

Seven Latin American intellectuals and researchers provide different critiques of the "conservative" notion of interculturality and explore the more radical possibilities of decolonization. Most essays focus on questions of philosophy and epistemology, though Esteban Ticona's chapter provides a more concrete discussion of the contribution of Aymara educators.

1658 Kohl, Benjamin H. and **Linda C. Farthing.** Impasse in Bolivia: neoliberal hegemony and popular resistance. London; New York: Zed Books, 2006. 236 p.: bibl., index, map.

Two long-time analysts of Bolivia provide an excellent critique of the rise and crisis of neoliberal governance in Bolivia. This book offers an especially well-informed account of the "neoliberal wars" (around water, gas, and taxes) that were turning points in the political and economic trajectories of the country.

1659 Laserna, Roberto. El caudillismo fragmentado. (*Nueva Soc.*, 209, mayo/junio 2007, p. 100–117, graphs)

Though some expected social mobilization to decrease once Evo Morales entered office, Laserna argues that the frequency of social protest has only increased. While some of this may be due to opposition, even sectors close to the government see mobilization as the central avenue to getting their demands heard. While some may see this as a continuation of social movement politics, Laserna sees the prospect of undemocratic caudillo style of governance.

1660 Lazar, Sian. El Alto, rebel city: self and citizenship in Andean Bolivia. Durham, N.C.: Duke Univ. Press, 2008.

328 p.: bibl., ill., index. (Latin America otherwise)

Based on ethnographic fieldwork conducted between 1997 and 2004, this book offers an in-depth examination of one of the central sites of contestation against neoliberalism. Putting forth a provocative conceptualization of citizenship (communal and place-based), this book is a challenge to liberal theory and also a valuable ethnographic study of neighborhood, union, and religious organizations of Bolivia's youngest and fastest growing indigenous city.

1661 Mansilla, H.C.F. Problemas de la autonomía en el oriente boliviano: la ideología de la nación camba en el espejo de las fuentes documentales. Santa Cruz de la Sierra, Bolivia: Editorial El País, 2007. 94 p.: bibl. (Col. Ciencias sociales; 8)

A polemical yet social-scientifically informed essay on autonomy. Rather than explore the actual contours of the project of the *nación camba*, the author reconstructs the ideas coming from Santa Cruz autonomy movements into a critique of the "antimodern" MAS political project. The author offers an alternative camba project (based on direct access to hydrocarbon rents, access to markets, and regional autonomy) that he suggests has broad support in Bolivia.

1662 Marinkovic Úzqueda, Vesna. Memoria de un conflicto urbano: el dilema autonomic y la prensa en la crisis del 11 de enero de 2007. Santa Cruz, Bolivia: El País, 2009. 181 p.: bibl.

Using the clash between pro- and antigovernment forces in Cochabamba on Jan. 11, 2007, as a case study, this book explores state crisis, the debate over autonomies, and the role of the press in Bolivian politics. Though uneven in its treatment of these themes, this is a useful exploration of one of the major challenges to the Morales presidency.

1663 Martínez, Emilio. Ciudadano X: la historia secreta del evismo. 2a. ed. Santa Cruz de la Sierra, Bolivia: Editorial El País, 2008. 409 p.: bibl., index, maps.

Though written as a fictionalized set of interviews with a "Deep Throat"-like informant, this book provides an accessible introduction to many of the critiques of the government of Evo Morales. Though often overly conspiratorial, the work provides provocative discussions of many of the more controversial policies and events in the first two years of the Morales regime.

1664 MAS-IPSP: instrumento político que surge de los movimientos sociales.
Entrevistas de Marta Harnecker y Federico Fuentes. Entrevista colectiva con Santos Ramírez *et al.* Entrevistas individuales a Leonilda Zurita *et al.* Caracas: Centro Internacional Miranda, 2008. 225 p.: bibl.

Organized thematically, this is a collection of various testimonies from MAS deputies, senators, party officials, one opposition senator, and a few intellectuals. It documents the rise of MAS and provides a generally positive picture. Nevertheless, as it presents a lively set of conversations, it is not without moments of tension.

1665 Mayorga, Fernando. Antinomias: el azoroso camino de la reforma política. Cochabamba, Bolivia: CESU/UMSS, 2009. 289 p.: bibl., tables.

A collection of essays written in 2008 and 2009 by one of Bolivia's leadings sociologists, this is a coherent and useful account of the changes in the Bolivian political system. Tracing the collapse of the old party system and the emergence of a new one dominated by the Movimiento al Socialismo (MAS), it examines multiple tensions in the MAS, the opposition, the military, and regional geopolitics.

1666 Mujeres grafiteando más. Recopilación de María Galindo. La Paz: Ediciones Mujeres Creando, 2009. 180 p.: ill.

Bolivia's best-known feminist organization, famous for the political commentary they leave on the major cities of the country, offers another photographic compilation of their work. Their anarchistic, feminist critique is leveled against left and right: "There is nothing more similar to a machista from the right as a machista from the left."

1667 La permanente construcción de lo cruceño: un estudio sobre la identidad en Santa Cruz de la Sierra. 2 ed. La Paz: UAGRM; CEDURE; PIEB, 2009. 173 p.: bibl., ill., tables.

Originally published in 2003 (see *HLAS 62:1750*), this examination of identity in Santa Cruz misses an opportunity to integrate recent autonomy demands but remains a useful guide into contemporary invention of camba traditions. Usefully combines a historical exploration of *cruceño* identity with survey research that sheds light on the construction and limits of camba identity.

1668 Postero, Nancy Grey. Andean utopias in Evo Morales's Bolivia. (*Lat. Am. Caribb. Ethn. Stud.*, 2:1, April 2007, p. 1–28)

Examining the political use of Andean culture and symbols, the author suggests that these framings have the potential to build new bridges between popular sectors but also carry the risk of alienating those who are outside the boundaries of the Andean imaginary. These Andean-centric discourses also risk fueling anti-indigenous racism and regional tensions.

1669 Postero, Nancy Grey. Now we are citizens: indigenous politics in post-multicultural Bolivia. Stanford, Calif.: Stanford Univ. Press, 2007. 294 p.: bibl., ill., index, map.

This book offers an ethnography of Guarani cultural politics in Santa Cruz and an overview of indigenous contention in Bolivia from 2000 to 2005. Examining the consequences of "neoliberal multicultural" policies, the book suggests that Guaranís and other Bolivians have inaugurated a new more inclusive "postmulticultural" age, though there are dangers of a backlash.

1670 Prada Alcoreza, Raúl. Subversiones indígenas. La Paz: CLACSO: Muela del Diablo Editores: Comuna, 2008. 151 p.: bibl.

Written by one of Bolivia's leading critical theorists, this provocative book examines indigenous movements through a philosophical lens shaped by the ideas of *inter alia* Deleuze, Foucault, Negri, Laclau, and Derrida. Though often abstract, it provides fascinating explorations of the meanings of community, ayllu, and multitude in Bolivia.

1671 Quispe Quispe, Ayar. Los tupakataristas revolucionarios. 2. ed. La Paz: Ediciones Pachakuti, 2009. 193 p.: bibl., ill.

A very sympathetic account of the Tupak Katari Revolutionary Army (EGTK) based on interviews with EGTK leaders, primary documents, and secondary sources. A mix of history and manifesto, it concludes with a call for armed struggle as the only path to indigenous liberation.

1672 Rojas Ríos, César Armando. Democracia de alta tensión: conflictividad y cambio social en la Bolivia del siglo XXI. La Paz: Plural Editores, 2007. 298 p.: bibl.

Engaging social scientific theories on social movements, governability, and revolution, this book offers a theoretically informed account of social conflicts from 2000 to 2006. Careful to distinguish between the causes and consequences of different kinds of conflicts, this account of "high tension" democracy strikes a nice balance between the risks and rewards of contention.

1673 Seleme Antelo, Susana; Claudia Peña Claros; and Fernando Prado Salmón. Poder y elites en Santa Cruz: tres visiones sobre un mismo tema. Santa Cruz de la Sierra, Bolivia: CEDURE: CORDAID: Editorial El País, 2007. 210 p.: bibl. (Col. ciencias sociales; 10)

In this useful and integrated collection, three authors contribute separate essays on the question of power and elites in Santa Cruz. Seleme provides a conceptual framework that owes much to Gramsci, Pareto, and Zavaleta. Peña provides a historical exploration of cruceño elites from the 19th to the 21st century. Prado concludes the volume with an examination of the mechanisms through which elite exercise power in contemporary Santa Cruz.

1674 Sierra, Malú and Elizabeth Subercaseaux. Evo Morales: primer indígena que gobierna en América del Sur. Santa Cruz de la Sierra, Bolivia: Editorial El País, 2007. 154 p.: ill., ports.

Authored by a Chilean journalist, this is a breezy and occasionally interesting account of the rise of Evo Morales. As evidenced by the questionable subtitle (many indigenous people have "governed" on local and national levels), this book's strength is not in the political analysis. Interviews with government and opposition figures, though, do provide some insights into the tensions of the current moment.

1675 Soruco Sologuren, Ximena; Wilfredo Plata; and Gustavo Medeiros. Los barones del oriente: el poder en Santa Cruz ayer y hoy. Santa Cruz, Bolivia: Fundación

TIERRA, 2008. 283 p.: bibl., col. ill., maps (some col.).

The three essays in this book explore the historical roots as well as the political and economic dimensions of the autonomy project of some Santa Cruz elites. Though there is a palpable ideological and normative position against that autonomist project, the essays provide an interesting and empirically informed critique.

1676 Stefanoni, Pablo and Hervé do Alto. La revolución de Evo Morales: de la coca al palacio. Buenos Aires: Capital Intelectual, 2006. 111 p.: bibl. (Claves para todos)

To date, this is the best political biography of Evo Morales. Written by a team of (Argentine and French) writers that worked closely with the campaign, this book provides a highly readable account of the rise of Evo Morales without falling into the traps of hagiography.

1677 Tapia, Luis. Pensando la democracia geopolíticamente. La Paz: CLACSO; CIDES; Muela del Diablo; Comuna, 2009. 115 p.

Drawing on an eclectic set of sources that include Talcott Parsons, Antonio Gramsci, and John Murra, this essay makes an argument for a rethinking of democracy as a geopolitical possibility beyond the nation-state. While some empirical support may have helped make this proposal seem less utopian, it is nevertheless a provocative work by a leading Bolivian critical scholar.

1678 Valverde Barbery, Carlos. ¿Qué pasó? Santa Cruz, Bolivia: El Paíz, 2009. 1 v.: ill.

Written by a popular television host who initially was supportive of the Morales presidency, this book asks why, despite President Morales' promise of a "government without deaths," there have been so many deaths during this presidency. Though the author claims to provide an objective description of events, the book forms part of a rising opposition, especially in the eastern lowlands. This book offers insights into the tenor of anti-Morales sentiment.

1679 Van Cott, Donna Lee. Radical democracy in the Andes. Cambridge; New York: Cambridge Univ. Press, 2009. 261 p.: bibl., index.

The final book by one of the leading scholars of indigenous politics, this work offers a comparative examination of indigenous politics on the local level in Bolivia and Ecuador. Van Cott suggests that institutional and organizational contexts are important to the success of indigenous municipalities, but that equally important are mayoral leadership and charisma, something she argues has been underemphasized in previous studies. Published posthumously.

1680 Veltmeyer, Henry and **James F. Petras.** Bolivia and the political dynamics of change. (*Rev. Eur. Estud. Latinoam. Caribe,* 83, Oct. 2007, p. 105–119, bibl.)

The authors provide an account of the "precarious balancing act" of the Morales administration as it makes concessions to business sectors and social movements. Suggesting that the Morales administration is less radical than widely reported, the authors describe a mix of continuity and change with previous governments. Based mostly on secondary sources, this provides a reasonable summary of some of the challenges faced by the Morales government.

1681 Viaña Uzieda, Jorge. La interculturalidad como herramienta de emancipación: hacia una redefinición de la interculturalidad y de sus usos estatales. La Paz: Instituto Internacional de Integración, Convenio Andrés Bello, 2009. 159 p.: bibl.

Using empirical material from the constitutional debates in Ecuador and Bo-

livia, this book offers a critique of the use of the concept of interculturality and offers a more radical reinterpretation through often extended engagements with various critical theorists like Raúl Fornet and Max Horkheimer.

1682 Waldmann, Adrián. El hábitus camba: un estudio etnográfico sobre Santa Cruz de la Sierra. Santa Cruz de la Sierra, Bolivia: Editorial El País, 2008. 318 p.: bibl., ill. (Col. Ciencias sociales; 12)

A rich ethnographic portrait of contemporary Santa Cruz. Divided in two section, the first (Ethnography) uses "collages" of interviews divided thematically to explore such themes as identity, status, gender, power, ritual, religion, government, and taste, while the second offers a theoretical analysis of the tensions in Santa Cruz which the author labels provocatively *"feudernidad,"* a hybrid feudal/modern social formation.

1683 Zalles Cueto, Alberto Augusto. Una pieza más en el rompecabezas boliviano: el proyecto autonomista de Santa Cruz. (*Nueva Soc.,* 201, enero/feb. 2006, p. 20–32, bibl.)

A helpful description of the autonomy discourse emerging from Santa Cruz. This article goes beyond the standard dualisms of camba versus kolla (or lowlands versus highlands) by examining how Santa Cruz itself is a product of national processes such as migration and development.

PERU

PHILIP MAUCERI, *Dean, College of Social and Behavioral Sciences, University of Northern Iowa*

PERUVIANS CONTINUE TO STRUGGLE with the legacy of President Alberto Fujimori. In November 2005, Fujimori was detained in Chile after leaving his self-imposed exile in Japan to return to Peru as a candidate for the presidency in the 2006 elections. Following a prolonged extradition process he was sent to Peru in 2007 to face trial on charges involving his complicity in human rights violations and corruption during his presidency. This marked the first time in Peru's history that a former president was put on trial for criminal activities carried out during his government. Convicted of abuse of authority in December 2007, Fujimori was sentenced to six years in prison. Beginning in 2008 he stood trial for the most serious human rights violations, including crimes against humanity stemming from the activities of the paramilitary organization *Grupo Colina* and illegal detentions, as well as bribery and embezzlement charges. The trial itself was hailed for the professionalism of the judges and as an indication of institutional improvements in the judicial system. In April 2009, the Supreme Court convicted Fujimori of human rights abuses, sentencing him to 25 years in prison.

As Fujimori's extradition and trial proceeded, the new government of Alan García Perez showed little inclination to support broader investigations. Indeed, President García announced that the government would provide lawyers to defend former military officials accused of human rights violations, and investigations of human rights organizations were opened. At the same time, support for Fujimori in public opinion polls rose; a not-surprising outcome given that many Peruvians identify him as the president who "defeated terrorism." With a fragmented Congress, pro-Fujimori parties were often courted by others, including members of the PPC and the ruling APRA Party. It is clear that political figures linked to Fujimori will continue to play a role in Peruvian politics in the coming years and his legacy will continue to influence political debates.

Midway through his presidency, Alan García faced rising social protests, corruption scandals, and declining approval ratings. With 9.8 percent growth in 2008, Peru achieved the fastest growth rate in 14 years, propelled by rising commodity prices. However, social protests lead by unions, regional movements, and peasant communities have centered on what was widely seen as a lack of effort to reduce poverty and distribute the benefits of growth equitably. The pattern of commodity export-based growth combined with persistent social inequities characterized the Toledo, and until now, the García administrations. This pattern helps explain the continued political divisions that have developed between the Andean departments and Lima, stoking resentment over the limited benefits received from the export boom. During an October 2008 cabinet reshuffle, President García appeared to recognize these trends in appointing Yehude Simón as Prime Minister. Simón spent time in prison during the Fujimori regime for alleged ties to the Movimiento Revolucionario Tupac Amaru (MRTA) insurgency and has strong ties to regional-based movements. The difficulties in promoting greater efficiencies and social equity are nonetheless significant and include deep rooted clientelism among political parties, a lack of accountability and transparency in the public sector, and ethnic and regional cleavages.

Even as efforts to strengthen democratic norms and institutions at a national level face continued difficulties, there is much ferment at the local and regional level. No fewer than seven of the works under review examine new forms of local participation or decentralization policies. Both Ávila and Panfichi and Dammert analyze the Mesas de Concertación, or committees to foster dialogue among local actors, noting the possibilities for overcoming socioeconomic barriers while questioning the ultimate impact on policy (items **1685** and **1709**). On the other hand, Arroyo and *Democracia participativa en los Andes* examine the ways in which municipalities have used decentralization processes to increase citizen participation (items **1684** and **1694**). Together, these and other studies suggest innovation at the local level aimed at enhancing democratic participation. But as many of the essays in Zárate point out, this is neither easy nor without problems, especially when these efforts are only loosely connected to the institutions of representative democracy (item **1710**).

Efforts to foster democratic norms in Peru continue to confront several authoritarian legacies from the Fujimori administration. Boesten discusses the ways by which the population policies of Fujimori targeted poor indigenous women, reinforcing racial and gender stereotypes (item **1687**). Burt ascribes the weakness of civil society to the intimidation and social control of the regime, while Uceda offers extensive evidence of the Fujimori regime's complicity in human rights violations (items **1688** and **1718**). Durand focuses on the responsibility of the business sector in perpetuating the regime, given its emphasis on promoting its sectoral interests over other values (item **1699**). Two works offer fresh perspectives centered on institutional factors in the rise of Fujimori. Murakami argues that the pre-existing authoritarian structure of institutions paved the way for Fujimori, an analysis centered on the historical determinism of authoritarian caudillos in Peru (item **1707**). By contrast, Dietz and Myers focus more specifically on party system collapse as a reason for the rise of Fujimori, comparing Peru's collapse to a similar dynamic in Venezuela (item **1697**).

There are now several new works examining the post-Fujimori period, particularly aspects of the Toledo administration (2001–2006) and the 2006 presidential elections. Basombrio and Rospigliosi offer an overview of security policies of the Toledo period, noting the intense efforts to reform the police, the military, and intelligence agencies (item **1686**). Cornejo Ramírez and Ferrero Costa provide general political analyses of the period (items **1692** and **1702**), while Taylor analyzes what he sees as significant political learning on the part of a political elite intent on not repeating the mistakes of the 1980s (item **1717**). Durand and Godard review the demographic breakdown of the 2006 elections and *Elecciones 2006 en el Perú* reviews the role of women as both voters and candidates in the 2006 campaign (items **1699** and **1700**). McClintock offers an overview of the electoral dynamics at work, particularly the rise of Ollanta Humala (item **1705**).

Finally, the last several years have seen important new sources of information on Peruvian politics accessible through the web, which are reviewed in the annotations. For example, some data and official documents from ministries, state agencies, and local and regional governments are all accessible via the *Portal del Estado Peruano* (item **1714**). Among NGOs, the defense portal *Defensa y Reforma Militar* offers a comprehensive review of civil-military relations and related issues, while the website of the *Coordinadora de Derechos Humanos* provides information on human rights issues (items **1691** and **1693**).

Albó, Xavier. Movimientos y poder indígena en Bolivia, Ecuador y Perú. See item **1639**.

1684 Arroyo Laguna, Juan. Desafíos de la democracia participativa local en la descentralización: una lectura a partir de doce experiencias. Lima: CARE Perú: Ministerio Británico para el Desarrollo Internacional, 2005. 207 p.: bibl., ill.

An examination of 12 cases of decentralization at the municipal level, focusing on cases that are considered at an advanced stage of development, such as Curahuasi in Apurímac and Azángaro in Puno, to draw out lessons of successful processes. Book is divided in half, between a general overview of issues, such as the role of gender and NGOs, and a review of the individual cases.

1685 Ávila, Javier. Gobiernos locales, participación y exclusión social en cuatro distritos rurales de Apurímac y el Cusco. (*Debate Agrar.*, 37, dic. 2004, p. 1–21)

Author argues that debates about civil society in Peru assume a degree of common interests and outlooks that do not always exist in reality due to social and economic cleavages. Examining the use of Mesas de Concertación in two rural areas, author suggests that while they can help overcome some barriers, the extreme poverty in rural districts remains an important impediment to full social and political participation.

1686 Basombrío Iglesias, Carlos and **Fernando Rospigliosi.** La seguridad y sus instituciones en el Perú a inicios del siglo XXI: reformas democráticas o neo-militarismo. Lima: IEP, Instituto de Estudios Peruanos, 2006. 488 p.: bibl., ill. (Perú problema; 32)

Authors trace efforts to reform the armed forces, police, and intelligence agencies during the administration of Alejandro Toledo (2001–06). Author Rospigliosi played a pivotal role in these efforts as minister of defense and thus is able to bring important insight to these actions and events. Many proposals to increase civilian control were adopted in the early years of the Toledo administration, but authors conclude that the impetus for reform faded as the Toledo government lost interest and political capital. By the end of the administration, civil-military relations were back to where they had been in the 1980s, with the military asserting more autonomy.

1687 Boesten, Jelke. Free choice or poverty alleviation?: population politics in Peru under Alberto Fujimori. (*Rev. Eur. Estud. Latinoam. Caribe*, 82, April 2007, p. 3–20)

Author argues that the rhetoric of Fujimori regarding population policies, centered on a woman's right to choose, clashed with the ultimate goal of these policies, which was to rapidly reduce fertility among poor Andean women. In practice, forced birth control, including sterilization, was viewed as a way to reduce poverty among a target population that consisted of poor indigenous women in the rural Andes, underlining both racial and gender inequalities.

1688 Burt, Jo-Marie. "Quien habla es terrorista": the political use of fear in Fujimori's Peru. (*LARR*, 41:3, 2006, p. 32–62, bibl.)

Excellent analysis of the ways by which the Fujimori regime manipulated fear and played on insecurity while using coercive methods to create a "consensual façade" behind which lay authoritarianism. The weakness of civil society and the popu-larity of the regime during the 1990s, often attributed to economic factors, are additionally explained as functions of intimidation and control of social and political organizations emanating from state agencies.

1689 Ceccoli, Silvano. Il ritorno di Sendero Luminoso: conflitti sociali e "guerra popolare" in Perù dal 2001 al 2005. Introduzione di Nerio Nesi. San Marino: AIEP, 2006. 633 p.: bibl., ill., maps. (Riflessioni sulla storia; 6)

This journalistic account of the majority of the Toledo presidency views the shifting paths of power in the context of the continued activities of Sendero Luminoso in Peru. Based on the current print and electronic media reports in the country, the author argues that the inaction of the Toledo regime and the inability of organized labor to give direction to the simple demands of the popular sector for jobs made the continued activity of what is left of the Senderistas all the more important. Periodical-driven narrative gives extraordinary weight to Senderismo and discusses the Humala movement in the context of the heavy hand of the US and its adversary, Hugo Chávez. Does not foresee the return of Alan García. Good narrative with thoughtful analysis. [V. Peloso]

1690 Congreso de la República del Perú. Lima: Congreso de la República, 2009. http://www.congreso.gob.pe/

The official Web site of Peru's Congress provides links to individual congresspersons, congressional committees, current legislative agenda and proposed legislation, the daily record of congressional sessions, among others. Some of the pages are available in English translation.

1691 Coordinadora Nacional de Derechos Humanos. Lima: Coordinadora Nacional de Derechos Humanos Perú, 2009. http://dhperu.org/

The umbrella organization for 67 human rights-related organizations in Peru, the Coordinadora's Web site provides current information on human rights issues throughout the country and links to past reports issued by the organization.

1692 Cornejo Ramírez, Enrique. La respuesta y la propuesta: balance de treinta meses de política económica del gobierno de Perú Posible y propuestas para salir de la crisis. Lima: CEPEA, 2004. 498 p.

A collection of newspaper and periodical titles critiquing the economic policies of President Alejandro Toledo by a noted APRA official who served in President Alan García's cabinet. Most of the articles focus on growing income inequalities and the book ends with policy recommendations to address poverty during the next presidential administration.

1693 Defensa y Reforma Militar. Lince, Peru: Defensa y Reforma Militar, 2009. http://www.defensaidl.org.pe/

Designed and maintained by the Instituto de Defensa Legal, a Lima-based NGO focusing on civil-military issues, justice and law issues, and human rights, this Web site provides up-to-date information on civil-military relations, including recent legislation, military spending, organizational changes within the military, and military strategy and doctrine, as well as links to the Ministry of Defense and other organizations.

1694 Democracia participativa en los Andes: la experiencia de cuatro municipalidades rurales en el Perú. Lima: CICDA: REMURPE: Oxfam: DFID, 2003. 157 p.: bibl., ill.

Useful study of four rural municipalities in Peru—Limatambo, Santo Domingo, Haquira, and Castrovirreyna—coordinated by NGOs and governmental organizations, focusing on ways participation in local decision making have been increasing in rural municipal governments, which constitute 60 percent of municipalities in Peru. While a number of similar political mechanisms have arisen in different towns, such as local assemblies, the lack of a concluding chapter drawing general lessons is a significant limitation of the work.

1695 La descentralización en el Perú: un balance de lo avanzado y una propuesta de agenda para una reforma imprescindible. Comité operativo, Javier Azpur *et al.* Lima: Grupo Propuesta Ciudadana, 2006. 51 p. (Cuadernos descentralistas; 18)

Useful evaluation of the decentralization policies and processes launched during the Toledo administration. The report is particularly critical of a lack of focus on economic development and broader citizen participation in the decentralization process. Separate sections of the report offer suggestions to address the shortcomings outlined.

1696 Díaz-Albertini Figueras, Javier. Espacios ciudadanos: experiencias de participación en la gestión concertada para el desarrollo local y regional. Colaboración de Javier Díaz-Albertini Figueras y Humberto Lozada Castro. Lima: Escuela para el Desarrollo: EED, Evangelischer Entwicklungsdienst, 2006. 132 p.: bibl.

Results of a very structured study done between 2002 and 2006 examining citizen participation in 24 local organizations engaged in education, health care, environmental protection and other local development issues. Because of the rigid structure of the report, a function of reporting criteria to the sponsoring organization, the results are brief and they are not discussed in any depth.

1697 Dietz, Henry A. and **David J. Myers.** From thaw to deluge: party system collapse in Venezuela and Peru. (*Lat. Am. Polit. Soc.,* 49:2, Summer 2007, p. 59–86, tables)

Argues that "party system collapse" is a distinct category of party system change and uses case studies of Peru and Venezuela to examine how this occurs. Authors identify three preconditions of system collapse: a prolonged crisis across policy areas that challenges the ability of parties to govern; either extremely high or extremely low levels of party institutionalization; and the rise of an "anti-establishment" figure who has credibility to appear as an alternative to the existing party system. Analysis notes that in both cases collapse took hold across three presidential election cycles and efforts by party leaders to strengthen the system proved ineffectual and often counterproductive.

1698 Durand, Francisco. Cleptocracia y empresariado en el Perú. (*Nueva Soc.,* 194, nov./dic. 2004, p. 119–132)

Article examines notable corruption cases and the ways in which Fujimori advisor Vladimiro Montesinos established ties with the business sector. Author argues that the business sector as a whole bears significant responsibility for the authoritarian regime of President Alberto Fujimori given the strong support it offered that regime.

1699 Durand, Mathieu and Henri Godard. Las elecciones presidenciales en el Perú en 2006: un indicador de la segregación socioespacial y de la protesta social. *(Bull. Inst. fr. étud. andin.*, 36:1, 2007, p. 165–170, bibl., maps)

Useful overview of the demographic cleavages evident in the voting patterns of the 2006 presidential elections. Authors conclude that the results demonstrate profound social and economic divisions in Peruvian society that gave rise to a strong protest vote in the form of support for Ollanta Humala.

1700 Elecciones 2006 en el Perú: la agenda de género y los planes de gobierno. Coordinación de Diana Miloslavich Túpac. Lima: C.M.P. Flora Tristán, 2006. 65 p.: graphs, ill., tables. (Nexos feministas; 2)

With Peru having adopted a quota system to achieve gender balance in legislative elections, this work offers a useful examination of the role of gender in the 2006 elections, including party platforms on such issues as human rights, education, sexual rights, equality, and violence against women. Graphs and tables relying on data from the Oficina Nacional de Procesos Electorales (ONPE) provide statistics on female candidates and elected congresswomen. The report finds that parties met quota goals at the national level and 28 percent of the officials elected to the 2006 Congress were women.

1701 Elguera Valega, Luis. La descentralización y sus instituciones. Lima: Fondo Editorial UCSS: Regione Lombardia: IRER, Instituto Regionale di Ricerca della Lombardia, 2006. 306 p.: appendices, bibl.

A useful guide to the institutions and policy processes that govern the decentralization process in Peru, covering such issues as the roles of national ministries, public finance, economic development, and social policies in decentralization. Appendices include texts of key legislation governing decentralization.

1702 Ferrero C., Raúl. La consolidación democrática: escritos y estudios, 2001–2005. Lima: Nomos & Thesis, 2005. 1097 p.: bibl, indexes.

A collection of newspaper columns from various Lima papers by a noted Peruvian lawyer and journalist. The collection covers important topics discussed or proposed during the Toledo administration, such as constitutional reforms, human rights, and election procedures.

1703 Garreta, Jaime. Defensa pública: aportes para la gestión de la política de defensa. Lima: Instituto de Defensa Legal, IDL, 2006. 131 p.: bibl., ill. (Serie Democracia y fuerza armada; 7)

Collection of papers presented at 2006 conference at Lima's Instituto de Defensa Legal on the eve of presidential elections that analyzes civilian control of the armed forces. Useful overview of defense policy making and administration with reform suggestions for a new administration.

1704 Laplante, Lisa J. and Kimberly Susan Theidon. Truth with consequences: justice and reparations in post-truth commission Peru. *(Hum. Rights Q.*, 29:1, Feb. 2007, p. 228–250)

Analyzes the period after Peru's Truth Commission submitted its report, focusing on how nongovernmental organizations, state actors, and civil society groups struggled over the implications of the report and the steps they needed to take in light of the report's findings. Examining the experience of Peru in light of other cases such as South Africa, the authors conclude that although truth telling can have "temporary cathartic effects," systematic reparations are needed to serve as a form of justice, provide an important symbolic effect, and hold the state accountable.

1705 McClintock, Cynthia. An unlikely comeback in Peru. *(J. Democr.*, 17:4, Oct. 2006, p. 95–109, table)

Good overview of the 2006 presidential elections, covering the legacy of the Toledo administration, major campaign issues and the dynamics of both the first and second rounds of voting. Author argues that the election represented the success of the "right left" (pro-free market, pro-democracy and committed to social justice) candidacy of Alan García over the "wrong left" (nationalist, authoritarian and committed to social justice) candidacy of Ollanta Humala, and could help to reinvigorate democratic values in Peru.

1706 Miró Quesada Rada, Francisco. La democracia hacia el tercer milenio: Perú y América Latina. Lima: Univ. Ricardo Palma, Editorial Universitaria, 2005. 154 p.: bibl.

Collection of essays by noted Peruvian intellectual reflecting on Peruvian politics, including balancing human needs and economic competition, the role of women in politics, the politics of Mario Vargas Llosa, and constitutional reforms.

1707 Murakami, Yusuke. Perú en la era del chino: la política no institucionalizada y el pueblo en busca de un salvador. Lima: IEP, 2007. 715 p.: bibl., ill., maps. (Serie Ideología y política, 27)

An interpretation of Peruvian politics in the 1990s that de-emphasizes both Fujimori as a political actor and debates about regime type by focusing on institutional behavior and conflict as the primary force at work in this period. Author argues that authoritarianism was the result of institutions, such as political parties, which historically were structured and operated in authoritarian ways, allowing Fujimori to emerge as a traditional authoritarian caudillo. With Fujimori as a passive actor, the weight of historic continuity is seen as more determinant than individual decisions and policies in shaping Peruvian politics during that decade.

1708 Oficina Nacional de Procesos Electorales. Lima: Oficina Nacional de Procesos Electorales, 2009. http://www.web.onpe.gob.pe/

The ONPE is the national state agency responsible for vote counting during all electoral processes. ONPE's Web site provides official electoral results since 2001, information on political parties, electoral laws and regulations, and general information regarding current electoral campaigns.

1709 Panfichi, Aldo and Juan Luis Dammert. Participación, concertación y confrontación en espacios locales: el caso de la Mesa de Concertación para la Lucha Con-

tra la Pobreza del departamento de Puno. (*Debate Agrar.*, 40/41, julio 2006, p. 325–348)

Examination of a new institution, the Mesa de Concertación para la Lucha Contra la Pobreza (MCLP), developed during the provisional government of President Valentín Paniagua to facilitate dialogue between government officials, civil society representatives, and elected officials on policies and procedures addressing poverty. Authors review the MCLP in Puno, finding that while it has promoted increased cooperation and coordination between social and political actors, its representation has become increasingly narrow over time and its impact on policy-making has been limited.

1710 Participación ciudadana y democracia: perspectivas críticas y análisis de experiencias locales. Edición de Patricia Zárate Ardela. Lima: Instituto de Estudios Peruanos, 2005. 251 p.: ill. (Serie Ideología y política; 25)

Collection of four essays that raise important theoretical and empirical issues on the tensions between representative democracy and participatory democracy in Peru. Grompone offers an incisive discussion on the role participation plays in democracy while the chapter by Hernández Asencio offers a rare quantitative analysis of citizen participation using data from several regional research institutes. Finally, Tanaka and Melendez argue that the success of citizen participation depends on such factors as the goals pursued and the role of external actors.

1711 Páucar Mariluz, Felipe Ascención. La guerra oculta en el Huallaga, Monzón y Aguaytía: la política y el poder corruptor del narcotráfico—30 años de violencia en Huánuco, San Martín, Ucayali. Tingo María, Peru: Centro de Estudios y Promoción para el Desarrollo Agroindustrial, CEDAI, 2006. 234 p.: ill.

Detailed review of major violence carried out since the late 1970s in the Amazonian regions of Huánuco, San Martín, and Ucayali by state security forces, insurgent groups MRTA and the Shining Path, and drug traffickers. Chapters on insurgent violence since the capture of Shining Path leader Abimael Gúzman are especially useful, as is the chronology of human rights violations carried out during the 1980s and 1990s.

1712 Perfil del policía peruano. Lima: Instituto de Defensa Legal, 2004. 72 p.: ill.
Study provides a profile of the national police, providing data on their socioeconomic status, area of origin, region of service, gender, rank, and other information. Assessing the state of the police force in light of reforms carried out in 2001, the study finds that the police continue to suffer from lack of resources, including low pay for most personnel, as well as low technical abilities. Concludes by calling for greater attention to be paid to the needs of employees on the force.

1713 Peru Election 2006. Vancouver, British Columbia, Canada: Dept. of Political Science, Univ. of British Columbia, 2009. http://weblogs.elearning.ubc.ca/peru/
Developed and maintained by Dr. Maxwell Cameron at the Univ. of British Columbia, this Web site provides useful links to media stories, political parties, state agencies, civil society organizations, and blogs about Peruvian politics. The Web site is updated periodically with information on events since the 2006 elections.

1714 Portal del Estado Peruano: directorio de instituciones y organismos del estado. Surco, Peru: Presidencia del Consejo de Ministros (PCM); Oficina Nacional de Gobierno Electrónico e Informática (ONGEI), 2009. http://www.peru.gob.pe/
This Web site provides links to all the ministries of the national government, as well as to regional and local governments and autonomous organizations such as the Central Bank and the Constitutional Tribunal.

1715 Presidencia de la República del Perú. Lima: Presidencia de la República del Perú, 2009. http://www.presidencia.gob.pe/
Official Web site of the presidential office, the site provides information on the president's cabinet, agenda, speeches, and other activities of the executive.

1716 La reforma del sector defensa y las relaciones civiles-militares en el Perú. Lima: Comisión Andina de Juristas: Ministerio de Defensa: Embajada de Finlandia, 2005. 126 p.: appendices, maps. (Serie Democracia; 11)
Five useful essays examine the role of the military in a democratic post-Fujimori

era, including the impact of current international relations on Peru's geopolitical situation, potential military threats and the impact of the Truth and Reconciliation Commission's recommendations on the armed forces. The introductory chapter by Castro Contreras outlines ways by which the military can ensure it is no longer subject to the "interests of the government of the moment." Appendices contain PowerPoint presentations on Peru's military and geopolitical situation.

1717 Taylor, Lewis. Politicians without parties and parties without politicians: the foibles of the Peruvian political class, 2000–2006. (*Bull. Lat. Am. Res.*, 26:1, Jan. 2007, p. 1–23)
Excellent analysis of post-Fujimori politics arguing that "core" leaders of Peru's political class have been measured and rational in political actions, especially on legislative matters during the Toledo administrations. This is largely attributed to an effort to avoid the conflicts and "political decadence" that gave rise to Fujimori. Even so, many members in Congress, motivated by self-interest and double-dealing, created enough turbulence to taint the political class as a whole. Author suggests that efforts by political elites to reduce the role of outsiders and "exotic" movements offer some hope of stability, although clientelist traditions and the individualist strain in politics developed during the Fujimori administration remain strong.

1718 Uceda, Ricardo. Muerte en el Pentagonito: los cementerios secretos del Ejército Peruano. Bogotá: Planeta, 2004. 477 p.: bibl., ill.
Extensive interviews with soldiers, intelligence agents and Shining Path militants form the basis for a narrative about a series of human rights atrocities carried out between 1982 and 1993, written by an award winning investigative journalist. Riveting accounts point to official government complicity in this period as well as efforts to cover up evidence.

1719 Vargas León, Carlos. El retorno de los partidos a la democracia: las elecciones peruanas del 2001. Suita, Osaka: Japan Center for Area Studies, National Museum of Ethnology, 2005. 32 p.: bibl., ill., maps.

(*JCAS occasional paper*; no. 24) (JCAS-IEP series; 7)

Useful overview of the 2001 elections. After reviewing changes in electoral laws and policies in the aftermath of the Fujimori administration, author provides a summary of major campaign events and issues, along with an analysis of electoral outcomes.

1720 Wise, Carol. Reinventing the state: economic strategy and institutional change in Peru. Ann Arbor: Univ. of Michigan Press, 2003. xiii, 290 p.: bibl., index. (Development and inequality in the market economy)

An excellent examination of the links between economic development and state intervention in Peru since the early 1980s. Author provides an overview of three periods in Peru's economic policy making: developmentalism, state retreat and streamlined state intervention. She suggests that the economic turnaround in Peru since the mid-1990s is largely the result of both internal state reform and institutional modernization.

1721 Youngers, Coletta A. and **Susan C. Peacock.** Peru's Coordinadora Nacional de Derechos Humanos: a case study of coalition building. Washington, D.C.: Washington Office on Latin American (WOLA), 2002. 39 p.: bibl., ill. (WOLA special report)

This case study looks at one of Latin America's most successful country-based human rights organizations and examines how it has developed into a major civil society actor during a period of intense violence. Starting with its formation in 1985, authors examine the challenges it faced confronting human rights violations from state actors as well as insurgent groups. They offer 16 factors to explain how the Coordinadora was so successful, including a focus on human rights education, strong leadership within the organization, nonpartisanship and effective media strategies.

CHILE

MICHAEL FLEET, *Professor of Political Science, Marquette University*

CHILEAN POLITICS DURING THE BIENNIUM 2004–2006 have been less stressful and less uncertain when compared to previous periods. With markedly improved civil-military relations, and the constitutional reforms approved in 2005, Chile's lengthy transition to democracy appears to be close to an end. The continuing operation of an electoral system that inflates the representation of the political right remains, in the minds of most observers, however, a significant flaw in the country's democratic character.

The period's most important single political event was the election, in January 2006, of Michelle Bachelet, the first woman in Latin American history to be elected in her own right, and not just on the heels of a politically prominent husband. Bachelet served a year as Minister of Health under Ricardo Lagos, before being named his Minister of Defense in January 2002. She served in that capacity for two years, during which time she gained the trust and cooperation of senior military officers, helped them to embrace the concept of civilian supremacy, and in the process became a leading candidate to succeed Lagos as president. Ironically, her political ascent coincided with the equally dramatic decline of the political fortunes of the UDI's Joaquín Lavín, whom Lagos had narrowly defeated in the 2001 run-off, and who was expected to be a formidable candidate the next time around.

Bachelet's victory over eventual right-wing standard bearer Sebastian Piñera catapulted her into international political prominence, but saddled her government with high expectations. The first several years of her presidency were disappointing to both supporters and observers alike, as the economy faltered, party leaders bickered, and her government earned low marks for its management of Santiago's new metropolitan bus network (*el Trans-Santiago*) and its handling of secondary students who were protesting educational policies. Toward the end of her term, however, her handling of the Chilean economy in a period of global recession, and her unassuming, and yet graciously personal style, enabled her to recover her footing and to approach the end of her term with relatively high popularity ratings.

The literature on Chilean government and politics for this biennium reflects the increasingly normalized character of the country's political life. Perhaps the sharpest contrast with preceding periods is the marked decline of interest in Pinochet himself and in the issues and divisions generated by his almost 17 years in power. With the discovery of his US bank accounts, Pinochet's image and reputation suffered irreparable political damage. The revelations clearly helped the Concertation in the 2005/2006 elections, but both the political right and the public at large seemed willing, if not eager, to move beyond the coup and its continuing aftermath. Accordingly, national debate and discussion have revolved around more mundane political topics, and the political literature has followed suit. During the biennium, scholars and observers have focused on President Bachelet herself, the 2005/2006 elections, executive-legislative relations, civil-military relations, decentralization, and policy initiatives in areas such as health care, tax exemptions, and gender equality, rather than on historical divisions and disjunctures.

Reflecting the increasingly normalized state of Chilean politics, most of the material published during this biennium deal with either elections or contemporary political developments. In their coverage of the 2005/2006 elections, Angell and Reig point to elements of both continuity and departure vis-à-vis elections of previous years (item **1723**). Gamboa and Segovia (item **1737**) stress the continuing importance of the democratic/authoritarian divide in both the parliamentary and presidential elections. Huneeus analyzes Bachelet's meteoric rise in the polls, Lavin's equally dramatic decline, and the problems facing the PDC and UDI (item **1743**). And Morales, finally, offers a detailed analysis of Bachelet's victory, relating her vote totals, and those of other candidates, to voter attitudes towards the Lagos government, and to the gender, household status, and income level of individual voters as well (item **1750**).

In other articles dealing with election-related issues: Astorga argues that the country's merely "electoral" democracy is a perfect political fit for its neoliberal economic model (item **1724**); Carey and Siavelis explain how the Concertation uses the prospect of an administration appointment to persuade strong candidates to run in a district in which their coalition may not receive enough votes to win both seats (item **1728**); Garrido and Navia challenge this "insurance policy" explanation (item **1739**); Fuentes and Villar discuss the pros and cons of obligatory registration and voting (item **1765**); Rojas and Navia offer evidence that the binomial system was explicitly designed to favor forces sympathetic to the right (item **1753**); Siavelis proposes an open-list, small-district based proportional system in place of both the current binomial system and mixed-member systems to which some countries have been turning of late (item **1757**); and Bonilla and Gatica review efforts to develop a spatial theory of voting based on realistic assumptions and capable of predicting outcomes (item **1726**).

Among the many publications dealing with contemporary politics, the following are worthy of note: Buchanan's comparison of the Uruguayan and Chilean labor movements (item **1727**); Ferraro's depiction of the considerable influence that Senators and Deputies enjoy in their dealings with public-sector officials (item **1734**); Fuentes' book-length analysis of the difficulties in curbing police violence in postmilitary Argentina and Chile (item **1736**); the publication in English of Huneeus' earlier study of the Pinochet regime (item **1744**); and Huneeus' reflections on the enduring limitations of the 1980 Constitution (item **1745**). Additionally, Rodríguez Fisse's informative account of interest groups and lobbying activity in Chile (item **1752**), Ruiz-Rodríguez's analysis of polarization in the country's party system over the years (item **1754**), Santa-Cruz's discussion of international involvement in the plebiscite of 1989 (item **1755**), and Uggla's analysis of the negotiations that led to the 1989 reform of the 1980 Constitution (item **1764**), are of interest. And, finally, a number of people have ventured opinions as to what should be done to revitalize citizen involvement in the country's political process: the Águila collection brings together essays from veteran and younger Concertation Party members on how to reshape and revitalize their coalition's strategic objectives (item **1731**); Lahera calls for additional job creation, an extension of social benefits beyond existing levels, and more effective integration and representation of the "non-parliamentary" left (item **1747**); Walker and Jouannet urge the Christian Democratic Party to embrace the role of junior partner in a broader and explicitly social democratic Concertation (item **1766**); Garretón urges the Concertation to incorporate the non-parliamentary left and move beyond blandly social democratic initiatives (item **1738**); and Wilke proposes new, neocorporatist networks that link citizens, interest groups, and the policy-making process (item **1767**).

During this biennium, observers and analysts also looked at developments in the area of political decentralization, a topic that has attracted considerable interest of late in Chile as in other countries. Cleuren, for example, has written on the potentially destabilizing effects of such initiatives in a country (Chile) in which inter-elite accommodation has worked so well to this point (item **1729**). Durston, on the other hand, stresses the potential for local clients to play more active, less dependent roles if they are included in discussion between government agencies and local power brokers (item **1732**). Eaton emphasizes the long-term political risks to national policymakers of even modest concessions (item **1733**). Mardones Z. also points to the uncertain and unintended impact that decentralization can have on a party's political fortunes at the local level (item **1748**). And, finally, Kubal examines the effects of efforts to improve the country's schools and health care facilities through decentralization (item **1746**).

As might be imagined under a government headed by a popular female president, gender politics have also been a recurrent aspect of political life and debate during the period. Blofield and Haas' article looks at the challenges faced by initiatives that challenge traditional gender roles (item **1725**). Hardy has surveyed and interviewed women leaders in the political and nongovernmental sectors (item **1741**). Álvarez argues that the women's movement has been co-opted and weakened by its close association with recent Concertation governments (item **1722**); Pribble compares welfare policies affecting women (as opposed to men or people generally) in Chile and Uruguay (item **1751**). Franceschet suggests that Bachelet's election is a reflection of cultural changes that have already taken place, and an opportunity for the country to move even further (item **1735**). And, finally, Guzmán and Rojas Donoso have written an informative biography of Bachelet based on interviews of the candidate, her mother, and two of her children (item **1740**).

Among studies dealing with specific thematic or policy issues, Tokman *et al.*'s proposal for a new approach to tax-exemption policy might be of interest to political economists (item **1763**), while those interested in the political implications of Catholic values and beliefs might wish to examine Stewart-Gambino's interviews of pobladoras who feel abandoned by an increasingly conservative Church (item **1761**), the Summer 2006 issue of *Estudios Públicos* containing several articles on Catholic teaching and the papacy of John Paul II, and Thayer's reflections on Christian humanism in Chile (item **1762**).

And, finally, in contrast with previous biennia, only two studies of the once central, and potentially explosive, topic of civil-military relations appeared during this period: Montes and García Pino's account of the breakthroughs in the Concertation's relations with the military in the late 1990s and early 2000s (item **1749**), and Week's study of civil-military relations through 2002 (*HLAS 63:2359*).

1722 Álvarez San Martín, Roberto. La institucionalización de la perspectiva de género en las políticas públicas en Chile: una reflexión crítica. (*Polít. Gest.*, 10, 2007, p. 45–63, bibl.)

Looking at public policy in gender-related matters, the author reaches a number of paradoxical conclusions: the success of SERNAM (the cabinet-level agency, Servicio Nacional de la Mujer) in overseeing and coordinating initiatives has actually prevented other public services from assuming more active roles; the initiation of public discussion and debate with civil societal organizations has been used largely for political co-optation and has yielded little in the way of programs and policies; and while the public sector has been forming knowledgeable experts in gender-related matters, many of these professionals have left for either the private sector or an academic institution, and have neither permeated nor greatly influenced other state agencies.

1723 Angell, Alan and Cristóbal Reig. Change or continuity?: the Chilean elections of 2005/2006. (*Bull. Lat. Am. Res.*, 25:4, Oct. 2006, p. 481–502, tables)

An assessment of the 2005–06 general elections that stresses the country's impressive record of electoral stability and continuity. The authors credit Bachelet's second-round victory by a relatively comfortable margin to favorable economic conditions, the high approval rating enjoyed by outgoing President Ricardo Lagos, and the remarkable appeal of the candidate herself. Among other features, the article contains a useful assessment of the effects of the country's binomial electoral system, and of arguments for and against its reform.

1724 Astorga Lira, Enrique. La democracia agoniza voto a voto: la política en la era transnacional. Santiago, Chile: Editorial Univ. de Santiago, 2006. 311 p.: bibl., ill. (Col. Ciencias sociales)

A highly critical analysis of Chilean politics by an economist who once worked for the ILO and was a consultant to the UN's Economic Commission for Latin America. In his view, the country's merely "electoral" democracy has been made safe for its neoliberal economic model; voters are allowed to choose, and to delegate their sovereignty to, the people who will "represent" them, but not the policies they will pursue. Unfortunately, he does not address other, less critical analyses of Concertación policies, nor does he adequately explain why the increased social tensions that should flow from policies designed to protect the model have failed to materialize, or why a conservative candidate whose own enormous wealth is a product of these same free market policies is favored to win the next (2009) presidential election by a substantial margin.

1725 Blofield, Merike Helena and Liesl Haas. Defining a democracy: reforming the laws on women's rights in Chile, 1990–2002. (*Lat. Am. Polit. Soc.*, 47:3, Fall 2005, p. 35–68, bibl., tables)

A very useful analysis of the country's gender politics, e.g., dealing with education, children's rights, family policy, women's health, and human life issues. Traces the fate of 38 bills that both do and do not challenge traditional gender roles and do and do not entail economic redistribution. The authors focus on the strategic calculations of leftist parties (e.g., whether to present moderate or more radical proposals), and the crucial role played by Christian Democrats, whose ranks include both conservative and more liberal Catholics who face competition from the right-wing UDI, to which the party leaders do not want to lose more votes than they already have.

1726 Bonilla, Claudio A. and Leonardo A. Gatica. Una nota sobre la teoría espacial del voto. (*Estud. Públicos*, 102, otoño 2006, p. 113–146, bibl., graph)

Two economists, one who is Chilean, offer a review of efforts to develop and refine a spatial theory of voting that is both realistic in its assumptions regarding party and voter choices and capable of predicting actual outcomes. Unfortunately, the authors do not attempt to apply any of the refined versions or models to Chile, nor does their lengthy (11 p.) bibliography mention works that have used institutionalized versions of rational-choice theory to analyze the behavior of either Chilean voters or parties (e.g., Siavelis and Carey).

1727 Buchanan, Paul G. Preauthoritarian institutions and postauthoritarian outcomes: labor politics in Chile and Uruguay. (*Lat. Am. Polit. Soc.*, 50:1, Spring 2008, p. 59–89, bibl.)

Compares Uruguayan and Chilean labor movements. The author explains the former's reemergence as a formidable player in its country's post-authoritarian politics as a function of the greater autonomy it enjoyed prior to the period of military rule in its dealings with both state authorities and party hierarchies, making it more difficult for the country's military to dismantle it, or to prevent it from resuming its customary role and influence in the political system. In contrast, and despite Chile's vaunted democratic heritage, its labor movement was dependent on ideologically congenial political parties and vulnerable to state regulation and interference in the period leading up to military rule, which have limited its range of movement and influence in the post-military political arena.

1728 Carey, John M. and Peter Siavelis. Insurance for good losers and the survival of Chile's Concertación. (*Lat. Am. Polit. Soc.*, 47:2, Summer 2005, p. 1–21, bibl., tables)

Writing in early 2005, two close observers of Chile's party and electoral politics speculate about the future of the center-left Concertación coalition now that presidential elections have become much more competitive. Since 1989, they argue, the coalition's presumed capture of the presidency gave its leaders the means with which to persuade candidates to run in districts that were important to the coalition (where it would try to "double up," for example), albeit suboptimal for the candidates themselves, by rewarding them with a ministerial or ambassadorial appointment in the event that they failed to win the seat. It is not clear how well this strategy will work in the 2009 elections, in which the rightist candidate is the front-runner, or whether it worked at all in 2005, when people had to decide whether to run for a legislative seat long before the likely outcome of the presidential contest was known.

1729 Cleuren, Herwig. Local democracy and participation in post-authoritarian Chile. (*Rev. Eur. Estud. Latinoam. Caribe*, 83, Oct. 2007, p. 3–18, bibl.)

Examines political participation at the local level in Chile in the context of a broader debate over the depth and quality of Chilean democracy. The author points to a number of obstacles on the road to fuller democracy, among them widespread citizen apathy, and a reluctance on the part of both elected and bureaucratic officials to accept the risks and costs involved in greater popular participation. In the end, however, the author sides with those who argue that the current arrangement of inter-elite accommodation and politically isolated, largely technocratic policy-making have worked well in terms of both economic payoff and political stability, and would be jeopardized by potentially destabilizing reforms.

1730 Codoceo, Fernando. Demokratische Transition in Chile: Kontinuität oder Neubeginn? Berlin: WVB, Wissenschaftlicher Verlag Berlin, 2007. 420 p.: bibl., ill., tables.

Study about the Chilean transition to democracy from 1980–90. Author's thesis is that political economic and social changes introduced during the military regime from 1973 on led to a slow cultural transformation of the country, thus facilitating later democratization processes after the 1988 elections. Concluding chapter shows that the later juridical preoccupation with Pinochet and with his regime's human rights infractions did not create a nation-wide consensus about the past. [F. Obermeier]

1731 Los desafíos del progresismo: hacia un nuevo ciclo de la política chilena. Recopilación de Ernesto Águila Z. Santiago, Chile: Catalonia, 2005. 272 p.: bibl., ill.

A collection of essays by self-styled "progressives," including Ricardo Ffrench-Davis, Alfredo Joignant, Soledad Alvear, Alvaro Briones, and younger scholars and activists, offering a variety of proposals, on the eve of the 2005 elections, for reshaping the Concertación's strategic objectives (reversing inequality and reinvigorating political participation) and organizational structure (e.g., bringing the PS, the PPD, and the PRSD into a political federation if not a single party). None of the proposals gained sufficient traction or support to materialize during Bachelet's government, but they provide a useful assessment of the state of Chilean politics by a number of the center-left alliance's most important protagonists.

1732 Durston, John. Concertación local y clientelismo rural en el "norte chico" de Chile: los campesinos, el PRODECOP y los CDL. (*Debate Agrar.*, 40/41, julio 2006, p. 349–379)

Offers a useful discussion of the practice of clientelism, differentiating among classic and contemporary versions, and describing its evolution in changing political contexts. The author reports on forms and developments in three *comunas* in the Norte Chico region, near Coquimbo, where peasant communities, government agencies,

and local power brokers (councilors, mayors, and deputies) exchange favors, resources, and commitments in complex interactions in which the "clients" play more active and less dependent roles than in earlier times.

1733 Eaton, Kent. Risky business, decentralization from above in Chile and Uruguay. (*Comp. Polit./New York*, 37:1, Oct. 2004, p. 1–22)

Relates political decentralization in Chile and Uruguay to that in other Latin American countries over the last 20 years. The literature dealing with Argentina, Brazil, Colombia, Mexico, and Venezuela has explained outcomes as a function of the need for national party officials to accommodate important subnational power brokers (Willis, Garman, and Haggard, 1999), or the strategic calculations of national leaders whose party's prospects seemed more promising at the subnational than at the national level (O'Neill, 1999). Eaton sees these explanations as less persuasive in the Chilean and Uruguayan cases. In Uruguay, he argues, the national leadership of the more conservative Liberal and National parties supported decentralization in an effort to stem the rise of the left-wing Frente Amplio. In Chile, on the other hand, national party leaders on both the right and left favored local-level democratization (electing rather than appointing mayors), but for different reasons: the right concluded that its electoral prospects were better at the municipal level, while Concertación officials believed that they would do well at both levels, and might as well help local leaders to strengthen their political bases. Eaton wisely observes that modest changes agreed to for short-term political gains may result in more important concessions, and much more significant decentralization, in the longer term.

1734 Ferraro, Agustín. Friends in high places: congressional influence on the bureaucracy in Chile. (*Lat. Am. Polit. Soc.*, 50:2, Summer 2008, p. 101–129, bibl.)

In a detailed survey of work on presidential power in Chile, the author describes the controversy between those (Shugart and Carey, 1992; Shugart and Mainwaring, 1997; and Shugart and Haggard, 2001) who point to the vast array of formal powers at the disposal of Chilean presidents in their dealings with other branches, and those (Siavelis, 2002 and 2006) who argue that a variety of "informal" mechanisms and practices enable the Chilean Congress to exercise substantial influence on the political process, effectively preventing the executive from enjoying the full effects or benefits of its constitutional prerogatives. In support of Siavelis, he offers the findings of his own confidential interviews of 29 informants, including five experts on public administration, six career civil servants, and 18 political appointees presently holding bureaucratic positions to which they were appointed on the recommendation of either a Senator or a Deputy. On the basis of their testimony, he describes the widespread practice of legislative patronage, the extensive network of bureaucratic contacts that virtually every Concertación legislator enjoys, the frequent meetings they hold with policy-makers in many different areas, and the restraints on presidential power that stem from the system of *el cuoteo político* (proportional distribution of bureaucratic posts among the Concertación's member parties).

1735 Franceschet, Susan. El triunfo de Bachelet y el ascenso político de las mujeres. (*Nueva Soc.*, 202, marzo/abril 2006, p. 13–22)

The author views Bachelet's election as both a reflection of cultural changes that have already taken place, and an opportunity for the country to move further in this direction. She cautions, however, that the Concertación's decision to run a woman for president may have been a politically astute ploy to appear more interested in change than it really was, and that Bachelet's commitment to maintain the economic policies of her predecessors may make progress on gender equality more difficult. Pointing to evidence that Chile may be moving away from its traditional cultural conservatism, e.g., high-level public support for the legalization of divorce, a decline in the number of those believing that men make better leaders than women and that women should devote themselves to their home and families, and the apparently declining appeal of the UDI and the PDC within their respective coalitions, she urges feminists and others to continue pressuring Bachelet to

push for greater gender equality. It is hard to imagine, however, that those strongly committed to this goal could plausibly threaten to go elsewhere politically.

1736 Fuentes, Claudio. Contesting the iron fist: advocacy networks and police violence in democratic Argentina and Chile. New York: Routledge, 2005. 221 p.: bibl., ill., index. (Latin American studies: social sciences and law)

A neoinstitutional study of efforts to expand citizens' rights and limit police powers in post-authoritarian Argentina and Chile. The author focuses on the opportunities and resources available to pro-order and civil-rights coalitions when raising issues, introducing, passing, enforcing, and in some cases reversing, legislation in the face of citizen ambivalence, governmental priorities, and levels of corporateness among the police agencies involved. Comparing the single Chilean experience (1990–2002) with those of both the city and the province of Buenos Aires, the author explains the lack of meaningful progress in strengthening civil rights in Chile (aside from a 1998 judicial reform bill that has failed to alter police behavior) and the very modest advances that have been made in Argentina.

1737 Gamboa, Ricardo. Las elecciones presidenciales y parlamentarias en Chile, diciembre 2005–enero 2006. (*Rev. Cienc. Polít./Santiago*, 26:1, 2006, p. 84–113, bibl., graphs, tables)

An analysis of the 2005–06 elections that sets the political context in which they took place and describes the selection of candidates and the campaigns. Work divides its attention equally between the parliamentary elections that concluded in Dec. 2005, and the presidential elections whose second round took place in mid-Jan. 2006, and resulted in Michelle Bachelet's election. The authors argue that the principal determinant of outcomes in both cases remained, as in all preceding elections in the postmilitary period, the democratic-authoritarian divide, i.e., voter attitudes regarding the Pinochet regime. They also stress changes in the political balance and weight within each of the major blocs, the challenges which such changes pose to their political futures, and the disenfranchisement which the binomial electoral system imposes on the so-called extra-parliamentary left (essentially the Communist Party), which gained over 7 percent of the vote without winning a single congressional seat.

1738 Garretón Merino, Manuel Antonio. Reflexiones en torno de la(s) izquierda(s) chilena(s) y el proyecto de país. (*Nueva Soc.*, 197, mayo/junio 2005, p. 159–171, bibl., ill.)

Garretón has long been critical of the slowness and incompleteness of Chile's transition to democracy, and of the limited social agenda of the ruling Concertación. He proposes a broadening of the coalition to include unrepentantly Marxist socialist forces (e.g., the country's Communist Party and other radical groups), which are prevented by the electoral system from holding seats in the national legislature, and an abandonment of the current social and economic policies which he regards as a blandly and harmlessly social democratic version of neoliberalism.

1739 Garrido, Carolina and Patricio Navia. Candidatos fuertes en la Concertación: ¿seguro para subcampeones o prevalencia de los dos tercios? (*Estud. Públicos*, 99, invierno 2005, p. 1–29, bibl., tables)

Challenges Carey and Siavelis' argument that the Concertación presents more lists with two strong candidates than the rival Alliance because its occupancy of the presidency enables it to offer effective consolation to potentially losing candidates. According to Garrido and Navia, such insurance is neither necessary nor sufficient. The Concertación is in a better position to field more strong candidates, they argue, because of the larger number of coalition parties from which to draw them, and thanks to the persistence of the country's three-thirds party system, which apparently assures more reliable support for both centrist and left-wing candidacies in many districts. The authors offer empirical support for their explanation, but concede that it is no more plausible statistically than that of Carey and Siavelis. But they do point to the absence of any direct relationship between the number of years remaining in a president's term at the time of a parliamentary election and that of Concertación lists with two strong candidates in the 1989, 1993, 1997, and 2001 elections.

1740 Guzmán Bravo, Rosario and Gonzalo Rojas Donoso. La hija del tigre. Santiago, Chile: RiL Editores, 2005. 234 p.: ill. (Serie Identikit)

A readable and informative portrait of Michelle Bachelet published during the campaign that culminated in her election as president in the Jan. 2006 run-off. Written by two Chilean journalists on the basis of extensive interviews with Bachelet herself, her mother, and two of her three children, the early chapters contain interesting material concerning her father, Air Force General Alberto Bachelet, who died in custody in 1974 while awaiting trial on unspecified charges. Later chapters chronicle her rapid rise to political prominence, initially as an advisor in the defense ministry under President Frei Ruiz-Tagle and later as minister of both health and defense under President Lagos. Of particular interest is a brief psychological profile from popular psychologist Giorgio Agostini, and Bachelet's response to it.

1741 Hardy Raskovan, Clarisa. Eliterazgo: liderazgos femeninos en Chile. Santiago: Catalonia, 2005. 188 p.: bibl., ill.

Hardy, a psychologist, social policy analyst, and media personality, approaches gender inequality through a study of women holding important positions in social and political organizations (unions, guilds, parties, legislatures, and in executive positions at both national, regional, and municipal levels). On the basis of 570 questionnaires and 32 in-depth interviews, she compares the generally privileged socioeconomic, educational, and family backgrounds of these elite women with those of Chilean women generally, laying bare the inadequacies of analyses that emphasize their allegedly intrinsic virtues and defects. Particularly striking is the evidence Hardy presents of the costs that many of these career women have had to bear in terms of their marriages and relationships with their children.

1742 Heiss, Claudia and Patricio Navia. You win some, you lose some: constitutional reforms in Chile's transition to democracy. (*Lat. Am. Polit. Soc.*, 49:3, Fall 2007, p. 163–190, ill.)

The authors explain the constitutional amendments to which the opposition agreed in Aug. 1989 as a way for the outgoing military government to gain additional autonomy vis-à-vis new civilian authorities, shorten the presidential term which the opposition candidate would probably win, and strengthen the legislature in which promilitary would likely enjoy significant influence, in exchange for eliminating what the authors view as secondary limitations, such as the outlawing of Marxist parties.

1743 Huneeus, Carlos. Las elecciones presidenciales y parlamentarias de 2005 en Chile. (*Estud. Int./Santiago*, 39:153, abril/junio 2006, p. 69–94, graphs, tables)

An informative analysis that uses both public opinion and electoral data to assess the significance of the 2005–06 elections. It traces and accounts for Bachelet's extraordinary surge in popularity and political regard during her tenure as minister of defense (Jan. 2002 to Oct. 2004), the equally dramatic decline in Lavín's political image and prospects during 2004 and 2005, and shifting ideological identities and party-support levels. Additional coverage is provided for a number of Senate and Chamber of Deputies races and challenges (e.g., the lack of attractive new, i.e., younger, personalities facing the Christian Democratic Party in particular, and differences between the UDI and Renovación Nacional, which did not help the right's presidential aspirations and may have cost it several legislative seats).

1744 Huneeus, Carlos. The Pinochet regime. Translated by Lake Sagaris. Boulder, Colo.: Lynne Rienner Publishers, 2007. 558 p.: bibl., index.

Perhaps the most complete and well-argued single treatment of Pinochet's enormous, and yet now rapidly declining, impact on Chilean politics, this is an updated, English-language version of *Régimen de Pinochet* (2000; see *HLAS 62:1787*). Using a wide array of primary and secondary sources, it places Pinochet's regime in the context of other authoritarian governments that followed breakdowns in democratic rule, and includes material dealing with the 2004 discovery of well-stocked bank accounts in Washington, D.C., and the resulting damage to the former dictator's still substantial political credibility at the time. Especially informative are Huneeus'

discussions of Pinochet's overall "legitimation" strategy, and chapters on the roles played by the armed forces, Jaime Guzmán and his *gremialista* movement, and the Chicago Boys economists. Also of note is the 27 p. bibliography; many of the entries are referred to in the text as background or context for the author's analysis.

1745 Huneeus, Carlos. El problema constitucional de la democracia en Chile: la ausencia de una genuina constitución. (*Pers. Soc.*, 18:2, agosto 2004, p. 121–142, bibl., graph)

Argues that a country with as traumatically conflictive a past as Chile's cannot afford a majority-rule system of the sort established by the 1980 Constitution. Points to the conflict between the latter's authoritarian enclaves and an electoral system that produces two-bloc politics while inflating the representation of both. Huneeus also notes developments that have pulled politics in a more "consociative" direction: the 1989 reforms that legalized the Communist Party, reduced the influence of both the military and the designated senators, and strengthened the ability of courts to hear cases involving human rights abuses under the military government; agreements making the Boards of Directors of the Central Bank, the Constitutional Tribunal, and the National Television Network more pluralistic; legislative approval of legal initiatives designed to modernize state institutions; and the agreement between the UDI and the PDC to elect the latter's Gabriel Valdés president of the Senate in exchange for political concessions. Huneeus would no doubt approve of the additional reforms made in Aug. 2005, but would still argue that the continued operation of the binomial electoral system discourages voter participation, and renders the political system disturbingly unrepresentative.

1746 Kubal, Mary Rose. Contradictions and constraints in Chile's health care and education decentralization. (*Lat. Am. Polit. Soc.*, 48:4, Winter 2006, p. 105–135, bibl.)

Offers an account and assessment of efforts undertaken by the Aylwin, Frei Ruiz-Tagle, and Lagos governments to improve the country's schools and health-care facilities, each of which had been theoretically decentralized, i.e., "municipalized" under military rule, but with limited fiscal autonomy and cuts in budget resources that adversely affected equal access to, and the quality of, their services. Stresses the tensions that invariably arise in these areas between considerations of equity and efficiency, and describes several strategies for holding national and local officials accountable for their actions, e.g., local public choice, principal-agent, and hybrid accountability mechanisms. Argues that many of the deficiencies and inequities stemming from the Pinochet era have been corrected, not because of greater local autonomy, fiscal devolution, or administrative decentralization, but thanks to the willingness of central governments to spend greater amounts of their expanding public revenues in these areas, and to provide subsidies and target their spending to improve both the quality of services and greater equity of access to them.

1747 Lahera, Eugenio. ¿Qué está pasando en Chile? (*Nueva Soc.*, 197, mayo/junio 2005, p. 69–99, bibl., ill.)

An economist and former advisor to several Concertación governments calls for bolder socioeconomic policy initiatives and political reforms now that the skepticism and excessive concern for compromise and consensus of the early postauthoritarian period appear to be abating, and right wing forces are at least rhetorically embracing the need for more effective regulation, greater market transparency and competitiveness, and a strategy of development based on something other than profits dependent on stock transactions, natural resource exploitation, social exclusion, and unequal economic opportunity. Lahera specifically calls for new efforts at job creation; the extension of basic social services to all needing them; political party reform; the adoption of a one-person, one-vote electoral system; and automatic voter registration.

1748 Mardones Z., Rodrigo. Descentralización y transición en Chile. (*Rev. Cienc. Polít./Santiago*, 26:1, 2006, p. 3–24, bibl., tables)

This article, an updated version of the author's dissertation (NYU), is another of those focusing on the decentralization

of social services in postmilitary Chile. It looks at the effects of democratic restoration, electoral calculations, the interplay between top-down and bottom-up influences, and the divisions and financial constraints that have stunted efforts under each of the four Concertación governments. Mardones argues that the Chilean experience confirms the jump-starting impact of democratization, and underscores the uncertain and often unintended impact that it has on political fortunes at the municipal level, the threat posed to national legislators by the increased prominence of elected mayors, and the looming potential of regional officials (*consejeros regionales*) and greater regional autonomy.

1749 Montes, Juan Esteban and **Gonzalo García Pino.** ¿Y qué pasó con los militares?: Chile, 1990–2002. Santiago: Centro de Estudios para el Desarrollo, 2003. 146 p.: bibl., index. (Ediciones del segundo centenario)

An account of the remarkable progress in civil-military relations in the late-1990s and early 2000s that stresses the importance of Pinochet's waning influence and prestige, the emergence of a new generation of military leaders, most notably Army Generals Izurieta and Cheyre, and the willingness of Concertación authorities to facilitate military modernization even as they insisted on civilian supremacy, democratic control, and fuller acknowledgment of the military's role in human rights violations during the years of military rule.

1750 Morales Quiroga, Mauricio. La primera mujer presidenta de Chile: ¿qué explicó el triunfo de Michelle Bachelet en las elecciones de 2005–2006? (*LARR*, 43:1, 2008, p. 7–32, bibl., graphs, tables)

Morales combines general political, survey, and electoral data to explain Michelle Bachelet's historic capture of the Chilean presidency in Jan. 2006. He first describes the context of Chile's traditional tripartite party system, and then looks to public opinion polls for potential "support" variables, finding both longer-term and shorter-term variables affecting candidate preferences. Of note in this regard is his use of regression analysis to identify the relative weights of longer-term variables such as gender, age, socioeconomic level, education, religious affiliation, and ideological identity. And finally, he looks at Bachelet's actual vote totals, relative to those of rival candidates, in relation to attitudes toward Lagos, and to gender, household status, and income level, concluding that voters favorably disposed towards Lagos, yet those who were female heads of low income households were markedly more likely to vote for Bachelet.

1751 Pribble, Jennifer. Women and welfare: the politics of coping with new social risks in Chile and Uruguay. (*LARR*, 41:2, 2006, p. 84–111, bibl.)

Describes and attempts to account for differences in welfare policies affecting women in Chile and Uruguay. Finds that while the levels of overall social spending in the two countries are generally comparable, benefits are more evenly distributed between men and women in Uruguay, and family allowance, maternity leave, and childcare benefits are markedly more generous as well. Like Buchanan's study of Chilean and Uruguayan labor movement influence (see item **1727**), Pribble attributes these variations to a combination of historical differences, i.e., levels of female labor force participation, women's mobilization and female insertion in the country's party system and politics, and the impact of each country's military regime. Of the several interesting implications to be drawn from the study, the author observes that there may be greater flexibility within the open-market economic model with respect to degrees and patterns of social protection.

1752 Rodríguez Fisse, Hernán. Grupos de interés y lobby en Chile. Santiago: Ediciones Zéjel, 2006. 121 p.: bibl.

Originally an MA thesis in Political Science, this study focuses on the country's interest, pressure, and lobbying groups. Using standard secondary accounts (Lagos, Arriagada, Boenninger, Silva, and Valdés), the author pieces together an informative summary of the activities and influence of the leading peak associations since the 1960s, presents useful survey data on lobbying activities generallly, and provides information on 14 specific groups, including the SNA, the SOFOFA, the CPC and others.

Concludes with a discussion of the Lagos government's 2005 lobbying regulation bill which a joint Committee of Congress was still attempting to hammer out four years later (Oct. 2009).

1753 Rojas, Priscilla and **Patricio Navia.** Representación y tamaño de los distritos electorales en Chile, 1988–2002. (*Rev. Cienc. Polít./Santiago,* 25:2, 2005, p. 91–116, bibl., graphs, tables)

As the postmilitary period began, the binomial electoral system that was left in place by the military was widely perceived as having been designed to favor forces loyal to it. The authors provide compelling evidence that this was, in fact, the case, i.e., that districts were designed to reflect plebiscite ("sí" and "no") voting patterns, and to inflate the representation of those that had favored "sí," and, in the future, would likely favor the parties that had also supported Pinochet. In support, they point to the refusal of military government officials to consider adjusting downward the over-representation of three of the four regions (VII, IX, and X) in which "sí" vote totals exceeded the national average (43.0 percent), and that the average population in the 15 districts in which there were more "sí" votes was less than 100,000, while in the 45 districts in which votes for the "no" prevailed it was about 132,000. They also contend that population shifts since 1988 have further strengthened this tendency, and that more heavily populated districts continued to be more favorable to the Concertación in the 1999 presidential elections and the 2001 parliamentary elections, although the positive correlation between district size and Concertación strength has disappeared.

1754 Ruiz-Rodríguez, Leticia M. Polarization in the Chilean party system: changes and continuities, 1990–1999. Barcelona: Institut de Ciències Polítiques i Socials, 2005. 67 p.: bibl., tables. (Working Papers; 236)

This working paper offers an extensive analysis of political polarization in the postmilitary period (1990–99). Based entirely on secondary literature, it is not likely to alter or resolve the controversies surrounding the issue. But its treatment of the subject is exceptionally thorough and abounds in thoughtful insights. The author argues that polarization between the two main coalitions remains substantial, but is less marked among the parties within each of them, at least in relation to earlier periods in Chilean politics. She adds, however, that significant convergence has developed between and within the two camps with respect to socioeconomic issues, but that they are still very far apart on both religious and politico-institutional matters. And depending on the issue (e.g., religious values, socioeconomic issues, or the authoritarian/democratic cleavage), polarization is greater at times between, and at times within, the right-wing and center-left camps. Several additional observations should be noted, such as that the willingness to negotiate may be more important than the cleavage itself, that cross-cutting cleavages are less a problem than overlapping cleavages, and that while Chile's transition is widely regarded as having been successfully managed by its elites, polarization appears more pronounced among the elite than at the mass level.

1755 Santa-Cruz, Arturo. Redefiniendo la soberanía, creando una red: la observación internacional del plebiscito chileno de 1988. (*Foro Int./México*, 45:3, julio/sept. 2005, p. 489–516, bibl.)

This account of the 1988 Chilean plebiscite highlights the role played by foreign consultants and observers. While offering little new information, the author sees the event as making important inroads into what had previously been an area of presumably unquestionable national sovereignty, in which foreign-based NGOs not only had a hand in the outcome, but then passed judgment on the process. He doesn't believe that this could have happened outside of "the Americas," where apparently the "Western Hemisphere Idea" that seeks to balance a commitment to representative democracy with respect for individual national sovereignty encourages mutual accountability among member states.

1756 Seminario, a Diez Años de la Creación de los Gobiernos Regionales: evaluación y proyecciones. Santiago: Ministerio del Interior, Subsecretaría de Desarrollo Regional y Administrativo, 2003. 233 p.: ill.

Papers and proceedings from a seminar held in May 2003 attended by govern-

ment officials, intendants, and university rectors on the advances achieved, and challenges that remain, after 10 years of efforts to coordinate policy at the regional level.

1757 Siavelis, Peter. Electoral reform doesn't matter, or does it?: a moderate proportional representation system for Chile. (*Rev. Cienc. Polít./Santiago*, 26:1, 2006, p. 216–225)

Siavelis calls for an electoral reform offering incentives that will encourage Chile's party system to perform better. After pointing to the undesirable consequences of both single-member systems (which deny representation to smaller parties) and mixed-member systems (that complicate decisions for both parties and voters and create unhealthy differences between constituent and at-large representatives), he recommends an open-list proportional representation system based on relatively small (4- to 6-member) districts. It would not change the number of parties, but would give all significant parties some representation, produce real competition between, and greater democracy within them, make the candidate selection process more transparent, ensure greater accountability on the part of legislators, and offer long-term governability (stability) that does not depend solely on the ability of a president to attract support for his or her legislative agenda.

1758 Siavelis, Peter. The end of the unfinished transition. (*in* Constructing democratic governance in Latin America. Edited by Jorge I. Domínguez and Michael Shifter. Baltimore, Md.: Johns Hopkins Univ. Press, 2008, p. 177–208)

This informative book chapter analyzes the current state and future prospects of Chile's *estado de compromiso* politics following a number of highly significant developments in recent years: the election of Michelle Bachelet as the first Latin American woman who did not follow her politically prominent husband into the presidency, and the fourth consecutive Concertación candidate to win a presidential election; the "far-reaching" constitutional reforms of 2005 (eliminating non-elected Senators, restoring presidential authority over military promotions, and making it easier to modify the constitution); and significant improvements in civil-military relations. The author warns, however, that persistent socioeconomic inequality and a failure to reform the binomial electoral system are fault lines that could undermine the current climate of stability and consensus.

1759 Siavelis, Peter. La lógica oculta de la selección de candidatos en las elecciones parlamentarias chilenas. (*Estud. Públicos,* 98, otoño 2005, p. 1–32, bibl., tables)

In this revised and updated version of a 2002 article written just before the 2005–06 elections, Siavelis traces the twists and turns required in force-fitting Chile's multiparty system (five major parties plus at least that many smaller ones) into its two-member (binomial) electoral system. Complex negotiations take place among party leaders, and between them and candidates, at both the national and local levels in which potential votes are often sacrificed at the local level in order to keep smaller parties in a coalition, and thereby enhance the coalition's national vote and seat total. Siavelis sees the resulting system as undemocratic, overly informal, prone to strategic error on the part of both politicians and voters, and ultimately harmful to the legitimacy of the electoral process.

1760 Silva, Sergio G. La inculturación del evangelio: un desafío crucial de la Iglesia Católica. (*Estud. Públicos,* 101, verano 2006, p. 45–70)

A Chilean theologian argues that the Catholic Church is far from resolving the problem of the inculturation of faith in the modern era. To advance in this regard, he suggests, it needs a laity that is more mature in its faith and an institutional Church that looks upon the modern age with greater empathy. This issue of *Estudios Públicos* includes three additional articles, written by Joaquin Fermandois, the sociologist Pedro Morandé, and Fr. Richard John Neuhaus of the US on the subject of Pope John Paul II and the impact of his papacy.

1761 Stewart-Gambino, Hannah W. Las pobladoras y la iglesia despolitizada en Chile. (*Am. Lat. Hoy/Salamanca,* 41, dic. 2005, p. 121–138, bibl.)

Questions why Chilean women who had played important roles in the democratic struggles of the 1980s left the coun-try's political arena in the same patriarchal, elitist, and party-dominated condition that it had been in prior to military rule. From in-depth interviews with 50 former activists and leaders of parish-level human rights and survival organizations, the author concludes that the withdrawal by Chile's Catholic Church from its once-substantial social engagement and commitments has left these women without access to the financial and organizational resources that had helped them to become active and influential forces within civil society. The interviews capture the frustration and disappointment of these women, but the analysis does not shed much additional light on either the extent or the forces driving the Church's social withdrawal or "depoliticization."

1762 Thayer Arteaga, William. Humanismo cristiano chileno, 1931–2001: sus inspiradores, sus seguidores, sus polémicas y luchas. Santiago, Chile: Zig-Zag, 2002. 238 p.: bibl., index.

An analysis of Chilean politics from the 1930s through the end of the Pinochet years by a self-styled Christian humanist whose antipathy towards the left led him to sit out the 1970 election, accept the 1973 coup, and serve the ensuing military government in an effort to help to create a center-right alternative to which Pinochet might relinquish power. Thayer "assesses" the quality of the Christian humanism of some 15 historical Chilean political figures on the basis of his own recollections and the judgments of "informed observers."

1763 Tokman R., Marcelo; Jorge Rodríguez C.; and Cristóbal Marshall S. Las excepciones tributarias como herramienta de política pública. (*Estud. Públicos,* 102, otoño 2006, p. 69–112, bibl., tables)

Three economists, two of them Chilean government advisors, argue for a more systematic approach to the use of tax exemptions as instruments of public policy. Pointing to a recent upsurge in the number of exemptions granted, 25 of the 116 considered in the last several years, for example, they propose that individual exemptions be authorized only if they can be shown to be superior to alternative policy instruments in terms of ease of access for beneficiaries, administrative costs, the possibilities of abuse, flexibility, transparency, accountability, cost control, effectiveness, and equity.

1764 Uggla, Fredrik. "For a few senators more"?: negotiating constitutional changes during Chile's transition to democracy. (*Lat. Am. Polit. Soc.*, 47:2, Summer 2005, p. 51–75, bibl.)

A detailed analysis of the negotiations that led to an agreement in 1989 between the Pinochet regime and the Concertación por la Democracia to amend the 1980 Constitution prior to the latter's likely assumption of power following the elections in Dec. of that year. Concludes that each side was obliged to make significant concessions to the other, although those made by the opposition were far more substantial. The government was willing to accept secondary modifications to make its constitution a more likely permanent legacy; the Concertación, on the other hand, would only insist on those reforms that would not give the military a pretext for remaining in power, and thus jeopardize the transition itself. Uggla stresses the important role played by *Renovación Nacional*, some of whose leaders assured Concertación leaders that they would support additional reforms once democracy was restored. This commitment was later repudiated, and 15 years would elapse before significant reforms were approved.

1765 Voto ciudadano: debate sobre la inscripción electoral. Recopilación de Claudio Fuentes e Andrés Villar. Santiago: FLACSO Chile, 2005. 132 p.: bibl., ill. (Nueva serie)

In 2005, President Lagos proposed making Chile's very cumbersome voter registration system automatic, but making voting itself voluntary, i.e., no longer mandatory. The measure stimulated vigorous discussion and debate, but failed to pass at the time largely, it seems, because most parties preferred the status quo (characterized by low levels of registration and voter participation, especially among the young) to the uncertain consequences of change (the measure was finally approved in Jan. 2010). This collection of short essays compares Chilean laws and practices with those of other countries, speculates about

the likely consequences of several different scenarios, and features arguments for and against reform by Carlos Huneeus, Tomas Chuaqui, Clarisa Hardy, Patricio Navia, and Luis Sierra.

1766 Walker, Ignacio and **Andrés Jouannet.** Democracia cristiana y concertación: los casos de Chile, Italia y Alemania. (*Rev. Cienc. Polít./Santiago*, 26:2, 2006, p. 77–96, bibl.)

Addressing the PDC's discomfort with its reduced prominence and influence within the Concertación, the authors, one of them a former Christian Democratic Congressman and cabinet minister, argue that the party's earlier dominant role in Chilean politics was a function of the absence of a social democratic left, and that in the current political context the "middle of the road" has disappeared, the right remains tied to its authoritarian and neoliberal roots, and most of the once-Marxist left has embraced social democracy, leaving the party no other option than to remain in the "social democratic" coalition to which it has belonged since 1990. In support of this view, Walker and Jouannet point to the ruling Social Democratic/Christian Democratic coalitions that at the time of the article's publication were governing in both Italy and Germany.

1767 Wilke, Helmut. La transformación de la democracia como modelo de orientación de las sociedades complejas. (*Estud. Públicos*, 102, otoño 2006, p. 179–201, bibl.)

Wilke, a German social theorist, calls for the formation of neocorporatist networks that bring public and private sector groups together to deal with issues such as environmental pollution without requiring a sacrifice of the autonomy of those involved. This essay, published in German in 1995, does not deal directly with Chilean politics, but may influence future discussions and debate dealing with political reform. The center-right Instituto de Estudios Públicos chose to publish a Spanish-language version of the essay in its journal *Estudios Públicos*, and it will be interesting to see how Chile's political forces react to the author's German perspective on public-private cooperation.

ARGENTINA, PARAGUAY, AND URUGUAY

BRIAN TURNER, *Professor and Chair, Department of Political Science, Randolph-Macon College*

A FOCUS ON POLITICAL INSTITUTIONS characterizes much of the writing on the region. The rather striking recovery of institutional procedures in Argentina drew scholars' attention, as did the evolution of the Uruguayan political system at the 20th anniversary of the return to democracy, marked by the taking of office of that country's first left-wing government.

Most of the works on Argentina's institutions focus on the weakness of those institutions (for example, see item **1770**). The diversity of electoral arrangements and the problems with representation caused by many of these arrangements are the focus of Calvo and Escolar (item **1774**), *Democracia local* (item **1777**), Escolar and Calcagno (item **1781**), Melo (item **1787**), and Tula (item **1768**). Studies of campaigns and elections include D'Adamo and García Beaudoux (item **1776**) on the impact of television "spots," and Seligson (item **1796**) on voting choice in the 1990s.

A number of works discuss the early success of the Kirchner government and the evolution of Peronism. Iazzetta (item **1784**) and Ollier (item **1790**) assess President Kirchner's notable ability to govern after winning the presidency with just 22 percent of the vote in 2003. Levitsky's study of the Peronist Party shows how flexibility is both its strength and its weakness (item **1786**). Cavarozzi notes the partial disarticulation of the party system (item **1775**).

Mustapic (item **1789**) and Ollier (item **1790**) take distinct positions on the problem of presidential instability. Mustapic allows that early resignation may be an informal institutional adaptation of presidentialism to the permanence of a democratic regime structure, while Ollier points to the problem of party factionalism as a cause of presidential crises. *Broken Promises* details the causes and results of the crisis of 2001 (item **1773**).

Scholars have turned to assessing the state of civil society and associational life in the wake of the crisis of 2001. Quintar sees promise for the democratization of society in the new forms of associational life (item **1793**). Bonner discusses how human rights groups have opened spaces that have permitted them to take advantage of the evolution of international law in favor of pursuing prosecutions from the "Dirty War" (item **1772**). Quiroga is less optimistic about the quality of civic engagement in Argentina (item **1794**), while Hinton (item **1783**) and Armony (item **1771**) see signs of "uncivil society" in those organizations that confront but are unable to articulate with state institutions, in part because those institutions are poorly designed to channel interests.

Works on Paraguay have also focused on institutional features, but the apparent lack of change leads analyses to depend less on political choice and more on deep-seated political cultural and structural explanations (items **1800, 1801, 1803, 1804**, and **1805**). Publications thus far addressing the end of 61 years of rule by the Colorado Party have been journalistic, or recommendations for policy change.

Uruguayan scholars have turned their attention to deeper historical analysis of the roots of the victory of the Frente Amplio-Encuentro Progresista-Nueva Mayoría in 2004, and have arrived at a general consensus. Buquet (item **1809**),

Garcé (item **1814**), Lanzaro (item **1815**), and Yaffé (item **1819**), and even Arocena (item **1808**) from a more partisan position, argue that pragmatism and political strategy made possible by the internal dynamics of factional competition within the left explain the victory. Rico also might agree, but from a more critical stance (item **1816**). Similar considerations are found in scholarship on Argentina, but with significantly different results.

Claramunt Abbate (item **1810**) and Veneziano (item **1818**) argue that decentralization in Montevideo has altered some patterns of popular political participation, but has not delinked participation from partisan politics or fundamentally reshaped state-civil society relations.

ARGENTINA

**1768 Aportes para la discusión de la re-
forma política bonaerense.** Recopilación de María Inés Tula. Buenos Aires: Prometeo Libros, 2004. 211 p.: bibl., ill., maps.

Part of a series of volumes to be produced by the Centro de Implementación de Políticas Públicas para la Equidad y el Crecimiento (CIPPEC) that will discuss political reform in the provinces as part of a project to promote public consideration of reforms. The authors propose reforms of the closed list system; malapportionment in elections for municipal councils, the provincial legislature, and the federal Chamber of Deputies; electronic voting; provincial bicameralism; and open primaries.

**1769 Argentina 2020: propuestas para
profundizar la transformación.** Recopilación de Nicolás A. Trotta. Textos de Juan Manuel Abal Medina *et al.* Prólogo de Alberto Fernández. Buenos Aires: Lumiere, 2006. 349 p.: bibl., ill.

With optimism regarding the new political vision brought about by the successes of the early years of the Kirchner government, Trotta, director of the state public administration institute, the Escuela Nacional de Gobierno, brings together essays by elected and appointed government officials that analyze the functional changes that seem to be needed in institutions, economic policy, and civil society-state relations in order to overcome the cycles of crisis that have characterized Argentina since 2001–2003.

**1770 Argentine democracy: the politics
of institutional weakness.** Edited by Steven Levitsky and María Victoria Murillo. University Park: Pennsylvania State Univ. Press, 2005. 325 p.: bibl., ill., index.

This thoughtfully organized collection analyzes Argentine politics in light of theories drawn from the wider field of comparative politics. The central theme is the causes and consequences of institutional weakness, by which the editors mean that the "rules of the game" are unstable and poorly enforced. In spite of its characteristic institutional weakness, the democratic regime structure has survived severe crises and notable changes in economic policy and performance, the party system, and state-society relations.

1771 Armony, Ariel C. The dubious link: civic engagement and democratization. Stanford, Calif.: Stanford Univ. Press, 2004. 297 p.: bibl., index.

Using diverse methodologies and drawing on comparative cases (Weimer Germany, the US in the era of "massive resistance," Argentina, and others), the author explores those conditions under which active civic engagement does not promote democratization. Armony's ethnographic study of Argentina's human and civil rights groups of the 1990s finds that these groups' activities did not strengthen connections between society and the state, and group members demonstrated low levels of tolerance and willingness to compromise. Their frustration with unresponsive and corrupt institutions promoted high levels of cynicism and disengagement, contributing in turn to the social explosion of Dec. 2001.

1772 Bonner, Michelle D. Defining rights in democratization: the Argentine government and human rights organizations, 1983–2003. (*Lat. Am. Polit. Soc.,* 47:4, Winter 2005, p. 55–76, bibl., table)

The 10 "historical" human rights organizations have used the frame of the family to advance their rights claims to the state. The Asociación de Abuelas de Plaza de Mayo have had the most success with this frame in Argentine courts, as the emphasis on recovering stolen children and returning them to their families elides the question of the status of the disappeared parents as "subversives." However, the increasing use of international courts to press claims is reducing the need to frame these claims in terms of family.

1773 Broken promises?: the Argentine crisis and Argentine democracy. Edited by Edward C. Epstein and David Pion-Berlin. Lanham. Md.: Lexington Books, 2006. 288 p.: bibl., index.

The volume's essays detail the causes, events, and responses by various actors to the political crisis of 2001. With the exception of the editors, all contributors are Argentine-based scholars.

1774 Calvo, Ernesto and Marcelo Escolar. La nueva política de partidos en la Argentina: crisis política, realineamientos partidarios y reforma electoral. Buenos Aires: Prometeo: Pent, 2005. 389 p.: bibl., ill., maps. (Col. Democracia, partidos y elecciones)

A detailed empirical study of voting patterns through 2003. The authors argue that the data show a territorialization of the vote as parties seek to manipulate rules and organize coalitions primarily at the provincial rather than the national level. This has led to a markedly differentiated electoral system, since the electoral rules vary notably among the provinces. This has potentially negative consequences for the capacity of the electoral system to aggregate interests and to legitimize national political institutions.

1775 Cavarozzi, Marcelo. Autoritarismo y democracia, 1955–2006. 2a ed. Buenos Aires: Ariel, 2006. 229 p.: bibl.

This edition updates Cavarozzi's 1983 book by adding a third chapter (p. 71–169) to cover the period 1983 to 2006. The author finds that old habits of authoritarianism in the culture have been overcome, but the twin processes of decline of state capacity and partial disarticulation of the party system have led to a political system with limited ability to resolve conflicts and assure its future legitimacy. For review of

1st ed., see *HLAS 47:6510.* For review of earlier ed., see *HLAS 63:1847.*

1776 D'Adamo, Orlando J. and Virginia García Beaudoux. Campañas electorales y efectos sobre la decisión de voto: un análisis de la campaña para las elecciones presidenciales 2003 en Argentina. (*Am. Lat. Hoy/Salamanca,* 38, dic. 2004, p. 163–179, bibl., tables)

A survey conducted immediately after the 2003 presidential elections in the city of Buenos Aires shows that campaign "spots" on television were the most memorable to voters, and that campaign materials convinced over one-third of survey respondents (37 percent) to vote for a candidate other than their initial preference. However, in spite of receiving the most media attention and largely positive coverage, Carlos Menem's campaign was unable to reverse negative opinions of him. The authors argue that a larger voting pool of independent and relatively disengaged voters, in an increasingly intense media environment, corresponds with the professionalization and personalization of campaigns in the style of US elections.

1777 Democracia local: clientelismo, capital social e innovación política en la Argentina. Recopilación de Samuel Amaral y Susan C. Stokes. Buenos Aires: Editorial de la Univ. Nacional de Tres de Febrero, 2005. 286 p.: bibl., ill., maps.

This volume brings together detailed case studies of municipal politics in the 1990s in Misiones, Córdoba, and Provincia Buenos Aires. The various authors discuss the problems of party factionalism, clientelism, the election system such as the "sublemas" used in Misiones, and the party ballot, all of which call into question the quality of democracy at the local level. On the other hand, the essays highlight voters' support for "good governance" over clientelism, especially in Córdoba, and the capacity for local government innovation, as in the case of Mar del Plata.

1778 Dinatale, Martín; Alejandra Gallo; and Damián Nabot. La escalera invisible: mecanismos de ascenso en la clase política. Buenos Aires: Konrad Adenauer Stiftung: La Crujía Ediciones, 2005. 187 p.: bibl., ill.

Three journalists identify the patterns and problems in political careers that depend on trading votes for access to state resources, poorly regulated campaign financing, and professionalized media campaigns. The authors argue that these developments reduce the capacity of the political parties to compete on programmatic terms and undermine the quality of democracy.

1779 Donatello, Luis Miguel. Catolicismo liberacionista y política en la Argentina: de la política insurreccional en los setenta a la resistencia al neoliberalismo en los noventa. (*Am. Lat. Hoy/Salamanca*, 41, dic. 2005, p. 77–97, bibl.)

This work traces the roots of Catholic activists' opposition to neoliberal policies of the 1990s to "liberation Catholicism" of the 1960s and 1970s. The author argues that "liberation Catholicism," with its integralism and antiliberalism, shares origins with the earlier 20th-century integralists within the Church and in the political sphere who found political expression in support of Peronism, in some cases, and of military regimes, in others.

1780 Entre tecnócratas globalizados y políticos clientelistas: derrotero del ajuste neoliberal en el Estado argentino. Recopilación de Mabel Thwaites Rey y Andrea López. Buenos Aires: Prometeo, 2005. 254 p.: bibl.

This volume weaves together several complex themes regarding the role of state "reform" in the politics of class domination. The "good government" thesis of technocratic public administration, several essays argue, is certainly not free of the politics that create winners and losers. Technocratic administration is rhetorically in opposition to the "politicized" clientelism traditional to Argentine public administration, but each form of administration is inherently political in its design. True state "refounding," as argued in the conclusion, requires a democratic and participatory national project.

1781 Escolar, Marcelo and Natalia Calcagno. Reforma electoral nacional y reforma electoral federal: elementos para el análisis y discusión del caso argentino. (*Estud. Soc./Santa Fe*, 14:27, segundo semestre 2004, p.9–37, bibl., graphs, tables)

The authors demonstrate statistically the extreme diversity of electoral arrangements in Argentina's provinces and municipalities. They argue that electoral reforms that would address the problems of excessive majoritarianism and lack of legislator accountability to the electorate would have to address this diversity of arrangements.

1782 Frávega, Oscar E. Historia de la Unión Cívica Radical de Córdoba, 1890–2000. Córdoba, Argentina: Editorial Brujas, 2006. 488 p.: bibl., ill., maps.

This work is a highly detailed history of the Unión Cívica Radical political party (UCR) in the province of Córdoba. Concludes that the UCR is the only party that is national in scope, democratic in structure, and with the moderation and potential for the ideological coherence necessary to confront Argentina's deep problems. However, the UCR, like other parties, has been subject to excessive factionalism and the decline of the party system generally. The author is himself a member of the UCR.

Fuentes, Claudio. Contesting the iron fist: advocacy networks and police violence in democratic Argentina and Chile. See item **1736.**

1783 Hinton, Mercedes S. The state on the streets: police and politics in Argentina and Brazil. Boulder, Colo.: Lynne Rienner Publishers, 2006. 235 p.: bibl., ill., index.

As both the perception and reality that public safety was declining took hold in the democratic period, both Argentina and Brazil embarked on police reforms. The author focuses on Buenos Aires and Rio de Janeiro, where field research included 165 interviews with subjects from across the political and social spectrum, and visits to police training institutions, government programs, and community forums. She concludes that police reform in Buenos Aires suffered from police resistance, but most importantly from negative characteristics of the Argentine political culture and political system: tolerance for corruption, low levels of political accountability, an "uncivil" society prone to street protests and deep cynicism but unaccustomed to using public information to press for reform, and the "politics of destruction" where politicians seek to tear down opponents and where the public safety issue has been used as a political football without serious institutional commitment to its improvement.

1784 Iazzetta, Osvaldo Miguel. El gobierno de Kirchner y los desafíos democráticos pendientes. (*Td Temas Debates*, 9:10, nov. 2005, p. 35–55, bibl.)

President Kirchner's first two years in office were successful in restoring basic institutional and macroeconomic order. However, the author argues that Argentina's social and institutional deficits are profound and intertwined, and reform needs to confront the problem of these twin deficits. Poverty and inequality have increased dramatically in the democratic period since 1983, and public safety has deteriorated, with police often implicated in criminal activity. Only Peronist governments have been able to complete their terms in office, while the linkage between civic action and party governance is of low quality and rife with conflict. Kirchner has addressed the immediate crisis in ways that have exacerbated the institutional problem of "hyper-presidentialism" at the expense of strengthening the institutions of governance.

1785 Jozami, Eduardo. Final sin gloria: un balance del Frepaso y de la Alianza. Prólogo de Horacio González. Buenos Aires: Biblos, 2004. 164 p.: bibl. (Ensayo argentino)

The author, an economist and one-time Frepaso legislator in Buenos Aires, writes a postmortem of Frepaso, placing much of the blame for the party's demise on the failure of party leader Carlos "Chacho" Álvarez to maintain the party's oppositional stance to neoliberalism and Menemism. The party failed to cultivate organized working-class support, and by entering as a junior partner into the Alliance government led by Radical President Fernando de la Rúa, Frepaso lost all credibility as a force for alternative policies. Álvarez failed to use his resignation as vice president as an opportunity to move Frepaso back into the opposition.

1786 Levitsky, Steven. Transforming labor-based parties in Latin America: Argentine Peronism in comparative perspective. Cambridge, U.K.; New York: Cambridge Univ. Press, 2003. 290 p.: bibl., index.

An important book, cited by a number of titles listed here. The author explains how the informal and poorly institutionalized structures of the Peronist Party (also known as the Partido Justicialista or PJ) allowed the party to transform itself from "a de facto labor party into a predominantly patronage-based party" in less than a decade (p. 107). Those same characteristics allowed the PJ to support Menem without becoming neoliberal in orientation. The author provides detailed survey-based evidence of the attitudes and activities of Peronist local party leaders and precinct captains (*punteros*) from the federal capital and Buenos Aires province.

1787 Melo, Julián A. Federalismo y democracia: un análisis en torno de la transición democrática y el debate constituyente de 1994. (*Polít. Gest.*, 8, 2005, p. 97–129, bibl.)

The 1994 constitutional reform is best known for its provisions allowing immediate reelection of the president. This article focuses instead on the debate in the constitutional convention regarding the direct, popular election of senators and of the presidential ticket. The author argues that direct election was seen as a democratizing reform in that it makes senators accountable to the electorate and respects the principle of "one person, one vote" in both senate and presidential elections. However, the author argues that direct election undermines the principle that federalism is based on equality among the constitutive federal entities. Direct presidential election theorizes a single, homogenous national electorate rather than a president who is representative of a federation consisting of different polities. Direct senatorial election weakens the power of the provinces in the federal system by removing senators from accountability to the provinces' political institutions.

1788 Mocca, Edgardo. El incierto futuro de los partidos políticos argentinos. (*Estud. Soc./Santa Fe*, 15:29, segundo semestre 2005, p. 9–24, bibl.)

Appearing just before the congressional elections of 2005, the article reviews the status of the political parties at that particular political moment. Although cautioning against referencing all Argentine political history in Peronist terms, the author correctly identifies the uncertainties regarding the Senate race between then-first lady Cristina Fernández de Kirchner and former first lady Hilda González de Duhalde as a critical indicator of whether an entirely new party system was in formation.

1789 Mustapic, Ana María. Inestabilidad sin colapso, la renuncia de los presidentes: Argentina en el año 2001. (*Desarro. Econ.*, 45:178, julio/sept. 2005, p. 263–280, bibl., tables)

Taking the cases of presidents de la Rúa and Rodríguez Saá in 2001, the author explores the proposition that presidential resignation is becoming a mechanism for the "flexibilization" of the fixed term that is characteristic of presidential systems. As the possibility of military intervention becomes more remote, and legislatures become more important as bases of support for the president, resignation may be a developing informal institution that allows for the resolution of crises without destabilizing the democratic regime. An intriguing observation is that none of the four presidential resignations (add those of Alfonsín in 1989 and Duhalde in 2003) was accompanied by a sitting vice president with ambition to become president.

1790 Ollier, María Matilde. Hacia un patrón argentino de inestabilidad presidencial. (*Estud. Soc./Santa Fe*, 14:27, segundo semestre 2004, p. 39–70, bibl.)

While the successive resignations of Presidents de la Rúa, Rodríguez Saá, and Duhalde in 2001–02 have multiple causes, this work focuses on the impact of party fragmentation on presidential instability. In the period after 1997, neither the Peronists nor the Alliance (Radicals and Frepasistas) could count on clear party leadership. This left President de la Rúa to face a Congress controlled by the opposition and a majority of the provinces governed by Peronists, without a clear leader of the Peronists with whom to articulate accords. Nor was de la Rúa the authoritative leader of the Alliance or even his own party, the UCR. The author also suggests that the political ability of the particular president is itself an important variable, and this ability was found lacking in the cases of de la Rúa and Rodríguez Saá.

1791 Ollier, María Matilde. Liderazgo presidencial y jefatura partidaria: entre la confrontación y el pacto, 2003–2005. (*Td Temas Debates*, 9:10, nov. 2005, p. 7–32, bibl.)

On assuming the presidency, Néstor Kirchner faced many of the same structural weaknesses as did his predecessors. In his first year of office, Kirchner chose confrontation with his Peronist Party and his political patron, former President Duhalde, basing his power on an alliance of center-left politicians from various parties, *piquetero* leaders, and public opinion. In the second year, Kirchner moved successfully to consolidate his position, and weaken that of Duhalde, within the Peronist Party. The author asks whether Kirchner's successes at mid-term of his presidency suggest an individual and charismatic ability on the part of this particular president, or if Peronism itself is in the process of constructing a new type of party leadership.

1792 Problemas de política social en la Argentina contemporánea. Recopilación de Luciano Andrenacci. Textos de Ana Luz Abramovich *et al.* Buenos Aires: Prometeo Libros; Los Polvorines, Argentina: Univ. Nacional de General Sarmiento, 2005. 337 p.: bibl., ill.

This collection of essays reviews social policy in contemporary Argentina in light of theories about the relationship between state and civil society: the state as a means of construction (and deconstruction) of identities, and the state as guarantor of a particular mode of production. Contributions also consider the role of policy evaluation in political decision-making about social policy, and how policy could support alternative models of social organization, such as those described by the concepts of "social economy" and "popular economy" based on voluntary association.

1793 Quintar, Aída. Prácticas asociativas en la región metropolitana de Buenos Aires. (*Veredas*, 4/5, 2002, p. 225–238, bibl.)

Written shortly after the events of Dec. 2001, this article reviews the new types of associational life that were central to those events. The roots of these new forms of association can be found in the decline of industrial unionism and partisan organizations, so that by the late 1980s urban squatter movements and self-assistance organizations became more common forms of civic organization. By the late 1990s, organizational life had become more politicized, as *piqueteros* and popular assemblies articulated more sweeping visions of political change. At the same time, local groups supported by international governmental organizations like the World Bank, as well as the state and NGOs, were also becoming more common, as these outside institutions channeled assistance through organizational structures that promoted dependency and clientelism.

1794 Quiroga, Hugo. Ciudadanía y espacio público: debate y perspectivas. (*Rev. Venez. Cienc. Polít.*, 27, enero/junio 2005, p. 5–32, bibl.)

Argues that associational life in Argentina is "thin," in that a large portion of the citizenry is excluded from a sense of belonging in the community. This translates into low levels of political participation of all forms. Unemployment, even more than poverty, and the precariousness of employment, have created a dual society that is poorly integrated into a single civic community.

1795 Remmer, Karen L. The political economy of patronage: expenditure patterns in the Argentine provinces, 1983–2003. (*J. Polit.*, 69, 2007, p. 363–377)

Convincing analysis of provincial-level distributive politics in Argentina during its most recent period of democratization. Highlights several key variables, such as electoral cycles and the source of government revenues, in explaining fluctuations in patronage across Argentine provinces. [J. Hiskey]

1796 Seligson, Amber L. Disentangling the roles of ideology and issue positions in the rise of third parties: the case of Argentina. (*Polit. Res. Q.*, 56:4, Dec. 2003, p. 465–475, bibl., graphs, tables)

Statistical analysis of 1996 Latinbarometer data is used to assess what motivated FREPASO voters to shift support from the PJ or the UCR. The author finds that voters' self-identification on a left-right ideological scale was predictive of voting choice independent of the impact of issues. FREPASO voters were significantly drawn from those with left-wing ideology.

Tuozzo, María Fernanda. World Bank, governance reforms and democracy in Argentina. See item **2395**.

1797 Weitz-Shapiro, Rebecca. Partisanship and protest: the politics of workfare distribution in Argentina. (*LARR*, 41:3, 2006, p. 122–147, bibl., tables)

Constructs a measure of "deviation from ideal spending" for the Trabajar workfare program, which operated from 1996–2001, to assess hypotheses regarding the political reasons for deviations in spending at the provincial level. "Ideal spending" is measured by the distribution criteria set for the program itself, which was based on each province's number of unemployed poor. The findings do not support the hypothesis that either Menem or de la Rúa distributed funds to reward allied governors or to influence future voting in "swing" provinces. However, the data do suggest that Menem was responsive to *piquetero* demands, and that de la Rúa was only responsive to these demands in the second year, not the first, of his administration. The author correctly concludes that efforts to measure the politicization of distributional programs should be sensitive to variations across time within, as well as between, administrations.

PARAGUAY

1798 Cultura política y gobernabilidad democrática 2005. Recopilación de Alejandro Vial. Asunción: Fundación CIRD, 2005. 71 p.: ill.

This is a report of a survey conducted in late 2005 by the Fundación CIRD and supported by USAID. A key finding was the lack of support for democratic leaders, as most support was found for political groups with roots in the Partido Colorado. This work was published five months before the appearance of Fernando Lugo on the political scene.

1799 Los dilemas de Lugo: análisis inéditos. Dirección editorial de Pablo León Burián. Coordinación editorial de Bernardo Neri Farina. Textos de Luis Bareiro et al. Asunción: Editorial El Lector, 2008. 138 p.: bibl. (Col. Sociedad y política (Editorial El Lector))

Thirteen journalists review the array of policy challenges facing the Lugo government as it takes power.

1800 Fregosi, Renée. ¿Hay salida al bipartidismo tradicional en el Paraguay? (*Estud. Parag.*, 22/23, dic. 2005, p. 87–97)

A reflection on the nature of bipartisan systems as distinct from party systems based on class cleavages that developed in 20th-century Europe. Applying this reflection to Paraguay, the author looks for evidence of a leftist party challenger to the traditional parties, similar to the developments in Uruguay. She finds some hints in the formation of a moderate and modern political party, Partido País Solidario, but correctly concludes that parallels with Uruguay are hard to draw.

1801 Jara Goiris, Fabio Aníbal. Paraguay, ciclos adversos y cultura política. Asunción: Servilibro, 2004. 315 p.: bibl.

This history of the development of Paraguay's political culture argues that the characteristics of an authoritarian culture are rooted in the class relations that developed after the War of the Triple Alliance (1864–70) in the Liberal state. The landed oligarchy supported a state based on militarism that nurtured a "fraudulent bourgeoisie" and a "culture of submission," which retains cultural hegemony today.

1802 Memorándum para el gobierno, 2008–2013. Recopilación de Dionisio Borda. Asunción: Centro de Análisis y Difusión de la Economía Paraguaya, 2008. 237 p.: bibl., ill.

Analytical essays prepared by various social scientists propose policy solutions to economic, social, and political problems. Diego Abente Brun and Enrique Sosa Arrúa offer proposals for sweeping changes of the constitution, especially in the judicial branch, and the design of a variety of corporate state agencies whose functioning has fallen well short of desired levels. Borda's essay argues for macroeconomic stability with modernization of the administration and pro-growth policies targeted at the private sector. Borda was subsequently named finance minister by the Lugo government. For economist's comment, see item **830.**

1803 Mendonça, Daniel. Corrupción: un estudio sobre la corrupción en Paraguay. Asunción: Intercontinental Editora, 2005. 121 p.: bibl.

The author, a lawyer and legal scholar, argues that corruption in Paraguay is systemic, as opposed to the lesser ills of incidental or systematic corruption, and that since the fall of the Stroessner regime corruption has become decentralized, which is even more harmful to economic development.

1804 Molinas, José et al. Political institutions, policymaking processes, and policy outcomes in Paraguay, 1954–2003. (*Rev. Cienc. Polít./Santiago*, 24:2, 2004, p. 67–93, bibl., graphs, tables)

An important contribution to the general literature on policy-making and veto players, and a rare contribution to the political science of Paraguay. Working from a database of all final legislation addressed by Congress from 1993 to 2003, the authors conclude that current political institutions have created a high number of veto players, making approval of broad regulatory or redistributive policies very difficult. The authors compare the policy-making environment since 1993 with the Stroessner regime and with the transitional Rodríguez government, and find that the constant across all periods is low levels of "public regardedness." Legislators prefer provision of particularistic benefits over broad public goods.

1805 Nickson, R. Andrew and Peter Lambert. State reform and the "privatized state" in Paraguay. (*Public Adm. Dev.*, 22:2, 2002, p. 163–174, bibl., table)

This useful article describes the "privatized" state as controlled by vested interests with ties to the Stroessner regime. Political will for needed state reform is mostly absent. The authors illustrate the difficulties of introducing state reform under these circumstances by reviewing the cases of privatization of state companies, civil service reform, and decentralization. In all cases, reform efforts have either failed or produced minimally positive results.

1806 Paredes, Roberto. Por qué cayó el Partido Colorado. Asunción: ServiLibro, 2008. 311 p.: bibl., ports.

The prolific Paredes, a journalist, writes a detailed history of the fall of the Colorado Party from power in 2008, dating from the beginnings of the fall to 1947. Also attributes the party's failure to the power structures the party created to stay in power, while lacking the political will to address the problems of governance and development that built up over six decades.

URUGUAY

1807 Altman, David. Intraparty and inter-party politics: factions, fractions, parties, and coalitions in Uruguay, 1985–1999. (*Iberoamericana/Stockholm*, 34:1/2, 2004, p. 15–42, bibl., graphs)

The essay provides interesting insights into the post-electoral negotiations between parties and party factions to obtain policy goals and political posts. It only treats the period up to 1999, thus it doesn't address the impact of the switch from *lemas* to party primaries with a run-off election. It also says little about the role played by the Frente Amplio in these negotiations.

1808 Arocena, Rodrigo. Uruguay en la nueva ola de las izquierdas latinoamericanas. (*Nueva Soc.*, 197, mayo/junio 2005, p. 146–158, bibl., ill.)

Argues that, in the democratic period, the left has returned to the historic national consensus supporting batllismo, while the Colorado Party abandoned Batlle's vision of a market-oriented welfare state in favor of neoliberalism. This explains the electoral success of the FA-EP-NM. The essay provides a rather positive assessment of the FA-EP-NM's management of factionalism.

1809 Buquet Corleto, Daniel. Elecciones uruguayas 2004: el largo camino del bipartidismo al bipartidismo. (*Iberoamericana/Stockholm*, 34:1/2, 2004, p. 65–90, bibl., graphs)

Data on electoral volatility and the effective number of parties, and on the growth of the FA-EP-NM's percentage of votes coming from the interior, are employed to argue that the party system has returned to a two-party system, with the FA-EP-NM replacing the Colorado Party. Not well explained is the reason that voters treat the first round of presidential elections as if it is the only round, or the reason that parties should be expected to moderate internal conflict in the primaries.

1810 Claramunt Abbate, Adela. Participación en políticas sociales descentralizadas: el impacto en los actores sociales.

Buenos Aires: Espacio Editorial, 2006. 192 p.: bibl. (Col. Ciencias sociales. Novedades)

An analysis of decentralized administration in Montevideo after 1990 to determine how the interaction between civil society and the state was affected. Finds little support for claims that decentralization improves the quality of democratic participation, but that civil society actors have expanded their role in the administration of policies, especially those targeting services to the poor.

1811 Las claves del cambio: ciclo electoral y nuevo gobierno, 2004–2005. Coordinación de Daniel Buquet. Textos de Diego Aboal *et al.* Montevideo: Ediciones de la Banda Oriental: Instituto de Ciencia Política, 2005. 359 p.: bibl., ill. (Col. Política viva.)

This valuable collection brings together some of Uruguay's top political scientists, with nine essays of analysis of the 2004 elections and eight more essays discussing the conformation, challenges, and future of the new government elected in 2004.

1812 Colección Liber Seregni. Vol. 1, La fundación del Frente Amplio y las elecciones de 1971. Vol. 2, El proceso previo al golpe de Estado, 1972–1973. Coordinación de Gerardo Caetano. Montevideo: Taurus, 2005–2006. 2 v.: ill. (Ciencias sociales)

The first two of a seven-volume collection of the papers of Gen. Líber Seregni, the founder of the Frente Amplio in 1971 and its president until 1996. The papers include speeches, writings, interviews, letters from prison, court records, and party documents and communiqués, all kept and indexed by Seregni until his death in 2004.

1813 Corbo Longueira, Daniel J. El plebiscito constitucional de 1980: la derrota del proyecto militar para legitimar un régimen autoritario. Montevideo: Ediciones Puerta del Sur: Fundación Ciudad de Montevideo, 2006. 239 p.: bibl., ill. (Col. Historia reciente)

Detailed history of the 1980 plebiscite in which 57 percent of voters rejected the military government's proposed constitution. Argues that the defeat of the military's project was both a rejection of that government's performance as well as Uruguayans' expression of a democratic-liberal political culture that resisted the formalization of an authoritarian regime structure.

Eaton, Kent. Risky business, decentralization from above in Chile and Uruguay. See item **1733**.

1814 Garcé, Adolfo. Donde hubo fuego: el proceso de adaptación del MLN-Tupamaros a la legalidad y a la competencia electoral, 1985–2004. Montevideo: Editorial Fin de Siglo, 2006. 254 p.: bibl., ill.

A fascinating analysis of the transition of the Tupamaros from an urban guerrilla movement to an important electoral force. The author attributes the capacity of the MLN to make this transition to strong internal currents of pragmatism and tolerance for ideological heterodoxy, but also to internal political victories, richly described, by those leaders who ultimately favored the electoral route to power.

1815 Lanzaro, Jorge Luis. La izquierda se acerca a los uruguayos y los uruguayos se acercan a la izquierda. (*Cah. Am. lat.*, 46, 2004, p. 21–46, bibl., table)

Argues that the Frente Amplio has successfully moderated to attract non-ideological voters in the center of the political spectrum, and has become a catch-all party. Suggests that the Frente Amplio in power will continue to look more like traditional Uruguayan parties, governing through compromise and moderation.

Pribble, Jennifer. Women and welfare: the politics of coping with new social risks in Chile and Uruguay. See item **1751**.

1816 Rico, Alvaro. Cómo nos domina la clase gobernante: orden político y obediencia social en la democracia posdictadura: Uruguay, 1985–2005. Montevideo: Ediciones Trilce, 2005. 208 p.: bibl. (Col. Desafíos)

According to the author, the "third defeat" of the left began after 1989 with its loss in the field of symbolic discourse. In the 1990s the "common sense" of Uruguayan political discourse made the critique

of society developed in the 1960s marginal and unspeakable, even by the left. While the argument is fascinating and believable, one wishes for empirical data to support it.

1817 20 años de democracia: Uruguay 1985–2005: miradas múltiples. Bajo la dirección de Gerardo Caetano. Textos de Hugo Achugar *et al.* Montevideo: Taurus, 2005. 582 p.: bibl., ill., maps. (Ciencias sociales)

Sprawling, but well-organized collection of 22 essays, grouped into those on politics and policy, society and economy, and culture, addressing the evolution of society in the democratic period. The volume fits well into the developing periodization of Uruguayan political history, which takes the coming to power of the Frente Amplio in 2005 as a watershed moment.

1818 Veneziano, Alicia. Reflexiones sobre una reforma orientada al ciudadano: la descentralización participativa de Montevideo. Madrid: Instituto Nacional de Administración Pública, 2005. 148 p.: bibl., ill., maps. (Col. Iberoamérica)

Decentralization under the Frente Amplio in Montevideo began as an ideological effort to mobilize the citizenry, but due to the influence of institutional variables, such as the national political party system, the characteristics of the governing coalition, and a party-centric political culture, decentralization has led instead to a relationship of negotiation between city government and party-based social actors.

1819 Yaffé, Jaime. Al centro y adentro: la renovación de la izquierda y el triunfo del Frente Amplio en Uruguay. Montevideo: Linardi y Risso, 2005. 209 p.: bibl., ill.

Detailed analysis of the internal politics of the Frente Amplio that allowed it to move towards programmatic moderation and electoral victory. The author reviews various possible explanations for the victory of the FA-EP-NM in 2004, and concludes that political strategy, played out within the Frente and in the context of electoral incentives, largely explains the result.

BRAZIL

ENRIQUE DESMOND ARIAS, *Associate Professor of Government, John Jay College of The City University of New York (CUNY)*

SCHOLARSHIP ON BRAZILIAN POLITICS has followed the same general patterns as in the previous *Handbook* volume. Publications cover a range of issues including state level politics, political history, and the overall conditions of democracy. Nevertheless, key research remains focused in a few areas. Much scholarly writing, especially journal articles rather than books, examines the deep mechanics of Brazilian political institutions and elections. A substantial amount of work is focused on civil society and, in particular, on the role of participatory budgeting in helping city administrations promote an engaged citizenry. Finally, a considerable amount of writing on Brazilian politics has looked at the evolutions and vicissitudes of electoral politics, and in particular the fortunes of the Lula administration and its relationship with the Partido das Trabalhadores (PT).

One of the most important issues in Brazilian politics today and the issue that has had, perhaps, the most profound impact on the ongoing political direction of the country is corruption. In his book *O operador: como (e a mando de quem) Marcos Valério irrigou os cofres do PSDB e do PT*, Lucas Figueiredo provides a vivid portrait of one of the key figures on the congressional kickback scandals that rocked the first Lula administration in 2005 (item **1845**). Figueiredo goes into some depth showing the mechanics and the complex ongoing relationships that gave rise to the scandal and that have curbed the political ambitions of some of the most distinguished politicians in the country. This book is a must read for all those interested in the Lula administration and for those studying corruption.

Beyond the debate on corruption during the Lula administration there has been a wide discussion in Brazil on the nature of the left in power and the direction of the PT and the Lula presidency. Many publications have addressed this topic in recent years. Francisco de Oliveira's article "Lula in the labyrinth" examines the paradoxes of a PT administration operating in a neoliberal world in which the working class is allowed to rule but not really to benefit collectively from that rule (item **1836**). Luiz Carlos Bresser Perreira contributes a similarly thoughtful piece entitled "O paradoxo da esquerda no Brasil" in which he argues that, despite support for leftist governments in Brazil, it is difficult to govern from the left (item **1897**). Vicente Palermo and Germán Feierherd have published an article entitled "El liderazgo como capital político temporal: Lula y el proceso de adaptación del PT a la hora de gobernar" that examines and contrasts Lula's experience as a leader with his predecessor Fernando Henrique Cardoso, arguing that Lula's political capital comes not from expertise but from long term respect for his leadership among certain segments of the population (item **1887**).

Those interested in a wider panorama of Brazilian politics should examine Renato Lessa's *Presidencialismo de animação, e outros ensaios sobre a política brasileira, 1993–2006* (item **1863**). This book covers a series of engaging newspaper columns and other writings in which this noted scholar discusses an array of issues in national politics ranging from the nature of the Brazilian presidency to institutional reform.

While regional and state level politics are often overlooked in the English-language literature on Brazil, analyses of state level politics receive substantial attention from Brazilian publishers. Among recently published books, Angela de

Castro Gomes' edited volume *Minas e os fundamentos do Brasil moderno* stands out (item **1872**). Bringing together a group of noted social and political historians from the state of Minas Gerais, this volume provides a detailed examination of the emergence of developmentalist thought within the Minas political elite. Chapters focus on a variety of historical periods from the late 19th up to the mid-20th century examining how an array of prominent state leaders helped set the stage for the political and economic structure of modern Minas Gerias and for national level development policy.

One critical issue in the debates about subnational policy-making and innovation is participatory budgeting, a program first initiated in Porto Alegre but which has expanded to numerous cities around the country. While many earlier analyses have principally focused on these efforts in Porto Alegre, more recent writings have broadened their focus to other parts of the country. Vera Schattan P. Coelho and Marcos Nobre have published an edited volume that brings together debates about participation and deliberation in democratic politics (item **1888**). Sergio de Azevedo and Rodrigo Barroso Fernandes have organized an edited volume that examines the participatory budgeting process in the city of Belo Horizonte in Minas Gerais (item **1884**). Finally, Terence Wood and Warwick E. Murray's interesting article compares participatory democratic efforts in Belo Horizonte and Porto Alegre (item **1931**).

A great many quality articles have been published on the structure of Brazilian political institutions and electoral processes. For some time Brazilian academics have worked to provide substantial insights into elections and activities in the chambers of Congress. A piece by Fabiano Santos and Acir Almeida provides insights into the choice of committee rapporteurs in Congress as a strategy for understanding how bills are shepherded through the legislature (item **1912**). The edited volume *La democracia brasileña: balance y perspectivas para el siglo XXI* provides a wide array of studies addressing institutional questions in the current political system (item **1837**). Licínio Velasco Junior has published an article examining coalition building and state reform during the Cardoso administration (item **1928**). Looking at elections, Lúcio Renno and Anthony Spanakos have published an interesting article on the role of economics in election decision-making and César Zucco has published an article on pragmatism and voting in the 2006 presidential elections that reflects on the advantages on incumbency and wealth transfers in securing a second Lula term (items **1904** and **1934**). Finally, perhaps one of the most dynamic issues in Brazilian elections is the role of the growing evangelical population. Two recent books contribute substantially to this debate. The first, edited by Joanildo A. Burity and Maria das Dores Campos Machado, brings together a series of essays examining issues related to the participation of evangelicals in politics and in particular in the 2002 election when Anthony Garotinho, the governor of Rio de Janeiro, ran third on the strength of support from this group (item **1929**). Machado has also published a separate monograph entitled *Política e religião: a participação dos evangélicos nas eleições* that provides analysis of evangelical participation in Rio de Janeiro through interviews with evangelical officials and observation of campaign events (item **1866**).

Finally, at the broadest level is Alfred P. Montero's *Brazilian Politics: Reforming a Democratic State In a Changing World* (item **1874**). This book offers a succinct yet sophisticated introduction to Brazil that should provide students and others seeking a deeper understanding of Brazilian politics with entry into this complex field. With regular revisions and updates this volume may become a key general reference source on Brazil for years to come.

1820 Ahnen, Ronald E. The politics of police violence in democratic Brazil. (*Lat. Am. Polit. Soc.*, 49:1, Spring 2007, p. 141–164, bibl., graphs, tables)

This interesting article shows that democratization has had only limited effects on police violence in various Brazilian states. The author argues that the limited nature of the improvements is a result of the effectiveness of right-wing law and order coalitions at preventing reform.

1821 Análise dos parlamentares paranaenses na entrada do século XXI. Organização de Ricardo Costa de Oliveira. Com assistencia de Luiz Demétrio Janz Laibida e Vanderlei Hermes Machado. Colaboração de Edimara Domingues de Oliveira et al. Curitiba, Brazil: APUFPR-SSind, 2002. 352 p.: bibl., ill.

This is a compilation of detailed information about current Senators and Federal and State Deputies from the state of Paraná.

1822 Araújo, Marcos Goursand de. O quê que é isso, ex-companheiro Lula?: uma avaliação psico-política do seu governo. Belo Horizonte, Brazil: s.n., 2004. 341 p.: bibl.

This self-published book provides a leftist critique of the Lula administration.

1823 Araújo, Odília Sousa de. A reforma da previdência social brasileira no contexto das reformas do estado, 1988 a 1998. Natal, Brazil: EDUFRN, Editora da UFRN, 2004. 321 p.: bibl. (Teses & pesquisas. Ciências sociais aplicadas)

This book offers a thorough examination of social security and welfare reform in Brazil. The book argues that 1990s era reforms were not beneficial to workers but that the problems that led to this went beyond the political and into the basic values of Brazilian society in an era of globalization.

1824 Barreira, Irlys Alencar Firmo. A política de perto: recortes etnográficos de campanhas eleitorais. (*Novos Estud. CEBRAP*, 74, março 2006, p. 177–194)

This piece provides important insights into the process and implications of political campaigns in Brazil. Through an ethnographic analysis of campaign events, the article argues that elections play an important role in building ties between citizens and the political system providing for a reestablishment of social compacts and reinforcing the legitimacy of the political system.

1825 Barreiro Lemos, Leany. El sistema de comisiones en el Senado brasileño: jerarquía y concentración de poderes en la década de 1990. (*Am. Lat. Hoy/Salamanca*, 43, agosto 2006, p. 155–182, bibl., graphs, tables)

The article offers a solid description of the committee system in the Brazilian Senate in the 1990s, arguing that the system is hierarchical with power concentrated in a small number of committees dominated by the Partido do Movimento Democratico Brasileira (PMDB) and the Partido do Frente Liberal (PFL).

1826 Beck Fenwick, Tracy. Avoiding governors: the success of Bolsa Família. (*LARR*, 44:1, 2009, p. 102–131, bibl., graphs, table)

Study of Brazil's Bolsa Família program under President Lula. Argues that several key institutional features of Brazil's federal system are essential to understanding the relative success of the program and offers an optimistic assessment of the ongoing evolution of Brazilian federal institutions. [J. Hiskey]

1827 Bisilliat, Jeanne. Lá onde os rios refluem: Diadema: 20 anos de democracia e poder local. Traduçao de Helena Glória Ferreira e Wanda Caldeira Brant. Diadema, Brazil: Idem, Instituto Diadema de Estudos Municipais; São Paulo: Editora Fundação Perseu Abramo, 2004. 181 p.: bibl.

Diadema, a city on the São Paulo periphery, has become a center of policy innovation. This book looks at the city's political history since democratization.

1828 Braga, Maria do Socorro Sousa. O processo partidário-eleitoral brasileiro: padrões de competição política, 1982–2002. São Paulo: Associação Editorial Humanitas, 2006. 305 p.: bibl., ill. (some col.), col. maps.

This book argues that the Brazilian party system is becoming stronger over time as small parties disappear and larger parties consolidate power and create national level strategies.

1829 Castro, Marcus Faro de and **Maria Izabel Valladão de Carvalho.** Globalization and recent political transitions in Brazil. (*Int. Polit. Sci. Rev.*, 24:4, 2003, p. 465–490, bibl., graphs, tables)

This article looks at democratization in Brazil in the context of global economic change. The author argues that resistance to economic changes under the authoritarian regime opened up a pluralistic system with the capacity to deal with some of the social challenges facing the country.

1830 Caten, Odécio Ten. Forma(s) de governo nas reduções Guaranis. Porto Alegre, Brazil: S.A. Fabris Editor, 2003. 200 p.: bibl.

This book provides an interesting assessment of the forms of government that emerged in the areas of Guaraní settlement during the 17th and 18th centuries and the interactions between these areas and the wider Hispanic political system.

1831 Cavalheiro, Maria Eloisa. Imprensa e poder: o caso sui generis de Carazinho, RS. Passo Fundo, Brazil: UPF Editora, Universidade de Passo Fundo, 2005. 215 p.: bibl., ill.

This book examines the complexities of politics in one town in Rio Grande do Sul during the Estado Novo period. The author looks at how the mayor of this town held on to power for 12 years despite his opposition to the Estado Novo, not being a member of the party in power, and the intense opposition of other local elites.

1832 Chaves, Christine de Alencar. Festas da política: uma etnografia da modernidade no sertão, Buritis, MG. Rio de Janeiro: Relume Dumará: Núcleo de Antropologia da Política, 2003. 175 p.: bibl. (Coleção Antropologia da política; 19)

This well-written political ethnography examines the role of political parties and patronage in the social order in northern Minas Gerais.

1833 Controle parlamentar na Alemanha, na Argentina e no Brasil. Organização de Mariana Llanos e Ana María Mustapic. Rio de Janeiro: Konrad-Adenauer-Stiftung, 2005. 259 p.: bibl., ill.

This interesting edited volume brings together a series of comparative essays on legislative oversight of executive functions.

1834 Dantas Neto, Paulo Fábio. Tradição, autocracia e carisma: a política de Antonio Carlos Magalhães na modernização da Bahia, 1954–1974. Belo Horizonte, Brazil: Editora UFMG; Rio de Janeiro: IUPERJ, 2006. 587 p. (Origem)

This book provides a detailed history of the political rise of Antonio Carlos Magalhães, the leading figure in Bahian politics over the last half century, that focuses on the relations between Magalhães and the national government.

1835 Das ruas às urnas: partidos e eleições no Brasil contemporâneo. Organização de Helcimara de Souza Telles e João Ignacio Pires Lucas. Caxias do Sul, Brazil: EDUCS, 2003. 189 p.: bibl., ill.

This edited volume examines the trajectories of the PT and the PSDB at the national level and in the state of Rio Grande do Sul.

1836 De Oliveira, Francisco. Lula in the labyrinth. (*New Left Rev.*, 42, Nov./Dec. 2006, p. 5–22, graphs, map)

This article provides a political analysis of the Lula government after the 2006 election, arguing that innovative populist policies have been effective in building support for the government. At the same time, the author argues that the Lula administration creates a situation in which the poor may control the political system, but do so in a way that does not question the domination of the upper classes creating conditions for maintaining the existing class and social relations.

1837 La democracia brasileña: balance y perspectivas para el siglo XXI. Recopilação de Manuel Alcántara Sáez e Carlos Ranulfo Melo. Salamanca, Spain: Ediciones Univ. de Salamanca, 2008. 378 p.: bibl., ill. (Biblioteca de América; 39)

This book brings together chapters by a variety of prominent scholars of Brazil. The pieces touch on the history of democracy in Brazil, the institutional structure of the current democracy, the 2006 elections, participatory democracy, and dilemmas of Brazilian democracy.

1838 Democracia e participação: os conselhos gestores do Paraná. Organização de Mario Fuks, Renato M. Perissinotto e Nelson Rosário de Souza. Curitiba, Paraná, Brazil: Editora UFPR, 2004. 246 p.: bibl. (Série Pesquisa; n. 103)

This edited volume examines the activities of Conselhos Gestores, a type of participatory democratic institution, in various regions of Paraná.

1839 Diniz, Simone. O desempenho dos congressos argentino e brasileiro em perspectiva comparada. (*Contexto Int.*, 27:1, jan./junho 2005, p. 159–215, bibl., graphs, tables)

This article, which is well engaged in the international literature on institutional performance, offers a comparative analysis of the function of the Brazilian and Argentine political systems. Building on complex analyses of the legislative agendas in each country, the author argues that the limited power of the executive in the Argentine case reduces its ability to pass legislation. Nonetheless, the author shows that parties, especially those allied with the executive, have the ability to change bills in the legislative process.

1840 Domingues, José Maurício. Instituições formais, cidadania e solidariedade complexa. (*Lua Nova*, 66, 2006, p. 9–22, bibl.)

This piece provides a theoretical analysis of the gap between formal democratic institutions modeled after similar institutions built in Europe and the reality of citizenship in Brazil.

1841 Duriguetto, Maria Lúcia. Sociedade civil e democracia: um debate necessário. São Paulo: Cortez Editora, 2007. 240 p.: bibl.

This book provides a theoretical and historical analysis of the role of civil society in contemporary Brazilian democracy, arguing that civil society plays an important role in offering an alternative to the neoliberal model of social and political relationships.

1842 A era FHC e o governo Lula: transição? Organização de Denise Rocha e Maristela Veloso Campos Bernardo. Brasília: INESC, 2004. 485 p.: bibl., ill.

This volume provides a comprehensive analysis of a group of major policy areas

and the transition they underwent in the government change of 2002.

1843 Ferreira, Mary. As caetanas vão à luta: feminismo e políticas públicas no Maranhão. São Luís, Brazil: EDUFMA: Grupo de Mulheres da Ilha, 2007. 270 p.: bibl., ill.

This book provides an extremely detailed history of the women's movement in Maranhão, Brazil, in the late 20th century. The book grounds this study in a discussion of the wider feminist movements in Brazil and social movements during the democratization period. A valuable resource for scholars working on feminism and women's movements in Northeastern Brazil.

1844 Figueiredo, Argelina Maria Cheibub. Agendas, instituições, políticas e desempenho do governo na democracia brasileira. (*in* Retratos do Brasil. Organização de Elisa P. Reis and Regina Zilberman. Porto Alegre, Brazil: EDIPUCRS, 2004, p. 71–84, bibl., tables)

Through a comparison of the 1946 and 1988 Constitutions, the author argues that there is little evidence to support the hypothesis that Brazilian institutions have little ability to change the "status quo." Using comparative data from the time periods 1949–64 and 1989–2000, the chapter shows that the executive was much more effective in passing proposed legislation during the latter period. Data presented also shows a high degree of coalition discipline on post-1988 governments.

1845 Figueiredo, Lucas. O operador: como (e a mando de quem) Marcos Valério irrigou os cofres do PSDB e do PT. Rio de Janeiro: Editora Record, 2006. 250 p.: bibl., ill., index.

The book offers a narrative examination of the career of an important political fundraiser who was at the center of a major corruption scandal in the da Silva administration.

1846 Genosko, Gary. The party without bosses: lessons on anti-capitalism from Félix Guattari and Luis Inácio 'Lula' da Silva. Winnipeg, Canada: Arbeiter Ring Pub., 2003. 87 p.: bibl. (Semaphore series)

This very brief book offers an interesting analysis of the relevance of Félix

Guattari's theories of popular mobilization to Brazilian politics and the recent successes of the Partido dos Trabalhadores (PT). The book concludes with the reprint of a 1982 interview of Lula by Guattari that was previously unavailable in English.

1847 Genro, Luciana. A falência do PT e a atualidade da luta socialista: ensaios sobre a falência do PT e a urgência de uma alternativa de esquerda. Porto Alegre, Brazil: L&PM Editores, 2006. 159 p.: bibl.

Published in the year of the last national elections, this book discusses the "death" of the Worker's Party from the perspective of dissidents who have joined the Socialist Party. The Socialist candidate, Heloisa Helena, ran a surprisingly vigorous campaign that year coming in third in the first round of voting. The book contains an interview with Helena.

1848 Goiás: sociedade e estado. Organização de Dalva Borges Souza. Goânia, Brazil: Cânone, 2004. 230 p.: bibl.

This edited volume on an important but understudied region of Brazil contains chapters on Goiás politics from 1930–60, politics in the run up to and during the dictatorship, and in the recent period of democracy. The book contributes to greater knowledge about this region and also to understanding the complexities of the relationship between Brazil's traditional elite and the military dictatorship.

1849 Governo, políticas públicas e elites políticas nos estados brasileiros. Organização de Celina Souza e Paulo Fábio Dantas Neto. Brazil: Editora Revan, 2006. 310 p.: ill., maps.

This interesting set of essays takes on the critical question of state-level policymaking in Brazil. The chapters take up issues such as social spending, fiscal adjustment, and school reform.

1850 Guimarães, Juarez. A esperança equilibrista: o governo Lula em tempos de transição. Prefácio de Marilena Chaui. São Paulo: Editora Fundação Perseu Abramo, 2004. 166 p. (Col. Cadernos da Fundação Perseu Abramo; 3)

This book, published by a press affiliated with the Partido dos Trabalhadores, offers a progressive theory on how the relationship between state and economy needs

to be reorganized to build towards a new republicanism under the da Silva government.

1851 História do anarquismo no Brasil. Organização de Rafael Borges Deminicis e Daniel Aarão Reis Filho. Rio de Janeiro: Mauad X; Niterói, Brazil: EdUFF, 2006. 1 v.: bibl., ill. (Biblioteca EdUFF)

This book brings together a series of chapters on the history of anarchism in Brazil. The chapters cover such issues as the "roots of anarchism" in Brazil, anarchism and police in the Old Republic, immigration and anarchism, and particular anarchists in the period up to the end of the Estado Novo.

1852 Htun, Mala and **Timothy J. Power.** Gender, parties, and support for equal rights in the Brazilian Congress. (*Lat. Am. Polit. Soc.*, 48:4, Winter 2006, p. 83–104, bibl., tables)

This article offers an analysis of the opinions of Brazilian legislators on gender issues. The authors argue that there is substantial variance on these issues across Congress with parties on the left supporting more progressive orientations on gender issues. While there are women spread across parties that "share some interests," those interests "may be trumped by partisan, class, regional, and other cleavages."

1853 O jeito petista de governar: o exemplo de Porto Alegre. Contribuções de Alfonso Garcia *et al.* Organização de Jandira Feijó e Plínio Zalewski. Porto Alegre, Brazil: Mercado Aberto, 2002. 204 p. (Série Novas perspectivas)

This edited volume offers a very critical assessment of the 14 years of Worker's Party government in Porto Alegre between 1988 and 2002. Chapters assess such issues as social exclusion in Porto Alegre, growing crime and violence there, and movement towards a more enterprising city.

1854 Jesus Oliveira, Andréa Cristina de. Breve histórico sobre o desenvolvimento do *lobbying* no Brasil. (*Rev. Inf. Legis.*, 42:168, out./dez. 2005, p. 29–43, bibl.)

The title accurately describes this piece, which offers a concise history of lobbying in the Brazilian political system and its place in the wider international context of writing about lobbying in other democratic political systems.

1855 Küster, Angela. Democracia e sustentabilidade: experiências no Ceará, Nordeste do Brasil. Tradução e revisão de Tito Livio Cruz Romão. Fortaleza, Brazil: Fundação Konrad Adenauer, 2003. 279 p.: bibl., ill.

A close and detailed analysis of the implementation of sustainable development reforms in Ceará under the government of Tasso Jeressati and Ciro Gomes. The author concludes that reforms in that state provide evidence of the success of sustainable and participatory development policies, even under conditions that are not favorable to democracy.

1856 Lamounier, Bolivar. Da independência a Lula: dois séculos de política brasileira. São Paulo: Augurium, 2005. 320 p.: bibl., ill., index.

This book offers a concise and innovative political history of Brazil that seeks to reinterpret the place of different historical phases of Brazilian political life to more effectively tell the story, not just of the origins of Brazil's contemporary political system, but also of the system's context and possible future evolutionary path.

1857 Lattman-Weltman, Fernando. A política domesticada: Afonso Arinos e o colapso da democracia em 1964. Rio de Janeiro: FGV Editora, 2005. 260 p.: bibl.

This book is a political and intellectual biography of a prominent mid-century politician that highlights contradictions and tensions in the Estado Novo and the Second Republic.

1858 Leal, Murilo. À esquerda da esquerda: Trotskistas, comunistas e populistas no Brasil contemporâneo, 1952–1966. São Paulo: Paz e Terra, 2004. 280 p.: bibl.

This book provides a detailed analysis of the Trotskiite party in mid-20th century Brazil.

1859 Leal, Paulo Roberto Figueira. O PT e o dilema da representação política: os deputados federais são representantes de quem? Rio de Janeiro: FGV Editora, 2005. 126 p.: bibl.

Based on a solid theoretical and empirical analysis, this work examines the beliefs of the Worker's Party federal deputies to understand how they operate. The final chapter discusses a survey in which Worker's Party deputies reported their thoughts about the party and their participation in the federal legislature. The author argues that the PT generally operates as a cohesive bloc in the legislature with increasing internal dissent as a result of the policy choices of the da Silva government.

1860 Leal, Suely. Fetiche da participação popular: novas práticas de planejamento, gestão e governança democrática no Recife, Brasil. Recife, Brazil: Editora CEPE; Paris: Programa UNESCO Gestão das Transformações Sociais, 2003. 351 p.: bibl., ill. (some col.), maps (some col.).

This book provides an interesting look at the policies of participatory governance during the mayorships of Jarbas Vasconcelos between 1986 and 1988 and between 1993 and 1996. The author comprehensively examines the successes and failures of these efforts, concluding with an argument for the expansion of participatory democracy as a response to neoliberalism.

1861 Lemgruber, Julita; Leonarda Musumeci; and Ignacio Cano. Quem vigia os vigias?: um estudo sobre controle externo da polícia no Brasil. Com Ana Paula Miranda e Sonia Travassos. Rio de Janeiro: Record, 2003. 317 p.: bibl., ill.

This book is on the exceptionally important topic of police accountability and administration. For some time policing and crime have been top issues on the Brazilian agenda. This book brings together three important scholars of Brazilian policing to discuss police oversight. The book focuses on *ouvidorias*, a type of police ombudsman's office that exists in a number of Brazilian states, the problems with policing in Brazil and other forms of internal oversight, and examines statistics from *ouvidorias* and the results of a survey "applied directly to denouncers and denounced." The book outlines the limitations of the existing *ouvidoria* system and outlines a new and more effective way to build *ouvidorias*.

1862 Leonelli, Domingos and Dante de Oliveira. Diretas já: 15 meses que abalaram a ditadura. Edição de imagens de Orlando Brito. Rio de Janeiro: Editora Record, 2004. 639 p.: bibl., ill., index.

This book offers a very detailed history of the Diretas Já movement between

1983 and 1984 that challenged the dictatorship to reestablish the direct election of executives in the Brazilian government. Written from the perspective of two active participants in this movement, the book provides an interesting window on this time period in Brazilian history.

1863 Lessa, Renato. Presidencialismo de animação, e outros ensaios sobre a política brasileira, 1993–2006. Rio de Janeiro: Vieira & Lent, 2006. 269 p.: index, tables.

This series of essays by a noted Brazilian political scientist addresses a variety of issues, including examinations of the governments of Fernando Collor, Itamar Franco, Fernando Henrique Cardoso, and Luis Inácio Lula da Silva. The book also takes up issues related to political reform, the electoral process, policing, and history. The introduction addresses in part the evolution of political science in Brazil.

1864 Lucas, Luiz Paulo Vellozo. Qualicidades: poder local e qualidade na administração pública. Em entrevista a Carlos Pousa, Ricardo Murce e Ciça Guedes. Coordenação editorial de Ricardo Murce e Carlos Pousa. Contribuição técnica e revisão de Antonio Fernando Doria Porto. Rio de Janeiro: Qualitymark, 2006. 217 p.: col. ill., col. maps.

Building on an analysis of urban governance strategies in Vitória, Espirito Santo, this book seeks to offer comprehensive strategies that Brazilian municipal administrators can use to address the challenges facing Brazilian cities at the beginning of the 21st century.

1865 Luzes na floresta: o governo democrático e popular em Belém, 1997–2001. Organização de Edmilson Brito Rodrigues, Jurandir Santos de Novaes. Contribuções de Aclemilda Sousa Ferreira et al. 2a ed. rev. e ampliada. Belém do Pará, Brazil: Prefeitura Municipal de Belém, 2002. 255 p.: bibl., ill.

Printed by the city government and edited in part by the mayor who led many of the reforms discussed here, this book seeks to explain a variety of different policies adopted during the Worker's Party administration. The opening chapter is very useful in outlining the breadth of programs adopted, but the later chapters are clearly written by people predisposed to support these efforts.

1866 Machado, Maria das Dores Campos. Política e religião: a participação dos evangélicos nas eleições. Rio de Janeiro: Editora FGV, 2006. 179 p.: bibl.

This book provides a close analysis of the role of evangelical religiosity in elections in early 21st century Rio de Janeiro. Based on a substantial number of interviews with evangelical elected officials as well as campaign observation, the book addresses such topics as gender in evangelical politics, religion as a path into politics, clientelism and religious politics, and the relation between evangelical political leaders and those of other faiths.

1867 Martins Filho, João Roberto. The Brazilian armed forces and Plan Colombia. (*J. Polit. Mil. Sociol.*, 33:1, Summer 2005, p. 107–123, bibl.)

Analyzing official Brazilian discourse around national sovereignty in the Amazon and the impact of US policy in the region, the author argues that Plan Colombia has sharpened Brazilian policy in the region around not just abstract notions of a First World intervention in the region but also as a concrete response to the instability associated with the Colombian Civil War. In this response, the Brazilian government seeks to differentiate its position towards the conflict from that of the US.

1868 Melo, Marcus André Barreto Campelo de. O sucesso inesperado das reformas de segunda geração: federalismo, reformas constitucionais e política social. (*Dados/ Rio de Janeiro*, 48:4, 2005, p. 845–888, bibl., graphs)

This thoughtful piece is based on a historical institutional analysis of social reforms under the administration of Fernando Henrique Cardoso. The piece argues that the institutional power of the presidency and political incentives contributed to conditions that enabled the federal government to reshape the delivery of social benefits to the population.

1869 Menezes, Alfredo da Mota. Momento brasileiro: do fim do regime militar à eleição do Lula. Rio de Janeiro: Gryphus, 2006. 212 p.: bibl.

This book places the election of Luis Inácio Lula da Silva in the historical context of the postdictatorship period. The author argues that there is a relationship between economy and politics, and offers solutions to avoid future political problems.

1870 Messenberg, Débora. A elite parlamentar do pós-constituinte: atores e práticas. São Paulo: Editora Brasiliense, 2002. 175 p.: bibl., ill.

Based on interviews with Brazilian legislators who served in the national legislature during the five years immediately after the approval of the current constitution, this book seeks to describe and explain the practice of elite legislators. The author gives special attention to regional differences among this elite and their differing practices.

1871 Miguel, Luis F. Political representation and gender in Brazil: quotas for women and their impact. (*Bull. Lat. Am. Res.*, 27:2, April 2008, p. 197–214, tables)

The author shows that quotas have had relatively little effect in increasing the number of women holding elected office in Brazil, but suggests that quotas may have more effect in the future as party leaders learn how they work within the complexities of the party system.

1872 Minas e os fundamentos do Brasil moderno. Organização de Angela de Castro Gomes. Belo Horizonte, Brazil: Editora UFMG, 2005. 348 p.: bibl., ill. (Humanitas; 125)

This book, which brings together the work of a number of prominent scholars, tells the story of the emergence of developmentalism in Brazil from the perspective of intellectual and political trends in Minas Gerais.

1873 Moisés, José Álvaro. Cidadania, confiança e instituições democráticas. (*Lua Nova*, 65, 2005, p. 71–94, bibl.)

The article provides a theoretical examination of the relationship between confidence in institutions and citizenship. The author argues that where institutions function effectively and where individuals are treated equally before the law, there will be a greater degree of confidence in government that will allow for the resolution of collective problems.

1874 Montero, Alfred P. Brazilian politics: reforming a democratic state in a changing world. Cambridge, UK; Malden, Mass.: Polity, 2005. 167 p.: bibl., ill., index, map.

The volume offers a comprehensive introduction to Brazilian politics, taking up an array of issues including national history, the dilemmas of a weak state and a powerful oligarchy, economic inequality, integration into the international economy, and impact of the Lula government. Provides a comprehensive and digestible overview of politics in Latin America's largest republic.

1875 As mulheres e o poder legislativo no Estado do Rio de Janeiro: lugares, perfis e experiências municipais. Coordinação de Clara Araújo, Isabel Miranda e Maria América Pires. Rio de Janeiro: CEDIM, Conselho Estadual dos Direitos da Mulher, 2003. 73 p.: bibl., ill. (Cadernos do CEDIM. Série Pesquisas; 2)

This project provides a series of short chapters offering an analysis of the number and characteristics of women elected to the state legislature and municipal councils in Rio de Janeiro. This short volume, which contains a substantial number of charts and data, should be a valuable resource to scholars studying gender in state and local politics.

1876 Neto, Octavio Amorim; Gary W. Cox; and Mathew D. McCubbins. Agenda power in Brazil's Câmara dos Deputados, 1989–98. (*World Polit.*, 55:4, July 2003, p. 550–578, graph, tables)

This article offers a solid discussion of the Brazilian legislative structure and process in the context of a theoretical discussion of agenda cartels. Using data on "roll-call votes on projects and on agenda-setting motions," this article argues that Brazilian presidents choose different types of strategies to govern the country. Authors argue that while Cardoso chose a majority governance strategy that established control over the major veto points in the Brazilian legislative process, other presidents since the 1980s have chosen minority strategies of government based on rule by decree and shifting coalitions.

1877 Netto, J. Paulo. Marxismo impenitente: contribuição à história das idéias marxistas. São Paulo: Cortez Editora, 2004. 256 p.: bibl.

This volume covers a history of Marxist thought from Marx to Lukács. It concludes with a series of chapters on the impact of Marxism on Brazilian thought.

1878 Nogueira, Marco Aurélio. Más allá de lo institucional: crisis, partidos y sociedad en el Brasil de hoy. (*Nueva Soc.*, 202, marzo/abril 2006, p. 31–44)

This article offers a narrative analysis of the crisis in the Lula presidency arguing that the challenges facing the government in the wake of the corruption charges reflect not so much on the president himself, but rather on the structure of the Brazilian state and the use of the Worker's Party as an electoral machine to hold public office.

1879 Novo Contexto Internacional e a Social-Democracia, *Câmara dos Deputados,* *2002.* Seminário. 26 de março de 2002 na Câmara dos Deputados, Brasília. Organização de Yeda Crusius. Textos de Celso Lafer, Gilberto Dupas e José Augusto Guilhon Albuquerque. Brasília: Inst. Teotônio Vilela, 2003. 101 p.: bibl. (Col. Brasil 2010; 5)

This brief volume, a product of a seminar sponsored by the PSDB in the national legislature, discusses the role of and challenges facing social democracy in Brazil today.

1880 Oliva, Aloízio Mercadante. Brasil: primeiro tempo: análise comparativa do governo Lula. São Paulo: Editora Planeta do Brasil, 2006. 286 p.: ill.

This book, written by the leader of the PT in the Senate and with a preface by President da Silva, offers a favorable assessment of the first da Silva administration covering a wide range of government policy from international affairs to the economy. The book concludes with a series of annexes which offer a graphic comparison of initiatives during the da Silva and Cardoso administrations, a summary of economic statistics during the da Silva administration, and a list of significant laws passed during the da Silva administration.

1881 Oliveira, José Ribeiro de. A corrupção entrava o Brasil. Imperatriz, Brazil: Ética, 2005. 206 p.: bibl.

This book provides a broad overview of corruption in Brazil, beginning with a history of corruption in the country and covering different processes of corruption, such as corruption in government, crime and corruption, and responses to corruption.

1882 Oliveira, Luzia Helena Herrmann de. A reforma política no Brasil: propostas, temores e controvérsias. (*Estud. Soc./*

Santa Fe, 14:27, segundo semestre 2004, p. 71–90, bibl.)

This article addresses the evolution of reform proposals in the Brazilian political system over the last 30 years, arguing that reform efforts were focused on broadly reforming the entire system, for example by shifting to a parliamentary system, through the early 1990s, but in recent years have focused on more specific efforts designed to strengthen existing parties.

1883 Orçamento participativo: análise das experiências desenvolvidas em Santa Catarina. Organização de Julian Borba, Lígia Helena Hahn Lüchmann. Contribuições de Aline Maria da Campo *et al.* Florianópolis, Brazil: Editora Insular, 2007. 224 p.: bibl., ill.

This interesting volume offers a systematic comparison of participatory budgeting policies in several municipalities in Santa Catarina. The chapters employ similar modes of analysis to provide pictures of varying local programs.

1884 Orçamento participativo: construindo a democracia. Organização de Sérgio de Azevedo e Rodrigo Barroso Fernandes. Rio de Janeiro: Editora Revan; Belo Horizonte, Brazil: Observatório das Metrópoles, Núcleo Minas Gerais, PROEX-PUC Minas/ FASE, 2005. 222 p.: bibl., ill., map.

This edited volume offers a detailed account of the impact of participatory budgeting in Belo Horizonte, the capital of Minas Gerais. It includes two concluding chapters by Renato Boschi and Leonardo Avritzer.

1885 O orçamento público e a transição do poder. Coordenação de Fernando Rezende e Armando Cunha. Colaboração de Argelina Cheibub Figueiredo *et al.* Rio de Janeiro: FGV Editora, 2003. 156 p.: bibl., ill. (Série Contribuintes e cidadãos; 2)

This edited volume examines the complexities of the budgeting process in Brazil and suggests that the rigidity of the process interferes with efforts to bring about needed reforms in the state. Chapters examine such issues as the relationship between social security and fiscal budgeting, health care budgeting, and the nature of contemporary budgeting restrictions.

1886 Ottmann, Goetz. Cidadania mediada: processos de democratização da política municipal no Brasil. (*Novos Estud. CEBRAP,* 74, março 2006, p. 155–175)

Through a close analysis of politics in three Brazilian municipalities, the author suggests that citizenship in contemporary Brazil is mediated through clientelistic ties at the local level. Successful reforms often find ways of incorporating the clientelist structures into efforts to deliver resources to the population.

1887 Palermo, Vicente and **Germán Feierherd.** El liderazgo como capital político temporal: Lula y el proceso de adaptación del PT a la hora de gobernar. *(Rev. Arg. Cienc. Polít.*, 9/10, 2005, p. 31–59, appendix, bibl., graphs)

This article offers a narrative and insightful analysis of the origins of Lula's political capital and its impact on the structure and activities of his presidency. The authors argue that Lula's political capital was built over 25 years as a popular leader. This source of power provided Lula with a stable base of support that created different challenges for him from those faced by his predecessor who accumulated political capital more rapidly, but whose capital was based on a belief in his technical expertise.

1888 Participação e deliberação: teoria democrática e experiências institucionais no Brasil contemporâneo. Organização de Vera Schattan P. Coelho e Marcos Nobre. São Paulo: Editora 34, 2004. 367 p.: bibl.

With a preface by John Gaventa, this book brings together a number of the most important Brazilians and Brazilianists studying deliberative democracy. For some time Brazil has been on the leading edge of these types of reforms. It has begun to influence these debates in other countries. This book brings together sophisticated analyses of the processes that should be a useful resource for scholars working on these issues in Brazil.

1889 Participação feminina na construção da democracia: levantamento do resultado das eleições municipais (1992 a 2000), estaduais e federais (1994 a 2002). 4a ed. Rio de Janeiro: IBAM; Brasília: UNDP, 2004. 61 p.: bibl., ill., map.

This book provides extensive charts detailing the percentage of women elected to various political offices in Brazil over the course of the last two decades. The book also contains a short chapter on the demographic characteristics of women elected to mayorial positions, based on public data as well as on the comments of the mayors themselves.

1890 Partidos e coligações eleitorais no Brasil. Organização de Silvana Krause e Rogério Schmitt. Rio de Janeiro: Konrad Adenauer Stiftung; São Paulo: Editora Unesp, 2005. 143 p.: bibl., ill.

This edited volume provides an analysis of electoral alliances between parties that builds on both historical and contemporary data. Chapters cover a theory of party alliances, alliances between 1954 and 1962, the impact of proportional representation on alliances, and an analysis of party alliances in the 1990s and the new century.

1891 Partidos e comportamento político no Brasil. Organização de Rosana Katia Nazzari. Cascavel, Brazil: EDUNIOESTE, 2006. 193 p.: bibl., ill.

This series of essays examines the evolution of the Brazilian democratic system from the perspective of changes in the political system over the last century.

1892 Partidos, eleições e voto: o comportamento político e eleitoral em Santa Catarina. Organização de Monica Hass. Chapecó, Brazil: Argos Editora Universitária, 2003. 250 p.: bibl., map. (Debates)

This edited volume provides a history of electoral behavior in the southern state of Santa Catarina and covers such issues as behavior in the 2000 elections in the west of the state, behavior in presidential elections, political conflict in one town in 1969, and women's participation.

1893 Os partidos na política catarinense: eleições, processo legislativo, políticas públicas. Organização de Yan de Souza Carreirão e Julian Borba. Florianópolis, Brazil: Editora Insular, 2006. 224 p.: bibl., col. ill.

This edited volume offers a comprehensive and interesting set of essays on the party system and institutional politics in the southern state of Santa Catarina.

1894 Penna, Lincoln de Abreu. Imprensa e política no Brasil: a militância jornalística do proletariado. Rio de Janeiro: E-papers, 2007. 171 p.: bibl.

This book provides an analysis of left-wing media outlets in Brazil in the 19th and 20th centuries.

1895 Pereira, Anthony W. The dialects of the Brazilian military regime's political trials. (*Luso-Braz. Rev.*, 41:2, 2005, p. 162–183, bibl.)

Analyzing the Nunca Mais archive, this article provides important insights into the jurisprudence of the Brazilian military dictatorship. The author argues that courts adopted "schizophrenic" and inconsistent interpretations of laws, thus creating spaces through which defense attorneys were able to roll back some of the more "draconian" provisions of laws enacted by the authoritarian regime.

1896 Pereira, Carlos and **Bernardo Mueller.** The cost of governing: strategic behavior of the president and legislators in Brazil's budgetary process. (*Comp. Polit. Stud.*, 37:7, Sept. 2004, p. 781–815, bibl., graphs, tables)

The authors of this article argue that while existing literature predicts that Brazilian governance would be a politically costly or unmanageable enterprise—given factors such as federalism, presidentialism, and large-district proportional representation—efforts to govern Brazil are in fact much more manageable. This finding is the result of budgetary mechanisms that facilitate executive efforts to pass legislation through Congress. The executive's control of the budgeting process provides a basis for relatively inexpensive negotiations with the legislature that help the executive obtain the approval of other proposals in Congress.

1897 Pereira, Luiz Carlos Bresser. O paradoxo da esquerda no Brasil. (*Novos Estud. CEBRAP*, 74, março 2006, p. 25–45, table)

This article examines the complex question addressing the notion that Brazilian governments tend not to govern from a left of center perspective even though the left tends to win elections. The author argues that while this paradox exists, it is possible to have a government from the left in Brazil.

1898 Perondi, Regina Heurich. Partidos políticos e terceiro setor. Brasília: Fundação Ulysses Guimarães, 2007. 185 p.: bibl.

Built on a case study of the Partido do Movimento Democratico Brasileiro (PMDB), this book looks at the involvement of non-profit and advocacy groups in the Brazilian political process. Perondi points to the ways this reorientation with society has affected political activity in the country and raises an important counterpoint to both scholarship on social movements and institutional analyses of politics.

1899 Pívaro Stadniky, Hilda. Mulheres sem mordaça X tropa de choque: estratégias de lutas políticas no contexto das greves policiais no estado do Paraná. (*Prohistoria/Rosario*, 10:10, primavera 2006, p. 113–132, photos)

This article examines the role of the wives of police officers in supporting a police officers strike in southern Brazil.

1900 Poletto, Ivo. Brasil, oportunidades perdidas: meus dois anos no governo Lula: crônicas de um brasileiro aprendente. Rio de Janeiro: Garamond, 2005. 140 p.

Poletto memoirs document his participation in the first Lula administration at the head of some social policy efforts. Coming from the experience of a social organizer, the book offers an important outsider's look at Brazilian politics and suggests that real change in Brazilian social conditions is not possible without a different state of economic policies.

1901 Políticas culturais: diálogo indispensável. Organização de Lia Calabre. Rio de Janeiro: Edições Casa de Rui Barbosa, 2005. 80 p.: bibl., ill. (Col. FCRB. Aconteceu; 1)

This slim volume emerged from a conference and discusses cultural policies of the Brazilian government from the Vargas era onwards. The first essay briefly covers a broad history of cultural policy and provides a chronology of major government initiatives in culture from the 1930s through 1991. The second essay examines the intellectual history of the emergence of Brazil's ministry of culture. The third essay examines the impact of national security concerns on television in Brazil in the 1970s.

1902 A química da cidadania: Sindicato dos Químicos e Plásticos de São Paulo: 20 anos de lutas, democracia e conquistas. Organização de Paulo Fontes. São

Paulo: Sindicato dos Químicos e Plásticos de São Paulo: Viramundo, 2002. 255 p.: bibl., ill.

This edited volume, which begins with a preface by Aloísio Mercadante, offers a history of the political and social actions of the Chemical and Plastic Workers Union, a politically important component of the Central Único de Trabalhadores (CUT). The book's publication was supported by the union.

1903 Renault, Letícia. Comunicação e política nos canais de televisão do poder legislativo no Brasil. Belo Horizonte, Brazil: ALMG, 2004. 162 p.: bibl., ill.

This project analyzes the role of legislative television channels, akin to C-SPAN, in strengthening democracy in Brazil.

1904 Rennó, Lucio R. and Anthony P. Spanakos. Fundamentos de economia, mercado financeiro e intenção de voto: as eleições presidenciais brasileiras de 1994, 1998 e 2002. (*Dados/Rio de Janeiro*, 49:1, 2006, p. 11–40, bibl., tables)

This article takes up the important question of the impact of the economy on election results in Brazil. Using data from the 1994, 1998, and 2002 elections, the authors argue that incumbent party candidates at the national level are negatively affected by poor economic conditions.

1905 Retorno ao republicanismo. Organização de Sérgio Cardoso. Belo Horizonte, Brazil: Editora UFMG, 2004. 231 p.: bibl. (Humanitas; 102)

This book brings together a variety of authors of political thought discussing the question of republicanism in Brazil.

1906 Reznik, Luís. Democracia e segurança nacional: a polícia política no pós-guerra. Rio de Janeiro: FGV, 2004. 187 p.: bibl.

This well researched and thought out volume examines the evolution and role of political policing in the Brazilian Second Republic (1945–64). The author argues that political policing was critical in some ways to democratic practice during that period as a result of the concern in Brazil and other countries about the role of Communists in the political system. The author raises questions about the ongoing role of political policing in contemporary Brazil.

1907 Ribeiro, Luiz Cesar de Queiroz and Orlando Alves dos Santos. Democracia e cidade: divisão social da cidade e cidadania na sociedade brasileira. (*Anál. Soc./Lisboa*, 40:174, primavera 2005, p. 87–109, bibl.)

This very interesting article provides geographic and social analysis of the production of urban space and the concept of citizenship and democratic practice in Brazil. Building a strong theoretical argument, the authors suggest that spatial segregation in Brazil has the effect of undermining citizenship and producing a limited type of democracy that is not open to the types of civic organizing necessary to resolve collective problems or to deal with the needs of the poor.

1908 Rodrigues, Leôncio Martins. Mudanças na classe política brasileira. São Paulo: PubliFolha, 2006. 181 p.: bibl.

This book examines the shifting composition of the Brazilian Câmara dos Deputados finding that as the PT increases its control of seats in the legislature, the percentage of seats held by legislators from the middle and lower classes of Brazilian society increases.

1909 Rolim, Francisco Cartaxo. Do bico de pena à urna eletrônica. Recife, Brazil: Edições Bagaço, 2006. 368 p.: bibl.

This book provides a history of politics in the northeastern town of Cajazeira, Paraíba, focusing on the evolution of populist and clientelist practices in the area from the 1930s through the present day. The author has an informal writing style and provides important information on an understudied region of the country.

1910 Sader, Emir. Taking Lula's measure. (*New Left Rev.*, 33, May/June 2005, p. 59–79)

This article provides a well-written, engaging, and clear-eyed assessment of the first Lula administration. The author in particular is critical of the Worker's Party's move to the center over the last decade and raises questions about the future of the Brazilian left.

1911 Santos, Fabiano Guilherme Mendes. O poder legislativo no presidencialismo de coalizão. Belo Horizonte, Brazil:

Editora UFMG; Rio de Janeiro: IUPERJ, 2003. 251 p.: bibl., ill. (Col. Origem; 16)

Presents a collection of previously published works on the role of the legislature in the context of presidencies of coalitions. Using rational choice modeling, historical data, and statistical analysis, the book considers a series of issues such as the role of Congress in federal trade and patronage in Brazil to build a model of legislative behavior for Brazilian political conditions. Argues that the electoral environment in which deputies operate leads to conditions in which the Congress develops relatively little expertise on issues and, as a result, must look to the executive branch for guidance in passing legislation. Members of Congress realize that there are more opportunities to control legislation if they are able to move into executive posts. As a result, members often decide to leave their positions in Congress.

1912 Santos, Fabiano Guilherme Mendes and Acir Almeida. Teoria informacional e a seleção de relatores na Câmara dos Deputados. (*Dados/Rio de Janeiro*, 48:4, 2005, p. 693–735, bibl., table)

This article provides an argument for why legislative reporters with views divergent from the leadership of legislative committees are selected to report committee work to the House. Building on a solid empirical analysis, the authors suggest that these choices are made as a result of the strategic benefits they provide to the leadership of the committee.

1913 Santos, Maria Sirley dos. Democracia participativa no Brasil. (*Temas Nuestra Am.*, 41, julio/dic. 2004, p. 33–45, bibl., photo)

This piece offers a brief discussion of participatory practices and their historical roots in contemporary Brazil.

1914 Santos, Raimundo. La crisis en Brasil: izquierda y política en tiempos recientes. (*Nueva Soc.*, 200, nov./dic. 2005, p. 4–12, bibl.)

This article provides an interesting political analysis of the impact of the corruption scandals of the Worker's Party government on the Brazilian political scene. Noting the shifting currents within the

Brazilian party system, and the particular success of the Worker's Party coming from its outsider status, the author argues that while Luis Inácio Lula da Silva might still be in position to win reelection, his government would be greatly debilitated.

1915 Scotto, Gabriela. As difusas fronteiras entre a política e o mercado: um estudo antropológico sobre marketing político, seus agentes, práticas e representações. Rio de Janeiro: Relume Dumará, 2004. 205 p.: bibl., ill. (Col. Antropologia da política; 25)

This close examination of the political marketing in Brazil argues that there are no clear barriers between marketing and politics.

1916 Silva, Pedro Luiz Barros. Limites e obstáculos à reforma do Estado no Brasil: a experiência da previdência social na Nova República. Campinas, Brazil: Univ. Estadual de Campinas-UNICAMP, Inst. de Economia-IE, 2003. 238 p.: bibl., ill. (Col. Teses)

This book provides a comprehensive examination of the reform of social security in Brazil in the period between 1985 and 1988. The author suggests that reform policies in Brazil require a change in organization and in the "representation" of social interests in Brazil.

1917 Silva, Ricardo. A ideologia do Estado autoritário no Brasil. Chapecó, Brazil: Argos Editora Universitária, 2004. 363 p.: bibl. (Série Debates)

This interesting monograph examines the history of authoritarian political thought in Brazil. Demonstrates a recent evolution within the literature from a focus on supporting an authoritarianism of state-based institutions that emerged under the Estado Novo to a focus on rational economic claims positioned against forms of economic populism.

1918 Silveira, Alair. Memória social & processo eleitoral: as motivações do voto em Cuiabá e Várzea Grande, Mato Grosso. Cuiabá, Brazil: Entrelinhas, 2002. 156 p.: ill.

This book examines voting behavior in Cuiabá, the capital of Mato Grosso, and the neighboring city of Várzea Grande. Working through an analysis of theoretical

approaches to voting behavior and a survey
of residents of these cities, the author argues
that voting patterns are determined by a
combination of empathy for particular candidates and rational decision-making.

1919 Simpósio OBSERVANORDESTE, 5th,
Fortaleza, Brazil, 2004. Nordeste
2004: o voto das capitais: análises interpre-
tativas dos resultados eleitorais nas capitais
do Nordeste. Organização de Hugo Cortez
e Klaus Hermanns. Fortaleza, Brazil: Fundação Konrad Adenauer; Recife, Brazil: Inst.
de Pesquisas Sociais da Fundação Joaquim
Nabuco, 2005. 177 p.: bibl.

This volume offers a narrative analysis of election results in most of the state
capitals of the Brazilian Northeast: Salvador, Aracaju, Maceió, Recife, João Pessoa,
Natal, Fortaleza, and Teresina. In the introductory chapter, Jairo Nicolau argues that
the municipal elections in 2004 reflected a
polarization between the PSDB and the PT
that would likely lead to continuing parliamentary fragmentation at the national level
in 2006.

1920 Soares, Samuel Alves. Controles e
autonomia: as Forças Armadas e o
sistema político brasileiro, 1974–1999. São
Paulo: Editora Unesp, 2006. 222 p.: bibl.

This systematic historical institutional analysis of civilian control over
the military in the democratization and
post-transition period suggests that while
civilians have gained political control over
the military, the Brazilian military retains
substantial institutional autonomy over issues pertaining to its own organization and
governance.

1921 O sopro do minuano: transformações
societárias e políticas sociais: um
debate acadêmico. Organização de Carlos
Nelson dos Reis. Porto Alegre, Brazil:
EDIPUCRS, 2007. 355 p.: bibl.

This edited volume focuses on building a more sustainable and inclusive mode
of development in the contemporary world.
The authors focus on such issues as social
exclusion and social policy, health policy in
Brazil, worker health, rights to the city, and
"Fordism and flexibilization."

1922 Sousa, Vivaldo de. As coligações
partidárias: período 1986–94 versus
1954–62. Brasília: Plenarium, a Editora da

Câmara dos Deputados, 2006. 143 p.: bibl.,
ill. (Col. Parlamento em teses; 3)

This monograph takes up the question of formal party ties for electoral purposes in Brazil's current political system
and during the Second Republic. The author
concludes that legislative links are influenced by gubernatorial elections and efforts
to maximize electoral outcomes, and that
links are built more often to support election to the federal Congress than to support
election to state assembly.

1923 Taylor, Matthew M. and **Vinícius C.**
Buranelli. Ending up in pizza: accountability as a problem of institutional
arrangement in Brazil. (*Lat. Am. Polit. Soc.*,
49:1, Spring 2007, p. 59–87, bibl., tables)

The article offers an examination of
accountability structures within the Brazilian political system and explains the ineffi-
cacy of those institutions through their own
structure and the relationships between
those institutions.

1924 Teixeira, Alberto. Guia da cidadania
para a transparência: prevenção contra a corrupção. Fortaleza, Brazil: Fundação
Konrad Adenauer: Escola de Formação de
Governantes, 2006. 375 p.: bibl., ill., map.

This book is really a manual designed
to help citizens, principally in the state
of Ceará, but also in other parts of Brazil,
understand state mechanisms that can contribute to efforts to promote accountability
in the Brazilian political system. Among
the issues addressed is how to combat corruption through social action, legislative
processes, and with the help of international
actors.

1925 Transição e democracia: institu-
cionalizando a passagem do poder.
Coordenação de Ana Lucia Lobato e Wilson
Calvo. Brasília: Casa Civil, Presidência da
República, 2002. 276 p.: bibl.

This book provides an important
set of insights into the operation of the
presidency in Brazil. Much of the book is
devoted to the nature and dynamics of administrative transitions under a democratic
regime. Thus, the book examines, from
the perspective of insiders in the Cardoso
administration, including former President
Fernando Henrique Cardoso, the challenges
of shifting from one elected presidential

administration to another. Also includes detailed information about the operation of the Brazilian executive.

1926 Trotta, Miguel E.V. Cuestión social, movimientos sociales e integración regional: posibilidades de convergencia estratégica de los sujetos colectivos en el marco institucional del Mercosur. (*Rev. Arg. Cienc. Polít.*, 9/10, 2005, p. 69–80, bibl.)

This article examines the role of civil society and social movements in pushing forward a set of "social questions" in the context of regional integration in South America.

1927 Vasco, Ana. Aécio Neves: de fato e de direito. Prefácio de Fernando Henrique Cardoso. Belo Horizonte, Brazil: Soler Editora, 2005. 230 p.: bibl.

This book is a generally positive biography of the governor of Minas Gerais.

1928 Velasco Junior, Licínio. Congresso e política de reforma do estado no Brasil. (*Dados/Rio de Janeiro*, 49:2, 2006, p. 233–268, bibl., tables)

This article examines the complexities of ruling coalitions in the process of state reform in Brazil. Focusing on a systematic comparison of privatization of the Companhia do Vale do Rio Doce and the telecommunications reforms in the administration of Fernando Henrique Cardoso, the article argues that negotiations center around key members of Congress who may or may not support the effort. As the opposition comes around to support some measures it will tend to have the effect of bringing key coalition members into line. If the opposition does not support the reform, then the government would distribute resources to maintain the support of important deputies.

1929 Os votos de Deus: evangélicos, política e eleições no Brasil. Organização de Joanildo A. Burity e Maria das Dores C. Machado. Recife, Brazil: Fundação Joaquim Nabuco, Editora Massangana, 2005. 236 p.: bibl.

Examines one of the most interesting aspects of Brazilian politics: the rapidly growing evangelical Protestant vote. Chapters cover such issues as the history of evangelical participation in Brazil, the participation of evangelicals in the 2002 elections in Rio de Janeiro, the role of the neo-Pentecostal Igreja Universal in politics, the complexities of religion in a pluralist system, and general observations on the participation of evangelicals in the 2002 elections.

1930 Wampler, Brian and **Leonardo Avritzer.** Participatory publics: civil society and new institutions in democratic Brazil. (*Comp. Polit./New York*, 36:3, April 2004, p. 291–312, tables)

Building on different notions of participatory democracy, this important article seeks to contribute to the debates on democratization in Brazil by suggesting the role of what the authors refer to as "participatory publics" in deepening existing political regimes in Latin America. The article builds on a comparative analysis of participatory budgeting efforts in Porto Alegre, Belo Horizonte, and Recife to make this argument. The authors conclude by suggesting that political reform and progressive change in Brazil come not just from abstract institutional engineering, but also from the ways the institutions form relationships with civil society.

1931 Wood, Terence and **Warwick E. Murray.** Participatory democracy in Brazil and local geographies: Porto Alegre and Belo Horizonte compared. (*Rev. Eur. Estud. Latinoam. Caribe*, 83, Oct. 2007, p. 19–41, bibl., graph, tables)

This article offers a systematic comparison of participatory budgeting initiatives in Belo Horizonte and Porto Alegre. The authors argue that participatory budgeting enhances democratic governance and that important lessons can be learned from participatory democracy that may help strengthen national level representative democracy.

1932 Zaverucha, Jorge. FHC, forças armadas e polícia: entre o autoritarismo e a democracia, 1999–2002. Rio de Janeiro: Editora Record, 2005. 285 p.: bibl., ill.

This book goes to the heart of one of the most substantial problems facing contemporary Brazilian democracy, the general question of public security. The author documents the growing role of the military in public security and some of its negative impacts on democracy. The book is cogent and brings together important and interesting data on this issue.

1933 Zirker, Daniel. Property rights, democratization, and military politics in Brazil. (*J. Polit. Mil. Sociol.,* 33:1, Summer 2005, p. 125–139, bibl.)

This article suggests that growing tensions over landownership, the military's role as a land owner, and questions about state sovereignty in the Amazon region portend a larger, if politically difficult, role for the military in Brazilian national policy.

1934 Zucco, Cesar. The president's 'new' constituency: Lula and the pragmatic vote in Brazil's 2006 presidential elections. (*J. Lat. Am. Stud.,* 40:1, Feb. 2008, p. 29–49, graphs, maps, tables)

Building on historical municipal level elections data, this article argues that the shift in PT votes from more developed to less developed regions of the country reflects the effective use of the Bolsa Família to win votes and the advantages of incumbent parties in less developed parts of the country.

INTERNATIONAL RELATIONS

GENERAL

MARY K. MEYER McALEESE, *Professor of Political Science, Eckerd College*

THE SCHOLARLY WORKS ON INTERNATIONAL RELATIONS for the period under review reveal notable common themes and intellectual trends. The predominant general theme is regionalism in the context of continuing globalization. Secondary themes concern the role of the state in steering the new regionalism, multilevel governance issues, and the effectiveness of existing inter-American machinery. Very few works focus specifically on foreign policy making, comparative foreign policy analysis, or the more formal aspects of US-Latin American relations outside of these main themes. Constructivist and poststructuralist approaches are successfully joining the established intellectual and theoretical orientations in the field (item **2000**), while Latin American and European voices are far more prevalent than North American ones in the study of the general international relations of the Americas.

Most scholars under review see regionalism as a practical consequence of globalization. However, writers differ in their estimation of the nature, scope, or depth of the regionalization that has occurred, of states' strategies or capabilities in pursuing different forms of regionalization, and of the presumed benefits of regionalization *cum* globalization. While there continue to be generally critical views of neoliberal globalization processes (items **1939**, **1963**, and **1966**) and their links to US free trade policies (items **1943** and **1982**) or transnational investment patterns (items **1948** and **1952**), most scholars are focused on the econometric details, practical challenges, and strategic alternatives that Latin American states face in dealing with globalization.

Several scholars explore the "new regionalism" that is unfolding in the Western Hemisphere. Processes of globalization are producing new geographies based on new regional centers of economic, political, and normative power (items **1935**, **1961**, **1962**, and **1987**). NAFTA encompasses a powerful North American center or "zone" dominated by the US; however, other counterhegemonic centers and subregions are emerging, particularly Mercosur/l in the southern zone and a semiperipheral Andean subregion. The Central American and Caribbean subregions constitute dependent peripheral spaces pivoting toward the Northern zone but are susceptible to counterhegemonic forces. The "newness" of these zones and subregions may be questioned; however, the contemporary economic and political processes that define them, and the emerging Braudelian and constructivist discourses about them, do seem to be new to the field.

Scholars are divided on whether this new regionalism constitutes an opportunity or a challenge to Latin American states and whether these states are merely reacting to larger processes or are successfully influencing them; but most see Latin American states as active agents in this process. Several states are seizing opportunities to pursue an assertive regionalist and/or subregionalist agenda with the goal of lessening dependency and promoting development. Examples of such strategies include not just Mercosur/l or the revived Comunidad Andina de Naciones (CAN), but also the more political Comunidad Sudamericana de Naciones, spearheaded by Brazil's Cardoso, and the Alternativa Bolivariana para las Américas (ALBA), spearheaded by Venezuela's Chávez. These regional cooperation schemes represent significant counterhegemonic resistances to NAFTA, the US' "neo-pan-American" Free Trade Area of the Americas (FTAA) project, and the neoliberal agenda of the "Washington Consensus" (items **1941**, **1943**, **1945**, **1950**, **1960**, **1962**, **1967**, **1976**, and **1988**). Despite such resistances, however, the hemispheric patchwork of free trade agreements cobbled together in the past decade signals a widespread practical recognition of the pressures to open regional and subregional trade and investment flows in the face of globalization.

Several studies examine the regional economic integration experiments recently undertaken by Latin American states, assessing their depth, breadth, and prospects for success compared to previous Latin American integration efforts or to the European Union (EU) model of regional integration (items **1941**, **1976**, **1988**, and **1998**). Sandoval Peña examines the functioning of NAFTA mechanisms (item **1993**). Economist José Antonio Ocampo presents an excellent edited volume comparing regional financial cooperation in different parts of the world, with especially interesting chapters on Mercosur and the Andean, Central American, and Caribbean subregions (item **1986**). Ocampo sees regional financial cooperation as a key step in promoting South-South cooperation and development and a key requirement in building a more representative global financial architecture.

As Latin American states pursue more *intra-* and *sub*-regional cooperation and integration schemes in navigating globalization, they are also participating in growing *inter-* and *trans*-regional ties spanning oceans. Numerous studies analyze Latin American states' bilateral or multilateral relations with the EU (items **1954**, **1955**, **1956**, **1958**, and **1968**). Several others focus on such relations with China or East Asia (items **1946**, **1949**, **1957**, **1971**, **1984**, and **1996**). Significantly, others study emergent transregional relations, such as Mercosur/l's relations with the EU (items **1983** and **1994**) or South Africa (item **1974**). A special issue of Chile's *Revista de Estudios Internacionales* explores Latin American relations with APEC and the Asia-Pacific Region (items **1959**, **1978**, **1991**, and **1995**). However, not all scholars are as optimistic about the prospects for successful economic integration and political cooperation among Latin American states or between Latin America and other regional organizations in other parts of the world (items **1953**, **1958**, and **1975**). Guadarrama González calls for a new, *sui generis* Latin American theory of regional integration (item **1963**).

A number of scholars question the salience of the state and state-centrism in the context of neoliberal globalization. Rivelois, Coronado, and Moloeznik contribute an edited volume that merits attention, both for its multilayered analysis of corruption and criminality (in drug trafficking) as the other side of the neoliberal coin and for its engaging call for strengthening the power and democratic accountability of the state (item **1951**). Several other writers study various aspects of local-global politics and local-transnational governance issues in light of neoliberal globalization, including gender violence at the US-Mexican border (item **1997**), the "paradiplomacy" of municipal governments (item **1938**), the domestic political effects of internationally funded NGOs (item **1942**), and the proliferation of translocal actors, flows and networks in the inter-American system that challenge our conventional thinking about power (item **1985**).

A few writers focus on the weaknesses of the formal inter-American machinery, particularly the OAS. They remain largely skeptical of the ability of the OAS to promote democratization (items **1936** and **1972**). Mace and Loiseau provide a helpful discussion of the emerging Summit of the Americas machinery compared to the existing OAS machinery while testing the concept of "cooperative hegemony" (item **1973**). It remains to be seen whether these parallel substructures of hemispheric institutions are competing with or complementing each other. Others remain hopeful about the role of inter-American institutions in promoting democratic norms (item **1992**), fighting corruption (item **2001**), and developing soft law in the areas of workers' rights and freedom of association (item **1947**) or indigenous peoples' rights (items **1948** and **1981**). However, Pevehouse's top-down statistical analysis of the role of regional organizations in promoting democracy among member states illustrates the pitfalls of quantitative approaches to IR without a strong grounding in comparative politics (item **1979**).

Some scholars bridge this inside/outside, second image versus third image (levels of analysis) problem through foreign or defense policy analysis. Faust demonstrates the value of careful second-image or state-level analysis in explaining how Chile gained a foreign policy advantage over other Latin American states in its economic and political relations with China/East Asia (item **1957**). Pion-Berlin and Trinkunas offer an interesting study of why Latin American politicians tend to ignore developing defense policy expertise of their own and instead focus on coup avoidance in managing domestic civil-military relations (item **1980**). Benítez provides a fascinating analysis of Latin American states' growing diplomatic and military participation in international peacekeeping missions, both in the circum-Caribbean region and around the world (item **1940**). He indicates that this new Latin American presence in the global security regime can partly be explained as a strategic move by civilian politicians in the 1990s to consolidate their countries' democratic transitions. Manzella illustrates this point by calling for a closer strategic partnership between Mercosur and South Africa (item **1974**). A collection of papers published by Spain's *Centro Superior de Estudios de la Defensa Nacional* discusses the opportunities for security cooperation between the EU and Latin American and includes a rare overview of Latin American defense industries in light of regional and global security regimes (item **1964**).

Very few scholarly studies of the formal aspects of US-Latin American relations appeared in the period under review. An important exception is Weeks' very solid undergraduate textbook on this topic, one of the better ones currently available (item **2002**). Nevertheless, there is an unusual silence of US-based scholars on such mainstay issues of US-Latin American relations as security policy, human rights, migration, or foreign aid. However, Laurienti asks whether the US military's human rights promotion efforts positively influenced Latin American militaries (item **1969**). Rosenblum investigates migration issues from the perspective of the elites in sending countries (item **1990**). Scholars like Leogrande and Prevost and Oliva Campo contribute very critical essays about recent US policies toward Latin America (items **1944**, **1970**, and **1977**). Taffet looks back 40 years to provide a critical historical assessment of the Alliance for Progress program (item **1999**). Meanwhile, Rodríguez Díaz presents a fresh Latin American perspective on Elihu Root's early 20th century travels and diplomatic writings on US-Latin American relations (item **1989**). Heredia goes back even further in his detailed diplomatic history of Latin America's international relations in the formative 1810–20 period (item **1965**).

The contours of the field are marked by disciplinary, theoretical, and geographical diversity even if its focal point is predominantly fixed on the "new regionalism" in the context of trade and neoliberal globalization. Largely missing from the field are studies on the regional aspects of such transnational issues as human trafficking, environment, public health, and human security, as well as studies on regional responses to such issues. It remains to be seen what direction the field will take in the wake of global recession and the advent of the Obama administration in the US.

1935 Les Amériques latines: unité et diversité des territoires. Sous la coordination de André Gamblin. Paris: Sedes, 2005. 175 p.: bibl., ill. (Dossiers des images économiques du monde)

An engaging French university geography textbook that identifies and analyzes four territorial sets in Latin America: Mexico, the "American Mediterranean" (which includes Central America, the Caribbean Islands, and the Guyanas), the Southern Cone and Brazil (forming the most developed region), and the Andean countries. The text's focus includes questions of economic and cultural spaces that are shifting as a result of globalization, producing new power centers and a new regionalism that challenges traditional political or geostrategic centers and spaces.

1936 Arceneaux, Craig L. and David Pion-Berlin. Issues, threats, and institutions: explaining OAS responses to democratic dilemmas in Latin America. (*Lat. Am. Polit. Soc.,* 49:2, Summer 2007, p. 1–31, appendix, bibl., tables)

The authors offer a skeptical and well-supported critique of the liberal institutionalist claim that international organizations can help promote democracy inside states. Specifically, the authors examine the OAS machinery, including the corpus of normative and bureaucratic tools of the OAS aimed at protecting and strengthening democracy in the region. Discussion includes attention to Resolution 1080 (passed by the OAS General Assembly in 1991) aimed at triggering immediate responses to any threats to democracy and the Inter-American Democratic Charter signed in 2001. After examining numerous cases

from Haiti in 1991 to Ecuador and Bolivia in 2004–2005, the authors find that the OAS defends democracy selectively. Its responses are ambiguous and depend on the clarity of the threat that a given democratic challenge poses. Given such behavior, the authors ask whether the OAS actually legitimates the persistence of low-quality democracies.

1937 Arias, Julio. China "redescubre" América Latina. (*Polít. Exter./Madrid,* 19:105, mayo/junio 2005, p. 127–138, graph, photo, table)

Arias offers a table on China-Latin American trade circa 2004, asserts that US free trade agreements in the region may convert it into a privileged destination for Chinese foreign direct investment, and considers the implications of Sino-Latin American trade relations for Spain, which could use its privileged position within Latin America as a spring board to improve its relations with China.

1938 Asociación Mexicana de Estudios Internacionales. Congreso. *18th, Tuxtla Gutiérrez, Mexico,2004.* La paradiplomacia: las relaciones internacionales de los gobiernos locales. Coordinación de Sergio Rodríguez Gelfenstein. México: Cámara de Diputados, LIX Legislatura, Estados Unidos Mexicanos: Gobierno de Chiapas: M.A. Porrúa, 2006. 147 p.: bibl. (Conocer para decidir)

This text gathers six papers/lectures delivered at a panel of the 18th Congress of the Mexican International Studies Association (2004). Chapter authors are scholars, diplomats, and local politicians who discuss the theoretical and practical emergence of "paradiplomacy," or the insertion of local, provincial, and substate governments in international relations. Framed as the "other side of the coin" of the growing regionalism in the context of globalization, "paradiplomacy" offers greater opportunities for cross-border and multilevel cooperation in many issue areas such as economic and social development, human rights, environmental sustainability, migration, and more. Chapters also offer interesting insights into how multilevel diplomacy fits into a post-Cold War and post- 9/11 world.

1939 Barbosa, Walmir. América Latina sob nova ordem imperial. (*Estudos/Goiânia*, 32:5, maio 2005, p. 849–870, bibl.)

Historical structuralist/neo-Marxist critique of what the author describes as the development of neomercantilist imperialism and progressive militarization of political and social relations in Latin America, from the second term of former US President Clinton to Sept. 11, 2001. Discusses the limits of the Washington Consensus and resistance to it in Latin America.

1940 Benítez, Raúl. América Latina: operaciones de paz y acciones militares internacionales de las fuerzas armadas. (*Foro Int./México*, 47:1, enero/marzo 2007, p. 99–116, appendix, tables)

Very interesting analysis of the different forms of Latin American diplomatic and military participation in conflict mediation and peacekeeping operations since the early 20th century, and especially since the end of the Cold War. The participation of Latin American countries in various UN, OAS, and ad hoc regional peace missions is highlighted, ending with an analysis of the UN mission in Haiti (2004 onward) in which Argentina, Brazil, Chile, and Uruguay play a leading role. The Haiti mission represents a significant shift in thinking about regional humanitarian intervention and an important shift in fulfilling regional security responsibilities. Latin America's growing diplomatic and military participation in peace operations, both in the circum-Caribbean region and around the world, signals a change in the international division of labor in global security matters and a new presence of Latin America in the global security regime. This shift is also the result of a strategic move by politicians in the 1990s to give their militaries something constructive to do.

1941 Bittencourt, Gustavo and Rosario Domingo. Los determinantes de la IED y el efecto del Mercosur. (*Trimest. Econ.*, 71:281, enero/marzo 2004, p. 73–128, bibl., graphs, tables)

A solid econometric analysis of the effects of regional integration processes on foreign direct investment (FDI), looking specifically at Mercosur/l. This study identifies a model of Mercosur/l's FDI receipts in which internal market dynamism, export performance, and macroeconomic stability are key determinants. The study finds "significant and positive net effects" of the regional integration process on FDI.

1942 Brown, David S.; J. Christopher Brown; and Scott W. Desposato. Promoting and preventing political change through internationally funded NGO activity. (*LARR*, 42:1, 2007, p. 126–138, bibl., tables)

Joining a growing literature studying the political effects of NGOs at the national and local levels, this study asks whether international NGO funding promotes change or the status quo. The authors conduct a statistical (regression) analysis of voting behavior in Brazil to investigate whether the World Bank program Planaflora, which distributed development funds to local NGOs in the Amazonian state of Rondônia, impacted voting patterns for a conservative governor and a leftist president in the 1994–98 period. The authors find that NGO political effects depend on the design and implementation of NGO-centered aid programs as well as which politicians claim credit for the program.

1943 Brunelle, Dorval. Estados Unidos, el ALCA y los parámetros de gobierno global. (*Relac. Int./México*, 94, enero/abril 2006, p. 33–44)

A critique of the Free Trade Area of the Americas (FTAA) project and a review of regional resistances to it. FTAA's model is NAFTA, but the latter's free trade governance model reflects only US (and Canadian) interests.

1944 The Bush doctrine and Latin America. Edited by Gary Prevost and Carlos Oliva Campos. New York: Palgrave Macmillan, 2007. 261 p.: bibl., ill., index, maps.

Collection of essays presenting leftist intellectuals' critiques of the George W. Bush administration's policies in the region. Bibliography includes many Spanish and Portuguese language sources that may be useful to those interested in critical leftist and socialist thinking in Latin America during the G. W. Bush administration.

1945 Cardozo, Elsa. La gobernabilidad democrática regional y el papel (des)integrador de la energía. (*Nueva Soc.*, 204, julio/agosto 2006, p. 136–149, bibl.)

Considers two views of energy politics—energy as a power resource and energy as a sociopolitical resource—and which is more important for regional democratic governance.

1946 China y América Latina: nuevos enfoques sobre cooperación y desarrollo: una segunda ruta de la seda? Compilación de Sergio M. Cesarin y Carlos Moneta. Buenos Aires: BID-INTAL: Red de Centros de Estudios de Asia y el Pacífico de América Latina y el Caribe (REDEALAP); Washington, D.C.: Banco Interamericano de Desarrollo, Depto. de Integración y Programas Regionales, División de Integración, Comercio y Asuntos Hemisféricos, 2005. 312 p.: bibl., ill.

Edited volume draws together Latin American experts (researchers, academics, government advisers) specializing in China at REDEALAP, Latin America's leading network of East Asia specialists. China represents both better opportunities and potential competition for Latin American countries; therefore, Latin American countries must strengthen their bargaining power and negotiating skills by developing their human resources and expertise on China. Contributors in Part I provide analyses of the economic and political realities inside China, while contributors in Part II consider Sino-Latin American relations with a view to identifying an agenda for cooperation. Useful tables, bibliography, and the chapter on internet usage in China and its implications for future Latin American bilateral and regional relations with China will interest many researchers. Published through a joint project of the IADB, the Instituto para la Integración de America Latina y el Caribe (INTAL), and REDEALAP.

1947 Citroni, Gabriella. La libertad de asociación y reunión en la Convención Europea y en la Convención Americana sobre Derechos Humanos. (*Agenda Int.*, 10:20, 2004, p. 113–148)

Useful discussion comparing the jurisprudence of the Inter-American and European courts on human rights concerning the freedoms of association and assembly. While the European Court's jurisprudence is far more developed, both courts offer original and innovative decisions that can provide important references for each other.

1948 Community rights and corporate responsibility: Canadian mining and oil companies in Latin America. Edited by Liisa L. North, Timothy David Clark, and Viviana Patroni. Toronto: Between the lines, 2006. 253 p.: bibl., index.

Interesting collection of papers first presented at a conference held at York Univ. (Toronto) in Spring 2002 that brought together academics, NGO activists, and Canadian government representatives. Chapters critically analyze the impact and challenges of the growing foreign direct investment of Canadian mining corporations in Latin America since the 1990s (dubbed the region's "third mining boom"). Particularly valuable is that issues of indigenous and rural peoples' rights, environmental degradation, and dependent development within the neoliberal framework are addressed.

1949 Cornejo, Romer. China: un nuevo actor en el escenario latinoamericano. (*Nueva Soc.*, 200, nov./dic. 2005, p. 13–24, bibl.)

Very interesting review of Sino-Latin American relations with particular reference to official perspectives from the US, Latin America, and China. Whether one considers China's new importance for Latin America to be a threat or an opportunity, China is clearly in the driver's seat, while Latin American and US responses are merely reactive.

1950 Creamer, Germán. Regionalismo abierto en la Comunidad Andina: ¿creación o desviación de comercio? (*Trimest. Econ.*, 71:281, enero/marzo 2004, p. 45–71, bibl., tables)

Solid economic analysis showing that

the establishment of the Andean Community's free trade zone and its common external tariff has led to trade creation, as the hypothesis of "open regionalism" posits. The author concludes with policy considerations for deepening integration and open regionalism in the Andean Community.

1951 Criminalización de los poderes: corrupción y tráfico de drogas. Compilación de Jean Rivelois, Jaime Preciado Coronado y Marcos Pablo Moloeznik. Guadalajara, Mexico: Univ. de Guatemala, Centro Universitario de Ciencias Sociales y Humanidades; Zapopan, Mexico: Centro Universitario de Ciencias Económico Administrativas, 2004. 300 p.: bibl., ill., map.

This thoughtful and interesting edited volume considers the theoretical and practical dilemmas in addressing drug trafficking and closing the spaces of corruption that allow it to flourish in the context of a globalized free market. The territoriality of powerful drug cartels and official corruption at local and state levels contrasts with the deterritorialized nature of drug trafficking, money laundering operations, and tax havens in the global free market. Globalization creates a power vacuum in which these problems flourish while they also skew development. As a result, the state is unable to act without a militarized response that further undermines respect for the rule of law, guarantees of public security based on human rights, democratic politics, and equitable development. Contributors offer multidisciplinary and multitheoretical approaches, drawing on empirical evidence from across Latin America while challenging the local-state-interstate-global levels of analysis framework of mainstream international relations. The editors call for an integrated policy approach that places the role of the state—based on the rule of law and democratic debate—at the forefront of political solutions.

1952 Deblock, Christian; Dorval Brunelle; and **Michèle Rioux.** Globalización, competencia y gobernanza: el surgimiento de un espacio jurídico transnacional en las Américas. (*Foro Int./México*, 44:1, enero/marzo 2004, p. 66–102)
Very densely written (or poorly

translated) constructivist musing on the challenges of creating effective governance structures for investment and competition within neoliberal globalization processes, with specific attention to the Americas. A new model of international economic integration has emerged that is centered upon multinational corporations and their networks rather than states. This model results in an "impossible triangle" of international economic cooperation, that is, the impossibility of reconciling the autonomy of markets, international regulation, and state sovereignty.

1953 Deustua C., Alejandro. Perú, Bolivia y Chile: por una nueva relación trilateral. (*Polít. Int./Lima*, 75, enero/marzo 2004, p. 15–32)
Thoughtful consideration of the prospects for deeper cooperation between Peru, Bolivia, and Chile, despite a history of conflict and rivalry among these three states. Presents an analysis of the political, economic, and security dimensions of their relations, both bilaterally and as a group.

1954 Escribano Úbeda-Portugués, José. La dimensión europea de la política exterior española hacia América latina: política internacional de los primeros gobiernos socialistas. Madrid: Visión Net, 2005. 335 p.: bibl.
A very detailed diplomatic history describing the political, economic, and commercial aspects of Spain's activist role in promoting closer relations between the EU and "Iberoamérica," a term coined by the Spanish government in pursuing this policy from the mid-1980s to the mid-1990s. The period corresponds to the first Socialist governments led by D. Felipe González (1982–96) and Spain's accession to the European Community in 1986. This book provides a detailed chronology and description of events as well as extensive governmental, EU, and other diplomatic sources and several useful empirical tables.

1955 Escribano Úbeda-Portugués, José. El espacio eurolatinoamericano: perspectivas para la cooperación y el comercio. Madrid: CIDEAL, 2007. 233 p.: bibl.
Drawing from fields of law, political science, and economics, the author consid-

ers the deepening cooperative relations between the EU and Latin America as an example of the "new regionalism" in international relations and constitutive of a distinct Euro-Latin American "space." Political and security cooperation, trade, and other aspects of EU-Latin American relations are examined, supported by interesting conceptual tables, an extensive bibliography, and an appendix with documents from recent EU-Latin American meetings and summits.

1956 Europa y América Latina: el otro diálogo transatlántico. Dirección de José María Beneyto. Coordinación de Patricia Argerey. Madrid: Biblioteca Nueva: Instituto Univ. de Estudios Europeos de la Univ. CEU San Pablo, 2006. 324 p: bibl., ill., maps. (Col. La Sociedad internacional contemporánea; 2)

An interesting collection of Spanish and Latin American scholars, diplomats, and governmental officials specialized in EU-Latin American Relations, economics, and integration processes. As both the EU and Latin American countries have been interested in fostering closer economic, political, and cultural cooperation since the 1990s, many obstacles remain, including EU tariff and non-tariff barriers to Latin American products, the overvaluation of the Euro (from 2002–2005), the continuing dominance of the US in Latin America, and growing economic ties between Latin America and East Asia, particularly China. Numerous tables and figures offer a useful snapshot of EU-Latin American economic relations since the 1990s.

1957 Faust, Jörg. Latin America, Chile and East Asia: policy-networks and successful diversification. (*J. Lat. Am. Stud.*, 36:4, Nov. 2004, p. 743–770, tables)

Solid article focusing on the development of relations between Latin America and East Asia, with a particular focus on Chile's successful diversification of external relations with that region through the development of policy networks. Inter-regional relations between Latin America and East Asia are not sufficiently explained by neo-realist, structural-economic, or cultural-historical approaches. Rather, domestic or second-level explanations are more salient, both for Latin America generally and for

Chile particularly, given the profound economic and political transformations occurring across Latin America at the domestic level in recent years in the context of neoliberal globalization. In periods of political and economic realignment, the rearrangement of political coalitions and conflicts has a significant impact on foreign policy strategies.

1958 Fazio Vengoa, Hugo. La Unión Europea y América Latina: una historia de encuentros y desencuentros. Bogotá: Univ. de Los Andes, Facultad de Ciencias Sociales, CESO, 2006. 134 p.: bibl.

The author presents a critical historical-structural approach to EU-Latin American relations in the context of globalization that differs from more optimistic accounts. The "EU-phoria" of the early 1990s about cultivating new inter-regional relations between the EU and Latin America and the Caribbean has given way to indifference and skepticism today.

1959 Gálvez, Eduardo. Estrategias de desarrollo y políticas públicas en la Comunidad del Pacífico. (*Estud. Int./Santiago*, 36:144, enero/marzo 2004, p. 51–65)

Part of an interesting special issue focused on APEC and the Pacific region, this leading Chilean scholar on the topic considers four lessons or points of comparison between Latin America and Asian-Pacific states, including: development strategies, processes of democratization, free trade agreements, and preventing and coping with financial crises. Countries on each side of the Pacific region can learn useful and important lessons from each other.

1960 Giacalone, Rita. La Comunidad Sudamericana de Naciones: ¿una alianza entre izquierda y empresarios? (*Nueva Soc.*, 202, marzo/abril 2006, p. 74–86, bibl., ill.)

Helpful review of the emergence of the Comunidad Sudamericana de Naciones (CSN), established between Brazil, Argentina, and Venezuela in Dec. 2004, one year after the Andean Community of Nations and Mercosur/l concluded negotiations to establish a free trade treaty between the two groups. This was Brazil's (President Cardoso's) idea, posed as an alternative to NAFTA and a vehicle to challenge Mexico's regional diplomatic leadership. It is based on an alliance between private business and government in Brazil, and will help Brazil achieve its regional geopolitical goals.

1961 Girault, Christian A. Del TLCAN al Área de Libre Comercio de las Américas: perspectivas geopolíticas de la integración. (*Foro Int./México*, 44:1, enero/marzo 2004, p. 103–125)

Very interesting article that offers a Braudellian geohistorical approach to integration and the "new regionalism" in the Western hemisphere in light of neoliberal globalization and post-Cold War changes. The traditional binary division of the hemisphere into the Anglo-Saxon North and the Latin South is giving way to three zones: The North American zone, which includes Mexico via NAFTA; the fragile Middle America zone, which encompasses the Central American and circum-Caribbean countries (including Colombia, Venezuela, and even Ecuador, given the latter's dollarization); and the South American zone, which is anchored by Brazil via Mercosur/l. Middle America's ties to and dependency on the North American zone make it vulnerable to economic crisis and political fragmentation as well as populist backlash. The South American zone has tighter ties with the European Union and the Asia-Pacific region, which concern the US.

1962 Grabendorff, Wolf. Relaciones triangulares en mundo unipolar: America del Norte, la Unión Europea. (*Estud. Int./Santiago*, 38:149, abril/junio 2005, p. 21–49, bibl.)

An interesting analysis by an authoritative scholar of inter-American relations focused on the functioning of the "Atlantic Triangle" in the process of globalization. Latin America seems to be fragmenting itself geopolitically even further into North and South subregions along the fault lines of NAFTA and Mercosur/l. Discussion includes attention to regional issues pertinent to the three different parts of the triangle: the South American (Brazil-Argentina) "Consenso de Buenos Aires" as a challenge to the North American "Washington Consensus"; the political demise of the US-led FTAA negotiations; and the emergence of environmental issues as an area of South American-EU cooperation that further challenges US or North American positions.

1963 Guadarrama González, Pablo. El pensamiento de la integración latinoamericana ante la globalización. (*Cuad. Am./México*, 1:103, enero/feb. 2004, p. 34–59)

A sophisticated and engaging historical-structuralist (Marxist) consideration of past Latin American thinking about regional integration in the context of the global expansion of capitalism and of current directions for contemporary Latin American thinking about regional integration in the context of neoliberal globalization. This thoughtful Cuban academic calls for the development of new Latin American thinking that analyzes the current challenges of social development in a globalized/globalizing world, much as the region's thinkers had previously done in developing dependency theory, liberation theology, and a philosophy of human liberation.

1964 Hacia una política de cooperación en seguridad y defensa con Iberoamérica. Madrid: Ministerio de Defensa, Secretaría General Técnica, 2006. 222 p.: bibl., ill., maps. (Monografías del CESEDEN; 84)

Unusual but interesting collection of papers by Spanish defense intellectuals (based in the Spanish military and academia) who discuss the present and future opportunities for security cooperation between the EU and Latin America. Chap. 6 offers a rare assessment of the defense industries in Latin America in light of regional and global security regimes and proposes a model of EU-Latin American defense industry cooperation that "can promote economical (sic) and social development" in Latin America "without altering the geostrategic balance in the region" (p. 214).

1965 Heredia, Edmundo A. Relaciones internacionales latinoamericanas. Vol. 1, Gestación y nacimiento. Buenos Aires: Nuevohacer, Grupo Editor Latinoamericano, 2006. 346 p.: bibl.

Heredia presents a scholarly diplomatic history of the earliest years of Latin America's international relations, focusing on the formative decade of 1810–20. His study includes attention to the region's commercial, politico-diplomatic, and security concerns vis-à-vis European powers, the emerging power of the US, and other nascent Latin American states. The region's first independence-era treaties, early integrationist ideas, and the origins of the region's territorial conflicts are also considered. Valuable bibliography based on archival research in Spain and several Latin American countries, but not Brazil.

1966 Herrera, Beethoven. Globalización: el proceso real y financiero. Bogotá: Univ. Nacional de Colombia, Sede Bogotá, Facultad de Ciencias Económicas, 2005. 351 p.: bibl., ill.

A thoughtful, critical scholarly analysis of the theories of neoliberal globalization measured against the realities its practice has generated for Latin America. Clearly written without polemics by a respected emeritus professor of political economy at the Univ. Nacional de Colombia, Herrera shows the limits, contradictions, and challenges that neoliberal (or "semi-liberal") globalization poses for Colombia and other countries of the region. He calls for greater emphasis on developing Latin America's human resources (via education and professional development) as well as a new debate and social consensus on what development means in Colombia and beyond.

1967 Katz, Claudio. El rediseño de América Latina: ALCA, MERCOSUR y ALBA. Buenos Aires: Ediciones Luxemburg, 2006. 136 p.: bibl.

Neo-Marxist critical analysis of neoliberalism in Latin America with a particular focus on comparing three alternative economic cooperation schemes in the Americas: the neoliberal Free Trade Area of the Americas (and its subsequent patchwork of bilateral free trade agreements with the US); Mercosur/1; and the Alternativa Bolivariana para Nuestra América. The first provides only neoliberal domination without integration. The second offers only regulatory capitalism with reformist rhetoric. Only the third offers emancipatory content that can move the region beyond capitalism. Katz's analysis offers insights into the emergent crisis of neoliberalism since the 1990s and, significantly, the weakening of its domestic proponents in Latin America.

1968 Klaveren, Alberto van. Las relaciones políticas europeo-latinoamericanas. (*Nueva Soc.*, 189, enero/feb. 2004, p. 54–68)

Authoritative consideration of issues and common interests in the biregional relationship between the European Union (EU) and Latin America by a leading Chilean IR scholar, foreign policy official, and (then) Chilean ambassador to the EU. He argues that there is potential for far deeper relations between the two regions. Part of a special issue focused on EU-Latin American relations, with other essays by Lawrence Whitehead, Wolf Grabendorf, and other notable Latin American and European specialists in the field.

1969 Laurienti, Jerry M. The U.S. military and human rights promotion: lessons from Latin America. Westport, Conn.: Praeger Security International, 2007. 185 p.: bibl., index.

Hoping to fill a large gap in the literature, the author offers three case studies—Bolivia, Colombia, and Venezuela—to argue that the US military's human rights promotion efforts can serve as a positive influence on Latin American militaries, but the key to success rests with the level of democratic development in the countries in question.

1970 Leogrande, William M. A poverty of imagination: George W. Bush's policy in Latin America. (*J. Lat. Am. Stud.*, 39:2, May 2007, p. 355–385)

A commentary by a leading liberalist scholar of inter-American relations charging that George W. Bush put Latin American policy in the hands of neoconservative "cold warriors," leading to a dramatic deterioration of Washington's reputation and a worsening of relations with the region.

1971 León-Manríquez, José Luis. China-América Latina: una relación económica diferenciada. (*Nueva Soc.*, 203, mayo/junio 2006, p. 28–47, ill.)

This article provides an interesting and useful discussion of the different effects of growing Sino-Latin American trade in recent years, with some winners (Venezuela, Chile, Brazil, Argentina, and Peru) and some losers (Mexico and Central America). The difference depends on the nature or structure of trade relations and investments. Includes attention to Cuba.

1972 Levitt, Barry S. A desultory defense of democracy: OAS resolution 1080 and the Inter-American Democratic Charter.

(*Lat. Am. Polit. Soc.*, 48:3, Fall 2006, p. 93–123, bibl.)

Persuasively challenging the thesis on the democratizing role of regional intergovernmental organizations, Levitt argues that the application of OAS Resolution 1080 and/or the Inter-American Democratic Charter in various cases between 1991 and 2002 shows a very mixed record of OAS responses to democratic crises in the region. Domestic politics rather than structural or systemic traits of the inter-American system best explain the foreign policy responses to crises of democracy in the region.

1973 Mace, Gordon and **Hugo Loiseau.** Cooperative hegemony and summitry in the Americas. (*Lat. Am. Polit. Soc.*, 47:4, Winter 2005, p. 107–134, bibl., tables)

The authors examine the periodic Summits of the Americas since 1994 to test the concept of "cooperative hegemony." Specifically, two dimensions of "power-sharing" under cooperative hegemony in the inter-American system are considered: agenda setting and institutionalization. The authors' results are mixed. They find broader and deeper agenda-setting via an interesting content analysis of Summit documents that supports the cooperative hegemony thesis. However, the institutionalization measure is not supported, as the summits actually undermined or challenged OAS mechanisms, relegating the latter as "technical arms" of the Summit of the Americas substructures. Perhaps most useful is the authors' discussion of the two "parallel substructures" of hemispheric regionalism—the Summit of the Americas machinery and the OAS machinery.

1974 Manzella, Daniel Gustavo. South Africa-Mercosur: "a strategic partnership." (*Unisa Lat. Am. Rep.*, 20:1, 2004, p. 20–38, tables)

The author is an Argentine navy officer who discusses common interests between South Africa and Mercosur member countries and presents a model of a strategic partnership. His participation in the Executive National Security Programme at the South African National Defense College in 2003 is an interesting example of Mercosur's outreach to South Africa and of the internationalist turn of some Latin American militaries in recent years.

1975 Martins, Estevão Chaves de Rezende. O alargamento da União Européia e a América Latina. (*Rev. Bras. Polít. Int.*, 47:2, 2004, p. 5–24, tables)

A skeptical assessment of the possibility of closer EU-Latin American relations, partly because the identity of "Latin America" is so vague. However, the EU may choose to develop closer relations with similar economic integration blocs such as Mercosul or the Andean Community.

1976 Mayobre, Eduardo. El sueño de una compañía energética sudamericana: antecedentes y perspectivas políticas de Petroamérica. (*Nueva Soc.*, 204, julio/agosto 2006, p. 159–175)

The author discusses Petroamérica and other petroleum-related regional cooperative schemes initiated recently by Venezuela. The author holds that Petroamérica is an idea that in other circumstances might have been well received, fulfilling SELA's earlier vision of a Latin American multinational enterprise. The article provides a valuable review of the history of other regional cooperation and integration schemes, both formal and informal, in Latin America.

1977 Nieto, Clara. Los amos de la guerra: el intervencionismo de Estados Unidos en América Latina: de Eisenhower a G.W. Bush. México: Debate, 2006. 649 p.: bibl., index. (Debate historias)

Highly critical journalistic account of US-Latin American relations from the Cuban Revolution up to the George W. Bush administration, now in its sixth edition outside of the US. Nieto served as Colombian ambassador to Cuba from 1977–80 and as head of UNESCO's regional office for Latin America based in Havana from 1984–86. An eclectic collection of leftist sources can be found in the bibliography.

1978 Pérez Le-Fort, Martín. APEC y la seguridad energética: una visión desde América Latina. (*Estud. Int./Santiago*, 36:144, enero/marzo 2004, p. 139–159)

Part of an interesting special issue focused on APEC and the Pacific region, this article considers the implications of APEC's attention to energy security for Latin America.

1979 Pevehouse, Jon C. Democracy from above: regional organizations and democratization. Cambridge, U.K.; New York: Cambridge Univ. Press, 2005. 248 p.: bibl., ill., index.

Based on his PhD dissertation, the author presents a highly quantitative statistical analysis testing the hypothesized links between regional intergovernmental organizations and the transition to and survival of democracy in member states. The author seeks to contribute to the international organization literature and draws on global data sets and cases from Europe and Latin America. However, little depth is offered in his top-down view of the role of Latin American regional organizations such as the OAS and Mercosur in democratization within states. The author's disconnect with the political and institutional realities on the ground in Latin America goes so far as to assert that Guatemala "successfully completed a transition to democracy in the 1982–1983 period" (p. 186). This work is of minimal empirical or theoretical usefulness to students of inter-American relations or Latin American politics.

1980 Pion-Berlin, David and Harold Trinkunas. Attention deficits: why politicians ignore defense policy in Latin America. (*LARR*, 42:3, 2007, p. 76–100, bibl., tables)

The authors consider various reasons why Latin American civilian politicians tend to ignore defense policy issues (goal setting, policy formulation and implementation, etc.) and even the development of any defense policy expertise, and instead focus their attention on coup avoidance. A useful second-image contribution to an understudied aspect of civilian-military relations.

1981 Ponte Iglesias, María Teresa. Los pueblos indígenas ante el derecho internacional. (*Agenda Int.*, 10:20, 2004, p. 149–172)

Interesting discussion of the history of international human rights law regarding indigenous peoples, from the Spanish Natural Law tradition to more recent efforts in international and regional forums to define particular juridical rights and protections for indigenous peoples. The author traces the emergence of soft law that progressively recognizes the identity and collective rights of indigenous peoples. In particular, recent UN and OAS declarations on the rights of indigenous peoples are discussed along with a look at their application in Peru.

1982 Prevost, Gary and Robert Weber. The Free Trade Area of the Americas in the context of U.S.-Latin American relations. (*in* Globalization and development in Latin America. Edited by Richard L. Harris. Whitby, Canada: De Sitter, 2005, p. 24–45, bibl., tables)

This book chapter is highly critical of the FTAA and other neoliberal free trade agreements such as NAFTA. It includes useful tables comparing partisan votes in the US Congress on international trade and fast track authorization as well as a discussion of Latin American skepticism about free trade agreements in light of broader economic and political interests.

1983 Ramírez Díaz, Karina. Las relaciones comerciales entre la Unión Europea y América Latina: especial referencia al MERCOSUR y a la Comunidad Andina. (*Integr. Comer.*, 6:16, enero/junio 2002, p. 3–30, bibl., graphs)

Provides a descriptive overview of EU-Latin American trade relations since the 1990s, with a special focus on Mercosur and the Andean Community.

Ramjas Saavedra, J.S. Gabriel Arthur. Las relaciones de Colombia y América Latina con Europa. See item **2123.**

1984 Ramos, Danielly Silva. A política externa chinesa para a América Latina. (*Estudos/Goiânia*, 31:5, maio 2004, p. 947–963, bibl.)

Historical overview of Sino-Latin American relations during the Cold War period (viz., 1949–89) from a Brazilian perspective, tracing China's foreign policy shift from North-South contestation to South-South cooperation.

1985 Redes transnacionales en la Cuenca de los Huracanes: un aporte a los estudios interamericanos. Coordinación de Francis Pisani *et al.* México: Cámara de Diputados, LX Legislatura, Estados Unidos Mexicanos: ITAM: Miguel Ángel Porrúa, 2007. 404 p.: bibl., ill., map. (Conocer para decidir)

Originally presented at a panel at the 2006 Latin American Studies Assn. (LASA) meeting, this interesting collection of papers cultivates a fresh approach to inter-American relations by focusing on transnational and translocal networks operating in the circum-Caribbean region. Through theoretical chapters and empirical case studies, contributors consider the proliferation of transnational relations, flows, and networks among non-state actors in the region and their impact on interstate relations. Such a multilevel revisioning of inter-American relations suggests that the US capacity to influence the region is less asymmetrical or unidimensional than traditional state-centric approaches to inter-American relations would see it.

1986 Regional financial cooperation. Edited by Jose Antonio Ocampo. Santiago: United Nations Economic Commission for Latin America and the Caribbean; Washington, D.C.: Brookings Institute Press, 2006. 375 p.: bibl., ill., index.

This is an outstanding and clearly written comparative study of the role of regional financial institutions and their potential for complementing and completing international financial regimes. Using the European Union experience as a model and measure of regional financial integration, this expertly edited volume analyzes the political economy of regional cooperation and integration schemes in Latin America, Africa, Asia, and the Middle East. Two chapters specifically devoted to Latin America assess the prospects for deeper cooperation in Mercosur and the experiences of financial cooperation in the Andean, Central American, and Caribbean subregions. This book envisions regional financial cooperation as a key step in promoting greater South-South cooperation and development as well as a key requirement for a more meaningful and representative global financial architecture. The text also offers an excellent introductory chapter by Ocampo and very thoughtful policy recommendations.

1987 Rivarola Puntigliano, Andrés. Global shift: the U.N. system and the new regionalism in Latin America. (*Lat. Am. Polit. Soc.*, 49:1, Spring 2007, p. 89–112, bibl.)

Rivarola, an economic historian, presents a brilliant, engaging, and theoretically eclectic analysis that explores the "new regionalism" as the other side of globalization in the post-Cold War period, with specific reference to the emergence of Latin American regionalism as "countercenter" in the emergence of new normative rules in the international system. Drawing from Rosenau's notion of alternative and shifting "spheres of authority" (SOAs) within globalization, Shils' approach to center-periphery relations and the formation of "countercenters," and constructivist attention to rules and processes of rulemaking in IR, Rivarola explores the "sophisticated articulation" in Latin American foreign policy today and the new economic and political networks and formal agreements through which Latin American countries try to expand their influence, refine their diplomacy, and protect their interests. While some may question the author's notion of the "UN System" as a site of a new global SOA and source of normative and moral legitimacy, others will appreciate this article's empirical and theoretical richness and especially its contribution to inserting "a Latin American perspective into the current theoretical debate"(s) in the field of IR (p. 105). A fascinating read for students of IR theory as well as Latin American foreign policy and inter-American relations.

1988 Rocha V., Alberto. Un dilema político en la encrucijada histórica del proceso de integración regional de América Latina y el Caribe. (*Sociologias/Porto Alegre*, 6:11, jan./junho 2004, p. 64–87, bibl.)

Somewhat polemical, quite skeptical, but useful summary of the status of various subregional integration schemes in Latin America and the Caribbean, which remain economically weak and politically in disarray. The autonomous, independent regional integration project of Latin America and the Caribbean is threatened by the hegemonic continental integration project of the US, raising the specter of a pernicious neo-Pan-Americanism for the 21st century. However, there is hope, as the author offers an alternative project for healthy regional integration.

1989 Rodríguez Díaz, María del Rosario. La misión diplomática de Elihu Root en América Latina y el Caribe, 1906. (*Rev. Antropol./São Paulo*, 47:2, julho/dez. 2004, p. 129–148, bibl.)

A fascinating study of Elihu Root's writings relating to this US Secretary of State's travels in Latin America and the Caribbean on his way to the Third Pan-American Conference in Rio de Janeiro in 1906. Root's vision of and discourse about the region reflect a benevolent, paternalistic imperialism struggling with how to handle the region's economic and political instability. Root's kinder, gentler approach represented the conservative wing of the Republican Party then in power, questioning Teddy Roosevelt's "Big Stick" policies and foreshadowing elements of FDR's Good Neighbor Policy.

1990 Rosenblum, Marc R. Moving beyond the policy of no policy: emigration from Mexico and Central America. (*Lat. Am. Polit. Soc.*, 46:4, Winter 2004, p. 91–125, bibl., graphs, tables)

Drawing on numerous interviews with elites in Mexico and other circum-Caribbean states, the author shows that migrant-sending or source states can and do influence US immigration policy. This understudied aspect of migration studies in the region suggests that migration policy-making is increasingly transnational, intermestic, multilevel, and regionalized in nature.

1991 Saavedra Rivano, Neantro. Las nuevas afinidades regionales en el Pacífico: ensayo de construcción de un marco conceptual. (*Estud. Int./Santiago*, 36:144, enero/marzo 2004, p. 67–80)

Part of an interesting special issue focused on APEC and the Pacific region, this article offers an engaging and eclectic—if unfinished—conceptual sketch that tries to make sense of the institutional dynamism and diversity of integration schemes in the Pacific region. The various "organizaciones de asociación económica" (OAEs) found in the region are part of broader political economic spaces and deeper political economic processes that constitute contemporary versions of ongoing geopolitical transformations rooted in human history.

1992 Sánchez Flores, Alejandro A. La cláusula democrática en el sistema interamericano como norma de *soft law*. (*Agenda Int.*, 11:21, 2004, p. 137–156)

Presents a thoughtful and interesting legal analysis of the inter-American soft law on the defense and promotion of democratic values. This soft law norm is programmatic, prospective, and aspirational but lacks directly binding or obligatory juridical effects.

1993 Sandoval Peña, Natalia. Balance y perspectivas del Tratado de Libre Comercio de América del Norte: el caso del tratamiento jurídico de la inversión extranjera. (*Agenda Int.*, 11:21, 2004, p. 47–103, tables)

Provides a thorough legal analysis of the juridical mechanisms of investment protection and promotion in Chapter 11 of NAFTA and evaluates their functioning in the resolution of conflicts in several specific cases. Also provides a useful table summarizing these cases of claims against the three states parties.

1994 Saraiva, Miriam Gomes. A União Européia como ator internacional e os países de Mercosul. (*Rev. Bras. Polít. Int.*, 47:1, 2004, p. 84–111, bibl., tables)

Excellent scholarly discussion of the development of relations between the European Union (EU) and Mercosur/l from 1991 to 2003, including helpful attention to prior EU relations with the Rio Group in the mid- to late 1980s. Saraiva provides a detailed analysis of the political dimension of the Inter-regional Framework Cooperation Agreement, signed by the EU and Mercosur/l in 1995.

1995 Scollay, Robert and **Fernando González-Vigil.** Los acuerdos comerciales en la Asia-Pacífico de cara a los objetivos de APEC. (*Estud. Int./Santiago*, 36:144, enero/marzo 2004, p. 7–29)

Part of an interesting special issue devoted to APEC and the Pacific region, this article considers whether preferential trade agreements are "building blocks" or "stumbling blocks" in achieving the Bogor Goals for trade liberalization in APEC. The uncoordinated proliferation of such agreements is the biggest challenge.

1996 Shixue, Jiang. Recent development of Sino-Latin American relations and its implications. (*Estud. Int./Santiago*, 38:152, enero/marzo 2006, p. 19–41, tables)

Very interesting and authoritative review of Sino-Latin American relations and China's economic and political interests in developing and deepening those relations by a leading scholar of Sino-Latin relations.

1997 Staudt, Kathleen A. Gender, governance, and globalization at borders: femicide at the US-Mexico border. (*in* Global governance: feminist perspectives. Edited by Shirin M. Rai and Georgina Waylen. New York: Palgrave MacMillan, 2008, p. 234–253)

Sobering book chapter that focuses on the murders of hundreds of women and girls in Ciudad Juárez since the creation of NAFTA. Staudt examines these murders in light of the neoliberal governance structures at the US-Mexican border and analyzes the cross-border organizing strategies by activists at local, national, and transnational levels aimed at trying to get governments to respond to this gender violence. Accountable governance structures on this issue remain elusive.

1998 Stuhldreher, Amalia. La regionalización como estrategia frente a la globalización: la concepción de política externa conjunta en los bloques de América Latina y el Caribe. (*Estud. Int./Santiago*, 37:145, abril/junio 2004, p. 25–50, bibl.)

Compares the advances of the Comunidad Andina de Naciones (CAN), the Mercado Común Centroamericano (MCCA), CARICOM, and Mercosur/l in conceiving and implementing a coordinated foreign policy as a test both of integration and of theories of integration. The author presents an interesting empirical discussion of the mechanisms, actions, and limitations of these subregional integration organizations in developing a coordinated foreign policy. Then she discusses these cases from the perspectives of various IR and integration theoretical frameworks, including Deutsch's transactionalism, functionalism and neofunctionalism, realism and neorealism, neoliberalism or liberal institutionalism, and constructivism. Curiously, (neo)Marxist, historical-structuralist, and IPE approaches are not included in the theoretical discussion.

1999 Taffet, Jeffrey F. Foreign aid as foreign policy: the Alliance for Progress in Latin America. New York: Routledge, 2007. 301 p., 8 p. of plates: bibl., ill., index.

Taffet offers a careful, scholarly historical assessment of the Alliance for Progress program, showing how it was neither a true "alliance" nor really about economic progress. Rather, the author soberly demonstrates how unclear goals, unclear means for its implementation, and lack of direction made the Alliance for Progress a political tool to "help friends, hurt enemies" and maintain US dominance in the region. Appendices include key documents; a rich selection of sources and citations can be mined in the 40 pages of endnotes.

2000 Tickner, Arlene B. Latin American IR and the primacy of "lo práctico." (*Int. Stud. Rev.*, 10:4, Dec. 2008, p. 735–748, bibl.)

An interesting review article of Latin American theoretical and practical approaches to IR since WWII. Taking up the question posed by critical IR theorists in North America and Europe as to whether IR "looks different" from peripheral regions, Tickner traces the scholarship of Latin American IR specialists, who have had to be more interested in questions of state autonomy, the role of the state, and practical foreign policy considerations than "theory for theory's sake." Tickner finds a significant melding of indigenous dependency theory (which was misunderstood when taken up by North American scholars) with imported North American IR theories such as Morganthauian realism and complex interdependence. Latin American IR scholars have also been more likely to blur the lines between "IR" and "comparative politics" than their northern counterparts. Includes a very helpful bibliography of key Latin American IR scholars since the 1960s.

2001 Vargas, Edmundo. La lucha contra la corrupción en la agenda regional e internacional: las convenciones de la OEA y de la ONU. (*Nueva Soc.*, 194, nov./dic. 2004, p. 133–148)

Provides an interesting discussion of inter-American and UN conventions aimed at stopping political corruption inside states. These conventions create innovative interstate definitions, obligations, and response mechanisms. However, states will also need to find more effective ways of punishing not only the public officials who engage in corrupt practices, but also the transnational businesses that initiate them.

2002 Weeks, Gregory Bart. U.S. and Latin American relations. New York: Pearson Longman, 2008. 290 p.: bibl., ill., index, maps.

This solid introductory college textbook to inter-American relations incorporates realist, liberal institutionalist, and dependency approaches as frameworks for explaining the historical background and current issues in US-Latin American relations. Weeks offers useful insights and helpful bibliographic resources for more specialized readers as well as a solid introduction for a more general audience. Chapters on current policy issues include free trade and neoliberal reform, immigration, human rights and democracy, and drug trafficking and terrorism.

MEXICO AND CENTRAL AMERICA

ANDREW D. SELEE, *Director, Mexico Institute, Woodrow Wilson International Center for Scholars*

ONE OF THE MOST NOTABLE FEATURES of this review period is a series of books and articles that analyze Mexico's foreign policy in a comprehensive way and look for alternatives for the future. This focused research is a natural outgrowth of Mexico's transition to democracy and the need to develop a new consensus around foreign policy in a multiparty system. An excellent starting point is the collection edited by Schiavon, Spenser, and Vázquez Olivera, which provides both historical context and current debates (item **2014**). The volumes edited by Herrera-Lasso (item **2024**) and Navarrete (item **2034**), along with Pellicer de Brody's contribution (item **2030**), provide analysis from scholars and diplomats involved in the debates around Mexico's foreign policy.

Several highly original contributions on Mexico's relationship with the US were recently published. An excellent starting point is Meyer's masterful article on the development of Mexico's defensive nationalism vis-à-vis the US (item **2027**). Aguayo's *Almanaque México-Estados Unidos* is a particularly useful source of information on the nature of the relationship between the two countries (item **2004**). Contreras' book (now available in both Spanish and English) is an insightful account of US influence in Mexico, though it often veers into the anecdotal (item **2010**). Laveaga's essay on the US Congress provides a practical way of understanding congressional influence on the complex relationship between the two countries (item **2021**).

Several excellent works address the US-Mexico border, including the truly comprehensive work by Anderson and Gerber which looks at both the integration and the inequalities of the border region (item **2008**), and a companion article by Anderson (item **2007**). Mendoza's article suggests that NAFTA has had different impacts at the border than elsewhere in Mexico, a useful contribution to understanding border economics (item **2023**). Edited volumes by Payán Alvarado and Tabuenca Córdoba (item **2016**) and Flores and Peña Medina (item **2031**) provide useful analyses of regional debates on cross-border integration and cooperation.

The book by Ramos García examines the way security cooperation at the border has changed after 9/11 (item **2033**). His edited volume with Woo Morales looks more broadly at how Mexico, the US, and Canada are rethinking national security after 9/11 (item **2039**). An article by Gabriel, Jimenez, and MacDonald explores the reasons why security regimes have developed differently along the Canada-US and Mexico-US borders (item **2015**).

Several works of varying quality look at Mexico and Central America's increasing economic integration with the US. Golob provides a theoretically sophisticated analysis of how the Mexican government overcame domestic resistance to negotiate NAFTA, while Dombois explores the very uneven performance of the labor side agreement (items **2017** and **2012**, respectively). Furthermore, Saxe-Fernández decries Mexico's submission to US capital (item **2037**). Contributions by Fumero Paniagua, Rodríguez Holkemeyer, and Flórez-Estrada and Hernández explore the implications of the Central American Free Trade Agreement for Costa Rica (items **2044**, **2047**, and **2049**, respectively). A particularly useful work, published by Comex, looks at the integration between Costa Rica and Mexico since the implementation of their free trade agreement (item **2050**).

A growing body of work on Mexico's relationships with Latin America, Asia, and Africa appears here. A well-written book by Tello Díaz (item **2040**) and two academically grounded articles by Velázquez Flores and Sánchez Ramírez (items **2041** and **2035**) examine Mexico's important but increasingly conflicted relationship with Cuba. Muñoz chronicles Mexico's relationship with the Caribbean as an often forgotten third border (**2028**). Two interesting articles by López Villafañe and Zeraoui trace Mexico's relationship with China and the Magreb, northern Africa, respectively (items **2022** and **2042**).

Some useful historical analyses of Mexico and Central America's relationship with Europe and Brazil were reviewed here. Domínguez Ávila probes the history of Brazil's influence in Central America (item **2043**). Cordero Olivero and González Ibarra examine Mexico's complicated relationship with Franco's Spain (items **2011** and **2018**), while Ojeda Revah addresses Mexico's support for the Republican government of Spain in the context of great power politics before World War II (item **2029**).

Finally, two works trace important issues in Central America's evolving peace process. Zamora addresses the US role in blocking the Esquilipas and Contadora peace processes, while Saxon tells a personal story about the disappearance of his wife, a human rights advocate, in a book that sheds light on the difficulties of consolidating peace in the region (items **2051** and **2048**, respectively).

MEXICO

2003 Adventures into Mexico: American tourism beyond the border. Edited by Nicholas Dagen Bloom. Lanham, Md.: Rowman & Littlefield, 2006. 231 p.: bibl., index. (Jaguar books on Latin America series)

This edited collection looks at the encounters between American tourists and Mexicans in the 20th century. Essays included cover a variety of topics, from American tourism in Mexico City in the 1940s and beatnik travels to Mexico in the 1950s to the contradictions of the development of Cancún and the emergence of long-term US communities in the Lake Chapala and San Miguel de Allende regions.

2004 Aguayo, Sergio. Almanaque México-Estados Unidos. Con la colaboración de María Yolanda Argüello, Alejandro Cabello y Javier Treviño. México: Fondo de Cultura Económica: Mexico: Ideas y Palabras, 2005. 326 p.: bibl., index. (Tezontle)

This is an ambitious effort to provide valuable data on the US-Mexico relationship. The only work of its kind in either country, it covers everything from trade to migration to education and culture, looking at both comparisons and interconnections between the two countries.

2005 Aguirre, Robert D. Informal empire: Mexico and Central America in Victorian culture. Minneapolis: Univ. of Minnesota Press, 2005. 198 p.: bibl., ill., index, 1 map.

This book looks at the multiple encounters that Britain had with Mexico and Central America during the 19th century. The author argues that it is important to understand not only economic interactions, but also the social and cultural encounters to determine how elites on both sides constructed views of each other.

2006 América del Norte: una integración excluyente. Coordinación de Delia Montero Contreras y María Antonia Correa Serrano. México: Univ. Autónoma Metropolitana, Unidad Iztapalapa, División de Ciencias Sociales y Humanidades: Plaza y Valdés, 2007. 200 p.: ill. (Col. Extensión universitaria)

This edited book provides a critical assessment of Mexico's integration in NAFTA at the beginning of the 21st century. The chapters on Monterrey corporations and labor inequality are particularly interesting.

2007 Anderson, Joan B. The U.S.-Mexico border: a half century of change. (*Soc. Sci. J./New York*, 40:4, 2003, p. 536–554, bibl., maps)

Analyzes demographic trends in the US-Mexico border region. Notes that the population has increased dramatically and educational and economic indicators have improved overall. To a large extent the region shows a greater socioeconomic convergence than the two countries as a whole since Mexican border communities generally rank higher than the national average on income and educational statistics, while US border communities tend to rank lower than the national average.

2008 Anderson, Joan B. and James Gerber. Fifty years of change on the U.S.-Mexico border: growth, development, and quality of life. Photographs by Lisa Foster. Austin: Univ. of Texas Press, 2008. 275 p.: bibl., ill., index, maps.

This may be the most comprehensive analysis of the border region published in recent years. The authors explore both the extent of cross-border integration and way that existing inequalities affect quality of life and the possibilities of cross-border cooperation.

2009 Canchola Gutiérrez, Ulises. Práctica de México respecto del derecho internacional: consideraciones sobre la elaboración de un repertorio. (*Rev. Mex. Polít. Exter.*, 78, oct. 2006, p. 9–49)

Seeks to systematize Mexico's historical positions on key issues of international law, a cornerstone of the country's foreign policy. Suggests key commitments that Mexico still needs to apply internally and current debates in international law require Mexican policymakers to develop new positions.

2010 Contreras, Joseph. Tan lejos de Dios: el México moderno a la sombra de Estados Unidos. Traducción de Elia Olvera. México: Grijalbo, 2006. 276 p.: bibl., ill., index. (Actualidad)

This interesting book (now available in both English and Spanish) by a former *Newsweek* bureau chief looks at the way proximity to the US is shaping Mexico. The argument sometimes falls short, but the analysis of key trends shaping contemporary Mexico is well worth the read.

2011 Cordero Olivero, Immaculada. El espejo desenterrado: España en México, 1975–1982. Sevilla, Spain: Fundación El Monte; Guadalajara, Mexico: El Colegio de Jalisco, 2005. 337 p.: bibl., ill. (Col. América; 6)

This beautifully illustrated book looks at the relationship between Mexico and Spain during the transition from Franquismo. Includes a strong overview of the relations between the two countries during Franco's rule and several chapters that chronicle the thawing in relations as Spain pursued its transition towards democracy after Franco.

2012 Dombois, Rainer. La regulación laboral internacional en los Tratados de Libre Comercio: el caso de Acuerdo de Cooperación Laboral de América del Norte entre México, Canadá y los Estados Unidos. (*Foro Int./México*, 46:4, oct./dic. 2006, p. 741–761, bibl.)

Looks at the first 12 years of operation of the North American Labor Agreement, one of the side accords of NAFTA.

The research suggests that the agreement has contributed to a few innovative encounters among civil society and governmental actors in the three NAFTA countries, but it has achieved little else. In particular, the agreement appears to have no effect on the implementation of labor laws in the three countries or the resolution of conflicts, and even its activities to promote research and dialogue seem to be on the decline in recent years.

2013 La economía global: márgenes de maniobra para México y América Latina. Coordinación de Rosa María Piñon Antillón. México: Facultad de Ciencias Políticas y Sociales, UNAM: Delegación de la Comisión Europea en México, 2002. 422 p.: bibl., ill.

Collection of essays on Mexico's external relations, focusing on the economic ties with the US, Canada, and the EU. Essays present research on the dynamics of trade flows between Mexico and other countries, the highlights of the negotiations preceding the signing of trade agreements, and the implications of international trade links for domestic social policies. Essays are of high quality, very informative, and relevant to other Latin American countries. [L.R. Cáceres]

2014 En busca de una nación soberana: relaciones internacionales de México, siglos XIX y XX. Recopilación de Jorge A. Schiavon, Daniela Spenser y Mario Vázquez Olivera. México: Centro de Investigación y Docencia Económicas, 2006. 644 p.

This collected volume presents a broad panorama of empirical work on Mexico's foreign policy since independence. Most chapters are well-researched and theoretically grounded, and the book provides a useful lens for viewing the sweep of Mexican foreign policy history and drawing conclusions about how notions and strategies of sovereignty have shifted over time. Particularly useful for scholars of contemporary international relations are the final chapters by Ana Covarrubias Velasco (principles of foreign policy), Jorge A. Schiavon (Mexico's relationship with the US), Guadalupe González González (Mexico's relationship with Latin America), Antonio Ortiz Mena (economic policy), and Manuel García y Griego (migration).

Feria Internacional del Libro de Guadalajara. Coloquio de Historia, *Guadalajara, Mexico, 2002.* México y Cuba, siglos de historia compartida. See item **2064.**

2015 Gabriel, Christina; Jimena Jiménez; and Laura Macdonald. Hacia las "fronteras inteligentes" norteamericanas: ¿convergencia o divergencia en las políticas de control de fronteras? (*Foro Int./México,* 46:3, julio/sept. 2006, p. 549–579, bibl., table)

The authors look at whether border policies between the US-Canada and US-Mexico borders are converging. They find that despite the rhetoric of North American integration and "smart borders," there are two quite different border policies in each case. Existing asymmetries, different levels of trust, and divergent histories of cooperation are driving separate processes of border management between Canada and the US, on one hand, and Mexico and the US, on the other.

2016 Gobernabilidad o ingobernabilidad en la región Paso del Norte. Recopilación de Luis Antonio Payán Alvarado y María Socorro Tabuenca Córdoba. Tijuana, Mexico: Colegio de la Frontera Norte; Las Cruces, N.M.: New Mexico State Univ.; Juárez, Mexico: Univ. Autónoma de Ciudad Juárez; México: Ediciones y Gráficos Eón, 2004. 282 p.: bibl., ill., maps. (Col. Paso del Norte)

This edited volume on the El Paso-Ciudad Juárez region presents an interesting set of essays on the life of these sister cities and their interaction. Chapters that focus on insecurity, the impact of federal policies, and the role of informality are particularly interesting.

2017 Golob, Stephanie R. Beyond the policy frontier: Canada, Mexico, and the ideological origins of NAFTA. (*World Polit.,* 55:3, April 2003, p. 361–398, table)

This theoretically grounded analysis of how Mexico's and Canada's policy elite chose to cross an existing "policy frontier" that proscribed deeper integration with the US suggests that a combination of exogenous economic shocks and related internal legitimacy crises shifted the balance of power among key actors within the states of each country. Challenges both structuralist and pluralist interpretations of changes in international relations.

2018 González Ibarra, Juan de Dios. La circunstancia franquista y el floreci-miento español en México: derecho y filoso-fía. Prólogo de Fernando Serrano Migallón. México: Univ. Autónoma del Estado de Morelos: Fontamara, 2006. 234 p.: bibl. (Col. Argumentos; 46)

Looks in detail at the context of Spanish immigration to Mexico during the Franquista takeover in Spain and the way that Spanish immigrants transformed intellectual and cultural life in Mexico, especially in law and philosophy. Provides a specific analysis of the contributions of several prominent Spanish immigrants in these fields.

2019 Ibarra Escobar, Guillermo. Migran-tes en mercados de trabajo globales: mexicanos y sinaloenses en Los Ángeles. Culiacán Rosales, Mexico: Univ. Autónoma de Sinaloa, Escuela de Estudios Internacio-nales y Políticas Públicas, 2005. 153 p.: bibl., ill., maps.

Examines the insertion of Mexican workers in three areas of Los Angeles and provides an overview on the role of Sina-loans in Los Angeles in particular.

2020 Laborde Carranco, Adolfo A. Re-flexiones sobre el fenómeno migra-torio de los mexicanos en Estados Unidos. México: Plaza y Valdés; Mexico: Coalición por los Derechos Políticos de los Mexicanos en el Extranjero: Milenio Hidalgo, 2006. 170 p.: bibl. (Ciencias sociales)

Presents a collection of articles origi-nally published in the *Milenio de Hidalgo* newspaper about migration issues. Written by a former migrant leader, who is also a journalist and scholar, it provides a useful collection of reflections about the way that migration is transforming both Mexico and the US and chronicles the major debates around key migration-related issues in the two countries in recent years.

2021 Laveaga R., Rafael. Mitos y realida-des del Congreso estadounidense: una perspectiva mexicana. (*Rev. Mex. Polít. Exter.*, 73, feb. 2005, p. 141–165, bibl.)

Discusses three key aspects of the way the US Congress addresses issues related to Mexico which are often mis-understood in Mexico. First, he suggests that there are no permanent "friends" or

"enemies" of Mexico in the US Congress, but that the same member of Congress may have different positions on different issues of interest to the Mexican government. Sec-ond, he notes that there is limited sustained attention to Mexico in the US Congress, but that some issues garner attention at stra-tegic moments. Finally, he notes that the professionalization of the US Congress has less to do with reelection than it does with the existence of a professional staff and a strong institutional framework.

2022 López Villafañe, Víctor. El creciente papel de China en los mercados de América del Norte. (*Estud. Int./Santiago*, 38:152, enero/marzo 2006, p. 5–17, bibl., graphs, table)

The author argues that China has be-come a kind of "fourth partner" in NAFTA without most people in Mexico realizing it. This scenario creates a real threat to Mexi-can manufacturing, which must compete with Chinese exports in the US market, but it also generates opportunities to attract Chinese investment.

2023 Mendoza Costa, Jorge Eduardo. El TLCAN y la integración económica de la frontera México-Estados Unidos: situa-ción presente y estrategias para el futuro. (*Foro Int./México*, 45:3, julio/sept. 2005, p. 517–544)

The study shows that NAFTA has accelerated the economic integration of the US-Mexico border region far more quickly than that of the two countries as a whole. Trade and FDI have been disproportion-ately concentrated in the border region, and other industries, including retail, tourism, and transportation, have also expanded significantly.

2024 México ante el mundo: tiempo de definiciones. Coordinación de Luis Herrera-Lasso M. Textos de Guadalupe Gon-zález G. *et al.* México: Fondo de Cultura Económica, 2006. 401 p.: bibl., ill. (Política y derecho)

This edited volume includes valuable chapters that examine Mexico's changing role in the world, including foreign policy, national security, and economic relations. Of particular interest are the introductory chapter on Mexico's relations abroad by Olga Pellicer, the chapter on the internal political bases of foreign policy by Guadalupe González, and the chapter on national security by Jorge Tello.

2025 México en el mundo: inserción eficiente. Coordinación de José Luis Calva. Textos de Jaime Cárdenas *et al.* México: UNAM, 2007. 248 p.: ill. (Agenda para el desarrollo; 3)

This edited volume generally deals with Mexico's attempts to position itself in the global economy and is mostly sharply critical of recent economic policy. The chapters on Mexico's options for development are particularly interesting.

2026 México y la economía atlántica, siglos XVIII-XX. Recopilación de Sandra Kuntz Ficker y Horst Pietschmann. México: Colegio de México, Cátedra Guillermo y Alejandro Humboldt, 2006. 337 p.: bibl., ill.

This edited volume analyzes the economic interactions between Mexico and Europe, especially Germany, during the 19th and first half of the 20th century.

2027 Meyer, Lorenzo. Estados Unidos y la evolución del nacionalismo defensivo mexicano. (*Foro Int./México,* 46:3, julio/sept. 2006, p. 421–464)

Offers an indispensable analysis of the way Mexico developed a defensive nationalism vis-à-vis the US. In examining how Mexico has defended its sovereignty since independence, the article shows how Mexico could create a more proactive strategy for defending its sovereignty in the future through constructive engagement.

2028 Muñoz, Laura. El Golfo-Caribe, de límite a frontera de México. (*Hist. Mex./México,* 57:2, oct./dic. 2007, p. 531–563, bibl.)

The author seeks to recover an understanding of Mexico's relationship with the Caribbean by addressing the history of Mexico's "third border" in the Gulf of Mexico. The article traces the shifting meanings this border has had for an understanding of Mexico's relationship with its neighbors in the Caribbean Basin.

2029 Ojeda Revah, Mario. El frente diplomático: defensa mexicana de España ante la Sociedad de las Naciones. (*Foro Int./México,* 46:4, oct./dic. 2006, p. 762–791)

The author examines Mexico's support of the Spanish government in the League of Nations and of other embattled democracies prior to WWII. He analyzes how this support also contributed to a warmer relationship with the US and the Allies leading up to WWII.

2030 Pellicer de Brody, Olga. México y el mundo: cambios y continuidades. Mexico: Miguel Ángel Porrúa, 2006. 189 p.: bibl.

This collection of articles from the author's newspaper and magazine columns provides a comprehensive analysis of Mexico's changing foreign policy. It provides considerable insight into the challenges that Mexico faces in rethinking its foreign policy generally to deal with emerging issues and specifically in its relationship with the US, Latin America, Europe, and the UN.

2031 Planeación binacional y cooperación transfronteriza entre México y Estados Unidos. Coordinación de César M. Fuentes Flores y Sergio Peña Medina. Juárez, Mexico: Univ. Autónoma de Ciudad Juárez; Tijuana, Mexico: Colegio de la Frontera Norte, 2005. 271 p.: bibl., ill., maps.

This edited book looks at planning across the US-Mexico border, especially concentrated in the El Paso-Ciudad Juárez area and the Arizona-Sonora border.

2032 La política exterior mexicana en la transición. México: Secretaría de Relaciones Exteriores: FCE, 2005. 281 p.: ill., maps. (Col. Editorial del gobierno del cambio)

Published by Mexico's Foreign Relations Ministry under then-Secretary Luis Ernesto Derbez, this book looks at Mexico's official positions on key foreign policy issues. A useful primary source for those studying the evolution of Mexico's foreign policy.

2033 Ramos García, José María. Relaciones México-Estados Unidos: seguridad nacional e impactos en la frontera norte. Mexicali, Mexico: Univ. Autónoma de Baja California, 2005. 153 p.: bibl.

The author examines the ways that democracy in Mexico and 9/11 in the US reshaped the security relationship between the two countries. He places a special emphasis on how this relationship comes together at the border.

2034 La reconstrucción de la política exterior de México: principios, ámbitos, acciones: una colección de ensayos. Coordinación de Jorge Eduardo Navarrete. Textos de Antonio Gazol Sánchez *et al.* México: UNAM, Centro de Investigaciones Interdisciplinarias en Ciencias y Humanidades, 2006. 371 p.: bibl., ill. (Col. Prospectiva global)

This edited book brings together specialists in foreign policy, many of them former Mexican ambassadors, to evaluate challenges for Mexico's global engagement. The volume is generally quite critical of current directions in foreign policy, and the authors often seem to wish for the return of past times. However, some chapters, including the ones by Carlos Heredia (relations with the US), Cassio Luisselli and Rebeca Rodríguez (Mexico's relations with Latin America), and Olga Pellicer (emerging challenges) offer fresh perspectives on how Mexico could reposition itself in a changing world.

Respuesta social ante la movilidad poblacional y el VIH/Sida: experiencias en Centroamérica y México. See item **2046.**

2035 Sánchez Ramírez, Pablo Telman. Las oscilaciones y contradicciones en las relaciones México-Cuba. (*Relac. Int./ México*, 95, mayo/agosto 2006, p. 85–107)

Analyzes the history of relations between Mexico and Cuba. The first decades after the Cuban Revolution were characterized by close cooperation, which emerged from the perceived revolutionary character of both regimes and the desire of the Mexican government to legitimize its independence in foreign policy vis-à-vis the US. However, Mexico's democratic transition has put a strain on the relationship as other values, including democracy and human rights, come to the fore in Mexican foreign policy.

2036 Sandoval Mendiolea, Juan. La lucha contra la delincuencia organizada transnacional en las Américas: liderazgo de México en la OEA. (*Rev. Mex. Polít. Exter.*, 78, oct. 2006, p. 51–83)

The article looks at Mexico's role in developing an OAS system to promote co-

operation in dealing with organized crime and the challenges that still need to be addressed to strengthen this mechanism.

2037 Saxe-Fernández, John. La compraventa de México: una interpretación histórica y estratégica de las relaciones México-Estados Unidos. México: Plaza y Janés, 2002. 598 p.: bibl. (Temas de debate)

An extensive argument about the dominance of US capital in shaping the relationship between Mexico and the US through NAFTA and the peril this poses to Mexico's future.

2038 Saxe-Fernández, John. México-Estados Unidos: seguridad y colonialidad energética. (*Nueva Soc.*, 204, julio/agosto 2006, p. 187–199, ill.)

The author argues that the US government is using the Security and Prosperity Partnership to promote privatization of energy in Mexico in order to ensure a supply of oil to the US. The greater concentration of powers that the US president has in light of the 9/11 attacks have further contributed to this process.

2039 Seminario de Seguridad Nacional y Fronteriza en la Relación México-Estados Unidos-Canadá, *Guadalajara, Mexico, 2002.* Seguridad nacional y fronteriza en la relación México-Estados Unidos-Canadá. Coordinación de José María Ramos García y Ofelia Woo Morales. Guadalajara, Mexico: Univ. de Guadalajara, Centro Universitario de Ciencias Sociales y Humanidades, 2004. 171 p.: bibl., map.

This edited volume traces the ways that Mexico, Canada, and the US perceive national security in the 21st century. Chapters compare US and Mexican policy-making and address specific aspects of national security and border policies in each of the three countries.

Staudt, Kathleen A. Gender, governance, and globalization at borders: femicide at the US-Mexico border. See item **1997.**

2040 Tello Díaz, Carlos. El fin de una amistad: la relación de México con la Revolución cubana. México: Planeta, 2005. 204 p.: bibl., ill., index.

This well-researched and well-written book covers the history of the friendship between Cuba's revolutionary government and the Mexican government and the reasons that this relationship began to break down during the Fox administration.

Tratado de Libre Comercio entre Costa Rica y México: una evaluación a diez años de su vigencia (1995–2005). See item **2050.**

2041 Velázquez Flores, Rafael. Modelos de análisis de política exterior: el caso de la crisis diplomática entre México y Cuba. (*Rev. Antropol./São Paulo*, 47:2, julho/dez. 2004, p. 57–127, bibl.)

The author analyzes the breakdown of Mexico's relations with Cuba under President Fox. In a nuanced discussion of possible factors, he determines that the crisis in bilateral relations was influenced by geopolitical and internal political factors, but that the specific decisions made by the Mexican government that led to the withdrawal of ambassadors was largely a product of individual decision-making within the government. See also item **2040.**

2042 Zeraoui, Zidane. México y el Magreb: ¿el reencuentro? (*Rev. Mex. Polít. Exter.*, 74, junio 2005, p. 109–135, bibl., tables)

The author analyzes the reasons for the limited relationship between Mexico and northern Africa and suggests possible areas of opportunity to enhance the trade relationship.

CENTRAL AMERICA

2043 Domínguez Ávila, Carlos Federico. Brasil-Centroamérica: cien años de solidaridad y cooperación, 1906–2006. (*Cuad. Am./México*, 4:118, oct./dic. 2006, p. 125–143, table)

The author analyzes 100 years of history in Brazil's relations with Central America, including its role in the peace processes in Central America and more recent initiatives to extend commercial relations and deepen political ties.

2044 Fumero Paniagua, Gerardo; Salvador López Alfaro; and Juan Manuel Villasuso Estomba. TLC con Estados Unidos: desafío al modelo solidario de Costa Rica: el caso del ICE. Recopilación de Gerardo Fumero Paniagua. San José: Editorial Univ. Estatal a Distancia (EUNED), 2005. 256 p.: bibl., ill.

This edited book argues against Costa Rica approving a free trade agreement with

the US. It takes a detailed look at issues involving electricity and the telecommunications sector.

2045 Milla Reyes, Jorge. Costa Rica y Nicaragua: historias de un arreglo de fronteras. Managua: PAVSA, 2006. 168 p.: bibl., ill., index.

This book traces the way the two countries reached agreement on the limits of their border. It covers the legal and political context that led to the 1858 agreement and then to the Central American Court of Justice ruling in 1916.

Perla, Héctor. Si Nicaragua venció, El Salvador vencerá: Central American agency in the creation of the U.S.-Central American Peace and Solidarity Movement. See item **2587.**

2046 Respuesta social ante la movilidad poblacional y el VIH/Sida: experiencias en Centroamérica y México. Recopilación de René Leyva, Marta Caballero y Mario Bronfman. Cuernavaca, Mexico: Instituto Nacional de Salud Pública, 2005. 252 p.: bibl., ill., map.

This edited book looks at the rise of HIV/AIDS in Central America and Mexico (including both Belize and Chiapas) and the institutional responses to address it.

2047 Rodríguez Holkemeyer, Patricia. Poder y vulnerabilidad: la política comercial de los Estados Unidos y los países en desarrollo. San José: Fundación para la Paz y la Democracia, 2005. 173 p.: bibl. (Serie Desarrollo, comercio e integración)

The author seeks to understand the development of US trade policy and what this suggests about the impact of a free trade agreement with the US on Costa Rica's economic future.

2048 Saxon, Dan. To save her life: disappearance, deliverance, and the United States in Guatemala. Berkeley: Univ. of California Press, 2007. 306 p.: bibl., index.

This very accessible book tells the story of the author's efforts to save the life of his future wife, Maritza Urrutia, who was kidnapped in Guatemala in 1992. More than a history, however, it provides an analysis of the often contradictory ways in which government leaders and the human rights activists respond to rights violations and the impacts of their actions.

2049 TLC con Estados Unidos: contribuciones para el debate. Recopilación de María Flórez-Estrada y Gerardo Hernández. San José: Univ. de Costa Rica, 2004. 435 p.: bibl., ill.

This edited volume presents a set of detailed analyses of the (then) proposed TLC with the US from leading Costa Rican scholars who question the impact that the TLC will have on the future of the country.

2050 Tratado de Libre Comercio entre Costa Rica y México: una evaluación a diez años de su vigencia (1995–2005). Dirección de Aplicación de Acuerdos Comerciales Internacionales, Unidad de Monitoreo del Comercio y la Inversión. San José: COMEX, Ministerio de Comercio Exterior, 2005. 71 p.: ill.

This book provides excellent data and an overall analysis, from a Costa Rican government perspective, of the country's free trade agreement with Mexico. It argues that the 10-year old agreement has helped stimulate trade between the two countries significantly.

2051 Zamora R., Augusto. La paz burlada: los procesos de paz de Contadora y Esquipulas. Madrid: SEPHA, 2006. 520 p.: bibl. (Libros abiertos; 7)

A critical analysis of the Contadora and Esquilipas peace processes that traces the difficulty that Latin American countries faced to deal with the hegemony of the US in the region. Written by a former Sandinista government official and representative to the peace negotiations, it is a first-hand account of these processes.

THE CARIBBEAN AND THE GUIANAS

FRANK O. MORA, *Professor of National Security Strategy, National War College*
JACQUELINE ANNE BRAVEBOY-WAGNER, *Professor of Political Science, The City College and The Graduate School, and University Center, The City University of New York (CUNY)*

HISPANIC CARIBBEAN

ALTHOUGH CUBA CONTINUES TO DOMINATE the literature on Hispanic Caribbean international relations, this biennium, unlike previous ones, offers a more diverse set of studies focusing on the impact of globalization on the Dominican Republic and Haiti (items **2060** and **2067**, among others) and regional integration (items **2053**, **2054**, **2066**, and **2075**). More importantly, the theoretical and methodological approaches offered in the literature are much broader and more sophisticated (items **2061**, **2066**, and **2078**) than in previous years. Though one still notices the rather strong ideological undercurrents in most studies on Cuba and by Cubans on and off the island, these works remain good sources of data and analysis.

Some new research in the area of Cuban studies appears this biennium, such as a study of US-Cuban military relations prior to the Revolution (item **2077**), and another book-length study that examines current US-Cuban cooperation in the areas of drug trafficking and migration (item **2079**). At a time when the literature on US-Cuban relations is so ideologically charged, these studies offer more interesting and somewhat more delicate approaches. Of course, ideology—mostly an anti-imperialist/dependency approach delivered with either a heavy or light hand—continues to dominate the literature (items **2058**, **2059**, **2066**, **2071**, among others). Many of the works reviewed are historical and descriptive, although Cruz Herrera provides an interesting and systematic analysis of US-Cuban relations during the 1990s (item **2059**). This year, however, there are fewer works on Cuban foreign policy; the exceptions include a review of Cuba's policy toward Angola (item **2073**), a study of Cuban-Mexican economic relations (item **2064**), and a more nuanced article on Cuba's relations with Latin America (item **2063**) that addresses the important inroads made in the region by the Castro government.

As in previous volumes of *HLAS*, the literature on the Dominican Republic and Haiti is lacking in rigor. There are the usual surveys on Dominican-Haitian relations (item **2060**) and Dominican-US relations (item **2072**), but overall the quantity and quality of the work on non-Cuba international relations in the Caribbean remains deficient and void of theoretical rigor. [FOM]

NON-HISPANIC CARIBBEAN

Few works on the English-speaking Caribbean seem to be addressing the many facets of international relations per se—topics ranging from new security threats such as cyber and environmental threats to human rights, international institutions, or foreign policy. Instead the literature of the first decade of the 2000s concentrates on international political economy, primarily assessing the choices facing the region in an era of neoliberal globalization. This focus also means that there is a lack of theoretical development: the new thrust in international relations to constructivist theorizing seems not to have taken hold in the region. Nevertheless, among the small number of works reviewed, two stand out, both in an historical vein: one study offers fresh insights into immigration flows and policies (item **2076**), and the other into the West Indian events leading up to 1962 (item **2074**). [JBW]

Alonso Vázquez, Francisco Javier. La alianza de dos generalísimos: relaciones diplomáticas Franco-Trujillo. See *HLAS 64:1078.*

2052 Benetti, Raffaello. Survival of weak countries in the face of globalization: Puerto Rico and the Caribbean. San Juan: Editorial de la Univ. de Puerto Rico, 2003. 137 p.: bibl.

A short report in question-answer-comment format offering the author's views of the roles that firms, the government, and social actors need to play in order to help Caribbean small economies confront globalization. [JBW]

2053 Briceño Ruiz, José. El nuevo regionalismo caribeño y el proceso de integración en las Américas. (*Estud. Latinoam./ México*, 10:20, julio/dic. 2003, p. 93–109, bibl., graph, tables)

The integration schemes that emerged or were expanded in the 1990s such as the Association of Caribbean States and the Caribbean Community (CARICOM) are expressions of a new regionalism in the area.

According to the author, the new institutions and frameworks of this new regionalism in the Caribbean Basin are more a reaction than a complement to NAFTA and the Free Trade Area of the Americas (FTAA). In an era of growing asymmetries, the Caribbean area is in search of greater autonomy and subregional integration. [FOM]

2054 Building strategic partnerships for development: Dominican Republic-New York. Edited by María Elizabeth Rodríguez and Ramona Hernández. Santo Domingo: Fundación Global Democracia y Desarrollo; New York: CUNY Dominican Studies Institute at City College, 2004. 408 p.: bibl., index.

In this lengthy volume, the editors and authors provide not only data and analysis but recommendations as to how to strengthen and expand ties between the Dominican Republic and its citizens or diaspora in New York. Some of the areas covered are health, education, remittances, economic development, and culture. Some very useful tables and graphs on each of the areas under study are included. [FOM]

Byron, Jessica. "Singing from the same hymn sheet": Caribbean diplomacy and the Cotonou Agreement. See item **1540.**

2055 The Caribbean economies in an era of free trade. Edited by Nikolaos Karagiannis and Michael Witter. Aldershot, England; Burlington, Vt.: Ashgate, 2004. 203 p.: bibl., ill., index.

Contributions by economists on the economic choices facing the Caribbean under neoliberal globalization, particularly focusing on assessments of the advantages and disadvantages of hemispheric free trade. The contributors are generally pessimistic about the prospects for the Caribbean's small economies in this new economic era. [JBW]

2056 Caribbean integration and cooperation in the Americas: some contemporary issues. Edited by Sahadeo Basdeo and Heather N. Nicol. San Juan, Trinidad: Lexicon Trinidad, 2006. 223 p.: bibl., ill., index.

This volume contains informative contributions assessing various aspects of regionalism in the context of the neoliberalist agenda of the 2000s. Topics include both political and economic issues, such as the problems of drug trafficking and maritime disputes, the growing relations between the Caribbean Community and Cuba, and two chapters on the role of Canada in Haiti. Relations with the US and European Union are noticeably not addressed. [JBW]

2057 Caribbean survival and the global challenge. Edited by Ramesh Ramsaran. Boulder, Colo.: Lynne Rienner Publishers, 2002. 491 p.: bibl., ill., index.

A host of well-known contributors offer policy perspectives on a wide range of subjects, including the nature and impact of globalization, prospects for bilateral and regional cooperation, governance issues, the role of civil society, and trade and financial policies. This is a comprehensive and informative review of Caribbean issues. [JBW]

Castillo, Nelson. Presencia de Estados Unidos en la República Dominicana. See *HLAS* 64:937.

2058 Castro, Fidel. Cold war: warnings for a unipolar world. Melbourne; New York: Ocean Press: Consortium Book Sales and Distribution, 2003. 76 p.

This book contains reflections of the Cuban leader's understanding of the Cold War and Cuba's role in the East-West conflict. In this interview with CNN and BBC (March 1998), Castro provides an interesting analysis of the Cuban Missile Crisis. He also reiterates the point that Cuba was never a Soviet proxy, indicating that Cuban support for liberation movements in the Third World was a "constant source of disagreement" with Moscow. [FOM]

Clegg, Peter. Banana splits and policy challenges: the ACP Caribbean and the fragmentation of interest coalitions. See item **1542.**

2059 Cruz Herrera, Dulce Maria. États-Unis, Cuba: les interventions d'un empire, l'autodétermination d'un peuple. Québec: Presses de l'Univ. du Québec, 2007. 323 p.: bibl.

An historical overview is provided in this work, but the author's focus is the period since the early 1990s and the persistent and escalating US efforts to undermine the Cuban government. Much attention is devoted to the economic dimension of US interventionism with a focus on the extraterritorial aspects of the US embargo. [FOM]

2060 Despradel, Alberto. Comentarios sobre las relaciones dominico haitianas desde 1915 hasta nuestros días. Santo Domingo: Editora Manatí, 2004. 161 p.: bibl., ill., index.

The author—a Dominican diplomat serving as ambassador to Haiti—provides a survey of bilateral relations during the 20th century. This book is another in a long list of surveys by Dominican authors examining Dominican-Haitian relations. Examines relations primarily from a Dominican perspective. One chapter focuses on the influence of Dominican strongman Rafael Leonidas Trujillo in Haitian politics. There are several historical gaps. Much of the book centers on bilateral relations during the Trujillo era. [FOM]

Despradel, Alberto. El Consulado de Belladere en las relaciones dominicohaitianas. See *HLAS 64:1099.*

2061 Dilla Alfonso, Haroldo and **Sobeida de Jesús Cedano.** De problemas y oportunidades: intermediación urbana fronteriza en República Dominicana. (*Rev. Mex. Sociol.*, 67:1, enero/marzo 2005, p. 99–126, bibl., map)

This article was the initial publication of a subsequent book-length study published two years later (see item **2065**) on the challenges and opportunities prevalent on the Dominican-Haitian border. The authors (and later book editors) argue that much of the economy, population, and structures on the Haitian side of the border are being subordinated by a process of capitalist accumulation. The Haitian communities are gradually becoming marginal neighborhoods of Dominican metropoles. [FOM]

2062 The diplomacies of small states: between vulnerability and resilience. Edited by Andrew F. Cooper and Timothy M. Shaw. Basingstoke, England; New York: Palgrave Macmillan, 2009. 291 p.: bibl., ill., index. (International political economy series)

This book contends that, since the end of the Cold War, the previously cooperative nature of small state diplomacy has been eroded by heated competition in an increasingly globalized world such that differences between small states have been exacerbated, and further, that while some are growing, others seem to be left behind. [C.E. Griffin]

2063 Erikson, Daniel P. Castro and Latin America: a second wind? (*World Policy J.*, 21:1, Spring 2004, p. 32–40)

In this prescient piece, the author notes how the Castro regime's stock and influence in Latin America is on the rise. In addition to the rise of ideologically sympathetic regimes in Venezuela and elsewhere, other Latin American countries seem to have drawn closer to Havana due, in part, to the glaring unpopularity of the George W. Bush administration in the hemisphere. Despite the renewed appeal of Cuba as a symbol of independence from the US, few countries are eager to face the inevitable diplomatic tensions with Washington that would be provoked by seeking even warmer relations with Cuba. [FOM]

2064 Feria Internacional del Libro de Guadalajara. Coloquio de Historia, *Guadalajara, Mexico, 2002.* México y Cuba, siglos de historia compartida. Coordinación

de Gladys Lizama Silvia. Guadalajara, Mexico: Univ. de Guadalajara, Universitario de Ciencias Sociales y Humanidades, 2005. 343 p.: bibl.

This edited volume takes a unique approach to the study of Mexico-Cuba relations. The focus is on contact or interaction in three periods. The first section examines contact between colonists living in Cuba and New Spain in the very early period of the Spanish empire in the New World. The second "strategic" period of contact focuses on the production and commercialization of sugar when the migration of people and goods between both countries intensified as a result of the industry's global commercial importance. Finally, the contributors focus on the migration of people and the impact of exiles. Ends with an historiography of the key themes in the sociocultural relationship between the two countries. [FOM]

2065 Frontera en transición: diagnóstico multidisciplinario de la frontera dominico/haitiana. Coordinación de Haroldo Dilla Alfonso y Sobeida de Jesús Cedano. Santo Domingo: Yan Impresos, 2007. 363 p.: bibl., col. ill., col. maps.

In this ambitious and comprehensive volume, the editors and authors provide a multidisciplinary study of the very complex and often tumultuous Dominican-Haitian border. There are contributions on environmental degradation, trade, security, poverty, and demography. One of the key themes of the volume is that the border is fragmented and conflict-ridden, undermining the great potential that exists for local development and greater bilateral integration and cooperation. [FOM]

2066 Gortázar, Guillermo *et al.* Democracia, desarrollo y sociedad civil en Cuba: la Unión Europea frente al problema cubano. Selección y prólogo de Grace Giselle Piney Roche. Cádiz, Spain: Aduana Vieja, 2004. 207 p.: bibl. (Col. 1812)

This edited volume contains a series of essays by a distinguished group of academics, diplomats, and politicians on the political, economic, cultural, and diplomatic relations between Cuba and the European Union. The volume includes essays on post-Castro Cuba, EU-Cuban relations in relation to the Cotonou agreement, the impact of European political culture on Cuban civil society, and relations between Cuba and France. The context in which most of the chapters were written was the confrontation between Cuba and the EU when the latter took a common position demanding that Havana cease repression. [FOM]

2067 Gregory, Steven. The devil behind the mirror: globalization and politics in the Dominican Republic. Berkeley: Univ. of California Press, 2007. 285 p.: bibl., ill., index, map.

In this anthropological analysis of globalization applied to a specific and narrow context, the author analyzes the "distinct and uneven manner" in which transnational flows of capital, culture, and people impact a specific sociocultural and political context—namely the towns of Boca Chica and Andres on the southern coast of the Dominican Republic. Within this context, the author focuses on sex tourism, race, identity, transnational capital, and "structures of imagination." [FOM]

2068 Griffin, Clifford E. The race for fisheries and hydrocarbons in the Caribbean Basin: the Barbados-Trinidad and Tobago dispute, regional delimitation implications. Kingston: Ian Randle, 2007. 181 p.: bibl., maps.

With reference to the Barbados-Trinidad and Tobago Maritime Dispute and acknowledgement that "there exist among and between members of CARICOM a number of undefined maritime boundaries," this work examines issues germane to conflict management regarding Caribbean marine resources. Chapter topics are the following: "Maritime Disputes and Caribbean International Relations," "The Genesis of the Barbados-Trinidad and Tobago Dispute," "International Law and Maritime Boundary Delimitation," "Maritime Boundary Delimitation and Economic Interdependence," "Fisheries Development in Barbados and Trinidad and Tobago," "Deconstructing the Disputes," "The Arbitral Tribunal's Deliberations and Findings," "Maritime Boundary Delimitation and Regional Fisheries Management," and "Contending With Maritime Boundary Delimitation Within CARICOM." [J. Higbee]

2069 Laurent, Edwin. Understanding international trade: a CARICOM perspective. Kingston: Ian Randle, 2007. 108 p.: bibl., ill. (Integrationist)

Addresses challenges faced by the small economies constituting CARICOM and having "no options but to rely on and be open to the outside world for their survival and prosperity." The work discusses experiences of CARICOM countries and their economic production within regional and global trading systems. Also analyzes negotiations relevant to service sectors, including tourism. [J. Higbee]

2070 Martín Fadragas, Alfredo. Comunidad canaria de Cuba: síntesis histórica. La Habana: Ediciones Extramuros, 2004. 59 p.: bibl. (Ciudad)

In this short book, the author traces the migration and role of inhabitants of the Canary Islands in Cuba. According to the author, since the beginning Spaniards and their descendants from the Canary Islands played an active role in the cultural and sociopolitical life of Cuba. Much of the text focuses on the activities of Canary community in the 19th century. [FOM]

Matibag, Eugenio. Haitian-Dominican counterpoint: nation, state, and race on Hispaniola. See *HLAS 64:947.*

2071 Michaut, Maxime. Cuba, l'encadrement idéologique et social face à la politique de déstabilisation des États-Unis. Préface de Denis Rolland. Paris: Harmattan, 2006. 166 p.: bibl., ill. (International)

The author analyzes US-Cuban relations from the perspective of a small, weaker actor defending its sovereignty and honor against the aggression of a stronger state seeking to undermine the enduring principles of the nation and Revolution. Several examples from the last decade are examined to demonstrate the Cuban Revolution's strength and success in defending against the "subversive" activities of the hegemon. [FOM]

2072 Morillo, Pedro H. Las relaciones domínico-norteamericanas desde Báez a Leonel. Santo Domingo: Editorial Argos, 2006. 109 p.: bibl.

This survey of the Dominican Republic's diplomatic relations with the US attempts a review of the relationship during a 140-year (1865–2005) period in only 100 pages. There are a few pages devoted to the period prior to the US Civil War and the Dominican Republic's War of Restoration (1861–65); the bulk of the study focuses on the period of the post-1965 US intervention. The book's principal theme is the asymmetric relationship and systemic dependence of the Dominican Republic on the US. The author argues that the governments of Gen. Rafael Leonidas Trujillo and Juan Bosch (in power for only seven months) experienced greater levels of autonomy from Washington. [FOM]

Nieto, Clara. Los amos de la guerra: el intervencionismo de Estados Unidos en América Latina: de Eisenhower a G.W. Bush. See item **1977.**

2073 Othieno, Timothy. Cuba's foreign policy in Angola. (*Unisa Lat. Am. Rep.*, 21:1, 2005, p. 40–55, bibl., graphs)

This article provides a historical survey and analysis of Cuba's foreign policy goals and motivations in Angola. The author, somewhat confusingly, argues that Cuban foreign policy—specifically the deployment of troops to Angola—was driven by ideology and pragmatism. According to the author, Cuba's principled support for revolutionary movements and governments fighting against imperialism was tempered by a pragmatism that reflected changing dynamics of international politics. [FOM]

2074 Parker, Jason C. Brother's keeper: the United States, race, and empire in the British Caribbean, 1937–1962. Oxford; New York: Oxford Univ. Press, 2008. 248 p.: bibl., index, map.

This work provides an excellent historical treatment of the US-UK-West Indian triangle of relationships during the eventful period between 1937–62 when the region moved toward federation, followed by independence. The author's mining of the US Archives generates interesting historical insights into the Caribbean diplomacy of the US and the UK at this time as well as their perspectives on the role of key leaders (Williams, Bustamante, Manley). The author also nicely weaves developments in the region with those elsewhere in the world. The inclusion of the African diaspora perspective is also a plus. [JBW]

Pérez-López, Jorge F. Tiempo de cambios: tendencias del comercio exterior cubano. See item **758.**

Redes transnacionales en la Cuenca de los Huracanes: un aporte a los estudios interamericanos. See item **1985.**

2075 Sánchez Mendoza, Maria de Lourdes. Un acercamiento a la región del Caribe: su importancia estratégica y económica. (*Relac. Int./México,* 95, mayo/agosto 2006, p. 109–126)

As with many recent articles published by journals in Mexico and the Caribbean Basin, this essay emphasizes the Caribbean's continuing strategic relevance, though in the post-Cold War era its importance has shifted from the geostrategic to the geoeconomic. The author delves into the causes of this shift. The article provides a historical survey of the region's strategic relevance, underscoring the importance of the Caribbean finding its own solutions to regional problems. The region should not allow itself to be defined by others. [FOM]

Sánchez Ramírez, Pablo Telman. Las oscilaciones y contradicciones en las relaciones México-Cuba. See item **2035.**

2076 Szabó, Éva Eszter. U.S. foreign and immigration policies in the Caribbean Basin. Szombathely, Hungary: Savaria Univ. Press, 2007. 311 p.: bibl., ill., maps.

Presents a very good analysis of the immigration relationship between the US and the Dominican Republic and Cuba, based on a synthetic dual approach (the boomerang-effect theory) which essentially focuses on the domestic and foreign policies of the host country. There are nicely detailed sections on US foreign policy toward these Caribbean countries and on the different historical aspects of US visa policy. [JBW]

Tello Díaz, Carlos. El fin de una amistad: la relación de México con la Revolución cubana. See item **2040.**

2077 Valdés Sánchez, Servando. Cuba y
Estados Unidos: relaciones militares,
1933–1958. La Habana: Editora Política,
2005. 148 p.: bibl., maps.

The dearth of research on pre-
Revolution US-Cuba military relations is
as glaring as the extensive literature on
bilateral diplomatic and economic relations.
This study is an important contribution to
this specific area of the relationship prior to
the Cuban Revolution. It is based on documentary research completed at the Center
of Military History Studies of the Revolutionary Armed Forces (CEHM). Though the
author does mention the security imperative
in the asymmetrical and subordinated relationship, the book—like many studies on bilateral relations published in Cuba—focuses
on imperialist and ideological explanations
for the Cuban military's subordination to
the US government. [FOM]

Velázquez Flores, Rafael. Modelos de análisis de política exterior: el caso de la crisis
diplomática entre México y Cuba. See item
2041.

2078 Villarreal Ramos, Enrique. El impacto del final de la Guerra Fría en el
Caribe. (*Relac. Int./México*, 96, sept./dic.
2006, p. 67–85)

Argues that the Caribbean's relative
strategic importance declined over time
since the inception of the Cold War. Geopolitics during the first three decades of the
Cold War gave the Caribbean "some relative
international negotiation power"; however,
the intensification of the Cold War in the
1980s and the subsequent post-Cold War
period saw its international role decline. In
fact, the region has become more vulnerable
to the forces of globalization and the information technology revolution. As a result,
the Caribbean has become more dependent
on the US and Europe. [FOM]

2079 Ziegler, Melanie M. U.S.-Cuban
cooperation past, present, and future.
Gainesville: Univ. Press of Florida, 2007.
182 p.: bibl., index. (Contemporary Cuba)

Despite popular views of the intensive and persistent animosity in the US-
Cuban relationship, the author offers a more
strategic and nuanced view of bilateral ties
suggesting the multiple ways in which both
countries have sought security cooperation.
Specifically, "naked self-interest" has led
the US and Cuba to cooperate in four key
security areas: drug trafficking, decreasing
tension around Guantánamo Naval Base,
illegal immigration, and reducing the threat
of unintended war. The author asserts that
these and other areas of cooperation can
become the pathways toward avoiding future confrontation and for building a more
normal relationship. [FOM]

SOUTH AMERICA (EXCEPT BRAZIL)

ALDO C. VACS, *Professor of Government, Skidmore College*

THE PUBLICATIONS ON THE INTERNATIONAL RELATIONS of the South
American countries (except Brazil) reviewed in this section continue to demonstrate a high level of interest in nontraditional topics. Analyses of the processes
of integration, impact of free trade agreements, relations with extra-hemispheric
and global organizations, and the new approaches to regional security continue
to predominate in the literature. The rise and consolidation in power of a number of nationalist populist and left-of-center governments has generated new
concerns about the evolution of relations with the US and the possibility of intra-
regional conflicts, resulting in the need to formulate and implement common
policies aimed at promoting democratic stability and peaceful relations in the
region. Among the more traditional issues addressed in recent foreign policy stud-

ies are territorial disputes and historical confrontations. However, the number of works of this kind has declined, and the analyses have become less antagonistic and more solution oriented. Studies on bilateral relations continue to focus on neighboring countries and the US, but there has been a noticeable increase in studies dealing with European countries and organizations, China and Japan, and Africa. As in the past, most of the publications on international relations are still coming from the largest countries in the region, but there has been an important increase in publications from smaller countries and a distinct shift from a focus on the policies of individual countries to an emphasis on multilateral relations and international organizations.

A substantial number of publications are devoted to international economic issues, particularly the analysis of processes of regional and subregional integration and discussions of the negotiation of free trade agreements and their impact. Among those studies related to regional economic integration, a majority concentrate on Mercosur (Common Market of the South) and the Andean Community. The research on Mercosur has been focused on the recent institutional evolution and enlargement of the market (item **2091**), the role of presidents and parliaments in its consolidation (items **2084**, **2089**, **2094** and **2095**), and the possibilities for converting it from a free trade area to a customs union (item **2087**) and creating a common currency (item **2090**). Other works are focused on the Andean Community, analyzing its development (item **2080**) and exploring the prospects for cooperation that it creates (item **2088**). Another political economic topic that has generated great interest during this period is the possibility and convenience of signing free trade agreements with the US and creating a Free Trade Area of the Americas. In most cases, authors coincided in foreseeing negative consequences for their countries and the region (items **2127**, **2032**, **2135**, and **2182**), or had mixed opinions about the opportunity to sign these agreements (items **2085** and **2105**). One issue that became the focus of renewed attention was the establishment of relations with extrahemispheric organizations, particularly the EU, and its advantages for the region (items **2083**, **2092**, and **2111**).

In security terms, most of the attention has been concentrated on Colombia's internal conflict and relations with the US (items **2120**, **2122**, and **2124**), as well as its impact on the region, particularly on the security of the neighboring countries (items **2121**, **2125**, **2128**, and **2130**). In general, scholars criticize the growing militarization of the conflict and the role of the US, while stating their concern with the spillover effects of the Colombian conflict on neighboring countries. Traditional security issues and territorial disputes are no longer the focus of attention of most analysts, particularly as the Argentine-Chilean, Ecuadorian-Peruvian, and other conflictive situations appear to have been resolved peacefully. The main exception is the Bolivian-Chilean dispute over the perennial demands by Bolivia to regain access to the Pacific Ocean. This problem continues to generate discussions both on the Bolivian (item **2108**) and Chilean (items **2112**, **2113**, **2114**, and **2117**) sides, while in some cases the studies also include the role of the third actor historically involved in the dispute, Peru (items **2109** and **2115**). Recently the rise of national populism in Bolivia and the issue of the exportation of Bolivian natural gas seem to have generated a worsening of relations, although both sides still insist that they are looking for a peaceful resolution of the dispute.

The relations between individual countries and regional organizations with extrahemispheric counterparts have also generated some interesting analyses focused on reviewing the evolution of these relations and exploring the opportunities for mutually advantageous links. In this regard, the focus of attention seems to be on relations with the EU (items **2083, 2092,** and **2111**); Asian organizations and countries, particularly Japan and China whose economic importance is recognized (items **2104, 2116,** and **2137**); and, in the case of Argentina, on relations with Africa (items **2097** and **2100**).

A number of studies are also devoted to the historical and more recent evolution of the foreign policies of some countries in the region, including Argentina (items **2098, 2101,** and **2102**), Bolivia (item **2106**), Colombia (items **2118** and **2119**), Ecuador (item **2131**), Peru (items **2133** and **2136**), Uruguay (item **2138**), and Venezuela (item **2142**). Most of these works offer informative examinations of the evolution of the international relations of the respective countries and updated critical analyses of recent foreign policy approaches and initiatives.

GENERAL

2080 Casas Gragea, Angel María. La economía política internacional de la nueva integración regional de las Américas: el caso de la Comunidad Andina. (*Integr. Comer.*, 6:16, enero/junio 2002, p. 97–163, bibl., graph, tables)

Excellent analysis of the emergence of the Andean Community places the process into the context of the development of the "new regionalism" in Latin America and offers a detailed review of the features of the community and the characteristics of its regional and international insertion.

2081 Centro de Estudios Unión para la Nueva Mayoría (Argentina). Balance militar de América del Sur. Dirección de Daniel Reimundes. Buenos Aires: Nueva Mayoría Editorial, 2004. 428 p.: bibl., ill. (some col.), maps. (Col. Estudios; 44)

Very useful and detailed study of the military balance in South America as of 2004. The volume contains country-by-country and regional information about military expenditures; armed forces personnel; organization, weapons and equipment of the land, air, and naval military forces as well as other militarized security organizations. It also includes well-informed reports on the different countries' strategic doctrines; their participation in multinational organizations, joint operations, and peace missions; the nature of civilian-military relations; their attitude concerning terrorism; and the British military presence in the Falklands-Malvinas.

2082 Centro de Investigaciones de la Economía Mundial (Havana, Cuba). ALCA: proyecto neoliberal de anexión. La Habana: Editora Política, 2005. 228 p.: bibl., ill.

Collection of extremely critical essays published by Cuba's Research Center of the World Economy attacking the proposal for a Free Trade Area of the Americas Agreement as a neoliberal project to reinforce the US imperialistic domination of Latin America. Nine articles denounce the potential negative effects of a free trade agreement on the economic, social, political, environmental, and strategic conditions of Latin America. Clear presentation of Cuba's arguments for opposing a hemispheric free trade agreement, a position that has been shared by other countries in the region.

2083 El diseño de la asociación estratégica birregional. Santiago: Centro Latinoamericano para las Relaciones con Europa, 2005. 245 p.: bibl., ill.

Useful study of the association agreements signed between the European Union and several Latin American countries and regional organizations. The book includes a general examination of the commercial relations between the members of the Latin American Integration Association (ALADI) and the European Union between 1997 and 2003, analyses of the developments in the bilateral association between the Union and Chile and Mexico, and of the agreements with Mercosur, the Andean Community, and Central America.

2084 La encrucijada política del Mercosur: parlamentos y nueva institucionalidad. Recopilación de Gerardo Caetano y Rubén M. Perina. Textos de Alvaro Coronel *et al.* Montevideo: Centro Latinoamericano de Economía Humana; Washington, D.C.: Organización de los Estados Americanos, U.P.D., 2003. 332 p.: bibl., ill.

Interesting collection of articles produced by the Mercosur Regional Program for Inter-Parliamentary Cooperation and Legislative Modernization discussing the role of the national parliaments in the process of integration and the prospects for the creation of an integrated parliament. Authors coincide on the need to strengthen the parliamentary role in incorporating regional norms into the national legislation, acting as institutional links with civil society and promoting democratic consolidation, while exploring the possibilities of transforming the existing Joint Parliamentary Commission into a Mercosur Parliament.

2085 Fairlie Reinoso, Alan. Costos y beneficios del TLC con Estados Unidos. Lima: Friedrich Ebert Stiftung: Red Latinoamericana de Comercio Internacional, 2005. 124 p.: bibl., ill.

Informative empirical analysis of the costs and benefits for the Andean countries (Bolivia, Colombia, Ecuador, Peru, and Venezuela) of signing free trade agreements with the US. After examining the evolution of the Andean trade with the US, the convergent and divergent commercial interests, the impact of the Andean Trade and Drug Eradication Preferences, and the existing effective protection, the author concludes that neither the signing of an agreement nor its rejection would have significant impact on the economic situation of the Andean countries.

2086 Gomez Mera, Laura. Explaining Mercosur's survival: strategic sources of Argentine-Brazilian convergence. (*J. Lat. Am. Stud.*, 37:1, Feb. 2005, p. 109–140, tables)

Addresses the question of why Mercosur has survived despite repeated crises and pessimistic forecasts. Argues that the main explanation for its continuous survival after 1999—when many economic factors had become less important—can be attributed to three types of strategic interests held by Argentina and Brazil: defensive interest arising from a common sense of vulnerability before external actors; offensive interests, particularly on the part of Brazil, to foster regional cooperation; and positive incentives resulting from the increased interactions.

2087 Hacia una política comercial común del Mercosur. Coordinación de Julio Berlinski, Honório Kume y Marcel Vaillant. Buenos Aires: Red Mercosur: Siglo XXI, 2006. 247 p.: bibl., ill. (Serie Red Mercosur y centros; 5)

Insightful collection of articles written by members of the Network of Economic Research of Mercosur exploring the possibility of establishing a common commercial policy for the group. The authors discuss the creation of common import duties, the existing deviations from the common external tariff and the special commercial regimes, commercial defense policies in Mercosur, and the cost of the effective rate of protection in order to promote the transformation of Mercosur from a free trade area into a customs union.

2088 Kundmüller Caminiti, Franz and Salvador Martín Herencia Carrasco. Estrategias para la agenda económico-social de la Comunidad Andina. Lima: Comisión Andina de Juristas, 2006. 323 p.: bibl., ill.

Valuable study sponsored by the Andean Commission of Jurists examining the existing conditions and prospects for cooperation between the Andean Community countries on economic issues, development of a common social agenda, defense of human rights and democracy, and fight against corruption. After assessing the current state of development and cooperation in these different areas, the study advances a number of policy recommendations concerning institutional, economic, social, and extra-Andean relations agendas aimed at strengthening the integration process.

2089 Malamud, Andrés. Presidential diplomacy and the institutional underpinnings of Mercosur: an empirical examination. (*LARR*, 40:1, 2005, p. 138–164, bibl.)

Excellent article discusses the role and relative importance of presidential diplomacy in consolidating Mercosur and solving intra-organization disputes. After analyzing the negotiations concerning three issues: the automobile and sugar special regimes and the aftermath of the 1999 Brazilian devaluation crisis, the author concludes that the concentration of power in the executive has facilitated the expansion of the role played by presidents in the integration process, especially through their engagement in face-to-face diplomacy at the summit level, making presidential intervention in the management of Mercosur a structural component of the decision-making process.

2090 Menéndez, Lisandro. El Mercosur— debe tener una moneda común? Colaboración de Edgardo Torija Zane, Demián Tupac Panigo y Diego Nicolás Moccero. Buenos Aires: EDICON, Consejo Profesional de Ciencias Económicas de la Ciudad Autónoma de Buenos Aires, 2006. 208 p.: bibl., ill.

Technical study of the convenience of creating a Mercosur common currency particularly focused on the monetary situations affecting Argentina and Brazil. Authors conclude that there could be some advantages in terms of stability associated with the creation of a common currency in comparison to the maintenance of national autonomous currencies or the adoption of the dollar, but they emphasize that political factors and decisions are paramount in determining the chances of a monetary union.

2091 El Mercosur en la integración latino- americana y caribeña: contextos, dimensiones y procesos. Coordinación de Enrique Amayo et al. Guadalajara, Mexico: Univ. de Guadalajara: Puebla, Mexico: Benemérita Univ. Autónoma de Puebla, 2006. 392 p.: bibl., ill.

Interesting collection of articles focused on the importance of Mercosur's institutional, contextual, developmental, legal, ethnic, and educational aspects. Most valuable essays address state reform issues; Mercosur and the negotiations for the Free Trade Area of the Americas Agreement; Mercosur and the global economic crisis; and labor, indigenous, and environmental factors in the process of integration. In general well-researched and documented contributions that highlight the importance of recent developments.

2092 Moura, Heitor et al. Acordo Mercosul- União Européia: além da agricultura. Organização de Mário Antonio Marconini e Renato Flôres. Rio de Janeiro: CEBRI, Centro Brasileiro de Relações Internacionais: Konrad-Adenauer-Stiftung, 2003. 269 p.: bibl., ill. (Série Pesquisas; 28)

Collection of well-researched articles exploring the non-agricultural aspects of the negotiations between Mercosur and the European Union for a possible free trade agreement. Authors examine how the institutional-juridical complexity of the EU and its recent enlargement affect the negotiations, the opportunities for liberalization in services trade and the provision of professional services, and the chances of exporting manufactures to the European market.

2093 Mullins, Martin. In the shadow of the generals: foreign policy making in Argentina, Brazil and Chile. Aldershot, England; Burlington, Vt.: Ashgate, 2006. 169 p.: bibl., index, maps.

Thoughtful analysis of the formation and characteristics of Argentine, Brazilian, and Chilean foreign policies particularly focused on the most recent authoritarian regimes and the emerging democratic governments. The author argues convincingly that a Realist power-centered interpretation of foreign policy formation in the Southern Cone countries should be supplemented by a careful consideration of the national identity politics and historical narratives in each country. Interesting theoretical and comparative contribution to the understanding of recent foreign policies pursued by the three countries regarding regional integration, bilateral relations, and relations with the US.

2094 Presidentes e o Mercosul: reflexões sobre a integração. Organização de Fábio Magalhães. São Paulo: Fundação Memorial da América Latina, 2002. 298 p.

Interesting set of interviews granted by the former presidents of Argentina (Raúl Alfonsín), Brazil (José Sarney), and Uruguay (Julio María Sanguinetti)—each of whom were involved in the creation of Mercosur—and by President Eduardo Frei of Chile, a country that became an associate member of the organization. Each interview was conducted by a panel of experts and was followed by a discussion among the participants, providing a timely record of the motivations, objectives, and expectations held by each of them regarding the process of integration.

Saludjian, Alexis. Critiques du régionalisme ouvert à partir de l'économie géographique appliquée au Mercosur. See item 1186.

2095 **Seminario: "Instituciones, Democracia e Integración Regional," 2nd, Alma Mater Studiorum-Università di Bologna. Representación en Bs. As., 2003.** Instituciones, democracia e integración regional en el MERCOSUR. Compilación de Giorgio Alberti, Elsa Esther Llenderrozas y Julio Pinto. Buenos Aires: Prometeo: Univ. di Bologna, Buenos Aires, Bononiae Libris, 2006. 294 p.: bibl.

Collection of interesting papers delivered at a 2003 seminar on institutions, democracy, and regional integration in the context of Mercosur and the European Union. The first part includes articles on the impact of values, cultural identities, and institutions in the conformation of the European Union and Mercosur. Second part studies economic competitiveness, labor policies, trade unions, and higher education in the context of integration agreements. Third part considers the impact of South American integration on security policies and cooperation as well as on democratic stability and consolidation.

ARGENTINA

2096 **Argentina-Chile y sus vecinos.** Vol. 2, Argentina y Chile en la región. Recopilación de Pablo Lacoste. Iquique, Chile: Univ. Arturo Prat, Instituto de Estudios Internacionales; Mendoza, Argentina: Caviar Bleu, 2005. 1 v.: bibl. (Col. Cono sur)

Second volume of a collective work on the relations between Argentina, Chile, and their neighbors is focused on specific aspects of the bilateral relations and regional insertion of the two countries. Relatively disorganized collection contains some pertinent analyses of bilateral migrations, regional integration policies, and the respective policies of regional and global insertion.

2097 **Buffa, Diego.** El Africa subsahariana en la política exterior argentina: las presidencias de Alfonsín y Menem. Córdoba, Argentina: Centro de Estudios Avanzados, Univ. Nacional de Córdoba, 2006. 200 p.: bibl. (Col. Africa; 1)

Valuable contribution to the study of a relatively neglected aspect of Argentina's foreign policies: its relations with sub-Saharan Africa. First part presents a brief review of the political and economic evolution of the region since decolonization. Well-researched and informative second part offers an historical analysis of the evolution of Argentine-African relations focusing on the developments during the Alfonsín and Menem administrations, including the break with South Africa's apartheid regime and support for democratization, cooperation in multilateral organizations, new diplomatic and economic links, participation in UN peace operations, and attempts to create a Zone of Peace and Cooperation in the South Atlantic.

2098 **Congreso Nacional de Ciencia Política (Argentina), 7th, Córdoba, Argentina, 2005.** La política exterior del gobierno de Kirchner. Textos de Alfredo Bruno Bologna *et al.* Edición preparada por el CERIR, Centro de Estudios en Relaciones Internacionales de Rosario. Rosario, Argentina: UNR Editora, Univ. Nacional de Rosario, 2006. 2 v.: bibl. (Col. Académica)

Comprehensive and insightful examination of the foreign policies implemented during the first two years of the Néstor Kirchner administration (2003–05) published by the Center of Studies in International relations of the Univ. of Rosario (Argentina). The authors highlight the relative autonomy exhibited by Argentina's foreign policy under Kirchner (in contrast to the "automatic alignment" with the US characteristic of the Menem and de la Rua administrations) examining a number of issues such as the financial negotiations after the 2001 default, Antarctic policy, regional integration, and the question of the Malvinas-Falklands as well as the bilateral relations with different countries (US, Russia, China, Japan, Brazil, Chile, and Uruguay) and regions (Africa, European Union, and the Middle East).

2099 Gardini, Gian Luca. Making sense of rapprochement between Argentina and Brazil, 1979–1982. (*Rev. Eur. Estud. Latinoam. Caribe*, 80, April 2006, p. 57–71, bibl.)

Case study designed to identify and disclose three misrepresentations of the Itaipú quarrel involving Argentina and Brazil between 1979 and 1982. [D. Dent]

2100 Lechini de Alvarez, Gladys. Argentina y África en el espejo de Brasil: política por impulsos o construcción de una política exterior? Buenos Aires: CLACSO, 2006. 279 p.: bibl., ill. (Col. Sur-Sur)

Excellent study by the foremost specialist in the study of Argentine-African relations analyzes the evolution of Argentina's foreign policy toward the African states and contrasts it with Brazil's approach since the 1960s. Author discusses in detail the evolution of the "unstable and impulsive" African policies implemented by Argentina in the last 50 years comparing them to the more coherent and incremental strategy followed by Brazil that resulted in the deepening of advantageous commercial, political, and cultural ties with the African countries.

2101 Miranda, Roberto Alfredo. ¿Por qué cambia la política exterior de un mismo gobierno?: algunas consideraciones sobre la gestión internacional de Néstor Kirchner. (*Td Temas Debates*, 9:10, nov. 2005, p. 95–108, bibl.)

Interesting article explores why the Kirchner administration foreign policy changed direction during its first two years. Argues that domestic weaknesses combined with international pressures forced the Kirchner administration to accommodate Brazil's decision to try to establish a Community of South American Nations under its leadership (instead of strengthening Mercosur as the Argentine government desired) and to participate in the Haitian multinational peace force (instead of refusing to join as the government initially wanted).

2102 Parish, Randall R. Democrats, dictators, and cooperation: the transformation of Argentine-Chilean relations. (*Lat. Am. Polit. Soc.*, 48:1, Spring 2006, p. 143–174, bibl.)

Well-documented and thoughtful article discusses the reasons why Argentina and Chile left aside their rivalry in 1984 and moved in the direction of cooperation and partnership. Reviews the evolution of the conflictive bilateral relations that culminated in the 1978 confrontation over the Beagle Channel and analyzes the factors that led to the peace agreements that resolved the territorial disputes and cleared the way for growing cooperation. Argues that the crucial factor was the existence in both countries of relatively strong executives that could sustain cooperation over weak and divided opposition forces.

2103 Zanatta, Loris. Auge y declinación de la tercera posición: Bolivia, Perón y la Guerra Fría, 1943–1954. (*Desarro. Econ.*, 45:177, abril/junio 2005, p. 25–53, bibl.)

Interesting historical study of the Argentine government's intervention in Bolivia between 1943–55 and the reasons why this attempt to promote Perón's "Third Position" doctrine (nonalignment) at the regional level failed. Highlights the importance in determining this failure not only of the US opposition and the economic and diplomatic weaknesses of Argentina, but also the distrust within neighboring countries of Peron's hegemonic intentions.

BOLIVIA

2104 Bösenhofer, Manuela. El dragón despierta: desarrollo económico de China y su impacto en las economías latinoamericanas—enfoque especial, Bolivia. Switzerland: Secretaría de Estado de Economía; La Paz: Instituto Boliviano de Comercio Exterior, 2004. 144, 50 p.: bibl., ill., map.

Short study of the People's Republic of China's economic transformation and its rise as an significant actor in the international market is followed by an analysis of the economic opportunities that Latin America and, in particular, Bolivia, have with China. The work examines Bolivian-Chinese commercial relations and the export opportunities of different Bolivian sectors that could contribute to reducing the large trade deficit.

2105 Núñez del Prado, José and Marco Antonio F. Romay Hochkofler. Tratado de libre comercio Bolivia-Estados Unidos: dos miradas del impacto en el agro campesino indígena. La Paz: Centro de Investigación y Promoción del Campesinado, 2005. 233 p.: bibl., ill.

Two interesting studies of the likely impact on Bolivia's peasant-indigenous sector of the signing of a free trade agreement with the US. Núñez del Prado's analysis, focused on Bolivia's emerging agricultural production networks, concludes that the current deficiencies in terms of productivity and competitiveness of the agricultural peasant-indigenous sector makes it unadvisable to enter into a free trade agreement that would result in the removal of protection. On the other hand, Romay Hochkofler focuses on the characteristics of the Bolivian agricultural trade composition, origins, and destination to argue that a free trade treaty involving the US would not have the negative consequences some peasant-indigenous producers expect and could generate opportunities for certain exports.

2106 Política exterior boliviana a inicios del siglo XXI. Textos de Edgar Camacho Omiste *et al.* La Paz: CAF, UDAPEX, 2005. 242 p.: bibl.

Collection of articles published by Bolivia's Ministry of Foreign Relations and Culture addressing a number of issues considered crucial in the context of 21st-century Bolivian foreign policy. The book includes analyses of the natural gas export project and relations with Chile, Bolivia's trade policies and its approach to the World Trade Organization, relations with Brazil and the European Union, positions concerning South American integration, and possibilities for Ibero-American cooperation. Written by experts, former government officials, and diplomats, the collection is somewhat unsystematic, but highlights important components of Bolivia's international relations strategy and policy making.

2107 Política exterior en materia de recursos hídricos. La Paz: Ministerio de Relaciones Exteriores y Culto: PNUD, 2005. 231 p.: bibl., ill.

Informative analyses of Bolivia's international rivers and shared water resources aimed at establishing the technical and conceptual basis of a foreign policy revolving around national interests and the possibilities of cooperation with neighboring countries. Particularly interesting

considering Bolivia's landlocked condition are the articles devoted to the opportunities associated with transnational cooperation with Chile, Peru, and Paraguay, the development of the Paraguay-Parana rivers' link, and the binational and trinational projects with Argentina and Paraguay.

2108 Salazar Paredes, Fernando. Bolivia y Chile: desatando nudos: propuesta de salida al mar para Bolivia basada en el equilibrio de intereses y una nueva racionalidad política. Bolivia: CERID; La Paz: Plural Editores, 2006. 193 p.: bibl., ill., index, maps.

Brief study of the recent evolution of the perennial territorial dispute between Bolivia and Chile and a well-conceived proposal aimed at "unknotting" the diplomatic tangle that has prevented Bolivia from attaining access to the Pacific Ocean. Bolivian diplomat and former minister recommends leaving aside the notion of territorial sovereignty and negotiating the creation of a land corridor from the Bolivian border to the Chilean port of Arica in which Bolivia would have "territorial supremacy"—similar to the extra-territorial rights granted to embassies and other legal foreign entities—in the context of a bilateral treaty of friendship, justice, security, and development.

2109 Seminario Internacional sobre las Relaciones entre Bolivia, Chile y Perú, *Caracas, Venezuela, 2000.* Hacia un enfoque trinacional de las relaciones entre Bolivia, Chile y Perú. Vol. 1. La Paz: Centro de Estudios Estratégicos para la Integración Latinoamericana: Instituto PRISMA: Univ. Andina Simón Bolívar; Santiago: Corporación Tiempo 2000: FLACSO-Chile; Lima: Centro Peruano de Estudios Internacionales; Caracas: Corporación Andina de Fomento, 2001. 1 v.: bibl.

Collection of papers by Bolivian, Chilean, and Peruvian authors discussing the prospects for cooperation between their countries followed by a brief report on the deliberations and conclusions of the seminar sponsored by the Andean Corporation of Promotion in Venezuela. Interesting contribution highlights the views and attitudes of civil society actors (business groups, intellectuals, religious institutions, mass media, etc.) concerning the recent evolution of relations between the three countries and prospects for cooperation particularly in terms of the integrated development of southern Peru, northern Chile, and western Bolivia and its projection toward the Asian-Pacific basin. For comment on Vol. 2, see item **2110**.

2110 Seminario Internacional sobre las Relaciones entre Bolivia, Chile y Perú, Caracas, Venezuela, 2000. Hacia un enfoque trinacional de las relaciones entre Bolivia, Chile y Perú. Vol. 2. La Paz: Centro de Estudios Estratégicos para la Integración Latinoamericana: Instituto PRISMA: Univ. Andina Simón Bolívar; Santiago: Corporación Tiempo 2000: FLACSO-Chile; Lima: Centro Peruano de Estudios Internacionales; Caracas: Corporación Andina de Fomento, 2002. 1 v.: bibl.

In this second volume, the authors discuss more specific aspects of the trinational relations from the different national perspectives, as well as the prospects for sectoral integration. It includes national analyses of the impact of regional and global changes on the trilateral integration project. Also focuses on the impact that the export of Bolivia's natural gas may have on the integrated development of the region and on facilitating the country's access to the sea. For comment on Vol. 1, see item **2109**.

Vargas Aguirre, Oscar Patricio and **Juan Carlos Montecinos Luque.** Trayectoria de la diplomacia boliviana: 179 años de internacionalismo. See *HLAS 64:1374*.

CHILE

Argentina-Chile y sus vecinos. See item **2096**.

2111 Blanc Altemir, Antonio. Los tres pilares del acuerdo de asociación Chile-Unión Europea: diálogo político, cooperación y comercio. (*Estud. Int./Santiago*, 38:151, oct./dic. 2005, p. 73–116, bibl.)

Analyzes the three main components of the association agreement signed by Chile and the European Union in 2002: political dialogue, cooperation, and trade. Author is optimistic about the prospects for the agreement to further political coincidences; the growth of scientific-technological and educational cooperation; and an increase in trade, investment, and financial flows.

2112 Bustos, Carlos. Chile y Bolivia: un largo camino. Chile: Editorial Puerto de Palos, 2003. 303 p.: bibl.

Former Chilean diplomat who was consul general in Bolivia and president of Chile's commission on boundaries analyzes the evolution of Bolivian-Chilean relations and suggests some possible solutions to the secular dispute. Although defending Chile's positions, the author attempts to present a balanced treatment of the issues. He recommends making this problem a Chilean foreign policy priority, while reinitiating bilateral negotiations without pre-conditions and considering the possibility of some territorial concessions to Bolivia.

2113 Hormazábal Díaz, Fernando. El libro blanco de Chile: el problema marítimo boliviano. Santiago: Ediciones Centro de Estudios Bicentenario, 2005. 524 p.: bibl., ill., maps.

"White Book" written by Chilean general in response to the "Blue Book" published in 2004 by the Bolivian government asserting its rights to the territory lost to Chile in the War of the Pacific and requesting international support for its demands. As expected, this book affirms the complete justice of the Chilean positions and rejects the Bolivian contentions. Nevertheless, it is useful in offering a comprehensive treatment of the Chilean historical, legal, diplomatic, and political arguments in the long dispute with its neighbor.

2114 Maira, Luis and **Javier Murillo de la Rocha.** El largo conflicto entre Chile y Bolivia: dos visiones. Santiago: Taurus, 2004. 196 p.: bibl. (Taurus historia)

Two essays by Chilean and Bolivian foreign relations experts and diplomats highlight the differences between both sides in the historical analysis and current interpretation of the secular territorial dispute that remained unsolved by the treaty of 1904. Includes a concluding essay by Monica Hirst—Brazilian expert in international relations who resides in Argentina—that recommends the use of multilateral mediation to overcome the bilateral diplomatic impasse.

2115 Milet, Paz V. Chile-Perú: las raíces de una difícil relación. (*Estud. Int./Santiago*, 38:150, julio/sept. 2005, p. 59–73, bibl., table)

Discusses the factors contributing to the difficult relationship between Chile and Peru, focusing on the impact of the historical distrust prevalent since the War of the Pacific, the existence of cultural differences, and public opinion and mutual perceptions.

Parish, Randall R. Democrats, dictators, and cooperation: the transformation of Argentine-Chilean relations. See item **2102.**

2116 Ross, César. Chile y Japón: pragmatismo y negocios internacionales, 1973–1989. (*Ciclos Hist. Econ. Soc.*, 15:29, primer semestre 2005, p. 163–204, bibl., tables)

Informative study of the evolution of Chilean-Japanese relations during the Pinochet dictatorship. Well-documented analysis of the bilateral commercial, investment, and financial relations between the two countries. Also treats the emergence and consolidation of the Entrepreneurial Committee Chile-Japan leading to growing cooperation between private firms of both countries.

2117 Witker Barra, Iván. Bolivia 2003: percepciones de la crisis en la prensa chilena y su impacto en la seguridad subregional y relaciones bilaterales. Chile: Academia Nacional de Estudios Políticos y Estratégicos, Ministerio de Defensa Nacional, 2005. 172 p.: bibl., ill., maps. (Col. Investigaciones Academia Nacional de Estudios Políticos y Estratégicos; 11)

Interesting study published by the National Academy of Political and Strategic Studies of Chile's Ministry of National Defense about Chilean perceptions of and reactions to the Bolivian crisis of 2003 that culminated in the resignation of President Sánchez de Lozada and revealed the popularity of Evo Morales. It shows the growing concern of the Chilean mainstream press with the crisis, particularly concerning the nationalistic opposition toward building a natural gas pipeline across Chile and the renewed Bolivian demands for access to the sea. It also points out that from the Chilean perspective, this Bolivian hostility not only worsened bilateral relations, but combined with the rise of violence and secessionist threats, created an atmosphere of subregional instability.

COLOMBIA

2118 Colombia y su política exterior en el siglo XXI. Recopilación de Martha Ardila, Diego Cardona y Socorro Ramírez. Bogotá: Friedrich Ebert Stiftung en Colombia: Fondo Editorial CEREC, 2005. 393 p.: bibl., ill.

Excellent collection of articles discussing the impact of intermestic issues on the international insertion and foreign policies of Colombia. The book contains analyses of the repercussions of Colombia's international situation and foreign policies on civil conflict (Alcides Costa Vaz), migration (Martha Ardila), economic integration and free trade (Edgar Vieira Posada), environmental problems (Manuel Rodríguez Becerra), peace and human rights issues (Iván Orozco Abad), drug traffic (Francisco E. Thoumi), and foreign service and foreign policy instruments (Diego Cardona).

2119 Fernández de Soto, Guillermo. La ilusión posible: un testimonio sobre la política exterior colombiana. Bogotá: Grupo Editorial Norma, 2004. 591 p.: bibl., ill. (Col. Actualidad)

Valuable memoir by former Colombian minister of foreign relations during the administration of President Andrés Pastrana (1998–2002). Very interesting testimony addressing some of the central issues facing Colombia's foreign policy during that period, including the peace negotiations and the formulation of Plan Colombia, the evolution of relations with the US and Venezuela, territorial disputes, the drug problem, human rights, regional integration, multilateral cooperation, relations with other Latin American countries, and insertion into the global system. Useful source of information for anyone interested in understanding the recent vicissitudes of Colombia's foreign policies.

2120 Una fuerza preventiva de la ONU: opción para Colombia. Colombia: Fundación Seguridad & Democracia, 2003. 84 p.: bibl. (Ensayos de seguridad y democracia)

Interesting and timely analysis of the internationalization of the Colombian civil conflict, especially considering the recent clashes between Colombia, Ecuador, and Venezuela. The first part discusses the "passive" aspects of the internationalization of the conflict with its transborder impact on neighboring countries and the rise of intermestic problems such as immigration and refugees, the humanitarian crisis, and drug traffic. Work then turns to the "active" dimension of the process, examining the militarization of the conflict and the introduction of foreign troops during the Uribe administration. The second part discusses different options such as the US "intervention by invitation" and the possibility of a regional force before making the case for the creation of a UN-led multilateral preventive force with military, police, and civilian components to be located in the border areas.

Gallardo Román, José. El Plan Colombia y sus efectos sobre el Ecuador: ensayo. See item **2130**.

2121 Moreano Urigüen, Hernán. Colombia y sus vecinos frente al conflicto armado. Quito: Abya Yala: FLACSO Ecuador, 2005. 224 p.: bibl., maps. (Tesis)

Critical study of the likely impact of Plan Colombia and the US antidrug policies on the security of Colombia and its neighboring countries (Brazil, Ecuador, Peru, and Venezuela). Most interesting portion of the book is focused on the evolution of US and Colombian security policies after 9/11 and the possible impact on Ecuador's security and, to a lesser extent, on the other three countries. Suggests that the hard-line militarized security approaches followed by presidents George W. Bush and Uribe have generated security problems in neighboring countries and have not only been unsuccessful in promoting security cooperation in the region, but have generated perceptions of threat and growing friction. Concludes that the divergent security interests of the actors would prevent the emergence of a cooperative security community, but that there are possibilities of improving policy coordination through regional and hemispheric agreements and initiatives.

2122 Parada Fernández, Alvaro. Ironía histórica cínica: E.U. & U.E. en Colombia: la democracia más antigua de América

en guerra suCIA de baja intensidad. Bogotá: Univ. Autónoma de Colombia, 2004. 464 p.: bibl., ill.

Highly critical analysis of the strategy adopted by the Colombian government in its fight against internal enemies with the support of the US and the European Union. Author denounces Plan Colombia as generating a low intensity "dirty war" that, in his view, has resulted in the surge of neofascist paramilitary groups, human rights violations, massacres, socioeconomic crisis, decline of democracy, and erosion of the rule of law and national sovereignty. The US and European countries are accused of supporting President Uribe's repressive, militaristic, and neoliberal policies in order to serve their imperialistic interests and undermine President Chávez's revolutionary initiatives.

Peceny, Mark and **Michael Durnan.** The FARC's best friend: U.S. antidrug policies and the deepening of Colombia's Civil War in the 1990s. See item **1606**.

2123 Ramjas Saavedra, J.S. Gabriel Arthur. Las relaciones de Colombia y América Latina con Europa. Bogotá: Univ. Externado de Colombia, Facultad de Finanzas, Gobierno y Relaciones Internacionales, 2006. 411 p.: bibl.

General historical study of the relations between Europe and Latin America, especially between the European Union and Colombia. The first two parts, which address European-Latin American relations, are informative at an introductory level and highlight the recent inter-regional agreements as well as the bilateral relations between some individual Western European and the largest Latin American countries. The third part offers a more in-depth survey of Colombian relations with the European Union, the western European countries and the Central-Eastern European nations, particularly in terms of economic relations and cooperation agreements.

2124 Sandoval Robayo, Mary Luz. El papel de las ONGs internacionales en los conflictos armados internos, caso Colombia. Bogotá: Univ. Libre, Facultad de Derecho y Ciencias Políticas, Centro de Investigaciones Sociojurídicas, 2003. 458 p.: bibl., maps.

Extensive study of the presence of international NGOs in Colombia and their humanitarian role in relation to the internal armed conflict. After a review and discussion of the emergence and evolution of international NGOs since 1945 and their humanitarian intervention in crises such as Gulf War, former Yugoslavia, African conflicts, and Afghanistan, the analysis is focused on the legal situation of these organizations in Colombia and the legal project to regulate their activities. The second part of the book offers a detailed analysis of the characteristics, history, geographical location, objectives, activities, and relations established by 34 NGOs in Colombia, including peace, religious, human rights, developmental, refugee, and other international organizations.

2125 Seguridades en construcción en América Latina. Vol. 1, El círculo de Colombia: Brasil, Ecuador, Panamá, Perú y Venezuela. Textos de Rubén Sánchez D. *et al.* Bogotá: Centro Editorial Univ. del Rosario, 2005. 1 v.: bibl., ill., indexes, maps (some col.).

Collective work analyzing the security interests and policies of the states located in what the authors define as the "circle of Colombia," that is Brazil, Ecuador, Panama, Peru, and Venezuela. Interesting analysis from the Colombian perspective of the security issues and strategies of these neighboring countries. Pays special attention to the repercussions that these diverse security problems and policies could have on Colombia's national security and on the possibility of building a new system of security cooperation in the Americas.

2126 Stokes, Doug. America's other war: terrorizing Colombia. London; New York: Zed Books: Palgrave Macmillan, 2004. 147 p.: bibl., index.

Highly critical examination of US foreign policy in Colombia conducted against the background of the general US objectives in Latin America argues that in pursuing the stabilization of a given set of favorable social, economic, and political arrangements, the US intervention in Colombia has resulted in continuous violations of human rights and the consolidation of a system of state terror imposed on the population.

2127 Umaña, Germán and Soraya Caro. El juego asimétrico del comercio: el tratado de libre comercio Colombia-Estados Unidos. Bogotá: Viva la Ciudadanía: Univ.

Nacional de Colombia, Facultad de Ciencias Económicas, Centro de Investigaciones para el Desarrollo, 2004. 247 p.: bibl., ill.

Detailed examination of the Colombia-US free trade treaty as proposed in 2004 analyzes its contents and likely impact on Colombia in terms of goods and services trade, intellectual property, and public sector purchases. Well-researched and informative study concludes that the asymmetrical nature of the bilateral negotiations results in an agreement that would be favorable to US interests, Colombian importers, and groups associated with multinational companies, while negatively affecting small producers and workers, and weakening the Colombian state, its sovereignty, and its capacity to control macroeconomic policies.

2128 La vecindad colombo-venezolana: imágenes y realidades. Coordinación de Socorro Ramírez y José G. María Cadenas. Colombia: Univ. Nacional de Colombia, IEPRI; Venezuela: UCV; Bogotá: CAB, 2003. 447 p.: bibl., ill.

Comprehensive examination of the evolution of Colombian-Venezuelan relations conducted by members of the Grupo Académico Binacional sponsored by universities of both countries. This comprehensive set of articles includes a study of binational academic integration; an in-depth analysis of mutual images and perceptions concerning issues such as international politics, security, human rights, migrations, drugs, borders, trade and economic relations, education, and culture; a historical analysis of the binational relations; studies of the recent evolution of the bilateral economic relations and the process of integration; an examination of bilateral environmental issues; and a linguistic and ethnic study of the border populations.

ECUADOR

2129 Emigración y política exterior en Ecuador. Recopilación de Javier Ponce Leiva. Quito: Centro de Estudios Internacionales: FLACSO, Sede Académica de Ecuador: Abya Yala, 2005. 255 p.: bibl., ill. (Ágora)

Compilation of articles discussing the causes, composition, and destination of Ecuadorian emigration that increased exponentially in the 1990s, as well as the foreign policies implemented in this regard by the Ecuadorian state. Includes articles examining Ecuador's policies toward its migrants in different countries, the impact of international remittances on the country's economy, and specific analysis of the migration flows to the US, Italy, and the European Union. The authors recommend the creation of a specific agency focused on migration, development of adequate legislation, elaboration of a migration policy aimed to support residents abroad, and the creation of cultural, financial, and educational cooperation programs.

2130 Gallardo Román, José. El Plan Colombia y sus efectos sobre el Ecuador: ensayo. Quito: Eskeletra Editorial, 2005. 280 p.: bibl.

Former defense minister and general commander of the Ecuadorian army examines the history of armed conflict in Colombia and analyzes its impact on Ecuador. First part offers an even-handed study of the Colombian civil war that assesses the responsibility of both the government and the guerrilla movement, while arguing for a negotiated solution. Second part briefly examines the possible impact of Colombia instability on Ecuador's border regions in terms sovereignty, violence, drug traffic, refugees, destruction of productive activities, environmental degradation, and spill-over of the armed conflict. Recommends a number of domestic and foreign policies to prevent negative effects.

2131 Las relaciones Ecuador-Estados Unidos en 25 años de democracia, 1979–2004. Recopilación de Javier Ponce Leiva. Quito: Abya-Yala: FLASCO, 2005. 307 p.: bibl. (Agora)

Valuable collection of articles produced in 2004 for a Project for the Actualization of Diplomats sponsored by FLACSO-Ecuador and the International Studies Center of the Univ. de Barcelona examining the evolution of Ecuador-US relations since democratization in 1979. Five articles are focused on successive Ecuadorian administrations of this period (Roldós-Hurtado, Febres Cordero, Borja, and Bucaram-Alarcón), while four others are devoted to topics such as the US and the Ecuador-Peru conflict, the International Criminal Court controversies,

the bilateral free trade agreement, and the role of US religious organizations in Ecuador. Excellent source for anyone interested in understanding the growing disagreements affecting the relations between the two countries.

2132 TLC, más que un tratado de libre comercio. Recopilación de Alberto Acosta y Falconí Benítez Fander. Quito: FLACSO, Ecuador: ILDIS-Friedrich Ebert Stiftung, 2005. 255 p.: bibl. (Serie Foro)

Collection of critical articles discussing the features, prospects, and expected consequences for Latin America of the free trade treaties negotiated between the US and the Andean countries and the possible impact of an eventual Free Trade of the Americas Agreement. First part of the book compares unfavorably free trade treaties with regional integration agreements and negatively assesses the impact of these treaties on Mexico, Chile, and the Andean Community. Second part includes a detailed analysis of the negative consequences expected for Ecuador of signing a free trade agreement with the US in terms of human development, poverty and inequality, food production, employment, medicine access, intellectual property, and cultural industry.

PERU

2133 Bákula, Juan Miguel. El Perú en el reino ajeno: historia interna de la acción externa. Lima: Univ. de Lima, Fondo Editorial, 2006. 694 p.: bibl.

Authoritative and detailed study by an experienced diplomat of the features and evolution of Peru's foreign service from independence to the early 2000s. Analyzes the gradual institutionalization of the country's foreign service from its emergence until the promulgation of the 2003 diplomatic service law, offers portraits and personal recollections of different foreign relations ministers, discusses the impact of the formation of the Peruvian nation-state and nationalistic ideologies on its national identity, and examines Peru's attitude toward Latin American integration, the role of the consultative commission on foreign relations, and the national maritime policies.

2134 Congreso Internacional "Dos Mundos, Dos Culturas: la Huella Peruana en la Ciencia Española," Lima, 1999. Dos mundos, dos culturas, o, De la historia (natural y moral) entre España y el Perú. Coordinación de Fermín del Pino Díaz. Frankfurt: Vervuert; Madrid: Iberoamericana, 2004. 334 p.: bibl. (Textos y estudios coloniales y de la independencia; 11)

Collection of papers delivered at a 1999 international congress on cultural relations between Peru and Spain. The articles are mostly centered on interactions during the conquest and colonial period. The articles highlight the impact of such interactions on the development of nautical, botanical, mineralogical, linguistic, historical, and anthropological knowledge and methods in both countries.

2135 Libre comercio y TLC Perú-EEUU: realidades y consecuencias del Tratado de Libre Comercio con EEUU. Textos de Alberto Acosta *et al.* Caricaturas e ilustraciones de Deborah Vázquez Tejada. Recopilación de César Cornejo Román. Peru: Ediciones Populares FORJA, 2004. 308 p.: bibl., ill. (Col. Alerta que camina!)

Collective work critically analyzes from a leftist perspective the possible impact of free trade agreements on Latin America, the results of NAFTA and the Chilean-US free trade agreement, and the expected consequences of the signing of a free trade treaty between Peru and the US. Authors coincide in pointing out that although free trade might lead to economic growth and export increases, its negative effects include growing income concentration and poverty as well as the decline of national producers and social welfare. Particularly interesting are the uniformly negative assessments of the impact of a commercial agreement with the US on Peru's agriculture and food production, public education and services, national culture, and biodiversity. The assessments help explain the opposition to the agreement and the call for a popular referendum before the agreement's ratification.

2136 McClintock, Cynthia and Fabian Vallas. The United States and Peru: cooperation at a cost. New York: Routledge, 2003. 222 p.: bibl., index. (Contemporary inter-American relations)

Best comprehensive study in English about the recent evolution of US-Peruvian relations. After a brief review of the bilateral relations from independence to the Cold War period, the authors offer a detailed and well-documented analysis of the evolution of relations since the 1980s focused on issues of national security, economic reform, drug traffic, and democracy and human rights. The study offers a convincing analysis of the reasons why the priority assigned by the Clinton administration to national security, narcotics control, and free-market reform led to tolerating the Fujimori regime's authoritarianism, human rights violations, and corruption until its demise in late 2000.

Milet, Paz V. Chile-Perú: las raíces de una difícil relación. See item **2115**.

2137 Murakami, Yusuke. Sueños distintos en un mismo lecho: una historia de desencuentros en las relaciones Perú-Japón durante la década de Fujimori. Lima: Instituto de Estudios Peruanos; Japan: Japan Center of Area Studies, 2004. 161 p.: bibl. (Serie Ideología y política; 20)

Japanese political scientist analyzes the relations between Japan and Peru throughout the Fujimori period and its aftermath (1990–2003) focusing on the Japanese approach to the 1990 presidential election, the establishment of the financial support group for Peru in 1991, the Fujimori coup in April 1992, the 1996–97 hostage crisis in the Japanese ambassador's residence in Lima, economic relations during the 1990s, and Fujimori's asylum and Peruvian extradition request in the early 2000s. Argues that, despite the sympathy stated by the Japanese mass media and public opinion toward Fujimori, the generally supportive attitude of the Japanese government was relatively restrained and based on realistic economic and diplomatic considerations.

URUGUAY

2138 Batalla, Isabel Clemente. La política exterior del primer gobierno de izquierda en Uruguay. (*Iberoamericana/Stockholm,* 34:1/2, 2004, p. 323–351, bibl., graph)

Excellent analysis of the formulation and first foreign policy initiatives implemented by the Tabaré Vázquez administration inaugurated in 2005 in Uruguay. Argues that the leftist government followed a pragmatic and incremental approach aimed at strengthening Uruguay's international position and autonomy by privileging regional integration policies, closer relations with the European Union, the G20 and the Cairns group, and bilateral links with Chile, Spain, and Germany.

VENEZUELA

2139 Briceño Ruiz, José. La posición de Venezuela frente al ALCA y las relaciones de la CAN con Estados Unidos y la UE. (*Aldea Mundo*, 8:16, nov. 2003/abril 2004, p. 59–66, bibl.)

Argues that the Chávez administration foreign policy has affected the design of the Andean Community's foreign common policy towards the US and the European Union, particularly because the Venezuelan governments strong opposition to free trade agreements has fragmented the Andean Community weakening its capacity to develop an effective common approach.

2140 Cardozo, Elsa. Venezuela en la comunidad andina: retrocesos en tres escalas. (*Aldea Mundo*, 8:16, nov. 2003/abril 2004, p. 29–39, appendix, bibl., graphs, tables)

Argues that Venezuela's relations with the Andean Community have experienced backwards movement since 1999 under the Chávez administration. In particular, the author points out the widening ideological and strategic rift between Venezuela and some Andean countries (especially Colombia and Peru), and the relative decline in Venezuelan participation and economic interaction with the Community.

2141 Golinger, Eva. Bush versus Chávez: Washington's war on Venezuela. New York: Monthly Review Press, 2008. 175 p.: bibl., ill., index.

Highly critical analysis of the Bush administration foreign policy toward Venezuela under Hugo Chávez. Based on declassified US documents and international sources, the author denounces US attempts to undermine and overthrow the Chávez administration employing the National Endowment for Democracy and USAID to support the Venezuelan opposition and destabilize the regime. Arguments could benefit from gathering more solid evidence of US intervention.

2142 Mora Brito, Daniel. La política exterior de Hugo Chávez en tres actos, 1998–2004. (*Aldea Mundo*, 8:16, nov. 2003/ abril 2004, p. 76–85, bibl.)

Critical examination of the evolution of Venezuela's foreign policy under the Chávez administration between 1998 and 2004. Argues that there were three stages of development of Chávez's Bolivarian foreign policy: the preparation phase of the revolutionary policy (1998–2001), the consolidation phase (2001–02), and the confrontation and radicalization phase (since 2002). The article points out that although Chávez continues to fulfill the obligations and commitments made by previous administrations, the country has implemented a policy aimed at establishing alternative centers of power to displace US hegemony and transform the international system.

La vecindad colombo-venezolana: imágenes y realidades. See item **2128**.

2143 Venezuela en el ALCA: entre realidades y fantasías. Compilación de Rita Giacalone. Mérida, Venezuela: Grupo de Integración Regional, GRUDIR: Univ. de los Andes, Vicerrectorado Académico, Publicaciones, 2005. 209 p.: bibl., ill., maps. (Ciencias sociales y humanidades/Universidad de los Andes)

Interesting study of the proposal to create a Free Trade Area of the Americas that analyzes the evolution of the negotiations until 2005 and its possible impact on Venezuela. First part includes three articles discussing the state of the negotiations, a theoretical-conceptual analysis of the proposal, and a review of special treatment and structural funds components of the potential agreement. Second part is focused on Venezuela, discussing the potential commercial effects, the impact on agricultural producers, the evolution of the country's negotiation positions, the possible political and geopolitical costs of participating or not in the free trade area, and the approach to the Andean Community and Mercosur. In general, the authors see the rejection of the agreement as disadvantageous for Venezuela but seem to be too optimistic about the chances of reaching a successful conclusion to the negotiations.

BRAZIL

THOMAZ GUEDES DA COSTA, *Professor of National Security, Center for Hemispheric Defense Studies, National Defense University*

WORKS REVIEWED THIS BIENNIUM offer the casual reader and professional researcher alike an analytical picture of Brazil's foreign policy. The two dominant challenges for Brazil are regional relations and globalization. Most of the works reviewed date from 2002. This period roughly corresponds to President Lula da Silva's first administration.

International integration continues to be a dominant issue in Brazil's foreign policy. Unlike the enthusiastic drive seen in the 1990s, this collection focuses on the dilemmas of the subregional integration process observed in South America (items **2148**, **2155**, **2166**, and **2169**), and hemispheric trade negotiations of the Free Trade Area of the Americas (items **2153**, **2160**, and **2172**). Furthermore, integration provides an incentive for Brazil to expand its relations globally, absorbing the impact and opportunities of the recent economic globalization (items **2144**, **2147**, **2150**, **2164**, **2168**, and **2170**) and establishing new ties aimed at fostering Brazilian economic interests (items **2159**, **2161**, and **2167**).

Another significant component of this collection are the publications that present facets of Brazil's foreign policy formulation, either by portraying the interests and actions of national actors (items **2149**, **2156**, **2169**, and **2171**), or by describing policy processes within the government in general, and the foreign ministry, in particular (items **2146**, **2165**, **2173**, and **2174**).

Noteworthy are some publications that could be helpful to readers interested in the relations between Brazil and the US. These works (items **2145** and **2153**) provide historical evaluations that may help readers understand the underlying and enduring factors present in bilateral relations.

2144 Almeida, Paulo Roberto de. O Brasil e a construção da ordem econômica internacional contemporânea. (*Contexto Int.*, 26:1, jan./junho 2004, p. 7–63, bibl.)

This is a very useful survey of Brazil's participation in the construction of the international economic order during the 20th century. The author argues that Brazil is one of the few peripheral countries that has had a significant role in international negotiations and in the generation of initiatives for financial, trade, and investment political order in global politics. Using diplomatic sources, the articles lists the active presence of Brazil in international conferences and organizations, and in advanced multilateral negotiation processes to foster what is perceived as a cooperative democratization of international relations.

2145 Alves, Vágner Camilo. Ilusão desfeita: a "aliança especial" Brasil-Estados Unidos e o poder naval brasileiro durante e

após a Segunda Guerra Mundial. (*Rev. Bras. Polít. Int.*, 48:1, 2005, p. 151–177, bibl.)

The author studied the shaping of a "special alliance" between Brazil and the US at the end of WW II. Using naval cooperation, purchases, and support from the US, the article illustrates the initial political hopes and the later disappointment in the relationship. The subordination in doctrine and equipment of the Brazilian navy to US influence did not result in Brazil's goal of regional maritime superiority, and may have caused the divergences of recent decades in military collaboration.

2146 Barreto Filho, Fernando Paulo de Mello. Os sucessores do Barão: relações exteriores do Brasil. v. 2, 1964 a 1985. Prefácio de Celso Lafer. São Paulo: Paz e Terra, 2006. 1 v.: bibl., ill., index.

In an earlier work, this Brazilian diplomat surveyed Brazilian foreign policy from 1912 to 1964. Now, the author turns his attention to the period of the military regime from 1964–85. The structure of the book follows the tenure of six foreign ministers, describing issues, policies, processes, and leadership styles for each period. As Ambassador Rubens Ricupero points out in the preface, the choice of evaluating Brazilian foreign policy through the administration of each minister shows the organizational culture and management style within the foreign ministry as an institution and its preponderant role in the conduct of foreign policy over the military and any other national institution or interest group. The book reveals a strong sense of continuity in Brazilian foreign policy, not just as observed by each minister during the period but also in preserving principles and values traditional to Brazil foreign policy. This permits the author to observe that the ministers are officially and figuratively successors of the Baron of Rio Branco, José Maria da Silva Paranhos Júnior. Nevertheless, the author points out that each foreign minister wished to provide his own imprimatur with a particular label in foreign relations (i.e., Fidelity of the West, Security and Development, Responsible Pragmatism, etc.).

2147 Batista Júnior, Paulo Nogueira. O Brasil e a economia internacional: recuperação e defesa da autonomia nacional. Rio de Janeiro: Elsevier, Editora Campus, 2005. 154 p.: bibl., index.

One of the foremost Brazilian economists of his time analyzes the evolution of the Brazilian economy and its presence in global markets. His approach defends a "national idea" for Brazil to conduct its financial and economic affairs and trade with greater autonomy and independence from the international forces of the liberal market approaches.

2148 Brasil e Argentina hoje: política e economia. Organização de Brasilio Sallum Júnior. Bauru, Brazil: EDUSC, 2004. 290 p.: bibl., ill. (Ciências sociais)

This book collects essays delivered at a seminar that focused on the relationship between Argentina and Brazil, and their economic and political development during the 2002 Argentine crisis. The essays, though skeptical about the possibilities for social-economic development within the current liberal, capitalist globalization process, conclude that political stability is a crucial factor for societies to aiming to reduce the distance between expectations and results of governments and markets.

Bueno, Clodoaldo. Política externa da primeira república: os anos de apogeu, de 1902 a 1918. See *HLAS 64:1667.*

2149 Ciência, política e relações internacionais: ensaios sobre Paulo Carneiro. Organização de Marcos Chor Maio. Rio de Janeiro: Editora Fiocruz; Brasília: UNESCO Representação no Brasil, 2004. 339 p.: bibl., ill.

This book surveys the life of the Brazilian scientist Paulo Estevão de Berrêdo Carneiro. Paulo Carneiro was a renowned researcher, educator, diplomat, and promoter of the sciences in Brazil and abroad, especially during his service for the Pasteur Institute and UNESCO, both in France. The work provides many insights on the history of science and public policy in Brazil during the 20th century.

2150 Crise e oportunidade: o Brasil e o cenário internacional. Organização de Antônio Corrêa de Lacerda. São Paulo: Lazuli Editora, 2006. 328 p.: bibl., ill.

This collection of essays written by economists evaluate Brazil's performance in the globalizing economy and describe its economic relationship with foreign markets. It covers foreign direct investments, capital flow, macroeconomics, competitiveness, and foreign trade. The book is especially useful for readers seeking to learn about Brazil's political economy by taking advantage of each author's individual perspectives and projections using economic data. The results inform the reader about Brazil's potential future performance in the global economy.

2151 Cronologia da política externa do governo Lula, 2003–2006. Edição de Ministério das Relações Exteriores, Secretaria de Planejamento Diplomático e Fundação Alexandre de Gusmão. Coordenação de Eliane Miranda Paiva. Brasília: FUNAG, Fundação Alexandre de Gusmão, 2007. 163 p.: index.

This is an official, diplomatic chronology edited by the Brazilian Foreign Ministry listing events of President Lula da Silva's administration and foreign policy. Index provides entries on countries, organizations, individuals, and themes.

2152 De Negri, Fernanda. O perfil dos exportadores industriais brasileiros para a China. *(Rev. Bras. Comér. Exter.*, 19:84, julho/set. 2005, p. 22–35, bibl., graphs, tables)
With a variety of data and information, the author records Brazilian industrial sales to China from 1996 to 2003. The author concludes that there is still greater space for increasing Brazilian exports of higher aggregated value products.

2153 Deblock, Christian and **Sylvain F. Turcotte.** Estados Unidos, Brasil y las negociaciones hemisféricas: el ALCA en modalidad bilateral. *(Foro Int./México*, 45:1, enero/marzo 2005, p. 5–35, bibl., tables)
Between 1994 and 2003, the US led negotiations to establish a free trade area in the Americas. By 2003, the multilateral negotiations had come to a stand still. During the period, the US and Brazil were two of the main protagonists in projecting the structures, negotiation mechanisms, and strategies to advance such a project. The attempt to build a free trade in the Americas reveals the clash between two different approaches: the US preference for an overall negotiation including all countries (except Cuba), and Brazil's choice for negotiating block-by-block of countries and issue-by-issue. This difference resulted in deadlock and eventual dissipation of interest and efforts for advancing the continental free trade area as a common strategy among all countries in the Western Hemisphere. In this work, the authors describe the FTAA negotiation process with particular emphasis on the US and Brazil given their important roles in the debate.

Domínguez Ávila, Carlos Federico. Brasil-Centroamérica: cien años de solidaridad y cooperación, 1906–2006. See item **2043.**

2154 Encontro de História Brasil Paraguai, *1st, Salvador, Brazil, 2001.* Anais. Salvador, Brazil: Instituto Geográfico e Histórico da Bahia, 2002. 356 p.: bibl.
This report of an event coordinated by national history research institutions gathers essays and papers written by authors from Brazil and Paraguay. The collection reviews events, chronicles, and historical developments of the history shared by the two countries, mostly during the 19th century and especially during the Paraguayan War. For those interested in this history, the work collects many references to primary sources and analyses of developments.

2155 Flores, Maria Candida Galvão. O Mercosul nos discursos do governo brasileiro, 1985–1994. Rio de Janeiro: FGV Editora, 2005. 125 p.: bibl.
This well-documented work with a carefully crafted methodology studies the discourse of three Brazilian presidents (Sarney, Collor, and Franco). The author presents and evaluates how each president conveyed ideas, proposals, and decisions regarding the MERCOSUL effort for regional integration amidst challenges of national agendas and debates and international negotiation processes.

2156 Goes Filho, Paulo de. O clube das nações: a missão do Brasil na ONU e o mundo da diplomacia parlamentar. Rio de Janeiro: Relume Dumará: NuAP, 2003. 230 p.: bibl. (Col. Antropologia da política; 23)
This is a unique work that reveals routines, principles, and processes of the bureaucratic and political performance of the Brazilian mission to the UN in New York. It results from personal observations of diplomatic work. The analysis is particularly useful for those interested in Brazil's diplomatic organizational culture and institutions in terms of style and decision-making processes.

2157 Internacionalização e desenvolvimento da indústria no Brasil. Organização de Mariano Francisco Laplane, Luciano Coutinho e Célio Hiratuka. Campinas, Brazil: UNICAMP, Instituto de Economia; São Paulo: Editora UNESP, 2004. 349 p.: bibl., ill. (Col. Economia contemporânea)
This collection of essays evaluates many facets of Brazil's industrial development, from the role of foreign capital, internal consumption and markets, national and foreign companies, and of the flow of capital. More than providing a sense of unity and synthesis for the readers, individual chapters stand alone with causal arguments and insights about trends.

2158 Lima, Maria Regina Soares de. Aspiração internacional e política externa. *(Rev. Bras. Comér. Exter.*, 19:82, jan./março 2005, p. 4–19)
The work is an historical evaluation

of Brazil's design and implementation of strategies in international politics. The author recognizes the desires of national elites and diplomats to legitimize the country's foreign policy to sustain an autonomous position in political and economic issues in international relations. In her analysis, official discourse reveals that elites sought to increase Brazil's influence within the international sphere while advancing its own national interests. The article is a robust synthesis of foreign relations concepts and discourse during the 20th century.

2159 Lima, Maria Regina Soares de.
A política externa brasileira e os desafios da cooperação Sul-Sul. (*Rev. Bras. Polít. Int.*, 48:1, 2005, p. 24–59, bibl., graphs)
The author evaluates the possibilities, challenges, and obstacles for greater South-South cooperation, especially for India, Mexico, Brazil, Indonesia, and other South American countries. Special attention is given to Brazil's past and current official efforts to explore the political and economic benefits of such collaboration. Article available in English in the *American Historical Review*, vol. 111, no. 2, April 2006, p. 4–29.

2160 O Nordeste frente à ALCA: impactos potenciais, interesses de negociação e desafios de política. Coordenação de Pedro da Motta Veiga. Fortaleza, Brazil: Banco do Nordeste do Brasil, 2003. 163 p.: bibl.
This work reviews the economic relations of Brazilian Northeastern states with the countries of the North American Free Trade Agreement (NAFTA). It seeks to evaluate the terms of trade, the potential for investments, and the prospects for local industrial projects that can be integrated to the needs of an eventual Free Trade Area of the Americas (FTAA). The review is based on extensive statistical aggregation covering the regional economic performance in the late nineties.

2161 Oliveira, Henrique Altemani de.
Brasil-China: trinta anos de uma parceria estratégica. (*Rev. Bras. Polít. Int.*, 47:1, 2004, p. 7–30, bibl., tables)
This is a brief analytical review of Brazil's relations with the People's Republic of China, including considerations of events before 1974. In that year, Brazil recognized the PRC in the context of expanding South-

South relations. The author uses mainly trade relations as central evidence of the expansion of bilateral relations. Unique in this relationship is the technological cooperation for satellite technology taking place during the 1990s. This is another evaluation of a "strategic partnership," a term commonly used but with unclear operational value. The author does a fine job of illustrating the discourse of political cooperation accompanying an expanding economic partnership.

2162 A política externa brasileira na visão dos seus protagonistas. Organização de Henrique Altemani de Oliveira e José Augusto Guilhon Albuquerque. Colaboração de Bruno Ayllón Pino *et al.* Rio de Janeiro: Editora Lumen Juris, 2005. 239 p.: bibl.
This keenly constructed publication results from a research project that collected information in interviews conducted with leading figures of the Brazilian government, including bureaucrats, high ranking military officers, politicians, and diplomats. The analysis of the data reports on different sessions covering Brazil's bilateral and regional relations and thematic challenges, especially between 1960 and 1980.

2163 Raffaelli, Marcelo. A monarquia e a república: aspectos das relações entre Brasil e Estados Unidos durante o Império. Rio de Janeiro: CHDD; Brasília: FUNAG, 2006. 289 p.: bibl., index.
This book presents a richly documented narrative of the diplomatic relations between Brazil and the US, from 1822 until 1889—the period of the Brazilian Empire. The author, a Brazilian career diplomat, ably uses diplomatic and governmental records from the Foreign Ministry's historical archive and other sources to produce an attractive and gripping description of the relationship between the two countries. This work promises to be very useful for those interested in the roots of the official relationship between Brazil and the US, especially in shaping Brazilian views about the US.

2164 Relações sul-sul: países da Ásia e o Brasil. Organização de Alberto do Amaral Júnior e Michelle Ratton Sanchez. São Paulo: Aduaneiras, 2004. 318 p.: bibl.
Another collection of essays focusing their analysis on political and economic developments in Asia and on Brazilian

bilateral relations with countries in the East, demonstrating the global reach of its interests. This set of essays is particularly useful for readers interested in learning more about the country's relations with Japan, India, South Korea, and China.

2165 Saraiva, José Flávio Sombra. A busca de um novo paradigma: política exterior, comércio externo e federalismo no Brasil. *(Rev. Bras. Polít. Int.,* 47:2, 2004, p. 131–162, bibl., graph, tables)

This article provides unique insights into the shaping of Brazil's foreign policy by analyzing the interests and interference of Brazilian states (i.e., provinces) in national politics and agendas. As a federal state, the Brazilian central government struggles in aggregating the demands and forces of interest groups and of subnational political forces. The structure of national production, especially of agricultural products, conditions the value of actors and items in the national agenda. The federal government's efforts to promote foreign trade and investments correlate with the dynamics of the internal markets and politics. This unique perspective enriches the understanding of the formation of Brazil's foreign policy as it brings forth enduring factors, actors, and dimensions of national politics and politicking.

2166 Seminário Brasil-Argentina, *Brasília, Brazil and Buenos Aires, Argentina,* **2002.** Brasil-Argentina: a visão do outro: soberania e cultura política. Organização de Carlos Henrique Cardim e Monica Hirst. Brasília: Instituto de Pesquisa de Relações Internacionais-IPRI/FUNAG, 2003. 438 p.: bibl., ill.

This is another collection of essays edited by the Brazilian Foreign Ministry's Institute for International Relations Research. In a well-structured pairing of Brazilian and Argentine scholars, the authors analyze the historical evolution and current perspectives of sovereignty and political culture in both Argentina and Brazil regarding national and international developments and repercussions. The book gathers the proceedings of two seminars aimed at understanding how convergences of tendencies and the uniqueness of processes impact regional integration and wider international relations of both countries.

2167 Seminário "Comunidade dos Países de Língua Portuguesa-CPLP: Oportunidades e Perspectivas," *Brasília, Brazil,* **2002.** CPLP: oportunidades e perspectivas Organização de Carlos Henrique Cardim e João Batista Cruz. Brasília, DF: IPRI, FUNAG 2002. 541 p.: bibl., ill., maps. (Col. Países e regiões)

This publication is the proceedings of the seminar "The Community of Portuguese-Speaking Countries—CPLP: Opportunities and Perspectives" that took place in Brasília in 2002. The event gathered diplomats, government officials, scholars, and representatives of nongovernmental and international organizations. This is a very diverse collection of chapters that present dissimilar perspectives, problems, and solutions for countries that have in common the language and heritage of Portugal's colonialism. It provides insights into socioeconomic development, the possibilities of collaborative projects, and the value in promoting the use of the Portuguese language as a factor of integration. The work provides a glimpse of a unique facet of Brazil's foreign policy in using cultural elements to promote multilateral diplomacy with geographically distant countries.

2168 Seminário Internacional Hegemonia e Contra-hegemonia: os Impasses da Globalização e os Processos de Regionalização, *Rio de Janeiro, Brazil, 2003.* Globalização: dimensões e alternativas. Tradução de Noéli Correia de Melo Sobrinho. Coordenação de Theotonio dos Santos. Organização de Carlos Eduardo Martins, Fernando Sá e Mónica Bruckmann. Rio de Janeiro: Editora PUC Rio: REGGEN; São Paulo: Edições Loyola, 2004. 363 p.: bibl., ill., maps. (Hegemonia e contra-hegemonia; 2)

A 2003 seminar featured a number of papers written by renowned scholars, now collected in this book. This collection focuses on analyses of the economic and social implications of globalization. According to the editor, it represents the counter-hegemonic thinking of the forces promoting capitalist globalization. This Marxist criticism is directed towards the George W. Bush administration and the European industrialized countries, claiming that these political actors seek the expansion of capitalist properties and accumulation. Additionally, the authors evaluate the impact of capitalist globalization on the economies and social structure in Latin America. The work is significant for its evaluation of different academic paradigms and political perspectives on economic growth and development in Latin America in general, and Brazil in particular.

2169 Seminário Internacional Regional de Estudos Interdisciplinares, 1st, Univ. Federal de Santa Catarina, 2002. Condição humana e modernidade no Cone Sul: elementos para pensar Brasil e Argentina. Organização de Héctor Ricardo Leis, Caleb Faria Alves e Denis Rosenfield. Florianópolis, Brazil: Cidade Futura, 2003. 382 p.: bibl.

This multi-author volume analyzes Brazil and Argentina in terms of historical and current human development and social conditions as each attempts greater regional integration while facing modernity and globalization. The authors are reputable scholars working in academia in Brazil and Argentina. The point of departure for the analysis is the socio-philosophical assertion that societies in both countries display features of both barbaric and modern behavior in their polities. The chapters show that Brazilians and Argentinians endure the legacies of colonialism, imperfect political socialization, and significant clashes between popular images and local reality with democracy and industrialization, on one hand, and social cleavages and despair, on the other. The collection provides enriching insights for those interested in studying regional integration and its development from the perspective of sociologists and philosophers.

2170 Seminário "Política Externa do Brasil para o Século XXI," *Câmara dos Deputados*, 2002. Coletânea de textos apresentados no Seminário "Política Externa do Brasil para o Século XXI," realizado nos dias 13, 14 e 15 de agosto de 2002, na Câmara dos Deputados. Organização de Aldo Rebelo, Luis Fernandes e Carlos Henrique Cardim. 2a. ed. Brasília: Centro de Documentação e Informação, Coordenação de Publicações, 2004. 457 p.: bibl. (Série Ação parlamentar; 254)

The book collects the proceedings of a seminar organized by Brazil's Federal Chamber of Deputies to survey current and prospective developments of Brazilian foreign policy at the beginning of the 21st century. Congressmen and distinguished scholars (e.g., Celso Lafer, Letícia Pinheiro, Oliveiros S. Ferreira, Mônica Hirst, José Flávio S. Saraiva among others) contributed to the eight-part work. The resulting collection has a regional geographic perspective (Brazilian relations with the US, the North America Free Trade Area, South America, and Europe) and an issues-based approach (regional powers, Portuguese-speaking countries, and international organizations). Demonstrates Brazil's wide reach in foreign relations in economic, security, cultural, and environmental initiatives, and contrasts different visions of Brazil's foreign policy goals.

2171 Silva, Alex Giacomelli da. Poder inteligente: a questão do HIV/AIDS na política externa brasileira. (*Contexto Int.*, 27:1, jan./junho 2005, p. 127–158, bibl.)

The author argues that Brazil has employed its traditional approaches to international relations, negotiating and diplomatic abilities, and the achievements in fighting HIV/AIDS as an example of smart power in promoting its foreign policy agenda. The argument posed—that the example of what Brazil has achieved in negotiating with countries and multinational corporations holding patents to medicines—is not an isolated case of Brasilia advancing its public diplomacy for concrete gains, but rather the successful result of a larger strategy, especially in multilateral diplomacy, to mobilize other countries and to promote Brazil as an alternative leading player in global issues.

2172 Souza, Ielbo Marcus Lobo de. A Área de Livre Comércio das Américas e o Brasil: questões geopolíticas e disputas hegemônicas subjacentes. (*Rev. Inf. Legis.*, 42:167, julho/set. 2005, p. 15–26, bibl.)

The author argues that for Brazil, the Free Trade Area of the Americas is one of many negotiations that have taken place in the country's global trade agenda. Brazil joins in the FTAA negotiations to prevent the US from taking hegemonic control of trade in the Americas.

2173 Vizentini, Paulo Gilberto Fagundes. Relações exteriores do Brasil, 1945–1964: o nacionalismo e a política externa

independente. Petrópolis, Brazil: Editora
Vozes, 2004. 279 p.: bibl. (Col. Relações
internacionais)

This survey of Brazilian diplomacy
from 1945–64 is put forth by one the country's foremost international relations scholars. It covers what the author considers the
populism period of foreign policy. It features
Brazil's efforts at balancing international
alignment, in managing the needs of foreign
financing and national development, and
the launching of an independent foreign
policy initiating Brazil's multilateral diplomatic age.

2174 Vizentini, Paulo Gilberto Fagundes.
Relações internacionais do Brasil: de
Vargas a Lula. São Paulo: Editora Fundação
Perseu Abramo, 2003. 117 p.: bibl., ill. (His-
tória do povo brasileiro)

The book is a description, with many
chronologies, of Brazilian foreign policy
from the end of Vargas administration to the
Cardoso administration. The book briefly
evaluates several different periods, including the "independent foreign policy," "Brazil
as a rising power," and the duality nationalist and internationalist approaches to conducting the country's international affairs.

POLITICAL ECONOMY

GENERAL

JONATHAN HISKEY, *Associate Professor of Political Science, Vanderbilt University*

WITH THE ONSET OF THE GLOBAL FINANCIAL CRISIS in 2008, scholarship on the political economy of Latin America is almost certain to continue to pursue with vigor many of the same questions that have occupied scholars over the past several years. Dominant among these lines of inquiry is the impact that globalization and the neoliberal model have had on the economic and political development prospects of Latin American countries. Running through this common research agenda, however, is a stark dividing line between those who see the region's increasing economic integration and turn toward market-based development strategies as an obstacle to Latin American prosperity, and those who see these phenomena as essential to the region's economic development. Given the developed country origins of the global financial crisis, those scholars that have long warned of the heightened vulnerabilities of Latin America to international instability that come with globalization will surely feel vindicated. Conversely, the *relatively* optimistic growth projections emerging in 2009 that forecast a weathering of the storm for Latin America would seem to offer support to those who have seen the region's economic reforms as critical in providing it with much needed economic stability and growth. The majority of the works reviewed here, reflective of broader trends in recent Latin American political economy research, tend toward one or the other of these general orientations.

Somewhat more common in past years have been those works that focus on the flaws of the neoliberal model and its principal strategy of more fully inserting Latin American economies into the global economy. Recent research continues this pattern, but offers a far more nuanced, analytical approach to the question of the impact of globalization and neoliberalism on the region, moving away from the more broad-brushed critiques prevalent during the 1990s. Deere's (item **2183**) innovative analysis of how the neoliberal restructuring of the rural economy across the region has affected women and their role in the agricultural sectors of their countries is exemplary of this trend. Rhoads and Torres' edited volume (item **2199**) also offers an indication of the increasingly fine-tuned critiques of the neoliberal paradigm through analysis of its (and globalization's) impact on higher education in Latin America. A similarly novel perspective on the consequences of neoliberalism emerges from Lucer-Graffigna's study (item **2192**) of how the dominant conceptions of poverty in the World Bank influence the general approach to its development programs.

Even those works that offer more general critiques of years past reveal the advances in political economy research over the past two decades. Rather than attributing to globalization all of Latin America's ills, with only scant support for such claims, these recent works access and analyze data on the actual outcomes of specific market-based reforms in supporting their generally pessimistic assessments of the model. Solimano's (item **2196**) assessment of social policies in the region over the past 25 years, for example, offers a compelling point of departure for his call to move away from the "growth-based" strategy for poverty reduction. Gabaldón (item **2187**) takes a similar approach in positing the need for a set of policy alternatives oriented more toward sustainable development. In a similar vein, Farrari (item **2186**) argues rather optimistically for the viability of a new political economy in Latin America. Bouzas and Ffrench-Davis (item **2178**) also assess Latin America's economic prospects moving forward, and in the process call for a reestablishment of control over domestic economic policy in order to better manage the consequences of the clearly unstable global economy. Tulchin and Bland's (item **2189**) edited volume centers around the theme of fixing the flaws of globalization that have been so evident in Latin America's development patterns of the past two decades. Though still offering largely negative assessments of the economic changes over the past 20 years, these works represent a significant shift away from prior tendencies to merely focus on the problems of globalization and neoliberalism, moving instead toward a more prescriptive, policy-oriented research agenda that seeks to shape future policy directions of Latin America's political economy.

Across the divide from research that highlights the flaws of globalization and neoliberalism stand those works that find global integration and market-based development as essential elements of Latin America's recent economic successes, relative stability, and its chances for surviving the current global economic downturn. As with the works discussed above, this research also represents a departure from its predecessors of the 1980s and 1990s. Early works on the merits of the neoliberal model in general shared the assumption that reducing the role of the ineffective Latin American states from the region's economic development process represented a positive step. A lesson that emerged from that period, however, is that although the state was in dire need of reform throughout Latin America, it still had to play a critical role in fostering the conditions conducive to stable economic growth.

Works such as Treisman's study (item **2198**) of the different types of anti-inflation strategies implemented during the 1980s and 1990s highlight the various ways that such "neoliberal sins" as distributive politics and cooptive strategies in fact played critical roles in the successful achievement of broader neoliberal goals. The work of Kurtz and Brooks (item **2191**) and Remmer (item **1795**) also highlight the somewhat counterintuitive role of partisan-based policies in shaping the reform strategy pursued by a particular country and its likelihood of attaining relatively successful outcomes.

Adding to this body of work is research that re-establishes a place for the Latin American citizenry in politics during the neoliberal era. The conventional view of the public's role in the market-driven, emerging democracies of the last 20 years has been one characterized by a limited voice that at times might be given to sporadic, violent outbursts. Arce and Bellinger (item **2176**) challenge this view, instead finding that when compared with previous periods of political participation, Latin Americans of the last decades of the 20th century were in fact quite participatory. Gans-Morse and Nichter (item **2188**) provide a similar reassessment of the impact of neoliberalism on Latin American democracies more generally, offering evidence in support of the notion that the region's market-based reforms and integration with the global market ultimately served to strengthen emerging democratic political systems. A challenge to these findings, however, emerges from Holzner's study (item **2219**) of political participation among the poor of Mexico. At least for this case and this population, he finds steadily declining rates of political involvement as the country moved ahead with its economic reform agenda during the 1990s. When taken together, though, these works offer a much more complete picture of how and where the neoliberal reforms in particular, and globalization more generally, have affected Latin American economic and political developments.

A final related strand of research reviewed here concerns variations in the specific policy designs and outcomes of Latin America's reform agenda. Weyland's work on the diffusion of certain policies across the region (item **2200**), Bichara's comparative study of financial reforms in Latin America and Asia (item **2177**), and Carstens and Jácome's (item **2179**) overview and analysis of the various central bank reforms carried out in Latin America are among the more notable works in this area. Also worthy of mention is the continuation of research on social policy, in particular social security programs (item **2190**), during the neoliberal era, and the various effects that these policies have had for the quality of life of Latin Americans. As the region struggles through the global financial storm over the next several years, such works on the consequences of globalization and the market-based reforms seem certain to flourish as scholars continue to examine successes and failures over the past 20 years.

2175 América Latina a comienzos del siglo XXI: perspectivas económicas, sociales y políticas. Coordinación de Gilberto Dupas. Textos de Luis Fernando Ayerbe *et al.* Rosario, Argentina: Obreal Eularo: Instituto de Estudios Económicos e Internacionales: Homo Sapiens Ediciones, 2005. 374 p.: bibl., ill., map.

One of many edited volumes seeking to offer a comprehensive assessment of the impact that neoliberalism and globalization have had on various aspects of Latin America's economic and political development. A mixed but useful assortment of chapters that include analyses of structural change in Mexico and the political and economic challenges faced by Lula in Brazil.

2176 Arce, Moisés and **Paul T. Bellinger.** Low-intensity democracy revisited: the effects of economic liberalization on political activity in Latin America. (*World Polit.*, 60:1, Oct. 2007, p. 97–121)

Challenges the conventional view that recent economic reforms have led to "low intensity citizenship." Rather, through analysis of economic liberalization and social protests across 17 Latin American coun-

tries between 1970 and 2000, the authors find no significant declines in political participation during the economic reforms of the past 20 years.

Artigas, Alvaro. Amérique du Sud: les démocraties inachevées. See *HLAS 64:473.*

Benton, Lauren. No longer odd region out: repositioning Latin America in world history. See *HLAS 64:375.*

2177 Bichara, Julimar da Silva; André Moreira Cunha; and **Marcos Tadeo Caputi Lélis.** Integración monetaria y financiera en América del Sur y en Asia. (*LARR*, 43:1, 2008, p. 84–112, bibl., graphs, tables)

An innovative comparative analysis of capital and monetary reforms in Asia's ASEAN+3 and South America's Mercosur. Seeks to understand those conditions that influence economic convergence among member countries of regional economic organizations.

2178 Bouzas, Roberto and **Ricardo Ffrench-Davis.** Globalización y políticas nacionales: ¿cerrando el círculo? (*Desarro. Econ.*, 45:179, oct./dic. 2005, p. 323–348, bibl.)

Provides an overview of the political and economic dimensions of globalization and then explores the abilities of countries to alter the course of globalization and its impact through a strengthening of domestic control over economic policy.

2179 Carstens, Agustín and **Luis I. Jácome H.** La reforma de los bancos centrales latinoamericanos. (*Trimest. Econ.*, 72:288, oct./dic. 2005, p. 683–732, bibl., graphs, tables)

An informative assessment of central bank reforms in Latin America during the 1990s. The authors argue that these reforms were critical in anti-inflationary efforts across the region. Includes several useful country-by-country charts of exchange rate and inflationary trends between 1990 and 2000s.

Casas Gragea, Angel María. La economía política internacional de la nueva integración regional de las Américas: el caso de la Comunidad Andina. See item **2080**.

2180 Castiglioni, Rossana. Reforma de pensiones en América Latina: orígenes y estrategias, 1980–2002. (*Rev. Cienc. Polít./Santiago*, 25:2, 2005, p. 173–189, bibl.)

A useful and concise overview and assessment of pension reform in Latin America over the past two decades. Examines variations in these reforms and concludes that each case represents a complex combination of such factors as international institutions, veto players within each case, and the particular institutional makeup of the relevant political system.

2181 Cinquetti, Carlos Alberto. The debt crisis: a re-appraisal. (*Rev. Econ. Polít.*, 25:3, julho/set. 2005, p. 209–223, bibl., graphs, tables)

An empirical challenge to conventional views of the roots of Latin America's debt crisis. Results suggest a far less important role for domestic conflict management institutions in explaining variations in developing country debt during the 1980s. Analysis is based on a somewhat limited sample of 33 countries.

2182 De La Reza, Germán A. La integración económica entre países dispares: un caso de sistema complejo. (*Perf. Latinoam.*, 13:27, enero/junio 2006, p. 87–105, bibl.)

Analysis of the complexities involved in determining the effects of economic integration between countries of differing size economies. Author highlights deficiencies of current theoretical work on the issue, calling for more interdisciplinary work.

2183 Deere, Carmen Diana. The feminization of agriculture?: economic restructuring in rural Latin America. Geneva, Switzerland: United Nations Research Institute for Social Development, 2005. 67 p.: ill. (Occasional paper; 1)

Compelling exploration of an understudied by-product of the neoliberal era—the growth in women's participation in the agricultural wage labor force of Latin America. Author offers strong evidence connecting these trends to the heightened need for family income diversification during times of economic crisis.

2184 La economía mundial y América Latina: tendencias, problemas y desafíos. Compilación de Jaime Estay Reyno. Textos de Theotonio Dos Santos *et al.* Buenos Aires: CLACSO, 2005. 411 p.: bibl., ill. (Col. Grupos de trabajo)

Covering a wide range of regions and countries, this edited volume offers another diverse set of perspectives on the oft-asked question of how globalization and economic integration have affected the development of Latin America. Volume includes general assessments of regional development trends and sector-specific case studies of how certain Latin American countries have fared over the past 20 years.

2185 Ellner, Steve. Globalization, macroeconomic policies, and Latin American democracy. (*Lat. Am. Polit. Soc.*, 48:1, Spring 2006, p. 175–187, bibl.)

A critical review of recent scholarship on Latin American political and economic development in an era of globalization. Offers a useful synthesis of views during the early 2000s on the seeming permanence of many features of globalization and its mixed effects on Latin America.

2186 Farrari, César. Hacia un nuevo consenso de política económica en América Latina. (*Nueva Soc.*, 199, sept./oct. 2005, p. 60–79, bibl., photo)

An optimistic assessment of the

chances for a "new political economy" across Latin America that challenges a status quo fiscal policy shaped in large part by defenders of monopolies. Calls for a reorientation of the redistributive policy in an effort to reduce inequality while enhancing the competitiveness of the region through a strengthening of its human capital.

2187 Gabaldón, Arnoldo. La salida de América Latina: desarrollo sustentable. Caracas: Grijalbo, 2006. 489 p.: bibl., ill.

An in-depth analysis of the concept of sustainable development as it applies across Latin America provides the basis for an extensive development policy prescription for the region that the author sees as a viable strategy for such development in the future.

2188 Gans-Morse, Jordan and **Simeon Nichter.** Economic reforms and democracy: evidence of a j-curve in Latin America. (*Comp. Polit. Stud.*, 41:10, Oct. 2008, p. 1398–1426)

A revisiting of the question of how neoliberal economic reforms have affected Latin American democracies. Authors offer an innovative, nonlinear accounting of how these reforms ultimately improved the chances for democracy in the region.

2189 Getting globalization right: the dilemmas of inequality. Edited by Joseph S. Tulchin and Gary Bland. Boulder, Colo.: Lynne Rienner Publishers, 2005. 261 p.: bibl., ill., index.

A diverse collection of case studies, including South Africa, South Korea, Brazil, and Mexico, examines progress—or the lack thereof—in efforts to reduce economic inequalities during an era of globalization. A common theme of many of the contributions focuses on the need to have an inclusive policy-making process for newly democratic countries.

2190 Gill, Indermit Singh; Truman Packard; and Juan Yermo. Keeping the promise of social security in Latin America. With the assistance of Todd Pugatch. Palo Alto, Calif.: Stanford Economics and Finance, Stanford Univ. Press; Washington, DC: World Bank, 2005. 341 p.: bibl., ill., index. (Latin American development forum series)

An important contribution to research on social security innovations in Latin America over the past 30 years. Extensively researched and well supported, the authors highlight the need to address poverty as a key to social security success.

2191 Kurtz, Marcus J. and **Sarah M. Brooks.** Embedding neoliberal reform in Latin America. (*World Polit.*, 60:2, Jan. 2008, p. 231–280)

Using time series cross-national analyses of 17 Latin American countries between 1985 and 2003, the authors develop a model to explain the type of economic reform model pursued by countries across the region over the past three decades. Postwar economic regimes combined with partisan politics in a country are strong predictors of whether a country employs one of the two methods of economic liberalization.

2192 Lucero-Graffigna, Marcelo. Empleo y pobreza en la estrategia del Banco Mundial. (*Polít. Cult.*, 24, otoño 2005, p. 153–167, bibl.)

Discourse analysis of neoliberal conceptions of poverty and employment as manifested in World Bank public works programs applied across Latin America. The consequences of this translation of British and US "workfare" programs into Latin America are then discussed.

2193 Montero, Alfred P. Macroeconomic deeds, not reform words: the determinants of foreign direct investment in Latin America. (*LARR*, 43:1, 2008, p. 55–83, appendix, tables)

One of many recent works on determinants of foreign direct investment levels in Latin America. Employing a quantitative cross-national time series analysis of 15 countries in the region between 1985 and 2003, this study finds that stable macroeconomic conditions serve as the most robust variables in FDI models.

2194 Reyes, Giovanni E. and **José Briceño Ruiz.** Actualidad de la integración en América Latina y el Caribe: viejos dilemas, nuevos desafíos. Mérida, Venezuela: Centro de Estudios de Fronteras e Integración: Publicaciones Vicerrectorado Académico: Grupo de Regionalismo, Integración y Desarrollo, 2006. 269 p.: bibl., ill. (Col. Ciencias sociales y humanidades)

Incisive and comprehensive assessment of trends in economic integration across the Americas over the past decade. Authors also consider the global integration efforts of the region as a whole.

2195 Roberts, Kenneth M. The mobilization of opposition to economic liberalization. (*Annu. Rev. Polit. Sci.*, 11, June 2008, p. 327–349)

Comparative analysis of popular opposition to economic reforms. Study finds that in comparison to the backlash against previous periods of economic liberalization, current popular opposition movements are more heterogeneous with more pluralistic and decentralized organizational structures.

2196 Solimano, Andrés. Reassessing social polices in Latin America: growth in middle classes and social rights. (*CEPAL Rev.*, 87, dic. 2005, p. 45–60, bibl., tables)

Critical analysis of "growth-led poverty reduction" strategies that have characterized many social policy regimes of Latin America over the past 25 years. The dismal results of these policies form the basis for a new social policy agenda in the region oriented more to income distribution and greater attention to the lower middle class populations.

2197 Think tanks y políticas públicas en Latinoamérica: dinámicas globales y realidades regionales. Recopilación de Adolfo Garcé y Gerardo Uña. Textos de Donald E. Abelson *et al.* Buenos Aires: Prometeo: Centro de Implementación de Políticas Públicas para la Equidad y el Crecimiento: International Development Research Centre: Konrad Adenauer Stiftung, 2006. 316 p.: bibl., ill.

An eclectic, somewhat disjointed, collection of chapters focusing on the compelling question of the role that think tanks play in policy-making across South America. Most of the studies assess this question in the context of Argentina, but Uruguay and (oddly enough) Canada are also examined.

2198 Treisman, Daniel. Stabilization tactics in Latin America: Menem, Cardoso, and the politics of low inflation. (*Comp. Polit./New York*, 36:4, July 2004, p. 399–419, graphs, table)

A study of the political strategies behind the anti-inflation policies of Brazil and Argentina during the 1990s. As with many other neoliberal policies, the author finds classic political devices such as pork and cooptation as keys to the policy successes in both cases.

2199 The university, state, and market: the political economy of globalization in the Americas. Edited by Robert A. Rhoads and Carlos Alberto Torres. Stanford, Calif.: Stanford Univ. Press, 2006. 360 p.: bibl., index.

A compelling collection of critiques and analyses of the impact that neoliberal-based development strategies, and globalization more generally, have had on higher education across Latin America. Includes insightful essays on current trends toward commodification of higher education in such cases as Argentina, Brazil, and Mexico.

2200 Weyland, Kurt. Theories of policy diffusion: lessons from Latin American pension reform. (*World Polit.*, 57:2, Jan. 2005, p. 262–295, graphs, table)

An important contribution to scholarship on the mechanisms of policy diffusion. Poses a significant challenge to works that emphasize the determinitive role of globalization in shaping developing country policies in areas such as pension reform. Through innovative theoretical and empirical analysis, the author offers convincing support for a "cognitive-psychological" basis to policy diffusion.

MEXICO

PAMELA K. STARR, *Senior Fellow in Public Diplomacy and Senior Lecturer in International Relations, University of Southern California*

THE LITERATURE ON MEXICAN POLITICAL ECONOMY has undergone a gradual shift in recent years away from the process of economic reform and toward the economic performance of the reforms. While some analysts continue to focus their research on explaining the particular design and implementation of Mexico's economic reforms, the bulk of research attention is now focused on a more immediate policy problem—why these reforms have not fulfilled their economic promise. This expanding body of research aims to identify the forces that have undermined market efficiency and effective economic policy-making in Mexico and how these obstacles to growth and development might be overcome. This new wave of research has thus begun to focus carefully on microeconomic activity in Mexico and the operation of the country's distinct regional economies. It has also fostered some outstanding research projects carried out by analysts working in regional universities whose work has often been overlooked and underappreciated.

Looking first at new research on the politics of economic reform, two works stand out for their high-quality attention to the role of individuals in the policy process. During the past two decades, a rich body of research has been developed to explain the central role of economic structure and institutions in shaping policy choice and implementation. The dominance of this research agenda, however, tended to reduce the amount of analytic attention given to other important drivers of policy outcomes, including the role of individual policymakers. Sarah L. Babb's analysis of the rise of neoliberal economic thinking among Mexican policymakers (item **2204**) and Jonathan T. Hiskey's case study of President Carlos Salinas' striking skill as a politician (item **2218**) remind us that at the end of the day it is individuals, with their personal biases and skills, who operate within the constraints imposed by the structures and institutions that shape the policy-making environment to formulate and implement policy.

Research on Mexico's postreform economy, meanwhile, has produced an impressive array of studies that together make an important contribution to explaining why reforms that shifted economic decisions from the state to the market while democratizing policy-making have failed to result in rapid growth and development. Although there remains a strong current of analytic opinion that identifies global capitalism as the culprit, recent literature reveals a broad consensus among both Mexican and non-Mexican analysts that the problem is not the capitalist market model per se but instead how it has operated in Mexico. This finding has produced a new research agenda focused on government and market failures, the ways they have hindered market efficiency, and policy recommendations for reducing their negative impact.

This research includes an excellent volume published by Mexico's UNAM (item **2207**) that couples a comprehensive set of analyses of the macroeconomic sources of Mexico's weak economic performance during the past 20 years with studies focusing on weaknesses inherent to specific economic sectors and regions. A series of in-depth studies of the financial, information technology, and social policy sectors, the provision of public services, and the economies of Sinaloa,

Veracruz, Estado de México, and Puebla deepen and further enrich this research agenda.

These studies identify a complex mix of variables that help explain limited growth, job creation, and increased inequality. Yet in the process, several of them reach strikingly similar conclusions: the Mexican government has been unable or unwilling to mitigate the negative impact of market failures operating in the national, regional, and sectoral economies and of government failures of its own making. Specifically, this literature points to the absence of supportive public policies to promote emerging sectors (item **2212**) or to mitigate the negative impact of reform in regions that are highly dependent on nonmodern agriculture (items **2202** and **2228**). Other works identify the challenge created by institutions that developed in an authoritarian political environment and are operating perversely in Mexico's current democratic setting (items **2215** and **2223**). One title illuminates the continuing ability of powerful societal actors to protect their interests even at the price of harming national well-being (item **2229**). And two studies show how policy "solutions" often derive from a purely political logic and thereby actually increase inefficiencies rather than reduce them (items **2216** and **2221**).

By shifting analytic focus from the macro level to the regional and sectoral and from past policy decisions and economic models to the future of the Mexican political economy, recent research has helped to identify some of the obstacles to effective market operations in the Mexican context. By pointing to the government as a key culprit in failing to respond effectively to market failures and to avoid policies that generate additional distortions, these studies have also directed the Mexican political economy research agenda on a path that leads "back to the future"—back to a focus on the drivers of policy choice and implementation.

2201 Acosta Barradas, Rey. Los desafíos de la globalización en México: una perspectiva regional. Xalapa, Mexico: Univ. Veracruzana, 2005. 298 p.: bibl., ill., maps. (Biblioteca)

Argues that understanding the operation of Mexico's market economy requires analysis of its regional and microeconomic impact. In Veracruz state, economic restructuring heavily damaged key agricultural sectors, created a strong rural-to-urban labor migration, and did not promote investment in manufacturing or leading service industries. Concludes that the market economy's success may depend on state intervention to generate favorable externalities and investment.

2202 Avilés Ochoa, Ezequiel. Crecimiento y política económica: Sinaloa frente a Mexico. Sinaloa, Mexico: Univ. de Occidente, 2006. 342 p.: bibl.

Argues that Sinaloa state's significant drop in per capita income from 1983 to 1994 was not due to Mexico's economic liberalization. Instead, finds that the main drivers were the economy's heavy reliance on agriculture, the lack of competitiveness and weak response to market signals in the large traditional agricultural sector, and the absence of effective government action to mitigate the negative impact of these market failures.

2203 Ayala Espino, José. Instituciones para mejorar el desarrollo: un nuevo pacto social para el crecimiento y el bienestar. México: Fondo de Cultura Económica, 2003. 448 p.: bibl. (Sección de obras de economía latinoamericana)

Presents a detailed analysis of Mexican institutions and their role in facilitating—and limiting—socioeconomic development. After a review of the literature on institutions and economic growth, the author examines the trajectory of Mexico's development during the last two decades. Examines Mexico's judiciary, legislative, and executive sectors, and assesses the banking and finance, rural development, and international trade sectors, identifying their weaknesses and strengths and recommending measures for their restructuring. Contains an extensive analysis of the literature on institutions and their role in development. [L.R. Cáceres]

2204 Babb, Sarah L. Managing Mexico: economists from nationalism to neoliberalism. Princeton, N.J.: Princeton Univ. Press, 2001. 295 p.: bibl., ill., index.

Babb shines analytic light on an important and often overlooked driver of Mexico's economic reforms of the 1980s and 1990s—the transformation of the economics profession in Mexico. Presents a detailed analysis of the sociological transition of Mexican economists from lawyers and self-taught politicians inspired by Keynes and Marx to US trained, free-market technocrats. Describes how this shift influenced Mexico's decision to adopt neoliberalism.

2205 Basurto, Jorge. La vida política del Sindicato de Trabajadores de la UNAM. México: UNAM, Instituto de Investigaciones Sociales, 2006. 300 p.: bibl. (Cuadernos de investigación; 34)

Basurto presents the internal politics of one of Mexico's most prominent independent unions as it adjusted to the country's shift from protectionist and statist economic policies to neoliberalism. The book illuminates the distinct internal currents within the union, how their behavior weakened the opponents of union leadership, and how the Sindicato de Trabajadores de la UNAM (STUNAM) adapted itself—albeit imperfectly—to its new operating environment.

2206 Chiquiar, Daniel and **Gordon H. Hanson.** International migration, self-selection, and the distribution of wages: evidence from Mexico and the United States. (*J. Polit. Econ.*, 113:2, April 2005, p. 239–281, bibl., graphs)

The statistical model employed in this essay provides theoretic support for recent empirical evidence of rising education levels among Mexican migrants entering the US. The authors show that, contrary to the expectations of standard economic theory, Mexican migrants tend to be better educated and possess greater skills than their counterparts who remain in Mexico.

2207 Coloquio "La Globalización de México: Opciones y Contradicciones," Mexico City, 2005. La globalización

de México: opciones y contradicciones. Coordinación de Rolando Cordera Campos. México: UNAM, Facultad de Economía, 2006. 334 p.: bibl., ill., maps.

Based on a 2005 UNAM conference, this volume analyzes why Mexico's market economy has not generated strong growth and job creation and how it can be improved. Following a clear introduction and summary of the conference debate, the individual articles identify the need to promote internal growth, improve fiscal receipts, direct more credit toward productive investment, and implement industrial policy with a regional focus.

2208 La economía política de la migración internacional en Puebla y Veracruz: siete estudios de caso. Recopilación de Leigh Binford. Puebla, Mexico: Benemérita Univ. Autónoma de Puebla, 2004. 331 p.: bibl., ill., map.

This volume presents seven case studies of international migration from towns in the new migrant-sending regions of Puebla and Veracruz. The cases demonstrate the complicated interplay of global, national, regional, and local forces that encourage migration and their differential impact according to each locality's political and economic characteristics. They also show migration increased during the mid-1990s when deep recession coincided with contracting government assistance.

2209 Experiencias de crisis y estrategias de desarrollo: autonomía económica y globalización. Edición de Alejandro Nadal y Francisco Aguayo. México: El Colegio de México, 2006. 549 p.: bibl.

Based on a 2003 conference, this volume presents a series of critical analyses of Mexico's market economy. Individual articles are divided between theoretic and empirical approaches that place the Mexican experience in historical and comparative perspective. The volume concludes that Mexico's economic crisis reflects its integration with the flawed global capitalist system.

2210 Financiamiento de los mercados emergentes ante la globalización. Coordinación de María Luisa Quintero Soto y Emilio Aguilar Rodríguez. México: Cámara de Diputados: UNAM, Facultad de Estudios

Superiores Aragón: Miguel Ángel Porrúa, 2006. 306 p.: bibl., ill. (Conocer para decidir) (Las ciencias sociales)

Critical analysis of how international financial institutions have managed emerging market financial crises. By employing both theoretic analysis and empirical investigation of the Mexican case, the contributors point to flaws in international financial markets that produce volatility, generate dependency, and undermine growth, and offer suggestions for modifying ISI's crisis management to promote national development instead of protecting global capital markets.

2211 Fuentes, Rolando and Reynaldo Lozano. De populistas, neoliberales y otros demonios: el proyecto económico de Andrés Manuel López Obrador bajo la Lupa. Mexico: Libros para Todos, 2006. 317 p.: bibl. (Col. "Política")

Written during the 2006 presidential campaign, this book presents a detailed, highly critical analysis of the economic program of left-leaning presidential candidate Andrés Manuel López Obrador. The authors conclude that rather than presenting a coherent alternate vision for the country, the proposals simply embody opposition to the existing economic model.

2212 Gallagher, Kevin P. The enclave economy: foreign investment and sustainable development in Mexico's Silicon Valley. Cambridge, Mass.: MIT Press, 2007. 214 p.: bibl., ill., index, maps. (Urban and industrial environments)

A critical analysis of Mexico's heavy reliance on foreign direct investment that shows the failure of this strategy to promote sustainable development. The authors employ an illuminating account of the information technology sector to identify the main cause of this failure—the absence of "supportive public policies" such as investments in human capital and efforts to develop domestic markets.

2213 Garza Cantu, Vidal. Los estados mexicanos: sus activos y su dinamismo económico y social. México: Cámara de Diputados, LIX Legislatura: Miguel Angel Porrua; Monterrey, Mexico: Instituto Tecnológico y de Estudios Superiores de Monterrey, 2005. 178 p.: ill. (Conocer para decidir)

Motivated by the lack of comprehensive information on regional development in Mexico, this volume (and its companion CD-ROM) presents a comparative database of human and natural resources and economic and social policy performance in Mexico's 32 federal entities. The methodology measures the situation statically (end of 1990s) and dynamically (change during the 1990s) and creates a ranking that identifies the relative developmental status of each entity.

2214 Girón González, Alicia and Noemí Levy Orlik. México: los bancos que perdimos: de la desregulación a la extranjerización del sistema financiero. Mexico: UNAM, Instituto de Investigaciones Económicas: UNAM, Facultad de Economía, 2005. 131 p.

Argues that financial globalization in combination with its associated process of deregulation of national financial systems has had several pernicious consequences for Mexico: financial crises, inefficient lending, and foreign ownership of the banking sector. The result is a financial system that operates according to the demands of international finance and has thus limited the supply of funds channeled to productive investment.

Globalización y alternativas incluyentes para el siglo XXI. See item 676.

2215 Haber, Stephen H. Por qué importan las instituciones: la banca y el crecimiento económico en México. (*Trimest. Econ.*, 73:290, abril/junio 2006, p. 429–478, bibl., graphs, tables)

Haber argues that Mexico's historically weak financial system is due to the weak development of the political institutions that limit the authority and discretion of the state. The centrality of executive power in an authoritarian system and the public's resulting fear of state power weakened property rights, the legal system, and police capacity essential to protecting the contracts that are the essence of financial transactions.

2216 Hernández Trillo, Fausto and Juan Manuel Torres Rojo. Definición de responsabilidades, rendición de cuentas y eficiencia presupuestaria en una federación:

el caso mexicano. (*Rev. Mex. Sociol.*, 68:1, enero/marzo 2006, p. 1–47, bibl., graphs, tables)

Case study analysis disproving the argument that decentralization, by bringing service provision closer to voters and thereby increasing accountability, leads to higher quality public services. This outcome did not develop for Mexican education and health care because reform produced a complicated distribution of responsibilities that prevented citizens from identifying what level of government to hold accountable.

2217 Hernández Vicencio, Tania. Los empresarios tijuanenses: evolución y vínculo con el poder político. (*Rev. Mex. Sociol.*, 66:1, enero/marzo 2004, p. 99–139, bibl.)

Through a historic analysis of the Tijuana business sector, Hernández explains their unusual concentration in services and commerce rather than industry, their inability to form a regional economic group, and their surprising political flexibility. She argues that this condition was largely due to Tijuana's geographic, and hence economic and political, isolation from Mexico City and its close ties with the US.

2218 Hiskey, Jonathan T. Political entrepreneurs and neoliberal reform in Mexico: the Salinas Requisa of the port of Veracruz. (*Lat. Am. Polit. Soc.*, 45:2, Summer 2003, p. 105–132, bibl.)

Hiskey analyzes the 1991 restructuring of the port of Veracruz to illuminate the role of political entrepreneurship in the process of economic reform. He argues that even in an authoritarian setting a political strategy that reframes the issue and thereby weakens the opposition and invests supporters in the policy is often key to a successful policy outcome.

2219 Holzner, Claudio A. The poverty of democracy: neoliberal reforms and political participation of the poor in Mexico. (*Lat. Am. Polit. Soc.*, 49:2, Summer 2007, p. 87–122, bibl., graphs, tables)

A study of how the poor in Mexico responded to the country's economic reform agenda. Findings support work by others noting that economic reforms may produce short-term bursts of political participation

but over the longer term will tend to be associated with declines in participation by the lower income strata. [J. Hiskey]

2220 Huerta González, Arturo. Por qué no crece la economía mexicana y cómo puede crecer. Mexico: Diana, 2006. 214 p.: bibl., ill.

Clearly written and organized critique of Mexico's current development strategy. This essay is a cogent reminder of the shortcomings associated with a stable exchange rate and excessive reliance on international markets as the driver of development. But its policy recommendations calling for a significant increase in government spending behind a national industrial policy are apt to be controversial.

2221 Levy, Santiago. Good intentions, bad outcomes: social policy, informality, and economic growth in Mexico. Washington, D.C.: Brookings Institution Press, 2008. 357 p.: bibl., ill., index, map.

An illuminating analysis of the interplay between the formal institutions of social policy and the informal operation of labor markets in Mexico that explains how well-intentioned decisions produced inefficient and fiscally unsustainable social policies while undermining economic productivity and growth. Levy argues that the only viable solution is to scrap existing policies and replace them with a single, universal health care system.

2222 Madrid Hurtado, Miguel de la. Una mirada hacia el futuro. México: Fondo de Cultura Económica, 2006. 188 p.: bibl., ill. (Vida y pensamiento de México)

The president who initiated Mexico's process of liberalization reflects on its political and economic impact. Discusses Mexico's current challenges and offers broad counsel rather than specific policy solutions. Argues that democratic legitimacy depends on providing for public welfare and that rescuing from the past values and institutions "that affirm our nation" may be the keys to future advancement.

2223 México, democracia ineficaz. Coordinación de Luis Rubio y Susana Kaufman. México: Cámara de Diputados, LIX Legislatura: CIDAC: M.A. Porrúa, 2006. 240 p.: bibl. (Conocer para decidir)

Translation of the book *Mexico under Fox* (see *HLAS 63:1939*), the individual chapters in this volume present a useful overview of the changes, and in some cases lack of change, in politics, the economy, and foreign policy that took place in Mexico during the first half of the administration of Vicente Fox, Mexico's first democratically elected president.

2224 Mexico's democracy at work: political and economic dynamics. Edited by Russell Crandall, Guadalupe Paz, and Riordan Roett. Boulder, Colo.: Lynne Rienner Publishers, 2005. 231 p.: bibl., ill., index.

This series of essays authored by both Mexican and American academics provides an overview of Mexico's political and economic liberalization during the 1990s. Looking at political, economic, and foreign policy reforms, it illuminates their status half way through Mexico's first democratically elected presidential administration and the remaining policy challenges produced by this uniquely Mexican process of reform.

2225 Minns, John. The politics of developmentalism: the Midas states of Mexico, South Korea, and Taiwan. Houndmills, England; New York: Palgrave Macmillan, 2006. 310 p.: bibl., index. (International political economy series)

Minns offers a new twist on an established idea: greater state autonomy helps explain superior growth rates in South Korea and Taiwan compared with Latin America (1950–80). He argues instead that Mexico's development trajectory mirrors its Asian counterparts. An initially autonomous state promotes industrialization and growth, and this success strengthens the business and middle classes who ultimately and inevitably demand economic liberalization and democracy leading to reduced rates of growth.

2226 Ortega Riquelme, Juan Manuel. Acuerdos tripartitas y gobernanza económica en el México de fin de siglo. (*Foro Int./México,* 46:2, abril/junio 2006, p. 227–262, bibl.)

Explanation of the use of economic policy pacts among government, business, and labor in Mexico, from 1987 to 1997, which eased the implementation of economic reform and their ensuing absence. Ortega argues that this trajectory is due to the Mexican government's relative credibility as a partner as democracy weakened corporatism and undercut presidential autonomy, power, and governing experience and economic actors adjusted to this new institutional setting.

2227 Pastor, Manuel and Carol Wise. The lost *sexenio*: Vicente Fox and the new politics of economic reform in Mexico. (*Lat. Am. Polit. Soc.,* 47:4, Winter 2005, p. 135–160, bibl., graphs)

The authors acknowledge the economic and political restraints on Fox's efforts to implement economic reform, ranging from budgetary problems to an unfavorable congressional situation. However, they stress that the "policy gridlock" affecting economic reform resulted to a great extent from what they describe as Fox's lack of "statecraft" (compromise, negotiation, alliance building). [D. Coerver]

2228 Rivera Herrejón, Gladys. La reforma rural y los productores maiceros: el caso de dos comunidades del Estado de México. Toluca, Mexico: Univ. Autónoma del Estado de México, 2005. 292 p.: bibl., ill.

Well-structured, detailed case analysis of the impact of Mexico's market-based rural reforms of the early 1990s on two corn-growing peasant communities in Mexico state. Rivera concludes that the failure of these reforms to reduce corn production despite declining prices is due to a series of social and market structures—nonmarket uses for corn, corn storage as food security, and lack of irrigation—that impeded the expected supply response.

2229 Sandoval, Irma Eréndira. Intervencionismo neoliberal y desregulación financiera: evolución institucional del sector bancario en México. (*Rev. Mex. Sociol.,* 67:3, julio/sept. 2005, p. 593–631, bibl.)

Drawing on evidence from the nationalization, privatization, and government bailout of the Mexican banking sector from 1982 to 1995, Sandoval argues that market failures are inherent in the neoliberal model as is the influence of societal actors in economic policy-making. Instead of decreasing state intervention in the economy, therefore, market reform merely changes its character to match the interests of newly dominant economic actors.

2230 Teichman, Judith A. The World Bank and policy reform in Mexico and Argentina. (*Lat. Am. Polit. Soc.*, 46:1, Spring 2004, p. 39-74, bibl.)

Teichman examines the role of social learning and international policy networks in the process of economic reform by analyzing World Bank activities in Mexico and Argentina during the 1990s. The Bank's resulting policy influence varied with the institutional context. Although high in democratic Argentina, Mexico's one-party political system and close relationship with the US permitted more policy autonomy.

2231 Zapata, Francisco. Tiempos neoliberales en México. México: El Colegio de México, Centro de Estudios Sociológicos, 2005. 163 p.: bibl.

Zapata analyzes the negative repercussions of economic restructuring (1982–2002) on the social foundations of unionization and its resulting political implications. Although developments such as increased informality, fewer state sector and manufacturing workers, the geographic dispersal of manufacturing, and weakened state-union ties have diluted union power, Mexico's traditional corporatist unions continue to control strategic economic sectors and to have a surprising degree of influence over government policy.

CENTRAL AMERICA AND THE CARIBBEAN

DANIEL MASÍS-IVERSON, *Professor of Political Science, American University*

CENTRAL AMERICA

2232 Liderazgos femeninos y desarrollo local: sistematización de las experiencias de las liderezas de la región central de las Mélidas. El Salvador: Asociación Movimiento de Mujeres "Mélida Anaya Montes", 2001. 80 p.: bibl., ill.

This publication of the "Mélida Anaya Montes" Women's Movement, an autonomous feminist association, reports on the progress made in terms of women's participation in local public service in El Salvador's central region. Describes the political platform and justification of the movement and identifies the obstacles to successful local development (not just in El Salvador, but globally) as both economic and cultural, including addressing the difficulty of overcoming vertical and authoritarian power structures which have been culturally embedded and which are socially reproduced by women themselves. Offers several recommendations to provide training to young women leaders in critical thinking and argument, the development of tolerance,

and increasing their capacity for negotiation and delegation of responsibilities.

2233 Lizano Fait, Eduardo. Visión desde el Banco Central, 1998–2002. San José: Academia de Centroamérica, 2003. 360 p.: bibl., ill.

This collection of essays is clearly the work of a policymaker who is also a scholar. The contributions were written when Lizano was the president of Costa Rica's Central Bank and chairman of its board, during 1998–2002. Covers a wide array of topics including the role of central banks, different tools for economic policy-making, evolution of the world economy and its influence on Costa Rica, as well as the limitations placed on the country's Central Bank by domestic political conditions. Although the intended audience was, at the time, the enlightened public of the country, the care given to the construction of clear and logical arguments, and the scholarly references to global economic literature as well as the author's wise and witty reflections on the vicissitudes of economic policy-making for a small, open economy make the book interesting to a much wider readership.

2234 Molina, Francisco. Reforma institucional: el desafío del nuevo milenio. San Salvador: Facultad Latinoamericana de Ciencias Sociales (FLACSO), 2005. 44 p.: bibl. (Debates Serie de Investigación; 1)

Using a "New Institutional Economics" framework, the author provides a brief report in favor of taking seriously the importance of institutions for economic and social development. He describes, using World Bank data, the link in Latin America between institutional performance and per capita income. He then focuses on El Salvador and examines the factors that explain the slow evolution of institutions to strengthen the rule of law and implement the reforms of the "Washington Consensus" as well as the effects of slow institutional evolution on growth, investment, and social conditions. Finally, the author estimates the economic impact of weak institutions and rule of law in El Salvador and offers his reflections regarding its current institutional reform challenges.

2235 Participación ciudadana y desarrollo local en Centroamérica. Recopilación de Ricardo Córdova Macías y Leslie Quiñónez Basagoitia. Textos de Nuria Cunill Grau *et al.* San Salvador: FundaUngo, 2003. 508 p.: bibl., ill.

This valuable collection of essays on citizen participation and local development in Central America is divided into five major topics: a discussion of the concept of citizen participation, its basic elements, limitations, and possible changes based on an expansion of the public sphere; political representation and citizenship as currently debated in Latin America with a special focus on Central America; an examination of cases in citizen participation in the isthmus; public opinion and attitudes in local government; and community participation in social development projects.

2236 Ríos Morales, Ruth Muriel. Globalización: democracia y mercado en conflicto: la experiencia nicaragüense. Zaragoza, Spain: Editorial Combra, 2001. 173 p.: bibl.

This book seeks to answer the question of whether the recent transition towards democratic economic systems that developing countries have been undergoing has produced an end to poverty. The author looks at Nicaragua, focusing on the years of Sandinista rule and the subsequent administration of President Violeta Chamorro, who was elected in a democratic transition. The FSLN enjoyed political power for 11 years (1979–90) but not economic power; nevertheless the Sandinistas did manage to transform the socioeconomic landscape. President Chamorro, in turn, faced with the need to stabilize the Nicaraguan economy, had no choice but to follow structural adjustment prescriptions which then, as no safety net was present, threatened the poorest sectors of the population and endangered the democratic transition itself.

2237 Saldomando, Angel and **Rokael Cardona.** Descentralización, desarrollo local y gobernabilidad en Centro América. San Salvador: Coordinación Técnica CONFEDELCA: Cooperación Técnica Alemana, 2005. 214 p.: bibl., ill.

This publication is the product of research carried out by the authors and several collaborators for the Central American Conference for State Decentralization and Local Development (CONFEDELCA) on state decentralization, local development, and democratic governance in Central America. Begins with a theoretical discussion of the relationship between the three variables; includes perspectives on states that are large and interventionist but ineffective, on national states that are as yet an unfinished project, and on state reform and decentralization. Offers a comparative analysis of decentralization in Central American countries from 1980 to 2004 in the context of difficult transitions to democracy for some, evaluates overall progress towards decentralization, and proposes national public debates in each country on the topic for which the authors provide a basic framework.

Solano, Luis. Guatemala: petróleo y minería en las entrañas del poder. See item **1012.**

Spalding, Rose J. Civil society engagement in trade negotiations: CAFTA opposition movements in El Salvador. See item **2606.**

2238 Umaña Cerna, Carlos. Tendencias y actores del desarrollo local en Centroamérica. San Salvador: FUNDAUNGO, 2002. 162 p.: bibl., ill.

This report seeks to identify the main local development actors in Costa Rica, El Salvador, Guatemala, Honduras, and Nicaragua, including their beginnings and their purposes and proposals for action, and to provide an inventory of their documentary output. Finds that the origins of the current notion of local development are found in the transitions to peace in the region in the 1990s, in turn influenced by international governmental and NGOs. Classifies local development actors in six sectors: central government, municipalities, civil society, international cooperation agencies, private enterprise, and academic centers, and identifies several municipal and nongovernmental networks. A valuable sourcebook for anybody seeking to understand local development as a trend in Central America.

CARIBBEAN

2239 Alonso Tejada, Aurelio. El laberinto tras la caída del muro. La Habana: Editorial de Ciencias Sociales, 2006. 414 p.: bibl. (Política)

A collection of thoughtful essays written by a Marxist Cuban sociologist of a Gramscian persuasion between 1990 and 2006. The topics are quite varied, including, e.g., a history of Marxist ideas and their debate in Cuba since the late 19th century, problems of poverty in the Spanish-speaking Caribbean, new hegemonic myths in the hemisphere, the debate over the concept of civil society, religious adaptation and conformity in a globalized world, conditionality and the international financial institutions, and Cuban society in the 1990s.

2240 Blackman, Courtney N. The practice of economic management: a Caribbean perspective. Kingston; Miami: Ian Randle, 2006. 422 p.: bibl., ill., index.

This clearly and beautifully written book is a compilation of essays written over the span of 30 years, from the standpoint of a Caribbean manager—not economist—and scholar, who examines development problems and proposes solutions with a focus on small states. The author takes issue with right and left: with statist and autarchic policies of some Caribbean state leaders, with the industrialized country and international financial institution (IFI) policies that forced less developed countries to as-

sume the burden of the debt crisis, and with "market-fundamentalist" programs codified in the "Washington Consensus." The author remains optimistic regarding the capacity of small states to be managerially nimble and to adopt development policies according to their own needs.

Bridging the gaps: faith-based organizations, neoliberalism, and development in Latin America and the Caribbean. See item **2616.**

2241 Brittain-Catlin, William. Offshore: the dark side of the global economy. New York: Farrar, Straus and Giroux, 2005. 272 p.: index.

The author embarks on a denunciation of offshore financial transactions by large corporations, with special emphasis on Caribbean island financial centers. He describes the web of interests woven between the corporations and their offshore host countries, and the attempts by governments (especially the US and the European Union) to obtain access to information about their corporation's foreign accounts, and the ensuing economic development dilemmas for Caribbean countries that have hosted offshore financial centers. The author's style as an investigative journalist makes for fast-paced reading, but he also includes notes documenting his assertions. A serious book.

2242 Cao-García, Ramón J. Impuestos en Puerto Rico: treinta años de experiencias y estudios. San Juan: Grupo Editorial Akron, 2004. 247 p.: bibl., ill.

The author, a professor of Economics at the Univ. de Puerto Rico who has also been a government and legislative advisor in Puerto Rico on tax issues, contributes to the debate on the island regarding tax reform. After a detailed analysis of the evolution of the Puerto Rican tax system since 1950, the author agrees that reform is needed, but at the same time argues against abrupt shifts in policy. He cautions that tax policies are not only about revenue collection. Any proposed reforms to the tax structure will affect the demand of different sectors of the population for government services and the distribution of their cost; hence, changes must be carefully and individually studied. The tax structure should be kept simple and with low administrative costs, although the author warns that a single tax is not a good idea. The system should be fair across social sectors and, very interestingly, across generations.

Corrales, Javier. The gatekeeper state: limited economic reforms and regime survival in Cuba, 1989–2002. See *HLAS 64:1095.*

2243 Cuba en el siglo XXI: ensayos sobre la transición. Coordinación de Marifeli Pérez-Stable. Madrid: Colibrí, 2006. 345 p.

The authors of this book, which has also been released in English as *Looking Forward: Comparative Perspectives on Cuba's Transition* (2007), seek to envision the nature and course of Cuba's change after Fidel Castro's rule. They address institutions, social relations, and ideology as they compare political and economic transitions over the course of the last 20 years in Latin America, the former Soviet bloc, and East Asia, and outline possible and desirable outcomes. The vast array of topics include, inter alia, democracy, civil-military relations, the Cuban constitution, gender equality, welfare policies, corruption, the future relation of the Cuban diaspora with the island, and Cuba-US relations. All contributors are experts in their respective fields. This volume is an excellent sourcebook on Cuba today.

2244 Cuba: sociedad, cultura y política en tiempos de globalización. Recopilación de Mauricio de Miranda Parrondo. Bogotá: Centro Editorial Javeriano, 2003. 202 p.: bibl. (Col. Biblioteca del profesional)

The nine authors in this provocative volume examine, from different political perspectives, the social, political, and cultural effects of globalization on Cuba including: the construction of national and citizen identities, the role of the family in preserving social values; the displacement of Marxist-Leninist discourse for revolutionary nationalism; pluralism, especially as manifested in the existence of Catholicism as a major component of Cuban culture; the "uncertain transition" in the country's governance; the possible legacies to be bequeathed by today's Cuba; and the possibilities for Cuban emigrés to play a role in the construction of a new society.

2245 Curet, Eliezer. Economía política de Puerto Rico: 1950 a 2000. San Juan: Ediciones M.A.C., 2003. 393 p.: ill.

A valuable contribution to the study of Puerto Rican economic history over the second half of the 20th century, this book combines a wealth of empirical data with a thorough knowledge of the economic and welfare policies adopted at each stage and the ideas, interests, and politics behind them. At times polemical, but never lacking in data and arguments, the author goes beyond traditional economics to include the analysis of the effects of institutions and politics on economic growth and welfare.

2246 Domínguez, Jorge I. Cuba hoy: analizando su pasado, imaginando su futuro. Madrid: Editorial Colibrí, 2006. 418 p.: bibl.

This volume gathers articles and book chapters originally published in English, although several were translated into Spanish, since the author's book *Cuba: Order and Revolution* (1978; see *HLAS 41:3058, 42:2598,* and *43:6265*). The essays are divided into three periods regarding Cuban politics and society: 1959–90, 1990–2000, and 2000 onward. The author offers a profound and nuanced examination of Cuban institutions, society, and political processes. Among other topics, he discusses the relationship between political power and social support after the crisis caused by the collapse of the Soviet Union, successes in fighting the economic crisis in the first half of the 1990s, increasing social and economic inequality in the country and its implications for political institutions, and whether the political elite, after an early revolutionary use of increasingly centralized power to further egalitarian ends, is now helping or hindering the reforms necessary for economic reactivation and to fight an increase in poverty unseen for decades.

2247 Ferriol Muruaga, Ángela; Rita Castiñeiras; and Göran Therborn. Politica social: el mundo contemporáneo y las experiencias de Cuba y Suecia. Sweden: Agencia Sueca de Cooperación Internacional para el Desarrollo; La Habana, Cuba: Instituto Nacional de Investigaciones Económicas; Montevideo: Depto. de Economía, Facultad de Ciencias Sociales, Univ. de la República Uruguay, 2004. 278 p.: bibl., ill.

This book, by two Cuban and one Swedish economist, compares social policy in Sweden and Cuba. The authors explain the meaning of social policy and the increasing importance it has acquired for both academic pursuits and actions on the part of global and regional international governmental organizations, detailing how the problématique is variously approached by the latter. They then describe social policy in Cuba and Sweden, and conclude with some final comparative reflections. The book is valuable in its theoretical discussion and in the detailed description of the Swedish and Cuban experiences in social policy-making and implementation.

2248 Pantin, Dennis A.; Dennis Brown; and Michelle Mycoo. Feasibility of alternative, sustainable coastal resource-based enhanced livelihood strategies: people and the Caribbean Coast. St. Augustine, Trinidad and Tobago: Sustainable Economic Development Unit, SEDU, Univ. of the West Indies, St. Augustine Campus, 2003–2005. 92 p.: bibl., ill. (some col.).

This study begins by reviewing the debate over the concepts of sustainable development (SD) and sustainable livelihoods (SL), subjecting the SL framework to a critique. It offers an overview of macro-trends in the Caribbean, including economic structure, unemployment, debt, risks for exporters, and vulnerability to natural disasters. Although reference is made especially to Belize, Guyana, Jamaica, St. Lucia, St. Vincent & the Grenadines, and Trinidad & Tobago, the study focuses chiefly on St. Lucia and Belize. The authors, in their application of the sustainable livelihoods approach (SLA), find that in both countries there is a need for improved credit access, new production techniques, marketing tools, adequate infrastructure, specific policies for the promotion of small-scale tourism, along with the need to overcome weak governance and inadequate, unenforceable legislation.

2249 Ramón, José Luis de. Volver a crecer: propuesta para el desarrollo dominicano tras la crisis del año 2003. Santo Domingo: Editora Corripio, 2004. 192 p.: bibl., ill.

The author begins by dismissing defeatist attitudes regarding Latin American development on the grounds of cultural backwardness or geography. He argues that the difference in growth rates between Latin America and sub-Saharan Africa with East Asia are to be explained in terms of fertility rates, human capital, the portion of government spending in GDP, terms of trade, and the rule of law. He suggests that good economic and welfare policies are needed for successful development. Using this framework, the author studies the Dominican Republic's development bottlenecks as he sees them and provides a series of recommendations for the country to "grow again."

2250 Stewart, Taimoon. An empirical examination of competition issues in selected Caricom countries: towards policy formulation. Research assistance by Elsa Roker et al. St. Augustine, Trinidad: Sir Arthur Lewis Institute of Social and Economic Studies, Univ. of the West Indies, St. Augustine Campus, 2004. 218 p.: bibl., ill.

The area of competition and competition law is fraught with misunderstandings between developed countries that encourage the adoption of competition laws with small or micro-developing countries that in turn perceive a lack of understanding of their social and economic peculiarities on the part of the industrial nations. This study comparatively examines competition issues for the larger countries of Trinidad & Tobago, Jamaica, and the Bahamas, along with the smaller states of St. Lucia, St. Vincent & the Grenadines, and Belize, examining limitations on competition as products of the historical political economy of the region and of problems of scale. Sectors examined include banking, tourism, and utilities. The authors favor the introduction of competition law but warn that this law must take into consideration the risks associated with the countries' insertion in the global economy, inequalities in the world trading system, and the need to protect certain sectors. This is a serious and valuable study, a good antidote to abstract theoretical thinking about the relationship between competition, growth, and welfare in small developing countries.

VENEZUELA

DANIEL HELLINGER, *Professor of Political Science, Webster University*

THE STUDIES REVIEWED here were published in Venezuela between 2002 and 2006, years of political strife that included a short-lived coup, a management-organized work stoppage in the vital oil industry (December 2002–February 2003), and, finally, a hotly contested recall referendum in August 2004. All were failed attempts by the opposition to oust controversial President Hugo Chávez from office.

Most of these studies, then, preceded the subsequent years of renewed economic growth, substantial poverty reduction, and mass mobilizations (*misiones*) that were all aided by steep rises in oil prices and consequently a boost in government shares of oil profits. The studies are based on data and experiences gathered during a period when statistics showed the economy and poverty near their nadir. Both the decline and subsequent prosperity had as much to do with political conditions as with any policy successes or failures on the part of the government. The exception may be the fiscal reform of November 2001, which has significantly boosted government revenues. Unfortunately the reform receives little attention in these works.

Several of the edited volumes here emanate from the leading private university and the leading state university. The former, the Universidad Católica Andrés Bello, reflecting the Catholic corporatist traditions, published several volumes purporting to seek a common vision, stressing the need for harmony born of a new social pact. The latter, through the Centro de Estudios de Desarrollo (CENDES), offered a less coherent, but in some ways more realistic vision of actual political economic conditions.

Notable in both approaches is a desire for more institutionalized planning. Several volumes here seem to be relics of a bygone era in a Venezuela when most intellectuals, heavily influenced by positivism, placed their faith in planning. While the Chávez administration was rolling out huge new social programs in health, education, and subsidized markets, young planners seemed more intent on reviewing the lifeless pages of ministry plans long discarded in the pre-Chávez era. The country might very well benefit from a marriage between the kind of professional planning urged in these books and the political will to address poverty shown by the government.

Lacking here is an examination of the economic warfare that broke out during the oil industry shutdown, in particular, an analysis of the reasons that the government survived the assault on its fiscal base. The CENDES anthology (*Venezuela visión plural*, item **2263**) offers the reader interested in the achievements and shortcomings of first five years of the Chávez administration the best overall view of the complex interplay between political conflict and social outcomes.

2251 Castellano B., Hercilio. La planificación del desarrollo sostenible: contenidos, entorno y método. Caracas: Centro de Estudios del Desarrollo del Univ. Central de Venezuela, 2005. 195 p.: bibl., ill.

Argues for incorporating "eco-philosophy," defined as taking a more integral view, one more harmonious with nature, and a more "hybrid" methodological approach into planning for sustainable development. Lacks any specific analysis of Venezuela, but does suggest how such an approach might be employed in general.

2252 Castillo, Nelson Antonio. Venezuela en el siglo XXI: visiones de futuro. Caracas: Centro de Estudios del Desarrollo, Univ. Central de Venezuela: Instituto Venezolano de Planificación, 2006. 330 p.: bibl., ill.

Yet another broad-brush study of planning that aims to summarize the attitudes and priorities of major actors in the past and project them into the future. One hundred forty eight tables and graphs, some running over multiple pages, tend to overwhelm the analysis. Relies heavily on views of institutional actors; views of social movements are noticeably absent.

2253 Guayana sustentable 5: ponencias. Montalbán, Venezuela: Univ. Católica Andrés Bello: Fundación Konrad Adenauer Stiftung, 2004. 181 p.: bibl., ill.

A series of short (some only four pages) proposals and ideas for implementing participatory democracy and sustainable development in the heavy industrial zone of Ciudad Guayana, with a long, rambling introduction reviewing political history and contemporary issues on the national level.

2254 Guerra, José. Venezuela endeudada: de Carlos Andrés Pérez a Hugo Chávez. Caracas: De la A a la Z Ediciones, 2006. 101 p.: bibl. (Col. E)

Venezuela's public debt became significant during the oil boom of 1974–1982 and continued its unabated increase through the following periods of rising and falling oil prices, changing domestic fiscal regimes, and political vicissitudes. The Chávez government has shifted indebtedness away from the external sources toward the internal private sector, reducing incentive to deal with inflation. Author believes the government has used borrowing to finance production cooperatives and a militia to prepare for eventual confrontation with its internal enemies.

2255 Hernández, Carlos Raúl and Luis Emilio Rondón. La democracia traicionada: grandeza y miseria del Pacto de Punto Fijo, Venezuela 1958–2003. Caracas: Rayuela, Taller de Ediciones, 2005. 384 p.: bibl., ill.

Two functionaries of the regime displaced by the ascent of Hugo Chávez to the presidency in 1998 blame its demise upon the failures to support political reform.

The new regime represents a kind of punishment for this failure. Little new here; no original research.

2256 Herrera Escorcha, Juan Rafael. Planificación estratégica agrícola y su aplicación en lo institucional. Caracas: Centro de Estudios del Desarrollo, Universidad Central de Venezuela, 2003. 61 p.: bibl. (Serie Mención publicación)

Readers familiar with Venezuela will hardly be surprised at the main finding: Between 1989 and 1998 the Ministry of Agriculture displayed an institutional failure of formulation and execution, largely due to acute disorganization. As a result, the sector made little progress achieving production goals or competitiveness.

2257 Machado N., Gustavo E. and Alberto G. Castellano M. La tasa de interés real y la inversión privada en Venezuela: ¿una relación causal? (*Rev. Cienc. Soc./ Maracaibo*, 11:3, sept./dic. 2005, p. 475–484, bibl., tables)

Secular decline in private investment in Venezuela since 1978 is explained by the exhaustion (a premature conclusion by the authors, given the commodity boom of 2001–2008) of the rentier capitalism, as demonstrated by the absence of any link between real rates of interest and investment.

2258 Mata Mollejas, Luis. Los límites de la revolución: petróleo y gobernabilidad. Caracas: Ediciones FaCES/UCV, 2006. 128 p.: bibl., ill.

This book first reviews how the combination of extraordinary rents during boom times and political pacts among parties has limited the capacity of civil society in Venezuela, a well-trodden path. The author does, however, introduce financial speculation and resultant bubbles during boom as recurrent factors, extending the analysis into the Chávez period, suggesting more historical continuity than change in the government's management of the boom. The solution, according to the author, is to apply public choice theory to management decisions— even if that means deciding to leave OPEC.

2259 Una mirada sobre Venezuela: reflexiones para construir una visión compartida. Caracas: Univ. Católica Andrés Bello: Fundación Centro Gumilla, 2006. 253 p.: bibl., ill.

A compilation of articles prepared for use in the Jesuit Order's "Program of Civic-Political Training," purporting to offer a "humanistic-Christian" vision of social, economic, and political issues facing the country. Rather than a "shared vision," the overall thrust of the articles points toward a process of compromise and, in general, corporatist solutions in the context of the country's highly polarized politics.

2260 Mujica Chirinos, Norbis and **Sorayda Rincón González.** Caracterización de la política social y la política económica del actual gobierno venezolano: 1999–2004. (*Rev. Venez. Econ. Cienc. Soc.*, 12:1, enero/ abril 2006, p. 31–57, bibl.)

Authors characterize the early years of the Chávez administration as a superficial shift from "open neoliberalismo" to "silent adjustment." The post-2001 period showed a shift toward greater commitment to social assistance and a focus upon reducing social exclusion in more of an attempt to find a model to harmonize accumulation and distribution through state intervention.

2261 Seminario Globalización, Integración Económica y Seguridad Alimentaria, *Maracay, Venezuela, 2004.* Globalización, integración económica y seguridad alimentaria. Compilación de Leonardo Taylhardat, Ricardo Castillo y Agustín Morales. Maracay: Univ. Central de Venezuela, Facultad de Agronomía; Caracas: Fondo Editorial Tropykos, 2005. 301 p.: bibl., ill., map.

Chapters consist of a highly heterogeneous group of papers presented in June 2004 in Maracay, an important agroindustrial commercial center. Early chapters deal more broadly and critically with the impact of globalization on nutrition in Latin America and the Third World. Other chapters critically or sympathetically examine government policies, both in production and distribution, and their impact on consumers, the poor, and producers. Most useful are chapters examining tendencies in the Venezuelan diet compared to other countries in the region.

2262 Venezuela: un acuerdo para alcanzar el desarrollo. Caracas: Instituto de Investigaciones Económicas y Sociales, UCAB, 2006. 572 p.: bibl., ill.

Dense series of chapters urging a range of public policies predicated upon the construction of a social pact. Though the specific content may vary, its fundamental parameters are to be based upon liberal democracy with guarantees of social inclusion. According to the author of the book's conclusion, the path toward such an outcome is a foundational pact similar to those that have permitted progress in Chile and Spain.

2263 Venezuela visión plural: una mirada desde el CENDES. CENDES, Centro de Estudios del Desarrollo, Univ. Central de Venezuela. Caracas: bid & co.: CENDES, UCV, 2005. 2 v. (804 p.): bibl., ill. (Col. Intramuros. Serie académica)

A "plural vision" affirms that the authors of this book value "pluralism" politically; the term pertains as well because the contributors are as politically divided as the country itself, and this is reflected in the diversity of attitudes toward the Chávez government and its putative accomplishments. The title reflects, therefore, a certain lack of coherence, but taken as a whole the volume offers the reader useful research and perspectives by many of the country's best and brightest scholars.

2264 Venezuela y los retos frente a la integración económica en el siglo XXI. Compilación de Eduardo Ortiz Ramírez y Marisela Díaz. Caracas: Univ. Central de Venezuela, Comisión de Estudios de Postgrado, Facultad de Ciencias Económicas y Sociales: Fondo Editorial Tropykos, 2006. 387 p.: bibl., ill.

As the title implies, this book goes far beyond the theme of "free trade" to review the possibilities for and obstacles to other forms of integration, exploring harmonization of investment laws and property, compatibility of subregional trade agreements with one another and with global agreements, and so forth. The author is in favor of greater integration, but calls for more attention to be given to the development of social nets and sustainability. Useful compendium and analysis, but lacks attention to the Chávez regime's Bolivarian scheme, the main Venezuelan initiative in the area of economic integration.

COLOMBIA AND ECUADOR

ERIC HERSHBERG, *Director, Center for Latin American and Latino Studies and Professor, Department of Government, American University*

SEVERAL THEMATIC CLUSTERS EMERGE from a review of the voluminous literature on the political economy of Colombia and from the less extensive material published over the past several years on Ecuador. Researchers analyzing both countries have devoted considerable attention to the forces of economic globalization. Frequently the theme is framed in terms of prospects for adapting to competitive pressures without exacerbating already dreadful levels of social inequality, which are generally portrayed as stagnant or worsening (item **2272**). Indeed, the putative tendency of market liberalization to aggravate social exclusion over the past quarter century is a common concern of many scholars, as are the implications of liberalization for environmental sustainability and community cohesion.

A welcome development in the literature on Colombia is the increasingly sophisticated treatment of issues relating to the knowledge economy and what elsewhere—though not for the most part in these writings—is commonly analyzed theoretically in terms of national systems of innovation (item **2291**). Technological change and adaptation, enterprise and sectoral competitiveness, human capital formation, and the adaptive capabilities of productive sectors are among the themes that emerge as prominent in this growing body of research. Some of this literature concentrates on local-level processes (item **2266**). Issues relating to innovation receive comparatively little attention in Ecuador, even while the challenge of productive upgrading is obviously central to that country's fortunes in petroleum exports as well as in a variety of other natural resource-based industries subject to global competition.

Not surprisingly given the inequalities that pervade both countries, social policy and equity are at the core of much of the political economy research on Colombia and Ecuador (items **2268, 2269, 2271, 2277, 2285, 2295, 2296, 2300, 2303, 2304,** and **2305**). Among the more interesting contributions are analyses of labor market dynamics, health and education expenditures, and institutional mechanisms for allocating public services. These works highlight, among other issues, the challenge of maximizing social welfare in an environment characterized by widespread labor informality (items **2285, 2295,** and **2300**). The production of work on these topics is quite comprehensive in Colombia, but rare in Ecuador, making the limited number of studies on these topics all the more valuable (item **2303**). With regard to both countries there is some consideration of the implication of bilateral and multilateral trade accords, though the centrality of these arrangements for the outcomes in question is never presented in an entirely convincing manner (item **2306**).

Addressing the social deficit requires fiscal solvency, a chronic problem in both Colombia and Ecuador during the 1990s. Fiscal questions remain a topic of concern in recent publications on Colombia (items **2275, 2282,** and **2294**), though the theme is not as ubiquitous as it was during the late 1990s and beginnings of the present decade. Where fiscal solvency does appear, there is analysis of the impact of significant reforms, particularly changes to Ley 100 governing transfers to subnational units of government, that have been undertaken during the Uribe presidency and that appear to have achieved some success. Despite the precarious fiscal situation in Ecuador as of this writing, none of the contributions included in this review address the budgetary situation in Quito or connect fiscal constraints to social policy options. It will be interesting to see whether this gap is redressed in studies that address these questions in the aftermath of Rafael Correa's election to the presidency in 2006.

As has been the case for many years, the political and economic underpinnings of persistent conflict represent an ongoing concern for Colombian social scientists. Some of this literature is disappointing, consisting of polemics or book-length op-ed pieces opining about "what is wrong with Colombia" (item **2281**). But for the most part the literature on Colombia's violence exhibits theoretical sophistication, reflecting in particular state-of-the-art social scientific research on the economic underpinnings of conflict systems (items **2265**, **2280**, and **2292**). Colombian scholars are producing work that will be of immense value to students of civil conflicts well beyond Latin America, and it is to be hoped that their research gains a wide following. The connection between drug trafficking and violence is a frequent topic for analysis, as are narcotics-related issues more generally, but many studies of conflict admirably resist the temptation to place narcotics at the core of their interpretations. An interesting development is the publication of several detailed empirical studies that examine the interplay between microeconomic factors and responses to violence in particular localities, and a focus on the ramifications of the Uribe government's strategy of "democratic security" (items **2265**, **2274**, **2276**, and **2280**). Also noteworthy are studies linking systems of violence to the presence of large scale foreign investment (items **2286** and **2289**).

In both Colombia and Ecuador studies of contemporary political economy assign prominence to heterogeneous circumstances within national boundaries. Questions of local development, community economic dynamics and subnational patterns of integration into both the national and global economies are addressed productively (items **2266**, **2273**, **2280**, **2287**, and **2288**). Conversely, and regrettably, there is a dearth of comparative work on the region. Here the political economy literature may well stand in contrast to that devoted to politics and governance, where the notion of an Andean region has gained greater salience. Arguably, analysts of political economy might be well advised to situate their studies in a broader regional context. Similarly, perhaps the time has come for students of political parties, state institutions, leadership styles, and social movements to engage more directly the questions of economic development that preoccupy political economists. There is much to be learned through an encounter between these two subfields, and this could prove particularly fruitful through cross-country comparisons (item 2284).

COLOMBIA

2265 Aristizábal García, José. Metamorfosis: guerra, estado y globalización en Colombia. Bogotá: Ediciones Desde Abajo, 2007. 267 p.: bibl. (Biblioteca Vértices colombianos)

This nuanced study situates Colombia's contemporary violent conflicts in historical context while exploring how the country's growing engagement with global processes has transformed both the nature and causes of ongoing violence. The global narcotics industry, transnational economic ties, and cultural trends that transcend Colombia's borders are among the forces that shape the character of internal conflict and the opportunities for its mitigation. Perceptive chapters consider features of the social landscape that fuel conflict as well as trends in Colombian civil society that propel movement toward peace and nonviolence. A particular strength of the volume is its consideration of the changes brought about under the democratic security programs implemented during the Uribe administrations.

2266 Banguero, Harold. Ensayos sobre desarrollo tecnológico y competitividad del Pacífico colombiano. Cali, Colombia: Univ. Autonoma de Occidente, 2004. 193 p.: bibl., ill.

This series of essays, written in 1998 and 1999, considers the challenges facing four departments along Colombia's Pacific coast as they seek to promote competitiveness of key tradable goods sectors. The book analyzes several underpinnings of competitiveness, including human capital, organizational capabilities, physical infrastructure, and technological development. The study devotes attention to innovation planning, sectoral agenda setting, education and innovation, and innovation management. The author concludes that science and technology in the region have received inadequate investment and that policy initiatives have lacked strategic coherence, consisting instead of isolated and piecemeal policy initiatives.

2267 Bedoya, Rocío. Hacia un balance de las cooperativas de trabajo asociado. Medellín, Colombia: Ediciones Escuela Nacional Sindical, 2006. 219 p.: bibl. (Ensayos laborales; 15)

Globalization poses risks and opportunities for economic actors throughout Latin America as elsewhere in the world, and this volume considers these from the perspective of cooperative producers in Colombia. Contributions include analysis of legal frameworks governing the operation of the growing number of cooperatives in the country, thorough discussion of precarious working conditions encountered by labor in the sector, and considerations of future prospects for cooperative producers.

2268 Bien-estar y macroeconomía 2002/ 2006: crecimiento insuficiente, inequitativo e insostenible. Coordinación de Ricardo Bonilla González y Jorge Iván González. Bogotá: Univ. Nacional de Colombia, Centro de Investigaciones para el Desarrollo, 2006. 170 p.: bibl., ill.

This review of economic performance and welfare during the first Uribe administration notes that the government presided over a period of steady economic expansion. However, drawing on careful analysis of the empirical record, the authors deem this trend insufficient, unsustainable, and associated with deepening inequality. Separate chapters address each of these criticisms, and a series of commentaries reflects on the significance of the findings and future lines of research. An interesting feature of the collection is a pointed critique from the co-Director of the Banco de la República, who offers a far rosier evaluation of government policies and their consequences.

2269 Bien-estar y macroeconomía: más allá de la retórica. Edición por Marcela Giraldo Samper. Coordinación editorial por Rosa Quintero Amaya. Bogotá: Univ. Nacional de Colombia—Seda Bogotá, Facultad de Ciencias Económicas: Centro de Investigaciones para el Desarrollo (CID), 2007. 310 p.: bibl., graphs.

Taking a heterodox, post-Keynesian approach, contributors to this collection of thoroughly documented essays consider macroeconomic performance and social welfare trends during the Uribe years, which they characterize as having followed a neoliberal paradigm rooted in policies advanced during the era of Thatcher and Reagan, and paralleled by the policy directions of the George W. Bush administration. In addition to a data-rich overview of macroeconomic policy, chapters are devoted to the health, education, poverty and employment consequences of social policies, the balance between bilateral and multilateral approaches to regional economic integration and trade, and the prospects for Colombia's petroleum industry.

2270 Caballero Argáez, Carlos. Memorias incompletas: crónica sobre el despertar del siglo XXI en Colombia. Bogotá: Grupo Editorial Norma, 2007. 359 p.: bibl. (Vitral)

This collection of short essays and newspaper columns published between 2000 and 2006 provides a personal perspective on issues related to Colombian democracy, armed conflict, the Uribe administration in power, economic performance, and energy policy. With regard to the latter, the author draws on his experience as Minister of Mines and Energy during the Pastrana administration. Here, as in most of the volume, the perspective is more testimonial than scholarly.

Cárdenas Santa-María, Mauricio; Roberto Junguito; and Mónica Pachón. Political institutions and policy outcomes in Colombia: the effects of the 1991 Constitution. See item **1590.**

2271 Colombia: diálogo pendiente. Dirección de Luis Jorge Garay Salamanca. Coordinación general de Adriana Rodríguez Castillo. Bogotá: Planeta Paz, 2005. 421 p.: bibl., ill. (Documentos de política pública para la paz)

A result of a series of forums designed to build societal consensus, this collection of essays focuses on possibilities for reform in policies relating to employment, wages, and housing. The five well-written chapters include a review of European active labor market policies as a potential model for Colombia, normative essays on the right to work and the right to decent housing, and empirical studies of the informal sector in Bogotá and of wages and occupational structure at the national level.

2272 Debates sobre globalización y derecho. Compilación de Carlos Julio Pineda. Bogotá: Politécnico Grancolombiano Editorial: Corporación Escenarios, 2006. 273 p.: ill.

This volume consists of 18 brief essays resulting from seminars held during 2003 and 2004 on Colombia's preparedness to respond to globalization. The strength of the collection lies in its consideration of social policies, economic competitiveness, and technological capabilities, themes that provide the focus for several chapters. The overall tone is one of pessimism, suggesting that Colombia has become inserted into processes of globalization at a pace that exceeds its capacity for adaptation, its mechanisms for cushioning the social dislocations occasioned by integration, and lacking the institutional foundations required to set the country on a course of knowledge-intensive development. Oddly, despite the book's title, issues relating to law are virtually absent.

2273 Economías locales en el Caribe colombiano: siete estudios de caso. Edición de María M. Aguilera Díaz. Bogotá: Banco de la República, 2005. 388 p.: bibl., ill., maps. (Col. de economía regional)

Decentralization measures over the past quarter century have augmented the significance of municipal governance which in turn highlights the importance of subnational public finance for advancing regional development. This series of comprehensive case studies of local economies along Colombia's Caribbean coast assesses government revenues and expenditures as well as the functioning of local governance institutions. In addition, the authors, all of whom are economists, outline the key historical, demographic, and social characteristics of each of the localities and identify their principal economic activities, which principally entail agro-fisheries, agro-industry, commerce, and tourism.

2274 Engel, Stefanie and Ana María Ibáñez. Displacement due to violence in Colombia: a household-level analysis. (*Econ. Dev. Cult. Change,* 55:2, Jan. 2007, p. 335–364, tables)

Colombia ranks among the countries with the highest number of displaced people, with estimates ranging between two million and four million people having left their homes to escape political violence. This sophisticated article deploys econometric analysis of household survey data in an effort to discover the precise determinants of decisions to leave one's place of residence. Whereas most migration literature emphasizes economic factors, the Colombian experience highlights the importance of perceptions of risk of violence. Yet economic factors do impinge on the capability of households confronting risk to make the decision to uproot themselves: a lack of opportunities for income generation or unmet basic needs is positively correlated with displacement.

2275 Esclava, Marcela. Ciclos políticos de la política fiscal con votantes opuestos al déficit: el caso colombiano. (*Trimest. Econ.,* 73:290, abril/junio 2006, p. 289–336, bibl., tables)

The political budget cycle has been studied in many countries, but rarely in

Colombia. Informed by the political science literature on the topic, this article evaluates levels and composition of public expenditures over time in order to assess whether and in what ways campaign calculations of elected officials impact public spending. The conclusion is that while levels of public expenditures remain constant over the course of electoral cycles, in the midst of campaigns spending is more likely to be targeted toward objectives that are visible and that elicit substantial support from prospective voters.

2276 González, María A. and **Rigoberto A. Lopez.** Political violence and farm household efficiency in Colombia. (*Econ. Dev. Cult. Change*, 55:2, Jan. 2007, p. 367–392, graphs, tables)

It is well known that political violence inhibits economic expansion, and it is also generally accepted that boosting farm productivity is a significant source of potential growth in developing economies. This study examines the impact of violence on agrarian household efficiency in Colombia, and highlights the disruptive impact of violence, particularly through its consequences for rural labor markets.

2277 Hábitat y financiación: una estrategia para la lucha contra la pobreza. Bogotá: UN-Hábitat: Ministerio de Ambiente, Vivienda y Desarrollo Territorial: Departamento Nacional de Planeación: First Initiative, 2007. 322 p.: bibl., ill. (some col.), 1 CD-ROM.

Inadequate housing and related infrastructure—potable water, green spaces, public transportation—are among the most pressing problems confronting the poor throughout Latin America. This book and accompanying CD-Rom, assembled by the Ministerio de Medio Ambiente, Vivienda y Desarrollo Territorial and based on materials prepared under the auspices of an IDB-funded initiative, offer a comprehensive treatment of measures undertaken by the Colombian government to address the need for improved housing for disadvantaged citizens. Chapters review topics such as access to credit, formalization of titles to property, territorial governance, and regulations concerning markets for rental housing. The central message is that the Colombian

government under the Uribe administration has made a concerted effort to attack the full range of obstacles to providing safe and secure housing to the citizenry as part of comprehensive strategies for overcoming poverty.

2278 Hernández Gamarra, Antonio. Una contraloría creíble y respetada. t. 1, Macroeconomía y políticas públicas. t. 2, Control fiscal, funciones de advertencia y lucha contra la corrupción. t. 3, Comentarios, coloquios y remembranzas. t. 4, Economía, políticas públicas y modernización del control fiscal. Bogotá: Contraloría General de la República, 2006. 4 v.: ill.

Vol. 1 of this four-volume collection published by the Contraloría General de la República compiles public declarations generated by that agency between 2002 and 2006. These include congressional testimony, speeches, and other documents, and the collection is presented as a signal of government commitment to transparency and accountability. Sections are devoted to the objectives of government policy as well as to assessments of its efficacy. Among the topics covered are macroeconomic policy, public finance, trade negotiations, social and sectoral policies, and the effectiveness of Plan Colombia.

Herrera, Beethoven. Globalización: el proceso real y financiero. See item **1966.**

2279 Hershberg, Eric. Technocrats, citizens and second generation reforms: reflections on Colombia's Andean malaise. (*in* State and society in conflict: comparative perspectives on the Andean crises. Edited by Paul W. Drake and Eric Hershberg. Pittsburgh, Pa.: Univ. of Pittsburgh Press, 2006, p. 134–156)

Repeated efforts to reform fiscal policies, transfers to subnational governments and both health and retirement programs were frustrated during the Pastrana administration of 1994–98. This book chapter attributes these failures in part to the absence of a political analysis on the part of policymakers. Reforms in these domains are portrayed as fundamentally political processes. Absent negotiations with relevant stakeholders, the author contends that the policies were doomed to fail.

2280 Holmes, Jennifer S.; Sheila Amin Gutiérrez de Piñeres; and Kevin M. Curtin. Drugs, violence, and development in Colombia: a department-level analysis. (*Lat. Am. Polit. Soc.*, 48:3, Fall 2006, p. 157–184, bibl., graphs, maps, tables)

Counter to the widespread assumption that coca production is an important source of violence in Colombia, this study finds that economic factors and coca eradication programs are more direct triggers of conflict. Drawing on data gathered at the departmental level, the authors find minimal physical overlap between coca production and guerrilla violence, and a powerful correlation between eradication programs and locally concentrated spikes in violence. Noting evidence that increases in legitimate exports are associated with declining violence, the authors advocate renewed attention to the promotion of labor-intensive export crops.

2281 Hommes, Rudolf *et al.* Colombia ante el siglo XXI: cómo sacar este país adelante. Bogotá: Ed. Oveja Negra, 2007. 256 p.

This collection of eleven essays, most of them polemics, takes as its point of departure that Colombia is "at an abyss," plagued by multiple crises that will be overcome only as a result of radical measures, what one contributor labels "a 180 degree turn." There is relatively little empirical analysis, with priority given instead to lamenting the myriad failures of leadership and of the Colombian citizenry, and to sketching objectives for a very different future.

2282 Iregui B., Ana María; Ligia Melo B.; and Jorge Ramos F. El impuesto predial en Colombia: evolución reciente, comportamiento de las tarifas y potencial de recaudo. (*Ens. Polít. Econ.*, 46:2, 2004, p. 259–301, bibl., graphs)

Property taxes are potentially significant sources of revenue for subnational governments, yet across much of Latin America rates tend to be low and collection uneven. This rigorous study of 309 Colombian municipalities assesses performance of local governments in collecting property taxes during the 1990s, and concludes that opportunities for raising revenue are substantial. Enforcement of existing legislation is deemed more important than establishing new regulations.

2283 Lafaurie Rivera, José Félix. Posconflicto y desarrollo: inversiones sustitutivas de impuestos: una propuesta de inclusión y desarrollo rural. Colaboración de Alfonso Santana Díaz, Sandra Castro Contreras y Ricardo Cortes Dueñas. Bogotá: Konrad-Adenauer-Stiftung: Federación Colombiano de Ganaderos: Corporación Pensamiento Siglo XXI, 2006. 495 p.: bibl., ill.

This lengthy tome, written by the President of the Federación Colombiana de Ganaderos (Colombian Ranchers Association), laments the profoundly antirural bias of development policies in Colombia, which is portrayed as having generated both social exclusion and rural conflict. The author considers a revival of the agrarian sector to be critical for the future of the democratic security policies promoted by the Uribe government, and for achieving a proposed "rural vision 2019." In pursuit of these objectives, he outlines a proposed system of tax credits to support rural investment, and the book cover features an endorsement of the idea from President Uribe.

2284 Moncayo Jiménez, Edgard. Neoliberalismo en los países andinos: balance de dos decenios. Bogotá: Oveja Negra; Guayaquil, Ecuador: Univ. Católica de Santiago de Guayaquil, Facultad de Especialidades Empresariales, 2006. 236 p.: bibl., ill.

This study offers a balanced assessment of the degree to which Andean economies adopted reforms proposed by the Washington Consensus, and a review of performance of Andean economies from 1991–2005. The book provides an invaluable comparative perspective on a region where neither growth nor distribution has developed as desired. The author effectively deploys empirical data to illustrate the primary arguments. The book concludes by exploring a number of theoretical insights to be derived from analysis of the past two decades and by advancing a policy agenda for decisionmakers during the next phase of the region's development.

2285 Montenegro, Armando and Rafeal Rivas. Las piezas del rompecabezas: desigualdad, pobreza y crecimiento. Bo-

gotá: Taurus, 2005. 341 p.: bibl., ill., index.
(*Pensamiento*)

This valuable book offers a review of social scientific understandings of the complex relationships between inequality, poverty, and growth, highlighting the difficulties of making improvements in all areas at one time. Applying these frameworks to the political economy of contemporary Colombia, the authors include chapters on education, employment, pensions, public services, and public expenditures, each of which offers a thorough analysis of the current situation and prospects for reform. A chapter analyzing demographic trends and their ramifications for inequalities is especially innovative.

2286 Montenegro, Santiago. Sociedad abierta, geografía y desarrollo: ensayos de economía política. Bogotá: Grupo Editorial Norma, 2006. 317 p.: bibl., ill., index. (Col. Vitral)

This collection of essays, written both before and during the author's tenure as Director of the Depto. de Planeación Nacional under the Uribe government, addresses a disparate series of issues relating to Colombia's political economy. Following a first section consisting of reflections on the writings of Karl Popper and Douglass North, the book turns to the political economy of Colombia during the 1990s and early 2000s. Section 2 examines territory, governability, and economy, with attention given to competitiveness across regions of the country, while the third section, perhaps the most valuable of the book, consists of separate chapters on labor market reforms and unemployment during the 1990s, the history of the political economy of petroleum and coffee, and a review of Colombia's shifting pattern of insertion into the global coffee markets.

2287 Pearce, Jenny. Más alla de la malla perimetral: el petróleo y el conflicto armado en Casanare, Colombia. Bogotá: Cinep, 2005. 103 p.: bibl.

Drawing on fieldwork carried out in the Department of Casanare in 1997, 2001, and 2002, this study analyzes the relationship between an expanding petroleum industry and armed conflict, highlighting the roles of the local and national state,

multinational companies, armed actors, and civilians. Focused on the experience of British Petroleum, the author argues that the company adapted over time to the complex environment in which its extractive activity was being carried out. Whereas initially the focus was on military protection of company assets, over time British Petroleum exhibited increasing concern with establishing the rule of law as a mechanism for protecting its economic interests.

2288 Ramírez Moreno, Humberto. Descentralización y desarrollo institucional en Colombia: análisis crítico. Ibagué, Colombia: Univ. del Tolima, 2006. 274 p.: bibl., ill. (Col. Univ. del Tolima 50 años; 11)

The roles, capabilities, and financing of subnational levels of government have been the subject of ongoing debate since enactment of the 1991 Colombian Constitution, and this valuable study explores these questions in detailed fashion, encompassing the Samper, Pastrana, and Uribe administrations. The topic is situated in the context of the organization of state institutions more generally, and the text takes into account the impact of subnational units on health, education, social infrastructure and other key areas of governance. While addressing these issues empirically, the study also draws insightfully on theoretical literature on institutions, and thus makes an important contribution to scholarship beyond the particular case of Colombia.

2289 Ramiro, Pedro; Erika González; and Alejandro Pulido. La energía que apaga Colombia: los impactos de las inversiones de Repsol y Unión Fenosa. Bogotá: Ediciones desde abajo, 2007. 247 p.: bibl., ill., map. (Pensamiento y futuro)

Studies of foreign direct investment in economic development in Colombia have typically focused on US-based enterprises. This book broadens the literature by examining Spanish investments, specifically of two major companies in the energy sector. The authors pose the question of whether the presence of Spanish companies in this strategic sector represents a "recolonization" of the region. Their conclusion is that this need not be the case, despite the aspirations of investors, given popular resistance to foreign enterprises and what the authors portray as their adverse impacts on human rights, indigenous peoples, and the environment.

2290 La reforma política del estado en Colombia: una salida integral a la crisis. Coordinación de Miguel Eduardo Cárdenas Rivera. Bogotá: Friedrich Ebert Stiftung en Colombia-Fescol: Fondo Editorial Cerec, 2005. 256 p.: bibl., ill.

Recent decades have witnessed fundamental legal and constitutional reforms in the Colombian political system, and these have affected governability and the prospects for resolving conflict. Changes encompass the territorial organization of representation, the nature of the party system, the institutions handling national security, and most recently, the possibility of presidential reelection. The eleven essays assembled in this volume explore the ramifications of these and other developments and assess their significance for diminishing conflict, strengthening legitimacy, and addressing the country's chronic social deficit. Although highly disparate in their thematic concerns, the eleven essays included here engage topics that are relevant to state-society relations in contemporary Colombia and that directly concern the organizer's aspiration to minimize polarization and articulate strategies for what is labeled civilized political debate.

2291 Restrepo Rivillas, Carlos Alberto; Jairo Guillermo Isaza Castro; and Clara Inés Acosta Niño. Competitividad y estructura de la economía colombiana. Bogotá: Univ. Externado de Colombia, Facultad de Administración de Empresas, 2005. 292 p.: bibl., ill.

Drawing on state-of-the-art literature on national competitiveness, this timely publication reviews Colombia's location in the global economic hierarchy, encompassing separate treatments of the primary, secondary, and tertiary sectors, within each of which specific sections are devoted to key industries. The analysis includes a review of patterns of change over time, and consideration of the geographic distribution of economic activity within Colombia. By focusing on sectoral productivity and generation of quality employment, the volume is highly relevant to debates about prospects for enhancing social welfare while engaging in global markets.

2292 Richani, Nazih. Multinational corporations, rentier capitalism, and the war system in Colombia. (*Lat. Am. Polit. Soc.*, 47:3, Fall 2005, p. 113–144, bibl.)

This theoretically ambitious article considers the role of multinational corporations in the configuration of a "war system" in Colombia, understood as a dynamic of violence that persists over a protracted period through a self-sustaining logic. Investment in extractive and security sectors is identified as a key source of sustaining the war system. The author engages literature on the so-called resource curse and its connection to violence and notes that, contrary to what this body of scholarship would predict, foreign investment has increased despite ongoing conflict. The flow of capital into extractive industries fueled conflict over land, while investors simultaneously allocated resources to private security to protect their assets. Finally, the article notes the role of these corporations as interest groups in the US, lobbying for increased military assistance to Colombia, a phenomenon that has further contributed to the persistence of that country's war system. For political scientist's comment, see item **1611**.

2293 Rincón García, John Jairo. Trabajo, territorio y política: expresiones regionales de la crisis cafetera, 1990–2002. Medellín, Colombia: La Carreta Editores, 2006. 158 p.: bibl., ill., map. (La Carreta histórica)

This slim volume inquires into the causes and nature of the crisis in Colombia's coffee sector during the 1990s, and the impact of the sector's difficulties on local socioeconomic circumstances. The first half of the book draws important distinctions between zones where technological upgrading has permitted continued dynamism and others where innovation has been lacking and where cultivation on marginal lands has been accompanied by poverty and social exclusion. The shift in some settings from coffee cultivation into production of coca and opium poppies is also noted. The second half of the book examines the crisis in a marginal producing area in the north of Colombia, and traces the protests that this development has engendered as well as the social consequences for households and communities.

2294 Rubiano, Néstor and Luis Mario López. Instituciones políticas y presupuesto público: el caso de Colombia, 1990–2003. (*Ens. Polít. Econ.*, 46:2, 2004, p. 307–357, bibl., graphs)

This study, anchored in the tradition of the new institutionalism, explores the relationship between public expenditures and the prevalence of informal institutions such as clientelism in Colombian politics, emphasizing the centrality of clientelism to the functioning of legislative politics. Tracing the phenomenon to the colonial period, the authors devote particular attention to how executive-legislative interactions concerning budgetary issues have reinforced the logic of clientelism following enactment of the 1991 Constitution and, in the process, have undermined fiscal balance. Strengthening political party discipline through reform is deemed essential to overcoming patterns of budgetary politics that undermine efforts to strategically allocate resources to deal with accumulated social deficits.

2295 Seminario: "Empleo, Reformas Estructurales y Desarrollo," 1st, Universidad de La Salle, Facultad de Economía, 2005. Empleo, reformas estructurales y desarrollo. Compilación de Luis Fernando Ramírez H. y Jairo Guillermo Isaza Castro. Centro de Investigaciones de Economía Social—CIDES, Grupo de Investigaciones de Economía Laboral, Facultad de Economía, Universidad de La Salle. Bogotá: Univ. de La Salle, 2006. 217 p.: bibl., ill.

Beginning with a lengthy assessment of changes in the labor market between 1984 and 2000, this book addresses the connections between employment and social welfare in contemporary Colombia. Stemming from a seminar held in 2005, the collection of essays considers the consequences of labor market trends for poverty, inequality, and social and collective rights. The ramifications of Colombia's high levels of informal sector employment receive particular attention. The series of chapters on social security reforms, encompassing the health sector as well as pensions, represents a significant contribution. There is also a lengthy section devoted to relationships between economic growth, violence, and employment.

2296 Sierra Montoya, Jorge Emilio. Qué hacemos con Colombia?: los grandes debates económicos con los principales dirigentes del país. Prólogo de Rudolf Hommes. Bogotá: Planeta, 2006. 269 p.

This book is a compilation of interviews with 28 prominent Colombian politicians that were published during 2005 in the Bogotá daily *La República*, and an additional set of 10 opinion pieces penned by prominent figures for publication in that newspaper. Interviews focus on topics ranging from social equity and combatting poverty to regional integration and trade and financing the state. Authors are predictably of mixed views regarding the performance of the incumbent Uribe government. The collection is a useful window onto the contours of political debate during the period in question.

2297 Sistemas de protección social: entre la volatilidad económica y la vulnerabilidad social. Coordinación de Óscar Rodríguez. Bogotá: Univ. Nacional de Colombia, Sede Bogotá, Facultad de Ciencias Económicas, Centro de Investigaciones para el Desarrollo, 2005. 283 p.: bibl., ill. (Col. Estudios sobre protección social; 1)

This analytically sophisticated and data-rich collection situates efforts to combat poverty in terms of reducing social vulnerability and the impacts of macroeconomic, and particularly financial, volatility. The book details the failures of health and pension policies advanced during the 1990s and shows how free market reforms exacerbated existing dynamics of social exclusion. A key conclusion is that sufficient financing of the health and social security systems is essential in order to extend social citizenship to the entire population. The authors contend that this financing is crucial given Colombia's heightened integration into the global economy.

2298 Suárez Montoya, Aurelio. El modelo agrícola colombiano y los alimentos en la globalización. Bogotá: Ediciones Aurora, 2007. 221 p.: bibl., ill., map.

This interesting volume provides an overview of Colombian agriculture since independence from Spain, devoting more than half of an initial historical section to developments beginning in the 1990s. The second section of the book focuses on the ramifications of the proposed free trade agreement with the US, portrayed as the country's definitive integration into globalization. A lengthy appendix reviews trends in global markets for key agricultural products of relevance to Colombia. The author concludes that a series of handicaps, encompassing technological backwardness, highly concentrated land tenure, inequality-generating agricultural support policies, and the generalized poverty of agrarian producers, combine to portend difficult times for Colombian agriculture as the country exposes itself as never before to foreign competition.

2299 Tabares, Elizabeth and **Ramón Rosales.** Políticas de control de oferta de coca: "la zanahoria" y "el garrote". (*Desarro. Soc.*, 55, primer semestre 2005, p. 211–253, bibl., tables)

Crop substitution and coca eradication represent the "carrots" and "sticks" that policymakers have employed in an effort to reduce cultivation of coca in Colombia. This study draws on econometric techniques to measure the impact of both strategies, and determines that while the promotion of alternative crops has had a small positive impact, eradication has failed to reduce the volume of coca production. The response of illicit producers to fumigation and other repressive strategies has been to relocate cultivation elsewhere.

2300 Uribe G., José I. and **Carlos Humberto Ortiz.** Informalidad laboral en Colombia, 1988–2000: evolución, teorías y modelos. Cali, Colombia: Programa Editorial Univ. del Valle, 2006. 210 p.: bibl., ill. (Col. Libros de Investigación)

It is widely understood that urban labor markets in Colombia are characterized by high levels of informality, yet there is a dearth of theoretically informed and empirically rich literature on the topic. This study fills the gap through a series of chapters that grapple with competing definitions of infomality and their salience for the Colombian case, followed by analyses of labor market segmentation during the 1990s. The book concludes with an empirical assessment of trends in ten metropolitan areas during that decade and a series of propos-

als for public policies to improve labor conditions.

2301 Valencia, Germán. Los grupos de interés en la regulación de la industria eléctrica colombiana. (*Lect. Econ.*, 62, enero/junio 2005, p. 123–155, bibl.)

The role of the Latin American state is increasingly one of regulation rather than direct control over economic activity. This is especially evident in infrastructure and public services. This study, focusing on the electricity sector, analyzes the role of interest groups in shaping the regulatory functions of the Colombian state and finds that elites deploy organizational and financial resources to encourage state interventions that maximize their ability to capture rents while the citizenry as a whole exercises relatively little influence over the substance of regulation. The article concludes with recommendations for strengthening the regulatory system, maximizing the independence of public authorities and thus their ability to regulate in the public interest.

ECUADOR

2302 Acosta, Alberto. Ecuador: ecos de la rebelión de los forajidos. (*Nueva Soc.*, 198, julio/agosto 2005, p. 42–54, bibl.)

This descriptive article opens by noting that the abrupt overthrow of Col. Lucio Gutiérrez from the presidency in 2005 occurred despite relatively favorable macroeconomic indicators. Nonetheless, this essay argues, economic factors figured prominently in his removal. Economic stability had come at the expense of social expenditures, which were curtailed in order to satisfy demands of external creditors and international financial institutions. In order to sustain this bias, the author contends, the Gutiérrez government systematically violated institutional norms, governing by decree and running roughshod over the judicial and legislative branches of government.

2303 Asedios a lo imposible: propuestas económicas en construcción. Edición de Alberto Acosta y Falconí Benítez Fander. Quito: FLACSO Ecuador: ILDIS-FES, 2005. 269 p.: bibl. (Serie Foro)

This book consists of 11 chapters written by leading Ecuadorian social scientists, including future President Rafael

Correa, in an effort to provide heterodox responses—portrayed as diverse but counter to neoclassical formulations—to failed neoliberal strategies of the 1990s. There are particularly insightful contributions covering social policy, development finance, ecological sustainability, and international economic relations. The prologue accurately captures the common point of departure, which is that Ecuador suffers from inefficient insertion into global markets and from public policies that reflect private rather than public interests. In response, the authors provide broad overviews of crucial policy domains and concrete recommendations for reforms.

2304 Foro sobre la Democracia, el Bienestar y el Crecimiento Económico (Ecuador). Textos de Augusto Barrera *et al.* Quito: FLACSO Ecuador: Terranueva, Gestión Social: UNICEF, 2006. 192 p.: bibl., ill. (some col.). (Cuadernos de trabajo)

This edited collection includes empirically thorough and theoretically informed essays on social exclusion and economic growth, fiscal policy and equity, ethnicity and poverty, territoriality and public policy, and contemporary legacies of past experiences with democratic governance in Ecuador. Empirical data used in the key articles extend through 2004. The authors situate their contributions in the context of the need for democratically generated responses to Ecuador's stubborn patterns of inequality and social exclusion.

2305 Hacia un modelo alternativo de desarrollo histórico: Comité Nacional por la Renovación de la Izquierda. Compilación de Rafael Quintero López y Erika Silva Charvet. Quito: Ediciones La Tierra, 2005. 477 p.: bibl., ill. (Ediciones La tierra; 26)

A seminar held during July 2004 gave rise to this collection of roughly 30 contributions from progressive intellectuals, including future President Rafael Correa,

devoted to outlining an alternative model of development, encompassing perspectives from diverse currents of the Ecuadorian left. Contributors articulate a shared commitment to identifying paths toward socioeconomic development and state strengthening consistent with the quest for national independence, expanded employment, social welfare enhancement, and economic competitiveness. The book is organized in six sections, corresponding to themes covered during the seminar: the historical context; territorial dimensions; prospects for industry; external economic relations; development finance; and new challenges, including advancing science and technology and maximizing returns from migration. Taken as a whole, the volume offers an especially rich if inevitably uneven set of reflections on the challenges and opportunities facing advocates of equitable and sustainable development in Ecuador.

2306 Romero Cevallos, Marco. Los desafíos de una nueva integración andina: una agenda desde los jóvenes. Quito: Corporación Editora Nacional: Univ. Andina Simón Bolívar, Sede Ecuador, 2007. 231 p.: bibl., ill. (Biblioteca de ciencias sociales; 56)

Despite the disappointing results of neoliberal reforms, these are uncertain times for the alternative represented by regional integration schemes in South America. In that context, and in light of the limited civic participation in integration efforts to date, this book considers the role of civil society in promoting regional integration in the Andes, with particular attention to the attitudes and potential contributions of youth. Drawing on interviews and focus group sessions with young Ecuadorians, the study concludes that greater involvement of the citizenry in articulating the objectives and content of integration efforts will help to overcome the democratic deficit that has constrained integration to date.

BOLIVIA AND PERU

BARBARA KOTSCHWAR, *Research Associate, Peterson Institute for International Economics, and Adjunct Professor, Center for Latin American Studies, Georgetown University*

WHILE MUCH OF THE POLITICAL ECONOMY LITERATURE of the 1990s and early 2000s focused on complimenting or critiquing the results of the Washington Consensus reforms implemented in the 1980s and 1990s, subsequent works have begun to look at specific economic issues—energy and environment being major topics of interest—and at the future direction of economic policy.

Bolivia and Peru have confronted many similar economic and political challenges. Both countries suffered from extremely high levels and volatility of inflation and high levels of external debt—Bolivia with inflation rates of over 10,000 percent per year with external debt stocks exceeding 150 percent of GDP in the mid-1980s, while Peru by 1990 had inflation rates of over 7000 percent, with debt stocks over 100 percent of GDP. Both experienced dramatic shifts in economic policy from state-centered capitalism to a neoliberal embrace of the free market model: Bolivia in 1985 under President Paz Estenssoro (with Planning Minister and future-President Gonzalo Sánchez de Lozada), and Peru under Alberto Fujimori, who dramatically overturned many of the populist economic policies implemented by his predecessor (and Peru's current President) Alan García.

Both have recently experienced relatively high levels of economic growth. Both also continue to suffer from high levels of poverty in their respective countries and have instituted propoverty programs as a response: Peru's *Juntos* program, a conditional cash transfer program established under President Alejandro Toledo and Bolivia's much more recent efforts to use increased hydrocarbon tax revenues resulting from high oil prices for social protection programs.

Another significant factor is the countries' demographic composition: Bolivia and Peru are the two South American countries with the highest percent of indigenous peoples in their population. In both countries indigenous peoples are more likely to be poor and traditionally have less access to political power. These combined factors have been elemental in recent elections in both countries. In Peru this was manifested in bringing Alejandro Toledo, an economist of Quechua heritage from the north coast of Peru, to power in 2001. This demographic situation also played a role in the last election, with Alan García's narrow victory over opposition candidate Ollanta Humala, who has been associated with the indigenista movement. In Bolivia current President Evo Morales came into power through his Movimiento al Socialismo (MAS) in December 2005. Morales' legitimacy stems in part from his ethnicity: in a country that is over 50 percent indigenous, he is Bolivia's first indigenous head of state. His popularity has steadily increased since being elected, despite instituting controversial policies such as nationalizing the hydrocarbons sector, gaining more than two thirds of the vote in a 2008 recall referendum.

While both countries have seen great improvements in their macroeconomic picture, each faces serious economic and political challenges. Each has seen an increase in inequality over the past two decades, with Gini coefficients rising from about 42 in 1990 to 58 for Bolivia and 52 for Peru in 2005. Whereas in 1990 17 percent of Bolivia's population was living on less than two dollars per day (PPP) this percentage rose to 30 by 2005. In Peru the percentage increased from 5 to 19 during the same time period. The challenge is how to translate the significant improvement in macroeconomic stability and the gains from high commodity prices into better welfare for the population. Both countries also face a dilemma in their wealth model and will soon need to reconcile their dependence on natural resource extraction with the environmental impacts thereof.

The works reviewed here reflect these challenges. CEDLA's *Legitimando el orden neoliberal: 100 días de gobierno de Evo Morales* (item **2310**) criticizes the Morales government for maintaining neoliberal economic policies despite its critical rhetoric. They especially find fault with continued ties to transnational corporations. Amparo Ergueta echoes this fear of foreign investment in her assessment of the role of Spanish investment in Bolivia (item **2308**). While she recognizes that Spanish investment has improved the quality of service in certain sectors, she also sees them holding monopoly power and worries that foreign investors are interested more in their profits than in the welfare of the Bolivian people. McGuigan (item **2311**) evaluates the costs and benefits of privatizing the hydrocarbons sector, using the period 1999–2004 as reference. She finds limited gains and finds that costs were incurred to the poor in the form of higher consumer prices. These critiques illustrate a dilemma for the Morales government, which must strike a balance between satisfying its power base and maintaining economic stability. The UNICEF document tracking Bolivia's spending on youth (item **2307**) shows that Bolivia has made progress in addressing youth poverty (even while overall poverty has increased) but that much more progress needs to be made in order to meet Bolivia's Millennium Development goal of alleviating poverty.

Natural resources provide much of Bolivia's prosperity and are also a source of great political contention, both internal and external. This debate, particularly the internal component, is detailed in *Gas: debate nacional*, a collection of stories from the *El Pulso del País* newspaper (item **2309**). Zeballos Hurtado and Quiroga Crespo (item **2313**) examine the potential for alternative energy in Bolivia, recognizing the political complications of such an endeavor. Mamerto Pérez Luna cautions about the overreliance on soya in *No todo grano que brilla es oro: un análisis de la soya en Bolivia* (item **2312**).

In Peru the situation is also complex. Economic reforms have stabilized the economy but without increased prosperity or opportunities for large segments of the population. Moisés Arce studies the interaction between societal groups and economic reforms in "The Societal Consequences of Market Reform in Peru" (item **2314**), arguing that while political space was largely closed during the Fujimori years, neoliberal reforms did stimulate new groups to act and those groups impacted the implementation (or not) of different policies. Ruiz Torres (item **2319**) discusses the lengthy implementation of the neoliberal model in Peru and points to various factors that led to the internalization of globalization in Peru, including the economic crisis, a political system lacking in legitimacy, and the large swaths of poor and unemployed Peruvians. The role of economic elites is explored by Figueroa (item **2317**). He criticizes the current government for continuing with the current model, stating that it has not led to economic development and has simply reinforced inequality. He attributes this continuity to a lack of opposition, brought about by Fujimori's transformation of the state. Víctor Vich (item **2321**) also criticizes the neoliberal model, accusing President Toledo of acting as a glorified tour guide and pandering to international media with a view to influencing investors' perceptions of Peru. Vich also accuses Toledo of exploiting indigenous Peru. Juan Martín Sánchez's "Hatun Willakuy, importancia del relato en la política" (item **2320**) assesses the results of Peru's Truth and Reconciliation commission, arguing that the main importance of this work is in its transparency and its ability to stimulate dialogue among Peruvians. Sánchez sees this as an important step in Peru's future. Azpur cites political centralization as one element that has maintained the structure of inequality in Peru (item **2315**).

María Isabel Remy examines the associations of small coffee producers (item **2318**) and concludes that while this is a sector that has been largely left out from the state's support, it has managed to create a strong dynamism, partly through external factors such as the emergence of the fair trade market and partly through internal factors, particularly the spirit of cooperativism among the small producers. Finally, Paula Castro, Javier Coello, and Liliana Castillo examine an emerging sector—biodiesel (item **2316**). They examine the current debates on biodiesel versus traditional energy sources and place these debates within a Peruvian context.

Overall, these works point to a continuing evaluation of the successes and failures of the past economic models and identify some important current issues whose treatment by policymakers no doubt will be discussed and debated in the next tranche of political economy analyses. As pointed out by the books and articles reviewed here, Bolivia and Peru each face major challenges in the areas of poverty alleviation and unequal access to political and economic resources. How they deal with these compelling societal issues will help determine their success in tackling the important challenges in issues such as energy and the environment facing them in the short and medium term.

BOLIVIA

2307 Bolivia—gasto social funcional y gasto social para la niñez, 2000–2004. La Paz: Ministerio de Planificación del Desarrollo, UDAPE: UNICEF, 2006. 215 p.: bibl., col. ill.

UNICEF reviews Bolivia's progress towards complying with the Millennium Development Goals related to alleviating child poverty. The authors employ two measures, the "functional social expenditure" and the "social expenditure for children" to gauge and measure the impact of the amount of resources directed at youth. An initial finding was that, although total public spending fell 4.5 percent during the time period examined, both social functional spending and social spending on youth rose. Another improvement was in terms of equality of access: the Gini coefficient of the distribution of consumption improved. In terms of composition, education is the top spending priority (65 percent) and health second (16 percent). The report recommends continued monitoring of social spending on youth, with greater efforts toward increasing access to and quality of information with a goal to increasing the priority level of enhancing social expenditure on youth.

2308 Ergueta Tejerina, Amparo. El retorno de Colón: inversión española en el sector eléctrico de Bolivia. La Paz: CEDLA, 2006. 94 p.: bibl., ill.

Ergueta selects the time period 1994–2004 and the electrical sector to test her hypothesis that foreign investors affect national policy. The bulk of the volume is devoted to an extensive description of foreign direct investment (FDI) in Bolivia, Spanish FDI and Spanish investment in the electricity sector. The conclusions, that Spanish investment has improved the quality of service in some aspects of the electrical sector, but that monopolies are difficult to avoid in sectors such as electricity are interesting. The study could have benefitted from more comparative analysis, for example, looking at whether Spanish companies behaved differently than other foreign companies in this sector or identifying investment in this sector that differed from those in other sectors, for example. The evidence presented in the book does not fulfill the promise of the title, which hints that

Spanish investment in the electrical sector represents a return to Spanish colonialism.

Fernández Terán, Roberto. Gas, petróleo e imperialismo en Bolivia. See item **1650**.

2309 Gas: debate nacional. La Paz: Ediciones El Pulso del País, 2004. 199 p.

This volume collects articles and editorials published in the newspaper *PULSO* during the period 2002–04 that reflect the heated debate in Bolivia on the topic of gas. Articles address the issue of private investment and nationalization, exports, the new hydrocarbons law, the 2003 gas war that forced President Gonzalo Sánchez de Lozada to resign, the referendum on the future of natural gas reserves held in 2004, and relations with Chile and Peru (including, of course, the issue of Bolivia's maritime access). An interesting collection of timely pieces on a topic important to Bolivian politics and economics.

Kohl, Benjamin H. and **Linda C. Farthing.** Impasse in Bolivia: neoliberal hegemony and popular resistance. See item **1658**.

2310 Legitimando el orden neoliberal: 100 días de gobierno de Evo Morales. 2. ed. La Paz: Centro de Estudios para el Desarrollo Laboral y Agrario, 2006. 122 p.: bibl. (Documento de Coyuntura; 12)

This booklet was prepared by the Center for the Study of Labor and Agrarian Development (CEDLA). The document's thesis is that, although Evo Morales was elected on an anti-neoliberal platform, once in office, President Morales adopted neoliberal economic policies through "other paths." Morales' "other path" to neoliberalism, according to this book, is the forging of a social pact with exporters and transnational corporations. The Movimiento al Socialismo (MAS), which brought Morales to power, has its power base in two main groups with contradictory objectives: the "masses" who railed against the entrenched power of the political oligarchy, whose objective is to change the system, and the small urban bourgeoisie, whose objective is to maintain stability. The tension between these groups' objectives explains Morales' policies.

2311 McGuigan, Claire. Los beneficios de la inversión extranjera: ¿cuáles fueron sus resultados en el sector de petróleo y gas en Bolivia? La Paz: Centro de Estudios para el Desarrollo Laboral y Agrario, 2007. 177 p.: bibl., ill.

This volume is the result of collaboration between Christian Aid and CEDLA. McGuigan assesses the costs and benefits of foreign investment in the hydrocarbons sector in Bolivia during the period 1999–2004 and quantifies the contribution of this sector to the economy since its privatization in 1996.

2312 Pérez Luna, Mamerto. No todo grano que brilla es oro: un análisis de la soya en Bolivia. La Paz: Centro de Estudios para el Desarrollo Laboral y Agrario, 2007. 216 p.: bibl.

Soy has been a dynamic and main component of Bolivia's exports during the last quarter century. Pérez Luna holds that previously optimistic assessments of the sector's potential failed to take into account important non-economic activities affecting its competitiveness. Key developments include the impact on the environment, as soy production expands into areas of primary forest; the introduction of genetically modified soy; and social conditions, particularly labor conditions and the distribution of gains from the sector. Pérez Luna attributes Bolivia's competitive advantage in soy to artificially low land and labor costs, partially attributable to lax environment and labor standards. This advantage could be erased with additional liberalization, both with ALADI and non-ALADI countries which may have more productive soy sectors.

2313 Zeballos Hurtado, Hernán and **Eduardo Quiroga Crespo.** Política y economía de los recursos naturales renovables en Bolivia. La Paz: COSUDE: SIRENARE, 2003. 241 p.: bibl., col. ill., col. maps.

The history of Bolivia is dominated by the exploitation of nonrenewable resources: gas tends to dominate the discussion of Bolivia's economic potential. This volume makes an important contribution in examining the potential for alternative energy in Bolivia. Bolivia's current dilemma is whether to maximize the exploitation of its considerable energy resources or move more toward conservation of its rich biodiversity. Zeballos and Quiroga Crespo attempt to demonstrate how conservation can be of economic benefit for Bolivia, setting out a methodology for valuing Bolivia's natural resources, including water and forest (wood products as well as non-timber environmental services including the purification of air and water) resources.

PERU

2314 Arce, Moisés. The societal consequences of market reform in Peru. (*Lat. Am. Polit. Soc.*, 48:1, Spring 2006, p. 27–54, bibl., tables)

Arce holds that a more complex dynamic is at work than just one between winners and losers, that reforms can have a variable impact on interactions between the state and civil society. He holds that different sets of policy reforms induce different types of societal responses depending on the content and the distribution of costs and benefits of the policy. He focuses on Peru, whose deep 1980s economic crisis was compounded by ongoing guerrilla activity. He looks at tax and pension reforms (with narrowly distributed costs and benefits; resulting in the emergence of opposition groups); poverty reforms (widespread costs and benefits, thus the interests of state actors figured more prominently); and health reforms (narrowly concentrated costs give rise to the emergence of opposition and support groups, with the government as arbiter). Arce exhorts analysts to disaggregate the concept of reform to take into account the interactive process between the government and civil society who, while not initiating reforms, will have an impact on how they are implemented.

2315 Azpur, Javier. Descentralización y regionalización en el Perú. (*Ecuad. Debate*, 65, agosto 2005, p. 137–154, bibl.)

Azpur discusses the difficulties inherent in the proposal to decentralize Peru. He cites local identities, political fragmentation, and the tradition of centralization as important obstacles.

2316 Castro P., Paula; Javier Coello; and Liliana Castillo. Opciones para la producción y uso de biodiésel en el Perú. Miraflores, Peru: Soluciones Prácticas, ITDG, 2007. 173 p.: bibl., ill. (Serie Libros; 51)

Castro, Coello, and Castillo set out a panorama of the possibilities of and obstacles to biodiesel production in Peru. The authors examine current debates on energy and the environment including the benefits of diversifying into renewable energy, as well as the balance of gases in global warming, the polluting effect of producing biodiesel and the relative merits of different materials for producing biofuel. Much of the book is focused on the world biofuel market and on different ways of producing biodiesel and is at times rather technical in its analysis, sometimes reading like a science manual. The study on the biodiesel market in Colombia, Ecuador, and Peru included as an annex gives the volume a regional scope.

2317 Figueroa, Adolfo. Competencia y circulación de las elites económicas: teoría y aplicación al caso del Perú. (*Economía/Lima*, 27:53/54, junio/dic. 2004, p. 255–291, bibl., tables)

This article focuses on a topic often cited as a factor in the emergence of Fujimori and the economic policies adopted afterwards: the behavior of Peruvian economic elites. Figueroa finds, using statistical analysis, that the Peruvian case is consistent with elite theory.

2318 Remy, María Isabel. Cafetaleros empresarios: dinamismo asociativo para el desarrollo en el Perú. Colaboración de Marisa Glave Remy. Lima: Oxfam Internacional: IEP, Instituto de Estudios Peruanos, 2007. 135 p.: bibl., ill., maps. (Estudios de la sociedad rural; 31)

This book addresses the problem of volatility in the coffee market for small producers which, according to Oxfam, produce close to three fourths of the world's coffee. Remy details the history of coffee associations and cooperatives in Peru and provides four compelling case studies of existing associations that will serve students of the Peruvian coffee sector as well as of small business and entrepreneurship in Peru. The authors identify four key factors that have helped to stimulate entrepreneurship among these small coffee growers: the world coffee market; the market for "fair trade" coffee; the phenomenon of cooperativism; and, finally, the Junta Nacional del Café, the national coffee union which represents the cooperatives. The author points out an important missing element: the state, which has so far largely ignored this potentially dynamic sector.

2319 Ruiz Torres, Guillermo. Neoliberalism under crossfire in Peru: implementing the Washington Consensus. (*in* Internalizing globalization: the rise of neoliberalism and the decline of national varieties of capitalism. Edited by Susanne Soederberg, Georg Menz and Philip G. Cerny. New York: Palgrave Macmillan, 2005, p. 200–218)

Ruiz Torres argues that the Peruvian state's double goal of implementing neoliberal economic reforms and maintaining President Fujimori's power shaped the transformation of the state. While the authoritarian regime undoubtedly helped in implementing neoliberal reforms, the assertion that the main goal of the state was attracting international capital downplays the demands of domestic Peruvian society for economic and security stability. The article contributes to the literature through its analysis of political, economic, and societal variables that allowed the Fujimorazo to take place and the subsequent consequences thereof.

2320 Sánchez, Juan Martín. Hatun Willakuy: importancia del relato en la política. (*Nueva Soc.*, 197, mayo/junio 2005, p. 54–68, bibl.)

The final report of Peru's Truth and Reconciliation Commission (Hatun Willakuy, a Quechua phrase, can be translated loosely as "gran relato" or great story), documents 20 years of armed conflict, detailing interviews with survivors and perpetrators and documenting the stories of victims, and places responsibility for the conflict at the feet of the Sendero Luminoso and, to a lesser extent the armed forces. The report is presented by Juan Martín Sánchez as a central document for analyzing 20th-century Peru, a key basis for democracy and justice in the Peru of the future and an example for other countries undergoing a similar process. Sánchez concludes that the importance of the report lies not in its truths or recommendations, but rather in its transparency, a component essential to democracy and justice.

2321 Vich, Víctor. Magical, mystical: "The Royal Tour" of Alejandro Toledo. (*J. Lat. Am. Cult. Stud.*, 16:1, March 2007, p. 1–10, bibl.)

Vich's starting point is that in "late capitalism" all sovereign states are merely cogs in the wheels of machinery set in place by transnational corporations. Vich illustrates this theory by showing Peru's President Toledo operating as an "amateur tour guide" to an American journalist in the hope of raising Peru's profile to investors. Vich sees the Peruvian government's sponsorship of this tourism documentary, which promotes Peru's exoticism by showing indigenous peoples, nature, and the Peruvian country presented by President Toledo, as promoting a new colonialism with the country now subject to the global market.

CHILE

PETER M. SIAVELIS, *Associate Professor of Political Science, Wake Forest University*

MICHELLE BACHELET'S HISTORIC 2006 VICTORY as Latin America's first self-made woman president with no connection to a political husband fit well with the story of Chile as a rapidly modernizing polity and economy. While inequalities in income and access to social security, health care, and education have been recognized, most of the economic news out of Chile in the early 2000s continued a trend of casting the country as a success story, particularly given many of its comparative regional referents. However, the early missteps of the Bachelet government (2006–2010) revealed some problems in this otherwise positive economic story. The disastrous launch of the Transantiago transport reform, widespread student and labor protests, and criticisms of Bachelet's Finance Minister Andrés Velasco for alleged penny-pinching in his management of the country's copper reserve, left the administration open to charges of incompetence and insensitivity to the country's stark inequalities. Velasco resisted intense political pressure, mostly from workers and students, to spend some of the copper windfall. When copper prices abruptly fell due to the 2007–2009 financial crisis, accumulated funds were used to support a comprehensive stimulus package which has spared Chile the depth of economic crisis experienced by other countries in the region. Bachelet's (and Velasco's) popularity have rebounded, and the country is again being praised for its wise economic management and relative regional economic success.

Part of the reason for this success is a general consensus across the political spectrum, with the exception of the far left, regarding Chile's economic model. Literature in the past spent a good deal of energy attempting to place credit or blame either with former dictator Augusto Pinochet or with the center-left Concertación governments that have ruled Chile since the return of democracy in 1990. With the passage of years, constant tinkering with the model and the moderate left's acceptance of a market-oriented economy make it difficult to say who deserves credit for successes or blame for failures. The frequently cited idea that there is no difference among Chile's mainstream political parties when it comes to economic policy is, however, also misleading. As Waissbluth and Inostroza (item **2339**) note, there is disagreement between the country's two major coalitions regarding the particular type of market capitalism to follow. The right is generally more sympathetic to the growth-oriented American model characterized by low taxation and high influence for corporations and the moderate left more likely to support a greater role for the state and be more concerned about inequality. In addition, the non-Concertación left remains marginalized and unrepresented as noted by Lischetti (item **2329**).

Even though most literature has moved beyond debate on the model per se, however, several recent works have looked at the development of Chile's successful economy through new interpretive lenses. González (item **2327**), in his comparative study of Chile and Mexico, points to the longer term political variables which were permissive contextual conditions of Chile's success, including an agreed upon electoral framework and constitution and the existence of institutionalized parties and a strong executive. Silva (item **2336**), on the other hand, explores another longer term, yet largely unexplored, cause for the periods of relative peace and prosperity in Chile interrupted occasionally by authoritarian politics. In particular, he shows how Chile's technocrats, who often are linked to authoritarian governments in the literature, historically contributed to the development of party programs and often played a mediating role that helped to sustain democracy in Chile. Finally, Taylor (item **2337**) argues that Chile's free market orientation has grown from the development of a new and specific normative theory of society that grew out of the military's transformative project.

Numerous other recent works have similarly left behind the debate on the "Chilean model," raising the perhaps more important questions of Chile's position in the global economy and the impact of globalization on the country. Cademártori (item **2323**) points to the changing nature of global capitalism and analyzes its impact on Chile, proposing that a new model of global capitalism has developed, characterized by the domination of a limited number of transnational corporations. This new model has affected all major aspects Chile's economy including agriculture and mining, and has shaped the development of trade policy, particularly with the US. Fazio takes a contrasting view (item **2326**). He argues, rather, that the effects of globalization cannot be understood by analyzing only a particular moment in time. He points to globalization as a centuries' long process that has affected economic policy-making in Chile, pitting global forces against Chile's tendency to organize its economy around a state-centered matrix.

Given Chile's extraordinary inequality in income and access to education and social services, distributional concerns continue to be a dominant theme in the political economy literature. However, many works have gone beyond general analyses of inequality to focus on the nuts and bolts of the causes and consequences of it. Matear's study of educational inequality is a good example (item **2331**). She uncovers the economic, class, and cultural forces that have helped to drive the development of inequality in the educational system. Two excellent studies of labor also introduce more nuanced accounts of the causes, nature, and consequences of inequality. Berg (item **2322**) explores the impact of free trade on Chilean wages, presenting a much more comprehensive analysis than most previous works. Contrary to some studies, she finds that firms do not necessarily shift production in ways that benefit low-skilled labor where labor is cheap. Sehnbruch (item **2335**) moves beyond the usual approach of measuring the quality of labor market in terms of unemployment or wage levels. Instead, she develops a comprehensive quality-of-employment measure that better captures the objective conditions of Chilean workers. Posner (item **2333**), on the other hand, is concerned with the impact of inequality on political representation. He finds that the social and economic transformations associated with neoliberalism have diminished the capacity of the marginal poor to engage in collective action, while enhancing the economic and political leverage of business elites.

A series of very engaging and innovative studies explores the strengths and weaknesses of the Chilean economy (item **2325**), the pension system (item **2338**), efforts aimed at improving virtual government (item **2334**), and efforts at eliminating patrimonialism and promoting technocratic orientations in state agencies (item **2332**). This is all very good and promising work. The biggest lacuna in the political economy literature on Chile, however, is a perspective on the broader issues of where the Chilean economy needs to go to maintain its dynamism. Unfortunately, just like governing elites, much of the literature fails to explore where Chile fits in the emerging global economy as a country with a middle level of development, relatively expensive labor in developing world terms, few energy resources, and little in the way of a comprehensive national industrial policy. Research on this important topic is much needed.

2322 Berg, Janine. Miracle for whom?: Chilean workers under free trade. New York: Routledge, 2006. 194 p.: bibl., ill., index. (New political economy)

Berg's study focuses on the impact of free trade on the wages of Chilean workers. In particular, it analyzes how the accepted free trade regime has led to industrial restructuring, and in turn, a transformation in firms' uses of labor. The author presents a much more comprehensive analysis of the causes of growing wage inequality under free trade than previous works. She does so by analyzing the multifaceted processes that lead to wage dispersion, directly challenging the argument that where labor is cheap, firms shift production in ways that benefit low-skilled workers. The work provides in-depth case studies in two particular industries chosen for a variety of theoretical and empirical reasons: cosmetics and agro-industry.

2323 Cademártori, José. La globalización cuestionada. Santiago: Editorial de la Universidad de Santiago de Chile, 2004. 186 p.: bibl. (Col. Ciencias sociales. Economía)

This work, written by a former economy minister of the Salvador Allende government (1970–73), is divided into two parts. The first explores the development of a new form of transnational capitalism. Rather than the national monopoly capitalism that characterized the 1960s and 1970s, the author proposes a new brand of capitalism, characterized by the domination of a limited number of transnational corporations. The second part of the book examines the consequences of this new form of capitalism for Chile, with a special focus on agriculture, mining, external debt, and trade policy with the US.

2324 De Gregorio, José. Bonanza del cobre: impacto macroeconómico y desafíos de política. (*Estud. Públicos*, 102, otoño 2006, p. 17–42, graphs)

The economic bonanza reaped by Chile due to high copper prices is one of the most important narratives in the political economy literature in recent years. Former minister and vice-president of the Central Bank of Chile, De Gregorio asks why Chile has not grown as rapidly during this copper bonanza as it had during previous ones. He finds a number of features that explain this reality, but argues that macroeconomic policy aimed at stabilization of the economy is the primary reason and this is probably a positive economic reality. De Gregorio goes on to explore ways to dampen the potentially negative impact that a rapid increase in spending might have, proposing that areas that simultaneously enhance social spending and have a positive macroeconomic impact, such as unemployment insurance, are good spending candidates to ensure that Chile retains economic stability and growth.

2325 De Gregorio, José. Crecimiento económico en Chile: evidencia, fuentes y perspectivas. (*Estud. Públicos*, 98, otoño 2005, p. 19–86, bibl., graphs, tables)

In this lengthy, yet carefully executed analysis, De Gregorio begins by tracing the evolution of Chilean economic growth, with special emphasis on the period following the deep economic crisis of the early 1980s. Even more usefully, he provides a sophisticated and complete overview of the strengths and weaknesses of the Chilean growth experience. On the plus side, he finds low inflation, solid fiscal policies, a strong financial sector, an economy open to international business, and strong regulatory institutions. On the negative side, the elements of the economy that could stall growth include insufficient research and development, inequality, a lower quality educational system than is usually supposed, and low levels of intraregional trade. For economist's comment, see item **795**.

2326 Fazio Vengoa, Hugo. La globalización en Chile: entre el Estado y la sociedad de mercado. Bogotá: Univ. Nacional de Colombia, Instituto de Estudios Políticos y Relaciones Internacionales (IEPRI), 2004. 233 p.: bibl. (Col. Sede; 18)

The effect of globalization broadly considered is the focus of Fazio's study. His study is innovative in its exploration of globalization conceived as a multidimensional, not just economic, process. In addition, rather than simply exploring the effect of globalization on a particular economy at a specific juncture, this well-researched work analyzes the impact of globalization as a longer term evolutionary process that stretches back to the colonial period. Fazio argues that there is a central and long-standing tension in Chile between the tendency for society to organize itself around a strong state and the globalizing force of market economics.

2327 González González, Francisco Enrique. Dual transitions from authoritarian rule: institutionalized regimes in Chile and Mexico, 1970–2000. Baltimore, Md.: Johns Hopkins Univ. Press, 2008. 286 p.: bibl., ill., index.

This comparative analysis of Mexico and Chile (with additional insights from Brazil, Hungary, Taiwan, and South Korea) analyzes how two ideologically distinct authoritarian regimes crafted policies that allowed them to survive the financial turmoil of the early 1980s and experience relatively successful dual political and economic transitions. González's excellent study argues that, despite their differing ideologies, the authoritarian regimes of Mexico and Chile possessed institutional bases that provided building blocks for successful economic and political reforms. These building blocks included stable constitutional frameworks, agreed-upon calendars for electoral contestation, institutionalized parties, and strong executives.

Lahera, Eugenio. ¿Qué está pasando en Chile? See item **1747.**

2328 Leight, Jessica. The political dynamics of agricultural liberalisation in the US-Chile free trade agreement. (*J. Lat. Am. Stud.*, 40:2, May 2008, p. 225–250, bibl.)

The point of departure for Leight's essay is the widely held notion that the US-Chile Free Trade Agreement was easily ratified in Chile with little controversy. Rather, the author underscores the significant controversy the treaty generated in the agricultural sector. The key finding is that it was actually Chile's political right that supported agricultural protection despite its purported preference for a general market agenda. The author proposes that one of the most significant challenges for future trade strategy will be the Concertación's ability to manage the promotion of a free trade agenda, while avoiding accusations of a lack of concern for the disadvantaged in Chile's largely rural agricultural sector.

2329 Lischetti, Mirtha *et al.* Contra-hegemonía y clase trabajadora en una comuna chilena. (*Polít. Cult.*, 25, primavera 2006, p. 143–174, graph)

Employing a Gramscian approach, the author argues that the experience of military rule provided fertile ground for the spread of globalization, which in turn has transformed the "subjectivities of individuals." In particular, Chile's working class had traditionally been Communist, yet this sector was violently suppressed during the military government and failed to recover. The author argues that Concertación governments have failed to represent this class, and indeed, have been preferred by the business community because they have kept popular demands and mobilization at bay.

2330 Macroeconomic policies for sustainable growth: analytical framework and policy studies of Brazil and Chile. Cheltenham, UK; Northampton, Mass.: Edward

Elgar Publishing, 2006. 349 p.: bibl., ill., index. (Munasinghe Institute for Development (MIND) series on growth and sustainable development)

This edited volume's research was undertaken by a team of international scholars and is part of a series dedicated to economic sustainability, supported by the World Bank and the Munasinghe Institute for Development in Colombo, Sri Lanka. The book's core concern is the sustainability of growth-oriented macroeconomic policies. It presents two detailed case studies of Chile and Brazil that demonstrate the unsustainable outcomes that emerge from the tension between economic growth and economic imperfections. The book relies on a sophisticated set of economic models to underscore this core thesis and explores various policy options to help ameliorate the problems raised by the volume. A very comprehensive review of the literature is only one of this book's many cutting edge contributions.

2331 Matear, Ann. Tensions between state and market in Chile: educational policy and culture. (*Rev. Eur. Estud. Latinoam. Caribe*, 83, Oct. 2007, p. 61–82, bibl., tables)

Despite some success, Chile's educational system is suffering from segmentation and growing inequality between public and private schools. As a public good, education in Chile has been characterized by long-standing tensions generated by the country's market orientation. This article explores three areas of tension, beginning with an analysis of shared public-private funding systems, which have driven children increasingly into privately run schools. The second area of tension is growing social class differentiation between public and private schools, where stratification by income has become the norm. The third area is cultural, with a growing, but only partly accurate, perception that there is a wide performance gap between public and private schools.

2332 Nelson, Roy C. Transnational strategic networks and policymaking in Chile: CORFO's high technology investment promotion program. (*Lat. Am. Polit. Soc.*, 49:2, Summer 2007, p. 149–181, bibl., graphs, tables)

Nelson analyzes CORFO (Corporación de Fomento de la Producción), Chile's main economic development agency, arguing that it had often fallen prey to patrimonial practices. The article shows how these practices were overcome, allowing the agency to develop toward technocratic independence. By establishing a high technology investment promotion program aimed at attracting foreign investment, CORFO connected with transnational strategic actors who helped them learn standard business practices and allowed the institution to better understand and attract the types of FDI (foreign direct investment) best suited to Chile's businesses and markets.

2333 Posner, Paul W. State, market, and democracy in Chile: the constraint of popular participation. New York: Palgrave Macmillan, 2008. 246 p.: bibl., index.

Like many of the works included here, Posner's book explores the impact of neoliberalism on the poor. In particular, the focus is on the impact of free market reforms on the potential for political participation of the marginalized urban poor. Based on extensive interviews with political elites and shantytown dwellers, Posner's work finds that neoliberal reforms have undermined the capacity of the poor to hold public officials accountable, ultimately eroding the quality of Chilean democracy. The book explores the changing nature of the state, business-labor relations, democratic participation and transformations in the social welfare system that pose impediments to collective action. While the power and influence of the marginalized have been diminished, Posner finds that business elites have enhanced economic and political leverage. Brief, yet useful treatments of the Argentine and Mexican case complement the analysis.

2334 Rivera Urrutia, Eugenio. Nueva economía, gobierno electrónico y reforma del Estado: Chile a la luz de la experiencia internacional. Santiago: FLACSO-Chile: Editorial Universitaria, 2003. 285 p.: bibl., ill. (Estudios)

Rather than focusing on political economy writ large, this study focuses on the impact of the new economy and the role of what the author terms the "information society." This very functionally focused study explores the confluence of new technology with new management theories and its effect on government. After reviewing debates on state reform and the new economic role of technology generally, Rivera analyzes the concept of "virtual government" and its implications for state reform. He reviews proposals made during Concertación governments for reforming the state structure and explores how virtual government can play an important role. Finally, the book analyzes concrete case studies of efforts towards virtual government including the Internal Revenue Service, the Customs Agency, and the National Welfare Institute. The author is generally positive about the role that technology can play in improving government services and responsiveness to citizens.

2335 Sehnbruch, Kirsten. The Chilean labor market: a key to understanding Latin American labor markets. New York: Palgrave Macmillan, 2006. 339 p.: bibl., ill., index.

This pathbreaking book applies Amartya Sen's capability approach to the study of labor markets in Chile. Rather than focusing on more conventional measures of labor market performance like unemployment or wage levels, Sehnbruch develops a "quality of employment" indicator that better captures the objective conditions of Chilean workers. The study finds that the quality of employment has changed dramatically over time, something traditional statistics may not capture. In particular, quality of employment has varied with respect to number of workers that have contracts, the types of contracts they have, business contributions to social security systems, and employment stability. For economist's comment, see item **810**.

2336 Silva, Patricio. In the name of reason: technocrats and politics in Chile. University Park, Pa.: Pennsylvania State Univ. Press, 2008. 254 p.: bibl., index.

Silva's seminal work challenges the conventional wisdom on the role of technocrats in Chile. While the neoliberal "Chicago Boys" usually come to mind when technocrats are mentioned in Chile, the author shows that technocrats have a much longer historical trajectory, dating from the late 19th century. More importantly,

Silva demonstrates that despite the non-democratic image of technocrats, they have been central to the mediation of conflict in Chile by acting as neutral arbiters between sometimes hostile social adversaries. In addition, he demonstrates that technocrats have often been quintessential representatives of Chile's core middle class values, and that they played a crucial role in the development of political party programs. While political parties have historically been considered the most important actors in Chilean politics, Silva shows that technocrats have played a central, albeit little analyzed, role.

2337 Taylor, Marcus. From Pinochet to the "third way": neoliberalism and social transformation in Chile. London; Ann Arbor, Mich.: Pluto Press, 2006. 224 p.: bibl., ill., index.

Taylor argues that rather than just a simple model of economic management, neoliberalism in Chile instead represents a specific normative theory of society, based on efficiency, rationality, and a desire to remake the social bases of society. This chronologically organized study traces the evolution of neoliberalism in its various phases and examines the social implications of the neoliberal model during each of the periods. The final section of the study argues that, despite their often being lauded, the policies of Concertación governments have had mixed results for the majority of Chileans. This is the case largely because the Concertación made a somewhat contradictory attempt to transform certain aspects of the neoliberal model without changing the fundamental institutional basis on which it was built.

2338 Valdés Prieto, Salvador. Para aumentar la competencia entre las AFP. (*Estud. Públicos*, 98, otoño 2005, p. 87–142, bibl., graph, table)

This very lengthy, but expertly executed, journal article provides a comprehensive overview of the competitive status of Chile's AFP (Administradoras de Fondos de Pensiones) pension system. The author argues that the tendency for the state to intervene asymmetrically among different providers has produced a type of neocorporatist structure. He proposes very detailed reforms to the system to better spur competition and provide the most benefits for AFP customers. This is essential reading to understand the structure and functioning of the AFP system, and to study the areas where its performance is lacking.

2339 Waissbluth, Mario and **José Inostroza Lara.** ¿Pueden la empresa y la izquierda convivir y no morir en el intento?: la experiencia chilena, 1990–2005. (*Nueva Soc.*, 202, marzo/abril 2006, p. 98–111)

The concepts of left and right are increasingly losing their meaning for these authors who advocate a distinct way to view different economic models and apply them to Chile. Two models for structuring state-society relations are most prevalent today: the American style characterized by pro-growth, pro-market, and pro-business capitalism, and the European-Asian model characterized by a larger state and more concern with eliminating inequality. The authors suggest that the first view of capitalism most corresponds with the vision of the traditional right in Chile, while the second is more characteristic of the contemporary center-left.

ARGENTINA, PARAGUAY, AND URUGUAY

ANA MARGHERITIS, *Assistant Professor of Political Science, University of Florida, Gainesville*

ACADEMIC WORKS ON THE POLITICAL ECONOMY of the Latin American Southern Cone in the last few years have been overwhelmingly influenced by national and regional economic developments, most notably the Argentine debacle in December 2001. The need to explain the causes and implications of that dramatic crisis prompted a number of analytical studies, as well as some normative accounts that pass judgment on apparent policy mistakes and advance recommendations for the future. The bulk of these works focuses on the financial and banking aspects of the crisis, touching only tangentially on social and political dimensions. From a strictly political economy point of view, a few volumes stand out in terms of their scope and contribution. They address either relatively novel, less-explored phenomena, or controversial topics, such as the role of the state in a market economy.

Of the former group, a good example is the 2005 journal article by Armony and Armony (item **2345**) on popular mobilization. The authors emphasize cognitive and psychological factors to explain the effects of the Argentine economic crisis on citizens' behavior and notions of national identity and collective projects. Another example is the volume edited by Susana Hintze (item **2373**) on the expansion of the informal economy in Argentina and some new forms of economic relations that defy traditional political economy assumptions, such as the barter clubs that proliferated as economic recession deepened. This book gathers contributions by both scholars and practitioners to a one-day workshop and includes reflections on why the networks of barter clubs eventually declined. Also, the volume by Esteban Magnani, entitled *El cambio silencioso: empresas y fábricas recuperadas por los trabajadores en la Argentina* (item **2379**), uses several case studies of workers' taking over of firms in the aftermath of the crisis to illustrate the innovative social responses to a critical situation of unprecedented magnitude. It emphasizes the subtle underlying (and usually unintended) processes that are often neglected in the analysis of how an economy is restructured after a dramatic crisis. Along similar lines, the volume compiled by Floreal Forni (*Caminos solidarios de la economía argentina*) (item **2354**) gathers several cooperative experiences of lower social sectors that emerged as alternatives to either market- or state-centered economic models. Also, the book edited by Neffa and Pérez, entitled *Macroeconomía, mercado de trabajo y grupos vulnerables: desafíos para el diseño de políticas públicas* (item **2378**), compiles a number of contributions concerning the impact of macroeconomic transformations on labor markets in general and the most vulnerable social sectors in particular. The authors' perspective is one of public policy; they aim to identify ways in which the state could ameliorate poverty and unemployment.

This last point is a shared concern with some authors who make the case for bringing back the state and its role in the new politico-economic context. The volume by Thwaites Rey and López, *Fuera de control: la regulación residual de los servicios privatizados* (item **2393**), is a case in point. This is the saga of a number of critical studies by the same authors on the regulatory capacities of the Argentine state following controversial privatizations in the 1990s. Using examples from the public utilities sector, they argue in favor of regulation guided by social efficiency and collective needs. From a more comprehensive and theoretical perspective, the volume by Vilas *et al.*, entitled *Estado y política en la Argentina actual* (item **2366**), also places the state as the focal point of analysis and conceptualizes it as a problem, with particular emphasis on some misleading accounts of the crucial role the Argentine state played in structuring economic and political forces.

Finally, a large number of academic sources provide us with a historical analysis of the evolution and troubles of Argentine political economy. They tend to be largely descriptive and very ambitious in terms of scope and time frame. Several of them focus on two issues: public debt and the evolution of the manufacturing sector. A remarkable piece is Mónica Peralta-Ramos' *La economía política argentina: poder y clases sociales (1930–2006)* (item **2385**), which compiles and synthesizes previous works by the author on the connections among global trends, domestic social conflicts, and economic policies in contemporary Argentina. Likewise, Roberto Cortés Conde's *La economía política de la Argentina en el siglo XX* (item **2360**) provides a comprehensive overview of the frustrated path to development taken by Argentina between 1880 and 1990.

The number of works on Uruguay and Paraguay is very low. Studies on the latter are usually immersed in broader analysis that frames developments within the Paraguayan economy in regional and global trends. For instance, Fleitas' *Integraciones regionales: el MERCOSUR y Paraguay* (item **2402**), using a colloquial and normative tone, or Borda's *Globalización y crisis fiscal: casos de Argentina, Brasil y Paraguay* (item **2403**), based on research studies on the three cases. As for Uruguay, two volumes stand out from a political economy perspective. On the one hand, the book edited by Aboal *et al.* (*Economía política en Uruguay: instituciones y actores políticos en el proceso económico*) (item **2406**) aims to fill a gap in the literature by examining the impact of political actors and institutions on the making of different economic policy initiatives, such as monetary, fiscal, and commercial. The underlying theme that links all chapters is the question of long-term economic growth and development. On the other hand, Bergara's work, entitled *Las reglas de juego en Uruguay: el entorno institucional y los problemas económicos* (item **2404**), also emphasizes the role of the institutional framework on economic processes. The author points out the serious obstacles to maintain, implement, and enforce norms in Uruguayan society. Overall, the study of the political economy of these two countries would benefit from further exploration of how political and economic processes are shaping public policies in the context of the ongoing global economic crisis.

I am grateful to Brian Readout for his efficient research assistance.

ARGENTINA

2340 Abeles, Martín; Karina Forcinito; and Martín Schorr. El oligopolio telefónico argentino frente a la liberalización del mercado: de la privatización de ENTel a la conformación de los grupos multimedia. Presentación de Daniel Azpiazu. Bernal, Argentina: Univ. Nacional de Quilmes, 2001. 276 p.: bibl. (Col. Economía política argentina)

A critical examination of the privatization of ENTel, the state telephone company, and the structural and regulatory changes that resulted. The authors claim this process has generated an oligopoly status for the company that will result in higher incomes for executives and higher prices for customers.

2341 Acosta, Pablo and Leonardo Gasparini. Capital accumulation, trade liberalization, and rising wage inequality: the case of Argentina. (*Econ. Dev. Cult. Change*, 55:4, July 2007, p. 793–812, bibl., graphs, tables)

Examines the relationship between capital investment and wage inequality in Argentina. The study compares wages among skilled and unskilled workers using cross-sectional income data from 1985 to 2001. The authors conclude that capital accumulation can increase the wage gap between skilled and unskilled workers.

2342 Alvarez de Celis, Fernando. Inversión, concentración y desindustrialización: la nueva configuración geográfica de la industria en la Región Metropolitana de Buenos Aires, en la década del noventa. Buenos Aires: Cooperativa de Trabajo Cultural El Farol, 2007. 185 p.: bibl., maps.

An analysis of the state of the industrial sector in Buenos Aires in the 1990s. A wide range of factors are considered, such as the history of metropolitan industry, the growth of the services sector, the extent and distribution of investment in industrial enterprises, and the role of the state in industrial promotion.

2343 Los años de Alfonsín: el poder de la democracia o la democracia del poder? Coordinación de Alfred Raúl Pucciarelli. Buenos Aires: Siglo Veintiuno Editores, 2006. 510 p.: bibl., ill. (Sociología y política)

A collection of essays examines the challenges of democratic politics during the 1980s. Contributors engage in the difficulties confronting the Alfonsín administration in the aftermath of military rule and the complexity of meeting popular demands during a period of diminished stability in electoral politics. See also *HLAS 63:3240.*

Argentina 2020: propuestas para profundizar la transformación. See item **1769**.

2344 Arias, César. Deuda externa y Banco Central: instrumentos estratégicos del poder: enfoque político económico sobre la crisis en el mundo globalizado. Buenos Aires: De Los Cuatro Vientos Editorial, 2006. 300 p.: bibl., ill.

A comprehensive analysis of the role of foreign debt in Argentine political economy over the last few decades. Chapters focus on the role of the Banco Central with an emphasis on globalization, the effects of debt on monetary and fiscal policy, and the factors that contributed to the 1980s debt crisis.

2345 Armony, Ariel C. and Victor Armony. Indictments, myths, and citizen mobilization in Argentina: a discourse analysis. (*Lat. Am. Polit. Soc.,* 47:4, Winter 2005, p. 27–54, bibl., tables)

The turmoil of the 2001 economic crisis in Argentina is often attributed to a flawed financial environment, imprudent policy-making, and institutional weaknesses. Instead, the authors describe the

ensuing citizen mobilization and indictment of the political class in terms of cultural frameworks, social psychology, and long-standing conceptions of national identity.

2346 Azcuy Ameghino, Eduardo. La carne vacuna argentina: historia, actualidad y problemas de una agroindustria tradicional. Buenos Aires: Imago Mundi, 2007. 319 p.: bibl., ill.

A 20th century economic history of the meat industry in Argentina and the wider economic circumstances surrounding its development. Chapters establish various phases of growth and decline, and the author concludes with an examination of the recent fall in exports, the diminishing output of the industry, and the rise of the Brazilian market.

2347 Azpiazu, Daniel and Martín Schorr. Crónica de una sumisión anunciada: las renegociaciones con las empresas privatizadas bajo la administración Duhalde. Buenos Aires: Siglo Veintiuno Editores Argentina, 2003. 295 p.: bibl., ill. (Economía política argentina)

An examination of the renegotiation of contracts with recently privatized firms in the aftermath of the 2001 economic crisis. The authors perform case studies of various privatized industries and conclude that such businesses made only minor concessions and may have benefitted from new state subsidies and the dollarization of salaries.

2348 Azpiazu, Daniel; Eduardo M. Basualdo; and Miguel Khavisse. El nuevo poder económico en la Argentina de los años 80. Ed. definitiva. Buenos Aires: Siglo Veintiuno Editores Argentina, 2004. 231 p.: bibl., ill. (Economía política argentina)

An examination of economic policy in Argentina during the military dictatorship, which lasted from 1976 to 1983. The author illustrates the implications of structural changes in the economy, society, and politics during military rule, concluding that it resulted in the concentration of capital and wealth in the hands of a few economic elites.

2349 Beccaria, Luis and Fernando Groisman. Income instability, mobility and distribution in Argentina. (*CEPAL Rev.,* 89, Aug. 2006, p. 123–144, bibl., graph, tables)

A study on workers' income instability in Buenos Aires from 1988 to 2001, evaluating its effect on different individual and household groups. This time period includes a range of varying macroeconomic conditions, allowing the authors to examine the adverse effects of labor wage instability on social welfare.

2350 Benbenaste, Narciso. La madurez política en el argentino: psicología y economía del populismo. Colaboración de Gisela Delfino. Buenos Aires: Eudeba, 2004. 188 p.: ill. (Materiales de cátedra)

This work analyzes the revitalization of populist discourse in the late 1990s and the backlash against neoliberal policies. Chapters examine the nature of contemporary political power and market economics while criticizing populist proclivities to blame neoliberalism for what are in fact failures at the local level.

2351 Berlinski, Julio. Los impactos de la política comercial: Argentina y Brasil, 1988–1997. Buenos Aires: Siglo Veintiuno de Argentina Editores, 2004. 190 p.: bibl., ill.

An analysis of commercial relations between Argentina and Brazil, focusing on particular arrangements and protections, their impact on economic incentives, and their effects on productive activities. The work focuses on the evolution of commercial agreements and negotiations between the two countries as well as prospects for future relations.

2352 Bielsa, Rafael; Roberto Lavagna; and Horacio Rosatti. Estado y globalización: el caso argentino. Buenos Aires: Rubinzal-Culzoni, 2005. 156 p.: ill.

Ministers from the Néstor Kirchner government provide a varied range of analysis on the topic of Argentina's reemergence into the global economy. Essays focus on a series of relevant issues such as globalization, the export sector, debt financing strategies, and domestic and international law.

2353 Bruno, Eugenio Andrea. El default y la reestructuración de la deuda. Prólogo de Rosendo Fraga. Colaboración especial de Juan A. Bruno y Lucas A. Piaggio. Buenos Aires: Nueva Mayoría Editorial, 2004. 392 p., 32 leaves of plates: ill.

A comprehensive study of debt default and restructuring in Argentina. The author discusses the nation's history of public debt, examining the nature of its current debt situation, the legal institutions involved in financing, and the dynamics of restructuring with the IMF, the government, and Wall Street.

2354 Caminos solidarios de la economía argentina: redes innovadoras para la integración. Recopilación de Floreal H. Forni. Textos de Lucrecia Barreiro et al. Buenos Aires: Ediciones CICCUS, 2004. 312 p.: bibl., ill.

A collection of essays examining the social consequences of recent economic policy. The work analyzes economic theory in the context of various contemporary case studies in urban and rural areas, and it attempts to inform cooperatives and NGOs about present social conditions and challenges.

2355 Cardoza, Guillermo; Julián Díaz; and Adriana Ángel. Institutional determinants of the Argentinean crisis: a systemic approach. (*Lat. Am. Bus. Rev.*, 7:1, 2006, p. 1–32, bibl., graphs, tables)

Contemporary analyses often emphasize economic variables in understanding the 2001 economic crisis. This study examines other negative factors such as institutional frailty, the absence of transparency, poor political management, and institutional obsolescence that hindered economic reform consolidation. The authors analyze how economic and political agents resolved the crisis in a new framework.

2356 Castillo, Victoria et al. Labour mobility in Argentina since the mid-1990s: the hard road back to formal employment. (*CEPAL Rev.*, 89, Aug. 2006, p. 145–164, bibl., graph, tables)

A research study on the magnitude and characteristics of labor mobility in Argentina from 1996 to 2004 and the duration of employment for workers in the primary sector. Labor mobility significantly correlates with economic instability, resulting in high unemployment among skilled laborers and low job retentions rates.

2357 Centrángolo, Oscar and Juan Pablo Jiménez. The relations between different levels of government in Argentina.

(*CEPAL Rev.*, 84, Dec. 2004, p. 115–132, bibl., graphs, tables)

A historical review of institutional conflict between Argentina's federal and provincial governments over the last 15 years. The authors analyze the functionality of the federal tax system and criticize the use of transitory pacts and bilateral agreements that have usurped the presence of transparent and stable rules.

2358 Conocimiento y competitividad: tramas productivas y comercio exterior. Recopilación de Gabriel Yoguel. Textos de Darío Milesi *et al.* San Miguel, Argentina: Univ. Nacional de General Sarmiento, Instituto de Industria, 2002. 107 p.: bibl., ill. (Col. Investigación. Serie Informes de investigación; 14)

Two research essays examine new configurations in the automotive sector and the development of internal competition and successful export activity among small businesses. Both essays highlight the importance of domestic competition through innovation and expansion of industrial capacity, as well as the role of public policy in such industries.

2359 Corrales, Javier. Technocratic policy making and parliamentary accountability in Argentina, 1983–2002. Geneva: United Nations Research Institute for Social Development, 2004. 23 p. (Democracy, governance and human rights programme paper; 13)

A concise examination of the "technocratic capacity" of the Argentine legislature to interpret and challenge complex economic bills. The author concludes that the relationship between political parties and the executive branch affects the nature and extent of congressional oversight, and the acquisition of technical expertise can enhance such oversight functions.

2360 Cortés Conde, Roberto. La economía política de la Argentina en el siglo XX. Buenos Aires: Edhasa, 2005. 353 p.: bibl., ill.

A comprehensive economic history of 20th century Argentina. The work demonstrates how the long-term prospects of the economy were transformed by mid-century, examining how factors like persistent inflation, growing public debt, state inefficiency,

a weak financial system, and diminished competitiveness precluded the country from sustaining economic growth.

2361 Damill, Mario; Roberto Frenkel; and Roxana Maurizio. Argentina: una década de convertibilidad: un análisis del crecimiento, el empleo y la distribución del ingreso. Santiago, Chile: Oficina Internacional del Trabajo, 2002. 157 p.: bibl., ill.

This work details how recent years of macroeconomic stability contributed to problems with unemployment and income inequality. The use of intensive antiinflationary policies is claimed to be the source of economic vulnerability from the frequent external shocks of the 1990s, resulting in significant shifts in job markets.

2362 Di Pietro, Sergio Ramón. Seis décadas de políticas económicas en la República Argentina, 1943/2003: señales—logros, dudas y peligros de cada período. Rosario, Argentina: Pueblos del Sur; Buenos Aires: Belgrano Complejo Educativo, 2004. 854 p.: bibl., ill.

An extensive, ambitious analysis of the gap between economic theory and reality. The work thoroughly examines the effects of wider political developments on the formation and the effectiveness of economic policy. Quantitative data is frequently used to establish various economic and political trends over the period.

2363 Economía y sociedad en la región metropolitana de Buenos Aires en el contexto de la reestructuración de los 90. Organización de Alberto Federico Sabaté. Textos de Ana Luz Abramovich *et al.* Buenos Aires: Ediciones al Margen; Los Polvorines, Argentina: Instituto del Conurbano, Univ. Nacional de General Sarmiento, 2002. 294 p.: bibl., ill., map.

A collection of interdisciplinary essays examining the economy of metropolitan Buenos Aires with an emphasis on socioeconomic implications. Primary themes include privatizations, foreign debt, changes in the job market, the rise of income inequality, social imbalances, productive activities and services, transportation, and the concentration of financial capital.

2364 Empresas sociales y economía social: una aproximación a sus rasgos fundamentales. Textos de Ana Luz Abramovich *et al.* San Miguel, Argentina: Univ. Nacional de General Sarmiento, Instituto del Conurbano, Programa de Desarrollo Local, 2003. 122 p.: bibl. (Cartilla de desarrollo local; 6) (Col. Comunidad)

Essays on the role of social business in economic activities previously abandoned or economically disadvantaged. This work provides a critique of current social business legislation, analysis on particular projects in Buenos Aires, and a delineation of the relevant aspects that should be considered when creating new legislation.

2365 Encuentro Internacional de Economía, *5th, Córdoba, Argentina, 2005.* Desequilibrios en el mercado de trabajo argentino: los desafíos de la posconvertibilidad. Textos de Julio César Neffa *et al.* Buenos Aires: Asociación Trabajo y Sociedad: CEIL-PIETTE CONICET, 2005. 128 p.: bibl., ill.

A collection of essays on the challenges facing the job market in the coming years. The authors illuminate various aspects of the structures of job markets, the persistence of long-term unemployment among some workers, the social impact of structural adjustments, and the acquisition of knowledge through work processes.

2366 Estado y política en la Argentina actual. Textos de Carlos M. Vilas *et al.* Prólogo de Fernando Falappa y Germán Soprano. Los Polvorines, Argentina: Univ. Nacional de General Sarmiento; Buenos Aires: Prometeo Libros, 2005. 129 p.: bibl.

A collection of essays from interdisciplinary perspectives evaluating the origins and consequences of globalization, its effects on the autonomy of the state, and its impact on the democratic system and its citizens. The work largely examines the shortcomings of government regulation and the expectations society places on the state.

2367 Fanelli, José María. Estrategias para la reconstrucción monetaria y financiera de la Argentina. Buenos Aires: CEDES (Centro de Estudios de Estado y Sociedad): Siglo Veintiuno Editores Argentina: Fundación OSDE, 2003. 106 p.: bibl., ill.

An integral analysis of strategies for sustaining economic growth in capital markets with an emphasis on macroeconomics and global integration. Chapters establish

the necessity of building controls in the financial and monetary systems to avoid the "stop-and-go" economic volatility of the recent past.

2368 Giuliano, Héctor Luis. Problemática de la deuda pública argentina. Vol. 1, La deuda bajo la administración Kirchner. Buenos Aires: Grupo Editor del Encuentro, 2006. 1 v.

A compilation of articles analyzing the nature and problems of public debt under the Kirchner administration. The author examines various dimensions of the new relationship with the IMF, the nation's exit from default status, the accumulation of new debt, and the reemergence of inflation.

2369 González Fraga, Javier and Martín Lousteau. Sin atajos: de la ciclotimia a la madurez del desarrollo. Buenos Aires: Temas Grupo Editorial, 2005. 203 p.: bibl., ill.

An account of the failure of dynamic economic policies to create stable economic growth in Argentina. Chapters clinically examine the origins of such instability, emphasizing reliance on foreign debt, energy needs, the propensity for international trade over internal market development, and an overextended financial sector.

2370 González-Rozada, Martín and Alicia Menendez. Why have urban poverty and income inequality increased so much?: Argentina, 1991–2001. (*Econ. Dev. Cult. Change,* 55:1, Oct. 2006, p. 109–138, bibl., graphs, tables)

Despite economic growth in the 1990s, Argentina experienced rising unemployment. This work explores the ways that the labor market affected poverty and income inequality with two distinct approaches. The authors use microeconometric decompositions to understand this relationship and methodological analysis to determine the statistical significance of this model.

2371 Heredia, Mariana. Reformas estructurales y renovación de las élites económicas en Argentina: estudio de los portavoces de la tierra y del capital. (*Rev. Mex. Sociol.,* 65:1, enero/marzo 2003, p. 77–115, bibl.)

This study of the emergence of economic elites in Argentina focuses on the development of two business corporations: the Sociedad Rural Argentina (SRA) and the Asociación de Bancos de la Argentina (Adeba-ABA). These organizations have strongly supported the liberal economic policies and market reforms of the 1990s.

2372 Jornada "El Desarrollo Económico de la Argentina en el Mediano y Largo Plazo: Hacia la Construcción de Consensos," Buenos Aires, 2004. El desarrollo económico de la Argentina en el mediano y largo plazo: hacia la construcción de consensos. Recopilación de Chacho Álvarez. Textos de Víctor Beker *et al.* Buenos Aires: Centro de Estudios Políticos, Económicos y Sociales: Prometeo, 2005. 256 p.: bibl., ill.

A collection of essays delineating various economic proposals from different organizations and their potential impact on financial systems, global and regional integration, industry, social welfare, and state politics. The editor concludes that the state must strengthen industrial production while developing a strong domestic market and improving income distribution.

2373 Jornada Nacional sobre Trueque y Economía Solidaria, *Universidad Nacional de General Sarmiento, 2002.* Trueque y economía solidaria. Recopilación de Susana Hintze. Buenos Aires: Prometeo: Univ. Nacional de General Sarmiento, 2003. 324 p.: bibl.

This collaborative work between the Univ. Nacional de General Sarmiento and the UN Development Program in Argentina provides reflections and proposals on the informal exchange sector of the economy. Contributors examine its role in economic development and the potential impact on different social sectors.

2374 Jornadas de Desarrollo Rural en su Perspectiva Institucional y Territorial, *1st, Buenos Aires, 2005.* Desarrollo rural: organizaciones, instituciones y territorios. Recopilación de Mabel Manzanal, Guillermo Neiman, y Mario Lattuada. Buenos Aires: CONICET: Agencia Nacional de Promoción Científica y Tecnológica: Ediciones CICCUS, 2006. 449 p.: bibl., ill. (Col. "Trabajo, integración y sociedad")

A series of academic essays analyzing various aspects of rural development and current institutional policies. The entries are divided into three main sections: theoretical and methodological analysis, case studies and research, and development fieldwork and experiences. The authors emphasize territorial identity as a necessary focus for development institutions.

2375 Lederman, Daniel. Income, wealth, and socialization in Argentina. (*Cuad. Econ./Santiago*, 42:125, mayo 2005, p. 3–30, bibl., graphs, tables)

This sociological study analyzes level of participation in social organizations and level of trust in members of the community. Extensive quantitative research investigates rates of participation and trust in terms of age, household income, rural communities, individual trust, and community unemployment rates and inequality.

2376 Lenz, Maria Heloisa. Crescimento econômico e crise na Argentina de 1870 a 1930: a Belle Époque. Porto Alegre, Brazil: UFRGS Editora: Fundação de Economia e Estatística Sigfried Emanuel Heuser, 2004. 327 p.: bibl., maps. (Col. Estudos e pesquisas IEPE)

A multidisciplinary study of economic history, focusing on the Belle Époque and its characteristically strong economic growth. The work analyzes early indications of globalization, the growth of infrastructure, the proliferation of export markets, the development of financial institutions, the country's relationship with Great Britain, and its eventual economic decline.

2377 Lo Vuolo, Rubén Mario. Estrategia económica para la Argentina. Buenos Aires: Siglo Veintiuno Editores Argentina, 2003. 430 p.: bibl. (Sociología y política)

A comprehensive work that identifies recent shortcomings of economic policy and proposes new strategies for economic development. Chapters discuss important issues like income distribution, the status of various productive sectors, Argentina's position within the global economy, and the need for reforms on socioeconomic policy.

2378 Macroeconomía, mercado de trabajo y grupos vulnerables: desafíos para el diseño de políticas públicas. Coordinación de Julio César Neffa y Pablo Pérez. Textos de Mariana Busso *et al.* Buenos Aires: Asociación Trabajo y Sociedad: CEIL-PIETTE CONICET, 2006. 342 p.: bibl., ill.

A collection of essays utilizing sociological, anthropological, and economic perspectives to analyze recent changes and challenges in labor markets. The work evaluates the impact of macroeconomic developments, the effects of recent changes on different social groups, and the role of the public sector in fighting poverty and unemployment.

2379 Magnani, Esteban. El cambio silencioso: empresas y fábricas recuperadas por los trabajadores en la Argentina. Buenos Aires: Prometeo, 2003. 230 p.: bibl.

A journalistic examination of worker movements to keep problematic industrial facilities functioning during the economic recession of 2001–2002. The work includes case studies of some of these businesses which are presently growing and providing valuable jobs. There are several personal interviews with workers and management.

2380 Marcolini, Walther Alberto. La política económica anticíclica de Perón, 1946–1955. Mendoza, Argentina: W. Marcolini, 2004. 251 p.: bibl.

A historical analysis of economic policy under Perón in a period of exceptional financial and economic conditions following WWII. Primary topics include the economic legacy of the Great Depression, interventionism in monetary policy, nationalizations, agrarian and industrial policies, and economic integration in Latin America.

2381 Míguez, Eduardo José. "El fracaso argentino": interpretando la evolución económica en el "corto siglo XX." (*Desarro. Econ.*, 44:176, enero/marzo 2005, p. 483–514, bibl.)

An analysis of Argentina's failure to sustain significant economic growth in the 20th century, examining the political economy, institutions, and macroeconomic structures that generated this economic reality. The author uses a historical perspective to analyze global economic development in order to identify problems in Argentina's own economic evolution.

2382 Mortimore, Michael and **Leonardo Stanley.** Obsolescencia de la protección a los inversores extranjeros después de la crisis argentina. (*Rev. CEPAL/Santiago*, 88, abril 2006, p. 17–34, bibl., graph)

During the 2001 Argentine economic crisis, foreign investors and creditors faced decidedly unfavorable terms of protection. The author examines the diminished power of the international financial institutions and whether or not these circumstances are an indication of a weakening in protection for foreign investment.

2383 El país que queremos: principios, estrategia y agenda para alcanzar una Argentina mejor. Compilación de Sergio Berensztein, Horacio Rodríguez Larreta, y Federico Sturzenegger. Buenos Aires: Temas, 2006. 195 p.: ill., 1 CD-ROM.

A series of institutional recommendations and strategies for improving public spending, the development of institutional infrastructure, and economic policy. The work explains Argentina's current economic dilemmas and proposes a number of public policy ideas to generate social mobility through dynamic institutional reforms.

2384 Parodi Trece, Carlos. La crisis argentina: lecciones para América Latina. Lima: Univ. del Pacífico, Centro de Investigación, 2003. 243 p.: bibl.

A work that utilizes economic, social, political, historical, and institutional perspectives to detail the collapse of the Argentine economy in late 2001. The author examines numerous aspects of the crisis and its important contributing factors as a means of understanding how Latin America may prevent such crises in the immediate future.

2385 Peralta-Ramos, Mónica. La economía política argentina: poder y clases sociales (1930–2006). Buenos Aires: Fondo de Cultura Económica, 2007. 453 p.: bibl. (Sección de obras de economía)

An updated compilation of previously published essays (see *HLAS 53:5519*) analyzes the power structures that generated particular social and political conflicts and their influence on economic policy-making during the period. The author emphasizes the role of Peronism in altering social relations and changing the nature of political power struggles for future decades.

2386 Por qué sucedió?: las causas económicas de la reciente crisis argentina. Textos de Mercedes Botto *et al.* Compilación de Carlos Bruno y Daniel Chudnovsky. Buenos Aires: Siglo Veintiuno de Argentina Editores: CENIT, 2003. 219 p.: bibl., ill.

A compilation of essays offering perspectives on the origins of the recent economic crisis. Special attention is given to the political-economic climate resulting from the recent recession. Contributors consider how to respond to challenges in international export markets, domestic industrial development, and relations within Mercosur.

2387 Rapoport, Mario. El viraje del siglo XXI: deudas y desafíos en la Argentina, América Latina y el mundo. Buenos Aires: Norma, 2006. 430 p.: bibl., ill. (Tiempos de cambio)

A broad, diverse collection of essays analyzing geopolitical factors, national economic history, international debt policies, regional and international commerce, the education system, and global economic integration. The work engages such topics to generate a comprehensive understanding of Argentina's current position in the global economy.

2388 Rougier, Marcelo. Industria, finanzas e instituciones en la Argentina: la experiencia del Banco Nacional de Desarrollo, 1967–1976. Bernal, Buenos Aires: Univ. Nacional de Quilmes, 2004. 350 p.: bibl., ill. (*Col. Convergencia.* Entre memoria y sociedad)

Utilizes complementary historical perspectives on political economy, state institutions, and business to understand state-industrial relationships and the sources of economic instability. The work focuses on the role of the Banco Nacional de Desarrollo in industrial development along with the industrial policies enacted by the Peronist governments and the military administrations that followed.

2389 La salida del laberinto neoliberal: la búsqueda de vías políticas alternativas. Recopilación de Edgar G. Fernández Suárez. Textos de Pablo C. Riberi *et al.* Córdoba, Argentina: Facultad de Derecho y Ciencias Sociales, Univ. Nacional de Córdoba, 2004. 130 p.: bibl.

A compilation of essays providing different perspectives on the exclusionary effects of globalization and neoliberal policies in social, political, and economic realms. Special emphasis is given to the role of the private sector and private citizens in determining the viability and success of a new economic model.

2390 Schorr, Martín. Industria y nación: poder económico, neoliberalismo y alternativas de reindustrialización en la Argentina contemporánea. Prólogo de Daniel Azpiazu. Buenos Aires: Edhasa: IDAES, 2004. 360 p.: bibl. (Ensayo Edhasa)

An historical analysis of the industrial sector leading up to the recession of 2001 to 2002. The chapters analyze elements like structural reforms, distribution of income in the manufacturing sector, characteristics of manufacturing markets, and international trade. The author argues that a new industrial model can maximize capacity and improve social welfare.

2391 Spiller, Pablo Tomas and **Mariano Tommasi.** The institutional foundations of public policy in Argentina. New York: Cambridge Univ. Press, 2007. 237 p.: bibl., index. (Political economy of institutions and decisions)

The work develops a model of public policy-making, utilizing game theory, transaction cost theory, Douglass North's institutional arguments, and contract theory to determine which conditions result in high-quality policies. Using statistical evidence, the authors detail why Argentina has been unable to design and implement high-quality public policies over time.

2392 Sturzenegger, Federico. La economía de los argentinos: reglas de juego para una sociedad próspera y justa. Buenos Aires: Planeta, 2003. 284 p.: ill.

An analysis of current economic problems in Argentina and possible solutions. The work highlights the rise of inequality, the convertibility crisis, the potential for monetary and fiscal policy to avoid recessions, the need for global integration, the role of Mercosur, and Argentina's economic expansionism in recent years.

Teichman, Judith A. The World Bank and policy reform in Mexico and Argentina. See item **2230.**

2393 Thwaites Rey, Mabel and **Andrea López.** Fuera de control: la regulación residual de los servicios privatizados. Buenos Aires: Temas, 2003. 158 p.: bibl.

A critical analysis of the privatization

of public utilities companies in the 1990s. The authors criticize past inefficiencies of those firms and the self-interests of private enterprises. The work addresses the need for a new government role in providing basic public goods like health, education, and welfare services.

2394 Todesca, Jorge. El mito del país rico: economía y política en la historia argentina. Buenos Aires: Emecé, 2006. 412 p.

The work challenges the widely accepted image of Argentina as a wealthy nation. The author contends that such perceptions are derived from the late 19th century until WWI, when the country was a major exporter and recipient of substantial foreign investment, but crises and missed opportunities have precluded substantial economic achievement since that period.

2395 Tuozzo, María Fernanda. World Bank, governance reforms and democracy in Argentina. (*Bull. Lat. Am. Res.*, 23:1, Jan. 2004, p. 100–118, bibl., table)

An examination of the nature of the World Bank's endorsement of institutional reforms in the 1990s and its influence on political and civil society structures in Argentina. The author argues that attempts to reform governance problems have created policies and practices that have proven problematic to the consolidation of democracy.

2396 Vicente, Ricardo. El gobierno de la "revolución libertadora" y un nuevo relacionamiento económico internacional argentino, 1955–1958. (*Ciclos Hist. Econ. Soc.*, 14:28, segundo semestre 2004, p. 175–207, bibl., tables)

The provisional government that emerged from the 1955 coup rejected a number of international economic and financial strategies that were initiated by the Perón government. The article illustrates how the efforts to increase exports and gain a greater share in capital markets were troubled by an unfavorable international economic environment.

2397 Vilas, Carlos María. Pobreza, desigualdad y sustentabilidad democrática: el ciclo corto de la crisis argentina. (*Rev. Mex. Sociol.*, 67:2, enero/marzo 2005, p. 229–269, bibl., graphs)

The adoption of certain financial and monetary policies in 2001 resulted in a popular uprising and the overthrow of a government. The author analyzes this movement in terms of rising poverty and inequality, concluding that new social welfare policies and economic reforms reflected some of the more virulent popular demands.

2398 Whitson, Risa. Beyond the crisis: economic globalization and informal work in urban Argentina. (*J. Lat. Am. Geogr.*, 6:2, 2007, p. 121–136, bibl.)

A study of the ascent of informal labor following the 2001 economic crisis. The author conducts interviews with informal workers in Buenos Aires to examine the nature of informal work in the present economy, criticizing the lack of formal work, the use of probationary labor, and the increase in contractual arrangements. For geography specialist's comment, see item **1214**.

2399 Wibbels, Erik. Federalism and the market: intergovernmental conflict and economic reform in the developing world. Cambridge; New York: Cambridge Univ. Press, 2005. 276 p.: bibl., index.

This academic research analyzes intergovernmental bargaining among state-level bureaucracies in the developing world as it relates to economic policy reform. Using cross-sectional time-series and case study analysis of Argentina, the author illustrates how political pressures create challenges for bargaining between national and regional leaders, making complex reforms difficult to implement.

2400 Wogart, Jan Peter. Argentina and the global capital roller coaster of the 1990s. (*Rev. Econ. Polít.*, 24:3, julho/set. 2004, p. 370–385, bibl., tables)

An analysis of the "Currency Board" experiment of the 1990s, which attempted to control inflation with a quasi-fixed exchange rate and led to the breakdown of the Argentine economy in 2001. The author argues that Chilean economic policy was markedly more pragmatic and prudent, helping it avoid a similar downfall.

PARAGUAY

2401 Centurión López, Aldo. Competitividad: factores e indicadores de la competitividad en Paraguay. Asunción: Mix, 2004. 290 p.: bibl., ill.

A study on competitiveness and the

competitive deficiencies of various productive sectors in the Paraguayan economy.
The work attempts to alert private citizens and high government officials of the
need to make competition a primary focus
in an increasingly globalized economic
environment.

2402 Fleitas, Ovidio. Integraciones regionales: el MERCOSUR y Paraguay. Asun-
ción: El Lector, 2004. 467 p.: map.

A broad analysis of the complexities
of regional integration and its failure to
produce positive results in Paraguay in the
last few decades. The author criticizes the
nation's failure to modify administrative
structures, reorganize the judicial system,
and develop domestic industries, contributing to diminished competitiveness in the
region. For geography specialist's comment,
see *HLAS 63:1752*.

**2403 Globalización y crisis fiscal: casos
de Argentina, Brasil y Paraguay.**
Compilación de Dionisio Borda. Asunción:
Centro de Análisis y Difusión de Economía
Paraguaya, CADEP, 2003. 155 p.: bibl. (Serie
Políticas públicas)

Paraguay's fiscal deficit and foreign
indebtedness began increasing rapidly after
1995. The authors delineate the causes of
fiscal crisis in terms of developments in
the region's political economy, illustrating
how the nation has become increasingly
characterized by susceptibilities to external
shocks, pro-cyclical fiscal policies, weaknesses in budgetary institutions, and unconventional debt policies. For additional
comment, see *HLAS 63:3019*.

URUGUAY

2404 Bergara, Mario. Las reglas de juego
en Uruguay: el entorno institucional
y los problemas económicos. Montevideo:
Ediciones Trilce: CIIIP-UPAZ: Univ. de la
República, Facultad de Ciencias Sociales,
Depto. de Economía, 2003. 160 p.: bibl.
(Serie (H)ojeadas)

An analysis of government institutions as a means of understanding and
evaluating economic problems in Uruguay.
The author explains such problems in the
context of the financial system, the regulation of public services, the need for institutional competency, the financial regulation

system, the tax system, and the banking
sector.

2405 Bittencourt, Gustavo. Uruguay 2006:
desarrollo esquivo o ruptura con la
historia. (*Am. Lat. Hoy/Salamanca*, 43, dic.
2006, p. 15–39, bibl., graphs, tables)

The article explains Uruguay's
low long-term economic growth in terms
of its specialization in low-demand products
and its static technological progress. The
author claims that recent decades of neoliberal policies have supported a productive
structure based in natural resources, yet
this could be improved through regional
integration.

**2406 Economía política en Uruguay: ins-
tituciones y actores políticos en el
proceso económico.** Recopilación de Diego
Aboal y Juan Andrés Moraes. Textos de
Alvaro Forteza *et al.* Montevideo: Ediciones
Trilce, 2003. 215 p.: bibl., ill.

A collection of academic essays analyzing various financial, monetary, and
exchange policies and the larger structural
issues of social security and commerce. The
contributions emphasize the fiscal deficit,
significant political changes over time,
debt policies, and other major issues with
the intent of encouraging further study on
Uruguayan political economy.

**2407 La industria audiovisual uruguaya:
realidad o ficción?: su impacto sobre
las PYMES.** Textos de Luis Stolovich *et al.*
Colaboración de Sylvia Barreiro y Valeria
Stolovich. Montevideo: Ediciones IDEAS,
2004. 238 p.: bibl., ill.

An analysis of the potential economic
impact that could result from the development of an audio-visual industry (i.e., film,
television, cable, video, advertising, etc.)
among small businesses. Chapters examine other industries around the world, the
process of initiating such an industry, its
economic characteristics, and its economic
potential and limitations.

**2408 Uruguay 2005: propuestas de política
económica.** Textos de Danilo Astori
et al. Montevideo: Ediciones de la Banda
Oriental, 2004. 197 p.: bibl.

An analysis of contemporary Uruguayan political economy from various
academic experts with a series of proposals

for alleviating significant problems. The authors examine recent structural reforms, macroeconomic issues, industrial produc-tion, income distribution, economic competitiveness, and financial and commercial integration at the international level.

BRAZIL

ANTHONY PETER SPANAKOS, *Assistant Professor, Montclair State University, and Adjunct Assistant Professor, New York University*

THE ELECTION OF LUIS INÁCIO "LULA" DA SILVA to the presidency in 2002 received considerable attention within and outside of Brazil. Since then debate centering on political economy has been primarily concerned with either the relative virtues or problems with liberalism and/or state intervention, and with explaining whether Lula's economic policies in either or both of his governments (2002–2006, 2006–2010) can be considered "left," "progressive," or "alternatives to liberalism."

The relative dearth of other subjects being explored in published works is disappointing. Political economists are largely continuing somewhat tired discussions to the same audiences. Although most of the works reviewed here are interesting and solid pieces of scholarship, few are written or will be read by partisans of "the other side." This is partially because their partisan perspective is clear and partially because they do not extend beyond the tradition in which they are writing to examine opposing viewpoints. Instead of considering the most interesting puzzles in political science and economics and rendering them in innovative ways, much of the political economy literature reviewed here relies on exploring issues through existing methodologies and, not surprisingly, coming to the same conclusions. This is not to say that the works below are unworthy of being read and challenged. Rather, one hopes that future works in the field will better create a more meaningful dialogue between this and new methodologies and conclusions.

There are two important new developments in the field. First, after many years of simply critiquing (being "pure opposition") neoliberalism, a tradition has developed of emphasizing not only social inclusion, but also social networks in the construction of "alternatives" to liberalism. The second development is that more works are studying problems of Brazilian political economy from a legitimately comparative lens.

Despite these shifts, the most consistent theme in the works reviewed here is a generalized critique of neoliberalism and globalization. Dall'Acqua's dissertation (item **2417**) offers an interesting examination of globalization by looking at productive chains and clusters of participation. Carvalho, consistent with his earlier work, returns to Keynes as a means of critiquing Brazil's policy of inflation-targeting, insisting that short-term interest rates affect long-term rates, and that monetary policy must focus on real, not nominal, issues (item **2415**). Souza *et al.* (item **2437**) is a collection of writings by Paul Singer's students on his contributions as a scholar activist. The work offers important insights into one of the most important economists of the Partido dos Trabalhadores (PT), but it needs to be updated or re-evaluated on the basis of Singer's participation in the Lula government.

The most ideologically driven of the books proposing critiques of liberalism and globalization are those by Sader (item **2448**) and Petras and Veltmeyer (item **2438**). Sader's short missive against globalization recalls the glory days of state intervention and rapid economic growth and then touches on World Social Forum issues and the landless movement in Brazil. Representing an even more radical critique of liberalism, Petras and Veltmeyer's *Cardoso's Brazil: A Land for Sale* attacks the Cardoso government as having worsened virtually every socioeconomic indicator in Brazil. These works should not be understood simply as academic critiques of liberalism, but also as efforts by the scholars involved to try to come to grips with the policy choices of the Lula government. Potential contradictions among the PT's economic policies are directly discussed in the volume edited by Tavares Soares (item **2426**). The contributions focus on various significant issues for the PT. A more critical approach to the same issue is seen in the compilation edited by Paula (item **2420**). Released shortly into Lula's first term, the volume contests policies of "continuismo," that is, continuing those of President Cardoso.

Cardoso's policies, and liberalism more generally, are not without their advocates. Giambiagi *et al.* (item **2419**) and editors Giambiagi, Reis, and Urani (item **2444**) are apologists for liberalism, defending the need to maintain inflation targeting and a liberal trade profile. The low growth of the "liberal era" of the 1980s and 1990s was the result of inflation generated earlier and then low investment, not the general macroeconomic policies of the Cardoso government. Bacha and Bonelli (item **2412**) support this claim by showing that the cost of investment increased in Brazil due to declining credibility for the monetary authority and the subsequent increase in inflation.

This liberal structuralist debate is also found in works on economic history, such as items **2419** and **2427**. The two offer vastly differing views of the causes and constraints on economic growth in 20th-century Brazil, with the former defending liberal analysis and the latter critiquing it. Political scientists looking at economic history and recent reforms have offered fewer apologetic works and more mainstream scholarship. Kohli's (item **2428**) study of development in South Korea, India, Brazil, and Nigeria argues that state strategy was most effected when states were strong and nations cohesive. Benevides, Vannuchi, and Kerche (item **2443**) assess a broad range of reforms in Brazil, including state reform, while editors Sola and Whitehead (item **2450**) evaluate the role of statesmanship and negotiation as Brazil democratized and reformed its economy. The essays in these books aim to address questions beyond Brazil through engaging theoretical work in the field, using Brazil as a case study to advance their arguments. Their work constitutes an important and compelling area of scholarship.

Another such area is largely a spin-off of critiques of globalization. Over the course of the decade, literature in this camp has argued that an alternative to neoliberalism and globalization was possible and Brazil has now developed some of these alternative arrangements. Senator Suplicy's collection (item **2451**) is a good starting point as it is a rather introductory collection of essays and interviews. Sachs (item **2447**) begins with a relatively well-rehearsed neostructural critique of liberalism and globalization, but uses this as a platform to argue on moral and empirical grounds that inclusion provides better growth patterns for Latin American countries. This literature is at its strongest when it offers case studies that aim to provide the foundations for the "alternative" project. Abramovay (item **2429**) brings together a strong collection of essays which shows how various social arrangements exist within different spaces and how they can be used to combat poverty. Finally, Arraes, Barreto, and Teles argue on behalf of broadening the understanding of development to include social and institutional accounts (item **2411**).

2409 Amaro, Meiriane Nunes. O processo de reformulação da previdência social brasileira, 1995–2004. (*Rev. Inf. Legis.*, 42:166, abril/junho 2005, p. 267–292, bibl., graphs)

Amaro offers a broad look at the process of social security reform. The original reform of 1995 is seen as incomplete but necessary, and effective given the time, in terms of long-term rationalization of the social security budget. The climate for passing the bill improved under Lula in 2003 and the reform passed very quickly.

2410 Araújo, João Lizardo de. Diálogos da energia: reflexões sobre a última década, 1994–2004. Organização de Adilson de Oliveira. Rio de Janeiro: 7 Letras, 2005. 271 p.: bibl., ill.

This book collects influential essays written about energy policy in Brazil during its most significant period of reform. The essays are of use as a reflection of the important policy reforms begun under the Cardoso administration and partially reformulated by the Lula administration. Many of the questions raised, particularly in the theoretical chapter, are of continued relevance especially with the rise of energy consumption in Brazil, Russia, India, and China, and the most recent boom in oil prices.

2411 Arraes, Ronaldo A.; Ricardo Candéa S. Barreto; and Vladimir Kühl Teles. Efeitos do capital social e do capital político no desenvolvimento econômico: simulações para países e estados brasileiros. (*Anál. Econ./Porto Alegre*, 22:41, março 2004, p. 211–239, bibl., tables)

Argues that liberal economics has erred by focusing on simple numbers in measuring development. Economists need to include social and institutional forces in discussions of development and growth. Similarly, practitioners need to improve social and institutional factors in order to raise GDP per capita in Brazil.

2412 Bacha, Edmar Lisboa and Regis Bonelli. Uma interpretação das causas da desaceleração econômica do Brasil. (*Rev. Econ. Polít.*, 25:3, julho/set. 2005, p. 163–189, bibl., graphs)

Why did growth, which had been 7 percent from 1940–80, decline to 2.5 per-cent since then? The question is generally answered by structuralist analysis and antiliberal rhetoric. Here, Bacha and Bonelli show that the increased cost of investment weakened the "purchasing power" of savings and led to lower levels of investment and, therefore, growth. The increased cost of investment, they argue, was the result of the inward-oriented policies since at least the 1970s, if not the 1950s.

2413 Boschetti, Ivanete. Seguridade social e trabalho: paradoxos na construção das políticas de previdência e assistência social no Brasil. Brasília: Letras Livres, Editora UnB, 2006. 322 p.: bibl.

Boschetti presents an evolutionary approach to social security and labor protection beginning with predemocratic Brazil and the assumption of moral but legally unprotected obligations towards social inclusion, and moving through the democratic period with the gradual development of a legal and policy framework to achieve greater inclusion. The Constitution of 1988 is especially important for framing the discussion and the policy and rhetorical space available for understanding social policy. Boschetti argues against social security benefits based on contribution given that the Brazilian labor force has a large a non-salaried component.

2414 Cabral Filho, Severino Bezerra. Brasil megaestado: nova ordem mundial multipolar. Rio de Janeiro: Contraponto, 2004. 226 p.: bibl.

The author studies the thought of two very different Brazilian intellectuals from the 1950s and ruminates on how their work speaks to the current shift towards multi-polarity in international relations. San Tiago Dantas was a strategist associated with the leftist Goulart regime and Golbery do Couto one of the chief intellectuals of the military dictatorship. Nevertheless, Cabral argues, their points of consensus over modernization and industrialization have contributed to Brazil being capable of claiming the states of a "megastate" in a new multipolar world order.

2415 Carvalho, Fernando J. Cardim de. Uma contribuição ao debate em torno da eficácia da política monetária e algumas implicações para o caso do Brasil. (*Rev.*

Econ. Polít., 25:4, out./dez. 2005, p. 323–336, bibl.)

Keynesians argue that monetary policy is not neutral in contrast to classical economists. Using a Keynesian logic, which says that short-term interest rates affect long-term interest rates (and investment), the author criticizes the inflation-targeting policy regime of Brazil. He also critiques the liberal view that monetary policy should be outside of the influence of politics.

2416 Costa, Paulo Roberto Neves. Como os empresários pensam a política e a democracia: Brasil, anos 1990. (*Opin. Públ.*, 11:2, out. 2005, p. 422–449, bibl.)

This paper examines how democratization has impacted the way businesspeople think about politics. According to opinion polls, democratization has brought few changes. Costa then examines two groups, the Commerical Association of São Paulo and the Federation of Commerce of the State of São Paulo (ACSP and DECOMERCIO SP), in the 1970s and 1990s and shows that businessmen continue to see politics as administrative, a form of public management, and that they continue to criticize the weakness of political parties, Congress and the national bureaucracy.

2417 Dall'Acqua, Clarisse Torrens Borges. Competitividade e participação: cadeias produtivas e a definição dos espaços geoeconômico, global e local. São Paulo: Annablume, 2003. 175 p.: bibl., ill. (some col.), maps (some col.).

Dall'Acqua's published doctoral thesis from the Univ. de São Paulo aims to advance understanding in the area of regional development by focusing on productive chains and clusters. She argues against globalization and in favor of more local production.

2418 Desenvolvimento e construção nacional: política econômica. Organização de Rogério Sobreira e Marco Aurélio Ruediger. Rio de Janeiro: FGV Editora, 2005. 203 p.: bibl., ill.

In early 2003, Tarso Genro formed a Counsel of Economic and Social Development to promote economic policies that were consistent with PT visions of growth with equity. This book is a collection of essays written by economists associated with that effort who pushed a shift away

from liberalism towards a post-Keynesian agenda. Critical to the perspective of the authors is the constriction on growth and its stop-and-go performance during the liberal era.

2419 Economia brasileira contemporânea. Organização de Fabio Giambiagi *et al.* 2 ed. Rio de Janeiro: Elsevier, Editora Campus, 2005. 425 p.: bibl., ill.

This is an excellent collection of writings by some of Brazil's most important policy-making economists. The book contains several historical chapters that evaluate the various strategies pursued by Brazilian governments between 1945 and 2004. The historical analyses are followed by chapters focusing on some of the most important sustainable development issues in Brazil, namely developmentalism, inflation, education, inequality, and the role of finance.

2420 A economia política da mudança: os desafios e os equívocos do início do governo Lula. Organização de João Antonio de Paula. Belo Horizonte, Brazil: Autêntica, 2003. 254 p.: bibl.

A number of prominent intellectuals on the left respond to the first few months of the Lula administration in this collected volume. It is highly critical of trends toward "continuation" of the policies associated with the Cardoso administration, particularly in terms of monetary policy.

2421 Fernandes, Marcelo and Juan Toro. O mecanismo de transmissão monetária na economia brasileira pós-Plano Real. (*Rev. Bras. Econ./Rio de Janeiro*, 59:1, jan./março 2005, p. 5–32, bibl., graphs, tables)

The paper uses a VAR model for real money stock to evaluate the monetary transmission mechanism in Brazil following the Real Plan. It finds three relationships: a negative one between the real output gap and the real interest rate; a second between international reserves and expansion of money; and a third between money stock and the basic interest rate (SELIC).

2422 Fonseca, Pedro Cezar Dutra. Credibilidade e populismo no Brasil: a política econômica dos governos Vargas e Goulart. (*Rev. Bras. Econ./Rio de Janeiro*, 59:2, abril/junho 2005, p. 215–243)

Presidents Vargas and Goulart are considered paradigmatic of irresponsible, irrational pursuit of populist policies but, according to Fonseca, there is a rationality to their policies. The problem is that this rationality corresponds to a less coherent response and a breakdown of stabilization efforts. Both governments engaged in economic orthodoxy but were unable to maintain these policies as developmentalist prescriptions became more popular. This policy choice led to a breakdown in credibility and the failure of stabilization programs.

2423 Fragoso Lugo, Lucero. Nuevos enfoques de desarrollo regional para América Latina: el caso de Ceará, Brasil. (*Foro Int./México*, 45:3, julio/sept. 2005, p. 382–408, bibl.)

This article looks at the new emphases for development in Latin America by examining the state of Ceará and new policies oriented towards the creation of human and physical capital. Fragos Lugo uses endogenous development theories to frame the case of development in Ceará and the emergence of a new elite in the 1980s. The article concludes with brief comparisons to southern Mexico.

2424 Getúlio Vargas e a economia contemporânea. Organização de Tamás Szmrecsányi y Rui G. Granziera. 2a. ed. rev. e ampliada. Campinas, Brazil: Editora Unicamp; São Paulo: Editora Hucitec, 2004. 207 p.: bibl.

This book claims to be a revised and expanded second edition of an important book published in 1985 following a conference on Getúlio Vargas. The panelists were leading political scientists, historians, and economic historians who were reconsidering the legacy of Getúlio Vargas in light of the military dictatorship and the beginning of the process of democratization. Unfortunately, the only updating to this edition is a thin preface which talks of the timeless strength of the articles. The book is designed for general audiences and lower level undergraduate courses and gives only hints of rigorous interrogations of the Vargas and post-Vargas era.

2425 Giambiagi, Fabio and **Marcio Ronci.** Las instituciones fiscales brasileñas: las reformas de Cardoso, 1995–2002. (*CEPAL Rev.*, 85, abril 2005, p. 61–80, bibl., graphs, tables)

Two leading liberal economists show that, after the 1998–99 crisis, fiscal austerity was as important as institutional fiscal reforms. Giambiagi and Ronci argue that the decline in production between 1995 and 1998 was not the result of interest rates, but rather of a reduction in the primary balance.

2426 Governo Lula: decifrando o enigma. Edição de Laura Tavares Soares. São Paulo: Viramundo, 2004. 190 p.: ill.

This collection of essays written by public intellectuals associated with the PT attempts to explain the party's policy shift once Lula took office. These essays were published online throughout 2003 and focus on themes important to the traditional progressive sector of the PT, particularly, social movements, economic policy, foreign policy, and social security/labor policy.

2427 Jaguaribe, Hélio. Urgências e perspectivas do Brasil. Brasília: Instituto Rio Branco: Fundação Alexandre de Gusmão, 2005. 109 p. (Col. Rio Branco)

This small book contains a number of essays written by public intellectual Helio Jaguaribe and an impassioned argument about economic stagnation in Brazil since 1980 which he identifies with liberalism. He critiques the Lula government heavily for following the same neoliberal policies of Cardoso and he longs for a return to Kubitschek-style developmentalist policies. Unfortunately, Jaguaribe does not properly identify the processes occurring under Kubitschek that led to the deterioration of credibility in monetary policy authority, and in turn to the hyperinflation that produced many of the constraints on growth that Brazil faced in the 1980s and 1990s. His essay also fails to acknowledge the cycle of growth that emerged in the second Lula administration.

2428 Kohli, Atul. State-directed development: political power and industrialization in the global periphery. Cambridge, UK; New York: Cambridge Univ. Press, 2004. 466 p.: bibl., ill., index.

Using South Korea, India, Brazil, and Nigeria as case studies, Kohli's highly regarded study attempts to identify when and how state intervention was productive in developing countries. He argues that the means by which states were created matters and that when effective states existed before industrialization, economic performance was better. Using a typology that separates neopatrimonial (Nigeria), cohesive-capitalist states (South Korea), and fragmented multiclass states (Brazil, India), he explains the poor, good, and inconsistent performance of his cases.

2429 Laços financeiros na luta contra a pobreza. Organização de Ricardo Abramovay. São Paulo: Annablume, 2004. 246 p.: bibl.

This book presents a policy and social agenda that emphasizes the importance of social capital and networking for the poor. Traditional development studies have not seen the contributions of these aspects or of poor people more generally. Instead, they have proposed public policies that are distant from the poor populations they are intended to benefit. Using cooperation and solidarity as the basis for analysis of economic activity among poor sectors, the authors look at financial and credit markets for low income populations.

2430 Leite, Sérgio Pereira. Estado, padrão de desenvolvimento e agricultura: o caso brasileiro. (*Estud. Soc. Agric.*, 13:2, out. 2005, p. 280–332, bibl.)

Leite examines the position of agriculture within the Brazilian economy during the national developmentalist phase of the 1930s–80s and the fiscal crisis phase that followed. While industrialization resulted in the diminished importance of agriculture, the fiscal crisis of the 1980s, in particular the currency policies of the era, coupled with the internationalization of Brazilian agro-industry, increased the importance of agricultural policies.

2431 Lion, Octávio Manuel Bessada; Claudio Barbedo; and Gustavo Araújo. Mercado de derivativos no Brasil. Rio de Janeiro: Editora Record, 2005. 366 p.: bibl., ill., index.

This book, aimed at both professionals and students, is largely an introduction to the derivatives market in Brazil. The chapters explain the concepts and structure of derivative markets, giving particular attention to the nature of contracts and opera-

tions and different strategies available to market agents. It includes modeling to give a practical sense of how professionals understand the market, but does not demand that readers have an extensive mathematical background.

2432 Melo, Carlos Ranulfo and Fátima Anastasia. A reforma da previdência em dois tempos. (*Dados/Rio de Janeiro*, 48:2, 2005, p. 301–331, bibl., tables)

Melo and Anastasia compare social security reforms under Cardozo and Lula. They see democracy as an iterative game played on many levels. Decisionmakers are constantly producing interdependent decisions (due, in this case, to deputies voting with leaders as the lowest cost option). However, when dealing with constitutional changes, party discipline is more difficult, and the costs increase. Under both administrations, the social security reforms took place during moments of discontinuity from iterative games.

2433 Minayo, Maria Cecília de Souza. De ferro e flexíveis: marcas do Estado empresário e da privatização na subjetividade operária. Rio de Janeiro: Garamond, 2004. 458 p.: bibl. (Garamond universitária)

This book presents an interesting analysis of the conditions of the mine workers in the Vale do Rio Doce Company in Itabira, and the mineral industry in Brazil and the world more broadly. Using the current situation of mineworkers as an "ideal type" to demonstrate the restructuring of national and international markets, Minayo investigates what the industry and performing labor in the industry mean in terms of subjective identity, state retreat, and privatization of state-labor relations.

2434 Moutinho, Lúcia Maria Goes; Paulo Fernando de Moura Bezerra Cavalcanti Filho; and Paulo Ortiz Rocha de Aragão. Estratégias empresariais e políticas regionais: as políticas de incentivos às grandes empresas calçadistas da Paraíba. (*REN Rev. Econ. Nordeste*, 36:4, out./dez. 2005, p. 541–558, bibl., graphs, tables)

Based on field research in the shoe industry in Paraíba, this article argues that public policies were not sufficient to bring about necessary changes. State strategies failed to attract large shoe companies because of their global strategies. States contemplating the tradeoff between attracting jobs and reducing tax revenue (to win over companies) must take into account local needs and company strategies (given national and international opportunities and restrictions).

2435 Niemeyer Neto, Luiz M. de. Dívida externa brasileira nos anos 90 em uma perspectiva histórica: créditos internacionais de curto prazo e "estatização da dívida." Tradução de Ines Archipovas de Niemeyer. São Paulo: EDUC, 2003. 245 p.: bibl., ill. (Scholae)

This book is the publication of Niemeyer's dissertation on external debt in Brazilian history. He compares the post-WWII period, when the maturity on external debt decreased, with the entry of portfolio investment in Brazil during the 1990s. He also compares the lending boom at the beginning of the 20th century with the way that the Brady bonds opened Latin America to investment. Finally, he compares debt-growth strategies to those pursued by the military government. The conclusions identify the use of foreign debt with its worst practices during the 20th century.

2436 Nobre, Osvaldo. Brasil, país do presente: o crescimento inevitável. Rio de Janeiro: EducaBem Editora, 2003. 140 p.: bibl., map.

With an ironic take on Brazil's long-term title as the "country of the future," Nobre argues that the current international moment augurs well for Brazilian growth. He challenges the idea of slowly putting together the building blocks for long-term growth, arguing that the time for growth is now. He argues that a colonized elite that is overly concerned with details of administration and does not think about the long-term has been bad for Brazil. The book's details and evidence are weak and are better read as rhetoric within a part of the left that has felt abandoned by Lula's administration.

2437 Uma outra economia é possível: Paul Singer e a economia solidária. Organização de André Ricardo de Souza, Gabriela Cavalcanti Cunha e Regina Yoneko Dakuzaku. São Paulo: Editora Contexto, 2003. 320 p.: bibl.

This book is a fetschrift for Paul Singer composed of essays by his former students. The essays focus on various aspects of interest of the important scholar-activist and founder of the Partido dos Trabalhadores (PT). The essays emphasize Singer's interests in socialism and solitary economics including cooperatives, barter, and alternative responses to the crisis of labor. The publication of the book occurred at the beginning of the first Lula administration, when Singer was a secretary of "solidary economics" and, unfortunately, the chapters do not speak about Singer's participation in a government that continued the liberal policies of the past.

2438 Petras, James F. and **Henry Veltmeyer.** Cardoso's Brazil: a land for sale. Lanham, Md.: Rowman & Littlefield Publishers, Inc., 2003. 143 p.: bibl., index. (Critical currents in Latin American perspective)

According to Petras and Veltmeyer, Brazil's Human Development Index and every other meaningful indicator (national production, unemployment, social inclusion, etc.) has worsened since Cardoso came to power. They argue that the lack of social development is due to the policies chosen and the class coalition that supports Cardoso. They write that Cardoso served international (IMF, bankers) and local capital (PFL) interests and that Brazil needs an entirely different strategy or a socialist revolution.

2439 Pinheiro, Armando Castelar and **Fabio Giambiagi.** Rompendo o marasmo: a retomada do desenvolvimento no Brasil. Colaboração de Sergio Guimarães Ferreira e Fernando Veloso. Rio de Janeiro: Elsevier, 2006. 312 p.: bibl., ill.

Two of the most important liberal economists in Brazil provide a strategy for ending the current situation of slow growth in Brazil. They insist on the importance of fiscal surplus and inflation targeting programs of the Cardoso government and reject any calls to loosen monetary policy, reduce participation in global markets, or impose capital controls. The stagnation of the 1980s, they argue, was the result of low levels of investment and productivity. While productivity increased during the 1990s, the levels of investment remain low. They propose a number of often-cited reforms that they believe are necessary to a path of sustainable growth.

2440 Prado, Maria Clara R.M. do. A real história do real. Rio de Janeiro: Record, 2005. 573 p.: bibl., index.

Economic journalist Maria Clara do Prado tells the behind-the-scenes story of the Brazilian currency, the real, from its introduction until just after it was floated in Jan. of 1999. The historical work is excellent and well-detailed, highlighting the considerable amount of uncertainty in a process which appears to be very intentional from the outside. The book, unfortunately, ends abruptly, moving from 1999 to 2004 with a few short paragraphs on the problems of public debt following the Real Plan. Given that the book was published in 2005, a more complete chapter on post-1999 monetary policies, one that included some analysis of Lula's continuation of the basic macroeconomic policy guidelines of the Cardoso government, would have strengthened the book.

2441 Prêmio Ipea, 40 anos: IPEA-CAIXA 2004: monografias premiadas. Brasília: IPEA, 2005. 576 p.: bibl., ill.

The Institute of Applied Economic Research (IPEA), one of Brazil's most trusted producers of statistics, celebrated its 40th anniversary by having a national essay competition to address questions of inequality, social policies, and growth policy. The essays here include contributions by students as well as economists and professionals. The chapters represent a number of diverse methodologies and perspectives and, taken together, are a strong contribution to studies of development in Brazil.

2442 Ramalho, José Ricardo. Novas conjunturas industriais e participação local em estratégias de desenvolvimento. (*Dados/Rio de Janeiro,* 48:3, 2005, p. 491–524, bibl.)

Economic literature examining the effect of regulation of labor markets often underspecifies the effectiveness of regulatory frameworks and laws. This paper interrogates the notion of the Brazilian labor inspection system as a way of determining the effectiveness of labor market regulation to effectively monitor behavior and punish transgressions.

2443 Reforma política e cidadania. Organização de Maria Victoria Benevides, Paulo Vannuchi e Fábio Kerche. São Paulo: Editora Fundação Perseu Abramo: Instituto Cidadania, 2003. 511 p.: bibl., ill.

In this excellent collection, some of Brazil's finest political scientists write about political reforms. Reforms considered range from radicalizing democracy to changing electoral rules and party system votes.

2444 Reformas no Brasil: balanço e agenda. Organização de Fabio Giambiagi, José Guilherme Reis e André Urani. Rio de Janeiro: Editora Nova Fronteira, 2004. 543 p.: bibl., ill., index.

This collection of essays, introduced by a preface from former President Cardoso, analyzes challenges for the reform agenda in Brazil focusing on growth, monetary policy, international relations, social policy, and political reforms. The chapters provide a justification for much of the agenda of the Cardoso administration, most of which was taken up by President Lula. Although there is little diversity of perspective, the book serves as an excellent evaluation by academics and policymakers of the state of the reform agenda one decade after it had entered mainstream Brazilian politics.

2445 Ricupero, Rubens. A ALCA. São Paulo: Publifolha, 2003. 96 p.: bibl. (Folha explica; 56. Economia)

In this concise book the former Brazilian Ambassador to the US explains the Free Trade Area of the Americas, the negotiation process within it, and the points of conflict and interest between Brazil and the other trade partners, particularly the US. The book is a very detailed handbook and is especially of use to journalists or policymakers who want a quick introduction to the FTAA.

2446 Rubio, Delia Ferreira. Financiamento de partidos e campanhas: fundos públicos *versus* fundos privados. (*Novos Estud. CEBRAP,* 73, nov. 2005, p. 5–15, bibl., graph, tables)

Here, Rubio argues that regulation depends on autonomy, efficiency of institutions, and political culture. This notion is critical since political parties are considered the most corrupt institutions in Latin America and throughout the world.

2447 Sachs, Ignacy. Desenvolvimento includente, sustentável, sustentado. Prefácio de Celso Furtado. Rio de Janeiro: Garamond: SEBRAE, 2004. 151 p.: bibl., ill. (Garamond universitária)

This short book aims to create a neostructural strategy for economic growth for Latin America. Sachs opposes the view that Latin American countries benefitted from liberal economics through low interest rates and state involvement in economic planning. Moreover, he makes an argument for the importance of social inclusion, not only on moral grounds, but also for achieving sustainable growth.

2448 Sader, Emir. Perspectivas. Rio de Janeiro: Editora Record, 2005. 135 p.: bibl. (Os porquês da desordem mundial)

Sader begins this small apology for alternatives to globalization by comparing the period of Keynesianism/state intervention with that of neoliberalism, arguing that the former was the greatest period of economic growth in the world, whereas the latter has been unsuccessful. The book emerges out of the World Social Forum meetings in Porto Alegre and it includes concise critiques of neoliberalism before offering an alternative focusing on the Movimento Sem Terra (Rural Landless Movement) in Brazil.

2449 Saraiva, José Flávio Sombra. La búsqueda de un nuevo paradigma: política exterior, comercio externo y federalismo en el Brasil. (*Ciclos Hist. Econ. Soc.*, 15:29, primer semestre 2005, p. 205–229, bibl., graphs, tables)

Saraiva argues for the importance of understanding federalism in the context of studying foreign policy. His primary case study is Ceará, but he also discusses the US, Switzerland, and Germany.

2450 Statecrafting monetary authority: democracy and financial order in Brazil. Edited by Lourdes Sol and Laurence Whitehead. Oxford: Centre for Brazilian Studies, 2006. 392 p.

This excellent book emphasizes the role of statecraft (actors and negotiations) in public policy-making. The chapters stand in contrast to institutionalist accounts that highlight the importance of institutional restraints on policymaker activity as central to the establishment of credibility. Using examples from both the Cardoso and first Lula governments, they show the role of political actors, and the importance of their discretion, in terms of creating a sound arena for economic policy-making.

2451 Suplicy, Eduardo Matarazzo. Renda de cidadania: a saída é pela porta. São Paulo: Cortez Editora: Editora Fundação Perseu Abramo, 2002. 367 p.: bibl.

PT Senator and one time presidential candidate Eduardo Suplicy makes an argument in favor of a law to ensure a minimum income to all Brazilians. The book shifts from moral and philosophical appeals (citing the Old and New Testaments, Confucius, Aristotle, and Marx) to more traditional pop-economy arguments. One particular feature of the book is that it contains several interviews with Suplicy and economists including Milton Friedman, Amartya Sen, James Tobin, Celso Furtado, and PT leader Lula. Unfortunately, the many different ways to justify a basic income for citizens ends up weakening what might otherwise be a persuasive argument and renders the book more appropriate for a general (and partisan) audience than an academic one.

SOCIOLOGY

GENERAL

2452 Aguirre, Benigno E. Los desastres en Latinoamérica: vulnerabilidad y resistencia. (*Rev. Mex. Sociol.*, 66:3, julio/sept. 2004, p. 485–510, bibl.)

Presents a critical analysis of the concept of social vulnerability as used in Latin America and suggests that incorporating the concept of capacity for resistance would allow a better understanding of disasters. It would also give greater importance to the process of community mobilizations and help establish more stable public administration models. [A. Ugalde]

Barquet, Mercedes and **Sandra Osses.** Governability and women's citizenship. See item **2463.**

2453 Conversion of a continent: contemporary religious change in Latin America. Edited by Timothy J. Steigenga and Edward L. Cleary. New Brunswick, N.J.: Rutgers Univ. Press, 2007. 290 p.: bibl., index.

An edited volume of 12 chapters focusing on the religious transformation of Latin America during the past few decades. The Catholic Church has lost its once near monopoly on religion to proponents of other faiths. Chapter authors explore topics such as the converts and the contexts for conversion and how conversion affects the life of the convert, his/her family, and the wider community in general. Authors present competing explanations for why the conversions occur. [S. Ramírez]

2454 Firmin, Joseph-Anténor. De l'égalité des races humaines: anthropologie positive. Édition présentée par Jean Métellus. Montréal: Mémoire d'encrier, 2005. 407 p.: bibl., ill.

The reprinting of this seminal work merits contemporary notice because of the analytical preface written by Jean Métellus. [J.F. Higbee]

Gaborit, Mauricio. Memoria histórica: revertir la historia desde las víctimas. See item **2564.**

Gender, sexuality, and power in Latin America since independence. See *HLAS* 64:480.

Multiculturalismo: perspectivas y desafíos. See item **2517.**

Women writing resistance: essays on Latin America and the Caribbean. See *HLAS* 64:2469.

MEXICO

ANTONIO UGALDE, *Professor of Sociology, The University of Texas at Austin*

DURING THIS BIENNIUM THE THEMATIC TREND from the last biennia has been reinforced. Gender studies have become a mainstream field among Mexican sociologists; women sociologists are very active at organizing conferences and symposia on gender issues. Organizers frequently make sure to publish a selection of the papers, which explains why some of the works reviewed for this *HLAS* volume contain a relatively large number of individual studies. By and large the collections include a variety of topics (see, for example, items **2481** and **2516**). Articles and monographs on gender examine many different topics such as female migration flows, disability statistics, shifts in male-female power relations (for an excellent study, see item **2511**), household and urban violence, the role of women in social movements, and participation and discrimination in the labor force. Cisneros and Luna's study of social stratification of women inmates in the prison system is an original topic and a valuable contribution to the literature on Mexican sociology (item **2470**).

An unusually large number of articles and books on Ciudad Juárez are included in this review. The city's location makes it an important transit area for drugs and migrants. In-fighting among drug cartels has led to unprecedented levels of violence to the extent that the federal government was forced to militarize the city in an attempt to control the take-over of the city by drug traffickers. In addition, Ciudad Juárez's many maquilas provide jobs for thousands of women from other parts of the country. The high number of women assassinated—about 400 in the last 12 years—has called the attention of the national and international media. Social scientists and investigative reporters have tried to explain the rising level of violence against women, mostly maquila workers, that, for the most part, appears unrelated to the drug trafficking. Ravelo and Domínguez have edited an excellent volume providing thoughtful insights into the problem (item **2482**). The literature also examines the response by NGOs both in Ciudad Juárez and in El Paso across the international border, including marches and protests.

Mexican sociologists are increasingly specializing in criminology. In recent years, drug-related violence in the country has, according to observers, severely weakened the very foundations of the state. Drug money is corrupting the judicial and political systems, the executive, the police, and even the army; and violence and corruption are responsible for the frequent use of torture. Of interest is the study of torture, commissioned by the Mexican Commission on Human Rights (item **2495**), that discusses documented cases of torture committed by the state. Interestingly, the study does not include cases perpetrated by the drug cartels. However, it is important to note that violence is not confined to drug trafficking alone. Studies on urban gang violent behavior, the victimization of prostitutes and gays, and even violence erupting at soccer games appear in this review. Some sophisticated qualitative research is presented on the police force (see the solid studies by Suárez de Garay in items **2544** and **2545**), the prison system, descriptive work on the cartels, the organization of urban gangs, the acceptance of drug lords by the poor, and studies that analyze citizens' concerns for safety and security.

Research on migration, both internal and international, continues to take place but, as with the last *HLAS* volume, there is a shift from demographic to ethnographic work. Examinations of international migration are beginning to focus on links between migrants and those left behind by studying place of origin alongside destination. Researchers are also looking at the positive and negative consequences of international migration for Mexican communities, analyzing the impact of remittances in rural development (see the excellent collection edited by Suárez and Zapata, item **2502**), the local impact of human resources drain, or the benefits on international migration in language acquisition. A valuable teaching tool is the outstanding book edited by López Castro (item **2478**) that combines photographs depicting international migration with scholarly chapters.

The tradition of political sociology, one of the strengths of Mexican sociology, continues. Materials reviewed in this section include research on the transition from a one-party to a multiparty system. Nevertheless, there is a vacuum of research on the performance and achievements of the PAN, the new party in power, as well as a lack of analysis on the impact of a multiparty system on democracy (for one exception see item **2486**). Readers interested in political behavior will find useful chapters in the edited volume by González (item **2523**). On the other hand, an abundance of research exists on social movements, including those with a transnational reach. The study of social movements includes case studies of student, labor, and urban movements, which examine the organizational characteristics, tactics used to achieve the objectives, and results. By and large the case studies are informative and of high quality.

In Mexico, studies of race relations have traditionally consisted of work that characterized the discrimination of indigenous communities. Occasionally, research on other minority groups such as Jews and Palestinians has been published. For the first time, we are seeing studies of Afro-Mexicans—research that stands out because of its novelty and quality.

The theoretical influence of French sociologists and thinkers is noticeable in a number of writings. The quantitative approach that has become dominant in US sociology has not taken root in Mexican sociology. At the same time, US reaction to the events of September 11, 2001, by tightening the border has made it difficult for Mexican sociologists to cross the border and participate in conferences in the US as frequently as in the past and to interact with their US colleagues; difficulties in obtaining visas have also played a role in distancing Mexican and US sociologists. As a result, more Mexican graduate students are studying in Europe. An example of the growing ties between Mexican and French sociologists is the volume edited by Gutiérrez (item **2517**).

2455 Aguilar Sánchez, Martin. Mouvements sociaux et démocratie au Mexique, 1982–1998: un regard du point de vue régional. Paris: Harmattan, 2005. 371 p.: bibl., ill. (Logiques politiques)

The People's Movement in Tabasco, the Coordinadora for the Defense of PEMEX and the Indígena Movement in Veracruz, and the Barzón Union in Zacatecas are studied in this monograph. Reasons for the movements, their organization and leadership characteristics, tactics, and results are well explained. Special attention is given to the complex relations between the PRI and social movements.

Alfaro-Velcamp, Theresa. Immigrant positioning in twentieth-century Mexico: Middle Easterners, foreign citizens, and multiculturalism. See *HLAS 64:729.*

Alfaro-Velcamp, Theresa. "Reelizing" Arab and Jewish ethnicity in Mexican film. See *HLAS 64:730.*

2456 Aranda Bezaury, Josefina. La experiencia organizativa de las mujeres cafetaleras de la CEPCO. (*Acervos/Oaxaca,* 7, verano 2004, p. 58–64, bibl., photos)

CEPCO is an independent coordinating institution that was created in 1989 to assist Oaxaca's small coffee growers. Today it includes 42 regional organizations with 16,000 producers. This paper describes the incorporation of women into CEPCO, their support role to increase household incomes, the organization of women's projects, and their achievements.

2457 Arias, Patricia and **Emma Peña.** Las mujeres de Guanajuato: ayer y hoy, 1970–2000. Guanajuato, Mexico: Univ. de Guanajuato: Instituto de la Mujer Guanajuatense, 2004. 254 p.: bibl., ill. (some col.), maps (some col.).

A demographic study of women in Guanajuato. Data come mostly from National Population Censuses, the state's Vital

Statistics, National Labor Surveys, and National Survey of Microenterprises. Data on population distribution, education, employment, and migration flows are divided by municipalities and then regrouped into the state's six regions. Data on fertility, mortality, and disability is presented at the state level.

2458 Arteaga Botello, Nelson. Una aproximación sociohistórica de la pobreza en tres comunidades de México. (*Rev. Mex. Sociol.*, 67:4, oct./dic. 2005, p. 661–685, bibl.)

A critique of the indexes used to measure poverty such as social vulnerability and urban marginalization. Interventions used to address poverty based on these indexes have not been successful. According to the author, interventions have failed because poverty has been considered a "condition." Suggests that we need to start looking at the sociohistorical relationship of the population to its surroundings and the processes that follow.

2459 Arteaga Botello, Nelson. Pobres y delincuentes: estudio de sociología y genealogía. México: Cámara de Diputados, LIX Legislatura: Univ. Autónoma del Estado de México, Facultad de Ciencias Políticas y Administración Pública: M.Á. Porrúa, 2006. 172 p.: bibl. (Conocer para decidir)

According to the author, today the poor and delinquents are blamed for their condition by public opinion, political parties, and civil society. Current individualism is responsible for such views, but individualism also shapes how society is organized and the prevailing solutions to overcome both problems. Argues that a recognition of society's own responsibility is required to reduce poverty and crime.

2460 Astorga Almanza, Luis Alejandro. El siglo de las drogas: el narcotráfico, del Porfiriato al nuevo milenio. México: Plaza y Janés, 2005. 197 p.: bibl.

Written for the general public, this account of drug-use changes in Mexico during the 20th century provides detailed information on drug preferences by social classes, links between traffickers and politicians, and violence associated with drug commerce. Information is mostly collected from newspapers from Sinaloa and Mexico City.

2461 Baca Tavira, Norma. Precarización ocupacional por género en Zona Metropolitana de la ciudad de Toluca. (*Convergencia/Toluca*, 12:37, enero/abril 2005, p. 289–326, bibl., graphs)

This article studies the occupational changes that occurred in the labor force in Toluca from 1990 to the beginning of the 21st century. Specifically examines the impoverishment of occupations by gender. Finds that the main shift has been from production to services, many of which are low-paying temporary jobs.

2462 Bandy, Joe. Paradoxes of transnational civil societies under neoliberalism: the Coalition for Justice in the Maquiladoras. (*Soc. Probl.*, 51:3, Aug. 2004, p. 410–431, bibl.)

The Coalition for Justice in the Maquiladoras (CJM) was organized for the purpose of reforming exploitative labor conditions at the maquilas. This research discusses CJM and its efforts to build a transnational civil society. Using extended participant observation, 30 in-depth interviews, and archival materials, the paper assesses the possibilities of transnational networks and movements. In spite of internal disunity and external forces of social control, CJM appears to succeed in creating transnational cultures of solidarity and opportunities for social change.

2463 Barquet, Mercedes and **Sandra Osses.** Governability and women's citizenship. (*J. Women Polit. Policy*, 27:1/2, 2005, p. 9–30, bibl., graph, tables)

Analyzes the insertion of Mexican women in the construction of citizenship, based on empirical material from the Second National Survey on Political Culture and Practice of Citizenship. For the authors, solidarity, responsibility, and tolerance are important democratic values that women possess and could contribute to strengthening fragile Latin American democracies if a new form of gendered citizenship is recognized and nurtured.

2464 Baschet, Jérôme. ¿Más allá de la lucha por la humanidad y contra el neoliberalismo? (*Chiapas/México*, 16, 2004, p. 31–50)

An essay that uses the EZLN political tenets to analyze different approaches to explain US neoliberal imperialism vis-à-vis

Mexico. Written shortly after the Sept. 11, 2001, attack, the paper is heavily influenced by the US military response and the Iraq War. The role of international agencies, the emerging economies, the interests of multinational corporations, and the weakened economy within the US are examined in this overview of changes taking place in the world order.

2465 Begné, Patricia. MujereS. Guanajuato, Mexico: Guanajuato, Gobierno del Estado, Instituto de la Mujer Guanajuatense, 2004. 148 p.: bibl. (Col. Estudios)

The first chapter presents an overview of women's changing status from ancient times to the 20th century. The next two chapters discuss the condition of women in Mexico from precolonial days to the present. Mini-chapters on efforts to modify Mexican laws and liberalize the status of women, women's movements, and the feminization of poverty close the volume. Written for the general public.

2466 Bendesky, León et al. La industria maquiladora de exportación en México: mitos, realidades y crisis. (*Estud. Sociol./México*, 22:65, mayo/agosto 2004, p. 283–314, bibl., tables)

Several theories attempt to explain the transformation that the maquila industry (Fordism, precaurious Toyotism) has undergone. This paper reviews a large number of variables, including capital distribution and value of equipment by industry size, percent of exports with US destination, sources of income, percent of income allocated to technology investments, unionization levels, type of employment and occupational categories by gender, income by operational categories, yearly shifts of productivity, aggregate value, and rates of benefits. Concludes that previous theories are not valid and that the maquila industry is not as different from other national industries as one might expect.

2467 Brickner, Rachel K. Mexican union women and the social construction of women's labor rights. (*Lat. Am. Perspect.*, 33:6, Nov. 2006, p. 55–74)

Examines the social construction of citizenship rights and their relationship to labor rights for women. Despite legal advances, women have been restricted in ex-

ercising full labor rights by the implementation of neoliberal economic reforms and by the corporatist and paternalistic structure of Mexican labor organizations. Author emphasizes the importance of women workers building alliances beyond union structures. [D. Coerver]

2468 Canales Cerón, Alejandro; Israel Montiel Armas; and Tarsicio Torres Chávez. Gente grande: situación actual y perspectivas del envejecimiento en Jalisco. Guadalajara, Mexico: Univ. de Guadalajara, Centro Universitario de Ciencias Económico Administrativas, Depto. de Estudios Regionales—INESER, Centro de Estudios de Población: Centro Universitario de Ciencias Sociales y Humanidades, Depto. de Estudios Sociourbanos, Centro de Estudios Estratégicos para el Desarrollo: Consejo Nacional de Ciencia y Tecnología, 2004. 182 p.: bibl., ill.

In Mexico, similar to other middle income countries, a demographic transition is taking place whereby the aging population will have an impact on the family, the economy, and society at large. The author presents a technical study projecting the aging of the population to the year 2030 in the state of Jalisco and considers the consequences.

2469 Castillo Berthier, Héctor. De las bandas a las tribus urbanas: de la transgresión a la nueva identidad social. (*Desacatos*, 9, primavera/verano 2002, p. 57–71, bibl., photos)

A brief account of gang organizations (*bandas*) among the youth. Reasons for the presence of gangs, behavioral patterns, and activities are included in the first part of the study. The author concludes by indicating that the gangs have been replaced by new youth groupings known as urban tribes (*tribus*). Several groups are identified and their interests and behaviors are described.

2470 Cisneros, José Luis and Hilario Anguiano Luna. Identidad, exclusión y espacio: autopercepción de la mujer en prisión. (*Veredas*, 4/5, 2002, p. 73–98, bibl.)

The article presents several organizational aspects of a women's prison in Mexico City. Wings are stratified in five types by social class and crime gravity. Upper class cells are comfortable with TVs, refrigerators, lamps, and other conveniences. Cleaning is contracted with lower-class prisoners. These relatively decent cells contrast with the dreadful conditions of cells for poor prisoners and high-security prisoners. Leadership roles, sexual behavior among inmates, and abuses are also discussed. An informative paper.

2471 Comercio sexual en La Merced: una perspectiva constructivista sobre el sexoservicio. Coordinación de Angélica Bautista López y Elsa Conde Rodríguez. México: Univ. Autónoma Metropolitana, Unidad Iztapalapa: Miguel Ángel Porrúa, 2006. 287 p.: bibl., ill. (Las ciencias sociales. Estudios de género)

This study of possibly the oldest and poorest red-light district in Mexico City is written by a team of social workers, social psychologists, and human rights activists. Ethnographic fieldwork, 23 in-depth interviews with sex workers, and one focal group with 10 steady clients inform the study. Provides information on different organizational forms of prostitution, clients' attitudes, and the victimization of workers.

2472 Contreras Montellano, Óscar F. and Alfredo Hualde Alfaro. El aprendizaje y sus agentes: los portadores del conocimiento en las maquiladoras del norte de México. (*Estud. Sociol./México*, 22:64, enero/abril 2004, p. 79-122, bibl.)

Most studies have concluded that maquilas are a source of cheap labor and criticize working conditions. Taking a unique approach, this paper looks at the training impact of maquilas on workers, middle-level technicians, and managers. It presents the positive learning experience and consequences for the local economy, the transfer of knowledge, and the opening of local businesses that follow. Low-level workers, as is the case in most national industries, have few possibilities of learning useful skills to increase employment opportunities.

2473 Curran, Sara R. and Estela Rivero-Fuentes. Engendering migrant networks: the case of Mexican migration. (*Demography/Washington*, 40:2, May 2003, p. 289-307, bibl., tables)

Authors compare the impact of family migrants and destination-specific networks in international migration. The study finds

that migrant networks are more important for international than for internal flows; female networks are more important than male networks for internal migration; and male migrant networks are more important for prospective male migrants than for female migrants. Distinguishing gender composition and destination contents of networks deepens our understanding of how cumulative causation affects patterns of Mexican migration.

2474 Danopoulos, Constantine P. Economic measurements and quality of life in Mexico. (*J. Polit. Mil. Sociol.*, 32:2, Winter 2004, p. 193-206, bibl., table)

Using the Genuine Progress Indicator, the article evaluates the quality of life in Mexico. The index includes the following indicators: per capita GDP, income distribution, health care costs due to air and water pollution, loss of wetlands, time spent on highways, loss of leisure time, and other social costs. Taking these factors into account, the purchasing power and quality of life of Mexicans are considerably lower than the per capita GDP would indicate.

2475 D'Aubeterre Buznego, María Eugenia. "Mujeres trabajando por el pueblo": género y ciudadanía en una comunidad de transmigrantes oriundos del estado de Puebla. (*Estud. Sociol./México*, 23:67, enero/abril 2005, p. 185-215, bibl., table)

The *cargo* system is a traditional form of community service and a system of selecting persons to serve ad honorem in community positions, both civil and religious. Traditionally, women had been excluded from these responsibilities—until recently. This article explores the consequences of women's participation in *cargo* positions such as gender conflicts. It also examines aspects of women's migration to the US.

2476 Delgado Wise, Raúl; Humberto Márquez Covarrubias; and Héctor Rodríguez Ramírez. Organizaciones transnacionales de migrantes y desarrollo regional en Zacatecas. (*Migr. Int.*, 2:4, julio/dic. 2004, p. 159-177, bibl., tables)

International migration has resulted in negative consequences for the communities left behind, including the drain of human resources that makes the local economy unsustainable. However, migration also has a positive side with the presence of actors that could foster the development of transnational activities through migrant organizations based in the US.

2477 Los desafíos del presente mexicano. Coordinación de Francisco Toledo, Enrique Florescano, y José Woldenberg. Mexico: Taurus Historia, 2006. 291 p.: bibl., ill. (Col. Pasado y presente)

This collection presents insightful analysis of various aspects of Mexico's social and political realities. Written by informed and knowledgeable authors, the chapters cover the political dilemmas of the new multiparty system that has emerged in Mexico, inequality and education problems, culture, and health. The chapter on health discusses the Seguro Popular (People's Insurance), which aims to achieve full health care coverage by 2010, a target unlikely to be achieved.

2478 Diáspora michoacana. Coordinación editorial de Gustavo López Castro. Zamora, Mexico: Colegio de Michoacán; Morelia, Mexico: Gobierno del Estado de Michoacán, 2003. 493 p.: bibl., ill., indexes, maps.

This deluxe volume is a collector's gem. It includes about 150 superb photographs related to migration scenes and 17 scholarly chapters written by experts mostly from the Colegio de Michoacán. All aspects of the international migration experience are covered: the migration flow and return, the impact of migration on families and religious practices, remittances, the maintenance of links between migrants and those left behind, encounters with migration authorities, and the joys and sorrows of life in the US.

2479 Dorantes, Gerardo L. Conflicto y poder en la UNAM: la huelga de 1999. México: UNAM, 2006. 185 p.: bibl.

Study of the longest (almost one year) and most conflictive strike at UNAM, Mexico's national university. The strike was a response to increases in student fees and attempts to privatize higher education. The author, the university's general director of information, conducted a random survey among the 250,000 students (sample size 760) at the beginning of the strike to assess knowledge of causes, information sources,

and respondents' opinion of the strike. Additional sources include participant observation and archival materials.

2480 Durand Ponte, Víctor Manuel and Leticia Durand Smith. Valores y actitudes sobre la contaminación ambiental en México: reflexiones en torno al posmaterialismo. (*Rev. Mex. Sociol.*, 66:3, julio/sept. 2004, p. 511–535, bibl., tables)

Examines the relationship between the values and attitudes concerning environmental pollution in Mexico and the change in values that has taken place with the shift from materialism to postmaterialism. Data show that the change is more evident among the upper classes, but environmental values are also emerging among the poor. Results qualify Ingleharth's classic hypothesis.

2481 Encuentro de Investigación sobre Mujeres y Perspectiva de Género, 1st, Zacatecas, Mexico, 2003. Memorias. Coordinación de Emilia Recéndez Guerrero. Zacatecas, Mexico: Univ. Autónoma de Zacatecas, Centro Interinstitucional de Investigaciones en Artes y Humanidades: Consejo Zacatecano de Ciencia y Tecnología, 2005. 274 p.: bibl., ill.

An unusual collection of articles of varied length and quality, grouped in three parts: historical studies on women (nine chapters), the presence of women in the arts (four chapters), and women in other settings (three). Most historical chapters deal with colonial times and include three studies of women in Zacatecas on dowry, systems of protection, and piety.

2482 Entre las duras aristas de las armas: violencia y victimización en Ciudad Juárez. Coordinación de Patricia Ravelo Blancas y Héctor Domínguez Ruvalcaba. México: CIESAS, 2006. 219 p.: bibl. (Publicaciones de la Casa Chata) (Antropologías)

An informative volume by academics on both sides of the border. The chapters discuss living and working conditions of women in Ciudad Juárez, a city that has attracted women to work in the maquilas. The city's culture of violence, machismo, the economic independence gained by female workers, and the presence of narcotraffickers all lead to violence against women.

2483 Escobar Hernández, Bogar Armando.
Los nodos del poder: ideología y
cambio social en Guadalajara. Guadalajara,
Mexico: Univ. de Guadalajara, 2004. 179 p.:
bibl., ill. (Serie Jalisco)
According to the author, the economic power of Mexico's third largest city
lays in the Chamber of Commerce. This
monograph studies the Chamber's history
and its transformation caused by the arrival
of large supermarkets and retail chains that
displaced local merchant elites. Also discusses the Chamber's role in urban development and modernization and its relations
with other power holders such as political
parties and the Catholic Church.

**2484 Espacios múltiples, horas intermina-
bles: quehaceres de mujeres.** Coordinación de Beatriz Martínez Corona y Emma
Zapata Martelo. Guanajuato, Mexico: Guanajuato, Gobierno del Estado, Instituto de la
Mujer Guanajuatense, 2003. 308 p.: bibl., ill.,
map. (Col. Estudios)
The first chapter presents the composition and organization of households
headed by women. The second chapter
addresses the experience of indigenous
women who are transforming their identities through empowerment and autonomy.
The subsequent chapter describes one
study of women who generate some income
through crafts, and another of women in
two rural municipalities who engage in a
variety of jobs to complement household
income. The last chapter offers insights
into women bakers, a demanding job that is
characterized by unusual working hours.

2485 Farr, Marcia. Rancheros in Chicagoacán: language and identity in a transnational community. Austin: Univ. of Texas
Press, 2006. 312 p.: bibl., ill., index.
An ethnolinguistic study of Mexican
migrants to Chicago from rural Michoacán.
Based on several years of participant observation and many hours of taped conversations of a Mexican network in Chicago and
relatives in Michoacán. Farr, an education
and linguistics professor, provides insights
to help teachers of Mexican-origin students
develop bilingual programs.

2486 Favela Gavia, Diana Margarita. Cambios en el sistema político y en la
protesta social en México, 1946–2000:

interacción entre instituciones y acción
social. (*Estud. Sociol./México*, 23:68, mayo/
agosto 2005, p. 535–599, bibl.)
Important changes have occurred in
the Mexican political system, creating new
possibilities for democratization. Among
the changes discussed are the autonomy
gained by the judicial system, the disman-
tling of some features of corporatist politics,
and the opening of the political system to
competitive party politics. These changes
were caused by pressures from civil society.
In turn, citizens' participation gained more
political space.

2487 Fernandez, Marcos and **Jean-
Christophe Rampal.** La ciudad de
las muertas. México: Grijalbo, 2006. 295 p.:
bibl., ill., maps. (Actualidad)
Based on interviews and secondary
sources and written by two French investigative reporters, this descriptive book
provides a large amount of information on
violence in general and violence against
women that Ciudad Juárez continues to
experience. Intended for a general audience.
(See also item **2549** for another work on this
topic by investigative reporters.)

2488 Gadea, Carlos A. Acciones colectivas
y modernidad global: el movimiento
neozapatista. Toluca, Mexico: Univ. Autónoma del Estado de México, 2004. 276 p.:
bibl., maps. (Col. Humanidades. Serie Estudios latinoamericanos) (Ciencias Sociales.
Política)
The analysis of the neo-Zapatista
movement in Chiapas allows the author to
theorize about today's collective phenomena, the tensions that both globalization
and the demands for diversity of cultural
identities create. Gadea reconceptualizes
the analytical categories linked to collective
actions and social movements in order to
understand the difference between today's
responses to social problems and those from
previous decades.

2489 Gall, Olivia. Identidad, exclusión y
racismo: reflexiones teóricas y sobre
México. (*Rev. Mex. Sociol.*, 66:2, abril/junio
2004, p. 221–259, bibl.)
The first part of this study presents
a theoretical overview of racism and exclusion in Mexico. Then the author discusses
the contradiction found in Mexico between

the claim of miscegenation *mestizaje* and the racism that segregates indigenous populations. The paper concludes with an examination of gender and race discrimination and reaches the conclusion that indigenous women are one of the groups with the least access to citizenship.

2490 García Rojas, Gustavo. Migración y desmemoria: la ciudadania étnica en Monterrey. (*Trayectorias/Monterrey*, 5:12, mayo/agosto 2003, p. 76–88, bibl.)

This paper presents the findings of recent migration to Monterrey of two indigenous groups: the Otomies and the Mixtecos. Patterns of urban settlement, the role of religion, and the acculturation process are all discussed. The education of monolingual children is one of the many social problems that the indigenous populations face in the process of adapting to the city.

2491 Gutiérrez, Natividad. Violencia estructural y masacre genocida en los pueblos indígenas de Chiapas, 1997, y Oaxaca, 2002. (*Estud. Sociol./México*, 22:65, mayo/agosto 2004, p. 315–348, bibl., tables)

The massacre in Agua Fria (Oaxaca) has not been attributed to any group but can be explained by unresolved land tenure problems, continuous fighting among rival political leaders, and the presence of the military and abuses perpetrated by them. In Acteal (Chiapas) religious antagonisms between Catholics and Evangelicals developed into mixed partisan political conflicts. In both places discrimination and racism contributed to confrontations and political violence.

2492 Guzmán Gómez, Elsa. Resistencia, permanencia y cambio: estrategias campesinas de vida en el poniente de Morelos. Cuernavaca, Mexico: Univ. Autónoma del Estado de Morelos; México: Plaza y Valdés, 2005. 314 p., 4 leaves of plates: bibl., col. maps. (Agricultura)

Monograph studies the transformation of four villages in the state of Morelos. Mexico's emphasis on industrial modernization and abandonment of rural development has produced unique consequences for peasants who live in states near Mexico City. This work describes survival adjustments to industrialization, labor linkages with out-

side opportunities, and the role of women in the new division of labor.

2493 Haber, Paul Lawrence. Power from experience: urban popular movements in late twentieth-century Mexico. University Park: Pennsylvania State Univ. Press, 2006. 280 p.: bibl., index.

Participation, leadership, organization, and cooptation by political parties are part of the analysis of two social movements in Mexico City and Durango. Additional study of Mexico's political developments allows the author to provide insightful analysis of the decade of the 1990s. Author concludes that social movements have an impact on reforms but not on transforming the political system.

2494 Héau Lambert, Catherine and **Gilberto Giménez.** La representación social de la violencia en la trova popular mexicana. (*Rev. Mex. Sociol.*, 66:4, oct./dic. 2004, p. 627–659, bibl.)

This study uses the concept of a sociogram as a tool for cultural analysis. The idea of violence in popular culture, particularly in the *corridos* songs about brave men concerning honor, and recently in the *narcocorridos*, has a different meaning than the one people normally assign to it. Lyrics that may seem to be an affirmation of honor or demand for rights in one case may have a sense of illegality in another situation.

2495 Hernández Forcada, Ricardo and **María Elena Lugo Garfias.** Algunas notas sobre la tortura en México. México: Comisión Nacional de los Derechos Humanos, 2004. 192 p.: bibl., ill.

Commissioned by the country's Commission on Human Rights, this is the first quantitative account of documented abuses based on reported violations from 1990 to 2003. Number and types of torture, those responsible (all security agents and police investigators), and location by sites and states are included. Also presents international treaties ratified by Mexico and national legislation against torture.

2496 Higgins, Michael J. and **Tanya L. Coen.** Rompiendo esquemas: el retrato etnográfico de una familia de travestíes en el Oaxaca urbano. (*Desacatos*, 9,

primavera/verano 2002, p. 89–95, bibl.,
photos)
This short paper presents the results
of a lengthy in-depth interview with members of a family of transvestites that are
prostitutes and leaders of a group of transvestite prostitutes in Oaxaca. The two leaders have created Grupo Unión, an organization of transvestite sex workers dedicated to
fighting HIV/AIDS by increasing education
and awareness about the disease.

2497 Hill, Kenneth and **Rebeca Wong.**
Mexico-US migration: views from
both sides of the border. (*Popul. Dev. Rev.*,
31:1, March 2005, p. 1–18, bibl., graphs,
tables)
Authors focus on overall migration
rather than solely on unauthorized migration, and obtain estimates of net emigration
from Mexico using data from both Mexico
and the US 1990 and 2000 population censuses. Results estimate an annual net migration between 324,000 and 440,000 persons of
ages 10 to 80—figures that are considerably
lower than other conservative estimates.

2498 Hirsch, Jennifer S. A courtship after
marriage: sexuality and love in Mexican transnational families. Berkeley: Univ.
of California Press, 2003. 376 p.: bibl., ill.,
index, maps.
Compares sexuality and reproduc-
tive practices of women in rural Jalisco and
migrants from the same village in Atlanta,
Georgia. In the US structural changes such
as increased education and greater economic opportunities for women influence
gender relations. Among women in Mexico,
lower fertility and change in attitudes towards a traditional marriage are caused by
modernization.

2499 Hoddinott, John and **Emmanuel
Skoufias.** The impact of Progresa
on food consumption. (*Econ. Dev. Cult.
Change*, 53:1, Oct. 2004, p. 37–61, bibl.,
graph, tables)
Progresa (now called Oportunidades)
is a World Bank-supported antipoverty
social program initiated in Mexico in 1997.
Women who send their children to school
and to health clinics receive cash transfers
and nutritional supplements, and participate
in discussions about nutrition and health. In
this evaluation, conducted under the aus-

pices of the World Bank, the authors recognize the complexity and limitations of the
methodology. The findings report a positive
significant relationship between consumption and caloric intake that is interpreted as
a nutritional improvement sign.

**2500 Hombres y masculinidades en Guada-
lajara.** Coordinación de Roberto Miranda Guerrero y Lucía Mantilla Gutiérrez.
Guadalajara, Mexico: Univ. de Guadalajara,
Centro Universitario de Ciencias Sociales y
Humanidades, 2006. 267 p.: bibl. (Col. Estudios de género)
A Jungean psychiatrist writes the first
chapter of this volume based on the experience of her practice. The next chapters
explore the shifting meaning of work in the
configuration of male identity by interviewing 22 males belonging to three generations,
and the impact on machismo as women
enter occupations that are considered exclu-
sively for men, specifically engineering and
the police force. The study of the figure of
the *charro* as a symbolic representation of
Mexican masculinity is included in the collection that ends with a review of authors
that have written about masculinity during
the 19th and first half of the 20th centuries.

2501 Huesca, Robert. Social aspects of labor organizing: maquiladora workers
in a grassroots development effort. (*in* Globalization and development in Latin America. Edited by Richard L. Harris. Whitby,
Canada: De Sitter, 2005, p. 135–175, bibl.)
The poor labor conditions at the
maquilas have been documented in many
studies. This paper looks at an NGO's effort
at organizing workers in three northern border cities. Management and existing labor
unions make difficult any organization that
will humanize work at the maquilas. Following Freire's educational approach and
grassroots participation, community organization promoters seem to have had some
success.

**2502 Ilusiones, sacrificios y resultados:
el escenario real de las remesas de
emigrantes a Estados Unidos.** Coordinación
de Blanca Suárez y Emma Zapata Martelo.
México: Grupo Interdisciplinario sobre
Mujer, Trabajo y Pobreza, 2007. 772 p.: ill.
(Serie PEMSA; 6)
Each lengthy chapter (50 p.) of this

voluminous collection merits an individual review. While the concern of the collection is remittances, the analysis is not the typical economic or quantitative approach, but rather a sociological and qualitative assessment. Authors discuss the impact of remittances on gender relations, family, community and social organization, health access, home improvements of recipients, and the creation of family enterprises. Some chapters analyze the role of women in the management of the funds received. The mechanisms used to send remittances are also examined. All chapters include a review of the migratory process itself, providing valuable information.

2503 Imperialismo, crisis de las instituciones y resistencia social. Coordinación de Ana Alicia Solís de Alba et al. México: Editorial Itaca, 2004. 370 p.: bibl., ill.

The authors of the 18 chapters of this volume are in agreement that neoliberal economic policies and globalization have caused Mexico to remain undeveloped to the benefit of wealthy nations. Each chapter discusses different themes. The reader will understand why the maquila industry has not promoted Mexico's industrial development, why the World Bank promoted the privatization of health care delivery, and learn the reasons behind the crisis of the PRI and the resistance of citizens against the new imperialism. Written by sociologists, economists, political scientists, and labor leaders.

2504 Jóvenes y niños: un enfoque socio-demográfico. Coordinación de Marta Mier y Terán y Cecilia Rabell. México: Cámara de Diputados, XIX Legislatura, Estados Unidos de México: IIS: FLACSO México: Porrúa, 2005. 373 p.: bibl., ill. (Conocer para decidir)

In the first part of this volume, five articles explore changes that have occurred and continue to occur among children and youth regarding labor participation, migration, courtship, marriage, and education. The changes are a reflection of family and societal changes. The five articles in the second part examine child and youth labor as strategies to increase family income and the process of selection of family members that are to be educated. Gender roles, social class, family organization, place of residence (urban-rural), and ethnicity all influence these life-defining decisions.

2505 Juárez Huet, Nahayeilli B. La santería à Mexico: ébauche ethnographique. (*Civilisations/Brussels*, 51:1/2, 2002, p. 61–79, bibl.)

The spreading of santería, originally an Afro-Cuban religion, is a recent phenomenon in Mexico that has not been studied much. This paper presents an ethnographic view of the current practices of santería in Mexico City.

2506 Jurado, Mario Alberto. Movilidad laboral y género: apuntes sobre el fenómeno en la zona metropolitana de Monterrey. (*Trayectorias/Monterrey*, 6:16, sept./dic. 2004, p. 81–98, bibl., graphs, tables)

This study focuses on highly educated persons in Monterrey; variables include gender, age, and employment types. Women have more labor stability; salaried employees change employment more frequently; and there is a tendency to less occupational distance between genders, except in the case of managerial positions. The National Survey of Urban Employment is the source of data.

2507 Lewis, Laura A. Negros, negros-indios, afromexicanos: raza, nación e identidad en una comunidad mexicana morena (Guerrero). (*Guaraguao/Barcelona*, 9:20, 2005, p. 49–73, bibl.)

The ambiguity of ethnic identity of blacks in Mexico is well explained in this article of San Nicolás, a town in Costa Chica, a Pacific coastal region that was settled by black slaves in colonial times. Findings slightly contrast with those found by Vaughn (see item **2547**) regarding the degree of common identity among Mexican blacks and cultural integration with the mestizo population.

2508 López, Flor and **Adrián Guillermo Aguilar.** Niveles de cobertura accesibilidad de la infraestructura de los servicios de salud en la periferia metropolitana de la Ciudad de México. (*Invest. Geogr./México*, 53, abril 2004, p. 185–209, bibl., maps, tables)

Explains the spatial distribution of health services that different public institutions offer in the municipalities surrounding Mexico City. The analysis shows that health policy lacks a territorial approach to the distribution of health facilities as measured by number of physicians, nurses, and health centers. There is a concentration of resources in urban areas.

2509 Lutz, Bruno. La apuesta democrática en una empresa social guerrerense, la Sanzekan Tinemi. (*Veredas*, 4/5, 2002, p. 100–116, bibl., graphs)

This interesting paper examines the conflicts between maximizing profits and democratizing decision-making in a rural social enterprise in Guerrero. Effective management demands professionally trained decisionmakers that at times must overrule decisions made democratically by organization members that have limited business knowledge. Author does not find an easy solution to this dilemma in spite of management's committed interest to increase democratic participation.

2510 Magazine, Roger. Golden and blue like my heart: masculinity, youth, and power among soccer fans in Mexico City. Tucson: The Univ. of Arizona Press, 2007. 223 p.: bibl., index.

Ethnography of the fan club of the Puma's soccer team, one of Mexico City's four major teams. According to author, the ideals that the team represents to the fans lead to behaviors that contradict the ideals. Fans engage in violence and machismo reflecting the national myths of urban Mexican men.

2511 Martínez García, Luz Elena et al. Género y poder en tres organizaciones rurales de la región lagunera. (*Rev. Mex. Sociol.*, 67:2, abril/junio 2005, p. 271–319, bibl., graphs, tables)

Authors observed the changes in gender identity and power relations between males and females in the three organizations studied. Findings suggest that globalization has altered the identities of women and men. Women are more empowered and men are modifying the traditional hegemonic masculinity. A solid contribution based on a careful analysis of fieldwork data.

2512 Mata García, Bernardino. Desarrollo rural centrado en la pobreza. Chapingo, Mexico: Univ. Autónoma Chapingo, 2002. 170 p.: bibl., ill., maps.

A professor at the agricultural Univ. Autónoma Chapingo offers models to rural development that are alternatives to those sponsored by international organizations. Based on community participation and empowerment and using case studies from Chiapas, the author outlines steps to be taken to improve the quality of life within the confines of the resources available in the community.

2513 Méndez González, Rosa María; Ana García de Fuentes; and María Dolores Cervera Montejano. Mortalidad infantil y marginación en la península de Yucatán. (*Invest. Geogr./México*, 54, agosto 2004, p. 140–163, bibl., graphs, maps, tables)

Article studies infant mortality and its relationship to social deprivation in the three states and the 125 municipalities in the Yucatán Peninsula. Sources include municipal data from the National Institute of Statistics and National Population Council (INEGI) between 1990 and 2000. While infant mortality rates have decreased in Mexico and in Yucatán, infant mortality has worsened in some municipalities in Yucatán in comparison to the national trend.

2514 Mendoza Pérez, Cristóbal. Circuitos y espacios transnacionales en la migración entre México y Estados Unidos: aportes de una encuesta de flujos. (*Migr. Int.*, 2:6, enero/junio 2004, p. 83–109, bibl. graphs, tables)

Quantitative study based on the Migration Survey in the Northern Border (EMIF). Examines mobility patterns from the interior to the border, network importance, and the role that northern cities play in the creation of transnational spaces to promote migration to the US.

2515 La migración en Oaxaca. Coordinación de Jacobo Arellano Amaya. Oaxaca, Mexico: Dirección General de Población de Oaxaca, 2004. 261 p.: bibl., ill., maps.

A technical demographic study of internal, external, and international migration based, among others, on the 2000 National Household Census, the 1992 and 1997 National Surveys of Demographic Dynamics, the 2002 the National Employment Survey, the 2000 CONAPO's Indexes of

Migration Density, and the Northern Border Migration Survey. Each of the eight chapters addresses one specific dimension of migration, including municipalities of origin and destination, comparisons with other states, and return migration.

2516 Una mirada de género a la Ciudad de México. Compilación de Alejandra Massolo. México: Univ. Autónoma Metropolitana, Unidad Azcapotzalco: Red de Investigación Urbana, AC, 2004. 309 p.: bibl., ill.

The nine articles in this collection examine a variety of themes from the perspective of gender. Topics covered include the organization of housework and use of space in the household, single mothers' access to public credit for home improvements, the experience of women who are street vendors, the role of women in social movements, new gender equality policies and the creation of institutions to assist women, household violence against women and public responses to reduce it, and characteristics of the increasing number of households headed by women.

2517 Multiculturalismo: perspectivas y desafíos. Coordinación de Daniel Gutiérrez Martínez. México: Colegio de México: UNAM: Siglo XXI, 2006. 322 p.: bibl., index. (Sociología y política)

Eleven essays by Mexican and French authors explore approaches to multiculturalism beyond ethnic relations. Religious affiliation, social class, political ideology, and ethnicity produce pluralities and diversity. Two chapters reflect on UNESCO's covenant on cultural rights and two on religious diversity. In addition to studies on Mexico's intercultural education and sociocultural adjustments of migrants, three chapters discuss broad aspects of the interaction between culture and society.

2518 Münch Galindo, Guido. Una semblanza del Carnaval de Veracruz. México: UNAM, Instituto de Investigaciones Antropológicas, 2005. 415 p.: bibl., ill.

After a historical chapter on the origins of the Veracruz carnival, this ethnology presents an account of daily activities, including social events and participants, negative implications such as violence and accidents, and the economic impact of four carnivals (from 2000 to 2003). The analysis of myths and of the parades themselves provides a better understanding of this civic ceremony with ancestral origins.

2519 Neri Contreras, Arturo. Migración, globalización y perspectiva poblacional en la zona indígena cuicateca, Oaxaca. (*Cotidiano/México*, 20:126, julio/agosto 2004, p. 121–132)

Author attributes increasing migration among indigenous populations to policies that were responding to global demands during the 1980s. Policy consequences include the destruction of subsistence agriculture, the reduction of agricultural prices, and the reduction of remittances from migrants due to unemployment. Unavailability of labor in the villages has increased migration, leaving behind the elderly. As a result, cultural survival of the Cuicateca is endangered.

2520 Oaxaca: escenarios del nuevo siglo: sociedad, economía, política. Coordinación de Víctor Raúl Martínez Vásquez. 2a ed., corr. y aum. Oaxaca, Mexico: Instituto de Investigaciones Sociológicas, Univ. Autónoma "Benito Juárez" de Oaxaca, 2004. 276 p.: bibl., maps.

The 19 chapters in this volume on Oaxaca, grouped under three headings (society, economy, and politics), provide insights into the state's demographics, indigenous language, education, agricultural resources, migration, employment, urban development, and political and electoral aspects. Overall, the volume provides a comprehensive view of changes and challenges faced by one of Mexico's poorest states.

2521 Oehmichen Bazán, Cristina. La multiculturalidad de la ciudad de México y los derechos indígenas. (*Rev. Mex. Cienc. Polít. Soc.*, 46:188/189, mayo/dic. 2003, p. 147–168, bibl.)

For many years, indigenous populations have migrated to other parts of the country and to the US. They have organized networks that help them to maintain their cultural identity and unity in their new destination. This study looks at the discrimination and racism that indigenous people suffer in Mexico City and the process of reconstructing their communities to survive in the new environment.

2522 Ortiz Hernández, Luis and **José Arturo Granados Cosme.** Violencia hacia bisexuales, lesbianas y homosexuales de la ciudad de México. (*Rev. Mex. Sociol.*, 65:2, abril/junio 2003, p. 265–303, bibl., tables)

In order to advance our understanding of violence experienced by homosexuals, bisexuals, and lesbians in Mexico City, the authors interviewed 506 persons who engage in sexual practices generally considered deviant. Findings show that homosexuals and bisexual men were victims of violence more often than bisexual and lesbian women.

2523 Pensando la política: representación social y cultura política en jóvenes mexicanos. Coordinación de Marco Antonio González Pérez. México: Plaza y Valdés, 2006. 390 p.: bibl.

Six social psychologists and sociologists present in 11 chapters the results of interesting, well-designed and executed research in Tlaxcala, Puebla, Querétaro, and the Federal District on the meaning and social representation of politics among youth ages 15 to 24. Useful for understanding the malaise that permeates Mexico's political system and the need for changes.

2524 Pérez-Akaki, Pablo and **Pedro L. Álvarez Colín.** Intermediación financiera y remesas en México. (*Migr. Int.*, 3:1, enero/junio 2005, p. 111–140, bibl., graphs, maps, tables)

This paper studies the role of formal financial intermediaries in transferring family remittances from the US to Mexico. Since the 1990s, the volume of remittances has increased greatly, and the channels of transferences have changed. Banks, mostly Spanish and US, have entered into the transfer business through electronic payments, credit and debit cards, and checking accounts providing a fast and safe service at a higher price than other more informal channels.

2525 Pérez García, Martha Estela. Las organizaciones no gubernamentales en Ciudad Juárez y su lucha contra la violencia de género. (*Nóesis/UACJ*, 15:28, julio/dic. 2005, p. 147–167, bibl., photos)

After a brief description of the development of NGOs in Ciudad Juárez, the article explores efforts of NGOs to find the perpetrators of the multiple assassinations of women in the city. Attention is also given to agreements and disagreements on tactics among NGOs. The paper ends with an explanation of the contact between NGOs and the government and a discussion of results of this interaction.

2526 Pimienta Lastra, Rodrigo. Tendencias de la migración indocumentada en la frontera norte de México. (*Veredas*, 6, 2003, p. 127–155, bibl., graphs, tables)

This paper studies migrant flows to the northern international border, and undocumented migration from there to the US. These numbers are compared to those of migrants deported by US authorities. Quantitative data from the Migration Survey to the Mexican Northern Border (EMIF) of the Colegio de la Frontera Norte (1994) shows that measures to reduce undocumented migration have not been effective, and have in fact shifted migration routes to deserts and remote rural centers, increasing risks of death while attempting to cross the border.

2527 Poblaciones y culturas de origen africano en México. Recopilación de María Elisa Velázquez Gutiérrez y Ethel Correa Duró. México: Instituto Nacional de Antropología e Historia, 2005. 454 p.: bibl., ill. (Col. Africanía; 1)

The study of Mexican blacks has not received much scholarly attention. This compilation is an exception. Most papers in this collection were presented at a 1997 international symposium held in Oaxaca on African cultures in Mexico. Papers in the first part discuss theoretical and methodological problems to be taken into account by researchers of blacks in Mexico. Poor archival records are one of the many problems. The second part, mostly historical, includes chapters on integration, culture, and labor in Puebla, Acapulco, Oaxaca, and Mexico City.

2528 Ponce, Patricia. Sexualidades costeñas: un pueblo veracruzano entre el río y la mar. México: CIESAS, 2006. 430 p.: bibl. (Publicaciones de la Casa Chata) (Antropologías)

During 11 months of ethnographic work, the author carried out a household survey, 13 testimonials, and 50 in-depth interviews. One life history and interviews with local leaders and older community members helped to reconstruct the town's history. These materials and the author's participant observation explain the meaning of family, love, sex, division of labor, the nature of social problems, and alternate lifestyles.

2529 Protestantismo en el mundo maya contemporáneo. Recopilación de Mario Humberto Ruz y Carlos Garma Navarro. México: UNAM, Instituto de Investigaciones Filológicas; Ixtapalapa, Mexico: Univ. Autónoma Metropolitana, Unidad Iztapalapa, 2005. 177 p.: bibl., ill. (Cuadernos del Centro de Estudios Mayas; 30)

The seven chapters provide an understanding of the complex reality of Protestantism in Mexico and Guatemala. Reasons for the expansion and retrenchment of various denominations and beliefs and behaviors of followers are well presented. There is a general agreement that more syncretism exists between precolonial beliefs and Protestantism than with Catholic dogma.

2530 Ramos García, José María. Seguridad ciudadana y la seguridad nacional en México: hacia un marco conceptual. (*Convergencia/Toluca*, 12:39, sept./dic. 2005, p. 33–52, bibl.)

Author analyzes public security from the perspective of Mexican common citizens and their need for safety and freedom. Looks at social security as a means to protect the civil rights of individuals and of organizations that can be affected by US national security policies and concerns. Also examines the national security policy as presented in the 2002–2006 National Development Plan.

2531 Ravelo Blancas, Patricia. Entre ángeles y demonios: construcción de la victimización en Ciudad Juárez. (*Chihuah. Hoy*, 2004, p. 107–123, bibl.)

The article provides insights about the process of blaming-the-victim to explain violence against women in Ciudad Juárez. Argues that the media, churches, and social and civic organizations are responsible for presenting a negative picture of women who were murdered or sexually violated.

2532 La realidad alterada: drogas, enteógenos y cultura. Recopilación de Julio Glockner y Enrique Soto. México: Debate, 2006. 210 p.: bibl., ill. (Arena abierta)

Among Mexican Amerindians, hallucinogenic drugs are legally allowed for ceremonial purposes. This collection presents information about the history and usage of a variety of psychotropic and mind-altering drugs among indigenous communities. Discussions about the transformation of plants into pills by Westerners and the rationale to legalize marijuana close the volume.

2533 Red de Investigadores del Fenómeno Religioso en el Centro Occidente de México. Encuentro. *6th, Colotlán, Mexico, 2003.* El fenómeno religioso en el occidente de México: VI encuentro de investigadores. Recopilación de Cristina Gutiérrez Zúñiga. Zapopan, Mexico: El Colegio de Jalisco; Guadalajara, Mexico: Univ. de Guadalajara, Centro Universitario de Ciencias Sociales y Humanidades, 2004. 244 p.: bibl., ill., maps.

The first three articles in this collection discuss theoretical and methodological aspects of the study of religion in Mexico. Two papers address the religious world of the wixaarika o huicholes, an ethnic group that has maintained its culture. For three years, the author observed the rites and ceremonies of the life cycle in that community, collecting data heretofore unknown. These essays are followed by four studies of Mexican saints and the devotional rituals and tourism that they created. Essays on the clergy's migration during and after the Mexican Revolution, the study of the Partido Católico Nacional, and the presence of the clergy in Mexican literature close the volume. An outstanding collection.

2534 Rivas Sánchez, Héctor Eloy. Entre la temeridad y la responsabilidad: masculinidad, riesgo y mortalidad por violencia en la Sierra de Sonora. (*Desacatos*, 15/16, otoño/invierno 2004, p. 69–89, bibl., photos)

Qualitative methods and quantitative data are used to explore the relationship among masculinity, risk behavior, and mortality through accidents and violence in rural communities in Sonora's highlands during the 20th century. Results show that only 30 percent of deaths by accidents and violent causes are due to alcoholism, high speed driving, or fights. Among the studied population, manhood means work and family responsibility, as well as deference to others—attitudes that are not compatible with risky behaviors.

2535 Rivera González, José Guadalupe. Nuevas estrategias familiares de trabajo en sectores medios de la Ciudad de México. (*Convergencia/Toluca*, 12:39, sept./dic. 2005, p. 151–178, bibl.)

Describes the survival strategies used by middle class families in Mexico City after the main income earner became temporarily or permanently unemployed. Food preparation and distribution, renting rooms in the house, opening small shops at home to sell clothing or cosmetics, and finding employment for other family members are examples of income-generating activities.

2536 Robledo Hernández, Gabriela Patricia and Jorge Luis Cruz Burguete. Religión y dinámica familiar en Los Altos de Chiapas: la construcción de nuevas identidades de género. (*Estud. Sociol./México*, 23:68, mayo/agosto 2005, p. 515–534, bibl.)

This ethnography focuses on women's identity changes caused by the Catholic pastoral movement and in Protestant groups such as Pentecostalism. While there are differences between the effects produced by joining one of these religious movements, commonalities exist. Most significant are a sense of personal liberation from patriarchal dominance, increased autonomy, freedom to select one's spouse, and breaking with old traditions that regulate gender interactions.

2537 Rojo Pons, Flavio A. and Saúl Salazar Barbosa. Mujeres y hombres con discapacidades en el estado de Guanajuato: una aproximación desde la estadística. Guanajuato, Mexico: Guanajuato, Gobierno del Estado, Instituto de la Mujer Guanajuatense, 2004. 105 p.: bibl., ill. (Col. Estudios)

A sample of the General Population and Household Census of 2000 collected basic information on disabled persons and nature of disability. Based on these data for the state of Guanajuato, authors cross demographic information (age, gender, marital status) by type of disability and access to care.

2538 Sánchez-Mejorada Fernández, María Cristina. De actores y programas sociales en la Ciudad de México: el caso del programa de vivienda en el lote familiar.

(*Andamios*, 1, otoño/invierno 2004, p. 77–108, bibl.)

The electoral triumph of the Partido de la Revolución Democrática (PRD) in the Federal District in Mexico in 1997 led to new, more transparent approaches to the governance of one of the largest cities in the world and its 1,352 territorial units. This paper describes the PRD's policies, the party's attempts to incorporate popular participation, the role of civic and social organizations, and successes and failures of social programs.

2539 Seguridad alimentaria, seguridad nacional. Coordinación de Felipe Torres Torres. Textos de Yolanda Trápaga Delfín *et al.* México: UNAM, 2003. 291 p.: bibl., ill., maps.

Torres brings together eight articles that analyze the impact of NAFTA on food accessibility among the poor, and that look at the political and social risks that Mexico could face in situations of food scarcity. The volume contains a large amount of quantitative data up to the year 2000 on food production, agricultural acreage, and food imports and exports.

2540 Ser padres, esposos e hijos: prácticas y valoraciones de varones mexicanos. Coordinación de Juan Guillermo Figueroa, Lucero Jiménez y Olivia Tena. México: Colegio de México, 2006. 401 p.: bibl., ill.

Brings together nine articles centered on male attitudes and values towards marriage, sexuality, and paternity. Most methodologies are qualitative, but the approach, the number of interviewees, and participants' social and ethnic characteristics are quite varied. One chapter includes a handful of interviewees; others study Mazahuas, the poor, middle-class professionals, and one explores households with disabled children.

2541 Singelmann, Peter. La transformación política de México y los gremios cañeros de PRI. (*Rev. Mex. Sociol.*, 65:1, enero/marzo 2003, p. 117–152, bibl.)

This paper was written at the time (ca. 2000) the Mexican political system was being transformed into a more open one. The author attempts to foresee the implications of the new political reality for the sugar plantation workers' unions that until then had worked within an authoritarian, one-party system. The data gathered suggest that the new system will continue to rely on existing political practices.

2542 Solís, Patricio. Cambio estructural y movilidad ocupacional en Monterrey, México. (*Estud. Sociol./México*, 23:67, enero/abril 2005, p. 43–74, bibl., tables)

Looking at social mobility from 1940 on, Solís defines two periods: the import substitution period until the 1980s crisis and the era of globalization. Monterrey developed a powerful industrial base that suffered significantly during and after the crisis. Mobility changes from one period to the next were not uniform among different social strata, suggesting that social mobility is more complex than previous studies have indicated.

Staudt, Kathleen A. Gender, governance, and globalization at borders: femicide at the US-Mexico border. See item **1997.**

2543 Suárez de Garay, María Eugenia. Armados, enrejados, desconfiados: tres breves lecturas sobre la cultura policial mexicana. (*Polít. Soc./Madrid*, 42:3, 2005, p. 87–102, bibl.)

Exposes corruption and police participation in criminal behavior. Author explains how the security forces utilize their knowledge of legality to organize their illegal activities. To understand police behavior, it is necessary to study its corporate culture, beliefs, and norms that rule the security institutions. Based on in-depth interviews.

2544 Suárez de Garay, María Eugenia. Los policías: una averiguación antropológica. Tlaquepaque, Mexico: ITESO; Guadalajara, Mexico: Univ. de Guadalajara, 2006. 487 p.: bibl., ill.

One of the few academic studies of Mexico's police. Participant observation, 25 semi-structured interviews of members or former members of the Guadalajara police force, and archival materials are the main sources of this interesting monograph. Author examines the culture and organization of the police force and the identity and experience of members, among other topics.

2545 Torres, Victor M. A cultural model of pregnancy: a comparison between Mexican physicians and working-class women in Tijuana, B.C. (*Soc. Sci. J./New York*, 42:1, 2005, p. 81–96, bibl., graph, tables)

This research examines the accuracy of the explanation that health-seeking behaviors among poor and working class Mexican women tend to focus on cultural beliefs. The author compares the cultural model of prenatal care of those women with the biomedical model of Mexican physicians. The findings, based on ethnographic interviews, show that the two share a similar model of prenatal care based on biomedicine.

2546 Valladares de la Cruz, Laura R. Democracia y derechos indios en México: la ciudadanía multicultural como modelo de paz. (*Rev. Mex. Cienc. Polít. Soc.*, 46:188/189, mayo/dic. 2003, p. 121–146)

Indigenous peoples in Mexico have been fighting for the recognition of their collective rights and the restoration of a political model that would allow them to live in a multicultural nation. According to author, the 2001 law on indigenous populations and the public aid programs make them dependent instead of recognizing them as political actors in their own right.

2547 Vaughn, Bobby. Afro-Mexico: blacks, indígenas, politics, and the greater diaspora. (*in* Neither enemies nor friends: Latinos, Blacks, Afro-Latinos. Edited by Anani Dzidzienyo and Suzanne Oboler. New York: Palgrave Macmillan, 2005, p. 117–136, bibl.)

Black Mexican Americans have not been identified by others or by themselves as a distinctive ethnic group. The study of predominately black communities in the Pacific Coast of Guerrero and Oaxaca confirms this statement. The author explains the reasons for the lack of a black culture in the region where historically a large number of blacks have mixed with mestizos but not with indigenous populations.

2548 Verdugo Córdova, Joel. El movimiento estudiantil en la Universidad de Sonora de 1970 a 1974: un enfoque socio-histórico a partir del testimonio oral. Hermosillo, Mexico: Colegio de Sonora, 2004. 244 p. (Cuadernos Cuarto creciente; 9)

This case study is a historical reconstruction of the student movement in

Sonora in the 1970s. Using information from archival materials and the media, as well as in-depth interviews with witnesses, the monograph provides detailed accounts of events. The analysis takes into consideration the cultural and political contexts within which the student movement occurred. A valuable monograph.

2549 Violencia sexista: algunas claves para la comprensión del feminicidio en Ciudad Juárez. Coordinación de Griselda Gutiérrez Castañeda. México: UNAM, Facultad de Filosofía y Letras, Programa Universitario de Estudios de Género, 2004. 166 p.: bibl.

About 400 women have been assassinated, many of them sexuality violated, and hundreds more disappeared during the last 12 years in Ciudad Juárez, a point of transit to the US for thousands of products, migrants, and drugs. Investigative reporters, one senator, one academic, and one human rights advocate attempt to explain gender violence, providing in the process a wealth of information on the events.

2550 Zamorano-Villarreal, Claudia Carolina. Naviguer dans le désert : itinéraires résidentiels à la frontière Mexique-Etats-Unis. Paris: IHEAL: CREDAL, 2003. 267 p.: bibl., ill., maps. (Travaux & mémoires de l'IHEAL; 73)

Ciudad Juárez, across the border from El Paso, Texas, has always been a city of migrants arriving in hopes of crossing the border or working in maquilas. This monograph examines the patterns of urban settlement and land acquisition, the adaptation of self-built houses to accommodate new family members, and labor alternatives. Family genealogies are one of the methodological techniques used.

2551 Zamudio, Francisco José; José Luis Romo; and Domingo Rosas. Análisis comparativo 1995–2000 del desarrollo humano de los estados de Colima, Jalisco y Nayarit. (*Espiral/Guadalajara*, 12:34, sept./ dic. 2005, p. 95–124, bibl., graphs)

Presents a comparative analysis of human development in three Mexican states based on modifications of the human development index. Includes three variations of the index—the first includes four indicators: life expectancy, literacy, number of literate children between 6–14 years old, and per capita gross domestic production; the second index incorporates access to drainage, potable water, and electricity; and the third looks at the participation of men and women in political and economic decision-making roles. An interesting exercise that reflects the measurement problems of using complex indexes.

CENTRAL AMERICA

HANNAH WITTMAN, *Assistant Professor of Sociology, Simon Fraser University*

CONTEMPORARY RESEARCH IN CENTRAL AMERICAN SOCIOLOGY continues to evolve methodologically, deepening a commitment to ethnography, extended qualitative interviewing, critical case-study research, and cultural/ historical analysis. Mirroring an international trend, mixed-method approaches that integrate quantitative and survey data with qualitative case studies are appearing more frequently in the literature.

Topically, following the recent trend, the largest volume of new works continues to analyze youth and gang violence in Central America. Studies in this area have moved from quantifying and identifying the geographic spread of violence, mainly to inform containment strategies, towards a more qualitative and historical understanding of the root and structural causes of youth violence.

This approach has involved the investigation of student rivalries and adolescent identity construction in schools (e.g., item **2601**) as well as demonstrating the socioeconomic characteristics that indicate conditions of vulnerability and social exclusion for youth (items **2560** and **2600**) caused by the removal of socioeconomic supports and stability precipitated by the imposition of neoliberalism in the 1980s and 1990s (item **2593**). Several studies reflect on the systematic presence of violence and fear in political, institutional, academic, and media discourses on gangs that dehumanize gang members and obscure institutional violence (cf. item **2576**), while others reflect on the internationalization of gang violence and the transition from youth gangs to adult crime networks. A comprehensive comparative study of civil society responses to gang violence across Central America provides useful insight into the role of social participation and civil rights in youth transformation (item **2554**).

Ongoing interest in subject and identity formation in postwar Central America also continues to be at the forefront of current research. This topic is represented by several notable studies that examine the complex navigation of indigenous and ladino identities in Guatemala, including a presentation of the concept of "neoliberal multiculturalism," which arguably has opened important spaces for indigenous empowerment while simultaneously reproducing Guatemala's racial hierarchy (item **2569**). In the same vein, other in-depth longitudinal studies investigate the dynamics of community building and identity formation among returned exiles in Ixcán and Petén (item **2608**) and other, less commonly researched diasporic communities in Central America, including Chinese immigrants in Panama (item **2604**) and Russian and other former Soviet immigrants in Costa Rica (item **2597**). Issues of identity, labor, and gender intersect in several notable works that look at processes of subject formation as shaped by participation in export production and consumption in contexts of structural and symbolic violence (items **2568** and **2590**).

In fact, almost a quarter of the items reviewed for this section revive and deepen recent forays into multifaceted aspects of gender and gendered social change in Central America, also in methodologically and substantively diverse ways. An outstanding study on gender and the media in Guatemala, for example, uses in-depth interviews and focus groups with women reporters and columnists from Guatemala's six major periodicals to analyze women's role in the media—as workers as well as subjects (item **2609**). Complementary studies on gender and revolution in Nicaragua and El Salvador analyze how and why women participated in revolutionary armies (item **2605**), or conversely, became positioned as Contra supporters (item **2561**). Both of these studies highlight revolution and counter-revolution as arenas of cultural struggle in which women must negotiate both gender and political identities. In the same vein, a comprehensive study on the women's movement in Guatemala from 1986–2003 demonstrates how movements and activists negotiated global restructuring, noting the institutionalization and NGO-ization of the women's movement as it moved from protest to policy (item **2558**). Notable for its careful acknowledgement of issues of ethnicity, class, and geographical location in transformation of gender identities, this study also delves into the fruitful areas of the redefinition of gendered citizenships. Overall, this growing research area highlights the various ways in which women's participation in political struggles has facilitated their repositioning within their communities in the postwar period, wherein they have developed new forms of political action that both utilize and transform gender roles. On a more applied note, a large group of quantitative surveys supported by case studies or targeted interviews inform demographic and public health programs in gender, health, and family planning policy, while a second group of studies analyzes issues of gender, incarceration and domestic violence in Guatemala as a basis for recommending specific reforms of the penal and judicial systems.

Several retrospective analyses of post-peace accord political reforms provide useful insights into perceptions of justice and processes of memory by examining the impact of truth commissions. For example, one rigorous comparative study of implementation processes and outcomes of peace negotiations in El Salvador, Nicaragua, Guatemala, and Colombia (item **2583**), concludes that despite the distinct trajectories of each peace process, successful peace accord negotiations produced common effects including the reduction of violence and the facilitation of more open political systems. Several other studies counter this conclusion, however, arguing that peace negotiations have in fact facilitated the imposition of neoliberal policies that failed to fundamentally restructure government and economic systems in favor of the poor. This policy failure is then linked to current levels of interpersonal and community or gang violence that may be even more pervasive than during the periods of war.

The subfield of environmental sociology, in Central America and beyond, has expanded exponentially since the late 1990s in response to growing concern about global environmental degradation, the relationship between livelihoods and conservation, and development- and conservation-induced displacement of rural and indigenous populations. Often in collaboration with local NGOs, development agencies, and long term ethnographic relationships with rural communities in Central America, many new sociological works examine issues including the discourse and practice of environmental sustainability and the social costs and benefits of the growing imposition of international conservation models to rural areas. Several of these studies are particularly important for the way in which they integrate qualitative and ethnographic data with quantitative land-use and satellite data to explore how nature shapes human relations and vice versa (cf. items **2567** and **2610**). Notable are identifications of the role of cultural values and beliefs in the social construction of distinct "environmentalisms" that emerge as a result of complex interactions between global environmental values and local historical, political, and environmental factors (cf. item **2602**).

While sociology of religion has mostly disappeared from the Central American research agenda, studies of migration (both to the US and within the region) is a continued solid area of focus, with particular attention paid not only to socioeconomic impacts, but also to the comparative cultural and political implications of demographic change. Persistent interest in transnational social movement organization has fostered several fruitful studies on the transformation of peace and antiwar activism characteristic of the last decades of the 20th century to contemporary antiglobalization and trade-oriented struggles. In this area, several notable contributions analyze power dynamics between activists in the global North and South to assess the creation and growth of transnational movements (items **2587** and **2614**), while another analyzes civil society networks that are opposed to the Central American Free Trade Agreement (CAFTA) in El Salvador, identifying two kinds of opposition coalitions: "critic negotiators" and "transgressive resisters" (item **2606**).

I would like to thank Rachel Elfenbein for assistance with the annotated bibliography.

2552 Abuso sexual y prostitución infantil y juvenil en Costa Rica durante los siglos XIX y XX. Recopilación de Eugenia Rodríguez Sáenz. San José: Plumsock Mesoamerican Studies, 2005. 222 p.: bibl., ill.

Edited volume provides a panoramic, sociohistorical analysis of perceptions and sanctions of child prostitution and sexual abuse in Costa Rica since the 19th century. Part of a growing wave of research on gender and sexuality in Costa Rica.

2553 Afflitto, Frank M. and **Paul Jesilow.** The quiet revolutionaries: seeking justice in Guatemala. Austin: Univ. of Texas Press, 2007. 206 p.: bibl., index.

Long-term ethnographic research (1990–99) with 80 survivors of state-sanctioned violence analyzes how the ambiguous nature and psychological uncertainty of disappearances motivated family members to become politically organized. The authors examine perceptions of justice, mechanisms that enabled a common sense of purpose to be built amongst them in spite of their diverse backgrounds, and how experiences of seeking justice inspired the formation of nationalist political goals. Author argues that such "quiet revolutionaries" helped to construct a pluralistic national identity based on the common experience of being survivors of state-sanctioned violence.

2554 Aguilar, Jeannete *et al.* Maras y pandillas en Centroamérica. Vol. 4, Las respuestas de la sociedad civil organizada. Recopilación de José Miguel Cruz. San Salvador: Univ. Centroamericana, 2006. 450 p. (Col. Estructuras y Procesos. Serie Mayor; 28)

Vol. 4 of comprehensive and highly respected comparative study of street gangs and violence in El Salvador, Nicaragua, Honduras, and Guatemala. This volume focuses on civil society responses to this growing phenomenon on a country-by-country basis, analyzing the work of NGOs, social movements, and other civil society organizations. Excellent concluding chapter synthesizes analysis and recommends rehabilitation with widespread societal participation and attention to civil rights, rather than continued repression of street violence. For comment on vols. 1–3, see *HLAS 63:3486.*

2555 Alvarenga Venutolo, Patricia. De vecinos a ciudadanos: movimientos comunales y luchas cívicas en la historia contemporánea de Costa Rica. San José: Editorial de la Univ. de Costa Rica; Heredia, Costa Rica: Editorial de la Univ. Nacional, 2005. 320 p.: bibl.

Social history of community organizing in Costa Rica since the 1950s, concentrating on the evolution from neighborhood and civil struggles to the consolidation of patterns of identity and citizenship. Highlight is an analysis of growing women's political mobilization and participation in gaining key concessions in public and social service provision. Demonstrates the "defensive character" of Costa Rican social movements in struggles to protect social welfare.

2556 Artiga-González, Álvaro. Las migraciones como manifestación de la globalización. (*Realidad/San Salvador*, 108, abril/junio 2006, p. 165–220, bibl., tables)

Analyzes the political effects of migration in El Salvador and receiving countries over the past two decades, arguing that current migratory fluxes have taken on new identities and political agendas. Asserts that migration in the age of globalization poses a series of challenges to the state related to sovereignty and political representation, arguing for the extension of the vote to Salvadorans in the diaspora.

2557 Baires, Sonia and **Lilian Vega.** Pobreza, género y desarrollo en el posconflicto salvadoreño. (*ECA/San Salvador*, 60, 681/682, julio/agosto 2005, p. 613–629, bibl., photo, tables)

Study analyzes 2002–2003 census data on persistent socioeconomic gender gaps in El Salvador. Contends that poverty continues to be a fundamental barrier in achieving equitable gender development. The authors critique traditional poverty indicators for their gender neutrality and biases and argue instead for the development of non-quantitative indicators that acknowledge the complexities of gender differences and assess interrelated causal factors and conditions of the feminization of poverty.

2558 Berger, Susan A. Guatemaltecas: the women's movement, 1986–2003. Austin: Univ. of Texas Press, 2006. 157 p.: bibl., index.

Excellent study by long-term scholar of Guatemalan politics and society on the formation and practice of the Guatemalan women's movement between 1986 and 2003. Investigates how the women's movement and activists negotiated global restructuring, and notes the institutionalization/NGO-ization of the movement as it moved from protest to policy. Also discusses the redefinition of citizenship, femininity and sexuality, and gender equity and rights. Notable for careful acknowledgement of issues of ethnicity, class, and geographical location in the transformation of gender identities.

2559 Coloquio "La Transnacionalización de la Sociedad Centroamericana: Nuevos Retos Planteados a Partir de la Migración Internacional," San Salvador, 2004. La transnacionalización de la sociedad centroamericana: visiones a partir de la migración. San Salvador: FLACSO El Salvador, 2005. 156 p.: bibl., ill.

Edited volume derived from a FLACSO-Programa El Salvador colloquium examining socioeconomic, cultural, and political impacts of labor migration in Central America. Provides some comparative analysis of migration experiences across Central America, but focuses primarily on El Salvador.

2560 Cruz, José Miguel. Los factores asociados a las pandillas juveniles en Centroamérica. (*ECA/San Salvador*, 60:685/686, nov./dic. 2005, p. 1155–1182, bibl., photos, table)

Reviews the literature on social factors explaining the emergence of youth gangs in Central America and collects youth gang member testimonies to counteract popular myths and misconceptions about why youth join gangs. Using an ecological model, the author argues that the appearance and reproduction of youth gangs is the result of a historically constructed interaction of social conditions, political decisions, and concurrent events. Suggests that a recent turn towards organized crime has been driven largely by state responses to organized juvenile violence.

2561 Cupples, Julie. Between maternalism and feminism: women in Nicaragua's counter-revolutionary forces. (*Bull. Lat. Am. Res.*, 25:1, Jan. 2006, p. 83–103)

Life history research in Waslala, Nicaragua, in 1999 and 2001 leads to an examination of circumstances that led a group of women to become Contra supporters, exploring construction of gender identities in relation to Contra activism. Uses Foucauldian discourse analysis to contextualize the revolution and counter-revolution as arenas of cultural struggle in which women must negotiate both gender and political identities and illustrates how women's subjectivity as Contras is partial and in constant flux.

2562 Durini Cárdenas, Edgar. Pobreza y problemas sociales en Guatemala: apuntes básicos y elementos quantitativos para el estudio del problema de la pobreza en Guatemala. Guatemala: Impresos Ramírez, 2006. 117 p.: bibl., map.

University textbook prepared for a course on "Socio-economic problems" at the Univ. de San Carlos de Guatemala. Useful as a primer on current social and political elements of poverty in Guatemala as well as offering useful tables of quantitative indicators based on recent census data.

2563 Gaborit, Mauricio. Los círculos de la violencia: sociedad excluyente y pandillas. (*ECA/San Salvador*, 60:685/686, nov./dic. 2005, p. 1145–1154, bibl., photo, table)

Contends that youth gangs have emerged in Central America as a result of exclusion on macro-structural and micro-structural levels, thus forming a vicious cycle in which youth are both victims and perpetrators of violence. Argues that breaking this cycle of violence requires state policies informed by research and based on the rights of youth to inclusion in cultural, educational, social, and economic life.

2564 Gaborit, Mauricio. Memoria histórica: revertir la historia desde las víctimas. (*ECA/San Salvador*, 61:693/694, julio/agosto 2006, p. 663–684, bibl., tables)

Comparative analysis of truth commission inquires in Latin America challenges official conflict histories using a victim-oriented perspective. Author constructs his argument regarding state obligations to provide social reparations and public commemorations emanating from victims' basic right to truth, which would reconstruct social relations damaged by the exclusion of certain victims from official history. Calls for a historicized praxis that elucidates truth from the point of view of victims, brings about justice, and provides space for the critical construction of a utopian ideological future.

2565 García, Sandra G. *et al*. Emergency contraception in Honduras: knowledge, attitudes, and practice among urban family planning clients. (*Stud. Fam. Plan.*, 37:3, Sept. 2006, p. 187–196, bibl.)

Multivariate analysis of pre- and post-intervention cross-sectional surveys from 2001-03 of 2,693 family planning clinic clients in two urban centers in Honduras assesses knowledge, attitudes, and practices of emergency contraception before and after outreach education. Respondents generally demonstrated a positive attitude toward and low rates of concern about emergency contraception.

2566 Gareau, Brian J. Class consciousness or natural consciousness?: socionatural relations and the potential for social change; suggestions from development in southern Honduras. (*Rethinking Marx.*, 20:1, Jan. 2008, p. 120–141, bibl., graphs, tables)

Innovative look at how nature shapes human relations, through class and political economic analysis of Honduran post-hurricane agrarian development case study. Proposes the idea of "socio-naturally determined classes" in which individual decisions are based on perceptions of situation, interests, and material conditions.

2567 Gareau, Brian J. Ecological values amid local interests: natural resource conservation, social differentiation, and human survival in Honduras. (*Rur. Sociol.*, 72:2, June 2007, p. 244–268, bibl., tables)

Qualitative survey and case study research with local residents in the Cerro Guanacuare protected area in southern Honduras demonstrates a disconnect between residents' understanding about natural space and the imposition of external natural resource management schemes that fail to acknowledge local conditions of social differentiation and power. Advocates increased local involvement in conservation initiatives.

2568 Guadarrama, Rocío. Identidades, resistencia y conflicto en las cadenas globales: las trabajadoras de la industria maquiladora de la confección en Costa Rica. (*Desacatos*, 21, mayo/agosto 2006, p. 67–82, bibl., photos)

Case study of the ambivalence experienced by 13 Costa Rican female maquiladora workers in regard to their reproductive work and engagement in paid productive labor, focusing on the family and solidarity networks that facilitate participation in both forms of work. Concludes that women engage in a double process of constructing their identity and subjectivity as women and as workers. Social networks reproduce patriarchal constraints but also create opportunities for women's resistance.

2569 Hale, Charles R. Más que un Indio = More than an Indian: racial ambivalence and neoliberal multiculturalism in Guatemala. Santa Fe, N.M.: School of American Research Press, 2006. 292 p.: bibl., ill., index.

Mixed-methods study carried out intermittently from 1994 to 2000 explores the paradox of "neoliberal multiculturalism" in Guatemala through an analysis of the words and actions of provincial ladinos who express racial ambivalence toward indigenous culture. Author argues that important spaces for indigenous empowerment have opened while simultaneously reproducing Guatemala's racial hierarchy. Volume highlights the contradictions of antiracist politics and the limits of multiculturalism in Guatemala.

2570 Horton, Lynn. Grassroots struggles for sustainability in Central America. Boulder: Univ. Press of Colorado, 2007. 215 p.: bibl., ill., index, maps.

Rigorous comparative ethnographic study on discourses and practices of environmental sustainability in three rural and indigenous communities in Nicaragua, Costa Rica, and Panama identifies the terrain of struggle over the meaning of sustainability. Welcome demonstration of how communities challenge sustainability as a dominant ideological project, while creating multiple pathways that enable both grassroots livelihoods provision and environmental conservation.

2571 Hume, Mo. "(Young) men with big guns": reflexive encounters with violence and youth in El Salvador. (*Bull. Lat. Am. Res.*, 26:4, Oct. 2007, p. 480–496)

Methodological article discusses shifting subjectivity, reflexivity, and positionality in fieldwork in San Salvador from 2000 to 2007. Provides a critical reflection on the research process in which insecurity, violence, and fear mark both the substance of the research and the gendered analytical process. Discusses how the author and the participants construct notions of danger and fear related to youth gangs on an everyday basis.

2572 Jos, Joseph. Guadeloupéens et Martiniquais au canal de Panama: histoire d'une émigration. Paris: Harmattan, 2004. 260 p.: bibl., ill., maps.

The author investigates migratory paths, strategies, and relationships of thousands of workers from Guadeloupe and Martinique who participated in the creation of the Panama Canal. Careful attention is paid to difficulties faced by West Indian workers, differences between Anglophone and Francophone Caribbean workforces, and the different receptions that these two groups received within Panama. Also studies the effects of acculturation within Panama upon workers from Martinique and Guadeloupe and their descendants. [J.F. Higbee]

2573 León, Federico R. *et al.* Providers' compliance with the balanced counseling strategy in Guatemala. (*Stud. Fam. Plan.*, 36:3, Sept. 2005, p. 117–126, bibl., graphs, ill., tables)

Experimental quantitative study in two clinics (one Mayan and one Ladino) of Guatemala assessing counseling and family planning. The research rejects a linear decision-making model of family planning counseling in favor of providing visual, verbal, and literary information to patients based on the contraceptive methods they choose.

2574 Lindstrom, David P. and **Elisa Muñoz-Franco.** Migration and the diffusion of modern contraceptive knowledge and use in rural Guatemala. (*Stud. Fam. Plan.*, 36:4, Dec. 2005, p. 277–288, bibl., tables)

Uses social network theory and secondary statistical data analysis from the 1995 Guatemalan Survey of Family Health to explore the impact of out-migration on modern contraceptive knowledge and use in rural Guatemala. Personal, familial, and community experiences of urban and international migration are associated with greater contraceptive knowledge and greater likelihood of modern contraceptive use among married women. Interestingly, the authors also find that social networks have a greater influence on modern contraceptive knowledge and use than family planning services.

2575 Lundgren, Rebecka Inga *et al.* Cultivating men's interest in family planning in rural El Salvador. (*Stud. Fam. Plan.*, 36:2, June 2005, p. 173–188, bibl., tables)

Community-based household survey in 13 rural villages in El Salvador assesses pilot project integrating family planning into resource management and community development. Authors find the integration of water and sanitation and family planning projects is both feasible and beneficial, finding significant changes in contraceptive knowledge, attitudes, and behavior amongst both female and male participants. Study demonstrates the power of informal networks for diffusion of family planning information amongst men.

2576 Martel Trigueros, Roxana. Las maras salvadoreñas: nuevas formas de espanto y control social. (*ECA/San Salvador*, 61:696, oct. 2006, p. 957–997, bibl., graph, photos, tables)

Foucauldian discourse analysis linking gang activity with historical events in El Salvador argues that colonization, military repression, and civil war have constructed an authoritarian culture anchored in fear. Essay reflects upon a systematic presence of violence in political, institutional, academic, and media discourses on gangs that dehumanizes gang members, obscures institutional violence and white-collar crimes, and thereby secures the existing order of hegemonic socioeconomic relations.

2577 Midré, Georges. Opresión, espacio para actuar y conciencia crítica: líderes indígenas y percepción de la pobreza en Guatemala. Guatemala: Instituto de Estudios Interétnicos, Univ. de San Carlos, 2005. 196 p.: bibl.

In Spanish translation, Norwegian sociologist analyzes the social construction of poverty through discourse analysis and grounded theory analysis of semi-structured interviews with 32 indigenous leaders. Study is critical of traditional measures and analyses of poverty, and rather than focusing strictly on material resources, Midré examines moral and emotional poverty and critical consciousness as equally important aspects of quality of life.

2578 Montalvo H., Patricia L. Recuperación de la memoria histórica: actitudes de la población salvadoreña. (*ECA/San Salvador*, 61:693/694, julio/agosto 2006, p. 685–700, bibl., graphs, tables)

Quantitative study carried out in 2004 in three different regions in El Salvador on attitudes and memories of the war period measures level of exposure to the armed conflict and stage of development of the individual when the conflict occurred. Study found that psychological distancing attitudes were greater for older respondents who were less likely to discuss the war with their children. Poses a theoretical framework about memory as the interplay of social, collective, and subjective forces, suggesting that respondents' different memories of the war are due to desires to maintain an equilibrium between traumatic experiences.

2579 Montoya, Aquiles. Relaciones de poder en la sociedad salvadoreña. (*ECA/San Salvador*, 61:695, sept. 2006, p. 869–881)

Theoretical essay uses a case study of El Salvador to contend that seizing power to transform society requires not only political power, but also other interrelated—particularly economic—forms of power. Analyzes the possible structures of an "economy of solidarity" that prioritizes basic needs of community members rather than seizing state power.

2580 Morales Gamboa, Abelardo and **Carlos Castro Valverde.** Migración, empleo y pobreza. San José: FLACSO Costa Rica, 2006. 274 p.: bibl., ill., maps.

Reports on a new phase of the continuing FLACSO-Costa Rica study of Nicaraguan immigrants to Costa Rica focusing on labor dynamics and impacts on poverty

in the context of broader migratory fluxes in Central America. Heavily based on 2000 census data, with some additional household interviews. Good analysis of the cultural and economic effects of changing labor pools, including labor market differentiation and gendered and ethnic differences in wage levels, health status, and the satisfaction of basic needs.

2581 Mujer y mercado laboral El Salvador, 2006. San Salvador: Fundación Nacional para el Desarrollo: Organización de Mujeres Salvadoreñas por la Paz, 2006. 223 p.: ill.

Comprehensive edited collection analyzing women and socially excluded workers in the labor market in El Salvador. Topics include self-employment, maquilas, domestic and service labor, and migration. The section on socially excluded laborers (sex workers, workers with HIV/AIDS, indigenous and gay/lesbian workers) is especially useful. Introductory chapters summarize current census data on labor and employment in El Salvador.

2582 Mujeres y prisión—: su tránsito conflictivo en la justicia penal. Coordinación de Lucía Morán. Equipo de investigación, Delmi Arriaza *et al.* Guatemala: ICCPG, 2004. 139 p.: bibl.

Innovative NGO-sponsored qualitative study of incarcerated women in Guatemala analyzes human rights abuses, gender, and the penal system. Volume concludes with well-reasoned recommendations for improving women's rights in Guatemala's penal and judicial systems.

2583 Nasi, Carlo. Cuando callan los fusiles: impacto de la paz negociada en Colombia y en Centroamérica. Bogotá: Grupo Editorial Norma: CESO, Ciencia Política, Univ. de los Andes, 2007. 347 p.: bibl., ill. (Col. Vitral)

Rigorous comparative study of implementation processes and outcomes of peace negotiations in Colombia, El Salvador, Nicaragua, and Guatemala. Analyzes structural changes produced by peace accords, concentrating on transformations in patterns of violence and democratic representation. Concludes that, despite the distinct trajectories of each peace process, successful peace accord negotiations produced common effects across countries including the reduction of violence and the facilitation of more open political systems.

2584 Oettler, Anika. Encounters with history: dealing with the "present past" in Guatemala. (*Rev. Eur. Estud. Latinoam. Caribe*, 81, Oct. 2006, p. 3–19, bibl.)

Essay applies "'communities of memory" concept to the Guatemalan truth commission experience, rejecting the idea of a single national subject dealing with the trauma of its past. Discusses the effect of truth commissions on national politics, individuals, and collective memory, and describes how primarily civil society actors, rather than state institutions, provided the context for truth telling and trauma work to occur in Guatemala. Concludes that commemorating the past is a constantly shifting process, emerging as a result of the complex interplay of unstable power relations.

2585 Ortega Hegg, Manuel; Malene Nissen Daza; and Marcelina Castillo Venerio. Diversidad, identidades y relaciones interétnicas en Nicaragua: la Costa Caribe y el Pacífico: conocimientos y percepciones interregionales. Managua: Univ. Centroamericana, 2006. 126 p.: bibl. (Cuadernos de investigación; 22. Col. Humanidades)

Comparative mixed-methods study on regional and ethnic identities in Nicaragua, including analysis of inter-regional identity conflicts, particularly between the Caribbean Autonomous regions and residents of the Pacific Coast. Based on 1,850 surveys, in addition to focus groups and in-depth interviews, shows how local and national identity constructions are related. Includes proposals to increase understanding of multi-ethnic diversity in Nicaragua.

2586 Peláez, Ana Victoria and Miguel A. Ugalde. ¿Cómo afectan las migraciones internacionales a la familia?: avances sobre estudios de caso en Guatemala. (*ECA/San Salvador*, 62:699/700, enero/feb. 2007, p. 89–120, bibl., graphs, tables)

Case study and grounded theory analysis of distinct impacts and microsocial processes of international immigration on 47 Guatemalan families in two Guatemalan municipalities from 2005 to 2006. Examines local causes of family member migration to the US (often due to debt) and its impacts

on family structure and integration, on the roles of women who stay, and on community and indigenous Maya cultures.

2587 Perla, Héctor. Si Nicaragua venció, El Salvador vencerá: Central American agency in the creation of the U.S.-Central American Peace and Solidarity Movement. (*LARR*, 43:2, 2008, p. 136–158, bibl.)

Article critiques past explanations of the emergence of the Central American Peace and Solidarity Movement in the 1970s and 1980s for neglecting the agency of Central America. Documents how Nicaraguans and Salvadorans played crucial roles in the transnational movement's creation, growth, and success, and develops a theoretical framework of "single flare strategy of transnational activism" by which subaltern populations use transnational substate actors to constrain foreign policy.

2588 Pfeffer, Max John et al. Population, conservation, and land use change in Honduras. (*Agric. Ecosystems Environ.*, 110:1/2, 2005, p. 14–28, bibl., graphs, maps, tables)

Analyzes the relationship between population change and agricultural intensification to understand the impacts of contemporary conservation policies on society. Mixed-method approach includes 600 household surveys and an analysis of satellite land-use data.

2589 Pfeffer, Max John; John W. Schelhas; and Catherine Meola. Environmental globalization, organizational form, and expected benefits from protected areas in Central America. (*Rur. Sociol.*, 71:3, Sept. 2006, p. 429–450, bibl., graph, map, tables)

Mixed-methods study uses interview and survey data to analyze resident perceptions of benefits from national park designation in Costa Rica and Honduras. Assesses efforts to adapt globally oriented conservation models (e.g., park designations as exclusionary or zoned) to local conditions.

2590 Pine, Adrienne. Working hard, drinking hard: on violence and survival in Honduras. Berkeley: Univ. of California Press, 2008. 253 p.: bibl., index.

Ethnography carried out from 1997–2003 analyzing the interconnection of violence, alcohol use, and the export processing industry to examine how identity, subjectivity, and daily relationships amongst Hondurans are mediated through processes of production and consumption, in the shadow of US hegemony and neoliberal globalization. Argues that processes of identity formation are shaped by a context of perpetual structural and symbolic violence.

2591 Porras, Ana Elena. Cultura de la interoceanidad: narrativas de identidad nacional de Panamá, 1990–2002. Panamá: Editorial Universitaria Carlos Manuel Gasteazoro, 2005. 309 p.: bibl.

Extended ethnographic and archival inquiry into historical and contemporary aspects of national identity in Panama. Offers an insightfully postmodern perspective on mentalities, customs, and ideologies, and summarizes a series of metaphorical "narrative identities" in Panama from "Banana Republic" to "Bridge of the World" to "Sovereignty Panama." Worthwhile investigation into tensions and resolutions of competing cultural processes that inform national identities.

2592 Ramsay, Paulette A. Soy una Feminista Negra': Shirley Campbell's feminist/womanist agenda. (*Lat. Am. Caribb. Ethn. Stud.*, 2:1, April 2007, p. 51–68)

Essay analyzes Shirley Campbell's redefinition of herself, as an Afro-Costa Rican woman of West Indian descent, in her poetry as marking an intersection of sexual, racial, and cultural politics. The author argues that while Campbell occupies a broad feminist position, she also undertakes a complex process and exercise of power, which the author identifies as a "feminist/womanist" agenda. Explores the importance of the experiences of multiple and intersecting forms of oppression that Afro-Hispanic women face in the struggle for agency and self-empowerment.

2593 Reguillo Cruz, Rossana. La mara: contingencia y afiliación con el exceso. (*Nueva Soc.*, 200, nov./dic. 2005, p. 70–84, bibl., ill.)

Document analysis of 500 press articles critiques the dominant discourse on youth gangs for being simplistic and historically and politically decontextualized. Argues that the emergence and extension of youth gangs throughout Central America

is, in large part, a result of and reaction to the absence of socioeconomic supports and stability precipitated by the neoliberal economic framework imposed on the region in the 1980s and 1990s, so that gangs came to be "parallel legal" alternatives for socialization and belonging for youth who were disenfranchised by neoliberalism.

2594 Rocha Gómez, José Luis. Mapping the labyrinth from within: the political economy of Nicaraguan youth policy concerning violence. (*Bull. Lat. Am. Res.*, 26:4, Oct. 2007, p. 533–549)

Exegesis of methodological issues with extensive (1999–2003) field research that mapped interactions of two main organizations dealing with youth violence in Nicaragua. Analyzes political interference from incongruent interest groups and discourses. Participant observation facilitated understanding institutional and organizational labyrinths, while Jürgen Habermas' theory of "legitimization" reveals a constitution of dynamics of Nicaraguan state practices around youth violence.

2595 Rodgers, Dennis. Joining the gang and becoming a *broder*: the violence of ethnography in contemporary Nicaragua. (*Bull. Lat. Am. Res.*, 26:4, Oct. 2007, p. 444–461)

Methodological analysis of doctoral fieldwork from 1996–97 in Managua which involved initiation into an urban youth gang. Author uses concrete practical, ethical, and epistemological dimensions of his research to discuss the "violence" of an ethnographic process in research settings imbued with chronic violence. Drawing on these experiences, the author argues that whether violence is a moral or an immoral act is not the issue; rather, the situational reasoning behind its deployment should be the focus of the investigation.

2596 Rodgers, Dennis. Living in the shadow of death: gangs, violence and social order in urban Nicaragua, 1996–2002. (*J. Lat. Am. Stud.*, 38:2, May 2006, p. 267–292)

Longitudinal ethnographic research in Managua from 1996–97 and in 2002 explores the transformation of youth gangs to challenge dominant discourse that gangs are anarchic. Contends that contemporary gangs are coherent modes of social structuration in the face of wider processes of state and social breakdown. Discusses the evolution of gang violence from collective social violence to a more individually and economically motivated type of violence tied to local drug trafficking and abuse. Notes the "social death" of traditional institutions of social solidarity in contemporary Nicaragua.

2597 Rodriguez, Leila and Jeffrey H. Cohen.
Generations and motivations: Russian and other former Soviet immigrants in Costa Rica. (*Int. Migr./Oxford,* 43:4, 2005, p. 147–165, bibl., tables)

Ethnographic survey conducted in 2003 examines social networks in the migration and settlement processes of Russian and other former Soviet immigrants to Costa Rica, critiquing traditional theories of migration that assume the centrality of migrant networks. The authors find significant differences in the form and function of social networks between immigrants who arrived before and after the fall of the Soviet Union, and that the period of arrival of Russian immigrants is more important in defining social networks than a common background and a shared cultural identity.

2598 Rubio, Mauricio. De la pandilla a la mara: pobreza, educación, mujeres y violencia juvenil. Bogotá: Univ. Externado de Colombia, 2007. 579 p.: bibl., ill., indexes.

Summary of Inter-American Development Bank consultancy reports on citizen security programs in Honduras, Nicaragua, and Panama. Discusses the phenomenon of "internationalization of gang violence," from a localized problem to one of international public order. Analyzes the change from "youth" to adult violence, identifies common mechanisms for youth recruitment and retention, and describes the evolution from a phenomenon the author characterizes as "neighborhood gangs" (pandillas) to a "criminal organization" (maras). Includes two final chapters of policy implications, including a critique of "economic strategies" in favor of social programs for at-risk youth.

2599 Sánchez Saavedra, Kevin Evandro.
Migración transfronteriza indígena en Darién, Panamá. (*ECA/San Salvador,* 62:699/700, enero/feb. 2007, p. 63–88, graph, map, photo)

Mixed-methods study with indigenous men on the Panama-Colombia border in 2005. Using a transnational circuit theoretical framework, study argues that cross-border migration of indigenous people between Chocó, Colombia and Darién, Panama in the last 20 years is more a result of the Colombian armed conflict and drug trafficking, environmental destruction, social exclusion, and extreme poverty than a cultural migratory practice. For economist's comment, see item **727.**

2600 Santacruz Giralt, María. Creciendo en El Salvador: una mirada a la situación de la adolescencia y juventud en el país. (*ECA/San Salvador,* 60:685/686, nov./dic. 2005, p. 1079–1099, bibl., graphs, photo, tables)

Analyzes 2003–2004 census data on economic, educational, public health, violence, unemployment, and political participation rates of Salvadoran youth to contextualize the situation of adolescents and youth, showing conditions of vulnerability and social exclusion. Author argues that sufficient and integrated efforts are lacking to address the multiple needs of El Salvador's majority youth population.

2601 Savenije, Wim and María Antonieta Beltrán. Compitiendo en bravuras: violencia estudiantil en el Área Metropolitana de San Salvador. San Salvador: FLACSO El Salvador, 2005. 269 p.: bibl., ill. (chiefly col.).

In-depth FLACSO study focusing on student rivalries, school violence, and adolescent identity construction in San Salvador's Area Metropolitana. Based on quantitative, qualitative, and participatory methodologies in 12 public and private schools, study identifies deficiencies in family and community structure, institutions, and public policies, and argues that student violence has links to, but must be classified as separate phenomenon from, gang violence. Also notes the increasing influence of a "street subculture" in the educational system. Includes recommendations for educational reform.

2602 Schelhas, John and Max J. Pfeffer.
Forest values of national park neighbors in Costa Rica. (*Hum. Organ.,* 64:4, Winter 2005, p. 386–398, bibl.)

Qualitative analysis of in-depth interviews with residents adjacent to Parque Internacional La Amistad in Costa Rica analyzes forest-related mental and cultural models, beliefs, and values, demonstrating that distinct "environmentalisms" are socially constructed through complex interactions between global environmental values and local historical, political, and environmental factors.

Schelhas, John and **Max John Pfeffer.** Saving forests, protecting people?: environmental conservation in Central America. See item **996.**

2603 Shiffman, Jeremy and **Ana Lucía Garcés Del Valle.** Political history and disparities in safe motherhood between Guatemala and Honduras. (*Popul. Dev. Rev.*, 32:1, March 2006, p. 53–80, bibl., tables)

Mixed-method study critiques past studies of safe motherhood in developing countries for ignoring historical and structural elements that may shape maternal mortality levels and interventions. Uses political history and social structure to explain cross-country variation in maternal mortality rates between Guatemala and Honduras, finding that, in these cases, geopolitical stability contributes more to safe motherhood than economic development does. The authors argue for complementing quantitative examinations of health services and demographic data with an analysis of history and social structure.

2604 Siu, Lok C.D. Memories of a future home: diasporic citizenship of Chinese in Panama. Stanford, Calif.: Stanford Univ. Press, 2005. 247 p.: bibl., ill., index, 1 map.

Ethnography and life narrative analysis from 1994–2000 on the diasporic Chinese experience of belonging in Panama as people forge transnational forms of community through migration and displacement amid shifting geopolitical relations and conditions of globalization. The book illustrates the manner in which the homeland state and diasporic Chinese sustain multilayered relations through mutual support and exchange, while Chinese citizenship is simultaneously challenged and transformed through these experiences.

2605 Soriano Hernández, Silvia. La organización de las mujeres a partir de la guerra: El Salvador y Nicaragua. (*Cuad. Am./México*, 2:120, abril/junio 2007, p. 189–204, bibl.)

Historical sociological article analyzes how and why women in Nicaragua and El Salvador participated in revolutionary armies, finding that women engaged in warfare to bring about changes in social relations, open political spaces, and improve living conditions, and notes a postwar emergence of new discourses on gender. As the wars progressed, women's political participation became more militant, breaking from the predominant feminine role, ideology, and practices, causing changes in identity and the ways in which women were perceived by male comrades.

2606 Spalding, Rose J. Civil society engagement in trade negotiations: CAFTA opposition movements in El Salvador. (*Lat. Am. Polit. Soc.*, 49:4, Winter 2007, p. 85–114, appendix, bibl., tables)

Analyzes civil society networks opposing the Central American Free Trade Agreement (CAFTA) in El Salvador to identify two kinds of opposition coalitions: "critic negotiators" and "transgressive resisters." Social movement theory and a mixed-method approach explores coalition resource mobilization, the role of movement entrepreneurs, strategic decision-making, mechanisms linking local and transnational activists, and the dynamics of intramovement competition.

2607 Sprenkels, Ralph. The price of peace: the human rights movement in postwar El Salvador. Amsterdam: Centre for Latin American Studies and Documentation, 2005. 120 p. (Cuadernos del CEDLA; 19)

Ethnographic testimonials document transformations in grassroots political identities from the 1970s to the late 1990s in El Salvador. Argues that the Salvadoran human rights movement was paralyzed by an implicit pact of impunity between the government and the FMLN, in which both political parties agreed to erase the truth of the past as the "price of peace," and that the employment of strategic essentialist identity politics limits the power of social movements and discusses the contradictory impacts of democratic transitions on social movements.

2608 Stølen, Kristi Anne. Guatemalans in the aftermath of violence: the refugees' return. Philadelphia: Univ. of Pennsylvania Press, 2007. 236 p.: bibl., index, maps. (The ethnography of political violence)

In-depth longitudinal study of the dynamics of community building and identity formation among returned exiles in Ixcán and Petén. Focuses on the interplay of migration, violence, and the establishment of new gender roles. General review of historic violence in Guatemala and refugee camp survival in Mexico is followed by a thoughtful analysis of new ways of "being indigenous" in relation to gender roles and relationships with the state.

2609 Trujillo, Silvia; Patricia Borrayo; and Wendy Santa Cruz. Espejos rotos: la intrincada relación de las mujeres y el periodismo impreso. Guatemala: FLACSO, Sede Académica Guatemala, 2006. 248 p.: bibl., ill.

Excellent qualitative study of gender and media in Guatemala, based on in-depth interviews and focus groups with women reporters and columnists from Guatemala's six major periodicals, as well as text-based content analysis of *El Periódico, Prensa Libre,* and *Nuestro Diario.* Analyzes women's role as media workers and the space given to "women's issues" in major periodicals, as well as general media representations of women. Concludes that women now have a greater role in media production, but are underrepresented in terms of salary and decision-making, and that sexist language prevails in media portrayals of women, while indigenous women are almost entirely ignored.

2610 Tucker, Catherine M. Changing forests: collective action, common property, and coffee in Honduras. Berlin: Springer, 2008. 258 p.: bibl., ill., maps.

Well-done study based on repeated visits over 15 years to La Campa, Honduras, involving participant observation, interviews, and analysis of land-use data. Author explores the complex relationships between people and natural resources through an analysis of social and forest transformations over several decades. Examines the impacts of market integration and globalization on communitarian traditions (communal labor, social solidarity, and common-pool resources), which include the privatization of communal land and other changes in community collective action.

2611 Vega, Lilian. Migraciones y dinámicas locales: diferentes dinámicas locales generadas por la migración en la región de los Nonualcos. (*ECA/San Salvador,* 61:690, abril 2006, p. 393–407, bibl., table)

Mixed-method study in eight different municipalities in the Nonualcos region of El Salvador provides a comparative analysis of economic and cultural aspects of out-migration on the region. Municipalities with similar economic and cultural conditions react differently to migration and conflicting discourses and identities around emigration exist in the region. Interestingly, the study finds that municipalities with more commercial activity are more likely to experience out-migration because money earned from migration assists in the establishment of local business and dynamizes the local economy but does not necessarily create enough employment to meet the regional labor market.

2612 Violencia contra las mujeres: tratamiento por parte de la injusticia penal de Guatemala. Coordinación de Andrea Diez. Subcoordinación de Kenia Herrera. Guatemala: Instituto de Estudios Comparados en Ciencias Penales de Guatemala, 2005. 148 p.: bibl. (Ediciones del Instituto)

Based on surveys and interviews conducted in 2003–2004, this study examines the impact of the reform of the Penal Code in Guatemala on violence against women (particularly sexual and domestic violence). Notes that while some advances have been made in terms of the creation of agencies dedicated to women's assistance, the penal system itself still fails to address adequately crimes against women.

2613 Walker, Lee Demetrius. Gender and attitudes toward justice system bias in Central America. (*LARR,* 43:2, 2008, p. 80–106, bibl., graphs, table)

Secondary statistical analysis of the 2003 Latinobarómetro analyzes gender differences in attitudes toward the performance of the criminal justice system in Costa Rica, El Salvador, and Nicaragua. Women are significantly more likely to believe that the justice system provides unequal treatment before the law than are men, perceiving unequal treatment to be due to women's subordinate socioeconomic position in these societies. Gendered attitudes are explained by a conflict model of criminal justice that links criminal justice processes to dominant economic and political interests.

2614 Weber, Clare. Visions of solidarity: U.S. peace activists in Nicaragua from war to women's activism and globalization. Lanham, Md.: Lexington Books, 2006. 153 p.: bibl., index.

Comparative feminist institutional ethnographic study carried out from 1997–98 by a US solidarity activist and sociologist analyzes responses by two US peace and social justice organizations to US-sponsored neoliberal development projects in Nicaragua. Discusses the transformation of peace activism from an antiwar struggle to an antiglobalization struggle; explores the power dynamics between activists in the global North and South; examines efforts at reframing issues of social justice over time; and highlights transnational feminist politics and agency at the local level.

THE CARIBBEAN AND THE GUIANAS

Alonso Tejada, Aurelio. El laberinto tras la caída del muro. See item **2239**.

2615 Beyond borders: cross-culturalism and the Caribbean canon. Edited by Jennifer Rahim and Barbara Lalla. Kingston: Univ. of the West Indies Press, 2009. 267 p.: ill.

The book is a collection of essays that explores cross-cultural themes and issues across a range of disciplines including literature, language, education, history and popular culture. [C.E. Griffin]

2616 Bridging the gaps: faith-based organizations, neoliberalism, and development in Latin America and the Caribbean. Edited by Tara Hefferan, Julie Adkins, and Laurie Occhipinti. Lanham, Md.: Lexington Books, 2009. 238 p.: bibl., index.

This work explores the various ways that faith-based organizations attempt to mend the fissures and mitigate the effects of neoliberal capitalism and development practices on the poor and powerless. Empirical case studies attempt to explain the meaning of "faith-based" development, evaluate faith-based versus secular approaches and the influence of faith-orientation on program formulation and delivery, and examine faith-based organizations' impacts on structural inequality and poverty alleviation. [C.E. Griffin]

2617 Caribbean perspectives on African history and culture. Edited by Richard Goodridge. St. Michael, Barbados: Dept.

of History and Philosophy, Univ. of the West Indies, Cave Hill Campus, 2004. 200 p.: bibl.

Presents research on Africa and African Diaspora Studies from the Univ. of the West Indies. Chapter one touches upon Afro-Asian Studies in the Dept. of History, St. Augustine Campus, Trinidad. [J.F. Higbee]

2618 CARICOM: single market and economy: genesis and prognosis. Edited by Kenneth O. Hall and Myrtle Chuck-A-Sang. Kingston: Ian Randle Publishers, 2007. 535 p.: ill.

Illuminating beyond its textual material, this book presents cover and contents divided by gender. Introductory matter touts this approach. Authorship is promoted as male ("traditional Caribbean, male predominant style") and female ("eminent academics of the feminine gender"). Men discuss CSME, governance, key factors, mechanisms, support needs, and the way forward. They are, ironically, concerned with "avoiding marginalization in the world." Women wrote one section only: "CSME: Putting Gender on the Agenda." Their topics and this book reflect an urgent need to do just that. The women address issues which include Caribbean sex trafficking with a reference to tourism, women's unequal position in the Caribbean labor market, and HIV/AIDS. [J.F. Higbee]

Changes in Cuban society since the nineties. See item **1582**.

Clarke, Colin G. Politics, violence and drugs in Kingston, Jamaica. See item **1566**.

Cultural identity and creolization in national unity: the multiethnic Caribbean. See item **1546**.

2619 **Guadeloupe, Francio.** Chanting down the new Jerusalem: calypso, Christianity, and capitalism in the Caribbean. Berkeley: Univ. of California Press, 2009. 255 p.: bibl., ill., index. (The anthropology of Christianity; 4)

This book probes the ethos and attitude created by radio disc jockeys on the binational Caribbean island of Saint Martin/Sint Maarten by examining the intersection of Christianity, calypso, and capitalism, and showing how a multiethnic and multireligious island nation, where livelihoods depend on tourism, has managed to encourage all social classes to transcend their ethnic and religious differences. [C.E. Griffin]

2620 **HIV-AIDS and social work practice in the Caribbean: theories, issues and innovation, Jamaica.** Jamaica: Ian Randle Publishers, 2009. 248 p.: bibl., index.

Using Trinidad and Tobago as a case study, this book demonstrates how social workers, working alongside heath care professionals, can contribute to the multidisciplinary intervention in the fight against HIV-AIDS in the Caribbean using the lived experiences of person affected by HIV-AIDS. [C.E. Griffin]

2621 **Muturi, Nancy** and **Patricia Donald.** Violence against women in the Caribbean: an intervention and lessons learned from Jamaica. (*Caribb. Q./Mona*, 52:2/3, June/Sept. 2006, p. 83–103, bibl.)

This paper describes the interagency campaign implemented in the Caribbean in 1998 that specifically addressed violence against women and girls, and documents the lessons learned, key findings of the intervention, as well as some implications. [C.E. Griffin]

2622 **Oliver, M. Cynthia.** Queen of the Virgins: pageantry and black womanhood in the Caribbean. Jackson: Univ. Press of Mississippi, 2009. 182 p., 8 p. of plates: bibl., ill., index. (Caribbean studies series)

This book maps the trajectory of pageantry in the Virgin Islands from its colonial precursors at tea meetings, dance dramas, and street festival parades to its current incarnation as the beauty pageant or "queen show," and uses pageantry as a lens through which to view the region's understanding of gender, race, sexuality, class, and colonial power. [C.E. Griffin]

2623 **Our Caribbean: a gathering of lesbian and gay writing from the Antilles.** Edited and with an introduction by Thomas Glave. Durham, N.C.: Duke Univ. Press, 2008. 405 p.: bibl.

This book is an anthology of lesbian and gay writings from across the Antilles reflecting and resulting in an unprecedented literary conversation on gay, lesbian, bisexual, and transgendered experiences throughout the Caribbean and its far-flung diaspora. [C.E. Griffin]

San Miguel, Pedro Luis. La guerra silenciosa: las luchas sociales en la ruralía dominicana. See *HLAS 64:1126*.

ECUADOR

JASON PRIBILSKY, *Associate Professor of Anthropology, Whitman College*

THE LAST 20 YEARS IN ECUADOR have been characterized by two seemingly different social currents. On the one hand, the country is in the midst of a diaspora; by most estimates, fully 10 percent of the country's population lives in the exterior, mainly Spain and the US. Despite the global security effects of September 11, 2001, out-migration continues largely unclipped, fueled by Ecuador's chronic poverty, under- and unemployment, and a languishing agricultural sector. On the other hand, Ecuador has seen an intensification of civil society participation and a move toward greater *inclusion* of once marginalized groups and constituencies. In late 2008, voters approved one of the most progressive constitutions in the world, including provisions to uphold *sumak kawsay,* an indigenous concept meaning "living well" which stipulates harmonious relationships between people, their immediate surroundings, and the environment. While the project of democracy has been far from perfect, and in no short supply of critics, there is little disputing the extreme importance of new democratic pulses.

Several themes related to these social currents show up during this review period. In addition to the steady coverage of migration, researchers have committed themselves to addressing issues of gender, Afro-Ecuadorian political engagement, and the conditions facing communities along the country's northern border with Colombia. Studies focused on bedrock issues such as poverty and health inequality also continue to shape the research agendas of both individual researchers and NGOs and aid groups (items **2627** and **2635**).

Since the election of President Rafael Correa in late 2006, issues surrounding international migration began to receive a public face and were accorded governmental acknowledgement. Correa named a coordinator of migration issues and drafted a "migration policy." Among its most ambitious positions, the policy proposed changing the constitution to grant Ecuadorians living overseas proportional representation in Congress. Previously in 2005, Ecuadorians living overseas were allowed to vote in presidential elections. During the presidential election of 2006, just over 84,000 Ecuadorians (living in 42 countries) cast their votes from afar. In short, there has been an official recognition of transnational migration politics and a greater recognition of the role migration and migrants abroad play in Ecuador's political and economic life. The political will to "bring migration back home" is reflected in a number of new studies. The productive use and potential of remittances in particular (items **2625, 2628, 2632,** and **2634**) has proven to be a major interest of a number of researchers. The new lexicon of migration studies focuses on the NGO-directed programs of *"codesarrollo"* (item **2624**), which look beyond remittance figures to identify ways to make migration sustainable and to search out alternatives to new migration. Similarly, borrowing sociologist Peggy Levitt's concept of "social remittances" (item **2634**), new attention seems to be pouring into explorations of the generative capacities of the earnings migrants are sending back home. What perhaps remains absent among the studies of migration are analyses attuned to Ecuador's own receipt of migrants, particularly Peruvians and Colombians. Especially with respect to the former group, almost no attention has been focused on the estimated 60,000 to 120,000 Peruvians now residing in Ecuador, most without legal permission and mostly concentrated in the country's southern provinces. Their story is the flipside of the migration and globalization story told elsewhere. Peruvians flock to Ecuador to take advantage of dollarization as well as the booming migration-related construction in *el austro.*

The absence of work on Colombian migration to Ecuador (mostly as political refugees) aside, this review period does reveal an uptick in attention paid to Ecuador's northern border and issues of warfare, security, and threats to both highland and Amazonian livelihoods (items **2636** and **2638**). The border region is at once an international issue, made combustible by the US' so-called War on Drugs and Plan Colombia, now in its ninth year. In April 2007, Plan Colombia was matched by Ecuadorian President Rafael Correa's announcement of Plan Ecuador, a five-province development initiative, including the northern frontier, expressly geared towards "replacing war with peace." The plan outlines initiatives to shore up local institutions, provide basic services, protect natural resources, and monitor human rights. While it is perhaps too early to furnish a prognosis on this ambitious project, these works provide a critical baseline for comparison. Vásconez's research (item **2638**) deserves special mention as it redirects readers toward the culture of fear on the border, reconstructed through media representations.

A final theme in studies examined this review period may be summed up as the remaking of civil society. The state of grassroots democracy and the importance of identity politics in Ecuador's political arena are arguably difficult to diagnose where contradictions abound. Flashes of novel political participation, such as the *"asembleas populares"* (item **2630**), point to parliamentary alternatives, yet, as the authors stress, not without compromises. To be sure, the country's new inclusionary constitution has already been tested by Correa's turn toward the conflicted role of *capitalista popular.* Support of indigenous peoples and other vulnerable groups has been shaken by recent concessions to mining and other extractive industries that disproportionately affect minority groups. During this review period, attention to issues of gender has remained of high priority with a variety of approaches represented, including histories of feminism (items **2631** and **2633**) and the intersection of gender and development (item **2628**). Lastly, important work takes aim at identity construction in the largest urban centers, including youth identities inside and outside the rapidly gentrifying neighborhoods of Guayaquil (item **2626**) and the popular perceptions of Afro-Ecuadorians in Quito (item **2637**).

2624 Acosta, Alberto *et al.* Crisis, migración y remesas en Ecuador: una oportunidad para el codesarrollo? Madrid: Cideal, 2006. 164 p.: bibl., ill.

The idea of *codesarrollo* (an integrated approach that channels the effects of migration into sustainable development) is the linking theme in a series of new articles on international migration from Ecuador to Spain. Along with overviews of the role of networks in determining where migrants go, remittance behavior, and a profile of fomenting female migration to Spain, the volume offers one of the most comprehensive overviews of the importance of remittances to the national economy, with a particular focus on the ways migrant earnings have helped relieve the problems of increased poverty and inflation stemming from the dollarization. Despite its inquiring subtitle, the volume does not provide programmatic ways to think about and assess the potential advantages of *codesarrollo.*

2625 Acosta, Alberto; Susana López; and **David Villamar.** La migración en el Ecuador: oportunidades y amenazas. Quito:

Centro Andino de Estudios Internacionales, Univ. Andina Simón Bolívar; Corporación Editora Nacional, 2006. 269 p.: bibl., ill. (Serie Estudios internacionales; 6)

An important contribution to a little-studied topic. Migration from Ecuador to Spain and the US accelerated in the late 1990s in response to deteriorating economic conditions. Chapter 3 examines the shift in migrant flows from the US to Spain which took place after the mid-1990s. Remittances now are second only to petroleum as a source of foreign exchange. Provides a good historical survey of migration, a considerable amount of data on its current dimensions, and a useful analysis of the impact of remittances on the Ecuadorian economy. Highly recommended.

2626 Andrade, Xavier. Jóvenes en Guayaquil: de las cuidadelas fortaleza a la limpieza del espacio público. (*Nueva Soc.,* 200, nov./dic. 2005, p. 85–95, bibl., ill.)

This article, rendered largely as a thought piece, considers the different ways urban renovation, gentrification, and the "privatization of space" in Ecuador's largest city, Guayaquil, has impacted "youth culture" in the city. Andrade explores the identities of two opposing groups affected by the structural conditions of the city: elite youth living in gated communities (*"chicos burbuja"*) and those living at the lowest rung of the labor class. Contrasting their experiences, the article inadvertently provides a way to assess the impact of globalization on residents of cities like Guayaquil where increasing poverty rubs against astronomical wealth.

2627 El desarrollo social en la década del 1990: los logros y desafíos del Ecuador frente a los compromisos de la Cumbre Mundial sobre Desarrollo Social y la Cumbre Mundial en favor de la Infancia. Quito: Ministerio de Bienestar Social, Secretaría Técnica del Frente Social, Unidad de Información y Análisis, Sistema Integrado de Indicadores Sociales del Ecuador, 2002. 129 p.: bibl. (Estudios e informes del SIISE; 3)

Report provides a detailed overview of various health and development indicators in Ecuador since the World Summit for Social Development in 1995. The report shows that the country, despite the 1999 economic crisis and 1997–98 El Niño, made significant steps in amplifying the political structures needed for positive development (gender equity, greater democratic participation by ethnic and other marginalized groups), yet still fell short on key sensitive indicators of overall development, including food security, infant malnutrition, and access to health services. The volume ends with a useful set of recommendations for future development efforts.

2628 Las displicencias de género en los cruces del siglo pasado al nuevo milenio en los Andes. Compilación de Nina Lauria y María Esther Pozo. Cochabamba, Bolivia: Univ. of Newcastle Upon Tyne: UMSS, CESU, 2006. 243 p.: bibl., ill.

Edited volume collecting together a number of a high quality articles on gender and development in the Andes, many originally published in English. The articles range from theoretical treatments of ethnodevelopment, gendered violence and coca production, to an analysis of discourse about masculinity in the Cochabamba water war.

2629 Handelsman, Michael H. Leyendo la globalización desde la mitad del mundo: identidad y resistencias en el Ecuador. Quito: Editorial El Conejo, 2005. 263 p.: bibl. (Ensayo)

This creative work "reads" globalization from the perspective of Ecuador while simultaneously positioning the country within processes of globalization. Concerned primarily with literature, film, documentary, and drama, the work understands the experiences of plurinationalism, indigenous and Afro-Ecuadorian identity, and migration through artistic expression. A notable addition to the work is an emphasis of the ways blanco-mestizos have experienced globalization.

2630 Hidalgo Flor, Francisco; Eloy Alfaro; and Luis Corral. El "Que se vayan todos" y las "Asambleas Populares" en Ecuador. (*Herramienta/Buenos Aires*, 29, junio 2005, p. 59–72)

Assesses the impact of the recent pattern of presidential removals and the call for popular assemblies to reform the Ecuadorian government. Popular assemblies are explored as a viable answer to the crisis of representation and legitimacy plaguing Ecuador's many political parties. While signaling the radical democratic potential of assemblies, the authors ultimately warn against the exclusionary aspects of a movement largely comprised of the middle class, lacking national coverage, and having little representation from workers' organizations and peasant and indigenous groups.

2631 Identidad y ciudadanía de las mujeres: la experiencia de cinco proyectos auspiciados por el Fondo para la Igualdad de Género, Ecuador. Edición de Erika Silva Charvet. Quito: Editorial Abya-Yala: 2005. 517 p.: bibl., index.

A collection of essays drawn from the Fondo para la Igualdad de Género (FIG), a program of the Canadian Agency for International Development. The papers bring together the results of five projects broadly aimed at gender equality in a context of sustainable development. The five studies range from the results of women's leadership training in Cuenca and Quito (focused on issues of local political action in marginalized neighborhoods) to identity construction among women living in the southern border regions with Peru. A useful historical introduction to the politics of feminism in Ecuador opens the book.

2632 La migración ecuatoriana: transnacionalismo, redes e identidades. Edición de Gioconda Herrera, María Cristina Carrillo y Alicia Torres. Quito: FLACSO Ecuador: Plan Migración, Comunicación y Desarrollo, 2005. 512 p.: bibl., ill. (Foro)

Compilation of articles originally presented at a FLACSO sponsored conference. The wide-ranging collection is the most comprehensive arrangement of works to date on Ecuadorian transnational migration by an international group of scholars. Particularly noteworthy sections of the book provide little-explored dimensions of migration focused on youth and indigenous Quichua migrants. Geographical coverage extends beyond the usual US and Spanish destinations to include receiving communities in Italy and France.

2633 Orígenes del feminismo en el Ecuador: antología. Compilación de Ana María Goetschel. Quito: Consejo Nacional de Las Mujeres, Presidencia de la Nación: FLACSO Ecuador: Secretaría de Desarrollo y Equidad Social, Quito, Alcaldía Metropolitana: Fondo de Desarrollo de las Naciones Unidas para la Mujer, 2006. 352 p.: bibl., ill.

The first volume of a larger collection plumbs the origins of feminist thought in the first decades of the 20th century through a diverse compilation of primary works written by female authors. Primarily essays and journalistic writing, rarely heard women's voices speak out on issues of education and political participation. A useful historical essay opens and frames the volume's themes.

2634 Parella, Sònia and Leonardo Cavalcanti. Una aproximación cualitativa a las remesas de los inmigrantes peruanos y ecuatorianos en España y a su impacto en los hogares transnacionales. (*Rev. Esp. Invest. Sociol.*, 116, oct./dic. 2006, p. 241–257, bibl.)

Built around interviews with Peruvian and Ecuadorian migrants living in Spain, this study aims to look at the impact of remittances on the formation of transnational households. The study does not provide substantial new information about the role of remittances, despite a careful attempt to tease out strictly economic functions of remittances from more social effects—a concept borrowed from sociologist Peggy Levitt's idea of "social remittances." The study is most useful in its comparisons between Peruvian and Ecuadorian contexts, pointing out ways the impact of remittances is never homogenous.

2635 Políticas sociales para la reducción de la pobreza: acción del Frente Social de Ecuador, 2003–2007. Elaboración de Marco Poso Z. *et al.* Edición de Ernesto Guerrero. Quito: Frente Social, STFS, 2004. 156 p.: bibl., ill.

A useful presentation and analysis of the problem of poverty in Ecuador, a reality for over 60 percent of households in the country. The information, compiled by the Politicas Sociales para la Reducción de la Pobreza en el Ecuador (PSRP), begins with a demographic overview of the poverty situation between 1990 and 2001, aggregated by region, gender, and ethnicity, among other categories. Subsequent chapters focus on ways to safeguard and fortify at-risk populations through analyses of social protection, human development, and inclusion into productive spheres of the economy.

2636 Ramón Valarezo, Galo. Frontera norte ecuatoriana: desafío de gobernabilidad. Quito: COMUNIDEC, Comunidades y Desarrollo en el Ecuador: Abya Yala, 2004. 127 p.: bibl., ill., maps.

General statistical, documentary, and ethnographic analysis of social, political, and economic conditions of the northern region of Ecuador along the Colombian border. The study serves to highlight the strengthening of local governments and civic activity amidst the challenges of dollarization, the spill-over of the Colombian armed conflict, and direct effects of Plan Colombia.

2637 Torre, Carlos de la. Afro-Ecuadorian responses to racism: between citizenship and corporatism. (*in* Neither enemies nor friends: Latinos, Blacks, Afro-Latinos. Edited by Anani Dzidzienyo and Suzanne Oboler. New York: Palgrave Macmillan, 2005, p. 61–74, bibl.)

Exploratory research project addressing recent political activism of Afro-

Ecuatorianos. Within Ecuador's racist society, blacks have often been associated with criminal behavior (males) and unbridled sexuality (females). De La Torre show that activists have combated these stereotypes through an accommodation to corporatist politics. Interesting parallels are drawn between indigenous politics of alterity and Afro-Ecuadorian efforts to carve out cultural autonomy in intercultural Ecuador.

2638 Vásconez Rodríguez, Belén. La construcción social del miedo: caso: Sucumbíos. Quito: Univ. Andina Simón

Bolívar: Abya-Yala: Corp. Editora Nacional, 2005. 76 p.: bibl. (Serie Magíster; 59)

This short book explores how the province of Sucumbíos in the northern Ecuadorian Amazon was transformed from a peaceful tourist destination into a place of fear and violence. Adjunct to the effects of Plan Colombia, Vásconez addresses how the exodus of Colombian civilians into the region extended the guerrilla war in Colombia into Ecuadorian territory. Along with emerging social changes, the development of a culture of fear is analyzed through local and national media representations.

PERU

KEITH JAMTGAARD, *Research Assistant Professor, Department of Rural Sociology & Office of Social and Economic Data Analysis, University of Missouri System*

2639 Calderón Cockburn, Julio. La ciudad ilegal: Lima en el siglo XX. Lima: Fondo Editorial de la Facultad de Ciencias Sociales UNMSM, 2005. 320 p.: bibl. (Serie Tesis)

This study examines the history of the city of Lima and its relationship to the shantytowns that grew with it during the 20th century. The growth of these slums has been the principal vehicle for the growth of Lima during this past century. The author focuses in particular on the practice of taking possession of land illegally in Lima through mechanisms such as land invasions and illegal purchases, and how these properties eventually re-enter the world of legitimate properties. Attention is given to the role of state policies in this process. The study places Lima in the context of the other large urban centers of Latin America.

2640 Maldonado Zambrano, Stanislao. Trabajo y discapacidad en el Perú: mercado laboral, políticas públicas e inclusión social. Lima: Comisión Especial de Estudio Sobre Discapacidad del Congreso de la República: Fondo Editorial del Congreso del Perú, 2006. 253 p.: bibl., ill. (Col. Estudios sobre discapacidad en el Perú; 4)

The goal of this study is to provide a frame of reference for the employment situation of people with disabilities in Peru. Statistical summaries are based on the Population Census of 1993 and the Housing Census from the third quarter of the 2002–2003 year, which was conducted by the Ministry of Work and Employment Promotion. Provides estimates regarding the extent of disabilities among Peru's indigenous population, along with estimates of the type of disabilities, type of employment, and distribution by department.

2641 Portocarrero Maisch, Gonzalo. Racismo y mestizaje y otros ensayos. Lima: Fondo Editorial del Congreso del Perú, 2007. 405 p.: bibl.

This series of essays discusses the forms of racism in Peru. What is interesting about Peru is the coexistence of racism with a tradition of mixed-race unions. Racism is examined from its association with religion during the colonial period, followed by a period of "scientific racism" which was the justification behind much of the European colonization. The contemporary form of racism is one which is more esthetic, in which features associated with Caucasians are perceived as more attractive than those of other races. Another feature of racism in Peru is that its existence had been denied, until recent times, because of the suggestion that all Peruvians shared an ancestry of mixed-race unions which made racism an impossibility. This book examines the

forms that racism takes in contemporary Peru.

Ramírez Bautista, Bernardino. Desarrollo urbano y desigualdad en el área periurbana de Carabayllo. See item **1146.**

BOLIVIA AND PARAGUAY

BOLIVIA

2642 Galindo, María and **Sonia Sánchez.** Ninguna mujer nace para puta: análisis feminista de la prostitución. La Paz: Ediciones Mujeres Creando, 2008. 210 p.: ill.

Published by a leading feminist Bolivian organization, this unorthodox and powerful exploration of sex work in Bolivia is perhaps best read as a primary document of the cutting edge of Bolivian feminism. Written as a dialogue between a prostitute and a lesbian, the work reflects the creative energies and political commitments of Mujeres Creando. [J.A. Lucero]

2643 Garcés, Fernando. ¿Colonialidad o interculturalidad?: representaciones de la lengua y el conocimiento quechuas. La Paz: PIEB, Univ. Andina Simón Bolívar, 2009. 257 p.: bibl., ill., tables.

Based on close readings of Quechua texts that formed part of two different projects, official state-produced textbooks and a newspaper published by an NGO in Cochabamba, the author examines the contradictions and possibilities of Quechua-language use in Bolivia. Combining broad theoretical analysis of the modern-colonial world-system with detailed ethnographic and linguistic research, this is an ambitious book of the varieties and consequences of language politics and ideologies in Bolivia. [J.A. Lucero]

García Linera, Álvaro. La potencia plebeya: acción colectiva e identidades indígenas, obreras y populares en Bolivia. See item **1652.**

Gustafson, Bret Darin. New languages of the state: indigenous resurgence and the politics of knowledge in Bolivia. See item **639.**

2644 Himpele, Jeffrey D. Circuits of culture: media, politics, and indigenous identity in the Andes. Minneapolis: Univ. of Minnesota Press, 2008. 246 p.: bibl., ill., index. (Visible evidence; 20)

A visual anthropologist offers a politically and culturally attuned tour of the history of Bolivian film and television. Using visual media to illustrate changing representations (and responses) of indigenous peoples, this book offers key insights into how local and global processes frame modernity and identity in contemporary Bolivia. The chapter on Carlos Palenque's *Tribuna Libre del Pueblo* is especially good. [J.A. Lucero]

PARAGUAY

2645 Fogel, Ramón B. La cuestión socioambiental en el Paraguay. Asunción: Centro de Estudios Rurales Interdisciplinarios (CERI), 2006. 220 p.: bibl., ill., maps.

A sociological investigation of environmental problems in rural Paraguay that also focuses on the relationship between the state and large agribusiness, which results in what the author calls "environmental neoliberalism." The author chronicles strategies of resistance employed by peasants and indigenous communities. For geography specialist's comment, see item **1267.** [B. Turner]

2646 Movimientos sociales y expresión política. Compilación de Mariella Palau y Arístides Ortiz. Asunción: BASE Investigaciones Sociales; Centro de Estudios Paraguayos Antonio Guasch; Sindicato de Periodistas del Paraguay, 2005. 278 p.: bibl.

The authors discuss Paraguay's major

social movements and their links to political movements, mainly those of the marginalized far left.

Security in Paraguay: analysis and responses in comparative perspective. See item **831**.

ARGENTINA, CHILE, AND URUGUAY

MARÍA ESPERANZA CASULLO, *Associate Professor, Universidad Nacional de Río Negro, Argentina*

THE SOCIOLOGICAL PRODUCTION OF THE 2002–2005 period in Argentina was marked by an overarching theme: the causes and effects of the social and economic crisis that ravaged Argentina in 2001–2002.

In 2001 the deterioration of the country's financial situation triggered a widespread economic crisis that caused the progressive deterioration of its social and economic indicators. Unemployment rose to over 40 percent, poverty climbed to almost 50 percent, and political unrest grew accordingly. The Argentine government decided to freeze all bank assets and to compulsively confiscate savings accounts. In December of 2001, then-president Fernando de la Rua was forced to resign in the midst of widespread protests, food riots, and police repression. In the two months that followed, Argentina changed five presidents, its currency devaluated over 300 percent, and there was a climate of unrest and uncertainty.

Understandably, in the immediate aftermath of the crisis, the social sciences focused on the responses that the Argentine civil society deployed to counterbalance the rising poverty, hunger and unemployment: neighbors who spontaneously opened soup kitchens, workers who opened and ran the factories that had been shut down by their owners, unemployed workers who organized politically. Argentine civil society showed remarkable creativity and resilience in its fight to survive.

Five years later, the situation is markedly different. Argentina's economy bounced back in 2003, when it began to grow at rates of over 8 percent a year. Néstor Kirchner, the serendipitous president who won the elections in 2003, applied a battery of measures that moved the country to a more center-left trajectory (relatively similar to the agendas pursued by Lula Da Silva's government in Brazil and Ricardo Lagos' government in Chile, for instance) and completed his four-year term in (relative) calm, at least for Argentine standards. Néstor Kirchner stepped down at the end of his term, and he was succeeded by his wife, Cristina Fernández de Kirchner, who won the election in 2007.

To a certain extent, the normalization of the Argentine political and economic life caused a change in the topics reflected in the sociological production. There is an obvious reduction in the number of studies on the *piqueteros* movement, recuperated factories, and other emergent phenomena.

As a matter of fact, the contemporary period of sociological production could be characterized as "the return of normal sociology." We encounter a surge in studies on such classic topics as demographic sociology, economic sociology, gender and family studies, and the like. There is a renewed interest in labor market dynamics, social stratification, and other more relatively mainstream topics.

However, we still find some newer topics, or at least some new angles from which to look at the social landscape. The first new issue has to do with the effects of the social crisis of 2001 and 2002 on Argentine social structure. Five years ago, sociology seemed to have a more optimistic tone, enamored as it was with the then-surging expressions of social resistance and creativity. But the current body of work seems more pessimistic, since it is faced with what can be labeled the "permanent" social crisis. New studies find that, even after seven years of sustained economic growth, Argentina is a changed country, and not for the better. The polarization of the social structure, the rise in inequality, the degradation of the labor market have all come to stay; and it is no longer possible to maintain the illusion that these problems will be solved by economic growth per se.

Argentina always took pride in being a country with relatively low poverty, medium inequality, and a labor market characterized by high levels of unionization and upward social mobility. Unemployment and poverty were very low (at least for Latin American standards) until the end of the 1980s decade. But now, even after almost a decade of breakneck economic growth, 30 percent of the population is poor and unemployment is 10 percent. This is the new social structure that scholars need to make sense of.

Another area in which original production is being done is what might be characterized as "rich people" studies. For one cannot forget this paradoxical finding: the Argentina of the post-crisis is at the same time a much poorer country and a much richer one. The sudden change in the structures of wealth distribution caused the impoverishment of vast sectors of the middle and lower-middle classes, but it also caused a sudden influx of wealth to a sliver of the upper middle class, especially to those groups connected to the financial services industries and the exportable agricultural businesses (these two economic sectors are intimately connected), on the other hand.

There are fascinating books that explore this new wealthy upper middle class, as well as their lifestyle, which is not identical either to the lifestyles of the older landed elites or of the older middle classes. For one, they are not urban, unlike "old" wealthy and middle class families. (These new upper middle classes have fled the urban centers, and have caused the explosive growth of the so-called countries (closed neighborhoods) in the outskirts of the city of Buenos Aires, an area that was much poorer.) This dynamic creates a new reality, in which wealthy closed neighborhoods coexist side-by-side with poor neighborhoods and even shantytowns. For another thing, they are delinked from the state, while "older" middle classes tended to be employed by the state. These new middle classes reject the old political parties, view all social relations through the prism of the market metaphor, and tend to vote for political entrepreneurs with a business background and no political expertise to represent them.

There is one topic, however, that is almost absent from this more recent body of sociological production, and it has to do with the violations to human rights committed by the last dictatorial regime (1976–83). There are some studies on the topic, but it does not seem to have the importance that it had in previous years. Interestingly, though, this one topic is central in the Chilean sociological production. Quite evidently, the scholarly debate on the causes and effects of Pinochet's dictatorship (1973–90) in Chile has begun more recently there, and it should continue for some years.

The other topic that resonates throughout Chilean sociology is the structural inequality of the Chilean society, a fact that has persisted even after years of diminishing poverty rates. There are studies on the relation between inequality and education, housing, and even the prison system.

To sum up, in both countries the sociological production of these last five years has less to do with the causes and effects of a sudden economic crisis and more to do with the structural challenges and limitations of Latin American social structures.

ARGENTINA

2647 Arizaga, Cecilia. El mito de comunidad en la ciudad mundializada: estilos de vida y nuevas clases medias en urbanizaciones cerradas. Buenos Aires: Cielo por Asalto: Distribuye Manantial, 2005. 223 p.: bibl., ill. (Col. Teoría, crítica y cultura urbana; 1)

In this book Arizaga enters into the peculiar life that takes place in the so-called countries, the closed urbanizations that surround the city of Buenos Aires, where the upper-middle class reside. Countries are a relatively recent phenomenon in Argentina and they are changing the social, economic, and cultural landscape of its cities.

2648 Auyero, Javier and Débora Alejandra Swistun. Inflamable: estudio del sufrimiento ambiental. Buenos Aires: Paidós, 2008. 234 p.: bibl., ill., map. (Tramas sociales; 45)

An ethnographic journey into one of the poorest and most environmentally degraded shantytowns (or *villas*) of the city of Buenos Aires.

2649 Beccaria, Luis and Roxana Maurizio. Movilidad ocupacional en Argentina. San Miguel, Argentina: Inst. de Ciencias, Univ. Nacional de General Sarmiento, 2003. 81 p.: bibl., ill. (Col. Investigación. Serie Informes de investigación; 18)

Offers a better understanding of the recent and deep changes in the Argentine labor market.

2650 Blanco, Alejandro. Razón y modernidad: Gino Germani y la sociología en la Argentina. Buenos Aires: Siglo Veintiuno Editores, 2006. 280 p.: bibl. (Historia y cultura; 23)

A very thorough examination of the beginnings of scientific sociology in Argentina and an intellectual biography of its founder, Gino Germani.

2651 Buenos Aires negra: identidad y cultura. Recopilación de Leticia Maronese. Buenos Aires: Comisión para la Preservación del Patrimonio Histórico Cultural de la Ciudad de Buenos Aires, 2006. 398 p.: bibl. (Temas de patrimonio cultural; 16)

This book attempts a reconstruction of the Afro-descendant identity in the city of Buenos Aires: its music, its dances, and its culture. Afro-descendant culture, once prominent in Buenos Aires, was subsequently denied by official narratives that stressed the "whiteness" of the Argentine society.

2652 Chiara, Magdalena and María Mercedes Di Virgilio. Gestión social y municipios: de los escritorios del Banco Mundial a los barrios del Gran Buenos Aires. Los Polvorines, Argentina: Univ. Nacional de General Sarmiento; Buenos Aires: Prometeo Libros, 2005. 231 p.: bibl., ill.

This book belongs to the young subfield of local development studies, focusing on municipal governance.

2653 Conflictos globales, voces locales: movilización y activismo en clave transnacional. Recopilación de Alejandro Grimson y Sebastián Pereyra. Geneva: UNRISD; Buenos Aires: Prometeo Libros, 2008. 269 p.: bibl.

Grimson and Pereyra's book presents several case studies of contentious social movements with an international agenda, such as organizations that protest external debt and the IMF, antiglobalization movements, etc.

2654 Conocimiento, periferia y desarrollo: los nuevos escenarios en la Patagonia Austral. Recopilación de Rubén Zárate y Liliana Artesi. Textos de Martín Buzzi *et al.* Buenos Aires: Biblos, 2004. 344 p.: bibl. (Col. Educación y sociedad)

An interesting study of the relation between education, labor, and wages in southern Patagonia.

2655 Cravino, María Cristina. Las villas de la ciudad: mercado e informalidad urbana. Buenos Aires: Univ. Nacional de General Sarmiento, 2006. 280 p.: bibl., ill.

This book offers an interesting and challenging reconstruction of the market dynamics at work in the *villas* (shantytowns) of the city of Buenos Aires.

2656 Educación en la Argentina: qué pasó en los '90. Coordinación de Inés Aguerrondo. Textos de María Esther Arrieta *et al.* Buenos Aires: Papers Editores, 2007. 197 p.: bibl. (Col. Educación)

This compilation of essays describes the (mostly negative) effects of the educational reforms that the Argentine state implemented during the 1990s.

2657 Efectos de las políticas de ajuste en la década del '90: salud, género, trabajo, educación. Recopilación de Myriam Barone y Lidia Schiavoni. Posadas, Argentina: Editorial Universitaria, Univ. Nacional de Misiones, 2005. 451 p.: bibl., ill. (Col. Contemporánea)

An interesting compilation on the impact of the structural adjustment policies of the 1990s on labor, gender, health, and education in several Argentine provinces. Studies that focus on the provincial level are not usually available.

2658 Entre el campo y la ciudad: desafíos y estrategias de la pluriactividad en el agro. Recopilación de Guillermo Neiman y Clara Craviotti. Textos de Silvia Bardomás *et al.* Buenos Aires: Ediciones CICCUS, 2006. 352 p.: bibl., ill. (Col. "Trabajo, integración y sociedad")

A study on multi-activity rural enterprises in Argentina.

2659 González Villar, Carlos; Lila Sintes; and Alina E. Báez. Pobreza y exclusión social en una ciudad intermedia: Posadas, Misiones. Posadas, Argentina: Editorial Universitaria, Univ. Nacional de Misiones, 2005. 342 p.: bibl., ill. (Cátedra)

A rich social and economic description of the city of Posadas, in the province of Misiones, in the Argentine North-East, one of the poorest regions of the country. This type of study, presenting a subnational

analysis, is a welcome addition to a literature that usually focuses only on the national level.

Hinton, Mercedes S. The state on the streets: police and politics in Argentina and Brazil. See item **1783**.

2660 Ideas, presencia y jerarquías políticas: claroscuros de la igualdad de género en el Congreso Nacional de la Argentina. Textos de Jutta Borner *et al.* Buenos Aires: Prometeo Libros: PNUD Argentina, 2009. 173 p. (Col. Democracia, partidos y elecciones)

This book contains rich data and interesting analysis on gender representation in the Argentine Congress.

Lederman, Daniel. Income, wealth, and socialization in Argentina. See item **2375**.

2661 Lodola, Germán. Protesta popular y redes clientelares en la Argentina: el reparto federal del Plan Trabajar (1996–2001). (*Desarro. Econ.,* 44:176, enero/marzo 2005, p. 515–535, bibl., graphs, tables)

This article explores the statistical relationship between social protests and the allocation of federal unemployment alleviation policies during the 1990s.

2662 Mercado de trabajo y equidad en Argentina. Recopilación de Luis Beccaria y Roxana Maurizio. Buenos Aires: Prometeo Libros, 2005. 269 p.: bibl.

Provides a thorough examination of the recent trends in employment and wages in Argentina. Contains rich data, especially for the topics of gender and labor, family income, and poverty.

2663 Patrimonio cultural gitano. Recopilación y coordinación de edición de Leticia Maronesey y Mira Tchileva. Buenos Aires: Comisión para la Preservación del Patrimonio Histórico Cultural de la Ciudad de Buenos Aires, 2005. 159 p. (Temas de patrimonio cultural)

An interesting and instructive first approximation to the cultural world of Roma (i.e., gypsy) populations in Argentina, a woefully understudied subject.

2664 Qué es una nación: la pregunta de Renan revisitada. Recopilación de Esteban Vernik. Buenos Aires: Prometeo Libros, 2005. 213 p.: bibl.

A collection of essays that reflects on the concepts of nation, state, and community, both in historical and purely theoretical terms. These essays focus on figures of Latin American thought that are commonly overlooked, such as José Carlos Mariátegui.

2665 Los significados de la pobreza. Coordinación de Amalia Eguía y Susana Ortale. Textos de Corina Aimetta *et al.* Buenos Aires: Editorial Biblos, 2007. 263 p.: bibl. (Sociedad)

A collection of essays that discusses the causes, consequences, and palliative strategies of poverty in Argentina.

2666 Todo sexo es político: estudios sobre sexualidades en Argentina. Recopilación de Mario Pecheny, Carlos Figari, y Daniel Jones. Buenos Aires: Libros del Zorzal, 2008. 301 p.: bibl. (Mirada atenta)

A book belonging to the relatively young subfield of Argentine queer and LGBT studies.

2667 El trabajo infantil no es juego: investigaciones sobre trabajo infanto-adolescente en Argentina (1900–2003). Dirección de Mariela Macri *et al.* Buenos Aires: Editorial Stella: La Crujía Editores, 2005. 317 p.: bibl. (Col. Itinerarios)

This book attempts to shed light on the problem of child labor in Argentina with the use of statistic, sociological, and anthropological information.

2668 Wortman, Ana. Construcción imaginaria de la desigualdad social. Buenos Aires: CLACSO, 2007. 232 p.: bibl., ill., maps. (Col. Becas de Investigación)

An interesting and original analysis of the social crisis of 2001–02, from the point of view of the influence of the "new cultural mediations," i.e., journalists and pundits from the mass media conglomerates.

CHILE

2669 Dávila León, Óscar; Felipe Ghiardo Soto; and Carlos Medrano Soto. Los desheredados: trayectorias de vida y nuevas condiciones juveniles. 2. ed. aum. Valparaíso, Chile: Ediciones CIDPA, 2006. 292 p.: bibl., ill.

A reconstruction of the institutional causes of unequal academic success in Chilean high schools.

2670 Sepúlveda Ruiz, Lucía. 119 de nosotros. Santiago, Chile: LOM Ediciones, 2005. 572 p.: bibl., ill. (Col. Septiembre)

A former Communist leader, Sepúlveda reconstructs the lives of the 119 "Miristas" (partisans in the MIR, the Communist guerrilla movement) that were kidnapped and killed by the dictatorship of Augusto Pinochet in 1975.

Silva, Sergio G. La inculturación del evangelio: un desafío crucial de la Iglesia Católica. See item **1760.**

2671 Stippel, Jörg Alfred. Las cárceles y la búsqueda de una política criminal para Chile: un estudio acerca de acceso a la justicia, la violación de derechos y el nuevo proceso penal. Santiago, Chile: LOM Ediciones, 2006. 303 p.: bibl., ill. (Ciencias humanas. Sociedad y justicia)

This book contains a systematic analysis of an overlooked subject: imprisonment policies in Chile and their effects.

2672 Thumala Olave, María Angélica. Riqueza y piedad: el catolicismo de la elite económica chilena. Santiago, Chile: Debate, 2007. 334 p.: bibl. (Arena abierta)

An unusual study about the religiosity of the Chilean economic elite, an understudied subject.

2673 Velasquez Almonacid, Marlen. Episcopado chileno y Unidad Popular. Santiago, Chile: Ediciones UCSH, 2003. 246 p.: bibl. (Col. Monografías y textos)

This book analyzes the relationship between the Chilean Catholic Church and the Socialist government of President Salvador Allende.

URUGUAY

2674 Graña, François. Nosotros, los del gremio: participación, democracia y elitismo en un movimiento social. Montevideo: Nordan-Comunidad, 2005. 118 p.: bibl. (Piedra libre; 24)

The author reconstructs the process by which an elite class was formed within the high school student movement in Montevideo in 1996.

2675 Porzecanski, Teresa. La vida empezó acá: inmigrantes judíos al Uruguay: historias de vida y perspectiva antro-pológica de la conformación de la

comunidad judía uruguaya, contrastes
culturales y procesos de enculturación.
Montevideo: Linardi y Risso, 2005. 198 p.:
bibl.

An ethnographic account of Jewish
immigration in Uruguay. Immigrants from
Eastern Europe and the Middle East tell
their stories.

BRAZIL

DANIEL HILLIARD, *Adjunct Assistant Professor, Georgetown Public Policy Institute, and Executive Director, Zoo Conservation Outreach Group*
MEREDITH DUDLEY, *Adjunct Assistant Professor, Department of Anthropology, Tulane University*

Sociology and the social sciences continue to play an important role in engaging with Brazil's ongoing social challenges: racism, sexism, extreme economic inequalities, poverty, rapid urbanization, and the degradation of rural environments, among others. Sociological research in Brazil has sought simultaneously to document the historical roots of these problems and to examine their complex interplay with globalization and emergent change. Furthermore, most studies have moved beyond mere documentation of Brazil's social problems and increasingly offer public policy recommendations based on research outcomes. The rich cultural heritage of Brazil also continues to provide fertile ground for the study of different aspects of identity, such as ethnicity, race, gender, sexuality, and religion. These various research interests are reflected in the large number of recent social science publications on Brazil, many of which are interdisciplinary in nature. The studies reviewed here represent only a small sample of this much larger body of sociological research.

The inequalities that characterize Brazilian society continue to engage social science scholarship. Documenting the fundamental forces driving socioeconomic disparity in Brazil remains a top research priority, and much of the resulting scholarship is dedicated to advancing a more nuanced understanding of the dynamics of poverty in the country. Recent social science research has focused on the intersection of poverty with violence, drugs, racial inequality, and programs that seek to remove exclusionary barriers.

The relationship between violence and poverty remains a particularly salient concern and a dominant theme in recent sociological scholarship (items **2690**, **2700**, and **2706**). As Brazil struggles with rates of violence comparable to some international conflict regions, criminology has emerged as a growing area of research. Homicides in particular are explored as a major public policy challenge. Most studies have documented a clear link between rates of violence and demographic variables such as poverty and race. In his ambitious treatise on violence in Brazil, Luís Mir (item **2690**) argues that violence in contemporary Brazil has clear historical roots and that the primary victims are the same as they always have been: poor, black, and segregated. Mir's study is highly critical of the role of the state, contending that it bears primary responsibility for failing to address the social, economic, and political mechanisms of violence, thereby leaving the country in what he refers to as "a permanent state of civil war for the past 500 years." A collection of ten empirical studies published in 2007 (item **2700**) likewise explores the diverse causes of Brazil's increasing homicide rates and highlights the paradox of military participation in public security.

Contemporary studies of violence in Brazil also explore the complex interaction of firearms and drug trafficking in urban areas. A collection of studies by the Organização de Rubem César Fernandes (item **2678**) examines the relationship between firearms and violence in contemporary Brazilian society. Several of the chapters focus on the high levels of gun violence in Rio de Janeiro and the impact of the illegal trafficking of firearms within the city's greater metropolitan area. Alba Zaluar's collection of articles (item **2706**) similarly examines the relationship between violence, poverty, and drug trafficking in Rio de Janeiro. Zaluar purposely moves beyond what he calls "the traditional ethnic and ideological debates that tend to dominate discussions about violence, poverty, and drugs," and instead places emphasis on the intersection of poverty and drug trafficking in relationship to mass consumer society, organized crime, and state actors involved in illicit criminal activities. Studies that explore the underground economies of firearms and drug trafficking offer new and interesting insights into violence and criminality in Brazilian society.

On a related note, the public health impact of violence on Brazilian society is a significant component of recent scholarship. As a medical doctor and historian, Luís Mir offers a public health perspective in his study about the history of homicide and violence in Brazil (item **2690**). The collection of essays in *Homicídios no Brasil* (item **2700**) and *Brasil: as armas e as vítimas* (item **2678**) directly explore the link between gun violence, crime, and public health in Brazil, and discuss public policy solutions.

Another emergent aspect within the scholarship on violence in Brazil is a focus on the situated experience of violence. For instance, the collection of empirical studies on homicide, *Homicídios no Brasil* (item **2700**), examines the symbolic components of violence affecting Brazilian youth as well as the perceived disproportionate impact of homicide on the country's black youth. In addition, Soares, Miranda, and Borges (item **2702**) offer a multidisciplinary look at the impact of violence on what the authors refer to as the "hidden" victims—the family, friends, and neighbors of individuals targeted by violence. Their study of the broader impact of violence in Rio de Janeiro is intended to provoke public policy debate on how to confront increasing levels of violence in Brazilian society. As in the past, most sociological studies about violence focus on urban areas like Rio de Janeiro, which is well-researched and symptomatic of metropolitan societies.

The sprawling slums or favelas of Rio de Janeiro remain a focus of social science research in Brazil, although sociologists are increasingly utilizing ethnographic and interview methodologies to document the experiences of individuals (items **2702** and **2683**). *A favela fala* (item **2683**) is a collection of testimonies provided by community leaders in four Rio de Janeiro favelas. By depicting the diverse socioeconomic and political realities of each community, the volume challenges some of the preconceived notions about favelas that helped create the city's segmented and separated civil society.

Contemporary racial and gender inequalities continue to engage many Brazilian sociologists. Most studies about race relations document the ongoing correlation between race, social exclusion, and poverty in Brazil (items **2677**, **2679**, **2681**, **2686**, **2692**, **2694**, **2695**, and **2698**). The article by Souza (item **2704**) begins with a review of the empirical and theoretical dimensions of racial discrimination and inequality in Brazil. The author critiques studies that correlate race with negative social indices like poverty, but which fail to clarify the role of race in the production of inequality. Souza suggests that the debate over inequality in Brazil should return to the question of social class, which has been relegated to a secondary theme of analysis as a "residual of the Marxist dialectic." While not denying the importance of race and racism in Brazil, Souza argues that race must be properly understood in the "hierarchy of causes" in order to combat both class-based and race-based prejudice.

Other sociologists are paying greater attention to the role of economic class after several decades of focusing largely on other aspects of identity, such as race or gender. Instead, a prevalent thread of contemporary social science scholarship in Brazil is examining the intersection of class with race or gender-based inequalities (items 2695, 2698, and 2704). In his analysis of the relationship between schooling, social mobility, and race in Brazil, Ribeiro (item 2695) concludes that opportunities for lower-class individuals are significantly marked by race, and that racial inequality likewise influences the odds of social mobility for persons of upper class origins. Ribeiro suggests that theories of stratification in Brazil be rethought, taking into account the observed interactions between race and class. Santos' (item 2698) study of the interaction between class and race-based inequalities in income provides another example of this trend. Santos utilizes linear regression analysis to examine the "moderating effect" of class on racial inequalities in income, and concludes that whites are favored in nearly all class categories, but that the racial effect is moderated significantly by class condition.

Several scholars have examined the impact of inequality in the workplace as a means of exploring the linkages between race, gender, and economic class in Brazil (items 2677, 2679, 2686, and 2694). For example, Cacciamali and Hirata (item 2679) analyze the labor markets in Bahia and São Paulo to test hypotheses of racial and gender discrimination, and find that significant discrimination exists against both blacks and women in the Brazilian labor market. Guimarães (item 2686) likewise analyzes salary patterns by race and gender and finds unequal salaries that reflect ongoing inequality, discrimination, and intolerance in the modern Brazilian workplace. In his study of discrepancies in personal income, Quadros (item 2694) concludes that these distortions of income result primarily from unequal access to better-remunerated positions based on race and gender. Brandão's study (item 2677) goes beyond basic correlations between poverty and racial inequality in Brazil to consider the effects of globalization on the job market in Rio de Janeiro. He discusses whether changes in employment patterns due to globalization have contributed to the development of a new and distinctly Brazilian form of poverty that continues to be grounded in racial discrimination.

Another trend in sociological studies on Brazil is the analysis of social exclusion and economic mobility barriers. The collection of articles published by the IPEA (Instituto de Pesquisa Econômica Aplicada) examines these impacts and concludes that race, gender, age, and place of residence function to make some groups of people more vulnerable to social exclusion (item 2681). The authors suggest that social inclusion programs may help groups overcome exclusionary barriers that prevent them from emerging from poverty. Other publications examine evidence of the success or shortcomings of existing social inclusion programs. For instance, *Políticas de inclusão social* presents and analyzes four years of data on the integrated social and political inclusion programs implemented in the greater São Paulo metropolitan area (item 2692). Preliminary evaluations demonstrate job generation and reductions in violence and school truancy, even in the most marginalized areas of the city. Rocha analyzes results of the 2004 Brazilian National Household Survey to document spatially differentiated reductions in poverty linked to Brazil's Plano Real (item 2696). She concludes that the reductions were most favorable in rural areas and less effective in the São Paulo metropolitan area.

Sociologists continue to document and analyze social movements in Brazil, and the sociology of gender and sexuality remains a dynamic area of research. Much of this research remains focused on the various dimensions and sources of gender inequality, including the intersection of gender and labor market dynamics, identity formation, and gay and lesbian identity politics. The volume *A mulher brasileira* provides a synthesis of the 2001 national survey of Brazilian woman and presents a series of essays that address the diverse political and socioeconomic realities in which contemporary women live (item **2691**). Facchini combines historical research and participant observation to explore the emergence, organization, and internal dynamics of Brazil's homosexual movement at the end of the 20th century (item **2682**). This study contributes to the literature on identity formation as well as social movement organization in Brazil.

Finally, religion remains a salient theme in sociological studies of contemporary Brazil. Much of this research focuses on the adaptation of religion and religious practices to globalization and contemporary social transformations in Brazil. Bittencourt Filho introduces the concept of the "Brazilian Religious Matrix" as a way of interpreting the historical relationship between the development of Brazilian society and diverse religious practices from Europe, Africa, and Native America (item **2676**). His book explores the rise of Protestant Pentacostalism as a recent challenge to the Brazilian Religious Matrix, and argues that globalization and attendant social transformations have lead to increased competition for religious hegemony in Brazil. The volume *Sociologia da religião e mudança social* brings together a number of specialists in the sociology of religion to examine the complex relations between religious phenomena, modernity, and social change in contemporary Brazil (item **2703**). The authors examine the ways in which both Catholicism and Protestantism have developed strategies to maintain their relevance. Prandi (item **2693**) explores the manner in which Afro-Brazilian religions likewise are adapting to changes in society in order to maintain their relevance in an expanding and increasingly competitive religious market in Brazil.

The studies reviewed, along with the larger body of literature on the sociology of Brazil, continue to advance our understanding of the nuances of Brazil's complex and changing society. Future research should continue to explore the articulation of race, gender, and class, as well as the ways in which they mediate the situated experience of globalization in Brazil.

HLAS Humanities Editor Katherine D. McCann contributed to this section.

2676 **Bittencourt Filho, José.** Matriz religiosa brasileira: religiosidade e mudança social. Petrópolis, Brazil: Editora Vozes; Rio de Janeiro: Koinonia, 2003. 260 p.: bibl. (Col. Religião e pesquisa)

Offers an interpretation of the relationship between religious phenomena and the historical formation of Brazilian society by introducing the concept of the "Brazilian Religious Matrix." Rooted in Iberian Catholicism, European magic, and indigenous and African religions, the Brazilian Religious Matrix is presented as the product of racial and cultural miscegenation that supplied diverse religious symbols, values, and practices. The book explores the rise of Protestant Pentecostalism as a recent challenge to the predominance of the Brazilian Religious Matrix, and argues that globalization and attendant societal transformations during the late 20th century have led to increased competition for religious hegemony in Brazil. [DH]

2677 **Brandão, André Augusto.** Miséria da periferia: desigualdades raciais e pobreza na metrópole do Rio de Janeiro. Niterói, Brazil: PENESB; Rio de Janeiro: Pallas, 2004. 215 p.: bibl.

Analyzes poverty and racial inequality in the Rio de Janeiro metropolitan area. Considers the effects of globalization on the Rio de Janeiro job market and discusses whether changes in employment patterns have contributed to the development of a new and distinctly Brazilian form of poverty. Uses empirical data to describe how racism and racial discrimination operate at the most marginalized socioeconomic ends of Brazilian society. [DH]

2678 Brasil: as armas e as vítimas. Coordinación de Rubem César Fernandes. Textos de Benjamin Lessing *et al.* Rio de Janeiro: ISER: 7 Letras, 2005. 295 p.: bibl., ill., maps.

Collection of studies that examine the relationship between firearms and violence in contemporary Brazilian society. Topics include the impact of firearms on public health in Brazil, firearms control legislation efforts from the Vargas to Lula administrations, and an overview of the Brazilian handgun manufacturing industry. Brazilian gun ownership is analyzed and mapped in a chapter by Pablo Dreyfus and Marcelo de Sousa Nascimento, and Rio de Janeiro, which suffers from exceedingly high levels of gun violence, receives special attention in chapters that examine the demand and illegal trafficking of firearms within the city's greater metropolitan area. [DH]

2679 Cacciamali, Maria Cristina and Guilherme Issamu Hirata. A influência da raça e do gênero nas oportunidades de obtenção de renda: uma análise da discriminação em mercados de trabalho distintos: Bahia e São Paulo. (*Estud. Econ./São Paulo,* 35:4, out./dez. 2005, p. 767–795, bibl., graphs, tables)

Tests the hypothesis of racial discrimination for men and women in the labor markets of Bahia and São Paulo. Statistical analyses demonstrate discrimination against blacks and women in the Brazilian labor market. [DH]

Chacon, Vamireh. A construção da brasilidade: Gilberto Freyre e sua geração. See *HLAS 64:3021.*

2680 Contins, Marcia. Lideranças negras. Rio de Janeiro: Aeroplano Editora: FAPERJ, 2005. 469 p.: bibl.

A compilation of interviews with 23 leaders of the black movement in Rio de Janeiro, including, among others, Abdias Nascimento and Éle Semog (see item **2701**). While the work is fairly bare bones, containing only a very brief contextualizing introduction, the personal narratives are nicely edited, readable essays with each figure describing his or her life story, the growing awareness of black consciousness, and the evolution to activism/militancy. Narratives also touch on the limits of the movement, the black movement and the state, and the role of women within the movement. [KDM]

2681 Exclusão social e mobilidade no Brasil. Organização de Estanislao Gacitúa-Marió e Michael Woolcock. Brasília: IPEA: Banco Mundial, 2005. 306 p.: bibl., ill.

Interdisciplinary collection of seven articles organized by the Insituto de Pesquisa Econômica Aplicada (IPEA) that examines the effects of social exclusion and the barriers to economic mobility on Brazil's poor. Concludes that groups are vulnerable to social exclusion processes as a function of race, age, gender, and place of residence. Programs focusing on improved access to job markets, developing human capital, and reducing discrimination are offered as a means of overcoming exclusionary barriers that prevent many social groups from emerging from poverty. [DH]

2682 Facchini, Regina. Sopa de letrinhas?: movimento homossexual e produção de identidades coletivas nos anos 90. Rio de Janeiro: Editora Garamond, 2005. 301 p.: bibl., ill. (Col. Sexualidade, gênero e sociedade. Homossexualidade e cultura) (Garamond universitária)

Examines identity formation within the Brazilian homosexual movement during the second half of the 1990s. Facchini combines historical research and direct participant observation to explore the emergence, organization, and internal dynamics of the movement in Brazil. The study makes a significant contribution to the literature on social movement organizations in Brazil, particularly the homosexual movement. [DH]

2683 A favela fala: depoimentos ao CPDOC. Organização de Dulce Chaves Pandolfi e Mario Grynszpan. Rio de Janeiro: FGV Editora, 2003. 360 p.: bibl., ill., map.

A rare and interesting look into four Rio de Janeiro favelas through the documented accounts of 12 community leaders. The collected testimonies provide unique insights into the daily lives of the favela inhabitants, depict the diverse socio-economic and political realities of each community, and call into question some of the preconceived notions about favelas that have helped to create a segmented and separated civil society in the city of Rio de Janeiro. [DH]

2684 Figueira, Ricardo Rezende. Pisando fora da própria sombra: a escravidão por dívida no Brasil contemporâneo. Fotografias de João Roberto Ripper. Rio de Janeiro: Civilização Brasileira, 2004. 445 p.: bibl., ill., maps.

A study of contemporary slavery on fazendas primarily in the states of Mato Grosso, Pará, and Piauí that reveals the culture of fear created by the fazenderos who use financial dependency and physical brutality to isolate, intimidate, and hold captive their work force. Based on interviews with workers and fazenderos, as well as primary and secondary resources, the author is a Catholic priest with a doctorate in social anthropology and years of experience working with human rights organizations. Appendix contains a list of 445 fazendas in Pará accused between 1969–2004 of enslaving their workers. [KDM]

Freeman, James. Great, good, and divided: the politics of public space in Rio de Janeiro. See item **1326**.

2685 Gomes, Nilma Lino. Sem perder a raiz: corpo e cabelo como símbolos da identidade negra. Belo Horizonte, Brazil: Autêntica, 2006. 411 p.: bibl., ill. (Col. Cultura negra e identidades)

The author, a social anthropologist, performed an ethnographic study of four "ethnic" hair salons in Belo Horizonte, interviewing 28 men and women about their hair, skin color, and idea of beauty. Understanding identity as a social and historical construct, the author looks at how hair style preferences and decisions contribute to the physical and symbolic expression of black identity in Brazil, a country with a high degree of racial miscegenation, but, which maintains, according to the author, an ideal of beauty that is European and white. Despite the

small size of the study, provides a window into the tensions and contradictions of personal and racial identity formation. Based on author's doctoral dissertation. [KDM]

2686 Guimarães, Nadya Araujo. Los desafíos de la equidad: reestructuración y desigualdades de género y raza en Brasil. (*Rev. Mex. Sociol.*, 65:4, oct./dic. 2003, p. 763–787, bibl., graphs, tables)

Documents the pattern of unequal salaries between groups of different color or sex in Brazil. Argues that physical differences are significant, though not exclusive, elements for explaining income gaps. Reflects on the links between inequality, discrimination, and intolerance in the modern Brazilian workplace. [DH]

Hoefle, Scott William. Twisting the knife: frontier violence in the Central Amazon of Brazil. See item **1336**.

2687 Hofbauer, Andreas. Uma história de branqueamento, ou, O negro em questão. São Paulo: FAPESP: Editora UNESP, 2006. 453 p.: bibl.

Hofbauer's work provides an historical analysis of the ideology of branqueamento in order to understand its significance to the history of racism in Brazil. The work begins with an examination of slavery in antiquity, the Middle Ages, and the era of discovery through the establishment of slavery in colonial Brazil, abolition, and the subsequent development of the homogenizing ideology of racial democracy. Drawing on historical, religious, and scientific writings, Hofbauer builds a case for the centrality of the notion of branqueamento in any discussion of Brazilian racism. [KDM]

2688 Lody, Raul Giovanni da Motta. O negro no museu brasileiro: construindo identidades. Rio de Janeiro: Bertrand Brasil, 2005. 335 p.: bibl., ill.

Anthropologist and museologist provides overviews of the Afro-Brazilian collections of 20 museums around Brazil. Brief descriptions include the history of each collection, the number of pieces at each museum, and a survey of the artifacts. Small sketches by the author accompany the descriptions. [KDM]

2689 Matta, Roberto da and **Elena Soárez.** Eagles, donkeys and butterflies: an anthropological study of Brazil's "animal game." Translated by Clifford E. Landers. Notre Dame, Ind.: Univ. of Notre Dame Press, 2006. 210 p.: bibl., ill., index. ("From the Helen Kellogg Institute for International Studies")

A long overdue English language translation of Matta and Soárez's 1999 *Aguias, burros e borboletas: um estudo antropológico do jogo do bicho.* The book is a fascinating examination of a distinctly Brazilian gambling game, which originated in the late 19th century. The authors provide insight into and analysis of the *jogo do bicho*'s unique rituals and symbols, while simultaneously exploring the structural, symbolic, and cultural significance of the animals and numbers that make up this quintessential and omnipresent Brazilian enterprise. The game's continued success is offered as a lens through which one can view important aspects of present-day Brazilian society, including the significance of gambling and the role of animal images in the country's cultural identity. [DH]

2690 Mir, Luís. Guerra civil: estado e trauma. São Paulo: Geração Editorial, 2004. 956 p.: bibl., ill., index.

An ambitious 900-page overview of the historical roots of homicide and violent death in Brazil. Mir, who is both a historian and a medical doctor, argues that violence in contemporary Brazil has a clear historical continuity and that the primary victims are the same now as they always have been: poor, black, and segregated. The massive treatise, which includes an examination of medical records from the country's five largest emergency rooms, is highly critical of the state's role in the violent deaths of Brazil's marginalized populations, contending that it bears primary responsibility for failing to address the social, economic, and political mechanisms of violence, thereby leaving the country in what he refers to as "a permanent state of civil war for the past 500 years." [DH]

2691 A mulher brasileira nos espaços público e privado. Textos de Margareth Rago *et al.* Organização de Gustavo Venturi, Marisol Recamán e Suely de Oliveira. São Paulo: Editora Fundação Perseu Abramo: Friedrich Ebert Stiftung, 2004. 247 p.: bibl., col. ill.

Synthesizes the results of a 2001 national survey of over 2,500 Brazilian women. Eleven essays delve into questions addressing some of the most relevant issues affecting women in contemporary Brazilian society. The cumulative result is a sociodemographic profile emphasizing the diverse political and socioeconomic realities in which contemporary Brazilian women live. [DH]

Poletto, Ivo. Brasil, oportunidades perdidas: meus dois anos no governo Lula: crônicas de um brasileiro aprendente. See item **1900.**

2692 Políticas de inclusão social: resultados e avaliação. Organização de Marcio Pochmann. São Paulo: Cortez Editora, 2004. 237 p.: bibl., ill., maps.

The third in a series of books about the integrated social and political inclusion programs implemented throughout the city of São Paulo in 2001 by its municipal government. Four years of program data are presented and analyzed. Preliminary evaluations demonstrate job generation and a reduction in measures of violence and school truancy in the most marginalized areas of the greater metropolitan area. [DH]

2693 Prandi, J. Reginaldo. Segredos guardados: orixás na alma brasileira. São Paulo: Companhia das Letras, 2005. 328 p.: bibl., ill. (some col.), index.

Discusses the future of Candomblé and other Afro-Brazilian religions in Brazil by analyzing how they have adapted to changes in society in order to maintain their relevance. In particular, these traditions are analyzed within the context of an expanding and increasingly competitive religious market in Brazil, which has led to a decline in the number of followers of Afro-Brazilian religions throughout Brazil. The capacity of Candomblé and other Afro-Brazilian religions to recover lost traditions and address contemporary societal demands and questions is examined. [DH]

2694 Quadros, Waldir. Gênero e raça na desigualdade social brasileira recente. (*Estud. Av.,* 18:50, jan./abril 2004, p. 95–117, bibl., graphs)

Presents the differences in personal income in Brazil as associated by race and gender. Concludes that distortions in income result primarily from inequality of access to better-remunerated positions. [DH]

2695 Ribeiro, Carlos Antonio Costa.
Classe, raça e mobilidade social no Brasil. (*Dados/Rio de Janeiro*, 49:4, 2006, p. 833–873, bibl., graphs, tables)
Analyzes the differences in intergenerational social mobility and schooling between white, mulatto, and black men in Brazil. Concludes that for individuals from lower social origins, inequality of opportunities is significantly marked by racial differences, and for persons of upper class origins, racial inequality influences the odds of social mobility. Results suggest that theories of stratification by race and class in Brazil should be rethought, taking into account the observed interactions between race and class. [DH]

2696 Rocha, Sonia. Pobreza e indigência no Brasil: algumas evidências empíricas com base no PNAD 2004. (*Nova Econ./Belo Horizonte*, 16:2, maio/agosto 2006, p. 265–299, tables)
Analyzes results of the 2004 Brazilian National Household survey relative to poverty and indigence. Concludes that there were demonstrable yet spatially differentiated reductions in poverty and indigence from 2003 to 2004—with the impact of the reductions being more favorable in rural areas and less so in the São Paulo metropolitan area. Net benefits to the poor were linked to Brazil's Plano Real. Poor individuals benefited from reduction in returns to education, real increases in minimum wage, and expansion of the social security net, which resulted in broader income increases at the lowest levels of distribution and led to a narrowing of inequality. [DH]

2697 Sansone, Livio. Negritude sem etnicidade: o local e o global nas relações raciais e na produção cultural negra do Brasil. Tradução de Vera Ribeiro. Salvador, Brazil: Edufba; Rio de Janeiro: Pallas, 2004. 335 p.: bibl., ill.
Portuguese translation of *Blackness without Ethnicity* (see *HLAS 63:3786*).

2698 Santos, José Alcides Figueiredo. Efeitos de classe na desigualdade racial no Brasil. (*Dados/Rio de Janeiro*, 48:1, 2005, p. 21–65, appendixes, bibl., tables)

Analyzes the conditioning exercised by class inequality on racial inequality in income between whites and non-whites. Uses linear regression analysis to examine the "moderating effect" of class categories in the attenuation or exacerbation of race effects on personal income. Concludes that racial gaps favor whites in nearly all class categories, but the effect is moderated significantly by class condition. [DH]

2699 Schwartzman, Simon. A agenda social brasileira. (*in* Retratos do Brasil. Organização de Elisa P. Reis and Regina Zilberman. Porto Alegre, Brazil: EDIPUCRS, 2004, p. 39–69, bibl., graphs, tables)
Well-developed essay that places post-2000 socioeconomic, demographic, and educational data in a 20th century historical context to help develop a comprehensive social public policy agenda for Brazil. Concludes that the competition between the "politics of social mobilization" and the "politics of social measures" will help define the form, philosophy, and outcomes of Brazil's public policy agenda for the next generation. [DH]

2700 Seminário Homicídios—Perspectivas e Experiências de Políticas Públicas, Belo Horizonte, Brazil, 2005. Homicídios no Brasil. Organização de Marcus Vinicius Gonçalves da Cruz e Eduardo Cerqueira Batitucci. Rio de Janeiro: FGV Editora, 2007. 252 p.: bibl., ill., maps.
A collection of 10 empirical studies that emerged from a May 2005 seminar entitled *Homicide—Public Policy Perspectives and Experiences*. The book explores the diverse causes of Brazil's increasing homicide rates and offers possible solutions to confront this complex public policy challenge. Among the issues examined are the symbolic components of violence affecting Brazilian youth, the regional demographics of homicide in Brazil, the perceived disproportionate impact of homicide on black youth, and the paradox of the growing participation of the armed forces in the public security of a country experiencing the consolidation of democracy. [DH]

2701 Semog, Ele and Abdias Nascimento.
Abdias Nascimento: o griot e as muralhas. Rio de Janeiro: Pallas, 2006. 235 p.: bibl., ill., index.

An (auto)biography of Abdias Nascimento, a leader of Brazil's black movement, written in collaboration with Nascimento's friend, the poet Éle Semog. The book focuses on Nascimento's early life exploring the roots of his racial consciousness by tracing his childhood, entrance into the military, and the founding of the Black Experimental Theater (TEN) in 1944. There is a comparatively brief discussion of his life in exile in the US during the military dictatorship and his subsequent return to political life in Brazil. Nascimento served in the Chamber of Deputies and the Senate, and the book reproduces several of his speeches from the late 1990s. Valuable work for the first-hand reflections of an important cultural and political figure. [KDM]

2702 Soares, Gláucio Ary Dillon; Dayse Miranda; and Doriam Borges. As vítimas ocultas da violência na cidade do Rio de Janeiro. Rio de Janeiro: Civilização Brasileira: CESeC, Centro de Estudos de Segurança e Cidadania, 2006. 238 p.: bibl., ill. (Col. Segurança e cidadania)

A multidisciplinary look at the impact of violence on what the authors refer to as Rio de Janeiro's "hidden" victims—the family, friends, and neighbors of individuals targeted by violence. The authors focus attention on these indirect or "forgotten" victims, interviewing 690 individuals, and recounting and analyzing the psychological, social, and economic impact on their daily lives. The study makes visible the broader impact of violence, gives voice to the struggles and concerns of its hidden victims, and provokes public policy debate on how to confront increasing levels of violence in contemporary Brazilian society. [DH]

2703 Sociologia da religião e mudança social: católicos, protestantes e novos movimentos religiosos no Brasil. Organização de Beatriz Muniz de Souza e Luis Mauro Sá Martino. São Paulo: Paulus, 2004. 173 p.: bibl. (Col. Sociologia e religião)

Sociology of religion specialists examine the complex relations between religious phenomena, modernity, and social change in contemporary Brazil. Essays discuss how Catholicism, Protestantism, and new religious movements have modernized and developed new strategies to maintain political and cultural significance in con-

temporary Brazilian society. Outlines the effects of globalization and rising economic and social inequality on religious movements in Brazil. [DH]

2704 Souza, Jessé. Raça ou classe sobre a desigualdade brasileira. (*Lua Nova,* 65, 2005, p. 43–69, bibl.)

A review of the empirical and theoretical dimensions of racial discrimination and inequality in Brazil. The article begins with a critique of empirical studies that correlate race with negative social indices but fail to clarify the role of race in the production of inequality, or which isolate race relations from broader dynamics of social inequality. Instead, the author seeks to redirect the debate over inequality to the question of social class, which has been relegated to a secondary theme of analysis as a "residual of the Marxist dialectic." While not denying the importance of race and racism in Brazil, the article concludes that race must be properly understood in the hierarchy of causes in order to combat both class-based and racial prejudice. [DH]

2705 Telles, Edward E. Racismo à brasileira: uma nova perspectiva sociológica. Tradução de Ana Arruda Callado, Nadjeda Rodrigues Marques, e Camila Olsen. Rio de Janeiro: Relume Dumará, 2003. 347 p.: bibl., ill., maps.

Portuguese translation of *Race in Another America* (see *HLAS 63:3807* and *HLAS 64:1776*).

2706 Zaluar, Alba. Integração perversa: pobreza e tráfico de drogas. Rio de Janeiro: Editora FGV, 2004. 438 p.: bibl., ill. (Violência, cultura, poder)

A collection of articles written over a 10-year period that examines the relationship between urban violence, poverty, and drug trafficking in Rio de Janeiro. The author purposely moves beyond what he calls "the traditional ethnic and ideological debates that tend to dominate discussions about violence, poverty, and drugs," and instead places emphasis on the intersection of poverty and drug trafficking in relationship to mass consumer society, organized crime, and state actors involved in illicit criminal activities. The book offers new and interesting insights into violence and criminality in Brazilian society. [DH]

ABBREVIATIONS AND ACRONYMS

Except for journal abbreviations which are listed: 1) after each journal title in the *Title List of Journals Indexed* (p. 541); and 2) in the *Abbreviation List of Journals Indexed* (p. 553).

ALADI	Asociación Latinoamericana de Integración
a.	annual
ABC	Argentina, Brazil, Chile
A.C.	antes de Cristo
ACAR	Associação de Crédito e Assistência Rural, Brazil
AD	Anno Domini
A.D.	Acción Democrática, Venezuela
ADESG	Associação dos Diplomados de Escola Superior de Guerra, Brazil
AGI	Archivo General de Indias, Sevilla
AGN	Archivo General de la Nación
AID	Agency for International Development
a.k.a.	also known as
Ala.	Alabama
ALALC	Asociación Latinoamericana de Libre Comercio
ALEC	*Atlas lingüístico etnográfico de Colombia*
ANAPO	Alianza Nacional Popular, Colombia
ANCARSE	Associação Nordestina de Crédito e Assistência Rural de Sergipe, Brazil
ANCOM	Andean Common Market
ANDI	Asociación Nacional de Industriales, Colombia
ANPOCS	Associação Nacional de Pós-Graduação e Pesquisa em Ciências Sociais, São Paulo
ANUC	Asociación Nacional de Usuarios Campesinos, Colombia
ANUIES	Asociación Nacional de Universidades e Institutos de Enseñanza Superior, Mexico
AP	Acción Popular
APRA	Alianza Popular Revolucionaria Americana, Peru
ARENA	Aliança Renovadora Nacional, Brazil
Ariz.	Arizona
Ark.	Arkansas
ASA	Association of Social Anthropologists of the Commonwealth, London
ASSEPLAN	Assessoria de Planejamento e Acompanhamento, Recife
Assn.	Association
Aufl.	Auflage (edition, edición)
AUFS	American Universities Field Staff Reports, Hanover, N.H.
Aug.	August, Augustan
aum.	aumentada
b.	born (nació)
B.A.R.	British Archaeological Reports
BBE	Bibliografia Brasileira de Educação
b.c.	indicates dates obtained by radiocarbon methods
BC	Before Christ

bibl(s).	bibliography(ies)
BID	Banco Interamericano de Desarrollo
BNDE	Banco Nacional de Desenvolvimento Econômico, Brazil
BNH	Banco Nacional de Habitação, Brazil
BP	before present
b/w	black and white
C14	Carbon 14
ca.	*circa* (about)
CACM	Central American Common Market
CADE	Conferencia Anual de Ejecutivos de Empresas, Peru
CAEM	Centro de Altos Estudios Militares, Peru
Calif.	California
Cap.	Capítulo
CARC	Centro de Arte y Comunicación, Buenos Aires
CARICOM	Caribbean Common Market
CARIFTA	Caribbean Free Trade Association
CBC	Christian base communities
CBD	central business district
CBI	Caribbean Basin Initiative
CD	Christian Democrats, Chile
CDHES	Comisión de Derechos Humanos de El Salvador
CDI	Conselho de Desenvolvimento Industrial, Brasília
CEB	comunidades eclesiásticas de base
CEBRAP	Centro Brasileiro de Análise e Planejamento, São Paulo
CECORA	Centro de Cooperativas de la Reforma Agraria, Colombia
CEDAL	Centro de Estudios Democráticos de América Latina, Costa Rica
CEDE	Centro de Estudios sobre Desarrollo Económico, Univ. de los Andes, Bogotá
CEDEPLAR	Centro de Desenvolvimento e Planejamento Regional, Belo Horizonte
CEDES	Centro de Estudios de Estado y Sociedad, Buenos Aires; Centro de Estudos de Educação e Sociedade, São Paulo
CEDI	Centro Ecumênico de Documentos e Informação, São Paulo
CEDLA	Centro de Estudios y Documentación Latinoamericanos, Amsterdam
CEESTEM	Centro de Estudios Económicos y Sociales del Tercer Mundo, México
CELADE	Centro Latinoamericano de Demografía
CELADEC	Comisión Evangélica Latinoamericana de Educación Cristiana
CELAM	Consejo Episcopal Latinoamericano
CEMLA	Centro de Estudios Monetarios Latinoamericanos, Mexico
CENDES	Centro de Estudios del Desarrollo, Venezuela
CENIDIM	Centro Nacional de Información, Documentación e Investigación Musicales, Mexico
CENIET	Centro Nacional de Información y Estadísticas del Trabajo, Mexico
CEOSL	Confederación Ecuatoriana de Organizaciones Sindicales LIbres
CEPADE	Centro Paraguayo de Estudios de Desarrollo Económico y Social
CEPA-SE	Comissão Estadual de Planejamento Agrícola, Sergipe
CEPAL	Comisión Económica para América Latina y el Caribe
CEPLAES	Centro de Planificación y Estudios Sociales, Quito
CERES	Centro de Estudios de la Realidad Económica y Social, Bolivia
CES	constant elasticity of substitution
cf.	compare
CFI	Consejo Federal de Inversiones, Buenos Aires
CGE	Confederación General Económica, Argentina
CGTP	Confederación General de Trabajadores del Perú
chap(s).	chapter(s)
CHEAR	Council on Higher Education in the American Republics

Cía.	Compañía
CIA	Central Intelligence Agency
CIDA	Comité Interamericano de Desarrollo Agrícola
CIDE	Centro de Investigación y Desarrollo de la Educación, Chile; Centro de Investigación y Docencias Económicas, Mexico
CIDIAG	Centro de Información y Desarrollo Internacional de Autogestión, Lima
CIE	Centro de Investigaciones Económicas, Buenos Aires
CIEDLA	Centro Interdisciplinario de Estudios sobre el Desarrollo Latinoamericano, Buenos Aires
CIEDUR	Centro Interdisciplinario de Estudios sobre el Desarrollo Uruguay, Montevideo
CIEPLAN	Corporación de Investigaciones Económicas para América Latina, Santiago
CIESE	Centro de Investigaciones y Estudios Socioeconómicos, Quito
CIMI	Conselho Indigenista Missionário, Brazil
CINTERFOR	Centro Interamericano de Investigación y Documentación sobre Formación Profesional
CINVE	Centro de Investigaciones Económicas, Montevideo
CIP	Conselho Interministerial de Preços, Brazil
CIPCA	Centro de Investigación y Promoción del Campesinado, Bolivia
CIPEC	Consejo Intergubernamental de Países Exportadores de Cobre, Santiago
CLACSO	Consejo Latinoamericano de Ciencias Sociales, Secretaría Ejecutiva, Buenos Aires
CLASC	Confederación Latinoamericana Sindical Cristiana
CLE	Comunidad Latinoamericana de Escritores, Mexico
cm	centimeter
CNI	Confederação Nacional da Indústria, Brazil
CNPq	Conselho Nacional de Pesquisas, Brazil
Co.	Company
COB	Central Obrera Boliviana
COBAL	Companhia Brasileira de Alimentos
CODEHUCA	Comisión para la Defensa de los Derechos Humanos en Centroamérica
Col.	Collection, Colección, Coleção
col.	colored, coloured
Colo.	Colorado
COMCORDE	Comisión Coordinadora para el Desarrollo Económico, Uruguay
comp(s).	compiler(s), compilador(es)
CONCLAT	Congresso Nacional das Classes Trabalhadoras, Brazil
CONCYTEC	Consejo Nacional de Ciencia y Tecnología (Peru)
CONDESE	Conselho de Desenvolvimento Econômico de Sergipe
Conn.	Connecticut
COPEI	Comité Organizador Pro-Elecciones Independientes, Venezuela
CORFO	Corporación de Fomento de la Producción, Chile
CORP	Corporación para el Fomento de Investigaciones Económicas, Colombia
Corp.	Corporation, Corporación
corr.	corrected, corregida
CP	Communist Party
CPDOC	Centro de Pesquisa e Documentação, Brazil
CRIC	Consejo Regional Indígena del Cauca, Colombia
CSUTCB	Confederación Sindical Unica de Trabajadores Campesinos de Bolivia
CTM	Confederación de Trabajadores de México
CUNY	The City University of New York
CUT	Central Unica de Trabajadores (Mexico); Central Unica dos Trabalhadores (Brazil); Central Unitaria de Trabajadores (Chile; Colombia); Confederación Unitaria de Trabajadores (Costa Rica)

CVG	Corporación Venezolana de Guayana
d.	died (murió)
DANE	Departamento Nacional de Estadística, Colombia
DC	developed country; Demócratas Cristianos, Chile
d.C.	después de Cristo
Dec./déc.	December, décembre
Del.	Delaware
dept.	department
depto.	departamento
DESCO	Centro de Estudios y Promoción del Desarrollo, Lima
Dez./dez.	Dezember, dezembro
dic.	diciembre, dicembre
disc.	discography
DNOCS	Departamento Nacional de Obras Contra as Secas, Brazil
doc.	document, documento
Dr.	Doctor
Dra.	Doctora
DRAE	*Diccionario de la Real Academia Española*
ECLAC	UN Economic Commision for Latin America and the Caribbean, New York and Santiago
ECOSOC	UN Economic and Social Council
ed./éd.(s)	edition(s), édition(s), edición(es), editor(s), redactor(es), director(es)
EDEME	Editora Emprendimentos Educacionais, Florianópolis
Edo.	Estado
EEC	European Economic Community
EE.UU.	Estados Unidos de América
EFTA	European Free Trade Association
e.g.	*exempio gratia* (for example, por ejemplo)
ELN	Ejército de Liberación Nacional, Colombia
ENDEF	Estudo Nacional da Despesa Familiar, Brazil
ERP	Ejército Revolucionario del Pueblo, El Salvador
ESG	Escola Superior de Guerra, Brazil
estr.	estrenado
et al.	*et alia* (and others)
ETENE	Escritório Técnico de Estudos Econômicos do Nordeste, Brazil
ETEPE	Escritório Técnico de Planejamento, Brazil
EUDEBA	Editorial Universitaria de Buenos Aires
EWG	Europaische Wirtschaftsgemeinschaft. *See* EEC.
facsim(s).	facsimile(s)
FAO	Food and Agriculture Organization of the United Nations
FDR	Frente Democrático Revolucionario, El Salvador
FEB	Força Expedicionária Brasileira
Feb./feb.	February, Februar, febrero, febbraio
FEDECAFE	Federación Nacional de Cafeteros, Colombia
FEDESARROLLO	Fundación para la Educación Superior y el Desarrollo
fev./fév.	fevereiro, février
ff.	following
FGTS	Fundo de Garantia do Tempo de Serviço, Brazil
FGV	Fundação Getúlio Vargas
FIEL	Fundación de Investigaciones Económicas Latinoamericanas, Argentina
film.	filmography
fl.	flourished
Fla.	Florida
FLACSO	Facultad Latinoamericana de Ciencias Sociales
FMI	Fondo Monetario Internacional

FMLN	Frente Farabundo Martí de Liberación Nacional, El Salvador
fold.	folded
fol(s).	folio(s)
FPL	Fuerzas Populares de Liberación Farabundo Marti, El Salvador
FRG	Federal Republic of Germany
FSLN	Frente Sandinista de Liberación Nacional, Nicaragua
ft.	foot, feet
FUAR	Frente Unido de Acción Revolucionaria, Colombia
FUCVAM	Federación Unificadora de Cooperativas de Vivienda por Ayuda Mutua, Uruguay
FUNAI	Fundação Nacional do Indio, Brazil
FUNARTE	Fundação Nacional de Arte, Brazil
FURN	Fundação Universidade Regional do Nordeste
Ga.	Georgia
GAO	General Accounting Office, Wahington
GATT	General Agreement on Tariffs and Trade
GDP	gross domestic product
GDR	German Democratic Republic
GEIDA	Grupo Executivo de Irrigação para o Desenvolvimento Agrícola, Brazil
gen.	gennaio
Gen.	General
GMT	Greenwich Mean Time
GPA	grade point average
GPO	Government Printing Office, Washington
h.	hijo
ha.	hectares, hectáreas
HLAS	*Handbook of Latin American Studies*
HMAI	*Handbook of Middle American Indians*
Hnos.	hermanos
HRAF	Human Relations Area Files, Inc., New Haven, Conn.
IBBD	Instituto Brasileiro de Bibliografia e Documentação
IBGE	Instituto Brasileiro de Geografia e Estatística, Rio de Janeiro
IBRD	International Bank for Reconstruction and Development (World Bank)
ICA	Instituto Colombiano Agropecuario
ICAIC	Instituto Cubano de Arte e Industria Cinematográfica
ICCE	Instituto Colombiano de Construcción Escolar
ICE	International Cultural Exchange
ICSS	Instituto Colombiano de Seguridad Social
ICT	Instituto de Crédito Territorial, Colombia
id.	*idem* (the same as previously mentioned or given)
IDB	Inter-American Development Bank
i.e.	*id est* (that is, o sea)
IEL	Instituto Euvaldo Lodi, Brazil
IEP	Instituto de Estudios Peruanos
IERAC	Instituto Ecuatoriano de Reforma Agraria y Colonización
IFAD	International Fund for Agricultural Development
IICA	Instituto Interamericano de Ciencias Agrícolas, San José
III	Instituto Indigenista Interamericana, Mexico
IIN	Instituto Indigenista Nacional, Guatemala
ILDIS	Instituto Latinoamericano de Investigaciones Sociales
ill.	illustration(s)
Ill.	Illinois
ILO	International Labour Organization, Geneva
IMES	Instituto Mexicano de Estudios Sociales
IMF	International Monetary Fund

Impr.	Imprenta, Imprimérie
in.	inches
INAH	Instituto Nacional de Antropología e Historia, Mexico
INBA	Instituto Nacional de Bellas Artes, Mexico
Inc.	Incorporated
INCORA	Instituto Colombiano de Reforma Agraria
Ind.	Indiana
INEP	Instituto Nacional de Estudios Pedagógicos, Brazil
INI	Instituto Nacional Indigenista, Mexico
INIT	Instituto Nacional de Industria Turística, Cuba
INPES/IPEA	Instituto de Planejamento Econômico e Social, Brazil
INTAL	Instituto para la Integración de América Latina
IPA	Instituto de Pastoral Andina, Univ. de San Antonio de Abad, Seminario de Antropología, Cusco, Peru
IPEA	Instituto de Pesquisa Econômica Aplicada, Brazil
IPES/GB	Instituto de Pesquisas e Estudos Sociais, Guanabara, Brazil
IPHAN	Instituto de Patrimônio Histórico e Artístico Nacional, Brazil
ir.	irregular
IS	Internacional Socialista
ITESM	Instituto Tecnológico y de Estudios Superiores de Monterrey
ITT	International Telephone and Telegraph
Jan./jan.	January, Januar, janeiro, janvier
JLP	Jamaican Labour Party
Jr.	Junior, Júnior
JUC	Juventude Universitária Católica, Brazil
JUCEPLAN	Junta Central de Planificación, Cuba
Kan.	Kansas
KITLV	Koninklijk Instituut voor Tall-, Land- en Volkenkunde (Royal Institute of Linguistics and Anthropology)
km	kilometers, kilómetros
Ky.	Kentucky
La.	Louisiana
LASA	Latin American Studies Association
LDC	less developed country(ies)
LP	long-playing record
Ltd(a).	Limited, Limitada
m	meters, metros
m.	murió (died)
M	mille, mil, thousand
M.A.	Master of Arts
MACLAS	Middle Atlantic Council of Latin American Studies
MAPU	Movimiento de Acción Popular Unitario, Chile
MARI	Middle American Research Institute, Tulane University, New Orleans
MAS	Movimiento al Socialismo, Venezuela
Mass.	Massachusetts
MCC	Mercado Común Centro-Americano
Md.	Maryland
MDB	Movimiento Democrático Brasileiro
MDC	more developed countries
Me.	Maine
MEC	Ministério de Educação e Cultura, Brazil
Mich.	Michigan
mimeo	mimeographed, mimeografiado
min.	minutes, minutos
Minn.	Minnesota

MIR	Movimiento de Izquierda Revolucionaria, Chile and Venezuela
Miss.	Mississippi
MIT	Massachusetts Institute of Technology
ml	milliliter
MLN	Movimiento de Liberación Nacional
mm.	millimeter
MNC	multinational corporation
MNI	minimum number of individuals
MNR	Movimiento Nacionalista Revolucionario, Bolivia
Mo.	Missouri
MOBRAL	Movimento Brasileiro de Alfabetização
MOIR	Movimiento Obrero Independiente y Revolucionario, Colombia
Mont.	Montana
MRL	Movimiento Revolucionario Liberal, Colombia
ms.	manuscript
M.S.	Master of Science
msl	mean sea level
n.	nació (born)
NBER	National Bureau of Economic Research, Cambridge, Massachusetts
N.C.	North Carolina
N.D.	North Dakota
NE	Northeast
Neb.	Nebraska
neubearb.	neubearbeitet (revised, corregida)
Nev.	Nevada
n.f.	neue Folge (new series)
NGO	nongovernmental organization
NGDO	nongovernmental development organization
N.H.	New Hampshire
NIEO	New International Economic Order
NIH	National Institutes of Health, Washington
N.J.	New Jersey
NJM	New Jewel Movement, Grenada
N.M.	New Mexico
no(s).	number(s), número(s)
NOEI	Nuevo Orden Económico Internacional
NOSALF	Scandinavian Committee for Research in Latin America
Nov./nov.	November, noviembre, novembre, novembro
NSF	National Science Foundation
NW	Northwest
N.Y.	New York
OAB	Ordem dos Advogados do Brasil
OAS	Organization of American States
OCLC	Online Computer Library Center
Oct./oct.	October, octubre, octobre
ODEPLAN	Oficina de Planificación Nacional, Chile
OEA	Organización de los Estados Americanos
OECD	Organisation for Economic Cooperation and Development
OIT	Organización Internacional del Trabajo
Okla.	Oklahoma
Okt.	Oktober
ONUSAL	United Nations Observer Mission in El Salvador
op.	opus
OPANAL	Organismo para la Proscripción de las Armas Nucleares en América Latina

OPEC	Organization of Petroleum Exporting Countries
OPEP	Organización de Países Exportadores de Petróleo
OPIC	Overseas Private Investment Corporation, Washington
Or.	Oregon
OREALC	Oficina Regional de Educación para América Latina y el Caribe
ORIT	Organización Regional Interamericana del Trabajo
ORSTOM	Office de la recherche scientifique et technique outre-mer (France)
ott.	ottobre
out.	outubro
p.	page(s)
Pa.	Pennsylvania
PAN	Partido Acción Nacional, Mexico
PC	Partido Comunista
PCCLAS	Pacific Coast Council on Latin American Studies
PCN	Partido de Conciliación Nacional, El Salvador
PCP	Partido Comunista del Perú
PCR	Partido Comunista Revolucionario, Chile and Argentina
PCV	Partido Comunista de Venezuela
PD	Partido Democrático
PDC	Partido Demócrata Cristiano, Chile
PDS	Partido Democrático Social, Brazil
PDT	Partido Democrático Trabalhista, Brazil
PDVSA	Petróleos de Venezuela S.A.
PEMEX	Petróleos Mexicanos
PETROBRAS	Petróleo Brasileiro
PIMES	Programa Integrado de Mestrado em Economia e Sociologia, Brazil
PIP	Partido Independiente de Puerto Rico
PLN	Partido Liberación Nacional, Costa Rica
PMDB	Partido do Movimento Democrático Brasileiro
PNAD	Pesquisa Nacional por Amostra Domiciliar, Brazil
PNC	People's National Congress, Guyana
PNM	People's National Movement, Trinidad and Tobago
PNP	People's National Party, Jamaica
pop.	population
port(s).	portrait(s)
PPP	purchasing power parities; People's Progressive Party of Guyana
PRD	Partido Revolucionario Dominicano
PREALC	Programa Regional del Empleo para América Latina y el Caribe, Organización Internacional del Trabajo, Santiago
PRI	Partido Revolucionario Institucional, Mexico
Prof.	Professor, Profesor(a)
PRONAPA	Programa Nacional de Pesquisas Arqueológicas, Brazil
PRONASOL	Programa Nacional de Solidaridad, Mexico
prov.	province, provincia
PS	Partido Socialista, Chile
PSD	Partido Social Democrático, Brazil
pseud.	pseudonym, pseudónimo
PT	Partido dos Trabalhadores, Brazil
pt(s).	part(s), parte(s)
PTB	Partido Trabalhista Brasileiro
pub.	published, publisher
PUC	Pontifícia Universidade Católica
PURSC	Partido Unido de la Revolución Socialista de Cuba
q.	quarterly
rev.	revisada, revista, revised

R.I.	Rhode Island
s.a.	semiannual
SALALM	Seminar on the Acquisition of Latin American Library Materials
SATB	soprano, alto, tenor, bass
sd.	sound
s.d.	*sine datum* (no date, sin fecha)
S.D.	South Dakota
SDR	special drawing rights
SE	Southeast
SELA	Sistema Económico Latinoamericano
SEMARNAP	Secretaria de Medio Ambiente, Recursos Naturales y Pesca, Mexico
SENAC	Serviço Nacional de Aprendizagem Comercial, Rio de Janeiro
SENAI	Serviço Nacional de Aprendizagem Industrial, São Paulo
SEP	Secretaría de Educación Pública, Mexico
SEPLA	Seminario Permanente sobre Latinoamérica, Mexico
Sept./sept.	September, septiembre, septembre
SES	socioeconomic status
SESI	Serviço Social da Indústria, Brazil
set.	setembro, settembre
SI	Socialist International
SIECA	Secretaría Permanente del Tratado General de Integración Económica Centroamericana
SIL	Summer Institute of Linguistics (Instituto Lingüístico de Verano)
SINAMOS	Sistema Nacional de Apoyo a la Movilización Social, Peru
S.J.	Society of Jesus
s.l.	*sine loco* (place of publication unknown)
s.n.	*sine nomine* (publisher unknown)
SNA	Sociedad Nacional de Agricultura, Chile
SPP	Secretaría de Programación y Presupuesto, Mexico
SPVEA	Superintendência do Plano de Valorização Econômica da Amazônia, Brazil
sq.	square
SSRC	Social Sciences Research Council, New York
STENEE	Empresa Nacional de Energía Eléctrica. Sindicato de Trabajadores, Honduras
SUDAM	Superintendência de Desenvolvimento da Amazônia, Brazil
SUDENE	Superintendência de Desenvolvimento do Nordeste, Brazil
SUFRAMA	Superintendência da Zona Franca de Manaus, Brazil
SUNY	State University of New York
SW	Southwest
t.	tomo(s), tome(s)
TAT	Thematic Apperception Test
TB	tuberculosis
Tenn.	Tennessee
Tex.	Texas
TG	transformational generative
TL	Thermoluminescent
TNE	Transnational enterprise
TNP	Tratado de No Proliferación
trans.	translator
UABC	Universidad Autónoma de Baja California
UCA	Universidad Centroamericana José Simeón Cañas, San Salvador
UCLA	University of California, Los Angeles
UDN	União Democrática Nacional, Brazil
UFG	Universidade Federal de Goiás

UFPb	Universidade Federal de Paraíba
UFSC	Universidade Federal de Santa Catarina
UK	United Kingdom
UN	United Nations
UNAM	Universidad Nacional Autónoma de México
UNCTAD	United Nations Conference on Trade and Development
UNDP	United Nations Development Programme
UNEAC	Unión de Escritores y Artistas de Cuba
UNESCO	United Nations Educational, Scientific and Cultural Organization
UNI/UNIND	União das Nações Indígenas
UNICEF	United Nations International Children's Emergency Fund
Univ(s).	university(ies), universidad(es), universidade(s), université(s), universität(s), universitá(s)
uniw.	uniwersytet (university)
Unltd.	Unlimited
UP	Unidad Popular, Chile
URD	Unidad Revolucionaria Democrática
URSS	Unión de Repúblicas Soviéticas Socialistas
UNISA	University of South Africa
US	United States
USAID	*See* AID.
USIA	United States Information Agency
USSR	Union of Soviet Socialist Republics
UTM	Universal Transverse Mercator
UWI	Univ. of the West Indies
v.	volume(s), volumen (volúmenes)
Va.	Virginia
V.I.	Virgin Islands
viz.	*videlicet* (that is, namely)
vol(s).	volume(s), volumen (volúmenes)
vs.	versus
Vt.	Vermont
W.Va.	West Virginia
Wash.	Washington
Wis.	Wisconsin
WPA	Working People's Alliance, Guyana
WWI	World War I
WWII	World War II
Wyo.	Wyoming
yr(s).	year(s)

TITLE LIST OF JOURNALS INDEXED

For journal titles listed by abbreviation, see *Abbreviation List of Journals Indexed*, p. 553.

Acervos: Boletín de los Archivos y Bibliotecas de Oaxaca. Asociación Civil Amigos de los Archivos y Bibliotecas de Oaxaca. Oaxaca, Mexico. (Acervos/Oaxaca)

Acta geographica. Société de Géographie. Paris. (Acta geogr.)

Agenda Internacional. Pontificia Univ. Católica del Perú, Instituto de Estudios Internacionales. Lima (Agenda Int.)

Agriculture, Ecosystems & Environment. Elsevier. New York. (Agric. Ecosystems Environ.)

Agroalimentaria. Univ. de los Andes, Facultad de Ciencias Económicas y Sociales, Centro de Investigaciones Agroalimentarias. Mérida, Venezuela. (Agroalimentaria)

Aldea Mundo: Revista sobre Fronteras e Integración. Univ. de los Andes-San Cristóbal, Centro de Estudios de Fronteras e Integración "Dr. José Briceño Monzillo." San Cristóbal, Venezuela. (Aldea Mundo)

Allpanchis. Instituto de Pastoral Andina. Cuzco, Peru. (Allpanchis/Cuzco)

Alternativa. Instituto de Ciencias Alejandro Lipschutz. Santiago, Chile. (Alternativa/Santiago)

Ambio. Royal Swedish Academy of Sciences. Stockholm. (Ambio/Stockholm)

América Latina Hoy: Revista de Ciencias Sociales. Univ. de Salamanca, Instituto de Estudios de Iberoamérica y Portugal. Salamanca, Spain. (Am. Lat. Hoy/Salamanca)

América Latina: Revista del Doctorado en el Estudio de las Sociedades Latinoamericana. Univ. ARCIS. Santiago, Chile. (Am. Lat./Santiago)

American Anthropologist. American Anthropological Assn. Washington, D.C. (Am. Anthropol.)

American Ethnologist. American Anthropological Assn., American Ethnological Society. Washington, D.C. (Am. Ethnol./Washington)

The Americas: A Quarterly Review of Inter-American Cultural History. Catholic Univ. of America, Academy of American Franciscan History; Catholic Univ. of America Press. Washington, D.C. (Americas/Washington)

Anais do Museu Paulista: História e Cultura Material. Museu Paulista. São Paulo. (An. Mus. Paul.)

Anales del Museo de América. Museo de América, Dirección General de Bellas Artes y Bienes Culturales, Ministerio de Educación, Cultura y Deporte. Madrid. (An. Mus. Am.)

Análise Econômica. Univ. Federal do Rio Grande do Sul, Faculdade de Ciências Econômicas. Porto Alegre, Brazil. (Anál. Econ./Porto Alegre)

Análise Social. Univ. de Lisboa, Instituto de Ciências Sociais. Lisboa. (Anál. Soc./Lisboa)

Ancient Mesoamerica. Cambridge Univ. Press. Cambridge, England; New York. (Anc. Mesoam.)

Andamios. Univ. de la Ciudad de México, Colegio de Humanidades y Ciencias Sociales. México. (Andamios)

Ankulegi. Ankulegi Antropologia Elkartea. Donostia, Spain. (Ankulegi)

Annals of the Association of American Geographers. Blackwell Publishers. Oxford, England; Malden, Mass. (Ann. Assoc. Am. Geogr.)

Annual Review of Entomology. Annual Reviews, Inc. Palo Alto, Calif. (Annu. Rev. Entomol.)

Annual Review of Political Science. Annual Reviews, Inc. Palo Alto, Calif. (Annu. Rev. Polit. Sci.)

Anthropological Quarterly. Catholic Univ. Press of America. Washington, D.C. (Anthropol. Q.)

Anthropology of Consciousness. American Anthropological Assn. Washington, D.C. (Anthropol. Consciousness)

Anthropos: International Review of Ethnology and Linguistics. Anthropos-Institut. Freiburg, Switzerland. (Anthropos/Freiburg)

Antípoda: Revista de Antropología y Arqueología. Depto. de Antropología, Facultad de Ciencias Sociales, Univ. de los Andes. Bogotá. (Antípoda)

Antipode. Basil Blackwell. Oxford, England; Cambridge, Mass. (Antipode)

Antiquity. Antiquity Publications Ltd. Cambridge, England. (Antiquity/Cambridge)

Anuario de Estudios Centroamericanos. Univ. de Costa Rica. San José. (Anu. Estud. Centroam.)

Anuario Demográfico de Cuba. Dirección de Estadísticas de Población, Dirección General de Estadística, JUCEPLAN. La Habana. (Anu. Demogr. Cuba)

Anuario Estadístico de Cuba. Dirección General de Estadística. La Habana. (Anu. Estad. Cuba)

Anuario IEHS. Univ. Nacional del Centro de la Provincia de Buenos Aires, Facultad de Ciencias Humanas, Instituto de Estudios Histórico-Sociales. Tandil, Argentina. (Anu. IEHS)

Applied Geography. Butterworths. Sevenoaks, Kent, England. (Appl. Geogr.)

Arqueologia. Univ. Federal do Paraná, Centro de Estudos e Pesquisas Arqueológicas (CEPA). Curitiba, Brazil. (Arqueologia/Curitiba)

Arqueología. Instituto Nacional de Antropología e Historia, Coordinación Nacional de Arqueología. México. (Arqueología/México)

Arqueología Mexicana. Instituto Nacional de Antropología e Historia; Editorial Raíces. México. (Arqueol. Mex.)

The Art Bulletin. College Art Assn. of America. New York. (Art Bull.)

Avá: Revista de Antropología. Programa de Posgrado en Antropología Social, Univ. Nacional de Misiones. Argentina. (Avá)

Belizean Studies. Belizean Institute of Social Research and Action; St. John's College. Belize City. (Belizean Stud.)

Biology Letters. The Royal Society. London. (Biol. Letters)

BioScience. American Institute of Biological Sciences. Washington, D.C. (BioScience)

Boletim do Museu Paraense Emílio Goeldi Série Ciências Humanas. Museu Paraense Emílio Goeldi. Belém, Brazil. (Bol. Mus. Para. Emílio Goeldi Sér. Ciênc. Hum.)

Boletín Cuatrimestral. Centro de Estudios de la Economía Cubana (CEEC). La Habana. (Bol. Cuatrimestral)

Boletín de Historia y Antigüedades. Academia Colombiana de Historia. Bogotá. (Bol. Hist. Antig.)

Boletín de Lima: Revista Cultural Científica. Asociación Cultural Boletín de Lima A.C. Lima. (Bol. Lima)

Boletín del Museo Chileno de Arte Precolombino. Santiago, Chile. (Bol. Mus. Chil. Arte Precolomb.)

Bulletin de l'Institut français d'études andines. Lima. (Bull. Inst. fr. étud. andin.)

Bulletin of Latin American Research. Blackwell Publishers. Oxford, England; Malden, Mass. (Bull. Lat. Am. Res.)

Caderno CRH. Univ. Federal da Bahia, Faculdade de Filosofia e Ciências Humanas, Centro de Recursos Humanos. Salvador, Brazil. (Cad. CRH/Salvador)

Cadernos de Estudos Sociais. Fundação Joaquim Nabuco, Instituto de Pesquisas Sociais. Recife, Brazil. (Cad. Estud. Sociais)

Cahiers des Amériques latines. Univ. de la Sorbonne nouvelle—Paris III, Institut des haute études de l'Amérique latine. Paris. (Cah. Am. lat.)

Caleidoscopio. Univ. Autónoma de Aguascalientes, Centro de Artes y Humanidades. Aguascalientes, Mexico. (Caleidoscopio/Aguascalientes)

The Canadian Mineralogist. Mineralogical Association of Canada. Ottawa. (Can. Mineralogist)

Caribbean Journal of Science. Univ. of Puerto Rico, College of Arts and Sciences. Mayagüez, Puerto Rico. (Caribb. J. Sci.)

Caribbean Quarterly: CQ. Univ. of the West Indies, Vice Chancellery, Cultural Studies Initiative. Mona, Jamaica. (Caribb. Q./Mona)

Caribbean Studies. Univ. of Puerto Rico, Institute of Caribbean Studies. Río Piedras, Puerto Rico. (Caribb. Stud.)

Catauro: Revista Cubana de Antropología. Fundación Fernando Ortiz. La Habana. (Catauro/Habana)

CEPAL Review. UN, Comisión Económica para América Latina (CEPAL). Santiago, Chile. (CEPAL Rev.)

Chiapas. UNAM, Instituto de Investigaciones Económicas. México. (Chiapas/México)

Chihuahua Hoy. Univ. Autónoma de Ciudad Juárez. Ciudad Juárez, Mexico. (Chihuah. Hoy)

Ciclos en la Historia, Economía y la Sociedad. Univ. de Buenos Aires, Facultad de Ciencias Económicas, Instituto de Investigaciones de Historia Económica y Social. Buenos Aires. (Ciclos Hist. Econ. Soc.)

Ciencia y Sociedad. Instituto Tecnológico de Santo Domingo. Santo Domingo. (Cienc. Soc./Santo Domingo)

Ciudad y Territorio Estudios Territoriales. Ministerio de Fomento, Centro de Publicaciones. Madrid. (Ciudad Territ. Estud. Territ.)

Civilisations. Univ. Libre de Bruxelles, Institut de Sociologie. Brussels. (Civilisations/Brussels)

Colombia Internacional. Univ. de los Andes, Centro de Estudios Internacionales. Bogotá(Colomb. Int.)

Comercio Exterior. Banco Nacional de Comercio Exterior. México. (Comer. Exter.)

Community Development: Journal of the Community Development Society. The Community Development Society. Columbus, Ohio. (Community Dev.)

Comparative Political Studies. Sage Publications. Thousand Oaks, Calif. (Comp. Polit. Stud.)

Comparative Politics. City Univ. of New York, Political Science Program. New York. (Comp. Polit./New York)

Conservation Biology. Blackwell Scientific Publications. Boston, Mass. (Conserv. Biol.)

Contexto Internacional. Pontifícia Univ. Católica, Instituto de Relações Internacionais. Rio de Janeiro. (Contexto Int.)

Convergencia: Revista de Ciencias Sociales. Univ. Autónoma del Estado de México, Facultad de Ciencias Políticas y Administración Pública. Toluca, Mexico. (Convergencia/Toluca)

Coral Reefs. Springer International. Berlin. (Coral Reefs)

El Cotidiano: Revista de la Realidad Mexicana Actual. Univ. Autónoma Metropolitana—Unidad Azcapotzalco, División de Ciencias Sociales y Humanidades. México. (Cotidiano/México)

Critique of Anthropology. Sage Publications. London. (Crit. Anthropol.)

Cuadernos Americanos. UNAM. México. (Cuad. Am./México)

Cuadernos de Antropología. Univ. de Costa Rica, Depto. de Antropología, Laboratorio de Etnología. San José. (Cuad. Antropol./San José)

Cuadernos de Economía: Latin American Journal of Economics. Pontificia Univ. Católica de Chile, Facultad de Ciencias Económicas y Administrativas, Instituto de Economía. Santiago. (Cuad. Econ./Santiago)

Cuba in Transition: Papers and Proceedings of the . . . Annual Meeting of the Association for the Study of the Cuban Economy. Assn. for the Study of the Cuban Economy. Washington, D.C. (Cuba Transit.)

Cuba Siglo XXI (Online). La Habana; http://www.nodo50.org/cubasigloXXI/. (Cuba Siglo XXI (online))

Cuban Affairs. Univ. of Miami, Institute for Cuban and Cuban-American Studies. Coral Gables, Fla. (Cuban Aff.)

Cuban Studies. Univ. of Pittsburgh Press. Pittsburgh, Pa. (Cuba. Stud.)

Cultural Anthropology: Journal of the Society for Cultural Anthropology. American Anthropological Assn., Society for Cultural Anthropology. Washington, D.C. (Cult. Anthropol.)

Culture & Agriculture: Bulletin of the Anthropological Study Group on Agrarian Systems. The Study Group. Corvallis, Ore. (Cult. Agric.)

Current Anthropology. Univ. of Chicago Press. Chicago, Ill. (Curr. Anthropol.)

Dados. Instituto Universitário de Pesquisas do Rio de Janeiro. Rio de Janeiro. (Dados/Rio de Janeiro)

Debate Agrario. Centro Peruano de Estudios Sociales. Lima. (Debate Agrar.)

Demography. Population Assn. of America. Washington, D.C. (Demography/Washington)

Desacatos. CIESAS, Centro de Investigaciones y Estudios Superiores en Antropología Social. México. (Desacatos)

Desarrollo Económico: Revista de Ciencias Sociales. Instituto de Desarrollo Económico y Social. Buenos Aires. (Desarro. Econ.)

Desarrollo y Sociedad. Univ. de los Andes, Facultad de Economía, Centro de Estudios sobre el Desarrollo Económico. Bogotá. (Desarro. Soc.)

Earth and Environmental Science Transactions of the Royal Society of Edinburgh. RSE Scotland Foundation. Edinburgh. (Earth Environ. Sci.)

ECA. Univ. Centroamericana José Simeón Cañas. San Salvador. (ECA/San Salvador)

Ecología Política: Cuadernos de Debate Internacional. Icaria Editorial; Fundación Hogar del Empleado. Barcelona. (Ecol. Polít./Barcelona)

Ecology and Society (online). Resilience Alliance Publications. Waterloo, Ontario, Canada. (Ecol. Soc. (online))

Economía. Pontificia Univ. Católica del Perú, Depto. de Economía. Lima. (Economía/Lima)

Economía, Sociedad y Territorio. El Colegio Mexiquense. Toluca, Mexico. (Econ. Soc. Territ.)

Economía Mexicana. Centro de Investigación y Docencia Económicas. México. (Econ. Mex.)

Economic Development and Cultural Change. Univ. of Chicago Press. Chicago, Ill. (Econ. Dev. Cult. Change)

Economic Geography. Clark Univ. Worcester, Mass. (Econ. Geogr.)

Economics Press Service. Havana Inter Press Service Tercer Mundo. Havana. (Econ. Press Serv.)

Ecuador Debate. Centro Andino de Acción Popular. Quito. (Ecuad. Debate)

Encuentro de la Cultura Cubana. Asociación Encuentro de la Cultura Cubana. Madrid. (Encuentro Cult. Cuba.)

Ensaios FEE. Governo do Rio Grande do Sul, Secretaria de Coordenação e Planejamento, Fundação de Economia e Estatística Siegfried Emanuel Heuser. Porto Alegre, Brazil. (Ensaios FEE)

Ensayos sobre Política Económica. Banco de la República, Subgerencia de Estudios Económicos. Bogotá. (Ens. Polít. Econ.)

Environment, Development and Sustainability. Kluwer Academic Publishers. Boston, Mass. (Environ. Dev. Sustain.)

Environment and Planning A. Pion Ltd. London. (Environ. Plann. A)

Environment and Planning: D, Society & Space. Pion Ltd. London. (Environ. Plann. D Soc. Space)

Environment and Urbanization. Human Settlements Programme, International Institute for Environment and Development. London. (Environ. Urban.)

Environmental Conservation. Cambridge Univ. Press. Cambridge, England. (Environ. Conserv./Cambridge)

Environmental Management. Springer-Verlag New York, Inc. New York. (Environ. Manag.)

Erdkunde: Archiv für Wissenschaftliche Geographie (Archive for Scientific Geography). Univ. Bonn, Geographisches Institut. Bonn, Germany. (Erdkunde/Bonn)

Espacio Laical. Consejo Arquidiocesano de Laicos de La Habana. La Habana. (Espacio Laical)

EspacioTiempo: Revista Latinoamericana de Ciencias Sociales y Humanidades. Univ. Autónoma de San Luis Potosi. San Luis Potosi, Mexico. (EspacioTiempo)

Espiral: Estudios sobre Estado y Sociedad. Univ. de Guadalajara, Centro Universitario de Ciencias Sociales y Humanidades. Guadalajara, Mexico. (Espiral/Guadalajara)

Estudios Atacameños. Univ. del Norte, Museo de Arqueología. San Pedro de Atacama, Chile. (Estud. Atacameños)

Estudios de Cultura Maya. UNAM, Instituto de Investigaciones Filológicas, Centro de Estudios Mayas. México. (Estud. Cult. Maya)

Estudios de Cultura Náhuatl. UNAM, Instituto de Investigaciones Históricas. México. (Estud. Cult. Náhuatl)

Estudios de Cultura Otopame. UNAM, Instituto de Investigaciones Antropológicas. México. (Estud. Cult. Otopame)

Estudios Fronterizos. Univ. Autónoma de Baja California, Instituto de Investigaciones Sociales. Mexicali, Mexico. (Estud. Front.)

Estudios Geográficos. Instituto de Economía y Geografía Aplicadas. Madrid. (Estud. Geogr./Madrid)

Estudios Internacionales. Univ. de Chile, Instituto de Estudios Internacionales. Santiago. (Estud. Int./Santiago)

Estudios Jaliscienses. El Colegio de Jalisco. Zapopan, Mexico. (Estud. Jalisc.)

Estudios Latinoamericanos. UNAM, Facultad de Ciencias Políticas y Sociales, División de Estudios de Posgrado, Centro de Estudios Latinoamericanos. México. (Estud. Latinoam./México)

Estudios Paraguayos. Univ. Católica Nuestra Señora de la Asunción. Asunción. (Estud. Parag.)

Estudios Políticos: Revista de Ciencias Políticas y Administración Pública. UNAM, Facultad de Ciencias Políticas y Sociales. México. (Estud. Polít./México)

Estudios Públicos. Centro de Estudios Públicos. Santiago, Chile. (Estud. Públicos)

Estudios Sociales: Revista Universitaria Semestral. Univ. Nacional del Litoral, Secretaría de Extensión, Centro de Publicaciones. Santa Fe, Argentina. (Estud. Soc./Santa Fe)

Estudios Sociológicos. El Colegio de México, Centro de Estudios Sociológicos. México. (Estud. Sociol./México)

Estudos Avançados. Univ. de São Paulo, Instituto de Estudos Avançados. São Paulo. (Estud. Av.)

Estudos Econômicos. Univ. de São Paulo, Faculdade de Economia, Administração e Contabilidade, Fundação Instituto de Pesquisas Econômicas. São Paulo. (Estud. Econ./São Paulo)

Estudos: Revista da Universidade Católica de Goiás. Univ. Católica de Goiás. Goiânia, Brazil. (Estudos/Goiânia)

Estudos Sociedade e Agricultura. Univ. Federal Rural do Rio de Janeiro, Instituto de Ciências Humanas e Sociais, Curso de Pós-Graduação em Desenvolvimento, Agricultura e Sociedade, Depto. de Letras e Ciências Sociais. Rio de Janeiro. (Estud. Soc. Agric.)

Ethnohistory: The Bulletin of the Ohio Valley Historic Indian Conference. American Society for Ethnohistory. Columbus, Ohio. (Ethnohistory/Columbus)

Ethnos. Statens Etnografiska Museum. Stockholm. (Ethnos/Stockholm)

EURE: Revista Latinoamericana de Estudios Urbano Regionales. Pontificia Univ. Católica de Chile, Facultad de Arquitectura y Bellas Artes, Instituto de Estudios Urbanos. Santiago. (EURE/Santiago)

The European Journal of Development Research. Frank Cass. London. (Eur. J. Dev. Res.)

Foro Internacional. El Colegio de México, Centro de Estudios Internacionales. México. (Foro Int./México)

Frontera Norte. El Colegio de la Frontera Norte. Tijuana, Mexico. (Front. Norte)

Gender, Place and Culture: A Journal of Feminist Geography. Carfax Pub. Co. Abingdon, England. (Gend. Place Cult.)

Geoarchaeology. John Wiley. New York. (Geoarchaeology/New York)

Geoderma. Elsevier Scientific Pub. Co. Amsterdam, N.Y. (Geoderma)

Geoforum. Pergamon Press. New York; Oxford, England. (Geoforum/New York)

Geographica Helvetica. Schweizerische Zeitschrift für Länder- und Völkerkunde; Kümmerly & Frey, Geographischer Verlag. Bern, Switzerland. (Geogr. Helv.)

The Geographical Journal. The Royal Geographical Society. London; Institute of British Geographers. Cambridge, England. (Geogr. J./London)

Geographical Review. American Geographical Society. New York. (Geogr. Rev.)

Geographische Rundschau. Westermann Schulbuchverlag GmbH. Braunschweig, Germany. (Geogr. Rundsch.)

Geography. Geographical Assn. London. (Geography/London)

Geography Compass. Blackwell Publishing. Oxford, England. (Geogr. Compass)

GeoJournal. D. Reidel Publishing Co. Boston, Mass. (GeoJournal/Boston)

Geopolitics. Frank Cass. London. (Geopolitics/London)

GIScience & Remote Sensing. V.H. Winston & Son, Inc. Palm Beach, Fla. (GIScience Remote Sensing)

Guaraguao: Revista de Cultura Latinoamericano. Univ. Autónoma de Barcelona, Centro de Estudios y Cooperación para América Latina. Barcelona. (Guaraguao/Barcelona)

Herramienta: Revista de Debate y Crítica Marxista. Editorial Antídoto. Buenos Aires. (Herramienta/Buenos Aires)

Hispanic American Historical Review. Duke Univ. Press. Durham, N.C. (HAHR)

História Ciências Saúde: Manguinhos. Fundação Oswaldo Cruz, Casa de Oswaldo Cruz. Rio de Janeiro. (Hist. Ciênc. Saúde Manguinhos)

Historia Mexicana. El Colegio de México, Centro de Estudios Históricos. México. (Hist. Mex./México)

Historia y Política. Univ. Complutense de Madrid, Depto. de Historia del Pensamiento y de los Movimientos Sociales y Políticos; Univ. Nacional de Educación a Distancia, Depto. de Historia Social y del Pensamiento Político. Madrid. (Hist. Polít.)

History Workshop Journal. Oxford Univ. Press. Oxford, England. (Hist. Workshop J.)

Hombre y Desierto: Una Perspectiva Cultural. Univ. de Antofagasta, Instituto de Investigaciones Antropológicas. Antofagasta, Chile. (Hombre Desierto)

Human Ecology. Kluwer Academic Publishers. Dordrecht, N.Y. (Hum. Ecol.)

Human Organization. Society for Applied Anthropology. Washington, D.C. (Hum. Organ.)

Human Rights Quarterly. Johns Hopkins Univ. Press. Baltimore, Md. (Hum. Rights Q.)

Iberoamericana: Nordic Journal of Latin American Studies/Revista Nórdica de Estudios Latinoamericanos. Stockholm Univ., Institute of Latin American Studies. Stockholm. (Iberoamericana/Stockholm)

ICONOS. FLACSO Ecuador. Quito. (ICONOS/Quito)

Informações Econômicas. Governo do Estado de São Paulo, Secretaria de Agricultura e Abastecimento, Instituto de Economia Agrícola. São Paulo. (Inf. Econ./São Paulo)

Integración & Comercio. Instituto para la Integración de América Latina, Depto. de Integración y Programas Regionales, Banco Interamericano de Desarrollo = Inter-American Development Bank. Buenos Aires. (Integr. Comer.)

Interciencia. Asociación Interciencia. Caracas. (Interciencia/Caracas)

International Journal of South American Archaeology. Syllaba Press. Miami, Fla. (Int. J. South Am. Archaeol.)

International Migration. International Organization for Migration. Geneva; Blackwell Publishers, Ltd. Oxford, England; Malden, Mass. (Int. Migr./Oxford)

International Political Science Review: IPSR. Sage Publications. Beverly Hills, Calif. (Int. Polit. Sci. Rev.)

International Regional Science Review. West Virginia Univ., Regional Research Institute. Morgantown. (Int. Reg. Sci. Rev.)

International Studies Quarterly. Blackwell Publishers. Malden, Mass.; Oxford, England. (Int. Stud. Q./Oxford)

International Studies Review. Blackwell Publishers for the International Studies Association. Malden, Mass. (Int. Stud. Rev.)

Investigaciones Geográficas. Univ. de Chile, Depto. de Geografía. Santiago. (Invest. Geogr./Santiago)

Investigaciones Geográficas: Boletín del Instituto de Geografía. UNAM, Instituto de Geografía. México. (Invest. Geogr./México)

Investigaciones Sociales: Revista del Instituto de Investigaciones Histórico Sociales. Univ. Nacional Mayor de San Marcos, Facultad de Ciencias Sociales. Lima. (Investig. Soc./San Marcos)

Journal of Agrarian Change. Blackwell Publishers. Oxford, England; Malden, Mass. (J. Agrarian Change)

Journal of Anthropological Archaeology. Academic Press. New York. (J. Anthropol. Archaeol.)

Journal of Anthropological Research. Univ. of New Mexico. Albuquerque. (J. Anthropol. Res.)

Journal of Archaeological Research. Plenum Press. New York. (J. Archaeol. Res.)

Journal of Archaeological Science. Academic Press. New York. (J. Archaeol. Sci.)

Journal of Biogeography. Blackwell Scientific Publications. Oxford, England. (J. Biogeogr.)

Journal of Caribbean Archaeology. Univ. of Florida, Florida Museum of Natural History. Gainesville, Fla. (J. Caribb. Archaeol.)

Journal of Democracy. National Endowment for Democracy, International Forum for Democratic Studies. Washington, D.C.; Johns Hopkins Univ. Press. Baltimore, Md. (J. Democr.)

Journal of Ethnobiology. Society of Ethnobiology; Tulane Univ., Dept. of Anthropology. New Orleans, La. (J. Ethnobiol.)

Journal of Ethnobiology and Ethnomedicine. Biomed Central. London. (J. Ethnobiol. Ethnomed.)

Journal of Field Archaeology. Boston Univ. Boston, Mass. (J. Field Archaeol.)

Journal of Geography. National Council of Geographic Education. Menasha, Wis. (J. Geogr.)

Journal of Historical Geography. Academic Press. London; New York. (J. Hist. Geogr.)

Journal of Island & Coastal Archaeology. Taylor & Francis Group. Philadelphia, Pa. (J. Island Coastal Archaeol.)

The Journal of Latin American and Caribbean Anthropology. Univ. of California Press, Journals Division. Berkeley, Calif. (J. Lat. Am. Caribb. Anthropol.)

Journal of Latin American Cultural Studies. Carfax Publishing. Abingdon, England. (J. Lat. Am. Cult. Stud.)

Journal of Latin American Geography. Conference of Latin Americanist Geographers. Tucson, Ariz. (J. Lat. Am. Geogr.)

Journal of Latin American Studies. Cambridge Univ. Press. Cambridge, England. (J. Lat. Am. Stud.)

The Journal of Peasant Studies. Frank Cass & Co. London. (J. Peasant Stud.)

Journal of Political and Military Sociology: JPMS. Northern Illinois Univ., Dept. of Sociology. DeKalb, Ill. (J. Polit. Mil. Sociol.)

Journal of Political Economy. Univ. of Chicago Press. Chicago, Ill. (J. Polit. Econ.)

The Journal of Politics. Blackwell Publishers. Abingdon, England; Williston, Vt.; Southern Political Science Assn.; Univ. of North Carolina. Chapel Hill. (J. Polit.)

Journal of Psychoactive Drugs. Haight-Ashbury Publications. San Francisco, Calif. (J. Psychoactive Drugs)

Journal of Public Health Policy. South Burlington, Vt. (J. Public Health Policy)

Journal of Regional Science. Regional Science Research Institute. Amherst, Mass. (J. Reg. Sci.)

The Journal of Socio-Economics. Elsevier Science, Inc. New York; Amsterdam. (J. Socio-Econ./New York)

Journal of Sustainable Forestry. Food Products Press. Binghamton, N.Y. (J. Sustain. For.)

The Journal of the Royal Anthropological Institute. London. (J. Royal Anthropol. Inst.)

Journal of the West. Sunflower Univ. Press. Manhattan, Kan. (J. West/Manhattan)

Journal of Transport Geography. Butterworth-Heinemann. London. (J. Transport Geogr.)

Journal of Urban Affairs. Division of Environment and Urban Systems, Virginia Polytechnic Institute and State Univ. Blacksburg, Va. (J. Urban Aff.)

Journal of Women, Politics & Policy. Haworth Press, Inc. Binghamton, N.Y. (J. Women Polit. Policy)

Land Use Policy. Butterworths. Guildford, England. (Land Use Policy)

Latin American and Caribbean Ethnic Studies. Taylor & Francis. Colchester, England. (Lat. Am. Caribb. Ethn. Stud.)

Latin American Antiquity. Society for American Archaeology. Washington, D.C. (Lat. Am. Antiq.)

Latin American Business Review. Business Assn. of Latin American Studies; International Business Press. Binghamton, N.Y. (Lat. Am. Bus. Rev.)

Latin American Indian Literatures Journal. Geneva College, Dept. of Foreign Languages. Beaver Falls, Pa. (Lat. Am. Indian Lit. J.)

Latin American Perspectives. Sage Publications, Inc. Thousand Oaks, Calif. (Lat. Am. Perspect.)

Latin American Politics and Society. Univ. of Miami, School of Interamerican Studies. Coral Gables, Fla. (Lat. Am. Polit. Soc.)

Latin American Research Review. Latin American Studies Assn.; Univ. of Texas Press. Austin. (LARR)

Lecturas de Economía. Univ. de Antioquia, Facultad de Ciencias Económicas, Depto. de Economía, Centro de Investigaciones Económicas. Medellín, Colombia. (Lect. Econ.)

Lua Nova. Centro de Estudos de Cultura Contemporânea. São Paulo. (Lua Nova)

Luso-Brazilian Review. Univ. of Wisconsin Press. Madison. (Luso-Braz. Rev.)

Maguaré. Univ. Nacional de Colombia, Depto. de Antropología. Bogotá. (Maguaré/Bogotá)

Mana: Estudos de Antropologia Social. Univ. Federal do Rio de Janeiro, Museu Nacional, Programa de Pós-Graduação em Antropologia Social. Rio de Janeiro. (Mana/Rio de Janeiro)

Mappemonde. RECLUS. Montpellier, France. (Mappemonde)

Mayab. Sociedad Española de Estudios Mayas. Madrid. (Mayab/Madrid)

Mesoamérica. Plumsock Mesoamerican Studies. South Woodstock, Vt.; Centro de Investigaciones Regionales de Mesoamérica. Antigua, Guatemala. (Mesoamérica/Antigua)

Metapolítica: Revista Trimestral de Teoría y Ciencia de la Política. Centro de Estudios de Política Comparada. México. (Metapolítica/México)

Mexican Studies/Estudios Mexicanos. Univ. of California Press. Berkeley. (Mex. Stud.)

Mexicon. Verlag Anton Saurwein. Markt Schwaben, Germany. (Mexicon/Germany)

Migraciones Internacionales. El Colegio de la Frontera Norte. Tijuana, Mexico. (Migr. Int.)

Nature: International Weekly Journal of Science. Macmillan Magazines. London. (Nature/London)

New Left Review. New Left Review, Ltd. London. (New Left Rev.)

Nóesis: Revista de Ciencias Sociales y Humanidades. Univ. Autónoma de Ciudad Juárez. Dirección General de Investigación y Posgrado. Ciudad Juárez, Mexico. (Nóesis/UACJ)

Nova Economia. Univ. Federal de Minas Gerais, Faculdade de Ciências Econômicas, Depto. de Ciências Econômicas. Belo Horizonte, Brazil. (Nova Econ./Belo Horizonte)

Novos Estudos CEBRAP. Centro Brasileiro de Análise e Planejamento. São Paulo. (Novos Estud. CEBRAP)

Nueva Sociedad. Fundación Friedrich Ebert. Caracas. (Nueva Soc.)

NWIG: New West Indian Guide/Nieuwe West Indische Gids. Royal Institute of Linguistics and Anthropology, KITLV Press. Leiden, The Netherlands. (NWIG)

Observatorio Social de América Latina. Consejo Latinoamericano de Ciencias Sociales. Buenos Aires. (Obs. Soc. Am. Lat.)

Opinião Pública. Univ. Estadual de Campinas, Centro de Estudos de Opinião Pública. Campinas, Brazil. (Opin. Públ.)

Papeles de Geografía. Univ. de Murcia, Facultad de Letras, Depto. de Geografía Física, Humana y Análisis Regional. Murcia, Spain. (Pap. Geogr.)

Peace Review. Peace Review Publications. Palo Alto, Calif. (Peace Rev.)

Perfiles Latinoamericanos. Facultad Latinoamericana de Ciencias Sociales (FLACSO). México. (Perf. Latinoam.)

Persona y Sociedad. Instituto Latinoamericano de Doctrina y Estudios Sociales. Santiago, Chile. (Pers. Soc.)

Pesquisas Antropologia. Instituto Anchietano de Pesquisas. São Leopoldo, Brazil. (Pesqui. Antropol.)

Philosophical Transactions of the Royal Society of London. Series B, Biological Sciences. Royal Society of London. London. (Philos. Trans.)

Política Exterior. Estudios de Política Exterior S.A. Madrid. (Polít. Exter./Madrid)

Política Internacional. Academia Diplomática del Peru. Lima. (Polít. Int./Lima)

Política y Cultura. Univ. Autónoma Metropolitana—Xochimilco, División de Ciencias Sociales y Humanidades, Depto. de Política y Cultura. México. (Polít. Cult.)

Política y Gestión. Univ. Nacional de General San Martín. Rosario, Argentina. (Polít. Gest.)

Política y Sociedad. Univ. Complutense, Facultad de Ciencias Políticas y Sociología. Madrid. (Polít. Soc./Madrid)

Political Research Quarterly. Univ. of Utah. Salt Lake City. (Polit. Res. Q.)

Political Science Quarterly. The Academy of Political Science. New York. (Polit. Sci. Q.)

Population and Development Review. Population Council. New York. (Popul. Dev. Rev.)

Population Research and Policy Review. Elsevier Scientific Pub. Co. Amsterdam. (Popul. Res. Policy Rev.)

Problems of Post-Communism. M.E. Sharpe. Armonk, N.Y. (Probl. Post-Communism)

Proceedings of the National Academy of Sciences of the United States of America. Washington, D.C. (Proc. Natl. Acad. Sci. U.S.A.)

The Professional Geographer. Assn. of American Geographers. Washington, D.C.; Blackwell Publishers. Abindgon, England; Williston, Vt. (Prof. Geogr.)

Prohistoria. Manuel Suárez Editor. Rosario, Argentina. (Prohistoria/Rosario)

Public Administration and Development.
Wiley. Sussex, England. (Public Adm. Dev.)

Rábida. Patronato Provincial del V Centenario del Descubrimiento de América. Huelva, Spain. (Rábida/Huelva)

Realidad: Revista de Ciencias Sociales y Humanidades. Univ. Centroamericana José Simeón Cañas. San Salvador. (Realidad/San Salvador)

REIS: Revista Española de Investigaciones Sociológicas. Centro de Investigaciones Sociológicas. Madrid. (Rev. Esp. Invest. Sociol.)

Relaciones. El Colegio de Michoacán. Zamora, Mexico. (Relaciones/Zamora)

Relaciones de la Sociedad Argentina de Antropología. Buenos Aires. (Relac. Soc. Argent. Antropol.)

Relaciones Internacionales. UNAM, Facultad de Ciencias Políticas y Sociales, Coordinación de Relaciones Internacionales. México. (Relac. Int./México)

REN: Revista Econômica do Nordeste. Banco do Nordeste do Brasil, Escritório Técnico de Estudos Econômicos do Nordeste. Fortaleza, Brazil. (REN Rev. Econ. Nordeste)

Res. Harvard Univ., Peabody Museum of Archaeology and Ethnology. Cambridge, Mass. (Res/Cambridge)

Rethinking Marxism. Association for Economic and Social Analysis. Amherst, Mass. (Rethinking Marx.)

Revista Argentina de Ciencia Política. Editorial Universitaria de Buenos Aires. Buenos Aires. (Rev. Arg. Cienc. Polít.)

Revista Brasileira de Comércio Exterior: RBCE. Fundação Centro de Estudos do Comércio Exterior. Rio de Janeiro. (Rev. Bras. Comér. Exter.)

Revista Brasileira de Economia. Fundação Getúlio Vargas, Escola de Pós-Graduação em Economia. Rio de Janeiro. (Rev. Bras. Econ./Rio de Janeiro)

Revista Brasileira de Estudos de População. Associação Brasileira de Estudos Populacionais. São Paulo. (Rev. Bras. Estud. Popul.)

Revista Brasileira de Política Internacional: RBPI. Instituto Brasileiro de Relações Internacionais. Brasília. (Rev. Bras. Polít. Int.)

Revista Centroamericana de Economía. Univ. Nacional Autónoma de Honduras,

Programa de Postgrado Centroamericano en Economía y Planificación del Desarrollo. Tegucigalpa. (Rev. Centroam. Econ.)

Revista Chilena de Historia y Geografía. Sociedad Chilena de Historia y Geografía. Santiago. (Rev. Chil. Hist. Geogr.)

Revista Colombiana de Antropología. Ministerio de Educación Nacional, Instituto Colombiano de Antropología. Bogotá. (Rev. Colomb. Antropol.)

Revista Crítica de Ciências Sociais. Centro de Estudos Sociais. Coimbra, Portugal. (Rev. Crít. Ciênc. Sociais)

Revista de Administração (RAUSP). Univ. de São Paulo, Faculdade de Ciências Econômicas e Administrativas, Instituto de Administração, Serviço de Documentação. São Paulo. (Rev. Adm./São Paulo)

Revista de Antropologia. Univ. de São Paulo, Faculdade de Filosofia, Letras e Ciências Humanas, Depto. de Antropologia. São Paulo. (Rev. Antropol./São Paulo)

Revista de Arqueologia. Sociedade de Arqueologia Brasileira. São Paulo. (Rev. Arqueol./São Paulo)

Revista de Arqueología Americana. Instituto Panamericano de Geografía e Historia. México. (Rev. Arqueol. Am./México)

Revista de Ciencia Política. Pontificia Univ. Católica de Chile, Instituto de Ciencia Política. Santiago. (Rev. Cienc. Polít./Santiago)

Revista de Ciencias Sociales: RCS. Univ. de Zulia, Facultad de Ciencias Económicas y Sociales, Instituto de Investigaciones. Maracaibo, Venezuela. (Rev. Cienc. Soc./Maracaibo)

Revista de Economia e Sociologia Rural = Brazilian Review of Agricultural Economics and Rural Sociology. Sociedade Brasileira de Economia e Sociologia Rural = Brazilian Society of Agricultural Economics and Rural Sociology. Brasília. (Rev. Econ. Sociol. Rural)

Revista de Economia Política = Brazilian Journal of Political Economy. Centro de Economia Política. São Paulo. (Rev. Econ. Polít.)

Revista de Geografía Norte Grande. Pontificia Univ. Católica de Chile, Facultad de Historia, Geografía y Ciencia Política, Instituto de Geografía. Santiago. (Rev. Geogr. Norte Gd.)

Revista de Indias. Consejo Superior de Investigaciones Científicas, Instituto de

Historia, Depto. de Historia de América. Madrid. (Rev. Indias)

Revista de Informação Legislativa. Senado Federal. Brasília. (Rev. Inf. Legis.)

Revista de la CEPAL. Naciones Unidas, Comisión Económica para América Latina (CEPAL). Santiago, Chile. (Rev. CEPAL/Santiago)

Revista de Planeación y Desarrollo. Depto. Nacional de Planeación. Bogotá. (Rev. Planeac. Desarro.)

Revista del Instituto Electoral del Estado de México Apuntes Electorales. Toluca, México. (Rev. Inst. Elect. Estado Méx. Apunt. Elect.)

Revista do Museu de Arqueologia e Etnologia. Univ. de São Paulo, Museu de Arqueologia e Etnologia. São Paulo. (Rev. Mus. Arqueol. Etnol.)

Revista Española de Antropología Americana. Univ. Complutense de Madrid, Facultad de Geografía e Historia, Depto. de Historia de América II (Antropología de América). Madrid. (Rev. Esp. Antropol. Am.)

Revista Europea de Estudios Latinoamericanos y del Caribe = European Review of Latin American and Caribbean Studies. Center for Latin American Research and Documentation = Centro de Estudios y Documentación Latinoamericanos. Amsterdam. (Rev. Eur. Estud. Latinoam. Caribe)

Revista Geográfica. Instituto Panamericano de Geografía e Historia. México. (Rev. Geogr./México)

Revista Geográfica Venezolana. Univ. de Los Andes, Facultad de Ciencias Forestales y Ambientales, Instituto de Geografía y Conservación de Recursos Naturales. Mérida, Venezuela. (Rev. Geogr. Venez.)

Revista Mexicana de Ciencias Políticas y Sociales. UNAM, Facultad de Ciencias Políticas y Sociales. México. (Rev. Mex. Cienc. Polít. Soc.)

Revista Mexicana de Economía y Finanzas = Mexican Journal of Economics and Finance: REMEF. Tecnológico de Monterrey, Campus Ciudad México. México. (Rev. Mex. Econ. Finanz.)

Revista Mexicana de Política Exterior. Instituto Matías Romero de Estudios Diplomáticos. México. (Rev. Mex. Polít. Exter.)

Revista Mexicana de Sociología. UNAM, Instituto de Investigaciones Sociales. México. (Rev. Mex. Sociol.)

Revista Mexicana del Caribe. Chetumal, Mexico. (Rev. Mex. Caribe)

Revista Vasca de Administración Pública. Instituto Vasco de Estudios de Administración Pública. Oñati, Spain. (Rev. Vasca Adm. Pública)

Revista Venezolana de Ciencia Política. Univ. de Los Andes, Facultad de Ciencias Jurídicas y Políticas, Centro de Estudios Políticos y Sociales de América Latina. Mérida, Venezuela. (Rev. Venez. Cienc. Polít.)

Revista Venezolana de Economía y Ciencias Sociales. Univ. Central de Venezuela, Facultad de Ciencias Económicas y Sociales, Instituto de Investigaciones Económicas y Sociales Dr. Rodolfo Quintero. Caracas. (Rev. Venez. Econ. Cienc. Soc.)

Revue Tiers monde. Univ. de Paris I—Panthéon-Sorbonne, Institut d'étude du Développement économique et social; Presses Universitaires de France. Paris. (Rev. Tiers monde)

Rural Sociology. Rural Sociological Society; Univ. of Missouri. Columbia, Mo. (Rur. Sociol.)

Science. American Assn. for the Advancement of Science. Washington, D.C. (Science/Washington)

Science & Society. S & S Quarterly, Inc.; Guildford Publications. New York. (Sci. Soc.)

Scientia Agrícola. Univ. de São Paulo, Campus de Piracicaba ESALQ/CENA. São Paulo. (Scientia Agrícola)

Secuencia: Revista de Historia y Ciencias Sociales. Instituto de Investigaciones Dr. José María Luis Mora. México. (Secuencia/México)

Signos Históricos. Univ. Autónoma Metropolitana, División de Ciencias Sociales y Humanidades, Depto. de Filosofía. México. (Signos Hist.)

Singapore Journal of Tropical Geography. Blackwell Publishers. Oxford, England; Malden, Mass. (Singap. J. Trop. Geogr.)

Small Axe: A Journal of Criticism. Ian Randle. Jamaica. (Small Axe)

Social Problems. Univ. of California Press. Berkeley. (Soc. Probl.)

The Social Science Journal. Elsevier Science, Inc. New York. (Soc. Sci. J./New York)

Social Science Quarterly. Univ. of Texas, Dept. of Government. Austin. (Soc. Sci. Q.)

Society & Natural Resources. Taylor & Francis. New York. (Soc. Nat. Resour.)

Sociologias. Univ. Federal do Rio Grande do Sul, Instituto de Filosofia e Ciências Humanas, Programa de Pós-Graduação em Sociologia. Porto Alegre, Brazil. (Sociologias/Porto Alegre)

Space & Polity. Carfax. Abingdon, England; Cambridge, Mass. (Space Polity)

Studies in Family Planning. Population Council. New York. (Stud. Fam. Plan.)

Suplemento Antropológico. Univ. Católica de Nuestra Señora de la Asunción, Centro de Estudios Antropológicos. Asunción. (Supl. Antropol.)

Tabula Rasa. Univ. Colegio Mayor de Cundinamarca. Bogotá. (Tabula Rasa)

Tareas. Centro de Estudios Latinoamericanos. Panamá. (**Tareas**)

Td: Temas y Debates. Univ. Nacional de Rosario, Facultad de Ciencia Política y Relaciones Internacionales. Rosario, Argentina. (Td Temas Debates)

Temas de Nuestra América. Univ. Nacional, Facultad de Filosofía y Letras, Instituto de Estudios Latinoamericanos, Campus Omar Dengo. Heredia, Costa Rica. (Temas Nuestra Am.)

Tempo Social: Revista de Sociologia da USP. Univ. de São Paulo, Faculdade de Filosofia, Letras e Ciências Humanas, Depto. de Sociologia. São Paulo. (Tempo Soc./São Paulo)

T'inkazos: Revista Boliviana de Ciencias Sociales. Programa de Investigación Estratégica en Bolivia. La Paz. (T'inkazos)

Tipití: Journal of the Society for the Anthropology of Lowland South America. Society for the Anthropology of Lowland South America (SALSA). New Orleans, La. (Tipití)

Tourism Geographies. Routledge. London. (Tour. Geogr.)

Transactions—Institute of British Geographers. Institute of British Geographers. Oxford, England. (Trans. Inst. Br. Geogr.)

Trayectorias. Univ. Autónoma de Nuevo León. Monterrey, Mexico. (Trayectorias/Monterrey)

El Trimestre Económico. Fondo de Cultura Económica. México. (Trimest. Econ.)

Unisa Latin American Report. Univ. of South Africa, Centre for Latin American Studies. Pretoria. (Unisa Lat. Am. Rep.)

Universum. Univ. de Talca. Talca, Chile. (Universum/Talca)

Urban Geography. V.H. Winston. Silver Spring, Md. (Urban Geogr.)

Veredas: Revista del Pensamiento Sociológico. Univ. Autónoma Metropolitana. Mexico. (Veredas)

Visible Language. Wayne State Univ. Detroit, Mich. (Visible Lang.)

Water Policy: Official Journal of the World Water Council. Elsevier Science Ltd. Oxford, England. (Water Policy)

Wicazo Sa Review. Indian Studies, Eastern Washington Univ. Cheney, Wash. (Wicazo Sa Rev.)

The World Bank Economic Review. World Bank. Washington, D.C. (World Bank Econ. Rev.)

World Development. Elsevier Science; Pergamon Press. Oxford, England. (World Dev.)

World Policy Journal. World Policy Institute. New York. (World Policy J.)

World Politics. Johns Hopkins Univ. Press. Baltimore, Md. (World Polit.)

Yaxkin. Instituto Hondureño de Antropología e Historia. Tegucigalpa. (Yaxkin/Tegucigalpa)

Zeitschrift für Geomorphologie = Annals of Geomorphology = Annales de Géomorphologie. Gebrüder Borntraeger. Berlin. (Z. Geomorphol.)

ABBREVIATION LIST OF JOURNALS INDEXED

For journal titles listed by full title, see *Title List of Journals Indexed*, p. 541.

Acervos/Oaxaca. Acervos: Boletín de los Archivos y Bibliotecas de Oaxaca. Asociación Civil Amigos de los Archivos y Bibliotecas de Oaxaca. Oaxaca, Mexico.

Acta geogr. Acta geographica. Société de Géographie. Paris.

Agenda Int. Agenda Internacional. Pontificia Univ. Católica del Perú, Instituto de Estudios Internacionales. Lima.

Agric. Ecosystems Environ. Agriculture, Ecosystems & Environment. Elsevier. New York.

Agroalimentaria. Agroalimentaria. Univ. de los Andes, Facultad de Ciencias Económicas y Sociales, Centro de Investigaciones Agroalimentarias. Mérida, Venezuela.

Aldea Mundo. Aldea Mundo: Revista sobre Fronteras e Integración. Univ. de los Andes-San Cristóbal, Centro de Estudios de Fronteras e Integración "Dr. José Briceño Monzillo." San Cristóbal, Venezuela.

Allpanchis/Cuzco. Allpanchis. Instituto de Pastoral Andina. Cuzco, Peru.

Alternativa/Santiago. Alternativa. Instituto de Ciencias Alejandro Lipschutz. Santiago, Chile.

Am. Anthropol. American Anthropologist. American Anthropological Assn. Washington, D.C.

Am. Ethnol./Washington. American Ethnologist. American Anthropological Assn., American Ethnological Society. Washington, D.C.

Am. Lat. Hoy/Salamanca. América Latina Hoy: Revista de Ciencias Sociales. Univ. de Salamanca, Instituto de Estudios de Iberoamérica y Portugal. Salamanca, Spain.

Am. Lat./Santiago. América Latina: Revista del Doctorado en el Estudio de las Sociedades Latinoamericana. Univ. ARCIS. Santiago, Chile.

Ambio/Stockholm. Ambio. Royal Swedish Academy of Sciences. Stockholm.

Americas/Washington. The Americas: A Quarterly Review of Inter-American Cultural History. Catholic Univ. of America, Academy of American Franciscan History; Catholic Univ. of America Press. Washington, D.C.

An. Mus. Am. Anales del Museo de América. Museo de América, Dirección General de Bellas Artes y Bienes Culturales, Ministerio de Educación, Cultura y Deporte. Madrid.

An. Mus. Paul. Anais do Museu Paulista: História e Cultura Material. Museu Paulista. São Paulo.

Anál. Econ./Porto Alegre. Análise Econômica. Univ. Federal do Rio Grande do Sul, Faculdade de Ciências Econômicas. Porto Alegre, Brazil.

Anál. Soc./Lisboa. Análise Social. Univ. de Lisboa, Instituto de Ciências Sociais. Lisboa.

Anc. Mesoam.   Ancient Mesoamerica. Cambridge Univ. Press. Cambridge, England; New York.

Andamios.   Andamios. Univ. de la Ciudad de México, Colegio de Humanidades y Ciencias Sociales. México.

Ankulegi.   Ankulegi. Ankulegi Antropologia Elkartea. Donostia, Spain.

Ann. Assoc. Am. Geogr.   Annals of the Association of American Geographers. Blackwell Publishers. Oxford, England; Malden, Mass.

Annu. Rev. Entomol.   Annual Review of Entomology. Annual Reviews, Inc. Palo Alto, Calif.

Annu. Rev. Polit. Sci.   Annual Review of Political Science. Annual Reviews, Inc. Palo Alto, Calif.

Anthropol. Consciousness.   Anthropology of Consciousness. American Anthropological Assn. Washington, D.C.

Anthropol. Q.   Anthropological Quarterly. Catholic Univ. Press of America. Washington, D.C.

Anthropos/Freiburg.   Anthropos: International Review of Ethnology and Linguistics. Anthropos-Institut. Freiburg, Switzerland.

Antípoda.   Antípoda: Revista de Antropología y Arqueología. Depto. de Antropología, Facultad de Ciencias Sociales, Univ. de los Andes. Bogotá.

Antipode.   Antipode. Basil Blackwell. Oxford, England; Cambridge, Mass.

Antiquity/Cambridge.   Antiquity. Antiquity Publications Ltd. Cambridge, England.

Anu. Demogr. Cuba.   Anuario Demográfico de Cuba. Dirección de Estadísticas de Población, Dirección General de Estadística, JUCEPLAN. La Habana.

Anu. Estad. Cuba.   Anuario Estadístico de Cuba. Dirección General de Estadística. La Habana.

Anu. Estud. Centroam.   Anuario de Estudios Centroamericanos. Univ. de Costa Rica. San José.

Anu. IEHS.   Anuario IEHS. Univ. Nacional del Centro de la Provincia de Buenos Aires, Facultad de Ciencias Humanas, Instituto de Estudios Histórico-Sociales. Tandil, Argentina.

Appl. Geogr.   Applied Geography. Butterworths. Sevenoaks, Kent, England.

Arqueol. Mex.   Arqueología Mexicana. Instituto Nacional de Antropología e Historia; Editorial Raíces. México.

Arqueologia/Curitiba.   Arqueologia. Univ. Federal do Paraná, Centro de Estudos e Pesquisas Arqueológicas (CEPA). Curitiba, Brazil.

Arqueología/México.   Arqueología. Instituto Nacional de Antropología e Historia, Coordinación Nacional de Arqueología. México.

Art Bull.   The Art Bulletin. College Art Assn. of America. New York.

Avá.   Avá: Revista de Antropología. Programa de Posgrado en Antropología Social, Univ. Nacional de Misiones. Argentina.

Belizean Stud.   Belizean Studies. Belizean Institute of Social Research and Action; St. John's College. Belize City.

Biol. Letters.   Biology Letters. The Royal Society. London.

BioScience.   BioScience. American Institute of Biological Sciences. Washington, D.C.

Bol. Cuatrimestral.   Boletín Cuatrimestral. Centro de Estudios de la Economía Cubana (CEEC). La Habana.

Bol. Hist. Antig.   Boletín de Historia y Antigüedades. Academia Colombiana de Historia. Bogotá.

Bol. Lima.   Boletín de Lima: Revista Cultural Científica. Asociación Cultural Boletín de Lima A.C. Lima.

Bol. Mus. Chil. Arte Precolomb. Boletín del Museo Chileno de Arte Precolombino. Santiago, Chile.

Bol. Mus. Para. Emílio Goeldi Sér. Ciênc. Hum. Boletim do Museu Paraense Emílio Goeldi Série Ciências Humanas. Museu Paraense Emílio Goeldi. Belém, Brazil.

Bull. Inst. fr. étud. andin. Bulletin de l'Institut français d'études andines. Lima.

Bull. Lat. Am. Res. Bulletin of Latin American Research. Blackwell Publishers. Oxford, England; Malden, Mass.

Cad. CRH/Salvador. Caderno CRH. Univ. Federal da Bahia, Faculdade de Filosofia e Ciências Humanas, Centro de Recursos Humanos. Salvador, Brazil.

Cad. Estud. Sociais. Cadernos de Estudos Sociais. Fundação Joaquim Nabuco, Instituto de Pesquisas Sociais. Recife, Brazil.

Cah. Am. lat. Cahiers des Amériques latines. Univ. de la Sorbonne nouvelle—Paris III, Institut des haute études de l'Amérique latine. Paris.

Caleidoscopio/Aguascalientes. Caleidoscopio. Univ. Autónoma de Aguascalientes, Centro de Artes y Humanidades. Aguascalientes, Mexico.

Can. Mineralogist. The Canadian Mineralogist. Mineralogical Association of Canada. Ottawa.

Caribb. J. Sci. Caribbean Journal of Science. Univ. of Puerto Rico, College of Arts and Sciences. Mayagüez, Puerto Rico.

Caribb. Q./Mona. Caribbean Quarterly: CQ. Univ. of the West Indies, Vice Chancellery, Cultural Studies Initiative. Mona, Jamaica.

Caribb. Stud. Caribbean Studies. Univ. of Puerto Rico, Institute of Caribbean Studies. Río Piedras, Puerto Rico.

Catauro/Habana. Catauro: Revista Cubana de Antropología. Fundación Fernando Ortiz. La Habana.

CEPAL Rev. CEPAL Review. UN, Comisión Económica para América Latina (CEPAL). Santiago, Chile.

Chiapas/México. Chiapas. UNAM, Instituto de Investigaciones Económicas. México.

Chihuah. Hoy. Chihuahua Hoy. Univ. Autónoma de Ciudad Juárez. Ciudad Juárez, Mexico.

Ciclos Hist. Econ. Soc. Ciclos en la Historia, Economía y la Sociedad. Univ. de Buenos Aires, Facultad de Ciencias Económicas, Instituto de Investigaciones de Historia Económica y Social. Buenos Aires.

Cienc. Soc./Santo Domingo. Ciencia y Sociedad. Instituto Tecnológico de Santo Domingo. Santo Domingo.

Ciudad Terr. Estud. Territ. Ciudad y Territorio Estudios Territoriales. Ministerio de Fomento, Centro de Publicaciones. Madrid.

Civilisations/Brussels. Civilisations. Univ. Libre de Bruxelles, Institut de Sociologie. Brussels.

Colomb. Int. Colombia Internacional. Univ. de los Andes, Centro de Estudios Internacionales. Bogotá.

Comer. Exter. Comercio Exterior. Banco Nacional de Comercio Exterior. México.

Community Dev. Community Development: Journal of the Community Development Society. The Community Development Society. Columbus, Ohio.

Comp. Polit./New York. Comparative Politics. City Univ. of New York, Political Science Program. New York.

Comp. Polit. Stud. Comparative Political Studies. Sage Publications. Thousand Oaks, Calif.

Conserv. Biol. Conservation Biology. Blackwell Scientific Publications. Boston, Mass.

Contexto Int. Contexto Internacional. Pontifícia Univ. Católica, Instituto de Relações Internacionais. Rio de Janeiro.

Convergencia/Toluca. Convergencia: Revista de Ciencias Sociales. Univ. Autónoma del Estado de México, Facultad de Ciencias Políticas y Administración Pública. Toluca, Mexico.

Coral Reefs. Coral Reefs. Springer International. Berlin.

Cotidiano/México. El Cotidiano: Revista de la Realidad Mexicana Actual. Univ. Autónoma Metropolitana—Unidad Azcapotzalco, División de Ciencias Sociales y Humanidades. México.

Crit. Anthropol. Critique of Anthropology. Sage Publications. London.

Cuad. Am./México. Cuadernos Americanos. UNAM. México.

Cuad. Antropol./San José. Cuadernos de Antropología. Univ. de Costa Rica, Depto. de Antropología, Laboratorio de Etnología. San José.

Cuad. Econ./Santiago. Cuadernos de Economía: Latin American Journal of Economics. Pontificia Univ. Católica de Chile, Facultad de Ciencias Económicas y Administrativas, Instituto de Economía. Santiago.

Cuba Siglo XXI (online). Cuba Siglo XXI (Online). La Habana; http://www.nodo5oorg/cubasigloXXI/.

Cuba. Stud. Cuban Studies. Univ. of Pittsburgh Press. Pittsburgh, Pa.

Cuba Transit. Cuba in Transition: Papers and Proceedings of the . . . Annual Meeting of the Association for the Study of the Cuban Economy. Assn. for the Study of the Cuban Economy. Washington, D.C.

Cuban Aff. Cuban Affairs. Univ. of Miami, Institute for Cuban and Cuban-American Studies. Coral Gables, Fla.

Cult. Agric. Culture & Agriculture: Bulletin of the Anthropological Study Group on Agrarian Systems. The Study Group. Corvallis, Ore.

Cult. Anthropol. Cultural Anthropology: Journal of the Society for Cultural Anthropology. American Anthropological Assn., Society for Cultural Anthropology. Washington, D.C.

Curr. Anthropol. Current Anthropology. Univ. of Chicago Press. Chicago, Ill.

Dados/Rio de Janeiro. Dados. Instituto Universitário de Pesquisas do Rio de Janeiro. Rio de Janeiro.

Debate Agrar. Debate Agrario. Centro Peruano de Estudios Sociales. Lima.

Demography/Washington. Demography. Population Assn. of America. Washington, D.C.

Desacatos. Desacatos. CIESAS, Centro de Investigaciones y Estudios Superiores en Antropología Social. México.

Desarro. Econ. Desarrollo Económico: Revista de Ciencias Sociales. Instituto de Desarrollo Económico y Social. Buenos Aires.

Desarro. Soc. Desarrollo y Sociedad. Univ. de los Andes, Facultad de Economía, Centro de Estudios sobre el Desarrollo Económico. Bogotá.

Earth Environ. Sci. Earth and Environmental Science Transactions of the Royal Society of Edinburgh. RSE Scotland Foundation. Edinburgh.

ECA/San Salvador. ECA. Univ. Centroamericana José Simeón Cañas. San Salvador.

Ecol. Polít./Barcelona. Ecología Política: Cuadernos de Debate Internacional. Icaria Editorial; Fundación Hogar del Empleado. Barcelona.

Ecol. Soc. (online). Ecology and Society (online). Resilience Alliance Publications. Waterloo, Ontario, Canada.

Econ. Dev. Cult. Change. Economic Development and Cultural Change. Univ. of Chicago Press. Chicago, Ill.

Econ. Geogr. Economic Geography. Clark Univ. Worcester, Mass.

Econ. Mex. Economía Mexicana. Centro de Investigación y Docencia Económicas. México.

Econ. Press Serv. Economics Press Service. Havana Inter Press Service Tercer Mundo. Havana.

Econ. Soc. Territ. Economía, Sociedad y Territorio. El Colegio Mexiquense. Toluca, Mexico.

Economía/Lima. Economía. Pontificia Univ. Católica del Perú, Depto. de Economía. Lima.

Ecuad. Debate. Ecuador Debate. Centro Andino de Acción Popular. Quito.

Encuentro Cult. Cuba. Encuentro de la Cultura Cubana. Asociación Encuentro de la Cultura Cubana. Madrid.

Ens. Polít. Econ. Ensayos sobre Política Económica. Banco de la República, Subgerencia de Estudios Económicos. Bogotá.

Ensaios FEE. Ensaios FEE. Governo do Rio Grande do Sul, Secretaria de Coordenação e Planejamento, Fundação de Economia e Estatística Siegfried Emanuel Heuser. Porto Alegre, Brazil.

Environ. Conserv./Cambridge. Environmental Conservation. Cambridge Univ. Press. Cambridge, England.

Environ. Dev. Sustain. Environment, Development and Sustainability. Kluwer Academic Publishers. Boston, Mass.

Environ. Manag. Environmental Management. Springer-Verlag New York, Inc. New York.

Environ. Plann. A. Environment and Planning A. Pion Ltd. London.

Environ. Plann. D Soc. Space. Environment and Planning: D, Society & Space. Pion Ltd. London.

Environ. Urban. Environment and Urbanization. Human Settlements Programme, International Institute for Environment and Development. London.

Erdkunde/Bonn. Erdkunde: Archiv für Wissenschaftliche Geographie (Archive for Scientific Geography). Univ. Bonn, Geographisches Institut. Bonn, Germany.

Espacio Laical. Espacio Laical. Consejo Arquidiocesano de Laicos de La Habana. La Habana.

EspacioTiempo. EspacioTiempo: Revista Latinoamericana de Ciencias Sociales y Humanidades. Univ. Autónoma de San Luis Potosi. San Luis Potosi, Mexico.

Espiral/Guadalajara. Espiral: Estudios sobre Estado y Sociedad. Univ. de Guadalajara, Centro Universitario de Ciencias Sociales y Humanidades. Guadalajara, Mexico.

Estud. Atacameños. Estudios Atacameños. Univ. del Norte, Museo de Arqueología. San Pedro de Atacama, Chile.

Estud. Av. Estudos Avançados. Univ. de São Paulo, Instituto de Estudos Avançados. São Paulo.

Estud. Cult. Maya. Estudios de Cultura Maya. UNAM, Instituto de Investigaciones Filológicas, Centro de Estudios Mayas. México.

Estud. Cult. Náhuatl. Estudios de Cultura Náhuatl. UNAM, Instituto de Investigaciones Históricas. México.

Estud. Cult. Otopame. Estudios de Cultura Otopame. UNAM, Instituto de Investigaciones Antropológicas. México.

Estud. Econ./São Paulo. Estudos Econômicos. Univ. de São Paulo, Faculdade de Economia, Administração e Contabilidade, Fundação Instituto de Pesquisas Econômicas. São Paulo.

Estud. Front. Estudios Fronterizos. Univ. Autónoma de Baja California, Instituto de Investigaciones Sociales. Mexicali, Mexico.

Estud. Geogr./Madrid. Estudios Geográficos. Instituto de Economía y Geografía Aplicadas. Madrid.

Estud. Int./Santiago. Estudios Internacionales. Univ. de Chile, Instituto de Estudios Internacionales. Santiago.

Estud. Jalisc. Estudios Jaliscienses. El Colegio de Jalisco. Zapopan, Mexico.

Estud. Latinoam./México. Estudios Latinoamericanos. UNAM, Facultad de Ciencias Políticas y Sociales, División de Estudios de Posgrado, Centro de Estudios Latinoamericanos. México.

Estud. Parag. Estudios Paraguayos. Univ. Católica Nuestra Señora de la Asunción. Asunción.

Estud. Polít./México. Estudios Políticos: Revista de Ciencias Políticas y Administración Pública. UNAM, Facultad de Ciencias Políticas y Sociales. México.

Estud. Públicos. Estudios Públicos. Centro de Estudios Públicos. Santiago, Chile.

Estud. Soc. Agric. Estudos Sociedade e Agricultura. Univ. Federal Rural do Rio de Janeiro, Instituto de Ciências Humanas e Sociais, Curso de Pós-Graduação em Desenvolvimento, Agricultura e Sociedade, Depto. de Letras e Ciências Sociais. Rio de Janeiro.

Estud. Soc./Santa Fe. Estudios Sociales: Revista Universitaria Semestral. Univ. Nacional del Litoral, Secretaría de Extensión, Centro de Publicaciones. Santa Fe, Argentina.

Estud. Sociol./México. Estudios Sociológicos. El Colegio de México, Centro de Estudios Sociológicos. México.

Estudos/Goiânia. Estudos: Revista da Universidade Católica de Goiás. Univ. Católica de Goiás. Goiânia, Brazil.

Ethnohistory/Columbus. Ethnohistory: The Bulletin of the Ohio Valley Historic Indian Conference. American Society for Ethnohistory. Columbus, Ohio.

Ethnos/Stockholm. Ethnos. Statens Etnografiska Museum. Stockholm.

Eur. J. Dev. Res. The European Journal of Development Research. Frank Cass. London.

EURE/Santiago. EURE: Revista Latinoamericana de Estudios Urbano Regionales. Pontificia Univ. Católica de Chile, Facultad de Arquitectura y Bellas Artes, Instituto de Estudios Urbanos. Santiago.

Foro Int./México. Foro Internacional. El Colegio de México, Centro de Estudios Internacionales. México.

Front. Norte. Frontera Norte. El Colegio de la Frontera Norte. Tijuana, Mexico.

Gend. Place Cult. Gender, Place and Culture: A Journal of Feminist Geography. Carfax Pub. Co. Abingdon, England.

Geoarchaeology/New York. Geoarchaeology. John Wiley. New York.

Geoderma. Geoderma. Elsevier Scientific Pub. Co. Amsterdam, N.Y.

Geoforum/New York. Geoforum. Pergamon Press. New York; Oxford, England.

Geogr. Compass. Geography Compass. Blackwell Publishing. Oxford, England.

Geogr. Helv. Geographica Helvetica. Schweizerische Zeitschrift für Länder- und Völkerkunde; Kümmerly & Frey, Geographischer Verlag. Bern, Switzerland.

Geogr. J./London. The Geographical Journal. The Royal Geographical Society. London; Institute of British Geographers. Cambridge, England.

Geogr. Rev. Geographical Review. American Geographical Society. New York.

Geogr. Rundsch. Geographische Rundschau. Westermann Schulbuchverlag GmbH. Braunschweig, Germany.

Geography/London. Geography. Geographical Assn. London.

GeoJournal/Boston. GeoJournal. D. Reidel Publishing Co. Boston, Mass.

Geopolitics/London. Geopolitics. Frank Cass. London.

GIScience Remote Sensing. GIScience & Remote Sensing. V.H. Winston & Son, Inc. Palm Beach, Fla.

Guaraguao/Barcelona. Guaraguao: Revista de Cultura Latinoamericano. Univ. Autónoma de Barcelona, Centro de Estudios y Cooperación para América Latina. Barcelona.

HAHR. Hispanic American Historical Review. Duke Univ. Press. Durham, N.C.

Herramienta/Buenos Aires. Herramienta: Revista de Debate y Crítica Marxista. Editorial Antídoto. Buenos Aires.

Hist. Ciênc. Saúde Manguinhos. História Ciências Saúde: Manguinhos. Fundação Oswaldo Cruz, Casa de Oswaldo Cruz. Rio de Janeiro.

Hist. Mex./México. Historia Mexicana. El Colegio de México, Centro de Estudios Históricos. México.

Hist. Polít. Historia y Política. Univ. Complutense de Madrid, Depto. de Historia del Pensamiento y de los Movimientos Sociales y Políticos; Univ. Nacional de Educación a Distancia, Depto. de Historia Social y del Pensamiento Político. Madrid.

Hist. Workshop J. History Workshop Journal. Oxford Univ. Press. Oxford, England.

Hombre Desierto. Hombre y Desierto: Una Perspectiva Cultural. Univ. de Antofagasta, Instituto de Investigaciones Antropológicas. Antofagasta, Chile.

Hum. Ecol. Human Ecology. Kluwer Academic Publishers. Dordrecht, N.Y.

Hum. Organ. Human Organization. Society for Applied Anthropology. Washington, D.C.

Hum. Rights Q. Human Rights Quarterly. Johns Hopkins Univ. Press. Baltimore, Md.

Iberoamericana/Stockholm. Iberoamericana: Nordic Journal of Latin American Studies/Revista Nórdica de Estudios Latinoamericanos. Stockholm Univ., Institute of Latin American Studies. Stockholm.

ICONOS/Quito. ICONOS. FLACSO Ecuador. Quito.

Inf. Econ./São Paulo. Informações Econômicas. Governo do Estado de São Paulo, Secretaria de Agricultura e Abastecimento, Instituto de Economia Agrícola. São Paulo.

Int. J. South Am. Archaeol. International Journal of South American Archaeology. Syllaba Press. Miami, Fla.

Int. Migr./Oxford. International Migration. International Organization for Migration. Geneva; Blackwell Publishers, Ltd. Oxford, England; Malden, Mass.

Int. Polit. Sci. Rev. International Political Science Review: IPSR. Sage Publications. Beverly Hills, Calif.

Int. Reg. Sci. Rev. International Regional Science Review. West Virginia Univ., Regional Research Institute. Morgantown.

Int. Stud. Q./Oxford. International Studies Quarterly. Blackwell Publishers. Malden, Mass.; Oxford, England.

Int. Stud. Rev. International Studies Review. Blackwell Publishers for the International Studies Association. Malden, Mass.

Integr. Comer. Integración & Comercio. Instituto para la Integración de América Latina, Depto. de Integración y Programas Regionales, Banco Interamericano de Desarrollo = Inter-American Development Bank. Buenos Aires.

Interciencia/Caracas. Interciencia. Asociación Interciencia. Caracas.

Invest. Geogr./México. Investigaciones Geográficas: Boletín del Instituto de Geografía. UNAM, Instituto de Geografía. México.

Invest. Geogr./Santiago. Investigaciones Geográficas. Univ. de Chile, Depto. de Geografía. Santiago.

Investig. Soc./San Marcos. Investigaciones Sociales: Revista del Instituto de Investigaciones Histórico Sociales. Univ. Nacional Mayor de San Marcos, Facultad de Ciencias Sociales. Lima.

J. Agrarian Change. Journal of Agrarian Change. Blackwell Publishers. Oxford, England; Malden, Mass.

J. Anthropol. Archaeol. Journal of Anthropological Archaeology. Academic Press. New York.

J. Anthropol. Res. Journal of Anthropological Research. Univ. of New Mexico. Albuquerque.

J. Archaeol. Res. Journal of Archaeological Research. Plenum Press. New York.

J. Archaeol. Sci. Journal of Archaeological Science. Academic Press. New York.

J. Biogeogr. Journal of Biogeography. Blackwell Scientific Publications. Oxford, England.

J. Caribb. Archaeol. Journal of Caribbean Archaeology. Univ. of Florida, Florida Museum of Natural History. Gainesville, Fla.

J. Democr. Journal of Democracy. National Endowment for Democracy, International Forum for Democratic Studies. Washington, D.C.; Johns Hopkins Univ. Press. Baltimore, Md.

J. Ethnobiol. Journal of Ethnobiology. Society of Ethnobiology; Tulane Univ., Dept. of Anthropology. New Orleans, La.

J. Ethnobiol. Ethnomed. Journal of Ethnobiology and Ethnomedicine. Biomed Central. London.

J. Field Archaeol. Journal of Field Archaeology. Boston Univ. Boston, Mass.

J. Geogr. Journal of Geography. National Council of Geographic Education. Menasha, Wis.

J. Hist. Geogr. Journal of Historical Geography. Academic Press. London; New York.

J. Island Coastal Archaeol. Journal of Island & Coastal Archaeology. Taylor & Francis Group. Philadelphia, Pa.

J. Lat. Am. Caribb. Anthropol. The Journal of Latin American and Caribbean Anthropology. Univ. of California Press, Journals Division. Berkeley, Calif.

J. Lat. Am. Cult. Stud. Journal of Latin American Cultural Studies. Carfax Publishing. Abingdon, England.

J. Lat. Am. Geogr. Journal of Latin American Geography. Conference of Latin Americanist Geographers. Tucson, Ariz.

J. Lat. Am. Stud. Journal of Latin American Studies. Cambridge Univ. Press. Cambridge, England.

J. Peasant Stud. The Journal of Peasant Studies. Frank Cass & Co. London.

J. Polit. The Journal of Politics. Blackwell Publishers. Abingdon, England; Williston, Vt.; Southern Political Science Assn.; Univ. of North Carolina. Chapel Hill.

J. Polit. Econ. Journal of Political Economy. Univ. of Chicago Press. Chicago, Ill.

J. Polit. Mil. Sociol. Journal of Political and Military Sociology: JPMS. Northern Illinois Univ., Dept. of Sociology. DeKalb, Ill.

J. Psychoactive Drugs. Journal of Psychoactive Drugs. Haight-Ashbury Publications. San Francisco, Calif.

J. Public Health Policy. Journal of Public Health Policy. South Burlington, Vt.

J. Reg. Sci. Journal of Regional Science. Regional Science Research Institute. Amherst, Mass.

J. Royal Anthropol. Inst. The Journal of the Royal Anthropological Institute. London.

J. Socio-Econ./New York. The Journal of Socio-Economics. Elsevier Science, Inc. New York; Amsterdam.

J. Sustain. For. Journal of Sustainable Forestry. Food Products Press. Binghamton, N.Y.

J. Transport Geogr. Journal of Transport Geography. Butterworth-Heinemann. London.

J. Urban Aff. Journal of Urban Affairs. Division of Environment and Urban Systems, Virginia Polytechnic Institute and State Univ. Blacksburg, Va.

J. West/Manhattan. Journal of the West. Sunflower Univ. Press. Manhattan, Kan.

J. Women Polit. Policy. Journal of Women, Politics & Policy. Haworth Press, Inc. Binghamton, N.Y.

Land Use Policy. Land Use Policy. Butterworths. Guildford, England.

LARR. Latin American Research Review. Latin American Studies Assn.; Univ. of Texas Press. Austin.

Lat. Am. Antiq. Latin American Antiquity. Society for American Archaeology. Washington, D.C.

Lat. Am. Bus. Rev. Latin American Business Review. Business Assn. of Latin American Studies; International Business Press. Binghamton, N.Y.

Lat. Am. Caribb. Ethn. Stud. Latin American and Caribbean Ethnic Studies. Taylor & Francis. Colchester, England.

Lat. Am. Indian Lit. J. Latin American Indian Literatures Journal. Geneva College, Dept. of Foreign Languages. Beaver Falls, Pa.

Lat. Am. Perspect. Latin American Perspectives. Sage Publications, Inc. Thousand Oaks, Calif.

Lat. Am. Polit. Soc. Latin American Politics and Society. Univ. of Miami, School of Interamerican Studies. Coral Gables, Fla.

Lect. Econ. Lecturas de Economía. Univ. de Antioquia, Facultad de Ciencias Económicas, Depto. de Economía, Centro de Investigaciones Económicas. Medellín, Colombia.

Lua Nova. Lua Nova. Centro de Estudos de Cultura Contemporânea. São Paulo.

Luso-Braz. Rev. Luso-Brazilian Review. Univ. of Wisconsin Press. Madison.

Maguaré/Bogotá. Maguaré. Univ. Nacional de Colombia, Depto. de Antropología. Bogotá.

Mana/Rio de Janeiro. Mana: Estudos de Antropologia Social. Univ. Federal do Rio de Janeiro, Museu Nacional, Programa de Pós-Graduação em Antropologia Social. Rio de Janeiro.

Mappemonde. Mappemonde. RECLUS. Montpellier, France.

Mayab/Madrid. Mayab. Sociedad Española de Estudios Mayas. Madrid.

Mesoamérica/Antigua. Mesoamérica. Plumsock Mesoamerican Studies. South Woodstock, Vt.; Centro de Investigaciones Regionales de Mesoamérica. Antigua, Guatemala.

Metapolítica/México. Metapolítica: Revista Trimestral de Teoría y Ciencia de la Política. Centro de Estudios de Política Comparada. México.

Mex. Stud. Mexican Studies/Estudios Mexicanos. Univ. of California Press. Berkeley.

Mexicon/Germany. Mexicon. Verlag Anton Saurwein. Markt Schwaben, Germany.

Migr. Int. Migraciones Internacionales. El Colegio de la Frontera Norte. Tijuana, Mexico.

Nature/London. Nature: International Weekly Journal of Science. Macmillan Magazines. London.

New Left Rev. New Left Review. New Left Review, Ltd. London.

Nóesis/UACJ. Nóesis: Revista de Ciencias Sociales y Humanidades. Univ. Autónoma de

Ciudad Juárez. Dirección General de Investigación y Posgrado. Ciudad Juárez, Mexico.

Nova Econ./Belo Horizonte. Nova Economia. Univ. Federal de Minas Gerais, Faculdade de Ciências Econômicas, Depto. de Ciências Econômicas. Belo Horizonte, Brazil.

Novos Estud. CEBRAP. Novos Estudos CEBRAP. Centro Brasileiro de Análise e Planejamento. São Paulo.

Nueva Soc. Nueva Sociedad. Fundación Friedrich Ebert. Caracas.

NWIG. NWIG: New West Indian Guide/Nieuwe West Indische Gids. Royal Institute of Linguistics and Anthropology, KITLV Press. Leiden, The Netherlands.

Obs. Soc. Am. Lat. Observatorio Social de América Latina. Consejo Latinoamericano de Ciencias Sociales. Buenos Aires.

Opin. Públ. Opinião Pública. Univ. Estadual de Campinas, Centro de Estudos de Opinião Pública. Campinas, Brazil.

Pap. Geogr. Papeles de Geografía. Univ. de Murcia, Facultad de Letras, Depto. de Geografía Física, Humana y Análisis Regional. Murcia, Spain.

Peace Rev. Peace Review. Peace Review Publications. Palo Alto, Calif.

Perf. Latinoam. Perfiles Latinoamericanos. Facultad Latinoamericana de Ciencias Sociales (FLACSO). México.

Pers. Soc. Persona y Sociedad. Instituto Latinoamericano de Doctrina y Estudios Sociales. Santiago, Chile.

Pesqui. Antropol. Pesquisas Antropologia. Instituto Anchietano de Pesquisas. São Leopoldo, Brazil.

Philos. Trans. Philosophical Transactions of the Royal Society of London. Series B, Biological Sciences. Royal Society of London. London.

Polít. Cult. Política y Cultura. Univ. Autónoma Metropolitana—Xochimilco,

División de Ciencias Sociales y Humanidades, Depto. de Política y Cultura. México.

Polít. Exter./Madrid. Política Exterior. Estudios de Política Exterior S.A. Madrid.

Polít. Gest. Política y Gestión. Univ. Nacional de General San Martín. Rosario, Argentina.

Polít. Int./Lima. Política Internacional. Academia Diplomática del Peru. Lima.

Polit. Res. Q. Political Research Quarterly. Univ. of Utah. Salt Lake City.

Polit. Sci. Q. Political Science Quarterly. The Academy of Political Science. New York.

Polít. Soc./Madrid. Política y Sociedad. Univ. Complutense, Facultad de Ciencias Políticas y Sociología. Madrid.

Popul. Dev. Rev. Population and Development Review. Population Council. New York.

Popul. Res. Policy Rev. Population Research and Policy Review. Elsevier Scientific Pub. Co. Amsterdam.

Probl. Post-Communism. Problems of Post-Communism. M.E. Sharpe. Armonk, N.Y.

Proc. Natl. Acad. Sci. U.S.A. Proceedings of the National Academy of Sciences of the United States of America. Washington, D.C.

Prof. Geogr. The Professional Geographer. Assn. of American Geographers. Washington, D.C.; Blackwell Publishers. Abindgon, England; Williston, Vt.

Prohistoria/Rosario. Prohistoria. Manuel Suárez Editor. Rosario, Argentina.

Public Adm. Dev. Public Administration and Development. Wiley. Sussex, England.

Rábida/Huelva. Rábida. Patronato Provincial del V Centenario del Descubrimiento de América. Huelva, Spain.

Realidad/San Salvador. Realidad: Revista de Ciencias Sociales y Humanidades. Univ. Centroamericana José Simeón Cañas. San Salvador.

Relac. Int./México. Relaciones Internacionales. UNAM, Facultad de Ciencias Políticas y Sociales, Coordinación de Relaciones Internacionales. México.

Relac. Soc. Argent. Antropol. Relaciones de la Sociedad Argentina de Antropología. Buenos Aires.

Relaciones/Zamora. Relaciones. El Colegio de Michoacán. Zamora, Mexico.

REN Rev. Econ. Nordeste. REN: Revista Econômica do Nordeste. Banco do Nordeste do Brasil, Escritório Técnico de Estudos Econômicos do Nordeste. Fortaleza, Brazil.

Res/Cambridge. Res. Harvard Univ., Peabody Museum of Archaeology and Ethnology. Cambridge, Mass.

Rethinking Marx. Rethinking Marxism. Association for Economic and Social Analysis. Amherst, Mass.

Rev. Adm./São Paulo. Revista de Administração (RAUSP). Univ. de São Paulo, Faculdade de Ciências Econômicas e Administrativas, Instituto de Administração, Serviço de Documentação. São Paulo.

Rev. Antropol./São Paulo. Revista de Antropologia. Univ. de São Paulo, Faculdade de Filosofia, Letras e Ciências Humanas, Depto. de Antropologia. São Paulo.

Rev. Arg. Cienc. Polít. Revista Argentina de Ciencia Política. Editorial Universitaria de Buenos Aires. Buenos Aires.

Rev. Arqueol. Am./México. Revista de Arqueología Americana. Instituto Panamericano de Geografía e Historia. México.

Rev. Arqueol./São Paulo. Revista de Arqueologia. Sociedade de Arqueologia Brasileira. São Paulo.

Rev. Bras. Comér. Exter. Revista Brasileira de Comércio Exterior: RBCE. Fundação

Centro de Estudos do Comércio Exterior. Rio de Janeiro.

Rev. Bras. Econ./Rio de Janeiro. Revista Brasileira de Economia. Fundação Getúlio Vargas, Escola de Pós-Graduação em Economia. Rio de Janeiro.

Rev. Bras. Estud. Popul. Revista Brasileira de Estudos de População. Associação Brasileira de Estudos Populacionais. São Paulo.

Rev. Bras. Polít. Int. Revista Brasileira de Política Internacional: RBPI. Instituto Brasileiro de Relações Internacionais. Brasília.

Rev. Centroam. Econ. Revista Centroamericana de Economía. Univ. Nacional Autónoma de Honduras, Programa de Postgrado Centroamericano en Economía y Planificación del Desarrollo. Tegucigalpa.

Rev. CEPAL/Santiago. Revista de la CEPAL. Naciones Unidas, Comisión Económica para América Latina (CEPAL). Santiago, Chile.

Rev. Chil. Hist. Geogr. Revista Chilena de Historia y Geografía. Sociedad Chilena de Historia y Geografía. Santiago.

Rev. Cienc. Polít./Santiago. Revista de Ciencia Política. Pontificia Univ. Católica de Chile, Instituto de Ciencia Política. Santiago.

Rev. Cienc. Soc./Maracaibo. Revista de Ciencias Sociales: RCS. Univ. de Zulia, Facultad de Ciencias Económicas y Sociales, Instituto de Investigaciones. Maracaibo, Venezuela.

Rev. Colomb. Antropol. Revista Colombiana de Antropología. Ministerio de Educación Nacional, Instituto Colombiano de Antropología. Bogotá.

Rev. Crít. Ciênc. Sociais. Revista Crítica de Ciências Sociais. Centro de Estudos Sociais. Coimbra, Portugal.

Rev. Econ. Polít. Revista de Economia Política = Brazilian Journal of Political

Economy. Centro de Economia Política. São Paulo.

Rev. Econ. Sociol. Rural. Revista de Economia e Sociologia Rural = Brazilian Review of Agricultural Economics and Rural Sociology. Sociedade Brasileira de Economia e Sociologia Rural = Brazilian Society of Agricultural Economics and Rural Sociology. Brasília.

Rev. Esp. Antropol. Am. Revista Española de Antropología Americana. Univ. Complutense de Madrid, Facultad de Geografia e Historia, Depto. de Historia de América II (Antropología de América). Madrid.

Rev. Esp. Invest. Sociol. REIS: Revista Española de Investigaciones Sociológicas. Centro de Investigaciones Sociológicas. Madrid.

Rev. Eur. Estud. Latinoam. Caribe. Revista Europea de Estudios Latinoamericanos y del Caribe = European Review of Latin American and Caribbean Studies. Center for Latin American Research and Documentation = Centro de Estudios y Documentación Latinoamericanos. Amsterdam.

Rev. Geogr./México. Revista Geográfica. Instituto Panamericano de Geografía e Historia. México.

Rev. Geogr. Norte Gd. Revista de Geografía Norte Grande. Pontificia Univ. Católica de Chile, Facultad de Historia, Geografía y Ciencia Política, Instituto de Geografía. Santiago.

Rev. Geogr. Venez. Revista Geográfica Venezolana. Univ. de Los Andes, Facultad de Ciencias Forestales y Ambientales, Instituto de Geografía y Conservación de Recursos Naturales. Mérida, Venezuela.

Rev. Indias. Revista de Indias. Consejo Superior de Investigaciones Científicas, Instituto de Historia, Depto. de Historia de América. Madrid.

Rev. Inf. Legis. Revista de Informação Legislativa. Senado Federal. Brasília.

Rev. Inst. Elect. Estado Méx. Apunt. Elect. Revista del Instituto Electoral del

Estado de México Apuntes Electorales. Toluca, México.

Rev. Mex. Caribe. Revista Mexicana del Caribe. Chetumal, Mexico.

Rev. Mex. Cienc. Polít. Soc. Revista Mexicana de Ciencias Políticas y Sociales. UNAM, Facultad de Ciencias Políticas y Sociales. México.

Rev. Mex. Econ. Finanz. Revista Mexicana de Economía y Finanzas = Mexican Journal of Economics and Finance: REMEF. Tecnológico de Monterrey, Campus Ciudad México. México.

Rev. Mex. Polít. Exter. Revista Mexicana de Política Exterior. Instituto Matías Romero de Estudios Diplomáticos. México.

Rev. Mex. Sociol. Revista Mexicana de Sociología. UNAM, Instituto de Investigaciones Sociales. México.

Rev. Mus. Arqueol. Etnol. Revista do Museu de Arqueologia e Etnologia. Univ. de São Paulo, Museu de Arqueologia e Etnologia. São Paulo.

Rev. Planeac. Desarro. Revista de Planeación y Desarrollo. Depto. Nacional de Planeación. Bogotá.

Rev. Tiers monde. Revue Tiers monde. Univ. de Paris I—Panthéon-Sorbonne, Institut d'étude du Développement économique et social; Presses Universitaires de France. Paris.

Rev. Vasca Adm. Pública. Revista Vasca de Administración Pública. Instituto Vasco de Estudios de Administración Pública. Oñati, Spain.

Rev. Venez. Cienc. Polít. Revista Venezolana de Ciencia Política. Univ. de Los Andes, Facultad de Ciencias Jurídicas y Políticas, Centro de Estudios Políticos y Sociales de América Latina. Mérida, Venezuela.

Rev. Venez. Econ. Cienc. Soc. Revista Venezolana de Economía y Ciencias Sociales. Univ. Central de Venezuela, Facultad de Ciencias Económicas y Sociales, Instituto de

Investigaciones Económicas y Sociales Dr. Rodolfo Quintero. Caracas.

Rur. Sociol. Rural Sociology. Rural Sociological Society; Univ. of Missouri. Columbia, Mo.

Sci. Soc. Science & Society. S & S Quarterly, Inc.; Guildford Publications. New York.

Science/Washington. Science. American Assn. for the Advancement of Science. Washington, D.C.

Scientia Agrícola. Scientia Agrícola. Univ. de São Paulo, Campus de Piracicaba ESALQ/CENA. São Paulo.

Secuencia/México. Secuencia: Revista de Historia y Ciencias Sociales. Instituto de Investigaciones Dr. José María Luis Mora. México.

Signos Hist. Signos Históricos. Univ. Autónoma Metropolitana, División de Ciencias Sociales y Humanidades, Depto. de Filosofía. México.

Singap. J. Trop. Geogr. Singapore Journal of Tropical Geography. Blackwell Publishers. Oxford, England; Malden, Mass.

Small Axe. Small Axe: A Journal of Criticism. Ian Randle. Jamaica.

Soc. Nat. Resour. Society & Natural Resources. Taylor & Francis. New York.

Soc. Probl. Social Problems. Univ. of California Press. Berkeley.

Soc. Sci. J./New York. The Social Science Journal. Elsevier Science, Inc. New York.

Soc. Sci. Q. Social Science Quarterly. Univ. of Texas, Dept. of Government. Austin.

Sociologias/Porto Alegre. Sociologias. Univ. Federal do Rio Grande do Sul, Instituto de Filosofia e Ciências Humanas, Programa de Pós-Graduação em Sociologia. Porto Alegre, Brazil.

Space Polity. Space & Polity. Carfax. Abingdon, England; Cambridge, Mass.

Stud. Fam. Plan. Studies in Family Planning. Population Council. New York.

Supl. Antropol. Suplemento Antropológico. Univ. Católica de Nuestra Señora de la Asunción, Centro de Estudios Antropológicos. Asunción.

Tabula Rasa. Tabula Rasa. Univ. Colegio Mayor de Cundinamarca. Bogotá.

Tareas. Tareas. Centro de Estudios Latinoamericanos. Panamá.

Td Temas Debates. Td: Temas y Debates. Univ. Nacional de Rosario, Facultad de Ciencia Política y Relaciones Internacionales. Rosario, Argentina.

Temas Nuestra Am. Temas de Nuestra América. Univ. Nacional, Facultad de Filosofía y Letras, Instituto de Estudios Latinoamericanos, Campus Omar Dengo. Heredia, Costa Rica.

Tempo Soc./São Paulo. Tempo Social: Revista de Sociologia da USP. Univ. de São Paulo, Faculdade de Filosofia, Letras e Ciências Humanas, Depto. de Sociologia. São Paulo.

T'inkazos. T'inkazos: Revista Boliviana de Ciencias Sociales. Programa de Investigación Estratégica en Bolivia. La Paz.

Tipití. Tipití: Journal of the Society for the Anthropology of Lowland South America. Society for the Anthropology of Lowland South America (SALSA). New Orleans, La.

Tour. Geogr. Tourism Geographies. Routledge. London.

Trans. Inst. Br. Geogr. Transactions—Institute of British Geographers. Institute of British Geographers. Oxford, England.

Trayectorias/Monterrey. Trayectorias. Univ. Autónoma de Nuevo León. Monterrey, Mexico.

Trimest. Econ. El Trimestre Económico. Fondo de Cultura Económica. México.

Unisa Lat. Am. Rep. Unisa Latin American Report. Univ. of South Africa, Centre for Latin American Studies. Pretoria.

Universum/Talca. Universum. Univ. de Talca. Talca, Chile.

Urban Geogr. Urban Geography. V.H. Winston. Silver Spring, Md.

Veredas. Veredas: Revista del Pensamiento Sociológico. Univ. Autónoma Metropolitana. Mexico.

Visible Lang. Visible Language. Wayne State Univ. Detroit, Mich.

Water Policy. Water Policy: Official Journal of the World Water Council. Elsevier Science Ltd. Oxford, England.

Wicazo Sa Rev. Wicazo Sa Review. Indian Studies, Eastern Washington Univ. Cheney, Wash.

World Bank Econ. Rev. The World Bank Economic Review. World Bank. Washington, D.C.

World Dev. World Development. Elsevier Science; Pergamon Press. Oxford, England.

World Policy J. World Policy Journal. World Policy Institute. New York.

World Polit. World Politics. Johns Hopkins Univ. Press. Baltimore, Md.

Yaxkin/Tegucigalpa. Yaxkin. Instituto Hondureño de Antropología e Historia. Tegucigalpa.

Z. Geomorphol. Zeitschrift für Geomorphologie = Annals of Geomorphology = Annales de Géomorphologie. Gebrüder Borntraeger. Berlin.

SUBJECT INDEX

Abused Children. *See* Child Abuse.

Abused Wives. *See* Abused Women.

Abused Women. Guatemala, 2612. Mexico, 2482. *See Also* Women.

Acanceh Site (Mexico), 107.

Achuar (indigenous group). Sex Roles, 590.

Aconcagua River (Chile), 1243.

Acre, Brazil (state). Environmental Policy, 1367. Environmental Protection, 1388. Excavations, 347. History, 365. Indigenous Peoples, 561. Land Use, 1367. Rubber Industry and Trade, 1388.

Adolescents. *See* Youth.

Aeronautics. Chile, 797.

African-Americans. *See* Blacks.

African Influences. Brazil, 2693. Caribbean Area, 2617. Material Culture, 932. *See Also* Africans; Candomblé (cult); Santería (cult); Umbanda (cult).

Africans. Brazil, 364. Cultural History, 2617. Mexico, 2547.

Afro-Americans. *See* Blacks.

Aged. Mexico, 2468.

Agrarian Reform. *See* Land Reform.

Agribusiness. Chile, 1247.

Agricultural Colonization. Brazil, 1340–1341. *See Also* Land Settlement.

Agricultural Development, 531. Argentina, 302, 1206, 2658. Brazil, 1293, 1407, 2658. Ecuador, 656. Mesoamerica, 44. Uruguay, 2658. *See Also* Agricultural Technology; Development Projects; Economic Development; Rural Development.

Agricultural Development Projects. *See* Development Projects.

Agricultural Ecology. Brazil, 1276. Chile, 1251. *See Also* Ecology.

Agricultural Geography. Brazil, 1273, 1333, 1359. Colombia, 1107. French Guiana, 432. *See Also* Geography.

Agricultural Industries. *See* Agroindustry.

Agricultural Labor. Argentina, 1190, 1205. Brazil, 1279, 1311, 1393, 2684. Caribbean Area, 672. Ecuador, 652.

Agricultural Policy. Bolivia, 1182. Brazil,

849, 1279, 1338. Caribbean Area, 672. Chile, 803. Costa Rica, 699. Cuba, 743, 749, 754. Honduras, 718. Mexico, 2228. Nicaragua, 721–722. Venezuela, 1090, 2256. *See Also* Land Reform.

Agricultural Productivity. Brazil, 1408. Chile, 1231. Colombia, 2276. Costa Rica, 698. Dominican Republic, 985. Globalization, 2261.

Agricultural Systems. Mexico, 536. Peru, 1145.

Agricultural Technology. Amazon Basin, 1294. Bolivia, 1165. Colombia, 2298. *See Also* Agricultural Development.

Agriculture. Archeological Surveys, 91, 129. Argentina, 1211–1212. Bolivia, 1182. Brazil, 858, 889, 897, 1392, 2430. Chile, 791. Colombia, 412, 1107, 2298. Costa Rica, 1005. Cuba, 750. Ecuador, 779, 782. Free Trade, 2328. Jamaica, 989. Mexico, 1033, 1058, 1065, 1068, 2202. Venezuela, 2256. Women, 2183. *See Also* Sustainable Agriculture.

Agroindustry. Brazil, 1409, 2430. Cuba, 752, 754. Ecuador, 1113. Venezuela, 582.

Aguada (indigenous group). Archeological Survey, 304. Ceramics, 309.

Aguascalientes, Mexico (state). Economic Conditions, 1447. Political Sociology, 1037.

AIDS, 2618, 2620. Brazil, 2171. Central America, 2046. Mexico, 2046, 2496.

Alcohol and Alcoholism. Chile, 801. Honduras, 2590.

Alcoholism. *See* Alcohol and Alcoholism.

Alfonsín, Raúl, 2097.

Algae. Precolumbian Civilizations, 86. *See Also* Plants.

Alianza Nacional Popular (ANAPO). *See* Alianza Nacional Popular (Colombia).

Alianza Nacional Popular (Colombia), 1587.

Alliance for Progress, 1999.

Amapá, Brazil (state). Ceramics, 395–396. Economic Development, 1314. Paleo-Indians, 396. Precolumbian Pottery, 353.

Credit. Andean Region, 693. Brazil, 2429. *See Also* Microfinance.

Creole Languages. Caribbean Area, 1544–1545, 1571. Cultural Identity, 1544–1546.

Creoles. Intellectuals, 930.

Crime and Criminals. Argentina, 1783. Brazil, 918, 1783, 2678, 2702. Caribbean Area, 2241. Central America, 2613. Chile, 1261, 2671. El Salvador, 1501, 2576. Guatemala, 1501. Jamaica, 1567, 1569. Mexico, 2036, 2459. Nicaragua, 1527. Paraguay, 831. Women, 2582.

Criminals. *See* Crime and Criminals.

Cuauhtémoc, Emperor of Mexico, 479.

Cuban Missile Crisis (1962), 2058.

Cuban Revolution (1959), 2059, 2071.

Cuenca, Ecuador (city). Women, 2631.

Cuernavaca, Mexico (city). Environmental Degradation, 1045.

Cuicatec (indigenous group). Mexico, 2519.

Cuicuilco Site (Mexico). History, 89.

Cults. Mexico, 164.

Cultural Contact. Argentina/Spain, 327. Caribbean Area, 284. Cuba/Mexico, 2064. France/Peru, 461. Indigenous Peoples, 561. Taino/Spaniards, 271.

Cultural Development. Amazon Basin, 417, 562. Brazil, 359, 362.

Cultural Geography. Brazil, 1331, 1339. Cuba, 986. *See Also* Human Geography.

Cultural History. Argentina, 327. Bolivia, 332. Caribbean Area, 273. Mexico, 2005. Nicaragua, 1026. Peru, 446.

Cultural Identity, 2517. Blacks, 2697. Bolivia, 1645. Cuba, 986. Dance, 618. Ecuador, 648. Guatemala, 1517, 2569. Mexico, 1041, 1063, 2511, 2521, 2536. Nicaragua, 2585. Panama, 2591, 2604.

Cultural Policy. Brazil, 1901. Colombia, 427.

Cultural Property. Colombia, 1095. Mayas, 18. Peru, 1139.

Cultural Relations. Cuba, 263. Mexico/US, 2476. Peru/Spain, 2134.

Culture. Indigenous Peoples, 552. Peru, 816.

Cuna (indigenous group). Cultural Contact, 548. Social Life and Customs, 548.

Cundinamarca, Colombia (dept.). Precolumbian Civilizations, 414.

Curicó, Chile (city). Gender Relations, 791.

Curitiba, Brazil (city). Ecology, 1390.

Currency. *See* Money.

Curripaco (indigenous group). Myths and Mythology, 583.

Cusco, Peru (city). *See* Cuzco, Peru (city).

Cuzco, Peru (city). Archeology, 449. Con-servation, 440–441. Ethnohistory, 442. Excavations, 467. Indigenous Peoples, 661. Social Classes, 1685. Social Conditions, 1685.

Cuzco, Peru (dept.). Kinship, 657.

Cyclones. *See* Hurricanes.

Dams. Argentina, 1196. Brazil, 1351.

Dance. Mexico, 479.

Davidson, William V., 937.

Death. Brazil, 2700. Precolumbian Civilizations, 436. *See Also* Mortality.

Debt. *See* External Debt; Public Debt.

Debt Conversion. *See* Debt Relief.

Debt Crisis, 2181. Argentina, 2353.

Debt Relief. Argentina, 2353.

Decentralization. Andean Region, 1077. Bolivia, 1640. Central America, 2237. Chile, 1733, 1748, 1756. Colombia, 2288. Dominican Republic, 1556. Economic Conditions, 2273. Honduras, 1524. Mexico, 2216. Paraguay, 1805. Peru, 1684, 1695, 1701, 2315. Uruguay, 1733, 1810, 1818. Venezuela, 1627.

Decolonization. Bolivia, 1657. Caribbean Area, 2074. Cuba, 980. Trinidad and Tobago, 1553.

Defense Budgets, 1980.

Defense Industries, 1964.

Deforestation, 965. Amazon Basin, 1286, 1294, 1319, 1363. Belize, 999. Brazil, 908, 1277, 1295–1296, 1322–1323. Chile, 1223. Costa Rica, 1002. Cuba, 978–979. Easter Island, 1227–1228. Ecuador, 1123, 1127. El Salvador, 1006. Farms, 1319. Guatemala, 999, 1009. Honduras, 1019. Mexico, 1066, 1068.

Democracy, 1417–1418, 1420, 1936, 2176, 2185, 2188–2189. Andean Region, 1679. Argentina, 1770, 1777, 1795. Bolivia, 1677, 2253. Brazil, 1837, 1840–1841, 1843, 1848, 1855–1856, 1888, 1891, 1903, 1925, 1931–1932, 2450. Chile, 796, 1724, 1729, 1731, 1738, 1742. Colombia, 1594, 1609, 1615, 2127, 2290. Costa Rica, 1505–1506, 1508. Cuba, 1585, 2243. El Salvador, 1501. Guatemala, 1501, 1520. Haiti, 1561. Honduras, 1523–1524. Mexico, 1445–1446, 1449, 1456, 1458, 1460, 1463–1464, 1471, 1478, 1485, 1492, 2033, 2219, 2224. Paraguay, 1798. Peru, 1702, 1706, 1710, 2136. Uruguay, 1816. Venezuela, 1618, 1622, 1626–1627, 1630, 2262.

Democratization, 1420, 1432, 1434, 1959, 1972, 1979. Andean Region, 1643. Argentina, 1772–1773, 1775, 2395. Bolivia,

1648, 1651. Brazil, 1820, 1837, 1920. Caribbean Area, 1550. Chile, 643, 645, 1730, 1748–1749, 1758, 2327. Ecuador, 2304. Elites, 1499. Guatemala, 1517. Haiti, 1558, 1560, 1562. Mexico, 1470, 1474–1475, 1495, 2327, 2455, 2486. Nicaragua, 2236. Panama, 1538. Paraguay, 828. Public Opinion, 2416. Uruguay, 1813–1814, 1817.
Demography. Argentina, 1166. Bolivia, 1159, 1166. Brazil, 1366, 1371, 1374, 1376. Cuba, 731. Mexico, 2468. Peru, 597. Precolumbian Civilizations, 351. Venezuela, 1088.
Demonstrations. *See* Protests.
Dental Studies. Brazil, 364.
Dependency. Dominican Republic, 2072. Martinique, 1571.
Deregulation. Mexico, 2214, 2229.
Desaparecidos. *See* Disappeared Persons.
Description and Travel. Amazon Basin, 570, 1401. Brazil, 565. Ecuador, 1114. Peru, 1137. Venezuela, 565.
Devaluation of Currency. *See* Exchange Rates.
Development, 668, 1439, 1936, 1942, 1959, 2616. Brazil, 842, 846, 882, 2167, 2173. Caribbean Area, 982, 2240, 2616. Central America, 982, 2235, 2237–2238. Colombia, 1966. Ecuador, 651, 775, 2635. Mexico, 1042, 1463, 2551. Peru, 1696.
Development Projects, 667.
Diaguita (indigenous group), 318.
Dialectology. *See* Anthrolinguistics.
Dictatorships. Brazil, 1848, 1862. Chile, 1264. *See Also* Authoritarianism.
Dieties. Mexico, 19, 229.
Diplomacy, 1938, 1940. Brazil, 2171. Caribbean Area, 1540. Cuba, 740.
Diplomatic History, 1954, 1965, 1989. Dominican Republic, 2072. Peru, 2133. Southern Cone, 2089.
Diplomats. Brazil, 2156, 2158, 2162, 2167, 2173.
Disappeared Persons. Argentina, 1772. Chile, 2670. Guatemala, 2048, 2553. Social Movements, 926.
Disaster Relief, 2452.
Discovery and Exploration. Andean Region, 1082. Chile, 1235. Ecuador, 966.
Discrimination. Brazil, 2679. Guatemala, 715. Labor Market, 2679. Mexico, 2489, 2491, 2521.
Diseases. Colombia, 421.
Displaced Persons. Brazil, 1350.
Dissertations and Theses. Geography, 938.

Distribution of Wealth. *See* Income Distribution.
Doctors. Cuba, 740.
Dollarization. Ecuador, 777–778, 783.
Domestics. Mexico, 38.
Dos Pilas Site (Guatemala), 148.
Droughts. Argentina, 1193. Precolumbian Civilizations, 155.
Drug Abuse. Jamaica, 1566.
Drug Enforcement, 1951. Chile, 801. Colombia, 1606, 2126, 2130. Ecuador, 2130.
Drug Traffic, 950. Brazil, 2706. Colombia, 2119, 2128, 2265, 2280. Ecuador, 2130. Globalization, 1951. Mexico, 2460. Nicaragua, 2596. Peru, 1711.
Drug Use. *See* Drug Utilization.
Drug Utilization. Indigenous Peoples, 542, 586. Mexico, 542, 2460. Precolumbian Civilizations, 261.
Drugs and Drug Trade. *See* Drug Abuse; Drug Enforcement; Drug Traffic; Drug Utilization.
Dzibilchaltún Site (Mexico). Artifacts, 107.
Earthworks. Brazil, 349. Indigenous Peoples, 204, 432. *See Also* Excavations; Mounds.
East Indians. Cultural Identity, 1579.
Easter Island. El Niño Current, 1227–1228.
Ecological Crisis. *See* Environmental Protection.
Ecology. Amazon Basin, 1401. Bolivia, 331. Brazil, 349, 1291, 1315, 1330, 1357, 1396. Caribbean Area, 998. Economic Development, 785. Ecuador, 596, 1118. History, 598. Jamaica, 981. Mexico, 1039. Peru, 589, 597, 1134. Precolumbian Civilizations, 415.
Economic Anthropology. Mesoamerica, 6.
Economic Assistance, US, 1999.
Economic Conditions, 678, 2189. Argentina, 2355, 2360, 2665. Bolivia, 1646. Brazil, 834, 843, 857, 861, 893, 908, 914, 1874, 1904, 2175, 2424. Central America, 2593. Chile, 643, 788, 793, 813. Colombia, 2273, 2291, 2302. Cuba, 738, 761, 2246. Ecuador, 777. El Salvador, 714, 2234, 2611. Honduras, 1016. Mexican-American Border Region, 2008. Mexico, 2010, 2215. Panama, 725. Paraguay, 827, 832, 2401. Peru, 816, 1688. Uruguay, 2406. Venezuela, 2254.
Economic Crises, 2403. Argentina, 1773, 2345, 2353, 2355, 2384, 2386, 2400. Brazil, 897. Ecuador, 783. Paraguay, 2403.
Economic Destabilization. *See* Economic Stabilization.

2210, 2212. Venezuela, 1085. *See Also* Investments.
Foreign Investment, Canadian, 1948.
Foreign Investment, Chinese, 1937.
Foreign Investment, Spanish. Bolivia, 2308. Colombia, 2289.
Foreign Policy, 1957, 1987, 1998. Argentina, 2093, 2098, 2101, 2103. Bolivia, 2106. Brazil, 2093, 2146–2147, 2150–2151, 2158–2159, 2162–2163, 2165, 2167, 2170–2171, 2173–2174. Caribbean Area, 2056. Central America, 2587. Chile, 2093. Colombia, 2118–2119. Costa Rica, 1508. Cuba, 2063, 2073. Ecuador, 2129. Mexico, 2009, 2014, 2024, 2030, 2032, 2034–2035, 2224. Peru, 818, 2133. Research, 2000. Sovereignty, 1552. Uruguay, 2138. US, 1970, 1999, 2163. Venezuela, 2142.
Foreign Trade. *See* International Trade.
Forest Restoration. *See* Reforestation.
Forests and Forest Industry. Amazon Basin, 1346. Belize, 999. Brazil, 1291, 1295, 1335, 1379–1380. Central America, 996. Chile, 1222, 1265. Costa Rica, 1002, 2602. Ecuador, 1117, 1122. El Salvador, 1006–1007. Guatemala, 999, 1009. Honduras, 1015, 1020, 1022, 2610. Mexico, 1039, 1057, 1067. Monopolies, 1295. Nicaragua, 1025. Peru, 597. Venezuela, 1086. Women, 1335.
Forgery. Artifacts, 191. Precolumbian Art, 191.
Fortifications. Uruguay, 1271.
Fox Quesada, Vicente, 1483, 2227.
Franciscans. Florida, 277.
Free Trade, 666, 687, 1186, 1937, 1943, 1959–1960, 1982, 2082, 2085, 2445. Agriculture, 2298. Andean Region, 687. Brazil, 849, 2153, 2172. Caribbean Area, 2055. Central America, 697, 721. Chile, 796, 2322, 2328. Costa Rica, 702, 2044, 2047, 2049–2050. Ecuador, 2132. El Salvador, 2606. Honduras, 718. Mexico, 2050. Nicaragua, 721. Peru, 824, 2135. Venezuela, 2143. *See Also* Economic Integration.
Free Trade Area of the Americas (FTAA), 851, 1943, 1967, 1982, 2082, 2139, 2143, 2153, 2172, 2445.
French Influences. Peru, 461.
Frente Amplio (Uruguay), 1812, 1815, 1819.
Frente Nacional (Colombia), 1587.
Frente Sandinista de Liberación Nacional. *See* Sandinistas (Nicaragua).
FREPASO (Argentina), 1785, 1796.

Frontier and Pioneer Life. Brazil, 1293. *See Also* Frontiers.
Frontiers. Argentina, 318. Bolivia, 1174. Brazil, 1336, 1341, 1356, 1399. *See Also* Frontier and Pioneer Life.
Fruit Trade. Brazil, 1393.
FTAA. *See* Free Trade Area of the Americas (FTAA).
Fuentes, Octavio, 1451.
Fuerzas Armadas Revolucionarias de Colombia, 1588, 1600, 1606.
Fujimori, Alberto, 658, 1687–1688, 1698, 1707.
Furniture Industry and Trade. Brazil, 839.
Galápagos Islands. *See* Galápagos Islands, Ecuador.
Galápagos Islands, Ecuador. Conservation, 1120. Ecotourism, 1120. Environmental Protection, 1125. Human Ecology, 1125. Tourism, 1125.
Galicians. Brazil, 1289.
Gallegans. *See* Galicians.
Gambling. Brazil, 2689.
Gangs. Central America, 2554, 2560, 2563, 2593, 2598. El Salvador, 2571, 2576, 2601. Mexico, 2469. Nicaragua, 2595–2596. Social Structure, 2596.
Garbage. *See* Refuse and Refuse Disposal.
García Linera, Álvaro, 1653.
Gardens. Argentina, 1190. Precolumbian Civilizations, 109.
Garifuna (indigenous group). *See* Black Carib (indigenous group).
Gated Communities. Argentina, 1210, 2647. Brazil, 1304, 1309.
Gay, Claudio, 1235.
Gê (indigenous group). Indigenous Languages, 560.
Gender Relations, 3. Bolivia, 1644. Brazil, 1852, 2679, 2686, 2694. Caribbean Area, 1539, 1555, 2622. Cuba, 731. Economic Development, 2628. Ecuador, 429. El Salvador, 1516, 2605. Mesoamerica, 63. Mexico, 2511. Nicaragua, 2605. *See Also* Sex and Sexual Relations.
Gender Roles. Andean Region, 45. Archeology, 63. Chile, 1725. Costa Rica, 2568. El Salvador, 2557. Guatemala, 2558, 2608–2609. Mesoamerica, 8, 45. Mexico, 46, 2461, 2473, 2475, 2500, 2511, 2516, 2536. Nicaragua, 2561. Toba, 619. *See Also* Sex Roles.
Generals. Uruguay, 1812.
Genetics. *See* Human Genetics.

Herders and Herding. Peru, 1145.
Hidalgo, Mexico (state). Archeological Surveys, 36, 42. Ethnohistory, 36. Obsidian, 187.
Hieroglyphics. *See* Writing.
Higher Education. Paraguay, 830, 1802.
Higueras, Mexico (town). *See* Las Higueras, Mexico (town).
Hilbert, Peter Paul, 358.
Historic Sites. Brazil, 1358.
Historical Demography. Mexico, 96.
Historical Geography, 954, 967, 1089. Brazil, 1306, 1383. Colombia, 1100, 1104, 1109–1110. El Salvador, 997. Honduras, 997. Peru, 1136, 1152.
Historiography. Honduras, 495.
History. Environmental Degradation, 1028.
HIV. *See* AIDS.
Holguín, Cuba (prov.). Geomorphology, 974.
Homosexuality. Argentina, 2666. Brazil, 2682. Mexico, 2496, 2522. Violence, 2522.
Hospital Real de San Andrés (Peru), 449.
Households. Colombia, 427. Ecuador, 651, 655. Mexico, 1044, 2484. Peru, 662.
Housing, 673. Colombia, 1102, 2277. Cuba, 759. Mexico, 2550. Peru, 1144, 2639. Social Movements, 928.
Housing Policy. Argentina, 1215. Brazil, 1372, 2696. Colombia, 2277. Mexico, 1215. Peru, 1132.
Huaca de la Luna Site (Peru). Architecture, 448.
Huamanga, Peru (prov.). Water Distribution, 665.
Huarpe (indigenous group). Argentina, 617. Ethnicity and Ethnic Groups, 617.
Huastec (indigenous group). Cultural Identity, 58. Ethnohistory, 58. Land Use, 1072. Precolumbian Sculpture, 42. Sex and Sexual Relations, 61.
Huasteca Region (Mexico). Agriculture, 58. Cultural Identity, 58. Indigenous Peoples, 510.
Huehuetenango, Guatemala (dept.). Borderlands, 488.
Huichol (indigenous group). Religious Life and Customs, 499, 537.
Human Capital. *See* Human Resources.
Human Ecology, 927, 954. Amazon Basin, 1278. Bolivia, 1169. Brazil, 1292, 1316, 1354, 1377, 1381, 1389. Caribbean Area, 279, 288. Colombia, 1091, 1110. Ecuador, 1125. Paraguay, 1267, 2645.
Human Fertility. Brazil, 1391. Ecuador, 653.

Human Genetics, 653.
Human Geography, 958. Andean Region, 1130. Bolivia, 1174. Brazil, 1272, 1298, 1303, 1329, 1331, 1342, 1385, 1404. Colombia, 948, 1091, 1100. Mexico, 948. Venezuela, 1088. *See Also* Cultural Geography.
Human Remains, 293. Archeological Dating, 189. Brazil, 363–364, 373, 377, 382, 392, 399. Caribbean Area, 274. Colombia, 423. Mexico, 72, 144, 189, 200. Peru, 439, 452, 455, 466. *See Also* Bones.
Human Resources, 1966, 2186. Andean Region, 1081. Chile, 793. El Salvador, 713. Paraguay, 826, 828.
Human Rights, 1421, 1430, 1947, 1969. Argentina, 1736, 1771–1772. Caribbean Area, 1555. Chile, 1736. Colombia, 1604, 2119, 2126, 2128, 2271. Costa Rica, 1505. Ecuador, 648. El Salvador, 2607. Guatemala, 2048, 2553. Indigenous Peoples, 1981. Mexico, 1448, 2495, 2546. Peru, 1691, 1693, 1700, 1702, 1704, 1718, 1721, 1981, 2136, 2320.
Human Sacrifice. *See* Sacrifice.
Humanism. Chile, 1762.
Humboldt, Alexander von, 940, 1082, 1137.
Hunting. Indigenous Peoples, 587, 629. Paleo-Indians, 287.
Hurricanes. British Caribbean, 1049. Caribbeans, 998. Honduras, 1023. Mexico, 1040, 1049. *See Also* Natural Disasters.
Hydration Rind Dating. *See* Archeological Dating.
Hydroelectric Power. Brazil, 1350–1351. Honduras, 720.
Hydrology. Brazil, 1348. Mexico, 1047, 1064.
Hygiene. *See* Public Health.
Iconography. Argentina, 326. Chile, 407, 411. Mayas, 57. Mexico, 35. *See Also* Precolumbian Art.
Illness. *See* Diseases.
Immigration. *See* Migration.
Imperialism, 1939. US/Puerto Rico, 1575.
Import Substitution, 692.
Import Substitution Industrialization. *See* Import Substitution.
Imports and Exports. *See* International Trade.
Inca Influences. Agriculture, 402.
Incas. Architecture, 467. Human Remains, 449. Land Settlement, 402. Monuments, 467. Mummies, 449. Political Development, 442. Political Thought, 400. Preco-

Marine Resources. Bolivia, 1163. Caribbean Area, 272. Chile, 406.
Maritime History. Caribbean Area, 1568, 2068.
Marketing. Brazil, 1915.
Markets. Brazil, 2157. Economic Development, 596. Ecuador, 596. Indigenous Peoples, 596. Mesoamerica, 77.
Marriage. Brazil, 1899. Mexico, 2498, 2528.
Martí, José, 980.
Martinicans. Panama, 2572.
Marxism. Brazil, 1877. Cuba, 2239, 2244.
MAS. See Movimiento al Socialismo (Bolivia).
Mass Media. Bolivia, 641. Brazil, 1894. Chile, 2117. El Salvador, 1516. Jamaica, 1565. Political Ideology, 1429. Venezuela, 1636. See Also Journalism.
Massacres. Mexico, 2491.
Matacapán Site (Mexico). Artisanry, 95. Iconography, 23. Trade, 6.
Mataco (indigenous group). Food, 629.
Material Culture. Caribbean Area, 255, 265. Colombia, 419, 423, 427. Mesoamerica, 6, 26, 76. Mexico, 5. Peru, 460. Venezuela, 469.
Mato Grosso, Brazil (state). Archeology, 371. Excavations, 383. Land Settlement, 1340–1341. Museums, 558. Paleo-Indians, 383.
Mato Grosso do Sul, Brazil (state). Ceramics, 341. Precolumbian Civilizations, 366.
Matsigenka (indigenous group). See Machiguenga (indigenous group).
Mayan Influences, 240.
Mayas, 1009. Agricultural Production, 76. Archeological Surveys, 137, 160, 175, 179, 184, 217. Archeology, 139, 237. Architecture, 102, 130, 153, 160, 179, 199, 226. Artifacts, 169. Artisanry, 122, 124–125, 168, 170, 206. Belize, 126. Cacao, 165. Calendrics, 98, 152, 497. Canals, 165. Cave Paintings, 197. Caves, 207. Ceramics, 7, 126, 141, 153, 168, 170, 173, 175, 206, 212–213. Chronology, 179, 225. Cities and Towns, 81, 103, 155–156, 203, 215, 225. Colonial History, 145, 217. Cosmology, 13. Cultural Development, 506. Cultural Identity, 57, 102, 132, 140, 206, 524, 2569. Death, 37. Development, 539. Dieties, 13, 203, 227. Droughts, 155. Elites, 122, 124, 159, 180, 213. Ethnic Groups and Ethnicity, 221. Ethnography, 539. Fieldwork, 1010. Food Industry and Trade, 143, 145, 193. Food Supply, 194, 222. Globalization, 513. Government Relations, 22, 490.

History, 532. Households, 45. Hydrology, 165. Iconography, 37, 57, 80. Kings and Rulers, 163, 212, 236. Land Settlement, 130. Massacres, 481. Medicine, 475, 494. Midwives, 475, 494. Migration, 1011. Monuments, 102. Mortuary Customs, 37, 137, 153, 207. Myths and Mythology, 13. Obsidian, 124. Philosophy, 57. Political Anthropology, 481. Political Geography, 190. Political Institutions, 22. Political Structure, 140, 156–157, 169–171, 193, 196. Precolumbian Architecture, 215. Religion, 207, 491, 523, 539. Religion and Politics, 171, 506. Research, 140, 237. Rites and Ceremonies, 80, 157, 203, 206. Roads, 196. Sacrifice, 80. Sculpture, 153, 159, 212. Sex Roles, 497, 539. Social Conditions, 2569. Social History, 26. Social Life and Customs, 497, 513. Social Structure, 26, 168–169. Stone Implements, 122, 124, 149. Symbolism, 57. Textiles and Textile Industry, 136, 158, 213. Time, 98. Vernacular Architecture, 1008. Warfare, 66, 123, 160, 213. Women, 136, 213, 490, 497. Writing, 13, 37, 57, 80, 159, 168, 227, 239, 241.
Mayo (indigenous group), 529.
Mayors. Brazil, 1860, 1889.
Mazatlán, Mexico (city). Archeological Surveys, 105.
Mbya (indigenous group). Social Structure, 625.
MCCA. See Mercado Común Centroamericano.
Meat Industry. Argentina, 2346. See Also Cattle Raising and Trade.
Medellín, Colombia (city). Corruption, 1598. Precolumbian Civilizations, 424. Social Conditions, 1111.
Media. See Mass Media.
Medical Anthropology. Amazon Basin, 585. Colombia, 585. Guatemala, 525. Mexico, 540.
Medical Care. Chile, 1746. Guatemala, 2574. Mexico, 2508, 2537, 2545. See Also Medicine.
Medical Policy. Mexico, 2508.
Medicinal Plants. Mexico, 521, 1053.
Medicine. Indigenous Peoples, 609, 612.
Mendoza, Argentina (city). Obsidian, 305.
Mendoza, Argentina (prov.). Precolumbian Civilizations, 321.
Menem, Carlos Saúl, 1776, 2097.
Mercado, Patricia, 1457.
Mercado Común Centroamericano, 1998.

1832. Politicians, 1927. Return Migration, 1327. Social Structure, 1832.

Minerals and Mining Industry, 1948. Brazil, 2433. Peru, 1150.

Mining. *See* Minerals and Mining Industry.

Miscegenation. Peru, 2641.

Miskito Coast (Nicaragua and Honduras). *See* Mosquitia (Nicaragua and Honduras).

Miskito (indigenous group). *See* Mosquito (indigenous group).

Missionaries. Brazil, 381.

Missions, 491. Brazil, 575. Florida, 277.

Mixtec (indigenous group). Archeological Surveys, 67, 119. Artifacts, 232. Calendrics, 243. Codices, 230. Cultural History, 62. Cultural Studies, 108. Ethnography, 119. Ethnohistory, 119. Genealogy, 230, 245. Historiography, 84. Land Settlement, 245. Marriage, 231. Migration, 2490. Pictographs, 234, 242, 245–246. Religious Life and Customs, 231. Rites and Ceremonies, 232. Social Structure, 62. Symbolism, 232. Writing, 234, 238.

Moche (indigenous group). *See* Mochica (indigenous group).

Mochica (indigenous group). Architecture, 448. Ceramics, 444. Costume and Adornment, 444. Religious Art, 436.

Mocoví (indigenous group). Ethnicity, 618. Linguistics, 622. Myths and Mythology, 618. Oral History, 622.

Modernity. Intellectuals, 922.

Modernization. Brazil, 2414. Chile, 1254.

Monarchs. *See* Kings and Rulers.

Monbeig, Pierre, 1342.

Monetary Policy, 679, 2179. Argentina, 2367, 2400. Brazil, 869, 2415, 2421, 2427, 2440, 2444, 2450. Cuba, 767, 770. Uruguay, 2406.

Monetary Unions. Andean Region, 681. Southern Cone, 2090.

Money. Brazil, 2440.

Money Supply. Brazil, 2421.

Monsiváis, Carlos, 1451.

Monte Albán Site (Mexico), 147, 151, 201. Precolumbian Architecture, 34.

Monterrey, Mexico (city). Industry and Industrialization, 2542. Labor Market, 2506. Migration, 2490.

Montesinos, Vladimiro, 1698.

Montevideo, Uruguay (city). Political Ideology, 1818.

Monuments. Chile, 410. Colombia, 425. Mexico, 27.

Morales, Evo, 1644, 1649, 1651, 1663, 1674, 1676, 1678, 2310.

Morals. *See* Ethics.

Morelos, Mexico (state). Agricultural Development, 2492. Ceramics, 186. Obsidian, 198. Precolumbian Architecture, 7, 27.

Mormons. Argentina, 611.

Mortality. Chile, 799. Mexico, 2534. *See Also* Death.

Mortuary Customs, 293. Argentina, 302, 329. Bolivia, 330. Mayas, 80. Mesoamerica, 76. Mexico, 14, 25, 70, 113, 492. Peru, 466. Precolumbian Civilizations, 326, 353. Puerto Rico, 270. *See Also* Cemeteries; Tombs.

Mosquitia (Nicaragua and Honduras). Cultural History, 1026. Cultural Identity, 1018. Ethnic Groups and Ethnicity, 1018. Forests and Forest Industry, 1016.

Mosquito (indigenous group), 1533. Cultural Identity, 534.

Motherhood. Guatemala, 2603. Honduras, 2603.

Motion Pictures. *See* Film.

Mounds. Bolivia, 331. Brazil, 350, 363, 387, 390, 394, 399. Chile, 405. French Guiana, 432. Guyana, 433. Precolumbian Architecture, 204.

Movimento dos Trabalhadores Rurais Sem Terra (Brazil), 1329, 1410.

Movimiento al Socialismo (Bolivia), 947, 1422, 1664–1665.

Movimiento de Izquierda Revolucionaria (Chile), 2670.

Movimiento de Liberación Nacional (Uruguay), 1814.

Movimiento Nacional Justicialista (Argentina), 1786.

Muisca (indigenous group). *See* Chibcha (indigenous group).

Multiculturalism, 1424, 2517. Bolivia, 1640, 1657, 1669, 1681. Guatemala, 2569. Mexico, 2521, 2546. Nicaragua, 2585.

Multinational Corporations, 1952. Caribbean Area, 1543. Colombia, 1611, 2289, 2292.

Mummies. Peru, 449.

Municipal Government. Andean Region, 1643. Argentina, 1768, 1777, 2652. Brazil, 1368, 1864, 1883, 1886, 1919, 1934. Central America, 2235, 2238. Colombia, 1591, 2282. Costa Rica, 1507. Dominican Republic, 1556. International Relations, 1938. Mexico, 1474, 1484. Peru,

Nukak (indigenous group). Land Settlement, 581.

Nutrition. Ecuador, 2627. Mexico, 2499, 2539. Venezuela, 2261.

OAS. *See* Organization of American States (OAS).

Oaxaca, Mexico (city). Architecture, 192.

Oaxaca, Mexico (state). Archeological Dating, 67, 146, 154. Archeological Surveys, 92, 154, 195. Artifacts, 154. Artisanry, 38. Ceramics, 5, 151, 201. Colonial History, 202. Cultural Development, 118. Cultural Identity, 519. Economic Conditions, 2520. Ethnography, 512, 542. Ethnohistory, 5. Excavations, 146. Gender Relations, 45. Human Remains, 146. Indigenous Peoples, 154, 509, 1441. Land Tenure, 478. Material Culture, 40. Migration, 2515. Mixtec, 84, 108, 118, 202, 243. Monuments, 202. Mortuary Customs, 146. Municipal Government, 1446. Political Conditions, 2520. Political Participation, 487. Precolumbian Architecture, 34. Precolumbian Civilizations, 51. Religion, 118, 478. Social Conditions, 2520. Social Life and Customs, 166, 478. Social Structure, 118.

Obsidian. Argentina, 305. Artifacts, 30, 305, 308. Mesoamerica, 56, 181. Mexico, 134, 187–188. Teotihuacán Influences, 133.

Occupational Education. Maquiladoras, 2472.

Occupational Training. Argentina, 2649. Mexico, 2472.

Offshore Assembly Industry. *See* Maquiladoras.

Olancho, Honduras (dept.). History, 1014.

Older People. *See* Aged.

Olmec Influences. Mexico, 117.

Olmecs (indigenous group). Archeological Dating, 99. Artifacts, 116. Ceramics, 201. Cultural Development, 94. Cultural Identity, 29, 142. Economic Anthropology, 117. Iconography, 110. Inter-Tribal Relations, 40. Jade, 110. Material Culture, 41, 116. Political Culture, 117. Political Development, 142. Precolumbian Sculpture, 41. Research, 219. Social Structure, 40, 94.

Operación Cóndor, 1427.

Opposition Groups. Bolivia, 1678. Venezuela, 1623.

Oral History. Mexico, 543.

Organization of American States. (OAS), 1936, 1940, 1972–1973, 1981, 2036.

Orinoco River Region (Venezuela and Colombia). Land Use, 1084.

Ortega, Daniel, 1532.

Otavalo, Ecuador (town). Economic History, 775.

Otomi (indigenous group). Cultural History, 36, 551. Cultural Identity, 492, 551. Ethnography, 492. Kinship, 502. Language and Languages, 492. Migration, 2490. Precolumbian Art, 492. Social Structure, 551.

Oxkintok Site (Mexico). Chronology, 107.

Pachacamac Site (Peru), 458. Ceramics, 445. Precolumbian Textiles, 445. Quipu, 443.

Palenque Site (Mexico). Writing, 163, 179.

Paleo-Indians, 293. Agricultural Systems, 412. Amazon Basin, 370, 379, 598. Andean Region, 296. Argentina, 321. Bioarcheology, 185. Brazil, 337, 376, 399. Caribbean Area, 259, 274, 282, 286, 290. Caves, 376. Ceramics, 285. Colombia, 412. Cosmology, 578. Cuba, 263. Food Supply, 71. Land Settlement, 378, 598. Mesoamerica, 43, 71. Mexico, 115. Migration, 71. Origins, 85, 282, 299, 452. Patagonia, 296. Peru, 439, 452. Puerto Rico, 256. Saint Kitts and Nevis, 291. Stone Implements, 43. Tools, 472. Venezuela, 471–472.

Paleobotany. Brazil, 383. Caribbean Area, 260.

Paleoclimatology, 416. Amazon Basin, 368.

Paleoecology. Brazil, 365. El Salvador, 1006. Mayas, 216.

Paleogeology. Venezuela, 471.

Paleoindians. *See* Paleo-Indians.

Palms. Amazon Basin, 1274.

Palynology. Colombia, 416. Mexico, 216.

Pampas, Argentina (region). Archeology, 307, 316. Economic Development, 1203. Environment, 1209. Ethnic Groups and Ethnicity, 307. Natural Resources, 1206. Precolumbian Civilizations, 316.

PAN. *See* Partido Acción Nacional (Mexico).

Pan-Americanism, 1989.

Panama Canal. Migration, 2572.

Pantanal, Brazil (region). Paleoecology, 393. Precolumbian Civilizations, 393.

Papermaking. Mexico, 128.

Pará, Brazil (state). Agriculture, 2684. Archeological Dating, 340. Archeological Surveys, 352, 381. Dairy Industry, 1320. Land Tenure, 1275, 1399. Land Use, 1277. Minerals and Mining Industry, 894. Rock Art, 380. Slaves and Slavery, 1275. Violence, 2684.

Paracas Site (Peru). Research, 465.

Paraguayan War (1865–1870), 2154.

AUTHOR INDEX